# Lecture Notes in Computer Science 3896

*Commenced Publication in 1973*
Founding and Former Series Editors:
Gerhard Goos, Juris Hartmanis, and Jan van Leeuwen

### Editorial Board

David Hutchison
  *Lancaster University, UK*
Takeo Kanade
  *Carnegie Mellon University, Pittsburgh, PA, USA*
Josef Kittler
  *University of Surrey, Guildford, UK*
Jon M. Kleinberg
  *Cornell University, Ithaca, NY, USA*
Friedemann Mattern
  *ETH Zurich, Switzerland*
John C. Mitchell
  *Stanford University, CA, USA*
Moni Naor
  *Weizmann Institute of Science, Rehovot, Israel*
Oscar Nierstrasz
  *University of Bern, Switzerland*
C. Pandu Rangan
  *Indian Institute of Technology, Madras, India*
Bernhard Steffen
  *University of Dortmund, Germany*
Madhu Sudan
  *Massachusetts Institute of Technology, MA, USA*
Demetri Terzopoulos
  *New York University, NY, USA*
Doug Tygar
  *University of California, Berkeley, CA, USA*
Moshe Y. Vardi
  *Rice University, Houston, TX, USA*
Gerhard Weikum
  *Max-Planck Institute of Computer Science, Saarbruecken, Germany*

3896

Yannis Ioannidis   Marc H. Scholl
Joachim W. Schmidt   Florian Matthes
Mike Hatzopoulos   Klemens Boehm
Alfons Kemper   Torsten Grust
Christian Boehm (Eds.)

# Advances in Database Technology – EDBT 2006

10th International Conference on Extending Database Technology
Munich, Germany, March 26-31, 2006
Proceedings

Springer

Volume Editors

Yannis Ioannidis
E-mail: yannis@di.uoa.gr
Marc H. Scholl
E-mail: Marc.Scholl@uni-konstanz.de
Joachim W. Schmidt
E-mail: j.w.schmidt@tu-harburg.de
Florian Matthes
E-mail: matthes@in.tum.de
Mike Hatzopoulos
E-mail: mike@di.uoa.gr
Klemens Boehm
E-mail: boehm@ipd.uka.de
Alfons Kemper
E-mail: Alfons.Kemper@in.tum.de
Torsten Grust
E-mail: grust@in.tum.de
Christian Boehm
E-mail: boehm@dbs.ifi.lmu.de

Library of Congress Control Number: 2006922026

CR Subject Classification (1998): H.2, H.4, H.3, C.2.4, K.4.4

LNCS Sublibrary: SL 3 – Information Systems and Application, incl. Internet/Web and HCI

| | |
|---|---|
| ISSN | 0302-9743 |
| ISBN-10 | 3-540-32960-9 Springer Berlin Heidelberg New York |
| ISBN-13 | 978-3-540-32960-2 Springer Berlin Heidelberg New York |

This work is subject to copyright. All rights are reserved, whether the whole or part of the material is concerned, specifically the rights of translation, reprinting, re-use of illustrations, recitation, broadcasting, reproduction on microfilms or in any other way, and storage in data banks. Duplication of this publication or parts thereof is permitted only under the provisions of the German Copyright Law of September 9, 1965, in its current version, and permission for use must always be obtained from Springer. Violations are liable to prosecution under the German Copyright Law.

Springer is a part of Springer Science+Business Media

springer.com

© Springer-Verlag Berlin Heidelberg 2006
Printed in Germany

Typesetting: Camera-ready by author, data conversion by Scientific Publishing Services, Chennai, India
Printed on acid-free paper   SPIN: 11687238   06/3142   5 4 3 2 1 0

# Preface

The series of International Conferences on Extending Database Technology (EDBT) is an established and prestigious forum for the exchange of the latest research results in data management. It provides unique opportunities for database researchers, practitioners, developers, and users to explore new ideas, techniques, and tools, and to exchange experiences. This volume contains the proceedings of the 10th EDBT Conference, held in Munich, Germany, March 27-29, 2006. The conference included 3 keynote talks, 56 full-size and 4 half-size research papers in 20 sessions, 8 industrial presentations in 3 sessions, 1 panel session, 5 tutorials in 7 sessions, and 20 demonstrations in 4 sessions. All of the research papers as well as papers and abstracts from most of the other sessions are included here.

Distinguished members of the database and information-retrieval communities delivered the three keynotes, which were all in the spirit of the banner theme chosen for EDBT 2006: "From Database Systems to Universal Data Management." Martin Kersten, a pioneer in the area of database support for ambient application environments and the investigator of several kernel database architectures, discussed various hard issues that arise in organic database systems, i.e., systems that can be embedded in several hardware applications and have autonomic behavior. Alan Smeaton, a leader in content-based retrieval of information in a wide variety of media, introduced us to the world of digital video libraries and challenged us with several open problems associated with their effective management. Finally, David Maier, whose introduction of object-oriented concepts to the field has been pivotal for the establishment of object-relational databases as the current state of the art, used the Lewis and Clark expedition as an analogy to discuss the problems faced when trying to deploy dataspace systems, i.e., systems that manage enterprise data in the entire spectrum from fully structured to completely unstructured.

The Research Program Committee consisted of 76 members and was chaired by Yannis Ioannidis (University of Athens). It accepted 60 papers (56 regular-size and 4 half-size) out of 352 submissions, both of which are the largest numbers ever for EDBT. Papers were submitted from 37 countries. The reviewing process was managed by the Microsoft Conference Management Toolkit, developed and supported by Surajit Chaudhuri and the CMT team (from Microsoft Research).

The Industrial and Applications Program was assembled by a small committee under Alfons Kemper (Technical University of Munich). The 8 short papers that appear in the proceedings were selected from 28 submissions.

One panel session was solicited by Klemens Böhm (University of Karlsruhe), who also selected five tutorials out of ten submissions.

Christian Böhm (University of Munich) led a 14-member committee in putting together the Demonstrations Program, consisting of 20 demonstrations selected from 52 submitted proposals.

Mike Hatzopoulos (University of Athens) edited the proceedings. He also produced an electronic version for inclusion in the SIGMOD digital library and for posting on the Web prior to the conference.

The program and social activities of EDBT 2006 are the result of a huge effort by many hundreds of authors, reviewers, presenters, and organizers. We thank them all for helping to make the conference a success. In particular, we want to thank Gisela Krügel and Josef Lankes (both from the Technical University of Munich) for the smooth local organization.

Finally, this 10th edition of the EDBT Conference series coincides with the year of retirement of Joachim Schmidt, who was one of the "fathers" of EDBT. The success of the EDBT Association, its conferences, and services to the community is largely due to the effort and expertise that its founders invested. As a tribute to Joachim's commitment and dedication to EDBT, the organizers invited Joachim as an Honorary Chair of this year's conference. Thank you Joachim for all these years!

| | |
|---|---|
| Yannis Ioannidis | Program Chair |
| Marc H. Scholl | General Chair |
| Florian Matthes | Executive Chair |
| Michael Hatzopoulos | Proceedings Chair |
| Klemens Böhm | Panel and Tutorial Chair |
| Alfons Kemper | Industrial and Applications Chair |
| Torsten Grust | Workshop Chair |
| Christian Böhm | Demonstrations Chair |

# Table of Contents

## Invited Lectures

Database Architecture Fertilizers: Just-in-Time, Just-Enough, and Autonomous Growth
  *Martin Kersten* ............................................................. 1

Digital Video: Just Another Data Stream?
  *Alan F. Smeaton* ............................................................ 2

Charting a Dataspace: Lessons from Lewis and Clark
  *David Maier* ................................................................ 3

## Data Streams

Fast Approximate Wavelet Tracking on Streams
  *Graham Cormode, Minos Garofalakis,
  Dimitris Sacharidis* ......................................................... 4

Resource Adaptive Periodicity Estimation of Streaming Data
  *Michail Vlachos, Deepak S. Turaga,
  Philip S. Yu* ............................................................... 23

On Futuristic Query Processing in Data Streams
  *Charu C. Aggarwal* ......................................................... 41

## Semantic Heterogeneity

Detecting Similarities in Ontologies with the SOQA-SimPack Toolkit
  *Patrick Ziegler, Christoph Kiefer,
  Christoph Sturm, Klaus R. Dittrich,
  Abraham Bernstein* .......................................................... 59

Holistic Schema Matching for Web Query Interfaces
  *Weifeng Su, Jiying Wang,
  Frederick Lochovsky* ........................................................ 77

Data Mapping as Search
  *George H.L. Fletcher, Catharine M. Wyss* ................................... 95

## Distributed Databases

Parallelizing Skyline Queries for Scalable Distribution
  *Ping Wu, Caijie Zhang, Ying Feng, Ben Y. Zhao, Divyakant Agrawal,
  Amr El Abbadi* .................................................. 112

Replication, Load Balancing and Efficient Range Query Processing in
DHTs
  *Theoni Pitoura, Nikos Ntarmos, Peter Triantafillou* ............... 131

IQN Routing: Integrating Quality and Novelty in P2P Querying and
Ranking
  *Sebastian Michel, Matthias Bender, Peter Triantafillou,
  Gerhard Weikum* ................................................... 149

## Multidimensionality and Nearest-Neighbor Searches

Efficient Quantile Retrieval on Multi-dimensional Data
  *Man Lung Yiu, Nikos Mamoulis, Yufei Tao* ......................... 167

Fast Nearest Neighbor Search on Road Networks
  *Haibo Hu, Dik Lun Lee, Jianliang Xu* ............................. 186

Approximation Techniques to Enable Dimensionality Reduction for
Voronoi-Based Nearest Neighbor Search
  *Christoph Brochhaus, Marc Wichterich,
  Thomas Seidl* ..................................................... 204

## Privacy and Security

Authorization-Transparent Access Control for XML Under the
Non-Truman Model
  *Yaron Kanza, Alberto O. Mendelzon, Renée J. Miller,
  Zheng Zhang* ...................................................... 222

On Honesty in Sovereign Information Sharing
  *Rakesh Agrawal, Evimaria Terzi* .................................. 240

## Temporal Data Management

Multi-dimensional Aggregation for Temporal Data
  *Michael Böhlen, Johann Gamper,
  Christian S. Jensen* .............................................. 257

Similarity Search on Time Series Based on Threshold Queries
  *Johannes Aßfalg, Hans-Peter Kriegel, Peer Kröger, Peter Kunath,
  Alexey Pryakhin, Matthias Renz* .................................. 276

Supporting Temporal Slicing in XML Databases
  *Federica Mandreoli, Riccardo Martoglia, Enrico Ronchetti* .......... 295

## Text Databases and Information Retrieval

Indexing Shared Content in Information Retrieval Systems
  *Andrei Z. Broder, Nadav Eiron, Marcus Fontoura,
  Michael Herscovici, Ronny Lempel, John McPherson, Runping Qi,
  Eugene Shekita* .................................................... 313

Feedback-Driven Structural Query Expansion for Ranked Retrieval of
XML Data
  *Ralf Schenkel, Martin Theobald* .................................... 331

Expressiveness and Performance of Full-Text Search Languages
  *Chavdar Botev, Sihem Amer-Yahia,
  Jayavel Shanmugasundaram* ........................................... 349

## Schema Management

Model-Independent Schema and Data Translation
  *Paolo Atzeni, Paolo Cappellari, Philip A. Bernstein* ............... 368

Physical Design Refinement: The "Merge-Reduce" Approach
  *Nicolas Bruno, Surajit Chaudhuri* .................................. 386

Online, Non-blocking Relational Schema Changes
  *Jørgen Løland, Svein-Olaf Hvasshovd* ............................... 405

## Approximation and Estimation

Deferred Maintenance of Disk-Based Random Samples
  *Rainer Gemulla, Wolfgang Lehner* ................................... 423

Exploiting Cluster Analysis for Constructing Multi-dimensional
Histograms on Both Static and Evolving Data
  *Filippo Furfaro, Giuseppe M. Mazzeo,
  Cristina Sirangelo* ................................................. 442

HASE: A Hybrid Approach to Selectivity Estimation for Conjunctive
Predicates
*Xiaohui Yu, Nick Koudas, Calisto Zuzarte* .......................... 460

## Data and Query Patterns

On High Dimensional Skylines
*Chee-Yong Chan, H.V. Jagadish, Kian-Lee Tan, Anthony K.H. Tung,
Zhenjie Zhang* ................................................ 478

From Analysis to Interactive Exploration: Building Visual Hierarchies
from OLAP Cubes
*Svetlana Vinnik, Florian Mansmann* ............................. 496

DPTree: A Distributed Pattern Tree Index for Partial-Match Queries
in Peer-to-Peer Networks
*Dyce Jing Zhao, Dik Lun Lee, Qiong Luo* ........................ 515

## XML Queries and Updates

A Decomposition-Based Probabilistic Framework for Estimating the
Selectivity of XML Twig Queries
*Chao Wang, Srinivasan Parthasarathy, Ruoming Jin* .............. 533

Conflicting XML Updates
*Mukund Raghavachari, Oded Shmueli* ........................... 552

Improving the Efficiency of XPath Execution on Relational Systems
*Haris Georgiadis, Vasilis Vassalos* ............................... 570

## Data Streams and Pub/Sub Systems

Bridging Physical and Virtual Worlds: Complex Event Processing for
RFID Data Streams
*Fusheng Wang, Shaorong Liu, Peiya Liu, Yijian Bai* .............. 588

On Concurrency Control in Sliding Window Queries over Data Streams
*Lukasz Golab, Kumar Gaurav Bijay, M. Tamer Özsu* ............. 608

Towards Expressive Publish/Subscribe Systems
*Alan Demers, Johannes Gehrke, Mingsheng Hong, Mirek Riedewald,
Walker White* ................................................. 627

## Data Mining and Knowledge Discovery

Finding Data Broadness Via Generalized Nearest Neighbors
  *Jayendra Venkateswaran, Tamer Kahveci,
  Orhan Camoglu* .................................................. 645

TrajPattern: Mining Sequential Patterns from Imprecise Trajectories of
Mobile Objects
  *Jiong Yang, Meng Hu* ........................................... 664

On Exploring the Power-Law Relationship in the Itemset Support
Distribution
  *Kun-Ta Chuang, Jiun-Long Huang, Ming-Syan Chen* ............... 682

## Images, Multimedia, and User Interfaces

Fast Query Point Movement Techniques with Relevance Feedback for
Content-Based Image Retrieval
  *Danzhou Liu, Kien A. Hua, Khanh Vu, Ning Yu* .................. 700

On Fast Non-metric Similarity Search by Metric Access Methods
  *Tomáš Skopal* .................................................. 718

Constructing a Generic Natural Language Interface for an XML
Database
  *Yunyao Li, Huahai Yang, H.V. Jagadish* ........................ 737

## XML Data Management

A New Design for a Native XML Storage and Indexing Manager
  *Jihad Boulos, Shant Karakashian* .............................. 755

XML Duplicate Detection Using Sorted Neighborhoods
  *Sven Puhlmann, Melanie Weis, Felix Naumann* ................... 773

Handling Interlinked XML Instances on the Web
  *Erik Behrends, Oliver Fritzen, Wolfgang May* .................. 792

## Query Optimization

Query Planning in the Presence of Overlapping Sources
  *Jens Bleiholder, Samir Khuller, Felix Naumann, Louiqa Raschid,
  Yao Wu* ........................................................ 811

Optimizing Monitoring Queries over Distributed Data
  *Frank Neven, Dieter Van de Craen* .............................. 829

Progressive Query Optimization for Federated Queries
  *Stephan Ewen, Holger Kache, Volker Markl,
  Vijayshankar Raman* ............................................ 847

## Data Structures and Indexing

Indexing Spatially Sensitive Distance Measures Using Multi-resolution Lower Bounds
  *Vebjorn Ljosa, Arnab Bhattacharya, Ambuj K. Singh* .............. 865

Indexing Incomplete Databases
  *Guadalupe Canahuate, Michael Gibas,
  Hakan Ferhatosmanoglu* .......................................... 884

FlexInd: A Flexible and Parameterizable Air-Indexing Scheme for Data Broadcast Systems
  *André Seifert, Jen-Jou Hung* ................................... 902

## Nontraditional Query Processing

Multi-query SQL Progress Indicators
  *Gang Luo, Jeffrey F. Naughton, Philip S. Yu* ................... 921

Finding Equivalent Rewritings in the Presence of Arithmetic Comparisons
  *Foto Afrati, Rada Chirkova, Manolis Gergatsoulis,
  Vassia Pavlaki* ................................................. 942

Fast Computation of Reachability Labeling for Large Graphs
  *Jiefeng Cheng, Jeffrey Xu Yu, Xuemin Lin, Haixun Wang,
  Philip S. Yu* ................................................... 961

## Spatial Data Management

Distributed Spatial Clustering in Sensor Networks
  *Anand Meka, Ambuj K. Singh* .................................... 980

SCUBA: Scalable Cluster-Based Algorithm for Evaluating Continuous Spatio-temporal Queries on Moving Objects
  *Rimma V. Nehme, Elke A. Rundensteiner* ......................... 1001

Caching Complementary Space for Location-Based Services
  *Ken C.K. Lee, Wang-Chien Lee, Baihua Zheng,*
  *Jianliang Xu* .................................................... 1020

## Extending Data Base Technology

Evolving Triggers for Dynamic Environments
  *Goce Trajcevski, Peter Scheuermann, Oliviu Ghica, Annika Hinze,*
  *Agnes Voisard* .................................................. 1039

A Framework for Distributed XML Data Management
  *Serge Abiteboul, Ioana Manolescu,*
  *Emanuel Taropa* ................................................. 1049

Querying and Updating Probabilistic Information in XML
  *Serge Abiteboul, Pierre Senellart* ............................... 1059

An ECA Rule Rewriting Mechanism for Peer Data Management Systems
  *Dan Zhao, John Mylopoulos, Iluju Kiringa,*
  *Verena Kantere* .................................................. 1069

## Industrial Session

## Business Intelligence

A Metric Definition, Computation, and Reporting Model for Business Operation Analysis
  *Fabio Casati, Malu Castellanos, Umeshwar Dayal,*
  *Ming-Chien Shan* ................................................. 1079

BISON: Providing Business Information Analysis as a Service
  *Hakan Hacıgümüş, James Rhodes, Scott Spangler,*
  *Jeffrey Kreulen* ................................................. 1084

The Design and Architecture of the $\tau$-Synopses System
  *Yossi Matias, Leon Portman, Natasha Drukh* ....................... 1088

## Database System Enhancements

Integrating a Maximum-Entropy Cardinality Estimator into DB2 UDB
  *Marcel Kutsch, Peter J. Haas, Volker Markl, Nimrod Megiddo,*
  *Tam Minh Tran* ................................................... 1092

Improving DB2 Performance Expert - A Generic Analysis Framework
*Laurent Mignet, Jayanta Basak, Manish Bhide, Prasan Roy, Sourashis Roy, Vibhuti S. Sengar, Ranga R. Vatsavai, Michael Reichert, Torsten Steinbach, D.V.S. Ravikant, Soujanya Vadapalli* .......................................................... 1097

Managing Collections of XML Schemas in Microsoft SQL Server 2005
*Shankar Pal, Dragan Tomic, Brandon Berg, Joe Xavier* .................................................................... 1102

## Business Data Processing

Enabling Outsourced Service Providers to Think Globally While Acting Locally
*Kevin Wilkinson, Harumi Kuno, Kannan Govindarajan, Kei Yuasa, Kevin Smathers, Jyotirmaya Nanda, Umeshwar Dayal* ................................................................. 1106

Another Example of a Data Warehouse System Based on Transposed Files
*Antonio Albano, Luca De Rosa, Lucio Goglia, Roberto Goglia, Vincenzo Minei, Cristian Dumitrescu* .............................................................. 1110

## Demonstration Papers

XG: A Grid-Enabled Query Processing Engine
*Radu Sion, Ramesh Natarajan, Inderpal Narang, Thomas Phan* ................................................................... 1115

Managing and Querying Versions of Multiversion Data Warehouse
*Robert Wrembel, Tadeusz Morzy* .................................. 1121

Natix Visual Interfaces
*A. Böhm, M. Brantner, C-C. Kanne, N. May, G. Moerkotte* ....... 1125

Hermes - A Framework for Location-Based Data Management
*Nikos Pelekis, Yannis Theodoridis, Spyros Vosinakis, Themis Panayiotopoulos* .......................................... 1130

TeNDaX, a Collaborative Database-Based Real-Time Editor System
*Stefania Leone, Thomas B. Hodel-Widmer, Michael Boehlen, Klaus R. Dittrich* ................................................. 1135

Synopses Reconciliation Via Calibration in the $\tau$-Synopses System
*Yariv Matia, Yossi Matias,
Leon Portman* .................................................. 1139

X-Evolution: A System for XML Schema Evolution and Document Adaptation
*Marco Mesiti, Roberto Celle, Matteo A. Sorrenti,
Giovanna Guerrini* ............................................. 1143

TQuEST: Threshold Query Execution for Large Sets of Time Series
*Johannes Aßfalg, Hans-Peter Kriegel, Peer Kröger, Peter Kunath,
Alexey Pryakhin, Matthias Renz* ................................ 1147

VICO: Visualizing Connected Object Orderings
*Stefan Brecheisen, Hans-Peter Kriegel, Matthias Schubert,
Michael Gruber* ................................................ 1151

XQueryViz: An XQuery Visualization Tool
*Jihad Boulos, Marcel Karam, Zeina Koteiche,
Hala Ollaic* ................................................... 1155

SAT: Spatial Awareness from Textual Input
*Dmitri V. Kalashnikov, Yiming Ma, Sharad Mehrotra,
Ramaswamy Hariharan, Nalini Venkatasubramanian,
Naveen Ashish* ................................................. 1159

MUSCLE: Music Classification Engine with User Feedback
*Stefan Brecheisen, Hans-Peter Kriegel, Peter Kunath,
Alexey Pryakhin, Florian Vorberger* ............................ 1164

iMONDRIAN: A Visual Tool to Annotate and Query Scientific Databases
*Floris Geerts, Anastasios Kementsietsidis,
Diego Milano* .................................................. 1168

The SIRUP Ontology Query API in Action
*Patrick Ziegler, Christoph Sturm, Klaus R. Dittrich* ............ 1172

Querying Mediated Geographic Data Sources
*Mehdi Essid, François-Marie Colonna, Omar Boucelma,
Abdelkader Betari* ............................................. 1176

FIS-by-Step: Visualization of the Fast Index Scan for Nearest Neighbor Queries
*Elke Achtert, Dominik Schwald* ................................. 1182

*ArHeX*: An Approximate Retrieval System for Highly Heterogeneous XML Document Collections
*Ismael Sanz, Marco Mesiti, Giovanna Guerrini, Rafael Berlanga Llavori* .................................... 1186

MonetDB/XQuery—Consistent and Efficient Updates on the Pre/Post Plane
*Peter Boncz, Jan Flokstra, Torsten Grust, Maurice van Keulen, Stefan Manegold, Sjoerd Mullender, Jan Rittinger, Jens Teubner* ............................................... 1190

STRIDER: A Versatile System for Structural Disambiguation
*Federica Mandreoli, Riccardo Martoglia, Enrico Ronchetti* ......... 1194

An Extensible, Distributed Simulation Environment for Peer Data Management Systems
*Katja Hose, Andreas Job, Marcel Karnstedt, Kai-Uwe Sattler* ....... 1198

# Panel

Data Management in the Social Web
*Karl Aberer* ................................................ 1203

**Author Index** ................................................ 1205

# Database Architecture Fertilizers: Just-in-Time, Just-Enough, and Autonomous Growth

Martin Kersten

CWI Amsterdam, The Netherlands
Martin.Kersten@cwi.nl

**Organic Databases**

Ambient application environments call for innovations in database technology to fulfill the dream of an organic database, a database system which can be embedded in a wide collection of hardware appliances and provides an autonomous self-descriptive, self-organizing, self-repairable, self-aware and stable data store-recall functionality to its environment.

The envisioned setting consists of a large collection of database servers holding portions of the database. Each server joins this assembly voluntarily, donating storage and processing capacity, but without a "contract" to act as an obedient agent for the user in coordination of access to all other servers. They are aware of being part of a distributed database, but do not carry the burden to make this situation transparent for the application.

Applications should be prepared that updates sent to a server are either accepted, rejected with referrals, or only partly dealt with. An active client is the sole basis to exploit the distributed system and to realize the desired level of ACID properties.

The query language envisioned for this system avoids the trap to allocate unbounded resources to semantically ill-phrased, erroneous, or simply too time-consuming queries. It limits the amount of resources spent and returns a partial answer together with referral queries. The user can at any point in time come back and use the referral queries to obtain more answers.

The topics presented are part of ongoing long-term research in novel database technology based on and extending MonetDB[1].

**Biography**

Martin Kersten is professor at the University of Amsterdam and head of the Information Systems department of CWI, Amsterdam. He founded the CWI database research group in 1985. He devoted most of his scientific career on the development of database kernel software. The latest incarnation is the open-source system MonetDB, which demonstrates maturity of the decomposed storage scheme as an efficient basis for both SQL and XQuery front-ends. In 1995 he co-founded the company Data Distilleries to commercialize the data mining technology based on MonetDB technology. The company was sold to SPSS in 2003. In recent years his focus has been shifting to the implications of high demanding applications on the next generation systems. He is a member emeritus of the VLDB Endowment.

---

[1] See http://monetdb.cwi.nl

# Digital Video: Just Another Data Stream?

Alan F. Smeaton

Centre for Digital Video Processing & Adaptive Information Cluster,
Dublin City University, Glasnevin, Dublin 9, Ireland
Alan.Smeaton@dcu.ie

Technology is making huge progress in allowing us to generate data of all kinds, and the volume of such data which we routinely generate is exceeded only by its variety and its diversity. For certain kinds of data we can manage it very *efficiently* (web searching and enterprise database lookup are good examples of this), but for most of the data we generate we are not good at all about managing it *effectively*. As an example, video information in digital format can be either generated or captured, very easily in huge quantities. It can also be compressed, stored, transmitted and played back on devices which range from large-format displays to portable handhelds, and we now take all of this for granted. What we cannot yet do with video, however, is *effectively* manage it based on its actual content. In this presentation I will summarise where we are in terms of being able to automatically analyse and index, and then provide searching, summarisation, browsing and linking within large collections of video libraries and I will outline what I see as the current challenges to the field.

## Biography

Alan Smeaton is Professor of Computing at Dublin City University where he is Director of the Centre for Digital Video Processing and a member of the Adaptive Information Cluster. He was Dean of the Faculty of Computing and Mathematical Sciences from 1998 to 2004 and was Head of the School of Computer Applications from January 1999 to December 2001. His early research interests covered the application of natural language processing techniques to information retrieval but this has broadened to cover the indexing and content-based retrieval of information in all media, text, image, audio and especially digital video. Currently his major research funding is in the area of indexing and retrieval of digital video where most of his work is in the area of analysis, indexing, searching, browsing and summarisation of digital video information. Alan Smeaton was program co-chair of the ACM SIGIR Conference in Toronto in 2003, general chair of CIVR which he hosted in Dublin in 2004, and co-chair of ICME in 2005. He is a founding coordinator of TRECVid, the annual benchmarking activity for content-based video analysis and searching, hehas published over 150 book chapters, journal and conference papers and he is on the editorial boards of four journals. He holds the B.Sc., M.Sc. and PhD degrees in Computer Science from the National University of Ireland.

# Charting a Dataspace: Lessons from Lewis and Clark

David Maier

Department of Computer Science, Portland State University,
PO Box 751, Portland, OR 97207-0751, USA
maier@cs.pdx.edu

## Learning from the Past

A dataspace system (DSS) aims to manage all the data in an enterprise or project, be it structured, unstructured or somewhere between. A fundamental task in deploying a DSS is discovering the data sources in a space and understanding their relationships. Charting these connections helps prepare the way for other DSS services, such as cataloging, search, query, indexing, monitoring and extension. In this, the bicentennial of the Lewis and Clark Expedition, it is enlightening to look back at the problems and issues they encountered in crossing an unfamiliar territory. Many challenges they confronted are not that different from those that arise in exploring a new dataspace: evaluating existing maps, understanding local legends and myths, translating between languages, reconciling different world models, identifying landmarks and surveying the countryside. I will illustrate these issues and possible approaches using examples from medication vocabularies and gene annotation.

The work I describe on dataspaces is joint with Mike Franklin and Alon Halevy. Nick Rayner, Bill Howe, Ranjani Ramakrishnan and Shannon McWeeney have all contributed to the work on understanding relationships among data sources.

## Biography

Dr. David Maier is Maseeh Professor of Emerging Technologies at Portland State University. Prior to joining PSU, he taught at the OGI School of Science & Engineering at Oregon Health & Science University, and at the State University of New York at Stony Brook. He is the author of books on relational databases, logic programming and object-oriented databases, as well as papers in database theory, object-oriented technology, query processing and scientific databases. He received the Presidential Young Investigator Award from the National Science Foundation in 1984 and was awarded the 1997 SIGMOD Innovations Award for his contributions in objects and databases. He is also an ACM Fellow. His current research interests include data stream processing, superimposed information management, data product generation and forensic system reconstruction. He holds a double B.A. in Mathematics and Computer Science from the University of Oregon (Honors College, 1974) and a Ph.D. in Electrical Engineering and Computer Science from Princeton University (1978).

# Fast Approximate Wavelet Tracking on Streams

Graham Cormode[1], Minos Garofalakis[2], and Dimitris Sacharidis[3]

[1] Bell Labs, Lucent Technologies
cormode@bell-labs.com
[2] Intel Research Berkeley
minos.garofalakis@intel.com
[3] National Technical University of Athens
dsachar@dblab.ntua.gr

**Abstract.** Recent years have seen growing interest in effective algorithms for summarizing and querying massive, high-speed data streams. Randomized sketch synopses provide accurate approximations for general-purpose summaries of the streaming data distribution (e.g., wavelets). The focus of existing work has typically been on minimizing *space requirements* of the maintained synopsis — however, to effectively support high-speed data-stream analysis, a crucial practical requirement is to also optimize: (1) the *update time* for incorporating a streaming data element in the sketch, and (2) the *query time* for producing an approximate summary (e.g., the top wavelet coefficients) from the sketch. Such time costs must be small enough to cope with rapid stream-arrival rates and the real-time querying requirements of typical streaming applications (e.g., ISP network monitoring). With cheap and plentiful memory, space is often only a secondary concern after query/update time costs.

In this paper, we propose the first fast solution to the problem of tracking wavelet representations of one-dimensional and multi-dimensional data streams, based on a novel stream synopsis, the *Group-Count Sketch (GCS)*. By imposing a hierarchical structure of groups over the data and applying the GCS, our algorithms can quickly recover the most important wavelet coefficients with guaranteed accuracy. A tradeoff between query time and update time is established, by varying the hierarchical structure of groups, allowing the right balance to be found for specific data stream. Experimental analysis confirms this tradeoff, and shows that all our methods significantly outperform previously known methods in terms of both update time and query time, while maintaining a high level of accuracy.

## 1 Introduction

Driven by the enormous volumes of data communicated over today's Internet, several emerging data-management applications crucially depend on the ability to continuously generate, process, and analyze massive amounts of data in real time. A typical example domain here comprises the class of *continuous event-monitoring systems* deployed in a wide variety of settings, ranging from network-event tracking in large ISPs to transaction-log monitoring in large web-server farms and satellite-based environmental monitoring. For instance, tracking the operation of a nationwide ISP network requires monitoring detailed measurement data from thousands of network elements across several different layers of the network infrastructure. The volume of such monitoring data can easily become overwhelming (in the order of Terabytes per day). To deal effectively with the massive volume and continuous, high-speed nature of data in such environments, the *data streaming* paradigm has proven vital. Unlike conventional database query-processing engines that require several (expensive) passes over a static, archived data image, streaming data-analysis algorithms rely on building concise, approximate (but highly accurate) *synopses* of the input stream(s) in real-time (i.e., in one pass over the streaming data). Such synopses typically require space that is significantly sublinear in the size of the data and can be used to provide *approximate query answers* with guarantees on the quality of the approximation. In many monitoring scenarios, it is neither desirable nor necessary to maintain the data in full; instead, stream synopses can be used to retain enough information for the reliable reconstruction of the key features of the data required in analysis.

The collection of the top (i.e., largest) coefficients in the *wavelet transform* (or, *decomposition*) of an input data vector is one example of such a key feature of the stream. *Wavelets* provide a mathematical tool for the hierarchical decomposition of functions, with a long history of successful applications in signal and image processing [16, 22]. Applying the wavelet transform to a (one- or multi-dimensional) data vector and retaining a select small collection of the largest wavelet coefficient gives a very effective form of lossy data compression. Such *wavelet summaries* provide concise, general-purpose summaries of relational data, and can form the foundation for fast and accurate approximate query processing algorithms (such as approximate selectivity estimates, OLAP range aggregates and approximate join and multi-join queries. Wavelet summaries can also give accurate (one- or multi-dimensional) *histograms* of the underlying data vector at multiple levels of resolution, thus providing valuable primitives for effective data visualization.

Most earlier stream-summarization work focuses on minimizing the *space requirements* for a given level of accuracy (in the resulting approximate wavelet representation) while the data vector is being rendered as a stream of arbitrary point updates. However, while space is an important consideration, it is certainly not the only parameter of interest. To effectively support high-speed data-stream analyses, two additional key parameters of a streaming algorithm are: (1) the *update time* for incorporating a streaming update in the sketch, and (2) the *query time* for producing the approximate summary (e.g., the top wavelet coefficients) from the sketch. Minimizing query and update times is a crucial requirement to cope with rapid stream-arrival rates and the real-time querying needs of modern streaming applications. Furthermore, there are essential tradeoffs between the above three parameters (i.e., space, query time, and update time), and it can be argued that space usage is often the *least* important of these. For instance, consider monitoring a stream of active network connections for the users consuming the most bandwidth (commonly referred to as the "top talkers" or "heavy hitters" [6, 18]). Typical results for this problem give a stream-synopsis space requirement of $O(1/\epsilon)$, meaning that an accuracy of $\epsilon = 0.1\%$ requires only a few thousands of storage locations, i.e., a few Kilobytes, which is of little consequence at all in today's off-the-shelf systems featuring Gigabytes of main memory[1]. Now, suppose that the network is processing IP packets on average a few hundred bytes in length at rates of hundreds of Mbps; essentially, this implies that the average processing time per packet must much less than one millisecond: an average system throughput of tens to hundreds of thousands of packets per second. Thus, while synopsis space is probably a non-issue in this setting, the times to update and query the synopsis can easily become an insurmountable bottleneck. To scale to such high data speeds, streaming algorithms must guarantee provably small time costs for updating the synopsis in real time. Small query times are also important, requiring near real-time response. (e.g., for detecting and reacting to potential network attacks). In summary, we need fast item processing, fast analysis, and bounded space usage — different scenarios place different emphasis on each parameter but, in general, more attention needs to be paid to the time costs of streaming algorithms.

**Our Contributions.** The streaming wavelet algorithms of Gilbert et al. [11] guaranteed small space usage, only polylogarithmic in the size of the vector. Unfortunately, the update- and query-time requirements of their scheme can easily become problematic for real-time monitoring applications, since the whole data structure must be "touched" for each update, and every wavelet coefficient queried to find the best few. Although [11] tries to reduce this cost by introducing more complex range-summable hash functions to make estimating individual wavelet coefficients faster, the number of queries does not decrease, and the additional complexity of the hash functions means that the update time increases further. Clearly, such high query times are not acceptable for any real-time monitoring environment, and pose the key obstacle in extending the algorithms in [11] to multi-dimensional data (where the domain size grows exponentially with data dimensionality).

In this paper, we propose the first known streaming algorithms for *space- and time-efficient tracking* of approximate wavelet summaries for both *one- and multi-dimensional data streams*. Our approach relies on a novel, sketch-based stream synopsis structure, termed the *Group-Count Sketch (GCS)* that allows us to provide similar space/accuracy tradeoffs as the simple sketches of [11], while guaranteeing: (1) small, logarithmic update times (essentially touching only a small fraction of the GCS for each streaming update) with simple, fast, hash functions; and, (2) polylogarithmic query times for computing the top wavelet coefficients from the GCS. In brief, our GCS algorithms rely on two key, novel technical ideas. First, we work *entirely in the wavelet domain*, in the sense that we directly sketch *wavelet coefficients*, rather than the original data vector, as updates arrive. Second, our GCSs employ *group structures based on hashing and hierarchical decomposition* over the wavelet domain to enable fast updates and efficient binary-search-like techniques for identifying the top wavelet coefficients in sublinear time. We also demonstrate that, by varying the degree of our search procedure, we can effectively explore the tradeoff between update and query costs in our GCS synopses. Our GCS algorithms and results also naturally extend to both the standard and non-standard form of the *multi-dimensional* wavelet transform, essentially providing the only known efficient solution for streaming wavelets in more than one dimension. As

---
[1] One issue surrounding using very small space is whether the data structure fits into the faster cache memory, which again emphasizes the importance of running time costs.

our experimental results with both synthetic and real-life data demonstrate, our GCS synopses allow very fast update and searching, capable of supporting very high speed data sources.

## 2 Preliminaries

In this section, we first discuss the basic elements of our stream-processing model and briefly introduce AMS sketches [2]; then, we present a short introduction to the Haar wavelet decomposition in both one and multiple dimensions, focusing on some of its key properties for our problem setting.

### 2.1 Stream Processing Model and Stream Sketches

Our input comprises a continuous stream of update operations, rendering a data vector $a$ of $N$ values (i.e., the data-domain size). Without loss of generality, we assume that the index of our data vector takes values in the integer domain $[N] = \{0, \ldots, N-1\}$, where $N$ is a power of 2 (to simplify the notation). Each streaming update is a pair of the form $(i, \pm v)$, denoting a net change of $\pm v$ in the $a[i]$ entry; that is, the effect of the update is to set $a[i] \leftarrow a[i] \pm v$. Intuitively, "$+v$" ("$-v$") can be seen as $v$ insertions (resp., deletions) of the $i^{th}$ vector element, but more generally we allow entries to take negative values. (Our model instantiates the most general and, hence, most demanding *turnstile model* of streaming computations [20].) Our model generalizes to multi-dimensional data: for $d$ data dimensions, $a$ is a $d$-dimensional vector (*tensor*) and each update $((i_1, \ldots, i_d), \pm v)$ effects a net change of $\pm v$ on entry $a[i_1, \ldots, i_d]$.[2]

In the data-streaming context, updates are only seen *once in the (fixed) order of arrival*; furthermore, the rapid data-arrival rates and large data-domain size $N$ make it impossible to store $a$ explicitly. Instead, our algorithms can only maintain a concise *synopsis* of the stream that requires only sublinear space, and, at the same time, can (a) be maintained in small, sublinear processing time per update, and (b) provide query answers in sublinear time. Sublinear here means polylogarithmic in $N$, the data-vector size. (More strongly, our techniques guarantee update times that are sublinear in the *size of the synopsis*.)

**Randomized AMS Sketch Synopses for Streams.** The randomized *AMS sketch* [2] is a broadly applicable stream synopsis structure based on maintaining randomized linear projections of the streaming input data vector $a$. Briefly, an *atomic AMS sketch* of $a$ is simply the *inner product* $\langle a, \xi \rangle = \sum_i a[i]\xi(i)$, where $\xi$ denotes a random vector of four-wise independent $\pm 1$-valued random variates. Such variates can be easily generated on-line through standard pseudo-random hash functions $\xi()$ using only $O(\log N)$ space (for seeding) [2, 11]. To maintain this inner product over the stream of updates to $a$, initialize a running counter $X$ to 0 and set $X \leftarrow X \pm v\xi(i)$ whenever the update $(i, \pm v)$ is seen in the input stream. An *AMS sketch* of $a$ comprises several independent

---

[2] Without loss of generality we assume a domain of $[N]^d$ for the $d$-dimensional case — different dimension sizes can be handled in a straightforward manner. Further, our methods do not need to know the domain size $N$ beforehand — standard adaptive techniques can be used.

atomic AMS sketches (i.e., randomized counters), each with a different random hash function $\xi()$. The following theorem summarizes the key property of AMS sketches for stream-query estimation, where $||v||_2$ denotes the $L_2$-norm of a vector $v$, so $||v||_2 = \sqrt{\langle v, v \rangle} = \sqrt{\sum_i v[i]^2}$.

**Theorem 1 ([1, 2]).** *Consider two (possibly streaming) data vectors $a$ and $b$, and let $Z$ denote the $O(\log(1/\delta))$-wise median of $O(1/\epsilon^2)$-wise means of independent copies of the atomic AMS sketch product $(\sum_i a[i]\xi_j(i))(\sum_i b[i]\xi_j(i))$. Then, $|Z - \langle a, b \rangle| \leq \epsilon ||a||_2 ||b||_2$ with probability $\geq 1 - \delta$.*

Thus, using AMS sketches comprising only $O(\frac{\log(1/\delta)}{\epsilon^2})$ atomic counters we can approximate the vector inner product $\langle a, b \rangle$ to within $\pm \epsilon ||a||_2 ||b||_2$ (hence implying an $\epsilon$-relative error estimate for $||a||_2^2$).

### 2.2 Discrete Wavelet Transform Basics

The *Discrete Wavelet Transform (DWT)* is a useful mathematical tool for hierarchically decomposing functions in ways that are both efficient and theoretically sound. Broadly speaking, the wavelet decomposition of a function consists of a coarse overall approximation together with detail coefficients that influence the function at various scales [22]. *Haar wavelets* represent the simplest DWT basis: they are conceptually simple, easy to implement, and have proven their effectiveness as a data-summarization tool in a variety of settings [4, 24, 10].

**One-Dimensional Haar Wavelets.** Consider the one-dimensional data vector $a = [2, 2, 0, 2, 3, 5, 4, 4]$ ($N = 8$). The Haar DWT of $a$ is computed as follows. We first average the values together pairwise to get a new "lower-resolution" representation of the data with the pairwise averages $[\frac{2+2}{2}, \frac{0+2}{2}, \frac{3+5}{2}, \frac{4+4}{2}] = [2, 1, 4, 4]$. This averaging loses some of the information in $a$. To restore the original $a$ values, we need *detail coefficients*, that capture the missing information. In the Haar DWT, these detail coefficients are the differences of the (second of the) averaged values from the computed pairwise average. Thus, in our simple example, for the first pair of averaged values, the detail coefficient is 0 since $\frac{2-2}{2} = 0$, for the second it is $-1$ since $\frac{0-2}{2} = -1$. No information is lost in this process – one can reconstruct the eight values of the original data array from the lower-resolution array containing the four averages and the four detail coefficients. We recursively apply this pairwise averaging and differencing process on the lower-resolution array of averages until we reach the overall average, to get the full Haar decomposition. The final Haar DWT of $a$ is given by $w_a = [11/4, -5/4, 1/2, 0, 0, -1, -1, 0]$, that is, the overall average followed by the detail coefficients in order of increasing resolution. Each entry in $w_a$ is called a *wavelet coefficient*. The main advantage of using $w_a$ instead of the original data vector $a$ is that for vectors containing similar values most of the detail coefficients tend to have very small values. Thus, eliminating such small coefficients from the wavelet transform (i.e., treating them as zeros) introduces only small errors when reconstructing the original data, resulting in a very effective form of lossy data compression [22].

A useful conceptual tool for visualizing and understanding the (hierarchical) Haar DWT process is the *error tree* structure [19] (shown in Fig. 1(a) for our example

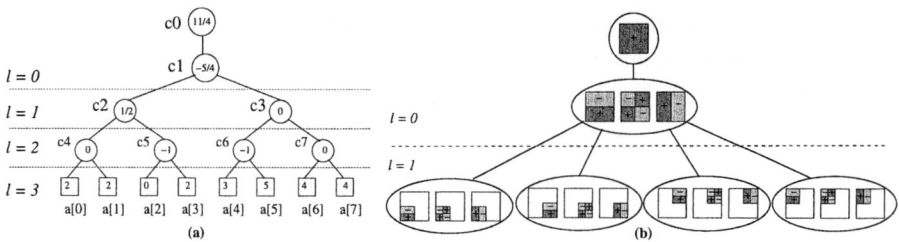

**Fig. 1.** Example error-tree structures for (a) a one-dimensional data array ($N = 8$), and (b) non-standard two-dimensional Haar coefficients for a $4 \times 4$ data array (coefficient magnitudes are multiplied by $+1$ ($-1$) in the "+" (resp., "-") labeled ranges, and 0 in blank areas)

array $a$). Each internal tree node $c_i$ corresponds to a wavelet coefficient (with the root node $c_0$ being the overall average), and leaf nodes $a[i]$ correspond to the original data-array entries. This view allows us to see that the reconstruction of any $a[i]$ depends only on the $\log N + 1$ coefficients in the path between the root and $a[i]$; symmetrically, it means a change in $a[i]$ only impacts its $\log N + 1$ ancestors in an easily computable way. We define the *support* for a coefficient $c_i$ as the contiguous range of data-array that $c_i$ is used to reconstruct (i.e., the range of data/leaf nodes in the subtree rooted at $c_i$). Note that the supports of all coefficients at resolution level $l$ of the Haar DWT are exactly the $2^l$ (disjoint) *dyadic ranges* of size $N/2^l = 2^{\log N - l}$ over $[N]$, defined as $R_{l,k} = [k \cdot 2^{\log N - l}, \ldots, (k+1) \cdot 2^{\log N - l} - 1]$ for $k = 0, \ldots, 2^l - 1$ (for each resolution level $l = 0, \ldots, \log N$). The Haar DWT can also be conceptualized in terms of vector inner-product computations: let $\phi_{l,k}$ denote the vector with $\phi_{l,k}[i] = 2^{l - \log N}$ for $i \in R_{l,k}$ and 0 otherwise, for $l = 0, \ldots, \log N$ and $k = 0, \ldots, 2^l - 1$; then, each of the coefficients in the Haar DWT of $a$ can be expressed as the inner product of $a$ with one of the $N$ distinct Haar *wavelet basis vectors*:

$$\{\frac{1}{2}(\phi_{l+1, 2k} - \phi_{l+1, 2k+1}) : l = 0, \ldots, \log N - 1; k = 0, \ldots, 2^l - 1\} \cup \{\phi_{0,0}\}$$

Intuitively, wavelet coefficients with larger support carry a higher weight in the reconstruction of the original data values. To equalize the importance of all Haar DWT coefficients, a common normalization scheme is to scale the coefficient values at level $l$ (or, equivalently, the basis vectors $\phi_{l,k}$) by a factor of $\sqrt{N/2^l}$. This normalization essentially turns the Haar DWT basis vectors into an *orthonormal basis* — letting $c_i^*$ denote the normalized coefficient values, this fact has two important consequences: (1) The *energy* of the $a$ vector is preserved in the wavelet domain, that is, $||a||_2^2 = \sum_i a[i]^2 = \sum_i (c_i^*)^2$ (by Parseval's theorem); and, (2) Retaining the $B$ largest coefficients in terms of *absolute normalized value* gives the (provably) best $B$-term approximation in terms of Sum-Squared-Error (SSE) in the data reconstruction (for a given budget of coefficients $B$) [22].

**Multi-Dimensional Haar Wavelets.** There are two distinct ways to generalize the Haar DWT to the multi-dimensional case, the *standard* and *nonstandard* Haar decomposition [22]. Each method results from a natural generalization of the one-dimensional decomposition process described above, and both have been used in a wide variety of applications. Consider the case where $a$ is a $d$-dimensional data array, comprising $N^d$

entries. As in the one-dimensional case, the Haar DWT of $a$ results in a $d$-dimensional wavelet-coefficient array $w_a$ with $N^d$ coefficient entries. The non-standard Haar DWT works in $\log N$ phases where, in each phase, *one step* of pairwise averaging and differencing is performed across each of the $d$ dimensions; the process is then repeated recursively (for the next phase) on the quadrant containing the averages across all dimensions. The standard Haar DWT works in $d$ phases where, in each phase, a *complete* 1-dimensional DWT is performed for each one-dimensional row of array cells along dimension $k$, for all $k = 1, \ldots, d$. (full details and efficient decomposition algorithms are in [4, 24].) The supports of non-standard $d$-dimensional Haar coefficients are $d$-dimensional hyper-cubes (over dyadic ranges in $[N]^d$), since they combine 1-dimensional basis functions from the same resolution levels across all dimensions. The cross product of a standard $d$-dimensional coefficient (indexed by, say, $(i_1, \ldots, i_d)$) is, in general a $d$-dimensional hyper-rectangle, given by the cross-product of the 1-dimensional basis functions corresponding to coefficient indexes $i_1, \ldots, i_d$.

Error-tree structures can again be used to conceptualize the properties of both forms of $d$-dimensional Haar DWTs. In the non-standard case, the error tree is essentially a quadtree (with a fanout of $2^d$), where all internal non-root nodes contain $2^{d-1}$ coefficients that have the same support region in the original data array but with different quadrant signs (and magnitudes) for their contribution. For standard $d$-dimensional Haar DWT, the error-tree structure is essentially a "cross-product" of $d$ one-dimensional error trees with the support and signs of coefficient $(i_1, \ldots, i_d)$ determined by the product of the component one-dimensional basis vectors (for $i_1, \ldots, d$). Fig. 1(b) depicts a simple example error-tree structure for the non-standard Haar DWT of a 2-dimensional $4 \times 4$ data array. It follows that updating a single data entry in the $d$-dimensional data array $a$ impacts the values of $(2^d - 1)\log N + 1 = O(2^d \log N)$ coefficients in the non-standard case, and $(\log N + 1)^d = O(\log^d N)$ coefficients in the standard case. Both multi-dimensional decompositions preserve the orthonormality, thus retaining the largest $B$ coefficient values gives a provably SSE-optimal $B$-term approximation of $a$.

## 3 Problem Formulation and Overview of Approach

Our goal is to continuously track a compact $B$-coefficient wavelet synopsis under our general, high-speed update-stream model. We require our solution to satisfy all three key requirements for streaming algorithms outlined earlier in this paper, namely: (1) sublinear synopsis space, (2) sublinear per-item update time, and (3) sublinear query time, where sublinear means polylogarithmic in the domain size $N$. As in [11], our algorithms return only an *approximate* synopsis comprising (at most) $B$ Haar coefficients that is provably near-optimal (in terms of the captured energy of the underlying vector) assuming that our vector satisfies the *"small-B property"* (i.e., most of its energy is concentrated in a small number of Haar DWT coefficients) — this assumption is typically satisfied for most real-life data distributions [11].

The streaming algorithm presented by Gilbert et al. [11] (termed "GKMS" in the remainder of the paper) focuses primarily on the one-dimensional case. The key idea is to maintain an AMS sketch for the streaming data vector $a$ (as discussed in Sec. 2.1). To produce the approximate $B$-term representation, GKMS employs the constructed sketch of $a$ to estimate the inner product of $a$ with all wavelet basis vectors, essentially performing an exhaustive search over the space of all wavelet coefficients to identify important ones. Although techniques based on range-summable random variables constructed using Reed-Muller codes were proposed to reduce or amortize the cost of this exhaustive search by allowing the sketches of basis vectors to be computed more quickly, the overall query time for discovering the top coefficients remains superlinear in $N$ (i.e., at least $\Omega(\frac{1}{\epsilon^2} N \log N)$), violating our third requirement. For large data domains, say $N = 2^{32} \approx 4$ billion (such as the IP address domain considered in [11]), a query can take a very long time: over an hour, even if a million coefficient queries can be answered per second! This essentially renders a direct extension of the GKMS technique to multiple dimensions infeasible since it implies an exponential explosion in query cost (requiring at least $O(N^d)$ time to cycle through all coefficients in $d$ dimensions). In addition, the update cost of the GKMS algorithm is *linear in the size of the sketch* since the whole data structure must be "touched" for each update. This is problematic for high-speed data streams and/or even moderate sized sketch synopses.

**Our Approach.** Our proposed solution relies on two key novel ideas to avoid the shortcomings of the GKMS technique. First, we work *entirely in the wavelet domain*: instead of sketching the original data entries, our algorithms sketch the wavelet-coefficient vector $w_a$ as updates arrive. This avoids any need for complex range-summable hash functions. Second, we employ *hash-based grouping* in conjunction with *efficient binary-search-like techniques* to enable very fast updates as well as identification of important coefficients in polylogarithmic time.

– *Sketching in the Wavelet Domain.* Our first technical idea relies on the observation that we can efficiently produce sketch synopses of the stream *directly in the wavelet domain*. That is, we translate the impact of each streaming update on the relevant wavelet coefficients. By the linearity properties of the DWT and our earlier description, we know that an update to the data entries corresponds to only polylogarithmically many coefficients in the wavelet domain. Thus, on receiving an update to $a$, our algorithms directly convert it to $O(\text{polylog}(N))$ updates to the wavelet coefficients, and maintain an approximate representation of the wavelet coefficient vector $w_a$.

– *Time-Efficient Updates and Large-Coefficient Searches.* Sketching in the wavelet domain means that, at query time, we have an approximate representation of the wavelet-coefficient vector $w_a$ and need to be able to identify all those coefficients that are "large", relative to the total energy of the data $\|w_a\|_2^2 = \|a\|_2^2$. While AMS sketches can give us these estimates (a point query is just a special case of an inner product), querying remains much too slow taking at least $\Omega(\frac{1}{\epsilon^2} N)$ time to find which of the $N$ coefficients are the $B$ largest. Note that although a lot of earlier work has given efficient streaming algorithms for identifying high-frequency items [5, 6, 18], our requirements here are quite different. Our techniques must monitor items (i.e., DWT coefficients) whose values increase and decrease over time, and which may very well be *negative* (even if all the data entries in $a$ are positive). Existing work on "heavy-hitter" tracking focuses solely on non-negative frequency counts [6] often assumed to be non-decreasing over time [5, 18]. More strongly, we must find items whose *squared value* is a large

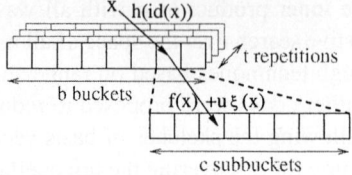

**Fig. 2.** Our Group-Count Sketch (GCS) data structure: $x$ is hashed ($t$ times) to a bucket and then to a subbucket within the bucket, where a counter is updated

fraction of the total vector energy $||w_a||_2^2$: this is a stronger condition since such "$L_2^2$ heavy hitters" may not be heavy hitters under the conventional sum-of-counts definition. [3]

At a high level, our algorithms rely on a *divide-and-conquer* or *binary-search-like* approach for finding the large coefficients. To implement this, we need the ability to efficiently estimate sums-of-squares for *groups* of coefficients, corresponding to dyadic subranges of the domain $[N]$. We then disregard low-energy regions and recurse only on high-energy groups — note that this guarantees no false negatives, as a group that contains a high-energy coefficient will also have high energy as a whole. Furthermore, our algorithms also employ *randomized, hash-based grouping* of dyadic groups and coefficients to guarantee that each update only touches a small portion of our synopsis, thus guaranteeing very fast update times.

## 4 Our Solution: The GCS Synopsis and Algorithms

We introduce a novel, hash-based probabilistic synopsis data structure, termed *Group-Count Sketch (GCS)*, that can estimate the energy (squared $L_2$ norm) of fixed groups of elements from a vector $w$ of size $N$ under our streaming model. (To simplify the exposition we initially focus on the one-dimensional case, and present the generalization to multiple dimensions later in this section.) Our GCS synopsis requires small, sublinear space and takes sublinear time to process each stream update item; more importantly, we can use a GCS to obtain a high-probability estimate of the energy of a group within additive error $\epsilon||w||_2^2$ in *sublinear time*. We then demonstrate how to use GCSs as the basis of efficient streaming procedures for tracking large wavelet coefficients.

Our approach takes inspiration from the AMS sketching solution for vector $L_2$-norm estimation; still, we need a much stronger result, namely the ability to estimate $L_2$ norms for a (potentially large) number of *groups of items* forming a partition of the data domain $[N]$. A simple solution would be to keep an AMS sketch of each group separately; however, there can be *many* groups, linear in $N$, and we cannot afford to devote this much space to the problem. We must also process streaming updates as quickly as possible. Our solution is to maintain a structure that first partitions items of $w$ into their group, and then maps groups to buckets using a hash function. Within each bucket, we apply a second stage of hashing of items to sub-buckets, each containing an atomic AMS sketch counter, in order to estimate the $L_2$ norm of the bucket. In our

---

[3] For example, consider a set of items with counts $\{4, 1, 1, 1, 1, 1, 1, 1, 1\}$. The item with count 4 represents $\frac{2}{3}$ of the sum of the squared counts, but only $\frac{1}{3}$ of the sum of counts.

analysis, we show that this approach allows us to provide accurate estimates of the energy of any group in $w$ with tight $\pm \epsilon ||w||_2^2$ error guarantees.

**The GCS Synopsis.** Assume a total of $k$ groups of elements of $w$ that form a partition of $[N]$. For notational convenience, we use a function id that identifies the specific group that an element belongs to, $\text{id}: [N] \rightarrow [k]$. (In our setting, groups correspond to fixed dyadic ranges over $[N]$ so the id mapping is trivial.) Following common data-streaming practice, we first define a basic randomized estimator for the energy of a group, and prove that it returns a good estimate (i.e., within $\pm \epsilon ||w||_2^2$ additive error) with constant probability $> \frac{1}{2}$; then, by taking the median estimate over $t$ independent repetitions, we are able to reduce the probability of a bad estimate to exponentially small in $t$. Our basic estimator first hashes groups into $b$ buckets and then, within each bucket, it hashes into $c$ sub-buckets. (The values of $t$, $b$, and $c$ parameters are determined in our analysis.) Furthermore, as in AMS sketching, each item has a $\{\pm 1\}$ random variable associated with it. Thus, our GCS synopsis requires three sets of $t$ hash functions, $h_m : [k] \rightarrow [b]$, $f_m : [N] \rightarrow [c]$, and $\xi_m : [N] \rightarrow \{\pm 1\}$ ($m = 1, \ldots, t$). The randomization requirement is that $h_m$'s and $f_m$'s are drawn from families of pairwise independent functions, while $\xi_m$'s are four-wise independent (as in basic AMS); such hash functions are easy to implement, and require only $O(\log N)$ bits to store.

Our GCS synopsis $s$ consists of $t \cdot b \cdot c$ counters (i.e., atomic AMS sketches), labeled $s[1][1][1]$ through $s[t][b][c]$, that are maintained and queried as follows:

UPDATE$(i, u)$. Set $s[m][h_m(\text{id}(i))][f_m(i)] + = u \cdot \xi_m(i)$, for each $m = 1, \ldots, t$.

ESTIMATE(GROUP). Return the estimate $\text{median}_{m=1,\ldots,t} \sum_{j=1}^{c} (s[m][h_m(\text{GROUP})][j])^2$ for the energy of the group of items GROUP $\in \{1, \ldots, k\}$ (denoted by $||\text{GROUP}||_2^2$).

Thus, the update and query times for a GCS synopsis are simply $O(t)$ and $O(t \cdot c)$, respectively. The following theorem summarizes our key result for GCS synopses.

**Theorem 2.** *Our Group-Count Sketch algorithms estimate the energy of item groups of the vector $w$ within additive error $\epsilon ||w||_2^2$ with probability $\geq 1 - \delta$ using space of $O\left(\frac{1}{\epsilon^3} \log \frac{1}{\delta}\right)$ counters, per-item update time of $O\left(\log \frac{1}{\delta}\right)$, and query time of $O\left(\frac{1}{\epsilon^2} \log \frac{1}{\delta}\right)$.*

*Proof.* Fix a particular group GROUP and a row $r$ in the GCS; we drop the row index $m$ in the context where it is understood. Let BUCKET be the set of elements that hash into the same bucket as GROUP does: BUCKET $= \{i \mid i \in [1, n] \land h(\text{id}(i)) = h(\text{GROUP})\}$. Among those, let COLL be the set of elements other than those of GROUP: COLL $= \{i \mid i \in [1, n] \land \text{id}(i) \neq \text{GROUP} \land h(\text{id}(i)) = h(\text{GROUP})\}$. In the following, we abuse notation in that we refer to a refer to both a group and the set of items in the group with the same name. Also, we write $||S||_2^2$ to denote the sum of squares of the elements (i.e. $L_2^2$) in set $S$: $||S||_2^2 = \sum_{i \in S} w[i]^2$.

Let $est$ be the estimator for the sum of squares of the items of GROUP. That is, $est = \sum_{j=1}^{c} est_j$ where $est_j = (s[m][h_m(\text{GROUP})][j])^2$ is the square of the count in sub-bucket SUB$_j$. The expectation of this estimator is, by simple calculation, the sum of squares of items in sub-bucket $j$, which is a fraction of the sum of squares of the bucket. Similarly, using linearity of expectation and the four-wise independence of the $\xi$ hash functions, the variance of $est$ is bounded in terms of the square of the expectation:

$$\mathsf{E}[est] = \mathsf{E}[||\text{BUCKET}||_2^2] \qquad\qquad \mathsf{Var}[est] \leq \tfrac{2}{c}\mathsf{E}[||\text{BUCKET}||_2^4]$$

To calculate $\mathsf{E}[||\text{BUCKET}||_2^2]$, observe that the bucket contains items of GROUP as well as items from other groups denoted by the set COLL which is determined by $h$. Because of the pairwise independence of $h$, this expectation is bounded by a fraction of the total energy. Therefore:

$$\mathsf{E}[||\text{BUCKET}||_2^2] = ||\text{GROUP}||_2^2 + E[||\text{COLL}||_2^2] \leq ||\text{GROUP}||_2^2 + \tfrac{1}{b}||w||_2^2$$
$$\text{and } \mathsf{E}[||\text{BUCKET}||_2^4] = ||\text{GROUP}||_2^4 + E[||\text{COLL}||_2^4] + 2||\text{GROUP}||_2^2 E[||\text{COLL}||_2^2]$$
$$\leq ||w||_2^4 + \tfrac{1}{b}||w||_2^4 + 2||w||_2^2 \cdot \tfrac{1}{b}||w||_2^2 \leq (1+\tfrac{3}{b})||w||_2^4 \leq 2||w||_2^2$$

since $||\text{GROUP}||_2^2 \leq ||w||_2^2$ and $b \geq 3$. The estimator's expectation and variance satisfy
$$\mathsf{E}[est] \leq ||\text{GROUP}||_2^2 + \tfrac{1}{b}||w||_2^2 \qquad\qquad \mathsf{Var}[est] \leq \tfrac{4}{c}||w||_2^4$$

Applying the Chebyshev inequality we obtain $\Pr\left[|est - \mathsf{E}[est]| \geq \lambda||w||_2^2\right] \leq \dfrac{4}{c\lambda^2}$ and by setting $c = \tfrac{32}{\lambda^2}$ the bound becomes $\tfrac{1}{8}$, for some parameter $\lambda$. Using the above bounds on variance and expectation and the fact that $|x-y| \geq ||x|-|y||$ we have,

$$|est - \mathsf{E}[est]| \geq \left|est - ||\text{GROUP}||_2^2 - \tfrac{1}{b}||w||_2^2\right| \geq \left||est - ||\text{GROUP}||_2^2| - \tfrac{1}{b}||w||_2^2\right|.$$

Consequently (note that $\Pr[|x| > y] \geq \Pr[x > y]$),

$$\Pr\left[\left|est - ||\text{GROUP}||_2^2\right| - \tfrac{1}{b}||w||_2^2 \geq \lambda||w||_2^2\right] \leq \Pr\left[|est - \mathsf{E}[est]| \geq \lambda||w||_2^2\right] \leq \tfrac{1}{8}$$

or equivalently, $\Pr\left[\left|est - ||\text{GROUP}||_2^2\right| \geq (\lambda + \tfrac{1}{b})||w||_2^2\right] \leq \tfrac{1}{8}$. Setting $b = \tfrac{1}{\lambda}$ we get $\Pr\left[\left|est - ||\text{GROUP}||_2^2\right| \geq 2\lambda||w||_2^2\right] \leq \tfrac{1}{8}$ and to obtain an estimator with $\epsilon ||w||_2^2$ additive error we require $\lambda = \tfrac{\epsilon}{2}$ which translates to $b = O(\tfrac{1}{\epsilon})$ and $c = O(\tfrac{1}{\epsilon^2})$.

By Chernoff bounds, the probability that the median of $t$ independent instances of the estimator deviates by more than $\epsilon ||w||_2^2$ is less than $e^{-qt}$, for some constant $q$. Setting this to the probability of failure $\delta$, we require $t = O\left(\log \tfrac{1}{\delta}\right)$, which gives the claimed bounds. □

**Hierarchical Search Structure for Large Coefficients.** We apply our GCS synopsis and estimators to the problem of finding items with large energy (i.e., squared value) in the $w$ vector. Since our GCS works in the wavelet domain (i.e., sketches the wavelet coefficient vector), this is exactly the problem of recovering important coefficients. To efficiently recover large-energy items, we impose a regular tree structure on top of the data domain $[N]$, such that every node has the same degree $r$. Each level in the tree induces a partition of the nodes into groups corresponding to *r-adic ranges*, defined by the nodes at that level. [4] For instance, a binary tree creates groups corresponding to dyadic ranges of size 1, 2, 4, 8, and so on. The basic idea is to perform a search over the tree for those high-energy items above a specified energy threshold, $\phi ||w||_2^2$. Following the discussion in Section 3, we can prune groups with energy below the threshold and, thus, avoid looking inside those groups: if the estimated energy is accurate, then these cannot contain any high-energy elements. Our key result is that, using such a hierarchical search structure of GCSs, we can provably (within appropriate probability bounds) retrieve all items above the threshold plus a controllable error quantity $((\phi+\epsilon)||w||_2^2)$, and retrieve no elements below the threshold minus that small error quantity $((\phi-\epsilon)||w||_2^2)$.

---

[4] Thus, the id function for level $l$ is easily defined as $\text{id}_l(i) = \lfloor i/r^l \rfloor$.

**Theorem 3.** *Given a vector $w$ of size $N$ we can report, with high probability $\geq 1-\delta$, all elements with energy above $(\phi+\epsilon)\|w\|_2^2$ (where $\phi \geq \epsilon$) within additive error of $\epsilon\|w\|_2^2$ (and therefore, report no item with energy below $(\phi-\epsilon)\|w\|_2^2$) using space of $O\left(\frac{\log_r N}{\epsilon^3} \cdot \log \frac{r \log_r N}{\phi \delta}\right)$, per item processing time of $O\left(\log_r N \cdot \log \frac{r \log_r N}{\phi \delta}\right)$ and query time of $O\left(\frac{r}{\phi \epsilon^2} \cdot \log_r N \cdot \log \frac{r \log_r N}{\phi \delta}\right)$.*

*Proof.* Construct $\log_r N$ GCSs (with parameters to be determined), one for each level of our $r$-ary search-tree structure. We refer to an element that has energy above $\phi\|w\|_2^2$ as a "hot element", and similarly groups that have energy above $\phi\|w\|_2^2$ as "hot ranges". The key observation is that all $r$-adic ranges that contain a hot element are also hot. Therefore, at each level (starting with the root level), we identify hot $r$-adic ranges by examining only those $r$-adic ranges that are contained in hot ranges of the previous level. Since there can be at most $\frac{1}{\phi}$ hot elements, we only have to examine at most $\frac{1}{\phi} \log_r N$ ranges and pose that many queries. Thus, we require the failure probability to be $\frac{\log_r N}{\phi \delta}$ for each query so that, by the union bound, we obtain a failure probability of at most $\delta$ for reporting all hot elements. Further, we require each level to be accurate within $\epsilon\|w\|_2^2$ so that we obtain all hot elements above $(\phi+\epsilon)\|w\|_2^2$ and none below $(\phi-\epsilon)\|w\|_2^2$. The theorem follows. □

Setting the value of $r$ gives a tradeoff between query time and update time. Asymptotically, we see that the update time decreases as the degree of the tree structure, $r$, increases. This becomes more pronounced in practice, since it usually suffices to set $t$, the number of tests, to a small constant. Under this simplification, the update cost essentially reduces to $O(\log_r N)$, and the query time reduces to $O(\frac{r}{\epsilon^2 \phi} \log_r N)$. (We will see this clearly in our experimental analysis.) The extreme settings of $r$ are 2 and $N$: $r=2$ imposes a binary tree over the domain, and gives the fastest query time but $O(\log_2 N)$ time per update; $r=N$ means updates are effectively constant $O(1)$ time, but querying requires probing the whole domain, a total of $N$ tests to the sketch.

**Sketching in the Wavelet Domain.** As discussed earlier, given an input update stream for data entries in $a$, our algorithms build GCS synopses on the corresponding wavelet coefficient vector $w_a$, and then employ these GCSs to quickly recover a (provably good) approximate $B$-term wavelet representation of $a$. To accomplish the first step, we need an efficient way of "translating" updates in the original data domain to the domain of wavelet coefficients (for both one- and multi-dimensional data streams).

– *One-Dimensional Updates.* An update $(i,v)$ on $a$ translates to the following collection of $\log N + 1$ updates to wavelet coefficients (that lie on the path to leaf $a[i]$, Fig. 1(a)):

$$\left(0, 2^{-\frac{1}{2}\log N} v\right), \left\{\left(2^{\log N - l} + k, (-1)^{k \mod 2} 2^{-\frac{l}{2}} v\right): \text{for each } l=0,\ldots,\log N - 1\right\},$$

where $l = 0, \ldots, \log N - 1$ indexes the resolution level, and $k = \lfloor i 2^{-l} \rfloor$. Note that each coefficient update in the above set is easily computed in constant time.

– *Multi-Dimensional Updates.* We can use exactly the same reasoning as above to produce a collection of (constant-time) wavelet-coefficient updates for a given data update in $d$ dimensions (see, Fig. 1(b)). As explained in Section 2.2, the size of this collection of updates in the wavelet domain is $O(\log^d N)$ and $O(2^d \log N)$ for standard and non-standard Haar wavelets, respectively. A subtle issue here is that our search-tree structure operates over a linear ordering of the $N^d$ coefficients, so we require a fast method for linearizing the multi-dimensional coefficient array — any simple linearization technique will work (e.g., row-major ordering or other space-filling curves).

**Using GCSs for Approximate Wavelets.** Recall that our goal is to (approximately) recover the $B$ most significant Haar DWT coefficients, without exhaustively searching through all coefficients. As shown in Theorem 3, creating GCSs for for dyadic ranges over the (linearized) wavelet-coefficient domain, allows us to efficiently identify high-energy coefficients. (For simplicity, we fix the degree of our search structure to $r = 2$ in what follows.) An important technicality here is to select the right threshold for coefficient energy in our search process, so that our final collection of recovered coefficients provably capture most of the energy in the optimal $B$-term representation. Our analysis in the following theorem shows how to set this threshold, an proves that, for data vectors satisfying the "small-B property", our GCS techniques can efficiently track near-optimal approximate wavelet representations. (We present the result for the standard form of the multi-dimensional Haar DWT — the one-dimensional case follows as the special case $d = 1$.)

**Theorem 4.** *If a d-dimensional data stream over the $[N]^d$ domain has a B-term standard wavelet representation with energy at least $\eta ||a||_2^2$, where $||a||_2^2$ is the entire energy, then our GCS algorithms can estimate an at-most-B-term standard wavelet representation with energy at least $(1 - \epsilon)\eta ||a||_2^2$ using space of $O(\frac{B^3 d \log N}{\epsilon^3 \eta^3} \cdot \log \frac{Bd \log N}{\epsilon \eta \delta})$, per item processing time of $O(d \log^{d+1} N \cdot \log \frac{Bd \log N}{\epsilon \eta \delta})$, and query time of $O(\frac{B^3 d}{\epsilon^3 \eta^3} \cdot \log N \cdot \log \frac{Bd \log N}{\epsilon \eta \delta})$.*

*Proof.* Use our GCS search algorithm and Theorem 3 to find all coefficients with energy at least $\frac{\epsilon \eta}{B}||a||_2^2 = \frac{\epsilon \eta}{B}||w||_2^2$. (Note that $||a||_2^2$ can be easily estimated to within small relative error from our GCSs.) Among those choose the highest $B$ coefficients; note that there could be less than $B$ found. For those coefficients selected, observe we incur two types of error. Suppose we choose a coefficient which is included in the best $B$-term representation, then we could be inaccurate by at most $\frac{\epsilon \eta}{B}||a||_2^2$. Now, suppose we choose coefficient $c_1$ which is not in the best $B$-term representation. There has to be a coefficient $c_2$ which is in the best $B$-term representation, but was rejected in favor of $c_1$. For this rejection to have taken place their energy must differ by at most $2\frac{\epsilon \eta}{B}||a||_2^2$ by our bounds on the accuracy of estimation for groups of size 1. Finally, note that for any coefficient not chosen (for the case when we pick fewer than $B$ coefficients) its true energy must be less than $2\frac{\epsilon \eta}{B}||a||_2^2$. It follows that the total energy we obtain is at most $2\epsilon \eta ||a||_2^2$ less than that of the best $B$-term representation. Setting parameters $\lambda, \epsilon', N'$ of Theorem 3 to $\lambda = \epsilon' = \frac{\epsilon \eta}{B}$ and $N' = N^d$ we obtain the stated space and query time bounds. For the per-item update time, recall that a single update in the original data domain requires $O(\log^d N)$ coefficient updates. □

The corresponding result for the non-standard Haar DWT follows along the same lines. The only difference with Theorem 4 comes in the per-update processing time which, in the non-standard case, is $O(d 2^d \log N \cdot \log \frac{Bd \log N}{\epsilon \eta \delta})$.

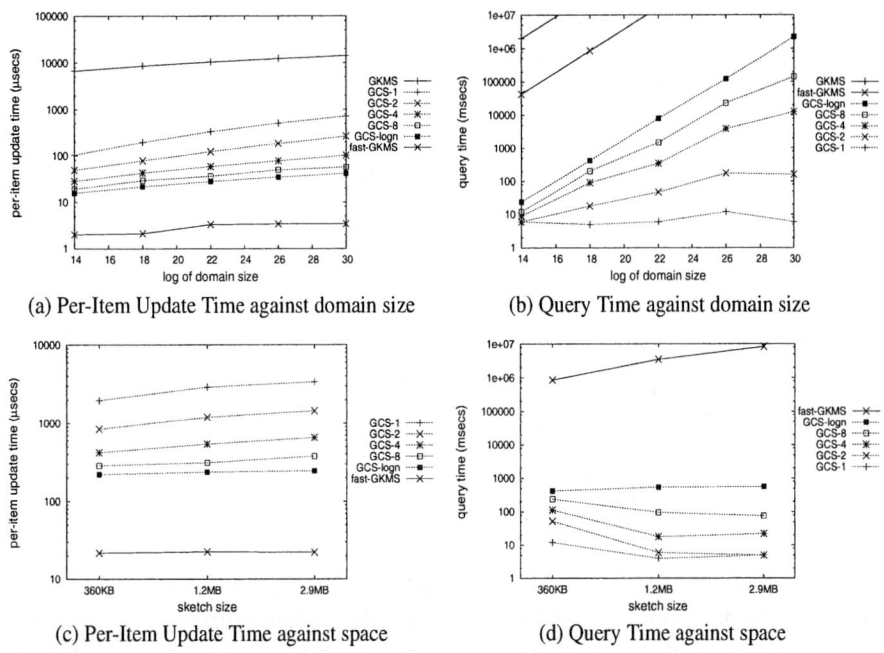

**Fig. 3.** Performance on one-dimensional data

## 5 Experiments

**Data Sets and Methodology.** We implemented our algorithms in a mixture of C and C++, for the Group-Count sketch (GCS) with variable degree. For comparison we also implemented the method of [11] (GKMS) as well as a modified version of the algorithm with faster update performance using ideas similar to those in the Group-Count sketch, which we denote by fast-GKMS. Experiments were performed on a 2GHz processor machine, with 1GB of memory. We worked with a mixture of real and synthetic data:

- *Synthetic Zipfian Data* was used to generate data from arbitrary domain sizes and with varying skewness. By default the skewness parameter of the distribution is $z = 1.1$.
- *Meteorological data set*[5] comprised of $10^5$ meteorological measurements. These were quantized and projected appropriately to generate data sets with dimensionalities between 1 and 4. For the experiments described here, we primarily made use of the AirTemperature and WindSpeed attributes to obtain 1- and 2-dimensional data streams.

In our experiments, we varied the domain size, the size of the sketch[6] and the degree of the search tree of our GCS method and measured (1) per-item update time, (2) query

---
[5] http://www-k12.atmos.washington.edu/k12/grayskies/
[6] In each experiment, all methods are given the same total space to use.

time and (3) accuracy. In all figures, GCS-k denotes that the degree of the search tree is $2^k$; i.e. GCS-1 uses a binary search tree, whereas GCS-logn uses an $n$-degree tree, and so has a single level consisting of the entire wavelet domain.

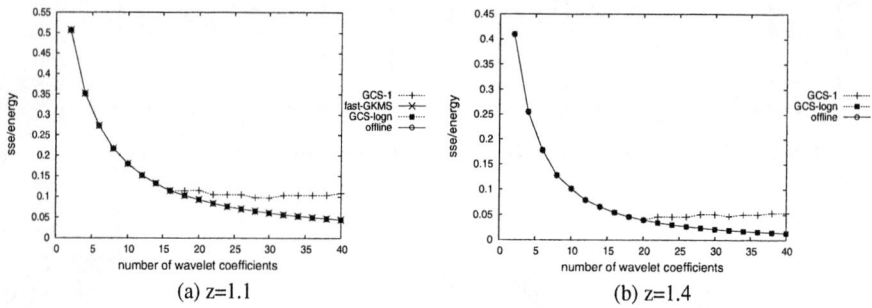

(a) z=1.1            (b) z=1.4

**Fig. 4.** Accuracy of Wavelet Synopses

**One-Dimensional Experiments.** In the first experimental setup we used a synthetic 1-dimensional data stream with updates following the Zipfian distribution ($z = 1.1$). Space was increased based on the log of the dimension, so for $\log N = 14$, 280KB was used, up to 600KB for $\log N = 30$. Figure 3 (a) shows the per-item update time for various domain sizes, and Figure 3 (b) shows the time required to perform a query, asking for the top-5 coefficients. The GKMS method takes orders of magnitude longer for both updates and queries, and this behavior is seen in all other experiments, so we do not consider it further. Apart from this, the ordering (fastest to slowest) is reversed between update time and query time. Varying the degree of the search tree allows update time and query time to be traded off. While the fast-GKMS approach is the fastest for updates, it is dramatically more expensive for queries, by several orders of magnitude. For domains of size $2^{22}$, it takes several hours to recover the coefficients, and extrapolating to a 32 bit domain means recovery would take over a week. Clearly this is not practical for realistic monitoring scenarios. Although GCS-logn also performs exhaustive search over the domain size, its query times are significantly lower as it does not require a sketch construction and inner-product query per wavelet coefficient.

Figures 3 (c) and (d) show the performance as the sketch size is increased. The domain size was fixed to $2^{18}$ so that the fast-GKMS method would complete a query in reasonable time. Update times do not vary significantly with increasing space, in line with our analysis (some increase in cost may be seen due to cache effects). We also tested the accuracy of the approximate wavelet synopsis for each method. We measured the SSE-to-energy ratio of the estimated $B$-term synopses for varying $B$ and varying zipf parameter and compared it against the optimal $B$-term synopsis computed offline. The results are shown in Figures 4 (a) and (b), where each sketch was given space 360KB. In accordance to analysis (GCS requires $O(\frac{1}{\epsilon})$ times more space to provide the same guarantees with GKMS) the GCS method is slightly less accurate when estimating more than the top-15 coefficients. However, experiments showed that increasing the size to 1.2MB resulted in equal accuracy. Finally we tested the performance of our methods

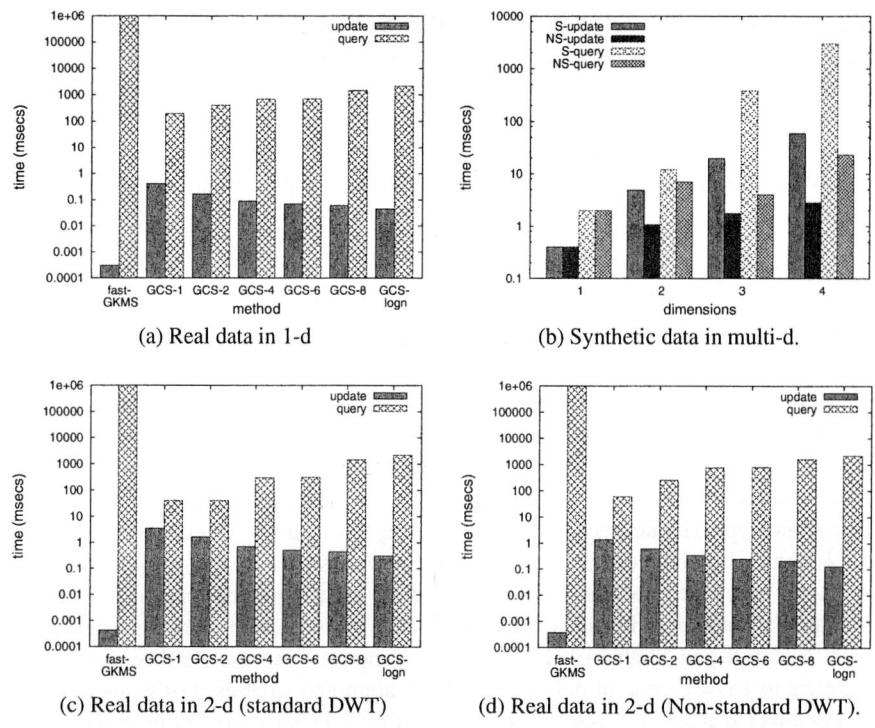

**Fig. 5.** Performance on 1-d Real Data and multi-d Real and Synthetic Data

on single dimensional meteorological data of domain size $2^{20}$. Per-item and query times in Figure 5 (a) are similar to those on synthetic data.

**Multi-Dimensional Experiments.** We compared the methods for both wavelet decomposition types in multiple dimensions. First we tested our GCS method for a synthetic dataset ($z = 1.1$, $10^5$ tuples) of varying dimensionality. In Figure 5 (b) we kept the total domain size constant at $2^{24}$ while varying the dimensions between 1 and 4. The per-item update time is higher for the standard decomposition, as there are more updates on the wavelet domain per update on the original domain. The increase in query time can be attributed to the increasing sparseness of the domain as the dimensionality increases which makes searching for big coefficients harder. This is a well known effect of multidimensional standard and non-standard decompositions. For the real dataset, we focus on the two dimensional case; higher dimensions are similar. Figure 5(c) and (d) show results for the standard and non-standard respectively. The difference between GCS methods and fast-GKMS is more pronounced, because of the additional work in producing multidimensional wavelet coefficients, but the query times remain significantly less (query times were in the order of hours for fast-GKMS), and the difference becomes many times greater as the size of the data domain increases.

**Experimental Summary.** The Group-Count sketch approach is the only method that achieves reasonable query times to return an approximate wavelet representation of data drawn from a moderately large domain ($2^{20}$ or larger). Our first implementation is capable of processing tens to hundreds of thousands of updates per second, and giving the answer to queries in the order of a few seconds. Varying the degree of the search tree allows a tradeoff between query time and update time to be established. The observed accuracy is almost indistinguishable from the exact solution, and the methods extend smoothly to multiple dimensions with little degradation of performance.

## 6 Related Work

Wavelets have a long history of successes in the signal and image processing arena [16, 22] and, recently, they have also found their way into data-management applications. Matias et al. [19] first proposed the use of Haar-wavelet coefficients as synopses for accurately estimating the selectivities of range queries. Vitter and Wang [24] describe I/O-efficient algorithms for building multi-dimensional Haar wavelets from large relational data sets and show that a small set of wavelet coefficients can efficiently provide accurate approximate answers to range aggregates over OLAP cubes. Chakrabarti et al. [4] demonstrate the effectiveness of Haar wavelets as a general-purpose approximate query processing tool by designing efficient algorithms that can process complex relational queries (with joins, selections, etc.) entirely in the wavelet-coefficient domain. Schmidt and Shahabi [21] present techniques using the Daubechies family of wavelets to answer general polynomial range-aggregate queries. Deligiannakis and Roussopoulos [8] introduce algorithms for building wavelet synopses over data with multiple measures. Finally, I/O efficiency issues are studied by Jahangiri et al. [15] for both forms of the multi-dimensional DWT.

Interest in data streams has also increased rapidly over the last years, as more algorithms are presented that provide solutions in a streaming one-pass, low memory environment. Overviews of data-streaming issues and algorithms can be found, for instance, in [3, 20]. Sketches first appeared for estimating the second frequency moment of a set of elements [2] and have since proven to be a useful summary structure in such a dynamic setting. Their application includes uses for estimating join sizes of queries over streams [1, 9], maintaining wavelet synopses [11], constructing histograms [12, 23], estimating frequent items [5, 6] and quantiles [13]. The work of Gilbert et al. [11] for estimating the most significant wavelet coefficients is closely related to ours. As we discuss, the limitation is the high query time required for returning the approximate representation. In follow-up work, the authors proposed a more theoretical approach with somewhat improved worst case query times [12]. This work considers an approach based on a complex construction of range-summable random variables to build sketches from which wavelet coefficients can be obtained. The update times remain large. Our bounds improve those that follow from [12], and our algorithm is much simpler to implement. In similar spirit, Thaper et al. [23] use AMS sketches to construct an optimal $B$-bucket histogram of large multi-dimensional data. No efficient search techniques are used apart from an exhaustive greedy heuristic which always chooses the next best bucket to include in the histogram; still, this requires an exhaustive search over a huge space. The idea of using *group-testing* techniques to more efficiently find heavy items appears in several prior works [6, 7, 12]; here, we show that it is possible to apply similar ideas to groups under $L_2$ norm, which has not been explored previously. Recently, different techniques have been proposed for constructing wavelet synopses that minimize non-Euclidean error metrics, under the time-series model of streams [14, 17].

## 7 Conclusions

We have proposed the first known streaming algorithms for space- and time-efficient tracking of approximate wavelet summaries for both one- and multi-dimensional data streams. Our approach relies on a novel, Group-Count Sketch (GCS) synopsis that, unlike earlier work, satisfies all three key requirements of effective streaming algorithms, namely: (1) polylogarithmic space usage, (2) small, logarithmic update times (essentially touching only a small fraction of the GCS for each streaming update); and, (3) polylogarithmic query times for computing the top wavelet coefficients from the GCS. Our experimental results with both synthetic and real-life data have verified the effectiveness of our approach, demonstrating the ability of GCSs to support very high speed data sources. As part of our future work, we plan to extend our approach to the problem of extended wavelets [8] and histograms [23].

## References

1. N. Alon, P. B. Gibbons, Y. Matias, and M. Szegedy. "Tracking join and self-join sizes in limited storage". In *ACM PODS*, 1999.
2. N. Alon, Y. Matias, and M. Szegedy. "The space complexity of approximating the frequency moments". In *ACM STOC*, 1996.
3. B. Babcock, S. Babu, M. Datar, R. Motwani, and Jennifer Widom. "Models and issues in data stream systems". In *ACM PODS*, 2002.
4. K. Chakrabarti, M. N. Garofalakis, R. Rastogi, and K. Shim. "Approximate query processing using wavelets". In *VLDB*, 2000.
5. M. Charikar, K. Chen, and M. Farach-Colton. "Finding frequent items in data streams". In *ICALP*, 2002.
6. G. Cormode and S. Muthukrishnan. "What's hot and what's not: Tracking most frequent items dynamically". In *ACM PODS*, 2003.
7. G. Cormode and S. Muthukrishnan. "What's new: Finding significant differences in network data streams". In *IEEE Infocom*, 2004.
8. A. Deligiannakis and N. Roussopoulos. "Extended wavelets for multiple measures". In *ACM SIGMOD*, 2003.
9. A. Dobra, M. N. Garofalakis, J. Gehrke, and R. Rastogi. "Processing complex aggregate queries over data streams". In *ACM SIGMOD*, 2002.
10. M. Garofalakis and A. Kumar. "Deterministic Wavelet Thresholding for Maximum-Error Metrics". In *ACM PODS*, 2004.
11. A. Gilbert, Y. Kotidis, S. Muthukrishnan, and M. Strauss. "One-pass wavelet decomposition of data streams". *IEEE TKDE*, 15(3), 2003.
12. A. Gilbert, S. Guha, P. Indyk, Y. Kotidis, S. Muthukrishnan, and M. Strauss. "Fast, small-space algorithms for approximate histogram maintenance". In *ACM STOC*, 2002.
13. A. Gilbert, Y. Kotidis, S. Muthukrishnan, and M. Strauss. "How to summarize the universe: Dynamic maintenance of quantiles". In *VLDB*, 2002.
14. S. Guha and B. Harb. "Wavelet Synopsis for Data Streams: Minimizing non-Euclidean Error" In *KDD*, 2005.

15. M. Jahangiri, D. Sacharidis, and C. Shahabi. "Shift-Split: I/O efficient maintenance of wavelet-transformed multidimensional data". In *ACM SIGMOD*, 2005.
16. B. Jawerth and W. Sweldens. "An Overview of Wavelet Based Multiresolution Analyses". *SIAM Review*, 36(3), 1994.
17. P. Karras and N. Mamoulis. "One-pass wavelet synopses for maximum-error metrics". In *VLDB*, 2005.
18. G.S. Manku and R. Motwani. "Approximate frequency counts over data streams". In *VLDB*, 2002.
19. Y. Matias, J.S. Vitter, and M. Wang. "Wavelet-based histograms for selectivity estimation". In *ACM SIGMOD*, 1998.
20. S. Muthukrishnan. Data streams: algorithms and applications. In *SODA*, 2003.
21. R.R. Schmidt and C. Shahabi. "Propolyne: A fast wavelet-based technique for progressive evaluation of polynomial range-sum queries". In *EDBT*, 2002.
22. E. J. Stollnitz, T. D. Derose, and D. H. Salesin. *"Wavelets for computer graphics: theory and applications"*. Morgan Kaufmann Publishers, 1996.
23. N. Thaper, S. Guha, P. Indyk, and N. Koudas. "Dynamic multidimensional histograms". In *ACM SIGMOD*, 2002.
24. J.S. Vitter and M. Wang. "Approximate computation of multidimensional aggregates of sparse data using wavelets". In *ACM SIGMOD*, 1999.

# Resource Adaptive Periodicity Estimation of Streaming Data

Michail Vlachos, Deepak S. Turaga, and Philip S. Yu

IBM T.J. Watson Research Center,
19 Skyline Dr, Hawthorne, NY

**Abstract.** Streaming environments typically dictate incomplete or approximate algorithm execution, in order to cope with sudden surges in the data rate. Such limitations are even more accentuated in mobile environments (such as sensor networks) where computational and memory resources are typically limited. This paper introduces the first "resource adaptive" algorithm for periodicity estimation on a continuous stream of data. Our formulation is based on the derivation of a closed-form incremental computation of the spectrum, augmented by an intelligent load-shedding scheme that can adapt to available CPU resources. Our experiments indicate that the proposed technique can be a viable and resource efficient solution for real-time spectrum estimation.

## 1 Introduction

Spectrum estimation, that is, analysis of the frequency content of a signal, is a core operation in numerous applications, such as data compression, medical data analysis (ECG data) [2], pitch detection of musical content [4], etc. Widely used estimators of the frequency content are the periodogram and the autocorrelation [5] of a sequence. For statically stored sequences, both methods have an $O(n \log n)$ complexity using the Fast Fourier Transform (FFT). For dynamically updated sequences (streaming case), the same estimators can be computed incrementally, by continuous update of the summation in the FFT computation, through the use of Momentary Fourier Transform [12, 9, 15].

However, in a high-rate, data streaming environment with multiple processes 'competing' over computational resources, there is no guarantee that each running process will be allotted sufficient processing time to fully complete its operation. Instead of blocking or abandoning the execution of processing threads that cannot fully complete, a desirable compromise would be for the system to make provisions for *adaptive* process computation. Under this processing model every analytic unit (e.g., in this case the 'periodogram estimation unit') can provide partial ('coarser') results under tight processing constraints.

Under the aforementioned processing model and given limited processing time, we are not seeking for results that are accurate or perfect, but only 'good-enough'. Since a typical streaming application will require fast, 'on-the-fly' decisions, we present an intelligent sampling procedure that can decide whether to retain or discard an examined sample. Our technique is based on a lightweight linear predictor, which records a sample only if its value cannot be predicted by previously seen sequence values.

Due to the sampling process, the retained data samples (a subset of the examined data window) are not guaranteed to be equi-spaced. Hence, we also elaborate on a *closed-form* periodogram estimation given *unevenly spaced* samples. We should note that the proposed method for periodogram reconstruction based on irregularly spaced samples is significantly more lightweight than the widely used Lomb periodogram [13] (which incurs a very high computational burden).

Other recent work on periodicity estimation on data streams has appeared in [6], where the authors study sampling techniques for period estimation using sublinear space. [8] proposes sampling methods for retaining (with a given approximation error) the most significant Fourier coefficients. In [11] Papadimitriou, et al., adapt the use of wavelet coefficients for modeling a data stream, providing also a periodicity estimator using logarithmic space complexity. However, none of the above approaches address the issue of resource adaptation which is one of the main contributions of our work.

In the sections that follow we will illustrate the main concepts behind the adaptive computation of the spectrum. In section 3 we describe our intelligent 'on-the-fly' sampling, and in section 4 we elaborate on the closed-form incremental computation of the periodogram from unevenly spaced data samples. Finally, section 5 provides extensive experiments that depict the accuracy and effectiveness of the proposed scheme, under given complexity constraints.

## 2 Overview of Our Approach

Considering a data streaming scenario, our goal is to provide efficient mechanisms for estimating and updating the spectrum[1] within the current data window. We use the periodogram as an estimate of the spectrum. A schematic of our resource-adaptive methodology is provided in Fig. 1.

At any given time, there might not be enough processing capacity to provide a periodogram update using all the samples within the data window. The first step toward tackling this problem is the reduction of points using an 'on-the-fly' load-shedding scheme. Sub-sampling can lead to data aliasing and deteriorate the quality of the estimated periodogram. Therefore our sampling should not only be fast but also intelligent, mitigating the impact of the sub-sampling on the squared error of the estimated periodogram. Sampling is based on a linear predictor, which retains a sample only if its value cannot be predicted by its neighbors. An estimator unit is also employed, which changes over time the 'elasticity' of the linear predictor, for proper adaptation to the current CPU load.

If there is enough CPU time to process the final number of retained samples, the spectrum is computed. Otherwise, more samples are dropped randomly and the new estimate is computed on the remaining samples.

---

[1] Note that during the course of the paper, we may use the terms periodicity estimation, spectrum estimation and periodogram estimation interchangeably.

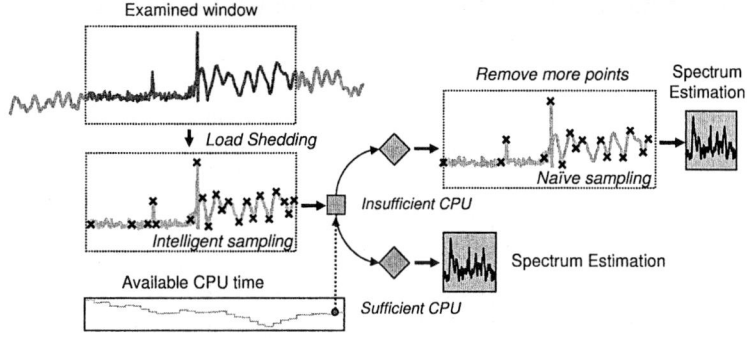

**Fig. 1.** Visual depiction of our methodology

The computation of the approximate periodogram is based on a formulation of the DFT and the periodogram using unevenly spaced samples, a necessary step due to the sampling process. Under a sliding window model, some of the previously used samples are discarded, while new samples are added in the window. The proposed periodicity estimation algorithm possesses a very simple update structure, requiring only subtraction of contributions from discarded samples and addition of contributions due to the newly included samples.

The contributions of this paper are summarized below:

- We provide an abstraction of the resource adaptation problem for periodicity estimation.
- We propose an intelligent *load-shedding* scheme along with a *parameter estimator unit* that tunes the adaptation to the current CPU load.
- We present a *closed-form Fourier approximation* using unevenly spaced samples and we show how to update it incrementally.

We analyze the performance of our proposed approach under CPU constraints, and we measure the complexity abstractly, in terms of the number of multiplications, additions and divisions involved (making the analysis independent of the underlying processor architecture). Even though our model is very spartan in its memory utilization, we do not explicitly impose any memory constraints, since this work focuses primarily on CPU adaptation. However, inclusion of potential memory constraints is a straightforward addition to our model.

### 2.1 Notation

The Discrete Fourier Transform is used to analyse the frequency content in a discrete and evenly sampled signal. In particular for a discrete time signal $x[n]$ the DFT $X[m]$ is defined for all samples $0 \leq m, n \leq N - 1$ as:

$$X[m] = \frac{1}{\sqrt{N}} \sum_{n=0}^{N-1} x[n] e^{-j\frac{2\pi nm}{N}} \quad (1)$$

The periodogram $P$ of a signal corresponds to the energy of its DFT:

$$P[m] = ||X[m]||^2 \qquad (2)$$

Consider now, a continuous signal $x(t)$ sampled unevenly at discrete time instants $\{t_0, t_1, \ldots, t_{N-1}\}$. We show an example of this in Fig. 2.

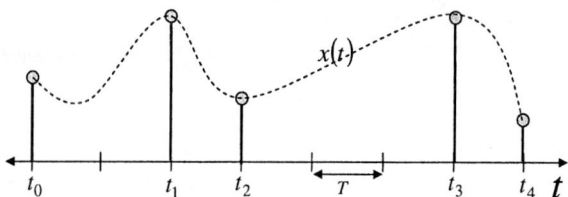

**Fig. 2.** Unevenly sampled signal

We write this unevenly sampled signal using the discrete notation as $x[k_n]$ where $t_i = k_i T (k_i \epsilon \mathbb{Z}^+)$ and $T$ corresponds to the sampling interval with all sampling instants as multiples. This is also shown in Fig. 2. In the remainder of this paper we will describe an adaptive load-shedding algorithm that retains unevenly spaced samples and we will also provide an incremental DFT estimation for such discrete signals.

We measure the complexity of all our algorithms in terms of the number of additions (subtractions), multiplications and divisions involved in the computations. Thus, we label the complexity of a single multiplication as $\xi_{Mul}$, of a division as $\xi_{Div}$ and of a sum/subtraction as $\xi_{Sub}$.

## 3 Load-Shedding Scheme

We consider the typical problem of running spectral analysis where we slide a window across the temporal signal and incrementally update the signal's DFT (and the respective periodogram). We start with an evenly sampled signal, with sampling interval $T$. Consider that the window slides by a fixed amount $Width \times T$. As a result of this sliding we discard $n_1$ points from the beginning of the signal and add $n_2$ points to the end. However, if the available CPU cycles do not allow us to update the DFT using all the points, we can adaptively prune the set of added points using uneven sub-sampling to meet the CPU constraint while minimizing the impact on the accuracy of the updated DFT.

### 3.1 Intelligent Sampling Via a Linear Predictor

We now present an algorithm (with linear complexity) for the adaptive pruning of the newly added samples. In order to decide whether we can retain a particular sample, we determine whether it can be linearly[2] predicted from its neighbors.

---

[2] Higher order predictors are also possible, but result in higher complexity.

In particular, to make a decision for sample $k_i$ we compare the interpolated value $x^{int}[k_i]$ with the actual value $x[k_i]$, where the interpolated value is computed as:

$$x^{int}[k_i] = \frac{x[k_{i-1}](k_{i+1} - k_i) + x[k_{i+1}](k_i - k_{i-1})}{k_{i+1} - k_{i-1}} \quad (3)$$

where sample $k_{i-1}$ is the last retained sample before sample $k_i$ and sample $k_{i+1}$ is the immediately following sample. If $|x^{int}[k_i] - x[k_i]| \leq \frac{Thresh \times |x[k_i]|}{100}$ we can discard the sample $k_i$, otherwise we retain it. The parameter $Thresh$ is an adaptive threshold that determines the quality of the approximation. If the threshold is large, more samples are discarded, and similarly if the threshold is small fewer samples are discarded[3]. We show an example of this interpolation scheme in Fig. 3.

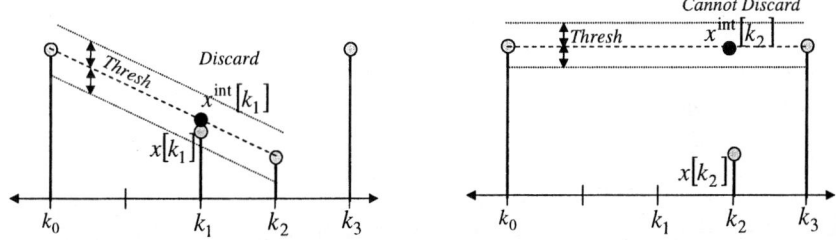

**Fig. 3.** Linear interpolation scheme for adaptive pruning of samples

In Fig. 3, we show two steps of the algorithm. In the first step, we decide that we can discard sample $k_1$ as it can be interpolated by samples $k_0$ and $k_2$. In the next step, we decide that we cannot discard sample $k_2$, as it cannot be interpolated using samples $k_0$ and $k_3$, its neighbors. If we start out with $n_2$ samples that we need to prune, the complexity of this algorithm is:

$$\xi^{interp} = (2\xi_{Mul} + 4\xi_{Sub} + \xi_{Div})(n_2 - 2) \quad (4)$$

In Section 3.2 we discuss how to tune the threshold $Thresh$ in order to obtain the desired number of $\hat{n}_2$ samples, out of the $n_2$ samples added by the sliding window.

In Fig. 4 we illustrate on a stream that measures web usage, a comparison of our intelligent sampling method against the equi-sampling technique, which samples data at a specified time interval. We execute our algorithm for a specific threshold and reduce the data points within a window from $M$ down to $N$

---

[3] Note that the squared approximation error due to this sub-sampling scheme cannot be bounded in general for all signals, however we select it for its computational simplicity. In particular, for the wide variety of signals we consider in our experiments, we do not observe squared error significantly larger than the absolute squared threshold value. Modification of this scheme to guarantee bounds on the approximation error is a direction for future research.

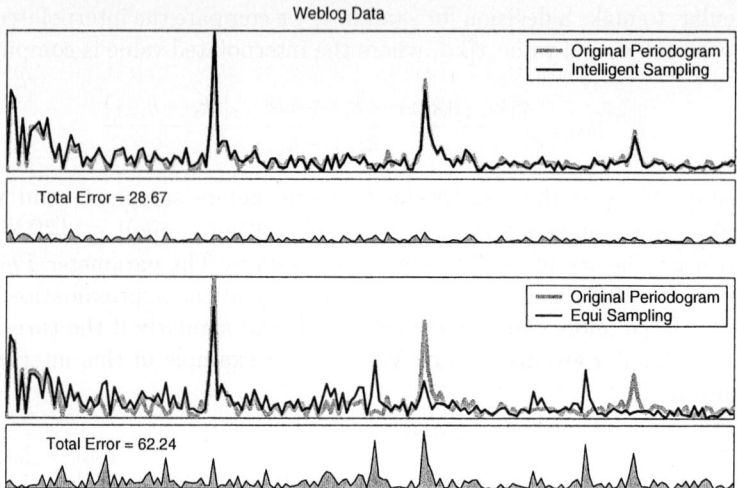

**Fig. 4.** Comparison of spectrum estimation errors for intelligent sampling and equi-sampling techniques

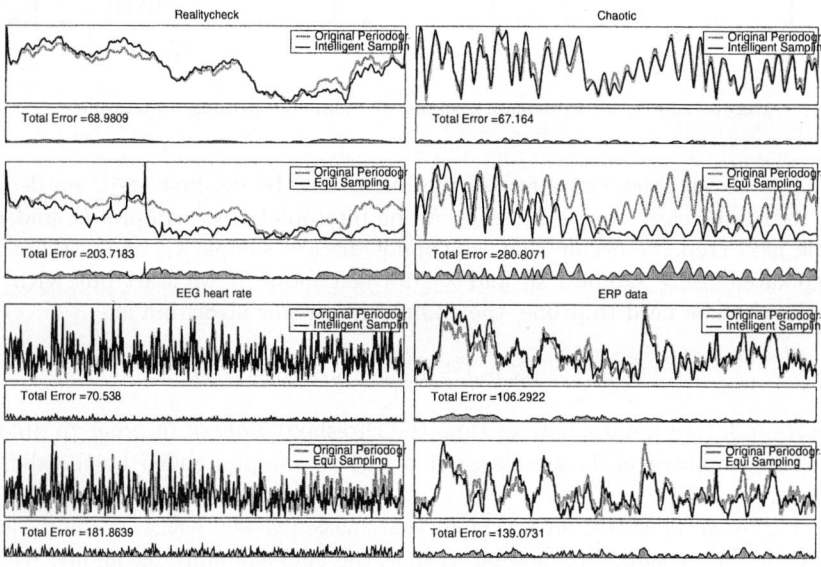

**Fig. 5.** Estimation comparisons for additional datasets

(unevenly spaced). We estimate the resulting periodogram (see section 4) as well the periodogram derived by equi-sampling every $N/M$ points. It is apparent from the figure that intelligent sampling provides a much higher quality reconstruction of the periodogram, because it can retain important features of the data stream. Additional examples on more datasets are provided in Fig. 5.

## 3.2 Threshold Estimator

The load-shedding algorithm assumes the input of a threshold value, which directly affects the resulting number of retained points within the examined window. The desirable number of final points after the thresholding is dictated by the available CPU load. An optimal threshold value would lead to

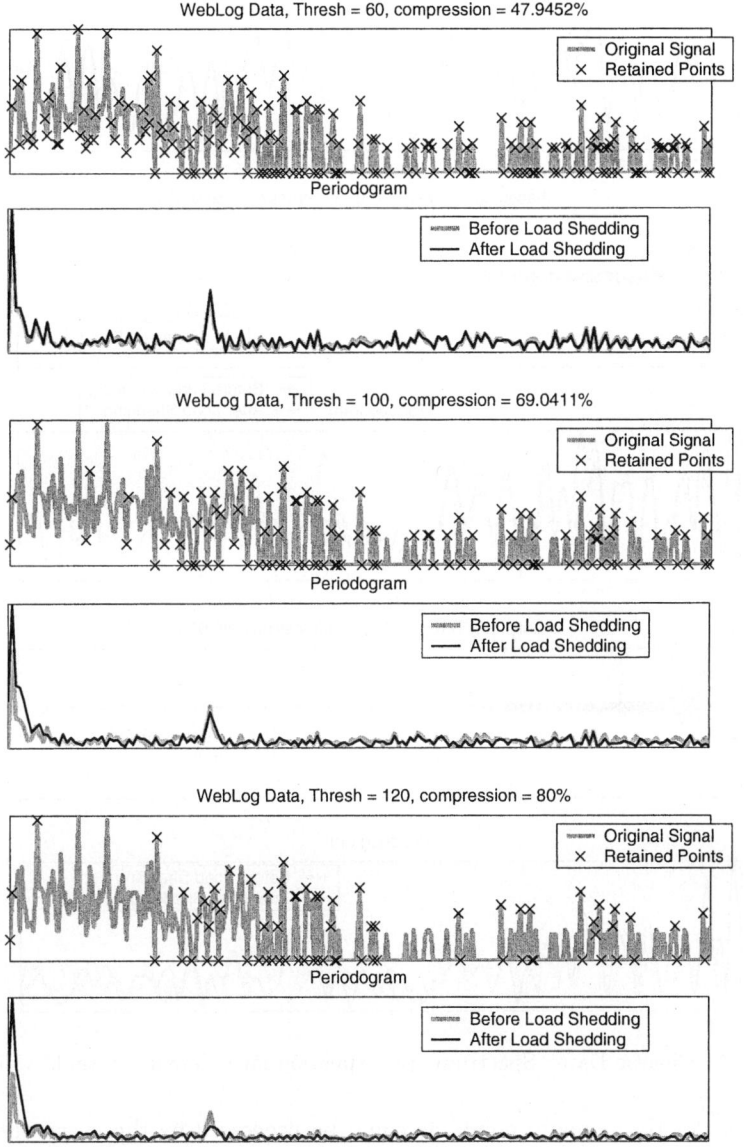

**Fig. 6.** [Weblog Data]: Spectrum approximation for different threshold values

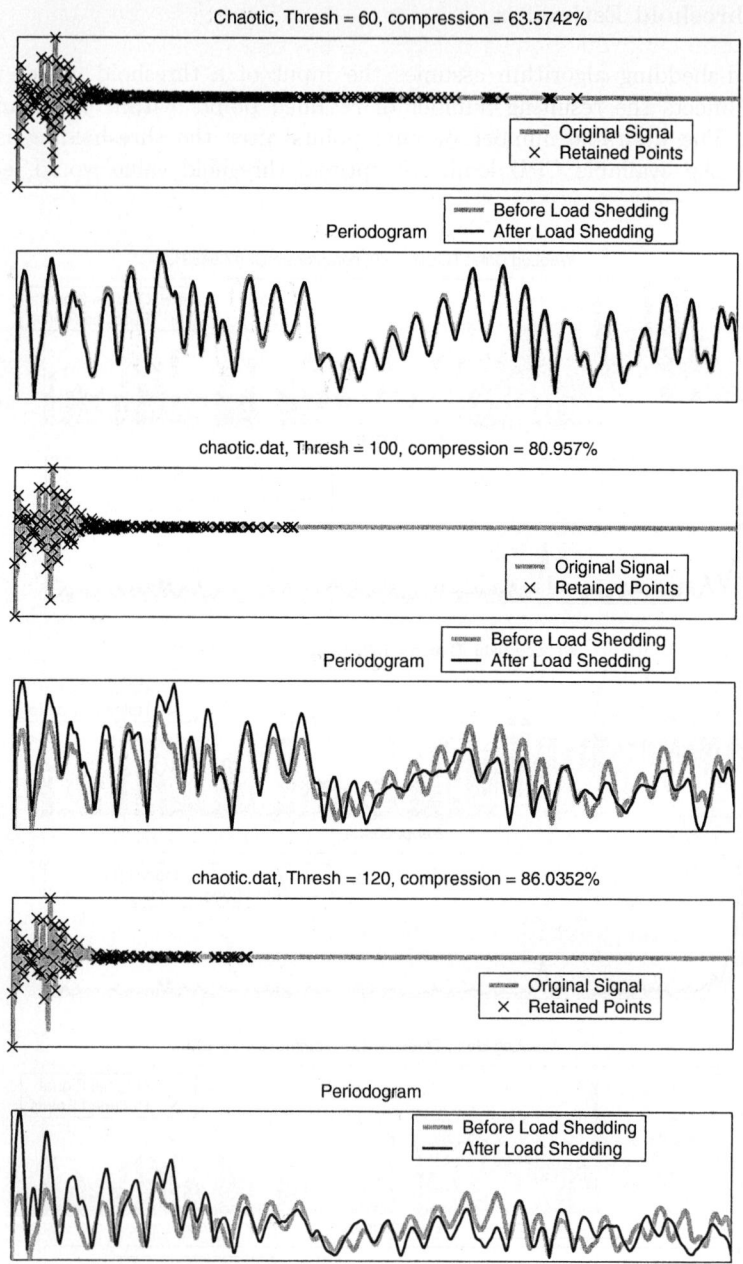

**Fig. 7.** [Chaotic Data]: Spectrum approximation for different threshold values

sampling exactly as many points as could be processed by the currently available CPU time. However, there is no way of predicting accurately the correct threshold without having seen the complete data, or without resorting to an expensive processing phase. In Figures 6 and 7 we provide various examples of the spectrum approximation for different parameters of the load-shedding threshold value.

We will provide a simple estimator of the threshold value with constant complexity, which is derived by training on previously seen portions of the data stream. The expectation is that the training will be performed on a data subset that captures a sufficient variation of the stream characteristics. The estimator will accept as input the desired number of final samples that should remain within the examined window, along with a small subset of the current data characteristics, which -in a way- describe its 'shape' or 'state' (e.g. a subset of the data moments, its fractal dimensionality, etc.). The output of the estimator is a threshold value that will lead (with high expectation) to the desirable number of window samples.

The estimator is not expected to have zero error, but it should lead *approximately* to the desired compression ratio. In the majority of cases the selected threshold will lead either to higher or lower compression ratio. Intuitively, higher compression (or *overestimated* threshold) is preferable. This is the case, because then one does not have to resort to the additional phase of dropping randomly some of the retained samples (a sampling that is 'blind' and might discard crucial points, such as important local minima or maxima). In the experiments, we empirically verify that this desirable feature is true for the threshold estimator that is presented in the following section.

## 3.3 Training Phase

Assume that $\mathcal{F}$ is a set of features that capture certain desirable characteristics of the examined data window $w$, and $\mathcal{P} \in \{0, 1, \ldots, |w|\}$ describes how many points can be processed at any given time. The threshold estimator will provide a mapping $\mathcal{F} \times \mathcal{P} \mapsto \mathcal{T}$, where $\mathcal{T}$ is a set of threshold values.

It is not difficult to imagine, that data whose values change only slightly (or depict small variance of values) do not require a large threshold value. The reverse situation exists for sequences that are 'busy', or exhibit large variance of values. With this observation in mind, we will use the *variance* within the examined window as a descriptor of the window state. Higher order moments of the data could also be used in conjunction with the variance for improving the accuracy of the predictor. However, for simplicity and for keeping the computational cost as low as possible, we select to use just the variance in our current prototype implementation.

The training phase proceeds as follows; given the training data we run a sliding window on them. For each data window we compute the variance and we execute the load-shedding algorithm for different threshold values (typically, $20, 40, \ldots, 100, 120$). After the algorithm execution the remaining number of data points is recorded. This process is repeated for all the extracted data windows. The result of this algorithm will be a set of triplets: [threshold, variance, number of points]. Given this, we can construct the estimator as a mapping $f(numPoints, variance) \mapsto Thresh$, where the actual estimator is essentially stored as a 2-dimensional array for constant retrieval time. An example of this mapping is shown in Fig. 8.

It is clear that the training phase is not performed in real-time. However it happens only once (or periodically) and it allows for a very fast prediction step.

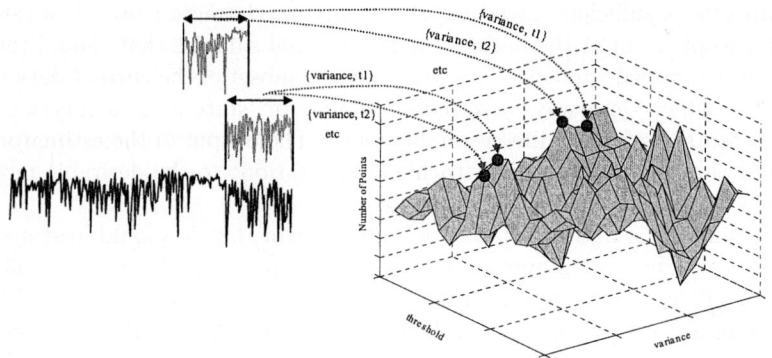

**Fig. 8.** Training phase for the threshold estimator

### 3.4 Additional Notes

There are a couple of points that we would like to bring to the attention of the reader:

1. Even though we assume that the training data will provide 'sufficient' clues on the data stream characteristics, the estimator might come upon an input of [variance, numPoints] that has not encountered during the training phase. In this case, we can simply provide the closest match, e.g. the entry that has the closest distance (in the Euclidean sense) to the given variance and number of points. Alternatively, we could provide an extrapolation of the values, in other words, explicitly learn the mapping function. This can be achieved by constructing an RBF network [1] based on the training triplets. Since this approach is significantly more expensive and could present over-fitting problems, in our experiments we follow the former alternative.
2. Over the period of time, the stream characteristics may gradually change, and finally differ completely from the training data, hence leading to inconsistent predictions. We can compensate for this by 'readjusting' the predictor, by also recording the observed threshold error during the algorithm execution. This will result in a more extended maintenance phase of the estimator, but this cost is bound to pay off in the long run for datasets that exhibit frequent 'concept drifts' [10, 7]. We do not elaborate more on this extension, but we note it as potential addition for a more complex version of the threshold estimator.

## 4 Incremental Spectrum Estimation for Unevenly Sampled Signals

Consider a signal $x[k_i], 0 \leq i \leq N-1$, as shown in Fig. 2. Since the DFT is defined only for evenly sampled signals, we implicitly recreate an evenly sampled signal before computing the DFT. For this, we again use a linear interpolator (that matches our sub-sampling algorithm), thereby reconstructing a piece-wise linear evenly sampled signal. The DFT of this evenly sampled signal may be computed in terms of the sum of contributions of each of the individual line segments that constitute it. Due to the nature of the linear interpolator the contribution of each line segment to the DFT may be analytically derived in terms of only the endpoints of the segment (i.e. samples in the original unevenly sampled signal) and the distance between them. This means that we do not actually need to interpolate the unevenly sampled signal but can derive a closed form expression for the DFT under the assumption of a linear interpolation scheme. Similar approaches to ours have also been followed in [2]. Note that while the time domain signal consists of only $N$ (uneven) samples, in order to compute the Discrete Fourier Transform (DFT) of this signal, we need to sample the DFT at least $M = k_{N-1} - k_0$ times to avoid time domain aliasing. If we denote by $X_n[m]$ the contributions to the Fourier Transform from each of the $N-1$ line segments that make up the implicitly recreated evenly sampled signal, then the DFT of the whole signal can be written as:

$$X[m] = \sum_{n=1}^{N-1} X_n[m] \qquad (5)$$

where for $m = 1, \ldots, M-1$

$$X_n[m] = \frac{1}{(k_n - k_{n-1})(\frac{2\pi m}{M})^2}[(x[k_{n-1}] - x[k_n])(e^{-j\frac{2\pi m k_{n-1}}{M}} - e^{-j\frac{2\pi m k_n}{M}}) \\ + j\frac{2\pi m}{M}(x[k_n]e^{-j\frac{2\pi m k_n}{M}} - x[k_{n-1}]e^{-j\frac{2\pi m k_{n-1}}{M}})] \qquad (6)$$

and for $m = 0$

$$X_n[0] = \frac{1}{2}(x[k_{n-1}] + x[k_n])(k_n - k_{n-1}) \qquad (7)$$

A significant benefit that equation (5) brings is that the DFT for such unevenly sampled signals can be evaluated incrementally. Hence, if we shift the window by a fixed width such that the first $n_1$ points are discarded, and $n_2$ points are added at the end, then the DFT of the signal may be updated as follows:

$$X^{new}[m] = X^{old}[m] - \sum_{n=1}^{n_1} X_n[m] + \sum_{n=N}^{N+n_2-1} X_n[m] \qquad (8)$$

We now consider the complexity of computing this update. As with several papers that analyze the complexity of the FFT, we assume that the complex exponentials $e^{\frac{j2\pi m k_n}{M}}$ (and the intermediate value $\frac{2\pi m k_n}{M}$) are considered precomputed for all $m$ and $n$. Using our labels for complexity as defined in the notation, the complexity of computing one single update coefficient $X_n[m]$ for $m = 1, \ldots, M-1$ may be represented as:

$$\hat{\xi} = 6\xi_{Mul} + 5\xi_{Sub} + \xi_{Div} \tag{9}$$

and for $m = 0$ as

$$\hat{\xi} = 2\xi_{Mul} + 2\xi_{Sub} \tag{10}$$

Finally, the complexity of updating all the $M$ DFT coefficients in this scenario is:

$$\xi^{update}(M, n_1, n_2) = (n_1 + n_2)[(M-1)(6\xi_{Mul} + 5\xi_{Sub} + \xi_{Div}) \\ + (2\xi_{Mul} + 2\xi_{Sub}) + M\xi_{Sub}] + 2M\xi_{Sub} \tag{11}$$

### 4.1 Benefit of Sub-sampling Algorithm

Using our sub-sampling algorithm we can reduce the number of samples that need to be used to update the DFT. Consider that as a result of the pruning, we can reduce $n_2$ samples into a set of $\hat{n}_2$ samples ($\hat{n}_2 \leq n_2$). While the reduction in the number of samples directly translates to a reduction in the complexity of the update, we also need to factor in the additional cost of the sub-sampling algorithm. Comparing equations (11) and (4) we realize that the overall complexity of the update (including the sub-sampling) is reduced when:

$$\xi^{update}(M, n_1, n_2) \geq \xi^{update}(M, n_1, \hat{n}_2) + \xi^{interp} \tag{12}$$

To determine when this happens, consider a simple case when $\hat{n}_2 = n_2 - 1$, i.e. the sub-sampling leads to a reduction of one sample. The increase in complexity for the sub-sampling is $(2\xi_{Mul} + 4\xi_{Sub} + \xi_{Div})(n_2 - 2)$ while the corresponding decrease in the update complexity is $(M-1)(6\xi_{Mul} + 5\xi_{Sub} + \xi_{Div}) + (2\xi_{Mul} + 2\xi_{Sub}) + M\xi_{Sub}$ (from equation (11)). Clearly, since $\hat{n}_2 < n_2 \leq M$, one can easily realize that the reduction in complexity far outweighs the increase due to the sub-sampling algorithm. In general, equation (12) is always true when the sub-sampling algorithm reduces the number of samples (i.e., when $\hat{n}_2 < n_2$).

If, at a certain time, the CPU is busy, thereby imposing a computation constraint of $\xi^{limit}$, we need to perform our DFT update within this constraint. If $\xi^{update}(M, n_1, n_2) > \xi^{limit}$ we cannot use all the samples $n_2$ for the update, and hence we need to determine the optimal number of samples to retain $\hat{n}_2$, such that $\xi^{update}(M, n_1, \hat{n}_2) + \xi^{interp} \leq \xi^{limit}$. Specifically, we may compute this as:

$$\hat{n}_2 \leq \frac{\xi^{limit} - \xi^{interp} - 2M\xi_{Sub}}{(M-1)(6\xi_{Mul} + 5\xi_{Sub} + \xi_{Div}) + (2\xi_{Mul} + 2\xi_{Sub}) + M\xi_{Sub}} - n_1 \tag{13}$$

Finally, we can achieve this by tuning the sub-sampling threshold $Thresh$ based on the algorithm described in Section 3.2.

## 5 Experiments

The usefulness of the proposed resource-adaptive periodicity estimation depends on two factors:

- The accuracy of the approach, which is indicated by the quality of the DFT approximation and its respective periodogram. If the periodogram after the load-shedding closely resembles the original one, then the provided estimate is meaningful.
- The adaptiveness of the proposed methodology, which is highly dependent on the quality of the threshold estimator. An accurate estimator will lead to sampling rates that closely adapt to the current CPU loads.

We examine separately those two factors in order to provide a more thorough and clear evaluation.

### 5.1 Quality of DFT Estimation

The quality of the approximated Fourier coefficients is measured on a variety of periodic datasets obtained from the time-series archive at UC Riverside [14]. These datasets only have a length of 1024, therefore it is difficult to provide a meaningful evaluation on the streaming version of the algorithm. However, by providing the whole sequence as input to the periodicity estimation unit we can evaluate the effectiveness of the load-shedding scheme in conjunction with the closed-form DFT computation on the unevenly spaced samples. We compute the accuracy by comparing the estimated periodogram against the actual one (had we not discarded any point from the examined data window). We run the above experiment on different threshold values $Thresh = 20\ldots 120$. For example, a value of $Thresh = 20$ signifies that the predicted value (using the linear predictor) does not differ more than 20% from the actual sequence value.

Note that the original periodogram is evaluated on a window of $M$ points ($M = 1024$), while the one based on uneven sampling uses only the $N$ remaining samples ($N \leq M$). In order to provide a meaningful comparison between them we evaluate the latter periodogram on all $M/2$ frequencies -see equation 6-, even though this is not necessary on an actual deployment of the algorithm.

We compare the accuracy of our methodology against a naive approach that uses equi-sampling every $N/M$ points (i.e., leading again to $N$ remaining points within the examined window). This approach is bound to introduce aliasing and distort more the original periodogram, because (unlike the intelligent load-shedding) it does not adapt according to the signal characteristics.

Figures 9, 10 indicate the periodogram error introduced by the intelligent and the equi-sampling techniques. On top of each bar we also portray the compression achieved using the specific threshold $Thresh$, computed as $100 * (1 - N/1024)$.

The results suggest that the load-shedding scheme employed by our technique can lead to spectrum estimates of much higher quality than competing methods. In two cases (Fig. 9, Reality Check) the equi-sampling performs better than the linear interpolator, but this occurs only for minute compression ratios (i.e.,

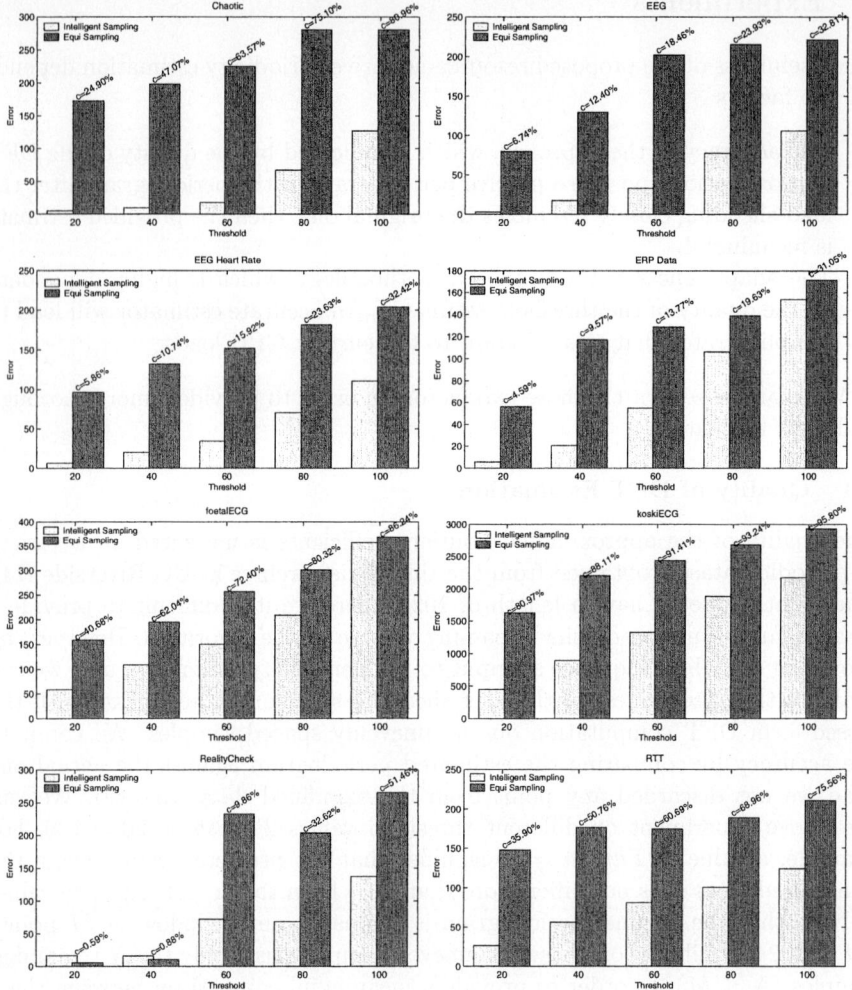

**Fig. 9.** Spectrum estimation comparison for various compression rates. The proposed intelligent sampling provides spectrum reconstruction of higher quality given the same number of samples.

when the threshold discards less than 10 samples per 1024 points). In general the observed reduction in the estimation error compared to equi-sampling, can range from 10% to more than 90% on the 14 datasets examined in this paper.

## 5.2 Threshold Estimator Accuracy

For testing the accuracy of the threshold estimator we need longer datasets, which could be used for simulating a sliding window model execution and additionally provide a training subset. We utilize real datasets provided by the

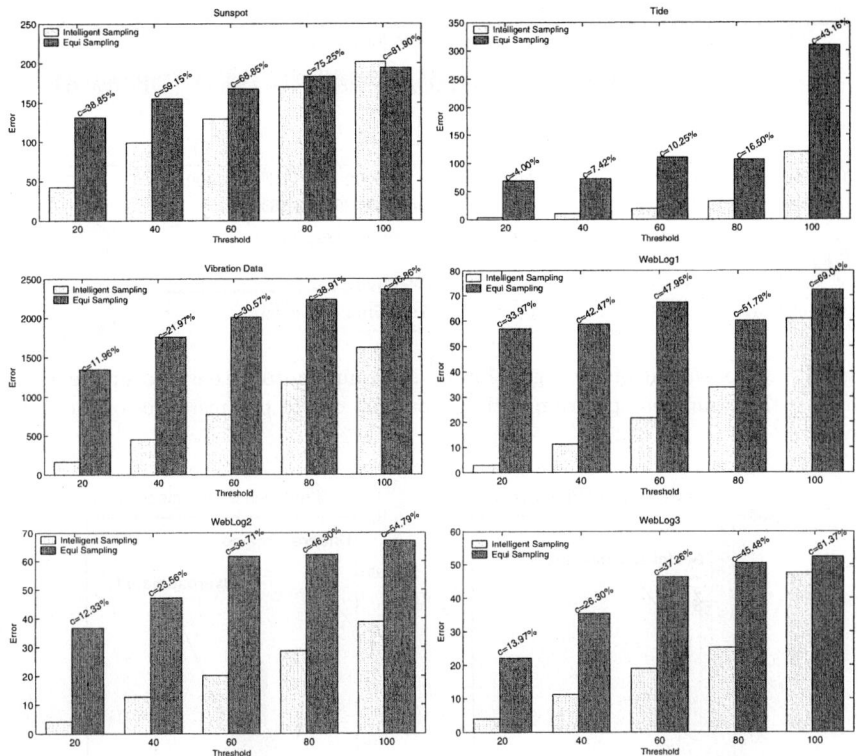

**Fig. 10.** Again the intelligent sampling outperforms equi-sampling techniques for the same compression rates

automotive industry. These are diagnostic measurements that monitor the evolution of variables of interest during the operation of a vehicle. Examples of such measurements could be the engine pressure, the torque, vibration patterns, instantaneous fuel economy, engine load at current speed, etc.

Periodic analysis is an indispensable tool in automotive industry, because predictive maintenance can be possible by monitoring the changes in the spectrum of the various rotating parts. Therefore, a change in the periodic structure of the various engine measurements can be a good indicator of machine wear and/or of an incipient failure.

The measurements that we use have length of 50000 points and represent monitoring of a variable over an extended period of time[4]. On this data we use a sliding window of 1024 points. We generate a synthetic CPU load, which is provided as input to the periodicity estimation unit. Based on the synthetic CPU trace, at any given point in time the periodicity unit is given adequate time for processing a set of points with cardinality within the range of 50 to 1024

---

[4] We have not provided the name of the specific engine measurement, because it is provided to us unlabeled by our automotive partner.

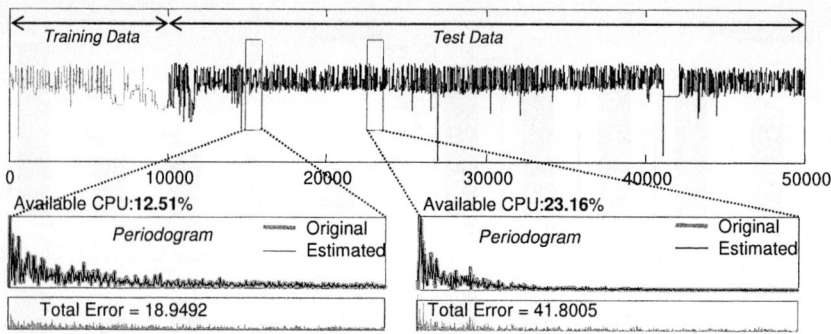

**Fig. 11.** A deployment of our algorithm on streaming automotive measurements. We constrast the estimated spectrum with the original one at two instances of the sliding window.

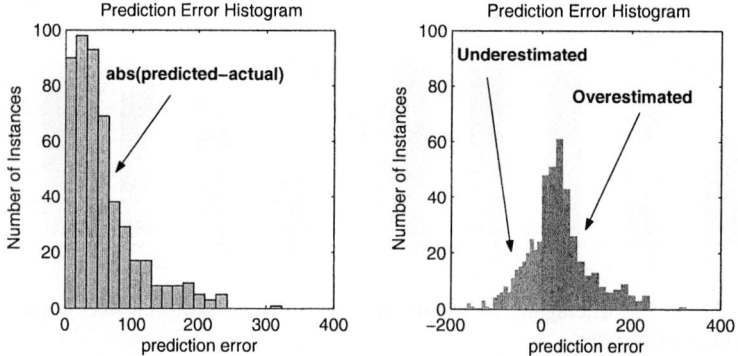

**Fig. 12.** *Left*: Histogram of the threshold estimator error. *Right*: Cases of *overestimated threshold* (fewer remaining samples -more desirable) are more frequent than instances of underestimated threshold

(1024 being the length of the window). In Fig. 11 we show two instances of the approximated spectrum under limited CPU resources. On the first instance the indicated available CPU of 12.41% means that only 12.41% of the total window points should remain after the load-shedding, given the available processing time.

Executing our algorithm on the complete data stream, we monitor the accuracy of the threshold estimator. The estimator is fed with the current CPU load and provides a threshold estimate $Thresh_{est}$ that will lead with high probability to $\hat{P}$ remaining points (so that they could be sufficiently processed given the available CPU load). Suppose that the actual remaining points after the application of the threshold $Thresh_{est}$ are $P$. An indicator of the estimator accuracy is provided by contrasting the estimated number of points $\hat{P}$ against the actual remaining ones $P$ (error = $|\hat{P} - P|$).

The experimental results are very encouraging and indicate an average error on the estimated number of points in the range of 5% of the data window.

For this experiment, if the predicted number of points for a certain threshold is 250 points, the actual value of remaining points could be (for example) 200 points. This is the case of an *overestimated threshold* which compressed more the flowing data stream. As mentioned before, this case is more desirable (than an underestimated threshold), because no additional points need to be subsequently dropped from the current data window (which is not bound to introduce additional aliasing problems).

A histogram of the estimator approximation error is given on the left part of Fig. 12. We observe that for the majority of data windows the estimation error is small, while fewer instances of the algorithm execution report a large error in the threshold estimation. On the right part of Fig. 12 we also provide how many cases of overestimated thresholds we have and how many underestimated. The overestimated ones (more desirable) are higher than the underestimated, which again indicates many of the attractive properties of the proposed threshold predictor.

## 6 Conclusion

We have presented the first resource-adaptive method for periodicity estimation. The key aspects of the proposed method are: (1) An intelligent load-shedding scheme that can adapt to the CPU load using a lightweight predictor. (2) A DFT estimation that utilizes unevenly spaced samples, provided by the previous phase. We have shown the quality of the approximated DFT and we also demonstrated that our scheme can adapt closely to the available CPU resources. We compare our intelligent load-shedding scheme against equi-sampling and we show improvements in the periodogram estimation ranging from 10% to 90%. As part of future work, we plan to examine whether it is possible to reduce even further the computational cost. This could be achieved by investigating the possibility of a 'butterfly' structure [3] in the incremental spectrum computation. We also plan to modify the sub-sampling algorithm in order to support provable bounds on the periodogram approximation error.

## References

1. D. Broomhead and D. Lowe. Multivariate functional interpolation and adaptive networks. In *Complex Systems, 2: 321:355*, 1988.
2. P. Castiglioni, M. Rienzo, and H. Yosh. A Computationally Efficient Algorithm for Online Spectral Analysis of Beat-to-Beat Signals. In *Computers in Cardiology:29, 417:420*, 2002.
3. J. W. Cooley and J. W. Tukey. An algorithm for the machine calculation of complex Fourier series. In *Math. Comput. 19, 297:301*, 1965.
4. P. Cuadra, A. Master, and C. Sapp. Efficient Pitch Detection Techniques for Interactive Music. In *International Computer Music Conference*, 2001.
5. M. G. Elfeky, W. G. Aref, and A. K. Elmagarmid. Using Convolution to Mine Obscure Periodic Patterns in One Pass. In *EDBT*, 2004.
6. F. Ergün, S. Muthukrishnan, and S. C. Sahinalp. Sublinear methods for detecting periodic trends in data streams. In *LATIN*, 2004.

7. W. Fan. StreamMiner: A Classifier Ensemble-based Engine to Mine Concept-drifting Data Streams. In *Proc. of VLDB*, pages 1257–1260, 2004.
8. A. C. Gilbert, S. Guha, P. Indyk, S. Muthukrishnan, and M. Strauss. Near-optimal Sparse Fourier Representations via Sampling. In *STOC*, pages 152–161, 2002.
9. M. Kontaki and A. Papadopoulos. Efficient similarity search in streaming time sequences. In *SSDBM*, 2004.
10. M. Lazarescu, S. Venkatesh, and H. H. Bui. Using Multiple Windows to Track Concept Drift. In *Intelligent Data Analysis Journal, Vol 8(1)*, 2004.
11. S. Papadimitriou, A. Brockwell, and C. Faloutsos. Awsom: Adaptive, hands-off stream mining. In *VLDB*, pages 560–571, 2003.
12. A. Papoulis. *Signal Analysis*. McGraw-Hill, 1977.
13. W. H. Press, B. P. Flannery, S. A. Teukolsky, and W. T. Vetterling. *Numerical Recipes: The Art of Scientific Computing*. Cambridge University Press, 1992.
14. Time-Series Data Mining Archive. http://www.cs.ucr.edu/ eamonn/TSDMA/.
15. Y. Zhu and D. Shasha. Statstream: Statistical monitoring of thousands of data streams in real time. In *VLDB*, 2002.

# On Futuristic Query Processing in Data Streams

Charu C. Aggarwal

IBM T.J. Watson Research Center,
19 Skyline Drive, Hawthorne, NY 10532
charu@us.ibm.com

**Abstract.** Recent advances in hardware technology have resulted in the ability to collect and process large amounts of data. In many cases, the collection of the data is a continuous process over time. Such continuous collections of data are referred to as *data streams*. One of the interesting problems in data stream mining is that of *predictive query processing*. This is useful for a variety of data mining applications which require us to estimate the future behavior of the data stream. In this paper, we will discuss the problem from the point of view of *predictive summarization*. In predictive summarization, we would like to store statistical characteristics of the data stream which are useful for estimation of queries representing the behavior of the stream in the future. The example utilized for this paper is the case of selectivity estimation of range queries. For this purpose, we propose a technique which utilizes a local predictive approach in conjunction with a careful choice of storing and summarizing particular statistical characteristics of the data. We use this summarization technique to estimate the future selectivity of range queries, though the results can be utilized to estimate a variety of futuristic queries. We test the results on a variety of data sets and illustrate the effectiveness of the approach.

## 1 Introduction

A number of technological innovations in recent years have facilitated the automated storage of data. For example, a simple activity such as the use of credit cards or accessing a web page creates data records in an automated way. Such dynamically growing data sets are referred to as data streams. The fast nature of data streams results in several constraints in their applicability to data mining tasks. For example, it means that they cannot be re-examined in the course of their computation. Therefore, all algorithms need to be executed in only one pass of the data. Furthermore, if the data stream evolves, it is important to construct a model which can be rapidly updated during the course of the computation. The second requirement is more restrictive, since it needs us to design the data stream mining algorithms while taking temporal evolution into account. This means that standard data mining algorithms on static data sets cannot be easily modified to create a one-pass analogue for data streams. A number of data mining algorithms for classical problems such as clustering and classification have been proposed in the context of data streams in recent years [1-8, 14].

An important problem in data stream computation is that of query selectivity estimation. Such queries include, but are not limited to problems such as selectivity estimation of range queries. Some examples of such queries are as follows:

- Find the number of data points lying in the range cube $\mathcal{R}$. (Range Query)
- For a target point $\overline{X}$, find the number of data points within a given radius $r$. (Radius Query)

A more general formulation of the above queries is to find the number of data points which satisfy a user-specified set of constraints $\mathcal{U}$. While this includes all standard selectivity estimation queries, it also allows for a more general model in which the selectivity of arbitrary constraints can be determined. For example, the constraint $\mathcal{U}$ could include arbitrary and non-linear constraints using some combinations of the attributes. This model for selectivity estimation is significantly more general than one which supports particular kinds of queries such as range queries.

Consider an aggregation query on a data stream for a given window of time $(T_1, T_2)$. While the query processing problem has been explored in the context of data streams [6, 7, 10, 11, 13, 15], these methods are designed for processing of *historical* queries. These correspond to cases in which $T_1$ and $T_2$ are less than the current time $t_0$. In this paper, we examine the problem of *predictive* query estimation. In the predictive query estimation problem, we attempt to estimate the selectivity of queries in a *future* time interval by making use of the current trends of the data stream. Thus, the generic data stream predictive selectivity estimation problem is defined as follows:

**Definition 1.** *Estimate the number of points in a data stream in the* **future** *time interval* $(T_1, T_2)$, *which satisfy the user-specified set of constraints* $\mathcal{U}$.

We note that predictive query processing is a significantly more difficult problem than historical query processing. This is because the historical behavior of the stream is already available, whereas the future behavior can only be estimated from the evolution trends in the data stream. This creates significant challenges in deciding on the nature of the summary information to be stored in order to estimate the responses to predictive queries. Some work has been done on performing high-level regression analysis to data cubes, but this work is designed for finding unusual trends in the data, and cannot be used for estimation of the selectivity of arbitrary user queries.

In order to solve the predictive querying problem, we use an approach in which we utilize local regression analysis in conjunction with storage of the summary covariance structure of different data localities. The local predictive approach stores a sufficient amount of summary statistics that it is able to create effective predictive samples in different data localities. These predictive samples can then be used in order to estimate the accuracy of the underlying queries. The sizes of the predictive samples can be varied depending upon the desired level of accuracy. We will show that such a local approach provides significant advantages over the technique of global regression. This is because the latter cannot generate the kind of refined summary constructed by the local approach. The refined summary from the local approach provides the ability to perform significantly superior estimation of the future data points. Thus, this approach is not only flexible (in terms of being able to handle arbitrary queries) but is also more effective over a wide variety of data sets. Furthermore, the summaries can be processed very efficiently because of the small size of the data stored. Thus, the paper presents a flexible, effective and efficient approach to predictive data summarization.

This paper is organized as follows. In the next section, we will discuss the overall framework for the approach. We will also discuss the summary statistics which are required to be stored in order to implement this framework. In section 3, we will discuss the algorithms in order to create the summary statistics, and the process of performing the estimation. The empirical sections are discussed in section 4. Section 5 contains the conclusions and summary.

## 2 The Overall Summarization Framework

In order to perform predictive selectivity estimation, we need to store a sufficient amount of summary statistics so that the overall behavior of the data can be estimated. One way of achieving this goal is the use of histograms in order to store the summary information in the data. While traditional methods such as histograms and random sampling are useful for performing data summarization and selectivity estimation in a static data set, they are not particularly useful for *predicting* future behavior of high dimensional data sets. This is because of several reasons:

(1) Histograms are not very effective for selectivity estimation and summarization of multi-dimensional sets. It has been estimated in [12] that for higher dimensional data sets, random sampling may be the only effective approach. However, random sampling is not very effective for predictive querying because the samples become stale very quickly in an evolving data stream.
(2) Since the data may evolve over time, methods such as histograms are not very effective for data stream summarization. This is because when the behavior of the data changes substantially, the summary statistics of the current histograms may not effectively predict future behavior.
(3) In this paper, we propose a very general model in which queries of *arbitrary* nature are allowed. Thus, the geometry of the queries is not restricted to particular kinds of rectangular partitions such as range queries. While summarization methods such as histograms are effective for rectangular range queries, they are not very effective for arbitrary queries. In such cases, random sampling is the only effective approach for static data sets. However, our empirical results will show that the random sampling approach is also not very useful in the context of an evolving data stream.

The overall approach in this paper emphasizes *predictive pseudo-data generation*. The essential idea in predictive pseudo-data generation is to store a sufficient amount of summary statistics so that representative pseudo-data can be generated for the *future* interval $(T_1, T_2)$. The summary statistics include such parameters as the number of data points arriving, the mean along each dimension as well as relevant second order statistics which encode the covariance structure of the data. While such statistics are stored on a historical basis, they are used to estimate the corresponding statistics for any future time horizon $(T_1, T_2)$. Such estimated statistics can then be used to generate the sample pseudo-data records within the desired horizon $(T_1, T_2)$. We note that while the sample records (which are generated synthetically) will not represent the true records within the corresponding future time horizon, their aggregate statistics will continue to reflect the selectivity of the corresponding queries. In other words, the aggregation queries can be resolved by determining the number of pseudo-data points which satisfy the user query. The advantage of using pseudo-data is that it can be leveraged to estimate the selectivity of arbitrary queries which are not restricted to any particular geometry or form. This is not the case for traditional methods such as histograms which work with only a limited classes of queries such as rectangular range queries.

We will now describe the statistics of the data which are maintained by the stream summarization algorithm. The summary statistics consist of the first order statistics as well as the co-variance structure of the data. In order to introduce these summary statistics, we will first introduce some further notations and definitions. Let us consider a set of $N$ records denoted by $\mathcal{D}$, each of which contains $d$ dimensions. The records in the database $\mathcal{D}$ are denoted by $\overline{X_1} \ldots \overline{X_N}$. The dimensions of each individual record $\overline{X_i}$ are denoted by $(x_i^1 \ldots x_i^d)$. For a subset of records $\mathcal{Q}$ from the database $\mathcal{D}$, we define the summary statistics $\overline{Stat}(\mathcal{Q}) = (\overline{Sc(\mathcal{Q})}, \overline{Fs(\mathcal{Q})}, n(\mathcal{Q}))$, which defines the complete covariance structure of $\mathcal{Q}$. Specifically, $\overline{Sc(\mathcal{Q})}$ corresponds to the second order statistics of $\mathcal{Q}$, $\overline{Fs(\mathcal{Q})}$ corresponds to the first order structure, and $n(\mathcal{Q})$ corresponds to the number of data points. Each of these statistics are defined as follows:

**(1) Product Sum (Second Order Covariance) Statistics.** For each pair of dimensions $i$ and $j$, we store the sum of the product for the corresponding dimension pairs. For the sake of convention (and to avoid duplication), we assume that $i \leq j$. The product sum for the dimension pairs $i, j$ and record set $\mathcal{Q}$ is denoted by $Sc_{ij}(\mathcal{Q})$. The corresponding value is defined as follows:

$$Sc_{ij}(\mathcal{Q}) = \sum_{k \in \mathcal{Q}} x_i^k \cdot x_j^k \tag{1}$$

The second order statistics is useful in computing covariance structure of the data records in $\mathcal{Q}$. We note that a total of $d \cdot (d+1)/2$ values (corresponding to different values of $i$ and $j$) need to be maintained in the vector $\overline{Sc(\mathcal{Q})}$.

**(2) First Order Statistics.** For each dimension $i$ we maintain the sum of the individual attribute values. Thus, a total of $d$ values are maintained. The value for the dimension $i$ is denoted by $Fs_i(\mathcal{Q})$, and is defined as follows:

$$Fs_i(\mathcal{Q}) = \sum_{k \in \mathcal{Q}} x_i^k \qquad (2)$$

We denote the vector $(Fs_1(\mathcal{Q}) \dots Fs_d(\mathcal{Q}))$ by $\overline{Fs(\mathcal{Q})}$.

**(3) Zero Order Statistics.** The zero order statistics $n(\mathcal{Q})$ contains one value and is equal to the number of records in $\mathcal{Q}$.

Thus, the total number of values which need to be stored in the vector $\overline{Stat(\mathcal{Q})}$ is equal to $d^2/2 + 3 \cdot d/2 + 1$. We make the following observations about the statistics which are stored:

**Observation 21.** *Each of the statistical values in $\overline{Stat(\mathcal{Q})}$ can be expressed as a linearly separable and direct sum of corresponding functional values over individual records.*

**Observation 22.** *The covariance $C_{ij}$ between the dimensions $i$ and $j$ can be expressed in the following form:*

$$C_{ij} = Sc_{ij}(\mathcal{Q})/n(\mathcal{Q}) - Fs_i \cdot Fs_j/(n(\mathcal{Q}) \cdot n(\mathcal{Q})) \qquad (3)$$

The first observation is important because it ensures that these statistical values can be efficiently maintained in the context of a data stream. This is because $\overline{Stat(\mathcal{Q})}$ can be computed as the simple arithmetic sum over the corresponding functional values over individual records. The second observation is important because it ensures that the covariance between the individual dimensions can be computed in terms of the individual statistical values. Thus, the statistical values provide a comprehensive idea of the covariance structure of the data. This is achieved by the method of principal component analysis. Since we will use this technique in our paper, we will discuss this method in detail below.

Let us assume that the covariance matrix of $\mathcal{Q}$ is denoted by $\mathcal{C}(\mathcal{Q}) = [C_{ij}]$. Therefore, $C_{ij}$ is equal to the covariance between the dimensions $i$ and $j$. This covariance matrix is known to be positive-semidefinite and can be diagonalized as follows:

$$\mathcal{C}(\mathcal{Q}) = P(\mathcal{Q}) \cdot \Delta(\mathcal{Q}) \cdot P(\mathcal{Q})^T \qquad (4)$$

Here the columns of $P(\mathcal{Q})$ represent the orthonormal eigenvectors, whereas $\Delta(\mathcal{Q})$ is a diagonal matrix which contains the eigenvalues. The eigenvectors and eigenvalues have an important physical significance with respect to the data points in $\mathcal{Q}$. Specifically, the orthonormal eigenvectors of $P(\mathcal{Q})$ represent an axis system in which the second order correlations of $\mathcal{Q}$ are removed. Therefore, if we were to represent the data points of $\mathcal{Q}$ in this new axis system, then the covariance between every pair of dimensions of the transformed data set would be zero. The eigenvalues of $\Delta(\mathcal{Q})$ would equal the variances of the data $\mathcal{Q}$ along the corresponding eigenvectors. Thus, the orthonormal columns of the matrix $P(\mathcal{Q})$ define a new axis system of transformation on $\mathcal{Q}$, in which $\Delta(\mathcal{Q})$ is the new covariance matrix.

We note that the axis system of transformation represented by $\mathcal{Q}$ is a particularly useful way to regenerate a sample of the data from the distribution represented by these statistics. This is because of the pairwise (second-order) independence between the dimensions of the transformed system. As a result, the data values along each of the transformed dimensions can also be generated independently of one another.[1] Thus, the covariance matrix serves the essential purpose of summarizing the hidden structure of the data.

This structural description can be used to estimate and generate *future* samples of the data. In order to do so, we use the historical statistics in order to estimate the future statistics. The aim of this approach is to effectively re-generate the data samples, while taking into account the evolution of the data. In the next section, we will discuss the details of the approach and its application to the predictive query estimation problem. In order to actually store the statistics, we use both a *global* and a *local* predictive approach. In the global approach, the summary statistics of the *entire* data are stored at regular intervals. Let us denote the data points which have arrived till time $t$ by $\mathcal{DS}(t)$. As each data point $\overline{X_t}$ arrives, we add the corresponding values of $\overline{Fs(\{X_t\})}$ and $\overline{Sc_{ij}(\{X_t\})}$ to $\overline{Fs(\mathcal{DS}(t))}$ and $\overline{Sc(\mathcal{DS}(t))}$ respectively. The value of $n(\mathcal{DS}(t))$ is incremented by one unit as well. Thus, the additivity property of the statistics ensures that they can be maintained effectively in a fast stream environment.

In order to improve the accuracy of prediction, we use a *local* approach in which the prediction is performed separately on each data locality. In the local predictive approach, the statistics are maintained separately for each data locality. In other words, the data stream $\mathcal{DS}(t)$ is segmented out into $q$ local streams which are denoted by $\mathcal{DS}_1(t), \mathcal{DS}_2(t), \ldots \mathcal{DS}_q(t)$ respectively. We note that the statistics for each local segment are likely to be more refined than the statistics for the entire data stream. This results in more accurate prediction of the future stream summaries. Correspondingly, we will show that the selectivity results are also more accurate in the local approach. We note that the local predictive approach degenerates to the global case when the value of $q$ is set to 1. Therefore, we will simply present the predictive query estimation method for the local case. The global case can be trivially derived from this description.

The process of maintaining the $q$ local streams is illustrated in Figure 1. The first step is to create the initial set of statistics. This is achieved by storing an initial portion of the stream onto the disk. The number of initial data points stored on disk is denoted by *Init*. A $k$-means algorithm is applied to this set of points in order to create the initial clusters. Once the initial clusters $\mathcal{DS}_1(t) \ldots \mathcal{DS}_q(t)$ have been determined, we generate the corresponding statistics $\overline{Stat(\mathcal{DS}_1(t))} \ldots \overline{Stat(\mathcal{DS}_q(t))}$ from these clusters. For each incoming data point, we determine its distance to the centroid of each of the local streams. We note that the centroid of each local stream $\mathcal{DS}_i(t)$ can be determined easily by dividing the first order statistics $Fs(\mathcal{DS}_i(t))$ by the number of points $n(\mathcal{DS}_i(t))$. We determine the closest centroid to each data point. Let us assume that the index of the closest centroid is $min \in \{1, \ldots q\}$. We assign that data point to the corresponding local stream. At the same time, we update $\overline{Stat(\mathcal{DS}_{min}(t))}$

---

[1] This results in a second-order approximation which is useful for most practical purposes.

**Algorithm.** *MaintainLocalStream*(Data Stream: $\mathcal{DS}(t)$,
            TimeStamp: $t$);
**begin**
   Store the first *Init* points from the data stream;
   Apply $k$-means clustering to create $l$ clusters;
   Denote each cluster by $\mathcal{DS}_i(t)$ for $i \in \{1, \ldots q\}$;
   Compute $\overline{Stat(\mathcal{DS}_i(t))}$ for $i \in \{1, \ldots q\}$;
      **for** each incoming data point $\overline{X}$ **do**
   **begin**
      Compute centroid of each $\mathcal{DS}_i(t)$ using $Stat(\mathcal{DS}_i(t))$;
      Compute closest centroid index $min \in \{1, \ldots q\}$;
      Assign $\overline{X}$ to closest centroid and update
         corresponding statistics $\mathcal{DS}_i(t)$;
   **end**
**end**

**Fig. 1.** Local Stream Maintenance

by adding the statistics of the incoming data point to it. At regular intervals of $r$, we also store the corresponding state of the statistics to disk. Therefore, the summary statistics at times $0, r, 2 \cdot r, \ldots t \cdot r \ldots$ are stored to disk.

## 3 The Predictive Query Estimation Method

In this section, we will discuss the predictive query estimation technique. Let us assume that the user wishes to find a response to the query $\mathcal{R}$ over the time interval $(T_1, T_2)$. In order to achieve this goal, a statistical sample of the data needs to be generated for the interval $(T_1, T_2)$. This sample needs to be sufficiently predictive of the behavior of the data for the interval $(T_1, T_2)$. For this purpose, we also need to generate the summary statistics which are relevant to the future interval $(T_1, T_2)$.

Let us assume that the current time is $t_0 \leq T_1 < T_2$. In order to generate the statistical samples in the data, we utilize a history of length $T_2 - t_0$. In other words, we determine $p$ evenly spaced snapshots in the range $(t_0 - (T_2 - t_0), t_0)$. These $p$ evenly spaced snapshots are picked from the summary statistics which are stored on disk. In the event that the length of the stream is less than $(T_2 - t_0)$, we use the entire stream history and pick $p$ evenly spaced snapshots from it. Let us assume that the time stamps for these snapshots are denoted by $b_1 \ldots b_p$. These snapshots are also referred to as the *base snapshots*. Then, we would like to generate a *functional form* for $\overline{Stat(\mathcal{DS}_i(t))}$ for all values of $t$ that are larger than $t_0$. In order to achieve this goal, we utilize a local regression approach for each stream $\mathcal{DS}_i(t)$. Specifically, each component of $\overline{Stat(\mathcal{DS}_i(t))}$ is generated using a polynomial regression technique.

The generation of the *zeroth* order and first order statistics from $\overline{Stat(\mathcal{DS}_i(t))}$ is done slightly differently from the generation of second order statistics. A bursty data stream can lead to poor approximations of the covariance matrix. This is because rapid changes in the covariance values could occur due to either changes in the speed of arriving data points, or due to changes in inter-attribute correlations. In order to improve the accuracy further, we use the *correlation matrix* for the period between $(t_0 - (T_2 - t_0), t_0)$ as a more usable predictor of future behavior. We note that the *correlation matrix* is far less sensitive to the absolute magnitudes and rate of arrival of the data points, and is therefore likely to vary more slowly with time. The correlation between the dimensions $i$ and $j$ for a set of data points $\mathcal{Q}$ is denoted by $\theta_{ij}(\mathcal{Q})$ and is essentially equal to the scaled covariance between the dimensions. Therefore, if $Cov_{ij}(\mathcal{Q})$ be the covariance between the dimensions $i$ and $j$, we have:

$$\theta_{ij}(\mathcal{Q}) = \frac{Cov_{ij}(\mathcal{Q})}{\sqrt{Cov_{ii}(\mathcal{Q}) \cdot Cov_{jj}(\mathcal{Q})}} \qquad (5)$$

We note that unlike the covariance, the correlation matrix is scaled with respect the absolute magnitudes of the data values, and also the number of data points. This ensures that the correlation between the data points remains relatively stable for a bursty data stream with noise in it. The value of $\theta_{ij}(\mathcal{Q})$ lies between 0 and 1 for all $i, j \in \{1, \ldots d\}$.

The local predictive approach works on each local stream $\mathcal{DS}_i(t)$ separately, and determines the values of certain statistical variables at the base snapshot times $b_1 \ldots b_p$. These statistical variables are as follows:

(1) For each local stream $\mathcal{DS}_i(t)$ and $j \in \{1 \ldots p-1\}$ we determine the number of data points arriving in the time interval $[b_j, b_{j+1}]$. This can be derived directly from the summary statistics stored in the snapshots, and is equal to $n(\mathcal{DS}_i(b_{j+1})) - n(\mathcal{DS}_i(b_j))$. We denote this value by $\eta(i, b_j)$.
(2) For each local stream $\mathcal{DS}_i(t)$, $j \in \{1 \ldots p-1\}$, and $k \in \{1 \ldots d\}$, we determine the mean of the data points which have arrived in the time interval $[b_j, b_{j+1}]$. This can again be estimated from the summary statistics stored in the snapshots at $b_1 \ldots b_p$. The corresponding value is equal to $(Fs_k(\mathcal{DS}_i(b_{j+1})) - Fs_k(\mathcal{DS}_i(b_j)))/(n(\mathcal{DS}_i(b_{j+1})) - n(\mathcal{DS}_i(b_j)))$. We denote this value by $\mu_k(i, b_j)$.
(3) For each local stream $\mathcal{DS}_i(t)$, $j \in \{1 \ldots p-1\}$, and dimension $k \in \{1 \ldots d\}$, we determine the variance of the data points which have arrived in the time interval $[b_j, b_{j+1}]$. This is estimated by using a two step process. First we compute the second order moment of dimension $k$ in interval $[b_j, b_{j+1}]$. This second order moment is equal to $(Sc_{kk}(\mathcal{DS}_i(b_{j+1})) - Sc_{kk}(\mathcal{DS}_i(b_j)))/(n(\mathcal{DS}_i(b_{j+1})) - n(\mathcal{DS}_i(b_j)))$. We denote this value by $SquareMoment_{kk}(i, b_j)$. Then, the variance in interval $[b_j, b_{j+1}]$ is equal to $SquareMoment_{kk}(i, b_j) - \mu_k(i, b_j)^2$. We denote this variance by $\sigma_k^2(i, b_j)$.
(4) For each local stream $\mathcal{DS}_i(t)$, $j \in \{1 \ldots p-1\}$, and dimension pairs $k, l \in \{1 \ldots d\}$, we determine the correlation between these dimension pairs. The correlation is determined by the expression $(SquareMoment_{kl}(i, b_j) - \mu_k(i, b_j) * \mu_l(i, b_j))/(\sigma_k(i, b_j) * \sigma_l(i, b_j))$. The correlation is denoted by $\phi_{kl}(i, b_j)$.

For each of the statistical values $\eta(i, b_j)$, $\mu_k(i, b_j)$, $\sigma_k^2(i, b_j)$, and $\phi_{kl}(i, b_j)$, we have $(p-1)$ different instantiations for different values of $k$ and $l$. Therefore, for each of the different values, we would like to define a functional form in terms of the time $t$. In the following discussion, we will discuss the general approach by which the functional form is that of the expression $\eta$. Let us assume that the functional form is determined by the expression $H(\eta, i, t)$. Note that the value of $H(\eta, i, t)$ refers to the number of data points in an interval of length $(b_2 - b_1)$ and starting at the point $t$ for data stream $\mathcal{DS}_i(t)$. We also assume that this functional form $H(\eta, i, t)$ is expressed polynomially as follows:

$$H(\eta, i, t) = a_m \cdot t^m + a_{m-1} \cdot t^{m-1} + \ldots + a_1 \cdot t + a_0 \qquad (6)$$

The coefficients $a_0 \ldots a_m$ define the polynomial function for $H(\eta, i, t)$. These coefficients need to be approximated using known instantiations of the function $H(\eta, i, t)$. The order $m$ is chosen based on the number $(p-1)$ of known instantiations. Typically, the value of $m$ should be significantly lower than the number of instantiations $(p-1)$. For a particular data stream $\mathcal{DS}_i(t)$, we know the value of the function for $(p-1)$ values of $t$ which are given by $t = b_1 \ldots b_{p-1}$. Thus, for each $j = 1 \ldots (p-1)$, we would like $H(\eta, i, b_j)$ to approximate $\eta(i, b_j)$ as closely as possible. In order to estimate the coefficients $a_0 \ldots a_m$, we use a linear regression technique in which we minimize the mean square error of the approximation of the known instantiations. The process is repeated for each data stream $\mathcal{DS}_i(t)$ and each statistical[2] variable $\eta$, $\mu_k$, $\sigma_k$, and $\phi_{kl}$. Once these statistical variables have been determined, we perform the predictive estimation process. As mentioned earlier, it is assumed that the query corresponds to the future interval $(T_1, T_2)$. The first step is to estimate the total number of data points in the interval $(T_1, T_2)$. We note that the expression $H(\eta, i, t)$ corresponds to the number of points for data stream $i$ in an interval of length[3] $(b_2 - b_1)$. Therefore, the number of data points $s(i, T_1, T_2)$ in stream $i$ for the interval $(T_1, T_2)$ is given by the following expression:

$$s(i, T_1, T_2) = \int_{t=T_1}^{T_2} \frac{H(\eta, i, t)}{b_2 - b_1} dt \qquad (7)$$

The value of $(b_2 - b_1)$ is included in the denominator of the above expression, since the statistical parameter $\eta$ has been estimated as the number of data points lying in an interval of length $(b_2 - b_1)$ starting at a given moment in time. Once the number of data points in the time interval $(T_1, T_2)$ for each stream $\mathcal{DS}_i(t)$ have been estimated, the next step is to generate $N_{samp}(i)$ sample points using the statistics $\eta$, $\mu$, $\sigma$, and $\phi$. The value of $N_{samp}(i)$ is chosen proportionally to $s(i, T_1, T_2)$ and should at least be equal to the latter. Larger values of $N_{samp}(i)$ lead to greater accuracy at the expense of greater computational costs. We will

---

[2] We note that the fitting method need not have the same order for all the polynomials. For the zero$th$, first order, and second order statistics, we used second order, first order and zero$th$ order polynomials respectively. This turns out to be more useful in a bursty data stream in which these parameters can vary rapidly.

[3] Since the intervals are evenly spaced, we note that $(b_j - b_{j-1})$ is equal to $(b_2 - b_1)$ for each value of $j \in \{1, \ldots (p-1)\}$.

discuss the process of generating each sample point slightly later. Each of these sample points is tested against the user-defined query predicate, and the fraction of points $f(i,\mathcal{U})$ which actually satisfy the predicate $\mathcal{U}$ from data stream $\mathcal{DS}_i(t)$ is determined. The final estimation $ES(\mathcal{U})$ for the query $\mathcal{U}$ is given by the sum of the estimations over the different data streams. Therefore, we have:

$$ES(\mathcal{U}) = \sum_{i=1}^{q} s(i, T_1, T_2) \cdot f(i, \mathcal{U}) \qquad (8)$$

It now remains to describe how each sample point from stream $i$ is generated using the summary statistics.

The first step is to generate the time stamp of the sample point from stream $\mathcal{DS}_i(t)$. Therefore, we generate a sample time $t_s \in (T_1, T_2)$ from the relative density distribution $\eta(i, T)$. Once the sample time has been determined, all the other statistical quantities such as mean, variance, and correlation can be instantiated to $\mu_k(i, t_s)$, $\sigma_k^2(i, t_s)$, and $\phi_{kl}(i, t_s)$ respectively. The covariance $\sigma_{kl}(i, t_s)$ between each pair of dimensions $k$ and $l$ can be computed as:

$$\sigma_{kl}(i, t_s) = \sqrt{\sigma_k^2(i, t_s) \cdot \sigma_l^2(i, t_s)} \cdot \phi_{kl}(i, t_s) \qquad (9)$$

The equation 9 relates the covariance with the statistical correlation by scaling appropriately with the product of the standard deviation along the dimensions $k$ and $l$. This scaling factor is given by $\sqrt{\sigma_k^2(i, t_s) \cdot \sigma_l^2(i, t_s)}$. Once the covariance matrix has been computed, we generate the eigenvectors $\{\overline{e_1} \ldots \overline{e_d}\}$ by using the diagonalization process. Let us assume that the corresponding eigenvalues are denoted by $\{\lambda_1 \ldots \lambda_d\}$ respectively. We note that $\lambda_i$ denotes the variance along the eigenvector $\overline{e_i}$. Since the eigenvectors represent the directions of zero correlation[4], the data values can be generated under the independence assumption in the transformed axis system denoted by $\{\overline{e_1} \ldots \overline{e_d}\}$. We generate the data in each such dimension using the uniform distribution assumption. Specifically, the offset from the mean $\overline{\mu(i, t_s)}$ of stream $\mathcal{DS}_i(t)$ along $\overline{e_j}$ is generated randomly from a uniform distribution with standard deviation equal to $\sqrt{\lambda_j}$. While the uniform distribution assumption is a simplifying one, it does not lead to an additional loss of accuracy. Since each data stream $\mathcal{DS}_i(t)$ represents only a small locality of the data, the uniform distribution assumption within a locality does not affect the *global* statistics of the generated data significantly. Once the data point has been generated using this assumption, we test whether it satisfies the user query constraints $\mathcal{U}$. This process is repeated over a number of different data points in order to determine the fraction $f(i, \mathcal{U})$ of the data stream satisfying the condition $\mathcal{U}$. The overall process of query estimation is illustrated in Figure 2. It is important to note that the input set of constraints $\mathcal{U}$ can take on any form, and are not restricted to any particular kind of query. Thus, this approach can also be used for a wide variety of problems that traditional selectivity estimation

---

[4] We note that the eigenvectors represent the directions of zero *second-order* correlation. However, a second-order approximation turns out be effective in practice.

**Algorithm.** *EstimateQuery(Local Statistics:* $\overline{Stat(\mathcal{DS}_i(b_j))}$,
   *Query Interval:* $(T_1, T_2)$, *Query:* $\mathcal{U}$);
**begin**
  Derive $\eta(i, b_j)$, $\mu_k(i, b_j)$, $\sigma_k^2(i, b_j)$, $\phi_{kl}(i, b_j)$ from
     $\overline{Stat(\mathcal{DS}_i(b_j))}$;
  Use local polynomial regression to generate
     functional forms $H(\eta, i, t)$, $H(\mu, i, t)$, $H(\sigma, i, t)$,
     and $H(\phi, i, t)$ for each stream $i$;
  $s(i, T_1, T_2) = \int_{t=T_1}^{T_2} \frac{H(\eta, i, t)}{b_2 - b_1} dt$;
  Generate $s(i, T_1, T_2)$ pseudo-points for each stream
     using statistics $\eta$, $\mu$, $\sigma$ and $\phi$;
  Let $f(i, \mathcal{U})$ be the fraction of data points satisfying
     predicate $\mathcal{U}$ from data stream $\mathcal{DS}_i$;
  $ES(\mathcal{U}) = \sum_{i=1}^{q} s(i, T_1, T_2) . f(i, \mathcal{U})$;
  **report**($ES(\mathcal{U})$);
**end**

**Fig. 2.** The Query Estimation Algorithm

methods cannot solve. For example, one can use the pseudo-points to estimate statistical characteristics such as the mean or sum across different records. We note that we can reliably estimate most first order and second order parameters because of the storage of second-order covariance structure. A detailed description of these advanced techniques is beyond the scope of this paper and will be discussed in future research. In the next section, we will discuss the effectiveness and efficiency of the predictive summarization procedure for query selectivity estimation.

## 4 Empirical Results

We tested our predictive summarization approach over a wide variety of real data sets. We tested our approach for the following measures:

**(1)** We tested the accuracy of the estimation procedure. The accuracy of the estimation was tested in various situations such as that of a rapidly evolving data stream or a relatively stable data stream. The aim of testing different scenarios was to determine how well these situations adjusted to the predictive aspect of the estimation process.
**(2)** We tested the rate of summarization of the stream processing framework. These tests determine the workload limits (maximum data stream arrival rate) that can be handled by the pre-processing approach.
**(3)** We tested the efficiency of the query processing approach for different data sets. This is essential to ensure that individual users are able to process offline queries in an efficient manner.

The accuracy of our approach was tested against two techniques:
**(1)** We tested the technique against a random sampling approach. In this method, we estimated the query selectivity of $\mathcal{U}$ corresponding to future in-

terval $(T_1, T_2)$ by using a sample of data points in the most recent window of size $(T_2 - T_1)$. This technique can work poorly in a rapidly evolving data stream, since the past window may not be a very good reflection of future behavior.

(2) We tested the local technique against the global technique in terms of the quality of query estimation. The results show that the local technique was significantly more effective on a wide variety of data sets and measures. This is because the local technique is able to estimate parameters which are specific to a given segment. This results in more refined statistics which can estimate the evolution in the stream more effectively.

### 4.1 Test Data Sets

We utilized some real data sets to test the effectiveness of the approach. A good candidate for such testing is the KDD-CUP'99 Network Intrusion Detection stream data set. The Network Intrusion Detection data set consists of a series of TCP connection records from two weeks of LAN network traffic managed by MIT Lincoln Labs. Each record can correspond to a normal connection, an intrusion or an attack. This data set evolves rapidly, and is useful in testing the effectiveness of the approach in situations in which the characteristics of the data set change rapidly over time.

Second, besides testing on the rapidly evolving network intrusion data stream, we also tested our method over relatively stable streams. The KDD-CUP'98 Charitable Donation data set shows such behavior. This data set contains 95412 records of information about people who have made charitable donations in response to direct mailing requests, and clustering can be used to group donors showing similar donation behavior. As in [9], we will only use 56 fields which can be extracted from the total 481 fields of each record. This data set is converted into a data stream by taking the data input order as the order of streaming and assuming that they flow-in with a uniform speed.

The last real data set we tested is the *Forest CoverType* data set and was obtained from the UCI machine learning repository web site [16]. This data set contains 581012 observations and each observation consists of 54 attributes, including 10 quantitative variables, 4 binary wilderness areas and 40 binary soil type variables. In our testing, we used all the 10 quantitative variables.

### 4.2 Effectiveness Results

We first tested the prediction accuracy of the approach with respect to the global approach and a random sampling method. In the sampling method, we always maintained a random sample of the history of the data stream. When a query was received, we used the random sample from the most recent history of the stream in order to estimate the effectiveness of the queries. The queries were generated as follows. First, we randomly picked $k' = d/2$ dimensions in the data with the greatest standard deviation. From these dimensions, we picked $k$ dimensions randomly, where $k$ was randomly chosen from $(2, 4)$. The aim of preselecting widely varying dimensions was to pick queries which were challenging to the selectivity estimation process. Then, the ranges along each dimension were

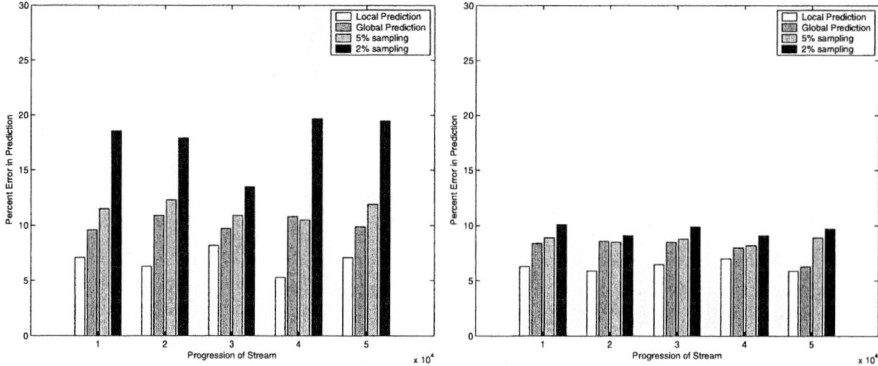

**Fig. 3.** Predictive Error of Different Methods with Stream Progression (Network Intrusion Data Set)

**Fig. 4.** Predictive Error of Different Methods with Stream Progression (Charitable Donation Data Set)

generated from a uniform random distribution. In each case, we performed the tests over 50 such randomly chosen queries and presented the averaged results.

In Figure 3, we have illustrated the predictive error of the Network Intrusion data set with stream progression. In each group of stacked bars in the chart, we have illustrated the predictive error of each method. Different stacks correspond to different time periods in the progression of the stream. The predictive accuracy is defined as the difference between the true and predictive selectivity as a percentage of the true value. On the X-axis, we have illustrated the progression of the data stream. The predictive error varied between 5% and 20% over the different methods. It is clear that in each case, the local predictive estimation method provides the greatest accuracy in prediction. While the local method is consistently superior to the method of global approach, the latter is usually better than pure random sampling methods. This is because random sampling methods are unable to adjust to the evolution in the data stream. In some cases, the 5% random sampling method was slightly better than global method. However, in all cases, the local predictive estimation method provided the most accurate result. Furthermore, the 2% sampling method was the least effective in all cases. The situations in which the 5% sampling method was superior to global method were those in which the stream behavior was stable and did not vary much over time.

In order to verify this fact, we also performed empirical tests using the charitable donation data set which exhibited much more stable behavior than the Network Intrusion Set. The results are illustrated in Figure 4. The stable behavior of the charitable donation data set ensured that the random sampling method did not show much poorer performance than the predictive estimation methods. However, in each case, the local predictive estimation method continued to be significantly superior to other techniques. In some cases, the 5% sampling method was slightly better than the global estimation method. Because of the lack of evolution of the data set, the sampling method was relatively more robust. However, it was still outperformed by the local predictive method in all cases.

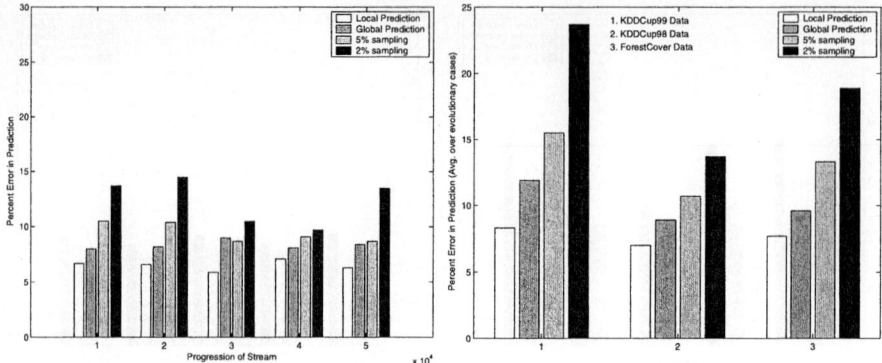

**Fig. 5.** Predictive Error of Different Methods with Stream Progression (Forest Cover Data Set)

**Fig. 6.** Predictive Error of Different Methods with Stream Progression (High Evolution Cases)

Finally, the results for the forest cover data set are illustrated in Figure 5. This data set showed similar relative trends between the different methods. However, the results were less skewed than the network intrusion data set. This is because the network intrusion data set contained sudden bursts of changes in data behavior. These bursts correspond to the presence of intrusions in the data. These intrusions also show up in the form of sudden changes in the underlying data attributes. While the forest cover data set evolved more than the charitable donation data set, it seemed to be more stable than the network intrusion data set. Correspondingly, the relative performance of the sampling methods improved over that for the network intrusion data set, but was not as good as the charitable donation data set. As in the previous cases, the predictive estimation approach dominated significantly over other methods.

We also tested the effectiveness of the approach in specific circumstances where the data was highly evolving. In order to model such highly evolving data sets, we picked certain points in the data set at which the class distribution of the data stream showed a shift. Specifically, when the percentage presence of the dominant class in successive blocks of 1000 data points showed a change of greater than 5%, these positions in the data stream were considered to be highly evolving. All queries to be tested were generated in a time interval which began at a lag of 100 data points from the beginning of the shift. This ensured that the queries followed a region with a very high level of evolution. For each data set, ten such queries were generated using the same methodology described earlier. The average selectivity error over the different data sets was reported in Figure 6. Because of the greater level of evolution in the data set, the absolute error values are significantly higher. Furthermore, the random sampling method performed poorly for all three data sets. The results were particularly noticeable for the network intrusion data set. This is because the random sampling approach uses only the history of past behavior. This turned out to be poor surrogate in this case. Since the random sampling approach relied exclusively on the history

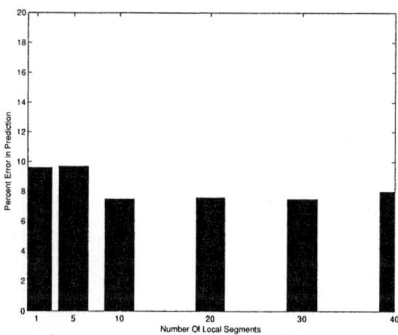 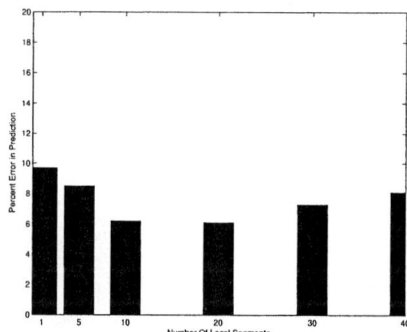

**Fig. 7.** Predictive Error with Increasing Number of Local Segments (Network Intrusion Data Set)

**Fig. 8.** Predictive Error with Increasing Number of Local Segments (Charitable Donation Data Set)

of the data stream, it did not provide very good results in cases in which the stream evolved rapidly. These results show that the predictive estimation technique was a particularly useful method in the context of a highly evolving data stream.

We also tested the effectiveness of the predictive estimation analysis with increasing number of segments in the data stream. The results for the network intrusion data set are presented in Figure 7. These results show that the error in estimation reduced with the number of segments in the data stream, but levelled off after the use of 7 to 8 segments. This is because the use of an increasing number of segments enhanced the power of data locality during the parameter estimation process. However, there was a limit to this advantage. When the number of clusters was increased to more than 20, the error rate increased substantially. In these cases, the number of data points from each cluster (which were used for the polynomial fitting process) reduced to a point which leads to a lack of statistical robustness. The results for the charitable donation data set are presented in Figure 8. While the absolute error numbers are slightly lower in each case, the trends are quite similar. Therefore, the results show that it is a clear advantage to use a large number of segments in order to model the behavior of each data locality.

## 4.3 Stream Processing and Querying Efficiency

In this section, we will study the processing efficiency of the method, and its sensitivity with respect to the number of segments used in the data stream. The processing efficiency refers to the online rate at which the stream can be processed in order to create and store away the summary statistics generated by the method. The processing efficiency was tested in terms of the number of data points processed per second with stream progression. The results for the case of the network intrusion and charitable donation data sets are illustrated in Figure 9. On the X-axis, we have illustrated the progression of the data stream.

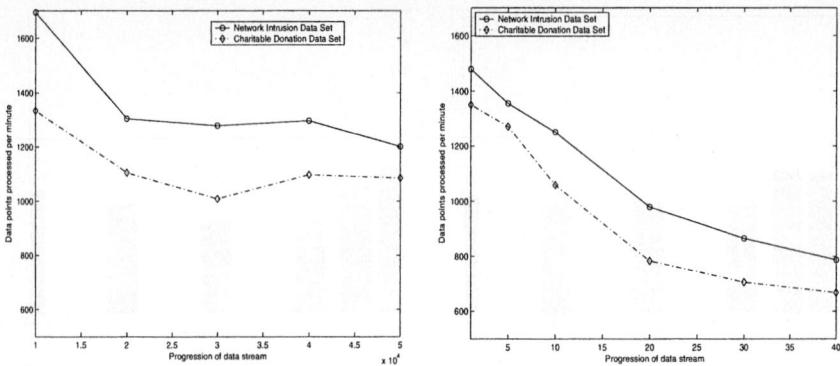

**Fig. 9.** Stream Processing Time with Data Stream Progress

**Fig. 10.** Stream Processing Time with Increasing Number of Local Segments

The Y-axis depicts the processing rate of the stream in terms of the number of data points processed every minute. It is clear that the algorithm was stable throughout the execution of the data stream. The processing rate for the network intrusion data set was higher because of its lower dimensionality. Furthermore, the execution times were relatively small, and several thousand data points were processed per minute. This is because the stream statistics can be updated using relatively straightforward additive calculations on each point. We have drawn multiple plots in Figure 9 illustrating the effect of using the different data sets.

In order to illustrate the effect of using different number of segments, we have illustrated the variation in processing rate with the number of stream segments in Figure 10. Both data sets are illustrated in this figure. As in the previous case, the lower dimensionality of the network intrusion data set resulted in higher processing efficiency. It is clear that the number of data points processed per second reduces with increasing number of segments. This is because of the fact that the time for finding the closest stream segment (in order to find which set of local stream segment statistics to update) was linear in the number of local stream segments. However, the majority of the time was spent in the (fixed) cost of updating stream statistics. This cost was independent of the number of stream segments. Correspondingly, the overall processing rate was linear in the number of stream segments (because of the cost of finding the closest stream segment), though the fixed cost of updating stream statistics (and storing it away) tended to dominate. Therefore, the results of Figure 10 illustrate that the reduction in processing rate with increasing number of stream segments is relatively mild.

Finally, we studied the efficiency of querying the data stream. We note that the querying efficiency depends upon the number of segments stored in the data stream. This is because the statistics need to be estimated separately for each stream segment. This requires separate processing of each segment and leads to increased running times. We have presented the results for the Charitable Donation and Network Intrusion Data data set in Figure 11. In order to improve the accuracy of evaluation, we computed the running times over a batch of one

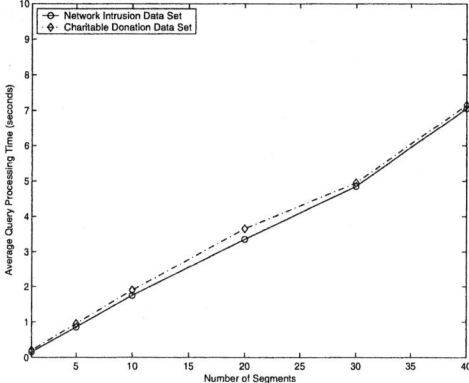

**Fig. 11.** Stream Query Time with Increasing Number of Local Segments

hundred examples and reported the *average* running times per query on the $Y$-axis. On the $X$-axis, we have illustrated the number of stream segments used. It is clear that in each case, the running time varied between 0.3 and 8 seconds. A relevant observation is that the most accurate results for query responses is obtained when about 7-10 segments were used in these data sets. For these cases, the query response times were less than 2 seconds in all cases. Furthermore, we found the running time to vary linearly with the number of stream segments. The network intrusion and the charitable donation data sets showed similar results except that the running times were somewhat higher in the latter case. This is because of the higher dimensionality of the latter data set which increased the running times as well.

## 5 Conclusions and Summary

In this paper, we discussed a method for predictive query estimation of data streams. The approach used in this paper can effectively estimate the changes in the data stream resulting from the evolution process. These changes are incorporated in the model in order to perform the predictive estimation process. We note that the summarization approach in this paper is quite general and can be applied to arbitrary kinds of queries as opposed to simple techniques such as range queries. This is because the summarization approach constructs pseudo-data which can be used in conjunction with an arbitrary query. While this scheme has been developed and tested for query estimation, the technique can be used for any task which requires predictive data summarization. We tested the scheme on a number of real data sets, and compared it against an approach based on random sampling. The results show that our scheme significantly outperforms the method of random sampling as well as the global approach. The strength of our approach arises from its careful exploitation of data locality in order to estimate the inter-attribute correlations. In future work, we will utilize the data summarization approach to construct visual representations of the data stream.

# References

1. Aggarwal C. C.: A Framework for Diagnosing Changes in Evolving Data Streams, ACM SIGMOD Conference, (2003) 575–586.
2. Aggarwal C. C., Han J., Wang J., Yu P.: A Framework for Clustering Evolving Data Streams, VLDB Conference, (2003) 81–92.
3. Babcock B., Babu S., Datar M., Motwani R., Widom J.: Models and Issues in Data Stream Systems, ACM PODS Conference, (2002) 1–16.
4. Chen Y., Dong G., Han J., Wah B., Wang J.: Multi-Dimensional Regression Analysis of Time Series Data Streams, VLDB Conference, (2002) 323–334.
5. Cortes C., Fisher K., Pregibon D., Rogers A., Smith F.: Hancock: A Language for Extracting Signatures from Data Streams, ACM KDD Conference, (2000) 9–17.
6. Dobra A., Garofalakis M., Gehrke J., Rastogi R.: Processing Complex Aggregate Queries over Data Streams, ACM SIGMOD Conference, (2002) 61–72.
7. Dobra A., Garofalakis M., Gehrke J., Rastogi R.: Sketch Based Multi-Query Processing Over Data Streams, EDBT Conference, (2004) 551–568.
8. Domingos P., Hulten G.: Mining High-Speed Data Streams, ACM KDD Conference, (2000) 71–80.
9. Farnstrom F., Lewis J., Elkan C.: Scalability for Clustering Algorithms Revisited, ACM SIGKDD Explorations, Vol. 2(1), (2000) 51–57.
10. Gilbert A. C., Kotidis Y., Muthukrishnan S., Strauss M. J.: Surfing Wavelets on Streams: One-pass Summaries for Approximate Aggregate Queries, VLDB Conference, (2001) 79–88.
11. Gilbert A. C., Kotidis Y., Muthukrishnan S., Strauss M. J.: How to Summarize the Universe: Dynamic Maintenance of Quantiles. VLDB Conference, (2002) 454–465.
12. Gunopulos D., Kollios G., Tsotras V., Domeniconi C.: Approximating Multi-Dimensional Aggregate Range Queries over Real Attributes. ACM SIGMOD Conference, (2000) 463–474.
13. Manku G. S., Motwani R.: Approximate Frequency Counts over Data Streams. VLDB Conference, (2002), 346–357.
14. O'Callaghan L., Mishra N., Meyerson A., Guha S., Motwani R.: Streaming-Data Algorithms For High-Quality Clustering, IEEE ICDE Conference, (2002) 685–696.
15. Vitter J., Wang M.: Approximate Computation of Multidimensional Aggregates of Sparse Data using Wavelets. ACM SIGMOD Conference, (1999) 193–204.
16. http://www.ics.uci.edu/~mlearn.

# Detecting Similarities in Ontologies with the SOQA-SimPack Toolkit

Patrick Ziegler, Christoph Kiefer, Christoph Sturm,
Klaus R. Dittrich, and Abraham Bernstein

DBTG and DDIS, Department of Informatics, University of Zurich,
Winterthurerstrasse 190, CH-8057 Zürich, Switzerland
{pziegler, kiefer, sturm, dittrich, bernstein}@ifi.unizh.ch

**Abstract.** Ontologies are increasingly used to represent the intended real-world semantics of data and services in information systems. Unfortunately, different databases often do not relate to the same ontologies when describing their semantics. Consequently, it is desirable to have information about the similarity between ontology concepts for ontology alignment and integration. This paper presents the SOQA-SimPack Toolkit (SST), an ontology language independent Java API that enables generic similarity detection and visualization in ontologies. We demonstrate SST's usefulness with the SOQA-SimPack Toolkit Browser, which allows users to graphically perform similarity calculations in ontologies.

## 1 Introduction

In current information systems, ontologies are increasingly used to explicitly represent the intended real-world semantics of data and services. Ontologies provide a means to overcome heterogeneity by providing explicit, formal descriptions of concepts and their relationships that exist in a certain universe of discourse, together with a shared vocabulary to refer to these concepts. Based on agreed ontological domain semantics, the danger of semantic heterogeneity can be reduced. Ontologies can, for instance, be applied in the area of data integration for data content explication to ensure semantic interoperability between data sources.

Unfortunately, different databases often do not relate to the same ontologies when describing their semantics. That is, schema elements can be linked to concepts of different ontologies in order to explicitly express their intended meaning. This complicates the task of finding semantically equivalent schema elements since at first, semantic relationships between the concepts have to be detected to which the schema elements are linked to. Consequently, it is desirable to have information about the similarity between ontological concepts. In addition to schema integration, such similarity information can be useful for many applications, such as ontology alignment and integration, Semantic Web (service) discovery, data clustering and mining, semantic interoperability in virtual organizations, and semantics-aware universal data management.

The task of detecting similarities in ontologies is aggravated by the fact that a large number of ontology languages is available to specify ontologies. Besides traditional ontology languages, such as Ontolingua [5] or PowerLoom[1], there is a notable number of ontology languages for the Semantic Web, such as SHOE[2], DAML[3], or OWL[4]. That is, data semantics can often be described with respect to ontologies that are represented in various ontology languages. In consequence, mechanisms for effective similarity detection in ontologies must be capable of coping with heterogeneity caused by the use of different ontology languages. Additionally, it is desirable that different similarity measures can be employed so that different approaches to identify similarities among concepts in ontologies can be reflected.

For instance, assume that in an example scenario, a developer of an integrated university information system is looking for semantically similar elements from database schemas that relate to the following ontologies to describe their semantics: (1) the Lehigh University Benchmark Ontology[5] that is represented in OWL, (2) the PowerLoom Course Ontology[6] developed in the SIRUP project [21], (3) the DAML University Ontology[7] from the University of Maryland, (4) the Semantic Web for Research Communities (SWRC) Ontology[8] modeled in OWL, and (5) the Suggested Upper Merged Ontology (SUMO)[9], which is also an OWL ontology. Assume further that there are schema elements linked to all of the 943 concepts which these five ontologies are comprised of. Unless suitable tools are available, identifying semantically related schema elements in this set of concepts and visualizing the similarities appropriately definitely turns out to be time-consuming and labor-intensive.

In this paper, we present the SOQA-SimPack Toolkit (SST), an ontology language independent Java API that enables generic similarity detection and visualization in ontologies. Our main goal is to define a Java API suitable for calculating and visualizing similarities in ontologies for a broad range of ontology languages. Considering the fact that different databases often do not relate to the same ontologies, we aim at calculating similarities not only within a given ontology, but also between concepts of *different* ontologies. For these calculations, we intend to provide a generic and extensible library of ontological similarity measures capable of capturing a variety of notions of "similarity". Note that we do not focus on immediate ontology integration. Instead, we strive for similarity detection among different pre-existing ontologies, which are separately used to explicitly state real-world semantics as intended in a particular setting.

---

[1] http://www.isi.edu/isd/LOOM/PowerLoom/
[2] http://www.cs.umd.edu/projects/plus/SHOE/
[3] http://www.daml.org
[4] http://www.w3.org/2004/OWL/
[5] http://www.lehigh.edu/~zhp2/univ-bench.owl
[6] http://www.ifi.unizh.ch/dbtg/Projects/SIRUP/ontologies/course.ploom
[7] http://www.cs.umd.edu/projects/plus/DAML/onts/univ1.0.daml
[8] http://www.ontoware.org/projects/swrc/
[9] http://reliant.teknowledge.com/DAML/SUMO.owl

This paper is structured as follows: Section 2 gives an overview of the foundations of the SOQA-SimPack Toolkit and Section 3 presents SST's functionality and architecture in detail. In Section 4, the SOQA-SimPack Toolkit Browser is illustrated, which allows users to graphically perform similarity calculations in ontologies. Section 5 discusses related work and Section 6 concludes the paper.

## 2  Foundations of the SOQA-SimPack Toolkit

In this section, the SIRUP Ontology Query API [22] and SimPack [2] are presented, which form the basis for the SOQA-SimPack Toolkit.

### 2.1  The SIRUP Ontology Query API

To overcome the problems caused by the fact that ontologies can be specified in a manifold of ontology languages, the SIRUP Ontology Query API (SOQA) [22] was developed for the SIRUP approach to semantic data integration [21]. SOQA is an ontology language independent Java API for query access to ontological metadata and data that can be represented in a variety of ontology languages. Besides, data of concept instances can be retrieved through SOQA. Thus, SOQA facilitates accessing and reusing general foundational ontologies as well as specialized domain-specific ontologies through a uniform API that is independent of the underlying ontology language.

In general, ontology languages are designed for a particular purpose and, therefore, they vary in their syntax and semantics. To overcome these differences, the SOQA Ontology Meta Model [22] was defined. It represents modeling capabilities that are typically supported by ontology languages to describe ontologies and their components; that is, concepts, attributes, methods, relationships, instances, and ontological metadata. Based on the SOQA Ontology Meta Model, the functionality of the SOQA API was designed. Hence, SOQA provides users and applications with unified access to metadata and data of ontologies according to the SOQA Ontology Meta Model. In the sense of the SOQA Ontology Meta Model, an ontology consists of the following components:

- Metadata to describe the ontology itself. This includes name, author, date of last modification, (header) documentation, version, copyright, and URI (Uniform Resource Identifier) of the ontology as well as the name of the ontology language the ontology is specified in. Additionally, each ontology has extensions of all concepts, attributes, methods, relationships, and instances that appear in it.
- Concepts which are entity types that occur in the particular ontology's universe of discourse — that is, concepts are descriptions of a group of individuals that share common characteristics. In the SOQA Ontology Meta Model, each concept is characterized by a name, documentation, and a definition that includes constraints;[10] additionally, it can be described by attributes,

---

[10] In SOQA, axioms/constraints are subsumed by the definitions of the particular meta model elements.

methods, and relationships. Further, each concept can have direct and indirect super- and subconcepts, equivalent and antonym concepts, and coordinate concepts (that are situated on the same hierarchy level as the concept itself). For example, ontology language constructs like `<owl:Class...>` from OWL and `(defconcept...)` from PowerLoom are represented as concepts in the SOQA Ontology Meta Model.
- Attributes that represent properties of concepts. Each attribute has a name, documentation, data type, definition, and the name of the concept it is specified in.
- Methods which are functions that transform zero or more input parameters into an output value. Each method is described by a name, documentation, definition, its parameters, return type, and the name of the concept the method is declared for.
- Relationships that can be established between concepts, for instance, to build taxonomies or compositions. Similar to the other ontology components, a name, documentation, and definition can be accessed for each relationship. In addition, the arity of relationship, i.e., the number of concepts it relates, as well as the names of these related concepts are available.
- Instances of the available concepts that together form the extension of the particular concept. Each instance has a name and provides concrete incarnations for the attribute values and relationships that are specified in its concept definition. Furthermore, the name of the concept the instance belongs to is available.

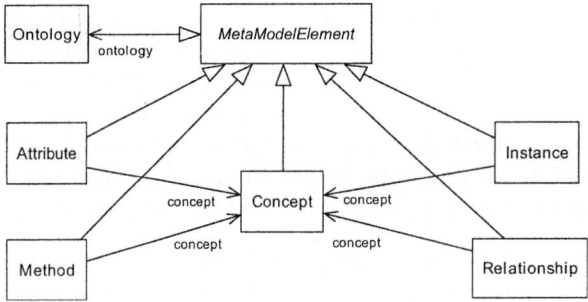

**Fig. 1.** Overview of the SOQA Ontology Meta Model as a UML Class Diagram

A UML class diagram of the SOQA Ontology Meta Model is shown in Figure 1. Note that the SOQA Ontology Meta Model is deliberately designed not only to represent the least common denominator of modeling capabilities of widely-used ontology languages. In deciding whether or not to incorporate additional functionality that is not supported by some ontology languages, we opted for including these additional modeling capabilities (e.g., information on methods, antonym concepts, ontology authors, etc.), provided that they are useful for users of the SOQA API and available in important ontology languages.

Architecturally, the SOQA API reflects the Facade [6] design pattern. That is, SOQA provides a unified interface to a subsystem that retrieves information from ontologies, which are specified in different ontology languages. Through the SOQA Facade, the internal SOQA components are concealed from external clients; instead, a single point for unified ontology access is given (see Figure 2). For example, the query language SOQA-QL [22] uses the API provided by the SOQA Facade to offer declarative queries over data and metadata of ontologies that are accessed through SOQA. A second example for an external SOQA client is the SOQA Browser [22] that enables users to graphically inspect the contents of ontologies independent of the ontology language they are specified in. Last, but not least, (third-party) Java applications can be based on SOQA for unified access to information that is specified in different ontology languages. Possible application areas are virtual organizations, enterprise information and process integration, the Semantic Web, and semantics-aware universal data management.

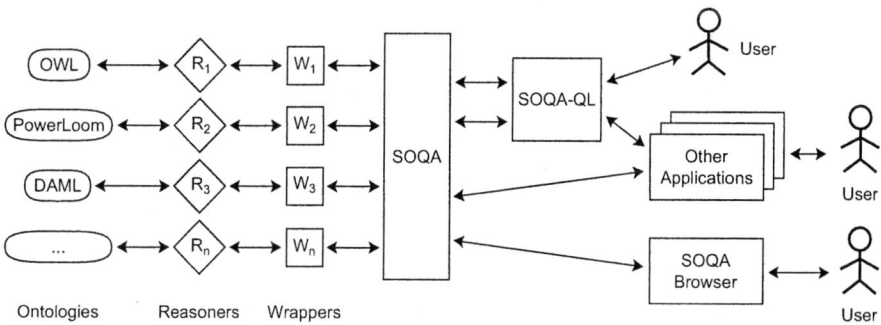

**Fig. 2.** Overview of the SOQA Software Architecture

Internally, ontology wrappers are used as an interface to existing reasoners that are specific to a particular ontology language (see Figure 2). Up to now, we have implemented SOQA ontology wrappers for OWL, PowerLoom, DAML, and the lexical ontology WordNet [11].

## 2.2 SimPack

SimPack is a generic Java library of similarity measures for the use in ontologies. Most of the similarity measures were taken from the literature and adapted for the use in ontologies. The library is generic, that is, the measures can be applied to different ontologies and ontology formats using wrappers. The question of similarity is an intensively researched subject in the computer science, artificial intelligence, psychology, and linguistics literature. Typically, those studies focus on the similarity between vectors [1, 17], strings [14], trees or graphs [18], and objects [7]. In our case we are interested in the similarity between resources in ontologies. Resources may be concepts (classes in OWL) of some type or individuals (instances) of these concepts. The remainder of this section will discuss different types of similarity measures, thereby explaining a subset of the measures implemented in SimPack.[11]

**Vector-Based Measures.** One group of similarity measures operates on vectors of equal length. To simplify their discussion, we will discuss all measures as the similarity between the (binary) vectors $\mathbf{x}$ and $\mathbf{y}$, which are generated from the resources $R_x$ and $R_y$ of some ontology $O$. The procedure to generate these vectors depends on how one looks at the resources. If the resources are considered as sets of features (or properties in OWL terminology), finding all the features for both resources results in two feature sets which are mapped to binary vectors and compared by one of the measures presented in Equation 1 through 3. For instance, if resource $R_x$ has the properties *type* and *name* and resource $R_y$ *type* and *age*, the following vectors $\mathbf{x}$ and $\mathbf{y}$ result using a trivial mapping $M_1$ from sets to vectors:

$$\mathbb{R}_x = \{type, name\} \Rightarrow \mathbf{x}' = \begin{pmatrix} 0 \\ name \\ type \end{pmatrix} \Rightarrow \mathbf{x} = \begin{pmatrix} 0 \\ 1 \\ 1 \end{pmatrix}$$

$$\mathbb{R}_y = \{type, age\} \Rightarrow \mathbf{y}' = \begin{pmatrix} age \\ 0 \\ type \end{pmatrix} \Rightarrow \mathbf{y} = \begin{pmatrix} 1 \\ 0 \\ 1 \end{pmatrix}$$

Typically, the cosine measure, the extended Jaccard measure, and the overlap measure are used for calculating the similarity between such vectors [1]:

$$sim_{cosine}(\mathbf{x}, \mathbf{y}) = \frac{\mathbf{x} \cdot \mathbf{y}}{||\mathbf{x}||_2 \cdot ||\mathbf{y}||_2} \qquad (1)$$

$$sim_{jaccard}(\mathbf{x}, \mathbf{y}) = \frac{\mathbf{x} \cdot \mathbf{y}}{||\mathbf{x}||_2^2 + ||\mathbf{y}||_2^2 - \mathbf{x} \cdot \mathbf{y}} \qquad (2)$$

$$sim_{overlap}(\mathbf{x}, \mathbf{y}) = \frac{\mathbf{x} \cdot \mathbf{y}}{\min(||\mathbf{x}||_2^2, ||\mathbf{y}||_2^2)} \qquad (3)$$

In these equations, $||\mathbf{x}||$ denotes the $L^1$-norm of $\mathbf{x}$, i.e. $||\mathbf{x}|| = \sum_{i=1}^{n} |x_i|$, whereas $||\mathbf{x}||_2$ is the $L^2$-norm, thus $||\mathbf{x}||_2 = \sqrt{\sum_{i=1}^{n} |x_i|^2}$. The cosine measure quantifies the similarity between two vectors as the cosine of the angle between the two vectors whereas the extended Jaccard measure computes the ratio of the number of shared attributes to the number of common attributes [19].

---
[11] We have also introduced a formal framework of concepts and individuals in ontologies but omit it here due to space limitations. Please refer to [2] for further details about the formal framework.

**String-Based Measures.** A different mapping $M_2$ from the feature set of a resource makes use of the underlying graph representation of ontologies. In this mapping, a resource $R$ is considered as starting node to traverse the graph along its edges where edges are properties of $R$ connecting other resources. These resources in turn may be concepts or, eventually, data values. Here, these sets are considered as vectors of strings, $\mathbf{x}$ and $\mathbf{y}$ respectively. The similarity between strings is often described as the edit distance (also called the Levenshtein edit distance [9]), that is, the minimum number of changes necessary to turn one string into another string. Here, a change is typically either defined as the insertion of a symbol, the removal of a symbol, or the replacement of one symbol with another. Obviously, this approach can be adapted to strings of concepts (i.e., vectors of strings as the result of mapping $M_2$) rather than strings of characters by calculating the number of insert, remove, and replacement operations to convert vector $\mathbf{x}$ into vector $\mathbf{y}$, which is defined as $xform(\mathbf{x}, \mathbf{y})$. But should each type of transformation have the same weight? Is not the replacement transformation, for example, comparable with a deleting procedure followed by an insertion procedure? Hence, it can be argued that the cost function $c$ should have the behavior $c(delete) + c(insert) \geq c(replace)$. We can then calculate the worst case (i.e., the maximum) transformation cost $xform_{wc}(\mathbf{x}, \mathbf{y})$ of $\mathbf{x}$ to $\mathbf{y}$ by replacing all concept parts of $\mathbf{x}$ with parts of $\mathbf{y}$, then deleting the remaining parts of $\mathbf{x}$, and inserting additional parts of $\mathbf{y}$. The worst case cost is then used to normalize the edit distance resulting in

$$sim_{levenshtein}(R_x, R_y) = \frac{xform(\mathbf{x}, \mathbf{y})}{xform_{wc}(\mathbf{x}, \mathbf{y})} \qquad (4)$$

**Full-Text Similarity Measure.** We decided to add a standard full-text similarity measure $sim_{tfidf}$ to our framework. Essentially, we exported a full-text description of all concepts in an ontology to their textual representation and built an index over the descriptions using Apache Lucene[12]. For this, we used a Porter Stemmer [13] to reduce all words to their stems and applied a standard, full-text TFIDF algorithm as described in [1] to compute the similarity between concepts.

TFIDF counts the frequency of occurrence of a term in a document in relation to the word's occurrence frequency in a whole corpus of documents. The resulting word counts are then used to compose a weighted term vector describing the document. In such a TFIDF scheme, the vectors of term weights can be compared using one of the vector-based similarity measures presented before.

**Distance-Based Measures.** The most intuitive similarity measure of concepts in an ontology is their distance within the ontology [15], defined as the number of sub-/super-concept (or *is-a*) relationships between them. These measures make use of the hierarchical ontology structure for determining the semantic similarity between concepts. As ontologies can be represented by rooted, labeled and unordered trees where edges between concepts represent relationships, distances

---

[12] http://lucene.apache.org/java/docs/

between concepts can be computed by counting the number of edges on the path connecting two concepts. Sparrows, for example, are more similar to blackbirds than to whales since they reside closer in typical biological taxonomies. The calculation of the ontology distance is based on the specialization graph of concepts in an ontology. The graph representing a multiple inheritance framework is not a tree but a directed acyclic graph. In such a graph, the ontology distance is usually defined as the shortest path going through a common ancestor or as the shortest path in general, potentially connecting two concepts through common descendants/specializations.

One possibility to determine the semantic similarity between concepts is $sim_{edge}$ as given in [16] (but normalized), which is a variant of the edge counting method converting from a distance (dissimilarity) into a similarity measure:

$$sim_{edge}(R_x, R_y) = \frac{2 * MAX - len(R_x, R_y)}{2 * MAX} \quad (5)$$

where $MAX$ is the length of the longest path from the root of the ontology to any of its leaf concepts and $len(R_x, R_y)$ is the length of the shortest path from $R_x$ to $R_y$.

A variation of the edge counting method is the conceptual similarity measure introduced by Wu & Palmer [20]:

$$sim_{con} = \frac{2 * N_3}{N_1 + N_2 + 2 * N_3} \quad (6)$$

where $N_1$, $N_2$ are the distances from concepts $R_x$ and $R_y$, respectively, to their Most Recent Common Ancestor $MRCA(R_x, R_y)$ and $N_3$ is the distance from $MRCA(R_x, R_y)$ to the root of the ontology.

**Information-Theory-Based Measures.** The problem of ontology distance-based measures is that they are highly dependent on the (frequently) subjective construction of ontologies. To address this problem, researchers have proposed measuring the similarity between two concepts in an ontology in terms of information-theoretic entropy measures [16, 10]. Specifically, Lin [10] argues that a class (in his case a word) is defined by its use. The information of a class is specified as the probability of encountering a class's (or one of its descendants') use. In cases where many instances are available, the probability $p$ of encountering a class's use can be computed over the instance corpus. Alternatively, when the instance space is sparsely populated (as currently in most Semantic Web ontologies) or when instances are also added as subclasses with is-a relationships (as with some taxonomies), then we propose to use the probability of encountering a subclass of a class. The entropy of a class is the negative logarithm of that probability. Resnik [16] defined the similarity as

$$sim_{resnik}(R_x, R_y) = \max_{R_z \in S(R_x, R_y)} [-\log_2 p(R_z)] \quad (7)$$

where $S(R_x, R_y)$ is the set of concepts that subsume both $R_x$ and $R_y$, and $p(R_z)$ is the probability of encountering a concept of type $z$ (i.e., the frequency of concept type $z$) in the corresponding ontology.

Lin defined the similarity between two concepts slightly differently:

$$sim_{lin}(R_x, R_y) = \frac{2 \log_2 p(MRCA(R_x, R_y))}{\log_2 p(R_x) + \log_2 P(R_y)} \qquad (8)$$

Intuitively, this measure specifies similarity as the probabilistic degree of overlap of descendants between two concepts.

## 3 The SOQA-SimPack Toolkit

The SOQA-SimPack Toolkit (SST) is an ontology language independent Java API that enables generic similarity detection and visualization in ontologies. Simply stated, SST accesses data concerning concepts to be compared through SOQA; this data is then taken as an input for the similarity measures provided by SimPack. That is, SST offers ontology language independent similarity calculation services based on the uniform view on ontological content as provided by the SOQA Ontology Meta Model. SST services that have already been implemented include:

- Similarity calculation between two concepts according to a single similarity measure or a list of them.
- Similarity calculation between a concept and a set of concepts according to a single or a list of similarity measures. This set of concepts can either be a freely composed list of concepts or all concepts from an ontology taxonomy (sub)tree.
- Retrieval of the $k$ most similar concepts of a set of concepts for a given concept according to a single or a list of similarity measures. Again, this set of concepts can either be a freely composed list of concepts or all concepts from an ontology taxonomy (sub)tree.
- Retrieval of the $k$ most *dis*similar concepts of a set of concepts for a given concept according to a single or a list of similarity measures. As before, a freely composed list of concepts or all concepts from an ontology taxonomy (sub)tree can be used to specify the set of concepts.

Note that for all calculations provided by SST, the concepts involved can be from *any* ontology that is connected through SOQA.[13] That is, not only is it possible to calculate similarities between concepts from a single ontology (for example, Student and Employee from the DAML University Ontology) with a given set of SimPack measures, but also can concepts from different ontologies be used in the very same similarity calculation (for example, Student from the Power-Loom Course Ontology can be compared with Researcher from WordNet). For all SST computations, the results can be output textually (floating point values or sets of concept names, depending on the service). Alternatively, calculation results can automatically be visualized and returned by SST as a chart.

---

[13] Generally, this is every ontology that can be represented in an ontology language. In fact, it is every ontology that is represented in a language for which a SOQA wrapper is available.

Using concepts from different ontologies in the same similarity calculation is enabled by the fact that in SST, all ontologies are incorporated into a single ontology tree. That is, the root concepts of the available ontologies (e.g., owl:Thing) are direct subconcepts of a so-called Super_Thing root concept. This makes it possible that, for instance, not only vector- and text-based similarity measures, but also distance-based measures that need a contiguous, traversable path between the concepts can be applied to concepts in SST. Alternatively, we could have replaced all root concepts of all ontologies with one general Thing concept. This, however, is a first step into the direction of ontology integration by mapping semantically equivalent concepts from different ontologies and not our goal in this research (consequentially, the ontologies should then completely be merged). Moreover, replacing the roots with Thing means, for example for OWL ontologies, that all direct subconcepts of owl:Thing from arbitrary domains are put directly under Thing and, thus, become immediate neighbors, blurring which ontology and domain a particular concept originates from. This is illustrated in Figure 3: Whereas the university domain of ontology$_1$ and the ornithology domain of ontology$_2$ remain separated in the first case, they are jumbled in the second. However, not mixing arbitrary domains is essential for distance-based similarity measures which found their judgments on distances in graphs (in Figure 3(b), Student is as similar to Professor as to Blackbird, due to the equality of the graph distances between Student, Professor, and Blackbird). Hence, we opted for introducing the Super_Thing concept as the root of the tree of ontologies in the SOQA-SimPack Toolkit.

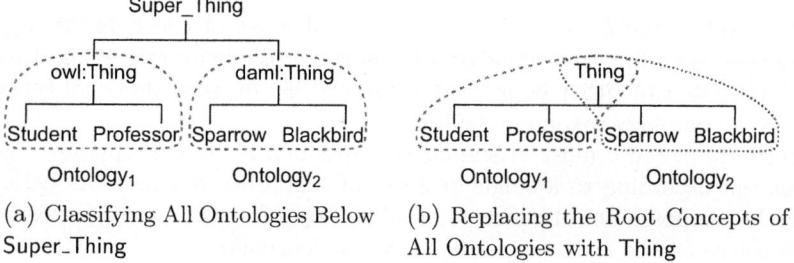

**Fig. 3.** Comparison of Approaches to Building a Single Tree for a Set of Ontologies

Like SOQA, the SOQA-SimPack Toolkit architecturally reflects the Facade design pattern: SST provides a unified interface to a subsystem which is in charge of generic similarity calculations based on data from ontologies that are specified in different ontology languages. The SST Facade shields external clients from its internal components and represents a single access point for unified ontological similarity services (see Figure 4). External users of the services provided by the SST Facade include:

- The SOQA-SimPack Toolkit Browser that is a tool to graphically perform similarity calculations in ontologies independent of the ontology language they are specified in;

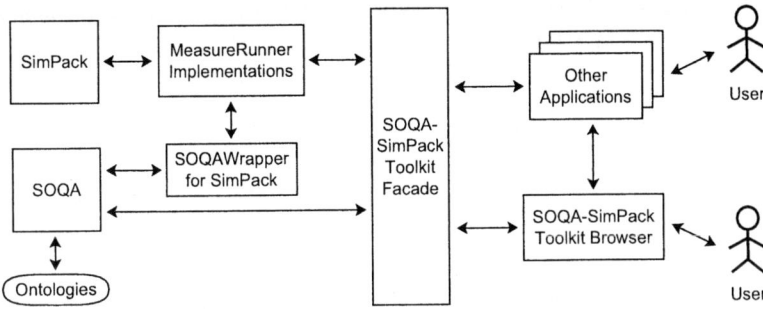

**Fig. 4.** Overview of the SOQA-SimPack Toolkit Software Architecture

– (Third-party) Java applications that use SST as a single point of access to generic similarity detection and visualization services as provided by the SST Facade. Possible application areas are ontology alignment and integration, Semantic Web (service) discovery, data clustering and mining, semantic interoperability in virtual organizations, and semantics-aware universal data management.

Behind the SOQA-SimPack Toolkit Facade, MeasureRunner implementations are used as an interface to the different SimPack similarity measures available. Each MeasureRunner is a coupling module that is capable of retrieving all necessary input data from the SOQAWrapper for SimPack and initiating a similarity calculation between two single concepts for a particular similarity measure. For example, there is a TFIDFMeasureRunner that returns a floating point value expressing the similarity between two given concepts according to the TFIDF measure. More advanced similarity calculations, such as finding the $k$ most similar concepts for a given one, are performed by tailored methods in the SOQA-SimPack Toolkit Facade itself based on the basic services supplied by underlying MeasureRunner implementations. By providing an additional MeasureRunner, SST can easily be extended to support supplementary measures (e.g., new measures or combinations of existing measures). Hence, the SOQA-SimPack Toolkit provides not only means for generic similarity detection, but can also be a fruitful playground for development and experimental evaluation of new similarity measures.

The SOQAWrapper for SimPack as another internal component of SST is in charge of retrieving ontological data as required by the SimPack similarity measure classes. This includes, for example, retrieval of (root, super, sub) concepts, provision of string sequences from concepts as well as depth and distance calculations in ontologies. Basically, all of this is done by accessing the necessary ontological data according to the SOQA Ontology Meta Model through SOQA and by providing the requested information as expected by SimPack. Summing up, the MeasureRunner implementations together with the SOQAWrapper for SimPack integrate both SOQA and SimPack on a technical level on behalf of the SST Facade.

Based on its Facade architecture, the SOQA-SimPack Toolkit provides a set of methods for ontology language independent similarity detection and visualization in ontologies. The following three method signatures (S1) to (S3) illustrate how similarities can be calculated with SST:

```
public double getSimilarity(String firstConceptName,           (S1)
    String firstOntologyName, String secondConceptName,
    String secondOntologyName, int measure)

public Vector<ConceptAndSimilarity> getMostSimilarConcepts     (S2)
    (String conceptName, String conceptOntologyName,
    String subtreeRootConceptName, String subtreeOntologyName,
    int k, int measure)

public Image getSimilarityPlot(String firstConceptName,        (S3)
    String firstOntologyName, String secondConceptName,
    String secondOntologyName, int[] measures)
```

In the examples given before, method signature (S1) provides access to the calculation of the similarity between the two given concepts — the similarity measure to be used is specified by an integer constant (e.g., SOQASimPackToolkitFacade.LIN_MEASURE for the measure by Lin). Note that in SST, for each concept we have to specify which ontology it originates from (parameters firstOntologyName and secondOntologyName, respectively). This is necessary since in SST's single ontology tree (into which all ontologies are incorporated), concept names are generally *not* unique anymore. For example, in case that more than one OWL ontology is used for similarity calculations, we have more than one owl:Thing concept as a direct subconcept of Super_Thing. Distinguishing which ontology the particular owl:Thing is the root of is essential (e.g., for graph-based measures) since the (direct) subconcepts for each owl:Thing concept differ. (S2) enables SST clients to retrieve the $k$ most similar concepts for the given one compared with all subconcepts of the specified ontology taxonomy (sub)tree. In the result set, ConceptAndSimilarity instances contain for each of the $k$ concepts the concept name, the name of its ontology, and the respective similarity value. Finally, (S3) computes the similarity between two concepts according to a set of measures and sets up a chart to visualize the computations.

Beyond access to similarity calculations, the SOQA-SimPack Toolkit Facade provides a variety of helper methods — for example, for getting information about a particular SimPack similarity measure, for displaying a SOQA Ontology Browser [22] to inspect a single ontology, or for opening a SOQA Query Shell to declaratively query an ontology using SOQA-QL [22].

Recall that in our running example from Section 1, a developer is looking for similarities among the concepts of five ontologies. In this scenario, the SOQA-SimPack Toolkit can be used, for instance, to calculate the similarity between the concept base1_0_daml:Professor from the DAML University Ontology and concepts from the other ontologies according to different SimPack similarity measures as shown in Table 1. Behind the scenes, SST initializes the necessary

**Table 1.** Comparisons of base1_0_daml:Professor with Concepts from Other Ontologies

| Concept | Conceptual Similarity | Leven-shtein | Lin | Resnik | Shortest Path | TFIDF |
|---|---|---|---|---|---|---|
| base1_0_daml:Professor | 0.7778 | 1.0 | 0.8792 | 2.7006 | 1.0 | 1.0 |
| univ-bench_owl:AssistantProfessor | 0.1111 | 0.1029 | 0.0 | 0.0 | 0.0588 | 0.3224 |
| COURSES:EMPLOYEE | 0.1176 | 0.0294 | 0.0 | 0.0 | 0.0625 | 0.0475 |
| SUMO_owl_txt:Human | 0.1 | 0.0028 | 0.0 | 0.0 | 0.0526 | 0.0151 |
| SUMO_owl_txt:Mammal | 0.0909 | 0.0032 | 0.0 | 0.0 | 0.0476 | 0.0184 |

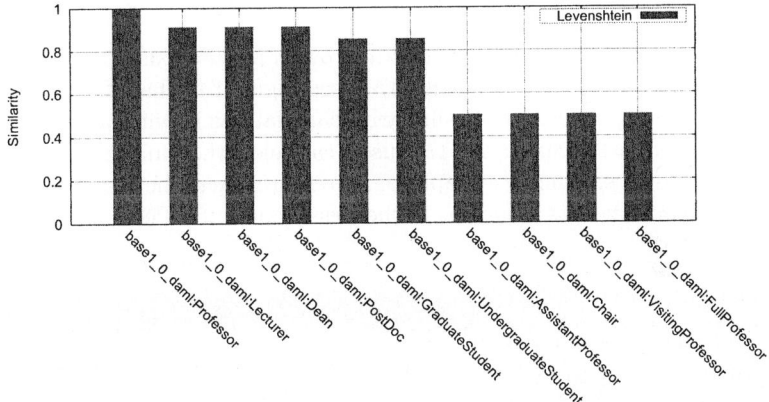

**Fig. 5.** SST Visualization of the Ten Most Similar Concepts for base1_0_daml:Professor

MeasureRunner instances which in turn manage the calculation of the desired similarity values by SimPack based on ontological information retrieved through SOQA. Note that for the plausibility of the calculated results, the SimPack measures as taken from the literature are responsible in general; in case that the available measures do not seem to be suitable for a particular domain, the set of available similarity measures can easily be extended by providing supplementary MeasureRunner implementations for further similarity measures.

In addition to numeric results, the SOQA-SimPack Toolkit is able to visualize the results of similarity calculations. For instance, our developer can retrieve the $k$ most similar concepts for base1_0_daml:Professor compared with all concepts from all five ontologies in our scenario. In response to this, SST can produce a bar chart as depicted in Figure 5. To generate the visualizations, SST creates data files and scripts that are automatically given as an input to Gnuplot[14], which then produces the desired graphics. Thus, the SOQA-SimPack Toolkit can effectively be employed to generically detect and visualize similarities in ontologies according to an extensible set of similarity measures and independently of the particular ontology languages in use.

---

[14] http://www.gnuplot.info

## 4 The SOQA-SimPack Toolkit Browser

The SOQA-SimPack Toolkit Browser is a tool that allows users to graphically perform similarity calculations and visualizations in ontologies based on the SOQA-SimPack Toolkit Facade. In general, it is an extension of the SOQA Browser [22] enabling users to inspect the contents of ontologies independently of the particular ontology language (i.e., according to the SOQA Ontology Meta Model). Based on the unified view of ontologies it provides, the SOQA-SimPack Toolkit Browser can be used to quickly survey concepts and their attributes, methods, relationships, and instances that are defined in ontologies as well as metadata (author, version, ontology language name, etc.) concerning the ontology itself.

In addition, the SOQA-SimPack Toolkit Browser provides an interface to all the methods of SST through its Similarity Tab (see Figure 6). That is, it is a tool for performing language independent similarity calculations in ontologies and for result visualization. In the Similarity Tab, users can select the similarity service to be run — for example, producing a graphical representation of the similarity calculation between two concepts according to the Resnik measure. Then, input fields are

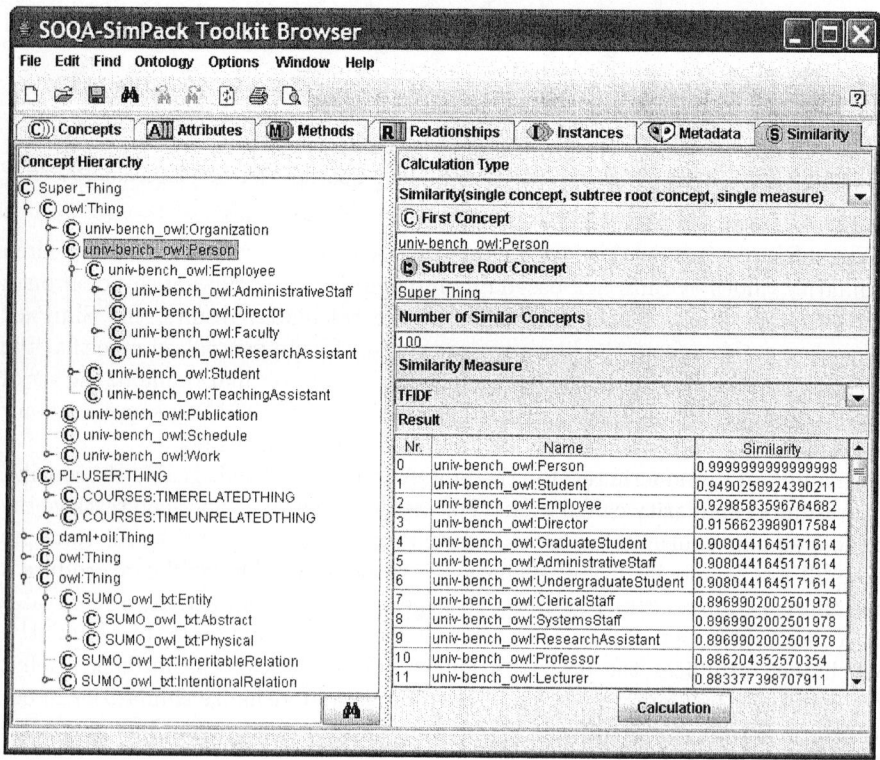

**Fig. 6.** The SOQA-SimPack Toolkit Browser and its Similarity Calculation Tab

inserted into the Similarity Tab so that all necessary input values can be entered; here, concept names can directly be mouse-dragged from the Concept Hierarchy view and dropped into the respective input field. In the end, the calculated results are shown in tabular or graphical form, depending on the selected service.

In our running example, the SOQA-SimPack Toolkit Browser can first be employed by the developer to quickly get a unified overview of the five ontologies represented in PowerLoom, OWL, and DAML respectively. Subsequently, he or she can use the Similarity Tab and calculate, for instance, the $k$ most similar concepts for univ-bench_owl:Person according to the TFIDF measure. The result is then presented in a table as shown in Figure 6. Thus, contrasting a conventional scenario where several ontology-language specific tools have to be employed for ontology access, the developer who takes advantage of SST does not have to cope with different ontology representation languages in use. Based on the unified view of ontologies as provided by the SOQA Ontology Meta Model, our developer can generically apply a rich and extensible set of SimPack similarity measures for similarity detection through the services offered by the SOQA-SimPack Toolkit. The results of these calculations can be presented as numerical values, textual lists (of concept names), or visualized in graphics. Hence, similarity detection in ontologies is facilitated and leveraged through the SOQA-SimPack Toolkit and its browser for the benefit of human users and applications.

## 5 Related Work

Closest to our work is the ontology alignment tool OLA presented by Euzénat et al. [4]. OLA is implemented in Java and relies on a universal measure for comparing entities of ontologies. Basically, it implements a set of core similarity functions which exploit different aspects of entities, such as textual descriptions, inter-entity relationships, entity class membership, and property restrictions. OLA relies on WordNet to compare string identifiers of entities. The main difference to our approach is OLA's restriction and dedication to the alignment of ontologies expressed in OWL-Lite. Using our generic approach, however, it is possible to compare and align entities of ontologies represented in a variety of ontology languages with the same set of similarity measures.

Noy and Musen's approach [12] follows similar goals: the comparison, alignment, and merging of ontologies to improve their reuse in the Semantic Web. The authors implemented a suite of tools called PROMPT that interactively supports ontology merging and the finding of correlations between entities to simplify the overall integration task. Compared to the SOQA-SimPack Toolkit, PROMPT is restricted to the comparison and merging of ontologies expressed in a few common ontology languages, such as RDF, DAML, and OWL. SST, on the other hand, offers the possibility to incorporate ontologies represented in a much broader range of languages. This includes not only ontologies described with recent Semantic Web languages, but also ones represented in traditional ontology languages, like PowerLoom. Furthermore, the SOQA-SimPack Toolkit supports ontologies supplied by knowledge bases, such as CYC [8], and by lexical ontology systems, such as WordNet.

Ehrig et al. [3] propose an approach that measures similarity between entities on three different layers (data layer, ontology layer, and context layer). Finally, an amalgamation function is used to combine the partial similarities of each layer and to compute the overall similarity between two entities. This approach differs from ours in its strong focus on entity layers and its amalgamation of individual layer-based similarity measures. Whilst it is easily possible to introduce such combined similarity measures through additional MeasureRunner implementations into the SOQA-SimPack Toolkit, we have left experiments with such measures for future work. In addition to this, we intend to extend the set of provided similarity measures in future, e.g., by incorporating measures from the SecondString project[15] which focuses on implementing approximate string-matching algorithms, and from SimMetrics[16] which presents similarity and distance metrics for data integration tasks.

## 6 Conclusions and Future Work

In this paper, we presented the SOQA-SimPack Toolkit, an ontology language independent Java API that enables generic similarity detection and visualization in ontologies. This task is central for application areas like ontology alignment and integration, Semantic Web (service) discovery, data clustering and mining, semantic interoperability in virtual organizations, and semantics-aware universal data management. SST is founded on (1) the SIRUP Ontology Query API, an ontology language independent Java API for query access to ontological metadata and data, and (2) SimPack, a generic Java library of similarity measures adapted for the use in ontologies.

The SOQA-SimPack Toolkit is extensible in two senses: First, further ontology languages can easily be integrated into SOQA by providing supplementary SOQA wrappers, and second, our generic framework is open to employ a multitude of additional similarity measures by supplying further MeasureRunner implementations. Hence, the extensible SOQA-SimPack Toolkit provides not only means for generic similarity detection, but can also be a fruitful playground for development and experimental evaluation of new similarity measures.

Contrasting a conventional scenario where several ontology-language specific tools have to be adopted for ontology access, users and applications taking advantage of the SOQA-SimPack Toolkit do not have to cope with different ontology representation languages in use. SST supports a broad range of ontology languages, including not only ontologies described with recent Semantic Web languages, but also ones represented in traditional ontology languages, like PowerLoom. Furthermore, ontologies supplied by knowledge bases, such as CYC, and by lexical ontology systems, such as WordNet, can be used in the SOQA-SimPack Toolkit.

Based on the unified view on ontologies as provided by the SOQA Ontology Meta Model, users and applications can generically apply a rich set of SimPack

---

[15] http://secondstring.sourceforge.net
[16] http://www.dcs.shef.ac.uk/~sam/simmetrics.html

similarity measures for similarity detection in SST services. By taking advantage of an extensible library of ontological similarity measures, a variety of notions of "similarity" can be captured. Additionally, for all calculations provided by SST, concepts can be used from *any* ontology that is connectible through SOQA. This is accomplished by incorporating all ontologies into a single ontology tree. The results of these calculations can be presented as numerical values, textual lists (of concept names), or visualized in graphics. As an application that is based on SST, we provide the SOQA-SimPack Toolkit Browser, a tool to graphically perform similarity calculations in ontologies independent of the ontology language they are specified in. Thus, similarity detection in ontologies is facilitated and leveraged through the SOQA-SimPack Toolkit and its browser for the benefit of human users and applications.

Future work includes the implementation of additional similarity measures (especially for trees) and the provision of more advanced result visualizations. Besides, we intend to do a thorough evaluation to find the best performing similarity measures in different task domains and to experiment with more advanced, combined similarity measures. In the end, a comprehensive assessment of SST in the context of data and schema integration is planned.

# References

1. R. Baeza-Yates and B. d. A. Ribeiro-Neto. *Modern Information Retrieval.* ACM Press, 1999.
2. A. Bernstein, E. Kaufmann, C. Kiefer, and C. Bürki. SimPack: A Generic Java Library for Similarity Measures in Ontologies. Technical report, University of Zurich, Department of Informatics. http://www.ifi.unizh.ch/ddis/staff/goehring/btw/files/ddis-2005.01.pdf, 2005.
3. M. Ehrig, P. Haase, N. Stojanovic, and M. Hefke. Similarity for Ontologies - A Comprehensive Framework. In *Workshop Enterprise Modelling and Ontology: Ingredients for Interoperability, PAKM 2004*, December 2004.
4. J. Euzénat, D. Loup, M. Touzani, and P. Valtchev. Ontology Alignment with OLA. In *3rd EON Workshop, 3rd Int. Semantic Web Conference*, pages 333–337, 2004.
5. A. Farquhar, R. Fikes, and J. Rice. The Ontolingua Server: A Tool for Collaborative Ontology Construction. *IJHCS*, 46(6):707–727, 1997.
6. E. Gamma, R. Helm, R. Johnson, and J. Vlissides. *Design Patterns. Elements of Reusable Object-Oriented Software.* Addison-Wesley, 1995.
7. D. Gentner and J. Medina. Similarity and the Development of Rules. *Cognition*, 65:263–297, 1998.
8. D. B. Lenat. CYC: A Large-Scale Investment in Knowledge Infrastructure. *Communications of the ACM*, 38(11):32–38, 1995.
9. V. I. Levenshtein. Binary Codes Capable of Correcting Deletions, Insertions and Reversals. *Soviet Physics Doklady*, 10:707–710, 1966.
10. D. Lin. An Information-Theoretic Definition of Similarity. In *15th International Conference on Machine Learning*, pages 296–304. Morgan Kaufmann, 1998.
11. G. A. Miller. WordNet: A Lexical Database for English. *Communications of the ACM*, 38(11):39–41, 1995.
12. N. F. Noy and M. A. Musen. The PROMPT Suite: Interactive Tools for Ontology Merging and Mapping. *IJHCS*, 59(6):983–1024, 2003.

13. M. F. Porter. An Algorithm for Suffix Stripping. *Program*, 14(3):130–137, 1980.
14. P.W.Lord, R. Stevens, A. Brass, and C.A.Goble. Investigating Semantic Similarity Measures Across the Gene Ontology: The Relationship Between Sequence and Annotation. *Bioinformatics*, 19(10):1275–83, 2003.
15. R. Rada, H. Mili, E. Bicknell, and M. Blettner. Development and Application of a Metric on Semantic Nets. In *IEEE Transactions on Systems, Man and Cybernetics*, pages 17–30, 1989.
16. P. Resnik. Using Information Content to Evaluate Semantic Similarity in a Taxonomy. In *IJCAI*, pages 448–453, 1995.
17. G. Salton and M. J. McGill. *Introduction to Modern Information Retrieval*. McGraw-Hill, 1983.
18. D. Shasha and K. Zhang. Approximate Tree Pattern Matching. In *Pattern Matching Algorithms*, pages 341–371. Oxford University Press, 1997.
19. A. Strehl, J. Ghosh, and R. Mooney. Impact of Similarity Measures on Web-page Clustering. In *17th National Conference on Artificial Intelligence: Workshop of Artificial Intelligence for Web Search*, pages 58–64. AAAI, July 2000.
20. Z. Wu and M. Palmer. Verb Semantics and Lexical Selection. In *32nd. Annual Meeting of the Association for Computational Linguistics*, pages 133–138, New Mexico State University, Las Cruces, New Mexico, 1994.
21. P. Ziegler and K. R. Dittrich. User-Specific Semantic Integration of Heterogeneous Data: The SIRUP Approach. In *First International IFIP Conference on Semantics of a Networked World (ICSNW 2004)*, volume 3226 of *Lecture Notes in Computer Science*, pages 44–64, Paris, France, June 17-19, 2004. Springer.
22. P. Ziegler, C. Sturm, and K. R. Dittrich. Unified Querying of Ontology Languages with the SIRUP Ontology Query API. In *Datenbanksysteme in Business, Technologie und Web (BTW 2005)*, volume P-65 of *Lecture Notes in Informatics*, pages 325–344, Karlsruhe, Germany, March 2-4, 2005. Gesellschaft für Informatik (GI).

# Holistic Schema Matching for Web Query Interfaces

Weifeng Su[1], Jiying Wang[2], and Frederick Lochovsky[1]

[1] Hong Kong University of Science & Technology, Hong Kong
{weifeng, fred}@cs.ust.hk
[2] City University, Hong Kong
wangjy@cityu.edu.hk

**Abstract.** One significant part of today's Web is Web databases, which can dynamically provide information in response to user queries. To help users submit queries to different Web databases, the query interface matching problem needs to be addressed. To solve this problem, we propose a new complex schema matching approach, Holistic Schema Matching (HSM). By examining the query interfaces of real Web databases, we observe that attribute matchings can be discovered from attribute-occurrence patterns. For example, **First Name** often appears together with **Last Name** while it is rarely co-present with **Author** in the Books domain. Thus, we design a count-based greedy algorithm to identify which attributes are more likely to be matched in the query interfaces. In particular, HSM can identify both *simple matching* i.e., 1:1 matching, and *complex matching*, i.e., 1:n or m:n matching, between attributes. Our experiments show that HSM can discover both simple and complex matchings accurately and efficiently on real data sets.

## 1 Introduction

Today, more and more databases that dynamically generate Web pages in response to user queries are available on the Web. These Web databases compose the *deep Web*, which is estimated to contain a much larger amount of high quality information and to have a faster growth than the static Web [1, 3].

While each static Web page has a unique URL by which a user can access the page, most *Web databases* are only accessible through a query interface. Once a user submits a query describing the information that he/she is interested in through the query interface, the Web server will retrieve the corresponding results from the back-end database and return them to the user.

To build a system/tool that helps users locate information in numerous Web databases, the very first task is to understand the query interfaces and help dispatch user queries to suitable fields of those interfaces. The main challenge of such a task is that different databases may use different fields or terms to represent the same concept. For example, to describe the genre of a CD in the MusicRecords domain, **Category** is used in some databases while **Style** is used in other databases. In the Books domain, **First Name** and **Last Name** are used in some databases while **Author** is used in others to denote the writer of a book.

In this paper, we specifically focus on the problem of matching across query interfaces of structured Web databases. The query interface matching problem is related to a classic problem in the database literature, *schema matching*, if we define an entry or field in a query interface as an *attribute* and all attributes in the query interface form a *schema* of the interface[1]. Schema matching maps semantically related attributes between pairs of schemas in the same domain. When matching the attributes, we call a 1:1 matching, such as Category with Style, a *simple matching* and a 1:n or m:n matching, such as First Name, Last Name with Author, a *complex matching*. In the latter case, attributes First Name and Last Name form a concept group before they are matched to attribute Author. We call attributes that are in the same concept group *grouping attributes* and attributes that are semantically identical or similar to each other *synonym attributes*. For example, attributes First Name and Last Name are grouping attributes, and First Name with Author or Last Name with Author are synonym attributes.

Discovering grouping attributes and synonym attributes in the query interfaces of relevant Web databases is an indispensable step to dispatch user queries to various Web databases and integrate their results. Considering that millions of databases are available on the Web [3], computer-aided interface schema matching is definitely necessary to avoid tedious and expensive human labor.

Although many solutions have been proposed to solve the schema matching problem, current solutions still suffer from the following limitations:

1. *simple matching*: most schema matching methods to date only focus on discovering simple matchings between schemas [2, 6, 9, 16].
2. *low accuracy on complex matching*: although there are some methods that can identify complex matchings, their accuracy is practically unsatisfactory [5, 12].
3. *time consuming*: some methods employ machine-learning techniques that need a lot of training time and some have time complexity exponential to the number of attributes [8, 10].
4. *domain knowledge required*: some methods require domain knowledge, instance data or user interactions before or during the matching process [2, 5, 8, 14, 16, 17].

In this paper, we propose a new interface schema matching approach, **Holistic Schema Matching** (HSM), to find matching attributes across a set of Web database schemas of the same domain. HSM takes advantage of the term occurrence pattern within a domain and can discover both simple and complex matchings efficiently without any domain knowledge.

The rest of the paper is organized as follows. Section 2 reviews related work and compares our approach to previous approaches. In section 3, we introduce our observations on Web database query interfaces and give an example that motivates our approach. Section 4, the main section of the paper, presents the holistic schema matching approach HSM. Our experiments on two datasets and the results are reported in section 5. Section 6 concludes the paper and discusses several further open research issues.

## 2 Related Work

Being an important step for data integration, schema matching has attracted much attention [2, 5-10, 12, 14, 16, 17]. However, most previous work either focuses on discovering simple matchings only or has un-satisfactory performance on discovering complex

---
[1] The terms "schema" and "interface" will be used in this paper interchangeably.

matchings. This is because complex matching discovery is fundamentally harder than simple matching discovery. While the number of simple matching candidates between two schemas is bounded by the product of the sizes of the two schemas, the number of complex matching candidates is exponential with respect to the size of the two schemas.

As a result, the performance of some existing complex matching discovery algorithms is not satisfactory. [5] tries to convert the problem of matching discovery into the problem of *searching* in the space of possible matches. [12] views the input schemas as graphs and designs a matching algorithm based on a fixpoint computation using the fact that two nodes are similar when their adjacent nodes are similar. Both approaches can handle simple matchings well (average accuracy around 78% in [5] and 58% in [12]), but their accuracy drops dramatically for complex matchings (around 55% in [5] and negative accuracy in [12]). [17] out performs [5, 12] by utilizing different kinds of information, such as linguistic similarity, type similarity and domain similarity between attributes. However, it also needs user interaction during the matching process to tune system parameters.

Different from most existing approaches, [2, 16] are notable in that they focus on exploiting instance-level information, such as instance-value overlapping. However, these two approaches can only handle simple matchings. In addition, data instances are very hard to obtain in the Web database environment.

[14, 10] are similar approaches in that they manage to combine multiple algorithms and reuse their matching results. [14] proposes several domain-independent combination methods, such as *max* and *average*, and [10] employs a weighted sum and adapts machine learning techniques to learn the importance of each individual component for a particular domain. Although the approach in [10] is able to learn domain-specific knowledge and statistics, it requires a lot of human effort to manually identify correct matchings as training data.

In contrast to the above works, our approach is capable of discovering simple and complex matchings at the same time without using any domain knowledge, data instances or user involvement. The HSM approach proposed in this paper can be considered as a single *matcher* that only focuses on exploiting domain-specific attribute occurrence statistics. HSM is specifically designed, and is thus more suitable, for the hidden Web environment where there are a large number of online interfaces to match whose attributes are usually informative in order to be understood by ordinary users. Compared with the above works, HSM is not suitable for a traditional database environment, where there are often only two schemas involved in the matching process and the attribute names could be very non-informative, such as attr1 and attr2, depending on the database designers.

Our HSM approach is very close to DCM developed in [7], which discovers complex matchings holistically using data mining techniques. In fact, HSM and DCM are based on similar observations that frequent attribute co-presence indicates a synonym relationship and rare attribute co-presence indicates a grouping relationship. However, HSM has two major differences (advantages) compared to DCM:

1. *measurement*: DCM defines a H-measure, $H = \frac{f_{01} f_{10}}{f_{+1} f_{1+}}$, to measure the negative correlation between two attributes by which synonym attributes are discovered. Such a measure may give a high score for rare attributes, while HSM's matching

score measure does not have this problem. Suppose there are 50 input schemas, where 25 schemas are $\{A_1, A_3\}$, 24 schemas are $\{A_1, A_4\}$ and the remaining one is $\{A_1, A_2, A_4\}$. In these schemas, $A_3$ and $A_4$ are actual synonym attributes appearing a similar number of times and $A_2$ is a rare and "noisy" attribute that only appears once. According to the negative measure of DCM, the matching score $H_{23} = \frac{1 \times 25}{1 \times 25} = 1$, and the matching score $H_{34} = \frac{25 \times 25}{25 \times 25}$, is also 1. In contrast, HSM measures the matching scores as $X_{23} = 0.96$ and $X_{34} = 12.5$ (see section 4.1). In this extreme case, DCM cannot differentiate frequent attributes from rare attributes, which affects its performance.

2. *matching discovery algorithm*: The time complexity of HSM's matching discovery algorithm is polynomial with respect to the number of attributes, $n$, while the time complexity of DCM is exponential with respect to $n$. DCM tries to first identify all possible groups and then discover the matchings between them. To discover grouping attributes, it calculates the positive correlation between all combinations of groups, from size 2 to size $n$ (the worst case). In contrast, HSM only considers the grouping score between every two attributes, and the complex matching is discovered by adding each newly found group member into the corresponding group incrementally. Consequently, HSM discovers the matchings much faster than DCM does.

Our experimental results in section 5.2 show that HSM not only has a higher accuracy than DCM, but is also much more efficient for real Web databases.

## 3 Intuition: Parallel Schemas

In this section, we first present our observations about interface schemas and interface attributes of Web databases in a domain, on which the HSM approach is based. Then, examples are given to motivate the intuition of HSM.

### 3.1 Observations

In Web databases, query interfaces are not designed arbitrarily. Web database designers try to design the interfaces to be easily understandable and usable for querying important attributes of the back-end databases. For Web databases in the same domain that are about a specific kind of product or a specific topic, their query interfaces usually share many characteristics:

1. Terms describing or labeling attributes are usually unambiguous in a domain although they may have more than one meaning in an ordinary, comprehensive dictionary. For example, the word title has ten meanings as a noun and two meanings as a verb in WordNet [13]. However, it always stands for "the name of a book" when it appears in query interfaces of the Books domain.
2. According to [8], the vocabulary of interfaces in the same domain tends to converge to a relatively small size. This indicates that the same concepts in a domain are usually described by the same set of terms.
3. Synonym attributes are rarely co-present in the same interface. For example, Author and Last Name never appeared together in any query interface that we investigate in the Books domain.

4. Grouping attributes are usually co-present in the same interface to form a "larger" concept. For example, in the Airfares domain, From is usually paired with To to form a concept, which is the same as the concept formed by another frequently co-present attribute pair, Departure city and Arrival city. This phenomenon is recognized as *collocation* in natural language [11] and is very common in daily life.

## 3.2 Motivating Examples

We use the query interfaces shown in Figure 1 to illustrate the main idea of HSM. Let us first consider the schemas in Figure 1(a) and 1(b). The two schemas are semantically equal[2], i.e., any single attribute or set of grouping attributes in one of them semantically corresponds to a single attribute or set of grouping attributes in the other. If we compare these two schemas by putting them in parallel and deleting the attributes that appear in both of them (according to observation 1), we get the matching correspondence between the grouping attributes {First Name, Last Name} and the attribute Author.

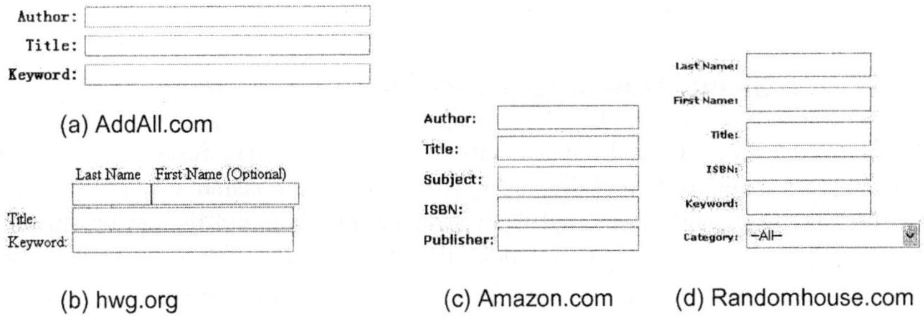

**Fig. 1.** Examples of query interfaces

**Definition 1.** *Given two schemas $S_1$ and $S_2$, each of which are comprised of a set of attributes, the two schemas form a **parallel schema** $Q$, which comprises two attribute sets $\{\{S_1 - S_1 \cap S_2\}$ and $\{S_2 - S_1 \cap S_2\}\}$.*

**Table 1.** Examples of parallel schemas

| AddAll.com | hwg.org |
|---|---|
| Author | First Name |
|  | Last Name |

(a)

| Amazon.com | RandomHouse.com |
|---|---|
| Author | First Name |
| Subject | Last Name |
| Publisher | Keyword |
|  | Category |

(b)

Table 1(a) shows the parallel schema formed by the schemas in Figure 1(a) and 1(b). The complex matching {First Name, Last Name}={Author} is directly available from this parallel schema. However, in most cases, matching is not so easy because

---

[2] We ignore the word "(Optional)" that appears in Figure 1(b) because it will be discarded during query interface preprocessing [7].

two target schemas may not be semantically equal, such as the schemas in Figure 1(c) and 1(d). After putting these two schemas in parallel and deleting common attributes, the parallel schema in Table 1(b) is obtained. Unfortunately, correct matchings are not directly available from this parallel schema.

To address this problem, we consider any two attributes cross-copresent in a parallel schema to be potential synonym attributes. For example Author with First Name and Author with Last Name in Table1(b) are potential synonym attributes. As a result, if two attributes are potential synonym attributes appearing in many parallel schemas, we may be statistically confident to find the synonym relationship between them (observation 3).

Furthermore, we also notice that First Name and Last Name are always co-present in the same query interface, which indicates that they are very likely to be grouping attributes that form a concept group (observation 4). Suppose we also know that Author with First Name and Author with Last Name are synonym attributes. We can compose an attribute group containing First Name and Last Name, with both of the two members matched to Author. That is, {First Name, Last Name}={Author} is discovered as a complex matching.

## 4 Holistic Schema Matching Algorithm

We formalize the schema matching problem as the same problem described in [7]. The input is a set of schemas $\mathcal{S} = \{S_1, \ldots, S_u\}$, in which each schema $S_i$ $(1 \leq i \leq u)$ contains a set of attributes extracted from a query interface and the set of attributes $\mathcal{A} = \cup_{i=1}^{u} S_i = \{A_1, \ldots, A_n\}$ includes all attributes in $\mathcal{S}$. We assume that these schemas come from the same domain. The schema matching problem is to find all matchings $\mathcal{M} = \{M_1, \ldots, M_v\}$ including both simple and complex matchings. A matching $M_j$ $(1 \leq j \leq v)$ is represented as $G_{j1} = G_{j2} = \ldots = G_{jw}$, where $G_{jk}$ $(1 \leq k \leq w)$ is a group of attributes[3] and $G_{jk}$ is a subset of $\mathcal{A}$, i.e., $G_{jk} \subset \mathcal{A}$. Each matching $M_j$ should represent the semantic synonym relationship between two attribute groups $G_{jk}$ and $G_{jl}$ $(l \neq k)$, and each group $G_{jk}$ should represent the grouping relationship between the attributes within it. More specifically, we restrict each attribute to appear no more than one time in $\mathcal{M}$ (observation 1 and 4).

A matching example is {First Name, Last Name} = {Author} in the Books domain, where attributes First Name and Last Name form an attribute group and attribute Author forms another group and the two groups are semantically synonymous. Besides this matching, suppose another matching {Author} = {Writer} is found. According to our restriction, we will not directly include the latter matching in the matching set $\mathcal{M}$. Instead, we may adjust the original matching to {First Name, Last Name} = {Author} = {Writer} or {First Name, Last Name, Writer} = {Author}, depending on whether the relationship found between Writer and {First Name, Last Name} is a grouping or a synonym relationship.

The workflow of the schema matching algorithm is shown in Figure 2. Before the schema matching discovery, two scores, *matching score* and *grouping score*, are calculated between every two attributes. The matching score is used to evaluate the possibility

---

[3] An attribute group can have just one attribute.

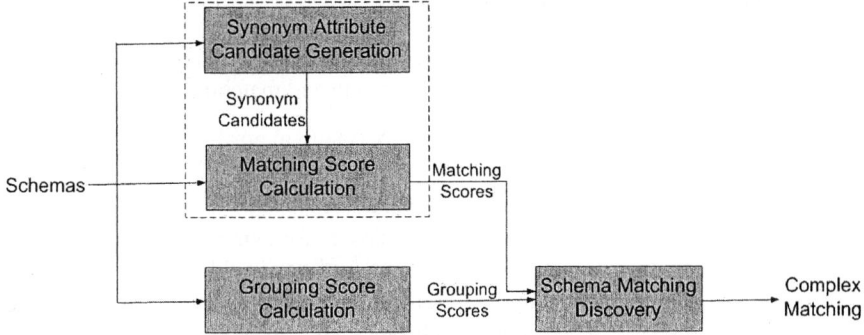

**Fig. 2.** Holistic Schema Matching Workflow

that two attributes are synonym attributes and the grouping score is used to evaluate the possibility that two attributes are in the same group in a matching.

The matching score is calculated in two steps. First, *Synonym Attribute Candidate Generation* takes all schemas as input and generates all candidates for synonym attributes based on the observation that synonym attributes rarely co-occur in the same interface schema. Then, *Matching Score Calculation* calculates matching scores between the candidates based on their cross-copresence count (see section 4.1) in the parallel schemas.

*Grouping Score Calculation* takes all schemas as input and calculates the grouping score between every two attributes based on the observation that grouping attributes frequently co-occur in the same schema.

After calculating the grouping and matching score between every two attributes, we use a greedy algorithm in *Schema Matching Discovery* that iteratively chooses the highest matching score to discover synonym matchings between pairs of attributes. At the same time, the grouping score is used to decide whether two attributes that match to the same set of other attributes belong to the same group. At the end, a matching list is outputted, including both simple and complex matchings. The overall time complexity of HSM is $O(un^2+n^3)$ where $n$ is the number of attributes and $u$ is the number of input schemas. We will explain the time complexity of HSM in detail later in this section.

The rest of this section is organized according to the workflow shown in Figure 2. Subsection 4.1 presents how to calculate the matching score between every two attributes. Subsection 4.2 shows how to calculate the grouping score between every two attributes, and finally subsection 4.3 describes how the matchings can be identified using the grouping and matching scores. In these subsections, the schemas in Table 2 will be used as examples of input schemas.

**Table 2.** Examples of input schemas

| $S_1$ | $S_2$ | $S_3$ | $S_4$ | $S_5$ |
|---|---|---|---|---|
| Title | Title | Title | Title | Title |
| First Name | Author | Author | First Name | Author |
| Last Name | Subject | Category | Last Name | Category |
| Category | Publisher | | | Publisher |
| Publisher | | | | |

## 4.1 Matching Score Calculation

As discussed above, in HSM, the matching scores between two attributes are calculated in two steps: Synonym attribute candidate generation and matching score calculation.

**Synonym Attribute Candidate Generation.** A synonym attribute candidate is a pair of attributes that are possibly synonyms. If there are $n$ attributes in the input schemas, the maximum number of synonym attribute candidates is $C_n^2 = \frac{n(n-1)}{2}$. However, not every two attributes from $\mathcal{A}$ can be actual candidates for synonym attributes. For example in the Books domain, attributes Title and Author should not be considered as synonym attribute candidates, while Author and First Name should. Recall that, in section 3.1, we observed that synonym attributes are rarely co-present in the same schema. In fact, Author and First Name do seldom co-occur in the same interface, while Title and Author appear together very often. This observation can be used to reduce the number of synonym attribute candidates dramatically.

**Example 1.** *For the four input schemas in Table 2, if we make a strict restriction that any two attributes co-present in the same schema cannot be candidates for synonym attributes, the number of synonym attribute candidates becomes 5 (shown in Table 3), instead of 21 when there is no restriction at all.*

**Table 3.** Synonym attribute candidates

| | |
|---|---|
| 1 | First Name, Author |
| 2 | First Name, Subject |
| 3 | Last Name, Author |
| 4 | Last Name, Subject |
| 5 | Category, Subject |

In HSM, we assume that two attributes $(A_p, A_q)$ are synonym attribute candidates if $A_p$ and $A_q$ are co-present in less than $\mathcal{T}_{pq}$ schemas. Intuitively, $\mathcal{T}_{pq}$ should be in proportion to the normalized frequency of $A_p$ and $A_q$ in the input schemas set $\mathcal{S}$. Hence, in our experiments, we set the co-presence threshold of $A_p$ and $A_q$ as

$$\mathcal{T}_{pq} = \frac{\alpha(C_p + C_q)}{u} \qquad (1)$$

where $\alpha$ is determined empirically, $C_p$ and $C_q$ are the count of attributes $A_p$ and $A_q$ in $\mathcal{S}$, respectively, and $u$ is the number of input schemas. In out experiments, $\alpha$ is empirically set to be 3. [4]

Suppose there are 50 input schemas and two attributes $A_1$ and $A_2$ that occur 20 and 25 times, respectively, then $\mathcal{T}_{12} = 2.7$. This means that $A_1$ and $A_2$ should be co-present in no more than two schemas to be synonym attribute candidates.

We use $\mathcal{L} = \{(A_p, A_q), p = 1..n, q = 1..n, p \neq q, C_{pq} < \mathcal{T}_{pq}\}$ to represent the set of synonym attribute candidates, where $C_{pq}$ is the count of the co-occurrences of $A_p$ and $A_q$ in the same schema.

---

[4] The experiments have the best performance when $\alpha \in [2, 4]$. We select a middle value of the range [2,4] here in our experiments.

**Matching Score Calculation.** For any two attributes $A_p$ and $A_q$, a matching score $X_{pq}$ measures the possibility that $A_p$ and $A_q$ are synonym attributes. The bigger the score, the more likely that the two attributes are synonym attributes.

**Definition 2.** *Given a parallel schema $Q$, we call $A_p$ and $A_q$ to be **cross-copresent** in $Q$ if $A_p \in S_1 - S_1 \cap S_2$ and $A_q \in S_2 - S_1 \cap S_2$.*

If we compare every two schemas, we can get $D_{pq} = (C_p - C_{pq})(C_q - C_{pq})$ parallel schemas in which $A_p$ and $A_q$ are cross-copresent. The bigger $D_{pq}$ is, i.e., the more often $A_p$ and $A_q$ are cross-copresent in a parallel schema, the more likely that $A_p$ and $A_q$ are synonym attributes. However $D_{pq}$ itself is not able to distinguish a scenario such as that in Example 2:

**Example 2.** *Suppose there are 50 input schemas, where 15 schemas are $\{A_1, A_3\}$, 15 schemas are $\{A_1, A_4\}$, 15 schemas are $\{A_1, A_5\}$ and the rest 5 are $\{A_2\}$. Our intuition is that the matching $A_3 = A_4 = A_5$ should be more preferred than matching $A_1 = A_2$ because it is highly like that $A_2$ is a noise attribute and occur randomly. $D_{pq}$ alone is not able to correctly catch this case because $D_{12} = D_{34} = D_{35} = D_{45} = 225$. Meanwhile, we also notice that $C_1 + C_2 = 50$ and $C_3 + C_4 = C_3 + C_5 = C_4 + C_5 = 30$. Hence if we divide $D_{pq}$ by $C_p + C_q$, we can reduce the problem caused by noise attributes, such as $A_2$ above.*

Hence, we formulate the matching score between $A_p$ and $A_q$ as:

$$X_{pq} = \begin{cases} 0 & \text{if } (A_p, A_q) \notin \mathcal{L} \\ \frac{(C_p - C_{pq})(C_q - C_{pq})}{(C_p + C_q)} & \text{otherwise,} \end{cases} \quad (2)$$

Specifically designed for the schema matching problem, this matching score has the following important properties:

1. *Null invariance* [15]. For any two attributes, adding more schemas that do not contain the attributes does not affect their matching score. That is, we are more interested in how frequently attributes $A_p$ and $A_q$ are cross co-present in the parallel schemas than how frequently they are co-absent in the parallel schemas.
2. *Rareness differentiation*. The matching score between rare attributes and the other attributes is usually low. That is, we consider it is more likely that a rare attribute is cross co-present with other attributes by accident. Example 3 shows that the matching scores for rare attributes, e.g., **Subject**, are usually small.

**Example 3.** *Matching scores between the attributes from the schemas in Table 2 are shown in Table 4, given the synonym attribute candidates in Table 3.*

In this example, the matching scores between all the actual synonym attributes are non-zero and high, such as the score between **First Name** and **Author** and the score between **Category** and **Subject**, which is desirable. The matching scores between some non-synonym attributes are zero, such as the score between **Title** and **Category** and the score between **Publisher** and **Author**, which is also desirable. However, the matching scores between some non-synonym attributes are also non-zero yet low, such as the score between **First Name** and **Subject**, which is undesirable. To tackle this problem,

**Table 4.** Matching scores

|  | Title | First Name | Last Name | Category | Publisher | Author | Subject |
|---|---|---|---|---|---|---|---|
| Title | | 0 | 0 | 0 | 0 | 0 | 0 |
| First Name | | | 0 | 0 | 0 | 1.2 | 0.67 |
| Last Name | | | | 0 | 0 | 1.2 | 0.67 |
| Category | | | | | 0 | 0 | 0.75 |
| Publisher | | | | | | 0 | 0 |
| Author | | | | | | | 0 |
| Subject | | | | | | | |

our matching discovery algorithm is designed to be greedy by considering the matchings with higher scores first when discovering synonym attributes (see section 4.3).

We use $\mathcal{X} = \{X_{pq}, p = 1..n, q = 1..n, p \neq q\}$ to denote the set of matching scores between any two different attributes.

### 4.2 Grouping Score Calculation

As mentioned before, a grouping score between two attributes aims to evaluate the possibility that the two attributes are grouping attributes. Recall observation 4 in section 3.1, attributes $A_p$ and $A_q$ are more liable to be grouping attributes if $C_{pq}$ is big. However using $C_{pq}$ only is not sufficient in many cases. Suppose there are 50 input schemas, where 8 schemas are $\{A_1, A_2\}$, 10 schemas are $\{A_1, A_3\}$, 10 schemas are $\{A_3, A_4\}$, and the rest are $\{A_4\}$. In this example, $C_{12} = 8$ and $C_{13} = 10$. Note that $A_2$ always appears together with $A_1$ and $A_3$ does not co-occur with $A_1$ half of the time, which indicates that $A_1$ and $A_2$ are more likely to be a group than $A_1$ and $A_3$. Given cases like this, we consider two attributes to be grouping attributes if the less frequent one usually co-occurs with the more frequent one. We propose the following grouping score measure between two attributes $A_p$ and $A_q$:

$$Y_{pq} = \frac{C_{pq}}{min(C_p, C_q)}. \tag{3}$$

We need to set a grouping score threshold $T_g$ such that attributes $A_p$ and $A_q$ will be considered as grouping attributes only when $Y_{pq} > T_g$. Practically, $T_g$ should be close to 1 as the grouping attributes are expected to co-occur most of the time. In our experiment, $T_g$ is an empirical parameter and the experimental results show that it has similar performance in a wide range (see section 5.2).

**Example 4.** *Grouping scores between the attributes from the schemas in Table 2 are shown in Table 5.*

In Table 5, the actual grouping attributes **First Name** and **Last Name** have a large grouping score, which is desirable. However, it is not very ideal that some non-grouping attributes also have large grouping scores, e.g., **Publisher** and **Subject**. This is not a problem in our matching discovery algorithm, which is designed to be matching score centric and always consider the grouping scores together with the matching scores when discovering grouping attributes (see section 4.3).

We use $\mathcal{Y} = \{Y_{pq}, p = 1..n, q = 1..n, p \neq q\}$ to denote the set of grouping scores between any two different attributes.

**Table 5.** Grouping scores between every two different attributes

|            | Title | First Name | Last Name | Category | Publisher | Author | Subject |
|------------|-------|------------|-----------|----------|-----------|--------|---------|
| Title      | 1     | 1          | 1         | 1        | 1         | 1      | 1       |
| First Name |       |            | 1         | 0.5      | 0.5       | 0      | 0       |
| Last Name  |       |            |           | 0.5      | 0.5       | 0      | 0       |
| Category   |       |            |           |          | 0.67      | 0.67   | 0       |
| Publisher  |       |            |           |          |           | 0.67   | 1       |
| Author     |       |            |           |          |           |        | 1       |
| Subject    |       |            |           |          |           |        |         |

The time complexity of both matching score calculation and grouping score calculation are $O(un^2)$ as there are $u$ schemas to go through and it takes a maximum of $O(n^2)$ time to go through each schema to obtain the co-occurrence counts for any two attributes in Equation (2) and (3).

### 4.3 Schema Matching Discovery

Given the matching score and grouping score between any two attributes, we propose an iterative matching discovery algorithm, as shown in Algorithm 1. In each iteration, a greedy selection strategy is used to choose the synonym attribute candidates with the highest matching score (Line 4) until there is no synonym attribute candidate available (Line 5). Suppose $X_{pq}$ is the highest matching score in the current iteration. We will insert its corresponding attributes $A_p$ and $A_q$ into the matching set $\mathcal{M}$ depending on how they appear in $\mathcal{M}$:

1. If neither $A_p$ nor $A_q$ has appeared in $\mathcal{M}$ (Lines 7 - 8), $\{A_p\} = \{A_q\}$ will be inserted as a new matching into $\mathcal{M}$.
2. If only one of $A_p$ and $A_q$ has appeared in $\mathcal{M}$ (Lines 9 - 16), suppose it is $A_p$ that has appeared in $M_j$ (the $j$-th matching of $\mathcal{M}$), then $A_q$ will be added into $M_j$ too if:
   - $A_q$ has non-zero matching scores between all existing attributes in $M_j$. In this case, $\{A_q\}$ is added as a new matching group into $M_j$ (Lines 11 - 12).
   - there exists a group $G_{jk}$ in $M_j$ where the grouping score between $A_q$ and any attribute in $G_{jk}$ is larger than the given threshold $T_g$, and $A_q$ has non-zero matching score between any attribute in the rest of the groups of $M_j$. In this case, $\{A_q\}$ is added as a member into the group $G_{jk}$ in $M_j$ (Lines 13 - 15).
   - If both $A_p$ and $A_q$ have appeared in $\mathcal{M}$, $X_{pq}$ will be ignored because each attribute is not allowed to appear more than one time in $\mathcal{M}$. The reason for this constraint is that if $A_p$ and $A_q$ have been added into $\mathcal{M}$ already, they must have had higher matching scores in a previous iteration.

Finally, we delete $X_{pq}$ from $\mathcal{X}$ (Line 17) at the end of each iteration.

One thing that is not mentioned in the algorithm is how to select the matching score if there is more than one highest score in $\mathcal{X}$. Our approach is to select a score $X_{pq}$ where one of $A_p$ and $A_q$ has appeared in $\mathcal{M}$, but not both. This way of selection makes full use of previously discovered matchings that have higher scores. If there is still more than one score that fits the condition, the selection will be random[5].

---
[5] Actually a tie occurs very seldom in our experiments.

**Algorithm 1.** Schema Matching Discovery

*Input*:
$\mathcal{A} = \{A_i, i = 1...n\}$: the set of attributes from input schemas
$\mathcal{X} = \{X_{pq}, p = 1...n, q = 1...n, p \neq q\}$: the set of matching scores between two attributes
$\mathcal{Y} = \{Y_{pq}, p = 1...n, q = 1...n, p \neq q\}$: the set of grouping scores between two attributes
$T_g$: the threshold of grouping score
*Output*:
$\mathcal{M} = \{M_j, j = 1...v\}$: the set of complex matchings where each matching $M_j$ is represented as $G_{j1} = ... = G_{jw}$, and $G_{jk}, k = 1...w$ stands for a group of grouping attributes in $\mathcal{A}$

1: **begin**
2:   $\mathcal{M} \leftarrow \emptyset$
3:   **while** $\mathcal{X} \neq \emptyset$ **do**
4:     choose the highest matching score $X_{pq}$ in $\mathcal{X}$
5:     **if** $X_{pq} = 0$ **then** break;
6:     **end if**
7:     **if** neither $A_p$ nor $A_q$ appears in $\mathcal{M}$ **then**
8:       $\mathcal{M} \leftarrow \mathcal{M} + \{\{A_p\} = \{A_q\}\}$
9:     **else if** only one of $A_p$ and $A_q$ appears in $\mathcal{M}$ **then**
10:       /*Suppose $A_p$ appears in $M_j$ and $A_q$ does not appear in $\mathcal{M}$*/
11:       **if** For each attribute $A_i$ in $M_j$, $X_{qi} > 0$ **then**
12:         $M_j \leftarrow M_j + (= \{A_q\})$
13:       **else if** there exists a matching group $G_{jk}$ in $M_j$ such that for any attribute $A_l$ in $G_{jk}, Y_{ql} > T_g$, and for any attribute $A_m$ in other groups $G_{jx}, x \neq k, X_{qm} > 0$ **then**
14:         $G_{jk} \leftarrow G_{jk} + \{A_q\}$
15:       **end if**
16:     **end if**
17:     $\mathcal{X} \leftarrow \mathcal{X} - X_{pq}$
18:   **end while**
19:   return $\mathcal{M}$
20: **end**

Example 5 illustrates the matching discovery iterations using the attributes from the schemas in Table 2.

**Example 5.** *Before the iteration starts, there is no matching among attributes (Figure 3(a)). In the first iteration,* First Name *with* Author *and* Last Name *with* Author *have the highest matching score from Table 4. As the matching set is empty now, we randomly select one of the above two pairs, say,* First Name *with* Author. *Hence,* {First Name}={Author} *is added to* $\mathcal{M}$ *(Figure 3(b)) and the matching score between* First Name *and* Author *is deleted from* $\mathcal{X}$. *In the second iteration,* Last Name *with* Author *has the highest matching score. Because* Author *has already appeared in* $\mathcal{M}$, Last Name *can only be added into the matching in which* Author *appears, i.e.,* {First Name}={Author}. *Suppose the grouping threshold* $T_g$ *is set to 0.9. We then let* Last Name *form a group with* First Name *as their grouping score is above the threshold (Table 5). Hence, the matching* {First Name}={Author} *is modified to be* {First Name, Last Name}={Author} *in* $\mathcal{M}$ *(Figure 3(c)). After the group is formed, the matching score of* Last Name *with* Author *is deleted from* $\mathcal{X}$. *In the third iteration,*

*Category* and *Subject* have the highest matching score. Accordingly, the matching {*Category*}={*Subject*} is added to $\mathcal{M}$ (Figure 3(d)) and the matching score between them is deleted from $\mathcal{X}$. In the fourth and fifth iterations, no more attributes are added to $\mathcal{M}$ because all attributes associated with the current highest matching score, such as *First Name* with *Subject*, have already appeared in $\mathcal{M}$, i.e., they have been matched already. After that, no matching candidates are available and the iteration stops with the final matching results shown in Figure 3(d).

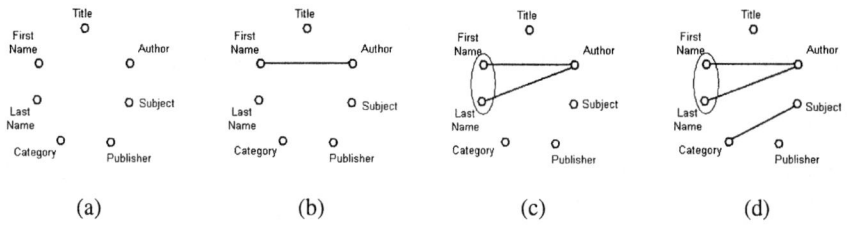

**Fig. 3.** Matching discovery iterations

The greediness of this matching discovery algorithm has the benefit of filtering bad matchings in favor of good ones. For instance, in the above example, even though the matching score between *First Name* and *Subject* is non-zero, the algorithm will not wrongly match these two attributes because their matching score is lower than the score between *First Name* and *Author*, and also lower than the score between *Category* and *Subject*.

Another interesting and beneficial characteristic of this algorithm is that it is matching score centric, i.e., the matching score plays a much more important role than the grouping score. In fact, the grouping score is never considered alone without the matching score. For instance in the above example, even though the grouping score between *Publisher* and *Subject* is 1, they are not considered by the algorithm as grouping attributes. Recall that a matching {*Category*}={*Subject*} is found in the early iterations. In order for *Publisher* to form a group with *Subject*, it must have a non-zero matching score with *Subject*'s matching opponent, i.e., *Category*. Obviously, this condition is not satisfied in the example. Similarly, although *Title* has high grouping scores with all the other attributes, it forms no groups as its matching score with all the other attributes is zero.

The time complexity of the matching discovery algorithm is $O(n^3)$ because a maximum of $n^2$ (i.e., the number of scores in $\mathcal{X}$) iterations are needed, and within each iteration a maximum of $n$ comparisons (i.e., the number of attributes in $\mathcal{M}$) are needed.

To conclude, the overall time complexity of HSM is $O(un^2 + n^3)$ since the time complexity of its three steps, matching score calculation, grouping score calculation and schema matching discovery are $O(un^2)$, $O(un^2)$ and $O(n^3)$, respectively.

## 5 Experiments

We choose two datasets, TEL-8 and BAMM, from the UIUC Web integration repository [4], as the testsets for our HSM matching approach. The TEL-8 dataset contains query interface schemas extracted from 447 deep Web sources of eight representative domains: Airfares, Hotels, Car Rentals, Books, Movies, Music Records, Jobs and Automobiles. Each domain contains about 20-70 schemas and each schema contains 3.6-7.2 attributes on average depending on the domain. The BAMM dataset contains query interface schemas extracted from four domains: Automobiles, Books, Movies and Music Records. Each domain has about 50 schemas and each schema contains 3.6-4.7 attributes on average depending on the domain.

In TEL-8 and BAMM, Web databases' query interfaces are manually extracted and their attribute names are preprocessed to remove some irrelevant information, e.g., "search for book titles" is cleaned and simplified to "title". In addition, the data type of each attribute is also recognized in TEL-8 which can be string, integer or datetime. For details of the preprocessing and type recognition, interested readers can refer to [4].

## 5.1 Metrics

We evaluate the set of matchings automatically discovered by HSM, denoted by $\mathcal{M}_h$, by comparing it with the set of matchings manually collected by a domain expert, denoted by $\mathcal{M}_c$. To facilitate comparison, we adopt the metric in [7], *target accuracy*, which evaluates how similar $\mathcal{M}_h$ is to $\mathcal{M}_c$. Given a matching set $\mathcal{M}$ and an attribute $A_p$, a *Closenym set* $Cls(A_p|\mathcal{M})$ is used to refer to all synonym attributes of $A_p$ in $\mathcal{M}$.

**Example 6.** *For a matching set* $\{\{A_1, A_2\}=\{A_3\}=\{A_4\}\}$, *the closenym set of* $A_1$ *is* $\{A_3, A_4\}$, *the closenym set of* $A_2$ *is also* $\{A_3, A_4\}$, *the closenym set of* $A_3$ *is* $\{A_1, A_2, A_4\}$ *and the closenym set of* $A_4$ *is* $\{A_1, A_2, A_3\}$. *If two attributes have the same closesym set, they are grouping attributes, such as* $A_1$ *with* $A_2$. *If two attribute have each other in their closenym sets, they are synonym attributes, such as* $A_1$ *with* $A_3$ *and* $A_3$ *with* $A_4$.

The target accuracy metric includes *target precision* and *target recall*. For each attribute $A_p$, the target precision and target recall of its closesym set in $\mathcal{M}_h$ with respect to $\mathcal{M}_c$ are:

$$P_{A_p}(\mathcal{M}_h, \mathcal{M}_c) = \frac{|Cls(A_p|\mathcal{M}_c) \cap Cls(A_p|\mathcal{M}_h)|}{|Cls(A_p|\mathcal{M}_h)|},$$

$$R_{A_p}(\mathcal{M}_h, \mathcal{M}_c) = \frac{|Cls(A_p|\mathcal{M}_c) \cap Cls(A_p|\mathcal{M}_h)|}{|Cls(A_p|\mathcal{M}_c)|}.$$

According to [7], the *target precision* and *target recall* of $\mathcal{M}_h$ (the matching set discovered by a matching approach) with respect to $\mathcal{M}_c$ (the correct matching set) are the weighted average of all the attributes' target precision and target recall (See equ. (4) and (5)). The weight of an attribute $A_p$ is set as $\frac{C_p}{\sum_{k=1}^{n} C_k}$ in which $C_p$ denotes the count of $A_p$ and $C_k$ denotes the count of attribute $A_k$ in $S$. The reason for calculating the weight in this way is that a frequently used attribute is more likely to be used in a query submitted by a user.

$$P_T(\mathcal{M}_h, \mathcal{M}_c) = \sum_{A_p} \frac{C_p}{\sum_{k=1}^{n} C_k} P_{A_p}(\mathcal{M}_h, \mathcal{M}_c), \qquad (4)$$

$$R_T(\mathcal{M}_h, \mathcal{M}_c) = \sum_{A_p} \frac{C_p}{\sum_{k=1}^{n} C_k} R_{A_p}(\mathcal{M}_h, \mathcal{M}_c). \qquad (5)$$

## 5.2 Experimental Results

Similar to [7], in our experiment we only consider attributes that occur more than an occurrence-percentage threshold $T_c$ in the input schema set $S$, where $T_c$ is the ratio of the count of an attribute to the total number of input schemas. This is because occurrence patterns of the attributes may not be observable with only a few occurrences. In order to illustrate the influence of such a threshold on the performance of HSM, we run experiments with $T_c$ set at 20%, 10% and 5%.

**Result on the TEL-8 dataset.** Table 6 shows the matchings discovered by HSM in the Airfares and CarRentals domains, when $T_c$ is set at 10%. In this table, the third column indicates whether the matching is correct: Y means fully correct, P means partially correct and N means incorrect. We see that HSM can identify very complex matchings among attributes. We note that destination in Airfares (the third row in Airfares) should not form a group by itself to be synonymous to other groups. The reason is that destination co-occurs with different attributes in different schemas, such as depart, origin, leave from to form the same concept, and those attributes are removed because their occurrence-percentages are lower than 10%.

**Table 6.** Discovered matchings for Airfares and CarRentals when $T_c = 10\%$

| Domain | Discovered Matching | Correct? |
|---|---|---|
| Airfares | {departure date (datetime), return date (datetime)} = {depart (datetime), return (datetime)} | Y |
| | {adult (integer), children (integer), infant (integer), senior (integer)} ={passenger (integer)} | Y |
| | {destination (string)} = {from (string), to (string)} ={arrival city (string), departure city (string)} | P |
| | {cabin (string)} = {class (string)} | Y |
| CarRentals | {drop off city (string), pick up city (string)} ={drop off location (string), pick up location (string)} | Y |
| | {drop off (datetime), pick up (datetime)= { pick up date (datetime), drop off date (datetime), pick up time (datetime), drop off time (datetime)} | Y |

**Table 7.** Target accuracy for TEL-8

| Domain | $T_c = 20\%$ | | $T_c = 10\%$ | | $T_c = 5\%$ | | Domain | $T_c = 20\%$ | | $T_c = 10\%$ | | $T_c = 5\%$ | |
|---|---|---|---|---|---|---|---|---|---|---|---|---|---|
| | $P_T$ | $R_T$ | $P_T$ | $R_T$ | $P_T$ | $R_T$ | | $P_T$ | $R_T$ | $P_T$ | $R_T$ | $P_T$ | $R_T$ |
| Airfares | 1 | 1 | 1 | .94 | .90 | .86 | Airfares | 1 | 1 | 1 | .71 | .56 | .51 |
| Automobiles | 1 | 1 | 1 | 1 | .76 | .88 | Automobiles | 1 | 1 | .93 | 1 | .67 | .78 |
| Books | 1 | 1 | 1 | 1 | .67 | 1 | Books | 1 | 1 | 1 | 1 | .45 | .77 |
| CarRentals | 1 | 1 | .89 | .91 | .64 | .78 | CarRentals | .72 | 1 | .72 | .60 | .46 | .53 |
| Hotels | 1 | 1 | .72 | 1 | .60 | .88 | Hotels | .86 | 1 | .86 | .87 | .38 | .34 |
| Jobs | 1 | 1 | 1 | 1 | .70 | .72 | Jobs | 1 | .86 | .78 | .87 | .36 | .46 |
| Movies | 1 | 1 | 1 | 1 | .72 | 1 | Movies | 1 | 1 | 1 | 1 | .48 | .65 |
| MusicRecords | 1 | 1 | .74 | 1 | .62 | .88 | MusicRecords | 1 | 1 | .76 | 1 | .48 | .56 |
| **Average** | 1 | 1 | .92 | .98 | .70 | .88 | **Average** | .95 | .98 | .88 | .88 | .48 | .58 |
| (a) HSM with $T_g = 0.9$ | | | | | | | (b) DCM | | | | | | |

Table 7(a) presents the performance of HSM on TEL-8 when the grouping score threshold $T_g$ is set to 0.9. As expected, the performance of HSM decreases when we reduce the occurrence-percentage threshold $T_c$ (from 20% to 5%), meaning that more rare attributes are taken into consideration. Moreover, we can see that the performance of HSM is almost always better than the performance of DCM, which was implemented with the optimal parameters reported in [7], especially for a small occurrence percentage threshold such as 5%, as shown in Table 7(b).

We note that the target recall is always higher than the target precision because we do not remove the less likely matchings, which are discovered in later iterations with small matching scores. These less likely matchings will reduce the target precision, while they are likely to improve the target recall. One reason that we do not set a threshold to filter lower score matchings is that the threshold is domain dependent. We also consider that it is much easier for a user to check whether a matching is correct than to discover a matching by himself/herself.

**Result on the BAMM dataset.** The performance of HSM on BAMM is shown in Table 8(a), when the grouping score threshold $T_g$ is set to 0.9, and the target accuracy of DCM on BAMM is listed in Table 8(b). For the BAMM dataset, HSM always outperforms DCM.

**Table 8.** Target accuracy for BAMM

(a) HSM with $T_g = 0.9$

| Domain | $T_c = 20\%$ | | $T_c = 10\%$ | | $T_c = 5\%$ | |
|---|---|---|---|---|---|---|
| | $P_T$ | $R_T$ | $P_T$ | $R_T$ | $P_T$ | $R_T$ |
| Automobiles | 1 | 1 | .56 | 1 | .75 | 1 |
| Books | 1 | 1 | .86 | 1 | .82 | 1 |
| Movies | 1 | 1 | 1 | 1 | .90 | .86 |
| MusicRecords | 1 | 1 | .81 | 1 | .72 | 1 |
| Average | 1 | 1 | .81 | 1 | .80 | .97 |

(b) DCM

| Domain | $T_c = 20\%$ | | $T_c = 10\%$ | | $T_c = 5\%$ | |
|---|---|---|---|---|---|---|
| | $P_T$ | $R_T$ | $P_T$ | $R_T$ | $P_T$ | $R_T$ |
| Automobiles | 1 | 1 | .56 | 1 | .45 | 1 |
| Books | 1 | 1 | .63 | 1 | .47 | .78 |
| Movies | 1 | 1 | 1 | 1 | .45 | .53 |
| MusicRecords | 1 | 1 | .52 | 1 | .36 | .55 |
| Average | 1 | 1 | .81 | 1 | .43.3 | .72 |

We note that the target precision in the Automobiles domain is low when $T_c = 10\%$. Again, the reason is that we do not remove the matchings with low matching scores, which are less likely to be correct matchings. We also note an exception that, in the Automobiles domain, the precision when $T_c = 5\%$ is much better than the precision when $T_c = 10\%$. This is because there are some incorrect matchings identified when $T_c = 10\%$, while most newly discovered matchings when $T_c = 5\%$ are correct.

**Influence of grouping score threshold.** The performance of HSM with different $T_g$ on TEL-8 is shown in Table 9(a). We can see that $T_g$ actually does not affect the performance of HSM much in a wide range. The target accuracy of HSM is stable with different $T_g$, except for the target accuracy in domain CarRentals. A similar phenomenon can be observed when we run experiments on BAMM using different $T_g$, as shown in Table 9(b). The explanation is as follows:

1. We use a greedy algorithm to always consider high matching scores first and the grouping score plays a minor role in the algorithm. Therefore, the change of grouping score threshold does not make much difference.
2. As we observed, an attribute usually co-occurs with the same set of attributes to form a larger concept. Hence, most grouping attributes have a grouping score equal to 1. This makes the grouping attribute discovery robust to the change of $T_g$. The reason why the target accuracy in domain CarRentals changes with $T_g$ is that some attributes in this domain co-occur with different sets of attributes to form the same concept, which makes their grouping scores less than 1 and thus the accuracy is affected by the threshold.

**Table 9.** Target accuracy of HSM with different grouping score thresholds when $T_c = 10\%$

(a) TEL-8

| Domain | $T_g = .7$ | | $T_g = .8$ | | $T_g = .9$ | | $T_g = .95$ | |
|---|---|---|---|---|---|---|---|---|
| | $P_T$ | $R_T$ | $P_T$ | $R_T$ | $P_T$ | $R_T$ | $P_T$ | $R_T$ |
| Airfares | 1 | .94 | 1 | .94 | 1 | .94 | 1 | .94 |
| Automobiles | 1 | 1 | 1 | 1 | 1 | 1 | 1 | 1 |
| Books | 1 | 1 | 1 | 1 | 1 | 1 | 1 | 1 |
| CarRentals | .69 | .71 | .75 | .81 | .89 | .91 | .86 | .88 |
| Hotels | .72 | 1 | .72 | 1 | .72 | 1 | .72 | 1 |
| Jobs | 1 | 1 | 1 | 1 | 1 | 1 | 1 | 1 |
| Movies | 1 | 1 | 1 | 1 | 1 | 1 | 1 | 1 |
| MusicRecords | .74 | 1 | .74 | 1 | .74 | 1 | .74 | 1 |
| **Average** | .89 | .96 | .90 | .97 | .92 | .98 | .92 | .98 |

(b) BAMM

| Domain | $T_g = .7$ | | $T_g = .8$ | | $T_g = .9$ | | $T_g = .95$ | |
|---|---|---|---|---|---|---|---|---|
| | $P_T$ | $R_T$ | $P_T$ | $R_T$ | $P_T$ | $R_T$ | $P_T$ | $R_T$ |
| Automobiles | .55 | 1 | .55 | 1 | .55 | 1 | .55 | 1 |
| Books | .86 | 1 | .86 | 1 | .86 | 1 | .92 | 1 |
| Movies | 1 | 1 | 1 | 1 | 1 | 1 | 1 | 1 |
| MusicRecords | 1 | 1 | 1 | 1 | 1 | 1 | 1 | 1 |
| **Average** | .85 | 1 | .85 | 1 | .85 | 1 | .87 | 1 |

**Table 10.** Actual execution time in seconds

| Dataset | BAMM | | | TEL − 8 | | |
|---|---|---|---|---|---|---|
| | 20% | 10% | 5% | 20% | 10% | 5% |
| DCM | 0.861 | 5.171 | 12.749 | 2.332 | 15.813 | 12624.5 |
| HSM | 0.063 | 0.202 | 0.297 | 0.207 | 0.781 | 2.313 |
| speedup ratio | 13.7 | 25.6 | 42.9 | 11.3 | 20.2 | 5458 |

**Actual Execution Time.** As we have pointed out, HSM discovers matchings in time polynomial to the number of attributes while DCM discovers matchings in time exponential to the number of attributes. In our experiments, both HSM and DCM are implemented in C++ and were run on a PC with an Intel 3.0G CPU and 1G RAM. Table 10 shows the actual execution time accumulated on TEL-8 and BAMM with different $T_c$. It can be seen that HSM is always an order of magnitude faster than DCM. The time needed by DCM grows faster when $T_c$ is smaller, i.e., when more attributes are considered for matching. As shown in Table 11, DCM takes more than three hours to generate all the matchings for the TEL-8 dataset when the occurrence-percentage threshold $T_c = 5\%$.

## 6 Conclusions and Future Work

In this paper, we present a holistic schema matching approach, HSM, to holistically discover attribute matchings across Web query interfaces. The approach employs several steps, including matching score calculation that measures the possibility of two attributes being synonym attributes, grouping score calculation that evaluates whether two attributes are grouping attributes, and finally a matching discovery algorithm that is greedy and matching score centric. HSM is purely based on the occurrence patterns of attributes and requires neither domain-knowledge nor user interaction. Experimental results show that HSM discovers both simple and complex matchings with very high accuracy in time polynomial to the number of attributes and the number of schemas.

However, we also note that HSM suffers from some limitations that will be the focus of our future work. In the Airfares domain in Table 6, although the matching {from, to}={arrival city, departure city} has been correctly discovered, HSM is not able to identify the finer matchings {from}={arrival city} and {to}={departure city}. To address this problem, we can consider to employ some auxiliary semantic information (i.e., an ontology) to identify the finer matchings.

We also plan to focus on matching the rare attributes for which HSM's performance is not stable. One promising direction may be to exploit other types of information, such as attribute types, linguistic similarity between attribute names, instance overlapping, and/or schema structures.

**Acknowledgment.** This research was supported by the Research Grants Council of Hong Kong under grant HKUST6172/04E.

## References

1. M.K. Bergman. Surfacing hidden value. http://www.brightplanet.com/technology/deepweb.asp, Dec. 2000.
2. A. Bilke and F. Naumann. Schema matching using duplicates. In *21st Int. Conf. on Data Engineering*, pages 69 – 80, 2005.
3. K. C.-C. Chang, B. He, C. Li, and Z. Zhang. Structured databases on the Web: Observations and implications. Technical Report UIUCDCS-R-2003-2321, CS Department, University of Illinois at Urbana-Champaign, February 2003.
4. K. C.-C. Chang, B. He, C. Li, and Z. Zhang. The UIUC Web integration repository. Computer Science Department, University of Illinois at Urbana-Champaign. http://metaquerier.cs.uiuc.edu/repository, 2003.
5. R. Dhamankar, Y. Lee, A. Doan, A. Halevy, and P. Domingos. imap: Discovering complex semantic matches between database schemas. In *ACM SIGMOD Conference*, pages 383 – 394, 2004.
6. A. Doan, P. Domingos, and A. Y. Halevy. Reconciling schemas of disparate data sources: A machine-learning approach. In *ACM SIGMOD Conference*, pages 509 – 520, 2001.
7. B. He and K. C.-C. Chang. Discovering complex matchings across Web query interfaces: A correlation mining approach. In *ACM SIGKDD Conference*, pages 147 – 158, 2004.
8. B. He, K. C.-C. Chang, and J. Han. Statistical schema matching across Web query interfaces. In *ACM SIGMOD Conference*, pages 217 – 228, 2003.
9. W. Li, C. Clifton, and S. Liu. Database Integration using Neural Networks: Implementation and Experience. In *Knowledge and Information Systems,2(1)*, pages 73–96, 2000.
10. J. Madhavan, P. Bernstein, A. Doan, and A. Halevy. Corpus-based schema matching. In *21st Int. Conf. on Data Engineering*, pages 57–68, 2005.
11. C. Manning and H. Schutze. *Foundations of Statistical Natural Language Processing*. MIT Press, May, 1999.
12. S. Melnik, H. Garcia-Molina, and E. Rahm. Similarity flooding: A versatile graph matching algorithm. In *18th Int. Conf. on Data Engineering*, pages 117–128, 2002.
13. G. Miller. *WordNet: An on-line lexical database*. International Journal of Lexicography, 1990.
14. E. Rahm and P. A. Bernstein. A survey of approaches to automatic schema matching. *The VLDB Journal*, 10:334–350, 2001.
15. P. Tan, V. Kumar, and J. Srivastava. Selecting the right interestingness measure for association patterns. In *ACM SIGKDD Conference*, pages 32 – 41, 2002.
16. J. Wang, J. Wen, F. Lochovsky, and W. Ma. Instance-based schema matching for Web databases by domain-specific query probing. In *30th Int. Conf. Very Large Data Bases*, pages 408–419, 2004.
17. W. Wu, C. Yu, A. Doan, and W. Meng. An interactive clustering-based approach to integrating source query interfaces on the deep Web. In *ACM SIGMOD Conference*, pages 95–106, 2004.

# Data Mapping as Search*

George H.L. Fletcher and Catharine M. Wyss

Computer Science Department, School of Informatics,
Indiana University, Bloomington, USA
{gefletch, cmw}@cs.indiana.edu

**Abstract.** In this paper, we describe and situate the TUPELO system for data mapping in relational databases. Automating the discovery of mappings between structured data sources is a long standing and important problem in data management. Starting from user provided example instances of the source and target schemas, TUPELO approaches mapping discovery as search within the transformation space of these instances based on a set of mapping operators. TUPELO mapping expressions incorporate not only data-metadata transformations, but also simple and complex semantic transformations, resulting in significantly wider applicability than previous systems. Extensive empirical validation of TUPELO, both on synthetic and real world datasets, indicates that the approach is both viable and effective.

## 1 Introduction

The data mapping problem, automating the discovery of effective mappings between structured data sources, is one of the longest standing problems in data management [17, 24]. Data mappings are fundamental in data cleaning [4, 32], data integration [19], and semantic integration [8, 29]. Furthermore, they are the basic glue for constructing large-scale semantic web and peer-to-peer information systems which facilitate cooperation of autonomous data sources [15]. Consequently, the data mapping problem has a wide variety of manifestations such as schema matching [31, 34], schema mapping [17, 26], ontology alignment [10], and model matching [24, 25].

Fully automating the discovery of data mappings is an "AI-complete" problem in the sense that it is as hard as the hardest problems in Artificial Intelligence [24]. Consequently, solutions have typically focused on discovering restricted mappings such as one-to-one schema matching [31]. More robust solutions to the problem must not only discover such simple mappings, but also facilitate the discovery of the *structural transformations* [18, 39] and *complex (many-to-one) semantic mappings* [8, 14, 29, 31] which inevitably arise in coordinating heterogeneous information systems. We illustrate such mappings in the following scenario.

**Example 1.** *Consider the three relational databases* Flights A, B, *and* C *maintaining cost information for airline routes as shown in Fig. 1. These databases, which exhibit three different natural representations of the same information, could be managed by independent travel agencies that wish to share data.*

---

* The current paper is a continuation of work first explored in poster/demo presentations (IHIS05 and SIGMOD05) and a short workshop paper [11].

```
FlightsA
Flights:
Carrier   Fee   ATL29   ORD17
AirEast   15    100     110
JetWest   16    200     220
```

```
FlightsB
Prices:
Carrier   Route   Cost   AgentFee
AirEast   ATL29   100    15
JetWest   ATL29   200    16
AirEast   ORD17   110    15
JetWest   ORD17   220    16
```

```
FlightsC
AirEast:                          JetWest:
Route   BaseCost   TotalCost      Route   BaseCost   TotalCost
ATL29   100        115            ATL29   200        216
ORD17   110        125            ORD17   220        236
```

**Fig. 1.** Three airline flight price databases, each with the same information content

Note that mapping between the databases in Fig. 1 requires (1) matching schema elements, (2) dynamic data-metadata restructuring, and (3) complex semantic mapping. For example, mapping data from `FlightsB` to `FlightsA` involves (1) matching the `Flights` and `Prices` table names and (2) promoting data values in the `Route` column to attribute names. Promoting these values will dynamically create as many new attribute names as there are `Route` values in the instance of `FlightsB`. Mapping the data in `FlightsB` to `FlightsC` requires (3) a complex semantic function mapping the sum of `Cost` and `AgentFee` to the `TotalCost` column in the relations of `FlightsC`.

### 1.1 Contributions and Outline

In this paper we present the TUPELO data mapping system for semi-automating the discovery of data mapping expressions between relational data sources (Section 2). TUPELO is an example driven system, generating mapping expressions for interoperation of heterogeneous information systems which involve schema matching, dynamic data-metadata restructuring (Section 2.1), and complex (many-to-one) semantic functions (Section 4). For example, TUPELO can generate the expressions for mapping between instances of the three airline databases in Fig. 1.

Data mapping in TUPELO is built on the novel perspective of mapping discovery as an example driven search problem. We discuss how TUPELO leverages Artificial Intelligence search techniques to generate mapping expressions (Sections 2 and 3). We also present experimental validation of the system on a variety of synthetic and real world scenarios (Section 5) which indicates that the TUPELO approach to data mapping is both viable and effective. We conclude the paper with a discussion of related research (Section 6) and directions for future work (Section 7).

## 2 Dynamic Relational Data Mapping with TUPELO

In this section we outline the architecture and implementation of the TUPELO system, illustrated in Fig. 2. TUPELO generates an effective mapping from a source relational

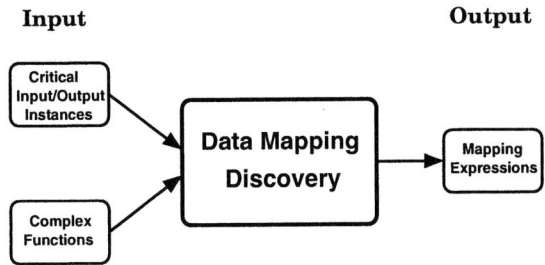

**Fig. 2.** Data Mapping in the TUPELO System

schema $S$ to a target relational schema $T$. The system discovers this mapping using (1) example instances $s$ of $S$ and $t$ of $T$ and (2) illustrations of any complex semantic mappings between the schemas. Mapping discovery in TUPELO is a completely syntactic and structurally driven process which does not make use of a global schema or any explicit domain knowledge [2, 16].

We first introduce the mapping language $\mathcal{L}$ used in TUPELO. This language focuses on simple schema matching and structural transformations. We then discuss the Rosetta Stone principle which states that examples of the same information under two different schemas can be used to discover an effective mapping between the schemas. We close the section by describing the idea that drives data mapping in the TUPELO system, namely that data mapping is fundamentally a search problem.

### 2.1 Dynamic Relational Transformations

TUPELO generates expressions in the transformation language $\mathcal{L}$, a fragment of the Federated Interoperable Relational Algebra (FIRA) [39]. FIRA is a query algebra for the interoperation of federated relational databases. The operators in $\mathcal{L}$ (Table 1) extend the relational algebra with dynamic structural transformations [18, 32, 39]. These include operators for dynamically promoting data to attribute and relation names, a simple merge operator [40], and an operator for demoting metadata to data values. The operators, for example, can express the transformations in Fig. 1 such as mapping the data from FlightsB to FlightsA.

**Example 2.** *Consider in detail the transformation from* FlightsB *to* FlightsA. *This mapping is expressed in $\mathcal{L}$ as:*

$R_1 := \uparrow_{\text{Route}}^{\text{Cost}} (\text{FlightsB})$
Promote Route values to attribute names with corresponding Cost values.

$R_2 := \mathcal{L}_{\text{Route}}(\mathcal{L}_{\text{Cost}}(R_1))$
Drop attributes Route and Cost.

$R_3 := \mu_{\text{Carrier}}(R_2)$
Merge tuples on Carrier values.

$R_4 := \rho_{\text{AgentFee} \to \text{Fee}}^{\text{att}}(\rho_{\text{Prices} \to \text{Flights}}^{\text{rel}}(R_3))$
Rename attribute AgentFee to Fee and relation Prices to Flights (i.e., match schema elements).

*The output relation $R_4$ is exactly* FlightsA.

**Table 1.** Operators for dynamic relational data mapping

| Operation | Effect |
|---|---|
| $\rightarrow_A^B (R)$ | *Dereference Column $A$ on $B$.* $\forall t \in R$, append a new column named $B$ with value $t[t[A]]$. |
| $\uparrow_B^A (R)$ | *Promote Column $A$ to Metadata.* $\forall t \in R$, append a new column named $t[A]$ with value $t[B]$. |
| $\downarrow (R)$ | *Demote Metadata.* Cartesian product of relation $R$ with a binary table containing the metadata of $R$. |
| $\wp_A(R)$ | *Partition on Column $A$.* $\forall v \in \pi_A(R)$, create a new relation named $v$, where $t \in v$ iff $t \in R$ and $t[A] = v$. |
| $\times(R, S)$ | *Cartesian Product* of relation $R$ and relation $S$. |
| $\amalg_A(R)$ | *Drop* column $A$ from relation $R$. |
| $\mu_A(R)$ | *Merge* tuples in relation $R$ based on compatible values in column $A$ [40]. |
| $\rho_{X \rightarrow X'}^{\text{att/rel}} (R)$ | *Rename* attribute/relation $X$ to $X'$ in relation $R$. |

FIRA is complete for the full data-metadata mapping space for relational data sources [39]. The language $\mathcal{L}$ maintains the full data-metadata restructuring power of FIRA. The operators in $\mathcal{L}$ focus on bulk structural transformations (via the $\rightarrow$, $\uparrow$, $\downarrow$, $\wp$, $\times$, $\amalg$, and $\mu$ operators) and schema matching (via the rename operator $\rho$). We view application of selections ($\sigma$) as a post-processing step to filter mapping results according to external criteria, since it is known that generalizing selection conditions is a nontrivial problem. Hence, TUPELO does not consider applications of the relational $\sigma$ operator. Note that using a language such as $\mathcal{L}$ for data mapping blurs the distinction between schema *matching* and schema *mapping* since $\mathcal{L}$ has simple schema matching (i.e., finding appropriate renamings via $\rho$) as a special case.

## 2.2 The Rosetta Stone Principle

An integral component of the TUPELO system is the notion of "critical" instances $s$ and $t$ which succinctly characterize the structure of the source and target schemas $S$ and $T$, respectively. These instances illustrate the same information structured under both schemas. The *Rosetta Stone principle* states that such critical instances can be used to drive the search for data mappings in the space of transformations delineated by the operators in $\mathcal{L}$ on the source instance $s$. Guided by this principle, TUPELO takes as input critical source and target instances which illustrate all of the appropriate restructurings between the source and target schemas.

**Example 3.** *The instances of the three airline databases presented in Fig. 1 illustrate the same information under each of the three schemas, and are examples of succinct critical instances sufficient for data mapping discovery.*

**Critical Instance Input and Encoding.** Critical instances can be easily elicited from a user via a visual interface akin to the Lixto data extraction system [13] or visual interfaces developed for interactive schema mapping [1, 3, 26, 37]. In TUPELO, critical

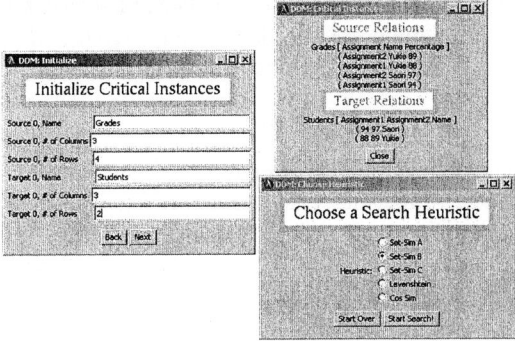

**Fig. 3.** TUPELO GUI

instances are articulated by a user via a front-end GUI that has been developed for the system (Figure 3). Since critical instances essentially illustrate one entity under different schemas, we also envision that much of the process of generating critical instances can be semi-automated using techniques developed for entity/duplicate identification and record linkage [2, 38].

Critical instances are encoded internally in *Tuple Normal Form* (TNF). This normal form, which encodes databases in single tables of fixed schema, was introduced by Litwin et al. as a standardized data format for database interoperability [23]. TUPELO makes full use of this normal form as an internal data representation format. Given a relation $R$, the TNF of $R$ is computed by first assigning each tuple in $R$ a unique ID and then building a four column relation with attributes TID, REL, ATT, VALUE, corresponding to tuple ID, relation name, attribute name, and attribute value, respectively. The table is populated by placing each tuple in $R$ into the new table in a piecemeal fashion. The TNF of a database is the single table consisting of the union of the TNF of each relation in the database.

**Example 4.** *We illustrate TNF with the encoding of database* FlightsC:

| TID | REL | ATT | VALUE |
|---|---|---|---|
| $t_1$ | AirEast | Route | ATL29 |
| $t_1$ | AirEast | BaseCost | 100 |
| $t_1$ | AirEast | TotalCost | 115 |
| $t_2$ | AirEast | Route | ORD17 |
| $t_2$ | AirEast | BaseCost | 110 |
| $t_2$ | AirEast | TotalCost | 125 |
| $t_3$ | JetWest | Route | ATL29 |
| $t_3$ | JetWest | BaseCost | 200 |
| $t_3$ | JetWest | TotalCost | 216 |
| $t_4$ | JetWest | Route | ORD17 |
| $t_4$ | JetWest | BaseCost | 220 |
| $t_4$ | JetWest | TotalCost | 236 |

The TNF of a relation can be built in SQL using the system tables. The benefits of normalizing the input instances in this manner with a fixed schema include (1) ease and uniformity of handling of the data, (2) both metadata and data can be handled directly in SQL, and (3) sets of relations are encoded as single tables, allowing natural multi-relational data mapping from databases to databases.

## 2.3 Data Mapping as a Search Problem

In TUPELO the data mapping problem is seen fundamentally as a search problem. Given critical instances $s$ and $t$ of the source and target schemas, data mapping is an exploration of the transformation space of $\mathcal{L}$ on the source instance $s$. Search successfully terminates when the target instance $t$ is located in this space. Upon success, the transformation path from the source to the target is returned. This search process is illustrated in Figure 4. The branching factor of this space is proportional to $|s| + |t|$; however intelligent exploration of the search space greatly reduces the number of states visited, as we discuss next.

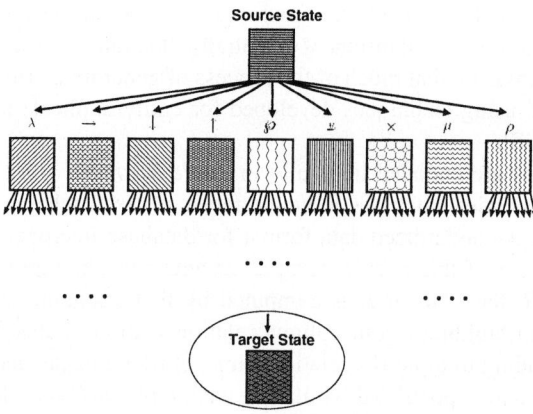

**Fig. 4.** Search space for data mapping discovery

**Heuristic Search Algorithms.** Due to their simplicity and effectiveness, we chose to implement the heuristic based *Iterative Deepening A\** (IDA) and *Recursive Best-First Search* (RBFS) search algorithms from the Artificial Intelligence literature [28]. In the heuristic exploration of a state space, both of these algorithms use a heuristic function to rank states and selectively search the space based on the rankings. The evaluation function $f$ for ranking a search state $x$ is calculated as $f(x) = g(x) + h(x)$, where $g(x)$ is the number of transformations applied to the start state to get to state $x$ and $h(x)$ is an educated guess of the distance of $x$ from the target state. Search begins at the source critical instance $s$ and continues until the current search state is a structurally identical superset of the target critical instance $t$ (i.e., the current state contains $t$). The transformation path from $s$ to $t$ gives a basic mapping expression in $\mathcal{L}$. After this expression has been discovered, filtering operations (via relational selections $\sigma$) must be applied if necessary according to external criteria, as discussed in Section 2.1. The final output of TUPELO is an expression for mapping instances of the source schema to corresponding instances of the target schema.

The two search algorithms used in TUPELO operate as follows. IDA performs a depth-bounded depth-first search of the state space using the $f$-rankings of states as the depth bound, iteratively increasing this bound until the target state is reached [28]. RBFS performs a localized, recursive best-first exploration of the state space, keeping track of a locally optimal $f$-value and backtracking if this value is exceeded [28]. Each of these algorithms uses memory linear in the depth of search; although they both perform redundant explorations, they do not suffer from the exponential memory use of basic A* best-first search which led to the ineffectiveness of early implementations of TUPELO. Furthermore, they both achieve performance asymptotic to A*.

**Simple Enhancements to Search.** To further improve performance of the search algorithms, we also employed the simple rule of thumb that "obviously inapplicable" transformations should be disregarded during search. For example if the current search state has all attribute names occurring in the target state, there is no need to explore applications of the attribute renaming operator. We incorporated several such simple rules in TUPELO.

## 3 Search Heuristics

Heuristics are used to intelligently explore a search space, as discussed in Section 2.3. A search heuristics $h(x)$ estimates the distance, in terms of number of intermediate search states, of a given database $x$ from a target database $t$. A variety of heuristics were implemented and evaluated. This section briefly describes each heuristic used in TUPELO.

**Set Based Similarity Heuristics.** Three simple heuristics measure the overlap of values in database states. Heuristic $h_1$ measures the number of relation, column, and data values in the target state which are missing in state $x$:

$$\begin{aligned} h_1(x) = \quad & |\pi_{\mathsf{REL}}(t) - \pi_{\mathsf{REL}}(x)| \\ + & |\pi_{\mathsf{ATT}}(t) - \pi_{\mathsf{ATT}}(x)| \\ + & |\pi_{\mathsf{VALUE}}(t) - \pi_{\mathsf{VALUE}}(x)|. \end{aligned}$$

Here, $\pi$ is relational projection on the TNF of $x$ and $t$, and $|x|$ is the cardinality of relation $x$. Heuristic $h_2$ measures the minimum number of data promotions ($\uparrow$) and metadata demotions ($\downarrow$) needed to transform $x$ into the target $t$:

$$\begin{aligned} h_2(x) = \quad & |\pi_{\mathsf{REL}}(t) \cap \pi_{\mathsf{ATT}}(x)| \\ + & |\pi_{\mathsf{REL}}(t) \cap \pi_{\mathsf{VALUE}}(x)| \\ + & |\pi_{\mathsf{ATT}}(t) \cap \pi_{\mathsf{REL}}(x)| \\ + & |\pi_{\mathsf{ATT}}(t) \cap \pi_{\mathsf{VALUE}}(x)| \\ + & |\pi_{\mathsf{VALUE}}(t) \cap \pi_{\mathsf{REL}}(x)| \\ + & |\pi_{\mathsf{VALUE}}(t) \cap \pi_{\mathsf{ATT}}(x)|. \end{aligned}$$

Heuristic $h_3$ takes the maximum of $h_1$ and $h_2$ on $x$:

$$h_3(x) = max\{h_1(x), h_2(x)\}.$$

**Databases as Strings: The Levenshtein Heuristic.** Viewing a database as a *string* leads to another heuristic. Suppose $d$ is a database in TNF with tuples

$$\langle k_1, r_1, a_1, v_1 \rangle, \ldots, \langle k_n, r_n, a_n, v_n \rangle.$$

For each tuple, let $s_i = r_i \star a_i \star v_i$, where $\star$ is string concatenation. Define $\texttt{string}(d)$ to be the string $d_1 \star \cdots \star d_n$, where $d_1, \ldots, d_n$ is a lexicographic ordering of the strings $s_i$, potentially with repetitions. The *Levenshtein distance* between string $x$ and string $y$, $L(x, y)$, is defined as the least number of single character insertions, deletions, and substitutions required to transform $x$ into $y$ [20]. Using this metric, we define the following *normalized Levenshtein heuristic*:

$$h_L(x) = round\left(k \frac{L(\texttt{string}(x), \texttt{string}(t))}{max\{|\texttt{string}(x)|, |\texttt{string}(t)|\}}\right)$$

where $|w|$ is the length of string $w$, $k \geq 1$ is a scaling constant (scaling the interval $[0, 1]$ to $[0, k]$), and $round(y)$ is the integer closest to $y$.

**Databases as Term Vectors: Euclidean Distance.** Another perspective on a database is to view it as a document vector over a set of terms [36]. Let $A = \{a_1, \ldots, a_n\}$ be the set of tokens occurring in the source and target critical instances (including attribute and relation names), and let

$$D = \{\langle a_1, a_1, a_1 \rangle, \ldots, \langle a_n, a_n\, a_n \rangle\}$$

be the set of all $n^3$ triples over the tokens in $A$. Given a search database $d$ in TNF with tuples $\langle k_1, r_1, a_1, v_1 \rangle, \ldots, \langle k_m, r_m, a_m, v_m \rangle$, define $\bar{d}$ to be the $n^3$-vector $\langle d_1, \ldots, d_{n^3} \rangle$ where $d_i$ equals the number of occurrences of the $i$th triple of $D$ in the list

$$\langle r_1, a_1, v_1 \rangle, \ldots, \langle r_m, a_m, v_m \rangle.$$

This term vector view on databases leads to several natural search heuristics. The standard Euclidean distance in term vector space from state $x$ to target state $t$ gives us a *Euclidean heuristic* measure:

$$h_E(x) = round\left(\sqrt{\sum_{i=1}^{n}(x_i - t_i)^2}\right)$$

where $x_i$ is the $i$th element of the database vector $\bar{x}$.

Normalizing the vectors for state $x$ and target $t$ gives a *normalized Euclidean heuristic* for the distance between $x$ and $t$:

$$h_{|E|}(x) = round\left(k\sqrt{\sum_{i=1}^{n}\left[\frac{x_i}{|\bar{x}|} - \frac{t_i}{|\bar{t}|}\right]^2}\right)$$

where $k \geq 1$ is a scaling constant and $|\bar{x}| = \sqrt{\sum_{i=1}^{n} x_i^2}$, as usual.

**Databases as Term Vectors: Cosine Similarity.** Viewing databases as vectors, we can also define a *cosine similarity heuristic* measure, with scaling constant $k \geq 1$:

$$h_{\cos}(x) = round\left(k\left[1 - \frac{\sum_{i=1}^{n} x_i t_i}{|\bar{x}||\bar{t}|}\right]\right)$$

Cosine similarity measures the cosine of the angle between two vectors in the database vector space. If $x$ is very similar to the target $t$, $h_{\cos}$ returns a low estimate of the distance between them.

## 4 Supporting Complex Semantic Mappings

The mapping operators in the language $\mathcal{L}$ (Table 1) accommodate dynamic data-metadata structural transformations and simple one-to-one schema matchings. However, as mentioned in Section 1, many mappings involve complex semantic transformations [8, 14, 29, 31]. As examples of such mappings, consider several basic complex mappings for bridging semantic differences between two tables.

**Example 5.** *A semantic mapping $f_1$ from airline names to airline ID numbers:*

| Carrier | | CID |
|---|---|---|
| AirEast | $\xmapsto{f_1}$ | 123 |
| JetWest | | 456 |

*A complex function $f_2$ which returns the concatenation of passenger first and last names:*

| Last | First | | Passenger |
|---|---|---|---|
| Smith | John | $\xmapsto{f_2}$ | John Smith |
| Doe | Jane | | Jane Doe |

*The complex function $f_3$ between $FlightsB$ and $FlightsC$ which maps $AgentFee$ and $Cost$ to $TotalCost$:*

| CID | Route | Cost | AgentFee | | CID | Route | TotalCost |
|---|---|---|---|---|---|---|---|
| 123 | ATL29 | 100 | 15 | | 123 | ATL29 | 115 |
| 456 | ATL29 | 200 | 16 | $\xmapsto{f_3}$ | 456 | ATL29 | 216 |
| 123 | ORD17 | 110 | 15 | | 123 | ORD17 | 125 |
| 456 | ORD17 | 220 | 16 | | 456 | ORD17 | 236 |

Other examples include functions such as date format, weight, and international financial conversions, and semantic functions such as the mapping from employee name to social security number (which can not be generalized from examples), and so on.

**Support for Semantic Mapping Expressions.** Any complex semantic function is unique to a particular information sharing scenario. Incorporating such functions in a non-ad hoc manner is essential for any general data mapping solution. Although there has been research on discovering specific complex semantic functions [6, 14], no general approach has been proposed which accommodates these functions in larger mapping expressions.

TUPELO supports discovery of mapping expressions with such complex semantic mappings in a straight-forward manner without introducing any specialized domain knowledge. We can cleanly accommodate these mappings in the system by extending $\mathcal{L}$ with a new operator $\lambda$ which is parameterized by a complex function $f$ and its input-output signature:

$$\lambda^{B}_{f,\bar{A}}(R).$$

**Example 6.** *As an illustration of the operator, the mapping expression to apply function $f_3$ in Example 5 to the values in the* Cost *and* AgentFee *attributes, placing the output in attribute* TotalCost:

$$\lambda^{\texttt{TotalCost}}_{f_3,\texttt{Cost, AgentFee}}(\texttt{FlightsB}).$$

The semantics of $\lambda$ is as follows: for each tuple $T$ in relation $R$, apply the mapping $f$ to the values of $T$ on attributes $\bar{A} = \langle A_1, \ldots, A_n \rangle$ and place the output in attribute $B$. The operator is well defined for any tuple $T$ of appropriate schema (and is the identity mapping on $T$ otherwise). Note that this semantics is independent of the actual mechanics of the function $f$. Function symbols are assumed to come from a countably infinite set $\mathbb{F} = \{f_i\}_{i=0}^{i=\infty}$.

**Discovery of Semantic Mapping Expressions.** TUPELO generates data mapping expressions in $\mathcal{L}$. Extending $\mathcal{L}$ with the $\lambda$ operator allows for the discovery of mapping expressions with arbitrary complex semantic mappings. Given critical input/output instances and indications of complex semantic correspondences $f$ between attributes $\bar{A}$ in the source and attribute $B$ in the target, the search is extended to generate appropriate mapping expressions which also include the $\lambda$ operator (Figure 4).

For the purpose of searching for mapping expressions, $\lambda$ expressions are treated just like any of the other operators. During search all that needs to be checked is that the applications of functions are well-typed. The system does not need any special semantic knowledge about the symbols in $\mathbb{F}$; they are treated simply as "black boxes" during search. The actual "meaning" of a function $f$ is retrieved during the execution of the mapping expression on a particular database instance, perhaps maintained as a stored procedure. Apart from what can be captured in search heuristics, this is probably the best that can be hoped for in general semantic integration. That is, all data semantics from some external sources of domain knowledge must be either encapsulated in the functions $f$ or somehow introduced into the search mechanism, for example via search heuristics.

This highlights a clear separation between semantic functions which interpret the symbols in the database, such as during the application of functions in $\mathbb{F}$, and syntactic, structural transformations, such as those supported by generic languages like $\mathcal{L}$. This separation also extends to a separation of labor in data mapping discovery: discovering particular complex semantic functions and generating executable data mapping expressions are treated as two separate issues in TUPELO.

Discovering complex semantic functions is a difficult research challenge. Some recent efforts have been successful in automating the discovery of restricted classes of complex functions [6, 14]. There has also been some initial research on optimization of mapping expressions which contain executable semantic functions [4].

Focusing on the discovery of data mapping expressions, TUPELO assumes that the necessary complex functions between the source and target schemas have been discovered and that these correspondences are articulated on the critical instance inputs to the system (Fig. 2). These correspondences can be easily indicated by a user via a visual interface, such as those discussed in Section 2.2. Internally, complex semantic maps are just encoded as strings in the VALUE column of the TNF relation. This string indicates the input/output type of the function, the function name, and the example function values articulated in the input critical instance.

## 5 Empirical Evaluation

The TUPELO system has been fully implemented in Scheme. In this section we discuss extensive experimental evaluations of the system on a variety of synthetic and real world data sets. Our aim in these experiments was to explore the interplay of the IDA and RBFS algorithms with the seven heuristics described in Section 3. We found that overall RBFS had better performance than IDA. We also found that heuristics $h_1$, $h_3$, normalized Euclidean, and Cosine Similarity were the best performers on the test data sets.

**Experimental Setup.** All evaluations were performed on a Pentium 4 (2.8 GHz) with 1.0 GB main memory running Gentoo Linux (kernel 2.6.11-gentoo-r9) and Chez Scheme (v6.9c). In all experiments, the performance measure is the number of states examined during search. We also included the performance of heuristic $h_0$ for comparison with the other heuristics. This heuristic is constant on all values ($\forall x, h_0(x) = 0$) and hence induces brute-force blind search. Through extensive empirical evaluation of the heuristics and search algorithms on the data sets described below, we found that the following values for the heuristic scaling constants $k$ give overall optimal performance:

|  | Norm. Euclidean | Cosine Sim. | Levenshtein |
|---|---|---|---|
| IDA | $k = 7$ | $k = 5$ | $k = 11$ |
| RBFS | $k = 20$ | $k = 24$ | $k = 15$ |

These constant $k$ values were used in all experiments presented below.

### 5.1 Experiment 1: Schema Matching on Synthetic Data

In the first experiment, we measured the performance of IDA and RBFS using all seven heuristics on a simple schema matching task.

**Data Set.** Pairs of schemas with $n = 2, \ldots, 32$ attributes were synthetically generated and populated with one tuple each illustrating correspondences between each schema:

$$\left\langle \begin{matrix} A1 & B1 \\ a1 & a1 \end{matrix} \right\rangle, \left\langle \begin{matrix} A1 & A2 & B1 & B2 \\ a1 & a2 & a1 & a2 \end{matrix} \right\rangle \cdots \left\langle \begin{matrix} A1 & \cdots & A32 & B1 & \cdots & B32 \\ a1 & \cdots & a32 & a1 & \cdots & a32 \end{matrix} \right\rangle$$

Each algorithm/heuristic combination was evaluated on generating the correct matchings between the schemas in each pair (i.e., A1↔B1, A2↔B2, etc.).

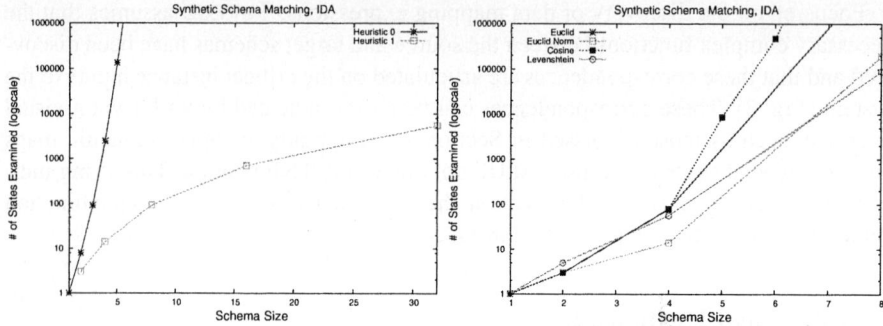

**Fig. 5.** Number of states examined using IDA for schema matching on synthetic schemas

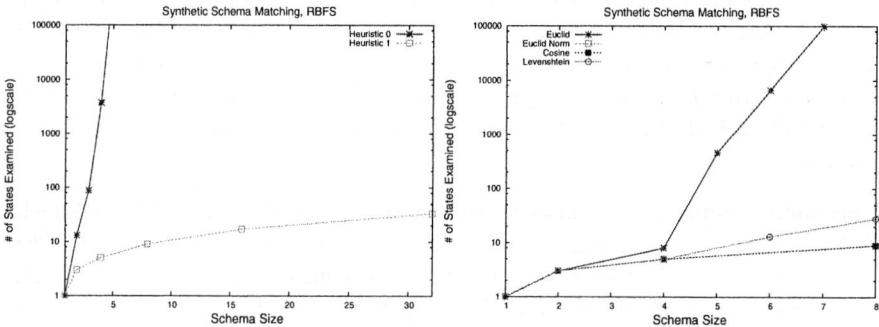

**Fig. 6.** Number of states examined using RBFS for schema matching on synthetic schemas. Note that the number of states examined using the normalized Euclidean and Cosine Similarity heuristics were identical.

**Results.** The performance of IDA on this data set is presented in Fig. 5, and the performance of RBFS is presented in Fig. 6. Heuristic $h_2$ performed identically to $h_0$, and heuristic $h_3$'s performance was identical to $h_1$. Hence they are omitted in Figs 5 and 6. RBFS had performance superior to IDA on these schemas, with the $h_1$, Levenshtein, normalized Euclidean, and Cosine Similarity heuristics having best performance.

### 5.2 Experiment 2: Schema Matching on the Deep Web

In the second experiment we measured the performance of IDA and RBFS using all seven heuristics on a set of over 200 real-world query schemas extracted from deep web data sources [5].

**Data Set.** The Books, Automobiles, Music, and Movies (BAMM) data set from the UIUC Web Integration Repository[1] contains 55, 55, 49, and 52 schemas from deep web query interfaces in the Books, Automobiles, Music, and Movies domains, respectively. The schemes each have between 1 and 8 attributes. In this experiment, we populated

---

[1] http://metaquerier.cs.uiuc.edu/repository, last viewed 26 Sept 2005.

the schemas of each domain with critical instances. We then measured the average cost of mapping from a fixed schema in each domain to each of the other schemas in that domain.

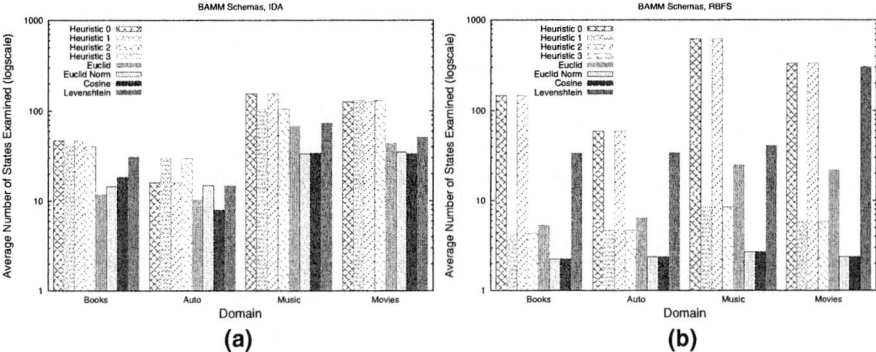

**Fig. 7.** Average number of states examined for mapping discovery in the four BAMM Domains using (a) IDA and (b) RBFS

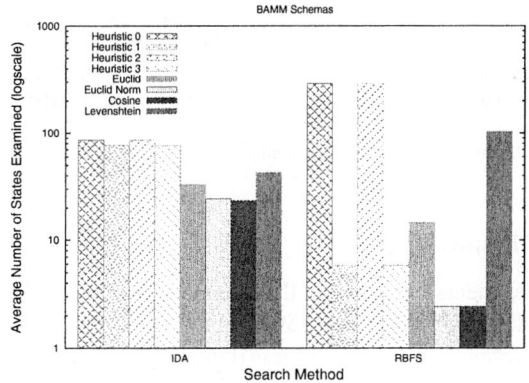

**Fig. 8.** Average number of states examined for mapping discovery across all BAMM domains

**Results.** The average performance of IDA on each of the BAMM domains is presented in Fig. 7 (a). Average RBFS performance on each of the BAMM domains is given in Fig. 7 (b). The average performance of both algorithms across all BAMM domains is given in Fig. 8. We found that RBFS typically examined fewer states on these domains than did IDA. Overall, we also found that the Cosine Similarity and normalized Euclidean heuristics had the best performance.

### 5.3 Experiment 3: Real World Complex Semantic Mapping

In the third experiment we evaluated the performance of TUPELO on discovering complex semantic mapping expressions for real world data sets in the real estate and business inventory domains.

**Data Set.** We measured performance of complex semantic mapping with the schemas for the Inventory and Real Estate II data sets from the Illinois Semantic Integration Archive.[2] In the Inventory domain there are 10 complex semantic mappings between the source and target schemas, and in the Real Estate II domain there are 12. We populated each source-target schema pair with critical instances built from the provided datasets.

**Results.** The performance on both domains was essentially the same, so we present the results for the Inventory schemas. The number of states examined for mapping discovery in this domain for increasing numbers of complex semantic functions is given in Fig. 9. On this data, we found that RBFS and IDA had similar performance. For the heuristics, the best performance was obtained by the $h_1$, $h_3$ and cosine similarity heuristics.

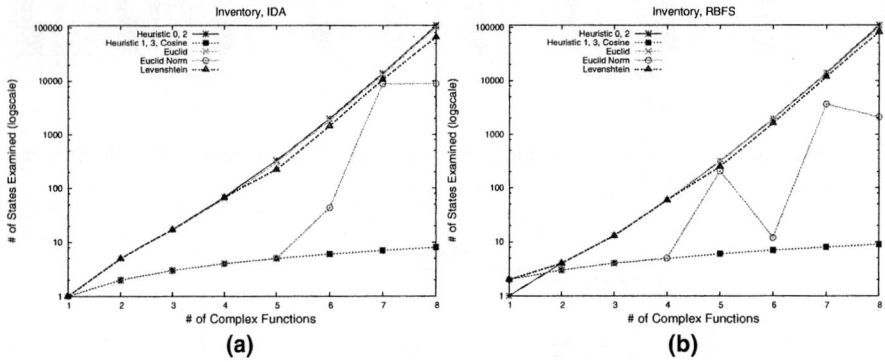

**Fig. 9.** Number of states for complex semantic mapping discovery in the Inventory domain using (a) IDA and (b) RBFS

### 5.4 Discussion of Results

The goal of the experiments discussed in this section was to measure the performance of TUPELO on a wide variety of schemas. We found that TUPELO was effective for discovering mapping expressions in each of these domains, even with the simple heuristic search algorithms IDA and RBFS. It is clear from these experiments that RBFS is in general a more effective search algorithm than IDA. Although we found that heuristic $h_1$ exhibited consistently good performance, it is also clear that there was no perfect all-purpose search heuristic. TUPELO has also been validated and shown effective for examples involving the data-metadata restructurings illustrated in Fig. 1 [11]. It was found in that domain that no particular heuristic had consistently superior performance. We can conclude from these observations that work still needs to be done on developing more intelligent search heuristics.

## 6 Related Work

The problem of overcoming structural and semantic heterogeneity has a long history in the database [8] and Artificial Intelligence [29] research communities. In Section 1

---
[2] http://anhai.cs.uiuc.edu/archive/, last viewed 26 Sept 2005.

we have already situated TUPELO in the general research landscape of the data mapping problem. We now briefly highlight related research not discussed elsewhere in the paper:

- *Schema Matching.* A wide variety of existing systems have leveraged Artificial Intelligence techniques for solving different aspects of schema matching and mapping. These include neural networks, Bayesian learning, and genetic programming approaches [7, 22, 27, 33]. The TUPELO view on data mapping as search complements this body of research; this view also complements the characterization of schema matching as constraint satisfaction proposed by Smiljanic et al. [35].
- *Data-Metadata Transformations.* Few data mapping systems have considered the data-metadata structural transformations used in the TUPELO mapping language $\mathcal{L}$. Systems that have considered some aspects of these transformations include [6, 9, 26].
- *Example-Driven Data Mapping.* The notion of example-based data mapping is an ancient idea, by some accounts dating back to the 4th century [30]. Recent work most closely related to the example driven approach of TUPELO include [21, 30, 33].
- *Executable Mapping Expressions.* Most schema matching systems do not address the issue of generating executable mapping expressions, which is in general considered to be an open hard problem [24]. Several notable systems that do generate such expressions include [1, 25, 26, 33].

TUPELO complements and extends this research by (1) attacking the data mapping problem as a basic search problem in a state space and by (2) addressing a broader class of mapping expressions including data-metadata transformations and complex semantics functions. We have also initiated a formal investigation of various aspects of the data mapping problem for relational data sources [12].

## 7 Conclusions and Future Work

In this paper we presented and illustrated the effectiveness of the TUPELO system for discovering data mapping expressions between relational data sources. Novel aspects of the system include (1) example-driven generation of mapping expressions which include data-metadata structural transformations and complex semantic mappings and (2) viewing the data mapping problem as fundamentally a sarch problem in a well defined search space. Mapping discovery is performed in TUPELO using only the syntax and structure of the input examples without recourse to any domain-specific semantic knowledge. The implementation of TUPELO was described and the viability of the approach illustrated on a variety of synthetic and real world schemas.

There are several promising avenues for future work on TUPELO. As is evident from the empirical evaluation presented in Section 5, further research remains on developing more sophisticated search heuristics. The Levenshtein, Euclidean, and Cosine Similarity based search heuristics mostly focus on the content of database states. Successful heuristics must measure both content and structure. Is there a good multi-purpose search heuristic? Also, we have only applied straightforward approaches to search with the

IDA and RBFS algorithms. Further investigation of search techniques developed in the AI literature is warranted. Finally, the perspective of data mapping as search is not limited to relational data sources. In particular, the architecture of the TUPELO system can be applied to the generation of mapping expressions in other mapping languages and for other data models. Based on the viability of the system for relational data sources, this is a very promising area for future research.

**Acknowledgments.** We thank the Indiana University database group, Alexander Bilke, Jan Van den Bussche, and Robert Warren for their helpful feedback and support.

# References

1. Bernstein, Philip A., et al. Interactive Schema Translation with Instance-Level Mappings (System Demo). *Proc. VLDB Conf.*, pp. 1283-1286, Trondheim, Norway, 2005.
2. Bilke, Alexander and Felix Naumann. Schema Matching using Duplicates. *Proc. IEEE ICDE*, pp. 69-80, Tokyo, Japan, 2005.
3. Bossung, Sebastian, et al. Automated Data Mapping Specification via Schema Heuristics and User Interaction. *Proc. IEEE/ACM ASE*, pp. 208-217, Linz, Austria, 2004.
4. Carreira, Paulo and Helena Galhardas. Execution of Data Mappers. *Proc. ACM SIGMOD Workshop IQIS*, pp. 2-9, Paris, France, 2004.
5. Chang, K. C.-C., B. He, C. Li, M. Patel, and Z. Zhang. Structured Databases on the Web: Observations and Implications. *SIGMOD Record*, 33(3):61-70, 2004.
6. Dhamankar, Robin, et al. iMAP: Discovering Complex Semantic Matches between Database Schemas. *Proc. ACM SIGMOD*, pp. 383-394, Paris, France, 2004.
7. Doan, AnHai, Pedro Domingos, and Alon Halevy. Learning to Match the Schemas of Databases: A Multistrategy Approach. *Machine Learning* 50(3):279-301, 2003.
8. Doan, A., N. Noy, and A. Halevy (Eds). Special Section on Semantic Integration. *SIGMOD Record* 33(4), 2004.
9. Embley, D. W., L. Xu, and Y. Ding. Automatic Direct and Indirect Schema Mapping: Experiences and Lessons Learned. In [8], pp.14-19.
10. Euzenat, Jérôme et al. State of the Art on Ontology Alignment. *Tech. Report D2.2.3, IST Knowledge Web NoE*, 2004.
11. Fletcher, George H.L. and Catharine M. Wyss. Mapping Between Data Sources on the Web. *Proc. IEEE ICDE Workshop WIRI*, Tokyo, Japan, 2005.
12. Fletcher, George H.L., et al. A Calculus for Data Mapping. *Proc. COORDINATION Workshop InterDB*, Namur, Belgium, 2005.
13. Gottlob, Georg, et al. The Lixto Data Extraction Project – Back and Forth between Theory and Practice. *Proc. ACM PODS*, pp. 1-12, Paris, France, 2004.
14. He, Bin, et al. Discovering Complex Matchings Across Web Query Interfaces: A Correlation Mining Approach. *Proc. ACM KDD*, 2004.
15. Ives, Zachary G., Alon Y. Halevy, Peter Mork, and Igor Tatarinov. Piazza: Mediation and Integration Infrastructure for Semantic Web Data. *J. Web Sem.* 1(2):155-175, 2004.
16. Kang, Jaewoo and Jeffrey F. Naughton. On Schema Matching with Opaque Column Names and Data Values. *Proc. ACM SIGMOD*, pp. 205-216, San Diego, CA, 2003.
17. Kolaitis, Phokion G. Schema Mappings, Data Exchange, and Metadata Management. *Proc. ACM PODS*, pp. 61-75, Baltimore, MD, USA, 2005.
18. Krishnamurthy, Ravi, et al. Language Features for Interoperability of Databases with Schematic Discrepancies. *Proc. ACM SIGMOD*, pp. 40-49, Denver, CO, USA, 1991.

19. Lenzerini, Maurizio. Data Integration: A Theoretical Perspective. *Proc. ACM PODS*, pp. 233-246, Madison, WI, 2002.
20. Levenshtein, Vladimir I. Binary codes capable of correcting deletions, insertions, and reversals. *Doklady Akademii Nauk SSSR* 163(4):845-848, 1965.
21. Levy, A.Y., and J.J. Ordille. An Experiment in Integrating Internet Information Sources. *Proc. AAAI Fall Symp. AI Apps. Knowl. Nav. Ret.*, pp. 92-96, Cambridge, MA, USA, 1995.
22. Li, Wen-Syan and Chris Clifton. SEMINT: A Tool for Identifying Attribute Correspondences in Heterogeneous Databases Using Neural Networks. *Data Knowl. Eng.* 33(1):49-84, 2000.
23. Litwin, Witold, Mohammad A. Ketabchi, and Ravi Krishnamurthy. First Order Normal Form for Relational Databases and Multidatabases. *SIGMOD Record* 20(4):74-76, 1991.
24. Melnik, Sergey. *Generic Model Management: Concepts and Algorithms, LNCS 2967*. Springer Verlag, Berlin, 2004.
25. Melnik, Sergey, et al. Supporting Executable Mappings in Model Management. *Proc. ACM SIGMOD*, Baltimore, MD, USA, 2005.
26. Miller, Renée J., Laura M. Haas, and Mauricio A. Hernández. Schema Mapping as Query Discovery, *Proc. VLDB Conf.*, pp. 77-88, Cairo, Egypt, 2000.
27. Morishima, Atsuyuki, et al. A Machine Learning Approach to Rapid Development of XML Mapping Queries. *Proc. IEEE ICDE*, pp.276-287, Boston, MA, USA, 2004.
28. Nilsson, Nils J. *Artificial Intelligence: A New Synthesis*. Morgan Kaufmann, San Francisco, 1998.
29. Noy, N.F., A. Doan, and A.Y. Halevy (Eds). Special Issue on Semantic Integration. *AI Magazine* 26(1), 2005.
30. Perkowitz, Mike and Oren Etzioni. Category Translation: Learning to Understand Information on the Internet. *Proc. IJCAI*, pp. 930-938, Montréal, Canada, 1995.
31. Rahm, Erhard and Philip A. Bernstein. A Survey of Approaches to Automatic Schema Matching. *VLDB J.* 10(4):334-350, 2001.
32. Raman, Vijayshankar, and Joseph M. Hellerstein. Potter's Wheel: An Interactive Data Cleaning System. *Proc. VLDB Conf.*, pp. 381-390, Roma, Italy, 2001.
33. Schmid, Ute and Jens Waltermann. Automatic Synthesis of XSL-Transformations from Example Documents. *Proc. IASTED AIA*, Innsbruck, Austria, 2004.
34. Shvaiko, Pavel and Jérôme Euzenat. A Survey of Schema-Based Matching Approaches. *J. Data Semantics* IV, 2005 (to appear).
35. Smiljanic, Marko, et al. Formalizing the XML Schema Matching Problem as a Constraint Optimization Problem. *Proc. DEXA*, Copenhagen, Denmark, 2005.
36. Stephens, D. Ryan. Information Retrieval and Computational Geometry. *Dr. Dobb's Journal* 29(12):42-45, Dec. 2004.
37. Wang, G., J. Goguen, Y.-K. Nam, and K. Lin. Critical Points for Interactive Schema Matching. *Proc. APWeb, Springer LNCS 3007*, pp. 654-664, Hangzhou, China, 2004.
38. Winkler, William E. The State of Record Linkage and Current Research Problems. U.S. Bureau of the Census, Statistical Research Division, Technical Report RR99/04, 1999.
39. Wyss, Catharine M. and Edward L. Robertson. Relational Languages for Metadata Integration. *ACM TODS* 30(2):624-660, 2005.
40. Wyss, Catharine M. and Edward L. Robertson. A Formal Characterization of PIVOT / UNPIVOT. *Proc. ACM CIKM*, Bremen, Germany, 2005.

# Parallelizing Skyline Queries for Scalable Distribution*

Ping Wu, Caijie Zhang, Ying Feng, Ben Y. Zhao, Divyakant Agrawal,
and Amr El Abbadi

University of California at Santa Barbara
{pingwu, caijie, yingf, ravenben, agrawal, amr}@cs.ucsb.edu

**Abstract.** Skyline queries help users make intelligent decisions over complex data, where different and often conflicting criteria are considered. Current skyline computation methods are restricted to centralized query processors, limiting scalability and imposing a single point of failure. In this paper, we address the problem of parallelizing skyline query execution over a large number of machines by leveraging content-based data partitioning. We present a novel distributed skyline query processing algorithm (DSL) that discovers skyline points progressively. We propose two mechanisms, recursive region partitioning and dynamic region encoding, to enforce a partial order on query propagation in order to pipeline query execution. Our analysis shows that DSL is optimal in terms of the total number of local query invocations across all machines. In addition, simulations and measurements of a deployed system show that our system load balances communication and processing costs across cluster machines, providing *incremental scalability* and significant performance improvement over alternative distribution mechanisms.

## 1 Introduction

Today's computing infrastructure makes a large amount of information available to consumers, creating an information overload that threatens to overwhelm Internet users. Individuals are often confronted with conflicting goals while making decisions based on extremely large and complex data sets. Users often want to optimize their decision-making and selection criteria across multiple attributes. For example, a user browsing through a real-estate database for houses may want to minimize the price and maximize the quality of neighborhood schools. Given such a multi-preference criteria, the system should be able to identify all potentially "interesting" data records. Skyline queries provide a viable solution by finding data records not "dominated" by other records in the system, where data record $x$ dominates $y$ if $x$ is no worse than $y$ in any dimension of interest, and better in at least one dimension. Records or objects on the skyline are "the best" under some monotonic preference functions[1].

A more general variant is the *constrained skyline query* [19], where users want to find skyline points within a subset of records that satisfies multiple "hard" constraints. For

---

* This work was supported in part by NSF under grants IIS 02-23022, IIS 02-20152, and CNF 04-23336.
[1] Without loss of generality, we assume in this paper that users prefer the minimum value on all interested dimensions.

example, a user may only be interested in car records within the price range of $10,000 to $15,000 and mileage between 50K and 100K miles. The discussion hereafter focuses on this generalized form of the skyline query.

Until recently, Skyline query processing and other online analytical processing (OLAP) applications have been limited to large centralized servers. As a platform, these servers are expensive, hard to upgrade, and provide a central point of failure. Previous research has shown common-off-the-shelf (COTS) cluster-based computing to be an effective alternative to high-end servers [3], a fact confirmed by benchmarks [4] and deployment in large query systems such as Google [6]. In addition, skyline queries are especially useful in the context of Web information services where user preference plays an important role. Integrating structured data from a large number of data sources, those services [2] help Web surfers formulate "structured" queries over large data sets and typically process considerable query load during peak hours. For these Web services, a scalable distributed/parallel approach can significantly reduce processing time, and eliminate high query load during peak hours.

Our paper is the first to address the problem of parallelizing progressive skyline queries on a share-nothing architecture. This paper makes four key contributions. First, we present a recursive region partitioning algorithm and a dynamic region encoding method. These methods enforce the skyline partial order so that the system pipelines participating machines during query execution and minimizes inter-machine communication. As a query propagates, our system prunes data regions and corresponding machines for efficiency, and progressively generates partial results for the user. In addition, we propose a "random sampling" based approach to perform fine-grain load balancing in DSL. Next, we perform analysis to show that our approach is optimal in minimizing number of local query invocations across all machines. Finally, we describe the cluster deployment of a full implementation on top of the CAN [21] content distribution network, and present thorough evaluations of its bandwidth, scalability, load balancing and response time characteristics under varying system conditions. Results show DSL clearly outperforms alternative distribution mechanisms.

The rest of the paper is organized as follows: Section 2 describes our design goals as well as two simple algorithms for distributed skyline calculation. We present our core algorithm (DSL) in Section 3. In Section 4, we address the query load-balancing problem in DSL. We then evaluate our system via simulation and empirical measurements in Section 5. Finally, we present related work in Section 6 and conclude in Section 7.

## 2 Design Goals and Proposals

In this section, we describe our design goals for parallel/distributed skyline query processing algorithms. We then present two simple solutions and discuss their limitations.

### 2.1 Goals

In addition to basic requirements for skyline processing, we describe three design goals for a distributed skyline algorithm. 1) *Progressiveness*. Similar to the requirements for centralized solutions [17], a distributed algorithm should be able to progressively produce the result points to the user: *i.e.*, the system should return partial results immediately without scanning the entire data set. Progressiveness in a distributed setting further requires that results be returned without involving all the nodes in the system. This eliminates the need for a centralized point for result aggregation. 2) *Scalability*. Incremental scalability is the primary goal for our system. In order to scale to a large number of participant machines, we require that internode communication be minimized, and processing load should be spread evenly across all nodes. It should also be easy to add more nodes into the system to handle increased data volume and/or heavier query load. 3) *Flexibility*. Our goal for flexibility has two components. First, the system should support *constrained skyline queries*, and find skyline records in arbitrarily specified query ranges during the runtime. Second, the distributed algorithm should not impose any restrictions on the local implementation on each machine, thus allowing easy incorporation of "state of the art" centralized skyline solutions.

## 2.2 Simple Solutions

In this section, we discuss two simple approaches towards distributing data and query processing across multiple machines. We analyze both proposals according to our stated goals.

*Naive partitioning.* One simple approach is to partition data records randomly across all machines, and to contact all nodes to process each query. Each node calculates a result set from local data, and all result sets are merged at a centralized node. To reduce congestion, we can organize the nodes into a multi-level hierarchy where intermediate nodes aggregate result sets from children nodes. We call this approach the *naive method*.

While easy to implement, this approach has several drawbacks. First, each query must be processed by *all* nodes even if the query range is very small, resulting in significant unnecessary computation. Second, most data points transmitted across the network are not in the final skyline, resulting in significant waste in bandwidth. Finally, this method is not progressive, since the final result set cannot be reported until all the nodes have finished their local computations. Note that using locally progressive algorithms does not produce globally progressive results.

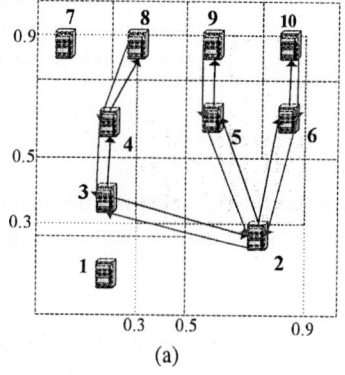
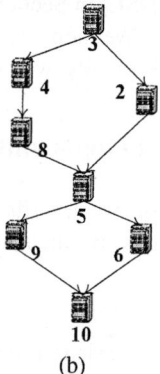

**Fig. 1.** (a) CAN multicast-based Method with in-network pruning. (b) Observation: partial order between nodes.

*CAN Multicast.* An improved algorithm utilizes the notion of content-based data partitioning. Specifically, we normalize the entire data space and directly map it to a virtual coordinate space. Each participating machine is also mapped into the same coordinate space and is responsible for a specific portion of that space. Then every machine stores all the data points that fall into its space. During query processing, a multicast tree is built to connect together all nodes overlapping with the query range, with the root at the node that hosts the bottom-left point of the query range[2]. The query propagates down the tree, nodes perform local computation, and result sets are aggregated up back to the root. Ineligible data points are discarded along the path to preserve bandwidth. Figure 1(a) illustrates how the tree is dynamically built at query time. Node 3 hosts the bottom-left point of the query range ((0.3, 0.3),(0.9, 0.9)), and acts as the multicast tree root. In this paper, we implement the content-based data partitioning scheme by leveraging the existing code base of the CAN [21] content distribution network. Therefore we call this approach the *CAN-multicast* method. While the following discussion is based on the CAN overlay network, our solutions do not rely on the specific features of the CAN network such as decentralized routing and are thus applicable to general cases of content-based data partition as well.

The CAN-multicast method explicitly places data so that constrained skyline queries only access the nodes that host the data within the query range. This prunes a significant portion of unnecessary data processing, especially for constrained skyline queries within a small range. However, its nodes within the query box still behave the same as those in the naive method. Thus it shares the bandwidth and non-progressiveness drawbacks.

## 3 Progressive Distributed Skylines

In this section, we begin by making observations from exploring the simple methods described in the last section. Based on these observations, we propose our progressive skyline query processing algorithm (DSL) and show the analytical results regarding its behavior.

### 3.1 Observations

Our progressive algorithm derives from several observations. Using the CAN multicast method, no result can be reported until results from *all* nodes in the query range are considered. We note that this strategy can be optimized by leveraging content-based data placement. Skyline results from certain nodes are guaranteed to be part of the final skyline, and can be reported immediately. For example, in Figure 1(a), no data points from other nodes can dominate those from node 3, and node 3 can reports its local results immediately. Meanwhile, node 8's calculations must wait for results from 3 and 4, since its data points can be dominated by those two nodes. On the other hand, data points in nodes 4 and 2 are mutually independent from a skyline perspective; that is, no points from node 2 can dominate points in node 4 and vice versa. Therefore, their

---

[2] The choice of the root will not impact the final result set as long as all the nodes in the query range are covered by the tree.

calculations can proceed in parallel. We summarize this observation as: any node in the virtual CAN space can decide whether its local skyline points are in the final result set or not by only consulting a *subset* of all the other nodes within the query range (***Observation 1***).

Based on the *Observation 1*, we visualize the computational dependency between nodes in Figure 1(b). Each edge in the graph captures the precedence relationship between CAN nodes. During query propagation, skyline points must be evaluated at all "upstream" nodes before "downstream" nodes can proceed. Based on this, we also observe that with skyline values from upstream nodes, some nodes within the query region do not need to execute the query(***Observation 2***). For example, in Figure 1(a), any skyline point from node 3 means that the query execution on nodes 5, 6, 9 and 10 should be skipped. In Theorem 4, our solution is proven to be optimal inthis sense.

### 3.2 Partial Orders over Data Partitions

We now formalize the notion of partial order over data partitions. According to CAN terminology, we call each data partition a *zone* in the CAN virtual space. Let $Q_{ab}$ be a $d$-dimensional query region in CAN space; $a(a_1, a_2, ..., a_d)$, $b(b_1, b_2, ..., b_d)$ be the bottom-left and top-right points, respectively. The *master node* of $Q_{ab}$, denoted as $M(Q_{ab})$, is the CAN node whose zone contains the point $a$ (*e.g.* Node 3 is the master node in Figure 1(a)).

Let point $x(x_1, x_2, ..., x_d)$ be the top-right point of $M(Q_{ab})$'s CAN zone (*e.g.* point (0.5,0.5) in Figure 1(a)). $M(Q_{ab})$ partitions the query region $Q_{ab}$ as follows: for each dimension $i(1 \leq i \leq d)$, if $x_i < b_i$, $M(Q_{ab})$ partitions $Q_{ab}$ into two halves on dimension $i$: namely the upper interval $[x_i, b_i]$ and the lower interval $[a_i, x_i]$; if $x_i \geq b_i$, the partition will not occur on this dimension since $M(Q_{ab})$ "covers" $Q_{ab}$ on dimension $i$. Thus, $M(Q_{ab})$ divides the query space $Q_{ab}$ into at most $2^d$ subregions (e.g., the query region in Figure 1(a) is partitioned into 4 subregions by node 3). We denote all the subregions resulting from the partition as the *region set* $RS(Q_{ab})$ and $|RS(Q_{ab})| \leq 2^d$.

*Example 1.* Figure 2 shows all four possibilities for region partitioning on a 2-d CAN space. $a$, $b$ determine the query box $Q_{ab}$ and $x$ represents the top-right point of $M(Q_{ab})$'s zone. In (a), $RS(Q_{ab})$ contains 4 subregions (denoted as $r_0, r_1, r_2, r_3$) since $x$ falls inside the query box and both dimensions are split. In (b) and (c), only one dimension is divided since $x$ is greater than $b$ in at least one dimension. Therefore, $RS(Q_{ab})$ contains 2 subregions (denoted as $r_0, r_1$) in both cases. Finally, in (d), the zone of $M(Q_{ab})$ covers the entire query space (on both dimensions), and no partitioning occurs. □

Given a query region $Q_{ab}$ and its master node's zone, the region partitioning process as well as its resulting region set $RS(Q_{ab})$ can be uniquely determined. It is important to note that the region partitioning process is *dynamically* determined, depending on 1) query region $Q_{ab}$ of the current skyline query; 2) the CAN zone of the node $M(Q_{ab})$ containing the virtual coordinate $a$. Furthermore, since there does not exist a "global" oracle in a distributed setting and each node only sees its own zone, this process is executed at the master node $M(Q_{ab})$. Next we define a partial order relation on $RS(Q_{ab})$.

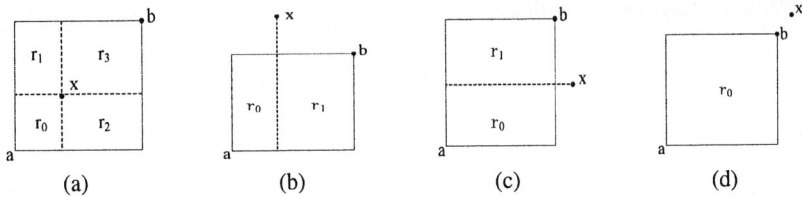

**Fig. 2.** Region partitions on 2-d CAN space

**Definition 1.** *(Skyline Dependent, $\ll$):* Relation *"Skyline Dependent, $\ll$"* is a relation over Region Set $RS(Q_{ab})$: region $r_i$ is *"Skyline Dependent"* on region $r_j$, i.f.f. $\exists p(p_1, p_2, ..., p_d) \in r_i, \exists q(q_1, q_2, ..., q_d) \in r_j$, s.t. $\forall k, 1 \leq k \leq d, q_k \leq p_k$, i.e., $q$ *"dominates"* $p$.

*Example 2.* In Figure 2(a), there are four subregions resulting from the partition of the query region $Q_{ab}$. Specifically, $RS(Q_{ab}) = \{r_0, r_1, r_2, r_3\}$. And according to Definition , $r_1 \ll r_0, r_2 \ll r_0, r_3 \ll r_0, r_3 \ll r_1$ and $r_3 \ll r_2$.

**Theorem 1.** *"Skyline Dependent, $\ll$" is a reflexive, asymmetric, and transitive relation over $RS(Q_{ab})$, and thus it defines a partial order over the region set $RS(Q_{ab})$.*

*Proof.* It is straightforward to show the reflectivity and transitivity of "Skyline Dependent". Asymmetry can be derived by the fact that all the subregions resulting from the region partitioning process are convex polygons. □

Intuitively, for each incoming query, if we can control the system computation flow to strictly satisfy the above partial order, then we can produce skyline results progressively. Hence nodes in a region would not be queried until they see the results from *all* "Skyline Dependent" regions. The reason for this is that with the aid of the partial order between regions, the local skyline on each participant node is only affected by the data in its "Skyline Dependent" regions, i.e. each region is able to determine its final result based *only* on the data from its "Skyline Dependent" regions and its own data records. This exactly captures our previous two observations.

### 3.3 Dynamic Region Partitioning and Encoding

We still face two remaining challenges. The first challenge involves generalizing the above approach to the case where subregions are distributed over multiple CAN zones. We call this the *Resolution Mismatch Problem*. We address this challenge with a *Recursive Region Partitioning* technique. Specifically, for a query range $Q_{ab}$, for each subregions in $RS(Q_{ab})$ resulting from a region partitioning based on master node $M(Q_{ab})$, the same region partitioning process is carried out recursively. Since after one region partitioning, at least the bottom-left subregion $r_0$ is entirely covered by the zone of $M(Q_{ab})$, we can resolve one part of the region $Q_{ab}$ at each step. Consequently, this recursive process will terminate when the entire query region is partitioned and matches the underlying CAN zones. Figure 3(a) shows that for the query range ((0.3,0.3),(0.9,0.9)), in total, region partitioning process is invoked three times on node 3, 2, and 6 sequentially until each of the resulting subregions is covered exactly by one CAN zone.

**Algorithm 1.** Successor Calculation

1: $Q_{ab}$: the "parent" region of $r_{cd}$;
2: $r_{cd}$: a region $\in RS(Q_{ab})$;
3: $ID(r_{cd})$: the code of $r_{cd}$;
4: $succ(r_{cd})$: successors of region $r_{cd}$;
5: $succ(r_{cd}) \longleftarrow \emptyset$; //Initialization
6: **foreach** $i$,s.t. $ID(r_{cd})[i]==$ '0'
7: **begin**
8: $oneSucessor.code[i] \longleftarrow$ '1'; // flip one '0' bit to '1'
9: $oneSucessor.region[i] \longleftarrow (d[i],b[i]$ ); // Set the corresponding region interval to the "upper interval"
10: $succ(r_{cd}) \longleftarrow succ(r_i) \bigcup oneSuccessor$;
11: **end**
12: Return $succ(r_{cd})$;
13: **END**

The second challenge that naturally arises is that the query range for a constrained skyline query is only given at *query time*. The recursive region partitioning and the partial order information are also computed at query time, since they are completely dependent on the query range. In order to enforce the partial order during the query propagation in a distributed setting, the master nodes in the subregions should know the predecessors they need to hear from before their own regions are activated, as well as their successive regions that it should trigger upon its own completion. Below, we present a *dynamic region encoding* scheme to capture this "context" information during the query processing time. In our solution, once a node receives its code from one of its predecessors, it obtains all the necessary information to behave correctly.

**Definition 2.** *(Dynamic Region Encoding) Given query region $Q_{ab}$, let $x$ be the top-right point of master node $M(Q_{ab})$'s CAN zone. For each d-dimensional region $r \in RS(Q_{ab})$, we assign a d-digit code $ID(r)$ to region $r$. where $ID(r)[i]$ equals to '0' if the interval of $r$ on the $i^{th}$ dimension $= [a_i, x_i]$; $ID(r)[i] =$ '1' if the interval of $r$ on the $i^{th}$ dimension $= [x_i, b_i]$; $ID(r)[i] =$ '\*' if during the region partition the original interval on $i^{th}$ dimension is not divided.*

Informally, the $i^{th}$ digit of $ID(r)$ encodes whether $r$ takes on the "lower half" ('0'), the "upper half" ('1') or the "original interval" ('\*') as the result of the corresponding region partitioning. Based on this region coding scheme, we define a "Skyline Precede" relation as follows:

**Definition 3.** *(Skyline Precede, $\prec$) Relation "Skyline Precede" ($\prec$) is a relation over region set $RS(Q_{ab})$: region $r_i$ "Skyline Precede" $r_j$, or $r_i \prec r_j$, i.f.f. code $ID(r_i)$ differs from $ID(r_j)$ in only one bit, say, the $k^{th}$ bit, where $ID(r_i)[k] =$ '0' and $ID(r_j)[k] =$ '1'. We denote $pred(r_i)$ as the set containing all the regions that "Skyline Precede" $r_i$, and $succ(r_i)$ as the set containing all the regions that $r_i$ "Skyline Precede".*

"Skyline Precede" precisely defines the order in which a distributed skyline query should be propagated and executed. In Algorithm 1 we describe how a specific

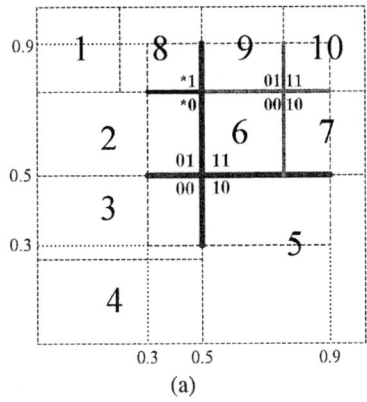 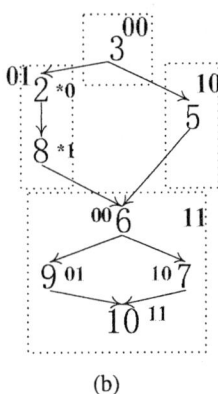

**Fig. 3.** (a) Finding the skyline points in range ((0.3,0.3),(0.9,0.9)). In total, region partitioning operation happens 3 times. (b) The query propagation order according to DSL.

region $r_{cd}$ calculates its successor set $succ(r_{cd})$ in $RS(Q_{ab})$ based on its code $ID(r_{cd})$ ($pred(r_{cd})$ is computed analogously). Basically, each successor is generated by flipping one single '0' bit to '1' (line 8) and adjust the region interval on that dimension to the "upper interval" accordingly (line 9). Therefore, the query coordinates $a, b$ of region $Q_{ab}$, and $c, d$ (its own region $r_{cd}$) and code $ID(r_{cd})$ are all the information that needs to be sent for correct query propagation. Figure 3(a) illustrates the region codes and the "Skyline Precede" relationship on a 2-d CAN network given the initial query range ((0.3,0.3),(0.9,0.9)). For example, node 5 is given code '10', its own query region ((0.5, 0.3),(0.9,0.5)), the whole query region ((0.3,0.3),(0.9,0.9)), it flips the '0' bit to '1' and adjust the y-interval from (0.3,0.5) to (0.5,0.9) and get its only successor region ((0.5,0.5), (0.9,0.9)) with code '11'.

The relationship between "Skyline Dependent, $\ll$" and "Skyline precede, $\prec$" is described by Lemma 1. Lemma 1 guarantees that, if we enforce that the query propagation follows the "Skyline Precede,$\prec$" relation, by the time a region starts, all and only its "Skyline Dependent, $\ll$" regions are completed.

**Lemma 1.** *For any two region $r_i$ and $r_j$ ($r_i, r_j \in RS(Q_{ab})$), $r_i \ll r_j$, i.f.f. there exists a sequence of regions, s.t.:$r_j \prec r_{j+1} ... \prec r_{i-1} \prec r_i$.*

**Proof.** According to Definition 2, in order for region $r_i$ to be Skyline Dependent on region $r_j$, for those bits in which $ID(r_i)$ differs from code $ID(r_j)$, $ID(r_i)$ must be '1' and $ID(r_j)$ must be '0'. This, together with Definition 3, ensures the correctness of Lemma 1. □

### 3.4 Algorithm Description

Now we present our system for **D**istributed **S**ky**L**ine query, or DSL. We assume that the data is injected into the system either by feeds from merchant's product databases [1] or from a Web database crawler that "pulls" structured data records from external Web sources [24]. The data space is normalized to [0, 1] on each dimension and every data object is stored at the corresponding CAN node. Starting from the global query region,

**Algorithm 2.** Distributed Skyline(DSL) Computation

1: $Q_{cd}$: current region to evaluate;   $Q_{ab}$: the "parent" region of $Q_{cd}$
2: $ID(Q_{cd})$: region code for $Q_{cd}$;   $skyline$: skyline results from upstream regions;
3: $M(Q_{cd})$: master node of $Q_{cd}$;
4:
5: QUERY($Q_{cd}$, $Q_{ab}$, $ID(Q_{cd})$, $skyline$)
6: **Procedure**
7: calculate predecessor set $pred(Q_{cd})$ and successor set $succ(Q_{cd})$;
8: **if** all regions in $pred(Q_{cd})$ are completed **then**
9:   **if** $skyline$ dominates $Q_{cd}$ **then**
10:     $M(Q_{cd})$.COMPLETE();
11:   **end if**
12:   $localresults \longleftarrow M(Q_{cd}).CalculateLocalSkyline(skyline, Q_{cd})$;
13:   $skyline \longleftarrow skyline \cup localresults$;
14:   **if** $M(Q_{cd}).zone$ covers $Q_{cd}$ **then**
15:     $M(Q_{cd})$.COMPLETE();
16:   **else**
17:     $M(Q_{cd})$ partitions $Q_{cd}$ into $RS(Q_{cd})$;
18:     **foreach** successor $Q_{gh}$ **in** $RS(Q_{cd})$
19:       $M(Q_{gh})$.QUERY($Q_{gh}$,$Q_{cd}$,$ID(Q_{gh})$,$skyline$);
20:   **end if**
21: **end if**
22: **End Procedure**
23:
24: COMPLETE()
25: **Procedure**
26: **if** $succ(Q_{cd})$ equals to NULL **then**
27:   $M(Q_{ab})$.COMPLETE();
28: **else**
29:   **foreach** successor $Q_{ef}$ **in** $succ(Q_{cd})$
30:     $M(Q_{ef})$.QUERY($Q_{ef}$, $Q_{ab}$, $ID(Q_{ef})$, $skyline$);
31: **end if**
32: **End Procedure**

DSL recursively applies the region partitioning process to match the underlying CAN zones and the query propagation between the resulting subregions strictly complies with the "Skyline Precede" relationship which is enforced using dynamic region coding.

On each node involved, the DSL computation is composed of two asynchronous procedures: QUERY and COMPLETE. These two procedures are described in Algorithm 2. To activate a subregion $Q_{cd}$ of $Q_{ab}$, a query message $q$ is routed towards point $c$ in the CAN virtual space using the CAN overlay routing mechanism. The node hosting $c$ becomes the master node of the region, or $M(Q_{cd})$. Upon receiving $q$, the QUERY procedure on $M(Q_{cd})$ is invoked. DSL's QUERY procedure on $M(Q_{cd})$ will be provided 4 parameters: 1) its region code $ID(Q_{cd})$; 2) its own query region $Q_{cd}$; 3) the skyline point set $skyline$ discovered from its "upstream" regions and 4) its "parent" query region $Q_{ab}$. Using this information, $M(Q_{cd})$ is able to calculate its position in the parent query region $Q_{ab}$, i.e. its immediate predecessors $pred(Q_{cd})$ (line 9) and successors

$succ(Q_{cd})$ (line 10). $M(Q_{cd})$ starts computation on its own query region $Q_{cd}$ only after hearing from *all* its predecessors in $pred(Q_{cd})$ (line 11). $M(Q_{cd})$ first checks whether its own zone covers region $Q_{cd}$ or whether $Q_{cd}$ has already been dominated by "upstream" skyline points in $skyline$ (line 14). If either is positive, $M(Q_{cd})$ will not further partition its query region $Q_{cd}$ and just directly call its local COMPLETE procedure meaning it finishes evaluating the region $Q_{cd}$ (line 15). Otherwise it recursively partitions $Q_{cd}$ into a new region set $RS(Q_{cd})$ (line 17), in which $M(Q_{cd})$ is responsible for the "first" subregion. For each successive region $Q_{gh}$ in the new region set of $RS(Q_{cd})$, $M(Q_{cd})$ activates $Q_{gh}$'s QUERY procedure by routing a query message $q'$ to the corresponding bottom-left virtual point $g$ (line 18-19).

In COMPLETE procedure, $M(Q_{cd})$ proceeds with the computation by invoking the QUERY procedures on its successors in $succ(Q_{cd})$ (line 29-30). If $Q_{cd}$ happens to be the last subregion in region set $RS(Q_{ab})$, i.e. set $succ(Q_{cd})$ contains no successive regions, $M(Q_{cd})$ will pass the control back to the master node $M(Q_{ab})$ of its "parent" region $Q_{ab}$ and invokes the COMPLETE procedure on $M(Q_{ab})$ (line 27), i.e. the recursion "rebounds". The entire computation terminates if the COMPLETE procedure on the master node of the global query region is invoked.

Figure 3(a) shows the recursive region partitioning process and its corresponding region codes of a constrained skyline query with initial query range $((0.3, 0.3), (0.9, 0.9))$. Figure 3(b) illustrates the actual query propagation order between machines according to DSL.

**Theorem 2.** *(Correctness and Progressiveness): For any constrained skyline query, DSL described above can progressively find all and only the correct skyline points in the system.*

### 3.5 Algorithm Analysis

In this subsection, we present two analytical results. First, in Theorem 3, we show DSL's bandwidth behavior, which measures the inter-machine communication overhead and is critical for the system scalability. Then we show in Theorem 4 DSL's optimality in terms of the total number of local skyline query invocation on each participating machine, which measures the I/O overhead and is important for its response time performance. We omit the proof here, please refer to a forthcoming technical report version for complete proofs.

**Theorem 3.** *(Bandwidth Behavior): In DSL, only the data tuples in the final answer set may be transmitted across machines.*

**Theorem 4.** *(Optimality): For a given data partitioning strategy, the total number of local skyline query invocations in DSL is minimized.*

## 4 Load Balancing

Load balancing plays an important role in the performance of any practical distributed query system. Some data storage load balancing techniques are described in [12], and specific data load balancing work for CAN-based systems can be found in [14]. This paper focuses only on addressing the query load imbalance issue inherent in DSL. We assume that compared to local query processing involving disk I/O, control messages consume negligible amounts of system resources. Therefore, our goal is to balance the number of local skyline queries processed on each node.

### 4.1 Query Load Imbalance in DSL

Our DSL solution leads to a natural query load imbalance. In DSL, query propagation always starts from the bottom-left part of the query box. An intermediate master node will not split its region if the region is dominated by "upstream" skyline points. When the region split does not take place, all nodes inside the region other than the master node will be left untouched which causes query load imbalance. Intuitively, for a given query range, nodes from the top-right regions are less likely to be queried than their "upstream" counterparts. In addition, real world query loads are more likely to be skewed, i.e. some query ranges are far more popular than others, which may further exacerbate this problem.

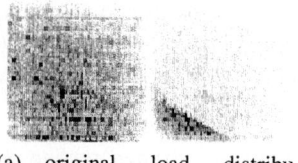

(a) original load distribution(independent and anticorrelated; random query)

(b) after zone replication (independent and anti-correlated; random query)

**Fig. 4.** Query Load Visualization

Figure 4(a) visualizes the original query load in a 2-$d$ CAN space without load balancing. The darkness level of each zone represents the number of times a local skyline calculation is invoked on the corresponding node. The darker a zone appears, the heavier its load. We use independent as well as anti-correlated data sets, both with cardinality of 1 million on a 5000 node system. The workload consists of 1000 constrained skyline queries with randomly generated query ranges (For more about experiment setting, please see Section 5). We see in Figure 4(a) that the query load exhibits strong imbalance among nodes with zones at the bottom-left corner being much heavier loaded.

### 4.2 Dynamic Zone Replication

To address the load imbalance problem, we propose a *dynamic zone replication* scheme. Our proposal is similar to the approach used in [26], but is tailored specifically to address the load imbalance in DSL.

Specifically, each node $p_i$ in the system periodically generates $m$ random points in the $d$ dimensional CAN space. We set $m$ equal to 10 by default. $p_i$ routes probes to these points to ask for the query load at the local node. After obtaining all the replies, $p_i$ compares its own load with the "random" probes. $p_i$ will *only* initiate the zone replication process when its load is heavier than some threshold $T$ of all samples. $T$ is a system parameter set to 0.5 by default. In zone replication, $p_i$ sends a copy of its zone contents to the least loaded node $p_{min}$ in the sample set, and records $p_{min}$'s virtual coordinates in its *replicationlist*.

If a node has performed zone replication, local query processing adjusts to take advantage. When calculating a local skyline query, $p_i$ picks a virtual coordinate $v_j$ from its *replicationlist* in a round-robin fashion. Then $p_i$ forwards the query to the node $p_j$ responsible for $v_j$ for actual processing. To avoid unnecessary load probing messages, we set the probing interval proportional to the rank of node's query load in its latest samples. By doing so, lightly loaded machines probe less frequently while nodes in heavily loaded zones probe and distribute their load more aggressively. Figure 4(b) visualizes the system load distribution on both data sets after dynamic zone replication. On both data sets, the load distribution is much "smoother" than in Figure 4(a).

## 5 Performance Evaluation

### 5.1 Experimental Setup

We evaluate our DSL system through both simulation and measurements of a real deployed system. Our system is implemented on the Berkeley PIER query engine [16], and uses PIER's CAN implementation and runtime environment. Because PIER uses identical interfaces for both discrete-event simulations and real deployment code, we used identical code in our simulations and cluster deployment. Our simulations ran on a Linux box with an Intel Pentium IV 2.4 GHz processor and 2 GB of RAM. The real measurement ran on a cluster composed of 20 Dell PowerEdge 1750 Servers, each with Intel 2.6Ghz Xeon CPUs and 2GBs of memory. We run 4 node instances on each server, for a total of 80 nodes. Since the cluster is shared with other competing applications, we ran the same experiment 10 times and the average response time is reported. In this experiment, the data space is static in the sense that neither deletion nor insertion is allowed during the query processing.

We summarize default parameters in Table 1. Specifically, we use both independent (uniform) and anti-correlated data sets with cardinality of 1 million and dimensionality from 2–5 [19]. For those experiments where the results reflect the same trend on both data sets, we only show one of them to save space. The number of nodes in the simulation varies from 100 to 10000. The default query load in simulation consists of 1000 sequential constrained skyline queries with the query range randomly generated. More specifically, for each dimension, both the starting point and the length of the interval are randomly distributed.

**Table 1.** Default setting

| Parameter | Domain | Default |
|---|---|---|
| Total nodes (Simulation) | [100,10000] | 5000 |
| Total nodes (Deployment) | 80 | 80 |
| Data cardinality | 1,000,000 | 1,000,000 |
| Dimensions (Simulation) | 2, 3, 4, 5 | 2 |
| Dimensions (Deployment) | 2, 3, 4, 5 | 3 |
| Query Range Pattern | random, biased | random |

We used three metrics in the experiment: percentage of nodes visited per query, number of data points transmitted per query and average query response time. All the response time results are from real measurement and the results of the other two metrics are based on simulation. Our experiments are divided into two groups: First, we show comparative results on the three distributed skyline query methods described in this paper. Second, we study the effects of different system parameters on DSL's performance.

## 5.2 Comparative Studies

**Scalability Comparison.** Figure 5 compares the three methods in terms of the number of node visited for each query on the anti-correlated data set. We show the cumulative density function (CDF) of percentage of queries (y-axis) against the percentage of nodes visited (x-axis). As expected, the naive method contacts all the nodes in the system for every incoming query, significantly limiting its scalability. The CAN-multicast method considerably improves upon the naive method: 90 percent of the queries will contact less than 40% of the nodes in the system. However, the remaining 10% of the queries still visit roughly 60% of all nodes. In a 5000 node system, this translates into visiting 3000 nodes for a single query! In contrast, DSL does a much better job of isolating the relevant data: no query involves more than 10% of the nodes, and roughly 90% of queries contact less than 1% of all nodes.

**Bandwidth Comparison.** Figure 6 shows the bandwidth performance of all three methods on the anti-correlated data set when varying system size from 100 to 10000 nodes. We measure for each query the average number of data tuples transmitted per node. The x-axis plots the total number of nodes in the system and y-axis shows the average number of data points transmitted for a single query divided by the total number of nodes. Here we use the number of data points to characterize the bandwidth consumption, because data points are the dominant factor in the overall bandwidth usage when compared to control messages. For all system sizes, DSL outperforms the other two methods by one order of magnitude. This validates our claim in Theorem 3 that DSL saves bandwidth by transmitting only the data points inside the final result set.

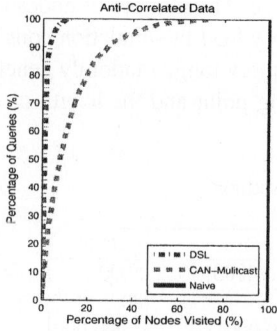
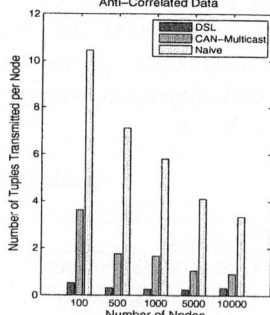

**Fig. 5.** Scalability comparison among all methods

**Fig. 6.** Bandwidth comparison among all methods

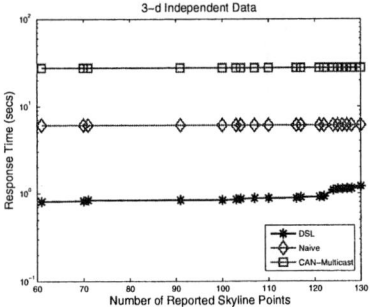
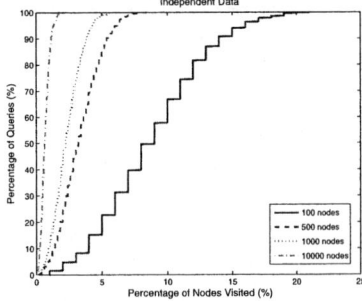

**Fig. 7.** Query response time comparison across three methods

**Fig. 8.** Effects of system size on scalability in DSL

**Query Response Time Comparison.** We compare DSL's query response latency with the naive method and the CAN-multicast method. Due to the space constraints, we only show a workload containing one global skyline query, *i.e.* find all skyline points in the entire data set[3]. There are a total of 130 skyline points in the result set. For each skyline point returned (x-axis), Figure 7 depicts the elapsed time of all three methods (y-axis). The progressive behavior of DSL is not clearly reflected here due to the logarithmic scale of the y-axis. In fact, the initial results of DSL are reported within 0.8 seconds, while the last skyline point is reported in less than 1.2 seconds. As expected, DSL demonstrates orders of magnitude performance improvement over the other two methods.

A surprising result is that CAN multicast method performs much worse than the naive method. There are two reasons for this. First, our query is a global skyline query without constraints. This means the CAN-multicast method has no advantage over the naive method. Second, the CAN-multicast method dynamically constructs a query propagation tree which is less efficient than the naive method where the entire tree is statically built at the beginning.

In summary, DSL is the clear winner over the other two alternative distribution methods in all the three metrics.

### 5.3 Performance Study of DSL

In this subsection, we study DSL's performance under different system settings.

**Scalability.** Figure 8 uses a CDF to illustrate the effect of system size on the number of nodes visited per query. We ran the simulation by varying the system size from 100 to 10000 nodes. Figure 8 shows a very clear trend: with the increase of the system size, the average number of participating nodes is quite stable. For example, when the system size is 100, most queries touches 15 machines. When the system size grows to 10000, all queries involve less than 3% of the node population; and among them, a large portion (80%) of the queries only touch less than 0.5% (or 50 in a 10000 node system)

---

[3] We have also tested several other query ranges and DSL is the consistent winner with the first several skyline points returned almost instantly (see Figure 13).

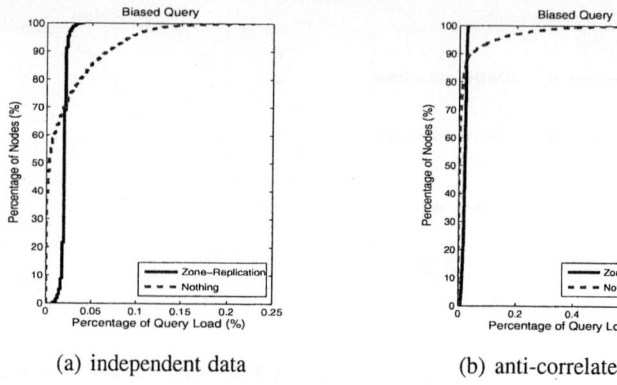

(a) independent data  (b) anti-correlated data

**Fig. 9.** Effectiveness of dynamic zone replication

of the nodes. The reason behind is that with the virtual space partitioned by more nodes, the average partition size on each node becomes smaller. The finer granularity of zone partitioning allows a more accurate pruning of relevant nodes and data points. This simulation shows that DSL can scale up to a fairly large number of machines.

**Effects of Dynamic Zone Replication on Load Balancing.** In this simulation, we study the effects of dynamic zone replication scheme on load balancing. We tested both the random query pattern as well as the biased query pattern. We only show the biased query load results because random query results were already visualized in Figure 4.

Figure 9 compares query load distributions before and after dynamic zone replication. The workload consists of 1000 constrained skyline queries evaluated on both anti-correlated and independent data sets. Each node reports the number of times its local skyline procedure is invoked. The x-axis represents the query load percentage and the y-axis plots the percentage of nodes with that load. In a perfectly balanced system with 5000 nodes, each node would perform 0.02% of the total number of local query operations.

The original load distribution is clearly imbalanced. In the anti-correlated data set, almost the entire query load is taken by 10% of the machines. 2% of the nodes are each responsible for more than 0.2% of the total query load, or overloaded by a factor of 10! After dynamic zone replication is used on both data sets, the query load is much more evenly distributed and closer to the ideal. Together with the previous visualization results, these results clearly show that dynamic zone replication is effective for balancing the query load in the system.

**Effects of Dimensionality on Bandwidth.** Now we study the effects of dimensionality on DSL's bandwidth overhead. We vary the dimensionality of queries from 2 to 5, which according to [7] satisfies most real world applications. Figure 10 shows the effect of dimensionality on the average bandwidth usage on the anti-correlated data set. The y-axis represents the average number of data points transmitted by every node for each query and the x-axis plots the dimensionality. Overall, the bandwidth usage steadily increases with the dimensionality. Specifically, on a 2-d data set, an average node only injects 1 data point into the network and this number grows to 20 on the 5-d data set. The

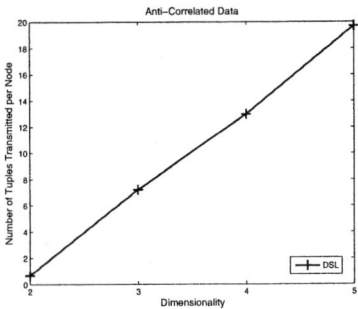 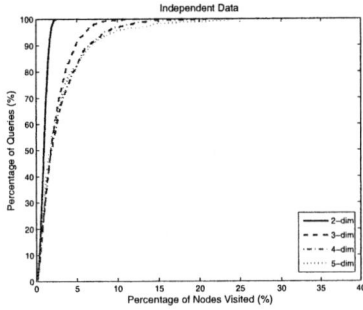

**Fig. 10.** Effects of dimensionality on bandwidth in DSL

**Fig. 11.** Effects of dimensionality on scalability in DSL

main reason for this increase is that the original size of the skyline result set increases rapidly with dimensionality and thus more result points need to be transmitted with the query message from the "upstream" machines to the "downstream" nodes, leading to greater bandwidth consumption.

**Effects of Dimensionality on Scalability.** Figure 11 shows the effects of dimensionality on the percentage of nodes visited per query on the independent data set. We vary the dimensionality from 2 to 5 and show the relationship between the query load percentage and node percentage involved. With the increase of the dimensionality, more nodes are involved in query processing. This is due to two reasons. First, as described above, with the increase in dimensionality, the skyline result size increases dramatically and thus more nodes are likely to store data points in the final result set. Second, with higher dimensionality, more virtual space needs to be visited while the number of machines used to partition the virtual spaces remains the same. However, even when the dimension number grows to as large as 5, most queries are evaluated across a small portion of the nodes. Specifically, more than 90% of queries each require less than 10% of all nodes. This demonstrates that DSL is scalable with the increase of dimensionality.

**Effects of Dimensionality on Response Time.** In Figure 12, we study the effects of dimensionality on the query response time on the independent data set. We still use one global skyline query as our query load. Under each dimensionality setting, Figure 12 shows the average response delay for all skyline results reported by DSL. Due to the progressiveness of DSL, initial result points are typically received much faster than this average number. As the number of dimensions grows, the average delay increases steadily. On the 2-d data set, the average response delay is 0.6 seconds. As the number of dimensions grows to 5, the average response time grows to roughly 2 seconds. This is explained by three factors. First, as was shown in Figure 10, DSL's bandwidth consumption increases with dimensionality, and therefore more time is spent on data transmission between nodes. Second, as was shown in simulations (Figure 11), the percentage of nodes visited per query also increases in the higher dimensional data sets. Since more machines are involved, it takes more time for the query to propagate to the "downstream" nodes. Finally, local skyline calculations at each node also becomes more expensive in higher dimension datasets.

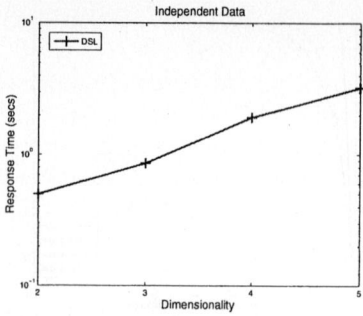 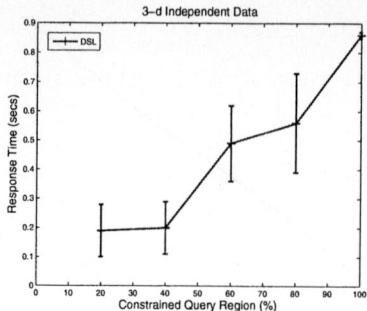

**Fig. 12.** Effects of dimensionality on DSL response time

**Fig. 13.** Effects of query box size on response time

**Effects of Query Range on Response Time.** In Figure 13, we investigate the effects of query box size on the response time. For each query box size, we generate 10 constrained skyline queries, each of which has a query range covering a certain percentage of the entire data space. We show the average response delay of 10 queries. For each point along the line, we also draw a bounding box that depicts the standard deviation of the response delay. Clearly, the average response delay increases with the growth of the query box size. In particular, when the query range equals 20%, the average delay is less than 0.2 seconds. The delay increases to 0.85 seconds when the query range grows to 100%.

## 6 Related Work

Skyline query processing algorithms have received considerable attention in recent database research. Early work [7] proposed the Block-nested loops, Divide and conquer, and B-tree solutions. Later work proposed the Indexing and Bitmaps solutions [23]. This was further improved in [17], where Nearest neighbor search (*NN*) was used on a R-tree indexed data set to progressively discover skyline points. The best centralized method, *BBS* [19], has been shown to be I/O optimal, and outperforms *NN*. Other work addresses continuous skyline queries over data streams [18], extends skyline query to categorical attribute domains where total order may not exist [8]. One latest work [13] introduces a new generic algorithm LESS with $O(n)$ average case running time. Similar results are presented in [25] and [20] on efficient computation methods of finding skyline points in subspaces. Huang et al. investigate efficient methods for supporting skyline queries in the context of Mobile Ad Hoc networks (MANETs) [15].

The notion of recursive partitioning of the data space in DSL is similar to *NN* and *BBS*. However, fundamental differences distinguish our effort from these two works. In *NN*, the order of the intermediate partitions will not influence its correctness and a distributed solution relying on NN queries is doomed to be inefficient. On the other hand, unlike *BBS*, there does not exist an "oracle" in the distributed environment to order the candidate partitions in a centralized priority queue. Moreover, DSL recursively partitions the query region *during run-time* to match the underlying node zones, since, unlike *BBS*, there does not exist certain *a-priori* "recursive" index structures like R-Tree.

The only previous work that calculates skyline query over distributed sources was presented in [5]. In this work, data is vertically distributed across different web information services. A centralized site is responsible for probing attribute values from each site to calculate the final skyline. This limits the scale of distribution and may result in intolerable response time due to round trip communications with multiple sources. Unlike this approach, DSL is targeted at cluster-based internet services, in which one integrates external data and has total control over the data placement. In addition, our solution provides incremental scalability, where performance is improved by adding additional machines to the cluster.

Parallel databases [9] and distributed database systems such as Mariposa [22] used multiple machines to efficiently process queries on partitioned data relations. In particular, previous research on parallel database systems have shown that "range partitioning" can successfully help query processing in share-nothing architectures(e.g. parallel sorting [10] and parallel join [11]). Skyline processing in these settings has not been studied, and is the problem addressed in this paper.

## 7 Conclusion and Future Work

In this paper, we address an important problem of parallelizing the progressive skyline queries on share nothing architectures. Central to our algorithm DSL, is the use of partial orders over data partitions. We propose two methods: namely recursive region partitioning and dynamic region encoding, for implementing this partial order for pipelining machines in query execution. We provide analytical and optimality result of our algorithm. Finally, we introduce the use of dynamic zone replication to distribute computation evenly across nodes. We implemented the DSL system on top of the PIER code base, and use the resulting code to perform extensive experiments on a simulation platform as well as a real cluster deployment. Our evaluation shows DSL to significantly outperform other distribution approaches, and that dynamic zone replication is extremely effective in distribution query load. As future work, we will further explore the resilience of query processing to node failures and replications, and DSL's bandwidth consumption in higher dimension data sets.

## References

1. Froogle data feeds. https://www.google.com/froogle/merchants/feed_instructions.html.
2. Yahoo! real estate. http://realestate.yahoo.com/.
3. T. E. Anderson, D. E. Culler, and D. A. Patterson. A case for NOW (network of workstations). *IEEE Micro*, 15(1):54–64, Feb 1995.
4. A. C. Arpaci-Dusseau, R. H. Arpaci-Dusseau, D. E. Culler, J. M. Hellerstein, and D. A. Patterson. High-performance sorting on networks of workstations. In *Proc. of SIGMOD*, Tucson, AZ, May 1997.
5. W. Balke, U. Guntzer, and X.Zheng. Efficient distributed skylining for web information systems. In *Proc. of EDBT*, 2004.
6. L. A. Barroso, J. Dean, and U. Holzle. Web search for a planet: The google cluster architecture. *IEEE Micro*, 23(2):22–28, March/April 2003.

7. S. Borzsonyi, D. Kossmann, and K. Stocker. The skyline operator. In *Proc. of ICDE*, 2001.
8. C.-Y. Chan, P.-K. Eng, and K.-L. Tan. Stratified computation of skylines with partially-ordered domains. In *Proc. of SIGMOD*, 2005.
9. D. Dewitt and J. Gray. Parallel database systems: The future of high performance database systems. *CACM*, 35(6), 1992.
10. D. Dewitt, J. Naughton, D. Scheneider, and S. Seshadri. Parallel sorting on a shared-nothing architecture. 1991.
11. D. Dewitt, J. Naughton, D. Schneider, and S. Seshadri. Practical skew handling in parallel joins. In *Proc. of VLDB*, 1992.
12. P. Ganesan, M. Bawa, and H. Garcia-Molina. Online balancing of range-partioned data with applications to peer-to-peer systems. In *Proc. of VLDB*, 2004.
13. P. Godfrey, R. Shipley, and J. Gryz. Maximal vector computation in large data sets. In *Proc. of VLDB*, 2005.
14. A. Gupta, O. D. Sabin, D. Agrawal, and A. E. Abbadi. Meghdoot: Content-based publish/subsribe over P2P networks. In *Proc. of Middleware*, 2004.
15. Z. Huang, C. S. Jensen, H. Lu, and B. C. Ooi. Skyline queries against mobile lightweight devices in manets. In *Proc. of ICDE*, 2006.
16. R. Huebsch, J. M. Hellerstein, N. L. Boon, T. Loo, S. Shenker, and I. Stoica. Querying the internet with pier. In *Proc. of VLDB*, 2003.
17. D. Kossmann, F. Ramsak, and S. Rost. Shooting stars in the sky: an online algorithm for skyline queries. In *Proc. of VLDB*, 2002.
18. X. Lin, Y. Yuan, W. Wang, and H. Lu. Stabbing the sky: Efficient skyline computation over sliding windows. In *Proc. of ICDE*, 2005.
19. D. Papadias, Y. Tao, G. Fu, and B. Seeger. An optimal and progressive algorithm for skyline queries. In *Proc. of SIGMOD*, 2003.
20. J. Pei, W. Jin, M. Ester, and Y. Tao. Catching the best views of skyline: A semantic approach based on decisive subspaces. In *Proc. of VLDB*, 2005.
21. S. Ratnasamy, P. Francis, M. Handley, R. Karp, and S. Schenker. A scalable content-addressable network. In *Proc. of SIGCOMM*, Aug 2001.
22. M. Stonebraker, P. M. Aoki, W. Litwin, A. Pfeffer, A. Sah, J. Sidell, C. Staelin, and A. Yu. Mariposa: A wide-area distributed database system. *VLDB Journal*, 5(1), 1996.
23. K. L. Tan, P. K. Eng, and B. C. Ooi. Efficient progressive skyline computation. In *Proc. of VLDB*, 2001.
24. P. Wu, J.-R. Wen, H. Liu, and W.-Y. Ma. Query selection techniques for efficient crawling of structured web sources. In *Proc. of ICDE*, 2006.
25. Y. Yuan, X. Lin, Q. Liu, W. Wang, J. X. Yu, and Q. Zhang. Efficient computation of the skyline cube. In *Proc. of VLDB*, 2005.
26. Y. Zhou, B. C. Ooi, and K.-L. Tan. Dynamic load management for distributed continous query systems. In *Proc. of ICDE*, 2005.

# Replication, Load Balancing and Efficient Range Query Processing in DHTs

Theoni Pitoura, Nikos Ntarmos, and Peter Triantafillou

Research Academic Computer Technology Institute, and Computer Engineering
and Informatics Department, University of Patras, Greece
{pitoura, ntarmos, peter}@ceid.upatras.gr

**Abstract.** We consider the conflicting problems of ensuring data-access load balancing and efficiently processing range queries on peer-to-peer data networks maintained over Distributed Hash Tables (DHTs). Placing consecutive data values in neighboring peers is frequently used in DHTs since it accelerates range query processing. However, such a placement is highly susceptible to load imbalances, which are preferably handled by replicating data (since replication also introduces fault tolerance benefits). In this paper, we present HotRoD, a DHT-based architecture that deals effectively with this combined problem through the use of a novel locality-preserving hash function, and a tunable data replication mechanism which allows trading off replication costs for fair load distribution. Our detailed experimentation study shows strong gains in both range query processing efficiency and data-access load balancing, with low replication overhead. To our knowledge, this is the first work that concurrently addresses the two conflicting problems using data replication.

## 1 Introduction

Structured peer-to-peer (P2P) systems have provided the P2P community with efficient and combined routing and location primitives. This goal is accomplished by maintaining a structure in the system, emerging by the way that peers define their neighbors. Different structures have been proposed, the most popular of which being: distributed hash tables (DHTs), such as CAN [17], Pastry [18], Chord [21], Tapestry [24], which use hashing schemes to map peers and data keys to a single, modular identifier space; distributed balanced trees, where data are stored at the nodes of a tree, such as P-Grid[1], PHT [16], BATON [11], etc.

One of the biggest shortcomings of DHTs that has spurred considerable research is that they only support exact-match queries. Therefore, the naïve approach to deal with range queries over DHTs would be to individually query each value in the range, which is greatly inefficient and thus infeasible in most cases. Although there are many research papers that claim to support range queries over DHTs more "cleverly" and, thus, efficiently ([2], [9], [19], [22]), all of them suffer from access load imbalances in the presence of skewed data-access distributions. Only a few approaches deal with both problems, i.e. load balancing and efficient range query processing, in DHTs ([5]), or other structures ([3], [7], [11]). However, these solutions are based on data migration which is sometimes inadequate in skewed data access distributions. This is more apparent in the case of a single popular data value which makes the peer that stores it heavily loaded. Transferring this value to another peer only transfers the problem. In such cases, access load balancing is best addressed using replication of popular values to distribute the access load among the peers storing such replicas.

In this work we propose solutions for efficiently supporting range queries together with providing a fair load distribution over DHTs using replication. Our approach is based on two key ideas. The first is to use locality-preserving data placement, i.e. to have consecutive values stored on neighboring peers; thus, collecting the values in a queried range can be achieved by single-hop neighbor to neighbor visits. The second is to replicate popular values or/and ranges to fairly distribute access load among peers. However, using data replication together with a locality-preserving data placement is not simple: if the replicas of a popular value are placed in neighboring peers, the access load balancing problem still exists in this neighborhood of peers that is already overloaded; On the other hand, if the replicas are randomly distributed, additional hops are required each time a replica is accessed during range query processing. Addressing these two conflicting goals is the focus of this paper.

Specifically, we make the following contributions:

1. We define a novel locality-preserving hash function, used for data placement in a DHT, which both preserves the order of values and handles value/range replication. The above can be applied to any DHT with slight modifications (we use Chord [21] for our examples and in our experiments).
2. We propose a tunable replication scheme: by tweaking the degree of replication, a system parameter, we can trade off replication cost for access load balancing. This is useful when we know, or can predict the characteristics of the query workload.
3. We develop a locality-preserving, DHT architecture, which we coin HotRoD, that incorporates the above contributions, employing locality-preserving replication to ensure access-load balancing, and efficient range query processing.
4. We comprehensively evaluate HotRoD. We propose the use of a novel load balancing metric, Lorenz curves and the Gini coefficient (which is being heavily used in other disciplines, such as economics and ecology), that naturally captures the fairness of the load distribution. We compare HotRoD against baseline competitors for both range query processing efficiency and load distribution fairness. Further, we study the trade-offs in replication costs vs. achievable load balancing.
5. Our results from extensive experimentation with HotRoD show that HotRoD achieves its main goals: significant speedups in range query processing and distributes accesses fairly to DHT nodes, while requiring only small replication overhead. Specifically, a significant hop count saving in range query processing, from 5% to 80% compared against standard DHTs. Furthermore, data-access load is significantly more fairly distributed among peers, with only a small number of replicas (i.e. less than 100% in total). As the range query spans, or data-access skewness increases, the benefits of our solution increase.

To our knowledge, this is the first work to concurrently address the issues of *replication-based data-access load balancing* and *efficient range query processing* in structured P2P networks and study in detail its performance features.

The rest of the paper is organized as follows: In section 2 we introduce the HotRoD architecture, its locality-preserving hash function, and the mechanisms for replica management, and in section 3 we present the algorithm for range query processing. In section 4 we experimentally evaluate HotRoD, and present its ability to tune replication. Finally, we discuss related work, in section 5, and conclude in section 6.

## 2 HotRoD: A Locality-Preserving Load Balancing Architecture

The main idea behind the proposed architecture is a novel hash function which: (a) preserves the ordering of data to ensure efficient range query processing, and, (b) replicates and fairly distributes popular data and their replicas among peers.

HotRoD is built over a locality-preserving DHT, i.e. data are placed in range partitions over the identifier space in an order-preserving way. Many DHT-based data networks are locality-preserving (Mercury [5], OP-Chord [22, 15], etc) in order to support range queries. However, this additional capability comes at a price: locality-preserving data placement causes load imbalances, whereas trying to provide load balancing, the order of data breaks. HotRoD strives for a uniform access load distribution by replicating popular data across peers in the network: its algorithms detect overloaded peers and distribute their access load among other, underloaded, peers in the system, through replication. (We should mention that instances of the algorithms run at each peer, and no global schema knowledge is required).

In the following sub-sections, we overview the underlying locality-preserving DHT, define a novel locality-preserving hash function, and algorithms to detect load imbalances and handle data replication and load balancing.

### 2.1 The Underlying Locality-Preserving DHT

We assume that data objects are the database tuples of a $k$-attribute relation $R(A_1, A_2, ..., A_k)$, where $A_i$ ($1 \leq i \leq k$) are $R$'s attributes. The attributes $A_i$ are used as single-attribute indices of any tuple $t$ in $R$. Their domain is $DA_i$, for any $1 \leq i \leq k$. Every tuple $t$ in $R$ is uniquely identified by a primary key, $key(t)$, which can be either one of its $A_i$ attributes, or calculated by more than one $A_i$ attributes.

In DHT-based networks, peers and data are assigned unique identifiers in an $m$-bit identifier space (here, we assume an identifier ring modulo-$2^m$). Traditional DHTs use secure hash functions to randomly and uniquely assign identifiers to peers and data. Here, a tuple's identifier is produced by hashing its attributes' *values* using k (at most[1]) order-preserving hash functions, $hash_i()$, to place tuples in range partitions over the identifier space. For fault tolerance reasons, a tuple is also stored at the peer mapped by securely hashing its $key(t)$. Thus, data placement requires $O((k+1) \cdot logN)$ hops - $N$ is the number of peers ([22]).

*Note: We may apply an additional level of indirection by storing pointers to tuples, as index tuples $I_i(t)$: $\{v_i(t)$ $key(t)\}$, instead of tuples themselves. At this point, we make no distinction.*

As most existing DHTs, tuples use consistent hashing ([12]): a tuple with identifier *id* is stored at the peer whose identifier is the "closest" to *id* in the identifier space (i.e. the successor function, $succ()$, of Chord [21]). Peers also maintain routing information

---
[1] Functions $hash_i()$ may be different for each one of the k different attributes $A_i$.

about peers that lie on the ring at logarithmically increasing distance (i.e. the *finger tables* of Chord [21]). Using this information, routing a message from one peer to another requires O(*logN*) hops in the worst case, where *N* is the number of peers. For fault-tolerance reasons, each peer also maintains a maximum of *logN* successors.

*Example 2.1. Fig. 1. illustrates data placement in a 14-bit order-preserving Chord-like ring, i.e. the id space is [0, 16383]. We assume single-attribute A tuples, DA=[0, 4096). Let N=7 peers inserted in the network with identifiers 0, 2416, 4912, 7640, 10600, 11448, and 14720. Each peer is responsible for storing a partition of the attribute domain DA, in an order-preserving way, as shown.*

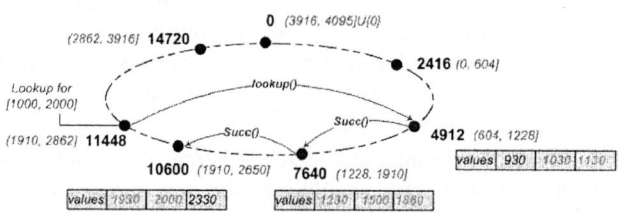

**Fig. 1.** The substrate locality-preserving DHT. (a) A tuple with value $v \in DA$ is stored on peer *succ(hash(v))*, (b) The range query [1000, 2000] is routed from peer *succ(hash(1000))*=4912, through the immediate successors, to peer *succ(hash(2000))*=10600.

A range query is pipelined through those peers whose range of index entries stored at them overlaps with the query range. It needs O(logN+ n') routing hops – n' is the number of these peers ([22]).

*Example 2.2. Fig. 1. also illustrates how the range query [1000, 2000] initiated at peer 11448 is answered. Using the underlying DHT network look up operation, lookup() (i.e. Chord lookup, if the underlying network is Chord), we move to peer succ(hash(1000)), which is peer 4912. Peer 4912 retrieves all tuples whose values fall into the requested range, and forwards the query to its successor, peer 7640. The process is repeated until the query reaches peer 10600 (i.e. succ(hash(2000))), which is the last peer keeping the requested tuples.*

Although it accelerates routing for range queries, this scheme cannot handle load balancing in the case of skewed data-access distributions. HotRoD, the main contribution of this work, deals with this problem while still attaining the efficiency of range query processing. From this point forward, we assume that R is a single-attribute index A relation, whose domain is *DA*. Handling multi-index attribute relations is straightforward ([14]), and beyond the scope of this paper.

### 2.2 Replication and Rotation

Each peer keeps track of the number of times, *a*, it was accessed during a time interval, and the average low and high bounds of the ranges of the queries it processed, at this time interval – *avgLow* and *avgHigh* respectively. We say that a peer is overloaded, or *"hot"* when its access count exceeds the upper limit of its resource capacity, i.e. when $\alpha > \alpha_{max}$. An arc of peers (i.e. successive peers on the ring) is *"hot"* when at least one of these peers is hot.

In our scheme, "hot" arcs of peers are replicated and rotated over the identifier space. Thus, the identifier space can now be visualized as a number of replicated, rotated, and overlapping rings, the Hot Ranges/Rings of Data, which we call HotRoD (see fig 2). A HotRoD instance consists of a regular DHT ring and a number of virtual rings where values are addressed using a multi-rotation hash function, *mrhf()*, defined in the following sub-section. By the term "virtual" we mean that these rings materialize only through *mrhf()*; there are no additional successors, predecessors or other links among the peers in the different rings.

## 2.3 Multi-rotation Hashing

We assume that $\rho_{max}(A)$ is the maximum number of instances that each value of an attribute $A$ can have (including the original value and its replicas). This parameter depends on the capacity of the system and the access load distribution of $A$'s values; indicative values for $\rho_{max}(A)$ are discussed in section 4.4. We also define the index variable $\delta \in [1, \rho_{max}(A)]$ to distinguish the different instances of $A$'s values, i.e. an original value $v$ corresponds to $\delta=1$ (it is the 1st instance of $v$), the first replica of $v$ corresponds to $\delta=2$ (it is the 2nd instance of $v$), and so on. Then, the $\delta^{th}$ instance of a value $v$ is assigned an identifier according to the following function, $mrhf()^2$.

**Definition 1: mrhf().** For every value, $v \in DA$, and $\delta \in [1, \rho_{max}(A)]$, the Multi-Rotation Hash Function (MRHF) $mrhf : DA \times [1, \rho_{max}(A)] \to \{0, 1, \ldots, 2^m - 1\}$ is defined as:

$$mrhf(v, \delta) = (hash(v) + random[\delta] \cdot s) \bmod 2^m \qquad (1)$$

where $s = \frac{1}{\rho_{max}(A)} \cdot 2^m$ is the rotation unit (or else, "stride"), and *random[]* is a pseudo-random permutation of the integers in $[1, \rho_{max}(A)]$ and $random[1]=0$.

It is obvious that for $\delta=1$, $mrhf()$ is a one-to-one mapping from $DA$ to $\{0, 1, \ldots, 2^m-1\}$ and a $\bmod 2^m$ order-preserving hash function. This means that, if $v$ and $v' \in DA$ and $v \leq v'$, then $mrhf(v,1) \leq_{\bmod 2^m} mrhf(v',1)$, which means that $mrhf(v,1)$ lies before $mrhf(v',1)$ in a clockwise direction over the identifier ring. For any $\delta>1$, HotRoD is also $\bmod 2^m$ order-preserving (the proof is straightforward and omitted for space reasons).

Therefore, a value $v$ is placed on the peer whose identifier is closer to $mrhf(v,1)$, according to the underlying DHT. When the $\delta^{th}$ instance of a value $v$ is created, or else the $(\delta-1)^{th}$ replica of $v$ (i.e. $\delta>1$), it will be placed on the peer whose identifier is closer to $mrhf(v,1)$ shifted by $\delta \cdot s$ clockwise. This can be illustrated as a clockwise rotation of the identifier ring by $\delta \cdot s$, and, thus, $s$ is called rotation unit, whereas $\delta$ is also referred as the number of rotations.

---

[2] Mapping data to peers (i.e. using consistent hashing) are handled by the underlying DHT.

*Example 2.3. Fig. 2. illustrates a HotRoD network with δ=2, where ring 1 is the network of fig 1. We assume that peers 4912 and 7640 are "hot", and, thus, have created replicas of their tuples in the peers 14720, and 0. Let s=8191 (i.e. half the identifier space). The partitions of the attribute domain that these peers are responsible to store in the ring 2 (i.e. the first replicas) are shown in the figure.*

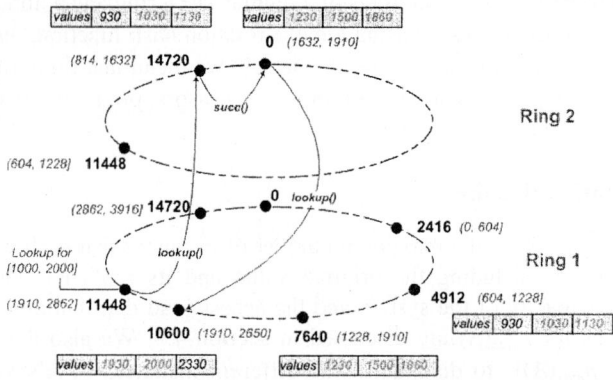

**Fig. 2.** HotRoD for δ=2. (a) The hot peers 4912, 7640 create replicas of their tuples at peers 14720, 0 of ring 2. (b) The range query [1000, 2000] initiated at peer 11448 is sent to peer mrhf(1000, 2)=14720 at ring 2, then to 0, and it jumps to ring 1, to complete.

*mrhf()* leverages the existence of a maximum of $\rho_{max}(A)$ replicas per value $v$, thus being able to choose one out of $\rho_{max}(A)$ possible positions for $v$ in the system. That way it fights back the effects of load imbalances caused by *hash()* (which are explained in [22]). Note that *randomly* selecting replicas, using *random[]*, leads to a uniform load distribution among replica holders. The result can be thought of as superimposing multiple rotated identical rings (as far as data is concerned) on each other, and projecting them to the original unit ring. Thus, "hot" (overloaded) and "cold" (underloaded) areas of the rings are combined through rotation, to give a uniform overall "temperature" across all peers.

## 2.4 Replicating Arcs of Peers: Implementation Issues

We assume that each peer keeps $\rho_{max}(A)$, the per-attribute maximum number of instances of a value of attribute $A$ (and, thus, it can calculate stride $s$)[3]. In addition, each peer can calculate the highest value of $DA$ that it is responsible to store at a specific ring; we call it *higherValue* (this is achieved through the reverse function of *mrhf()*, $mrhf^{-1}()$ ).

---

[3] We assume integer domains, whereas real domains can be handled in a similar way. Attribute domains other than integer/real valued can be handled by converting them to an appropriate integer/real form. Note that this conversion is also central to the design of range queries; e.g. range queries for string-valued attributes ought to define some sort of binary comparison operator between values of the attribute.

We also define $\rho(v(A))$ to be the replication factor for a value $v(A)$, i.e. the (current) number of its replicas, which should be equal to, or less than $\rho_{max}(A)$. Each peer must have "write" access to this measure during replication (see PutRho() below), or "read" access during query processing and data placement (see GetRho() below).

When a peer, p, is detected "hot", it starts replication. Instead of replicating a single peer, we decide to replicate arcs of peers, and specifically the arc consisting of p's successive neighbors that correspond to the range [avgLow, avgHigh]. In that way, costly jumps between rings during range query processing are reduced; jumps between rings happen when different replication factors exist between consecutive values (i.e. when two *non successive peers* store their replicas in one peer at a higher ring, whereas the peers that lie between them in the lower ring do not have replicas at the higher ring).

In terms of simplicity, in the algorithms presented below we assume that replication is only initiated at the original ring, i.e. ring 1.

Each peer periodically (or upon a request of another peer) runs the algorithm REPLICATE_ARC() which detects whether it is hot, or not (if $\alpha > a_{max}$); if it is hot, it creates replicas of its tuples, and sends replication messages, CREATE_REPLICA(), to both its successor *(succ())* and predecessor *(pred())*. The number of replicas that creates is equal to $rho = \max\{\lceil \alpha/\alpha_{max} \rceil, \{\rho(v(A)), v(A) \in [avgLow, avgHigh]\}\}$ (if rho$\leq \rho_{max}(A)$).

Upon receiving a replication message, a peer creates *rho* replicas of those tuples that have less than *rho* replicas, and sends replication messages to its successor (or predecessor, depending on which peer sent the message). Besides, each peer sets the replication factor $\rho(v(A))$ equal to *rho*, for all values $v(A) \in$ [avgLow, avgHigh] that had less than *rho* replicas. The message is sent to all peers that are responsible to store all values $v \in$ [avgLow, avgHigh], which form an arc on the identifier ring.

The pseudocode follows (it uses the inverse function of MRHF, $mrhf^{-1}$).

```
1.  REPLICATE_ARC()
2.    /* p is the current peer */
3.  BEGIN
4.    rho = ceiling(a / a_max);
5.    if (rho <= 1) exit;
6.    for each v(A) , v(A) >= avgLow and v(A) <= avgHigh {
7.        tmp = GetRho(v(A));
8.        rho = max(rho, tmp); }
9.    if (rho > p_max(A))  rho = p_max(A);
10.   for each tuple t in p, and v(A) ∈ t
11.       copy t to succ(mrhf(v(A), k)), for all k:ρ(v(A)) ≤ k ≤ rho;
12.   for each value v(A) in (avgLow, avgHigh) {
13.       if (ρ(v(A)) < rho) putRho(v(A), rho); }
14.   send create_replica(p, (avgLow, avgHigh), rho, 1) to succ(p);
15.   send create_replica(p, (avgLow, avgHigh), rho, 0) to pred(p);
16. END

17. CREATE_REPLICA(n, (low, high), rho, succ)
18.   /* n is the initiator peer; succ is equal to 1/0, if the
         message is  propagated through successsor/predecessor l
         inks; p is the current peer */
19. BEGIN
```

```
20.    higherValue = mrhf⁻¹(p, 1);
21.    if (succ==0 and higherValue<low)
22.        exit;
23.    for each tuple t in p, and v(A) ∈ t
24.        copy t to succ(mrhf(v(A), k)), for all k:ρ(v(A)) ≤ k ≤ rho;
25.    for each value v(A) in (avgLow, avgHigh) {
26.        if (ρ(v(A)) < rho) putRho(v(A), rho); }
27.    if (succ==1 and higherValue<high)
28.        send create_replica(n, (avgLow, avgHigh), rho, 1) to succ(p);
29.    else if (succ==0)
30.        send create_replica(n, (avgLow, avgHigh), rho, 0) to pred(p);
31. END
```

Functions GetRho(), PutRho() manipulate the replication factor, $\rho(v(A))$ of an attribute value $v(A)$ over the network; the former gets $\rho(v(A))$, while the latter sets $\rho(v(A))$ equal to a specific number. The replication factor, $\rho(v(A))$, is uniformly hashed in the underlying DHT architecture (using the secure hash function). The initial values for $\rho(v(A))$ is 1, for all $v(A) \in DA$. Since both functions use the underlying DHT architecture, their hop-count complexity is $O(logN)$.

Please note that we do not necessarily replicate all tuples that belong to a peer which is replicated. We replicate only the tuples whose values have fewer replicas than target *rho* (this concerns only the first and last peer of the arc). This reduces replication costs without affecting the efficiency of range query processing; we simply assume that each peer keeps track of the ranges that stores at each ring it belongs to.

### 2.5 Fault-Tolerance and High Availability

The existence of replicas in addition to being critical for load balancing purposes is instrumental in providing increased data availability and fault-tolerance during query processing. Although details are beyond the scope of this paper, HotRoD can straightforwardly provide fault tolerance as follows: when a peer storing a queried value does not respond, the requesting peer simply selects another ρ-value and redirects the query to the peer which keeps a replica of the queried values at a different ring. This continues until one available replica is retrieved.

### 2.6 Managing Tuple Updates

**Tuple Insertion.** The peer publishing the tuple stored the tuple at peer $succ(mrhf(v(A), 1))$, and checks if $\rho(v(A)) > 1$. If true, it creates $\rho(v(A))-1$ replicas of the tuple (or of its indices) and stores them to $succ(mrhf(v(A), k))$, for $2 \leq k \leq \rho(v(A))$.

This operation needs $O(logN)$ hops to retrieve $\rho(v(A))$ plus $O(\rho_{max}(A) \cdot logN)$ hops when $\rho(v(A)) > 1$, in the worst case (since $\rho(v(A)) \leq \rho_{max}(A)$).

**Tuple Deletion.** A tuple deletion message is sent to peer $succ(mrhf(v(A), 1))$ and to all $\rho(v(A))-1$ replica holders, if $\rho(v(A)) > 1$. In addition, peer $succ(mrhf(v(A),1))$ checks if there are other tuples having value $v(A)$, and if not, it sets $\rho(v(A))$ equal to 1.

The cost of a tuple deletion is, in the worst case, $O((\rho_{max}(A)+2)\cdot \log N)$ hops (including a GetRho() operation to get $\rho(v(A))$, and a PutRho() operation, to set $\rho(v(A))$ equal to 1, if needed).

**Tuple Update.** It consists of one tuple deletion and one tuple insertion operations.

Naturally, as with all data replication strategies, the load balancing and fault tolerance benefits come at the expense of dealing with updates. However, our experimental results (presented below) show that with a relatively small overall number of replicas our central goals can be achieved, indicating that the relevant replication (storage and update overheads) will be kept low.

## 2.7 Discussion

**Optimal $\rho_{max}$ Values**
The calculation of optimal $\rho_{max}(A)$ is important for the efficiency and scalability of HotRoD. This value should be selected without assuming any kind of global knowledge. Fortunately, the skewness of expected access distributions has been studied, and it can be given beforehand; for example, the skewness parameter (i.e. theta-value) for the Zipf distribution ([20]). Given this, and the fact that each additional replica created is expected through HotRoD to take on an equal share of the load, our present approach is based on selecting a value for $\rho_{max}(A)$ to bring the total expected hits for the few heaviest-hit peers (e.g., 2-3%) close to the expected average hits all peers would observe, if the access distribution was completely uniform.

**Data Hotspots at ρ-value Holders**
In order to avoid creating new data hotspots at the peers responsible for storing $\rho(v(A))$ of a value $v(A)$, our approach is as follows:

- $\rho_{max}(A)$ instances for this metadata information (ρ-value) of each value can be easily maintained, with each replica selected at random at query start time (recall that $\rho_{max}(A)$ is kept in each peer).
- The hottest values are values that participate in a number of range queries of varying span. Thus, all these queries may start at several different points.

## 3 Range Query Processing

Consider a range query $[v_{low}(A), v_{high}(A)]$ on attribute $A$ initiated at peer $p_{init}$. A brief description of the algorithm to answer the query follows: peer $p_{init}$ randomly selects a number, $r$ from 1 to $\rho(v_{low}(A))$, the current number of replicas of $v_{low}(A)$. Then, it forwards the query to peer $p_l$: $succ(mrhf(v_{low}(A), r))$. Peer $p_l$ searches for matching tuples and forwards the query to its successor, $p$. Peer $p$ repeats similarly as long as it finds replicas of values of $R$ at the current ring. Otherwise, $p$ forwards the range query to a (randomly selected) lower-level ring and repeats. Processing is finished when all values of $R$ have been looked up. The pseudocode of the algorithm follows:

```
1. PROCESS_RANGE_QUERY (p_init, (v_low(A), v_high(A)) )
2. BEGIN
3.     rho = GetRho(v_low(A));
4.     r = random(1, rho);
5.     send Forward_Range(p_init, (v_low(A), v_high(A)), r) to
                          succ(mrhf(v_low(A)), r);
6. END

7. FORWARD_RANGE (p_init, (v_l(A), v_h(A)), r)
8.     /* p is the current peer */
9. BEGIN
10.    Search p locally and send matching tuples to p_init;
11.    higherValue = mrhf^-1(p, r);
12.    if (higherValue < v_h(A)) {
13.       v_next(A) = higherValue+1;
14.       rho = GetRho(v_next(A));
15.       if (rho >= r)
16.          send Forward_Range(p_init, (v_next(A),v_h(A)),r) to succ(p);
17.       else {
18.          r_next=random(1, rho);
19.          send Forward_Range(p_init, (v_next(A), v_h(A)), r_next)
                              to succ(mrhf(v_next(A), r_next)); } }
20. END
```

*higherValue* of *p* is used to forward the query to the peer responsible for the lowest value of *DA* that is higher than *higherValue*. Let this value be $v_{next}(A)$. If there is such a peer in ring *r* (i.e. this happens when $\rho(v_{next}(A))$ is equal to, or higher than *r*), *p* forwards the query to its successor. Otherwise, *p* sends the query to a peer at a lower-level ring, selected randomly from 1 to $\rho(v_{next}(A))$ (using the lookup operation of the underlying DHT). This happens when the range consists of values with different number of replicas. The algorithm finishes when the current *higherValue* is equal to, or higher than $v_{high}(A)$.

*Example 3.1.* Fig. 2b illustrates how the range query of example 2.2 is processed in HotRoD. First, we assume that peer 11448 forwards the query to peer 14720, i.e. lookup(mrhf(1000, 2)). Moving through successors, the query reaches peer 0. But, the range partition (1910, 2000] is not found at ring 2. Therefore, the query "jumps" to ring 1, peer 10600 (i.e. lookup(mrhf(1911, 2))), where it finishes.

## 4 Experimental Evaluation

We present a simulation-based evaluation of HotRoD. The experiments have been conducted on a heavily modified version of the internet-available *Chord* simulator, extended to support relations, order-preserving hashing, replication, and range queries.

We compare the performance of HotRoD against:

- *Plain Chord (PC)*, as implemented by the original Chord simulator;
- an imaginary *enhanced Chord (EC)*, assuming that for each range the system knows the identifiers of the peers that store all values of the *range*;
- *OP-Chord*, a locality preserving Chord-based network ([22, 15])

The results are presented in terms of:
  a. *efficiency of query processing,* mainly measured by the number of hops per query, assuming that for each peer, the local query processing cost is O(1);
  b. *access load balancing,* measured by the cumulative access load distribution curves and the Gini coefficient (defined below);
  c. *overhead costs,* measured by the number of peers' and tuples' replicas.

### 4.1 Simulation Model

The experiments are conducted in a system with $N = 1,000$ peers, and a maximum of 10 (i.e. $\log N$) finger table entries and 10 immediate successors for each peer. We use a single-index attribute relation over a domain of 10,000 integers, i.e. $DA=[0, 10,000)$.

We report on 5,000 tuples and a series of 20,000 range queries generated as follows: the mid point of a range is selected using a Zipf distribution ([20]) over $DA$ with a skew parameter $\theta$ taking values 0.5, 0.8, and 1. The lower and upper bounds of a range are randomly computed using a *maximum* range span equal to $2 \cdot r$, for a given parameter $r$ (i.e. $r$ is equal to the average range span). In our experiments, $r$ ranges from 1 to 400, and, thus, yielding an average selectivity from 0.01% to 4% of the domain size $DA$.

Finally, we present experimental results of the HotRoD simulator with different maximum numbers of instances, $\rho_{\max}(A)$, ranging from 2, i.e. one replicated Chord ring, to 150 (in this section, $\rho_{\max}(A)$ is denoted as $\rho_{\max}$), to illustrate the trade-off load imbalances with replication overhead costs. We should mention here that the reported load imbalances are collected when the system has entered a *steady state* with respect to the peer population and the number of replicas.

### 4.2 Efficiency of Query Processing

Chord and OP-Chord resolve *equality queries* (i.e. $r = 1$) in $½ \cdot \log N$ hops, on average. In HotRoD, this becomes $\log N$ since two Chord lookup operations are needed: one for the GetRho() operation and one for the lookup operation on the selected ring.

Let a *range query RQ* of span $r$ (i.e. there are $r$ integer values in the query). We assume that the requested index tuples are stored on $n$ *peers* under Chord and enhanced Chord, and on $n'$ *peers* under OP-Chord. Thus, the average complexity of the range query processing is estimated as follows:

- *PC*: $r$ equality queries are needed to gather all possible results (one for each one of the values belonging to $RQ$) for an overall hop count of $O(r \cdot \log N)$.
- *EC*: $n$ equality queries must be executed to gather all possible results for an overall hop count of $O(n \cdot \log N)$.
- *OP-Chord* and *HotRoD:* one lookup operation is needed to reach the peer holding the lower value of $RQ$ ($\log N$ hops), and $n'-1$ forward operations to the successors ($n'-1$ hops), for a final overall hop count of $O(\log N + n')$; note that the constant factor hidden by the big-O notation is higher in HotRoD, due to the GetRho() operations needed to be executed first of all.

The experimental results in terms of hop counts per range query are shown in Table 1. Comparing HotRoD against OP-Chord, we conclude, as expected, that

HotRoD is more expensive; the extra hops incurred are due to the GetRho() operations, which facilitate load balancing. We should note, however, that HotRoD compares very well even against EC, ensuring hop-count savings from 4% to 78% for different $r$'s. As $r$ increases, the hop-count benefits of OP-Chord/HotRoD versus PC/EC increase.

**Table 1.** Average number of hops per query for different range spans $r$ ($\theta = 0.8$)

| $r$ | 50 | 100 | 200 | 400 |
|---|---|---|---|---|
| PC | 123 | 246 | 489 | 898 |
| EC | 25 | 48 | 87 | 190 |
| OP–Chord | 18 | 20 | 25 | 33 |
| HotRoD ($p_{max}=30$) | 24 | 27 | 31 | 41 |

### 4.3 Access Load Balancing

We compare load balance characteristics between OP-Chord and HotRoD. We use the access count, $a$, which, as defined above, measures the number of successful accesses per peer (i.e. *hits*). We illustrate results using the Lorenz curves and the Gini Coefficient, borrowed from economics and ecology because of their distinguished ability to capture the required information naturally, compactly, and adequately.

Lorenz curves ([6]) are functions of the cumulative proportion of ordered individuals mapped onto the corresponding cumulative proportion of their size. In our context, the ordered individuals are the peers ordered by the number of their hits. If all peers have the same load, the curve is a straight diagonal line, called the *line of equality*, or *uniformity* in our context. If there is any imbalance, then the Lorenz curve falls below the line of uniformity. Given $n$ ordered peers with $l_i$ being the load of peer $i$, and $l_1 \leq l_2 \leq \ldots \leq l_n$, the Lorenz curve is expressed as the polygon joining the points $(h/n, L_h/L_n)$, where $h=0, 1, 2, \ldots, n$, $L_0 = 0$, and $L_h = \sum_{i=1}^{h} l_i$.

The total amount of load imbalance can be summarized by the Gini coefficient ($G$) ([6]), which is defined as the relative mean difference, i.e. the mean of the difference between every possible pair of peers, divided by their mean load. It is calculated by:

$$G = \sum_{i=1}^{n}(2i-n-1)\cdot l_i \Big/ n^2 \cdot \mu, \qquad (2)$$

where $\mu$ is the mean load. $G$ also expresses the ratio between the area enclosed by the line of uniformity and the Lorenz curve, and the total triangular area under the line of uniformity. $G$ ranges from a minimum value of 0, when all peers have equal load, to a maximum of 1, when every individual, except one has a load of zero. Therefore, as $G$ comes closer to 0, load imbalances are reduced, whereas, as G comes closer to 1, load imbalances are increased.

We should mention here that $G=0$ if and only if *all* peers in the network have *equal* load. However, this is extremely rare in a P2P network. Therefore, we measured $G$ in different setups with different degrees of fairness in load distributions. We noticed that $G$ was very close to 0.5 in all setups with quite a fair load distribution. In general, in fair load distributions $G$'s values ranged from 0.5 to 0.65, whereas in very unfair load distribution, from 0.85 to 0.99. Therefore, our target is to achieve values of $G$ close to 0.5. Besides, $G$ is used as a summary metric to compare load imbalances between different architectures (i.e. PC, EC, etc) and different setups.

We ran experiments with different range spans, $r$'s, and Zipf parameters, $\theta$'s. In figure 3, hits distribution is illustrated for $r=200$ and $\theta=0.8$ (here, HotRoD ran with $\rho_{max} = 400$, and $\rho_{max}=15$). The Gini coefficient ($G$) in PC and EC is 0.78[4], in OP-Chord 0.87, and in HotRoD 0.53. $G$ in HotRoD is significantly reduced comparing to the other architectures, with a decrease of 32% comparing with PC/EC and 39% comparing to OP-Chord. The results of experiments with lower range spans are similar. As example, for $r=50$ and $\theta=0.8$, $G$ in PC and EC is 0.81, in OP-Chord 0.95, whereas in HotRoD ($\rho_{max}=100$, $\rho_{max}=50$) $G$ is 0.64, i.e. decreased by 20% and 32%, respectively (see figure 4). Both examples show clearly how HotRoD achieves a great improvement in access load balancing. All experiments have shown similar results.

Furthermore, the resulting Lorenz curves (figures 3 and 4) show that the top 3% heaviest-hit peers receive about an order of magnitude fewer hits in HotRoD than in OP-Chord. At the same time, the mostly-hit of the remaining (underutilized) 97% of the peers receive a hit count that is very slightly above the load they would receive if the load was uniformly balanced. The load balancing benefits and key philosophy of HotRoD are evident in Lorenz curves. HotRoD attempts to off-load the mostly-hit peers by involving the remaining least-hit peers. Thus, intuitively, we should expect to see a considerable off-loading for the heaviest-hit peers, while at the same time, we should expect to see an increase in the load of the least-hit peers.

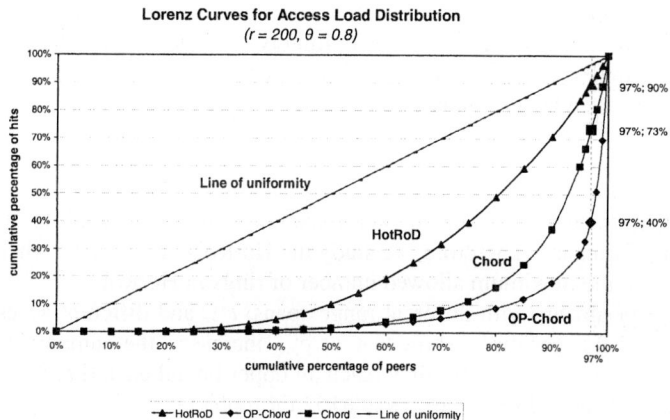

**Fig. 3.** In Chord, OP-Chord, HotRoD, the top 3% heaviest peers receive almost 27%, 60%, 10% of total hits

---

[4] Although Chord uniformly distributes values among peers (using consistent hashing), it does not succeed in fairly distributing access load in case of skewed query distributions.

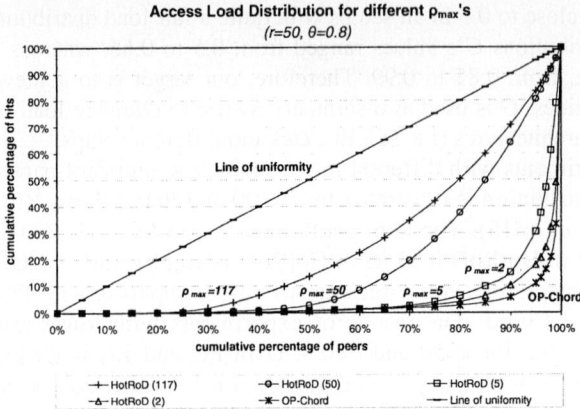

**Fig 4.** As ρmax increases, the Lorenz curves that illustrate the access load distribution come closer to the line of uniformity, which means that load imbalances and, thus, $G$ are decreased

We should mention that, in our experiments, the *upper access count threshold*, $\rho_{max}$, was set equal to the *average (value) access load* expected to be received by each peer in a uniform access load distribution. The latter is equal to $2 \cdot r$, as we briefly prove below.

*Proof sketch.* We assume that Q=20,000 queries request r values each, on average, and each peer is responsible for an average of |DA|/N=10 values. Therefore, we have $Q \cdot r \cdot N/|DA|$ hits uniformly distributed among N peers, and, thus an average of $Q \cdot r/|DA|$ hits per peer, which is equal to $2 \cdot r$, since |DA| = 10,000. □

In our experiments, $\rho_{max}$ was kept low (i.e. less than 50), which introduces a total of about 100% additional replicas. This is definitely realistic, given typical sharing network applications ([21], [24]); however, we stress that good load balancing can be achieved using even fewer replicas– see below.

### 4.4 Overhead Costs – Tuning Replication

An important issue is the degree of replication required to achieve a good load balancing performance. Therefore, we study the HotRoD architecture when tuning the parameter $\rho_{max}$, the maximum allowed number of rings in HotRoD.

We ran experiments with different range spans, $r$'s, and different access skew parameters, $\theta$'s. All experiments show that, as $\rho_{max}$ increases, the numbers of peers' and tuples' replicas are increased till they reach an upper bound each (i.e. for $r$=50, $\theta$=0.8, the upper bounds are 1449 for peers and 8102 for tuples).

Figure 5 illustrates how different $\rho_{max}$'s affect the number of peers' and tuples' replicas for $r$=50 and $\theta$=0.8. Specifically: for $\rho_{max}$=2, 11% of peers and 12% of tuples have been replicated; for $\rho_{max}$=5, 25% and 30% respectively; for $\rho_{max}$=10, 38% and 47%; for $\rho_{max}$=50, 85% and 103%. For high $\rho_{max}$'s, peers and replicas are heavily replicated, till $\rho_{max}$ reaches 117 (as it was experimentally proven), beyond which there is no replication and, thus, there are no further benefits in load balancing.

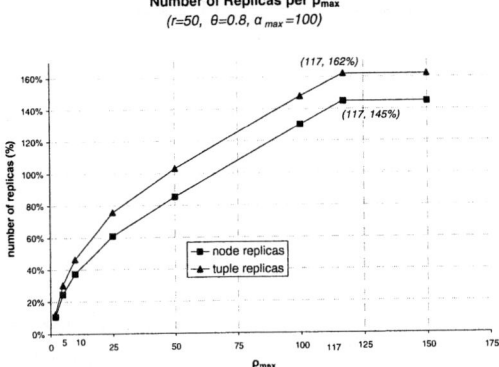

**Fig. 5.** Tuning replication degree by $\rho_{max}$

Similar conclusions are drawn from experiments with different $r$'s and $\theta$'s. In general, it holds that the lower the range span, $r$, or the higher the skew parameter, $\theta$, the higher the upper limit of $\rho_{max}$. For example, for $r=50$ and $\theta=0.5$, the upper limit of $\rho_{max}$ is 90; for $r=200$, $\theta=0.8$, it is 59; for $r=200$, $\theta=0.5$, it is 23.

Figures 4 and 5 illustrate the role that $\rho_{max}$ plays in the access load distribution. As $\rho_{max}$ increases, the load imbalances are decreased, and $G$ is decreased. Specifically, $G$ is decreased as follows: for $\rho_{max} = 2$, $G=0.92$; for $\rho_{max} = 5$, $G=0.88$; for $\rho_{max} = 50$, $G=0.64$; for $\rho_{max} \geq 117$, $G=0.50$. On the other hand, the degree of replication ($RD$) for the number of tuple replicas is increased as follows: for $\rho_{max} = 2$, $RD = 12\%$; for $\rho_{max} = 5$, $RD = 30\%$; for $\rho_{max} = 50$, $RD = 103\%$; for $\rho_{max} \geq 117$, $RD = 162\%$.

It is obvious that high values of $\rho_{max}$ provide diminished returns in load balancing, although the degree of replication is very high. This means that we can achieve a very good access load balancing with low values of $\rho_{max}$, and thus, low overhead costs.

To recap: In terms of average hop-counts per range query, HotRoD ensures significant savings, which increase as the range span $r$, or the access skew parameter $\theta$ increases. At the same time, with respect to load balancing, HotRoD achieves its goal of involving the lightest hit peers to offer significant help to the heaviest hit peers, while the total replication overhead is no more than 100%.

## 5 Related Work

There are quite a few solutions supporting range queries, either relying on an underlying DHT, or not. Some indicative examples of such DHTs solutions follow. Andrzejak and Xu ([2]) and Sahin, et al. ([19]) extended CAN ([17]) to allow for range query processing; however, performance is expected to be inferior compared to the other DHT-based solutions, since CAN lookups require $O(2 \cdot N^{1/2})$ hops, for a two-dimensional identifier space. Gupta et. al ([9]) propose an architecture based on Chord, and a hashing method based on a min-wise independent permutation hash function, but they provide only approximate answers to range queries. The system proposed in Ntarmos et al. ([14]) optimizes range queries by identifying and exploiting efficiently the powerful peers which have been found to exist in several environments. Ramabhadran et al ([16]) superimpose a trie (prefix hash tree – PHT) onto a DHT. Although their structure is generic and widely applicable, range queries are highly inefficient, since locality is not preserved. Triantafillou and Pitoura ([22]) outlined a Chord-based framework for complex query processing, supporting range queries. This was the substrate architecture of HotRoD, which we extended here to address replication-based load balancing with efficient range query processing. Although capable to support range queries, none of the above support load balancing.

Among the non-DHT solutions, the majority of them (such as Skip Graphs ([4]), SkipNet ([10]), etc) do not support both range queries and load balance. In a recent work ([3]), Aspnes et al provide a mechanism for providing load balancing using skip graphs. With the use of a global threshold to distinguish heavy from light nodes, they let the light nodes continue to receive elements whereas the heavy ones attempt to shed elements. However, many issues have been left unanswered, such as fault tolerance. Ganesan et al ([7]) propose storage load balance algorithms combined with distributed routing structures which can support range queries. Their solution may support load balance in skewed data distributions, but it does not ensure balance in skewed query distributions. BATON ([11]) is a balanced binary tree overlay network which can support range queries, and query load balancing by data migration between two, not necessarily adjacent, nodes. In their Mercury system ([5]), Bharambe et al support multi-attribute range queries and explicit load balancing, using random sampling; nodes are grouped into routing hubs, each of which is responsible for various attributes.

In all the above approaches, load balancing is based on transferring load from peer to peer. We expect that this will prove inadequate in highly-skewed access distributions where some values may be so popular that single-handedly make the peer that stores them heavy. Simply transferring such hot values from peer to peer only transfers the problem. Related research in web proxies has testified to the need of replication ([23]). Replication can also offer a number of important advantages, such as fault tolerance and high availability ([13]) albeit at the storage and update costs. Besides, we have experimentally shown that storage and update overheads can be kept low, since we can achieve our major goals with a relatively small number of replicas.

Finally, an approach using replication-based load balancing, as ours, is [8], where a replication-based load balancing algorithm over Chord is provided; however, it appears that knowledge about the existence of replicas is slowly propagated, reducing the impact of replication. Besides, it only deals with exact-match queries, avoiding the most difficult problem of balancing data access loads in the presence of range queries.

## 6 Conclusions

This paper presents an attempt at concurrently attacking two key problems in structured P2P data networks: (a) efficient range query processing, and (b) data-access load balancing. The key observation is that replication-based load balancing techniques tend to obstruct techniques for efficiently processing range queries. Thus, solving these problems concurrently is an important goal and a formidable task. Some researchers claim that existing DHTs are ill-suited to range queries since their property of uniform distribution is based on randomized hashing, which does not comply with range partitioning (i.e. [5]). However, HotRoD succeeded in combining the good properties of DHTs (simplicity, robustness, efficiency, and storage load balancing) with range partitioning using a novel hash function which is both locality-preserving and randomized (in the sense that queries are processed in randomly selected – replicated - partitions of the identifier space).

We have taken an encouraging step towards solving the two key aforementioned problems through the HotRoD architecture. HotRoD reconciles and trades-off hop-count efficiency gains for improved data-access load distribution among the peers. Compared to base architectures our detailed experimentation clearly shows that HotRoD achieves very good hop-count efficiency coupled with a significant improvement in the overall access load distribution among peers, with small replication overheads. Besides, in parallel with the evaluation of HotRoD, we have introduced novel load balancing metrics (i.e. the Lorenz curves and the Gini coefficient) into the area of distributed and p2p computing, a descriptive and effective way to measure and evaluate fairness of any load distribution. Finally, HotRoD can be superimposed over any underlying DHT infrastructure, ensuring wide applicability/impact.

# References

1. Aberer, K.: P-Grid: A self-organizing access structure for P2P information systems. In Proc of CoopIS (2001)
2. Andrzejak, A., and Xu, Z.: Scalable, efficient range queries for Grid information services. In Proc. of P2P (2002)
3. Aspnes, J., Kirsch, J., Krishnamurthy, A.: Load balancing and locality in range-queriable data structures. In Proc. of PODC (2004)
4. Aspnes, J., Shah, G: Skip graphs. In ACM-SIAM Symposium on Discrete Algorithms (2003)
5. Bharambe, A., Agrawal, M., Seshan, S.: Mercury: Supporting scalable multi-attribute range queries. In Proc. of SIGCOMM04 (2004)
6. Damgaard, C., and Weiner, J.: Describing inequality in plant size or fecundity. Ecology 81 (2000) pp. 1139-1142
7. Ganesan, P., Bawa, M., and Garcia-Molina, H.: Online balancing of range-partitioned data with applications to peer-to-peer systems. In Proc. of VLDB (2004)
8. Gopalakrishnan, V., Silaghi, B., Bhattacharjee, B., and Keleher, P.: Adaptive replication in peer-to-peer systems. In Proc. of ICDCS (2004)
9. Gupta, A., Agrawal, D., and Abbadi, A.E.: Approximate range selection queries in peer-to-peer systems. In Proc. of CIDR (2003)
10. Harvey, N., et al.: SkipNet: A scalable overlay network with practical locality preserving properties. In Proc.of 4th USENIX Symp. on Internet Technologies and Systems (2003)
11. Jagadish, H.V., Ooi, B.C., Vu, Q. H..: BATON: A balanced tree structure for peer-to-peer networks. In Proc. of VLDB (2005)
12. Karger, D., et al.: Consistent hashing and random trees: distributed caching protocols for relieving hot spots on the World Wide Web. In Proc. ACM STOC (1997)
13. Mondal, A., Goda, K., Kitsuregawa, M.: Effective Load-Balancing via Migration and Replication in Spatial Grids. In Proc of DEXA 2003 (2003)

14. Ntarmos, N., Pitoura, T., and Triantafillou, P.: Range query optimization leveraging peer heterogeneity in DHT data networks. In Proc. of DBISP2P (2005)
15. Pitoura, T., Ntarmos, N., and Triantafillou, P.: HotRoD: Load Balancing and Efficient Range Query Processing in Peer-to-Peer Data Networks. Technical Report No. T.R.2004/12/05, RACTI (2004)
16. Ramabhadran, S., Ratnasamy, S., Hellerstein, J., Shenker, S.: Brief Announcement: Prefix Hash Tree. In Proc. of PODC (2004)
17. Ratnasamy, S., Francis, P., Handley, M., Karp, R., and Shenker, S.: A scalable content-addressable network. In Proc. ACM SIGCOMM (2001)
18. Rowstron, A., Druschel, P.: Pastry: Scalable, decentralized object location and routing for large-scale peer-to-peer systems. In Proc. of Middleware (2001)
19. Sahin, O.D., Gupta, A., Agrawal, D., and Abbadi, A.E.: A peer-to-peer framework for caching range queries. In Proc. of ICDE (2004)
20. Saroiu, S., Gummadi, P., and Gribble, S.: A measurement study of peer-to-peer file sharing systems. In Proc. of MMCN (2002)
21. Stoica, I., Morris, R., Karger, D., Kaashoek, M.F., and Balakrishnan, H.: Chord: A scalable peer-to-peer lookup service for internet applications. In Proc. of SIGCOMM (2001)
22. Triantafillou, P., and Pitoura, T.: Towards a unifying framework for complex query processing over structured peer-to-peer data networks. In Proc. of DBISP2P (2003)
23. Wu, K., and Yu, P.S.: Replication for load balancing and hot-spot relief on proxy web caches with hash routing. Distributed and Parallel Databases, 13(2) (2003) pp.203-220.
24. Zhao, Y.B., Kubiatowitcz, J., Joseph, A.: Tapestry: An infrastructure for fault-tolerant wide-area location and routing. Technical Report UCB/CSD-01-1141 (2001)

# IQN Routing: Integrating Quality and Novelty in P2P Querying and Ranking

Sebastian Michel[1], Matthias Bender[1],
Peter Triantafillou[2], and Gerhard Weikum[1]

[1] Max-Planck-Institut für Informatik
{smichel, mbender, weikum}@mpi-inf.mpg.de
[2] RACTI and University of Patras
peter@ceid.upatras.gr

**Abstract.** We consider a collaboration of peers autonomously crawling the Web. A pivotal issue when designing a peer-to-peer (P2P) Web search engine in this environment is *query routing*: selecting a small subset of (a potentially very large number of relevant) peers to contact to satisfy a keyword query. Existing approaches for query routing work well on disjoint data sets. However, naturally, the peers' data collections often highly overlap, as popular documents are highly crawled. Techniques for estimating the cardinality of the overlap between sets, designed for and incorporated into information retrieval engines are very much lacking. In this paper we present a comprehensive evaluation of appropriate overlap estimators, showing how they can be incorporated into an efficient, iterative approach to query routing, coined *Integrated Quality Novelty (IQN)*. We propose to further enhance our approach using histograms, combining overlap estimation with the available score/ranking information. Finally, we conduct a performance evaluation in MINERVA, our prototype P2P Web search engine.

## 1 Introduction

### 1.1 Motivation

In recent years, the Peer-to-Peer (P2P) paradigm has been receiving increasing attention. While becoming popular in the context of file-sharing applications such as Gnutella or BitTorrent or IP telephony like Skype, the P2P paradigm is rapidly making its way into distributed data management and information retrieval (IR) due to its ability to handle huge amounts of data in a highly distributed, scalable, self-organizing way with resilience to failures and churn. Given the potentially very large set of peers storing relevant data, one of the key technical challenges of such a system is *query routing* (aka collection selection), which is the process of efficiently selecting the most promising peers for a particular information need. For example, in a file-sharing or publish-subscribe setting, a peer may issue a structured query about MP3 files with operas by the Greek composer Mikis Theodorakis referring to attributes like file type, music genre, and composer; and the P2P network should quickly and efficiently identify other peers that offer many such files and can deliver them with short latency. Another example would be a Web search engine based on a P2P overlay, where a peer initiates a multi-keyword search, and the query routing mechanism should forward this request to the best peers that offer highly scoring documents for IR-style top-k results. In this paper, we will primarily address the ranked retrieval setting for P2P Web search, but our solutions are also applicable to and beneficial for DB-style structured queries without ranking.

Several techniques borrowed from the literature on distributed IR [20, 12, 24, 28] could be employed for query routing, based on statistics about term frequencies (tf) and inverse document frequencies (idf) that reflect the relevance of documents to a query term and thus can be aggregated into measures reflect the wealth and quality of a peer's corpus. However, these strategies typically ignore the fact that popular documents are replicated at a significant number of peers. These strategies often result in promising peers being selected because they share the same high-quality documents. Consider a single-attribute query for all songs by Mikis Theodorakis. If, as in many of today's systems, every selected peer contributes its best matches only, the query result will most likely contain many duplicates (of popular songs), when instead users would have preferred a much larger variety of songs from the same number of peers. Other application classes with similar difficulties include P2P sensor networks or network monitoring [22]. What is lacking is a technique that enables the quantification of how many *novel* results can be contributed to the query result by each of the prospective peers.

## 1.2 Contribution

Contacting all prospective peers during query execution and exchanging the full information necessary to determine collection novelty is unacceptable due to the high cost in latency and network bandwidth. We envision an iterative approach based on compact statistical synopses, which all peers have precomputed and previously published to a (decentralized and scalable) directory implemented by a distributed hash table (DHT). The algorithm, coined *IQN routing* (for integrated quality and novelty), performs two steps in each iteration: First, the *Select-Best-Peer* step identifies the most promising peer regarding result quality *and* novelty based on the statistics that were posted to the directory. Then, the *Aggregate-Synopses* step conceptually aggregates the chosen peer's document collection with the previously selected peers' collections (including the query initiator's own local collection). This aggregation is actually carried out on the corresponding synopses obtained from the directory. It is important to note that this decision process for query routing does not yet contact any remote peers at all (other than for the, very fast DHT-based, directory lookups). The two-step selection procedure is iterated until some performance and/or quality constraints are satisfied (e.g., a predefined number of peers has been chosen).

The effectiveness of the IQN routing method crucially depends on appropriately designed compact *synopses* for the collection statistics. To support the Select-Best-Peer step, these synopses must be small (for low bandwidth consumption, latency, and storage overhead), yet they must offer low-error estimations of the novelty by the peers' collections. To support the Aggregate-Synopses step, it must be possible to combine synopses published by different peers in order to derive a synopsis for the aggregated collection.

In this paper we consider three kinds of synopses that each peer builds up and posts on a per-term basis, representing the global ids of documents (e.g., URLs or unique names of MP3 files) that a peer holds in its collection: Bloom filters [7], hash sketches [18], and min-wise permutations [9, 10]. These techniques have been invented for approximate, low-error representation of sets or multisets. In this paper we show how they can be adapted to a P2P setting and exploited for our highly effective IQN query routing. We assume that each peer locally maintains inverted index lists with entries of the form $< term, docId, score >$, and posts for each term (or attribute value in a structured data setting) a set synopsis that captures the docIds that the peer has for the term. These postings are kept in the DHT-based P2P directory for very efficient lookup by all peers in the network.

The specific contributions of this paper are as follows:

- We have conducted a systematic study of Bloom filters, hash sketches, and min-wise permutations to characterize the suitability for the specific purpose of supporting query routing in a P2P system.
- We have developed the new IQN query routing algorithm that reconciles quality and novelty measures. We show how this algorithm combines multiple per-term synopses to support multi-keyword or multi-attribute queries in an efficient and effective manner.
- We have carried out a systematic experimental evaluation, using real-life data and queries from TREC benchmarks, that demonstrate the benefits of IQN query routing (based on min-wise permutations) in terms of result recall (a standard IR measure) and query execution cost.

The rest of the paper is organized as follows. Section 2 discusses related work and gives general background on P2P IR. Section 3 introduces the different types of synopses and presents our experimental comparison of the basic techniques. Section 4 introduces our P2P testbed, coined MINERVA [5, 6]. Section 5 develops the IQN routing method in detail. Section 6 discusses special techniques for handling multi-dimensional queries. Section 7 describes extensions to exploit histograms on score distributions. Section 8 presents our experimental evaluation of the IQN routing method versus the best previously published algorithms, namely, CORI [13] and our prior method from [5].

## 2 Related Work

Many approaches have been proposed for collection selection in distributed IR, most notably, CORI [13], the decision-theoretic framework by [28], the GlOSS method presented in [20], and methods based on statistical language models [32]. In principle, these methods could be applied to a P2P setting, but they fall short of various critical aspects: they incur major overhead in their statistical models, they do not scale up to large numbers of peers with high dynamics, and they disregard the crucial issue of collection overlap.

The ample work on P2P networks, such as Chord [33], CAN [29], Pastry [31], or P-Grid [1], has developed scalable routing protocols for single-dimensional key-based requests only. How to map multidimensional data onto distributed hash tables (DHTs) and other overlay networks [3, 35] has not received enough attention, and these approaches do not work for the very-high-dimensional data spaces formed by text keywords and they do not provide any support for ranked retrieval either. P2P Web search has emerged as a new topic only recently. A variety of ongoing research projects are pursuing this direction [2, 37, 4, 14, 15, 30, 36, 22], including our MINERVA project [5]. Query routing has been identified as a key issue, but none of the projects has a fully convincing solution so far.

Fundamentals for statistical synopses of (multi-)sets have a rich literature, including work on Bloom filters [7, 17], hash sketches [18], and min-wise independent permutations [9, 10]. We will overview these in Section 3.

There is relatively little work on the specific issue of overlap and novelty estimation. [38] addresses redundancy detection in a centralized information filtering system; it is unclear how this approach could be made scalable in a highly distributed setting. [27, 21] present a technique to estimate coverage and overlap statistics by query classification and use a probing technique to extract features from the collections. The computational overhead of this technique makes it unsuitable for a P2P query routing setting where estimates must be made within the critical response-time path of an online query.

Our own prior work [5] addressed overlap estimation for P2P collections, but was limited to Bloom filters and used only a simple decision model for query routing. The current paper shows how to utilize also more sophisticated and flexible kinds of synopses like min-wise permutations, analyzes their advantages, and develops the novel IQN routing method. IQN outperforms the method of [5] by a large margin in terms of the ratio of query result recall to execution cost.

## 3 Collection Synopses for Information Retrieval

### 3.1 Measures

Consider two sets, $S_A$ and $S_B$, with each element identified by an integer key (e.g., *docID*). The *overlap* of these two sets is defined as $|S_A \cap S_B|$, i.e., the cardinality of the intersection.

The notions of *Containment* and *Resemblance* have been proposed as measures of mutual set correlation and can be used for our problem setting [8]. $Containment(S_A, S_B) = \frac{|S_A \cap S_B|}{|S_B|}$ is used to represent the fraction of elements in $S_B$ that are already known to $S_A$. $Resemblance(S_A, S_B) = \frac{|S_A \cap S_B|}{|S_A \cup S_B|}$ represents the fraction documents that $S_A$ and $S_B$ share with each other. If the intersection $|S_A \cap S_B|$ is small, so are containment and resemblance, and $S_B$ can be considered a useful information source from the viewpoint of $S_A$. Note that resemblance is symmetric, while containment is not. Also, given $|S_A|$ and $|S_B|$ and either one of Resemblance or Containment, one can calculate the other [11].

However, none of these notions can fully capture the requirements of our system model. Specifically, we expect peers to have widely varying index list sizes. Consider now, for example, two collections $S_A$ and $S_B$ with $|S_A| \ll |S_B|$ and a reference collection $S_C$. Since $|S_A|$ is small, so is $|S_A \cap S_C|$, yielding low containment and resemblance values, even if $S_A \subset S_C$. If we preferred collections with low containment or resemblance, we would prefer $S_A$ over $S_B$, even though $S_A$ might not add *any* new documents. To overcome this problem, we propose the notion of *novelty* of a set $S_B$ with regard to $S_A$, defined as $Novelty(S_B|S_A) = |S_B - (S_A \cap S_B)|$.

### 3.2 Synopses

In the following, we briefly overview three relevant statistical synopses methods from the literature, focusing on estimating resemblance. In Section 5.2 we will show how to use resemblance to estimate our proposed novelty measure.

**Bloom Filters.** A Bloom filter (BF) [7] is a data structure that compactly represents a set as a bit vector in order to support membership queries. Bloom filters can easily approximate intersections and unions by bit-wise *AND* and *OR*ing of two filters. The resemblance between two sets is derived from the cardinalities of their union and intersection.

**Min-Wise Independent Permutations (MIPs).** Min-Wise Independent Permutations, or MIPs for short, have been introduced in [9, 10]. This technique assumes that the set elements can be ordered (which is trivial for integer keys) and computes $N$ random permutations of the elements. Each permutation uses a linear hash function of the form $h_i(x) := a_i * x + b_i \bmod U$ where $U$ is a big prime number and $a_i$, $b_i$ are fixed random numbers. By ordering the resulting hash values, we obtain a random permutation. For each of the $N$ permutations, the MIPs technique determines the minimum hash value, and stores it in an $N$-dimensional vector, thus capturing the minimum set element under each of these random permutations. Its fundamental rationale is that each element has the same probability of becoming the minimum element under a random permutation.

An unbiased estimate of the pair-wise resemblance of sets using their $N$-dimensional MIPs vectors is obtained by counting the number of positions in

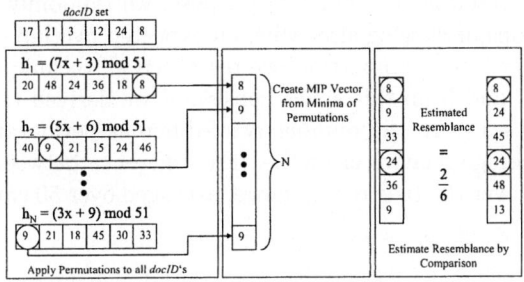

**Fig. 1.** Example of Min-Wise Permutations

which the two vectors have the same number and dividing this by the number of permutations $N$ [11]. Essentially, this holds as the matched numbers are guaranteed to belong to the intersection of the sets.

A heuristic form of approximating also the intersection and union of two sets would combine two MIPs vectors by taking, for each position, the maximum and minimum of the two values. The ratio of the number of distinct values in the resulting aggregated MIPs vector to the vector length $N$ provides an estimate for the intersection and union cardinalities, but in the intersection case, this is no longer a statistically sound unbiased estimator.

**Hash Sketches.** Hash sketches were first proposed by Flajolet and Martin in [18], to probabilistically estimate the cardinality of a multiset $S$. [19] proposes a hash-based synopsis data structure and algorithms to support low-error and high-confidence estimates for general set expressions. Hash sketches rely on the existence of a pseudo-uniform hash function $h() : S \to [0, 1, \ldots, 2^L)$. Durand and Flajolet presented a similar algorithm in [16] (*super-LogLog counting*) which reduced the space complexity and relaxed the required statistical properties of the hash function.

Hash sketches work as follows. Let $\rho(y) : [0, 2^L) \to [0, L)$ be the position of the least significant (leftmost) 1-bit in the binary representation of $y$; that is, $\rho(y) = min_{k \geq 0} bit(y, k) \neq 0$, $y > 0$, and $\rho(0) = L$. $bit(y, k)$ denotes the $k$th bit in the binary representation of $y$ (bit position 0 corresponds to the least significant bit). In order to estimate the number $n$ of distinct elements in a multiset $S$ we apply $\rho(h(d))$ to all $d \in S$ and record the results in a bitmap vector $B[0 \ldots L-1]$. Since $h()$ distributes values uniformly over $[0, 2^L)$, it follows that $P(\rho(h(d)) = k) = 2^{-k-1}$.

Thus, for an $n$-item multiset, $B[0]$ will be set to 1 approximately $\frac{n}{2}$ times, $B[1]$ approximately $\frac{n}{4}$ times, etc. Then, the quantity $R(S) = max_{d \in S}\rho(d)$ provides an estimation of the value of $\log n$. [18, 16] present analyses and techniques to bound from above the error introduced, relying basically on using multiple bit vectors and averaging over their corresponding $R$ positions.

### 3.3 Experimental Characterization

We evaluated the above synopses in terms of their general ability to estimate mutual collection resemblance. For this purpose, we randomly created pairs of synthetic collections of varying sizes with an expected overlap of 33%.

For a fair and realistic comparison, we restricted all techniques to a synopsis size of 2,048 bits, and from this space constraint we derived the parameters of the various synopses (e.g., the number $N$ of different permutations for MIPs). We report the average relative error (i.e., the difference between estimated and true resemblance over the true resemblance, averaged over 50 runs with different synthesized sets).[1]

---

[1] The expectation values, i.e., the averages over the estimated resemblance values, are more or less perfect (at least for MIPs and hash sketches) and not shown here. This is no surprise as the estimators are designed to be unbiased.

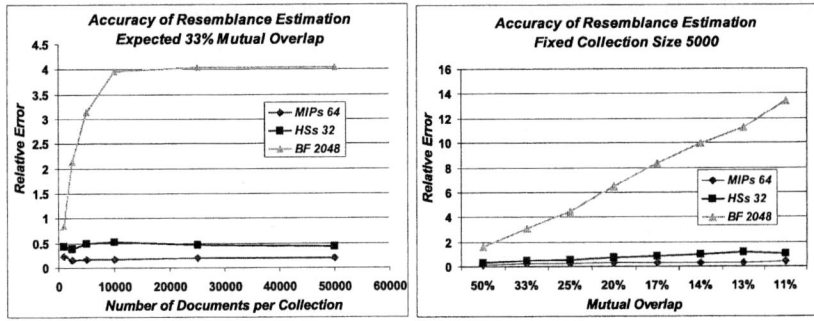

**Fig. 2.** Relative Error of Resemblance Estimation

Figure 2 shows, on the left side, the relative error as a function of the set cardinality. We see that MIPs offer accurate estimates with little variance and that their error is almost independent of the collection sizes. Hash sketches are also robust with respect to the collection sizes, but on average have a higher error. Bloom filters perform worse even with small collections, because (given their size of 2,048 bits) they are overloaded, i.e., they would require more bits to allow for accurate estimates.

Next, we created synthetic collections of a fixed size (10,000 elements), and varied the expected mutual overlap. We again report on average relative error. The results, shown in Figure 2 on the right side, are similar to the observations above: Bloom Filters suffer again from overload; MIPs and hash sketches offer accurate estimates with a low variance for all degrees of overlap.

### 3.4 Discussion

A qualitative comparison for selecting the most appropriate synopsis of the peer collections should be based on the following criteria: 1) low estimation error, 2) small space requirements for low storage and communication costs, 3) the ability to aggregate synopses for different sets in order to derive a synopsis for the results of set operations like union, intersection, or difference, and 4) the ability to cope with synopses of heterogeneous sizes, e.g., to combine a short synopsis for a small set with a longer synopsis for a larger set.

Bloom filters can provide tunably accurate estimations of resemblance between two sets. They also facilitate the construction of aggregate synopses for the union and intersection of sets, by simply taking the bit-wise $OR$ and bit-wise $AND$ of the filters of the two sets. ¿From these, it is in turn straightforward to derive a novelty estimator. A major drawback of Bloom filters is that they cannot work when different sets have used different size filters.

This leads either to very high bandwidth and storage overhead (when forcing all collections to be represented by an a-priori maximum filter size) or to high errors (when using inappropriately small size filters, due to very high false positive probability).

MIPs and hash sketches can offer set resemblance estimation with small errors with reasonable space and bandwidth requirements. For the numbers chosen in our experiments, MIPs work even more accurately (i.e., with a lower variance) than hash sketches for different combinations of collection sizes and degrees of overlap, for sets with cardinalities from a few thousand up to millions of elements.

For hash sketches, we are not aware of ways to derive aggregated synopses for the intersection of two sets (whereas union is straightforward by bit-wise $OR$). This somewhat limits their flexibility in some application classes with conjunctive multi-dimensional queries (cf. Section 6). Moreover, they share with Bloom filters the disadvantage that all hash sketches need to have the same bit lengths in order to be comparable.

MIPs are at least as good as the other two techniques in terms of error and space requirements. In contrast to both Bloom filters and hash sketches, they can cope, to some extent, with heterogeneous sizes for resemblance estimation. When comparing two MIPs vectors with $N_1$ and $N_2$ permutations, we can simply limit ourselves to the $min(N_1, N_2)$ common permutations and obtain meaningful estimates. Of course, the accuracy of the estimator may degrade this way, but we still have a working method and our experiments in Section 8 show that the accuracy is typically still good enough.

## 4 MINERVA Prototype for P2P Web Search

MINERVA is a fully operational distributed search engine that we have implemented and that serves as a testbed for our work. A conceptually global but physically distributed directory, which is layered on top of Chord [33], holds compact, aggregated information about the peers' local indexes, to the extent that the individual peers are willing to disclose. Unlike [23], we use the Chord DHT to partition the term space, such that every peer is responsible for the statistics and metadata of a randomized subset of terms within the directory. For failure resilience and availability, the responsibility for a term can be replicated across multiple peers. We do *not* distribute the actual index lists or even documents across the directory.

Directory maintenance, query routing, and query processing work as follows. Every peer publishes statistics, denoted as *Posts*, about every term in its local index to the directory. The peer onto which the term is hashed maintains a *PeerList* of all postings for this term from all peers across the network. Posts contain contact information about the peer who posted the summary together with statistics to calculate IR-style relevance measures for a term, e.g., the length of the inverted index list for the term, the maximum or average score among the term's inverted list entries, etc. A peer that initiates a multi-keyword query first retrieves the PeerLists for all query terms from the distributed directory. It combines this information to identify the most promising peers for the current query. For efficiency reasons, the query initiator can decide to not retrieve the complete PeerLists, but only a subset, say the top-$k$ peers from each list based on IR relevance measures, or more appropriately the top-$k$ peers over all lists, calculated by a distributed top-$k$ algorithm like [25].

## 5 Enhancing Query Execution Using Novelty Estimation

### 5.1 The IQN Query Routing Method

Good query routing is based on the following three observations:

1. The query initiator should prefer peers that are likely to hold highly relevant information for a particular query.
2. On the other hand, the query should be forwarded to peers that offer a great deal of *complementary results*.
3. Finally, this process should incur acceptable overhead.

For the first aspect, we utilize the statistical metadata about the peers' local content quality that all peers post to the distributed directory (based on local IR measures like tf*idf-based scores, scores derived from statistical language models, or PageRank-like authority scores of documents). For the second aspect, each peer additionally publishes term-specific synopses that can be used to estimate the mutual term-specific novelty. For the third aspect, we ensure that the synopses are as compact as possible and we utilize in a particularly cost-efficient way for making routing decisions.

The Integrated Quality Novelty (IQN) method that we have developed based on this rationale starts from the local query result that the query initiator can compute by executing the query against its own local collection and builds a synopsis for the result documents as a *reference synopsis* against which additionally considered peers are measured. Alternatively to the local query execution, the peer may also construct the reference synopsis from its already existing local per-term synopses. In this section we will simplify the presentation and assume that queries are single-dimensional, e.g., use only one keyword; we will discuss in Section 6 how to handle multi-keyword or multi-attributed queries.

IQN adds peers to the query processing plan in an iterative manner, by alternating between a *Select-Best-Peer* and an *Aggregate-Synopses* step.

The Select-Best-Peer step uses the query-relevant PeerList from the directory, fetched before the first iteration, to form a candidate peer list and identify the best peer that is not yet included in the execution plan. Quality is measured in terms of an IR relevance metric like CORI [13, 12]: CORI computes the collection score $s_i$ of the $i$-th peer with regard to a query $Q = \{t_1, t_2, ..., t_n\}$ as $s_i = \sum_{t \in Q} \frac{s_{i,t}}{|Q|}$ where $s_{i,t} = \alpha + (1-\alpha) \cdot T_{i,t} \cdot I_{i,t}$.

The computations of $T_{i,t}$ and $I_{i,t}$ use the *number of peers* in the system, denoted $np$, the *document frequency* ($cdf$) of term $t$ in collection $i$, and the *maximum document frequency* ($cdf^{max}$) for any term $t$ in collection $i$:

$$T_{i,t} = \frac{cdf_{i,t}}{cdf_{i,t} + 50 + 150 \cdot \frac{|V_i|}{|V^{avg}|}} \qquad I_{i,t} = \frac{\frac{log(np+0.5)}{cf_t}}{log(np+1)}$$

where the *collection frequency* $cf_t$ is the number of peers that contain the term $t$. The value $\alpha$ is chosen as $\alpha = 0.4$ [13].

CORI considers the size $|V_i|$ of the term space of a peer (i.e., the total number of distinct terms that the peer holds in its local index) and the average term space size $|V^{avg}|$ over all peers that contain term $t$.

In practice, it is difficult to compute the average term space size over all *peers in the system* (regardless of whether they contain query term $t$ or not). We approximate this value by the average over all *collections found in the PeerLists*.

Novelty is measured by the candidate peers' synopses, also fetched from the directory upfront, using the techniques of the previous section with further details provided below. The candidate list is sorted by the product of quality and novelty. Each IQN iteration selects the best quality*novelty peer, adds it to the query processing plan, and removes it from the candidate list.

The Aggregate-Synopses step aims to update the expected quality of the result under the condition that the query will be processed by all those peers that were previously selected including the one chosen in the current iteration. For this purpose, IQN aggregates the synopsis of the last selected peer and the references synopsis, where the latter already captures the results that can be expected from all peers chosen in previous iterations. The result forms the reference synopsis for the next iteration. The details of the synopses aggregation depend on the kind of synopsis structure and is discussed in the following subsection. Note that IQN always aggregates only two synopses at a time, and also needs to estimate only the novelty of an additionally considered peer against the reference synopsis. The algorithm is designed so that pair-wise novelty estimation is all it needs.

The two steps, Select-Best-Peer and Aggregate-Synopses, are iterated until some specified stopping criterion is satisfied. Good criteria would be reaching a certain number of maximum peers that should be involved in the query, or estimating that the combined query result has at least a certain number of (good) documents. The latter can be inferred from the updated reference synopsis.

## 5.2 Estimating Pair-Wise Novelty

We show how to utilize the synopses based on MIPs, hash sketches, and Bloom filters to select the next best peer in an iteration of the IQN method. For simplicity, *best* refers to highest novelty here. In a real-world application like MINERVA, the peer selection process will be based on a combination of novelty and quality as explained in the previous subsection.

**Exploiting MIPs.** MIPs can be used to estimate the resemblance $R$ between $S_A$ and $S_B$ as seen in Section 3.2. Given $|S_A|$ and $|S_B|$, we estimate the overlap between $S_A$ and $S_B$ as $|S_A \cap S_B| = \frac{R*(|S_A|+|S_B|)}{(R+1)}$ and can use this overlap estimation to calculate our notion of novelty using the equation from the definition: $Novelty(S_B|S_A) := |S_B - (S_A \cap S_B)| = |S_B| - |(S_A \cap S_B)|$. This assumes that the initial reference synopsis from which IQN starts is given in a form that we can estimate its cardinality (in addition to having its MIPs representation). This is guaranteed as the query initiator's local query result forms the seed for the reference synopsis.

**Exploiting Hash Sketches.** Hash sketches can be used to estimate the cardinality of the union of two sets. Using the equation $|S_A \cap S_B| = |S_A| + |S_B| - |S_A \cup S_B|$, we can derive the overlap $|S_A \cap S_B|$ and subsequently our notion of novelty. Given hash sketches for all candidate peers and an (initially empty) hash sketch representing the result space already covered, one can create a hash sketch for the union of two sets by a bit-wise $OR$ operation, as the document that is responsible for a set bit will also be present in the combined collection. Inversely, if none of the documents in either collection has set a specific bit, there will also be no document in the combined collection setting this particular bit: $HS_{A\cup B}[i] = HS_A[i] \; OR \; HS_B[i] \; \forall i : 1 \leq i \leq n$.

**Exploiting Bloom Filters.** Given Bloom filter representations of the reference synopsis and of the additionally considered peer's collection, we need to estimate the novelty of peer $p$ to the query result. For this purpose, we first compute a Bloom filter $bf$ for the set difference by taking the bit-wise difference, that is: $bf[i] := bf_p[i] \wedge /bf_{ref}[i]$. This is not an accurate representation of the set difference; the bit-wise difference may lead to additional false positives in $bf$, but our experiments did not encounter dramatic problems with false positives due to this operation (unless there were already many false positives in the operands because of short bitvector length). Finally, we estimate the cardinality of the set difference from the number of set bits in $bf$.

### 5.3 Aggregate Synopses

After having selected the best peer in an iteration of the IQN method, we need to update the reference synopsis that represents the result space already covered with the expected contribution from the previously selected peers. This is conceptually a *union* operation, since the previous result space is increased with the results from the selected peer.

**Exploiting MIPs.** By design of MIPs, it is possible to form the MIPs representation for the union of two MIPs-approximated sets by creating a vector, taking the position-wise $min$ of the vectors. This is correct as for each permutation, the document yielding the minimum for the combined set is the minimum of the two minima. More formally, given $MIPs_A[]$ and $MIPs_B[]$, one can form $MIPs_{A\cup B}[]$ as follows $MIPs_{A\cup B}[i] = min\{MIPs_A[i], MIPs_B[i]\} \; \forall i : 1 \leq i \leq n$.

A nice property of MIPs that distinguishes this technique from hash sketches and Bloom filters is that this MIPs-based approximation of unions can be applied even if the MIPs vectors of the two operands have different lengths, i.e., have used a different number of permutations. In a large-scale P2P network with autonomous peers and high dynamics, there may be many reasons why individual peers want to choose the lengths of their MIPs synopses at their own discretion. The only agreement that needs to be disseminated among and obeyed by all participating peers is that they use the same sequence of hash functions for creating their permutations. Then, if two MIPs have different lengths, we an always use the smaller number of permutations as a common denominator. This loses accuracy in the result MIPs, but still yields a viable synopsis that can be further processed by the IQN algorithm (and possibly other components of a P2P search engine).

**Exploiting Hash Sketches.** Similarly, one can create a hash sketch for the union of two sets by a bit-wise $OR$ operation, as described in Section 5.2.

**Exploiting Bloom Filters.** For Bloom filters, forming the union is straightforward. By construction of the Bloom filters, one can create the Bloom filter for the combined set from the Bloom filters of two collections by again performing a bit-wise $OR$ operation: $BF_{A \cup B}[i] = BF_A[i]\ OR\ BF_B[i]\ \forall i : 1 \leq i \leq n$.

## 6 Multi-dimensional Queries

As the synopses posted by the peers are per term, there is a need to combine the synopses of all terms or query conditions for a multi-dimensional query appropriately. This issue primarily refers to the Aggregate-Synopses step of the IQN method (once we have an overall synopsis for capturing multi-keyword result estimates, the Select-Best-Peer step is the same as before). We have developed two techniques for this purpose, a per-peer aggregation method and a per-term aggregation method. They will be discussed the following subsections. We start, however, by discriminating two kinds of queries, conjunctive and disjunctive ones, and discussing their requirements for synopses aggregation.

### 6.1 Conjunctive vs. Disjunctive Queries

Two query execution models are common in information retrieval: disjunctive queries and conjunctive queries. Conjunctive queries require a document to contain *all* query terms (or a file to satisfy all specified attribute-value conditions), while disjunctive queries search for documents containing *any* (and ideally many) of the terms. Both query types can be either with ranking of the results (and would then typically be interested only in the top-k results) or with Boolean search predicates. While conjunctive queries have become common in simple IR systems with human interaction such as Web search engines and are much more frequent in database querying or file search, disjunctive query models are often used in environments with large, automatically generated queries or in the presence of query expansion. The latter is often the case in intranet search, corporate knowledge management, and business analytics.

The choice for one of these query models has implications for the creation of per-peer synopses from the original term-specific synopses. In the Select-Best-Peer stage of IQN, a peer's novelty has to be estimated based on all terms of a specific query. For conjunctive queries, the appropriate operation on the per-term synopses would, thus, be an intersection. For Bloom filters this is straightforward: we represent the intersection of the two sets by simply combining their corresponding Bloom filters (i.e., bit vectors) using a bitwise $AND$. However, we are not aware of any method to create meaningful intersections between synopses based on hash sketches, and for MIPs the prior literature does not offer any solutions either. For hash sketches a very crude approach would be use unions also for conjunctive queries; this would at least give a valid synopsis as unions are superset of intersections. But, of course, the accuracy of the synopses would drastically degrade. This is certainly an inherent disadvantage of hash sketches for our P2P query routing framework. For MIPs the same crude technique would be applicable, too, but there is a considerably better, albeit somewhat ad hoc, heuristic solution. When combining the mininum values under the same permutation from two different MIPs synopses, instead of using the minimum of the two values (like for union) we could use the maximum for intersection. The resulting combined MIPs synopsis is no longer the MIPs representation that we would compute from the real set intersection, but it can serve as an approximation. It is a conservative representation because the true minumum value under a permutation of the real set intersection can be no lower than the maximum of the two values from the corresponding MIPs synopses.

For a disjunctive query model, in contrast, the *union* operation suffices to form an aggregated per-peer synopsis from the term-specific synopses of a peer. This follows since any document being a member of any of the peer's index lists qualifies for the result. In Section 5.3 we have introduced ways of creating such synopses from the synopses of both sets.

In the following, we present two strategies for combining per-term synopses of different peers to assess their expected novelty with respect to a reference set and its synopsis. For Bloom filters or MIPs, these can handle both conjunctive or disjunctive queries; for hash sketches a low-error aggregation method for conjunctions is left for future work.

## 6.2 Per-Peer Collection Aggregation

The per-peer aggregation method first combines the term-specific set representations of a peer for all query terms (using union or intersection, depending on the query type and the underlying type of synopsis). This builds one query-specific combined synopsis for each peer, which is used by IQN, to estimate the peer's novelty with respect to the aggregated reference synopsis of the previously covered result space. After selecting the most promising peer, its combined synopsis is aggregated with the reference synopsis of the current IQN iteration.

## 6.3 Per-Term Collection Aggregation

The per-term aggregation method maintains *term-specific* reference synopses of the previously covered result space, $\sigma_{prev}(t)$, one for each term or attribute-value condition of the query. The term-specific synopses $\sigma(p,t)$ of each peer $p$, considered as a candidate by IQN, are now used to calculate *term-specific* novelty values. For the entire query, these values are simply summed up over all terms in the query. The summation is, of course, a crude estimate of the novelty of the contribution of $p$ for the entire query result. But this technique leads to a viable peer selection strategy.

Per-peer aggregation, discussed in the previous subsection, seems to be more intuitive and accurate, but the per-term aggregation method offers an interesting advantage: there is no need for an intersection of set synopses, even in the conjunctive query model. Instead, the magic lies in the aggregation of the term-specific novelty values. We believe that this aggregation technique can be further extended, e.g., for exploiting term correlation measures mined from the P2P system. Our MINERVA testbed has implemented both of the two presented aggregation techniques, for all three kinds of synopses.

## 7 Extensions

### 7.1 Score-Conscious Novelty Estimation Using Histograms

In the previous sections we have focused on techniques that treat collections as a *set* of documents. This might be useful in P2P file sharing applications but in ranked retrieval we can do better. Observe that we are more interested in the mutual overlap that different peers have in the higher-scoring portions of an index list. We employ histograms to put documents of each index list into cells, where each cell represents a score range of an index list.

Synopses are now produced separately for each histogram cell. We calculate the weighted novelty estimate between two statistics by performing a pairwise novelty estimation over all pairs of histogram cells, i.e., we estimate the novelties of all histogram cells of a peer's synopses with regard to the cells of another peer's synopses and aggregate these novelty values using a weighted sum, where the weight reflects the score range (i.e., we assign a higher weight for overlap among high-scoring cells).

### 7.2 Adaptive Synopses Lengths

As mentioned before, a large-scale P2P setting with high churn dictates that different peers may want to use synopses of different lengths. The MIPs-based techniques do indeed support this option (although it has a price in terms of potential reduction of accuracy).

In P2P Web search, an important scenario is the situation where each peer wants to invest a certain budget $B$ for the total space that all its per-term synopses require together. This is primarily to limit the network bandwidth that is consumed by posting the synopses to the directory. Although each individual synopsis is small, peers should batch multiple posts that are directed to the same recipient so that message sizes do indeed matter. Especially when directory entries are replicated for higher availability and when peers post frequent updates, the network efficiency of posting synopses is a critical issue.

In this framework, a peer with a total budget $B$ has the freedom to choose specific a length $len_j$ for the synopsis of term $j$, such that $\sum_{j=1}^{M} len_j = B$ where $M$ is the total number of terms.

This optimization problem is reminiscent of a knapsack problem. A heuristic approach that we have pursued is to choose $len_j$ in proportion to a notion of *benefit* for term $j$ at the given peer. Natural candidates for the benefit weights could be the length of the index list for term $j$, giving higher weight to lists with more documents, or the number of list entries with a relevance score above some threshold, or the number of list entries whose accumulated score mass equals the 90% quantile of the score distribution.

## 8 Experiments

### 8.1 Experimental Setup

One pivotal issue when designing our experiments was the absence of a standard benchmark. While there are benchmark collections for centralized Web search, it is not clear how to distribute such data across peers of a P2P network. Some previous studies partitioned the data into many small and disjoint pieces; but we do not think this is an adequate approach for P2P search with no central coordination and highly autonomous peers. In contrast, we expect a certain degree of overlap, with popular documents being indexed by a substantial fraction of all peers, but, at the same time, with a large number of documents only indexed by a tiny fraction of all peers.

For our experiments we have taken the complete GOV document collection, a crawl of the .gov Internet domain used in the TREC 2003 Web Track benchmark (http://trec.nist.gov). This data comprises about 1.5 million documents (mostly HTML and PDF). All recall measurements that we report below are relative to this centralized reference collection. So a recall of $x$ percent means that the P2P Web search system with IQN routing found in its result list $x$ percent of the results that a centralized search engine with the same scoring/ranking scheme found in the entire reference collection.

For our P2P testbed, we partitioned the whole data into disjoint fragments, and then we form collections placed onto peers by using various strategies to combine fragments. In one strategy, we split the whole data into $f$ fragments and created collections by choosing all subsets with $s$ fragments, thus, ending up with $\binom{f}{s}$ collections each of which was assigned to one peer. In a second strategy, we have split the entire dataset into 100 fragments and used the following sliding-window technique to form collections assigned to peers: the first peer receives $r$ (subsequent) fragments $f_1$ to $f_r$, the next peer receives the fragments $f_{1+offset}$ to $f_{r+offset}$, and so on. This way, we systematically control the overlap of peers.

For the query workload we took 10 queries from the topic-distillation part of the TREC 2003 Web Track benchmark [34]. These were relatively short multi-keyword queries, typical examples being "forest fire" or "pest safety control".

All experiments were conducted on the MINERVA testbed described in Section 4, with peers running on a PC cluster. We compared query routing based on the CORI method which is merely quality-driven (see Section 5.1) against the quality- and novelty-conscious IQN method. Recall that CORI is among the very best database selection methods for distributed IR. We measured the (relative) recall as defined above, for a specified number of peers to which the query was forwarded. In the experiments we varied this maximum number of peers per query. This notion of recall directly reflects the benefit/cost ratio of the different query routing methods and their underlying synopses.

## 8.2 Experimental Results

Figure 3 shows the recall results (micro-averaged over all our benchmark queries), using the $\binom{f}{s}$ technique in the chart on the left side and the sliding-window technique on the right side. More specifically we chose $f = 6$ and $s = 3$ for the left chart, which gave us $\binom{6}{3} = 20$ collections for 20 peers, and we chose $r = 10$ and $offset = 2$ for 50 collections on 50 peers in the sliding-window setup.

The charts show recall results for 4 variants of IQN: using MIPs or Bloom filter synopses with two different lengths. The shorter synopsis length was 1024 bits (32 permutations); the longer one was 2048 bits (64 permutations).

Figure 3 clearly demonstrates that all IQN variants outperform CORI by a substantial margin: in some cases, the recall for a cost-efficient, small number of peers, e.g., 5 peers, was more than 3 times higher, a very significant gain. Also note that in the more challenging sliding-window scenario, the IQN methods needed about 5 peers to reach 50% recall, whereas CORI required more than 20 peers.

In the comparison of the two different synopses techniques, our expectation, from the stand-alone experiments in Section 3, that MIPs can outperform Bloom filters were fully reconfirmed, now in the full application setting of P2P Web search. Especially for the smaller synopsis length of 1024 bits, the MIPs-based IQN beats Bloom filters by a significant margin in terms of recall for a given number of peers. In terms of number of peers required for achieving a given recall target, again the improvement is even more prominent. For example, IQN with 1024-bit Bloom filters required 9 peers to exceed 60 % recall, whereas IQN with MIPs synopses of the same length used only 6 peers. Doubling the bit length improved the recall of the Bloom filter variant, and led to minor gains for MIPs.

As the network cost of synopses posting (and updating) and the network cost and load per peer caused by query routing are the major performance issues in a P2P Web search setting, we conclude that IQN, especially in combination with short MIPs synopses, is a highly effective means of gaining efficiency, reducing the network and per-peer load, and thus improving throughput and response times of the entire P2P system.

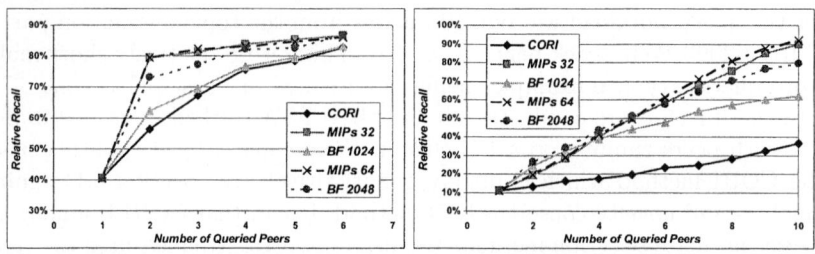

**Fig. 3.** Recall as a function of the number of peers involved per query

## 9 Conclusion and Future Work

This paper has developed the novel IQN query routing method for large-scale P2P systems, with applications in file and Web search. We have characterized and experimentally studied the strengths and weaknesses of three prominent types of statistical synopses, and we have shown how these basic techniques can be incorporated into and effectively leveraged for P2P query routing.

The experiments have proven the high potential of novelty-aware collection selection. It can drastically decrease the number of collections that have to be queried in order to achieve good recall. Depending on the actual degree of overlap between the collections, we have seen remarkable improvements especially at low numbers of queried peers. This fits exactly with our scenario of P2P Web search where we want to put low limits in the number of peers involved in a query.

Our future work will aim at further refinements and improvements of distributed statistics management in a highly dynamic P2P environment.

## References

[1] K. Aberer, M. Punceva, M. Hauswirth, and R. Schmidt. Improving data access in p2p systems. *IEEE Internet Computing*, 6(1):58–67, 2002.
[2] K. Aberer and J. Wu. Towards a common framework for peer-to-peer web retrieval. *From Integrated Publication and Information Systems to Virtual Information and Knowledge Environments*, 2005.
[3] D. Agrawal, A. E. Abbadi, and S. Suri. Attribute-based access to distributed data over p2p networks. *DNIS*, 2005.
[4] W.-T. Balke, W. Nejdl, W. Siberski, and U. Thaden. Dl meets p2p - distributed document retrieval based on classification and content. *ECDL*, 2005.
[5] M. Bender, S. Michel, P. Triantafillou, G. Weikum, and C. Zimmer. Improving collection selection with overlap awareness in p2p search engines. *SIGIR*, 2005.
[6] M. Bender, S. Michel, P. Triantafillou, G. Weikum, and C. Zimmer. Minerva: Collaborative p2p search. *VLDB*, 2005.
[7] B. H. Bloom. Space/time trade-offs in hash coding with allowable errors. *Commun. ACM*, 13(7):422–426, 1970.
[8] Broder. On the resemblance and containment of documents. *SEQUENCES*, 1997.
[9] A. Z. Broder, M. Charikar, A. M. Frieze, and M. Mitzenmacher. Min-wise independent permutations (extended abstract). *STOC*, 1998.
[10] A. Z. Broder, M. Charikar, A. M. Frieze, and M. Mitzenmacher. Min-wise independent permutations. *Journal of Computer and System Sciences*, 60(3), 2000.
[11] J. W. Byers, J. Considine, M. Mitzenmacher, and S. Rost. Informed content delivery across adaptive overlay networks. *IEEE/ACM Trans. Netw.*, 12(5):767–780, 2004.
[12] J. Callan. Distributed information retrieval. *Advances in information retrieval, Kluwer Academic Publishers.*, pages 127–150, 2000.
[13] J. P. Callan, Z. Lu, and W. B. Croft. Searching distributed collections with inference networks. *SIGIR*, 1995.
[14] P. Cao and Z. Wang. Efficient top-k query calculation in distributed networks. *PODC*, 2004.

[15] A. Crainiceanu, P. Linga, A. Machanavajjhala, J. Gehrke, and J. Shanmugasundaram. An indexing framework for peer-to-peer systems. *SIGMOD*, 2004.
[16] M. Durand and P. Flajolet. Loglog counting of large cardinalities. In G. Di Battista and U. Zwick, editors, *ESA, LNCS-2832*, 2003.
[17] L. Fan, P. Cao, J. M. Almeida, and A. Z. Broder. Summary cache: a scalable wide-area web cache sharing protocol. *IEEE/ACM Trans. Netw.*, 8(3), 2000.
[18] P. Flajolet and G. N. Martin. Probabilistic counting algorithms for data base applications. *Journal of Computer and System Sciences*, 31(2):182–209, 1985.
[19] S. Ganguly, M. Garofalakis, and R. Rastogi. Processing set expressions over continuous update streams. *SIGMOD*, 2003.
[20] L. Gravano, H. Garcia-Molina, and A. Tomasic. Gloss: text-source discovery over the internet. *ACM Trans. Database Syst.*, 24(2):229–264, 1999.
[21] T. Hernandez and S. Kambhampati. Improving text collection selection with coverage and overlap statistics. *WWW*, 2005.
[22] R. Huebsch, J. M. Hellerstein, N. L. Boon, T. Loo, S. Shenker, and I. Stoica. Querying the internet with Pier. *VLDB*, 2003.
[23] J. Li, B. Loo, J. Hellerstein, F. Kaashoek, D. Karger, and R. Morris. On the feasibility of peer-to-peer web indexing and search. *IPTPS*, 2003.
[24] W. Meng, C. T. Yu, and K.-L. Liu. Building efficient and effective metasearch engines. *ACM Computing Surveys*, 34(1):48–89, 2002.
[25] S. Michel, P. Triantafillou, and G. Weikum. KLEE: A framework for distributed top-k query algorithms. *VLDB*, 2005.
[26] M. Mitzenmacher. Compressed bloom filters. *IEEE/ACM Trans. Netw.*, 10(5):604–612, 2002.
[27] Z. Nie, S. Kambhampati, and T. Hernandez. Bibfinder/statminer: Effectively mining and using coverage and overlap statistics in data integration. *VLDB*, 2003.
[28] H. Nottelmann and N. Fuhr. Evaluating different methods of estimating retrieval quality for resource selection. *SIGIR*, 2003.
[29] S. Ratnasamy, P. Francis, M. Handley, R. Karp, and S. Schenker. A scalable content-addressable network. *SIGCOMM*, 2001.
[30] P. Reynolds and A. Vahdat. Efficient peer-to-peer keyword searching. *Middleware*, 2003.
[31] A. Rowstron and P. Druschel. Pastry: Scalable, decentralized object location, and routing for large-scale peer-to-peer systems. *Middleware*, 2001.
[32] L. Si, R. Jin, J. Callan, and P. Ogilvie. A language modeling framework for resource selection and results merging. *CIKM*, 2002.
[33] I. Stoica, R. Morris, D. Karger, M. F. Kaashoek, and H. Balakrishnan. Chord: A scalable peer-to-peer lookup service for internet applications. *SIGCOMM*, 2001.
[34] Text REtrieval Conference (TREC). http://trec.nist.gov/.
[35] P. Triantafillou and T. Pitoura. Towards a unifying framework for complex query processing over structured peer-to-peer data networks. *DBISP2P*, 2003.
[36] Y. Wang and D. J. DeWitt. Computing pagerank in a distributed internet search engine system. *VLDB*, 2004.
[37] J. Zhang and T. Suel. Efficient query evaluation on large textual collections in a peer-to-peer environment. *5th IEEE International Conference on Peer-to-Peer Computing*, 2005.
[38] Y. Zhang, J. Callan, and T. Minka. Novelty and redundancy detection in adaptive filtering. *SIGIR*, 2002.

# Efficient Quantile Retrieval on Multi-dimensional Data[*]

Man Lung Yiu[1], Nikos Mamoulis[1], and Yufei Tao[2]

[1] Department of Computer Science, University of Hong Kong,
Pokfulam Road, Hong Kong
{mlyiu2, nikos}@cs.hku.hk
[2] Department of Computer Science, City University of Hong Kong,
Tat Chee Avenue, Kowloon, Hong Kong
taoyf@cs.cityu.edu.hk

**Abstract.** Given a set of $N$ multi-dimensional points, we study the computation of $\phi$-quantiles according to a ranking function $F$, which is provided by the user at runtime. Specifically, $F$ computes a score based on the coordinates of each point; our objective is to report the object whose score is the $\phi N$-th smallest in the dataset. $\phi$-quantiles provide a succinct summary about the $F$-distribution of the underlying data, which is useful for online decision support, data mining, selectivity estimation, query optimization, etc. Assuming that the dataset is indexed by a spatial access method, we propose several algorithms for retrieving a quantile efficiently. Analytical and experimental results demonstrate that a branch-and-bound method is highly effective in practice, outperforming alternative approaches by a significant factor.

## 1 Introduction

We study quantile computation of a *derived measure* over multi-dimensional data. Specifically, given (i) a set $P$ of $N$ points in $d$-dimensional space, (ii) a continuous function $F : \mathbb{R}^d \to \mathbb{R}$, and (iii) a value $\phi \in [0, 1]$, a quantile query retrieves the $\phi N$-th smallest $F$-value of the objects in $P$. For instance, the median corresponds to the 0.5-quantile, whereas the maximum is the 1-quantile. Quantiles provide a succinct summary of a data distribution, finding application in online decision support, data mining, selectivity estimation, query optimization, etc.

Consider a mobile phone company that has conducted a survey on customers' preferences regarding their favorite service plans. The two dimensions in Figure 1a capture two properties of a monthly plan (e.g., the price and amount of air-time); each white point represents the preferences of a customer on these properties. Assume that the company is planning to launch a new plan corresponding to the black dot $q$. To evaluate the potential market popularity of $q$, the manager would be interested in the distribution of the similarity between $q$ and customers' preferences. For this purpose, $F$ may be defined as the Euclidean distance between $q$ and a white point and quantiles for various values of $\phi$ could be retrieved. As another (spatial) example, assume that point $q$ in Figure 1a is a pizza shop and the white points correspond to residential buildings. The

---
[*] Work supported by grants HKU 7380/02E and CityU 1163/04E from Hong Kong RGC, and SRG grant (Project NO: 7001843) from City University of Hong Kong.

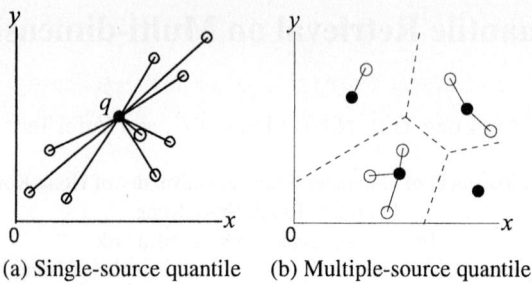

(a) Single-source quantile  (b) Multiple-source quantile

**Fig. 1.** Examples of quantiles based on derived Euclidean distances

*median* residential building distance (from the pizza shop) might be useful to the shop owner, in order to plan adequate number of staff for pizzadelivery.

The query in Figure 1a is a *single-source* query because the ordering of data points depends on one source only. A more complex scenario is shown in Figure 1b, where the white points correspond to residential areas, and the black dots represent supermarkets. Each dashed polygon is the "influence region" [21] of a supermarket, which covers those residential areas that find it as the nearest supermarket. A market analyst would like to obtain the distribution of the distance from a residential area to its nearest supermarket, in order to decide a suitable location to open a new supermarket. A quantile query in this case is a *multiple-source* one, because the ordering of the white points is determined by multiple sources (the supermarkets).

Our goal is to compute a quantile by accessing only a fraction of the dataset, *without knowing the ranking function $F$ in advance*. Previous research [1, 14, 15, 9, 8] in the database community focused on computing/maintaining approximate quantiles, whereas we aim at obtaining the *exact* results. Furthermore, our problem is completely different than the so-called "spatial quantiles" in computational geometry [12, 5]. For example, a *spatial center* is a location $p$ (not necessarily an actual point in the dataset) such that every hyperplane containing $p$ defines a "balanced" partitioning of the dataset (i.e., the numbers of points in the two partitions differ by less than a threshold). Our quantile, on the other hand, is a *one-dimensional* value in the output domain of $F$.

We develop several solutions that leverage a multi-dimensional index (e.g., R-tree) to prune the search space, starting with a variation of the incremental nearest neighbor (INN) algorithm [11]. This algorithm is not efficient as its cost linearly increases with $\phi$. We then present a faster algorithm, which iteratively approximates the $F$-distribution using linear functions. Our last solution combines the branch-and-bound framework with novel heuristics that minimize the I/O cost based on several problem characteristics. We analyze the relative performance of the proposed approaches, theoretically and experimentally. Finally, we generalize our algorithms to other variations of the problem including progressive retrieval, batch processing, etc.

The rest of the paper is organized as follows. Section 2 reviews related work. Section 3 formally defines the problem, while Section 4 presents the details of the proposed algorithms, and analyzes their performance. Section 5 extends our solutions to other types of quantile retrieval. Section 6 contains an experimental evaluation, and finally, Section 7 concludes the paper with directions for future work.

## 2 Related Work

We treat quantile computation of a derived measure as a spatial query. We review indexing and query evaluation for multidimensional data in Section 2.1. Section 2.2 surveys existing methods for retrieving quantiles on non-indexed data.

### 2.1 Spatial Query Processing

R-trees [10] have been extensively used for indexing spatial data. Figure 2a shows a set of points on the 2D plane, indexed by the R-tree in Figure 2b. The R-tree is balanced and each node occupies one disk page. Each entry stores the MBR (minimum bounding rectangle) that encloses all spatial objects in the corresponding sub-tree. Leaf nodes store object MBRs and their record-ids in the spatial relation that stores the objects. R-trees were originally designed for spatial range queries, but they can be used to process more advanced spatial queries, like nearest neighbors [11], spatial joins [4], reverse nearest neighbors [21], skyline queries [18], etc.

The aggregate R-tree (aR-tree) [13, 17] is a variant of the R-tree where each entry is augmented with an aggregate measure of all data objects in the sub-tree pointed by it. The aR-tree was originally designed for the efficient evaluation of spatial aggregate queries, where measures (e.g., sales, traffic, etc.) in a spatial region (e.g., a country, a city center) are aggregated. In Section 4, we show how aR-trees, augmented with COUNT measures, can be exploited for efficient quantile computation.

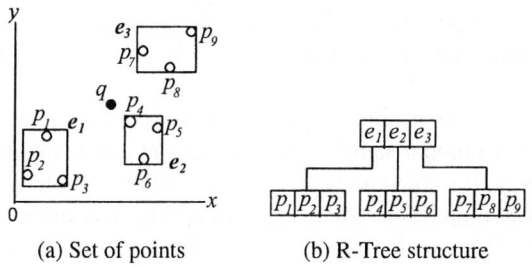

(a) Set of points     (b) R-Tree structure

**Fig. 2.** R-Tree example

Our work is also relevant to nearest neighbor (NN) queries. A NN query asks for the point closest to an input point $q$. INN, the state-of-the-art algorithm for NN search [11], retrieves the nearest neighbors of $q$ *incrementally* in ascending order of their distance to $q$. INN browses the R-tree and organizes the entries of the visited nodes in a min-heap based on their distances to $q$. First, all root entries are enheaped. When a non-leaf entry is dequeued, its child node is accessed and all entries in the child node are enheaped. When a leaf entry (data object) is dequeued, it is guaranteed to be the next nearest neighbor.

### 2.2 Quantile Computation

The computation of a quantile is known as the selection problem in the theory community. [19] is an overview of theoretical results on the selection problem. Sorting the elements is a straightforward solution but this requires $O(N \log N)$ comparisons. An early algorithm in [3] needs only $O(N)$ comparisons but it may access some elements multiple times. It was shown in [16] that $O(N^{\frac{1}{t}})$ memory is necessary and sufficient for solving the selection problem in $t$ passes of data.

This theoretical result implies that the *exact* quantile (selection) problem can only be answered in multiple passes with limited memory. Hence, the database community attempted to compute *approximate* quantiles with only one pass of the data. An element is an $\epsilon$-approximate $\phi$-quantile if its rank is within the range $[(\phi - \epsilon)N, (\phi + \epsilon)N]$. [1, 14, 15, 9, 8] presented algorithms for retrieving an approximate quantile with limited memory in at most one pass of data. The best result [9] requires only $O(\frac{1}{\epsilon} \log(\epsilon N))$ memory. Recently, [6] studied computation of biased (extreme) quantiles in data streams, which requires less space than the upper bound given by [9]. Observe that the memory required by the above methods is at least proportional to $1/\epsilon$. Thus, they are not appropriate for computing exact quantiles (or approximate quantiles with very small $\epsilon$).

In our problem setting, the ranking function $F$ is dynamic and only known at runtime. Due to this dynamic nature, pre-materialized results may not be used. In addition, we aim at utilizing existing indexes to minimize the data required to be accessed in order to compute the quantile, whereas existing techniques [1, 14, 15, 9, 8, 6] operate on non-indexed, one-dimensional data. Their focus is the minimization of error, given a memory budget, where one pass over the data is essential. The problem of computing quantiles on indexed one-dimensional data (i.e., by a $B^+$-tree) is not interesting, since the high levels of the tree are already an equi-depth histogram that can be easily used to derive the quantiles efficiently. On the other hand, there is no total ordering of multi-dimensional data, thus R-trees cannot be used directly for ad-hoc spatial ranking.

A viable alternative for handling dynamic ranking functions in multidimensional data is to maintain a random sample from the dataset and compute an approximate quantile value from it. It is known [2] that, for any random sample of size $O(\frac{1}{\epsilon^2} \log \frac{1}{\delta})$, the $\phi$-quantile of the sample is also an $\epsilon$-approximate quantile of the dataset with probability at least $1 - \delta$. The number of required samples directly translates to the required memory size. Thus, random sampling technique is inadequate for retrieving exact quantiles (where $\epsilon = 0$) or approximate quantiles with very small $\epsilon$. In this paper, we propose *index-based* methods for efficient computation of *exact* quantiles on derived ranking measures over multidimensional data.

## 3 Problem Definition

Let $P$ be a set of $N$ $d$-dimensional points and $F : \mathbb{R}^d \to \mathbb{R}$ be a continuous function on the domain of $P$. The continuity property implies that points close together have similar $F$ values. The coordinate of a point $p$ along the $i$-th dimension is denoted by $p(i)$. Given a real value $\phi$ in the range $[0, 1]$, a $\phi$-quantile query returns the $\phi N$-th smallest $F$ value among all points in the dataset. Without loss of generality, we assume that $\phi N$ is an integer.

We assume that the dataset is indexed by a COUNT aR-tree. Each entry in the tree is augmented with the number of points in its subtree. The ranking function $F$ is application-dependent. Moreover, we require two bounding functions $F_l$ and $F_u$, which take the MBR of a non-leaf entry $e$ as input and return the range $[F_l(e), F_u(e)]$ of possible $F$ values for any point in it. Given an entry $e$ of the aR-tree, the derived range $[F_l(e), F_u(e)]$ is used by our algorithms to determine whether the entry can be pruned or not from search. Computation of tight $F_l$ and $F_u$ bounds is essential for good query performance. Although our discussion assumes aR-trees, our framework is also applicable to other hierarchical spatial indexes (where non-leaf nodes are augmented with aggregate information [13]).

Our aim is to provide a generic framework for processing quantile queries using aR-trees. In the following, we provide examples of four ranking functions $F$. The first two define *single-source* quantile queries and take one (or zero) parameter (e.g., a query point). The last two define *multiple-source* quantile queries with multiple parameters.

**Distance ranking.** Each object in a dataset is associated with a rank based on its distance from a reference query point $q$. For an MBR $e$, we have $F_l(e) = mindist(q, e)$ and $F_u(e) = maxdist(q, e)$; the minimum and maximum distances [11], respectively, between any point in $e$ and $q$.

**Linear ranking.** A linear function combines coordinate values of a point into a single score. Such a function is the generalization of the SUM function used in top-$k$ queries [7]. Given $d$ weights $w_1, w_2, \cdots, w_d$, the ranking function $F$ is defined as $F(p) = \sum_{i \in [1,d]} w_i \cdot p(i)$. For an MBR $e$, we have $F_l(e) = \sum_{i \in [1,d]} w_i \cdot e^\vdash(i)$ and $F_u(e) = \sum_{i \in [1,d]} w_i \cdot e^\dashv(i)$, where $e^\vdash(i)$ and $e^\dashv(i)$ are the lower and upper bounds of the extent of $e$ on the $i$-th dimension.

**Nearest-site distance ranking.** This scenario is a generalization of simple distance ranking. We consider the ranking of objects based on their distances from their nearest query point in a given set. Given query points (sites) $q_1, q_2, \cdots, q_m$, the ranking function $F$ is defined as $F(p) = \min_{i \in [1,m]} dist(q_i, p)$, where $dist$ denotes the distance function (e.g., Euclidean distance). We have $F_l(e) = \min_{i \in [1,m]} mindist(q_i, e)$ and $F_u(e) = \min_{i \in [1,m]} maxdist(q_i, e)$, for an MBR $e$. We assume that the number $m$ of query points is small enough to fit in memory. For example, the data points represent users and the query points represent facilities (e.g., restaurants in the town).

**Furthest-site distance ranking.** Unlike the previous example, we consider the ranking of objects based on their distances from their furthest query point in a given set. For instance, a small group of people (modeled as query points) decide to meet at the same restaurant. The maximum distance of the restaurant from the group reflects their meeting time. Given query points (sites) $q_1, q_2, \cdots, q_m$, the ranking function $F$ is defined as $F(p) = \max_{i \in [1,m]} dist(q_i, p)$, where $dist$ denotes the distance function (e.g. Euclidean distance). For an MBR $e$, we have $F_l(e) = \max_{i \in [1,m]} mindist(q_i, e)$ and $F_u(e) = \max_{i \in [1,m]} maxdist(q_i, e)$. As in the previous example, we assume that the number $m$ of query points is small enough to fit in memory.

## 4 Quantile Computation Algorithms

In this section, we propose three quantile computation algorithms that apply on an aR-tree. The first method is a simple extension of a nearest neighbor search technique.

The second solution is based on iterative approximation. Section 4.3 discusses an optimized branch-and-bound method for computing quantiles. Finally, a qualitative cost analysis of the algorithms is presented in Section 4.4.

### 4.1 Incremental Search

The *incremental* quantile computation algorithm (INC) is a generalization of the incremental nearest neighbor (INN) algorithm [11]. It simply retrieves the point with the next lowest $F$ value until the $\phi N$-th object is found. A pseudocode for INC is shown in Figure 3. The algorithm employs a min-heap $H$ for organizing the entries $e$ to be visited in ascending order of their $F_l(e)$ value. A counter $cnt$ (initially 0) keeps track of the number of points seen so far. First, all entries of the root node are enheaped. When an entry $e'$ is deheaped, we check whether it is a non-leaf entry. If so, its child node is accessed and all entries in the node are enheaped. Otherwise ($e'$ is a leaf entry), $e'$ is guaranteed to have the next lowest $F$ value, and the counter $cnt$ is incremented by 1. The algorithm terminates when the counter reaches $\phi N$.

---

**Algorithm INC**(R-tree $R$, Function $F$, Value $\phi$)
1    $cnt:=0$;
2    $H:=\emptyset$;
3    **for each** entry $e \in R.root$
4        $Enheap(H, \langle e, F_l(e) \rangle)$;
5    **while** ($H \neq \emptyset$)
6        $e':=Deheap(H)$;
7        **if** ($e'$ is a non-leaf entry) **then**
8            read the node $n$ pointed by $e'$;
9            **for each** entry $e \in n$
10               $Enheap(H, \langle e, F_l(e) \rangle)$;
11       **else**
12           $cnt:=cnt+1$;
13           **if** ($cnt = \phi N$) **then**
14               **return** $F(e')$;

**Fig. 3.** The incremental search algorithm (INC)

---

Observe that the cost of INC is sensitive to $\phi$. For large values of $\phi$, many objects are accessed before the algorithm terminates. Next, we will present other quantile algorithms, which use the aggregate values stored at the high levels of the aR-tree and their performance is less sensitive to the value $\phi$.

### 4.2 Iterative Approximation

The motivation behind our second algorithm is to search the quantiles that correspond to some $F$ values and progressively refine an approximation for the desired $\phi$-quantile. Figure 4a illustrates an example distribution of $\phi$ as a function of $F$ values. Clearly, we do not know every value on this graph a priori as the ranking function $F$ is only known at runtime. Suppose we want to find the 0.25-quantile (i.e. $\phi = 0.25$). We initially obtain lower ($F_l(R)$) and upper bounds ($F_u(R)$) for the potential values of $F$ without any cost, according to the MBR of the aR-tree $R$. In the figure, $F_l(R)$ corresponds to point $a$ and $F_u(R)$ to point $b$. We reduce the computation of the 0.25-quantile to a numerical problem and apply *the interpolation method* [20] for solving it. The main idea is to approximate the distribution function as a straight line and *iteratively* "probe" for exact quantile values corresponding to the expected values based on the approximation, until the error is small enough for the $F$ value to correspond to an exact quantile.

Continuing with the example, we first connect points $a$ and $b$ by a straight line, and take the $F$-coordinate $\lambda_1$ of the intersection (see Figure 4a) between the line and a horizontal line at $\phi = 0.25$ (i.e., $\lambda_1$ is our estimate of the 0.25-quantile). Then, we compute the point $c$ on the *actual $\phi$-$F$ curve* whose $F$-coordinate is $\lambda_1$ (computation of $c$ will be explained shortly). Since the $\phi$-coordinate of $c$ is smaller than 0.25 (i.e., $\lambda_1$ *underestimates* the 0.25-quantile), we (i) obtain the $F$-coordinate $\lambda_2$ of the intersection between the horizontal line $\phi = 0.25$ and the line connecting $c$, $b$, and (ii) retrieve the point $d$ (Figure 4b) on the actual curve with $\lambda_2$ as the $F$-coordinate. As $\lambda_2$ *overestimates* the 0.25-quantile (the $\phi$-coordinate of $d$ is greater than 0.25), we perform another iteration by connecting $c$ and $d$, which leads to $e$ in Figure 4c. Since the $\phi$-coordinate of $e$ equals 0.25, the algorithm terminates.

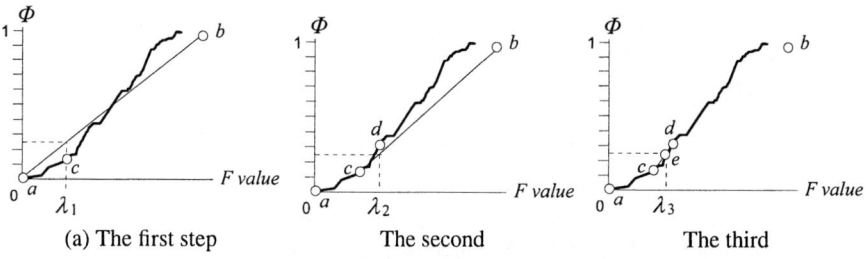

**Fig. 4.** Iterative approximation example

We now discuss how to use the aR-tree in order to find a point that corresponds to a value $\lambda$ for $F$. This is done using the RANGE_COUNT function shown in Figure 5, which counts the number of data points with $F$ values not greater than $\lambda$, while traversing the tree. The function is first invoked at the root node of an aR-tree. For an intermediate entry $e$, if $F_u(e) \le \lambda$, then all the points under the subtree fall in the range and the counter is incremented by COUNT($e$), the number of points under the subtree of $e$. note that COUNT($e$) can directly be retrieved from the tree node containing $e$. Otherwise ($F_u(e) > \lambda$), if $e$ is a non-leaf entry and $F_l(e) \le \lambda$, then it is possible that some points under $e$ lie in the query range. Thus, the function is called recursively to compute the remaining count of data points within the range.

Figure 6 shows the pseudocode of the iterative approximation algorithm (APX). First, the bounds $\lambda_l$ and $\lambda_u$ of the $F$-range that includes the $\phi$-quantile are initialized to $F_l(R)$ and $F_u(R)$, respectively. In addition, values $cnt_l$ and $cnt_u$ (conservative approximations of quantiles at the end-points of the range) are initialized to 0 and $N$ respectively. At Line 4, we link points ($\lambda_l, cnt_l$) and ($\lambda_u, cnt_u$) on the $\phi$-$F$ curve (like

```
Algorithm RANGE_COUNT(aR-tree node n, Function F, Value λ)
1    cnt:=0;
2    for each entry e ∈ n
3       if (F_u(e) ≤ λ) then
4          cnt:=cnt+COUNT(e);
5       else if (F_l(e) ≤ λ ∧ e is a non-leaf entry) then
6          read the node n' pointed by e;
7          cnt:=cnt+RANGE_COUNT(n', F, λ);
8    return cnt;
```

**Fig. 5.** Counting points in a generalized range

```
Algorithm Iterative_Approximation(aR-tree R, Function F, Value φ)
1    (λ_l, cnt_l):=(F_l(R), 0); // conservative lower end
2    (λ_u, cnt_u):=(F_u(R), N); // conservative upper end
3    do
4       λ:=λ_l + (λ_u−λ_l)/(cnt_u−cnt_l) · (φN − cnt_l); // linear approximation of quantile value
5       cnt:=RANGE_COUNT(R.root, F, λ); // actual rank for the estimated value
6       if (cnt > φN)
7          (λ_u, cnt_u):=(λ, cnt);
8       else
9          (λ_l, cnt_l):=(λ, cnt);
10   while (cnt ≠ φN);
11   return λ;
```

**Fig. 6.** The iterative approximation algorithm (APX)

the one of Figure 4) by a straight line, and use the line to estimate a value $\lambda$ for the $\phi$-quantile. Function RANGE_COUNT is then used to compute the number $cnt$ of points whose $F$ value is at most $\lambda$. After that, Lines 6–9 update the coordinates for the next iteration. The loop iterates until the count $cnt$ converges to $\phi N$.

### 4.3 Branch-and-Bound Quantile Retrieval

Although the iterative approximation algorithm is less sensitive to $\phi$, it is not very efficient as it needs to access the aR-tree multiple times. We now present a branch-and-bound algorithm for computing quantiles. Before we describe the algorithm, we introduce some notations and pruning rules employed by it.

**Definition 1.** *Let $S$ be a set of aR-tree entries. For any $e \in S$, $\omega_l(e, S)$ denotes the maximum possible number of objects whose $F$ value is at most $F_u(e)$ and $\omega_u(e, S)$ denotes the maximum possible number of objects whose $F$ value is at least $F_l(e)$. Formally:*

$$\omega_l(e, S) = \sum_{e' \in S, F_l(e') \leq F_u(e)} \text{COUNT}(e') \quad (1)$$

$$\omega_u(e, S) = \sum_{e' \in S, F_u(e') \geq F_l(e)} \text{COUNT}(e') \quad (2)$$

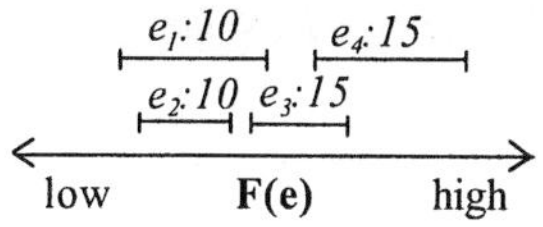

```
         e₁:10      e₄:15
       |------|    |------|
         e₂:10 e₃:15
       |------||------|
    <─────────────────────>
      low      F(e)     high
```

**Fig. 7.** Pruning example

Measures $\omega_l(e, S)$ and $\omega_u(e, S)$ form the basis of pruning rules for aR-tree entries during branch-and-bound traversal for quantile computation. When the context is clear, we sometimes drop the symbol $S$ and simply use $\omega_l(e)$ and $\omega_u(e)$. To illustrate the use of these measures, consider Figure 7, showing the $F$ range intervals of four aR-tree entries $S = \{e_1, \ldots, e_4\}$. Let $\phi = 0.5$ and $N = 50$. Note that $\omega_l(e_2) = 10 + 10 = 20 < \phi N$, which means that all objects $p$ in the subtree of $e_2$ have ranks lower than the quantile. Thus, we can safely prune $e_2$ and avoid accessing its subtree during quantile computation. On the other hand, we cannot prune entry $e_1$, since $\omega_l(e_1) = 10 + 10 + 15 = 35 \geq \phi N$. Symmetrically, by computing whether $\omega_u(e_i) < (1 - \phi)N + 1$, we can determine if an entry can be pruned due to the lower ranking bound of objects in it.

**The algorithm.** We can now describe in detail our branch-and-bound (BAB) quantile computation algorithm (shown in Figure 8). We initialize two variables $cur_l$ and $cur_u$, which capture the number of objects guaranteed to be before and after the $\phi$-quantile, respectively. The root of the aR-tree is visited and all entries there are inserted into set $S$. Lines 6–8 attempt to prune entries, all objects under which have rankings lower than $\phi N$. For this, we examine the entries ordered by their upper ranking bound $F_u(e)$. Lemma 1 (trivially proven) states the pruning condition. Lemma 2 suggests that $\omega_l$ values of entries can be incrementally computed. We can prune all entries $e$ satisfying $F_u(e) \leq F_u(e_l^*)$ where $e_l^*$ is the entry with the greatest $F_u$ value satisfying the pruning condition. Lines 12–14 perform symmetric pruning; entries are examined in descending order of their lower bounds in order to eliminate those for which all indexed objects have rankings higher than $\phi N$. Finally, in Lines 18–21, a heuristic is used to choose a (non-leaf) entry $e_c$ from $S$, visit the corresponding node, and update $S$ with its entries. Details on how to prioritize the entries will be discussed shortly. The algorithm terminates when the requested quantile is found (Line 10 or 16).

**Lemma 1.** *Pruning condition: Among the objects that were pruned, let $cur_l$ ($cur_u$) be the number of objects with $F$ values smaller (greater) than the quantile object. An aR-tree entry $e$ can be pruned if $cur_l + \omega_l(e) < \phi N$ or $cur_u + \omega_u(e) < N(1 - \phi) + 1$.*

**Lemma 2.** *Efficient computation: Let $l_1, l_2, \cdots, l_{|S|}$ ($u_1, u_2, \cdots, u_{|S|}$) be aR-tree entries in a set $S$ such that $F_u(l_i) \leq F_u(l_{i+1})$ ($F_l(u_i) \geq F_l(u_{i+1})$). We have $\omega_l(l_{i+1}, S) = \omega_l(l_i, S) + \sum_{e \in S, F_u(l_i) < F_l(e) \leq F_u(l_{i+1})} \text{COUNT}(e)$ and $\omega_u(u_{i+1}, S) = \omega_u(u_i, S) + \sum_{e \in S, F_l(u_i) > F_u(e) \geq F_l(u_{i+1})} \text{COUNT}(e)$.*

**Management of $S$.** We propose to use two main-memory B$^+$-trees ($T_l$ and $T_u$) for indexing the entries in $S$; one based on their $F_l$ values and another based on their $F_u$ values. Insertion (deletion) of an entry takes $O(log|S|)$ time in both trees. The rationale of using the above data structure is that it supports efficient pruning of entries. Lemma 2

**Algorithm BaB_Quantile**(aR-tree $R$, Function $F$, Value $\phi$)
1  $cur_l:=0$; $cur_u:=0$;
2  $S:=\varnothing$;
3  **for each** entry $e \in R.root$
4    $S:=S \cup \{e\}$;
5  **while** ($true$)
6    $e_l^* :=$ entry in $S$ with the greatest $F_u$ value satisfying $cur_l + \omega_l(e_l^*) < \phi N$ ;
7    **for each** entry $e \in S$ satisfying $F_u(e) \leq F_u(e_l^*)$ // pruning entries on the lower side
8      $S:=S - \{e\}$; $cur_l:=cur_l+\text{COUNT}(e)$;
9    $e_l :=$ entry in $S$ with the minimum $F_u$ value;
10   **if** ($cur_l = \phi N - 1 \land \omega_l(e_l) = 1 \land e_l$ is a leaf entry) **then**
11     **return** $F(e_l)$;
12   $e_u^* :=$ entry in $S$ with the least $F_l$ value satisfying $cur_u + \omega_u(e_u^*) < N(1 - \phi) + 1$ ;
13   **for each** entry $e \in S$ satisfying $F_l(e) \geq F_l(e_u^*)$ // pruning entries on the upper side
14     $S:=S - \{e\}$; $cur_u:=cur_u+\text{COUNT}(e)$;
15   $e_u :=$ entry in $S$ with the maximum $F_l$ value;
16   **if** ($cur_u = N(1 - \phi) \land \omega_u(e_u) = 1 \land e_u$ is a leaf entry) **then**
17     **return** $F(e_u)$;
18   **if** ($\phi \leq 0.5$) // heuristic for picking the next non-leaf entry to expand
19     set $e_c$ as the non-leaf entry, overlapping $e_l$'s $F$-interval, with the maximum count in $S$;
20   **else**
21     set $e_c$ as the non-leaf entry, overlapping $e_u$'s $F$-interval, with the maximum count in $S$;
22   $S:=S - \{e_c\}$;
23   access node $n'$ pointed by $e_c$;
24   **for each** entry $e \in n'$
25     $S:=S \cup \{e\}$;

**Fig. 8.** The branch-and-bound quantile computation algorithm (BAB)

suggests that $\omega_l$ ($\omega_u$) values of entries can be incrementally computed. Now, we discuss how to prune entries with rankings guaranteed to be lower than $\phi N$. First, we get the entry with lowest $F_u$ value from $T_u$ and then compute its $\omega_l$ value (by accessing entries in $T_l$ in ascending order). Next, we get the entry with the next lowest $F_u$ value from $T_u$ and compute its $\omega_l$ value (by accessing entries in $T_l$ in ascending order, starting from the last accessed location). The above process repeats until the current entry in $T_u$ does not satisfy the pruning condition in Lemma 1. Notice that entries (in $T_l$ and $T_u$) are accessed sequentially through sibling links in B$^+$-tree leaf nodes. Let $e_l^*$ be the entry with the greatest $F_u$ value satisfying the pruning condition. Then, we remove all leaf entries $e$ in $T_u$ satisfying $F_u(e) \leq F_u(e_l^*)$ and delete their corresponding entries in $T_l$. A symmetric procedure is applied to prune entries with rankings guaranteed to be greater than $\phi N$.

**Order of visited nodes.** We now elaborate on which non-leaf entry should be selected for further expansion (Lines 18–21 in Figure 8); the order of visited aR-tree nodes affects the cost of the algorithm. Before reaching Line 18, entries $e_l$ and $e_u$ have the minimum value of $\omega_l(e_l)$ and $\omega_u(e_u)$ respectively. Intuitively, we should attempt reducing the value $\omega_l(e_l)$ (or $\omega_u(e_u)$) so that entry $e_l$ (or $e_u$) can be pruned. For entry $e_l$, value $\omega_l(e_l)$ is determined by the count of other entries whose $F$-interval intersects that of the entry $e_l$. Thus, it suffices to identify the non-leaf entry that contributes the most to $w_l(e_l)$ (*maximum non-leaf component*). Lemma 3 guarantees that such a non-leaf component always exists. Similarly, we can also compute the maximum non-leaf component of $w_u(e_u)$. The question now is whether the removal of the maximum non-leaf component of $w_l(e_l)$ or that of $w_u(e_u)$ leads to lower overall I/O cost. Note that the algorithm terminates when the quantile result is found from either the lower side or the upper side. Hence, it is not necessary to expand non-leaf entries from both lower and upper sides. Based on this observation, a good heuristic is to select the maximum non-leaf component of $w_l(e_l)$ when $\phi \leq 0.5$, and that of $w_u(e_u)$, otherwise, in order to reach the requested quantile as fast as possible.

**Lemma 3. Non-leaf component:** *Let $e_l$ ($e_u$) be the entry in $S$ with the smallest $w_l$ ($w_u$) value. There exists a non-leaf entry among all entries $e' \in S$ satisfying $F_l(e') \leq F_u(e_l)$. Also, there exists a non-leaf entry among all entries $e' \in S$ satisfying $F_u(e') \geq F_l(e_u)$.*

*Proof.* We will prove the first statement; the proof for the second is symmetric. Consider two cases for the entry $e_l$. If $e_l$ is a non-leaf entry, then the statement is trivially true. If $e_l$ is a leaf entry (i.e. a data point), then we have $w_l(e_l) > 1$ as it is not pruned before. As there are no other leaf entries with $F$ value smaller than $e_l$, there must exist a non-leaf entry in $S$ whose interval of $F$ values intersects that of $e_l$.

## 4.4 Qualitative Cost Analysis

This section analyzes qualitatively the performance of the proposed algorithms. Our analysis considers only the number of (distinct) leaf nodes accessed by the algorithms, as the total cost is dominated by leaf node accesses (and a large enough memory buffer will absorb the effect of accessing nodes multiple times by the RANGE_COUNT queries of APX).

As discussed in Section 3, we assume that $F$ is a continuous function. Figure 9a shows a set of five exemplary *contours* on the data domain. Each of them connects the set of locations having the same $F$ value in the data domain. The continuity property of the ranking function implies that contours close together have similar $F$ values. In our example, inner contours have lower $F$ values than outer ones. Let $F^*$ be the $F$ value of the quantile corresponding to the *target contour* in bold. Note that the union of all

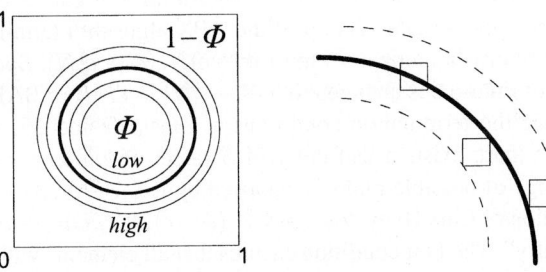

(a) Contours in data domain   (b) Region around the target contour

**Fig. 9.** Analysis example

contours with $F$ values at most $F^*$ enclose $\phi N$ data points. Figure 9b magnifies the region around the target contour. Observe that any algorithm that computes the quantile correctly must access the area enclosed by dotted curves which contain all leaf nodes (rectangles) intersecting the target contour.

We now examine the *search region* of the proposed algorithms. The branch-and-bound quantile algorithm (BAB) accesses the nodes intersecting the target contour, pruning at the same time a significant fraction of nodes which do not intersect the target contour. On the other hand, the incremental search algorithm (INC) accesses all nodes intersecting contours with $F$ values smaller than or equal to $F^*$. Clearly, INC is much more expensive than BAB. The iterative approximation algorithm (APX) employs an efficient range count algorithm so it only visits the nodes intersecting the target contour and a few other contours (due to multiple trials). Thus, APX is not as effective as BAB as APX accesses more space (i.e., more contours). Summarizing, BAB is expected to outperform both INC and APX in terms of I/O. Another observation is that different quantiles require different cost. This is obvious for INC. For APX and BAB, it is more expensive to compute the median than extreme quantiles because more nodes intersect the target contour of the median than that of extreme quantiles.

## 5 Variants of Quantile Queries and Problem Settings

In this section, we discuss variants of quantile query evaluation and cases where aR-trees may not be available. Section 5.1 discusses how the proposed algorithms can be adapted for approximate quantile queries. Section 5.2 examines efficient computation of *batch* quantile queries. Finally, Section 5.3 investigates quantile computation for cases where the data are indexed by simple (i.e., not aggregate) R-trees or when only spatial histograms are available.

### 5.1 Approximate and Progressive Quantile Computation

An $\epsilon$-approximate quantile query returns an element from the dataset with a rank in the interval $[(\phi - \epsilon)N, (\phi + \epsilon)N]$, where $N$ is the data size, $\phi$ and $\epsilon$ are real values in the range $[0, 1]$. The goal is to retrieve an accurate enough estimation, at low cost. For INC, the termination condition at Line 13 of the algorithm in Figure 3 is modified to $cnt = (\phi - \epsilon)N$. The approximate version of the APX algorithm terminates as soon as RANGE_COUNT returns a number within $[(\phi - \epsilon)N, (\phi + \epsilon)N]$. Specifically, the condition at Line 10 of Figure 6 is changed to $|cnt - \phi N| > \epsilon N$. For BAB (see Figure 8), we need to change the termination conditions at Lines 10 and 16, such that the algorithm stops when there exists a leaf entry in $S$ (a set of temporary entries to be processed) whose range of possible ranks is enclosed by $[(\phi - \epsilon)N, (\phi + \epsilon)N]$. Thus, we replace the condition of Line 10 by "$cur_l + 1 \geq (\phi - \epsilon)N \wedge cur_l + w_l(e_l) \leq (\phi + \epsilon)N \wedge e_l$ is a leaf entry". The first condition ensures that all elements with ranks lower than $(\phi - \epsilon)N$ have been pruned, while the second condition ensures that the maximum possible rank of $e_l$ does not exceed $(\phi + \epsilon)N$. Similarly, we replace the condition at Line 16 by "$N - cur_u \leq (\phi + \epsilon)N \wedge N + 1 - (cur_u + w_u(e_u)) \geq (\phi - \epsilon)N \wedge e_u$ is a leaf entry".

All three quantile algorithms can be adapted to generate progressively more refined estimates before the exact result is found. The progressive versions of the algorithms are identical to the methods described in Section 4, with only one difference. When the termination condition is checked, we compute and output the minimum value of $\epsilon$ (if any) for terminating, had the algorithm been approximate.

## 5.2 Batch Quantile Queries

A batch quantile query retrieves a set of quantiles $\phi_1, \phi_2, \cdots, \phi_m$ from the database, where $\phi_1 < \phi_2 < \cdots < \phi_m$ and each $\phi_i$ is a real value in the range $[0, 1]$. Batch quantiles offer a sketch of the underlying $F$ value distribution. A naive solution would process individual quantile queries separately. We aim at reducing the total cost by exploiting intermediate results from previous computation.

INC can directly be applied for a batch query. During search, an element is reported if its rank is exactly $\phi_i N$ for some $i \in m$. The algorithm terminates until the $\phi_m N$-th element is found. For APX, the first quantile (i.e. $\phi_1$) is computed as usual. In addition, we maintain a set $C$ for storing computed intermediate coordinates $(\lambda, cnt)$ (see Figure 6). These coordinates can be exploited to reduce the initial search space of the algorithm and improve the overall performance. Before computing the second quantile (i.e. $\phi_2$), the initial pair $(\lambda_l, cnt_l)$ is replaced by the pair in $S$ with the maximum count not greater than $\phi_2 N$. Similarly, the pair $(\lambda_u, cnt_u)$ is replaced by the pair in $S$ with the minimum count not smaller than $\phi_2 N$. Similarly, intermediate coordinates computed in this round are added to $C$ for reducing the search space of the next quantile.

We can also define an efficient version of BAB for batch quantile queries. We compute the quantiles in ascending order of their $\phi$ values. During the computation of the first quantile (i.e. $\phi_1$), any entry pruned on the upper side (i.e. at Lines 12–14 of Figure 8) is added to another set $S'$. After the first quantile is computed, we need not start the computation of the second quantile (i.e. $\phi_2$) from scratch. We simply reuse the content of $S$ in the last computation. Moreover, temporarily pruned entries in $S'$ are moved back to $S$. Finally, we initialize $cur_u$ to 0, reuse the previous value of $cur_l$, and begin the algorithm at Line 5 in Figure 8. The same procedure is repeated for subsequent quantiles. In this way, no tree nodes are accessed more than once.

## 5.3 Quantile Computation Without aR-Trees

R-trees are commonly used for indexing spatial data in GIS or as multi-attribute indexes in DBMS, in general. On the other hand, aR-trees are not as popular, as they are mainly used for aggregate queries. For the case where only an R-tree is available on a spatial dataset (not an aR-tree), we can still apply the BAB algorithm. For each non-leaf entry, we compute the *expected* the number of objects (i.e., the aggregate value) and use this value instead of the actual count. A rough estimate can be derived from the level of the entry in the tree and the average R-tree node occupancy (which is a commonly maintained statistic). Naturally, BAB will not compute exact quantiles in this case, but values which are hopefully close to the exact result. In Section 6, we experimentally evaluate the accuracy of BAB on R-trees, by comparing its results with the exact quantiles.

In some streaming applications (e.g., traffic monitoring, mobile services), spatial data could not be indexed effectively due to high update rates and/or constrained storage space. In such cases, a common approach is to maintain spatial histograms [22] for approximate query processing. A spatial histogram consists of a set of entries, each associated with a MBR and the number of points inside it. We can derive an approximate quantile from such histograms, by applying a single pass of the BAB algorithm to prune histogram entries $e$ that definitely do not containing the quantile. Based on the remaining (non-pruned) entries, we then compute the approximation and its respective error $\epsilon$ (in terms of rank).

## 6 Experimental Evaluation

In this section, we evaluate the proposed algorithms using synthetic and real datasets. Uniform synthetic datasets were generated by assigning random numbers to dimensional values of objects independently. The default cardinality and dimensionality of a synthetic dataset are $N = 200K$ and $d = 2$. We also used real 2D spatial datasets from Tiger/Line[1], LA (131K points) and TS (194K points). Attribute values of all datasets are normalized to the range $[0, 10000]$. Each dataset is indexed by a COUNT aR-tree [17] with disk page size of 1K bytes.

Unless otherwise stated, the default searched quantile is $\phi = 0.5$ (i.e., median) and the ranking function $F$ is defined as the Euclidean distance from a given query point, which follows the distribution of the dataset. All algorithms (INC for incremental search, APX for iterative approximation, BAB for branch-and-bound quantile) were implemented in C++. We also experimented with BAB-, a computationally cheaper variant of BAB that attempts pruning using only entries with upper bounds smaller than the quantile (i.e. Lines 12–17 in Figure 8 are not executed). All experiments were performed on a Pentium IV 2.3GHz PC with 512MB memory. The I/O cost corresponds to the number of aR-tree nodes accessed. A memory buffer of size 5% the number of aR-tree nodes is used by APX to avoid excessive number of page faults at repetitive RANGE_COUNT queries. For each experimental instance, the query cost is averaged over 100 queries with the same properties.

### 6.1 Experimental Results

Figure 10 shows the cost of the algorithms on real datasets LA and TS, as a function of $\phi$. The results verify the analysis in Section 4.4 that APX and BAB have higher cost in computing the median than in calculating extreme quantiles (with $\phi$ close to 0 or 1). The cost of INC grows linearly with $\phi$. APX is more efficient because it is based on RANGE_COUNT functions which can be answered effectively by the aR-tree. BAB incurs the lowest I/O overhead, indicating that the branch-and-bound approach only needs to explore a small fraction of the index. However, the CPU cost of BAB is slightly higher than APX because BAB requires considerable time computing the $\omega$ values of the intermediate entries. In practice, the I/O cost dominates, and thus BAB is by far the most efficient method.

Next, we study the effect of database size $N$ (Figure 11). As expected, BAB has the lowest I/O cost and outperforms the other two algorithms. BAB- has little I/O overhead

---

[1] www.census.gov/geo/www/tiger/

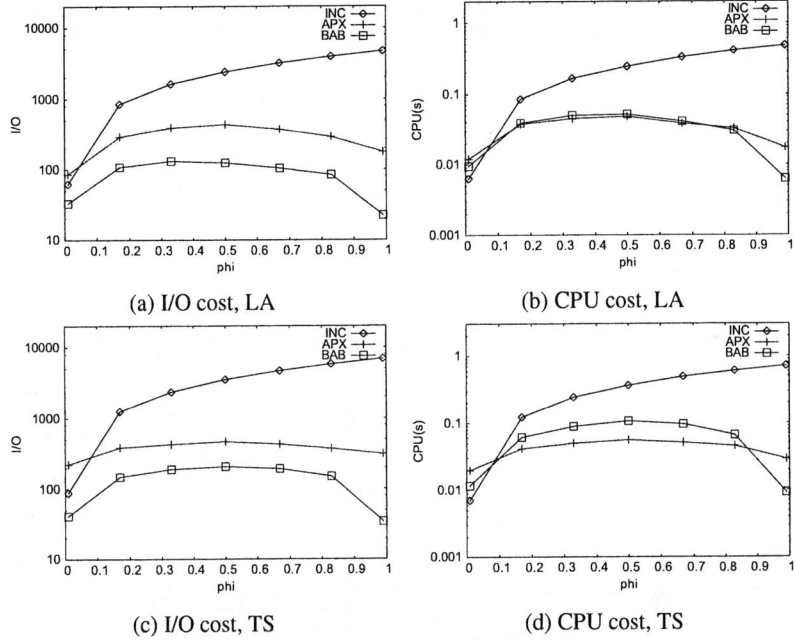

**Fig. 10.** Cost as a function of $\phi$

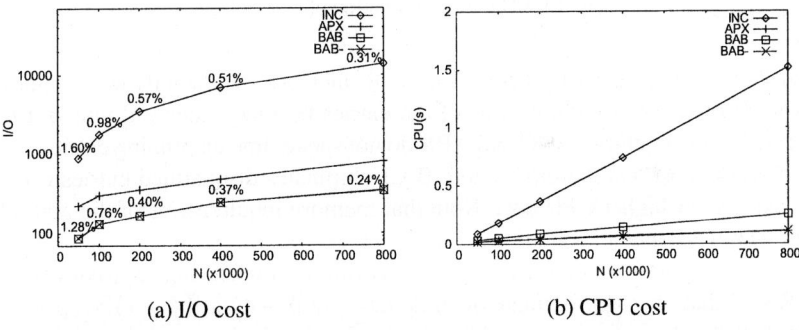

**Fig. 11.** Cost as a function of $N$, Uniform data, $d = 2$, $\phi = 0.5$

over BAB, although BAB- misses opportunities for pruning entries with rankings higher than the quantile. In addition, BAB- has the lowest CPU cost among all algorithms. The numbers over the instances of INC and BAB are the maximum memory requirements of the algorithms (for storing the heap and set $S$) as a percentage of aR-tree size. Note that they are very low and decrease with $N$.

Figure 12 shows the cost of the algorithms on uniform data as a function of dimensionality $d$ (together with the maximum memory requirements of INC and BAB). BAB remains the least expensive algorithm in terms of I/O. APX has the highest I/O cost at $d = 4$ because RANGE_COUNT becomes less efficient at higher dimensionality. On

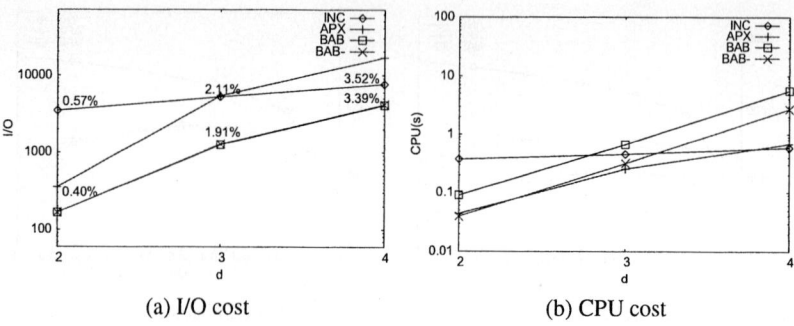

**Fig. 12.** Cost as a function of $d$, Uniform data, $N = 200K$, $\phi = 0.5$

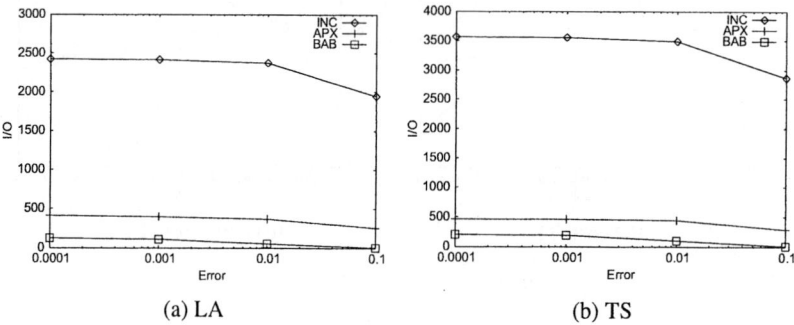

**Fig. 13.** I/O cost as a function of $\epsilon$, $\phi = 0.5$

the other hand, the CPU costs of BAB and BAB- increase significantly with dimensionality. As $d$ increases, the $F$-intervals of the entries become wider and intersect many $F$-intervals of other entries. INC and APX do not spend time on pruning entries so they incur high I/O cost. On the other hand, BAB eliminates disqualified entries carefully at the expense of higher CPU cost. Note that memory requirements of the algorithms remain within acceptable bounds, even at $d = 4$.

We also compared the efficiency of our algorithms in retrieving approximate quantiles. Recall that an $\epsilon$-approximate quantile has a rank within $[(\phi - \epsilon)N, (\phi + \epsilon)N]$, where $N$ is the data size. Figure 13 compares the algorithms for various values of $\epsilon$. As expected, all costs decrease with the increase of $\epsilon$, however, not at the same rate. The cost of BAB decreases by 95% when $\epsilon$ changes from 0.0001 to 0.1, while the corresponding rates for APX and INC are 40% and 20%, respectively. This implies that BAB is not only the best algorithm for exact quantiles, but also has the highest performance savings for approximate computation.

Figure 14 shows the progressiveness of the algorithms for a typical quantile query. As more disk page are accessed, all the algorithms continuously refine their intermediate results with decreasing error $\epsilon$. The values at $\epsilon = 0$ corresponds to the case when the exact answer is found. BAB is the most progressive algorithm, followed by APX and then INC. Thus, BAB provides informative results to users, very early and way before it converges to the exact result.

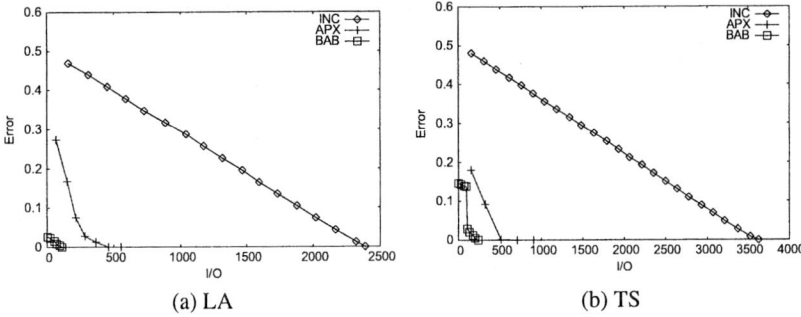

**Fig. 14.** Progressiveness of the algorithms for a typical query, $\phi = 0.5$

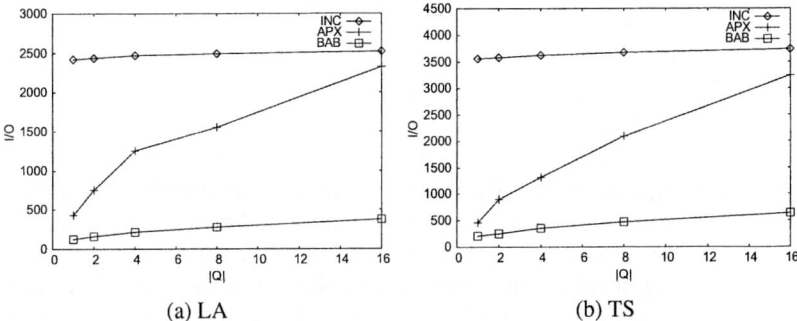

**Fig. 15.** I/O cost as a function of $|Q|$, $\phi = 0.5$

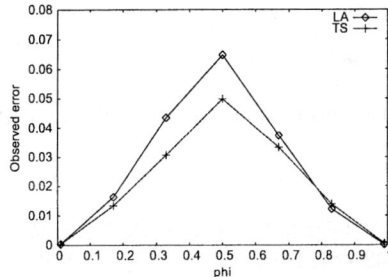

**Fig. 16.** Observed error of BAB as a function of $\phi$, on regular R-trees

We also investigated the cost of extracting quantiles based on nearest-site distance ranking; a problem discussed in Section 3. Given a set $Q = \{q_1, q_2, \ldots, q_m\}$ of query points (sites), the ranking of a data point $p$ is defined by $F(p) = \min_{i \in [1,m]} dist(q_i, p)$, where $dist$ denotes the Euclidean distance between two points. In the experiment, query points follow the distribution of data points. Figure 15 shows the cost of the algorithms as a function of the number of query points $|Q|$. As $|Q|$ increases, $F$-intervals of more entries overlap and the costs of all algorithms increase. The cost of BAB increases sublinearly with $|Q|$ and the algorithm outperforms its competitors by far.

Finally, we study the accuracy of the BAB algorithm on regular R-trees (i.e., not aR-trees), where the count of each entry is estimated from its level, as discussed in Section 5.3. Figure 16 shows the observed error of BAB as a function of $\phi$, on both real datasets LA and TS, indicating the difference of ranks (as a fraction of $N$) between the result and the actual quantile. Our solution produces fairly accurate results for real datasets indexed by regular R-trees. The maximum observed errors for LA and TS are just 0.07 and 0.05, respectively. The error is maximized at the median but it becomes negligible for extreme quantiles. As discussed, the I/O cost of BAB is maximized at $\phi = 0.5$. Higher I/O cost leads to higher error because counts of more entries need to be estimated.

# 7 Conclusion

We identified the problem of computing dynamically derived quantiles in multidimensional datasets. We proposed three quantile algorithms (INC, APX, and BAB) which operate on aggregate R-trees. Also, we analyzed their performance qualitatively and suggested solutions for handling variants of quantile queries. INC is very expensive for high values of $\phi$ (i.e., quantile value). Although the cost of APX is relatively insensitive to $\phi$, the algorithm accesses the aR-tree multiple times. BAB is the best algorithm as it traverses the tree carefully, pruning unnecessary nodes, and minimizing I/O cost.

In this paper we assume relatively low dimensionality, where aR-trees are effective. For high-dimensional spaces, however, the efficiency of aR-tree (as well as other space-partitioning access methods) drops significantly, in which case the algorithms may require accessing the entire dataset. Quantile computation in these environments is an interesting topic for future work.

# References

1. K. Alsabti, S. Ranka, and V. Singh. A One-Pass Algorithm for Accurately Estimating Quantiles for Disk-Resident Data. In *VLDB*, 1997.
2. Z. Bar-Yossef, R. Kumar, and D. Sivakumar. Sampling Algorithms: Lower Bounds and Applications. In *STOC*, 2001.
3. M. Blum, R. W. Floyd, V. R. Pratt, R. L. Rivest, and R. E. Tarjan. Time Bounds for Selection. *J. Comput. Syst. Sci.*, 7:448–461, 1973.
4. T. Brinkhoff, H.-P. Kriegel, and B. Seeger. Efficient Processing of Spatial Joins Using R-Trees. In *SIGMOD*, 1993.
5. K. Clarkson, D. Eppstein, G. Miller, C. Sturtivant, and S.-H. Teng. Approximating Center Points with Iterated Radon Points. *Int. J. Comp. Geom. and Appl.*, 6(3):357–377, 1996.
6. G. Cormode, F. Korn, S. Muthukrishnan, and D. Srivastava. Effective Computation of Biased Quantiles over Data Streams. In *ICDE*, 2005.
7. R. Fagin, A. Lotem, and M. Naor. Optimal Aggregation Algorithms for Middleware. In *PODS*, 2001.
8. A. C. Gilbert, Y. Kotidis, S. Muthukrishnan, and M. Strauss. How to Summarize the Universe: Dynamic Maintenance of Quantiles. In *VLDB*, 2002.
9. M. Greenwald and S. Khanna. Space-Efficient Online Computation of Quantile Summaries. In *SIGMOD*, 2001.

10. A. Guttman. R-Trees: A Dynamic Index Structure for Spatial Searching. In *SIGMOD*, 1984.
11. G. R. Hjaltason and H. Samet. Distance Browsing in Spatial Databases. *TODS*, 24(2): 265–318, 1999.
12. S. Jadhav and A. Mukhopadhyay. Computing a Centerpoint of a Finite Planar Set of Points in Linear Time. In *ACM Symposium on Computational Geometry*, 1993.
13. I. Lazaridis and S. Mehrotra. Progressive approximate aggregate queries with a multi-resolution tree structure. In *SIGMOD*, 2001.
14. G. S. Manku, S. Rajagopalan, and B. G. Lindsay. Approximate Medians and other Quantiles in One Pass and with Limited Memory. In *SIGMOD*, 1998.
15. G. S. Manku, S. Rajagopalan, and B. G. Lindsay. Random Sampling Techniques for Space Efficient Online Computation of Order Statistics of Large Datasets. In *SIGMOD*, 1999.
16. J. I. Munro and M. Paterson. Selection and Sorting with Limited Storage. *Theor. Comput. Sci.*, 12:315–323, 1980.
17. D. Papadias, P. Kalnis, J. Zhang, and Y. Tao. Efficient OLAP Operations in Spatial Data Warehouses. In *SSTD*, 2001.
18. D. Papadias, Y. Tao, G. Fu, and B. Seeger. An optimal and progressive algorithm for skyline queries. In *SIGMOD*, 2003.
19. M. Paterson. Progress in selection. *Technical Report, University of Warwick, Conventry, UK*, 1997.
20. W. H. Press, S. A. Teukolsky, W. T. Vetterling, and B. P. Flannery. *Numerical Recipes in C*. Cambridge University Press, second edition, 1992.
21. I. Stanoi, M. Riedewald, D. Agrawal, and A. E. Abbadi. Discovery of Influence Sets in Frequently Updated Databases. In *VLDB*, 2001.
22. N. Thaper, S. Guha, P. Indyk, and N. Koudas. Dynamic Multidimensional Histograms. In *SIGMOD*, 2002.

# Fast Nearest Neighbor Search on Road Networks*

Haibo Hu[1], Dik Lun Lee[1], and Jianliang Xu[2]

[1] Hong Kong Univ. of Science & Technology
{haibo, dlee}@cs.ust.hk
[2] Hong Kong Baptist University
xujl@comp.hkbu.edu.hk

**Abstract.** Nearest neighbor (NN) queries have been extended from Euclidean spaces to road networks. Existing approaches are either based on Dijkstra-like network expansion or NN/distance precomputation. The former may cause an explosive number of node accesses for sparse datasets because all nodes closer than the NN to the query must be visited. The latter, e.g., the Voronoi Network Nearest Neighbor ($VN^3$) approach, can handle sparse datasets but is inappropriate for medium and dense datasets due to its high precomputation and storage overhead. In this paper, we propose a new approach that indexes the network topology based on a novel network reduction technique. It simplifies the network by replacing the graph topology with a set of interconnected tree-based structures called SPIE's. An $nd$ index is developed for each SPIE and our new (k)NN search algorithms on an SPIE follow a predetermined tree path to avoid costly network expansion. By mathematical analysis and experimental results, our new approach is shown to be efficient and robust for various network topologies and data distributions.

## 1 Introduction

Nearest neighbor (NN) search has received intensive attention in spatial database community in the past decade, especially in high-dimensional Euclidean spaces [10, 1, 13, 15]. Recently, the research focus is brought to spatial network databases (SNDB) where objects are restricted to move on predefined roads [11, 6, 9, 8]. In SNDB, a road network is modeled as a graph $G$ ($< V, E >$), where a vertex (node) denotes a road junction and an edge denotes the road between two junctions; and the weight of the edge denotes the network distance. A nearest neighbor query on the road network is, given a query node $q$ and a dataset (e.g., restaurants, gas stations) distributed on the nodes $V$, to find a data object that is the closest to $q$ in terms of network distance.

Existing research falls into two categories. In the first category, NN search expands from the query node to adjacent nodes until a data object is found and further expansion cannot retrieve closer objects [6, 9]. Such network expansion originates from Dijkstra's algorithm that finds single-source shortest paths. The

---

* This work is supported by the Research Grants Council, Hong Kong SAR under grant HKUST6277/04E.

advantage of this approach is that the network distance, the key to NN search, is automatically obtained during the expansion. However, the disadvantage is that the "unguided graph traversal" during network expansion may cause an explosive number of node accesses, especially for sparse datasets. In the second category, solution-based indexes are built on the datasets. Kolahdouzan et al. proposed $VN^3$ to partition the network into cells by the *Network Voronoi Diagram* (NVD) [8]. Each cell contains one data object that is the closest object to all the nodes in this cell. These cells are indexed by an R-tree in the Euclidean space, and thus finding the first NN is reduced to a point location problem. To answer k-nearest-neighbor (kNN) queries, they showed that the $k$th NN must be adjacent to some $i$th NN ($i < k$) in the NVD. To speed up distance computation, they also precompute the distances between border points of adjacent cells. However, their approach is advantageous only for sparse datasets and small/medium $k$. Furthermore, if more than one dataset exists, NVD indexes and precomputed distances must be built and maintained separately for each dataset.

In this paper, we take a new approach by indexing the network topology, because compared with the datasets the topology is unique and less likely to change. To reduce index complexity and hence avoid unnecessary network expansion, we propose a novel technique called *network reduction* on road networks. This is achieved by replacing the network topology with a set of interconnected tree-based structures (called SPIE's) while preserving all the network distances. By building a lightweight $nd$ index on each SPIE, the (k)NN search on these structures simply follows a predetermined path, i.e., the tree path, and network expansion only occurs when the search crosses SPIE boundaries. By analytical and empirical results, this approach is shown to be efficient and robust for road networks with various topologies, datasets with various densities, and kNN queries with various $k$. Our contributions are summarized as follows:

– We propose a topology-based index scheme for kNN search on road networks. To reduce the index complexity, a network reduction technique is developed to simplify the graph topology by tree-based structures, called SPIE's.
– We propose a lightweight $nd$ index for the SPIE so that the (k)NN search in SPIE follows a predetermined tree path. With this index, the whole (k)NN search can avoid most of the costly network expansions.
– We develop cost models for the network reduction, NN and kNN search by our $nd$-based algorithms. These cost models, together with experimental results, show the efficiency of our approach and the performance impact of various parameters.

The rest of this paper is organized as follows. Section 2 reviews existing work of (k)NN search on SNDB. Section 3 presents the network reduction technique. Section 4 introduces the $nd$ index on the SPIE and NN search algorithms on the reduced network. The algorithms are extended to kNN search in Section 5. Section 6 develops the cost models, followed by the performance evaluation in Section 7. Finally, Section 8 concludes the paper.

## 2 Related Work

Nearest neighbor (NN) search on road networks is an emerging research topic in recent years [11, 6, 9, 8]. It is closely related to the single-source shortest path problem, which has been studied since Dijkstra [4]. He proposed to use a priority queue to store those nodes whose adjacent nodes are to be explored. Besides the Dijkstra algorithm, $A^*$ algorithm with various expansion heuristics was also adapted to solve this problem [5].

Among database researchers, Jensen et al. brought out the notion of NN search on road networks [6]. They proposed a general spatio-temporal framework for NN queries with both graph representation and detailed search algorithms. To compute network distances, they adapted the Dijkstra's algorithm to online evaluate the shortest path. Papadias et al. incorporated the Euclidean space into the road network and applied traditional spatial access methods to the NN search [9]. Assuming that Euclidean distance is the lower bound of network distance, they proposed *incremental Euclidean restriction* (IER) to search for NNs in the Euclidean space as candidates and then to compute their network distances to the query node for the actual NNs. However, IER cannot be applied to road networks where that distance bound does not hold, e.g., the network of transportation time cost. Although they proposed an alternative approach *incremental network expansion* (INE), it is essentially a graph traversal from the query point and thus performs poorly for sparse datasets.

Inspired by the Voronoi Diagram in vector spaces, Kolahdouzan et al. proposed a solution-based approach for kNN queries in SNDB, called *Voronoi Network Nearest Neighbor* ($VN^3$) [8]. They precompute the Network Voronoi Diagram (NVD) and approximate each Voronoi cell by a polygon called Network Voronoi Polygon (NVP). By indexing all NVP's with an R-tree, searching the first nearest neighbor is reduced to a point location problem. To answer kNN queries, they prove that the $k$th NN must be adjacent to some $i$th $(i < k)$ NN in NVD, which limits the search area. To compute network distances for an NN candidate, they precompute and store the distances between border nodes of adjacent NVP's, and even the distances between border nodes and inner nodes in each NVP. By these indexes and distances, they showed that $VN^3$ outperforms INE, by up to an order of magnitude. However, $VN^3$ heavily depends on the density and distribution of the dataset: as the dataset gets denser, both the number of $NVP$'s and the number of border points increase, causing higher precomputation overhead and worse search performance. Given that NN search by network expansion on dense datasets is efficient, $VN^3$ is only useful for sparse datasets.

Shahabi et al. applied graph embedding techniques to kNN search on road networks [11]. They transformed a road network to a high-dimensional Euclidean space where traditional NN search algorithms can be applied. They showed that KNN in the embedding space is a good approximation of the KNN in the road network. However, this technique involves high-dimensional (40-256) spatial indexes, which leads to poor performance. Further, the query result is approximate and the precision heavily depends on the data density and distribution.

Continuous nearest neighbor (CNN) query is also studied recently. Besides an efficient solution for NN query, CNN query on road network also requires to efficiently determine the network positions where the NN(s) change. Various approaches such as UBA [7], UNICONS [2] are proposed to solve this problem.

## 3 Reduction on Road Networks

The objectives for network reduction are: (1) to reduce the number of edges while preserving all network distances, and (2) to replace the complex graph topology with simpler structures such as trees. To achieve the objectives, we propose to use the *shortest path trees* (SPT). The basic idea is to start from a node (called *root*) in the road network $G$ and then to grow a shortest path tree from it by the Dijkstra's algorithm. During the execution, when a new node $n$ is added to the tree, we additionally check if its distances in $G$ to all the other tree nodes are preserved by the tree. This is completed by checking if there is any edge adjacent to $n$ in $G$ that connects $n$ to a tree node closer than the tree path. Such an edge is called a *shortcut*. If $n$ has no shortcuts, it is inserted to the tree as in Dijkstra's algorithm; otherwise $n$ becomes a new root and a new SPT starts to grow from it. The new SPT connects with some existing SPT's through the shortcuts of $n$. The whole process continues until the SPT's cover all nodes in network $G$. These SPT's form a graph— called an *SPT graph*— whose edges are the shortcuts from the root of an SPT to some node in another SPT. Figure 1 illustrates an SPT graph. Obviously the SPT graph is much simpler than the graph of road network. It is noteworthy that the reduction from a graph to a set

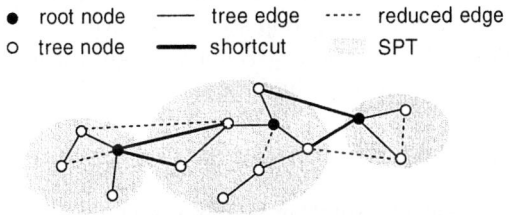

**Fig. 1.** An Example of Shortest Path Tree Graph

of interconnected trees is not generally beneficial. Nonetheless, road networks exhibit the following two properties that justify this approach: (1) the degree of a junction in the road network is normally equal to or greater than 3, some junctions serving as "hubs" of the network may have even higher degrees; (2) the *girth* of the network, i.e., the length of the shortest circuit in the network, is long, because small circuit means redundant paths between close-by nodes, which is normally avoided in network design. We show in the cost model (in Section 6.2) that these two properties lead to effective reduction on road networks.

In order to further reduce the shortcuts and thus the number of SPT's, we augment the SPT's to allow sibling-to-sibling edges. These edges are called *horizontal edges* and the SPT's that support such edges are called *shortest path tree with horizontal edges* (SPH). With horizontal edges, SPH's can store shortcuts between siblings and thus no new SPH needs to be created in such cases. Later in Section 4.2 we will prove that SPH still forms a hierarchy and the shortest path between any two nodes is still easy to allocate.

---
**Algorithm 1.** Network Reduction by SPH
---
**Input:** a network $G$ and a starting root $r$
**Output:** an SPH graph $\Gamma$
**Procedure:**
1: $starting\_node = r$;
2: **while** there is node in $G$ that is not covered in any SPH of $\Gamma$ **do**
3:    build a blank SPH $T$ and insert $T$ as a vertex into $\Gamma$;
4:    insert all the non-sibling shortcuts of $starting\_node$ as edges to $\Gamma$;
5:    build a blank priority queue $H$ and insert $<starting\_node, 0>$ to $H$;
6:    **while** $H$ is not empty **do**
7:      node $n = H.\text{pop}()$;
8:      **if** $n$ has no shortcuts to non-sibling tree nodes **then**
9:         insert $n$ into $T$;
10:      **else**
11:         break;
12:      relax the distances in $H$ according to Dijkstra's algorithm;

---

Algorithm 1 shows the procedure of network reduction. The inner *while* loop is modified from the Dijkstra's algorithm to build an individual SPH. Different from Dijkstra's algorithm, the inner loop stops whenever there are shortcuts to non-sibling tree nodes and then a new SPH starts to grow from this node. These shortcuts are stored as the edges in the SPH graph $\Gamma$.

## 4 Nearest Neighbor Search on SPH Graph

In this section, we present our solution to NN search on the reduced network, i.e., the SPH graph. The search starts from the SPH where the query node is located. By building a local index $nd$ on each SPH, this search is efficient. Searching into the adjacent SPH's in the graph continues until the distance to the SPH's already exceeds the distance to the candidate NN. In what follows, we first show the $nd$-based NN search on a tree. Then we extend it to the SPH and the SPH graph. Finally we present the index construction and maintenance algorithms. The extension to kNN search is shown in the next section.

### 4.1 NN Search on Tree

We begin with the NN search on a tree. To avoid network expansion that recursively explores the parent and child nodes from the current searching node, we

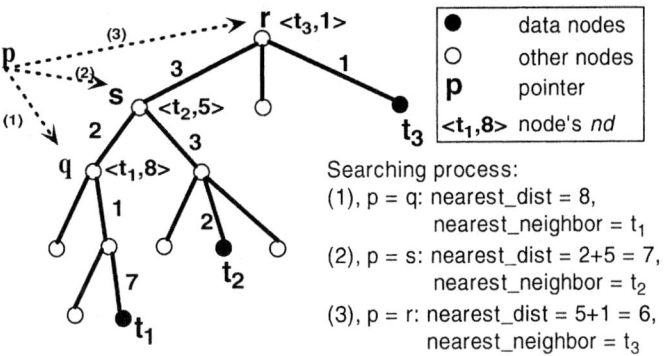

**Fig. 2.** Nearest Neighbor Search on Tree

store, for each node $v$, the nearest data object in its descendants (*nearest descendant* or *nd* for short). The object is denoted by $v.nd.object$ and its distance to $v$ is denoted by $v.nd.dist$. For example, in Figure 2, $s.nd$ is set to $<t_2, 5>$, as the $nd$ of $s$ is $t_2$ which is 5 units away. If a node have no data object in its descendants, its $nd$ is set to $<null, \infty>$.

The pointer to the current searching node, $p$, starts from the query node $q$. Based on the $nd$ index, if $p.nd$ is closer to $q$ than the current NN, $p.nd$ becomes the new NN and the current nearest distance, *nearest_dist*, is updated. Then $p$ proceeds to $q$'s parent, grandparent, $\cdots$, etc., until the distance between $p$ and $q$ exceeds *nearest_dist* or $p$ reaches the root. Figure 2 shows an example where $p$ starts at $q$ and then moves to $s$ and $r$, until it finds the NN. With the $nd$ index, the search path is at most as long as the tree path to the root. Therefore the number of node accesses is bounded by the height of the tree. In the next subsections, we extend the $nd$ index to the SPT and SPT graph.

### 4.2 SPIE: SPH with Triangular Inequality

An SPH is more complicated than a tree because there are multiple paths from the source to the destination. In this subsection, our objective is to modify the SPH obtained from Section 3 so that the weight of each edge (tree edge or horizontal edge) represents the shortest distance between the two adjacent nodes. In other words, we modify the SPH to satisfy the *triangular inequality*, that is, $\forall$ three edges $ab$, $bc$, $ac \in SPH.E$, $w(ac) \leq w(ab) + w(bc)$. The modified SPH is called an SPH with triangular inequality edges (SPIE).

The conversion from an SPH into an SPIE is a local operation. For each node $u$, we obtain its child nodes; the set of tree edges and horizontal edges between these nodes forms a weighted graph. We perform the *Floyd-Warshall* algorithm [3] to find all-pairs shortest paths in this graph. The distances of these shortest paths form the weights of tree edges and horizontal edges in the SPIE. The following theorem proves that SPIE guarantees that the shortest path of any two nodes $u$ and $v$ comprises one and only one horizontal edge which connects one of $u$'s ancestors and one of $v$'s ancestors.

**Theorem 1.** *For two nodes $u$ and $v$ in SPIE that are not descendant/ancestor of each other, their shortest path consists of the following nodes sequentially, $u_0, u_1, u_2, \cdots, u_s, v_t, \cdots, v_2, v_1, v_0$, where $u_0 = u$, $v_0 = v$, and $u_i$ ($v_i$) is the parent of $u_{i-1}$ ($v_{i-1}$); $u_s$ and $v_t$ are the child nodes of $lca_{u,v}$, the lowest common ancestor of $u$ and $v$.*

PROOF. In order to prove the theorem, we first introduce Lemma 1.

**Lemma 1.** *Any path from node $u$ to its descendant $v$ in an SPIE must include all the tree edges from $u$ to $v$. In other words, $v$'s parent, grandparent, $\cdots$, till $u$, must exist in any path from $u$ to $v$.*

PROOF. Let $level(i)$ denote the depth of node $i$ ($level(root) = 0$), and $n$ denote $level(v) - level(u) - 1$. By mathematical induction,

1. For $n = 1$, $v$'s parent node must be included in the path because otherwise there are more than one parent for node $v$, which is prohibited in an SPIE;
2. Assume the lemma holds for $n = k$. Thus for $n = k+1$, we only need to prove $t$, $u$'s child and $v$'s ancestor, is included in the path. By the assumption, all ancestors of $v$ that are below $t$ are already in the path, especially $s$, $t$'s child and $v$'s ancestor. Since $s$ is in the path, by the same reasoning as in 1, $t$ must be in the path.

Hereby, 1 and 2 complete the proof. □

We now prove the theorem. Let $p$ denote $lca_{u,v}$ for simplicity.

1. First, we prove that if all sibling edges among $p$'s children are removed, $p$ must exist in $path(u,v)$. Consider the two subtrees that are rooted at $p$'s two children and contain $u$ and $v$ respectively. Since the only edges linking them with the rest of the SPIE are the two tree edges adjacent to $p$, $p$ must exist in any path between the two subtrees. Thus, $p$ must exist in $path(u,v)$.
2. From Lemma 1, $u_1, u_2, \cdots, u_s$ must exist in $path(u,v)$. We only need to prove that they are the only nodes in the path.[1] By contradiction, if there were one node $x$ between $u_i$ and $u_{i+1}$, $x$ must be a sibling node of $u_i$. However, since all edge weights satisfy triangular inequality, i.e., $w(u_i, u_{i+1}) \leq w(u_i, x) + w(x, u_{i+1})$, removing node $x$ results in an even shorter path, which contradicts the shortest path condition. Therefore, $u_1, u_2, \cdots, u_s$ are the only nodes in the path.
3. Finally we prove that when adding back the sibling edges removed in 1, the path is the same except that $p$ is removed from $path(u,v)$. On the one hand, due to triangular inequality, $w(u_s, v_t) \leq w(u_s, p) + w(p, v_t)$, so $p$ should be removed from the shortest path. On the other hand, since all added edges are sibling edges, if any new node is to be added to the path, only sibling nodes are possible choices; but from 2, adding sibling nodes only increases the path distance. Therefore, no nodes should be added.

Hereby, 1, 2 and 3 complete the proof. □

---
[1] By symmetry, the proof is the same for the $v_1, v_2, \cdots, v_t$, and hence omitted.

## 4.3 NN Search on SPIE and SPIE Graph

By Theorem 1, a shortest path in an SPIE is the same as that in a tree except that a horizontal edge replaces two tree edges adjacent to the lowest common ancestor. Therefore, NN search in SPIE still starts from the query node $q$ and moves upward to its ancestors. The only difference is that, instead of $p$'s $nd$, the $nd$'s of $p$'s child nodes (except for the node pointed by the last $p$), are examined during the search. This is because if $p$ is the lowest common ancestor of $q$ and some possible NN, according to Theorem 1, one of $p$'s children, instead of $p$, appears in the path. Figure 3 illustrates the NN search on an SPIE. In this example, when $p = s$, the $nd$ of $u$, instead of $s$, is examined. Regarding

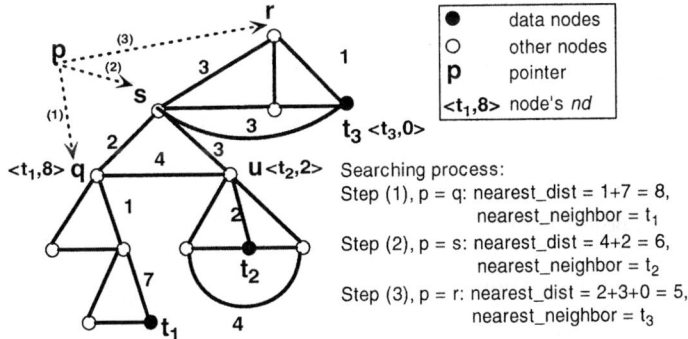

**Fig. 3.** NN search on SPIE

NN search on the SPIE graph, once the search is completed on the current SPIE, its shortcuts need to be considered. More specifically, the search should be propagated to those nodes that are adjacent to the shortcuts and are closer to $q$ than the current NN. With these nodes being query points, new NN searches on the SPIE's are started. These searches are processed similarly except that the distance is accumulated from $q$. Algorithm 2 shows the pseudo-code of the NN search on one SPIE. For NN search on the SPIE graph, this algorithm is invoked with the SPIE that contains $q$.

## 4.4 $nd$ Index Construction

The $nd$ index is independently constructed on each SPIE. As aforementioned, the $nd$ data structure of each node $n$ stores both the nearest descendant and its shortest distance to $n$. In addition, based on the fact that the nearest descendant of $n$ is also the nearest descendant of all nodes along the path from $n.nd$ to $n$, $n.nd$ also stores the child node of $n$ in this path to record the path to the nearest descendant. To build the $nd$ index, a bottom-up fashion is applied: the $nd$'s of $n$'s children are built and then the nearest $nd$ among them is elected as the $nd$ for $n$. Algorithm 3 shows the pseudo-code of the bottom-up $nd$ construction.

## Algorithm 2. NN Search on an SPIE

**Input:** an SPIE $\Gamma$, a query point $q$, accumulated distance $D$ from the global query point
**Global:** the candidate NN $r$, also the output when the entire search terminates
**Procedure:** NN_search_on_SPIE($\Gamma,q,D$)

1: $p = q$;
2: **while** $dist_{p,q} < dist_{r,q}$ **do**
3:     find the best NN object $u$ in $p$'s child nodes's $nd$;
4:     **if** u is better than r **then**
5:        update r;
6:     $p = p.parent$;
7: **for** each shortcut $s,t$ $(s \in \Gamma, t \in \Phi)$ **do**
8:     **if** $D + dist_{q,t} < dist_{r,q}$ **then**
9:        NN_search_on_SPIE($\Phi,t,D + dist_{q,t}$);

## Algorithm 3. Build $nd$ index on an SPIE

**Input:** an SPIE $\Gamma$, a node $p$
**Operation:** Build $p$'s $nd$ recursively
**Procedure:** build_nd($\Gamma,p$)

1: **if** $p$ is a data object **then**
2:     set $p.nd = p$;
3: **else if** $p$ is a leaf node **then**
4:     set $p.nd = null$;
5: **else**
6:     **for** each $p$'s child $v$ **do**
7:        build_nd($\Gamma, v$);
8:     find the nearest descendant $v^*$ among $p$'s child nodes' $nd$;
9:     set $p.nd = v^*$;

Regarding disk paging, the $nd$ index is paged in a top-down manner [14]: starting from the root, the SPIE is traversed in a breadth-first order, where $nd$ structure is greedily stored in a disk page until it is full. The breadth-first traversal guarantees that topologically close nodes are physically close on disk.

### 4.5 Handling Updates

This subsection copes with updates on both network topology and data objects.

**Updates on Network Topology.** Network updates include the insertion/deletion of nodes, insertion/deletion of edges, and change of edge weights.

- **node insertion:** the node is inserted to the SPIE that contains the adjacent node.
- **node deletion:** only the SPIE that contains this node needs to be rebuilt by Dijkstra's algorithm[2].

---

[2] If the SPHIE is no longer connected, the SPIE is split.

- **edge insertion:** if the edge is an intra-SPIE edge and provides a shorter distance between the two adjacent nodes, only this SPIE is rebuilt by Dijkstra's algorithm; otherwise if the edge is a shortcut, it is added to the SPIE graph, otherwise no operation is needed.
- **edge deletion:** if the edge is an intra-SPIE edge, this SPIE is rebuilt; otherwise if it is a shortcut, it is removed from the SPIE graph; otherwise no operation is needed.
- **increase edge weight:** same as *edge deletion*.
- **decrease edge weight:** same as *edge insertion*.

**Updates on Data Objects.** Updates on data objects include object insertion/deletion. These changes affect the $nd$ index only; the SPIE graph is not affected. Therefore, data objects updates are less costly than network updates. Moreover, the inserted/deleted object only affects the $nd$ index of this node and its ancestors in the SPIE. So the index update starts from the node where the object insertion/deletion occurs, and repeatedly propagates to the parent until the $nd$ no longer changes.

## 5 K-Nearest-Neighbor Search

To generalize NN search to KNN search, every time $p$ points at a new node, we not only examine the $nd$ of $p$ (or more precisely the $nd$'s of $p$'s children), but also search downwards to examine the $nd$ of $p$'s descendants for candidate NN farther than $p.nd$. The downward search terminates when all (or $k$, whichever is smaller) data objects in $p$'s descendants are found, or when the accumulated distance from $q$ exceeds the $k$th NN candidate distance from $q$. During the downward search, a priority queue $L$ is used to store the nodes to be examined, sorted by their accumulated distances from $q$.

Figure 4 shows an example of a 2NN search on the same SPIE as in Figure 3. $r$ denotes the current set of 2NN candidates, where $< t_1, 8 >$ means a candidate $t_1$ is 8 units from the query node $q$. In priority queue $L$, $< x, 1 >$ means that the $nd$ of node $x$ that is 1 unit from $q$ is to be examined. Every time $p$ moves upwards to a new node (e.g., $s$), the priority queue $L$ is initialized with $nd$ of $p$'s children (e.g., $u$). Then we repeatedly pop up the first node from $L$, examine its $nd$, and push its children to $L$ until $L$ is empty, or two objects have been found, or the accumulated distance exceeds the second NN distance to $q$. Afterwards $p$ moves upwards to its parent and the same procedure is repeated. The entire NN search terminates, as in Algorithm 2, when the distance from $p$ to $q$ already exceeds that from the $k$-th NN candidate to $q$.

## 6 Cost Models

In this section, we analyze the effectiveness of our proposed network reduction and $nd$-based nearest neighbor search algorithms. We develop cost models for the number of edges removed during the reduction and nodes accesses ($NA$)

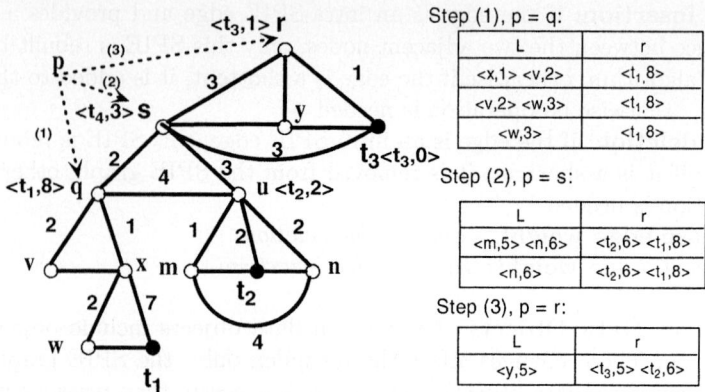

**Fig. 4.** KNN search on SPIE

during the NN and kNN search. We then compare the latter with the number of nodes accesses by the naive Dijkstra-like network expansion algorithm. Before we start the analysis, we first introduce some assumptions and notations.

### 6.1 Analytical Assumptions and Notations

To simplify the analytical model, we make the following assumptions on the network topology:

- The degree of each node is equal to $f$;
- The weight of each edge is equal to 1;
- There are $N$ nodes in the network and $M$ data objects are uniformly distributed in the network. Let $p = \frac{M}{N}$.

Table 1 summarizes all the notations, including those defined in the sequel.

**Table 1.** Notations for Cost Models

| Notation | Definition |
|---|---|
| $f$ | degree of each node |
| $N$ | number of nodes |
| $M$ | number of data objects |
| $p$ | probability of a node is an object, $p = \frac{M}{N}$ |
| $g$ | average length of the circuits in the network |
| $r$ | radius of the network |
| $NA$ | number of nodes accesses in the search |
| $\mathcal{D}$ | average distance between a node and its NN |
| $\mathcal{D}_k$ | average distance between a node and its $k$th NN |
| $n_d$ | cardinality of the $d$-th layer |
| $\mathcal{C}_d$ | sum of cardinality of all layers within the $d$-th layer |
| $P_i$ | probability that the NN is $i$ units away |

## 6.2 Cost Model for Network Reduction

We first estimate the number of edges remained after the network reduction. Let $g$ denote the average length of the circuits in the network. During the reduction process, each circuit leads to a new shortest path tree with two shortcuts (ref. Figure 5). Since there are $f \cdot N/2$ edges, the number of circuits is $\frac{fN}{2g}$. So the

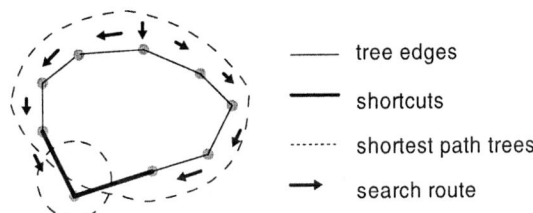

**Fig. 5.** A Circuit Leads to A New SPT with Two Shortcuts

number of tree edges and the number of shortcuts after reduction are $N - \frac{fN}{2g}$, and $\frac{2fN}{2g}$, respectively. Therefore, the ratio of the number of edges in the SPIE graph to the road network $\mathcal{R}$ is:

$$\mathcal{R} = \frac{(N - \frac{fN}{2g}) + \frac{2fN}{2g}}{fN/2} = \frac{2}{f} + \frac{1}{g} \quad (1)$$

An immediate observation from Equation 1 is that increasing $f$ and $g$ reduces the ratio and hence enlarges the performance gain of the network reduction. Nonetheless, the reduction is beneficial even when $f$ and $g$ are small. For example, in a network of 2D uniform grid, $f$ equals to 4 and $g$ equals to 4, $\mathcal{R} = 3/4 < 1$.

It is also noteworthy that, although SPIE does not further reduce the edges from SPT, it helps convert a shortcut to a tree edge, which reduces the NN search cost since the $nd$ index is built on tree edges.

## 6.3 Cost Model for NN Search

To derive the number of node accesses in an NN search, we first derive the *average distance* ($\mathcal{D}$) between a node and its NN. Let us define the *d-th layer* of node $q$ as the set of nodes that are $d$ units away from $q$. Let $n_d$ denote the cardinality of the $d$-th layer, and $\mathcal{C}_d$ denote the sum of cardinality of all layers within the $d$-th layer, i.e., $\mathcal{C}_d = \sum_{i=1}^{d} n_i$. Then we have:

$$\mathcal{C}_d = \sum_{i=1}^{d} n_i = 1 + f + f(f-1) + f(f-1)^2 + \ldots + f(f-1)^{d-1} \approx \frac{(f-1)^d}{f-2} \quad (2)$$

Let $P_i$ denote the probability that the NN is $i$ units away, and $r$ denote the radius of the network. Then we have:

$$\mathcal{D} = \sum_{i=0}^{r} i \times P_i \quad (3)$$

Since the data objects are uniformly distributed, we have:

$$P_i = (1-p)^{C_{i-1}}(1 - (1-p)^{C_i - C_{i-1}}) \qquad (4)$$

Replacing $P_i$ in (3) with (4) and $C_i$ with (2), we get:

$$\mathcal{D} \approx \sum_{i=0}^{r-1}(1-p)^{C_i} \approx \sum_{i=0}^{r-1}(1-p)^{\frac{(f-1)^i}{f-2}} \qquad (5)$$

Now we estimate the number of node accesses in the NN search. The naive algorithm searches all nodes within the $\lceil \mathcal{D} \rceil$-th layer. Therefore, $NA_{naive}$ is given by:

$$NA_{naive} = C_{\lceil \mathcal{D} \rceil} \approx \frac{(f-1)^{\lceil \mathcal{D} \rceil}}{f-2} \qquad (6)$$

Recall that in our $nd$-based algorithm, the pointer $p$ starts from $q$, examines the $nd$'s of $p$'s children (except for the child that $p$ previously points at), and moves upward (and possibly to other SPIE's through the shortcuts) until the distance from $p$ to $q$ exceeds $\lceil \mathcal{D} \rceil$. Therefore,

$$NA_{nd} = \sum_{i=0}^{\lceil \mathcal{D} \rceil}(f-1) = (f-1)(\lceil \mathcal{D} \rceil + 1) \qquad (7)$$

By comparing (6) and (7), $NA_{naive}$ is exponential to the average NN distance $\mathcal{D}$ while $NA_{nd}$ is linear to $\mathcal{D}$.

### 6.4 Cost Model for KNN Search

Similar to the derivation of NN search, we start by estimating $\mathcal{D}_k$, the *average distance* of the $k$th NN to $q$. Let $P_i$ denote the probability that the $k$th NN is $i$ units away. Then,

$$P_i = \binom{C_i}{k} p^k (1-p)^{C_i - k} \approx \frac{C_i^k p^k (1-p)^{C_i}}{k!(1-p)^k} \qquad (8)$$

Different from the NN search, we use the *maximum likelihood* (ML) estimation to derive $\mathcal{D}_k$, i.e., $\mathcal{D}_k = argmax_i P_i$. To get the maximum value of $P_i$ in 8, it is equivalent to solve the following equation on the derivatives.

$$\frac{\partial C_i^k (1-p)^{C_i}}{\partial i} = 0 \Longrightarrow \frac{\partial C_i^k (1 - C_i p)}{\partial i} = 0 \qquad (9)$$

The above derivation requires an additional assumption that $p \ll 1$. Solving (9) and replacing $C_i$ by (2), we obtain,

$$\mathcal{D}_k = argmax_i P_i = \frac{\log k(f-2) - \log p(k+1)}{\log(f-1)} \qquad (10)$$

Now we estimate the number of node accesses in the KNN search. For the naive algorithm, similar to (6), we have:

$$NA_{naive} = C_{\lceil \mathcal{D}_k \rceil} \approx \frac{(f-1)^{\lceil \mathcal{D}_k \rceil}}{f-2} \qquad (11)$$

Recall that in our $nd$-based algorithm, the pointer $p$ starts from $q$, examines the $nd$'s of $p$'s children (except for the child that $p$ previously points at), searches downwards, and moves upward (and possibly to other SPIE's through the shortcuts) until the distance from $p$ to $q$ exceeds $\lceil \mathcal{D} \rceil$. For each downward search, the number of node accesses, $NA_{down}$, is equivalent to the total length of the paths from the $k$ nearest descendants to $p$. Let $\beta$ denote the distance from the $k$th nearest descendant to $p$. We have the following two equations,

$$\sum_{i=1}^{\beta} (f-1)^i p = k$$

$$\sum_{i=1}^{\beta} (f-1)^i p \cdot i = NA_{down}$$

Solving these two equations, we have

$$NA_{down} \approx \frac{f \cdot \beta \cdot k}{p} \approx \frac{f \cdot k(\log k(f-2) - \log p)}{p \log(f-1)} \qquad (12)$$

Therefore,

$$NA_{nd} = \sum_{i=0}^{\lceil \mathcal{D}_k \rceil} NA_{down} \approx \frac{f \cdot k(\lceil \mathcal{D}_k \rceil + 1)(\log k(f-2) - \log p)}{p \log(f-1)} \qquad (13)$$

By comparing (11) and (13), we come to a similar conclusion as in Section 6.3 that $NA_{nd} \ll NA_{naive}$.

## 7 Performance Evaluation

In this section, we present the experimental results on network reduction, $nd$ index construction and (k)NN search. We used two road networks in the simulation. The first is synthetic for controlled experiments, which was created by generating 183,231 planar points and connecting them through edges with random weights between 1 and 10. The degree of nodes follows an exponential distribution with its mean denoted as $f$. $f$ is tuned to evaluate its effect on network reduction. The second is a real road network obtained from Digital Chart of the World (DCW). It contains 594,103 railroads and roads in US, Canada, Mexico. Among these line segments, we identified 430,274 unique nodes, and thus the average degree of nodes, $f$, is about 2.7. Similar to [9], we used the connectivity-clustered access method (CCAM) [12] to sort and store the nodes and their adjacent lists. The page size was set to 4K bytes. The testbed was implemented in C++ on a Win32 platform with 2.4 GHz Pentium 4 CPU, 512 MB RAM.

We compare our $nd$-based NN search algorithm with two competitors. The first is the Dijkstra-based naive network expansion algorithm which uses a priority queue to store the nodes to be searched and increasingly expands to their adjacent nodes on the network. The second is the Voronoi-based Network Nearest Neighbor ($NV^3$) algorithm [8] which computes the Network Voronoi Diagram for each dataset. So far, it is known to be the best algorithm for NN search in road networks.

Regarding the performance metrics, we measured the CPU time, the *number of disk page accesses* and the *number of node accesses*. The first two show the search cost while the last metric indicates the pruning capability of the network reduction and $nd$ index.

## 7.1 Network Reduction

We evaluated the performance of the network reduction by measuring the number of edges before and after the reduction. In Figure 6, the result from the synthetic networks shows the same trend as Equation 1: when $f$ increases from 2 to 10, the reduced edges increases from 5% to 60% of the total edges. However, when $f$ gets even larger, the average length $g$ of a circuit decreases, which partially cancels out the effect of $f$. Therefore, we expect the proportion of reduced edges to stabilize when $f > 10$. For the real road network, the average node degree $f$ is reduced from 2.7 to 2.05, which is very close to a tree structure. In fact, only 1571 shortest path trees were created out of the 430,274 nodes. These results confirm the feasibility and effectiveness of network reduction on large road networks.

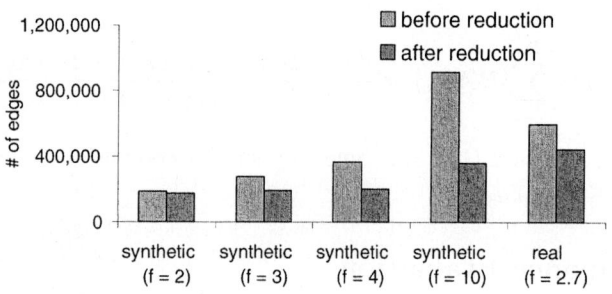

**Fig. 6.** Effect of Network Reduction

## 7.2 $nd$ Index Construction

We created three randomly distributed datasets with their cardinality set to 0.001, 0.01, 0.1 (denoted as $p$) to the total number of nodes on the real road network. We then built both $VN^3$ index (including the $NVP$ R-tree, $NVD$'s, $Bor-Bor$ distances, and OPC distances) and $nd$ index on these datasets. Table 2 shows the index sizes and the clock time for index construction. Note that for the $nd$ index, we do not count the size and construction time for the SPIE graph, which is 7.5 MB and 303 seconds respectively, because this one-time cost is shared by all datasets. The result shows that our $nd$ index has a constant size and almost constant construction time. It is more efficient to build than $VN^3$ index.

**Table 2.** Comparison on Index Construction

| Size (MB) | $p = 0.001$ | $p = 0.01$ | $p = 0.1$ | Time (s) | $p = 0.001$ | $p = 0.01$ | $p = 0.1$ |
|---|---|---|---|---|---|---|---|
| $VN^3$ | 347 | 92 | 67 | $VN^3$ | 2748 | 765 | 512 |
| $nd$ | 5.16 | 5.16 | 5.16 | $nd$ | 12 | 12 | 14 |

## 7.3 NN Search Result

We conducted experiments of NN search on the real road network for the three datasets and measured the CPU time, page accesses and node accesses[3]. All statistics were obtained from an average of 2,000 trials. In Figure 7(a), we observe that the number of page accesses for both the naive and $nd$ algorithms decreases as the density of the dataset $p$ increases, whereas the number of page accesses for $VN^3$ is almost constant. This is because the first two algorithms are based on graph traversal while $VN^3$ is based on point location on the NVP R-tree. Even though $VN^3$ precomputes the Network Voronoi Diagram and is thus efficient in finding the first nearest neighbor, our $nd$-based algorithm still outperforms it when $p > 0.01$, because more queries can be answered by visiting the $nd$ of a few nodes on a single SPIE. In this sense, $nd$ is more robust than $VN^3$ for datasets with various densities. Figure 7(b) confirms this argument: the $nd$-based algorithm reduces the node accesses of the naive algorithm by 2 orders of magnitude when $p = 0.001$ but it still reduces the nodes accesses by half when $p = 0.1$.

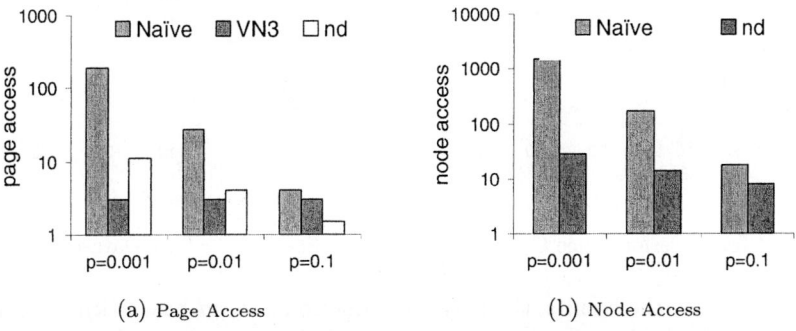

(a) Page Access    (b) Node Access

**Fig. 7.** Performance Comparison for NN Search

## 7.4 KNN Search Result

We conducted the kNN search for the $p = 0.01$ dataset on the real road network, where $k$ ranges from 1 to 50. We measured the page accesses and CPU time and plotted the results in Figures 8(a) and 8(b). The results show that when $k = 1$, $VN^3$ requires the fewest page accesses and the least CPU time, because $VN^3$

---

[3] Since CPU time was found neglectable in 1NN search, we omit it in this subsection.

optimizes the 1NN search by only requiring the search to locate the NVP that contains the query node. However, as $k$ increases, $VN^3$ still needs to traverse the NVD graph to search for candidate NNs; a major factor that contributes to the high cost of a kNN search by $VN^3$ is that the distance computation between each candidate and the query node is carried out separately and from scratch, while for network-expansion-based algorithms such as the naive and $nd$-based algorithms, the distance is computed accumulatively. This argument is supported by Figures 8(a) and 8(b) where the gap between $VN^3$ and the naive algorithm decreases as $k$ increases. On the other hand, the $nd$-based algorithm performs consistently well for a wide range of $k$. The reasons are four-folded. Firstly, recall that after network reduction, each SPIE contains hundreds of nodes on average, which means that for small $k$ it is likely that the search ends in one or two SPIE's. This explains why $nd$ outperforms $VN^3$ even for small $k$. Secondly, although kNN search on $nd$ index requires searching for the $nd$ of $p$'s descendants, these $nd$'s are likely stored in the same disk page that $p$ resides. Thirdly, since there are only 1571 SPIE's in the SPIE graph, looking for adjacent SPIE's to search is efficient. Last but not the least, thanks to the $nd$ index that avoids naive expansion within one SPIE, the $nd$ algorithm is the least affected by the increase of $k$. In Figures 8(a) and 8(b), both page accesses and CPU time of the $nd$ algorithm are sublinear to $k$.

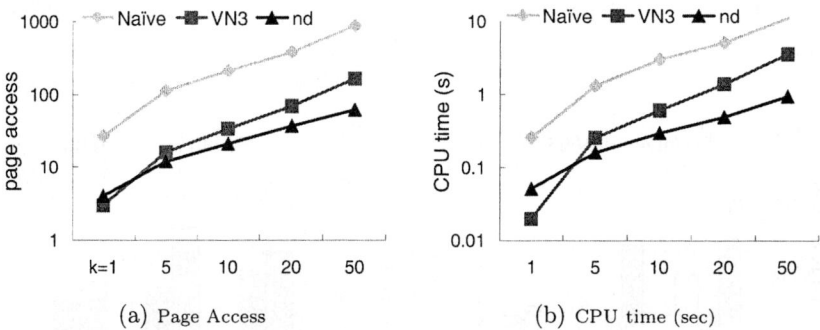

**Fig. 8.** Performance Comparison for KNN Search: $p = 0.01$ Dataset

To summarize the results, the network reduction and $nd$-based (k)NN search algorithms exhibit the following advantages: (1) the network topology is significantly simplified and the reduction is a one-time cost for multiple datasets; (2) the $nd$ index is lightweight in terms of storage and construction time; (3) the (k)NN search algorithm performs well for a wide range of datasets with different densities; (4) the kNN search algorithm performs well for a wide range of $k$.

## 8  Conclusion and Future Work

In this paper, we proposed a new kNN search technique for road networks. It simplifies the network by replacing the graph topology with a set of interconnected tree-based structures called SPIE's. An $nd$ index was devised on the SPIE so that our proposed kNN search on the SPIE follows a predetermined tree path. Both cost models and experimental results showed that our approach outperforms the existing network-expansion-based and solution-based kNN algorithms for most of the network topologies and data distributions.

In future work, we plan to devise structures other than SPIE to reduce the network topology. By striking a balance between the topological complexity of the structure and the kNN searching complexity on it, we can further improve the performance of our approach.

## References

1. Stefan Berchtold, Daniel A. Keim, Hans-Peter Kriegel, and Thomas Seidl. Indexing the solution space: A new technique for nearest neighbor search in high-dimensional space. *TKDE*, 12(1):45–57, 2000.
2. Hyung-Ju Cho and Chin-Wan Chung. An efficient and scalable approach to cnn queries in a road network. In *VLDB*, 2005.
3. T. H. Cormen, C. E. Leiserson, R. L. Rivest, and C. Stein. *Introduction to Algorithms, 2nd Edition*. McGraw Hill/MIT Press, 2001.
4. E. W. Dijkstra. A note on two problems in connection with graphs. *Numeriche Mathematik*, 1:269–271, 1959.
5. Eric Hanson, Yannis Ioannidis, Timos Sellis, Leonard Shapiro, and Michael Stonebraker. Heuristic search in data base systems. *Expert Database Systems*, 1986.
6. Christian S. Jensen, Jan Kolarvr, Torben Bach Pedersen, and Igor Timko. Nearest neighbor queries in road networks. In *11th ACM International Symposium on Advances in Geographic Information Systems (GIS'03)*, pages 1–8, 2003.
7. M. Kolahdouzan and C. Shahabi. Continuous k-nearest neighbor queries in spatial network databases. In *STDBM*, 2004.
8. Mohammad Kolahdouzan and Cyrus Shahabi. Voronoi-based k nearest neighbor search for spatial network databases. In *VLDB Conference*, pages 840–851, 2004.
9. D. Papadias, J. Zhang, N. Mamoulis, and Y. Tao. Query processing in spatial network databases. In *VLDB Conference*, pages 802–813, 2003.
10. Nick Roussopoulos, Stephen Kelley, and Frdric Vincent. Nearest neighbor queries. In *SIGMOD Conference, San Jose, California*, pages 71–79, 1995.
11. C. K. Shahabi, M. R. Kolahdouzan, and M. Sharifzadeh. A road network embedding technique for knearest neighbor search in moving object databases. In *10th ACM International Symposium on Advances in Geographic Information Systems (GIS'02)*, 2002.
12. S. Shekhar and D.R. Liu. Ccam: A connectivity-clustered access method for networks and network computations. *IEEE Transactions on Knowledge and Data Engineering*, 1(9):102–119, 1997.
13. Roger Weber, Hans-Jorg Schek, and Stephen Blott. A quantitative analysis and performance study for similarity-search methods in high-dimensional spaces. In *Proceedings of the 24rd International Conference on Very Large Data Bases*, pages 194–205, 1998.
14. J. Xu, X. Tang, and D. L. Lee. Performance analysis of location-dependent cache invalidation schemes for mobile environments. *IEEE Transactions on Knowledge and Data Engineering*, 15(2):474–488, 2003.
15. Cui Yu, Beng Chin Ooi, Kian-Lee Tan, and H. V. Jagadish. Indexing the distance: An efficient method to knn processing. In *VLDB Conference, Roma*, pages 421–430, 2001.

# Approximation Techniques to Enable Dimensionality Reduction for Voronoi-Based Nearest Neighbor Search

Christoph Brochhaus, Marc Wichterich, and Thomas Seidl

RWTH Aachen University, Germany
Data Management and Exploration Group
{brochhaus, wichterich, seidl}@informatik.rwth-aachen.de

**Abstract.** Utilizing spatial index structures on secondary memory for nearest neighbor search in high-dimensional data spaces has been the subject of much research. With the potential to host larger indexes in main memory, applications demanding a high query throughput stand to benefit from index structures tailored for that environment. "Index once, query at very high frequency" scenarios on semi-static data require particularly fast responses while allowing for more extensive precalculations. One such precalculation consists of indexing the solution space for nearest neighbor queries as used by the approximate Voronoi cell-based method. A major deficiency of this promising approach is the lack of a way to incorporate effective dimensionality reduction techniques. We propose methods to overcome the difficulties faced for normalized data and present a second reduction step that improves response times through limiting the dimensionality of the Voronoi cell approximations. In addition, we evaluate the suitability of our approach for main memory indexing where speedup factors of up to five can be observed for real world data sets.

## 1 Introduction

Research on the topic of nearest neighbor search in high-dimensional spaces traditionally has focused on secondary memory data structures. However, a growing number of applications stand to gain from a shift to main memory indexing as it promises to significantly reduce query response times and it becomes increasingly economically feasible to reserve a few hundred megabytes to do so. In addition, the volatile nature of main memory is not a disadvantage for semi-static data sets that are backed up on secondary memory and then read into main memory to be accessed at a high frequency. This scenario is often observed for server-based indexes where a large number of querying clients demands a low response time and thus a high query throughput on the server side. Furthermore, applications that use nearest neighbor queries as a base function for other algorithms such as classification and clustering fit this scenario. The interest in main memory indexing on the application side has been met by an increase in research activity in that domain over the past few years, which has resulted in several solutions to main memory indexing and shown that not all secondary memory indexing structures port well to main memory. Due to its low CPU-utilization, the approximate Voronoi cell approach to nearest neighbor search[1][2] subsumed in section 3.1 is a natural candidate for main memory indexing. Voronoi cells describe a covering of the

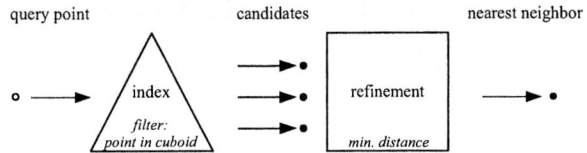

**Fig. 1.** Query processing using indexed Voronoi cell-bounding cuboids

underlying data space, so that each data object is assigned to a cell which contains all possible nearest neighbor locations of the corresponding object. A precomputation step is used to approximate the complex Voronoi cells with simpler high-dimensional axis-aligned bounding rectangles (i.e. cuboids) in order to enable low query response times. However, the approach resists attempts to incorporate effective dimensionality reduction techniques (cf. section 3.2) as it requires the boundaries of the data space to be taken into account. Straightforward solutions (bounding boxes, convex hulls) prove to be unsuitable. This severely limits the application domain of the approximate Voronoi approach as approximate Voronoi cells in high-dimensional spaces are neither feasible to compute nor efficient for indexing.

We therefore introduce new approximation-based methods in section 4 to efficiently overcome the difficulties faced during dimensionality reduction for normalized data such as size-invariant histograms common in image retrieval applications. A second reduction presented in section 5 improves response times through limiting the dimensionality of the Voronoi cell bounding cuboids themselves. The cuboids in the reduced dimensionality are indexed by facilitating either hierarchical or bitmap-based index structures in main memory as described in section 6. It is possible to find a complete set of nearest neighbor candidates for a querying point in a filtering step through simple point-in-cuboid tests (cf. figure 1). The significant performance improvements over other approaches achieved for the Voronoi-based technique through our two dimensionality reduction steps are shown in section 7 for real world data sets. These are made possible by the low number of CPU-intensive operations and the low amount of data transferred over the main memory bus.

## 2 Related Work

The idea to utilize the concept of precalculating the nearest neighborhood information with the help of Voronoi cells in order to support optimal worst-case query complexity was first adopted and investigated in [3]. The algorithm performs nearest neighbor queries on $N$ points in the 2-dimensional plane in $O(\log N)$ time by slicing the data space according to the Voronoi cell vertices and performing two binary searches on these slices. However, it does not extend well to higher dimensionalities.

In [1][2], a technique using approximations of Voronoi cells was introduced and enabled the use of data sets with a higher dimensionality. With increasing dimensionality and very large amounts of data this technique comes to its limits. Some methods presented in these papers (e.g. a limited amount of point insertions) can be facilitated for our work.

Multiple algorithms and data structures for computing the nearest neighbor of point $q$ by concentrating on the data space $D$ have been proposed in the past. The trivial solution is a linear scan over all points in $D$. The high CPU and memory bandwidth utilization make this approach unsuitable for multimedia database applications managing a large number of high-dimensional objects.

A variation of the simple linear scan is employed by the Vector Approximation File [4] which uses fewer bits per dimension of the data points. Each dimension is separated into $2^r$ bins. Thus, only $r$ bits are used to indicate the corresponding bin for each point. To find the nearest neighbor, the approximated vectors are scanned sequentially and an upper and a lower bound of the distance to the query point are computed. Only those points for which the lower bound is smaller than the smallest upper bound are then used to find the correct nearest neighbor.

Other approaches rely on a hierarchical, spatial division of the data space into regions. The data points are each associated with a region that is not further divided, mapping spatial proximity in the feature space to topological proximity in an index structure. A number of these structures use hierarchically nested (minimum) bounding rectangles (MBRs) for the inner directory nodes to manage the data points stored in the leaf nodes. The R-Tree [5] and its variants the $R^*$-Tree [6], the CR-Tree [7] and the X-Tree [8] are prime representatives of this paradigm. The CR-Tree compresses the MBR keys which occupy a large part of the index. The X-Tree was specifically designed to support high-dimensional searches and outperforms its predecessors in that scenario.

Nearest neighbor algorithms such as the Depth-first Traversal algorithm of [9] and the Priority Search algorithm described in [10] use these index structures to prune whole branches of the tree once the feature space region they represent can be guaranteed to not include the nearest neighbor.

Due to the continuing tendency of main memory becoming significantly larger and less expensive, research interest has been renewed on the creation and utilization of indexes in main memory. The above mentioned CR-Tree [7] is a modification of the R-Tree [5] which introduces cache-consciousness and holds the index in main memory. Other main memory index structures like the pkT-Tree/pkB-Tree [11] and the CSB+-Tree [12] have been investigated but are restricted to low-dimensional data.

## 3 Preliminaries

### 3.1 Voronoi Cells

The concept of space partitioning to describe nearest neighborhood information used in this work was developed in the early twentieth century by G. Voronoi [13] and is an n-dimensional generalization of the 2- and 3-dimensional diagrams already used by Dirichlet in 1850. It is still a widespread and important topic of extensive research in the field of computational geometry [14].

A Voronoi diagram for a set of points is a covering of the space by cells that indicate the nearest neighbor areas of the points and is thus directly tied to the problem of finding the nearest neighbor. Figure 2a shows such a partitioning for six points in the plane. For each point, the respective surrounding cell describes the area for which that point is closer than any of the other points. Given a query position $q$ in the plane, the nearest

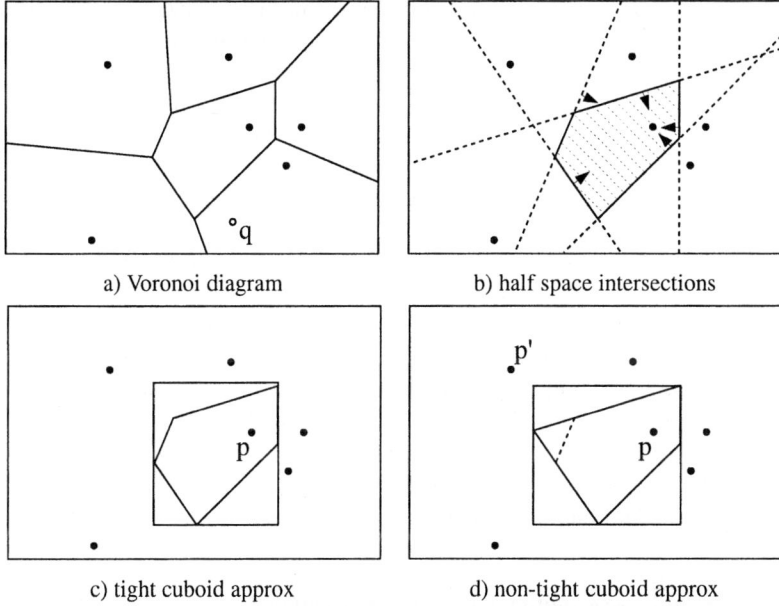

**Fig. 2.** Voronoi cells and their approximations

neighbor can be found by determining the cell that includes that position. As long as $q$ remains inside the same cell, its nearest neighbor does not change. The edges and vertices in the diagram describe positions for which more than one point is at minimal distance.

Formally, Voronoi cells can be described using half spaces as follows:

**Definition 1.** *Given a data space $S$, a metric distance function $\delta : S \times S \to \mathbb{R}$, a finite set of data points $D = \{p^1, ..., p^N\}$ with $D \subset S$ and half spaces $HS(p, p') = \{p'' \in S | \delta(p'', p) \leq \delta(p'', p')\}$, a **Voronoi cell** $VC_{S,D}(p^i)$ for point $p^i$ is defined as the intersection of $S$ and $(|D| - 1)$ half spaces:*

$$VC_{S,D}(p^i) = S \cap \left( \bigcap_{p \in (D-\{p^i\})} HS(p^i, p) \right)$$

**Definition 2.** *A **Voronoi diagram** $V_S(D)$ is simply defined as the set of the Voronoi cells:*

$$V_S(D) = \{VC_{S,D}(p^1), ..., VC_{S,D}(p^{|D|})\}$$

Thus, a Voronoi cell is a convex polytope. Figure 2b shows the half space intersections for a Voronoi cell where the half space separation lines are shown as dashed lines.

For the approximation approach to Voronoi cells chosen here, it is required that $S \subset \mathbb{R}^d$ be of convex shape such as the $d$-dimensional unit hypercube $[0, 1]^d$. Note that not only all points in $D$ but also all potential query points are located within $S$.

However, in more than two dimensions (as is the case in many multimedia applications) the cells become highly complex [15][16]. Due to that observation, neither computing nor storing or inclusion-testing is efficient for these Voronoi cells in nearest neighbor search. Therefore, our precalculation step determines approximations of Voronoi cells of lesser complexity without requiring the exact representations of the latter to be known while still allowing for fast nearest neighbor searches.

To reduce the complexity of the Voronoi cells, we approximate them by bounding shapes with fewer surfaces. To avoid false dismissals during nearest neighbor query processing, these shapes must include the whole data space of the respective Voronoi cells. We decided in favor of axis-aligned bounding cuboids which offer several advantages: they are storable in $O(dN)$ space for $N$ points in $d$ dimensions, enable inclusion tests in $O(d)$ time and are computable through well-studied standard algorithms like linear optimization [17]. Other methods like non-axis-aligned projections can also be used for determining cell approximations but are omitted here for simplicity. In linear optimization a linear objective function is maximized or minimized over a range of values restricted by a set of linear constraints.

In the context of Voronoi cell approximation, the required linear constraints are defined by

- the set of half spaces outlining the respective cell and
- the data space boundaries.

The objective functions are used to find the outermost points in each dimension $1, ..., d$ of a cell $VC(p)$ described by the linear constraints. For this purpose, functions $f_1$ to $f_d$ with $f_i(x_1, ..., x_d) = x_i$ are each minimized and maximized once per Voronoi cell. The extremal values directly represent the respective boundaries of the cuboid that tightly bounds the approximated Voronoi cell.

The data space boundaries must be added to the set of constraints to avoid that these extremal values extend outside the data space in certain dimensions.

To significantly speed up the calculation of the bounding cuboids, for each Voronoi cell, only a subset of all related half spaces can be used. Redundant half spaces can be left out without affecting the result of the cell approximation. Leaving out non-redundant half spaces only leads to a non-minimum bounding cuboid, which introduces more nearest neighbor candidates and slows down nearest neighbor searches but never misses a possible solution. Therefore the choice of the subset of half spaces is very important. In [1] some heuristics for the choice of an appropriate subset of half spaces are introduced. We concentrate on a heuristic which selects a number of nearest neighbor points for each data point $p \in D$ and uses the corresponding half spaces to approximate the original Voronoi cell $VC_{S,D}(p)$ since the half spaces defined by the nearest neighbors of $p$ are likely to actually restrict the cell. For the range of parameters in our experiments, a value of 2,000 neighbors has proven to yield good results.

Figure 2c shows the approximated cell belonging to object $p$ where all half spaces were used while in figure 2d the half space $HS(p, p')$ is left out, resulting in a slightly larger cuboid.

## 3.2 Dimensionality Reduction

The original data dimensionality can be high in multimedia applications. This complicates the nearest neighbor search via the Voronoi approach.

First, a high dimensionality results in the data space being sparsely populated with data points. Thus the bounding cuboids of the Voronoi cells become quite large as only comparatively few other cells are available to restrict each cell in all possible directions. In extreme cases, all cuboids overlap the complete data space as each cell includes points on both the upper and lower space boundary of each dimension. These unrestricted dimensions are useless for nearest neighbor searches, since they never cause any point to be dismissed as a nearest neighbor candidate for any query.

Second, computing the cell-bounding cuboids becomes more expensive as each dimension adds a new variable to the linear optimization process and more linear constraints are needed to describe the cells of points $D$ in $S$ as the total number of facets in $V_S(D)$ increases.

Finally, once the Voronoi cell approximations have been computed, they are to be indexed to answer future queries. For cuboids in a high dimensionality, hierarchical index structures such as the R-Tree or X-Tree are bound to experience a deteriorating efficiency caused by the effects of the "Curse of Dimensionality".

A partial solution to these problems lies in applying dimensionality reduction techniques as a special form of approximation. For the Voronoi approach, this can be performed on two levels as summarized by figure 3.

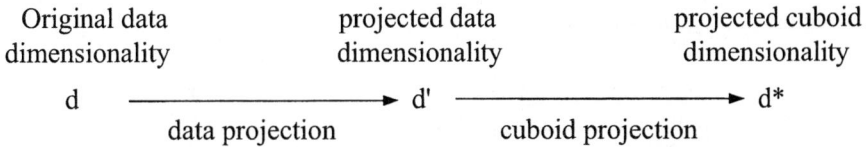

**Fig. 3.** Two-step strategy for reducing the dimensionality

All linear dimensionality reduction techniques (including Random Projection [18], Wavelet Transforms, Discrete Fourier Transform, etc) can be used as the first dimensionality reduction step in our approach, where data points are mapped to new data points with a lower dimensionality. We focus on the PCA due to its optimality regarding the mean squared error, its predominant position in practical applications and its beneficial two-part output (rotation matrix and variances) useful in section 5. Some of the nearest neighborhood information is given up in this step in order to more efficiently construct the Voronoi cell-bounding cuboids. Oftentimes, removing some dimensions in this way only introduces minor inaccuracies due to two properties of the similarity search framework based on feature vectors. The feature extraction process used can result in dimensions that are insignificant to the application at hand. This is the case when one dimension is dominated by other dimensions either due to differences in the variance of the dimensions or due to correlation effects. Additionally, the distance functions used to determine nearest neighbors only approximate a similarity concept that is often subjective. Introducing further minor inaccuracies through dimensionality reduction can go largely unnoticed in face of this observation and at the same time drastically increase the efficiency of the nearest neighbor search.

In the second dimensionality reduction step described in section 5, the dimensionality of the resulting cuboids can be further reduced prior to indexing.

## 4 The Bounding Constraints Problem

Unlike other nearest neighbor algorithms, the Voronoi approach using bounding cuboids depends on the data space being included in a polytope whose facets are used to define the outer constraints for the linear optimizations of the bounding cuboid computation. A direct application of dimensionality reduction techniques not taking this requirement into account is bound to fail.

We focus on normalized data where all points $p = (p_1, ..., p_d)$, $p_i \geq 0$, share a common sum $c = \sum_{i=1}^{d} p_i$. These conditions are frequently met for data used in multimedia similarity search. Two examples used for our experiments in section 7 include size-invariant image histogram representations and ratios ("1:3:2") in context of financial time series. For these data points, there is a suitable $(d-1)$-dimensional convex polytope with $d$ vertices and $d$ facets situated in a $(d-1)$-dimensional subspace. After rotating and projecting all points to eliminate the redundant dimension $p_d = c - \sum_{i=1}^{d-1} p_i$, the $d$ vertices of the polytope consist of the accordingly transformed unit vectors scaled by factor $c$. Figure 4 displays this for the case of $d = 3$ and $c = 1$ where all points are enclosed by the three lines between the three transformed unit vectors in the $d_1 d_2$ subspace.

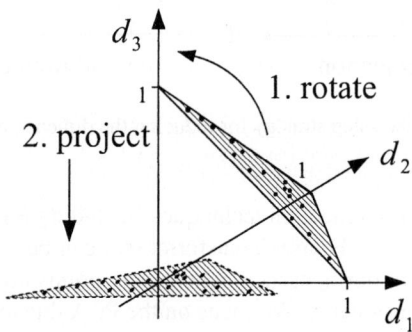

**Fig. 4.** 3-dimensional common-sum vectors bounded by three lines in a 2-dim. plane

In practical applications, the originally sum-normalized data is often linearly transformed. Scaling of individual dimensions is used to compute weighted distances and both rotations and projections are common in dimensionality reduction (PCA, DFT, Random Projection and others). The aim is to find the transformed convex polytope defining the data space - in particular after projections into a dimensionality $d' < d$. A linear transform of a convex polytope is another convex polytope where the vertices of the transformed polytope are (a subset of) the transformed original vertices. Thus, one

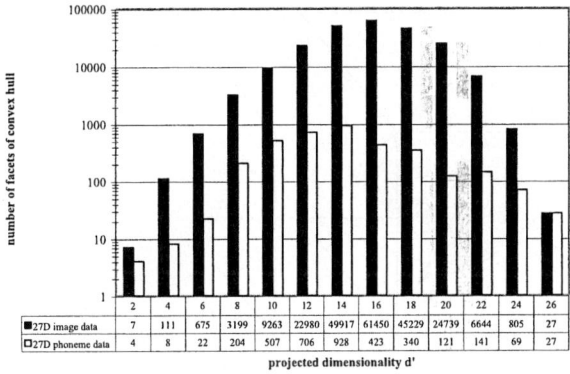

**Fig. 5.** Number of facets for convex hulls in the projected dimensionality d'

way to find the transformed polytope is to transform all original polytope vertices $P$ and then find the convex hull for those points $P'$. This has a worst-case time complexity of $O(n \log n + n^{\lfloor d'/2 \rfloor})$ for $n$ points in the (possibly lower) transformed dimensionality $d'$ [19]. Other approaches to find the projected polytope include the Fourier-Motzkin elimination with extensions to reduce the number of redundant constraints [20].

The potentially high complexity of the convex hull leads to another problem. Each facet of the resulting convex hull produces a constraint for the linear optimizations for each Voronoi cell. Hence, that number must be low for practical purposes. Contrary to that, a convex hull with $n$ vertices in $d'$ dimensions can have in the order of $O(n^{\lfloor d'/2 \rfloor})$ facets [19]. Figure 5 shows these values computed via the QHull algorithm [21] for two real world data sets used in section 7. While the convex hulls for the phoneme data set remain sufficiently simple, the image histogram data set quickly goes beyond values reasonable for a practical computation of the Voronoi cell-bounding cuboids. Due to that fact, we introduce a number of methods to conservatively approximate the convex hull. An approximation of a point set is called conservative in this context if all points inside the original point set are also contained in the approximation of the set.

**A bounding cuboid approximating the convex hull**

A simple way to conservatively approximate the convex hull of a point set $P'$ with $(d'-1)$-dimensional planes is to find a bounding cuboid for the hull. This can be done by determining the minimum and maximum values among the set $P'$ for each dimension. The resulting $2d'$ planes defined by the cuboid facets are suitable as constraints for the Voronoi cell approximations. However, the shape of the convex hull of $P'$ can be quite removed from an axis-aligned cuboid. If a larger precomputation cost is acceptable to better the selectivity for queries, it is worth finding more complex but closer approximations of the convex hull.

**Tilted planes approximating the convex hull**

A potentially closer approximation can be found by using the vertices of the bounding cuboid. For each of the $2^{d'}$ vertices, the adjacent $d$ vertices span a hyperplane with a normal vector $n$ as depicted in figure 6a for vertex $v$. Each such tilted hyperplane is

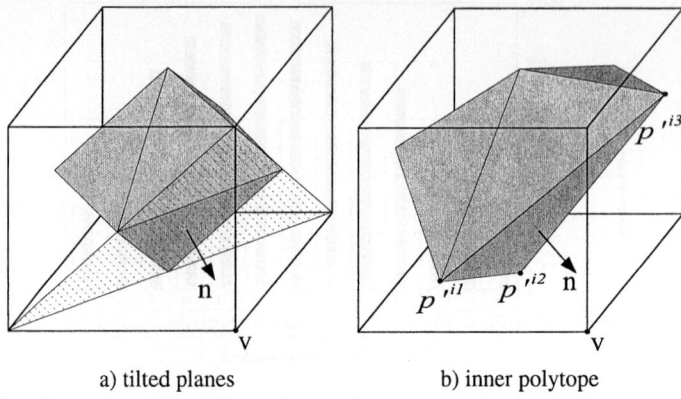

**Fig. 6.** Planes approximating a convex hull

then pushed outwards along its normal vector until all points in $P'$ are located either on the hyperplane or behind it as defined by the orientation of the normal vector. The plane-pushing algorithm has a time complexity of $O(d' \cdot |P'|)$.

**Inner polytopes approximating the convex hull**

Like the bounding cuboid approach, the tilted planes method makes little use of the geometric shape of the convex hull being approximated. The normal vectors of the hyperplanes are only influenced by the total extent of the convex hull. In this paragraph, a variation is proposed that attempts to calculate more suitable normal vectors for the fitting planes. The main idea is to define a convex polytope residing inside the convex hull of $P'$ that is less complex but still reflects its general shape. Once the facets of this polytope have been determined, they are pushed outwards along their respective normal vectors to include all the points in $P'$.

The polytope used in this proposal is defined through its vertices which form a subset of the vertices of the convex hull of $P'$.

**Definition 3.** *Let $R = \{r^1, r^2, ...\}$ be a finite set of k-dimensional points. The **set of extremal points Ext(R)** is defined as:*

$$Ext(R) = Ext_{min}(R) \cup Ext_{max}(R)$$

with

$$Ext_{min}(R) = \{r^i \in R | \exists k^* \in \{1, ..., k\} : \forall r^j \in R - \{r^i\} : \\ (r^i_{k^*} < r^j_{k^*}) \vee ((r^i_{k^*} = r^j_{k^*}) \wedge (i < j))\}$$

and

$$Ext_{max}(R) = \{r^i \in R | \exists k^* \in \{1, ..., k\} : \forall r^j \in R - \{r^i\} : \\ (r^i_{k^*} > r^j_{k^*}) \vee ((r^i_{k^*} = r^j_{k^*}) \wedge (i < j))\}$$

Intuitively, these are the points that are located on an axis-aligned minimum bounding cuboid of the set $R$. If more than one point is located on the same facet of the cuboid, only the one with the lowest index is used for that facet. For each vertex $v$ of the bounding cuboid, points $\{p'^{i_1}, ..., p'^{i_{d'}}\} \subseteq Ext(P')$ are selected as illustrated by figure 6b. These are the points that were included in $Ext(P')$ due to their position on a facet of the cuboid that has $v$ as one of its vertices. If none of the points are duplicate for vertex $v$, the $d'$ points define a facet of an inner polytope which can then be pushed outwards as in the tilted plane method. In higher dimensionalities with few points, it often happens that one point is extremal for more than one dimension and thus the maximum number of $2^{d'}$ facets is rarely reached for the inner polytope.

**Greedy point selection**

Further inner polytopes can be defined by using other methods to select a subset $T \subset P'$ and then constructing the less complex convex hull for $T$. The facets of the hull are then pushed outwards along their normal vectors. In order for $T$ to represent the general shape of $P'$, we used the following greedy heuristic for selecting points $\{t^1, ..., t^{|T|}\}$: choose any one point in $P'$ that is located on the convex hull of $P'$ as $t^1$. Then choose $t^{i+1}$ as the point $p$ from $(P' - \{t^1, ..., t^i\})$ with the greatest accumulated distance $\sum_{j=1}^{i} \delta(p, t^j)$. The greedy selection algorithm runs in $O(d' \cdot |P'| + d' \cdot |T|^2)$ time followed by the computation of the convex hull for $|T|$ points.

**Combinations and variations**

The strategies described for finding a convex polytope conservatively approximating the space in which data points potentially reside offer some practical alternatives to the extremes of the convex hull with its high facet count but small volume. A few more approaches can be directly derived from the prior approximations and shall be described here. An intersection of two conservative, convex approximations yields another conservative, convex approximation. Thus, all approaches can be combined by using constraining planes from more than one approach. Adding the $2d'$ axis-aligned facets of the convex hull-bounding cuboid to other constraints hardly induces any computational effort but helps to reduce the size of the also axis-aligned Voronoi cell-bounding cuboids and ensures that the data space is bounded in all directions. Similarly, the hyperplanes retrieved from a greedy point selection can be augmented by both the cuboid and the inner polytope hyperplanes.

## 5 Reducing the Bounding Cuboid Dimensionality

The dimensionality reduction discussed enables efficient computation of the bounding cuboids by projecting the data points from dimensionality $d$ to a subspace of dimensionality $d'$. However, it does so by sacrificing nearest neighborhood information. Though justifiable to some extent, it is often not viable to reduce the dimensionality to a level where indexing the cuboids is efficient while the data retains enough of the proximity information. Therefore, a further reduction to a dimensionality $d^* < d'$ (cf. figure 3) is proposed which nevertheless allows the nearest neighbor in the $d'$-dimensional space to be found.

After computing the Voronoi cell-bounding cuboids for the projected data points in dimensionality $d'$, those cuboids themselves are projected to dimensionality $d^*$ by dropping some of the dimensions. This produces the same nearest neighbor as in the case of the cuboids in dimensionality $d'$.

**Definition 4.** *Let $D \subset \mathbb{R}^d$ and $Q \subset \mathbb{R}^d$ be finite sets of d-dimensional points and $C = \{c^1, ..., c^{|D|}\}$ the set of Voronoi cell-bounding cuboids for data points in D defined by their respective lower and upper boundary vertices $L = \{l^1, ..., l^{|D|}\}$ and $U = \{u^1, ..., u^{|D|}\}$. Then the characteristic function*

$$include : Q \times \{1, .., |D|\} \times \mathcal{P}(\{1, ..., d\}) \to \{0, 1\}$$

$$include(q, i, E) = \begin{cases} 1 & : \quad \forall e \in E : l^i_e \le q_e \le u^i_e \\ 0 & : \quad otherwise \end{cases}$$

*determines if point q is inside all intervals defining the extent of the cuboid $c^i$ in the set of dimensions E.*

First, a query vector $q$ is transformed and projected to $q'$ in dimensionality $d'$ by the same method used to reduce the data dimensionality. Without the cuboid projection, vector $q'$ is then tested for inclusion in the Voronoi cell-bounding cuboids $c^i$ defined by their respective upper and lower boundary vertices $u^i$ and $l^i$. Each cuboid $c^i$ for which $include(q', i, \{1, ..., d'\})$ equals 1 indicates a nearest neighbor candidate. The cuboid dimensionality is reduced via dropping $(d' - d^*)$ of the dimensions of $q'$ and all $c^i$. The new inclusion test can then be performed as $include(q', i, E^*)$ with $E^* \subset \{1, ..., d'\}$. Whenever $q'$ is included in a cuboid, the same holds true for $q^*$ and the projected cuboid.

While no candidates are lost in this process, there might however be additional false positives. This results in a worsening selectivity of the filter step (cf. figure 1) as more dimensions are dropped. On the other hand, fewer dimensions can result in a faster filter step execution. Consecutively, the following question arises: Which dimensions are to be dropped and which ones are to be retained? Unfortunately, there are $\sum_{e=1}^{d'} \binom{d'}{e}$ combinations to consider in an exhaustive search. The search space must be vastly reduced by excluding combinations and using heuristics to find a combination of dimensions that produces a satisfyingly good solution.

**Using empirical selectivities to find dimensions to retain**

As a first simplification, average selectivity values from empirical queries are used to find dimensions with a good individual selectivity.

**Definition 5.** *Let D, Q, C be defined as in definition 4. The **empirical selectivity ES** for a set of dimensions $E \subseteq \{1, ..., d\}$ is defined as*

$$ES_{D,Q}(E) = \frac{1}{|Q|} \sum_{q \in Q} \frac{1}{|D|} \sum_{i=1}^{|D|} include(q, i, E).$$

Given a suitable query set $Q$, this reduces the workload considerably. For each dimension $k$ between 1 and $d'$, only $ES_{D,Q}(\{k\})$ must be computed. Using the worsening (i.e. increasing) selectivities as the order in which dimensions are retained makes sense if the underlying filtering events of the form "a cuboid is not dismissed as a candidate for a nearest neighbor query on grounds of its boundaries in dimension $k$" are statistically independent. In that case, the empirical selectivity of two combined dimensions is expected to be close to the product of both individual empirical selectivities. Thus, using the dimensions with the best (empirical) individual selectivities results in a good (empirical) combined selectivity for $k$ dimensions.

While statistic independence cannot be expected in general, the PCA removes linear dependencies of the data points by eliminating the covariances. For example, after PCA reduction to a dimensionality of 10 for the 27-dimensional image histogram data set from our experimental section the two dimensions with the highest variance exhibit an empirical selectivity of 15% and 10.8% respectively. The expected combined selectivity would be close to $15\% \cdot 10.8\% = 1.62\%$ in case of independence. The measured value was 1.95%. With an increasing number of dimensions, the relative gap widens to an expected 0.0027% for 10 dimensions and 0.0596% measured. Still, the proposed order of dropping dimensions resulted in empirical combined selectivities rarely beaten by spot samples of the same number of dimensions, which justifies using the simplification proposed in this section.

**Using variances to find dimensions to retain**

To avoid having to find a suitable query set $Q$ and compute empirical selectivities, another simplification can be employed when PCA has been used to reduce the data dimensionality. As a side effect of the PCA, the variances for each dimension of the rotated and projected data points are known. Instead of using the worsening selectivity order to pick dimensions to retain, the descending order of the variances can be used. While a high variance for a dimension does not necessarily imply a good selectivity for that dimension, it is a good indicator. Dimensions with a low variance tend to produce Voronoi cells that stretch far in said dimensions. Measured correlation coefficients for inverted variances and measured selectivities of individual dimensions were 0.957, 0.504 and 0.937 for the three real world data sets used in our experiments.

**On the number of dimensions to retain**

The question of how many dimensions are to be retained remains. This depends on the index structure used. One possibility would be to produce up to $d'$ indexes using 1 to $d'$ dimensions selected via the methods proposed above and then select the one index with the best average query performance. Without further information about the index structure, this might be the only method to pursue. Experiments in section 7 show that the X-Tree greatly benefits from the additional projection while the evaluated bitmap-based structure hardly does.

## 6 Main Memory Indexing

Data page access and read times are not the foremost cost factors of performing nearest neighbor queries when the index structure is stored in main memory. The querying time can be decomposed into a filter part (decide which points in $D$ need further

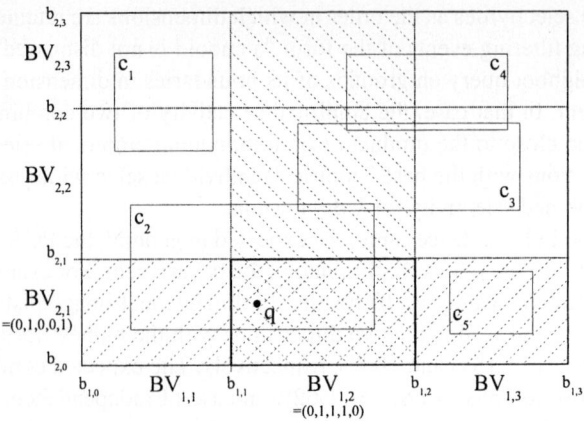

**Fig. 7.** Bitvector Index for 5 cuboids

examination) and a refinement part (compute the distances to the query point $q$). Both parts vary widely for the available algorithms and index structures. While the linear scan does not spend any time on filtering but computes the distances from $q$ to all data points in $D$, the Priority Search algorithm [10] for hierarchical index structures carefully considers which data points warrant a distance computation.

Since the Voronoi cell-bounding cuboids are axis-aligned, the usually secondary memory-based R-Tree family is an obvious candidate to support the filtering step in our approach. Due to its suitability for medium and higher dimensionalities, we chose to adapt the X-Tree variant[8] to run on main memory (with a space complexity of $O(N)$) for tests in section 7. In addition, we implemented a bitmap-based index structure described in [22]. The authors originally used the Bitvector Index for epsilon queries in a main memory-based similarity search system for audio samples but its design makes it an evident option for Voronoi-based nearest neighbor queries. For each dimension $i$ of the space to be indexed, the Bitvector Index stores a number $m$ of bitvectors $BV_{i,1}$, ..., $BV_{i,m}$ together with $m+1$ delimitation values $b_{i,0}, b_{i,1}$, ..., $b_{i,m}$. When indexing $N$ cuboids, each $BV_{i,j}$ has $N$ bit entries denoting which of the cuboids cover part of the interval $[b_{i,j-1}, b_{i,j}]$ in dimension $i$. In the example depicted in figure 7, only the cuboids $c_2$, $c_3$ and $c_4$ overlap the hatched interval belonging to $BV_{1,2}$.

When considering the query point $q$ in figure 7, only cuboids that overlap the crossed area are of interest during a nearest neighbor query using Voronoi cell-approximating cuboids. These can be found by a bit-wise 'and' operation for $BV_{1,2}$ and $BV_{2,1}$. A nearest neighbor algorithm using this index structure and Voronoi cell-approximating cuboids goes through four steps.

1. establish in which interval the query point falls per dimension, using binary search
2. combine the respective bitvectors via bitwise 'and'
3. retrieve a list of cuboid indices represented by the set bits in the resulting bitvector
4. scan over the data points belonging to the list of cuboids to find the nearest neighbor

On $N$ data points in $d'$ dimensions with cuboids of dimensionality $d^*$, the time complexity for this algorithm is $O(ld(m) \cdot d^* + d' \cdot N)$ while the space complexity is $O(d^* \cdot m \cdot N + d' \cdot N)$. While this is not lower than the complexity of the linear scan, it has the potential to show a significant performance boost through packing 32 bits of a bitvector each into an unsigned integer of that length. Thus, instead of computing $N$ floating point distances in $d'$ dimensions only $(d^* - 1) \cdot \lceil N/32 \rceil$ integer 'and' operations are required to create a bitvector that has its bits set to 1 for a superset of the cuboids which contain the point $q$. Only for the remaining cuboids the according point distances have to be computed. In addition to the lower CPU time requirement, the amount of data to be accessed in step 2 is limited to $d^*$ bits per cuboid compared to $d' \cdot 32$ or $d' \cdot 64$ bits per data point for the single and double precision floating points used by the linear scan. That reduction is important if the linear scan reaches the main memory throughput limits.

## 7 Experiments

To test the different proposed methods of producing outer constraints for the data space from section 4, various empirical selectivities were computed using a query set $Q$ consisting of 7,510 out of 207,510 image histograms projected from $d = 27$ to the first 10 principal components. This left 200,000 histograms for the data point set $D$. Before reducing the dimensionality to $d' = 10$, a linear transform was used in order to have the Euclidean distance values equal those of a similarity matrix-induced quadratic form as known from [23]. Figure 8a shows that the convex hull produced a total of 9,263 constraints. Using a higher dimensionality $d'$ significantly increased that number (cf. figure 5). The bounding cuboid with only 20 constraints suffered a selectivity increase of factor 55 compared to the convex hull that produced a selectivity of roughly 0.06%. Adding all 20 existing inner polytope planes to the cuboid helped reduce the increase to factor 24 while the 1,024 tilted planes resulted in a factor of 15. Using all three approaches together with 1,064 constraints brought this down further to factor 11. Compared to that, the greedy point selection using 11, 15, 19 and 23 points from left to right in figure 8a shows that it is a well-suited approach that allows for a favorable trade-off between the number of constraints and the resulting selectivity. For all further

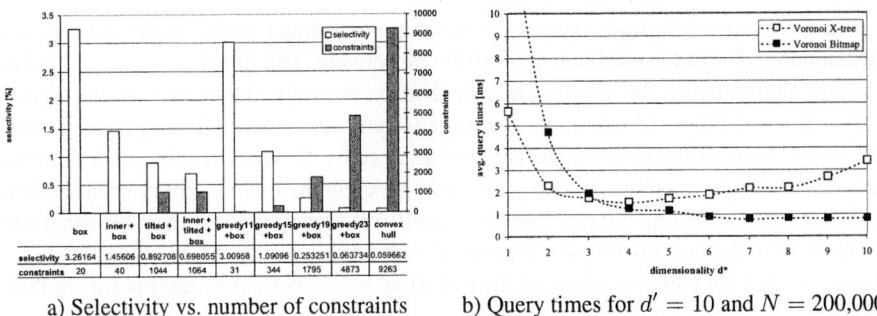

a) Selectivity vs. number of constraints    b) Query times for $d' = 10$ and $N = 200,000$

**Fig. 8.** Comparison of bounding constraints heuristics and the influence of $d^*$

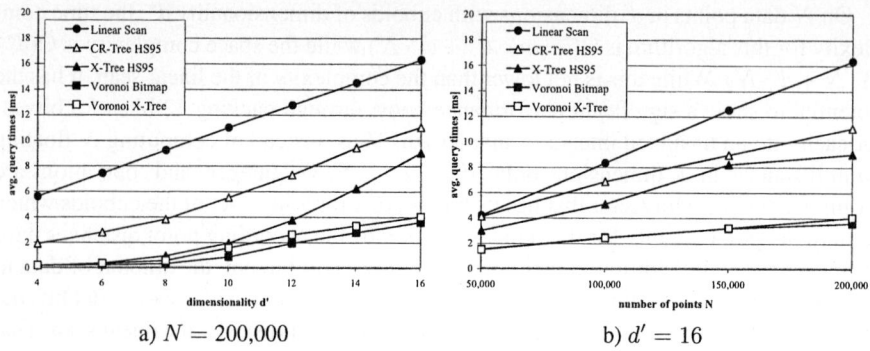

**Fig. 9.** Query times at varying dimensionality **d'** and cardinality **N**

experiments, we chose to use the box, inner polytope and greedy point selection combined in such a way that the number of constraints did not exceed 2,000 (e.g. 19 points in the 10-dimensional case).

All run-time benchmarks were performed using C++ implementations on a computer with a 2.4GHz Pentium 4 CPU (512 kilobytes of second level cache) with one gigabyte of 266MHz main memory hosting the respective index structure and data points for each measurement.

Using the variance-based heuristic from section 5, the axis-aligned projection of the Voronoi cell-bounding cuboids results in a definite advantage when indexing the cuboids in an X-Tree. With just four out of the ten dimensions, figure 8b displays a two-fold increase in the overall nearest neighbor querying speed. The Bitvector Index, on the other hand, hardly benefits from said projection. This can be explained by the relatively cheap computation of the final bitvector compared to a high computational cost of both decoding the vector in order to find the relevant data points (where bits are set to one) and computing their distances to the query point. The decoding part benefits from a sparsely populated bitvector which necessitates a low selectivity in the filtering step of the nearest neighbor search. Contrary to that, the selectivity using all ten dimensions was at 0.25% while it was twice that for the combination of only the five dimensions with the highest variances.

Figures 9a and 9b show average response times subject to the projected data dimensionality $d'$ and the cardinality $N$ of $D$ respectively. The linear scan is included as a trivial alternative to the various indexes. Nonsurprisingly, our tests with the Vector Approximation File [4] loaded into main memory never returned average query times faster than those of the linear scan. This is explained by the need to compute a minimal distance to the query point for each point in $D$ which in the main memory scenario was no faster than computing the exact distance itself. We thus dropped it from the diagrams for simplicity. Aside from the two Voronoi-based indexes explained in section 6, we included the X-Tree and a variation of the CR-Tree, which both store data points in their leaf nodes. The Priority Search algorithm [10] for those two hierarchical indexes outperformed the Depth-first Traversal algorithm of [9] in all our test runs. The latter was thus omitted. For the 200,000 image histograms of figure 9a, all remaining indexes out-

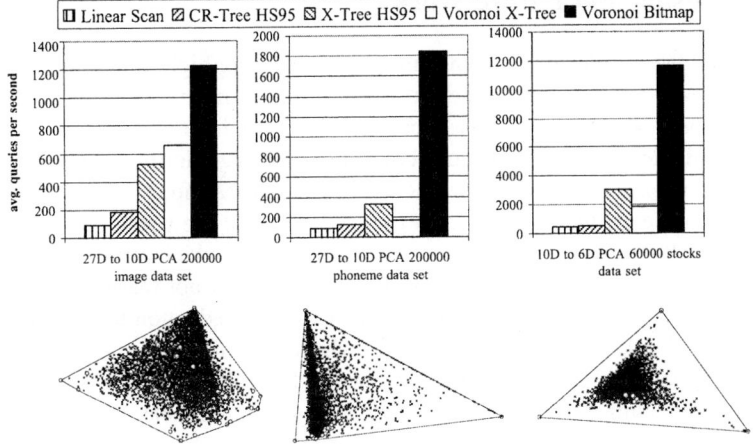

**Fig. 10.** Query throughputs per data set

performed the linear scan over the whole range of examined dimensionalities. Without exceptions, the Voronoi-based Bitvector Index has the lowest querying times followed by the Voronoi-based X-Tree. For the latter, the indexed dimensionality was optimal at $d^* = 4$ for $d' \in [4, 12]$ and $d^* = 3$ for the rest.

The same order of comparitive querying speeds was observed over the whole range of $N \in \{50000, 100000, 150000, 200000\}$ for a fixed $d' = 16$ as depicted by figure 9b. Here the point-based hierarchical indexes increasingly manage to outperform the linear scan as the number of data points grows. This is also true for the Voronoi-based X-Tree. Perhaps surprisingly at first, even the Bitvector Index with a linear time complexity displays a seemingly sub-linear behaviour. While this is of course not true in the strict theoretical sense, its slowing increase is explained by the decreasing selectivity that the approximation of the Voronoi cells exhibits with an increasing number of smaller cells. A linear behavior would be expected once that selectivity closes in on the ideal value of $1/N$ at the latest. At $d' = 16$ and $N = 200000$ the speedup factor comparing the bitmap-based Voronoi to the next fastest competing approach was over 2.5.

To finish our series of experiments, we varied the real world data set for all described indexes and algorithms. In addition to the 200,000 image histograms (all taken from TV screen shots), we used as many phoneme-based histograms extracted from 12,374 spoken and transcribed [24] sentences using resolution of 10ms for a sliding window of one second and a window-to-window overlap of 74% which resulted in a high number of non-unique vectors ($\approx$5%). Lastly, 60,000 ratios comparing the per-minute amount of money spent on 10 blue chip stocks traded were calculated from a subset of the data available in [25] and projected to the first six principal components. In order to visualize the distribution of the resulting vectors, we also projected all data sets to their first two respective principal components and show them together with the 2-dimensional convex hull in figure 10. The hierarchical methods were not as efficient for the later two data sets while the bitvector index enables a vastly increased query throughput for all three data sets with a speedup factor in excess of five for the phoneme data.

## 8 Conclusion and Future Work

In this paper we introduced a new technique for indexing high-dimensional data that allows for low nearest neighbor query response times in main memory environments, whose relevance grows steadily as prices for RAM continue to fall. The high query throughput supported by our approach outperforms existing priority-based search methods that use index structures like the CR-Tree or X-Tree as shown in the experimental section. We achieved this improvement by making use of the possibility to precalculate the nearest neighbor information using Voronoi cells, which can be performed efficiently for data with a low number of dimensions but is not reasonable for higher dimensionalities. A direct application of dimensionality reduction techniques fails to consider the complex data space boundaries which are important to the Voronoi concept. For high-dimensional multimedia data we additionally proposed new methods to efficiently approximate the data space boundaries and thus enable a significant reduction of the data dimensionality based on linear dimensionality reduction techniques. The cuboid-shaped Voronoi cell approximations are usually still not suitable for direct indexing. Our second reduction step removes less significant dimensions of the cuboids without sacrificing further proximity information of the data points. Our experiments on main memory indexing for the resulting low-dimensional cuboids using variants of the X-Tree and a bitmap-based index demonstrate a great response time speedup over competing approaches.

We plan to investigate the possibility of using non-axis-aligned projections in the dimensionality reduction step and accommodating our heuristics to further reflect the skewness of the underlying data. More research is intended on expanding the application domain beyond sum-normalized data, which we concentrated on in this paper and by investigating hybrid index structures that utilize both main and secondary memory.

**Acknowledgments.** We thank Eammon Keogh and Theodoros Folias for providing access to their Time Series Data Mining Archive [25] at the Computer Science & Engineering Department, University of California and Arne Theres for his work on the phoneme data set at the Chair of Computer Science VI, RWTH Aachen University.

## References

1. Berchtold, S., Ertl, B., Keim, D.A., Kriegel, H.P., Seidl, T.: Fast Nearest Neighbor Search in High-Dimensional Spaces. In: ICDE Conf. (1998) 209–218
2. Berchtold, S., Keim, D.A., Kriegel, H.P., Seidl, T.: Indexing the Solution Space: A New Technique for Nearest Neighbor Search in High-Dimensional Space. IEEE Trans. Knowl. Data Eng. **12** (2000) 45–57
3. Dobkin, D., Lipton, R.: Multidimensional Searching Problems. SIAM J. on Computing **5** (1976) 181–186
4. Weber, R., Schek, H.J., Blott, S.: A Quantitative Analysis and Performance Study for Similarity-Search Methods in High-Dimensional Spaces. In: VLDB Conf. (1998) 194–205
5. Guttman, A.: R-Trees: A Dynamic Index Structure for Spatial Searching. In: SIGMOD Conf. (1984) 47–57
6. Beckmann, N., Kriegel, H.P., Schneider, R., Seeger, B.: The R*-Tree: An Efficient and Robust Access Method for Points and Rectangles. In: SIGMOD Conf. (1990) 322–331

7. Kim, K., Cha, S.K., Kwon, K.: Optimizing Multidimensional Index Trees for Main Memory Access. In: SIGMOD Conf. (2001) 139–150
8. Berchtold, S., Keim, D.A., Kriegel, H.P.: The X-Tree: An Index Structure for High-Dimensional Data. In: VLDB Conf. (1996) 28–39
9. Roussopoulos, N., Kelley, S., Vincent, S.: Nearest Neighbor Queries. In: SIGMOD Conf. (1995) 71–79
10. Hjaltason, G.R., Samet, H.: Ranking in Spatial Databases. In: SSD. (1995) 83–95
11. Bohannon, P., McIlroy, P., Rastogi, R.: Main-Memory Index Structures with Fixed-Size Partial Keys. In: SIGMOD Conf. (2001) 163–174
12. Rao, J., Ross, K.A.: Making $B^+$-Trees Cache Conscious in Main Memory. In: SIGMOD Conf. (2000) 475–486
13. Voronoi, G.: Nouvelles applications des parametres continus la theorie des formes quadratiques. J. für die reine und angewandte Mathematik **138** (1908) 198–287
14. Aurenhammer, F., Klein, R. In: Handbook of Computational Geometry. Elsevier Science Publishers Amsterdam (2000) 201–290
15. Klee, V.: On the Complexity of d-dimensional Voronoi Diagrams. Archiv der Mathematik **34** (1980) 75–80
16. Seidel, R.: On the Number of Faces in Higher-Dimensional Voronoi Diagrams. In: Symposium on Computational Geometry. (1987) 181–185
17. Press, W.H., Teukolsky, S.A., Vetterling, W.T., Flannery, B.P.: Numerical Recipes in C: The Art of Scientific Computing. Cambridge University Press (1992)
18. Kaski, S.: Dimensionality Reduction by Random Mapping: Fast Similarity Computation for Clustering. In: IJCNN. (1998) 413–418
19. Edelsbrunner, H.: Algorithms in Combinatorial Geometry. Springer-Verlag (1987)
20. Jaffar, J., Maher, M.J., Stuckey, P.J., Yap, R.H.C.: Projecting CLP(R) Constraints. New Generation Computing **11** (1993) 449–469
21. Bradford Barber, C., Dobkin, D., Huhdanpaa, H.: The Quickhull Algorithm for Convex Hulls. ACM Trans. Math. Softw. **22** (1996) 469–483
22. Goldstein, J., Platt, J.C., Burges, C.J.C.: Indexing High Dimensional Rectangles for Fast Multimedia Identification. Technical Report MSR-TR-2003-38, Microsoft Research (2003)
23. Hafner, J., Sawhney, H.S., Equitz, W., Flickner, M., Niblack, W.: Efficient Color Histogram Indexing for Quadratic Form Distance Functions. IEEE Trans. PAMI **17** (1995) 729–736
24. Wahlster, W. In: Verbmobil: Foundations of Speech-to-Speech Translation. Springer-Verlag (2000) 537–631
25. Keogh, E., Folias, T.: The UCR Time Series Data Mining Archive, http://www.cs.ucr.edu/~eamonn/TSDMA/index.html (2002)

# Authorization-Transparent Access Control for XML Under the Non-Truman Model

Yaron Kanza, Alberto O. Mendelzon, Renée J. Miller, and Zheng Zhang

Department of Computer Science,
University of Toronto,
Toronto, Canada
{yaron, mendel, miller, zhzhang}@cs.toronto.edu

**Abstract.** In authorization-transparent access control, user queries are formulated against the database schema rather than against authorization views that transform and hide data. The Truman and the Non-Truman are two approaches to authorization transparency where in a Truman model, queries that violate the access restrictions are modified transparently by the system to only reveal accessible data, while in a Non-Truman model, such queries are rejected. The advantage of a Non-Truman model is that the semantics of user queries is not changed by the access-control mechanism. This work presents an access-control mechanism for XML, under the Non-Truman model. Security policies are specified as parameterized rules formulated using XPath. The rules specify relationships between elements, that should be concealed from users. Hence, not only elements, but also edges and paths within an XML document, can be concealed. The access-control mechanism authorizes only *valid queries*, *i.e.*, queries that do not disclose the existence of concealed relationships. The additional expressive power, provided by these rules, over element-based authorization techniques is illustrated. The proposed access-control mechanism can either serve as a substitute for views or as a layer for verifying that specific relationships are concealed by a view.

## 1 Introduction

Access control is a fundamental part of database systems. The purpose of access control is to protect private or secret information from unauthorized users. Given the status of XML as a standard for storing and exchanging data, the need for XML access control has been recognized and has received a lot of attention [3, 4, 9, 11, 14].

When an access-control model is *authorization transparent*, users formulate their queries against the database schema rather than against authorization views that transform and hide data [21]. Rizvi *et al.* [22] present two basic approaches to access control in authorization-transparent systems. The first approach is referred to as the *Truman model* and the second as the *Non-Truman model* [22]. In the Truman model, an access control language (often a view language) is used for specifying what data is accessible to a user. User queries are modified by the system so that the answer includes only accessible data. Suppose $Q$ is a user query, $D$ is a database and $D_u$ is the part of $D$ that the user is permitted to access, then $Q$ is modified to a safe query $Q_s$ such that $Q_s(D) = Q(D_u)$.

*Example 1.* Consider a database that contains information on courses in a university. For each course, the system stores information about the students who are enrolled, and the grades that they have received. Suppose that a Truman access control model is used to specify that each student is permitted to see only her grades (not the grades of other students). If student Alice poses a query that asks for the highest grade received in one of the courses in which she is enrolled, say *Databases 101*, the system will modify the query to return the highest grade that Alice has received in *Databases 101*.

As Rizvi et al. [22] point out, using a Truman access-control model, the answers to queries may be misleading. A user may wrongly assume that an answer to a query is correct over the entire database. In our example, Alice may be misled into thinking she is the best in the class (after all, she asked for the highest grade over all students).

Misleading answers are prevented by the Non-Truman model, an alternative, authorization-transparent model. In the Non-Truman model, a query that violates access-control specifications is rejected, rather than modified. Only *valid* queries, *i.e.*, queries that do not violate the access specifications, are answered. Hence, query answers are always the result of applying the user query to the entire database. The Non-Truman model has the desirable property that the semantics of a query is independent of the access-control specification. In Example 1, for instance, if the system uses a Non-Truman access-control model, then the query of Alice will be rejected. Alice will only receive answers to queries that are valid with respect to the access-control policy.

In a Non-Truman model, a fundamental question is the definition of validity. Rizvi et al. [22] use a mechanism in which the accessible data is defined using views. Given a database $D$, a query $Q$ is validated by checking whether it could be rewritten using only the authorized views $V$. The rewritten query needs to be equivalent to $Q$ either for all possible database states (referred to as *unconditional equivalence* [22] since it is independent of the current database state $D$) or for only those database states $D'$ for which $V(D) = V(D')$ (termed *conditional equivalence* [22]).

Certainly, such an approach is possible for XML as well. However, results on answering queries using views for small fragments of XML query languages are still emerging [28], and may be undecidable even for the relational model [22]. Furthermore, a view is a positive statement about what data is accessible and it is up to the designer of the view to decide what can be put in the view while still hiding the desired private data. Regardless of the form of the view or access control mechanism, we would like to be able to make statements about what information is *concealed* from a user. In our work, we will specifically consider what it means to conceal a relationship in an XML document.

*Example 2.* Consider an XML document $D$ that contains information about departments and employees in a company. There is an edge from each department element $d$ to an employee element $e$ whenever $e$ works in $d$. A company may have an access control policy that permits access to all employees and departments, but that restricts access to the works-in relationship. That is, a user should be able to ask queries about employees and departments, but the company may not wish to reveal who works in which department. Perhaps this information may reveal strategic information about the direction of the company.

Information disclosure has been studied formally. Miklau and Suciu [20], define disclosure as exposing information that increases the probability that a user can guess concealed information. There are cases, however, where rejecting a query just because its answer decreases the user's uncertainty about the concealed data is too restrictive [29]. If we consider a set of relationships, it may be sufficient to ensure that a user cannot distinguish between the current document and other documents that differ from the current document only in the concealed relationships.

Intuitively, a query conceals a relationship if the query answer does not reveal the presence (or absence) of a relationship in the document. To understand our semantics, consider the following example.

*Example 3.* Considering again Example 2 where the relationship between departments and employees is secret. Consider a query $Q_1$ that looks for all the employees in the company, regardless of their department, and a query $Q_2$ that looks for the employees in a specific department $d$. The query $Q_1$ conceals the relationships between departments and employees, while $Q_2$ does not.

In this work, we propose a precise semantics for what it means to *conceal* a relationship. We propose a mechanism for testing whether an XPath query *conceals* a relationship or set of relationships. In particular, we can test whether a view, specified by an XPath query, conceals a relationship.

Our model controls access to relationships. This approach provides a finer granularity than restricting access to elements. On one hand, restricting access to an element is possible in our approach. This is done by concealing all the relationships (edges and paths) to that element. On the other hand, in our approach it is possible to conceal a relationship without restricting access to any of the elements in the document. Returning to our example, our mechanism will permit access to employees and departments while restricting only access to the set of works-in relationships.

The main contributions of our work are the following.

- The first authorization-transparent, Non-Truman access-control model for XML. Our mechanism is fine-grained and enforces access control at the level of ancestor-descendant relationships among elements.
- A new semantics for concealing relationships in an XML document, where a relationship is defined by an edge or a path in the document. Our semantics uses a variation of $k$-anonymity [25]. To specify relationships in our mechanism, we use rules, each containing a pair of XPath expressions.
- We define two forms of query validity. A query is *locally valid* for a document and a set of rules, if it conceals all the relationships that are specified by the rules. Queries may be executed only if they are locally valid. For documents conforming to a schema, we define a stronger form of validity. A query is *globally valid* for a set of rules and a schema if the query is locally valid for the rules and each document that conforms to the schema.
- Finally, we show that indeed valid queries do not reveal information about concealed edges.

## 2 Related Work

Many non-authorization-transparent access-control models for XML have been proposed. Damiani et al. [9, 10] presented a model where restricted elements are identified using labels. These restricted elements are pruned from the document before queries are posed. A similar mechanism was proposed by Bertino et al. [2, 3] where the restricted parts of an XML document are encrypted rather than pruned. Encrypting the unauthorized data has also been used in the access-control model of Miklau and Suciu [18]. In their model the access control specifications are defined using a language that extends XQuery. Fan et al. [11] specified security by extending the document DTD with annotations and publishing a modified DTD. In their model, queries are formulated over the modified DTD and are rewritten by the system to befit the original DTD. The optimization of secure queries has also been given some attention [6, 30].

Fundulaki and Marx [13] survey a number of approaches that permit access control to be specified on elements within a document. Restricting access to elements has also been used in XACML [15] and XACL [16], two proposed industrial standards. An alternative approach of hiding element relationships was proposed by Finance et al. [12], however, their model is not authorization transparent. Authorization-transparent models have been proposed, so far, only for the relational model [21, 23, 24].

In contrast, we present the first authorization-transparent, Non-Truman model for XML. Queries are posed on the original document, thus, we do not present a model for publishing secure data. In our model, users simply specify the element relationships that should be concealed. For defining concealment we use a variation of $k$-anonymity. Various aspects of $k$-anonymity were studied in the relational model [1, 17, 25, 29]. To our knowledge, our work is the first to apply $k$-anonymity to XML. In Section 4, we define precisely the relationship of our model with $k$-anonymity. Our main focus is to provide a test of query validity for ensuring that valid queries effectively conceal secure relationships. This is important since unlike the non-authorization-transparent approaches, in our model, queries are posed on the entire document.

## 3 Data Model

In this section, we introduce our data model. We assume that the reader is familiar with the notion of a rooted labeled directed graph. We present a rooted labeled directed graph $G$, over a set $L$ of labels, by a 4-tuple $(V, E, r, \textit{label-of}_G)$, where $V$ is a set of nodes, $E$ is a set of edges, $r$ is the root of $G$ and $\textit{label-of}_G$ is a function that maps each node to an element of $L$.

**Document.** Let $L$ be a finite set of labels and $A$ be a finite set of atomic values. An *XML document* is a rooted labeled directed tree over $L$ with values of $A$ attached to atomic nodes (*i.e.*, to nodes that do not have outgoing edges). Formally, a document $D$ is a 5-tuple $(X, E_D, \textit{root}_D, \textit{label-of}_D, \textit{value-of}_D)$, where the tuple $(X, E_D, \textit{root}_D, \textit{label-of}_D)$ is a rooted labeled directed tree over $L$, and $\textit{value-of}_D$ is a function that maps each atomic node to a value of $A$. The nodes in $X$ are called *elements*. In order to simplify the model, we do not distinguish between elements and attributes and we assume that all the values on atomic nodes are of type PCDATA (*i.e.*, *String*).

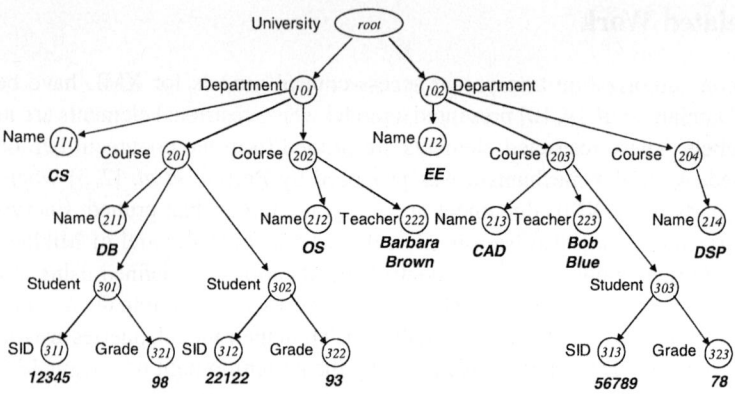

**Fig. 1.** A document that contains information on courses, students and grades in a university

*Example 4.* Figure 1 shows a document that contains information on courses, students and grades. Elements are represented by circles and are numbered, for easier reference. Atomic values appear below the atomic nodes and are written with a bold font.

**XPath.** In this work, we use XPath [8] for formulating queries and access control rules. XPath is a simple language for navigating in an XML document. XPath expressions are omnipresent in XML applications. In particular, XPath is part of both XSLT [7] and XQuery [5], the WWW-Consortium standards for querying and transforming XML.

In XPath there are thirteen types of axes that are used for navigating in a document. Our focus in this work is on the *child* axis (/) and the *descendant-or-self* axis (//) that are the most commonly used axes in XPath. Our model, however, can also be applied to queries that include the other axes.

## 4 Concealing Relationships

Before presenting our techniques, we first consider what it means to conceal a relationship. A *relationship* is a directed path between two elements. For example, in the university database shown in Figure 1, a student element is related to a grade element if there is an edge from the student element to the grade element.

A set of *relationships* is represented by a pair consisting of two sets of elements. For example, the pair $(S, G)$, where $S$ is the set of all elements labeled "Student" and $G$ is the set of all elements labeled "Grade", represents the set of relationships between student and grades. Concealing the relationships $(S, G)$ means that for every student $s$ and grade $g$ in the document, the user will not be able to infer (with certainty), from query answers, whether $g$ is the grade for $s$. We will want this to be true for all authorized queries (*i.e.*, all *valid queries*). Note that we are concealing the presence or absence of relationships, so we are concealing whether any of the set of pairs in $(S, G)$ exists in the document.

We also want to have some measure of the uncertainty that is gained by concealing relationships. Thus, we use a definition that is a variation of *k-anonymity* [25] applied to relationships in an XML document. In the $k$-anonymity model, the goal is to provide a guarantee that each element cannot be distinguished from at least $k-1$ other elements. In our case, suppose that we want to conceal a set of relationships $(A, B)$. Then, given the answer to a valid query and any element $b \in B$, the user will not be able to infer which element among some $k$ sized subset of $A$ is related to $b$. To make this more precise, we present a formal definition.

**Definition 1** ($k$-**Concealment**). *Consider a set of valid queries $Q$, a document $D$, and two sets $A$ and $B$ of elements in $D$. The relationships $(A, B)$ are $k$-concealed if for every $b \in B$ there exist $k$ elements $a_1, \ldots, a_k$ of $A$ and $k$ documents $D_1, \ldots, D_k$ over the element set of $D$, such that the following conditions hold for every $1 \leq i \leq k$.*

1. *In $D_i$, the element $b$ is a descendant of $a_i$. Furthermore, $b$ is not a descendant of any element among $a_1, \ldots, a_k$, except for $a_i$.*
2. $Q(D) = Q(D_i)$, *for every valid query $Q \in Q$.*

*Example 5.* Consider a university document $D$, similar to the document in Figure 1, and the set $(S, G)$ of relationships between students and grades. Suppose that $(S, G)$ is $k$-concealed, and let $Q$ be a set of authorized queries. Let $g$ be some grade element in $D$. Then, there are $k$ documents that provide the answer $Q(D)$ for every query $Q$ in $Q$ and in each one of these $k$ documents, $g$ is below a different student. That is, there is a set of $k$ students such that from the information revealed by answers to queries in $Q$, a user cannot tell which one among these $k$ students received $g$.

We consider a relationship to be concealed as long as *some* uncertainty remains about the ancestor-descendant relationships. Thus, in the rest of this paper, we will use the phrase "concealing relationships" for 2-concealment.

Given the definition of concealing relationships, we now turn to the logistics of specifying sets of relationships over XML documents. We will use pairs of XPath expressions for this purpose. Each pair will form an access-control rule. The two expressions will define a pair of sets, *i.e.*, a set of relationships that should be concealed.

## 5 Access Control Rules

Our approach to access control in XML documents is based on rules rather than views. While views are normally "positive" in the sense that they specify what the user is allowed to know, our rules are "negative" and specify what should be concealed from the user. Our access-control rules specify pairs of elements in the document and by this designate the relationships between these elements as being restricted. In this section, we first present the syntax of rules. Then, we explain why we use rules rather than views. We provide the semantics of rules in our model and define local and global validity. Finally, we briefly discuss the issue of testing validity.

### 5.1 The Syntax of Rules

Rules are formulated using XPath expressions. Each rule consists of two expressions specifying a set of ancestor and descendant elements. The rule specifies that the relationships between these two sets should be concealed.

**Definition 2 (Rule).** *An* access control rule *(or rule) is defined as:*

for $path_1$ exclude $path_2$

where $path_1$ and $path_2$ are XPath expressions. The path $path_2$ is a relative XPath expression with respect to $path_1$.

*Example 6.* Suppose that we want to prevent queries from disclosing information about what grades were given to which students. This restriction can be specified by the following rule: for //Student exclude /Grade.

*Example 7.* Suppose that in the CS department, relationships between students and grades and relationships between courses and grades should be concealed. To specify this restriction, two rules are used:

for /Department[Name='CS']//Student exclude //Grade, and
for /Department[Name='CS']/Course exclude //Grade.

In many scenarios, different users have different access permissions. For example, an institution could have a policy where a course teacher can have access to all the grades of the course while students can only see their own grades. To support this, the access control rules are parameterized. Parameterized variables are written with a preceding dollar sign. Common parameters include user ids, environment variables, time parameters, *etc.*

*Example 8.* Suppose that $userid is instantiated to be the current user identifier. Consider a policy where a student is permitted to see her own grades, but she should not see the student-grade relationships of other students. This policy is specified by the following rule:

for //Student[not(SID=$userid)] exclude /Grade.

Note that when $userid is null the comparison SID=$userid is false.

## 5.2 Rules Versus Views

We now explain why we use rules instead of views for XML access control in the Non-Truman model. The first reason is that there are many cases where using rules is simpler and requires a more succinct formulation than using views. The following example illustrates such a case.

*Example 9.* Suppose that we want to prevent users from knowing which student is enrolled in which course, but do not wish to conceal other information in the document. We can specify this using the rule: for //Course exclude //Student. If SID is identifying, we may also want to hide the relationship from course to a student's SID using the rule:

for //Course exclude //SID.

Note that these rules should not prevent evaluation of queries that "jump" over a restricted edge. For example, a query that returns the grades of a specific course does not violate the rules. Neither does a query that returns the grades of a specific student.

It is not easy to formulate an XQuery view that preserves all the relationships in the document except for the course-student and course-SID relationships. One example for such a view is a query $Q_{cut}$ that reconstructs the whole document with the following changes. First, student elements should be moved, with all their content, to be below their department element. This cuts the relationship between students and courses but keeps the relationships between departments and students. Second, grade elements may be copied and pasted below their ancestor course elements. We need to duplicate grades, because we need grades to be related to both courses and students. Note that $Q_{cut}$ would not work if in the original document, courses have an element named "Grade" as a child. It is cumbersome to formulate $Q_{cut}$ in XQuery. Hence, in many cases, defining access-control policies by views is more error-prone than using our rules. We consider in this example XQuery, however, the same problem occurs also in other languages for defining "positive" views.

The second reason for choosing rules instead of views is that with views it is difficult to verify that what we want to conceal is indeed concealed.

*Example 10.* Consider two views. One view contains students and their grades. The second view contains courses and for each course the grades that were given in the course. Do these views really conceal all the relationships between courses and students? Apparently not. Suppose that there is a grade, say 78, that appears only once in the document. Then, knowing who received this grade and in which course this grade was given, it is possible to infer a relationship between a student and a course.

Later in this paper we will present the notion of a coherent set of rules and we will show that when using a coherent set of rules, we can guarantee that restricted relationships are indeed concealed.

The third reason for not using authorization views is that in the Non-Truman model, when using views, testing validity is defined as the problem of answering-queries-using-views. However, answering-queries-using-views is not always decidable and may have a very high time complexity [22]. Note that the problem of answering-queries-using-views is different from the simpler problem of answering queries posed on views.

## 5.3 Local Validity

In the Non-Truman model, queries are evaluated only if they pass a validity test. We now define local validity for queries, given a document and a set of rules. We start by providing some necessary definitions and notation. Our first definition, of a document expansion, is a tool to help us define (later) the set of documents that should be indistinguishable from a given document, when using valid queries.

**Document Expansion.** Let $D = (X, E_D, root_D, label\text{-}of_D, value\text{-}of_D)$ be a document. An *expansion* of $D$, denoted $D''$, is a labeled directed graph that is created by replacing $E_D$ with a new set of edges $E'$ called *child edges*. In addition, we add to $D$ a second set $E_D''$ of edges, called *descendant edges*. Hence, the expansion of $D$ is a tuple $((X, E', root_D, label\text{-}of_D, value\text{-}of_D), E_D'')$, where $E'$ is a set of child edges and $E_D''$ is a set of descendant edges. Note that the expansion is not necessarily a tree and is not even required to be connected.

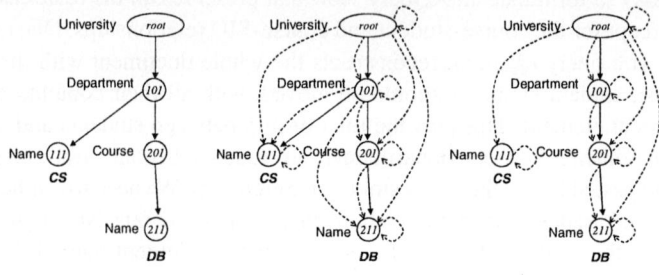

(a) Document $D_1$  (b) The transitive closure of $D_1$  (c) A document expansion

**Fig. 2.** A document $D_1$, the transitive closure of $D_1$ and a document expansion

To understand the role of the separate child and descendant edges, it is useful to consider one special expansion, the *transitive closure*, formed by adding to $D$ a descendant edge between any two connected nodes in $D$.

**Transitive Closure.** The *transitive closure* of a document $D$, denoted as $\bar{D}$, is a document expansion where $E' = E_D$. The transitive closure is $(D, E_D'')$, such that in $E_D''$ there is an edge between every two nodes that are connected by a directed path in $D$. The direction of the edge is the same as the direction of the path. Also, $E_D''$ contains an edge from every node to itself. Note that the original edge set of $D$ is not being replaced. As an example, Figure 2(b) shows the transitive closure of the document in Figure 2(a). Child edges are drawn with solid lines and descendant edges with dashed lines.

The evaluation of an XPath expression over a document expansion is by *following* a child edge whenever a child axis occurs and following a descendant edge whenever a descendant-or-self axis occurs. We explain this in the following example.

*Example 11.* Consider the XPath query //Department[Name='CS']//Course over a document expansion $D''$. This query returns course elements $c$ that satisfy the following. There are a department element $d$ and a descendant edge in $D''$ from the root to $d$. There is an element $n$ with label "Name", with value "CS" and there is a child edge in $D$ from $d$ to $n$. Finally, there is a descendant edge in $D''$ from $d$ to $c$. Note that to satisfy the // axis we require the existence of a descendant edge rather than the existence of a path between the relevant nodes.

It is easy to see that posing an XPath query $Q$ on a document $D$ is equivalent to evaluating $Q$ over the transitive closure of $D$. However, when evaluating $Q$ over a document expansion that is not the transitive closure of $D$, we may get an answer that is different from the answer to $Q$ over $D$.

**Pruning of a Document Expansion.** Given a set $R$ of access control rules, a *pruning* of a document expansion $D''$ is a new document expansion, denoted $prune_R(D'')$, that is created by removing from $D''$ all the edges (both child edges and descendant edges) that connect a *restricted* pair of nodes. By restricted pair, we mean two nodes whose relationship should be concealed according to $R$. For example, the pruning of the transitive closure of $D_1$ (Figure 2(b)) by the rule for //Department exclude //Name is depicted in Figure 2(c).

We represent a rule $\rho$ of the form for $x_1$ exclude $x_2$ as a pair $(x_1, x_2)$. By $x_1x_2$ we denote the XPath expression that is created by the concatenation of the expressions $x_1$ and $x_2$. In a document $D$, $\rho$ specifies as restricted all the pairs $(e_1, e_2)$ of elements of $D$ such that $e_1 \in x_1(D)$ (i.e., $e_1$ is in the answer to $x_1$ over $D$) and $e_2 \in x_1x_2(D)$. For example, the rule for //Student exclude //Grade specifies as restricted all the pairs of a student element and a grade of the student. A set of rules specify as restricted all the element pairs that are restricted according to at least one of the rules in the set.

Intuitively, given a rule $\rho = (x_1, x_2)$ we want to conceal whether (or not) there is a path between any two restricted elements. We can think of the existing paths in $D$ as defining a subset $P$ of $x_1(D) \times x_1x_2(D)$. We will define as valid only those queries that do not permit a user to distinguish whether $D$ contains the subset $P$ or another possible subset of $x_1(D) \times x_1x_2(D)$. This motivates the following definition.

**Universe of Expansions.** Consider a document $D$ and a set of access control rules $R$. Let $\bar{D}$ be the transitive closure of $D$ and let $prune_R(\bar{D})$ be the pruning of $\bar{D}$ using the rules of $R$. The *universe of expansions* (*universe*, for short) of $D$ under the concealment of $R$, is the set of all document expansions $D''$ such that $prune_R(\bar{D}) = prune_R(D'')$. In other words, the universe contains all the document expansions that are created by adding to $prune_R(\bar{D})$ some edges that connect restricted pairs of nodes. We denote the universe of $D$ by $\mathcal{U}_R(D)$.

**Definition 3 (Local Validity).** *Given a document $D$ and a set of rules $R$, a query $Q$ is locally valid if $Q(D) = Q(D'')$ for any document expansion $D''$ in the universe $\mathcal{U}_R(D)$.*

We now explain why we need to consider, in Definition 3, all the document expansions in the universe $\mathcal{U}_R(D)$ instead of applying a simpler test, called *pseudo-validity*, where we just consider the single document expansion $prune_R(\bar{D})$ (the pruning of the transitive closure of $D$), i.e., the document expansion that contains only edges between non-restricted pairs.

A query $Q$ is pseudo-valid if $Q(D) = Q(prune_R(\bar{D}))$. By Definition 3, the condition of pseudo-validity is necessary, but not sufficient for $Q$ to be locally valid. The following example demonstrates a situation where secure information may be leaked due to authorizing pseudo-valid queries.

*Example 12.* Consider the university document $D$ of Figure 1 and the rule $\rho$ in Example 6 that conceals relationships between students and grades. Suppose we authorize pseudo-valid queries such as $Q_i$ : //Student[SID='12345' and Grade=$i$], for $i = 0, 1, \ldots, 100$. In all the 100 cases where $i \neq 98$, the query will be authorized and return an empty result. For $i = 98$ (i.e., the grade of the student in the DB course), the query will not be authorized. This reveals the grade of a student in some course.

Such information leakage does not occur when only locally valid queries are authorized. To see why this is true, consider the document expansion $D''$ constructed as follows. Let $D''$ be the result of removing two edges and adding two new edges to the transitive closure $\bar{D}$. The removed edges are the two Student-Grade edges that connect Node 301 to 321 and Node 302 to 322. The two added edges are Student-Grade edges that connect Node 301 to 322 and Node 302 to 321. All these added and removed edges are Student-Grade edges and thus, are removed in a pruning w.r.t. $\rho$. That is, $prune_\rho(\bar{D}) = prune_\rho(D'')$. Yet, evaluating $Q_{93}$ w.r.t. $D''$ provides a different answer from the answer to $Q_{93}$ over $D$. Thus, $Q_{93}$ is not valid. $Q_{78}$ is also not valid by a similar construction. All the three queries $Q_{78}$, $Q_{93}$ and $Q_{98}$ are rejected. Thus, a user could only tell that the grade of Student '12345' is one of the grades 78, 93, 98; however, this is what she could have learned from the result of the valid query //Grade.

The definition of local validity has a number of properties that are important in practice. For example, if two documents are equal (that is, isomorphic) except for their restricted edges, then a locally valid query will not be able to distinguish between them.

**Proposition 1.** *Consider a set of rules $R$ and let $D_1$ and $D_2$ be two documents such that $prune_R(\bar{D}_1) = prune_R(\bar{D}_2)$. If a query $Q$ is locally valid w.r.t. $D_1$ and $R$ then $Q$ is also locally valid w.r.t. $D_2$ and $R$. Furthermore, $Q(D_1) = Q(D_2)$.*

### 5.4 Global Validity

For documents conforming to a schema, we define a more restrictive form of validity called *global validity*. First, we formally define the notion of a schema.

**Schema.** In our model, a *schema* is represented as a rooted labeled directed graph. Our schema representation is a simplification of common XML schema-definition languages such as DTD [26] and XSchema [27]. A schema can be used to provide a succinct description of a document structure, or as a constraint on the structure of documents in a repository. Formally, a schema $S$, over a finite set of labels $L$, is a rooted labeled directed graph $(Names_S, E_S, root_S, label\text{-}of_S)$ over $L$, where the nodes are uniquely labeled. A document *conforms* to a schema if there exists a *homomorphism* from the graph of the document to the schema. An example of a schema is given in Figure 3(c). The document in Figure 1 conforms to this schema.

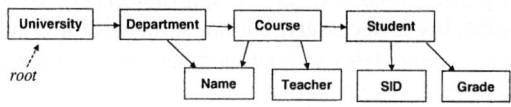

**Fig. 3.** A university schema

**Definition 4 (Global Validity).** *A query $Q$ is globally valid for a set of rules $R$ and a schema $S$, if, given $R$, $Q$ is locally valid for every document $D$ that conforms to $S$.*

*Example 13.* Let $R$ contain the rule given in Example 6. This rule rejects queries that use the relationship between students and grades. Suppose a query $Q$ that is asking for the grades of the student with id '00000' (*i.e.*, //Student[SID='00000']//Grade) is posed on the document in Figure 1. If there was a student with id '00000' in the document, then the query would not be considered locally valid and would not be authorized. Since there is no student with id '00000', there is no edge to prune and the query is locally valid. Note that the query does not reveal the grade of any existing student. Although $Q$ is locally valid, it is not globally valid if we consider the schema $S$ shown in Figure 3. It is possible to construct a document $D'$ that conforms to $S$ and contains a student with id '00000'. Hence, the query will not be locally valid for $D'$ and $R$. Thus, $Q$ is not globally valid for schema $S$.

In some cases, global validity could be too restrictive; however, it does have some advantages over local validity. Suppose that there is a collection of documents and all the documents conform to the same schema. In this case, if a query is globally valid, then we do not need to check the validity of the query over each document. Furthermore, after a document is updated, if the new document still conforms to the schema, we do not need to revalidate queries.

### 5.5 Testing Validity

Due to lack of space, presenting algorithms for efficient validity testing is beyond the scope of this paper. However, it is important to notice that our model has the following advantages. First, local validity is always decidable. This is because for any document $D$ and a set of rules $R$, the universe of expansions $\mathcal{U}_R(D)$ is finite. Secondly, for large classes of queries, local validity can be tested efficiently. Thirdly, there are important cases where global validity can be tested efficiently.

We now discuss one important case where testing local validity can be done efficiently. Consider XPath expressions that do not contain the logical operator not. Such queries are *monotone*. A query $Q$ is monotone, if for every two document expansions $D_1'' \subseteq D_2''$ holds $Q(D_1'') \subseteq Q(D_2'')$. For testing local validity of a monotone query, it is sufficient to compute the query over two specific document expansions and compare the answers. Given a document $D$ and a set of rules $R$, the document expansions on which the query should be computed are the following two. First, $prune_R(\bar{D})$. Second, the document expansion that is created from $prune_R(\bar{D})$ when connecting every restricted pair of elements, by both a child edge and a descendant edge.

## 6 A Coherent Set of Rules

Our goal is allowing users to conceal element relationships and let them be sure that what they want to conceal is truly concealed. Unfortunately, it is impossible to guarantee concealment for any arbitrary set of relationships. Sometimes, it is possible to infer a concealed relationship from the relationships that are not concealed. In this section, we characterize sets of rules whose designated relationships are indeed concealed.

We say that a set of rules is *coherent* if it is impossible to infer any concealed relationship from the relationships that are not pruned by the rules. Before providing the formal definition for a coherent set of rules, we give an example of two cases where a relationship can be inferred from a pair of non-concealed relationships.

*Example 14.* Suppose that in the university document it is known that the CAD course (Node 203) is given in the EE department (Node 102) and student 56789 (Node 303) is registered in the CAD course. In this case, the relationship between Node 102 and

Node 303 can be derived from the other two relationships, thus, there is no point in concealing it alone.

Suppose that the following is known. Student 12345 (Node 301) studies in the CS department (Node 101) and she is registered in the DB course (Node 211). Knowing that the document is a tree allows a user to infer that the DB course is given in the CS department (*i.e.*, Node 201 and Node 301 are related).

We now define when a set of rules is coherent. Consider a document $D$ and a set of rules $R$. The set $R$ has an *incomplete concealment* in a document $D$ if one of the following two cases occurs. *(1)* Lack of transitivity: $D$ has three elements $e_1$, $e_2$ and $e_3$ such that $prune_R(\bar{D})$ has an edge from $e_1$ to $e_2$ and an edge from $e_2$ to $e_3$, but $prune_R(\bar{D})$ does not have an edge from $e_1$ to $e_3$. *(2)* Lack of reverse transitivity: there are three elements $e_1$, $e_2$ and $e_3$ in $D$, such that $prune_R(\bar{D})$ has an edge from $e_1$ to $e_3$ and an edge from $e_2$ to $e_3$; however, $prune_R(\bar{D})$ does not have an edge from $e_1$ to $e_2$.

**Definition 5 (A Coherent Set of Rules).** *Given a document $D$, a set of rules $R$ is coherent if an incomplete concealment does not occur in $D$. Given a schema $S$, a set $R$ is coherent if $R$ is coherent for every document that conforms to $S$.*

### 6.1 Coherence for Documents

There is a simple and efficient test for verifying that a set of rules $R$ is coherent for a document $D$. The test starts by computing the pruning of the transitive closure of $D$ according to $R$, and considering the edge set of $prune_R(\bar{D})$ as a relation $r$. There is a lack of transitivity if and only if the algebraic expression $\pi_{\$1,\$4}(r \bowtie_{\$2=\$1} r) - r$ is not empty. There is a lack of reverse transitivity if and only if the algebraic expression $\pi_{\$1,\$3}(r \bowtie_{\$2=\$2} r) - r$ is not empty.

Next, we provide intuitive conditions for constructing coherent sets of rules. Our conditions consider how relationships specified by different rules are related. We say that an edge $(e_1, e_2)$ in a transitive closure $\bar{D}$ *encapsulates* an edge $(e'_1, e'_2)$ if there is a path $\phi$ in $\bar{D}$ that goes through the four nodes $e_1, e_2, e'_1, e'_2$, and one of the following three cases holds: *(1)* $e_1$ appears on $\phi$ before $e'_1$, and $e'_2$ appears before $e_2$. *(2)* $e_1 = e'_1$, and $e'_2$ appears on $\phi$ before $e_2$. *(3)* $e_1$ appears on $\phi$ before $e'_1$, and $e_2 = e'_2$. The following is a necessary condition for the coherency of a set of rules.

**Proposition 2.** *Given a document $D$, if a set of rules $R$ is coherent, then the following condition holds. For every descendant edge $(e_1, e_2)$ in $\bar{D}$, which is removed in the pruning of $\bar{D}$ by $R$, there is an edge $(e'_1, e'_2)$ in $\bar{D}$ such that $(e'_1, e'_2)$ is encapsulated by $(e_1, e_2)$ and $(e'_1, e'_2)$ is also removed in the pruning of $\bar{D}$.*

Consider two edges $(e_1, e_2)$ and $(e_1, e'_2)$ that are outgoing edges of the same node. We say that these two edges are *parallel* in $\bar{D}$ if either there is a path from $e_2$ to $e'_2$ or vice-versa. That is, these two edges do not lead to two disjointed parts of $\bar{D}$. We will use this definition in the next proposition to provide a sufficient condition for coherency.

**Proposition 3.** *Let $R$ be a set of rules and $D$ be a document. If the following condition holds, then $R$ is coherent w.r.t $D$. For every edge $(e_1, e_2)$ that is removed in the pruning of $\bar{D}$ w.r.t. $R$, all the edges $(e_1, e'_2)$ that are parallel to $(e_1, e_2)$ are also removed in the pruning of $\bar{D}$.*

## 6.2 Coherence for Schemas

Given a schema, we can generalize, using containment of XPath expressions, the condition presented in Proposition 3 for coherency. However, testing containment of XPath has high complexity [19]. Hence, the test is inefficient and we do not present it here. Yet, a special case of the generalized condition is that for every document $D$ that conforms to the schema, for each element $e$ in $D$, either all the outgoing edges of $e$ in $\bar{D}$ are removed in the pruning or none of them is removed.

A simple way to satisfy this condition is to allow only rules that have one of the following two forms: `for` *path* `exclude` `//*` or `for` *path* `exclude` `/`*label* `[`*condition*`]` `//*`, where *path* can be any XPath expression, *label* can be any label and *condition* can be any XPath condition.

*Example 15.* Consider the schema $S$ in Figure 3. Suppose that we want to conceal in courses all the information on students. We can apply the following two rules. The rule `for //Course exclude /Student` and the rule `for //Course exclude /Student//*`. These rules are coherent w.r.t. the schema $S$.

## 7 Effectiveness of Concealment

In this section, we prove the effectiveness of a coherent set of rules in concealing relationships. The presence of a schema and the fact that documents are trees impose limitations on the relationships that we are able to conceal. These limitations will be discussed in the first part of this section.

### 7.1 The Singleton-Source Disclosure

A *singleton-source disclosure* occurs when a user can infer that two elements $e_1$ and $e_2$ are related, from the following two pieces of information. *(1)* The path from the root to $e_2$ must go through an element of *type* $T$. *(2)* The only element in the document of type $T$ is $e_1$. The problem is illustrated by the following two examples.

*Example 16.* Consider a university document that conforms to the schema in Figure 3 and that contains only a single department element. Consider the rule

`for //Department exclude /Course`

which presumably conceals the relationships between departments and courses. A user that is familiar with the schema of the document and knows that the document contains only a single department can infer that every course element in the document is below the only department element.

*Example 17.* Consider the document in Figure 1 and the rule

`for //Department[Name='CS'] exclude /Course`

Suppose that $Q_1$ is a query that looks for all the courses in the document and $Q_2$ is a query that looks for all the courses in departments other than "CS". Both queries are locally valid w.r.t. the document and the rule. By applying set difference to the answers to $Q_1$ and to $Q_2$, it is possible to infer the set of courses in the "CS" department.

We use $k$-concealment (Definition 1) to define a singleton-source disclosure.

**Definition 6 (Singleton-Source Disclosure).** *Consider a document $D$ and a set of rules $R$. A singleton-source disclosure occurs when there is a rule $\rho = (x_1, x_2)$ in $R$ such that the set of relationships $(x_1(D), x_1x_2(D))$ is not 2-concealed.*

## 7.2 Verifying $k$-Concealment for a Coherent Set of Rules

We will describe now an algorithm that given a document $D$ and a coherent set of rules $R$, tests if a singleton-source disclosure occurs. Essentially, the algorithm computes, for each rule $\rho = (x_1, x_2)$ in $R$, the maximal $k$ for which the relationship $(x_1(D), x_1x_2(D))$ is $k$-concealed. If $k > 1$ for all the rules of $R$, then a singleton-source disclosure does not occur. Otherwise, a singleton-source disclosure does occur. Before presenting the algorithm that computes $k$, we provide an example that illustrates the algorithm.

*Example 18.* Consider the university document $D_u$ in Figure 1 and a coherent set of rules $R$. Suppose $R$ contains a rule $\rho$ that hides the relationships between courses and students. Also, we assume that $R$ does not hide the relationships between departments and students. We now discuss the computation of $k$ for $\rho$.

There are three students and four courses that we need to consider. For each student $s$, we need to count the number of courses $c$ for which $s$ might be related to $c$. The element $s$ might be related to $c$ if, and only if, there exists a document $D_{sc}$ for which the following conditions hold. *(1)* In $D_{sc}$, the element $s$ is a descendant of the element $c$. *(2)* For every locally valid query $Q$, holds $Q(D_{sc}) = Q(D_u)$.

Intuitively, we can think of a document $D_{sc}$ as a result of moving some subtrees of the original document, from one part of the document to another. Thus, for Node 301, we can either leave it below Node 201 or move it to be below Node 202. However, we cannot move Node 301 to be below Node 203. On the conceptual level, this is because Node 203 is a course that belongs to a different department from the department to which Node 301 is related. This is because if we move Node 301 to be below Node 203, we will have two ancestors to Node 301 (Node 101 and Node 102) that are not on the same path. In a tree this should not happen.

In the computation, we check for each student, how many courses it can be related to, as was done for Node 301. In our example, each student has two such courses. Thus, the relationships that $\rho$ defines are 2-concealed.

We present now the algorithm—Compute-$k$—that for any coherent set of rules $R$ and a document $D$, computes a maximal value $k$ such that $k$-concealment can be guaranteed for the relationships that are specified by the rules of $R$.

**Compute $k$ ($D$, $R$)**
**Input**: a document $D$ and a coherent set of rules $R$;
**Output**: a maximal $k$ such that there is a $k$-concealment for each rule in $R$;
Initially, we set $k = \infty$. We iterate over all the rules of $R$. Given a rule $\rho = (x_1, x_2)$ in $R$, we denote by $A$ the set $x_1(D)$; and by $B$ the set $x_1x_2(D)$. We iterate over all the elements of $B$. For each element $b \in B$ we count the number of nodes $a \in A$ such that we can move $b$ to be below $a$ (shortly, we will explain how). Let $k_b$ be this count. Then, if $k_b < k$, we set $k$ to be $k_b$. At the end of all the iterations, $k$ is returned.

We now explain how we count, for a given $b \in B$, the number of nodes $a \in A$ such that we can move $b$ to be below $a$. We iterate over the elements of $A$ and try to "attach" $b$ below each one of these elements. The test for $b$ and $a$ is as follows. We start by computing the pruning by $R$ of the transitive closure of $D$—$prune_R(\bar{D})$. We then try to connect $b$ to $a$ using only edges between restricted pairs, i.e., we add only edges that will be removed in the pruning by $R$. This produces an expansion $D''$ of $D$ such that $Q(D'') = Q(D)$ for every query $Q$ that is locally valid w.r.t. $R$ and $D$.

The following observations are important. First, for every $a' \in A$, in $prune_R(\bar{D})$ there does not exist any edge from $a'$ to $b$. This is because of the rule $\rho$. Furthermore, since $R$ is coherent, in $prune_R(\bar{D})$, there is no path from $a'$ to $b$, and no path from $a'$ to any ancestor or descendant of $b$. Hence, there is a subtree $T_b$ in $prune_R(\bar{D})$ that contains $b$ and is disconnected (i.e., not reachable by a directed path) from any $a' \in A$. What we need to test is the possibility to connect the root of $T_b$ to $a$ or to a descendant of $a$, using only edges that are removed in the pruning, such that *(1)* there is no element of $A$, other than $a$, on the path from $a$ to the root of $T_b$, and *(2)* the following two tests are passed. First, a test for making sure that we will eventually produce a tree or a graph that can be extended to be a tree. Secondly, a test for checking that by adding $T_b$ below $a$, we do not create a relationship (i.e., an ancestor-descendant pair) between two nodes that were not related in $D$ and do not form a restricted pair.

To ensure that we are able to extend the new graph $D''$ to be a tree, we need to verify that the nodes of $T_b$ do not have two ancestors that are not on one path. To that end, we define $X_b$ to be the nodes $x$ such that $x$ is not in $T_b$ and in $D''$ there is a descendant edge from $x$ to some node in $T_b$. For the node $a$ to be an ancestor of $b$, $a$ must be below all the nodes $X_b$ ($a$ cannot be above any one of the nodes $X_b$ since there is no path from $a$ to any node in $T_b$; also, $a$ must be on one path with all the nodes $X_b$). The test succeeds if one of the following cases occurs. *(1)* In $D''$, $a$ is below all the nodes $X_b$. *(2)* There is an ancestor $y$ of $a$ that does not have a parent in $D''$, such that $y$ can be connected to a node below the nodes $X_b$, using an edge that is removed in the pruning by $R$, without creating a path between a non-restricted pair.

In the second test, we simply check that for every pair of nodes connected by a path, after moving $T_b$, either they are connected by an edge in $prune_R(\bar{D})$ or they are a restricted pair according to $R$. If this test, or the previous test, fails, we do not increase $k_b$. Otherwise, we increase $k_b$ by one. □

An important advantage of the algorithm Compute-$k$ is that it has a polynomial time complexity. The following theorem shows the correctness of the algorithm Compute-$k$.

**Theorem 1.** *Given a document $D$ and a coherent set of rules $R$, Algorithm Compute-$k$ computes a value $k$ such that the followings hold.*

1. *All the relationships that are defined by rules of $R$ are $k$-concealed.*
2. *There is a rule in $R$ that defines a relationship which is not $k+1$-concealed.*

Theorem 1 shows that when a coherent set of rules is used, it can be tested for a given document $D$, whether 2-concealment, or even $k$-concealment for some $k > 2$, is provided. When $k$-concealment is provided for $D$ and $R$, the following holds. Suppose that $e_1$ and $e_2$ are two elements such that the association between them should be concealed, i.e., there is a rule in $R$ that specifies the relationship $(A, B)$, where $e_1 \in A$ and

$e_2 \in B$. Then, a user who sees the answers to locally valid queries will not be able to tell with certainty if the two elements $e_1$ and $e_2$ are connected in $D$. This is because 2-concealment guarantees that there are two documents $D_1$ and $D_2$ such that in $D_1$ the two elements $e_1$ and $e_2$ are connected, while in $D_2$, the two elements $e_1$ and $e_2$ are not connected. Furthermore, $Q(D_1) = Q(D_2)$, for any locally valid query.

## 8 Conclusion

We presented an authorization-transparent access-control mechanism for XML under the Non-Truman model. Our mechanism uses rules, which are formulated using XPath expressions, for specifying element relationships that should be concealed. We defined the semantics of rules with respect to a document and with respect to a schema. Coherency of a rule set was defined and discussed. A set of rules is coherent if concealed relationships cannot be inferred from non-concealed relationships. We showed how to construct a coherent set of rules. Finally, we presented the notion of $k$-concealment, which is a modification of $k$-anonymity to our model. We showed that when a coherent set of rules is used, $k$-concealment can be tested efficiently.

Traditionally, access control has been performed using views. Rules can be used either instead of views or in addition to views. There are cases where rules can be written concisely while using view is cumbersome. For example, when only a small fraction of the data should be concealed from users. Yet, when most of the data should be concealed, defining the policy using views might be easier than using rules. Rules, however, have the advantage that when the set is coherent, we can guarantee that concealed relationships cannot be inferred from the results of valid queries. Importantly, our solutions can be used to verify not only queries but also views.

Future work includes showing how to integrate our access-control rules with existing XPath query processors. Another important challenge is to adapt our mechanism to XQuery and XSLT.

## Acknowledgments

We thank the Natural Sciences and Eng. Research Council of Canada for their support, and the anonymous reviewers for their careful comments.

## References

1. R. J. Bayardo and R. Agrawal. Data privacy through optimal k-anonymization. In *Proc. of the 21st ICDE*, pages 217–228, 2005.
2. E. Bertino, S. Castano, and E. Ferrari. On specifying security policies for web documents with an XML-based language. In *Proc. of the 6th SACMAT*, pages 57–65, 2001.
3. E. Bertino and E. Ferrari. Secure and selective dissemination of XML documents. *ACM TISSEC*, 5(3):290–331, 2002.
4. L. Bouganim, F. Dang-Ngoc, and P. Pucheral. Client-based access control management for XML documents. In *Proc. of the 30th VLDB*, pages 84–95, 2004.

5. D. Chamberlin, J. Clark, D. Florescu, J. Robie, J. Siméon, and M. Stefanescu. XQuery 1.0, June 2001. W3C standard. Available at http://www.w3.org/TR/xquery.
6. SungRan Cho, S. Amer-Yahia, L. V.S. Lakshmanan, and D. Srivastava. Optimizing the secure evaluation of twig queries. In *Proc. of the 28th VLDB*, pages 490–501, 2002.
7. J. Clark. XSLT 1.0. W3C standard. Available at http://www.w3.org/TR/xslt, 1999.
8. J. Clark and S. DeRose. XPath 1.0. Available at http://www.w3.org/TR/xpath.
9. E. Damiani, S. De Capitani di Vimercati, S. Paraboschi, and P. Samarati. A fine-grained access control system for XML documents. *ACM TISSEC*, 5(3):169–202, 2002.
10. E. Damiani, S. Samarati, S. di Vimercati, and S. Paraboschi. Controlling access to XML documents. *IEEE Internet Computing*, 5(6):18–28, 2001.
11. W. Fan, C. Chan, and M. Garofalakis. Secure XML querying with security views. In *Proc. of the 23rd ACM SIGMOD*, pages 587–598, 2004.
12. B. Finance, S. Medjdoub, and P. Pucheral. The Case for access control on XML relationships. In *Proc. of the 14th CIKM*, pages 107–114, 2005.
13. I. Fundulaki and M. Marx. Specifying access control policies for XML documents with XPath. In *Proc. of the 9th ACM SACMAT*, pages 61–69, 2004.
14. A. Gabillon and E. Bruno. Regulating access to XML documents. In *Proc. of the 15th IFIP WG11.3*, pages 299–314, 2001.
15. S. Godik and T. Moses. eXtesible Access Control Markup Language (XACML) Version 1.0. Available at http://www.oasis-open.org/committees/xacml, 2003.
16. S. Hada and M. Kudo. XML Access Control Language: provisional authorization for XML documents. Available at http://www.trl.ibm.com/projects/xml/xacl.
17. A. Meyerson and R. Williams. On the complexity of optimal k-anonymity. In *Proc. of the 23rd PODS*, pages 223–228, 2004.
18. G. Miklau and D. Suciu. Controlling access to published data using cryptography. In *Proc. of the 29th VLDB*, pages 898–909, 2003.
19. G. Miklau and D. Suciu. Containment and equivalence for a fragment of XPath. *Journal of the ACM*, 51(1):2–45, 2004.
20. G. Miklau and D. Suciu. A formal analysis of information disclosure in data exchange. In *Proc. of the 23rd ACM SIGMOD*, pages 575–586, 2004.
21. A. Motro. An access authorization model for relational databases based on algebraic manipulation of view definitions. In *Proc. of the 5th ICDE*, pages 339–347, 1989.
22. S. Rizvi, A. O. Mendelzon, S. Sudarshan, and P. Roy. Extending query rewriting techniques for fine-grained access control. In *Proc. of the 23rd ACM SIGMOD*, pages 551–562, 2004.
23. A. Rosenthal and E. Scoire. View security as the basis for data warehouse security. In *Proc. of the 2nd DMDW*, Stockholm (Sweden), 2000.
24. A. Rosenthal and E. Scoire. Administering permissions for distributed data:factoring and automated inference. In *Proc. of the 15th IFIP WG11.3*, pages 91–104, 2001.
25. L. Sweeney. k-anonymity: a model for protecting privacy. *International Journal on Uncertainty, Fuzziness and Knowledge-based Systems*, 10(5):557–570, 2002.
26. XML. W3C standard. Available at http://www.w3c.org/XML.
27. XML Schema. W3C standard. Available at http://www.w3c.org/XML/Schema.
28. Wanhong Xu and Z. M. Özsoyoglu. Rewriting xpath queries using materialized views. In *Proc. of the 31st VLDB*, pages 121–132, 2005.
29. C. Yao, X. S. Wang, and S. Jajodia. Checking for k-anonymity violation by views. In *Proc. of the 31st VLDB*, pages 910–921, 2005.
30. T. Yu, D. Srivastava, L. V.S. Lakshmanan, and H. V. Jagadish. Compressed accessibility map: efficient access control for XML. In *Proc. of the 28th VLDB*, pages 363–402, 2002.

# On Honesty in Sovereign Information Sharing

Rakesh Agrawal[1] and Evimaria Terzi[1,2]

[1] IBM Almaden Research Center, San Jose, CA 95120, USA
[2] Department of Computer Science, University of Helsinki, Finland

**Abstract.** We study the following problem in a sovereign information-sharing setting: How to ensure that the individual participants, driven solely by self-interest, will behave honestly, even though they can benefit from cheating. This benefit comes from learning more than necessary private information of others or from preventing others from learning the necessary information. We take a game-theoretic approach and design a game (strategies and payoffs) that models this kind of interactions. We show that if nobody is punished for cheating, rational participants will not behave honestly. Observing this, our game includes an auditing device that periodically checks the actions of the participants and penalizes inappropriate behavior. In this game we give conditions under which there exists a unique equilibrium (stable rational behavior) in which every participant provides truthful information. The auditing device preserves the privacy of the data of the individual participants. We also quantify the relationship between the frequency of auditing and the amount of punishment in terms of gains and losses from cheating.

## 1 Introduction

There is an increasing requirement for sharing information across autonomous entities in such a way that only minimal and necessary information is disclosed. This requirement is being driven by several trends, including end-to-end integration of global supply chains, co-existence of competition and co-operation between enterprises, need-to-know sharing between security agencies, and the emergence of privacy guidelines and legislations.

Sovereign information sharing [1, 3] allows autonomous entities to compute queries across their databases such that nothing apart from the result is revealed. For example, suppose the entity $R$ has a set $V_R = \{b, u, v, y\}$ and the entity $S$ has a set $V_S = \{a, u, v, x\}$. As the result of sovereign intersection $V_R \cap V_S$, $R$ and $S$ will get to know the result $\{u, v\}$, but $R$ will not know that $S$ also has $\{a, x\}$, and $S$ will not know that $R$ also has $\{b, y\}$.

Several protocols have been proposed for computing sovereign relational operations, including [1, 3, 6, 8, 16]. In principle, sovereign information sharing can be implemented using protocols for secure function evaluation (SFE) [7]. Given two parties with inputs $x$ and $y$ respectively, SFE computes a function $f(x, y)$ such that the parties learn only the result.

The above body of work relies on a crucial assumption, that the participants in the computation are *semi-honest*. This assumption basically says that the participants follow the protocol properly (with the exception that they may keep a record of the intermediate computations and received messages, and analyze the messages). Specifically, it is assumed that the participants will not maliciously alter the input data to gain additional information. This absence of malice assumption is also present in work in which a trusted-third party is employed to compute sovereign operations.

In a real imperfect world, the participants may behave dishonestly particularly when they can benefit from such a behavior. This benefit can come from learning more than necessary private information of others or preventing others from learning the necessary information. In the sovereign intersection example given in the beginning, $R$ may maliciously add $x$ to $V_R$ to learn whether $V_S$ contains $x$. Similarly, $S$ may exclude $v$ from $V_S$ to prevent $R$ from learning that it has $v$.

## 1.1 Problem Addressed

We study the following problem in a sovereign information-sharing setting: *How to ensure that the individual participants, driven solely by self-interest, will behave honestly, even though they can benefit from cheating.*

We take a game-theoretic approach to address the problem. We design a game (i.e. strategies and payoffs) that models interactions in sovereign information sharing. Through this game, we show that if nobody is punished for cheating, it is natural for the rational participants to cheat. We therefore add an auditing device to our game that periodically checks the actions of the participants and penalizes inappropriate behavior. We derive conditions under which a unique equilibrium (stable rational behavior) is obtained for this game such that every participant provides truthful information. We also quantify the relationship between the frequency of auditing and the amount of punishment in terms of gains and losses from cheating.

The auditing device must have the following essential properties: (a) it must not access the private data of the participants and (b) it must be space and time efficient. The auditing device we provide has these properties.

## 1.2 Related Work

Notions from game theory are used widely in this paper. Game theory was founded by von Neumann and Morgenstern as a general theory of rational behavior. It is a field of study of its own, with extensive literature; see [17] for an excellent introduction.

Games related to our work include the interdependent security(IDS) games [10, 13]. They were defined primarily to model scenarios where a large number of players must make individual investment decisions related to a security - whether physical, financial, medical, or some other type - but in which the ultimate safety of every participant depends on the actions of the entire population. IDS games are closely related to summarization games [11] in which the players' payoff is a function of their own actions and the value of a global summarization function that is determined by the joint play of the population. Summarization games themselves are extensions of congestion games [15, 19] in which players compete for some central resources and every player's payoff is a decreasing function of the number of players selecting the resources. We have adopted some notions from the IDS games and used them to model information exchange. However, our problem is different from the one presented in [13], while at the same time we are not exploring algorithms for computing the equilibria of the games as in [10].

Inspection games [4, 5, 14, 21] are also related to our work. These are games repeated for a sequence of iterations. There is an inspector responsible for distributing a given number of inspections over an inspection period. Inspections are done so that possible illegal actions of an inspectee can be detected. The inspectee can observe the number of inspections the inspector performs. The question addressed is what are the optimal strategies for the inspector and the inspectee in such a game. The main difference between these games and the game we have designed is that in the inspection games the inspector is a player of the game. This is not true for our game, where the inspector acts as a referee for the players, helping them (via auditing) to achieve honest collaboration.

The modeling of private information exchange using game-theoretic concepts has received some attention recently. In [12], different information-exchange scenarios are considered and the willingness of the participants to share their private information is measured using solution concepts from coalition games. Our study is complementary to this work. We are interested in quantifying when people are willing to participate truthfully in a game, rather than the complementary question of whether they are willing to participate at all.

The work presented in [20] models information exchange between a consumer and a web site. Consumers want to interact with web sites, but they also want to keep control of their private information. For the latter, the authors empower the consumers with the ability to test whether a web site meets their privacy requirements. In the proposed games, the web sites signal their privacy policies that the consumers can test at some additional cost. The main conclusion of the study is that such a game leads to cyclic instability. The scenario we are modeling is completely different. Our players are all empowered with the same set of strategies. Our games also admit multiple players.

A recent work [22] addresses the problem of an adversary maliciously changing his input to obtain the private information from another party in a sovereign-intersection computation. They use concepts from non-cooperative games to derive optimal countermeasures for a defendant (and optimal attacking methods for the adversary) that balance the loss of accuracy in the result and the loss of privacy. These countermeasures involve the defendant also changing his input. Our approach is entirely different. We are interested in creating mechanisms so that the participants do not cheat and provide truthful information.

### 1.3 Road Map

The rest of the paper is structured as follows. In Section 2, we formally define the problem addressed in the paper, and also review the main game-theoretic concepts. In Section 3, we construct our initial game that captures two-party interactions in the absence of auditing and study its equilibria. The auditing device is introduced in Section 4 and its influence on the equilibria of the game is discussed. Section 5 shows how the observations from the two-player game generalize to multiple participants. An implementation of the auditing device is provided in Section 6. We conclude with a summary and directions for future work in Section 7.

## 2 Definitions

We first formally define the problem the paper addresses. We then review some basic concepts from game theory.

### 2.1 Problem Statement

First we give the classical sovereign information-sharing problem, which provided the setting for this work. Then we define the honest version of this problem, which is the concern of this paper. Finally, we specify the honest set-intersection problem, which is an important instantiation of the general problem.

*Problem 1 (Sovereign information sharing).* Let there be $n$ autonomous entities. Each entity $i$ holds a database of tuples $D_i$. Given a function $f$ defined on $D_i$'s, compute $f(D_1, \ldots, D_n)$ and return it to each entity. The goal is that in the end of the computation each entity knows $f(D_1, \ldots, D_n)$ and no additional information regarding the data of its peers.

The problem we are trying to tackle is more difficult. We want not only to guarantee that each participant in the end knows nothing more than the result, but also that each participant reports his true dataset. More formally:

*Problem 2 (Honest sovereign information sharing).* Let there be $n$ autonomous entities. Each party $i$ holds a database of tuples $D_i$. Each entity $i$ reports a dataset $\hat{D}_i$ so that a function $f(\hat{D}_1, \ldots, \hat{D}_n)$ is computed. The goal in the honest information sharing is to find a mechanism that can guarantee that all entities report $\hat{D}_i$ such that $\hat{D}_i = D_i$. As in Problem 1, in the end of the computation each entity knows only $f(\hat{D}_1, \ldots, \hat{D}_n)$ and no additional information regarding the data of its peers.

We use game-theoretic concepts to develop a general framework that can model different information-exchange scenarios and guarantee honest information exchange. For concreteness, we also consider:

*Problem 3.* [Honest computation of set intersection] Special case of Problem 2 in which $f(\hat{D}_1, \ldots, \hat{D}_n) = \cap_{i=1,\ldots,n} \hat{D}_i$.

The problem of honest computation of other relational operations (e.g. join, set-difference) can be defined analogously; the techniques presented in the paper apply to them as well.

## 2.2 Games and Equilibria

We mainly focus on *strategic games*. In each game there are $n$ players that can choose among a set of strategies $S_i$, $i = 1, 2, \ldots, n$. A function $u_i$ is associated with each player $i$ with $u_i : S_1, \ldots, S_n \to \mathbb{R}$. This is called a *payoff function* since it assigns a payoff to player $i$, for each combined strategy choices of the $n$ players. The basic question in game theory is what constitutes a rational behavior in such a situation. The most widely-used concept of rationality is the *Nash equilibrium*:

**Definition 1 (Nash equilibrium).** *A Nash equilibrium (NE) is a combination of strategies: $x_1 \in S_1 \ldots x_n \in S_n$ for which*

$$u_i(x_1, \ldots, x_i, \ldots x_n) \geq u_i(x_1, \ldots, x'_i, \ldots, x_n),$$

*for all $i$ and $x'_i \in S_i$.*

That is, a Nash equilibrium is a combination of strategies from which no player has the incentive to deviate. A game can have zero, one, or more than one Nash equilibrium and the payoffs of a player can be different in two different equilibria.

Another rationality concept is that of *dominant-strategy equilibrium*:

**Definition 2 (Dominant-strategy equilibrium).** *A dominant-strategy equilibrium (DSE) is a combination of strategies: $x_1 \in S1, \ldots, x_n \in S_n$ for which*

$$u_i(x'_1, \ldots, x_i, \ldots, x'_n) \geq u_i(x'_1, \ldots, x''_i, \ldots x'_n),$$

*for all $i$ and $x''_i \in S_i$ and for all $j \neq i$ and $x'_j \in S_j$.*

That is, the strategy of every player in a dominant-strategy equilibrium is the most profitable one (gives the highest payoff to every player) irrespective of what the other players' strategies are. A game need not have a dominant-strategy equilibrium. A dominant-strategy equilibrium is always a Nash equilibrium. The opposite is not true. Nash and dominant-strategy equilibria capture the behavior of selfish players who only care about maximizing their own payoffs without caring about the payoffs of the rest of the players. Nash equilibrium is widely used in many settings. However, there is no consensus on the best concept for rationality.

## 3 Dishonest Information Sharing

We now describe a real-world situation, but of course simplified, and use it to motivate the definition of a two-player game that can be used to analyze sovereign information-sharing interactions. Our goal is to formally show that when there is benefit from cheating that is not accompanied with any bad consequences, there is no guarantee for honesty. In fact, rational players driven solely by self-interest will cheat in such a situation.

Rowi and Colie are successful competitors. Though their products cover all segments of their industry, Rowi has a larger coverage in some while Colie is stronger in others. By finding the intersection of their customer lists, they both can benefit by jointly marketing to their common customers. This benefit accrues from business expansion as well as reduction in marketing costs with respect to these customers. Rowi has estimated that the benefit he will realize is $B_1$, whereas Colie's estimate is $B_2$.[1] Clearly, it is in the interest of both Rowi and Colie that they find their common customers without revealing their private customers, and can use sovereign set intersection for this purpose.

In practice, Rowi might be tempted to find more than just common customers. Rowi might try to find private customers of Colie by inserting some additional names in his customer database. By doing so, Rowi estimates that his benefit can increase to $F_1$. This temptation to cheat and find more holds for Colie too, and Colie's estimate of the increased benefit is $F_2$. Clearly, it must be that $F_1 > B_1$ and $F_2 > B_2$. We carry this assumption throughout the paper.

However, both Rowi and Colie may also incur some loss due to cheating. For example, from Rowi's perspective, Colie might succeed in stealing some of his private customers. Also, Rowi's customer database has become noisy as it now has some fake names. We use $L_{21}$ ($L_{12}$) to represent the player's estimate of the loss that Colie (Rowi) causes to Rowi (Colie) due to his cheating.

For now, let us consider the symmetric case: $B_1 = B_2 = B$, $F_1 = F_2 = F$, and $L_{12} = L_{21} = L$, and $F > B$.

We model the above situation as a two-player strategic game with payoffs described in Table 1. Both players have the same set of strategies: "Play Honestly" (**H**) or "Cheat" (**C**). Honest playing corresponds to reporting the true set of tuples, while cheating corresponds to alternating the reported dataset by adding extra tuples or removing real tuples.

**Table 1.** Payoff matrix for the two-player game where there is no punishment for cheating. Each entry lists the payoff of Rowi at the left-bottom, and the payoff of Colie at the right-top corner of the cell for the corresponding combination of strategies.

| Rowi \ Colie | Play Honestly (**H**) | Cheat (**C**) |
|---|---|---|
| Play Honestly (**H**) | $B$ \ $B$ | $F$ \ $B-L$ |
| Cheat (**C**) | $B-L$ \ $F$ | $F-L$ \ $F-L$ |

**Observation 1.** *For the strategic game described in Table 1 and given that there is extra benefit from cheating ($F > B$), the pair of strategies (**C**, **C**) is the only equilibrium (NE as well as DSE).*

To see that (**C**, **C**) is a Nash equilibrium, note that for Rowi $u(\mathbf{C},\mathbf{C}) > u(\mathbf{H},\mathbf{C})$ and for Colie $u(\mathbf{C},\mathbf{C}) > u(\mathbf{C},\mathbf{H})$. On the other hand, (**H**, **H**) is not a Nash equilibrium since $u(\mathbf{C},\mathbf{H}) > u(\mathbf{H},\mathbf{H})$ for Rowi.

---

[1] If the benefit is considered to be a function of the number of common customers, the latter can be determined (without revealing who the common customers are) by using the sovereign set intersection size operation.

Similarly, (**C,C**) is a dominant-strategy equilibrium since for Rowi $u(\mathbf{C},\mathbf{C}) > u(\mathbf{H},\mathbf{C})$ and $u(\mathbf{C},\mathbf{H}) > u(\mathbf{H},\mathbf{H})$ and for Colie $u(\mathbf{C},\mathbf{C}) > u(\mathbf{C},\mathbf{H})$ and $u(\mathbf{H},\mathbf{C}) > u(\mathbf{H},\mathbf{H})$. It is easy to see that (**H,H**) is not a dominant-strategy equilibrium.

Note that the above observation holds irrespective of the value of $L$. In other words, both Rowi and Colie will find it rational to cheat even if the loss from cheating makes $F - L$ less than $B$ for both of them.

## 4  Enforcing Honesty

We now extend the game described in the previous section with an auditing device that can check whether any player has cheated by altering the input. An implementation of such a device is discussed later in Section 6. Whenever the device finds out that a player has cheated, it penalizes the player. For a fixed penalty amount, we address the question of how often should the auditing be performed. We find a lower bound on the auditing frequency that guarantees honesty. Such a lower bound is important particularly in cases where auditing is expensive. Conversely, for fixed frequency of auditing we calculate the minimum penalty that guarantees honest behavior.

An auditing device can be characterized as follows, depending on the degree of honesty it can guarantee:

1. *Transformative:* It can induce equilibrium states where all players being honest is a dominant-strategy equilibrium (DSE). Recall that every dominant-strategy equilibrium is also a Nash equilibrium (NE), though the opposite is not true.
2. *Highly Effective:* It can induce equilibrium states where all participants being honest is the only Nash equilibrium of the game.
3. *Effective:* It can induce equilibria where all participants being honest is a Nash equilibrium of the game.
4. *Ineffective:* Nothing can be guaranteed about the honest behavior of the players. That is, the auditing device cannot induce equilibrium states where all players are honest.

We first study the symmetric case in which the players have identical payoffs. We then extend the analysis to study asymmetric payoffs.

### 4.1  The Symmetric Case

Consider the game with the payoff matrix given in Table 2. The semantics of the parameters $B, F$ and $L$ are the same as in the game described in Section 3. Two more parameters appear here. The first one, $P$, represents the penalty that the auditing device imposes on the cheating player once it detects the cheating. Parameter $f$, with $0 \le f \le 1$, corresponds to the *relative frequency* of auditing, and represents how often the device checks truthfulness of the data provided by the players. For brevity, from now on, we will use the term *frequency* to refer to relative frequency.

**Table 2.** Payoff matrix for the symmetric two-player game enhanced with the auditing device

| Rowi \ Colie | Play Honestly (**H**) | Cheat(**C**) |
|---|---|---|
| Play Honestly (**H**) | $B$ / $B$ | $(1-f)F - fP$ / $B - (1-f)L$ |
| Cheat (**C**) | $B - (1-f)L$ / $(1-f)F - fP$ | $(1-f)F - fP - (1-f)L$ / $(1-f)F - fP - (1-f)L$ |

In Table 2, when both players play honestly they each have benefit $B$. Since the auditing device checks with frequency $f$, the expected gain of a player that cheats is $(1-f)F$. That is, a cheating player gains amount $F$ only when he is not caught, which happens with probability $1-f$. A player who cheats and is not caught causes expected loss $(1-f)L$ to the other player. Finally, a cheating player may be caught with probability $f$ and pays penalty $P$, which gives an expected loss of $fP$ to the cheating player.

When both players are cheating their payoff is the expected cheating benefit $(1-f)F$ minus the expected cost of paying a penalty $fP$ as well as the expected loss caused from other player cheating $(1-f)L$. Note that $(1-f)L$ is the loss of a player due to the cheating behavior of the opponent, multiplied by the probability that the latter is not caught.

We now give some important observations from the analysis (details omitted) of this game. Assume first that all parameters are fixed except for $f$. In that case the auditing device gets as input the penalty amount $P$. The goal is to determine the corresponding frequency of auditing that can guarantee honest behavior. The following statement can be made in this case.

**Observation 2.** *For any fixed penalty amount $P$, there exists a checking frequency for which the auditing device is both transformative and highly effective. More specifically for fixed $P$, the equilibria of the game for different values of frequency $f \in [0,1]$ are:*

- *For $0 \leq f < \frac{F-B}{P+F}$, (**C**,**C**) is the only DSE and NE of the game. That is, for those frequencies the auditing device is ineffective.*
- *For $\frac{F-B}{P+F} < f \leq 1$, (**H**,**H**) is the only DSE and NE of the game. That is, for those frequencies the auditing device is transformative and highly effective.*
- *For $f = \frac{F-B}{P+F}$, (**H**,**H**) is among the NE of the game and therefore the auditing device is effective.*

The above observation is rather intuitive. The key quantity is $f = \frac{F-B}{P+F}$ that can be rewritten as $fP = (1-f)F - B$. The left-hand side corresponds to the expected loss due to the penalty imposed by the auditing device. The right-hand side is the net expected gain from cheating. Therefore the first case in observation 2 says that (**C**,**C**) is DSE and NE only when $fP < (1-f)F - B$; that is when the expected loss from the penalty is less than the expected gain from cheating. In this case, the auditing device does not provide enough deterrence to keep off the players from cheating. However, when the expected loss due to the penalty imposed by the device exceeds the expected gain, the players start behaving honestly.

The landscape of the equilibria for the different values of the checking frequency is shown in Figure 1. Notice that the above game for all the values of $f \neq \frac{F-B}{P+F}$ has only two equilibria in which either both players are honest or both of them are cheating.

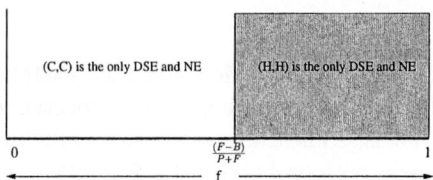

**Fig. 1.** Equilibria of the two-player symmetric game with auditing device for the different values of checking frequency $f$ and for fixed penalty amount $P$. Shaded region corresponds to (**H, H**) being both DSE and NE.

Alternatively, we can study the penalty-for-cheating versus frequency-of-checking trade off the other way round. What happens in the case where the auditing device is instructed to check at the specified frequencies? What is the minimum penalty amount it has to impose on cheating players so that honesty is ensured?

**Observation 3.** *For any fixed frequency $f \in [0, 1]$, the auditing device can be transformative and highly effective for wise choices of the penalty amount. Specifically:*

- *For $P > \frac{(1-f)F-B}{f}$, (**H, H**) is the only DSE and NE, and therefore the auditing device is both transformative and highly effective.*
- *For $P < \frac{(1-f)F-B}{f}$, (**C,C**) is the only DSE and NE, and therefore the auditing device is ineffective.*
- *For $P = \frac{(1-f)F-B}{f}$, (**H, H**) is among the NE of the game. That is for this penalty amount the auditing device is effective.*

The above observation is also intuitive as it says that the players will not be deterred by an auditing device that imposes penalties such that the expected loss due to them is smaller than the expected additional benefit from cheating. This is true no matter how often this device performs its checks.

On the other hand, note the following special case. When $f > \frac{F-B}{F}$, the auditing device does not have to impose any penalty on the cheating participants. The fact that the participants are aware of its existence is daunting by itself. Notice that this happens particularly in high frequencies and for the following reason. Due to high checking frequency, the expected gain from cheating $(1 - f)F$ becomes lower than the gain from honest collaboration $B$. Therefore, the players have incentive to play honestly.

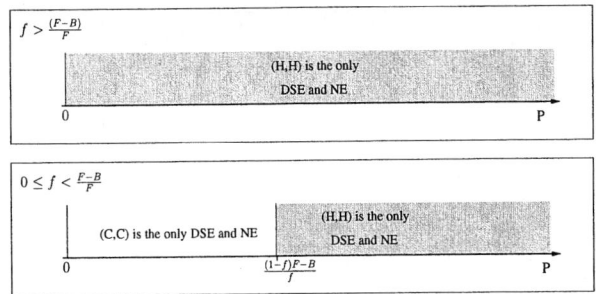

**Fig. 2.** Equilibria of the two-player symmetric game with auditing device for the different values of penalty regions $P$ for fixed checking frequency $f$. Shaded region corresponds to (**H**, **H**) being DSE as well as NE.

The equilibria of the game as a function of the penalty amount $P$ are given in Figure 2.

The above observations provide the game-designer the chance to decide, based on estimations of the players losses and gains, the minimum checking frequencies or penalty amounts that can guarantee the desired level of honesty in the system.

### 4.2 The Asymmetric Case

We now turn to the study of the asymmetric case where the payoffs of the two players are not necessarily the same. The payoff matrix of the game is given in Table 3. The easiest way to visualize the equilibria of such a game is by fixing the penalty amounts imposed on each player ($P_i$) and giving to the auditing device the freedom to select the frequency of checking each player ($f_i$). In this case, we get the landscape of the equilibria shown in Figure 3.

Again the auditing device becomes transformative and highly effective when it checks frequently enough so that the players cannot tolerate the extra losses from being caught cheating. Similar observations can be made by studying the game using the penalty amounts as the free parameters of the auditing device and fixing the checking frequencies.

Note that in contrast to the symmetric case, the current game exhibits equilibria in which the two players do not pick the same strategy. This is the case, for example, when the auditing device checks Colie very frequently and Rowi quite

**Table 3.** Payoff matrix for the asymmetric two-player game enhanced with the auditing device

| Rowi \ Colie | Play Honestly (**H**) | Cheat (**C**) |
|---|---|---|
| Play Honestly (**H**) | $B_1$ <br> $B_2$ | $B_1 - (1-f_2)L_{21}$ <br> $(1-f_2)F_2 - f_2P_2$ |
| Cheat (**C**) | $(1-f_1)F_1 - f_1P_1$ <br> $B_2 - (1-f_1)L_{12}$ | $(1-f_1)F_1 - f_1P_1 - (1-f_2)L_{21}$ <br> $(1-f_2)F_2 - f_2P_2 - (1-f_1)L_{12}$ |

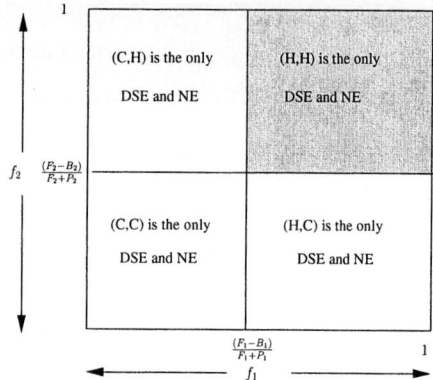

**Fig. 3.** Equilibria of two-player asymmetric game with auditing device for the different values of penalties $(P_1, P_2)$. Shaded region corresponds to (**H,H**) being both DSE and NE.

rarely (upper left-hand corner of the figure); the Nash equilibrium has poor Colie playing honestly while Rowi is cheating. This example brings out the need for careful choice of penalties and frequencies; otherwise, the rational players may be forced into unintuitive behaviors.

## 5 Generalization to Multiple Participants

More than two entities are often involved in an information-sharing situation. To model such situations we extend our two-player game to $n$ players.

Each player has again two possible strategies: to play honestly (**H**) or to cheat (**C**). We use indicator variable $h_i$ to denote the strategy of player $i$:

$$h_i = \begin{cases} 1, \text{ if player i is playing honestly} \\ 0, \text{ otherwise.} \end{cases}$$

We use vector $\boldsymbol{h}$ to represent the strategies of all $n$ players. The vector $\boldsymbol{h}_{-i}$ represents the strategies of all players except for player $i$. Motivated by [10], we design the $n$-player game by forming a *payoff function* that adequately describes: (a) the gains/losses a player has due to his own actions, and (b) the gains/losses due to the behavior of others.

The notation is along the same lines as used in the two-player game. We again assume the existence of an auditing device that checks on players with frequency $f$ and imposes penalty $P$ for cheating. We consider the case where the values of $f$ and $P$ are the same for all players. Assume that the benefit from honest collaboration for each player is $B$. The increased benefit of player $i$ due to his cheating is given by function $\mathcal{F}$, which is assumed to be the same for all players. The specific form of function $\mathcal{F}$ depends on the application domain. However, we do assume that it is monotonically increasing in the number of players that play honestly. That is, the larger the number of honest players in the game, the more the dishonest player gains by exploiting their honesty. Finally, assume that the loss a player $i$ experiences due to the cheating of another player $j$ is given by $L_{ji}$. The payoff of player $i$ is thus a function $u_i : \{\mathbf{H},\mathbf{C}\}^n \to \mathbb{R}$, which can be written as:

$$u_i(\mathbf{h}) = h_i B + (1-h_i)(1-f)\mathcal{F}(\|\mathbf{h}_{-i}\|) - (1-h_i)fP \\ - \sum_{j=1, j\neq i}^{n} (1-h_j)(1-f)L_{ji} \qquad (1)$$

The payoff $u_i$ of player $i$ depends on the strategies picked by the participating players and it consists of four terms. The first two terms correspond to the gains of the player and the last two correspond to his losses. The losses are due to either his own choices or the choices of the rest of the participants. More specifically, the first term is the gain player $i$ has in isolation (irrespective of the strategies of the rest $n-1$ players) when he plays honestly. The second term is his gain when he decides to cheat. This gain depends on the strategies of others as well. The third term, $(1-h_i)fP$, corresponds to his loss when he decides to cheat and he is caught. In that case, he experiences an expected loss of $fP$. The last term represents his loss due to the behavior of the other participants.

For building some intuition, consider the following special cases. When all players except player $i$ cheat, then the payoff of player $i$ would be:

$$u_i(\mathbf{h}_{-i} = \mathbf{0}, h_i = 1) = B - \sum_{j=1, j\neq i}^{n} (1-f)L_{ji}.$$

If player $i$ decides to cheat as well, his gain is:

$$u_i(\mathbf{h} = \mathbf{0}) = \mathcal{F}(0) - fP - \sum_{j=1, j\neq i}^{n} (1-f)L_{ji}.$$

Although it seems that the analysis of the auditing device in the presence of $n$ players could be more demanding, it turns out that some intuition and the results from the two-player game carry over.

Assume we fix the checking frequency $f$ with which the auditing device checks the participating players.

**Proposition 1.** *For the n-player game where the payoff of each player $i$ is given by $u_i$ as defined in equation 1, the following is true: For fixed frequencies $f \in [0,1]$ an auditing device that imposes penalty $P > \frac{(1-f)\mathcal{F}(n-1)-B}{f}$ is transformative and highly effective. That is, for those values of $f$ and $P$, ($\mathbf{H}, \mathbf{H}, \ldots, \mathbf{H}$) is the only combination of strategies that is DSE and NE.*

*Proof.* (Sketch) First we show that the auditing device is transformative. For this, we have to show that when $P > \frac{(1-f)\mathcal{F}(n-1)-B}{f}$ each player $i$ prefers $h_i = 1$ irrespective of the strategies of the other $n-1$ players. This comes down to proving that the inequality:

$$u_i(\mathbf{h}_{-i} = \mathbf{1}, h_i = 1) > u_i(\mathbf{h}_{-i} = \mathbf{1}, h_i = 0) \qquad (2)$$

is true for player $i$ (and thus for every player). If inequality 2 holds for $\boldsymbol{h}_{-i} = \boldsymbol{1}$, then it would also hold for any other $\boldsymbol{h}_{-i} \neq \boldsymbol{1}$. This means that even in the worst-case, where all $n-1$ other players are playing honestly (this is the case where player $i$ has the highest benefit from cheating), player $i$ still has more benefit from being honest than from cheating. This makes $h_i = 1$ dominant strategy. Indeed by solving inequality 2, we end up with a true statement.

Then we have to show that the auditing device is also highly effective. For this we need to show that when $P > \frac{(1-f)\mathcal{F}(n-1)-B}{f}$ there does not exist an equilibrium other than (**H,H,...,H**).

The proof is by contradiction. Assume there exists another equilibrium where $x$ players are playing honestly and $n - x$ players are cheating, with $x \neq n$. Now consider a player $i$ with $h_i = 1$. Since we have assumed an equilibrium state, the following should be true:

$$u_i(h_1 = 1, \ldots, h_i = 1, \ldots, h_x = 1, h_{x+1} = 0, \ldots, h_n = 0) >$$
$$u_i(h_1 = 1, \ldots, h_i = 0, \ldots, h_x = 1, h_{x+1} = 0, \ldots, h_n = 0).$$

This would mean that

$$B - \sum_{j=1, j \neq i}^{n} (1-h_j)(1-f)L_{ji} > (1-f)\mathcal{F}(x-1) - fP - \sum_{j=1, j\neq i}^{n}(1-h_j)(1-f)L_{ji},$$

and thus

$$P > \frac{(1-f)\mathcal{F}(x-1) - B}{f}. \tag{3}$$

Now consider a player $j$ from the set of $n - x$ cheating players. Due to the equilibrium assumption, the following should also hold:

$$u_j(h_1 = 1, \ldots, h_x = 1, h_{x+1} = 0, \ldots, x_j = 0, \ldots, h_n = 0) >$$
$$u_j(h_1 = 1, \ldots, h_x = 1, h_{x+1} = 0, \ldots, x_j = 1, \ldots, h_n = 0).$$

This would mean that

$$(1-f)\mathcal{F}(x) - fP - \sum_{i=1, l \neq j}^{n}(1-h_i)(1-f)L_{ij} > B - (1-f)\sum_{i=1, l \neq j}^{n}(1-h_i)(1-f)L_{ij}$$

and thus

$$P < \frac{(1-f)\mathcal{F}(x) - B}{f}. \tag{4}$$

However, inequalities 3, 4 and the constraint $P > \frac{(1-f)\mathcal{F}(n-1)-B}{f}$ cannot be satisfied simultaneously, due to the monotonicity property of $\mathcal{F}$. Therefore the auditing device is also highly effective. □

In a similar manner we can show the following proposition:

**Proposition 2.** *For the n-player game where the payoff of each player i is given by $u_i$ as defined in equation 1, the following is true: For fixed frequencies $f \in [0,1]$ an auditing device that imposes penalty $P < \frac{(1-f)\mathcal{F}(0)-B}{f}$ is ineffective. That is, for those values of f and P, (C, C, ..., C) is the only combination of strategies that is NE and DSE.*

Finally we can generalize the above propositions in the following theorem:

**Theorem 1.** *For the n-player game where the payoff of each player i is given by $u_i$, as defined in equation 1, the following is true: For $x \in 1, \ldots, n-1$ and for any $f \in [0,1]$, when the auditing device imposes penalty $\frac{(1-f)\mathcal{F}(x-1)-B}{f} < P < \frac{(1-f)\mathcal{F}(x)-B}{f}$, then the n-player game is in an equilibrium state where x players are honest and $n - x$ players are cheating.*

Consequently, the equilibria landscape looks as in Figure 4.

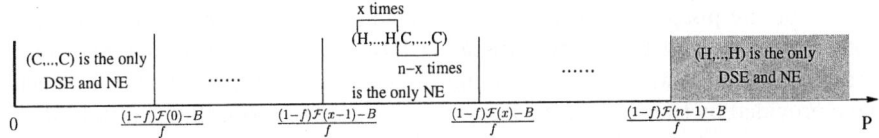

**Fig. 4.** Equilibria of the $n$-player symmetric game with auditing device for different values of penalty $P$. Shaded region corresponds to (**H,H**) being both DSE and NE.

## 6 Auditing Device

We turn now to a discussion of the feasibility of realizing the auditing device. The auditing service must be space as well as time efficient. It must also not see any private data of any of the participants.

### 6.1 Incremental Multiset Hash Functions

Our proposed auditing device makes use of incremental multiset hash functions [2], which are hash functions that map multisets of arbitrary finite size to hashes of fixed length. They are incremental in that when new members are added to the multiset, the hash can be quickly updated.

**Definition 3 (Multiset hash function [2]).** *Let $(\mathcal{H}, +_{\mathcal{H}}, \equiv_{\mathcal{H}})$ be a triple of probabilistic polynomial time algorithms. This triple is an incremental multiset hash function if it satisfies:*

- **Compression:** *$\mathcal{H}$ maps multisets of a domain $\mathcal{D}$ into elements of a set with cardinality $\approx 2^m$, where m is some integer. Compression guarantees that hashes can be stored in a small bounded amount of memory.*

- **Comparability:** *Since $\mathcal{H}$ can be a probabilistic algorithm, a multiset need not always hash to the same value. Therefore a means of comparison ($\equiv_\mathcal{H}$) is needed to compare hashes. For this it should hold that $\mathcal{H}(M) \equiv_\mathcal{H} \mathcal{H}(M)$, for all multisets of $M$ of $\mathcal{D}$.*
- **Incrementality:** *Finally, $\mathcal{H}(M \cup M')$ is computed efficiently using $\mathcal{H}(M)$ and $\mathcal{H}(M')$. The $+_\mathcal{H}$ operator makes this possible:*

$$\mathcal{H}(M \cup M') \equiv_\mathcal{H} \mathcal{H}(M) +_\mathcal{H} \mathcal{H}(M'),$$

*for all multisets $M$ and $M'$ of $\mathcal{D}$. In particular, knowing $\mathcal{H}(M)$ and an element $t \in \mathcal{D}$, one can easily compute $\mathcal{H}(M \cup \{t\}) = \mathcal{H}(M) +_\mathcal{H} \mathcal{H}(\{t\})$.*

Multiset hash functions are collision resistant in that it is computationally infeasible to find a multiset $M$ of $\mathcal{D}$ and a multiset $M'$ of $\mathcal{D}$ such that $M \neq M'$ and $\mathcal{H}(M) \equiv_\mathcal{H} \mathcal{H}(M')$.

### 6.2 Auditing

Auditing is provided by a secure network service, built using a secure coprocessor [9]. For the purposes of this paper, it is sufficient to observe that a certified application code can be securely installed into a secure coprocessor and, once installed, the application can execute untampered. The remote attestation mechanism provided by the secure coprocessor can be used to prove that it is indeed executing a known, trusted version of the application code, running under a known, trusted version of the OS, and loaded by a known, trusted version of the bootstrap code. Communication between the auditing device and the participants in the sovereign computation makes use of authenticated encryption that provides both message privacy and message authenticity [18].

The auditing device (AD) periodically checks the integrity of the data reported by the players, and hands over penalties if needed. As we shall see, AD accomplishes this check without accessing the private data of the players.

There is a tuple generator $\text{TG}_i$, associated with each player $i$. In the scenario given in Section 3, $\text{TG}_i$ may correspond to the customer registration process. $\text{TG}_i$ provides legal tuples to the player $i$ that should participate in sovereign computations. The player $i$ cannot influence $\text{TG}_i$ into generating illegal tuples[2] but can himself fabricate them. Each $\text{TG}_i$ operates as follows:

1. $\text{TG}_i$ picks $\mathcal{H}_i$ and announces it publicly.
2. For each new tuple $t$ entering the system and to be provided to player $i$:
   (a) $\text{TG}_i$ computes $\mathcal{H}_i(t)$.
   (b) $\text{TG}_i$ sends message $(\mathcal{H}_i(t), i)$ to AD.
   (c) $\text{TG}_i$ sends $t$ to player $i$.

AD maintains for each player $i$ a hash value $\text{HV}_i$. This is the hash value of all the tuples that player $i$ has received from $\text{TG}_i$. Upon receiving $(\mathcal{H}_i(t), i)$, AD

---

[2] If player $i$ can corrupt $\text{TG}_i$ into generating illegal tuples on his behalf, it can be shown that no automated checking device can detect this fraudulent behavior.

updates the hash value so that $HV_i = HV_i +_{\mathcal{H}_i} \mathcal{H}_i(t)$. Note that the auditing device does not know the actual tuples that each player $i$ has received. It only knows the hash value of this multiset of tuples, which it incrementally updates.

Finally, each player $i$ also maintains locally the hashed value of the set of tuples it has received, $\mathcal{H}(D_i)$. Therefore, upon receiving tuple $t$ from $TG_i$, the player $i$ updates the hash value so that $\mathcal{H}_i(D_i) = \mathcal{H}_i(D_i) +_{\mathcal{H}_i} \mathcal{H}_i(t)$.

For sovereign information-sharing computation, the players follow one of the standard protocols that guarantee correct and private computation of the result. These protocols require that each player $i$ reports $D_i$ (usually encrypted) to the other players or to a trusted third party. Here, we additionally require that along with the encrypted version of $D_i$, each player $i$ reports $\mathcal{H}_i(D_i)$.

Note that reporting $\mathcal{H}_i(D_i)$, along with the encrypted $D_i$, does not reveal anything about the actual $D_i$. This is due to the assumption that for a given multiset hash function $\mathcal{H}_i$, it is computationally infeasible to construct multisets $M$ and $M'$ such that $\mathcal{H}_i(M) \equiv_{\mathcal{H}_i} \mathcal{H}_i(M')$. Secondly, player $i$ will be reluctant to report $D_i$ along with $\mathcal{H}_i(D'_i)$ such that $D_i \neq D'_i$ because that will be a violation of the protocol and if the entity that received the encrypted $D_i$ along with $\mathcal{H}_i(D'_i)$ takes $i$ to court, the judge will be able to decide in polynomial time whether the hash value $\mathcal{H}_i(D'_i) \equiv_{\mathcal{H}_i} \mathcal{H}_i(D_i)$.

Given this communication model, the job of the auditing device is straightforward. If AD decides to audit player $i$, it requests the hash value that $i$ reported during the set-intersection computation. Let this hash value be $\mathcal{H}_i(D_i)$. Then AD can decide whether $i$ is cheating by checking whether $HV_i \equiv_{\mathcal{H}_i} \mathcal{H}_i(D_i)$.

## 7 Summary and Future Directions

A key inhibitor in the practical deployment of sovereign information sharing has been the inability of the technology to handle the altering of input by the participants. We applied game-theoretic concepts to the problem and defined a multi-party game to model the situation. The analysis of the game formally confirmed the intuition that as long as the participants have some benefit from cheating, honest behavior cannot be an equilibrium of the game. However, when the game is enhanced with an auditing device that checks at an appropriate frequency the integrity of the data submitted by the participants and penalizes by an appropriate amount the cheating behaviors, honesty can be induced not only as a Nash equilibrium but also as a dominant-strategy equilibrium. We addressed practical issues such as what should be the frequency of checking and the penalty amount and how the auditing device can be implemented as a secure network device that achieves the desired outcome without accessing private data of the participants.

In the future, we would like to study if appropriately designed incentives (rather than penalties) can also lead to honesty. We would also like to explore the application of game theory to other privacy-preservation situations.

*Acknowledgment.* We thank Alexandre Evfimievski for helpful discussions.

# References

1. R. Agrawal, A. V. Evfimievski, and R. Srikant. Information sharing across private databases. In *SIGMOD*, 2003.
2. D. Clarke, S. Devadas, M. van Dijk, B. Gassend, and G. E. Suh. Incremental multiset hash functions and their applications to memory integrity checking. In *Asiacrypt*, 2003.
3. C. Clifton, M. Kantarcioglu, X. Lin, J. Vaidya, and M. Zhu. Tools for privacy preserving distributed data mining. *SIGKDD Explorations*, 4(2):28–34, Jan. 2003.
4. T. Ferguson and C. Melolidakis. On the inspection game. *Naval Research Logistics*, 45, 1998.
5. T. Ferguson and C. Melolidakis. Games with finite resources. *International Journal on Game Theory*, 29, 2000.
6. M. J. Freedman, K. Nissim, and B. Pinkas. Efficient private matching and set intersection. In *EUROCRYPT*, Interlaken, Switzerland, May 2004.
7. O. Goldreich. *Foundations of Cryptography*, volume 2: Basic Applications. Cambridge University Press, May 2004.
8. B. A. Huberman, M. Franklin, and T. Hogg. Enhancing privacy and trust in electronic communities. In *Proc. of the 1st ACM Conference on Electronic Commerce*, Denver, Colorado, November 1999.
9. IBM Corporation. IBM 4758 Models 2 and 23 PCI cryptographic coprocessor, 2004.
10. M. Kearns and L. E. Ortiz. Algorithms for interdependent security games. In *NIPS*, 2004.
11. M. J. Kearns and Y. Mansour. Efficient Nash computation in large population games with bounded influence. In *UAI*, 2002.
12. J. Kleinberg, C. Papadimitriou, and P. Raghavan. On the value of private information. In *8th Conference on Theoretical Aspects of Rationality and Knowledge*, 2001.
13. H. Kunreuther and G. Heal. Interdependent security. *Journal of Risk and Uncertainty*, 2002.
14. M. Maschler. A price leadership method for solving the inspector's non-constant sum game. *Princeton econometric research program*, 1963.
15. D. Monderer and L. S. Shapley. Potential games. *Games and Economic Behavior*, 14, 1996.
16. M. Naor and B. Pinkas. Efficient oblivious transfer protocols. In *Proc. of the 12th Annual ACM-SIAM Symposium on Discrete Algorithms*, pages 448–457, Washington DC, USA, January 2001.
17. M. Osborne and A. Rubinstein. *A course in game theory*. MIT Press, 1994.
18. P. Rogaway, M. Bellare, and J. Black. OCB: A block-cipher mode of operation for efficient authenticated encryption. *ACM Transactions on Information and System Security*, 6(3):365–403, August 2003.
19. R. W. Rosenthal. A class of games possessing pure-strategy Nash equilibria. *International Journal of Game Theory*, 1973.
20. T.Vila, R. Greenstadt, and D. Molnar. Why we can't be bothered to read privacy policies: Models of privacy economics as a lemons market. In *Second International Workshop on Economics and Information Security*, 2003.
21. B. von Stengel. Recursive inspection games. *Technical Report S-9106, University of the Federal Armed Forces, Munich.*, 1991.
22. N. Zhang and W. Zhao. Distributed privacy preserving information sharing. In *VLDB*, 2005.

# Multi-dimensional Aggregation for Temporal Data

Michael Böhlen[1], Johann Gamper[1], and Christian S. Jensen[2]

[1] Free University of Bozen-Bolzano, Italy
{boehlen, gamper}@inf.unibz.it
[2] Aalborg University, Denmark
csj@cs.aau.dk

**Abstract.** Business Intelligence solutions, encompassing technologies such as multi-dimensional data modeling and aggregate query processing, are being applied increasingly to non-traditional data. This paper extends multi-dimensional aggregation to apply to data with associated interval values that capture when the data hold. In temporal databases, intervals typically capture the states of reality that the data apply to, or capture when the data are, or were, part of the current database state.

This paper proposes a new aggregation operator that addresses several challenges posed by interval data. First, the intervals to be associated with the result tuples may not be known in advance, but depend on the actual data. Such unknown intervals are accommodated by allowing result groups that are specified only partially. Second, the operator contends with the case where an interval associated with data expresses that the data holds for each point in the interval, as well as the case where the data holds only for the entire interval, but must be adjusted to apply to sub-intervals. The paper reports on an implementation of the new operator and on an empirical study that indicates that the operator scales to large data sets and is competitive with respect to other temporal aggregation algorithms.

## 1 Introduction

Real-world database applications, e.g., in the financial, medical, and scientific domains, manage temporal data, which is data with associated time intervals that capture some temporal aspect of the data, typically when the data were or is true in the modeled reality or when the data was or is part of the current database state. In contrast to this, current database management systems offer precious little built-in query language support for temporal data management.

In step with the increasing diffusion of business intelligence, aggregate computation becomes increasingly important. An aggregate operator transforms an argument relation into a summary result relation. Traditionally this is done by first partitioning the argument relation into groups of tuples with identical values for one or more attributes, then applying an aggregate function, e.g., sum or average, to each group in turn. For interval-valued databases such as temporal databases, aggregation is more complex because the interval values can also be used for defining the grouping of argument tuples.

In this paper we propose a new temporal aggregation operator, the Temporal Multi-Dimensional Aggregation (TMDA) operator. It generalizes a variety of previously proposed aggregation operators and offers orthogonal support for two aspects of aggregation: a) the definition of result groups for which to report one or more aggregate values and b) the definition of aggregation groups, i.e., collections of argument tuples that are associated with the result groups and over which the aggregate functions are computed. Our work builds on recent advances in multi-dimensional query processing [1, 2, 3] and is the first work to leverage these techniques to interval-valued data, in this paper exemplified by temporal data. We provide an efficient implementation of the TMDA operator with an average complexity of $n \log m$, where $n$ is the number of argument tuples and $m$ is the number of result groups. In experimental evaluations on large data sets, the operator exhibits almost linear behavior.

Aggregation of temporal data poses new challenges. Most importantly, the time intervals of result tuples can depend on the actual data and are not known in advance. Therefore, the grouping of the result tuples can only be specified *partially*. Next, aggregation should support what is termed *constant*, *malleable*, and *atomic* semantics of the association between data and time intervals. For example, the association of a time interval with an account balance is constant, meaning that the balance holds for each subinterval of the interval. In contrast, consider the association of a particular week with the number of hours worked by an employee during that week, e.g., 40 hours. Here, the association is malleable, as the 40 hours are considered an aggregate of the hours worked by the employee during each day during that week. An association is atomic if the data cannot be associated with modified timestamps. For example, chemotherapies used in cancer treatment often prescribe a specific amount of a drug to be taken over a specific time period. Neither the amount of the drug nor the time period can be modified without yielding a wrong prescription. All approaches so far support only constant semantics. Finally, a temporal aggregation result might be larger than the argument relation. Specifically, for instantaneous temporal aggregates that are grouped into so-called constant intervals, the result relation size can be twice that of the argument. To quantify the result size, the paper defines the notion of an aggregation factor; and to control the aggregation, the ability to specify fixed time intervals for the result tuples is included.

The rest of the paper is organized as follows. Section 2 studies related work and Sect. 3 covers preliminaries. In Sect. 4, after an analysis of some aggregation queries, we introduce the new TMDA operator. Section 5 presents the implementation of the operator. In Sect. 6, we discuss various properties of this operator including computational complexity and expressiveness. Section 7 reports on an experimental study; and Sect. 8 concludes and offers research directions.

## 2 Related Work

The notions of instantaneous and cumulative temporal aggregates have been reported previously. The value of an *instantaneous* temporal aggregate at chronon $t$ is computed from the set of tuples that hold at $t$. The value of a *cumulative* temporal aggregate (also called moving-window aggregate) at chronon $t$ is computed from the set of tuples that hold in the interval $[t-w, t]$, $w \geq 0$. Identical aggregate results with consecutive chronons are coalesced into so-called constant intervals. Most research has been done for instantaneous aggregates, e.g. [4, 5], and cumulative aggregates [6] and temporal aggregates with additional range predicates [7] have received only little attention.

An early proposal by Tuma [8] for computing temporal aggregates requires two scans of the input relation—one for the computation of the time intervals of the result tuples and one for the computation of the aggregates.

A proposal by Kline and Snodgrass [4] scans the input relation only once, building an *aggregation tree* in main memory. Since the tree is not balanced, the worst case time complexity is $O(n^2)$ for $n$ tuples. An improvement, although with the same worst case complexity, is the k-ordered aggregation tree [4]. This approach exploits partial ordering of tuples for garbage collection of old nodes.

Moon et al. [5] use a *balanced tree* for aggregation in main memory that is based on timestamp sorting. This solution works for the functions *sum*, *avg*, and *cnt*; for *min* and *max*, a merge-sort like algorithm is proposed. Both algorithms have a worst case complexity of $\mathcal{O}(n \log n)$. For secondary memory, an efficient bucket algorithm is proposed that assigns the input tuples to buckets according to a partitioning of the time line and also affords long-lived tuples special handling. Aggregation is then performed on each bucket in isolation. The algorithm requires access to the entire database three times.

The *SB-tree* of Yang and Widom [6] supports the disk-based computation and maintenance of instantaneous and cumulative temporal aggregates. An SB-tree contains a hierarchy of intervals associated with partially computed aggregates. With the SB-tree, aggregate queries are applied to an entire base relation—it is not possible to include selection predicates. The *multi-version SB-tree* [7] aims to support aggregate queries coupled with range predicates. A potential problem is that the tree might be larger than the input relation. Tao et al. [9] propose an approximate solution that uses less space than the multi-version SB-tree. Both approaches are restricted to range predicates over a single attribute, and the time interval of an input tuple is deleted once it is selected; hence the result is not a temporal relation.

The existing approaches share three properties. First, the temporal grouping process couples the partitioning of the time line with the grouping of the input tuples. The time line is partitioned into intervals, and an input tuple belongs to a specific partition if its timestamp overlaps that partition. Second, the result tuples are defined for time points and not over time intervals. Third, they allow the use of at most one non-temporal attribute for temporal grouping.

Our TMDA operator, which extends the multi-dimensional join operator [3] to support temporal aggregation, overcomes these limitations and generalizes the aggregation operators discussed above. It decouples the partitioning of the timeline from the grouping of the input tuples, thus allowing to specify result tuples over possibly overlapping intervals and to control the size of the result relation. Furthermore, it supports multiple attribute characteristics. For an efficient implementation we exploit the sorting of the input relation similar to what is done in the k-ordered tree approach [4].

## 3 Preliminaries

### 3.1 Notation

We assume a discrete *time domain*, $D^T$, where the elements are termed chronons (or time points), equipped with a total order $<^T$. Calendar months with the order $<$ satisfy these requirements, and we use these as our time domain. A timestamp (or time interval) is a convex set over the time domain and is represented by two chronons, $[T_s, T_e]$, denoting its inclusive starting and ending points, respectively. We will use $T$ as a shorthand for $[T_s, T_e]$. For timestamps, we introduce several relations: $t \in T$ means that chronon $t$ is included in timestamp $T$. For two timestamps $T$ and $T'$, $T' \subseteq T$ iff all chronons in $T'$ are also in $T$, and $T \cap T'$ returns the set of chronons in both timestamps. If $T \cap T' \neq \emptyset$, we say that the two intervals overlap (or intersect).

A *relation schema* is a three-tuple $S = (\Omega, \Delta, dom)$, where $\Omega$ is a non-empty, finite set of attributes, $\Delta$ is a finite set of domains, and $dom : \Omega \to \Delta$ is a function that associates a domain with each attribute. A *temporal relation schema* is a relation schema with at least one timestamp valued attribute (the domain of timestamps belongs to $\Delta$). For the purpose of this paper, we define temporal relation schemas $R = (A_1, \ldots, A_n, T)$ and $G = (B_1, \ldots, B_m, T)$. Note that the assumption that relations have a timestamp attribute $T$ is just for convenience. There is no implicit time attribute, and all definitions are parametrized with a timestamp attribute. As usual, the rename operator $\rho$ can be used to adjust schemas as appropriate.

A *tuple over schema* $S = (\Omega, \Delta, dom)$ is a function $r : \Omega \to \cup_{\delta \in \Delta} \delta$, such that for every attribute $A$ of $\Omega$, $r(A) \in dom(A)$. A tuple is temporal iff its schema is temporal. To simplify notation we assume an ordering of attributes and represent a tuple as $r = (v_1, \ldots, v_n, t)$. An *relation over schema* $R$ is a finite set of tuples over $R$, denoted as $\mathbf{r}$. We will also use a couple of shorthands: For a tuple $r$ and an attribute $A$ we write $r.A$ to denote the value of the attribute $A$ in $r$. For a set of attributes $A_1, \ldots, A_m$, $m < n$, we define $r[A_1, \ldots, A_m] = (r.A_1, \ldots, r.A_m)$.

## 3.2 Attribute Characteristics

We distinguish among three semantics of the association of a non-timestamp attribute with a timestamp attribute. For a relation with schema $(A_1, \ldots, A_n, T)$ the attribute characteristics wrt. $T$ are given as $C_T = (c_1, \ldots, c_n)$, where $c_i \in \{c, m, a\}$. The values $c$, $m$, and $a$ denote constant, malleable, and atomic characteristics, respectively. For example, $C_T = (c, m)$ for the schema $(N, H, T)$ means that $N$ has a constant characteristic and $H$ has a malleable characteristic. If several temporal attributes are used, e.g., valid time and transaction time, a non-timestamp attribute can have different characteristics for the two timestamps. For the rest of the paper, we use only one time attribute $T$, and $C$ refers to the characteristics wrt. $T$.

**Definition 1.** *(Adjustment of Attribute Values) Let $r = (v_1, \ldots, v_n, t)$ be a tuple over schema $(A_1, \ldots, A_n, T)$, $I$ be a timestamp, and let $C = (c_1, \ldots, c_n)$ be the attribute characteristics. The adjustment of attribute values is defined as follows:*

$$adj(r, I, C) = (adj(r.A_1, r.T, I, c_1), \ldots, adj(r.A_n, r.T, I, c_n), I)$$

$$adj(v, T, I, c) = \begin{cases} v & \text{iff } c = \text{'c'} \\ v * |I \cap T|/|T| & \text{iff } c = \text{'m'} \\ v & \text{iff } c = \text{'a'} \land T = I \\ UNDEF & \text{iff } c = \text{'a'} \land T \neq I \end{cases}$$

Considering the characteristics $C$, the $adj$ function adjusts each non-timestamp attribute value of $r$ to the time interval $I$ and returns the adjusted tuple. For example, for the tuple $(Jan, 2000, [2003/01, 2003/12])$, the characteristics $(c, m)$, and the time interval $[2003/01, 2003/06]$ the $adj$ function returns $(Jan, 1000, [2003/01, 2003/06])$.

## 4 The Temporal Multi-dimensional Aggregate Operator

### 4.1 Temporal Aggregate Examples

As a running example, consider the project database in Fig. 1. The relation EMPL captures project assignments by recording the name of an employee ($N$), a contract identifier ($CID$), the department responsible for an assignment ($D$), the name of a project ($P$), the hours an employee is assigned to a project ($H$), a monthly salary ($S$), and the valid time ($T$) over which a tuple holds true. The attribute $H$ is malleable, while all other attributes are constant. Figure 2 illustrates relation EMPL together with the intended results for the aggregation queries considered next.

EMPL

| | N | CID | D | P | H | S | T |
|---|---|---|---|---|---|---|---|
| r1 | Jan | 140 | DB | P1 | 2400 | 1200 | [2003/01,2004/03] |
| r2 | Jan | 163 | DB | P1 | 600 | 1500 | [2004/07,2004/09] |
| r3 | Ann | 141 | DB | P2 | 500 | 700 | [2003/01,2003/05] |
| r4 | Ann | 150 | DB | P1 | 1000 | 800 | [2003/06,2004/03] |
| r5 | Ann | 157 | DB | P1 | 600 | 500 | [2004/01,2004/12] |
| r6 | Sue | 142 | DB | P2 | 400 | 800 | [2003/01,2003/10] |
| r7 | Tom | 143 | AI | P2 | 1200 | 2000 | [2003/04,2003/10] |
| r8 | Tom | 153 | AI | P1 | 900 | 1800 | [2004/01,2004/06] |

**Fig. 1.** Relation EMPL of the Project Database

**Query 1:** *For each department, compute the total amount of hours spent in projects and the maximal monthly salary.* This instantaneous aggregation groups the result tuples by the non-temporal attribute $D$. The timestamps of the result tuples are not specified in the query, but are derived from the relation. Hence, the size of the result is data dependent and might exceed that of the input relation, as is the case here.

**Query 2:** *For each department and year, compute the total hours spent in projects and the maximal monthly salary.* This query differs from the previous one in that the result tuples are grouped according to fixed, user-specified time intervals. This query controls the size of the result relation, which is at the heart of aggregate functions. To the best of our knowledge, this type of query has not been studied previously.

**Query 3:** *Compute the moving average of hours spent for all six-month periods.* This moving-window query slides in steps of fixed duration over the time line, computing an aggregate for each six-month interval. Unlike for the traditional moving-window operator, the result tuples are valid over time intervals rather than at single time instants.

**Query 4:** *For the entire lifespan of each department, compute the total hours spent in projects and the maximal monthly salary.* This query specifies a single value for the entire lifespan of a relation.

## 4.2 Definition of Result Groups and Aggregation Groups

A general temporal aggregation operator should support the specification of two orthogonal aspects of aggregation: definition (1) of the result groups for which to report aggregate results and (2) of the sets of tuples, termed aggregation groups, to associate with each result group and over which to compute the aggregates result(s) to be reported for each group.

Each *result group* can be represented as a tuple in a temporal ("group") relation g with schema $(B_1, \ldots, B_m, T)$. Each $B_i$ is an attribute from the relation that is the argument of the aggregation operator, and the tuples assume values from $B_i$ that occur in the argument relation. For the timestamp, there are two cases: constant intervals and fixed intervals. With *constant intervals*, the timestamp attribute assumes as values the maximal, non-overlapping intervals over which the set of argument tuples is constant.

**Definition 2.** (Constant Intervals) *Let* r *be a temporal relation with timestamp attribute* $T$. *We define the constant intervals of* r *as*

$$CI(\mathbf{r}) = \{T \mid \forall r \in \mathbf{r}(r.T \supseteq T \vee r.T \cap T = \emptyset) \wedge \\ \forall T' \supset T(\exists r \in \mathbf{r}(r.T \not\supseteq T' \wedge r.T \cap T' \neq \emptyset))\}$$

The first line ensures that result intervals do not cross boundaries of argument intervals. The second ensures that the result intervals are maximal. The constant intervals for the EMPL relation grouped by department are shown in Fig. 2 (Result of Query 1).

**Theorem 1.** (Cardinality of Constant Intervals) *For a temporal relation* r *with* n *tuples*, $n > 0$, *the cardinality of constant intervals is limited by the following formula:*

$$\mid CI(\mathbf{r}) \mid \leq 2n - 1$$

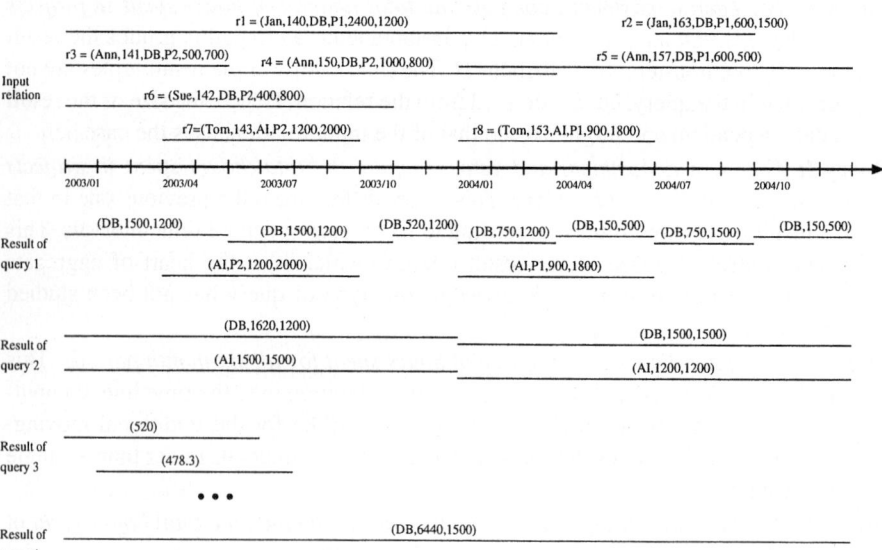

**Fig. 2.** Temporal Aggregation

*Proof.* The end points of the tuple's timestamps can be linearly ordered giving at most $2n$ timepoints. $n$ timepoints produce at most $n-1$ consecutive time interals.

The option *fixed intervals* is used when specifying fixed, possibly overlapping, time intervals. Queries 2 and 3 in our running example use different flavors of fixed intervals (see also Fig. 2).

**Definition 3.** (Fixed Intervals) *Let* $\mathbf{r}$ *be a temporal relation with timestamp attribute* $T$. *We define the fixed intervals as a user-specified set of timestamps,* $FI(\mathbf{r})$, *that satisfies the following condition:* $\forall T \in FI(\mathbf{r})(\exists r \in \mathbf{r}(r.T \cap T \neq \emptyset))$.

This condition states that fixed intervals must intersect with intervals in the argument relation. The explicit specification of result groups with fixed intervals allows control of the cardinality of the result relation. We use the following definition for quantifying the result size relative to the argument size.

**Definition 4.** (Aggregation factor) *The aggregation factor of a temporal aggregation operator is defined as the ratio between the cardinality of the result relation* $\mathbf{z}$ *and the cardinality of the argument relation* $\mathbf{r}$, *i.e.,* $af = |\mathbf{z}|/|\mathbf{r}|$.

This factor is between 0 and 1 if the result relation is smaller than the argument relation, 1 if the result relation has the same size as the argument relation, and $> 1$ if the result relation is larger than the argument relation. For instance, the aggregation factor is $9/8$ for Query 1 and $4/8$ for Query 2.

Having defined result groups, we associate a set of tuples from the argument relation, called *aggregation group*, with each result group. The aggregate(s) for each group is computed over this set. The aggregation groups can be defined by a condition $\theta(g, r)$ that for each input tuple $r$ decides whether it contributes to result group $g$ or not. The condition can involve non-temporal and timestamp attributes. Important classes of conditions are conjunctions of equality conditions for non-temporal attributes and the *overlaps* relationship for timestamps.

### 4.3 Definition of the TMDA Operator

The TMDA operator separates the specification of the result groups from the assignment of the input tuples to these result groups, thus providing an expressive framework for temporal aggregation.

**Definition 5.** (TMDA operator) *Let* $\mathbf{r}$ *and* $\mathbf{g}$ *be relations with timestamp attribute* $T$, $\mathbf{F} = \{f_{A_{i_1}}, \ldots, f_{A_{i_p}}\}$ *be a set of aggregate functions over attributes in* $\mathbf{r}$, $\theta$ *be a condition over attributes in* $\mathbf{g}$ *and* $\mathbf{r}$, *and let* $C$ *be attribute characteristics for* $\mathbf{r}$. *We define the temporal multi-dimensional aggregation operator as*

$$\mathcal{G}^T[\mathbf{F}][\theta][T][C](\mathbf{g}, \mathbf{r}) = \{x \mid g \in \mathbf{g} \land \\ \mathbf{r}_g = \{r' \mid r \in \mathbf{r} \land \theta(g,r) \land r' = adj(r, g.T, C)\} \land \\ x = g \circ (f_{A_{i_1}}(\pi[A_{i_1}](\mathbf{r}_g)), \ldots, f_{A_{i_p}}(\pi[A_{i_p}](\mathbf{r}_g)))\}$$

*where $\pi$ is a duplicate-preserving projection.*

Relation g is the group relation that defines the result groups, or (sub-) tuples that will be expanded into result tuples. Relation r is the (conventional) argument relation. Predicate $\theta$ associates an aggregation group, $\mathbf{r}_g \subseteq \mathbf{r}$, with each $g \in \mathbf{g}$. Thereby, the argument tuples are adjusted to the timestamp of the result group, which is also the timestamp of the result tuple. The aggregation functions $f_{A_{i_1}}, \ldots, f_{A_{i_p}}$ are then computed over each aggregation group. The schema of the result relation is the schema of g augmented with a column for each aggregate value, which for the scope of this paper are labeled $f_{A_{i_1}}, \ldots, f_{A_{i_p}}$.

*Example 1.* Query 2 can be expressed as follows: $\mathbf{z} = \mathcal{G}^T[\mathbf{F}][\theta][T][C](\mathbf{g}, \text{EMPL}/\mathbf{r})$, where

$\mathbf{g}$ : The two leftmost columns in Fig. 3
$\mathbf{F} = \{sum_H, max_S\}$
$\theta = (\mathbf{g}.D = \mathbf{r}.D) \wedge overlaps(\mathbf{g}.T, \mathbf{r}.T)$
$C = (c, c, c, c, m, c)$

The group relation g contains a tuple for each combination of department and year. Aggregate functions $sum$ and $max$ on hours and salary are used. The condition $\theta$ associates with a result group those argument tuples that have the same department value as the result group and overlap with the group's timestamp. For example, the aggregation group for the $DB$ department in 2003 consists of the tuples $r1, r3, r4$, and $r6$.

The attribute $H$ is malleable and is adjusted to the timestamp of the group specification before it is passed on to the aggregate functions. Therefore, $r1, r3, r4$, and $r6$ contribute to the sum of hours of the $DB$ department in 2003 with the values 1920, 500, 700, and 400, respectively. Attribute $S$ is constant, so the adjustment has no effect.

The result relation is shown in Fig. 3. Each result tuple is composed of a result group tuple extended by a value for each aggregate function. To improve readability these two parts are separated by a vertical line.

z

| D | T | $sum_H$ | $max_S$ |
|---|---|---|---|
| DB | [2003/01,2003/12] | 1620 | 1000 |
| DB | [2004/01,2004/12] | 1500 | 900 |
| AI | [2003/01,2003/12] | 1200 | 2000 |
| AI | [2004/01,2004/12] | 900 | 1800 |

**Fig. 3.** Temporal Aggregation with Fixed Interval Semantics

### 4.4 Partial Specification of Result Groups

The definition of the TMDA operator requires a completely specified group relation g. For the constant interval semantics, however, the timestamps of the result tuples are calculated from the argument tuples and are not available in advance. To handle this case, we pass on a relational algebra expression that computes the constant intervals, thus reducing constant intervals to fixed intervals.

$$\mathcal{G}^T[\mathbf{F}][\theta \wedge overlaps(\mathbf{g}.T, \mathbf{r}.T)][T][C](CI(\mathbf{g}', \mathbf{r}, \theta)/\mathbf{g}, \mathbf{r})$$

Now the group relation g is given as an expression $CI(\mathbf{g}', \mathbf{r}, \theta)$ that computes the constant intervals over the argument relation r based on a group relation $\mathbf{g}'$ that contains the non-temporal groups. This expression basically completes the non-temporal group relation $\mathbf{g}'$ with the constant intervals, i.e., $\mathbf{g} = \{g[B_1, \ldots, B_m] \circ T \mid g \in \mathbf{g}' \wedge T \in CI(\mathbf{g}', \mathbf{r}, \theta)\}$.

While this reduction of constant interval semantics to fixed interval semantics is sound from a semantic point of view, the computation of constant intervals in advance requires operations such as join and union that are computationally costly, as we will illustrate in the experimental section. To improve on the computational efficiency, we introduce partially specified result groups.

**Definition 6.** (Partially Specified Result Groups) *A result group with schema $G = (B_1, \ldots, B_m, T)$ is partially specified iff the value of the timestamp attribute is not specified. We represent a partially specified result tuple as $g = (v_1, \ldots, v_m, [*,*])$.*

With partially specified result groups in place, we push the completion of the result groups with constant intervals into the algorithm for the evaluation of the temporal multidimensional aggregation operator. The constant intervals are computed on the fly while scanning the data relation for the calculation of the aggregates. The partially specified result tuples are replicated to all constant intervals for the corresponding aggregation groups. The *overlaps* relation from condition $\theta$ that assigns the relevant data tuples to the constant intervals is applied implicitly by the evaluation algorithm.

*Example 2.* To express Query 1 we apply the constant interval semantics with a group relation g that contains the partially specified result groups $\{(DB, [*,*]), (AI, [*,*])\}$. The query is then expressed as $\mathbf{z} = \mathcal{G}^T[\mathbf{F}][\theta][T][C](\mathbf{g}, \text{EMPL}/\mathbf{r})$, where

$\mathbf{F} = \{sum_H, max_S\}$
$\theta = (\mathbf{g}.D = \mathbf{r}.D)$
$C = (c, c, c, c, m, c)$

The condition $\theta$ contains only non-temporal constraints. The aggregation group for department $DB$ contains six input tuples that induce seven constant intervals. For department $AI$, we have two input tuples and two constant intervals. The result relation is shown in Fig. 4. Unlike in previous approaches [10, 6], we do not coalesce consecutive tuples with the same aggregate values, as illustrated by the two first $DB$ tuples; we keep them separate since their lineage is different.

z

| D | T | $sum_H$ | $max_S$ |
|---|---|---|---|
| DB | [2003/01,2003/05] | 1500 | 1200 |
| DB | [2003/06,2003/10] | 1500 | 1200 |
| DB | [2003/11,2003/12] | 520 | 1200 |
| DB | [2004/01,2004/03] | 750 | 1200 |
| DB | [2004/04,2004/06] | 150 | 500 |
| DB | [2004/07,2004/09] | 750 | 1500 |
| DB | [2004/10,2004/12] | 150 | 500 |
| AI | [2003/04,2003/09] | 1200 | 2000 |
| AI | [2004/01,2004/06] | 900 | 1800 |

**Fig. 4.** Constant Interval Semantics with Partially Specified Result Groups

Converting the result set produced by the TMDA operator to the traditional format of result sets produced by temporal aggregation operators, where consecutive tuples with the same aggregate value are coalesced, can be achieved easily. Thus, the result sets produced by the TMDA operator retains lineage information, and this additional information is easy to eliminate.

## 5 Implementation of the TMDA Operator

### 5.1 Idea and Overview

The implementation of the TMDA operator for constant intervals is based on the following observation: if we scan the argument relation, which is ordered by the interval start

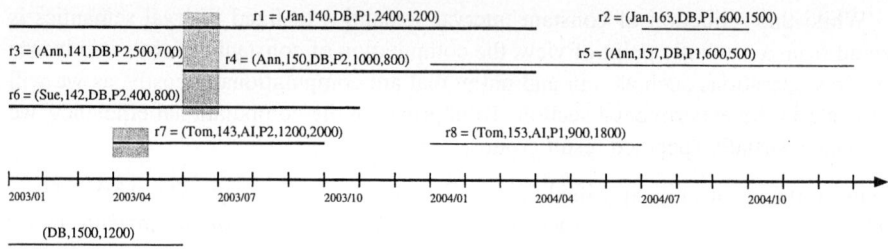

**Fig. 5.** Processing Input Tuples in TMDA-CI

values of the tuples, we can at any time point $t$ compute the result tuples that end before $t$ (assuming that no tuples that start after $t$ contribute to these result tuples). Hence, as the argument relation is being scanned, result tuples are produced, and old tuples are removed from main memory. Only the tuples that are valid at time point $t$, termed *open tuples*, are kept in main memory.

Figure 5 illustrates this evaluation strategy for Query 1, showing the situation after reading tuples $r1$, $r3$, $r6$, $r7$, and $r4$, in that order. Thick lines are used for open tuples, dashed lines are used for closed tuples, and solid lines are used for tuples not yet scanned. Grey rectangles indicate the advancement of time. For example, after reading $r4$, the first result tuple for the $DB$ department is computed, $r3$ is closed, and the current time instant for the $DB$ group is 2003/06; three tuples remain open, and two tuples have not yet been processed. For the $AI$ departement, one tuple is open and one tuple is to be processed.

For the use with fixed intervals, the timestamps of the result tuples are specified in the group relation. So, we do not need to maintain the data tuples in main memory, but can process them and update the aggregate values as we scan the data relation.

In the rest of this section we describe in detail two algorithms for the evaluation of TMDA with constant intervals and fixed intervals, respectively.

### 5.2 The TMDA-CI Algortihm for Constant Intervals

Figure 6 shows the algorithm, termed TMDA-CI, that evaluates $\mathcal{G}^T$ with constant intervals. The algorithm has five input parameters: the group relation **g**, the argument relation **r**, a list of aggregate functions $\mathbf{F} = \{f_{A_{i_1}}, \ldots, f_{A_{i_p}}\}$, a selection predicate $\theta$, and attribute characteristics $C$. The output is a temporal relation that is composed of **g** extended by the values of the aggregate functions in **F**.

The algorithm uses two types of data structures. A *group table* $gt$ stores each tuple $g \in \mathbf{g}$, together with a pointer to an end-point tree $\mathcal{T}$. An *end-point tree* $\mathcal{T}$ maintains the (potential) end points of the constant intervals together with the relevant attribute values of the currently open tuples. The tree is organized by the end points of the constant intervals, i.e., the end points $T_e$ of the data tuples plus the time points immediately preceding each data tuple. A node with time instant $t$ stores the attribute values $r.A_1, \ldots, r.A_p, r.T_s$ of all data tuples $r$ that end at $t$. For example, for Query 1 the aggregation tree for the $DB$ department contains a node with time instant 2004/03 that stores the attribute values of $r1$ and $r4$, i.e.,

**Algorithm:** TMDA-CI($\mathbf{g}, \mathbf{r}, \mathbf{F}, \theta, C$)
**if** $\mathbf{g} = \pi[A_1, \ldots, A_m](\mathbf{r})$ **then**
$\quad$ $gt \leftarrow$ empty group table with columns $B_1, \ldots, B_m, T, \mathcal{T}$;
**else**
$\quad$ Initialize $gt$ with $(g, empty\ \mathcal{T}), g \in \mathbf{g}$, and replace timestamp $T$ by $[-\infty, *]$;
Create index for $gt$ on attributes $B_1, \ldots, B_m$; $\mathbf{z} \leftarrow \emptyset$;
**foreach** *tuple* $r \in \mathbf{r}$ *in chronological order* **do**
$\quad$ **if** $\mathbf{g} = \pi[A_1, \ldots, A_m](\mathbf{r})$ and $r.A_1, \ldots, r.A_m$ *not yet in* $gt$ **then**
$\quad\quad$ Insert $(r.A_1, \ldots, r.A_m, [-\infty, *], empty\ \mathcal{T})$ into $gt$;
$\quad$ **foreach** $i \in$ LOOKUP($gt, r, \theta$) **do**
$\quad\quad$ **if** $r.T_s > gt[i].T_s$ **then**
$\quad\quad\quad$ Insert a new node with time $r.T_s - 1$ into $gt[i].\mathcal{T}$ (if not already there);
$\quad\quad\quad$ **foreach** $v \in gt[i].\mathcal{T}$ *in chronological order, where* $v.t < r.T_s$ **do**
$\quad\quad\quad\quad$ $gt[i].T_e \leftarrow v.t$;
$\quad\quad\quad\quad$ $\mathbf{z} \leftarrow \mathbf{z} \cup$ RESULTTUPLE($gt[i], \mathbf{F}, C$);
$\quad\quad\quad\quad$ $gt[i].T \leftarrow [v.t + 1, *]$;
$\quad\quad\quad\quad$ Remove node $v$ from $gt[i].\mathcal{T}$;
$\quad\quad$ $v \leftarrow$ node in $gt[i].\mathcal{T}$ with time $v.t = r.T_e$ (insert a new node if required);
$\quad\quad$ $v.open \leftarrow v.open \cup r[A_1, \ldots, A_p, T_s]$;

**foreach** $gt[i] \in gt$ **do**
$\quad$ **foreach** $v \in gt[i].\mathcal{T}$ *in chronological order* **do**
$\quad\quad$ Create result tuple, add it to $\mathbf{z}$, and close past nodes in $gt[i].\mathcal{T}$;
**return** $\mathbf{z}$;

**Fig. 6.** The Algorithm TMDA-CI for Constant Interval Semantics

$(2004/03, \{(2400, 1200, 2003/01), (1800, 800, 2003/06)\})$. A node that stores a potential end point $t$ of a constant interval, but with no tuples ending at $t$, has an empty data part. For example, tuple $r5$ terminates a constant interval and starts a new one; hence node $(2003/12, \{\})$ will be in the tree. In our implementation we use AVL-trees for end-point trees.

The first step of the algorithm is to initialize the group table $gt$. If $\mathbf{g}$ is a projection over $\mathbf{r}$, the group table is initially empty and will be populated while scanning the argument tuples. Otherwise, $gt$ is initialized with $\mathbf{g}$, with the start time of the entries set to $-\infty$, and an empty end-point tree is generated for each entry. Finally, an index over the non-temporal attributes is created.

The next step is to process the argument relation $\mathbf{r}$ chronologically with respect to the start times of the tuples. If the group relation is a relational algebra expression, we might have to extend the group table with a new entry before the function LOOKUP determines all result groups to which data tuple $r$ contributes. For each matching result group, two steps are performed: First, if $r$ advances the current time ($r.T_s > gt[i].T_s$), one or more constant intervals can be closed. Chronon $r.T_s - 1$ is a potential end point of a constant interval and is inserted into $gt[i].\mathcal{T}$. Then we process all nodes $v$ in $gt[i].\mathcal{T}$ with $v.t < r.T_s$ in chronological order. Thereby, the timestamp in the group table assumes the constant intervals. We compose the corresponding result tuples and remove the node from the tree. Second, we update the end-point tree with the new data tuple $r$.

The function LOOKUP gets as input parameters the group table $gt$, a tuple $r$, and the selection condition $\theta$. It evaluates the condition $\theta$ for all pairs $(g, r)$, $g \in gt$, and returns the indexes of the matching result groups. For the constant interval semantics, an AVL-tree on the non-timestamp attributes is used. For the fixed interval semantics (see algorithm TMDA-FI in Sect. 5.3), we use two AVL-trees, one on the start time and one on the end time of the timestamps. Fixed interval semantics allow us to combine indexes on the timestamps and the non-timestamp attributes.

The algorithm RESULTTUPLE gets as input an entry of the group table $gt[i]$, the set of aggregate functions $\mathbf{F}$, and the attribute characteristics $C$. It returns the result tuple for the constant interval $gt[i].T$, or the empty set if there are no open tuples in the interval $gt[i].T$. A result tuple is composed of the result group stored in $gt[i]$ extended by the values of the aggregate functions that are computed over all nodes in $gt[i].T$. The algorithm scans all nodes in the tree, adjusts the attribute values, and computes the aggregate values.

*Example 3.* We consider the evaluation of Query 1 with algorithm TMDA-CI. Having initialized the group table $gt$, relation EMPL is processed in chronological order: $r1, r3, r6, r7, r4, r5, r8, r2$. For $r1$, function LOOKUP returns the set $\{1\}$. A new node with time 2004/03 and the attribute values of $H$, $S$, and $T_s$ is inserted into $\mathcal{T}_1$, and the start time of the next constant interval is set to 2003/01 (see Fig. 7a).

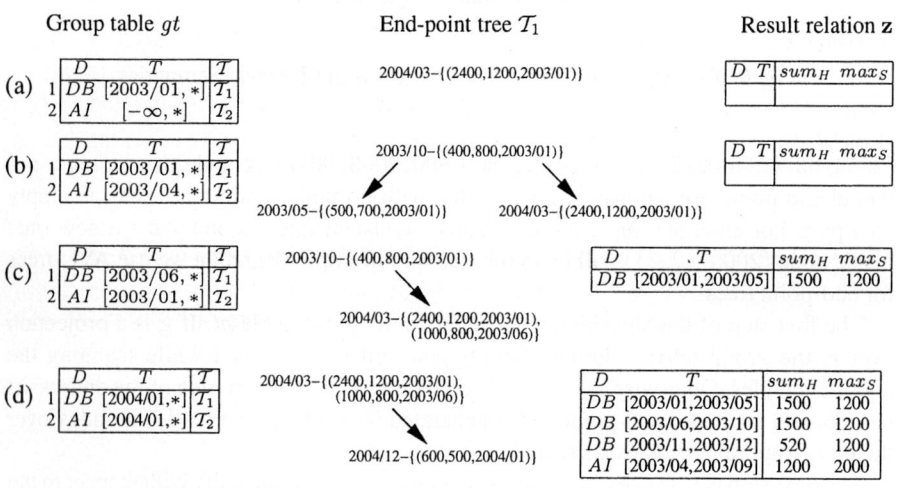

**Fig. 7.** Evaluation of TMDA-CI after processing $r1, r3, r6, r7, r4, r5$, and $r8$

Figure 7b shows the situation after processing $r1, r3, r6$, and $r7$. $\mathcal{T}_1$ contains three nodes, $\mathcal{T}_2$ contains one node, and the start time of the next constant interval for the $AI$ result group is set to the start time of $r7$.

The next input tuple is $r4$ for the $DB$ department. Since its start time advances in time, we close the currently open interval and get $[2003/01, 2003/05]$ as the first constant interval for which a result tuple is computed. The adjustment of the attribute values

**Algorithm:** TMDA-FI($\mathbf{g}, \mathbf{r}, \mathbf{F}, \theta, C$)
**if** $\mathbf{g} = \pi[A_1, \ldots, A_m, cast(T, G)](\mathbf{r})$ **then**
$\quad$ $gt \leftarrow$ empty group table with columns $A_1, \ldots, A_m, T, f_{A_{i_1}}, \ldots, f_{A_{i_p}}$;
**else**
$\quad$ Initialize $gt$ to $\mathbf{g}$ and extend it with columns $f_{A_{i_1}}, \ldots, f_{A_{i_p}}$ initialized to $NULL$;
Create index for $gt$ on attribute $T$;
**foreach** *tuple* $r \in \mathbf{r}$ **do**
$\quad$ **if** $\mathbf{g} = \pi[A_1, \ldots, A_m, T](\mathbf{r})$ **then**
$\quad\quad$ **foreach** $t \in cast(r.T, G)$ **do**
$\quad\quad\quad$ Insert $r.A_1, \ldots, r.A_m, t$ into $gt$ if not already there;
$\quad$ **foreach** $i \in \text{LOOKUP}(gt, r, \theta)$ **do**
$\quad\quad$ $r' \leftarrow \text{ADJUST}(r, gt[i].T, C)$;
$\quad\quad$ **foreach** $f_j \in \mathbf{F}$ **do** $gt[i].f_{A_{i_j}} \leftarrow gt[i].f_{A_{i_j}} \oplus r'.A_{i_j}$;
**return** $gt$;

**Fig. 8.** The Algorithm TMDA-FI for Fixed Interval Semantics

to the constant interval yields $800 + 500 + 200 = 1500$ for the *sum* function (attribute $H$ is malleable) and $max(1200, 700, 800) = 1200$ for the *max* function (attribute $S$ is constant). The node with time 2003/05 is removed from $\mathcal{T}_1$, and the start time of the next constant interval is set to 2003/06. Finally, the relevant data of $r4$ are added to the already existing node with time 2004/03. This situation is shown in Fig. 7c.

The next input tuples are $r5$ and $r8$, of which $r5$ contributes to the $DB$ group and gives rise to two result tuples. Tuple $r8$ contributes to the $AI$ group and gives rise to the first result tuple for that group. See Fig. 7d.

### 5.3 The TMDA-FI Algorithm for Fixed Intervals

Figure 8 shows the TMDA-FI algorithm for the evaluation of operator $\mathcal{G}^T$ with fixed interval semantics. The main data structure is the group table $gt$ that stores the group relation $\mathbf{g}$ and has an additional column labeled $f_{A_{i_j}}$ for each aggregate function $f_{A_{i_j}} \in \mathbf{F}$. The result groups, including their timestamps, are completely specified, so the data tuples need not be stored in an end-point tree, but can be processed as they are read, yielding an incremental computation of the aggregate values.

## 6 Properties

### 6.1 Complexity

For the complexity analysis of TMDA-CI, only the processing of the data relation $\mathbf{r}$ is relevant, which is divided into four steps: (possibly) update of the index, lookup in the index, production of result tuples, and insertion of the tuple in the end-point tree.

The update of the index and the lookup in the group table have complexity $\log n_g$, where $n_g$ is the cardinality of the group table. The production of a single result tuple is linear in the number $n_o$ of open tuples. The average number of result tuples induced by a data tuple depends on the aggregation factor $af = n_z/n_r$, where $n_z$ is the cardinality of the result relation and $n_r$ is the cardinality of the data relation, and on the number of result groups to which $r$ contributes, denoted as $n_{g,r}$. Finally, the insertion of a tuple in an end-point tree has complexity $\log n_o$. This yields an overall time complexity for TMDA-CI of $\mathcal{O}(n_r \max(\log n_g, n_{g,r}\, af\, n_o, \log n_o))$. In general, the size of the data relation $n_r$ might be very large, while all other parameters shall be small. The factor $n_{g,r}$ depends on the selectivity of the condition $\theta$, and is 1 for equality conditions. The aggregation factor, which is between 0 and 2, and the number of open tuples $n_o$ depend mainly on the temporal overlapping of the data tuples. The worst-case complexity is $\mathcal{O}(n_r^2)$ if the start and end points of all data tuples are different and there is a time instant where all tuples hold, hence $n_o = n_r$.

The support for different attribute characteristics comes at a price. For each result tuple, it requires a scan of the entire end-point tree and an adjustment of the attribute values, which becomes a major bottleneck in cases with a large number of open tuples and a high aggregation factor. If only constant attributes were used, the aggregate values could be calculated incrementally similar to [5], as we show later in our experiments.

In the TMDA-FI algorithm, there is no need to maintain the open data tuples, and the aggregate values can be calculated incrementally as the data relation is scanned. The time complexity of TMDA-FI is $\mathcal{O}(n_r\, max(\log n_g, n_{g,r}))$.

## 6.2 A Spectrum of Temporal Aggregation Operators

The TMDA operator is rather general. The group relation **g** is completely independent of the data relation **r** and has the only objective to group the results. This arrangement offers enormous flexibility in arranging the results according to various criteria, and it enables the formulation of a range of different forms of temporal aggregates, including the ones proposed previously.

**Lemma 1.** *(Aggregation Using Temporal Group Composition [10]) Let* $\mathbf{g}, \mathbf{r}, \mathbf{F}, \theta$, *and* $C$ *be as in Definition 5, SP be a selection predicate over* **r** *as in [10], and let* $\mathbf{ch}_G$ *be a relation with a single attribute CH that contains all chronons at granularity level G. The operator* $\mathcal{G}^T[\mathbf{F}][\theta][T][c,\ldots,c](\mathbf{g}, \mathbf{r})$ *with fixed interval semantics simulates aggregation using temporal group composition if* **g** *and* $\theta$ *are defined as follows:*

$$\mathbf{g} = \pi[CH, CH](\mathbf{r} \bowtie [overlaps(T, [CH, CH])]\mathbf{ch}_G)$$
$$\theta = SP(\mathbf{r}) \wedge overlaps(\mathbf{g}.T, \mathbf{r}.T)$$

If the partitioning of the timeline is at the smallest granularity level, temporal group composition simulates instantaneous aggregates [4]; and by transitivity, so does $\mathcal{G}^T$.

**Lemma 2.** *(Cumulative Temporal Aggregates [6]) Let* $\mathbf{g}, \mathbf{r}, \mathbf{F}, \theta$, *and* $C$ *be as in Definition 5, let* $w$ *be a window offset, and let* **ch** *be a relation with a single attribute CH that contains the set of chronons at the lowest granularity level supported by the relation. The operator* $\mathcal{G}^T[\mathbf{F}][\theta][T][c,\ldots,c](\mathbf{g}, \mathbf{r})$ *with fixed interval semantics simulates cumulative temporal aggregates if* **g** *and* $\theta$ *are defined as follows:*

$$\mathbf{g} = \pi[CH, CH](\mathbf{r} \bowtie [overlaps([T_s, T_e+w], CH)]\mathbf{ch})$$
$$\theta = overlaps([\mathbf{g}.T_e - w, \mathbf{g}.T_e], \mathbf{r}.T)$$

All temporal aggregates developed so far assume a partitioning of the timeline and compute aggregates at time instants. The TMDA operator is more expressive and allows the computation of additional flavors of temporal aggregates. For example, Query 3 is a kind of moving-window aggregate that computes aggregate values over overlapping time intervals. This form of temporal aggregate can easily be expressed by an appropriate group relation.

Another example is the calculation of quarter values that considers data tuples from the corresponding quarter in the past 5 years. In this query, data tuples that contribute to a result tuple are selected from non-contiguous intervals and from outside of the result tuple's timestamp. This functionality has not been addressed in previous temporal aggregation operators. The TMDA operator can afford for such queries by an appropriate $\theta$ condition.

## 7 Experimental Evaluation

We carried out a number of experiments with the TMDA-CI and TMDA-FI algorithms, investigating their performance for various settings. All experiments were run on an Intel Pentium workstation with a 3.6 GHz processor and 2 GB memory.

For the experiments, we use data relations that contain from $200,000$ to $1,000,000$ tuples. The lifespan of the data relations is $[0, 2^{25}]$, and we experiment with the following instances [11]:

- $\mathbf{r}^{seq}$: Sequential tuples with one open tuple at each time instant; $af = 1$.
- $\mathbf{r}^{equal}$: All tuples have the same timestamp; $af \in [0.000001, 0.000005]$.
- $\mathbf{r}^{random}$: Start time and duration of the tuples are uniformly distributed in $[0, 2^{25}]$ and $[1, 4000]$, respectively, with 33 open tuples on average; $af \in [1.940553, 1.987989]$.
- $\mathbf{r}^{worst}$: All start and end points are different, and there is a constant interval (in the middle) where all tuples are open; $af \in [1.999995, 1.999999]$.

The group relation contains one entry. This is a worst case since all timestamps end up in the same end-point tree. A group table with more tuples would yield smaller end-point trees and thus better performance.

### 7.1 Scalability of TMDA-CI and TMDA-FI

The first experiment investigates the scalability of TMDA-CI. Figure 9(a) shows how the time complexity depends on the number of open tuples and the aggregation factor. Relation $\mathbf{r}^{worst}$ with the largest possible number of open tuples and the maximal aggregation factor for constant intervals has a running time that is quadratic in the size of the data relation. For all other data sets, the running time exhibits a linear behavior. Relation $\mathbf{r}^{equal}$ has an aggregation factor close to 0 although the number of open tuples is maximal (however, they are scanned only once). Most of the time (60% for $\mathbf{r}^{random}$ and 97% for $\mathbf{r}^{worst}$) is spent in pruning the end-point tree and computing the result tuples. For each constant interval, the end-point tree must be scanned to adjust malleable attribute values and compute the aggregated value.

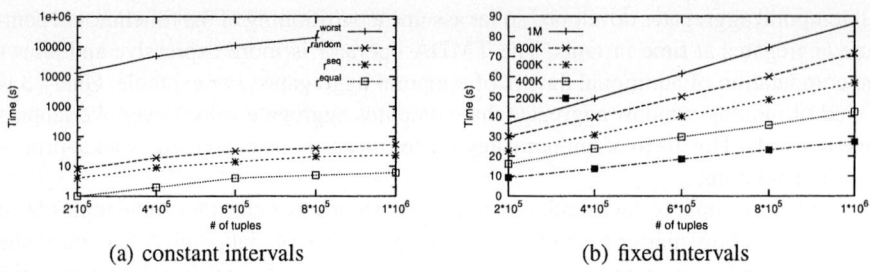

(a) constant intervals

(b) fixed intervals

**Fig. 9.** Evaluation of TMDA-CI and TMDA-FI

The performance of TMDA-FI is not affected by overlapping tuples since the aggregate result is computed incrementally. The key parameter in terms of performance is the number of result groups and the efficiency of the available lookup technique (for each tuple in **r**, we must find all groups that satisfy the $\theta$ condition and therefore have to be updated). Since we use AVL-trees for indexing result groups, the performance increases along with the number of groups, as illustrated in Fig. 9(b). If we used hashing, the lookup time would be constant. However, a hashing only supports equality conditions.

Figure 10 investigates the performance impact of varying the main parameters on the algorithms applied to data relation $\mathbf{r}^{rand}$. Figure 10(a) shows the running time when varying the number of open tuples. The performance decreases since with malleable attributes, all open tuples have to be stored in the end-point tree. As soon as a constant interval has been found, the end-point tree is traversed, the attribute values are adjusted, and the final aggregate is computed. We have also included the performance of a variation of TMDA-CI, denoted TMDA-CI$^c$, that supports constant attributes only. TMDA-CI$^c$ incrementally computes the aggregates, and its performance is independent of the number of open tuples.

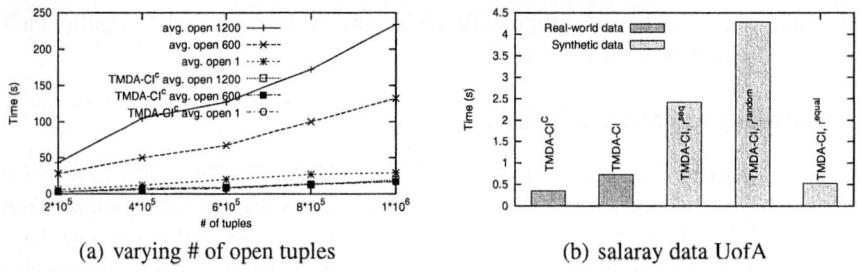

(a) varying # of open tuples

(b) salaray data UofA

**Fig. 10.** Evaluation of TMDA-CI: (a) different data sets, (b) real-world data

Figure 10(b) evaluates the performance for real-world salary data from the University of Arizona. The figure shows that the performance on the real-world data is much better than the performance on most syntetic data sets.

## 7.2 Constant Versus Fixed Intervals

Figure 11(a) shows the result of computing aggregates with constant interval semantics in two different ways: (1) TMDA-CI with partially specified result groups, and (2) CI-SQL + TMDA-FI, i.e., a priori computation of constant intervals using SQL followed by a call to TMDA-FI. The results confirm that TMDA-CI with partially specified result groups is indeed an efficient way of computing aggregates with constant interval semantics.

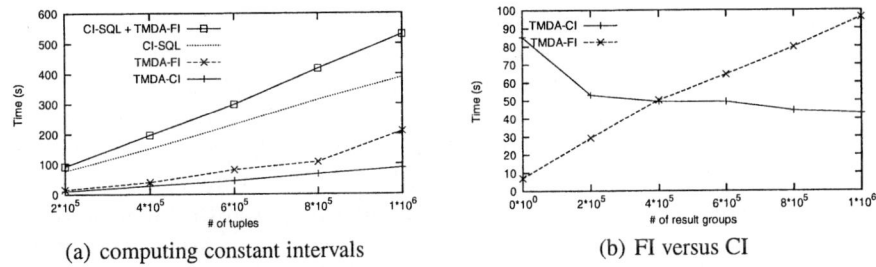

(a) computing constant intervals  (b) FI versus CI

**Fig. 11.** Constant versus Fixed Interval Semantics

Figure 11(b) evaluates TMDA-CI and TMDA-FI for varying result groups. As expected, the performance of TMDA-FI decreases as the number of groups increases. However, up to an aggregation factor of almost 50% FI outperforms CI. Thus, TMDA-FI is efficient for reasonable aggregation factors, and it permits to precisely control the aggregation factor.

## 7.3 Comparison with the Balanced Tree Algorithm

The last experiment compares TMDA-CI with the balanced-tree algorithm proposed in [5]. This is the most efficient algorithm developed so far, but note that it only handles $sum$, $cnt$, and $avg$—it does not support malleable attributes. Figure 12(a) compares the running time of the balanced-tree algorithm, TMDA-CI, and a modified version, called TMDA-CI$^c$, that supports only constant attributes and allows incremental computation

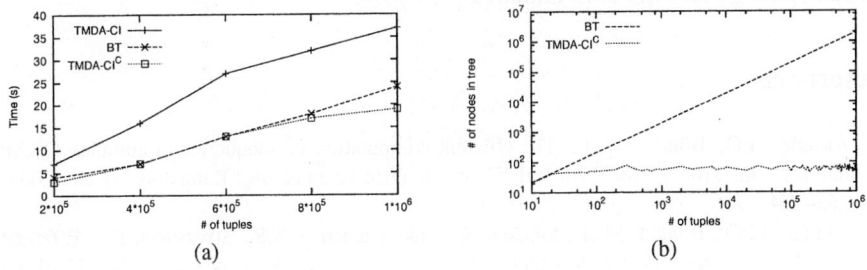

(a)  (b)

**Fig. 12.** TMDA-CI versus Balanced Tree

of aggregate values. While TMDA-CI$^c$ has the same performance as the balanced-tree algorithm, the experiments show that the support for multiple attribute characteristics in TMDA-CI is costly and that the DBMS should identify cases when no malleable attributes are present and TMDA-CI$^c$ can be used. The memory consumption of TMDA-CI depends only on the number of open tuples and is much smaller than for the balanced-tree algorithm (see Fig. 12(b)).

## 8 Conclusion

This paper presents a new aggregation operator, the Temporal Multi-Dimensional Aggregation (TMDA) operator, that leverages recent advances in multi-dimensional query processing [1, 2, 3] to apply to interval-valued data. The TMDA operator generalizes a variety of previously proposed aggregation operators. Most importantly, it clearly separates the definition of result groups from the definition of aggregation groups, i.e., the collections of argument tuples that are associated with the result groups and over which the aggregate functions are computed. This leads to a very expressive framework that allows also to control the size of the result relation. Next, the TMDA operator supports multiple attribute characteristics, including malleable attributes where an attribute value has to be adjusted if the tuple's timestamp changes. Finally, we provid two different algorithms for the evaluation of the TMDA operator with constant intervals and fixed intervals, respectively. Detailed experimental evaluations show that the algorithms are scalable with respect to data set size and compare well with other temporal aggregation algorithms. The evaluation also reveals that the support for multiple attribute characteristics comes at a cost.

Future work includes various optimization steps of the TMDA-CI and TMDA-FI algorithms, including the following ones: optimization rules for relational algebra expressions that interact with the TMDA operator, the initialization of the group table on the fly, indexes on the group table, and a variation of the end-point tree that does not require a totally sorted data relation.

## Acknowledgments

We thank Linas Baltrunas and Juozas Gordevicious for the implementation and evaluation of the algoritihms. The work was partially funded by the Municipality of Bozen-Bolzano through the eBZ-2015 initiative.

## References

1. Akinde, M.O., Böhlen, M.H.: The efficient computation of subqueries in complex OLAP queries. In: Proc. of the 19th Intl. Conf. on Data Engineering, Bangalore, India (2003) 163–174
2. Akinde, M.O., Böhlen, M.H., Johnson, T., Lakshmanan, L.V.S., Srivastava, D.: Efficient OLAP query processing in distributed data warehouses. In: Proc. of the 8th Intl. Conf. on Extending Database Technology, Prague, Czech Republic (2002) 336–353

3. Chatziantoniou, D., Akinde, M.O., Johnson, T., Kim, S.: MD-join: An operator for complex OLAP. In: Proc. of the 17th Intl. Conf. on Data Engineering, Heidelberg, Germany (2001) 524–533
4. Kline, N., Snodgrass, R.T.: Computing temporal aggregates. In: Proc. of the 11th Intl. Conf. on Data Engineering, Taipei, Taiwan (1995) 222–231
5. Moon, B., Vega Lopez, I.F., Immanuel, V.: Efficient algorithms for large-scale temporal aggregation. IEEE Trans. on Knowledge and Data Engineering **15**(3) (2003) 744–759
6. Yang, J., Widom, J.: Incremental computation and maintenance of temporal aggregates. The VLDB Journal **12** (2003) 262–283
7. Zhang, D., Markowetz, A., Tsotras, V., Gunopulos, D., Seeger, B.: Efficient computation of temporal aggregates with range predicates. In: Proc. of the 20th ACM SIGACT-SIGMOD-SIGART Symposium on Principles of Database Systems, Santa Barbara, CA (2001) 237–245
8. Tuma, P.A.: Implementing Historical Aggregates in TempIS. PhD thesis, Wayne State University, Detroit, Michigan (1992)
9. Tao, Y., Papadias, D., Faloutsos, C.: Approximate temporal aggregation. In: Proc. of the 20th Intl. Conf. on Data Engineering, Boston, USA (2004) 190–201
10. Vega Lopez, I.F., Snodgrass, R.T., Moon, B.: Spatiotemporal aggregate computation: A survey. IEEE Trans. on Knowledge and Data Engineering **17**(2) (2005) 271–286
11. Enderle, J., Hampel, M., Seidl, T.: Joining interval data in relational databases. In: Proc. of the ACM SIGMOD Intl. Conf. on Knowledge and Data Engineering, Paris, France (2004) 683–694

# Similarity Search on Time Series Based on Threshold Queries

Johannes Aßfalg, Hans-Peter Kriegel, Peer Kröger,
Peter Kunath, Alexey Pryakhin, and Matthias Renz

Institute for Computer Science, University of Munich
{assfalg, kriegel, kroegerp, kunath, pryakhin, renz}@dbs.ifi.lmu.de

**Abstract.** Similarity search in time series data is required in many application fields. The most prominent work has focused on similarity search considering either complete time series or similarity according to subsequences of time series. For many domains like financial analysis, medicine, environmental meteorology, or environmental observation, the detection of temporal dependencies between different time series is very important. In contrast to traditional approaches which consider the course of the time series for the purpose of matching, coarse trend information about the time series could be sufficient to solve the above mentioned problem. In particular, temporal dependencies in time series can be detected by determining the points of time at which the time series exceeds a specific threshold. In this paper, we introduce the novel concept of *threshold queries* in time series databases which report those time series exceeding a user-defined query threshold at similar time frames compared to the query time series. We present a new efficient access method which uses the fact that only partial information of the time series is required at query time. The performance of our solution is demonstrated by an extensive experimental evaluation on real world and artificial time series data.

## 1 Introduction

Similarity search in time series data is required in many application fields, including financial analysis, medicine, meteorology, analysis of customer behavior, or environmental observation. As a consequence, a lot of research work has focused on similarity search in time series databases recently.

In this paper, we introduce a novel type of similarity queries on time series databases called *threshold queries*. A threshold query specifies a query time series $Q$ and a threshold $\tau$. The database time series as well as the query sequence $Q$ are decomposed into time intervals of subsequent elements where the values are (strictly) above $\tau$. Now, the threshold query returns these time series objects of the database which have a similar interval sequence of values above $\tau$. Note, that the entire set of absolute values are irrelevant for the query. The time intervals of a time series $t$ only indicate that the values of $t$ within the intervals are above a given threshold $\tau$.

The novel concept of threshold queries is an important technique useful in many practical application areas.

**Application 1.** For the pharma industry it is interesting which drugs cause similar effects in the blood values of a patient at the same time after drug treatment. Obviously, effects such as a certain blood parameter exceeding a critical level $\tau$ are of particular interest. A threshold query can return for a given patient all patients in a database who show a similar reaction to a medical treatment w.r.t. a certain blood parameter exceeding the threshold $\tau$.

**Application 2.** The analysis of environmental air pollution becomes more and more important and has been performed by many European research projects in the recent years. The amount of time series data derived from environmental observation centers, increases drastically with elapsed time. Furthermore, modern sensor stations record many attributes of the observed location simultaneously. For example, German state offices for environmental protection maintain about 127 million time series each representing the daily course of several air pollution parameters. An effective and efficient processing of queries like "return all ozone time series which exceed the threshold $\tau_1 = 50\mu g/m^3$ at a similar time as the temperature reaches the threshold $\tau_2 = 25°C$" may be very useful. Obviously, the increasing amount of data to be analyzed poses a big challenge for methods supporting threshold queries efficiently.

**Application 3.** In molecular biology the analysis of gene expression data is important for understanding gene regulation and cellular mechanisms. Gene expression data contains the expression level of thousands of genes, indicating how *active* one gene is over a set of time slots. The expression level of a gene can be up (indicated by a positive value) or down (negative value). From a biologist's point of view, it is interesting to find genes that have a similar up and down pattern because this indicates a functional relationship among the particular genes. Since the absolute up/down-value is irrelevant, this problem can be represented by a threshold query. Each gene provides its own interval sequence, indicating the time slots of being up. Genes with similar interval sequence thus have a similar up and down pattern.

Time series (sometimes also denoted as time sequences) are usually very large containing several thousands of values per sequence. Consequently, the comparison of two time series can be very expensive, particularly when considering the entire sequence of values of the compared objects. However, the application examples above do not need the entire course of the time series, rather "qualitative" course information with respect to a certain threshold is sufficient to determine the correct query results. Consider again the query example of the second application. Let us assume, that we have the information when the ozone values are above $50\mu g/m^3$ for all ozone sequences in form of time intervals. Then, the processing of this query is reduced to compare sequences of time intervals. Usually, the number of intervals is much less than the number of ozone values per ozone sequence. With this aggregated information, obviously the query can be answered more efficiently compared to the approach where the time intervals are not given in advance.

As mentioned above, this is the first contribution to the novel concept of threshold queries for time series databases.

In summary, our contributions are the following:

- We introduce and formalize the novel concept of threshold queries on time series databases.
- We present a novel data representation of time series which support such threshold queries efficiently.
- We propose an efficient algorithm for threshold queries based on this new representation.
- We present a broad experimental evaluation including performance tests of our proposed algorithms and the evidence that the new type of query yields important information and is thus required in several application fields.

The remainder is organized as follows. We give a short overview of the field of similarity search in time series databases in Section 2. Section 3 formally introduces the notion of threshold queries. In Section 4, we show how time series can be represented in order to support threshold queries for arbitrary threshold values efficiently. Section 5 describes an efficient query algorithm based on the proposed representation. The effectiveness and efficiency of our algorithm are evaluated in Section 6. Section 7 concludes the paper with a summary of our findings and an outlook to future extensions.

## 2 Related Work

In the last decades, time series have become an increasingly prevalent type of data. As a result, a lot of work on similarity search in time series databases has been published. The proposed methods mainly differ in the representation of the time series; a survey is given in [1].

A time series X can be considered as a point in n-dimensional space. This suggests that time series could be indexed by spatial access methods such as the R-tree and its variants [2]. However, most spatial access methods degrade rapidly with increasing data dimensionality due to the "curse of dimensionality". In order to utilize spatial access methods, it is necessary to perform dimensionality reduction and/or to perform multi-step query processing. Standard techniques for dimensionality reduction have been applied successfully to similarity search in time series databases, including Discrete Fourier Transform (DFT) (e.g. [3]), Discrete Wavelet Transform (DWT) (e.g. [4]), Piecewise Aggregate Approximation (PAA) (e.g. [5]), Singular Value Decomposition (SVD) (e.g. [6]), Adaptive Piecewise Constant Approximation (APCA) [1], and Chebyshev Polynomials [7]. In [8], the authors propose the GEMINI framework, that allows to incorporate any dimensionality reduction method into efficient indexing, as long as the distance function on the reduced feature space fulfills the lower bounding property.

However, all techniques which are based on dimensionality reduction cannot be applied to threshold queries because necessary temporal information is lost. Usually, in a reduced feature space, the original intervals indicating that the time series is above a given threshold cannot be generated. In addition, the approximation generated by dimensionality reduction techniques cannot be used

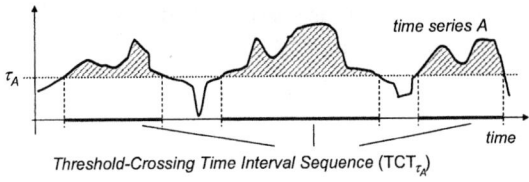

**Fig. 1.** Threshold-Crossing Time Intervals

for our purposes directly because they still represent the exact course of the time series rather than intervals of values above a threshold.

For many applications, the Euclidean distance may be too sensitive to minor distortions in the time axis. It has been shown, that Dynamic Time Warping (DTW) can fix this problem [1]. Using DTW to measure the distance between two time series $t_1$ and $t_2$, each value of $t_1$ may be matched with any value of $t_2$. However, DTW is not applicable to threshold queries because it considers the absolute values of the time series rather than the intervals of values above a given threshold.

In [9], a novel bit level approximation of time series for similarity search and clustering is proposed. Each value of the time series is represented by a bit. The bit is set to 1 if the value of the time represented by the bit is strictly above the mean value of the entire time series, otherwise it is set to 0. Then, a distance function is defined on this bit level representation that lower bounds the Euclidean distance and, by using a slight variant, lower bounds DTW. However, since this representation is restricted to a certain predetermined threshold, this approach is not applicable for threshold queries where the threshold is not known until query time.

To the best of our knowledge, there does neither exist any access method for time series, nor any similarity search technique which efficiently supports threshold queries.

## 3 Threshold Queries on Time Series

In this section, we introduce the novel concept of threshold queries and present techniques allowing for an efficient query processing. We define a time series $X$ as a sequence of pairs $(x_i, t_i) \in \mathbb{R} \times T : (i = 1..N)$, where $T$ denotes the domain of time and $x_i$ denotes the measurement corresponding to time $t_i$. Furthermore, we assume that the time series entities are given in such a way that $\forall i \in 1,..,N-1 : t_i < t_{i+1}$. Let us note, that in most applications the time series derive from discrete measurements of continuously varying attributes. However, commonly time series are depicted as continuous curves, where the missing curve values (i.e. values between two measurements) are estimated by means of interpolation. From the large range of appropriate solutions for time series interpolation, in this paper we assume that the time series curves are supplemented by linear interpolation which is the most prevalent interpolation method. In the rest of this paper, if not stated otherwise, $x(t) \in \mathbb{R}$ denotes the (interpolated) time series value of time series $X$ at time $t \in T$.

**Definition 1 (Threshold-Crossing Time Interval Sequence).** *Let $X = \langle (x_i, t_i) \in \mathbb{R} \times T : i = 1..N \rangle$ be a time series with $N$ measurements and $\tau \in \mathbb{R}$ be a threshold. Then the threshold-crossing time interval sequence of $X$ with respect to $\tau$ is a sequence $TCT_\tau(X) = \langle (l_j, u_j) \in T \times T : j \in \{1,..,M\}, M \le N \rangle$ of time intervals, such that*

$$\forall t \in T : (\exists j \in \{1,..,M\} : l_j < t < u_j) \Leftrightarrow x(t) > \tau.$$

*An interval $tct_{\tau,j} = (l_j, u_j)$ of $TCT_\tau(X)$ is called threshold-crossing time interval.*

The example shown in Figure 1 depicts the threshold-crossing time interval sequence of the time series $A$ which corresponds to threshold $\tau_A$.

**Definition 2 (Distance between Time Intervals).** *Let $t1 = (t1_l, t1_u) \in T \times T$ and $t2 = (t2_l, t2_u) \in T \times T$ be two time intervals. Then the distance function $d_{int} : (T \times T) \times (T \times T) \to \mathbb{R}$ between two time intervals is defined as:*

$$d_{int}(t1, t2) = \sqrt{(t1_l - t2_l)^2 + (t1_u - t2_u)^2}$$

Intuitively, two time intervals are defined to be similar if they have "similar" starting and end points, i.e. they are starting at similar times and ending at similar times.

Since for a certain threshold $\tau$ a time series object is represented by a sequence or a set of time intervals, we need a distance/similarity measure for sets of intervals. Let us note, that intervals correspond to points in a two-dimensional space, where the starting point corresponds to the first dimension and the ending point corresponds to the second dimension. This transformation is explained in more detail in the next section. Several distance measures for point sets have been introduced in the literature [10]. The Sum of Minimum Distances ($SMD$) most adequately reflects the intuitive notion of similarity between two threshold-crossing time interval sequences. According to the $SMD$ we define the *threshold-distance* $d_{TS}$ as follows:

**Definition 3 (Threshold-Distance).** *Let $X$ and $Y$ be two time series and $S_X = TCT_\tau(X)$ and $S_Y = TCT_\tau(Y)$ be the corresponding threshold-crossing time interval sequences.*

$$d_{TS}(S_X, S_Y) = \frac{1}{|S_X|} \cdot \sum_{s \in S_X} \min_{t \in S_Y} d_{int}(s,t) + \frac{1}{|S_Y|} \cdot \sum_{t \in S_Y} \min_{s \in S_X} d_{int}(t,s),$$

The idea of this distance function is to map every interval from one sequence to the closest (most similar) interval of the other sequence and vice versa. Time series having similar shapes, i.e. showing a similar behavior, may be transformed into threshold-crossing time interval sequences of different cardinalities. Since the above distance measure does not consider the cardinalities of the interval sequences, this distance measure is quite adequate for time interval sequences. Another advantage is that the distance measure only considers local similarity. This means, that for each time interval only its nearest neighbor (i.e. closest point) of the other sequence is taken into account. Other intervals of the counterpart sequence have no influence on the result.

Let us note that the threshold-distance between two time series according to a certain threshold $\tau$ is also called $\tau$-similarity.

**Definition 4 (Threshold Query).** *Let $TS$ be the domain of time series objects. The threshold query consists of a query time series $Q \in TS$ and a query threshold $\tau \in \mathbb{R}$. The threshold query reports the smallest set $TSQ_k(Q,\tau) \subseteq TS$ of time series objects that contains at least $k$ objects from $TS$ such that*

$$\forall X \in TSQ_k(Q,\tau), \forall Y \in TS - TSQ_k(Q,\tau):$$

$$d_{TS}(TCT_\tau(X), TCT_\tau(Q)) < d_{TS}(TCT_\tau(Y), TCT_\tau(Q)).$$

Let us note, that if not stated otherwise we assume $k = 1$ throughout the rest of this paper.

## 4 Efficient Management of Threshold-Crossing Time Intervals

The simplest way to execute a threshold query $TSQ_k(Q,\tau)$ is to sequentially read each time series $X$ from the database, to compute the threshold-crossing time interval sequence $S_X = TCT_\tau(X)$ and to compute the threshold-similarity function $d_{TS}(S_X, TCT_\tau(Q))$. Finally, we report the time series which yields the smallest distance $d_{TS}(S_X, TCT_\tau(Q))$. However, if the time series database contains a large number of objects and the time series are reasonably large, then obviously this type of performing the query becomes unacceptably expensive. For this reason we use a convenient access method on the time series data.

In this section, we present two approaches for the management of time series data, both of which efficiently support threshold queries. The key point is that we do not need to access the complete time series data at query time. Instead only partial information of the time series objects is required. At query time we only need the information at which time frames the time series is above the specified threshold. We can save a lot of I/O cost if we are able to access only the relevant parts of the time series at query time. The basic idea of our approach is to pre-compute the $TCT_\tau(X)$ for each time series object $X$ and store it on disk in such a way it can be accessed efficiently.

For the sake of clarity, we first present a simple approach with constant threshold value $\tau$ for all queries. Afterwards, we present the general approach which supports arbitrary choice $\tau$.

## 4.1 Representing Threshold-Crossing Time Intervals with Fixed $\tau$

Let us assume that the query threshold $\tau$ is fixed for all queries. Then, we can compute the corresponding $TCT_\tau(X)$ for each time series $X$. Consequently, each time series object is represented by a sequence of intervals. There are several methods to store intervals efficiently, e.g. the RI-Tree [11]. However, they only support intersection queries on interval data but do not efficiently support similarity queries on interval sequences. Besides, they cannot be used for the general approach when $\tau$ is not fixed. We propose a solution which supports similarity queries on intervals and which can be easily extended to support queries with arbitrary $\tau$.

Time intervals can also be considered as points in a 2-dimensional plane[12]. In the following we will refer to this plane as time interval plane. The 1-dimensional intervals (*native space*) are mapped to the time interval plane by taking their start and end points as two dimensional coordinates. This representations has some advantages for the efficient management of intervals. First, the distances between intervals are preserved. Second, the position of large intervals, which are located within the upper-left region, substantially differs from the position of small intervals (located near the diagonal). However, the most important advantage is that this plane preserves the similarity of intervals according to Definition 2. Let $t_1 = (x_1, y_1)$ and $t_2 = (x_2, y_2)$ be two time intervals, then the distance between $t_1$ and $t_2$ is equal to $d_{int}(t_1, t_2) = \sqrt{(x_1 - x_2)^2 + (y_1 - y_2)^2}$ which corresponds to the Euclidean distance in the time interval plane.

The complete threshold-crossing time interval sequence is represented by a set of 2-dimensional points in the time interval plane. The transformation chain from the original time series to the point set in the time interval plane is depicted in Figure 2. In order to efficiently manage the point sets of all time series objects, we can use a spatial index structure as for instance the R*-tree [13]. In particular, the R*-tree is very suitable for managing points in low-dimensional space which

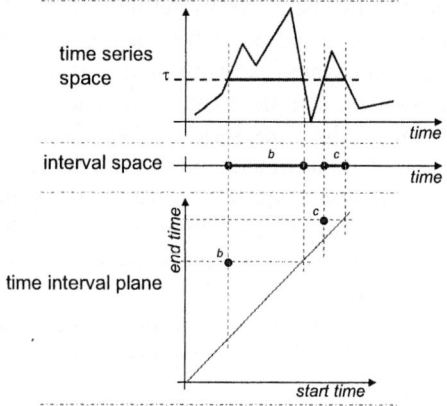

**Fig. 2.** Mapping of Time Intervals to the Time Interval Plane

are not equally distributed. Additionally, it supports the nearest neighbor query which will be required to perform the threshold queries efficiently (more details for the query process will be presented in Section 5). Let us note, that each object is represented by several points in the time interval plane. Consequently, each object is referenced by the index structure multiple times.

## 4.2 Representing Threshold-Crossing Time Intervals for Arbitrary $\tau$

In contrast to the first approach presented above we will now describe how to manage threshold queries for arbitrary threshold values $\tau$ efficiently. First, we have to extend the transformation task of the simple approach, in such a way that the time interval plane representations of the $TCT_\tau$s of the time series are available for all possible threshold values $\tau$. Therefore, we extend the time interval plane by one additional dimension which indicates the corresponding threshold values. In the following, we will call this space *parameter space*. A 2-dimensional plane along the threshold axis parallel to the (lower,upper)-plane at a certain threshold $\tau$ in the parameter space is called time interval plane of threshold $\tau$.

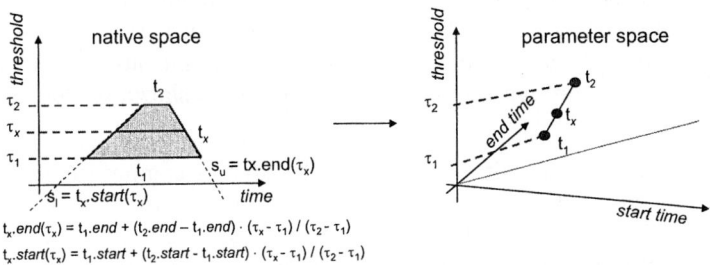

**Fig. 3.** Interval Ranges in Parameter Space

In the parameter space sets of threshold-crossing time intervals can be efficiently represented as follows. As shown in the example depicted in Figure 3, the set of all possible threshold-crossing time intervals of one time series which are left-bounded by the segment $s_l$ and right-bounded by the segment $s_u$ and whose threshold value is between $\tau_1$ and $\tau_2$ can be represented by the segment $t_1, t_2$ in the parameter space. The management of all threshold-crossing time intervals of a time series can be efficiently handled, as follows: We first identify all groups of *tct*-intervals which start and end at the same time series segment. Then, each group is represented by one segment in the parameter space, which can be efficiently organized by means of a spatial index structure, e.g. the R*-tree. At query time, the time interval plane coordinates of the threshold-crossing time intervals corresponding to the query threshold $\tau_q$ can be easily determined by computing the intersection of all segments of the parameter space with the time interval plane $P$ of threshold $\tau_q$.

## 4.3 Trapezoid Decomposition of Time Series

The set of all time intervals which start and end at the same time series segment can be described by a single trapezoid whose left and right bounds are each congruent with one single time series segment. Let $s_l = ((x_{l1}, t_{l1}), (x_{l2}, t_{l2}))$ denote the segment of the left bound and $s_r = ((x_{r1}, t_{r1}), (x_{r2}, t_{r2}))$ denote the segment of the right bound. The top-bottom bounds correspond to the two threshold-crossing time intervals $tct_{\tau_{top}}$ and $tct_{\tau_{bottom}}$ whose threshold values are computed as follows:

$$\tau_{top} = min(max(x_{l1}, x_{l2}), max(x_{r1}, x_{r2}));$$

$$\tau_{bottom} = max(min(x_{l1}, x_{l2}), min(x_{r1}, x_{r2}));$$

For our decomposition algorithm we can use the following property

**Lemma 1.** *Threshold-crossing time intervals always start at increasing time series segments (positive segment slope) and end at decreasing time series segments (negative segment slope).*

*Proof.* Due to Definition 1, all values of $X$ within the threshold-crossing time interval $tct_\tau(X)$ are greater than the corresponding threshold value $\tau$. Let us assume that the time series segment $s_l$ which lower-bounds the time interval at time $t_l$ has a negative slope. Then, all $x(t)$ on $s_l$ with $t > t_l$ are lower than $\tau$ which contradicts the definition of threshold-crossing time intervals. The validity of Lemma 1 w.r.t. the right bounding segment can be shown analogously.

Let us note that time series objects can be considered as half-open uni-monotone polygons in the time-amplitude plane. In the area of computational geometry there are known several sweep-line based polygon-to-trapezoid decomposition algorithms [14] which can be processed in $O(n \cdot log n)$ time w.r.t. the number of vertices. For this work we adopted one of these decomposition algorithms. Since the time series values are chronologically ordered, our decomposition algorithm can be processed in linear time w.r.t. the length of the sequence.

Figure 4 shows an example of how a time series is decomposed into the set of trapezoids. This algorithm works similar to polygon-to-trapezoid decomposition algorithms known from the area of computational geometry. As we can assume that the time series consist of chronologically ordered pairs $(x, t)$, our decomposition algorithm can be performed in linear time (linear w.r.t. the length of the time series).

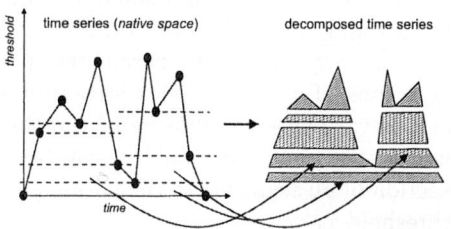

**Fig. 4.** Time Series Decomposition

## 4.4 Indexing Segments in the Parameter Space

We apply the R*-tree for the efficient management of the three-dimensional segments representing the time series objects in the parameter space. As the R*-tree index can only manage rectangles, we represent the 3-dimensional segments by rectangles where the segments correspond to one of the diagonals of the rectangles.

For all trapezoids which result from the time series decomposition, the lower bound time interval contains the upper bound time interval. Furthermore, intervals which are contained in another interval are located in the lower-right area of this interval representation in the time interval plane. Consequently, the locations of the segments within the rectangles in the parameter space are fixed. Therefore, in the parameter space the bounds of the rectangle which represents a segment suffice to uniquely identify the covered segment. Let $((x_l, y_l, z_l), (x_u, y_u, z_u))$ be the coordinates of a rectangle in the parameter space, then the coordinates of the corresponding segment are $((x_l, y_u, z_l), (x_u, y_l, z_u))$.

## 5 Query Algorithm

The query consists of a query time series $Q$ and a query threshold $\tau$ (cf. Definition 4). The first step of the query process is to determine the threshold-crossing time interval sequence $TCT_\tau(Q)$. Obviously, this can be done by one single scan through the query object $Q$. Next, we have to find those time series objects from the database which are most $\tau$-similar to $Q$ according to Definition 3.

### 5.1 Preliminaries

In this section, we assume that $Q$ denotes the query time series which is represented by its threshold-crossing time interval sequence $S_Q = TCT_\tau(Q)$. Furthermore, $S_X = v_1, .., v_n$ denotes the threshold-crossing time interval sequence $TCT_\tau(X)$ from any database time series $X$. Since the similarity query is performed in the parameter space (or time interval plane for a certain threshold $\tau$), $S_X$ denotes a set[1] of two-dimensional points.

### 5.2 Computation of the $\tau$-Similarity

At first, we will consider the computation of the $\tau$-similarities between time series objects in the time interval plane. As mentioned above, the threshold-crossing time interval sequence of a time series object corresponds to a set of points in the time interval plane. In the following, the point set of a time series denotes the time interval plane point representation which corresponds to the threshold-crossing time interval sequence of the time series object.

---

[1] In our approach it does not make any difference whether $S_X = TCT_\tau(X)$ denotes a sequence or a set of intervals or points, thus for simplicity we consider $S_X$ as a set of intervals or points.

Given a threshold-crossing time interval, the most similar threshold-crossing time interval in the time space (native space) (w.r.t. Definition 2) corresponds to the nearest-neighbor in the time interval plane.

**Definition 5 (k-Nearest Neighbor).** *Let $q$ be a point in the time interval plane and $S_X = \{v_1, ..., v_n\}$ be a set of points in the time interval plane. The k-nearest-neighbor $NN_{k,S_X}(q)$ $(k < n)$ of $q$ in the set $S_X$ is defined as follows:*

$$v = NN_{k,S_X}(q) \in S_X \Leftrightarrow$$

$$\forall v' \in S_X - \{NN_{l,S_X}(q) : l \leq k\} : d_{int}(q, v) \leq d_{int}(q, v').$$

*The distance $d_{int}(q, NN_{k,S_X}(q))$ is called k-nearest-neighbor distance. For $k = 1$, we simply call $NN_{1,S_X}(q) \equiv NN_X(q)$ the nearest-neighbor of $q$ in $S_X$. $NN_{l,.}(q)$ denotes the overall k-nearest neighbor of $q$, i.e. $NN_{l,.}(q) = NN_{l, \bigcup_{X \in DB} X}(q)$. The set $k - NN_X(q) = \{NN_{l,S_X}(q) : \forall l \leq k\}$ is called k-nearest-neighbors of $q$.*

In the time interval plane, the $\tau$-similarity between two time series objects $Q$ and $X$ can be determined by computing for all points of $S_Q$ the nearest neighbor points in $S_X$ and, vice versa, for all points in $S_X$ the nearest neighbor points in $S_Q$.

### 5.3 Efficient Query Processing

Let us assume that we are given any query threshold $\tau$ and the point set of the query object $Q$ in the time interval plane of $\tau$. A straightforward approach for the query process would be the following: First, we identify all parameter space segments of the database objects which intersect the time interval plane of threshold $\tau$. Then we determine the time interval plane point sets of all database objects by computing the intersection between the parameter space segments and the plane of $\tau$. For each database object, we compute the $\tau$-similarity to the query object. Finally, we report the object having the smallest $\tau$-distance to $Q$. Obviously, this is not a very efficient method since the respective parameter space segments of all time series objects have to be accessed. We can achieve a better query performance by using an R*-Tree index on the parameter space segments to filter out those segments which cannot satisfy the query. For this purpose, we require a lower bound criterion for the $\tau$-distance between two objects.

**Lower Distance Bound.** In the following, we will introduce a lower bound criterion for the threshold-distance $d_{TS}$ on the basis of partial distance computations between the query object and the database objects. This lower bound criterion enables the detection of false candidates very early, i.e. only partial information of the false candidates suffices to prune this object from the candidate list. The amount of information necessary for the pruning of an object depends on the location of the query object and the other candidates.

Let $S_Q = \{q_1, ..., q_n\}$ be the point set corresponding to the query object and $S_X = \{v_1, ..., v_m\}$ be the point set of any object $X$ from the database.

Furthermore, we reformulate the $\tau$-distance $d_{TS}(S_Q, S_X)$ between $S_Q$ and $S_X$ of Definition 3 as follows:

$$d_{TS}(S_Q, S_X) = \frac{1}{|S_Q|} \cdot D_1(S_Q, S_X) + \frac{1}{|S_X|} \cdot D_2(S_Q, S_X),$$

where $D_1(S_Q, S_X) = \sum_{i=1..n} d_{int}(q_i, NN_X(q_i))$
and $D_2(S_Q, S_X) = \sum_{i=1..m} d_{int}(v_i, NN_Q(v_i))$.

In the following, we use two auxiliary variables $K_l(q_i)$ and $\bar{K}_l(S_Q)$ which help to distinguish two classes of our objects. $K_l(q_i) \subseteq DB$ denotes the set of all objects $S_X$ which has at least one entity $x \in S_X$ within the set $k - NN_X(q_i)$. Furthermore, $\bar{K}_l(S_Q) \subseteq DB$ denotes the set of all objects which are not in any set $K_l(q_i)$ i.e. $\bar{K}_l(S_Q) = DB - (\bigcup_{i=1..n} K_l(q_i))$.

**Lemma 2.** *The following inequality holds for any object $S_X \in \bar{K}_l(S_Q)$:*

$$D_1(S_Q, S_X) \geq \sum_{i=1..n} d_{int}(q_i, NN_{l,.}(q_i)).$$

*Proof.* According to Definition 5 the following statement holds:

$$\forall i \in \{1,..,n\} : d_{int}(q_i, NN_{l,.}(q_i)) \leq d_{int}(q_i, NN_X(q_i)).$$

Therefore,

$$\sum_{i=1..n} d_{int}(q_i, NN_{l,.}(q_i)) \leq \sum_{i=1..n} d_{int}(q_i, NN_X(q_i)) = D_1(S_Q, S_X).$$

The following lemma is a generalization of Lemma 2 and defines a lower bound of $D_1(S_Q, S_X)$ for all database objects $S_X \in DB$ for any $l \in \mathbb{N}$.

**Lemma 3.** *Let $S_X \in DB$ be any database object and let $S_Q$ be the query object. The distance $D_1(S_Q, S_X)$ can be estimated by the following formula:*

$$d_{min}(S_Q, S_X) = \frac{1}{n} \sum_{i=1..n} \begin{cases} d_{int}(q_i, NN_X(q_i)), & \text{if } S_X \in K_l(q_i) \\ d_{int}(q_i, NN_{l,.}(q_i)), & \text{else} \end{cases} \leq D_1(S_Q, S_X).$$

*Proof.* Let $S_X \in DB$ be any database object and $S_Q$ be the query object. According to Definition 5 the following holds:

$$d_{int}(q_i, NN_{l,.}(q_i)) \leq d_{int}(q_i, NN_X(q_i)) \Leftrightarrow X \notin K_l(q_i).$$

Consequently, $d_{min}(Q, X) \leq \frac{1}{n} \sum_{i=1..n} d_{int}(q_i, NN_X(q_i)) = D_1(S_Q, S_X)$.

**Pruning Strategy.** By iteratively computing the $l$-nearest neighbors $NN_{l,.}(q)$ for all $q \in S_Q$ with increasing $l \in \mathbb{N}$, we can determine the lower bound distances for all objects. The maximal lower bound distance $d_{min}(S_Q, S_X)$ of an object $S_X$ has been achieved as soon as $S_X \in K_l(q_i) : \forall i \in 1,...,n$. Then, we refine the distance $d_{TS}(S_Q, S_X)$ by accessing the complete object $S_X$ in order to compute the distance $D_2(S_Q, S_X)$. The resulting distance $d_{TS}(S_Q, S_X)$ is then used as new pruning distance $d_{prun}$ for the remaining query process. All objects $Y \in DB - \{X\}$ whose current lower bound distance $d_{min}(S_Q, S_Y)$ exceeds $d_{prun}$ can be omitted from the remaining search steps. The search proceeds by continuing the iterative computations of the next nearest neighbors $NN_{l+1,.}$.

Let $S_X$ be the object with the lowest exact distance to $S_Q$, i.e. $d_{prun} = d_{TS}(S_Q, S_X)$. The pruning distance can be updated as soon as the next object $S_Y$ which has to be refined is found. In doing so, we have to consider two cases:

**Case 1:** $d_{TS}(S_Q, S_Y) \geq d_{prune} \rightarrow$ remove object $S_Y$ from the candidate set,
**Case 2:** $d_{TS}(S_Q, S_Y) < d_{prune} \rightarrow$ set $d_{prune} := d_{TS}(S_Q, S_Y)$ and remove object $S_X$ from the candidate set.

The search algorithm terminates as soon as all object candidates, except for the best one, have been pruned.

### 5.4 Query Algorithm

The query algorithm is depicted in Figure 5. The function *threshold-query* $(S_Q, DB, \tau)$ computes for a given query object $S_Q$ the database object $obj_{best}$

```
threshold-query(S_Q, DB, τ) {
    nn := ARRAY[1..—S_Q—];  /*array of current nn-objects*/
    d_min − tab := LIST of point ARRAY[1..|S_Q|]; /*d_min table*/
    obj_best := null;
    d_prune := +∞
    k := 0;
    LOOP
        k := k + 1;
        nn = fetch-next-nn(S_Q, DB, τ, d_prune);
        d_min − tab.update(nn);
        if ((o := d_min − tab.object_complete()) != null) then {
            load complete object o and compute d_TS(S_Q, o); /*refinement-step*/
            if (d_TS(S_Q, o) ≥ d_prune) then {
                obj_best := o;
                d_prune := d_TS(S_Q, o);
            } else { remove o from the candidate list in d_min − tab; }}
        for all objects obj ∈ d_min − tab do {
            if (D_1(S_Q, obj) ≥ d_prune) then {
                remove obj from the candidate list in d_min − tab; }}
        if (∑_{q_i ∈ S_Q} NN_{k,.}(q_i) ≥ d_prune) then {
            report o_best;
            break; }
    end LOOP; }
```

**Fig. 5.** The threshold query algorithm

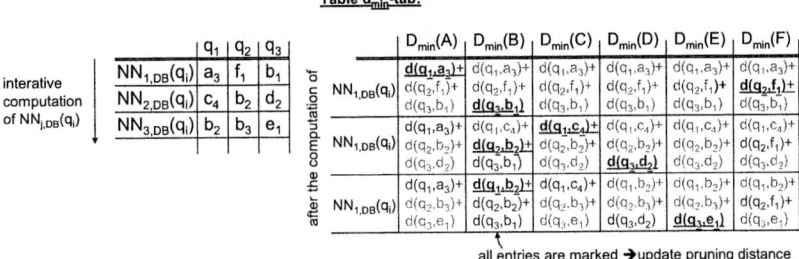

**Fig. 6.** Example of the query processing

having the smallest $\tau$-distance $d_{TS}(S_Q, S_X)$. The function *fetch-next-nn($S_Q$,DB)* is an iterator function which retrieves the next nearest neighbor for each $q_i \in S_Q$ in each iteration. The nearest neighbors can be efficiently computed by applying the nearest neighbor ranking method as proposed in [15]. Thereby, we maintain for each $q \in S_Q$ a priority queue, each storing the accessed R*-tree nodes in ascending order of their distances to the corresponding query point $q$.

In this section, we treated the objects as sets of points in the time interval plane. In fact, the database objects are organized within the three-dimensional parameter space (cf. Section 4.4). For the distance computation between the query point $q = (l_i, u_i, \tau)$ and an R*-tree rectangle $r = ((x_l, y_l, z_l), (x_u, y_u, z_u))$, we consider the horizontal distance at threshold $\tau$ only, i.e. $d_{int}(q_i, r) = d_{int}((l_i, u_i), ((x_l, y_l), (x_u, y_u)))$.

The basic functionality of the query algorithm can be explained by the following example which is depicted in Figure 6. In our example, the query consists of three time interval plane points $S_Q = \{q_1, q_2, q_3\}$. The upper table shows the results of the first three states of the incremental nearest-neighbor queries $NN_{1,.}(q_i)$, $NN_{2,.}(q_i)$ and $NN_{3,.}(q_i)$. The state of the corresponding $d_{min}$-table after each iteration is shown in the table below. The first iteration retrieves the points $a_3$, $f_1$ and $b_1$ of the time series objects $A$, $F$, and $B$, respectively. Consequently, the threshold-distance between $q$ and all objects $S_X \in DB$ can be restricted by the lower bound $d_{min} = \frac{1}{3}(d(q_1, a_3) + d(q_2, f_1) + d(q_3, b_1))$. Next, we insert the actual nearest neighbor distances into the $d_{min}$-table and mark the corresponding entries (marked entries are underlined in the figure). Let us note, that all unmarked distance entries correspond to the currently retrieved nearest neighbor distances, and thus, need not to be stored for each object separately. After the third query iteration, all nearest neighbor counterparts from $S_Q$ to $S_B$ are found. Consequently, we can update the pruning distance by computing the exact $\tau$-similarity $d_{prune} = d_{TS}(S_Q, S_B)$. We can now remove the column $D_{min}(B)$ from the $d_{min}$-table.

The runtime complexity of our threshold query algorithm is $O(n_q \cdot n_k \cdot log n_p)$, where $n_q$ denotes the size of the threshold-crossing time interval sequence $S_Q$, $n_k$ denotes the number of nearest-neighbor search iterations and $n_p$ denotes the overall number of segments in the parameter space. In the experiments (cf. Section 6) we will show that in average $n_q$ is very very small in comparison to the length of the time sequences. Furthermore, we will show that the number of required nearest-neighbor query iterations $n_k$ is very small, i.e. the query process terminates very early. The number $n_p$ of segments in the parameter space is quite similar to the sum $n_s$ of length of all time sequences in the database, but it is slightly smaller than $n_s$ which is also shown in the experiments.

## 6 Experimental Evaluation

In this section, we present the results of a large number of experiments performed on a selection of different time series datasets. In particular, we compared the efficiency of our proposed approach (in the following denoted by '$R_{Par}$') for answering threshold queries using one of the following techniques.

The first competing approach works on native time series. At query time the threshold-crossing time intervals (TCT) are computed for the query threshold and afterwards the distance between the query time series and each database object can be derived. In the following this method will be denoted by '$Seq_{Nat}$' as it corresponds to a sequential processing of the native data.

The second competitor works on the parameter space rather than on the native data. It stores all TCTs without using any index structures. As this storage leads to a sequential scan over the elements of the parameter space we will refer to this technique as the '$Seq_{Par}$' method.

All experiments were performed on a workstation featuring a 1.8 GHz Opteron CPU and 8GB RAM. We used a disk with a transfer rate of 100 MB/s, a seek time of 3 ms and a latency delay of 2 ms. Performance is presented in terms of the elapsed time including I/O and CPU-time.

### 6.1 Datasets

We used several real-world and synthetic datasets for our evaluation, one audio dataset and two scientific datasets. The audio dataset contains time sequences expressing the temporal behavior of the energy and frequency in music sequences. It contains up to 700000 time series objects with a length of up to 300 values per sequence. If not otherwise stated, the database size was set to 50000 objects and the length of the objects was set to 50. This dataset is used to evaluate the performance of our approach (cf. Section 6.2). In Section 6.3, we will show the effectiveness of threshold queries for the two scientific datasets. The scientific datasets are derived from two different applications: the analysis of environmental air pollution (cf. Application 2 in Section 1) and gene expression data analysis (cf. Application 3 in Section 1). The data on environmental air pollution is derived from the Bavarian State Office for Environmental Protection, Augsburg, Germany [2] and contains the daily measurements of 8 sensor stations distributed in and around the city of Munich from the year 2000 to 2004. One time series represents the measurement of one station at a given day containing 48 values for one of 10 different parameters such as temperature, ozone concentration,

---

[2] www.bayern.de/lfu

etc. A typical time series of this dataset contains 48 measurements of station $S$ during day $D$ of parameter $P$. The gene expression data from [16] contains the expression level of approximately 6,000 genes measured at only 24 different time slots.

## 6.2 Performance Results

To obtain more reliable and significant results, in the following experiments we used 5 randomly chosen query objects. Furthermore, these query objects were used in conjunction with 5 different thresholds, so that we obtained 25 different threshold queries. The presented results are the average results of these queries.

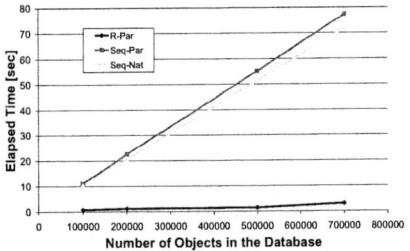

**Fig. 7.** Scalability against database size

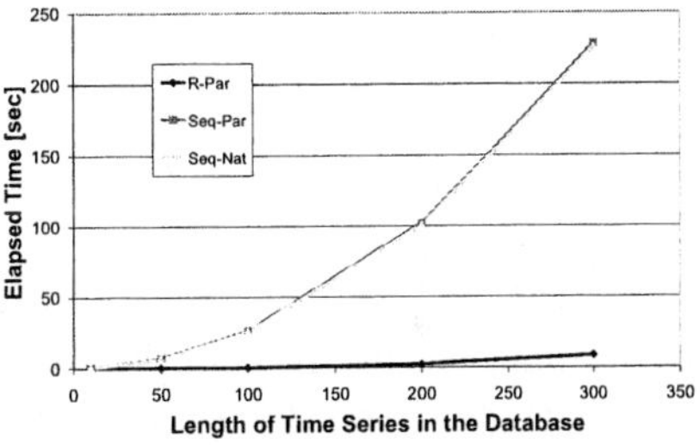

**Fig. 8.** Scalability against time series length

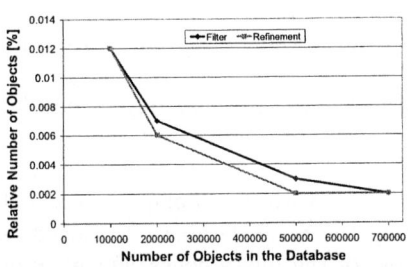
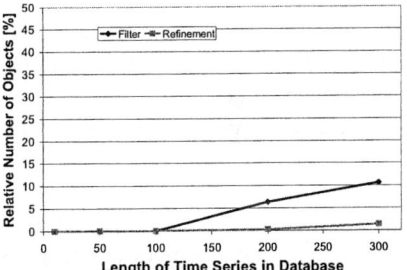

**Fig. 9.** Pruning power for varying database size

**Fig. 10.** Pruning power for varying time series length

First, we performed threshold queries against database instances of different sizes to measure the influence of the database size to the overall query time. The elements of the databases are time series of fixed length $l = 50$. Figure 7 exhibits the performance results for each database. It is shown that the performance of both approaches $Seq_{Nat}$ and $Seq_{Par}$ significantly decreases with increasing database size, whereas our approach scales very well even for large databases. Second, we explored the impact of the length of the query object and the time series in the database. The results are shown in Figure 8. Again, our technique outperforms the competing approaches whose cost increase very fast due to the expensive distance computations. In contrast our approach is hardly influenced by the size of the time series objects.

In the next experiment we present the speed-up of the query process caused by our pruning strategy. We measured the considered number of result candidates during the query processes and the number of finally refined objects. Figure 9 and Figure 10 show the results relatively to the database size and object size. Only a very small portion of the candidates has to be refined to report the result. An interesting point is that very large time series lead to lower pruning power than smaller time series.

Furthermore, we examined the number of nearest-neighbor search iterations which were required for the query process for varying length of the time series and varying size of the database. We observed, that the number of iterations was between 5 and 62. The number of iterations increases linear to the length of the time series and remains nearly constant w.r.t. the database size. Nevertheless, only a few iterations are required to report the result.

### 6.3 Results on Scientific Datasets

The results on the air pollution dataset were very useful. We performed 10-nearest neighbor threshold queries with randomly chosen query objects. Interestingly, when we choose time series as query objects, that were derived from rural sensor stations representing particulate matter parameters ($M_{10}$), we obtained only time series representing the same parameters measured also at rural stations. This confirms that the pollution by particle components in the city differs considerably from the pollution in rural regions. A second interesting result was produced when we used $M_{10}$ time series of working days as queries. The resulting time series were also derived from working days representing $M_{10}$ values.

The results on the gene expression dataset were also very interesting. The task was to find the most similar gene with $\tau = 0$ to a given query gene. The intuition is to find a gene that is functionally related to the query gene. We posed several randomized queries to this dataset with $\tau = 0$ and evaluated the results w.r.t. biological interestingness using the SGD database [3]. Indeed, we retrieved functionally related genes for most of the query genes. For example, for query gene CDC25 we obtained the gene CIK3. Both genes play an important role during the mitotic cell cycle. For the query gene DOM34 and MRPL17 we obtained two genes that are not yet labeled (ORF-names: YOR182C and YGR220C, respectively). However all four genes are participating in the protein biosynthesis. In particular, threshold queries can be used to predict the function of genes whose biological role is not resolved yet.

To sum up, the results on the real-world datasets suggest the practical relevance of threshold queries for important real-world applications.

---

[3] http://www.yeastgenome.org/

## 7 Conclusions

In this paper, we motivated and proposed a novel query type on time series databases called *threshold query*. Given a query object $Q$ and a threshold $\tau$, a *threshold query* returns time series in a database that exhibit the most similar threshold-crossing time interval sequence. The threshold-crossing time interval sequence of a time series represents the interval sequence of elements that have a value above the threshold $\tau$. We mentioned several practical application domains for such a query type. In addition, we presented a novel approach for managing time series data to efficiently support such threshold queries. Furthermore, we developed a scalable algorithm to answer *threshold queries* for arbitrary thresholds $\tau$. A broad experimental evaluation demonstrates the importance of the new query type for several applications and shows the scalability of our proposed algorithms in comparison to straightforward approaches.

For future work, we plan to develop suitable approximations which represent the novel time series data in a compressed form in order to apply efficient filter steps during the query process. Furthermore, we plan to extend our approaches to data mining tasks, such as clustering.

## References

1. Keogh, E., Chakrabati, K., Mehrotra, S., Pazzani, M.: "Locally Adaptive Dimensionality Reduction for Indexing Large Time Series Databases". In: Proc. ACM SIGMOD Int. Conf. on Management of Data (SIGMOD'01), Santa Barbara, CA. (2001)
2. Guttman, A.: "R-Trees: A Dynamic Index Structure for Spatial Searching". In: Proc. ACM SIGMOD Int. Conf. on Management of Data (SIGMOD'84). (1984)
3. Agrawal, R., Faloutsos, C., Swami, A.: "Efficient Similarity Search in Sequence Databases". In: Proc. 4th Conf. on Foundations of Data Organization and Algorithms. (1993)
4. Chan, K., Fu, W.: "Efficient Time Series Matching by Wavelets". In: Proc. 15th Int. Conf. on Data Engineering (ICDE'99), Sydney, Australia. (1999)
5. Yi, B.K., Faloutsos, C.: "Fast Time Sequence Indexing for Arbitrary Lp Norms". In: Proc. 26th Int. Conf. on Very Large Databases (VLDB'00), Cairo, Egypt. (2000)
6. Korn, F., Jagadish, H., Faloutsos, C.: "Efficiently Supporting Ad Hoc Queries in Large Datasets of Time Sequences". In: Proc. ACM SIGMOD Int. Conf. on Management of Data (SIGMOD'97), Tucson, AZ. (1997)
7. Cai, Y., Ng, R.: "Index Spatio-Temporal Trajectories with Chebyshev Polynomials". In: Proc. ACM SIGMOD Int. Conf. on Management of Data (SIGMOD'04), Paris, France). (2004)
8. Faloutsos, C., Ranganathan, M., Maolopoulos, Y.: "Fast Subsequence Matching in Time-series Databases". In: Proc. ACM SIGMOD Int. Conf. on Management of Data (SIGMOD'94), Minneapolis, MN. (1994)
9. Ratanamahatana, C.A., Keogh, E., Bagnall, A.J., Lonardi, S.: "A Novel Bit Level Time Series Representation with Implication for Similarity Search and Clustering". In: Proc. 9th Pacific-Asian Int. Conf. on Knowledge Discovery and Data Mining (PAKDD'05), Hanoi, Vietnam. (2005)

10. Eiter, T., Mannila, H.: "Distance Measure for Point Sets and Their Computation". In: Acta Informatica, 34. (1997) 103–133
11. Kriegel, H.P., Pötke, M., Seidl, T.: "Object-Relational Indexing for General Interval Relationships". In: Proc. Symposium on Spatial and Temporal Databases (SSTD'01), Redondo Beach, CA. (2001)
12. Gaede, V., Günther, O.: "Multidimensional Access Methods". Computing Surveys **30** (1984)
13. Beckmann, N., Kriegel, H.P., Seeger, B., Schneider, R.: "The R*-tree: An Efficient and Robust Access Method for Points and Rectangles". In: Proc. ACM SIGMOD Int. Conf. on Management of Data (SIGMOD'90), Atlantic City, NJ. (1990)
14. Fournier, A., Moniwno, D.Y.: "Triangulating simple polygons and equivalent problems". In: ACM Trans. Graph., 3, 2. (1984) 153–174
15. Hjaltason, G., Samet, H.: "Ranking in Spatial Databases". In: Proc. Int. Symp. on Large Spatial Databases (SSD'95), Portland, OR. (1995)
16. Spellman, P., Sherlock, G., Zhang, M., Iyer, V., Anders, K., Eisen, M., Brown, P., Botstein, D., Futcher, B.: "Comprehensive Identification of Cell Cycle-Regulated Genes of the Yeast Saccharomyces Cerevisiae by Microarray Hybridization". Molecular Biology of the Cell **9** (1998) 3273–3297

# Supporting Temporal Slicing in XML Databases*

Federica Mandreoli, Riccardo Martoglia, and Enrico Ronchetti

DII, Università degli Studi di Modena e Reggio Emilia,
via Vignolese, 905/b - I 41100 Modena
{fmandreoli, rmartoglia, eronchetti}@unimo.it

**Abstract.** Nowadays XML is universally accepted as the standard for structural data representation; XML databases, providing structural querying support, are thus becoming more and more popular. However, XML data changes over time and the task of providing efficient support to queries which also involve temporal aspects goes through the tricky task of time-slicing the input data. In this paper we take up the challenge of providing a native and efficient solution in constructing an XML query processor supporting temporal slicing, thus dealing with non-conventional application requirements while continuing to guarantee good performance in traditional scenarios. Our contributions include a novel temporal indexing scheme relying on relational approaches and a technology supporting the time-slice operator.

## 1 Introduction

Nowadays XML is universally accepted as the standard for structural data representation and exchange and its well-known peculiarities make it a good choice for an ever growing number of applications. Currently the problem of supporting structural querying in XML databases is thus an appealing research topic for the database community.

As data changes over time, the possibility to deal with historical information is essential to many computer applications, such as accounting, banking, law, medical records and customer relationship management. In the last years, researchers have tried to provide answers to this need by proposing models and languages for representing and querying the temporal aspect of XML data. Recent works on this topic include [5, 9, 10, 12].

The central issue of supporting most temporal queries in any language is time-slicing the input data while retaining period timestamping. A time-varying XML document records a version history and temporal slicing makes the different states of the document available to the application needs. While a great deal of work has been done on temporal slicing in the database field [8], the paper [9] has the merit of having been the first to raise the temporal slicing issue in the XML context, where it is complicated by the fact that timestamps are distributed throughout XML documents. The solution proposed in [9] relies on a

---

* This work has been supported by the MIUR-PRIN Project: "European Citizen in eGovernance: legal-philosophical, legal, computer science and economical aspects".

stratum approach whose advantage is that they can exploit existing techniques in the underlying XML query engine, such as query optimization and query evaluation. However, standard XML query engines are not aware of the temporal semantics and thus it makes more difficult to map temporal XML queries into efficient "vanilla" queries and to apply query optimization and indexing techniques particularly suited for temporal XML documents.

In this paper we propose a native solution to the temporal slicing problem. In other words, we address the question of how to construct an XML query processor supporting time-slicing. The underlying idea is to propose the changes that a "conventional" XML pattern matching engine would need to be able to slice time-varying XML documents. The advantage of this solution is that we can benefit from the XML pattern matching techniques present in the literature, where the focus is on the structural aspects which are intrinsic also in temporal XML data, and that, at the same time, we can freely extend them to become temporally aware. Our ultimate goal is not to design a temporal XML query processor from scratch but to put at the user disposal an XML query processor which is able to support non-conventional application requirements while continuing to guarantee good performance in traditional scenarios.

We begin by providing some background in Section 2, where the temporal slicing problem is defined. Our main contributions are:

- We propose a novel temporal indexing scheme (Section 3.1), which adopts the inverted list technology proposed in [14] for XML databases and changes it in order to allow the storing of time-varying XML documents. Moreover, we show how a time-varying XML document can be encoded in it.
- We devise a flexible technology supporting temporal slicing (Section 3.2 to Section 3.5). It consists in alternative solutions supporting temporal slicing on the above storing scheme, all relying on the holistic twig join approach [2], which is one of the most popular approaches for XML pattern matching. The proposed solutions act at the different levels of the holistic twig join architectures with the aim of limiting main memory space requirements, I/O and CPU costs. They include the introduction of novel algorithms and the exploitation of different access methods.
- Finally, in Section 4 we present experimental results showing the substantial performance benefits achievable by combining the proposed solutions in different querying settings.

We describe related work and concluding remarks in Section 5.

## 2  Preliminaries: Notation and Temporal Slicing Definition

A time-varying XML document records a version history, which consists of the information in each version, along with timestamps indicating the lifetime of that version [5]. The left part of Fig. 1 shows the tree representation of our reference time-varying XML document taken from a legislative repository of norms. Data

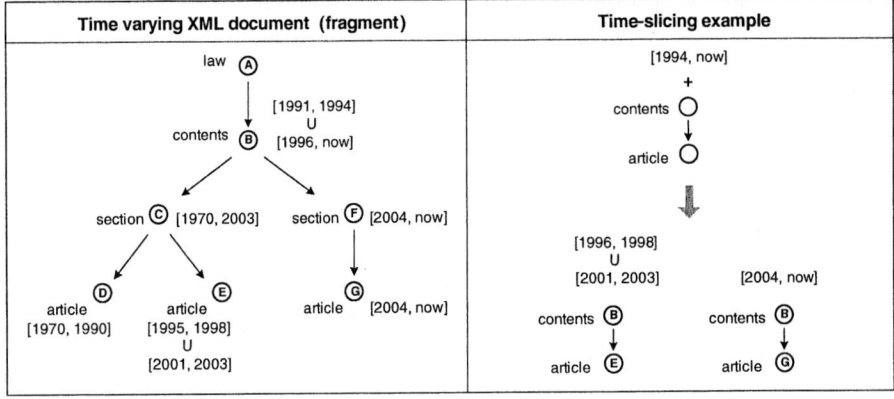

**Fig. 1.** Reference example

nodes are identified by capital letters. For simplicity's sake, timestamps are defined on a single time dimension and the granularity is the year. Temporal slicing is essentially the snapshot of the time-varying XML document(s) at a given time point but, in its broader meaning, it consists in computing simultaneously the portion of each state of time-varying XML document(s) which is contained in a given period and which matches with a given XML query twig pattern. Moreover, it is often required to combine the results back into a period-stamped representation [9] in the period [1994, $now$] and for the query twig contents//article. The right part of Fig. 1 shows the output of a temporal slicing example. This section introduces a notation for time-varying XML documents and a formal definition for the temporal slicing problem.

## 2.1 Document Representation

A temporal XML model is required when there is the need of managing temporal information in XML documents and the adopted solution usually depends on the peculiarities of the application one wants to support. For the sake of generality, our proposal is not bound to a specific temporal XML model. On the contrary, it is able to deal with time-varying XML documents containing timestamps defined on an arbitrary number of temporal dimensions and represented as temporal elements [8], i.e. disjoint union of periods, as well as single periods.

In the following, we will refer to time-varying XML documents by adopting part of the notation introduced in [5]. A *time-varying XML database* is a collection of XML documents, also containing time-varying documents. We denote with $D^T$ a *time-varying XML document* represented as an ordered labelled tree containing timestamped elements and attributes (in the following denoted as nodes) related by some structural relationships (ancestor-descendant, parent-child, preceding-following). The timestamp is a temporal element chosen from one or more temporal dimensions and records the lifetime of a node. Not all nodes are necessarily timestamped. We will use the notation $n^T$ to signify that node $n$ has been timestamped and $lifetime(n^T)$ to denote its lifetime. Sometimes it can be necessary to extend the lifetime of a node $n^{[T]}$, which can be either temporal or snapshot, to a temporal dimension not specified in its timestamp. In this case, we follow the semantics given in [6]: If no temporal semantics is provided, for each newly added temporal dimension we set the value on this dimension to the whole time-line, i.e. $[t_0, t_\infty)$.

The *snapshot* operator is an auxiliary operation which extracts a complete snapshot or *state* of a time-varying document at a given instant and which is particularly useful in our context. Timestamps are not represented in the snapshot. A snapshot at time $t$ replaces each timestamped node $n^T$ with its non-timestamped copy $x$ if $t$ is in $lifetime(n^T)$ or with the empty string, otherwise. The snapshot operator is defined as $snp(t, D^T) = D$ where $D$ is the snapshot at time $t$ of $D^T$.

## 2.2 The Time-Slice Operator

The time-slice operator is applied to a time-varying XML database and is defined as time-slice(twig,t-window). The twig parameter is a non-temporal node-labeled twig pattern which is defined on the snapshot schema [5] of the database through any XML query languages, e.g. XQuery, by specifying a pattern of selection predicates on multiple elements having some specified tree structured relationships. It defines the portion of interest in each state of the documents contained in the database. It can also be the whole document. The t-window parameter is the temporal window on which the time-slice operator has to be applied. More precisely, by default temporal slicing is applied to the whole time-lines, that is by using every single time point contained in the time-varying documents. With t-window, it is possible to restrict the set of time points by specifying a collection of periods chosen from one or more temporal dimensions.

Given a twig pattern twig, a temporal window t-window and a time-varying XML database $TXMLdb$, a *slice* is a mapping from nodes in twig to nodes in $TXMLdb$, such that: (i) query node predicates are satisfied by the corresponding document nodes thus determining the tuple $(n_1^{[T]}, \ldots, n_k^{[T]})$ of the database nodes that identify a distinct match of twig in $TXMLdb$, (ii) $(n_1^{[T]}, \ldots, n_k^{[T]})$ is *structurally consistent*, i.e. the parent-child and ancestor-descendant relationships between query nodes are satisfied by the corresponding document nodes, (iii) $(n_1^{[T]}, \ldots, n_k^{[T]})$ is *temporally consistent*, i.e. its lifetime $lifetime(n_1^{[T]}, \ldots, n_k^{[T]}) = lifetime(n_1^{[T]}) \cap \ldots \cap lifetime(n_k^{[T]})$ is not empty and it is contained in the temporal window, $lifetime(n_1^{[T]}, \ldots, n_k^{[T]}) \subseteq$ t-window. For instance, in the reference example, the tuple (B,D) is structurally but not temporally consistent as $lifetime(B) \cap lifetime(D) = \emptyset$. In this paper, we consider the temporal slicing problem:

> Given a twig pattern twig, a temporal window t-window and a time-varying XML database $TXMLdb$, for each distinct slice $(n_1^{[T]}, \ldots, n_k^{[T]})$, time-slice(twig,t-window) computes the snapshot $snp(t, (n_1^{[T]}, \ldots, n_k^{[T]}))$, where $t \in lifespan(n_1^{[T]}, \ldots, n_k^{[T]})$.

Obviously, it is possible to provide a period-timestamped representation of the results by associating each distinct state $snp(t, (n_1^{[T]}, \ldots, n_k^{[T]}))$ with its pertinence $lifetime(n_1^{[T]}, \ldots, n_k^{[T]})$ in t-window.

## 3 Providing a Native Support for Temporal Slicing

In this paper we propose a native solution to the temporal slicing problem. To this end, we addressed two problems: The indexing of time-varying XML databases and the definition of a technology for XML query processing relying on the above indexing scheme and efficiently implementing the time-slice operator.

Existing work on "conventional" XML query processing (see, for example, [14]) shows that capturing the XML document structure using traditional indices is a good solution, on which it is possible to devise efficient structural or containment join algorithms for twig pattern matching. Being timestamps distributed throughout the structure of XML documents, we decided to start from one of the most popular approaches for XML query processing whose efficiency in solving structural constraints is proved. In particular, our solution for temporal slicing support consists in an extension to the indexing scheme described in [14] such that time-varying XML databases can be implemented and in alternative changes to the holistic twig join technology [2] in order to efficiently support the time-slice operator in different scenarios.

### 3.1 The Temporal Indexing Scheme

The indexing scheme described in [14] is an extension of the classic inverted index data structure in information retrieval which maps elements and strings to inverted lists. The position of a string occurrence in the XML database is represented in each inverted list as a tuple (DocId, LeftPos,LevelNum) and, analogously, the position of an element occurrence as a tuple (DocId, LeftPos:RightPos,LevelNum) where (a) DocId is the identifier of the document, (b) LeftPos and RightPos can be generated by counting word numbers from the beginning of the document DocId until the start and end of the element, respectively, and (c) LevelNum is the depth of the node in the document. In this context, structural relationships between tree nodes can be easily determined: (i) *ancestor-descendant*: A tree node $n_2$ encoded as $(D_2, L_2 : R_2, N_2)$ is a descendent of the tree node $n_1$ encoded as $(D_1, L_1 : R_1, N_1)$ iff $D_1 = D_2$, $L_1 < L_2$, and $R_2 < R_1$; (ii) *parent-child*: $n_2$ is a child of $n_1$ iff it is a descendant of $n_1$ and $L_2 = L_1 + 1$.

As temporal XML documents are XML documents containing time-varying data, they can be indexed using the interval-based scheme described above and thus by indexing timestamps as "standard" tuples. On the other hand, timestamped nodes have a specific semantics which should be exploited when documents are accessed and, in particular, when the time-slice operation is applied. Our proposal adds time to the interval-based indexing scheme by substituting the

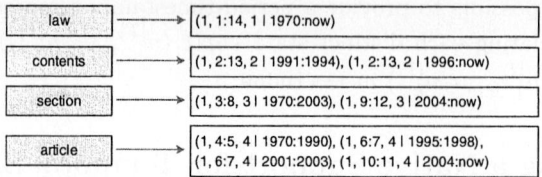

**Fig. 2.** The temporal inverted indices for the reference example

inverted indices in [14] with *temporal inverted indices*. In each temporal inverted index, besides the position of an element occurrence in the time-varying XML database, the tuple (DocId, LeftPos:RightPos,LevelNum|TempPer) contains an implicit temporal attribute [8], TempPer. It consists of a sequence of From:To temporal attributes, one for each involved temporal dimension, and represents a period. Thus, our temporal inverted indices are in 1NF and each timestamped node $n^T$, whose lifetime is a temporal element containing a number of periods, is encoded through as many tuples having the same projection on the non-temporal attributes (DocId, LeftPos:RightPos,LevelNum) but with different TempPer values, each representing a period. All the temporal inverted indices are defined on the same temporal dimensions such that tuples coming from different inverted indices are always comparable from a temporal point of view. Therefore, given the number $h$ of the different temporal dimensions represented in the time-varying XML database, TempPer is $From_1:To_1,\ldots,From_h:To_h$.

In this context, each time-varying XML document to be inserted in the database undergoes a pre-processing phase where (i) the lifetime of each node is derived from the timestamps associated with it, (ii) in case, the resulting lifetime is extended to the temporal dimensions on which it has not been defined by following the approach described in Subsec. 2.1. Fig. 2 illustrates the structure of the four indices for the reference example. Notice that the snapshot node A, whose label is law, is extended to the temporal dimension by setting the pertinence of the corresponding tuple to $[1970, now]$.

### 3.2 A Technology for the Time-Slice Operator

The basic four level architecture of the holistic twig join approach is depicted in Fig. 3. The approach maintains in main-memory a chain of linked stacks to compactly represent partial results to root-to-leaf query paths, which are then composed to obtain matches for the twig pattern (level SOL in Figure). In particular, given a path involving the nodes $q_1,\ldots,q_n$, the two stack-based algorithms presented in [2], one for path matching and the other for twig matching, work on the inverted indices $I_{q_1},\ldots,I_{q_n}$ (level L0 in Figure) and build solutions from the stacks $S_{q_1},\ldots,S_{q_n}$ (level L2 in Figure). During the computation, thanks to a deletion policy the set of stacks contains data nodes which are guaranteed to lie on a root-to-leaf path in the XML database and thus represents in linear space a compact encoding of partial and total answers to the query twig pattern. The skeleton of the two holistic twig join algorithms (HTJ algorithms in

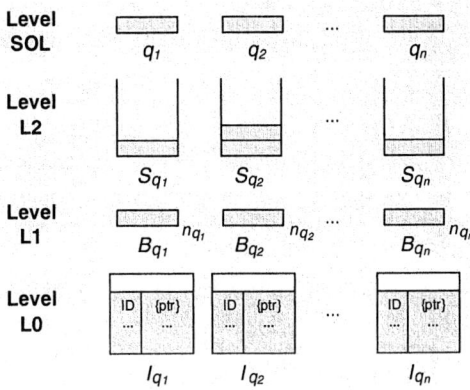

**Fig. 3.** The basic holistic twig join four level architecture

```
While there are nodes to be processed
(1) Choose the next node n_q̄
(2) Apply the deletion policy
(3) Push the node n_q̄ into the pertinence stack S_q̄
(4) Output solutions
```

**Fig. 4.** Skeleton of the holistic twig join algorithms (HTJ algorithms)

the following) is presented in Fig. 4. At each iteration the algorithms identify the next node to be processed. To this end, for each query node $q$, at level L1 is the node in the inverted index $I_q$ with the smaller LeftPos value and not yet processed. Among those, the algorithms choose the node with the smaller value, let it be $n_{\bar{q}}$. Then, given knowledge of such node, they remove partial answers form the stacks that cannot be extended to total answers and push the node $n_{\bar{q}}$ into the stack $S_{\bar{q}}$. Whenever a node associated with a leaf node of the query path is pushed on a stack, the set of stacks contains an encoding of total answers and the algorithms output these answers. The algorithms presented in [2] have been further improved in [3,11]. As our solutions do not modify the core of such algorithms, we refer interested readers to the above cited papers.

The time-slice operator can be implemented by applying minimal changes to the holistic twig join architecture. The time-varying XML database is recorded in the temporal inverted indices which substitute the "conventional" inverted index at the lower level of the architecture and thus the nodes in the stacks will be represented both by the position and the temporal attributes. Given a twig pattern twig, a temporal window t-window, a slice is the snapshot of any answer to twig which is temporally consistent. Thus the holistic twig join algorithms continue to work as they are responsible for the structural consistency of the slices and provide the best management of the stacks from this point of view. Temporal consistency, instead, must be checked on each answer output of the overall process. In particular, for each potential slice $((D, L_1 : R_1, N_1|T_1), \ldots, (D, L_k : R_k, N_k|T_k))$ it is necessary to intersect the periods represented by the values $T_1, \ldots, T_k$ and then check both that such intersection is not empty and that it is contained in the temporal window. Finally, the snapshot operation is simply a projection of the temporally consistent answers on the non-temporal attributes. In this way, we have described the "first step" towards the realization of a temporal XML query processor. On the other hand, the performances of this first solution are strictly related to the peculiarities of the underlying database. Indeed, XML documents usually contain millions of nodes and this is absolutely true in the temporal context where documents record the history of the applied changes. Thus, the holistic twig join algorithms can produce a lot of answers which are structurally consistent but which are eventually discarded as they are not temporally consistent. This situation implies useless computations due to an uncontrolled growth of the the number of tuples put on the stacks.

Temporal consistency considers two aspects: The intersection of the involved lifetimes must be non-empty (*non-empty intersection constraint* in the following) and it must be contained in the temporal window (*containment constraint* in the following). We devised alternative solutions which rely on the two different aspects of temporal consistency and act at the different levels of the architecture with the aim of limiting the number of temporally useless nodes the algorithms put in the stacks. The reference architecture is slightly different from the one presented in Fig. 3. Indeed, in our context, any timestamped node whose lifetime is a temporal element is encoded into more tuples (e.g. see the encoding of the timestamped node E in the reference example). Thus, at level L1, each node $n_q$ must be interpreted as the set of tuples encoding $n_q$. They are stored in buffer $B_q$ and step 3 of the HTJ algorithms empties $B_q$ and pushes the tuples in the stack $S_q$.

### 3.3 Non-empty Intersection Constraint

Not all temporal tuples which enter level L1 will at the end belong to the set of slices. In particular, some of them will be discarded due to the non-empty intersection constraint. The following Lemma characterizes this aspect. Without lose of generality, it only considers paths as the twig matching algorithm relies on the path matching one.

**Proposition 1.** *Let $(D, L : R, N|T)$ be a tuple belonging to the temporal inverted index $I_q$, $I_{q_1}, \ldots, I_{q_k}$ the inverted indices of the ancestors of $q$ and $TP_{q_i} = \bigcup \sigma_{LeftPos<L}(I_{q_i})|_{TempPer}$, for $i \in [1, k]$, the union of the temporal pertinences of all the tuples in $I_{q_i}$ having LeftPos smaller than $L$. Then $(D, L : R, N|T)$ will belong to no slice if the intersection of its temporal pertinence with $TP_{q_1}, \ldots, TP_{q_k}$ is empty, i.e. $T \cap TP_{q_1} \cap \ldots \cap TP_{q_k} = \emptyset$.*

```
Input: Twig pattern twig, the last processed node n←q̄
Output: Next node nq̄ to be processed
Algorithm Load:

(1) if all buffers are empty
(2)    start=root(twig);
(3) else
(4)    start=‾q̄;
(5) for each query node q from start to leaf(twig)
(6)    get n_q;
(7)    min_q is the minimum between n_q.LeftPos and min_{parent(q)};
(8)    if n_q.LeftPos is equal to min_q
(9)       load n_q into B_q;
(10)return the last node inserted into the buffers
```

Fig. 5. The buffer loading algorithm Load

Notice that, at each step of the process, the tuples having LeftPos smaller than $L$ can be in the stacks, in the buffers or still have to be read from the inverted indices. However, looking for such tuples in the three levels of the architecture would be quite computationally expensive. Thus, in the following we introduce a new approach for buffer loading which allows us to look only at the stack level. Moreover, we avoid accessing the temporal pertinence of the tuples contained in the stacks by associating a temporal pertinence to each stack (*temporal stack*). Such a temporal pertinence must therefore be updated at each push and pop operation. At each step of the process, for efficiency purposes both in the update and in the intersection phase, such a temporal pertinence is the smaller multidimensional period $P_q$ containing the union of the temporal pertinence of the tuples in the stack $S_q$.

The aim of our buffer loading approach is to avoid loading the temporal tuples encoding a node $n^{[T]}$ in the pertinence buffer $B_q$ if the inverted indices associated with the parents of $q$ contain tuples with LeftPos smaller than that of $n_q$ and not yet processed. Such an approach is consistent with step 1 of the HTJ algorithms as it chooses the node at level L1 with the smaller LeftPos value and ensures that when $n^{[T]}$ enters $B_q$ all the tuples involved in Prop. 1 are in the stacks. The algorithm implementing step 1 of the HTJ algorithms is shown in Fig. 5. We associate each buffer $B_q$ with the minimum $min_q$ among the LeftPos values of the tuples contained in the buffer itself and those of its ancestors. Assuming that all buffers are empty, the algorithm starts from the root of the twig (step 2) and, for each node $q$ up to the leaf, it updates the minimum $min_q$ and inserts $n_q$, the node in $I_q$ with the smaller LeftPos value and not yet processed, if it is smaller than $min_q$. The same applies when some buffers are not empty. In this case, it starts from the query node matching with the previously processed data node and it can be easily shown that the buffers of the ancestors of such node are not empty whereas the buffers of the subpath rooted by such node are all empty.

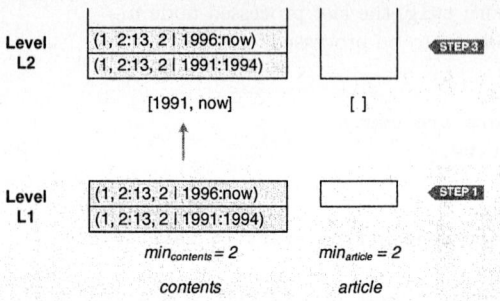

**Fig. 6.** State of levels L1 and L2 during the first iteration

**Lemma 1.** *Assume that step 1 of the HTJ algorithms depicted in Fig. 4 is implemented by the algorithm* Load. *The tuple* $(D, L : R, N|T)$ *in* $B_q$ *will belong to no slice if the intersection of its temporal pertinence $T$ with the multidimensional period* $P_{q_1 \to q_k} = P_{q_1} \cap \ldots \cap P_{q_k}$ *intersecting the periods of the stacks of the ancestors* $q_1, \ldots, q_k$ *of $q$ is empty.*

For instance, at the first iteration of the HTJ algorithms applied to the reference example, step 1 and step 3 produce the situation depicted in Fig. 6. Notice that when the tuple $(1, 4 : 5, 4|1970 : 1990)$ encoding node D (label article) enters level L1 all the tuples with LeftPos smaller than 4 are already at level L2 and due to the above Lemma we can state that it will belong to no slice.

Thus, the non-empty intersection constraint can be exploited to prevent the insertion of useless nodes into the stacks by acting at level L1 and L2 of the architecture. At level L2 we act at step 3 of the HTJ algorithms by simply avoiding pushing into the stack $S_q$ each temporal tuple $(D, L : R, N|T)$ encoding the next node to be processed which satisfies Lemma 1, i.e. such that $T \cap P_{q_1 \to q_k} = \emptyset$. At level L1, instead, we act at step 9 of the algorithm Load by avoiding loading in any buffer $B_q$ each temporal tuple encoding $n_q$ which satisfies Lemma 1. More precisely, given the LeftPos value of the last processed node, say $CurLeftPos$, we only load each tuple $(D, L : R, N|T)$ such that $L$ is the minimum value greater than $CurLeftPos$ and $T$ intersects $P_{q_1 \to q_k}$. To this purpose, our solution uses time-key indices combining the LeftPos attribute with the attributes $From_j : To_j$ in the TempPer implicit attribute representing one temporal dimension in order to improve the performances of range-interval selection queries on the temporal inverted indices. In particular, we considered two access methods: The B+-tree and a temporal index, the Multiversion B-tree (MVBT) [1].

An one-dimensional index like the B+-tree, clusters data primarily on a single attribute. Thus, we built B+-trees that cluster first on the LeftPos attribute and than on the interval end time $To_j$. In this way, we can take advantage of sequential I/O as tree leaf pages are linked and records in them are ordered. In particular, we start with the first leaf page that contains a LeftPos value greater than $CurLeftPos$ and a $To_j$ value greater than or equal to $P_{q_1 \to q_k}|From_j$, i.e.

the projection of the period $P_{q_1 \to q_k}$ on the interval start time $\texttt{From}_j$. Then we proceed by loading the records until the leaf page with the next LeftPos value or with a $\texttt{From}_j$ value greater than $P_{q_1 \to q_k}|_{\texttt{To}_j}$ is met. This has the effect of selecting each tuple $(D, L : R, N|T)$ where $L$ is the smaller value greater than $CurLeftPos$ and its period $T|_{\texttt{From}_j:\texttt{To}_j}$ intersect the period $P_{q_1 \to q_k}|_{\texttt{From}_j:\texttt{To}_j}$, as $T|_{\texttt{To}_j} \geq P_{q_1 \to q_k}|_{\texttt{From}_j}$ and $T|_{\texttt{From}_j} \leq P_{q_1 \to q_k}|_{\texttt{To}_j}$.

The alternative approach we considered is to maintain multiple versions of a standard B+-tree through an MVBT. An MVBT index record contains a key, a time interval and a pointer to a page and, thus, this structure is able to directly support our range-interval selection requirements.

### 3.4 Containment Constraint

The following proposition is the equivalent of Prop. 1 when the containment constraint is considered.

**Proposition 2.** *Let $(D, L : R, N|T)$ be a tuple belonging to the temporal inverted index $I_q$. Then $(D, L : R, N|T)$ will belong to no slice if the intersection of its temporal pertinence with the temporal window* t-window *is empty.*

It allows us to act at level L1 and L2, but also between level L0 and level L1. At level L1 and L2 the approach is the same as the non-empty intersection constraint; it is sufficient to use the temporal window t-window, and thus Prop. 2, instead of Lemma 1. Moreover, it is also possible to add an intermediate level between level L0 and level L1 of the architecture, which we call "under L1" (UL1), where the only tuples satisfying Prop. 2 are selected from each temporal inverted index, are ordered on the basis of their (DocId,LeftPos) values and then pushed into the buffers. Similarly to the approach explained in the previous section, to speed up the selection, we exploit $B^+$-tree indices built on one temporal dimension. Notice that this solution deals with buffers as streams of tuples and thus it provides interesting efficiency improvements only when the temporal window is quite selective.

### 3.5 Combining Solutions

The non-empty intersection constraint and the containment constraint are orthogonal thus, in principle, the solutions presented in the above subsections can be freely combined in order to decrease the number of useless tuples we put in the stacks. Each combination gives rise to a different scenario denoted as "X/Y", where "X" and "Y" are the employed solutions for the non-empty intersection constraint and for the containment constraint, respectively (e.g. scenario L1/L2 employs solution L1 for the non-empty intersection constraint and solution L2 for the containment constraint). Some of these scenarios will be discussed in the following. First, scenario L1/UL1 is not applicable since in solution UL1 selected data is kept and read directly from buffers, with no chance of additional indexing. Instead, in scenario L1/L1 the management of the two constraints can be easily combined by querying the indices with the intersection of the temporal pertinence of the ancestors (Proposition 1) and the required temporal window. All other combinations are straightforwardly achievable, but not necessarily advisable. In particular, when L1 is involved for any of the two constraints the L1 indices have to be built and queried: Therefore, it is best to combine the management of the two constraints as in L1/L1 discussed above. Finally, notice that the baseline scenario is the SOL/SOL one, involving none of the solutions discussed in this paper.

## 4 Experimental Evaluation

In this section we present the results of an actual implementation of our XML query processor supporting temporal slicing showing its behavior on different document collections and in different execution scenarios.

### 4.1 Experimental Setting

The document collections follow the structure of the documents used in [10], where three temporal dimensions are involved, and have been generated by a configurable XML generator. On average, each document contains 30-40 nodes, a depth level of 10, 10-15 of these nodes are timestamped nodes $n^T$, each one in 2-3 versions composed by the union of 1-2 distinct periods. We are also able to change the length of the periods and the probability that the temporal pertinence of the document nodes overlap. Finally, we investigate different kinds of probability density functions generating collections with different distributions, thus directly affecting the containment constraint.

Experiments were conducted on a reference collection (C-R), consisting of 5000 documents (120 MB) generated following a uniform distribution and characterized by not much scattered nodes, and on several variations of it. We tested the performance of the time-slice operator with different twig and t-window parameters. Due to the lack of space, in this article we will deepen the performance analysis by considering the same path, involving three nodes, and different temporal windows as our focus is not on the structural aspects.

The experiments have been performed on a Pentium 4 3Ghz Windows XP Professional workstation, equipped with 1GB RAM and an 160GB EIDE HD with NT file system (NTFS).

### 4.2 Efficiency Evaluation

We evaluated the performances of the time-slice operator in terms of execution time and number of tuples that are put in the buffers and in the stacks for each feasible computation scenario.

**Evaluation of the default setting.** We started by testing the time-slice operator with a default setting (denoted as TS1 in the following). Its temporal window has a selectivity of 20%, i.e. 20% of the tuples stored in the temporal inverted indexes involved by the twig pattern intersect the temporal window. The

**Table 1.** Evaluation of the computation scenarios with TS1

| Evaluation scenarios: | Execution Time (ms) | Non-Consistent Solutions (%) | Tuples (%) Buffer | Stack |
|---|---|---|---|---|
| L1/L1 | 1890 | 23.10 % | 7.99 % | 7.76 % |
| L2/L1 | 1953 | 23.10 % | 9.23 % | 7.76 % |
| SOL/L1 | 2000 | 39.13 % | 9.43 % | 9.17 % |
| L1/L2 | 2625 | 23.10 % | 17.95 % | 7.76 % |
| L2/L2 | 2797 | 23.10 % | 23.37 % | 7.76 % |
| SOL/L2 | 2835 | 39.13 % | 23.80 % | 9.17 % |
| L1/SOL | 12125 | 95.74 % | 88.92 % | 88.85 % |
| L2/SOL | 12334 | 95.74 % | 99.33 % | 88.85 % |
| SOL/SOL | 12688 | 96.51 % | 100.00 % | 100.00 % |

returned solutions are 5584. Table 1 shows the performance of each scenario when executing TS1. In particular, from the left: The execution time, the percentage of potential solutions at level SOL that are not temporally consistent and, in the last two columns, the percentage of tuples that are put in the buffers and in the stacks w.r.t. the total number of tuples involved in the evaluation. Notice that, the temporal inverted indices exploited at level L1 are B+-trees; the comparison of the performances between the $B^+$-tree and MVBT implementations will be shown in the following.

The best result is given by the computation scenario L1/L1: Its execution time is more than 6 times faster than the execution time of the baseline scenario SOL/SOL. Such a result clearly shows that combining solutions at a low level of the architecture, such as L1, avoids I/O costs for reading unnecessary tuples and their further elaboration cost at the upper levels. The decrease of read tuples from 100% of SOL/SOL to just 7.99% of L1/L1 and the decrease of temporally inconsistent solutions from 96.51% of SOL/SOL to 23.1% of L1/L1 represent a remarkable result in terms of efficiency. Let us now have a look to the other

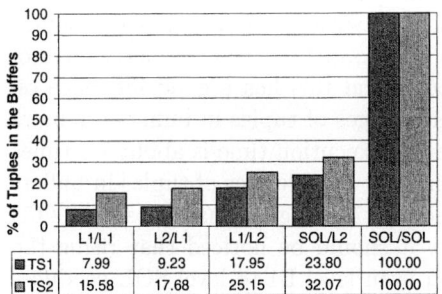
(a) Percentage of tuples in the buffers

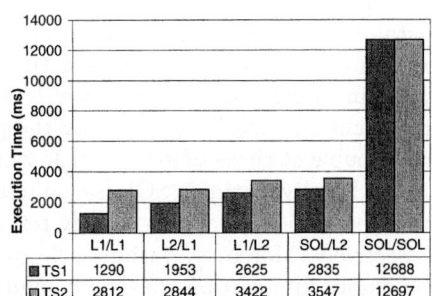
(b) Execution Time (ms)

**Fig. 7.** Comparison between TS1 and TS2

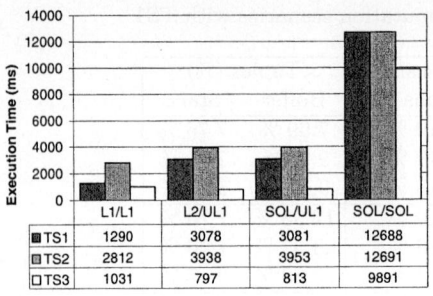
(a) UL1 scenarios performances

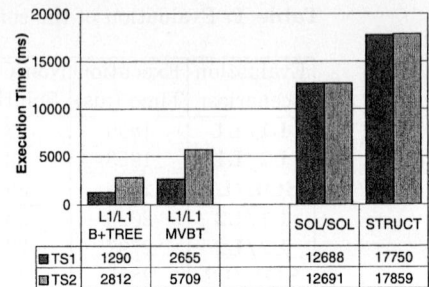
(b) MVBT and structural approach performances

**Fig. 8.** Additional execution time comparisons

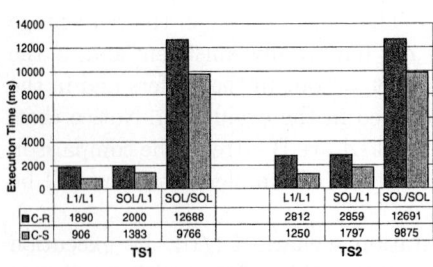
(a) Execution time

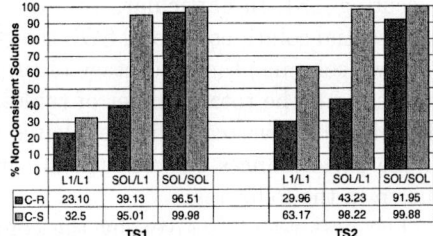
(b) Percentage of Non-Consistent Solutions

**Fig. 9.** Comparison between the two collections C-R and C-S

scenarios. TS1 represents a typical querying setting where the containment constraint is much more selective than the non-empty intersection constraint. This consideration induces us to analyse the obtained performances by partitioning the scenarios in three groups, */L1, */L2 and */SOL, on the basis of the adopted containment constraint solution. The scenarios within each group show similar execution time and percentages of tuples. In group */L1 the low percentage of tuples in buffers (10%) means low I/O costs and this has a good influence on the execution time. In group */L2 the percentages of tuples in buffers are more than double of those of group */L1, while the execution time is about 1.5 times higher. Finally, group */SOL is characterized by percentages of tuples in buffers and execution time approximately ten and six time higher than those in */T1, respectively. Moreover, within each group it should be noticed that rising the non-empty intersection constraint solution from level L1 to level SOL produces more and more deterioration in the overall performances.

**Changing the selectivity of the temporal window.** We are now interested in showing how our XML query processor responds to the execution of temporal slicing with different selectivity levels; to this purpose we considered a second time-slice (TS2) having a selectivity of 31% (lower than TS1) and returning 12873 solutions. Figure 7 shows the percentage of read tuples (Figure 7-a) and the execution time (Figure 7-b) of TS1 compared with our reference time-slice setting (TS1). Notice that the trend of growth of the percentage of read tuples along the different scenarios is similar. However, for TS1 the execution time follows the same trend as the read tuples whereas for TS2 the execution time of different scenarios are closer. In this case, the lower selectivity of the temporal window makes the benefits achievable by the L1 solutions less appreciable. Notice that, in the SOL/SOL scenario both queries have the same number of tuples in the buffers because no selectivity is applied at the lower levels; this explains also the same execution time.

**Evaluation of the performance of solution UL1.** In order to evaluate the results of exploiting access methods at level UL1 we considered a third time-slice (TS3) that is characterized by a highly selective temporal window (1%) and returns 123 solutions. Figure 8-a compares the execution time of the scenarios involving UL1 solutions (*/UL1) with the best and the baseline scenarios shown above (L1/L1 and SOL/SOL). As one would expect, it shows that */UL1 scenarios are inefficient for low-selectivity settings, while they are the best ones with high-selectivity setting. In particular the best computation scenario for TS3 is L2/UL1.

**Comparison with MVBT and purely structural techniques.** In Figure 8-b we compare the execution time for scenario L1/L1 when the access method is the B+-tree w.r.t. the MVBT. Notice that when MVBT indices are used to access data the execution time is generally higher than the B+-tree solution. This might be due to the implementation we used which is a beta-version included in the XXL package [7]. The last comparison involves the holistic twig join algorithms applied on the original indexing scheme proposed in [14] where temporal attributes are added to the index structure but are considered as common attributes. Notice that in this indexing scheme tuples must have different `LeftPos` and `RightPos` values and thus each temporal XML document must be converted into an XML document where each timestamped node gives rise to a number of distinct nodes equal to the number of distinct periods. The results are shown on the right of Figure 8-b where it is clear that the execution time of the purely structural approach (STRUCT) is generally higher than our baseline scenario and thus also than the other scenarios (13 times slower than the best scenario). This demonstrates that the introduction of our temporal indexing scheme alone brings significant benefits on temporal slicing performance. We refer the interested reader also to Section 5 where we provide additional discussion of state of the art techniques w.r.t. ours.

**Evaluation on differently distributed collections.** We also considered the performance of our XML query processor on another collection (C-S) of the same size of the reference one, but that is characterized by temporally scattered nodes. Figure 9 shows the execution time and the number of temporally inconsistent potential solutions of TS1 and TS2 on both collections. The execution time of scenarios L1/L1 and SOL/L1, depicted in Figure 9-a, shows that it is

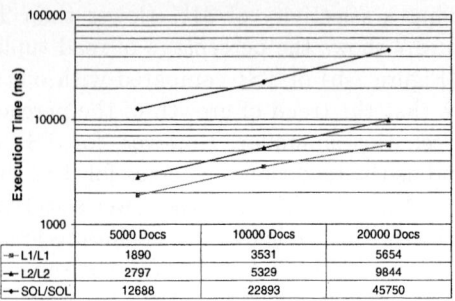

**Fig. 10.** Scalability results for TS1

almost unchanged for collection C-R, whereas the difference is more remarkable for both temporal slicing settings for collection C-S. Notice also that the percentage of temporally inconsistent potential solutions when no solution is applied under level SOL is limited in the C-R case but explodes in the C-S case (see for instance SOL/L1 in Fig. 9-b). The non-empty intersection constraint is mainly influenced by the temporal sparsity of the nodes in the collection: The more the nodes are temporally scattered the more the number of temporally inconsistent potential solutions increases. Therefore, when temporal slicing is applied to this kind of collections the best way to process it is to adopt a solution exploiting the non-empty intersection constraint at the lowest level, i.e. L1.

**Scalability.** Figure 10 (notice the logarithmic scales) reports the performance of our XML query processor in executing TS1 for the reference collection C-R and for two collections having the same characteristics but different sizes: 10000 and 20000 documents. The execution time grew linearly in every scenario, with a proportion of approximately 0.75 w.r.t. the number of documents for our best scenario L1/L1. Such tests have also been performed on the other temporal slicing settings where we measured a similar trend, thus showing the good scalability of the processor in every type of query context.

## 5 Discussion and Concluding Remarks

In the last years, there has been a growing interest in representing and querying the temporal aspect of XML data. Recent papers on this topic include those of Currim et al. [5], Gao and Snodgrass [9], Mendelzon et al. [12], and Grandi et al. [10] where the history of changes XML data undergo is represented into a single document from which versions can be extracted when needed. In [5], the authors study the problem of consistently deriving a scheme for managing the temporal counterpart of non-temporal XML documents, starting from the definition of their schema. The paper [9] presents a temporal XML query language, $\tau$XQuery, with which the authors add temporal support to XQuery by extending its syntax and semantics to three kinds of temporal queries: Current, sequenced, and representational. Similarly, the TXPath query language described in [12] extends XPath for supporting temporal queries. Finally, the main objective of the work presented in [10] has been the development of a computer system for the temporal management of multiversion norms represented as XML documents and made available on the Web.

Closer to our definition of `time-slice` operator, Gao and Snodgrass [9] need to time-slice documents in a given period and to evaluate a query in each time slice of the documents. The authors suggest an implementation based on a stratum approach to exploit the availability of XQuery implementations. Even if they propose different optimizations of the initial time-slicing approach, this solution results in long XQuery programs also for simple temporal queries and postprocessing phases in order to coalesce the query results. Moreover, an XQuery engine is not aware of the temporal semantics and thus it makes more difficult to apply query optimization and indexing techniques particularly suited for temporal XML documents. Native solutions are, instead, proposed in [4, 12]. The paper [4] introduces techniques for storing and querying multiversion XML documents. Each time one or more updates occur on a multiversion XML document, the proposed versioning scheme creates a new physical version of the document where it stores the differences w.r.t. the previous version. This leads to large overheads when "conventional" queries involving structural constraints and spanning over multiple versions are submitted to the system. In [12] the authors propose an approach for evaluating TXPath queries which integrates the temporal dimension into a path indexing scheme by taking into account the available continuous paths from the root to the elements, i.e. paths that are valid continuously during a certain time interval. While twig querying is not directly handled in this approach, path query performance is enhanced w.r.t. standard path indexing, even though the main memory representation of their indices is more than 10 times the size of the original documents. Moreover, query processing can still be quite heavy for large documents, as it requires the full navigation of the document collection structure, in order to access the required element tables, and the execution of a binary join between them at each level of the query path.

Similarly to the structural join approach [14] proposed for XML query pattern matching, the temporal slicing problem can be naturally decomposed into a set of temporal-structural constraints. For instance solving `time-slice(//contents// section//article,[1994,now])` means to find all occurrences in a temporal XML database of the basic ancestor-descendant relationships (`contents,section`) and (`section,article`) which are temporally consistent. In the literature, a great deal of work has been devoted to the processing of temporal join (see e.g. [13]) also using indices [15]. Given the temporal indexing scheme proposed in this paper, we could have extended temporal join algorithms to the structural join problem or vice versa. However the main drawback of the structural join approach is that the sizes of the results of binary structural joins can get very large, even when the input and the final result sizes obtained by stitching together the basic matches are much more manageable.

The native approach proposed in this paper extends one of the most efficient approaches for XML query processing and the underlying indexing scheme in order to support temporal slicing and overcome most of the previously discussed problems. Starting from the holistic twig join approach [2], which directly avoids the problem of very large intermediate results size by using a chain of linked stacks to compactly represent partial results, we proposed new flexible technologies consisting in alternative solutions and extensively experimented them in different settings. The resulting good efficiency is quite encouraging and induces us to continue in this direction.

# References

1. B. Becker, S. Gschwind, T. Ohler, B. Seeger, and P. Widmayer. An asymptotically optimal multiversion b-tree. *VLDB J.*, 5(4), 1996.
2. N. Bruno, N. Koudas, and D. Srivastava. Holistic twig joins: optimal XML pattern matching. In *Proc. of the ACM SIGMOD*, pages 310–321, 2002.
3. T. Chen, J. Lu, and T. Wang Ling. On boosting holism in xml twig pattern matching using structural indexing techniques. In *Proc. of the ACM SIGMOD*, 2005.
4. S. Chien, V. J. Tsotras, and C. Zaniolo. Efficient schemes for managing multiversionxml documents. *VLDB J.*, 11(4), 2002.
5. F. Currim, S. Currim, C. Dyreson, and R. T. Snodgrass. A Tale of Two Schemas: Creating a Temporal Schema from a Snapshot Schema with $\tau$XSchema. In *Proc. of EDBT*, pages 348–365, Heraklion, Greece, 2004.
6. C. De Castro, F. Grandi, and M. R. Scalas. Semantic interoperability of multitemporal relational databases. In *Proc. of ER*, 1993.
7. J. Van den Bercken, B. Blohsfeld, J. P. Dittrich, J. Krämer, T. Schäfer, M. Schneider, and B. Seeger. Xxl - a library approach to supporting efficient implementations of advanced database queries. In *Proc. of VLDB*, pages 39–48, 2001.
8. R. T. Snodgrass et al. *The TSQL2 Temporal Query Language*. Kluwer Academic Publishing, New York, 1995.
9. D. Gao and R. T. Snodgrass. Temporal slicing in the evaluation of xml queries. In *Proc. of VLDB*, pages 632–643, Berlin, Germany, 2003.
10. F. Grandi and F. Mandreoli. Temporal modelling and management of normative documents in xml format. *Data Knowl. Eng.*, 54(3), 2005.
11. H. Jiang, W. Wang, H. Lu, and J. Xu Yu. Holistic twig joins on indexed xml documents. In *Proc. of VLDB*, pages 273–284, 2003.
12. A. O. Mendelzon, F. Rizzolo, and A. A. Vaisman. Indexing temporal xml documents. In *Proc. of VLDB*, pages 216–227, 2004.
13. T. Bach Pedersen, C. S. Jensen, and C. E. Dyreson. Extending practical pre-aggregation in on-line analytical processing. In *Proc. of VLDB*, pages 663–674, 1999.
14. C. Zhang, J. F. Naughton, D. J. DeWitt, Q. Luo, and G. M. Lohman. On supporting containment queries in relational database management systems. In *Proc. of ACM SIGMOD*, 2001.
15. D. Zhang, V. J. Tsotras, and B. Seeger. Efficient temporal join processing using indices. In *Proc. of ICDE*, pages 103–114, 2002.

# Indexing Shared Content in Information Retrieval Systems

Andrei Z. Broder[1,*], Nadav Eiron[2], Marcus Fontoura[1], Michael Herscovici[3],
Ronny Lempel[3], John McPherson[4], Runping Qi[1], and Eugene Shekita[5]

[1] Yahoo! Inc
[2] Google Inc
[3] IBM Haifa Research Lab
[4] IBM Silicon Valley Lab
[5] IBM Almaden Research Center

**Abstract.** Modern document collections often contain groups of documents with overlapping or shared content. However, most information retrieval systems process each document separately, causing shared content to be indexed multiple times. In this paper, we describe a new document representation model where related documents are organized as a tree, allowing shared content to be indexed just once. We show how this representation model can be encoded in an inverted index and we describe algorithms for evaluating free-text queries based on this encoding. We also show how our representation model applies to web, email, and newsgroup search. Finally, we present experimental results showing that our methods can provide a significant reduction in the size of an inverted index as well as in the time to build and query it.

## 1 Introduction

Modern document collections such as e-mail, newsgroups and Web pages, can contain groups of documents with largely overlapping content. On the Web, for example, studies have shown that up to 45% of the pages are *duplicates* – pages with (nearly) identical content that are replicated in many different sites [6, 8, 22]. In e-mail collections, individual documents with significant amounts of overlapping content are naturally created as people reply to (or forward) messages while keeping the original content intact. E-mail exchanges often contain long chains or *threads* of replies to replies, causing early messages in the thread to be replicated over and over. Similar threading patterns are also common in newsgroup discussions.

Information Retrieval (IR) systems typically use an inverted text index to evaluate free-text queries. During indexing, most IR systems process each document separately, causing overlapping content to be indexed multiple times. This, in turn, leads to larger indexes that take longer to build and longer to query. In this paper, we describe a scheme where overlapping content is indexed just once

---

[*] Work done while this author was employed by IBM corporation.

and is logically *shared* among all documents that contain it. Thus, index space and index build times are greatly reduced. This does not come at the expense of any retrieval capabilities – queries can continue to be evaluated as if the full text of each document was indexed separately. Query evaluation is also faster due to the reduced index size.

Content is logically shared using a new *document representation model* where related documents are organized as nodes in a tree. Each node in a *document tree* can include content that it shares with all of its descendents as well as content and meta-data that is not shared with its descendents. The former is referred to as "shared content", while the latter is referred to as "private content". For example, in an e-mail or newsgroup thread, its document tree will mirror the history of the thread, with the root of the tree representing the first message of the thread whose text is quoted (and shared) with subsequent messages. We show how to encode our document representation model in a standard inverted index, and describe algorithms for evaluating free-text queries based on this encoding.

The basic operation of any inverted text index is the merging and intersection of *posting lists* - the lists of documents associated with each of the terms. The goal is to find the documents that contain terms appearing in a query. For efficiency, there are data structures and algorithms that allow skipping over the portions of the posting lists where no intersections might occur [5]. This operation is sometimes called a *zig-zag join* [11] and it is most useful for conjunctive queries. At its most basic, a zig-zag join of two lists proceeds by keeping two *index cursors* (also known as *posting list iterators*), one for each list. At every step, the cursor that points to a smaller document number is advanced at least as far as the other cursor. When the cursors meet, an intersection is reported, and one cursor is advanced to the next document in its list.

A key feature of our document representation model is that it can be easily encoded into an inverted index in such a way that the standard algorithms for evaluating free-text queries are still applicable. This is accomplished by defining virtual index cursors that are aware of our representation model and its encoding. In particular, the zig-zag join procedure uses virtual cursors as if they were normal physical cursors, and furthermore virtual cursors are relatively simple to implement on top of normal index cursors.

In the context of Web search, one may wonder why we opt to develop machinery for logically indexing all duplicates instead of simply retaining a single representative of any group of duplicates and discarding the rest. Some search engines (e.g., AltaVista as of 2000 [4]) adopted such a solution, which naturally also implies that they avoid returning duplicate content in their result sets. However, keeping a single representative is problematic for queries that include, in addition to some query terms, restrictions on meta-data such as URL, domain, or last-modified-date. Such meta-data is typically different for each duplicate. By sharing duplicate content and keeping the meta-data private, our representation model can support these queries, while at the same time indexing the duplicate content just once and preventing the return of multiple copies of it in the returned set of search results.

The main contributions of this paper include:

- A new document representation model where related documents are organized as a tree, allowing overlapping or shared content to be indexed just once.
- An encoding of our representation model that can easily support a standard zig-zag join for evaluating free-text queries on an inverted index.
- Descriptions of our representation model as applied to web, email, and newsgroup corpora, showing its usefulness in practical IR applications.
- Experimental results on large datasets showing that our representation model can provide a significant reduction in the size of an inverted index and in the time to build and query it.

## 2 Background

In this section we briefly review some basic IR concepts and terminology.

*Inverted Index.* Most IR systems use inverted indexes as their main data structure for full-text indexing [21]. There is a considerable body of literature on efficient ways to build inverted indexes (See e.g. [1, 3, 10, 13, 16, 21]) and evaluate full-text queries using them (See e.g. [5, 15, 21]).

In this paper, we assume an inverted index structure. The occurrence of a term $t$ within a document $d$ is called a *posting*. The set of postings associated to a term $t$ is stored in a *posting list*. A posting has the form <$docid, payload$>, where $docid$ is the document ID of $d$ and where the payload is used to store arbitrary information about each occurrence of $t$ within $d$. Here, we use part of the payload to indicate whether the occurrences of $t$ are shared with other documents and also to store the offsets of each occurrence.

Each posting list is sorted in increasing order of $docid$. Often, a B-tree [11] is used to index the posting lists [10, 16]. This facilitates searching for a particular $docid$ within a posting list, or for the smallest $docid$ in the list greater than a given $docid$. Similarly, within a posting, term occurrences are sorted by offset thus making intra-document searches efficient.

*Free-text Queries.* Most IR systems support free-text queries, allowing Boolean expressions on keywords and phrase searches. Support for mandatory and forbidden terms is also common, e.g. the query `+apple orange -pear` indicates that `apple` is mandatory, `orange` is optional, and `pear` is forbidden. Most systems also support *fielded* search terms, i.e. terms that should appear within the context of a specific field of a document, e.g. `+title:banana -author:plum`. Note that the queried fields are most often meta-data fields of the documents.

*Document at a Time Evaluation.* In this paper, we assume the document-at-a-time query evaluation model (DAAT) [20], commonly used in web search engines [3]. In DAAT, the documents that satisfy the query are usually obtained via a zig-zag join [11] of the posting lists of the query terms. To evaluate a free-text query using a zig-zag join, a *cursor* $C_t$ is created for each term $t$ in the query, and is used to access $t$'s posting list. $C_t.docid$ and $C_t.payload$ access the *docid* and *payload* of the posting on which $C_t$ is currently positioned. During a zig-zag join, the cursors are moved in a coordinated way to find the documents that satisfy the query. Two basic methods on a cursor $C_t$ are required to do this efficiently:

- $C_t.next()$ advances $C_t$ to the next posting in its posting list.
- $C_t.fwdBeyond(docid\ d)$ advances $C_t$ to the first posting in its posting list whose *docid* is greater than or equal to $d$. Since posting lists are ordered by *docid*, this operation can be done efficiently.

*Scoring.* Once a zig-zag join has positioned the cursors on a document that satisfies the query, the document is scored. The final score for a document usually contains a query-dependent textual component, which is based on the document similarity to the query, and a query-independent static component, which is based on the *static rank* of the document. In most IR systems, the textual component of the score follows an additive scoring model like $tf \times idf$ for each term, whereas the static component can be based on the connectivity of web pages, as in PageRank [3], or on other factors such as source, length, creation date, etc.

## 3 The Document Representation Model

In our document representation model each group of related documents is organized as a *document tree*; the corpus being indexed is therefore a forest of document trees.

Each node in a document tree corresponds to a document that can include shared and private content. The private content of a document $d$ is unique to $d$, whereas the shared content of $d$ is inherited by its descendants. Sharing occurs top-down. Therefore, the document at a particular node effectively contains the shared and private content of that node plus the union of all its ancestors' shared content.

Our representation model is illustrated in Figure 1. This might correspond to an email exchange starting with $d_1$. It was quoted by two independent replies $d_2$ and $d_4$. It turn, $d_2$ was quoted in full (including $d_1$) by $d_3$, while $d_4$ was quoted in full by $d_5$ and $d_6$.

In Figure 1, $d_i$ corresponds to the document whose $docid = i$, while $S_i$ and $P_i$ correspond to the shared and private content of document $d_i$, respectively. The content of $d_1$ is $S_1$ and $P_1$, while the content of $d_3$ is $S_3$ and $P_3$ plus $S_1$ and $S_2$.

We define a *thread* as the documents on a root-to-leaf path in a document tree. In Figure 1, there are three threads, $d_1$-$d_2$-$d_3$, $d_1$-$d_4$-$d_5$, and $d_1$-$d_4$-$d_6$.

Two functions on *docid* are needed for query evaluation:

- $root(docid\ d)$ returns the root of $d$'s document tree.
- $lastDescendant(docid\ d)$ returns the last descendant of the sub-tree rooted at $d$. If $d$ is a leaf, then $d$ itself is returned.

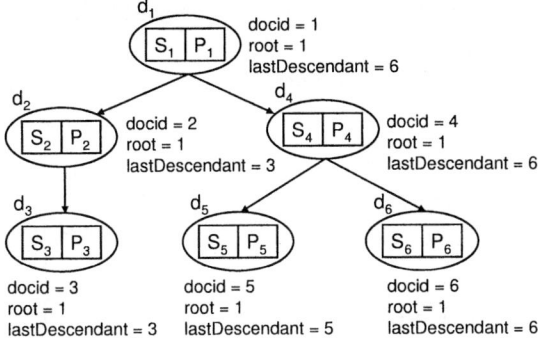

**Fig. 1.** Example of a document tree

Figure 1 shows the *root*() and *lastDescendant*() values for the documents in our example. In principle, our representation model does not impose any restriction on the assignment of *docid*'s across document trees. However, the query evaluation algorithm described is Section 5 requires the *docid*'s within a document tree to be assigned sequentially using a depth first traversal. This guarantees that all documents in the range $\{d_{i+1}, \ldots, lastDescendant(d_i)\}$ are descendants of document $d_i$, and this is the assumption we are making from now on.

The main limitation of our document representation model is that related documents can only share content in a top-down, hierarchical manner. Nonetheless, we will show that there are many applications such as web, email, and newsgroup search that can still benefit from our representation.

## 4 Index Encoding

To support our document representation model, we use a standard inverted index with a few additions. First, each posting within the inverted index needs to indicate whether it is shared or private. This can be done by adding one bit to the payload. Second, the *root*() and *lastDescendant*() functions need to be implemented, which can be done using an in-memory table or an external data structure that allows efficient access.

Figure 2 illustrates how the posting lists might look for an email thread matching $d_1$-$d_2$-$d_3$ in the previous example. In the posting lists, the letter "s" indicates a shared posting, while the letter "p" indicates a private posting. Document $d_1$ corresponds to the original message, while $d_2$ is a reply to $d_1$, and $d_3$ is a reply to $d_2$.

In Figure 2, the content in the header fields is treated as private, while the content in the body is shared. For example, the posting for "andrei" is private to $d_1$, since it appears in the "From" field, whereas the posting for "did" is shared, since it appears in the body. In the latter case, $d_1$ shares the posting for "did" with its descendants, that is, $d_2$ and $d_3$. More generally, a document $d_i$ *shares*

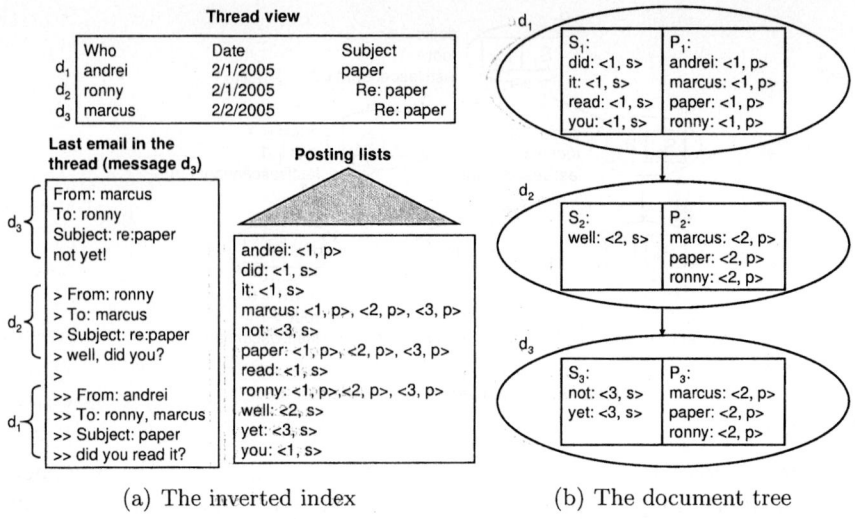

**Fig. 2.** An example of index encoding for a thread $d_1$-$d_2$-$d_3$

a posting for a term $t$ with document $d_j$ if the posting is marked as shared and $d_j \in \{d_i, \ldots, lastDescendant(d_i)\}$ or if the posting is marked as private and $d_i = d_j$.

One subtle point to notice in Figure 2 is that, although the terms "did" and "you" appear in both $d_1$ and $d_2$, only one posting for them is indexed, namely, the one for $d_1$. This is because $d_1$ already shares those postings with $d_2$, which in turn means it would be redundant to index them twice. The virtual cursor algorithms that we will present later assume that these redundant postings do not appear in the index. However, for scoring, their occurrences and an indication of which document they belong to are reflected in the payloads. For example, both occurrences of "did" (for $d_1$ and $d_2$) would appear in $d_1$'s payload, with an indication of the document they actually appear in. When scoring $d_1$ the system will ignore the occurence that is tagged with $d_2$, whereas when scoring $d_2$, both occurences will be taken into account.

## 5 Query Evaluation

We have described how our representation model can be encoded in an inverted index. Given this encoding, we now show how free-text queries can be evaluated using a standard zig-zag join. We allow queries to contain required, forbidden, and optional terms. The following high-level steps, which are described in the remainder of this section, are repeated during query evaluation:

- Enumerate candidates, that is, identify documents containing all required terms and none of the forbidden terms.

- Score the candidates, taking into account all occurrences of the query terms, including optional terms.
- Choose the next *docid* to resume searching for candidates.

## 5.1 Enumerating Candidates

A zig-zag join on required and forbidden terms is used to enumerate candidate documents. We define *virtual index cursors*, which look like normal cursors to a zig-zag join but are aware of our representation model and its encoding. A virtual cursor for a term $t$ enumerates the same documents that a physical cursor for $t$ would if shared content had been indexed multiple times. For example, in Figure 4, a virtual cursor for "well" would enumerate $d_2$ and $d_3$.

We create a "positive" virtual cursor for each required term, and a "negative" virtual cursor for each forbidden term. The latter allows a zig-zag join to treat forbidden terms the same as required terms.

Recall that two basic cursor methods are required for a zig-zag join, namely, *next()* and *fwdBeyond()*. The algorithms for the positive and negative versions of these methods are shown in Figure 3 and Figure 4, respectively. In the algorithms, *this.docid* corresponds to the virtual cursor's current position, while $C_p$ corresponds to the underlying physical cursor.

**Positive next() and fwdBeyond()**

Turning to Figure 3, the algorithm for positive *next()* is relatively straightforward, except when $C_p$ is on a shared posting. In that case, all of $C_p$'s descendants, which inherit the term from $C_p$, are enumerated (lines 2–4) before $C_p$ is physically moved (line 7).

The algorithm for positive *fwdBeyond(d)* relies on the physical cursor method *fwdShare()*, which will be describe shortly, to do most of its work. The call to $C_p$.*fwdShare(d)* tries to position $C_p$ on the next document that shares the term with $d$ (line 6). If there is no such document, *fwdShare()* returns with $C_p$ positioned on the first document beyond $d$.

**Negative next() and fwdBeyond()**

The algorithm for negative *next()* is shown in Figure 4. It works by trying to keep $C_p$ positioned ahead of the virtual cursor. The documents $d \in \{this.docid, \ldots, C_p - 1\}$, which do *not* contain the term, are enumerated until the virtual cursor catches up to $C_p$ (line 4). When that happens, the virtual cursor is forwarded past the documents that inherit the term from $C_p$ (lines 5–9), after which $C_p$ is moved forward (line 10). These steps are repeated until $C_p$ moves ahead of the virtual cursor again.

The algorithm for negative *fwdBeyond(d)* calls *fwdShare(d)* to position $C_p$ on the next document that shares the term with $d$ (line 6). Then *next()* is called to position the virtual cursor on the next document that does not contain the term (line 14).

## Physical fwdShare()

The algorithm for *fwdShare(d)* is shown in Figure 5. It keeps looping until the physical cursor moves beyond $d$ or to a posting that shares the term with $d$ (line 1). The movement of the physical cursor depends on whether the cursor lies outside $d$'s document tree (lines 5–7), within the tree but outside $d$'s thread (lines 9–11), or is on a private posting (lines 13–15).

```
PositiveVirtual::next()
   // Forward the virtual cursor to the next
   // document that contains the term.
   1. last = lastDescendant(Cp.docid);
   2. if (Cp.payload is shared and this.docid < last) {
   3.    // not done enumerating descendants of Cp
   4.    this.docid += 1;
   5. } else {
   6.    // advance Cp and reset docid
   7.    Cp.next();
   8.    this.docid = Cp.docid;
   9. }

PositiveVirtual::fwdBeyond(docid d)
   // Forward the virtual cursor to the next document
   // at or beyond document d that contains the term.
   1. if (this.docid >= d) {
   2.    // already beyond d, so nothing to do
   3.    return;
   4. }
   5. // try to forward Cp so it shares the term with d
   6. Cp.fwdShare(d);
   7. // set docid to Cp if it
   8. // is beyond d, else set it to d
   9. this.docid = max(Cp.docid, d);
```

**Fig. 3.** positive next() and fwdBeyond()

### 5.2 Correctness Proof for next() and fwdBeyond()

Because of space limitations, we can only provide a sketch of the correctness proof for virtual next() and fwdBeyond(). The proof follows from:

**Theorem 1.** *On a posting list generated from our representation model, the virtual next() and fwdBeyond() methods accurately simulate the behavior of next() and fwdBeyond() on a standard posting list.*

**Proof sketch:** The proof is based on proving the invariants we keep for the two types of virtual cursors, namely, for positive ones, that all *docid*'s between the current physical cursor position and its last descendant are valid return values,

```
NegativeVirtual::next()
  // Forward the virtual cursor to the
  // next document not containing the term.
  1. this.docid += 1;
  2. // keep incrementing the cursor until it
  3. // is on a document not containing the term
  4. while (this.docid >= Cp.docid) {
  5.     if (Cp.payload is shared) {
  6.         this.docid = lastDescendant(Cp.docid) + 1;
  7.     } else {
  8.         this.docid = Cp.docid + 1;
  9.     }
  10.    Cp.next();
  11. }

NegativeVirtual::fwdBeyond(docid d)
  // Forward the virtual cursor to the next
  // document at or beyond the document d
  // that does not contain the term.
  1. if (this.docid >= d) {
  2.     // already beyond d, so nothing to do
  3.     return;
  4. }
  5. // try to forward Cp so it shares the term with d
  6. Cp.fwdShare(d);
  7. this.docid = d;
  8. if (Cp.docid > d) {
  9.     // document d does not contain the term
  10.    return;
  11. }
  12. // document d contains the term
  13. // call next() to move the cursor and Cp
  14. this.next();
```

**Fig. 4.** negative next() and fwdBeyond()

and that in the negated case, all *docid*'s between the current virtual position and the physical cursor position are valid return values. These invariants guarantee that our methods do not return spurious results. We further prove that we never skip valid results, completing the proof. □

### 5.3 Scoring Candidates

Our representation model does not impose any restriction on the scoring function. However, the scoring function could take thread information into account. For example, documents toward the bottom of a document tree could be assigned a lower score.

Candidate enumeration returns with the virtual cursors positioned on postings for a candidate document $d$. Scoring usually needs to take into account all the

```
Physical::fwdShare(docid d)
   // Try to forward the physical cursor so it shares
   // the term with document d. If there is no such
   // document, return with the cursor positioned on
   // the first document beyond d.
1. while (this.docid <= d and this.docid
                does not share the term with d) {
2.     root = root(d);
3.     last = lastDescendant(this.docid);
4.     if (this.docid < root) {
5.         // the cursor is not in the
6.         // same document tree as d
7.         this.fwdBeyond(root);
8.     } else if (last < d) {
9.         // in the same document tree
10.        // but not in the same thread
11.        this.fwdBeyond(last + 1);
12.    } else {
13.        // in the same thread, but private
14.        // posting on a different document
15.        this.next();
16.    }
17. }
```

**Fig. 5.** fwdShare() on a physical cursor

occurrences of each query term $t$ in $d$, including optional terms. Given a virtual cursor $C_t$, this can be done by iterating all the occurrences of $t$ in the posting's payload. Since $C_t$ is virtual, the physical cursor $C_p$ associated with $C_t$ would be used to access the payload.

If the textual component of the scoring function is expensive to compute, we can remember the textual score of a document $d$ to speedup the scoring of other candidate documents in $d$'s thread. For example, suppose $d_i$ has been scored and now another candidate $d_j$ on the same thread needs to be scored. We can compute its textual score as:

$$Score_{text}(d_j) = PScore(d_j) + \sum_{d_k \in \text{path}(d_i, d_j)} SScore(d_k)$$

Here, $PScore()$ and $SScore()$ are the private and shared parts of the textual score, respectively, and $\text{path}(d_i, d_j)$ is the path from $d_i$ to $d_j$ in the document tree.

### 5.4 Choosing the Next Docid

After a candidate document $d$ has been scored, the next document to resume searching for candidates has to be chosen. This step depends on the retrieval policy of the system, which may be tuned for performance or a particular application's requirements. Possible choices include:

- Resume from the document $d+1$. This allows all the qualifying documents in a document tree to be returned.
- Resume from document $lastDescendant(root(d)) + 1$. This allows only the first qualifying document in a document tree to be returned.
- Resume from document $lastDescendant(d) + 1$. This is a hybrid of the first two approaches, allowing only the first qualifying document in a thread to be returned.

# 6 Applications

This section describes how our document representation model can be applied to web and email search, showing its usefulness in practical IR applications.

## 6.1 Web Search

Studies have shown that up to 45% of web pages are duplicates and near duplicates [6, 8]. On the web scale, repeated indexing of duplicate content is a huge waste of resources, and furthermore, users are seldom interested in seeing duplicates in the search results. Hence, web search engines need some way to identify and filter duplicates from results. To identify duplicates, a *signature* is typically computed for each document by hashing its content. These signatures are then used to identify groups of duplicate documents, that is, *duplicate groups*. To filter duplicates from search results, one of the following techniques is commonly used:

- Only the *master* of each duplicate group is indexed and returned in searches. The master of a duplicate group can be chosen arbitrarily or by using some heuristic, like picking the duplicate with the highest static rank. (This technique has been used in the *AltaVista* search engine.)
- All documents in a duplicate group are indexed. A post-processing filter is used to make sure that only one document per duplicate group appears in search results. Optionally the entire group is presented to the user.

By indexing only masters, the inverted index is kept small and query evaluation can ignore duplicates. However, queries that include restrictions on metadata become problematic. For example, suppose that for performance reasons, IBM has mirrored its main HR web page at us.ibm.com/hr.html and canada.ibm.com/hr.html, but the US version has been chosen by the US-centric search engine as the master. Then the query hr domain:canada.ibm.com that asks for web pages from IBM Canada that have the term "hr" in their content, will not return the main page. This type of domain restriction might be explicit in the query, or it might have been added to the query by the query interface without the user knowledge, based, say on user's location or IP address.

Conversely, if all the documents in a duplicate group are indexed, queries that include restrictions on meta-data do not pose a problem, but then the same content must be indexed multiple times and the query evaluation runtime has to filter duplicates from results. This filtering might be expensive, since it has to be done in a separate post-processing step.

Using our document representation model, it becomes possible to index duplicate content just once, while still allowing queries to be answered as if all the duplicates were indexed. This is done by creating a linear tree for each duplicate group, in which the master of the group serves as the root and is thus indexed with both its (shared) content and its private meta-data. The rest of the documents in the duplicate group follow in arbitrary order, where only the (private) meta-data of each duplicate (such as URL, creation date, geo-location, etc) is indexed. Note that this representation naturally applies to documents that have no duplicates, i.e. to duplicate groups of size 1.

Since duplicates are not returned in search results, an added benefit of using our representation is that the postings for all the remaining duplicates in a duplicate group can be skipped during query evaluation as soon as one of them has been returned. As our experimental results will show, this can dramatically improve query performance.

### 6.2 Email and Newsgroup Search

In most email and newsgroup clients replies include the full content of the original message. As illustrated earlier in Figure 4, our document representation model can support email or newsgroup search by simply creating a document tree for each message thread with a structure that mirrors the thread's history.

Unfortunately for our aims, most email and newsgroup clients allow users to edit the reply history, which potentially prevents any sharing between a message and its reply. Although such editing is common, our experimental results will show that 33% of the email messages in the Enron dataset [14] include an unedited reply history.

Another application for our document representation model is indexing on centralized email servers. For example, suppose an email message is sent to $N$ users on the same server. Rather than index the message and its attachments $N$ times, the message could be indexed as a two-level document tree, with the message body and attachments appearing as the shared root of the tree, and the meta-data of each recipient appearing as a separate, private leaf in the tree. Presumably, security information would be stored in the private meta-data and security meta-terms added to queries by the server to ensure that users could only search their own email.

## 7 Experimental Results

In this section, we present experimental results for web and email search. We implemented our algorithms on the Trevi search engine [10], which is currently used to support web searches on IBM's global intranet. Experiments were run on a two-way SMP with dual 2.4 Ghz Intel Xeon processors running Linux. The disk storage was configured as two physical RAID arrays, each with 6 drives.

**Table 1.** Index sizes with and without duplicates

| Num Docs (K) | Pct. Dups | Meta Data (GB) | Content Data (GB) | Index w/o Dups (GB) | Index w/ Dups (GB) | Expected Comp. | Actual Comp. |
|---|---|---|---|---|---|---|---|
| 500 | 36% | 1.2 | 3.7 | 2.5 | 3.6 | 72% | 69% |
| 1000 | 37% | 2.3 | 7.9 | 5.1 | 7.4 | 71% | 69% |
| 1500 | 41% | 3.5 | 11.1 | 7.1 | 11.0 | 69% | 64% |
| 2000 | 43% | 4.8 | 13.9 | 8.8 | 13.0 | 68% | 68% |
| 2500 | 44% | 6.0 | 19.9 | 11.0 | 16.0 | 66% | 69% |

## 7.1 Results for Web Search

For this set of experiments, we built a series of inverted indexes from snapshots of IBM's intranet, varying the corpus size between 500K to 2.5M documents[1]. These sizes are indicative since the actual IBM intranet has about 15M documents (before duplicate elimination). We built each index with and without duplicates, using our document representation model in the latter case, as described in Section 6.

For each dataset, Table 1 shows the percentage of duplicates in the index, the overall amount of meta-data, the overall amount of content data, the size of the index without duplicates, the size of the index with duplicates, the expected compression ratio of the index without duplicates to the index with duplicates, and the actual measured compression ratio. The expected compression ratio can be computed as:

$$ExpectedComp = \frac{MetaData + ContentData \cdot (1 - PctDups)}{MetaData + ContentData}$$

Table 1 shows that our representation model reduced index sizes by roughly 30% on the IBM intranet data. Note that the actual compression ratio was better than expected in some cases. This was because content tokens, which include payload and offset information, tended to be bigger than than meta-data tokens, whereas our calculation of the expected compression assumes all postings are of equal size.

The time to build an inverted index is an important metric in web search, since a decrease in the time to build an index allows it to be refreshed more frequently [10]. Table 2 shows the time to build each index on the IBM intranet data. Our indexing algorithm [10] is designed for batch builds of complete indexes, and hence a complete build was done for each experiment, rather than incrementaly growing an existing index. The build times reported do not include the time spent on separate analysis phase was run to identify duplicates. However, note that this phase would be necessary to filter duplicate results, regardless of whether our representation model was being used.

---

[1] When selecting a subset from the IBM intranet corpus we selected complete duplicate groups, so that the ratio of duplicate documents in all subsets has the same expectation, irrespective of the subset size.

**Table 2.** Index build performance

| Num Docs (K) | Index w/o Dups (sec) | Index w/ Dups (sec) | Pct. Decrease |
|---|---|---|---|
| 500 | 540 | 780 | 31% |
| 1000 | 1020 | 1440 | 29% |
| 1500 | 1500 | 2340 | 36% |
| 2000 | 1800 | 2940 | 39% |
| 2500 | 2160 | 3540 | 39% |

Table 2 reflects the time to scan the dataset (with duplicates) and then build the index (with or without duplicates). On average, it took about 30% to 40% less time to build an index without duplicates because of its smaller size. This is in keeping with the results in [10], which showed that the time to build an index is mostly I/O bound and a linear function of its size.

To study query performance, we ran one- and two-term queries on the dataset with 2.5M documents. We felt that this was a realistic set of experiments, since the average query on the IBM intranet contains only 1.2 terms. The single-term queries were on syntheticaly generated terms. 5 synthetic terms were added to the documents with selectivities that ranged from 20% to 100% (i.e., for each document, we added term $t_{20\%}$ with probability .2, a term $t_{40\%}$ with probability .4, etc.). We then used these five terms in five single-term queries. Note, however, that a query on such terms actually returned fewer documents than the expected fraction of the corpus size, because duplicates were filtered from the final result.

Query performance is strongly correlated to the number of physical cursor moves on the index – fewer moves translates into better query performance. Figure 6 shows the number of physical cursor moves and the execution time for single-term queries on a synthetic term. The results show that the number of cursor moves decreased by roughly 30% to 45% when our representation model was used. This is because the remaining postings in a duplicate group can be skipped as soon as one of them is returned. The improvement in execution time was even more pronounced, with a decrease of up to 80%. This was because of the combined effect of fewer cursor moves along with having a smaller index, which resulted in less CPU and I/O.

Figure 7 is provided to help understand the results in Figure 6. It illustrates how our representation model can decrease the number of physical cursor moves. As shown, there are two document groups $d_1$-$d_2$-$d_3$-$d_4$ and $d_5$-$d_6$. Using our representation model, duplicates $d_2$, $d_3$, and $d_4$ can be skipped as soon as $d_1$ is enumerated. In addition to decreasing I/O, this means that those documents do not need to be filtered from the final results by the upper layers of the system, which in turn decreases CPU requirements. Our representation model effectively allows the filtering of duplicates to be pushed down to the physical index level, rather than doing it in the upper layers of the system.

Figure 8 shows the number of physical cursor moves and the execution time for two-term queries. For variety, real query terms on both content and meta-data were used in this case. The results for two-term queries were similar to those for

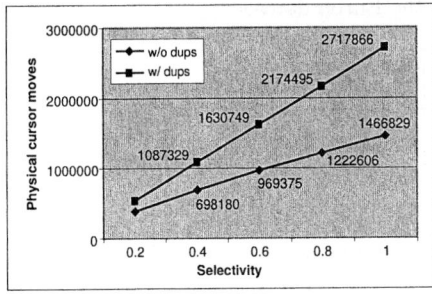 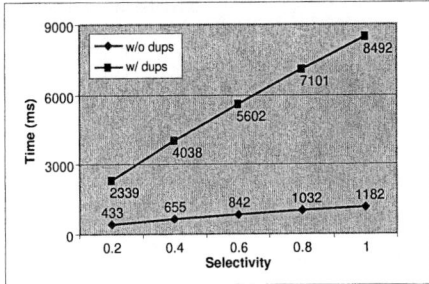

**Fig. 6.** Results for single-term queries

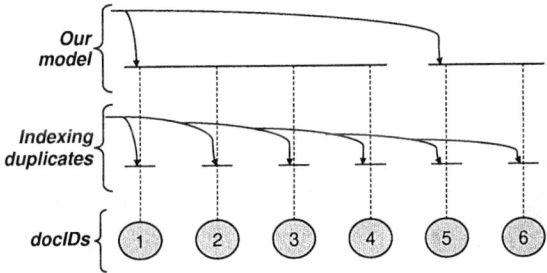

**Fig. 7.** Duplicate filtering at the index level

one-term queries, with improvements of up to 80% in execution time when our representation model was used. Again, this was because of the combined effect of fewer cursor moves on a smaller index.

## 7.2 Results for Email Search

We used the Enron email dataset [14] to study how well our document representation model can be applied to email search. This dataset contains 517,431 emails that were made public in the Enron fraud investigation. Unfortunately,

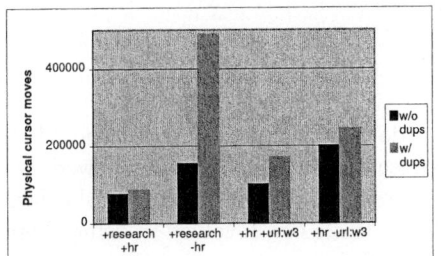 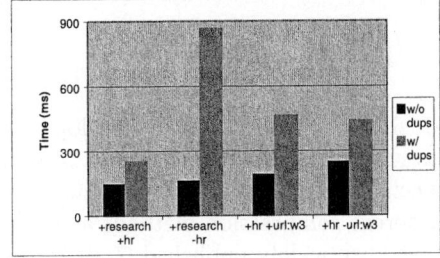

**Fig. 8.** Results for two-term queries

**Table 3.** Analysis of the Enron dataset

|               | Size (MB) |
|---------------|-----------|
| Meta Data     | 430       |
| Content Data  | 910       |
| Original Data | 580       |

we did not have an email search engine available to us that could be used for experimentation. Consequently, we only used the Enron dataset to judge the potential effectiveness of our method on a real email collection. As discussed in Section 6, the effectiveness of our method in email search depends on the percentage of email threads that include an unedited reply history.

An analysis of the Enron dataset showed that 61% of its email messages belong to some thread, and that 33% of the messages in a thread included an unedited reply history. In Table 3 we show the overall amount of meta-data, the overall amount of content data, and the amount of content data that was left when the reply history was removed (the "Original Data"). We treated anything that appeared in email headers as meta-data.

Comparing the size of an inverted index for the Enron dataset with our representation model to one without it, the expected compression ratio can be computed as:

$$ExpectedComp = \frac{MetaData + OriginalData}{MetaData + ContentData}$$

This works out to 75%. In other words, using our representation method, an inverted index for the Enron data set would be roughly 25% smaller, which is comparable to what was observed on the IBM intranet data. We believe that the improvement in query performance would be comparable as well, due to the combined effect of fewer cursor moves on a smaller index.

It worth noting that, for email search, Gmail [12] returns only one email message per thread. Using our document representation model, this would allow the remaining messages in a thread to be skipped during query evaluation as soon as one of them was returned. As our results on the IBM intranet data showed, this kind of skipping can dramatically improve query performance.

## 8 Related Work

Much of the motivation for developing our document representation model is to save index space. In this respect, our representation model can be viewed as a special type of an index compression that relies on explicit knowledge of the data. Different compression methods as well as the trade offs involved in using them, have been widely published [7, 9, 17, 18, 23]. However, we regard our scheme as independent of those methods, and indeed it can be used in combination with them.

This paper focused on the problem of efficiently building and querying an inverted index once the shared content has already been identified. How to identify the shared content is beyond the scope of this paper but is related to the problem of identifying duplicates in a text corpus [2, 4, 6]. In the case of email or newsgroup threads, identifying shared content may be aided by cross-reference information in message headers.

Our representation model is particularly effective in email or newsgroup search. Recently, email search like that provided by Gmail [12] and Bloomba [19] has become quite popular. Unfortunately, the Gmail architecture is not public, and although Bloomba is tailored for indexing and searching email, it does not seem to do anything special for the shared content in email threads.

## 9 Conclusions

In this paper, we described a new document representation model where related documents are organized as a tree, allowing shared content to be indexed just once. A key feature of our representation is that it can easily support the standard zig-zag join algorithm for processing free-text queries on an inverted index. We described how this can be accomplished by defining virtual index cursors that are aware of our representation model and its encoding.

Our model can be applied to practical IR applications such as web, email, and newsgroup search. Using data from the IBM intranet, we provided experimental results showing that our method was able to reduce the size of the inverted index by roughly 30% and improve the performance of one- and two-term queries by up to 80%. The improvement in query performance was due to the synergistic effect of fewer cursor moves on a smaller index.

For future research, we hope to extend this work to improving XML retrieval. In particular, we would like to index XML documents efficiently while enabling search at the individual *tag* level, i.e. to retrieve the tag within each document that is most relevant to the query. To that effect, we can represent each document using its DOM tree, and share the content of each node (tag) with the content of its ancestors (enveloping tags). Note that this down-up model of content sharing is exactly the opposite of the top-down sharing model discussed in this paper.

## References

[1] R. Baeza-Yates and B. Ribeiro-Neto. *Modern Information Retrieval*. Addison Wesley, 1999.
[2] M. Bilenko and R. J. Mooney. Adaptive duplicate detection using learnable string similarity measures. In *KDD '03*, pages 39–48, 2003.
[3] S. Brin and L. Page. The anatomy of a large-scale hypertextual Web search engine. In *WWW '98*, pages 107–117, 1998.
[4] A. Z. Broder. Identifying and filtering near-duplicate documents. In *CPM '00*, pages 1–10, 2000.
[5] A. Z. Broder, D. Carmel, M. Herscovici, A. Soffer, and J. Zien. Efficient query evaluation using a two-level retrieval process. In *CIKM '03*, pages 426–434, 2003.

[6] A. Z. Broder, S. C. Glassman, M. S. Manasse, and G. Zweig. Syntactic clustering of the web. In *WWW '97*, pages 1157–1166, 1997.
[7] D. Carmel, D. Cohen, R. Fagin, E. Farchi, M. Herscovici, Y. S. Maarek, and A. Soffer. Static index pruning for information retrieval systems. In *SIGIR '01*, pages 43–50, 2001.
[8] J. Cho, N. Shivakumar, and H. Garcia-Molina. Finding replicated web collections. In *SIGMOD '00*, pages 355–366, 2000.
[9] E. S. de Moura, C. F. dos Santos, D. R. Fernandes, A. S. Silva, P. Calado, and M. A. Nascimento. Improving web search efficiency via a locality based static pruning method. In *WWW '05*, pages 235–244, 2005.
[10] M. Fontoura, E. J. Shekita, J. Y. Zien, S. Rajagopalan, and A. Neumann. High performance index build algorithms for intranet search engines. In *VLDB '04*, pages 1158–1169, 2004.
[11] H. Garcia-Molina, J. Ullman, and J. Widom. *Database System Implementation*. Prentice Hall, 2000.
[12] Gmail. http://gmail.google.com/gmail/help/about.html.
[13] S. Heinz and J. Zobel. Efficient single-pass index construction for text databases. *JASIST*, 54(8), 2003.
[14] B. Klimt and Y. Yang. The Enron corpus: A new dataset for email classification research. In *European Conference on Machine Learning*, 2004.
[15] X. Long and T. Suel. Optimized query execution in large search engines with global page ordering. In *VLDB '03*, pages 129–140, 2003.
[16] S. Melnik, S. Raghavan, B. Yang, and H. Garcia-Molina. Building a distributed full-text index for the web. In *WWW '01*, pages 396–406, 2001.
[17] A. Moffat and J. Zobel. Compression and fast indexing for multi-gigabyte text databases. *Australian Computer Journal*, 26(1), 1994.
[18] F. Scholer, H. E. Williams, J. Yiannis, and J. Zobel. Compression of inverted indexes for fast query evaluation. In *SIGIR '02*, pages 222–229, 2002.
[19] R. Stata, P. Hunt, and M. G. Thiruvalluvan. The Bloomba personal content database. In *VLDB '04*, pages 1214–1223, 2004.
[20] H. Turtle and J. Flood. Query evaluation: strategies and optimizations. *Inf. Proc. Management*, 31(6):831–850, 1995.
[21] I. Witten, A. Moffat, and T. Bell. *Managing Gigabytes*. Morgan Kaufmann, 1999.
[22] Z. Zhang. The behavior of duplicate pages on the world wide web. Submitted to CIKM, 2005.
[23] J. Zobel and A. Moffat. Adding compression to a full-text retrieval system. *Software - Practice & Experience*, 25(8), 1995.

# Feedback-Driven Structural Query Expansion for Ranked Retrieval of XML Data

Ralf Schenkel and Martin Theobald

Max-Planck-Institut für Informatik, Saarbrücken, Germany
{schenkel, mtb}@mpi-inf.mpg.de

**Abstract.** Relevance Feedback is an important way to enhance retrieval quality by integrating relevance information provided by a user. In XML retrieval, feedback engines usually generate an expanded query from the content of elements marked as relevant or nonrelevant. This approach that is inspired by text-based IR completely ignores the semistructured nature of XML. This paper makes the important step from content-based to structural feedback. It presents an integrated solution for expanding keyword queries with new content, path, and document constraints. An extensible framework evaluates such query conditions with existing keyword-based XML search engines while allowing to easily integrate new dimensions of feedback. Extensive experiments with the established INEX benchmark show the feasibility of our approach.

## 1 Introduction

### 1.1 Motivation

With the proliferation of XML as a document format, information retrieval on XML data has recently received great attention. XML search engines employ the ranked retrieval paradigm for producing relevance-ordered result lists rather than merely using XPath or XQuery for Boolean retrieval. An important subset of XML search engines uses keyword-based queries [3, 9, 28], which is especially important for collections of documents with unknown or highly heterogeneous schemas.

Relevance Feedback is an important way to enhance retrieval quality by integrating relevance information provided by a user. In XML retrieval, existing feedback engines usually generate an expanded keyword query from the content of elements marked as relevant or nonrelevant. This approach that is inspired by text-based IR completely ignores the semistructured nature of XML. This paper makes the important step from content-based to structural feedback. We extend the well-established feedback approach by Rocchio [21] to expand a keyword-based query with additional structural constraints on result elements and on documents in which result elements reside, in addition to "standard" content-based query expansion. The resulting expanded query has weighted structural and content constraints and can be fed into a full-fledged XML search engine like our own TopX engine [24].

However, as there are many keyword-only search engines [3, 9] and some other engines allow only unweighted structural constraints, this approach is not generally applicable. Additionally, the correct choice of weights and the way the query is expanded depend on the underlying scoring model of the engine (like Rocchio's method initially requires that the vector space model is applied). To overcome these problems, this paper presents an extensible framework to extend existing keyword-based XML search engines with structure-based feedback. It reranks results of keyword-only queries according to additional scores induced by the structure of results that are marked as relevant (or nonrelevant).

This paper makes the following important contributions: (1) It presents a formal framework to integrate different dimensions of feedback, beyond content-based feedback, into XML retrieval, (2) it presents two structural query expansion techniques as important instances of new dimensions for query expansion, and (3) it shows how to effectively implement the framework, including structural constraints, with keyword-based XML search engines. We show that structural query expansion gives a huge gain in effectiveness with the established INEX benchmark [13].

To the best of our knowledge, this is the first paper that considers user relevance feedback for structural query expansion. The primary goal of this paper is to show that structural feedback helps to enhance result quality. The paper does not claim to present the ultimately best implementation of structural feedback, but opens a whole design space and presents variants that give reasonably good results.

## 1.2 Related Work

Relevance feedback has already been considered for document retrieval for a long time, starting with Rocchio's query expansion algorithm [21]. Ruthven and Lalmas [22] give an extensive overview about relevance feedback for unstructured data, including the assessment of relevance feedback algorithms.

Relevance feedback in XML IR is not yet that popular. Of the few papers that have considered it, most contentrate on query expansion based on the content of elements with known relevance [7, 15, 23, 27]. Some of these focus on blind ("pseudo") feedback, others on user feedback. Pan et al. [17, 18] apply user feedback to recompute similarities in the ontology used for query evaluation.

Even fewer papers have considered structural query expansion [8, 10, 11, 16, 19, 20]. Mihajlovic̀ et al. [16, 19, 20] proposed deriving the relevance of an element from its tag name, but could not show any significant gain in retrieval effectiveness. Additionally, they considered hand-tuned structural features specific for the INEX benchmark (e.g., the name of the journal to which an element's document belongs), but again without a significant positive effect. In contrast, we propose a general approach for feedback that can be applied with INEX, but does not rely on any INEX-specific things.

Hlaoua and Boughanem [10] consider common prefixes of relevant elements' paths as additional query constraints, but don't provide any experimental evaluation of their approach. Our path-based feedback supports path prefixes as one of six classes of path features.

Gonçalvez et al. [8] use relevance feedback to construct a restricted class of structured queries (namely field-term pairs) on structured bibliographic data, using a Bayesian network for query evaluation, but did not consider semistructured data like XML.

The work of Hsu et al. [11] is closest to our approach. They use blind feedback to expand a keyword-based query with structural constraints derived from a neighborhood of elements that contain the keywords in the original query. Our approach considers the whole document instead of only a fragment, can generate constraints with negative weight, and integrates also path- and content-based constraints.

### 1.3 Formal Model and Notation

We consider a fixed corpus of XML documents. For such a document $d$, $E(d)$ denotes the set of elements of the document; for an element $e$, $\text{tag}(e)$ denotes its tag name and $D(e)$ the document to which it belongs.

The *content* $c(e)$ of an element $e$ is the set of all terms (after stopword removal and optional stemming) in the textual content of the element itself and all its descendants. (Note that XML retrieval engines usually use this content model, while boolean languages like XPath or Xquery typically only use the content of the element itself.) For each term $t$ and element $e$, we maintain a weight $w_e(t)$. This can be a binary weight ($w_e(t) = 1$ if the term occurs in $e$'s content and 0 otherwise), a tf-idf style [14] or a BM25-based [1, 26] weight that captures the importance of $t$ in $e$'s content.

We represent elements in the well-known vector space model. Formally, with $T = \{t_1, ..., t_{|T|}\}$ the set of all terms occuring in the contents of elements, our vector space is $\mathcal{V} = \mathbb{R}^{|T|}$. Each element $e$ is assigned a vector $\boldsymbol{e} \in \mathcal{V}$ where $e_i = w_e(t_i)$ corresponds to the weight of term $t_i$ in $e$. Analogously, a query $\boldsymbol{q} \in \mathcal{V}$ is also a vector with nonzero entries for the requested keywords. The score of an element with respect to a query can then be defined as the cosine similarity [2]

$$s(\boldsymbol{q}, e) = \frac{<\boldsymbol{q}; \boldsymbol{e}>}{\|\boldsymbol{q}\| \cdot \|\boldsymbol{e}\|}$$

of the query and the element's vector (or any other distance measure), and the result to a query is then a list of elements sorted by descending score.

Note that, even though this paper uses the vector space model, the techniques for query expansion presented here can be carried over to other retrieval models, as long as they allow queries with structural constraints.

## 2 Dimensions for Query Expansion

In text-based IR and mostly also in XML IR, feedback has concentrated on the content of relevant documents or elements only. We propose to extend this text-driven notion of feedback with new structural dimensions for feedback that are more adequate to the semistructured nature of XML. Our framework for feedback supports the following three feedback dimensions:

- *content constraints* that impose additional conditions on the content of relevant elements,
- *path constraints* that restrain the path of relevant elements, and
- *document constraints* that characterize documents that contain relevant elements.

Another possible dimension for feedback is the quality of ontological expansions that is considered in [18].

In the remainder of this section, we give motivating examples for each of the dimensions and show how they can be formally expressed in the vector space model. The evaluation of queries that are expanded along these dimensions is presented in the following section.

For the remainder of this section, we consider a keyword query $q \in \mathcal{V}$ for which we know a set $E^+ = \{e_1^+, \ldots, e_r^+\}$ of relevant elements and a set $E^- = \{e_1^-, \ldots, e_n^-\}$ of nonrelevant elements, e.g., from user feedback. We assume boolean feedback, i.e., a single element can be relevant or nonrelevant, but not both. The models and formulae presented in the following can be extended to support weighted feedback (to capture vague information like 'somewhat relevant' or weighted relevance like in the different INEX quantizations), e.g. using the notion of probabilistic sets, but this is beyond the scope of this paper.

## 2.1 Content Constraints

Content-based feedback is widely used in standard IR and has also made its way into XML retrieval [15, 23]. It expands the original query with new, weighted keywords that are derived from the content of elements with known relevance. As an example, consider the keyword query "multimedia information" retrieval (this is topic 178 from the INEX topic collection). From the feedback of a user, we may derive that elements that contain the terms 'brightness', 'annotation', or 'rgb' are likely to be relevant, whereas elements with 'hypermedia' or 'authoring' are often irrelevant. An expanded query could include the former terms with positive weights and the letter terms with negative weights.

Formally, to expand our keyword query $q$ with new keywords, we apply a straight-forward extension of the well-known Rocchio method [21] to XML: We add new weighted keywords to the query that are taken from the contents of result elements for which we know the relevance. The weight $w(t)$ for a term $t$ is computed analogously to Rocchio with binary weights:

$$w_c(t) = \beta_c \cdot \frac{\sum_{e \in E^+} w_e(t)}{|E^+|} - \gamma_c \cdot \frac{\sum_{e \in E^-} w_e(t)}{|E^-|}$$

with adjustable tuning parameters $\beta_c$ and $\gamma_c$ between 0 and 1. We set $\beta_c = 0.5$ and $\gamma_c = 0.25$ which gave good results in our experiments. A term has a high positive weight if it occurs in many relevant elements, but only a few nonrelevant elements, so adding it to the query may help in dropping the number of nonrelevant results. Analogously, terms that are frequent among the nonrelevant elements' contents, but infrequent among the relevant elements', get a high negative weight. The expanded query $q^c$ is then a combination of $q$ with weighted terms from the candidate set, i.e., $q_i^c = \alpha \cdot q_i + w_c(t_i)$ for all $t_i \in T$.

Among the (usually many) possible expansion terms, we choose the $n_c$ with highest absolute weight, with $n_c$ usually less than 10. If there are too many with the same weight, we use the mutual information of the term's score distribution among the elements with known relevance and the relevance distribution as a tie breaker, which prefers terms that have high scores in relevant elements, but low scores (or are not present at all) in nonrelevant elements, or vice versa. If $E^+$ is empty, i.e., all elements with feedback are nonrelevant, mutual information cannot distinguish good from bad expansion terms as it is zero for all terms. We use the term's element frequency (the number of elements in which this term occurs) for tie breaking then, preferring terms that occur infrequently.

## 2.2 Path Constraints

Elements with certain tag names are more likely to be relevant than elements with other tag names. As an example, a keyword query may return entries from the index of a book or journal with high scores as they often contain exactly the requested keywords, but such elements are usually not relevant. Additionally, queries may prefer either large elements (such as whole articles) or small elements (such as single paragraphs), but rarely both. However, experiments show that tag names alone do not bear enough information to enhance retrieval quality, but the whole path of a result element plays an important role. As an example, the relevance of a paragraph may depend on whether it is in the body of an article (with a path like `/article/bdy/sec/p` from the root element), in the description of the vitae of the authors (with a path like `/article/bm/vt/p`), or in the copyright statement of the journal (with a path like `/article/fm/cr/p`).

As element tag names are too limited, but complete paths may be too strict, we consider the following seven classes of *path fragments*, with complete paths and tag names being special cases:

- $P_1$: prefixes of paths, e.g., `article/#`,`/article/fm/#`
- $P_2$: infixes of paths, e.g., `#/fm/#`
- $P_3$: subpaths of length 2, e.g., `#/sec/p/#`
- $P_4$: paths with wildcards, e.g, `#/bm/#/p/#`
- $P_5$: suffixes of paths, e.g., `#/fig`, `#/article`
- $P_6$: full paths, e.g, `/article/bdy/sec`

Mihajlovič et al. [16] used a variant of $P_5$, namely tag names of result elements, but did not see any improvement. In fact, only a combination of fragments from several classes leads to enhancements in result quality.

Formally, we consider for an element $e$ its set $P(e)$ of path fragments that are computed from its path. For each fragment that occurs in any such set, we compute its weight

$$w_p(p) = \beta_p \cdot \frac{|\{e \in E^+ : p \in P(e)\}|}{|E^+|} - \gamma_p \cdot \frac{|\{e \in E^- : p \in P(e)\}|}{|E^-|}$$

with adjustable tuning parameters $\beta_p$ and $\gamma_p$ between 0 and 1; we currently use $\beta_p = 1.0$ and $\gamma_p = 0.25$. This is a straightforward application of Rocchio's formula to occurrences of path features in result elements.

As we created new dimensions, we cannot use our initial vector space $\mathcal{V}$ to expand the initial query $\boldsymbol{q}$. Instead, we create a new vector space $\mathcal{V}_p = \mathbb{R}^{|P|}$ where $P = \{p_1, \ldots, p_{|P|}\}$ is the set of all path features of elements in the corpus. The components of the vector $e^p \in \mathcal{V}_p$ for an element $e$ are 1 for path features that can be computed from $e$'s path and 0 otherwise. The extended query $\boldsymbol{q^p}$ is then a vector in $\mathcal{V}_p$ with $q_i^p = w_p(p_i)$.

### 2.3 Document Constraints

Unlike standard text retrieval where the unit of retrieval is whole documents, XML retrieval focuses on retrieving parts of documents, namely elements. Information in other parts of a document with a relevant element can help to characterize documents in which relevant elements occur. A natural kind of such information is the content of other elements in such documents.

As an example, consider again INEX topic 178 (`"multimedia information" retrieval`). We may derive from user feedback that documents with the terms 'pattern, analysis, machine, intelligence' in the journal title (i.e., those from the 'IEEE Transactions on Pattern Analysis and Machine Learing') are likely to contain relevant elements. The same may hold for documents that cite papers by Gorkani and Huang (who are co-authors of the central paper about the QBIC system), whereas documents that cite papers with the term 'interface' in their title probably don't contain relevant elements (as they probably deal with interface issues in multimedia applications).

Formally, we consider for a document $d$ its set $S(d)$ of *structural features*, i.e., all pairs $(T(e), t)$ where $T(e)$ is the tag name of an element $e$ within $d$ and $t$ is a term in the content of $e$. For each feature $s$ that occurs in any such set, we compute its weight

$$w_s(s) = \beta_s \frac{|\{e \in E^+ : s \in S(D(e))\}|}{|E^+|}$$
$$- \gamma_s \frac{|\{e \in E^- : s \in S(D(e))\}|}{|E^-|}$$

with adjustable tuning parameters $\beta_s$ and $\gamma_s$ between 0 and 1; we currently use $\beta_s = \gamma_s = 1.0$. This is a straight-forward application of Rocchio weights to structural features. Note that we are using binary weights for each structural feature, i.e., a feature is counted only once per document. We experimented with using scores here, but the results were always worse than with binary weights; however, a more detailed study of different score functions is subject to future work. We select the $n_s$ features with highest absolute score to expand the query. If there are too many with the same weight, we use the mutual information of the feature's score distribution among the documents with known relevance and the relevance distribution as a tie breaker (like we did with content features). If there are no positive exampes and mutual information is zero for all features, we use the tag-term pair's document frequency (the number of documents in which this term occurs) for tie breaking then, preferring tag-term pairs that occur infrequently.

As with path constraints, we have to consider a new vector space $\mathcal{V}_s = \mathbb{R}^{|S|}$ where $S = \{s_1, ..., s_{|S|}\}$ is the set of all structural features of documents in the corpus[1]. Each element $e$ is assigned a vector $e^s \in \mathcal{V}_s$ such that $e_i^s = 1$ if $D(e)$ contains the structural feature $s_i$ and 0 otherwise. The extended query $q^s$ is then a vector in $\mathcal{V}_s$ with $q_i^s = w_s(s_i)$.

Other possible structural features include twigs, occurence of elements with certain names in a document, or combination of path fragments with terms. Further exploration of this diversity is subject to future work.

## 3 Expanding and Evaluating Queries

Once we have generated additional content, path, and document constraints, we want to evaluate the query and retrieve better results. There are three different ways to do this: (1) Evaluate the query in a combined vector space, (2) convert the generated constraints to the query language used in an existing XML retrieval engine (e.g., the engine used to compute the initial results) and evaluate the expanded query with that engine, (3) evaluate some part of the expanded query with an existing engine, the remaining part in the vector space model, and combine the resulting scores.

### 3.1 Combined Vector Space

As we have expressed each feedback dimension in a vector space, it is straightforward to combine the individual vector spaces and evaluate the query in the resulting combined vector space $\mathcal{V}' = \mathcal{V} \times \mathcal{V}_P \times \mathcal{V}_S$. The score of an element for an expanded query is then the similarity of the element's combined vectors and the corresponding combined vectors of the expanded query, measured for example with cosine similarity.

While this is an elegant solution from a theory point of view, it is not as elegant in practise. Even though we have a probably well-tuned XML search engine used to generate the initial set of results, we cannot use it here, but have to reimplement a specialized search engine for the new vector space. It is unsatisfactory to develop two independent, full-fledged search engines just to allow user feedback.

### 3.2 Engine-Based Evaluation

Standard feedback algorithms for text retrieval usually generate an expanded weighted keyword query that is evaluated with the same engine that produced

---

[1] Note that Carmel et al. [5] introduced a similar vector space with (tag, term) features for XML retrieval, but not for feedback.

the initial results. XML retrieval is different as expanded queries consist of more than simple keyword conditions. To benefit from the three dimensions of query expansion introduced in this paper (content, path, and document constraints), an XML search engine must support queries with weighted content and structural constraints that should be evaluated in a disjunctive mode (i.e., the more conditions an element satisfies, the better, but not conditions have to be strictly satisfied). Given such an engine with its query language, generating an expanded query is almost trivial.

As an example, consider again INEX topic 178 ("multimedia information" retrieval) already discussed in the previous section. We use INEX's query language NEXI [25] to explain how an expanded query is generated. NEXI basically corresponds to XPath restricted to the descendants-or-self and self axis and extended by an IR-style about predicate to specify conditions that relevant elements should fulfil. The initial query can be reformulated to the semantically identical NEXI query //*[about(.,"multimedia information" retrieval)], i.e., find any element that is "about" the keywords. Let's assume that the best content-based features were 'brightness' with weight 0.8 and 'hypermedia' with weight -0.7, and that the best document-based features (i.e., tagterm pairs) were 'bib[Gorkani]' with weight 0.9 and 'bib[interface]' with weight -0.85. Here 'bib[Gorkani]' means that the keyword 'Gorkani' occurs in an element with tag name 'bib'. Expanding the query with these features yields the following weighted query, formulated in NEXI with extensions for weights:

```
//article[0.9*about(.//bib,"Gorkani")
        -0.85*about(.//bib,'interface)]
    //*[about(.,0.8*brightness -0.7*hypermedia "multimedia
                information" retrieval)]
```

This query extends the initial keyword query with additional weighted constraints on the content of relevant elements. To specify document constraints, we have to somewhat abuse NEXI: We add an article element that has to be an ancestor of results; as the root of each INEX document is an article element, this is always true. We need it to specify the document constraints within its predicate. Such an expanded query can be submitted to any search engine that supports NEXI, possibly without the weights as they are not part of standard NEXI yet.

Path constraints cannot be easily mapped to a corresponding NEXI query as we cannot easily specify components of paths to result elements in NEXI. We evaluate path constraints therefore not with the engine, but externally; details are shown in the following subsection.

### 3.3 Hybrid Evaluation

The most promising approach for evaluating an expanded query is to evaluate as much of the expanded query with the existing search engine, evaluate the remaining part of the query separately, and combine the partial scores of each element. The result of the expanded query is then a ranked list of elements, sorted by combined score. Besides reusing the existing engine, this approach has the additional advantage that we can use different similarity measures for the different constraint dimensions and are not fixed to a single one (as with the extended vector space). On top of that, we can easily integrate new constraint dimensions.

As an example, assume we decide to evaluate the content-based part of the expanded query (i.e., $q^c$ in the notation of Section 2.1) with the engine and the remaining parts $q^p$ and $q^s$ in their corresponding vector spaces. The combined score of an element $e$ is then the sum of its score $S_c(e)$ computed by the engine for $q^c$, its score $S_p(e)$ for $q^p$ and its score $S_s(e)$ for $q^s$, where each of the additional scores is normalized to the interval $[-1.0, 1.0]$.

The score $S_S(e)$ is computed using standard cosine similarity of $e^s$ and $q^s$ in $\mathcal{V}_S$ (the same would hold for a content-based score if we decided to evaluate $q^c$ not with the engine, but separately). We could also use cosine similarity to compute $S_P(e)$; however, experiments have shown that using the following score function consistently gives better results:

$$S_P(e) = \frac{\sum q_i^p \cdot e_i^p}{|\{i : q_i^p \cdot e_i^p \neq 0\}|}$$

In contrast to cosine similarity, this normalizes the score with the number of dimensions where both vectors are nonzero. The rationale behind this is that path fragments that do not occur in either the query (i.e., in elements with known relevance) or in the current element should not modify the score.

This scoring model can easily integrate new dimensions for feedback beyond content, path and document constraints, even if they use a completely different model (like a probabilistic model). It only requires that the relevance of an element to a new feedback dimension can be measured with a score between -1 and 1. It is simple to map typical score functions to this interval by normalization and transformation. As an example, the transformation rule for a probability $p$, $0 \leq p \leq 1$, is $2 \cdot p - 1$.

## 4 Architecture and Implementation

### 4.1 Architecture

Figure 1 shows the high-level architecture of our extensible feedback framework. Each feedback dimension is implemented with a standard interface that allows a simple integration of new dimensions. For each dimension, there are methods to compute constraints, select the most important constraints, and compute the score of an element with respect to these constraints.

The initial results of a query are presented to the user who gives positive or negative feedback to some of the results. This feedback is sent together with the query and its initial results to the feedback framework which forwards them to the available feedback dimensions. Each dimension computes a number of

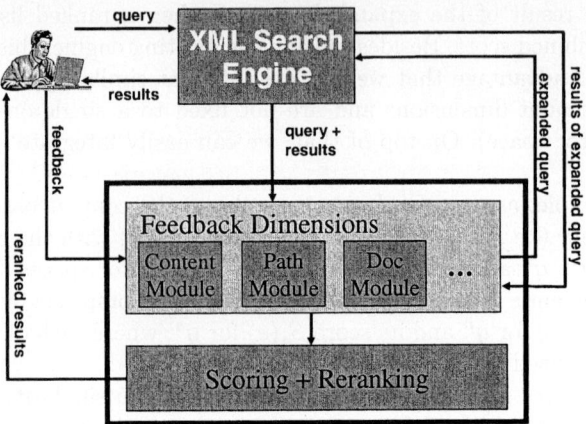

**Fig. 1.** Architecture of the feedback engine

constraints from the results with feedback. If the constraints for some dimensions are evaluated with the XML search engine, they are collected and transformed to an expanded query which is then evaluated with the engine; the results of this query are then the input for the remaining dimensions. For each element in the result of the expanded query, a score in the remaining dimensions is computed; the scores for each element are then aggregated, the list is sorted and returned to the user. The user may now again submit feedback for some of the new results, triggering another feedback cycle.

To facilitate an automatic assessment, the system can import queries and results from INEX (see Section 5.1) and automatically generate feedback for the top-k results, using the existing INEX assessments.

### 4.2 Implementation

We have implemented the framework in Java with content, path, and document constraints as examples for feedback dimensions and our TopX Search Engine [24]. For constraint generation we implemented the approaches presented in Section 2. Our implementation requires that important information about elements is precomputed:

- unique identifiers for the element (eid) and its document (did),
- its tag,
- its terms (after stemming and stopword removal), together with their score

This information is stored in a database table with schema (did,eid,tag,term, score) that contains one tuple for each distinct term of an element. We can reuse an existing inverted file of a keyword-based search engine that captures similar information, possibly after some transformation. On the database side, we provide indexes on (did,tag,term,score) (to efficiently collect all tag-term pairs of an element) and (eid,term,score) (to efficiently collect all distinct terms of an element). Inverse element frequency of terms and inverse document frequency of tag-term pairs that are used for tie breaking are derived from the base table if they are not available from the engine already.

Our current prototype reuses the `TagTermFeatures` table of TopX (see [24] that already provides did, eid, tag, term, and score, together with information on structural relationships of elements (like pre and post order) that is not used here.

The implementations of content-based and document-based feedback first load the content of elements with known relevance or the tag-term pairs of the corresponding documents, respectively, and compute the best features with respect to the score functions and tie breaking methods presented in the previous section. If content feedback is evaluated with the engine, an expanded query is created; otherwise, the implementation computes the additional content score of all candidate elements (i.e., the elements in the initial result list provided by the engine) with a database query. Analogously, the implementation of document-based feedback either builds an expanded query or computes the scores for documents itself, again using the database.

Unlike the others, path feedback does not require any information from the database; features and scores are computed only from the paths of elements. As this can be done very quickly and the scoring model for path-based feedback cannot be easily mapped to an expanded query for the engine, we always evaluate path-based scores within the framework.

## 5 Experimental Results

### 5.1 Settings

We use the well-known *INEX* [13] benchmark for XML IR that provides a set of 12,107 XML documents (scientific articles from IEEE CS), a set of queries with and without structural constraints together with a manually assessed set of results for each query, and an evaluation environment to assess the effectiveness of XML search engines. INEX provides a Relevance Feedback Track [12, 6] that aims at assessing the quality of different feedback approaches. As this paper concentrates on keyword-based queries (*content-only topics* or *CO* for short in INEX), we used the set of 52 CO queries from the 2003 and 2004 evaluation rounds with relevant results together with the *strict* quantization mode, i.e., an element was considered as relevant if it exactly answers the query. A *run* is the result of the evaluation of all topics with a search engine; it consists of 1500 results for each topic that are ranked by expected relevance. The measure of effectiveness is the *mean average precision* (MAP) of a run. Here, we first compute for each topic the average precision over 100 recall points (0.01 to 1.00) and then take the macro average over these topic-wise averages. Note that absolute MAP values are quite low for INEX (with 0.152 being the best MAP value of any participating engine in 2004). In addition to MAP values, we also measured precision at 10 for each run.

**Table 1.** Precision at $k$ for the baseline TopX run

| $k$ | 1 | 3 | 5 | 8 | 10 | 13 | 15 | 18 | 20 |
|---|---|---|---|---|---|---|---|---|---|
| prec@$k$ | 0.269 | 0.237 | 0.227 | 0.204 | 0.190 | 0.176 | 0.168 | 0.155 | 0.152 |

To assess the quality of feedback algorithms, we use the residual collection technique [22] that is also used in the INEX Relevance Feedback Track. In this technique, all XML elements that are used by the feedback algorithm, i.e., those whose relevance is known to the algorithm, must be removed from the collection before evaluation of the results with feedback takes place. This includes all $k$ elements "seen" or used in the feedback process regardless of their relevance. Under INEX guidelines, this means not only each element used or observed in the relevance feedback process but also all descendants of that element must be removed from the collection (i.e., the residual collection, against which the feedback query is evaluated, must contain no descendant of that element). All ancestors of that element are retained in the residual collection.

For all experiments we used our TopX Search Engine [24] that fully supports the evaluation of content-and-structure queries with weighted content constraints. The baseline for all experiments is a TopX run for all 52 INEX topics, with 1500 results for each topic. Table 1 shows the macro-averaged precision for this run for the top-$k$ ranked elements per topic, for different $k$.

The experiments were run on a Windows-based server with two Intel Xeon processors@3GHz, 4 gigabytes of RAM and a four-way RAID-0 SCSI disk array, running an Oracle 9i database on the same machine as the feedback framework.

### 5.2 Choice of Parameters

*Choice of Path Constraints.* We conducted experiments to assess the influence of the different classes of path constraints on the result quality. To do this, we examine how the MAP value and the precision at 10 of the baseline run change if we rerank the results based on feedback on the top-20 results with different combinations of path constraints enabled.

Table 2 shows the results of our experiments. It is evident that the best results are yielded with a combination of $P_1, P_3$, and $P_4$ (i.e., prefixes of paths, subpaths of length 2, and paths with wildcards), while adding infixes ($P_2$) is slightly worse.

**Table 2.** MAP and precision@10 values for some combinations of path fragments with the baseline TopX run

| classes | MAP | prec@10 |
|---|---|---|
| none | 0.0214 | 0.0706 |
| $P_1 - P_6$ | 0.0231 | 0.0745 |
| $P_1 - P_4$ | 0.0276 | 0.0824 |
| $P_1, P_3, P_4$ | **0.0281** | **0.0843** |
| $P_5$ | 0.0154 | 0.0569 |
| $P_6$ | 0.0157 | 0.0588 |

The absolute gain in MAP of about 0.0067 on average is small, but significant, as it corresponds to a relative gain of 31.3%. Using tag names alone ($P_5$) does not help and even hurts effectiveness (which was already shown in [16]), as does using the complete path ($P_6$). A similar influence of the different types of path constraints can be seen for the precision values.

*Number of content and document constraints.* We made some initial experiments to determine how many content and document constraints should be selected for expanding queries. Varying the number of content and/or document constraints from 1 to 10, we found that the MAP value didn't change a lot as soon as we had at least 3 content and 3 document constraints, even though results got slightly better with more constraints. For our experiments we choose the top 5 content and/or top 5 document constraints.

*Tuning parameters.* To calibrate the different tuning parameters introduced in Section 2, we made some initial experiments with varying parameter values. The best results were yielded with $\beta_c = 0.5$ and $\gamma_c = 0.25$ for content feedback, $\beta_p = 1.0$ and $\gamma_p = 0.25$ for path feedback, and $\beta_s = \gamma_s = 1.0$ for structural feedback. We used these values for our main series of experiments presented in the following subsections.

### 5.3 Engine-Based Feedback with TopX

We assessed the quality of document-based feedback with and without additional content-based feedback with our baseline run as input. Using relevance information for the top-k results for each topic from this run (for varying k), we computed the best five content-based and/or the best five document-based features features for each topic, created the corresponding expanded queries and evaluated them with TopX again.

Figure 2 shows the effect of content- and document-based feedback with the baseline TopX run, with known relevance of a varying number of elements from the top of the run. Our baseline is the TopX run on the corresponding residual collection (light dashed line in Figure 2),i.e., the run where the elements with known relevance and their descendants are virtually removed from the collection; its MAP value is not constant because the residual collection get smaller when elements are removed. Our implementation of content feedback (dark solid line) yields an absolute gain of about 0.02 in MAP which corresponds to roughly 70% relative gain when the relevance of at least the top-8 elements is known. Adding document-based constraints (dark dashed line) yields similar gains, but already with feedback for the top-ranked element. The combination of both approaches (light solid line) is best, yielding an absolute gain of up to 0.03 (corresponding to a relative gain of more than 100% for top-20 feedback).

The improvements for precision at 10 are less spectacular with document-based feedback (see Figure 3), especially compared to content-based feedback. On the other hand, this behaviour is not surprising as adding document-based constraints to a query gives a higher score to all elements in a matching document, regardless of their relevance to the query; hence document-based feedback

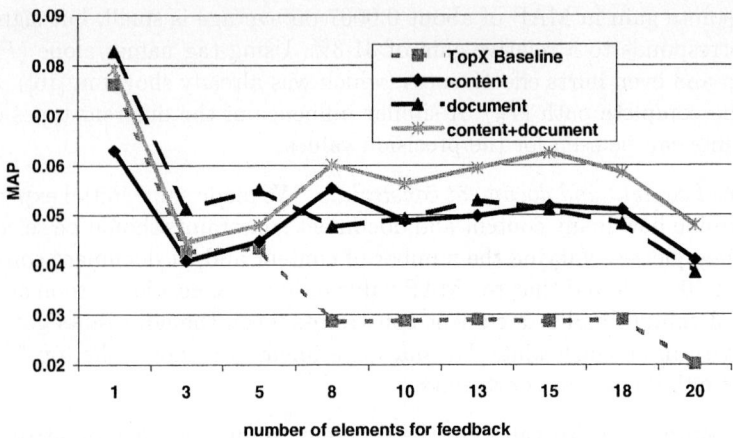

**Fig. 2.** MAP for document-based feedback on TopX

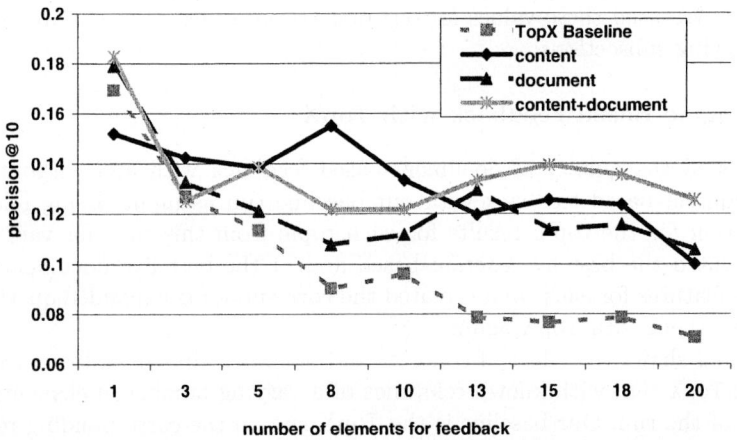

**Fig. 3.** Precision@10 for document-based feedback on TopX

is better in improving recall than precision. The combination of content-based and document-based feedback again beats the single dimensions, giving high scores to elements with good content in good documents.

Figure 4 shows the effect of additional path-based feedback in combination with document- and content-based feedback. The effect of path-based feedback alone (dark solid line in Figure 2) is mixed: While it slightly increases MAP for a medium number of elements with feedback, it downgrades results with feedback for a few or many elements. A similar effect occurs for the combination of path-based feedback with either content-based or document-based feedback; we omitted the lines from the chart for readability. However, combined with both content- and document-based feedback (dark dashed line), path constraints do result in a small gain in MAP.

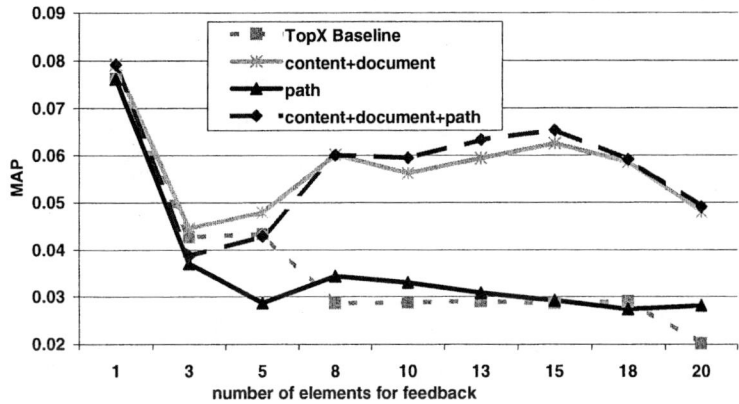

**Fig. 4.** MAP values for path-based feedback with TopX

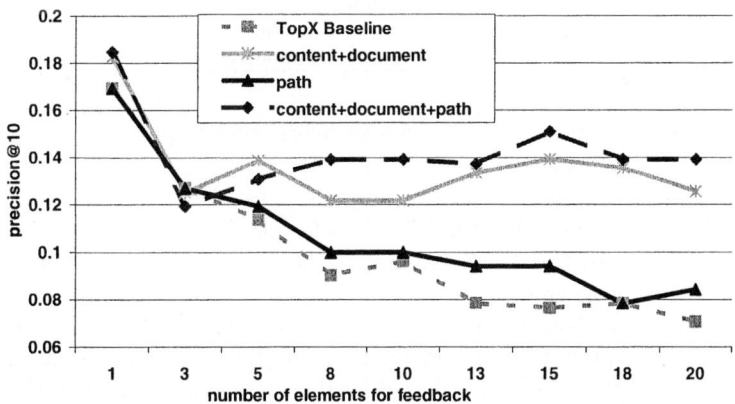

**Fig. 5.** Precision@10 values for path-based feedback with TopX

Regarding precision at 10 (shown in Figure 5), we find that path-based feedback alone always slightly increases precision over the baseline. The same holds for path feedback in combination with either document or content feedback (we omitted the lines in the chart for the sake of readability); the combination of all three dimensions of feedback yields the best precision if the relevance of at least the top-8 elements is known. The peak improvement (for top-20 feedback with all three dimensions) is about 100% over the baseline without feedback.

## 5.4 Hybrid Evaluation

To show that hybrid evaluation is a viable way of integrating structural feedback with keyword-based engines, we evaluated the effectiveness of content, path and document constraints with our hybrid evaluator and the TopX engine, using TopX only to compute the baseline run.

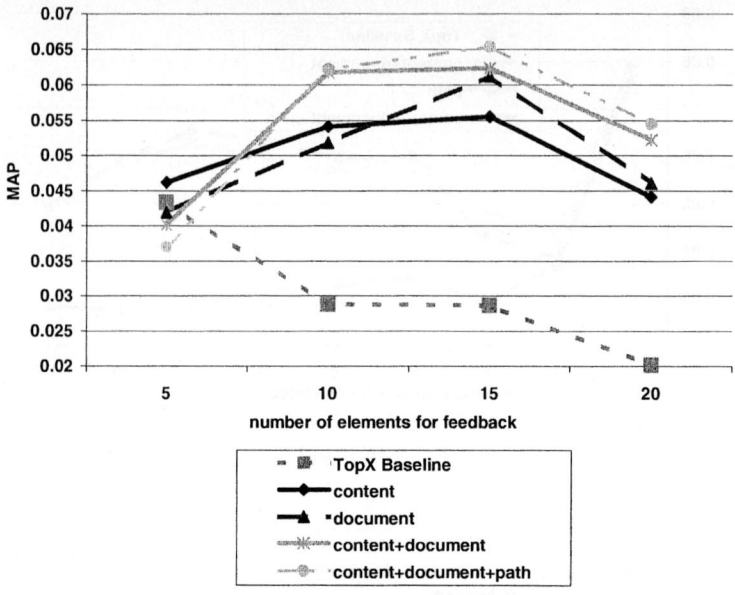

**Fig. 6.** MAP values for hybrid evaluation

Figure 6 shows the resulting MAP values for important combinations of feedback dimensions and the TopX baseline without feedback, measured with different numbers of elements with known relevance. The general trends are the same as with engine-based evaluation, which shows that our approach to evaluate feedback separately from the engine is viable. Interestingly, content feedback is slightly better than document-based feedback for small numbers of elements with known relevance, and slightly worse for large numbers; with engine-based evaluation we observed the inverse orders. Path based feedback in combination with a single, second dimension – which is again omitted from the chart – slightly outperformed the same dimension without path-based feedback. The combination of all feedback dimensions again outperforms all the others. The absolute MAP values are often slightly higher with hybrid evaluation; we attribute this to the fact that scores for each dimensions are normalized to the interval $[-1; 1]$ before aggregating them. The same effect could be obtained with engine-based evaluation if weights are selected more carefully; we plan to study this in future work. We also measured precision at 10 and got similar results that are omitted from the paper.

Even though execution times are not the focus of this paper, we measured the time needed for computing the best features for query expansion and reranking the list of 1500 results. On average, this took not more than 20 seconds per query with our preliminary, database-backed implementation, all three feedback dimensions and feedback for the top-20 results; we expect that this time will decrease a lot with a more performance-oriented implementation.

## 6 Conclusion and Future Work

This paper has made important steps from content-based to structural feedback in XML retrieval. It presented an integrated solution for expanding keyword queries with new content, path, and document constraints as a part of an extensible framework and showed huge performance gains with the established INEX benchmark of up to 150% for MAP and up to 100% for precision@10 under the evaluation method used in the INEX relevance feedback track.

Our future work will contentrate on adding new classes of document constraints (like paths, twigs, and the existence of elements or paths in a document) and integrating this work with our previous work on ontological query expansion [18]. We will also consider pseudo relevance feedback with paths and document constraints. We plan to evaluate our approach with the INEX Relevance Feedback Track where we will also examine the effect of feedback on queries with content and structural constraints.

## References

1. G. Amati, C. Carpineto, and G. Romano. Merging XML indices. In *INEX Workshop 2004*, pages 77–81, 2004. available from
http://inex.is.informatik.uni-duisburg.de:2004/.
2. R. A. Baeza-Yates and B. Riberto-Neto, editors. *Modern Information Retrieval*. Addison Wesley, 1999.
3. A. Balmin et al. A system for keyword proximity search on XML databases. In *VLDB 2003*, pages 1069–1072, 2003.
4. H. Blanken, T. Grabs, H.-J. Schek, R. Schenkel, and G. Weikum, editors. *Intelligent Search on XML Data*, volume 2818 of *LNCS*. Springer, Sept. 2003.
5. D. Carmel et al. Searching XML documents via XML fragments. In *SIGIR 2003*, pages 151–158, 2003.
6. C. Crouch. Relevance feedback at the INEX 2004 workshop. *SIGIR Forum*, 39(1):41–42, 2005.
7. C. J. Crouch, A. Mahajan, and A. Bellamkonda. Flexible XML retrieval based on the extended vector model. In *INEX 2004 Workshop*, pages 149–153, 2004.
8. M. A. Gonçalves, E. A. Fox, A. Krowne, P. Calado, A. H. F. Laender, A. S. da Silva, and B. Ribeiro-Neto. The effectiveness of automatically structured queries in digital libraries. In *4th ACM/IEEE-CS joint conference on Digital libraries (JCDL04)*, pages 98–107, 2004.
9. L. Guo et al. XRANK: ranked keyword search over XML documents. In *SIGMOD 2003*, pages 16–27, 2003.
10. L. Hlaoua and M. Boughanem. Towards context and structural relevance feedback in XML retrieval. In *Workshop on Open Source Web Information Retrieval (OSWIR)*, 2005. http://www.emse.fr/OSWIR05/.
11. W. Hsu, M. L. Lee, and X. Wu. Path-augmented keyword search for XML documents. In *ICTAI 2004*, pages 526–530, 2004.
12. INEX relevance feedback track.
http://inex.is.informatik.uni-duisburg.de:2004/tracks/rel/
13. G. Kazai et al. The INEX evaluation initiative. In Blanken et al. [4], pages 279–293.

14. S. Liu, Q. Zou, and W. Chu. Configurable indexing and ranking for XML information retrieval. In *SIGIR 2004*, pages 88–95, 2004.
15. Y. Mass and M. Mandelbrod. Relevance feedback for XML retrieval. In *INEX 2004 Workshop*, pages 154–157, 2004.
16. V. Mihajlovič et al. TIJAH at INEX 2004 modeling phrases and relevance feedback. In *INEX 2004 Workshop*, pages 141–148, 2004.
17. H. Pan. Relevance feedback in XML retrieval. In *EDBT 2004 Workshops*, pages 187–196, 2004.
18. H. Pan, A. Theobald, and R. Schenkel. Query refinement by relevance feedback in an XML retrieval system. In *ER 2004*, pages 854–855, 2004.
19. G. Ramirez, T. Westerveld, and A. de Vries. Structural features in content oriented xml retrieval. Technical Report INS-E0508, CWI,Centre for Mathematics and Computer Science, 2005.
20. G. Ramírez, T. Westerveld, and A. P. de Vries. Structural features in content oriented XML retrieval. In *CIKM 2005*, 2005.
21. J. Rocchio Jr. Relevance feedback in information retrieval. In G. Salton, editor, *The SMART Retrieval System: Experiments in Automatic Document Processing*, chapter 14, pages 313–323. Prentice Hall, Englewood Cliffs, New Jersey, USA, 1971.
22. I. Ruthven and M. Lalmas. A survey on the use of relevance feedback for information access systems. *Knowledge Engineering Review*, 18(1), 2003.
23. B. Sigurbjörnsson, J. Kamps, and M. de Rijke. The University of Amsterdam at INEX 2004. In *INEX 2004 Workshop*, pages 104–109, 2004.
24. M. Theobald, R. Schenkel, and G. Weikum. An efficient and versatile query engine for TopX search. In *VLDB 2005*, pages 625–636, 2005.
25. A. Trotman and B. Sigurbjörnsson. Narrowed Extended XPath I (NEXI). available at http://www.cs.otago.ac.nz/postgrads/andrew/2004-4.pdf, 2004.
26. J.-N. Vittaut, B. Piwowarski, and P. Gallinari. An algebra for structured queries in bayesian networks. In *INEX Workshop 2004*, pages 58–64, 2004.
27. R. Weber. Using relevance feedback in XML retrieval. In Blanken et al. [4], pages 133–143.
28. Y. Xu and Y. Papakonstantinou. Efficient keyword search for smallest LCAs in XML databases. In *SIGMOD 2005*, pages 537–538, 2005.

# Expressiveness and Performance of Full-Text Search Languages

Chavdar Botev[1], Sihem Amer-Yahia[2], and Jayavel Shanmugasundaram[1]

[1] Cornell University,
Ithaca, NY 14853, USA
cbotev@cs.cornell.edu,
jai@cs.cornell.edu
[2] AT&T Labs–Research,
Florham Park, NJ 07932, USA
sihem@research.att.com

**Abstract.** We study the expressiveness and performance of full-text search languages. Our motivation is to provide a formal basis for comparing full-text search languages and to develop a model for full-text search that can be tightly integrated with structured search. We design a model based on the positions of tokens (words) in the input text, and develop a full-text calculus (FTC) and a full-text algebra (FTA) with equivalent expressive power; this suggests a notion of completeness for full-text search languages. We show that existing full-text languages are incomplete and identify a practical subset of the FTC and FTA that is more powerful than existing languages, but which can still be evaluated efficiently.

## 1 Introduction

Full-text search is an important aspect of many information systems that deal with large document collections with unknown or ill-defined structure. The common full-text search method is to use simple keyword search queries, which are usually interpreted as a disjunction or conjunction of query keywords. Such queries are supported by traditional full-text search systems over "flat" text documents [1], over relational data [2, 16], and more recently over XML documents [9, 13, 25]. Many new and emerging applications, however, require full-text search capabilities that are more powerful than simple keyword search. For instance, legal information systems (e.g., LexisNexis®)[1] and large digital libraries (e.g., such as the Library of Congress (LoC))[2] allow users to specify a variety of full-text conditions such as the ordering between keywords and keywords distance. For example, a user can issue a query to find LoC documents that contain the keywords "assignment", "district", and "judge" in that order, where the keywords "district" and "judge" occur right next to each other (i.e., within a distance of 0 intervening words), and the keyword "judge" appears within 5 words of the keyword "assignment". In a recent panel at SIGMOD 2005,[3] a librarian at the LoC mentioned that support

---

[1] *http://www.lexisnexis.com/*
[2] *http://thomas.loc.gov/*
[3] *http://cimic.rutgers.edu/ sigmod05/*

for such "structured" full-text queries is one of the most important requirements for effectively querying LoC documents.

Given structured full-text queries, one of the practical problems that arises is being able to model, optimize and efficiently evaluate such queries. This problem has been studied for simple structured full-text queries in the information retrieval community [5], and more recently, for more complex structured full-text queries using text region algebras (TRAs) [10]. TRAs explicitly model keyword positions and pre-defined regions such as sentences and paragraphs in a document, and develop efficient evaluation algorithms for set operations between regions such as region inclusion and region ordering. While TRAs are an excellent first step, they have a fundamental limitation: they are not expressive enough to write certain natural structured full-text queries that combine inclusion and ordering of multiple regions. Further, since TRAs are based on a different algebraic model than the relational model, it is difficult to tightly integrate structured full-text search with structured search (which is usually relational).

To address the above issues, we propose a new model for structured full-text search. Specifically, we develop a Full-Text Calculus (FTC) based on first-order logic and an equivalent Full-Text Algebra (FTA) based on the relational algebra, and show how scoring can be incorporated into these models. Based on the FTC and FTA, we define a notion of completeness and show that existing query languages, including those based on TRAs, are incomplete with respect to this definition. The key difference that results in more expressive power for the FTA when compared to TRAs, is that the FTA deals with *tuples of one or more positions*, while TRAs only only keep track of the start and end positions of a region during query evaluation, and lose information about individual keyword positions within regions. Further, since the FTA is based on the relational algebra, it can be tightly integrated with structured query processing.

Our next focus in the paper is on efficiency: since the FTA (or equivalently, the FTC) is based on the relational algebra, not all queries can be efficiently evaluated in time that is linear in the size of the input database. To address this issue, we identify PPRED, a practical subset of the FTC, which strictly subsumes TRAs. We also propose an algorithm that can efficiently evaluate PPRED queries in a *single pass* over inverted lists, which are a common data structure used in information retrieval. We also experimentally evaluate the performance of the algorithm.

In summary, the main contributions of this paper are:

- We introduce a new formal model for structured full-text search and scoring based on first-order logic (FTC) and the relational algebra (FTA), and define a notion of completeness for full-text languages (Section 2).
- We show that existing languages are incomplete with respect to the above definition of completeness (Section 3).
- We define a practical subset of the FTC and FTA called PPRED, which subsumes TRAs and can be evaluated in a single pass over inverted lists (Section 4).
- We experimentally study the performance of the PPRED algorithm (Section 5).

## 2 Related Work

There has been extensive research in the information retrieval community on the efficient evaluation of full-text queries [1, 23, 27], including structured full-text queries [5].

However, the work on structured full-text queries only develops algorithms for specific full-text predicates (such as window) in isolation. Specifically, existing proposals do not develop a fully composable language for many full-text predicates, and also do not study the expressiveness and complexity of the language. This observation also applies to XML full-text search languages such as XQuery/IR [4], XSEarch [9], XIRQL [13], XXL [25] and Niagara [29]. Our proposed formalism is expressive enough to capture the full-text search aspects of these existing languages, and is in fact, more powerful (see Section 4.1).

More recently, there has been some work on using text region algebras (TRAs) to model structured full-text search [7, 10, 17, 20, 22, 28]. A text region is a sequence of consecutive words in a document and is often used to represent a structural part of a document (e.g., a chapter). It is identified by the positions of the first and the last words in the region. TRAs operate on sets of text regions which may contain overlapping regions ([7]) or strict hierarchies ([20]). Common operators are the set-theoretic operators, inclusion between regions and ordering of regions [28] as defined below:

- A region $s$ is represented as the ordered pair $(s.l, s.r)$, where $s.l$ is the left end-point of the region, and $s.r$ is its right end-point.
- A query operator has the form $\{s \in S \mid \exists d \in D\ Pred(s,d)\}$, where $S$ and $D$ are sets of regions and $Pred$ is a Boolean expression with the logical operators $\vee$ and $\wedge$ and containing clauses of the form $(x \odot y)$, where $\odot \in \{=, <, >, \leq, \geq\}, x \in \{s.l, s.r, s.l + const, s.l - const, s.r + const, s.r - const\}, y \in \{d.l, d.r\}$, and $const$ is a constant.

Efficient algorithms have been devised to evaluate TRA queries. However, while TRAs are useful in a number of scenarios (e.g. search over semi-structured SGML and XML documents), they have limited expressive power. Consens and Milo [10] showed that TRAs cannot represent simultaneously inclusion and ordering constraints. For example, the query: find a region that contains a region $s$ from a set $S$ and a region $t$ from a set $T$ such that $s$ comes before $t$, cannot be represented in TRAs. As we shall show in Section 4.2, similar queries arise in structured full-text search, for instance, when trying to find two windows nested inside another window.

Besides TRAs, there has also been a significant amount of work on using relational databases to store inverted lists, and in translating keyword queries to SQL [6, 12, 16, 18, 21, 29]; however, they do not study the completeness of languages and do not develop specialized one-pass query evaluation algorithms for structured full-text predicates.

## 3 The FTC and the FTA

Unlike SQL for querying relational data, there is no well-accepted language for expressing complex full-text search queries. In fact, many search systems use their own syntax for expressing the subset of complex queries that they support.[4] Instead of using one specific syntax, we adopt a more general approach and model full-text search

---

[4] http://www.lexisnexis.com/, http://www.google.com, http://thomas.loc.gov, http://www.verity.com

queries using calculus and algebra operations. Specifically, we use a Full-Text Calculus (FTC) based on first order logic and an equivalent Full-Text Algebra (FTA) based on the relational algebra.

The FTC and the FTA provide additional expressive power when compared to previous work on TRAs. The increased expressive power stems from the fact that the FTC and FTA deal with *tuples of positions*, instead of just start and end positions as in TRAs. Further, since the FTA is based on the relational algebra, it can be tightly integrated with structured relational queries.

### 3.1 Full-Text Search Model

We assume that full-text search queries are specified over a collection of *nodes* (which could be text documents, HTML documents, XML elements, relational tuples, etc.). Since our goal is to support structured full-text predicates such as distance and order, which depend on the position of a token (word) in a node, we explicitly model the notion of a *position* that uniquely identifies a token in a node. In Figure 1, we have used a simple numeric position for each token, which is sufficient to answer predicates such as distance and order. More expressive positions may enable more sophisticated predicates on positions such as sentence- and paragraph-distance predicates.

More formally, let $\mathcal{N}$ be the set of nodes, $\mathcal{P}$ be the set of positions, and $\mathcal{T}$ be the set of tokens. The function $Positions : \mathcal{N} \to 2^{\mathcal{P}}$ maps a node to the set of positions in the node. The function $Token : \mathcal{P} \to \mathcal{T}$ maps each position to the token at that position. In the example in Figure 1, if the node **it** is denoted by $n$, then $Positions(n) = \{410, ..., 423, ...\}$, $Token(412) = \text{``}judge\text{''}$, $Token(423) = \text{``}service\text{''}$, and so on.

We also have the following requirement for completeness: *The full-text search language should be at least as expressive as first-order logic formulas specified over the positions of tokens in a context node.* The above requirement identifies tokens and their positions as the fundamental units in a full-text search language, and essentially describes a notion of completeness similar to that of relational completeness [8] based on first-order logic. Other notions of completeness can certainly be defined based on higher-order logics, but as we shall soon see, defining completeness in terms of

```
<html> <head> ... </head>
<body>
   <p>HR-212-IH (104)</p>
   <p><center>109th(105) Congress (106)</center></p>
   <h3><center>January(107) 4(108), 2005(109)
      </center></h3>
   ...
   <h3>SEC (404). 7(405). ASSIGNMENT(406) OF(407)
      CIRCUIT(408) JUDGES(409).</h3>
      <p><it> Each (410) circuit (411) judge (412) of (413)
         the (414) former (415) ninth (416) circuit (417)
         who (418) is (419) in (420) regular (421) active (422)
         service (423) ...</it></p>
</body>
```

**Fig. 1.** Positions Example

first-order logic allows for both efficient evaluation and tight integration with the relational model. We also note that each context node is considered separately, i.e., a full-text search condition does not span multiple context nodes. This is in keeping with the semantics of existing full-text languages.

### 3.2 Full-Text Calculus (FTC)

The FTC defines the following predicates to model basic full-text primitives.

- $SearchContext(node)$ is true iff $node \in \mathcal{N}$
- $hasPos(node, pos)$ is true iff $pos \in Positions(node)$.
- $hasAsToken(pos, tok)$ is true iff $tok = Token(pos)$.

A full-text language may also wish to specify additional position-based predicates, $Preds$. The FTC is general enough to support arbitrary position-based predicates. Specifically, given a set $VarPos$ of position variables, and a set $Consts$ of constants, it can support any predicate of the form: $pred(p_1, ..., p_m, c_1, ..., c_r)$, where $p_1, ...p_m \in VarPos$ and $c_1, ..., c_r \in Consts$. For example, we could define

$$Preds = \{distance(pos_1, pos_2, dist), ordered(pos_1, pos_2), samepara(pos_1, pos_2)\}.$$

Here, $distance(pos_1, pos_2, dist)$ returns true iff there are at most $dist$ intervening tokens between $pos_1$ and $pos_2$ (irrespective of the order of the positions); $ordered(pos_1, pos_2)$ is true iff $pos_1$ occurs before $pos_2$; $samepara(pos_1, pos_2)$ is true iff $pos_1$ is in the same paragraph as $pos_2$.

An FTC query is of the form: $\{node|SearchContext(node) \land QueryExpr(node)\}$. Intuitively, the query returns $nodes$ that are in the search context, and that satisfy $QueryExpr(node)$. $QueryExpr(node)$, hereafter called the *query expression*, is a first-order logic expression that specifies the full-text search condition. The query expression can contain position predicates in addition to logical operators. The only free variable in the query expression is $node$.

As an illustration, the query below returns the context nodes that contain the keywords "district", "judge", and "assignment":

$\{node|SearchContext(node) \land \exists pos_1, pos_2, pos_3$
$\quad (hasPos(node, pos_1) \land hasAsToken(pos_1, 'district') \land$
$\quad hasPos(node, pos_2) \land hasAsToken(pos_2, 'judge') \land$
$\quad hasPos(node, pos_3) \land hasAsToken(pos_3, 'assignment'))\}$

In subsequent examples, we only show the full-text condition since the rest of the query is the same. The following query represents the query in the introduction (find context nodes that contain the keywords "assignment", "district", and "judge" in that order, where the keywords "district" and "judge" occur right next to each other, and the keyword "judge" appears within 5 words of the keyword "assignment"):

$\exists pos_1, pos_2, pos_3 (hasPos(node, pos_1) \land hasAsToken(pos_1, 'assignment') \land$
$\qquad hasPos(node, pos_2) \land hasAsToken(pos_2, 'district') \land$
$\qquad hasPos(node, pos_3) \land hasAsToken(pos_3, 'judge') \land$
$\qquad ordered(pos_1, pos_2) \land ordered(pos_2, pos_3) \land$
$\qquad distance(pos_2, pos_3, 0) \land distance(pos_1, pos_3, 5))$

## 3.3 Full-Text Algebra (FTA)

The FTA is defined based on an underlying data model called a *full-text relation*, which is of the form $R[node, att_1, ..., att_m]$, $m \geq 0$, where the domain of $node$ is $\mathcal{N}$ (nodes) and the domain of $att_i$ is $\mathcal{P}$ (positions). Each tuple of a full-text relation is of the form $(n, p_1, ..., p_m)$, where each $p_i \in Positions(n)$. Intuitively, each tuple represents a list of positions $p_1, ..., p_m$ that satisfy the full-text condition for node $n$. Since positions are modeled explicitly, they can be queried and manipulated.

An FTA expression is defined recursively as follows:

- $R_{token}(node, att_1)$, for each $token \in \mathcal{T}$, is an expression. $R_{token}$ contains a tuple for each $(node, pos)$ pair that satisfies: $node \in \mathcal{D} \land pos \in Positions(node) \land token = Token(pos)$. Intuitively, $R_{token}$ is similar to an inverted list, and has entries for nodes that contain $token$ along with its positions.
- If $Expr_1$ is an expression, $\pi_{node, att_{i_1}, ..., att_{i_j}}(Expr_1)$ is an expression. If $Expr_1$ evaluates to the full-text relation $R_1$, the full-text relation corresponding to the new expression is: $\pi_{node, att_{i_1}, ..., att_{i_j}}(R_1)$, where $\pi$ is the traditional relational projection operator. Note that $\pi$ *always* has to include node because we have to keep track of the node being queried.
- If $Expr_1$ and $Expr_2$ are expressions, then $(Expr_1 \bowtie Expr_2)$ is an expression. If $Expr_1$ and $Expr_2$ evaluate to $R_1$ and $R_2$ respectively, then the full-text relation corresponding to the new expression is: $R_1 \bowtie_{R_1.node=R_2.node} R_2$, where $\bowtie_{R_1.node=R_2.node}$ is the traditional relational equi-join operation on the node attribute. The join condition ensures that positions in the same tuple are in the same node, and hence can be processed using full-text predicates.
- If $Expr_1$ and $Expr_2$ are expressions, then $\sigma_{pred(att_1,...,att_m,c_1,...,c_q)}(Expr_1)$, $(Expr_1 - Expr_2)$, $(Expr_1 \cup Expr_2)$ are algebra expressions that have the same semantics as in traditional relational algebra.

An FTA query is an FTA expression that produces a full-text relation with a single attribute which, by definition, has to be node. The set of nodes in the result full-text relation defines the result of the FTA query.

We now show how two FTC queries in Section 3.2 can be written in the FTA:

$$\pi_{node}(R_{district} \bowtie R_{judge} \bowtie R_{assignment})$$

$$\pi_{node}(\sigma_{distance(att_2, att_3, 5)}(\\ \sigma_{ordered(att_3, att_1)}(\sigma_{ordered(att_1, att_2)}(\\ \sigma_{distance(att_1, att_2, 0)}(R_{district} \bowtie R_{judge}) \bowtie R_{assignment}))))$$

## 3.4 Equivalence of FTC and FTA and Completeness

**Theorem 1.** *Given a set of position-based predicates Preds, the FTC and FTA are equivalent in terms of expressive power.*

The proof of equivalence is similar to that of the relational algebra and calculus and is thus omitted (see [3]). We now formally define the notion of full-text completeness.

**Definition (Full-Text Completeness).** A full-text language $\mathcal{L}$ is said to be *full-text complete* with respect to a set of position-based predicates $Preds$ iff all queries that can be expressed in the FTC (or the FTA) using $Preds$ can also be expressed in $\mathcal{L}$.

The above definition of completeness provides a formal basis for comparing the expressiveness of full-text search languages, as we shall do in Section 4. To the best of our knowledge, this is the first attempt to formalize the expressive power of such languages for flat documents, relational databases, or XML documents.

## 3.5 Scoring

Scoring is an important aspect of full-text search. However, there is no standard agreed-upon method for scoring full-text search results. In fact, developing and evaluating different scoring methods is still an active area of research [13, 14, 15, 19, 25, 30]. Thus, rather than hard-code a specific scoring method into our framework, we describe a general scoring framework based on the FTC and the FTA, and show how some of the existing scoring methods can be incorporated into this framework. Specifically, we now show how TF-IDF [24] scoring can be incorporated, and refer the reader to [3] for how probability-based scoring [14, 30] can be incorporated. We only describe how scoring can be done in the context of the FTA; the extension to the FTC is similar.

Our scoring framework is based on two extensions to the FTA: (1) per-tuple scoring information and (2) scoring transformations. Per-tuple scoring information associates a score with each tuple in a full-text relation, similar to [14]. However, unlike [14], the scoring information need not be only a real number (or probability); it can be any arbitrary type associated with a tuple. Scoring transformations extend the semantics of FTA operators to transform the scores of the input full-text relations.

We now show how TF-IDF scoring can be captured using our scoring framework. We use the following widely-accepted TF and IDF formulas for a node $n$ and a token $t$: $tf(n,t) = occurs/unique\_tokens$ and $idf(t) = ln(1 + db\_size/df)$, where $occurs$ is the number of occurrences of $t$ in $n$, $unique\_tokens$ is the number of unique tokens in $n$, $db\_size$ is the number of nodes in the database, and $df$ is the number of nodes containing the token $t$. The TF-IDF scores are aggregated using the cosine similarity: $score(n) = \Sigma_{t \in q} w(t) * tf(n,t) * idf(t)/(||n||_2 * ||q||_2)$, where $q$ denotes query search tokens, $w(t)$, the weight of the search token $t$ and $||\cdot||_2$, the $L_2$ measure.

To model TF-IDF, we associate a numeric score with each tuple. Intuitively, the score contains the TF-IDF score for all the positions in the tuple. Initially, $R_t$ relations contain static scores: the $idf(t)$ for the token $t$ at that position divided by the product of the normalization factors $unique\_tokens * ||n||_2$. This is the $L_2$ normalized TF-IDF score for each position containing the token $t$. Thus, if we sum all the scores in $R_t$, we get exactly the $L_2$-normalized TF-IDF score of $t$ with regards to $n$.

We now describe the scoring transformations for some of the FTA operators. For traditional TF-IDF, the interesting operators that change the scores are the join and the projection. First, consider the relation $R$ that is the result of the FTA expression $(Expr_1 \bowtie Expr_2)$, where the scored full-text relations produced by $Expr_1$ and $Expr_2$ are $R_1$ and $R_2$, respectively. Then, for each tuple $t \in R$, formed by the tuples $t_1 \in R_1$ and $t_2 \in R_2$, $t.score = t_1.score/|R_2| + t_2.score/|R_1|$, where $|R|$ denotes the cardinality of $R$. We need to scale down $t_1.score$ and $t_2.score$ because their relevance decreases due to the increased number of tuples (solutions) in the resulting relation. For projections, the new relation should have the same total score as the original one. More formally, let the relation $R$ be the result of the expression $\pi_{\text{CNode,att}_1,\ldots,\text{att}_i}(Expr_1)$ and let $Expr_1$ produces the relation $R_1$. Then, for any tuple $t \in R$ which is the result of the aggregation of the tuples $t_1, \ldots, t_n \in R_1$, $t.score = \Sigma_{i=1,\ldots,n} t_i.score$.

It can be shown that the above propagation of scores preserves the traditional semantics of TF-IDF for conjunctive and disjunctive queries [3]. Further, this scoring method is more powerful than traditional TF-IDF because it can be generalized to arbitrary structured queries by defining appropriate scoring transformations for each operator. For instance, we can define a scoring transformation for distance selection predicates thereby extending the scope of TF-IDF scoring.

## 4 Incompleteness of Existing Full-Text Search Languages

We show the incompleteness of existing full-text languages, including TRAs.

### 4.1 Predicate-Based Languages

We first consider traditional full-text languages that have position-based predicates in addition to Boolean operators [1, 5]. A typical syntax, which we call DIST, is:

Query := Token | Query AND Query | Query OR Query | Query AND NOT Query | dist(Token,Token,Integer)

Token := StringLiteral | ANY

We can recursively define the semantics of DIST in terms of the FTC. If the query is a StringLiteral 'token', it is equivalent to the FTC query expression $\exists p(hasPos(n,p) \wedge hasAsToken(p,'token'))$. If the query is ANY, it is equivalent to the expression $\exists p(hasPos(n,p))$. If the query is of the form Query1 AND NOT Query2, it is equivalent to $Expr_1 \wedge \neg Expr_2$, where $Expr_1$ and $Expr_2$ are the FTC expressions for Query1 and Query2. If the query is of the form Query1 AND Query2, it is equivalent to $Expr1 \wedge Expr2$, where $Expr1$ and $Expr2$ are FTC expressions for Query1 and Query2 respectively. OR is defined similarly. The *dist(Token,Token,Integer)* construct is the equivalent of the *distance* predicate introduced in the calculus (Section 3.2), and specifies that the number of intervening tokens should be less than the specified integer. More formally, the semantics of *dist(token1,token2,d)* for some tokens $token1$ and $token2$ and some integer $d$ is given by the calculus expression: $\exists p_1(hasPos(n,p_1) \wedge hasAsToken(p_1,token1) \wedge \exists p_2(hasPos(n,p_2) \wedge hasAsToken(p_2,token2) \wedge distance(p_1,p_2,d)))$. If $token1$ or $token2$ is ANY instead of a string literal, then the corresponding $hasAsToken$ predicate is omitted in the semantics.

As an example, the query *dist('test','usability',3)* is equivalent to the FTC query expression: $\exists p_1 \exists p_2(hasPos(n,p_1) \wedge hasAsToken(p_1,'test') \wedge hasPos(n,p_2) \wedge hasAsToken(p_2,'usability') \wedge distance(p_1,p_2,3))$.

We now show that DIST is incomplete if $\mathcal{T}$ is not trivially small. We can also prove similar incompleteness results for other position-based predicates.

**Theorem 2.** *If $\mid \mathcal{T} \mid \geq 3$, there exists a query that can be expressed in FTC with $Preds = \{distance(p_1,p_2,d)\}$ that cannot be expressed by DIST.*

*Proof Sketch:* We shall show that no query in DIST can express the following FTC query: $\exists p_1, p_2, p_3(hasPos(n, p_1) \land hasAsToken(p_1, t_1) \land hasPos(n, p_2) \land hasAsToken(p_2, t_2) \land hasPos(n, p_3) \land hasAsToken(p_3, t_3) \land distance(p_1, p_2, 0) \land distance(p_2, p_3, 0))$ (find context nodes that contains a token $t_1$ that occurs right next to a token $t_2$ that in turn occurs right next to a token $t_3$). For simplicity, we use distances with at most 0 tokens but the example can be generalized to arbitrary distances. The proof is by contradiction. Assume that there exists a query $\mathcal{Q}$ in DIST that can express the calculus query. We now construct two context nodes $CN_1$ and $CN_2$ as follows. $CN_1$ contains the tokens $t_1$ followed by $t_2$ followed by $t_3$ followed by $t_1$. $CN_2$ contains the tokens $t_1$ followed by $t_2$ followed by $t_2$ followed by $t_3$ followed by $t_3$ followed by $t_1$. By the construction, we can see that $CN_1$ satisfies the calculus query, while $CN_2$ does not. We will now show that $\mathcal{Q}$ either returns both $CN_1$ or $CN_2$ or neither of them; since this contradicts our assumption, this will prove the theorem.

Let $C_Q$ be the calculus expression equivalent to $\mathcal{Q}$. We show that by induction on the structure of $C_Q$, every sub-expression of $C_Q$ (and hence $C_Q$) returns the same Boolean value for $CN_1$ and $CN_2$. If the sub-expression is of the form $\exists p(hasPos(n, p) \land hasAsToken(p, token))$, it returns the same Boolean value for both $CN_1$ and $CN_2$ since both documents have the same set of tokens. Similarly, if the sub-expression is of the form $\exists p(hasPos(n, p))$, it returns true for both $CN_1$ and $CN_2$. If the sub-expression is of the form $\neg Expr$, then it returns the same Boolean value for both $CN_1$ and $CN_2$ because $Expr$ returns the same Boolean value (by induction). A similar argument can also be made for the $\land$ and $\lor$ Boolean operators. If the sub-expression is of the form $\exists p_1(hasPos(n, p_1) \land hasAsToken(p_1, token1) \land \exists p_2(hasPos(n, p_2) \land hasAsToken(p_2, token2) \land distance(p_1, p_2, d)))$, there are two cases. In the first case, $token1 \notin \{t_1, t_2, t_3\} \lor token2 \notin \{t_1, t_2, t_3\}$, and it is easy to see that the sub-expression returns false for both $CN_1$ and $CN_2$. In the second case, $token1, token2 \in \{t_1, t_2, t_3\}$. Since $distance(token1, token2, 0)$ is true for both $CN_1$ and $CN_2$, and hence $distance(token1, token2, d)$ is true for $d \geq 0$, the sub-expression returns true for both $CN_1$ and $CN_2$. Since we have considered all sub-expressions, this is a contradiction and proves the theorem. □

### 4.2 Text Region Algebras

We now show that TRAs are incomplete.

**Theorem 3.** *There exists a query that can be expressed in FTC with $Preds = \{ordered(p_1, p_2), samepara(p_1, p_2)\}$ that cannot be expressed in TRA (as defined in [10]).*

*Proof Sketch:* The following FTC query cannot be expressed using TRA: $\exists pos_1, pos_2(hasPos(node, pos_1) \land hasAsToken(pos_1, t_1) \land hasPos(node, pos_2) \land hasAsToken(pos_2, t_2) \land ordered(pos_1, pos_2) \land samepara(pos_1, pos_2))$ (find context nodes that contain the tokens $t_1$ and $t_2$ in that order within the same paragraph). The proof is very similar to the proof by Consens and Milo [10], who have shown that TRAs cannot represent simultaneously inclusion and ordering constraints. In particular, they prove that the query: *find documents with regions $s \in S$ that contain two other regions $t \in T$ and $u \in U$ such that $t$ comes before $u$*, cannot be represented using TRA. When we consider $S$ to be the regions with the same start and end positions which correspond to the occurrences of the keyword $k_1$, and similarly for $T$ for keyword $k_2$, and set $U$ to be regions representing paragraphs, the theorem follows. □

## 5 PPRED: Language and Query Evaluation

The evaluation of FTC queries corresponds to the problem of evaluating Quantified Boolean Formulas (QBF), which is LOGSPACE-complete for data complexity (complexity in the size of the database) and PSPACE-complete for expression complexity (complexity in the size of the query) [26]. Since whether LOGSPACE is a strict subset of PTIME (polynomial time), and whether PSPACE is a strict subset of EXPTIME (exponential time) are open questions, we can only devise a query evaluation algorithm that is polynomial in the size of the data and exponential in the size of the query. This evaluation complexity is clearly unacceptable for large data sets and hence motivates the need to find efficient subsets of FTC.

In this section, we present PPRED (for Positive PREDicates), a subset of FTC which includes most common full-text predicates, such as *distance*, *ordered* and *samepara*, and is more powerful than existing languages such as DIST and TRAs. Further, PPRED queries can be evaluated in a single pass over inverted lists.

The key observation behind PPRED is that many full-text predicates are true in a contiguous region of the position space. For instance, *distance* applied to two position variables is true in the region where the position values of those variables are within the distance limit, and false outside this region. For *ordered*, a region specifies the part of the position space where the positions are in the required order. Other common full-text predicates such as *samepara*, and *window* also share this property. We call such predicates positive predicates. These predicates can be efficiently evaluated by scanning context nodes in *increasing order* of positions, which can be done in a single scan over the inverted list entries because they are typically stored in increasing order of positions.

We now formally define the PPRED language, and describe efficient query evaluation algorithms that also consider score-based pruning.

### 5.1 Positive Predicates

**Definition (Positive Predicates).** An n-ary position-based predicate *pred* is said to be a *positive predicate* iff there exist $n$ functions $f_i : \mathcal{P}^n \to \mathcal{P}$ ($1 \leq i \leq n$) such that:

$\forall p_1, ..., p_n \in \mathcal{P}\ (\neg pred(p_1, ..., p_n) \Rightarrow$
$\quad \forall i \forall p'_i \in \mathcal{P}\ p_i \leq p'_i < f_i(p_1, ..., p_n) \Rightarrow$
$\quad \quad \forall p'_1, ..., p'_{i-1}, p'_{i+1}, ..., p'_n \in \mathcal{P}$
$\quad \quad \quad p_1 \leq p'_1, ..., p_{i-1} \leq p'_{i-1},$
$\quad \quad \quad p_{i+1} \leq p'_{i+1}, ..., p_n \leq p'_n \Rightarrow \neg pred(p'_1, ..., p'_n)$
$\wedge$
$\exists j\ f_j(p_1, ..., p_n) > p_j)$

Intuitively, the property states that for every combination of positions that do not satisfy the predicate: (a) there exists a contiguous boundary in the position space such that all combinations of positions in this boundary do not satisfy the predicate; this contiguous area is specified in terms of the functions $f_i(p_1, ..., p_n)$, which specify the lower bound of the boundary for the dimension corresponding to position $p_i$, and (b) there is at least one dimension in the position space where the boundary can be advanced beyond the current boundary, i.e., at least one $f_i(p_1, ..., p_n)$ has value greater than $p_i$; this ensures that the boundary can be pushed forward in search of a combination of positions that do satisfy the predicate.

For example, for $distance(p_1, ..., p_n, d)$, we can define the $f_i$ functions as follows $f_i(p_1, ..., p_n) = max(max(p_1, ..., p_n) - d + 1, p_i)$. Similarly, for $ordered$, $f_i(p_1, ..., p_n) = max(p_1, ..., p_i)$. For $samepara$, $f_i(p_1, ..., p_n) = min\{p \in \mathcal{P} \mid para(p) = max(para(p_1), ..., max(para(p_n)))$ where $para$ is a function that returns the paragraph containing a position.

**Language Description.** We now define the PPRED language, which is a strict superset of DIST. Thus, simple queries retain the same conventional syntax, while new constructs are only required for more complex queries.

   Query := Token | Query AND Query | Query OR Query | Query AND NOT Query* | SOME Var Query | Preds
      Token := StringLiteral | ANY | Var HAS StringLiteral | Var HAS ANY
      Preds := distance(Var,Var,Integer) | ordered(Var,Var) | ...

The main additions to DIST are the HAS construct in Token and the SOME construct in Query. The HAS construct allows us to explicitly bind position variables (Var) to positions where tokens occur. The semantics for '$var_1$ HAS $tok$' in terms of the FTC, where $tok$ is a StringLiteral is: $hasAsToken(var_1, tok)$. The semantics for '$var_1$ HAS ANY' is: $hasPos(n, var_1)$. While the HAS construct allows us to explicitly bind position variables to token positions, the SOME construct allows us to quantify over these positions. The semantics of 'SOME $var_1$ Query' is $\exists var_1(hasPos(n, var_1) \wedge Expr)$, where $Expr$ is the FTC expression semantics for Query. Query* refers to a Query with no free variables.

For example, the following PPRED query expresses the second sample query from Section 3.2 SOME p1 HAS 'assignment' SOME p2 HAS 'district' SOME p3 HAS 'judge' ordered(p1,p2) AND ordered(pos2,pos3) AND distance(p2,p3) AND distance(p1,p3,5).

Although PPRED is not complete (e.g., it does not support universal quantification and arbitrary negation), it is still quite powerful. For instance, it can specify all of the queries used in the incompleteness proofs in Section 4 (since ordered, distance and samepara are all positive predicates). In fact, PPRED is a strict superset of DIST (since it contains all of the constructs of DIST) and of TRAs (see [3] for the proof).

## 5.2 Query Evaluation

We describe the PPRED query evaluation model and algorithm.

**Query Evaluation Model.** Each $R_{token}$ relation is represented as an inverted list associated to $token$. Each inverted list contains one or more *entries*. Each entry in $R_{token}$ is of the form: $(node, PosList, score)$, where $node$ is the identifier of a node that contains $token$, $PosList$ is the list of positions of $token$ in $node$, and $score$ is the score of $node$. We assume that the inverted lists are sorted on node identifiers. Note that they could be sorted on scores. Figure 2(a) shows example inverted lists for the words "district", "judge", and "assignment". Inverted lists are typically accessed sequentially using a *cursor*. Advancing the cursor can be done in constant time.

**Query Evaluation Overview.** We now illustrate how positive predicates enable efficient query evaluation. Consider the simple query $\pi_{node}(\sigma_{distance(att_1,att_2,1)}(R_{district} \bowtie R_{judge}))$ (return nodes that contain the words "district" and "judge" within at most 1 word of each other). The naïve evaluation approach over the inverted lists shown in Figure 2(a) would compute the Cartesian product of the positions for each node and then apply the distance predicate. For the node 1, this corresponds to computing 9 pairs of positions (3 in each inverted list), and then only selecting the final pair (139,140) that satisfies the distance predicate. However, using the property that distance is a positive predicate, we can determine the answer by only scanning 6 pairs of positions (3 + 3 instead of 3 * 3), as described below.

The query evaluation starts with the smallest pair of positions (80, 90) for node 1 and check whether it satisfies the distance predicate. Since it does not, we move *the smallest position* to get the pair (99, 90). Since this pair still does not satisfy the predicate, we again move the smallest position until we find a solution: (99, 105), (139, 105), (139, 140). Note that each position is scanned exactly once, so the complexity is linear in the size of the inverted lists. The reason the smallest position could be moved is because the distance predicate is true in a contiguous region, and if the predicate is false for the smallest position in the region, one can infer that it is also false for other positions without having to explicitly enumerate them.

Let us now consider a slightly more complex example using the *ordered* predicate: $\pi_{node}(\sigma_{ordered(att_1,att_2,att_3)}(R_{district} \bowtie R_{judge} \bowtie R_{assignment}))$ (return nodes that contain the words "district", "judge" and "assignment" in that order). For node 1, the first combination of positions (80, 90, 85) does not satisfy *ordered*. However, unlike the window predicate, we *cannot* move the cursor corresponding to the smallest position to get the combination (99, 90, 85); doing so will cause the solution (80, 90, 97) to be missed! (note that we cannot move a cursor back if we want a single scan over the positions). Rather, for *ordered*, we need to move the smallest position that *violates the order*. In our example, we should move the third cursor to get the combination (80, 90, 97).

In the above examples depending on the full-text predicate, different strategies may have to be employed to produce the correct results efficiently. This becomes harder with complex full-text queries (i.e., where different predicates are combined). Furthermore, the problem becomes even more complex when the query contains multiple predicates over possibly overlapping sets of positions. Which cursors should be moved in this case? Does the order in which cursors used by different predicates are moved matter? Is there a general strategy for evaluating arbitrary combinations of FTA queries with positive predicates? We answer these questions in the next section.

One aspect to note is that our query evaluation algorithms efficiently evaluate full-text predicates a node at a time before moving on to the next node. An important consequence of this is that our algorithms can be combined with any existing top-k evaluation technique (e.g. [11]), which prunes nodes from consideration based on their score (our algorithms will just not evaluate queries over the pruned nodes).

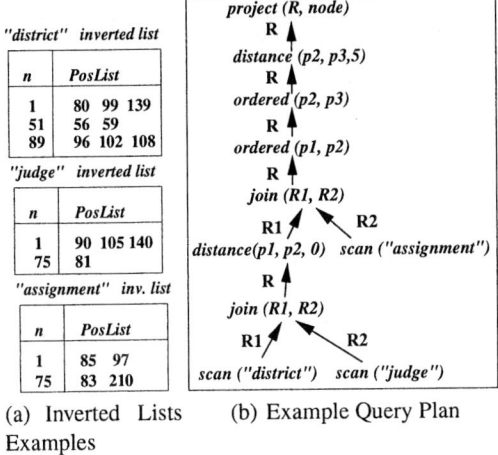

**Fig. 2.** Sample Inverted Lists and Query Plan

**Query Evaluation Algorithms.** A query is first converted to FTA operators and is rewritten to push down projections wherever possible so that spurious positions are not propagated. Figure 2(b) shows a sample FTA operator plan for the query in Section 1. Since we do not want to materialize the entire output full-text relation corresponding to an operator, each operator exposes a new API for traversing its output. This API ensures that successive calls can be evaluated in a single scan over the inverted list positions. We denote the output full-text relation for an operator $o$, $R$ which has $n$ position columns. The API, defined below, maintains the following state: $node$, which tracks the current node, and $p_1, ..., p_n$, which track the current positions in $node$.

- **advanceNode()**: On the first call, it sets $node$ to be the smallest value in $\pi_{node}(R)$ (if one exists; else $node$ is set to NULL). It also sets position values, $p_1, ..., p_n$ such that: $(node, p_1, ..., p_n) \in R \wedge \forall p'_1, ..., p'_n (node, p'_1, ..., p'_n) \in R \Rightarrow p'_1 \geq p_1 \wedge ... \wedge p'_n \geq p_n$ (i.e., it sets positions $p_1, ...p_n$ to be the smallest positions that appear in $R$ for that $node$; we will always be able to find such positions due to the property of positive predicates). On subsequent calls, $node$ is updated to the next smallest value in $\pi_{node}(R)$ (if one exists), and $p_1, ..., p_n$ are updated as before.
- **getNode()**: Returns the current value of $node$.
- **advancePosition(i, pos)**: It sets the values of $p_1, ..., p_n$ such that they satisfy: $(node, p_1, ..., p_n) \in R \wedge p_i > pos \wedge \forall p'_1, ..., p'_n (node, p'_1, ..., p'_n) \in R \wedge p'_i \geq pos \Rightarrow (p'_1 \geq p_1 \wedge ... \wedge p'_n \geq p_n)$ (i.e., the smallest values of positions that appear in $R$ and that satisfy the condition $p_i > pos$), and returns true. If no such positions exist, then it sets $p_i$s to be NULL and returns false.
- **getPosition(i)**: Returns the current value of $p_i$.

Given the operator evaluation tree in Figure 2(b), the general evaluation scheme proceeds as follows. To find a solution **advanceNode** is called on the top project operator which simply forward this call to the distance selection operator below it. The

**Algorithm 1.** Join Evaluation Algorithm

**Require:** $inp1, inp2$ are the two API inputs to the join, and have $c_1$ and $c_2$ position columns, respectively
1: Node advanceNode() {
2:   node1 = inp1.advanceNode(); node2 = inp2.advanceNode();
3:   **while** node1 != NULL && node2 != NULL && node1 != node2 **do**
4:     **if** node1 < node2 **then** node1 = inp1.advanceNode();
5:     **else** node2 = inp2.advanceNode(); **endif**
6:   **end while**
7:   **if** node1 == NULL || node2 == NULL **then** return NULL;
8:   **else** [node1 == node2]
9:     set $p_i$ ($i < c_1$) to inp1.getPosition(i);
10:    set $p_i$ ($i \geq c_1$) to inp2.getPosition($i - c_1$);
11:    node = node1;
12:    return node1; **endif** }
13:
14: boolean advancePosition(i,pos) {
15:   **if** ($i < c_1$)**then**
16:     result = inp1.advancePosition(i,pos);
17:     **if** (result)**then** $p_i$ = inp1.getPostion(i);**endif**
18:     return result;
19:   **else** //Similary for inp2 **end if** }

latter tries to find a solution by continuously calling **advancePosition** on the ordered predicate below it until it finds a satisfying tuple of positions. The ordered predicates behaves in a similar manner: it advances through the result of the underlying operator until it finds a tuple that satisfies it. The evaluation proceeds down the tree until the leaves (the scan operators) are reached. The latter simply advances through the entries in the inverted lists. The entire evaluation is pipelined and no intermediate relation needs to be materialized.

We now show how different PPRED operators can implement the above API. The API implementation for the inverted list scan and project operators are straightforward since they directly operate on the inverted list and input operator API, respectively. Thus, we focus on joins and selections. The implementation for set difference and union is similar to join, and is not discussed here.

Algorithm 1 shows how the API is implemented for the join operator. We only show the implementation of the **advanceNode** and **advancePos** methods since the other methods are trivial. Intuitively, **advanceNode** performs an equi-join on the *node*. It then sets the positions $p_i$ to the corresponding positions in the input.
**advancePosition(i, pos)** moves the position cursor on the corresponding input.

Algorithm 2 shows how the API is implemented for selections implementing predicate *pred* with functions $f_i$ defined in Section 5.1. Each call of **advanceNode**, advances *node* until one that satisfies the predicate is found, or there are no *cnodes* left. The satisfying node is found using the helper method **advancePosUntilSat**, which returns true iff it is able to advance the positions of the current *node* so that they satisfy the predicate *pred*. **advancePosition** first advances the position on its input, and then invokes **advancePosUntilSat** until a set of positions that satisfy *pred* are found.

**Algorithm 2.** Predicate Evaluation Algorithm

**Require:** $inp$ is API inputs to the predicate with $c$ position columns
1: Cnode advanceCnode() {
2:    cnode = inp.advanceCnode();
3:    **while** cnode != NULL && !advancePosUntilSat() **do**
4:       cnode = inp.advanceCnode();
5:    **end while**
6:    return cnode; }
7:
8: boolean advancePosition(i,pos) {
9:    success = inp.advancePosition(i,pos);
10:   **if** !success **then** return false; **endif**
11:   $p_i$ = inp.getPos(i); return advancePosUntilSat(); }
12:
13: boolean advancePosUntilSat () {
14:   **while** $!pred(p_1, ..., p_c)$ **do**
15:      find some $i$ such that $f_i(p_1, ..., p_c) > p_i$
16:      success = inp.advancePos($i, f_i(p_1, ..., p_c)$);
17:      **if** success **then** return false; **end if**
18:      $p_i$ = inp.getPosition(i);
19:   **end while**
20:   return true; }

**advancePosUntilSat** first checks whether the current positions satisfy *pred*. If not, it uses the $f_i$ functions to determine a position $i$ to advance, and loops back until a set of positions satisfying *pred* are found, or until no more positions are available. This is the core operation in selections: scanning the input positions until a match is found. Positive predicates enable us to do this in a single pass over the input.

**Correctness and Complexity.** We now present a sketch of the proof of correctness of the above algorithm (see [3] for the full proof). First, it is not hard to see that every answer returned by the algorithm results from evaluating the corresponding PPRED query. The **advancePosUntilSat** function of the predicate operator does not return until satisfying positions are found or the end of an inverted list is reached. The join operator only returns a tuple if both input tuples correspond to the same node. The union operator only returns a tuple if at least one of its inputs produces that tuple. The set-difference operator only returns tuples that are produced by the first input only.

We prove that the algorithm does not miss any query results inductively on each operator. The scan always moves the cursor to the first position of the node for **advanceNode** or to the first position that is after *pos* for **advancePosition(i, pos)**. Therefore, it is trivially correct. Selection only moves the cursor $p_i$ for which $p_i < f_i(p_1, ..., p_n)$, and the definition of positive predicates guarantees that we do not miss results. Similarly, the join operator moves the cursors only while one of the predicates is violated by a higher-level operator. The correctness of project, union, and set-difference can be proved similarly.

To calculate the query evaluation complexity, we define the following parameters: **entries_per_token** is the maximum number of scanned entries in a token inverted

list (this is either the entire inverted list in the case of regular query processing, or some subset in the case of top-k processing); pos_per_entry is the maximum number of positions in an entry in a token inverted list; toks_Q is the number of search keywords in a query $Q$; preds_Q is the number of predicates in a query $Q$; ops_Q is the number of operations in a query $Q$. The complexity of a PPRED query is:
$O(\text{entries\_per\_token} \times \text{pos\_per\_entry} \times \text{toks}_Q \times (\text{preds}_Q + \text{ops}_Q + 1))$ Intuitively, every node and every position within a node is processed at most once. For every combination of positions, we process each operator at most once.

## 6 Experiments

The main goal of our experiments is to study the performance of the PPRED query evaluation algorithm. We also compare its performance with two other techniques:

1. BOOL, which is a restriction of DIST with an empty set of position-based predicates; i.e. it only contains the Boolean operators and keyword matching. Such evaluation has been studied and optimized extensively in the IR community [27], and serves as a baseline because it does not incur the cost of predicate evaluation.
2. REL, which is a direct implementation of FTA using regular relational operators, such as proposed in [6, 12, 16, 18, 21, 29]. This helps illustrate the performance benefits of the PPRED query evaluation algorithm.

### 6.1 Experimental Setup

We used the 500MB INEX 2003 dataset,[5] which contains over 12000 IEEE papers represented as XML documents. Since we are interested in full-text search, we ignored the XML structure and indexed the collection as flat documents, i.e., each document corresponds to a context node. We also ran experiments using synthetic data; since the results were similar, we only report the results for the INEX collection.

We varied the data and query parameters described in Section 5.2 by appropriately varying the number of documents and the query keywords. To study the effect of each parameter on query performance, we varied only one parameter and fixed others at their default values. The range of values for each parameter are: entries_per_token took on the values 1000, 10000, 100000 (default 10000), pos_per_entry took on the values 25, 75, 125, 200 (default 125), toks_Q took on the values 1, 2, 3, 4, 5 (default 3) and preds_Q took on the values 0, 1, 2, 3, 4 (default 2). We used *distance* as the representative positive predicate. We only show the results for varying entries_per_token, pos_per_entry, toks_Q, and preds_Q since the other results are similar.

All the algorithms were implemented in C++ and used TF-IDF scoring. We ran our experiments on an AMD64 3000+ computer with 1GB RAM and one 200GB SATA drive, running under Linux 2.6.9.

### 6.2 Experimental Results

Figures 3(a) and 3(b) show the performance of the algorithms when varying toks_Q and preds_Q, respectively. The performance of BOOL and PPRED scales linearly,

---
[5] http://www.is.informatik.uni-duisburg.de/projects/inex03/

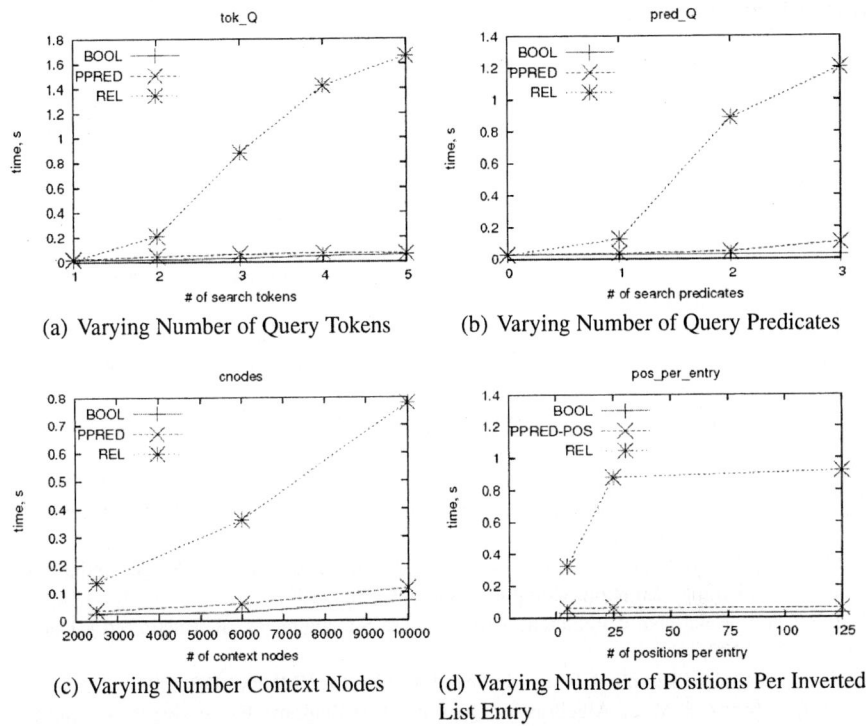

**Fig. 3.** Experiments on the INEX collection

while the performance of REL degrades exponentially. This is explained by the fact that REL uses traditional relational joins, which compute the entire Cartesian product of positions within a node, while PPRED and BOOL use single-pass evaluation algorithms. Interestingly, the performance of PPRED is only slightly worse than BOOL, which suggests that PPRED only introduces a slight additional overhead over the baseline.

Figures 3(c) and 3(d) show the performance of the algorithms when varying **entries_per_token** and **pos_per_entry**, respectively. PPRED and BOOL scale gracefully, while REL does not scale well. Again, PPRED performs only slightly worse than BOOL, suggesting that there is little overhead to evaluating positive predicates.

## 7 Conclusion

We introduced the FTC and FTA as a new formalism for modeling structured full-text search and showed that existing languages are incomplete in this formalism. We also identified a powerful subset of the FTC and FTA that can be evaluated efficiently in a single pass over inverted lists. As part of future work, we plan to capture more aspects such as stemming and thesauri; we believe that these can be modeled as additional predicates in the FTC. Since the FTA is based on the relational algebra, we also plan to explore the joint optimization of full-text and relational queries.

**Acknowledgements**

Chavdar Botev and Jayavel Shanmugasundaram were partially supported by the Cornell/AFRL Information Assurance Institute and NSF CAREER Award IIS-0237644.

# References

1. R. Baeza-Yates, B. Ribiero-Neto. Modern Information Retrieval. Addison-Wesley, 1999.
2. G. Bhalotia, A. Hulgeri, C. Nakhe, S. Chakrabarti, S. Sudarshan. Keyword Searching and Browsing in Databases using BANKS. ICDE 2002.
3. C. Botev, S. Amer-Yahia, J. Shanmugasundaram. "On the Completeness of Full-Text Search Languages". Technical Report, Cornell University, 2005. http://www.cs.cornell.edu/database/TeXQuery/Expressiveness.pdf
4. J. M. Bremer, M. Gertz. XQuery/IR: Integrating XML Document and Data Retrieval. WebDB 2002.
5. E. W. Brown. Fast Evaluation of Structured Queries for Information Retrieval. SIGIR 1995.
6. T. T. Chinenyanga, N. Kushmerick. Expressive and Efficient Ranked Querying of XML Data. WebDB 2001.
7. C. Clarke, G. Cormack, F. Burkowski. An Algebra for Structured Text Search and a Framework for its Implementation. Comput. J. 38(1): 43-56 (1995)
8. E.F. Codd. Relational Completeness of Database Sublanguages. R. Rustin (ed.), Database Systems, 1972.
9. S. Cohen et al. XSEarch: A Semantic Search Engine for XML. VLDB 2003.
10. M. P. Consens, T. Milo. Algebras for Querying Text Regions: Expressive Power and Optimization. J. Comput. Syst. Sci. 57(3): 272-288 (1998)
11. R. Fagin, A. Lotem, M. Naor. Optimal Aggregation Algorithms for Middleware J. of Comp. and Syst. Sciences 66 (2003)
12. D. Florescu, D. Kossmann, I. Manolescu. Integrating Keyword Search into XML Query Processing. WWW 2000.
13. N. Fuhr, K. Grossjohann. XIRQL: An Extension of XQL for Information Retrieval. SIGIR 2000.
14. N. Fuhr, T. Rölleke. A Probabilistic Relational Algebra for the Integration of Information Retrieval and Database Systems. ACM TOIS 15(1), 1997.
15. Y. Hayashi, J. Tomita, G. Kikui. Searching Text-rich XML Documents with Relevance Ranking. SIGIR Workshop on XML and Information Retrieval, 2000.
16. V. Hristidis, L. Gravano, Y. Papakonstantinou. Efficient IR-Style Keyword Search over Relational Databases. VLDB 2003.
17. J. Jaakkola, P. Kilpelinen. Nested Text-Region Algebra Report C-1999-2, Dept. of Computer Science, University of Helsinki, January 1999
18. J. Melton, A. Eisenberg. SQL Multimedia and Application Packages (SQL/MM). SIGMOD Record 30(4), 2001.
19. S.-H. Myaeng, D.-H. Jang, M.-S. Kim, Z.-C. Zhoo. A Flexible Model for Retrieval of SGML Documents. SIGIR 1998.
20. G. Navarro, R. Baeza-Yates. Proximal Nodes: a Model to Query Document Databases by Content and Structure. ACM Trans. Inf. Syst., 15(4), 1997.
21. A. Salminen. A Relational Model for Unstructured Documents. SIGIR 1987.
22. A. Salminen, F. Tompa. PAT Expressions: an Algebra for Text Search. Acta Linguistica Hungar. 41 (1-4), 1992
23. G. Salton, M. J. McGill. Introduction to Modern Information Retrieval. McGraw-Hill, 1983.

24. G. Salton. Automatic Text Processing: The Transformation, Analysis and Retrieval of Information by Computer. Addison Wesley, 1989.
25. A. Theobald, G. Weikum. The Index-Based XXL Search Engine for Querying XML Data with Relevance Ranking. EDBT 2002.
26. M. Vardi. The Complexity of Relational Query Languages. STOC 1982.
27. I. Witten, A. Moffat, and T. Bell. "Managing Gigabytes: Compressing and Indexing Documents and Images". Morgan Kaufmann Publishing, 1999.
28. M. Young-Lai, F. Tompa. One-pass Evaluation of Region Algebra Expressions. Inf. Syst., 28(3), 2003.
29. C. Zhang, J. Naughton, D. DeWitt, Q. Luo, G. Lohman. On Supporting Containment Queries in Relational Database Management Systems. SIGMOD 2001.
30. E. Zimanyi. Query Evaluations in Probabilistic Relational Databases. Theoretical Computer Science, 1997.

# Model-Independent Schema and Data Translation

Paolo Atzeni[1], Paolo Cappellari[1], and Philip A. Bernstein[2]

[1] Università Roma Tre, Italy
atzeni@dia.uniroma3.it, cappellari@dia.uniroma3.it
[2] Microsoft Research, Redmond,WA, USA
philbe@microsoft.com

**Abstract.** We describe MIDST, an implementation of the model management operator ModelGen, which translates schemas from one model to another, for example from OO to SQL or from SQL to XSD. It extends past approaches by translating database instances, not just their schemas. The operator can be used to generate database wrappers (e.g. OO or XML to relational), default user interfaces (e.g. relational to forms), or default database schemas from other representations. The approach translates both schemas and data: given a source instance $I$ of a schema $S$ expressed in a source model, and a target model TM, it generates a schema $S'$ expressed in TM that is "equivalent" to $S$ and an instance $I'$ of $S'$ "equivalent" to $I$. A wide family of models is handled by using a metamodel in which models can be succinctly and precisely described. The approach expresses the translation as Datalog rules and exposes the source and target of the translation in a generic relational dictionary. This makes the translation transparent, easy to customize and model-independent.

## 1 Introduction

### 1.1 The Problem

To manage heterogeneous data, many applications need to translate data and their descriptions from one model (i.e. data model) to another. Even small variations of models are often enough to create difficulties. For example, while most database systems are now object-relational (OR), the actual features offered by different systems rarely coincide, so data migration requires a conversion. Every new database technology introduces more heterogeneity and thus more need for translations. For example, the growth of XML has led to such issues, including *(i)* the need to have object-oriented (OO) wrappers for XML data, *(ii)* the translation from nested XML documents into flat relational databases and vice versa, *(iii)* the conversion from one company standard to another, such as using attributes for simple values and sub-elements for nesting vs. representing all data in sub-elements. Other popular models lead to similar issues, such as Web site descriptions, data warehouses, and forms. In all these settings, there is the need to translate both schemas and data from one model to another. A requirement of an even larger set of contexts is to be able to translate schemas only. This is called the *ModelGen* operator in [7].

Given two models $M_1$ and $M_2$ and a schema $S_1$ of $M_1$, *ModelGen* translates $S_1$ into a schema $S_2$ of $M_2$ that properly represents $S_1$. If data is of interest, it should translate that as well. Given a database instance $I_1$ of $S_1$ we want to produce an instance $I_2$ of $S_2$ that has the same information content as $I_1$.

As there are many different models, what we need is an approach that is generic across models, and can handle the idiosyncrasies of each model. Ideally, one implementation should work for a wide range of models, rather than implementing a custom solution for each pair of models.

We illustrate the problem with some of its major features by means of a short example (additional ones appear in Sec. 5). Consider a simple OR model whose tables have system-managed identifiers and tuples contain domain values as well as identifier-based references to other tables. Fig. 1 shows a database for this model with information about employees and departments: values for attribute Dept in relation EMPLOYEES contain a system managed identifier that refers to tuples of DEPARTMENTS. For example, E#1 in EMPLOYEES refers to D#1 in DEPARTMENTS.

|      | EMPLOYEES | | |
|------|-----|-------|------|
|      | EmpNo | Name | Dept |
| E#1  | 134 | Smith | D#1 |
| E#2  | 201 | Jones | D#2 |
| E#3  | 255 | Black | D#1 |
| E#4  | 302 | Brown | NULL |

| DEPARTMENTS | | |
|-----|------|---------------|
|     | Name | Address |
| D#1 | A | 5, Pine St |
| D#2 | B | 10, Walnut St |

**Fig. 1.** A simple object-relational database

To translate OR databases into the relational model, we can follow the well known technique that replaces explicit references by values. However, some details of this transformation depend upon the specific features in the source and target model. For example, in the object world, keys (or visible identifiers) are sometimes ignored; in the figure: can we be sure that employee numbers identify employees and names identify departments? It depends on whether the model allows for keys and on whether keys have actually been specified. If keys have been specified on both object tables, then Fig. 2 is a plausible result. Its schema has tables that closely correspond to the object tables in the source database. In Fig. 2 keys are underlined and there is a referential integrity constraint from the Dept attribute in EMPLOYEES to (the key of) DEPARTMENTS.

If instead the OR model does not allow the specification of keys or allows them to be omitted, then the translation has to be different: we use an additional attribute for each table as an identifier, as shown in Fig. 3. This attribute is visible, as opposed to the system managed ones of the OR model. We still have the referential integrity constraint from the Dept attribute in EMPLOYEES to DEPARTMENTS, but it is expressed using the new attribute as a unique identifier.

| EMPLOYEES | | |
|---|---|---|
| EmpNo | Name | Dept |
| 134 | Smith | A |
| 201 | Jones | B |
| 255 | Black | A |
| 302 | Brown | NULL |

| DEPARTMENTS | |
|---|---|
| Name | Address |
| A | 5, Pine St |
| B | 10, Walnut St |

**Fig. 2.** A translation into the relational model

| EMPLOYEES | | | |
|---|---|---|---|
| EmpID | EmpNo | Name | Dept |
| 1 | 134 | Smith | 1 |
| 2 | 201 | Jones | 2 |
| 3 | 255 | Black | 1 |
| 4 | 302 | Brown | NULL |

| DEPARTMENTS | | |
|---|---|---|
| DeptID | Name | Address |
| 1 | A | 5, Pine St |
| 2 | B | 10, Walnut St |

**Fig. 3.** A translation with new key attributes

The example shows that we need to be able to deal with the specific aspects of models, and that translations need to take them into account: we have shown two versions of the OR model, one that has visible keys (besides the system-managed identifiers) and one that does not. Different techniques are needed to translate these versions into the relational model. In the second version, a specific feature was the need for generating new values for the new key attributes.

More generally, we are interested in the problem of developing a platform that allows the specification of the source and target models of interest (including OO, OR, ER, UML, XSD, and so on), with all relevant details, and to generate the translation of their schemas and instances.

## 1.2 The MDM Approach

Given the difficulty of this problem, there is no complete general approach available to its solution, but there have been a few partial efforts (see Sec. 6). We use as a starting point the MDM proposal [3]. In that work a *metamodel* is a set of constructs that can be used to define models, which are instances of the metamodel. The approach is based on Hull and King's observation [18] that the constructs used in most known models can be expressed by a limited set of generic (i.e. model-independent) *metaconstructs*: lexical, abstract, aggregation, generalization, function. In MDM, a metamodel is defined by these generic metaconstructs. Each model is defined by its constructs and the metaconstructs they refer to. The models in the examples in Sec. 1.1 could be defined as follows:

- the relational model involves (i) aggregations of lexicals (the tables), with the indication, for each component (a column), of whether it is part of the key or whether nulls are allowed; (ii) foreign keys defined over components of aggregations;

– a simplified OR model has (i) abstracts (tables with system-managed identifiers); (ii) lexical attributes of abstracts (for example **Name** and **Address**), each of which can be specified as part of the key; (iii) reference attributes for abstracts, which are essentially functions from abstracts to abstracts (in the example, the **Dept** attribute in table EMPLOYEES).

A major concept in the MDM approach is the *supermodel*, a model that has constructs corresponding to all the metaconstructs known to the system. Thus, each model is a specialization of the supermodel and a schema in any model is also a schema in the supermodel, apart from the specific names used for constructs. The translation of a schema from one model to another is defined in terms of translations over the metaconstructs. The supermodel acts as a "pivot" model, so that it is sufficient to have translations from each model to and from the supermodel, rather than translations for every pair of models. Thus, a linear and not a quadratic number of translations is needed. Moreover, since every schema in any model is an instance of the supermodel, the only needed translations are those within the supermodel with the target model in mind; a translation is performed by eliminating constructs not allowed in the target model, and possibly introducing new constructs that are allowed.

Each translation in MDM is built from elementary transformations, which are essentially elimination steps. So, a possible translation from the OR model to the relational one is to have two elementary transformations (i) one that eliminates references to abstracts by adding aggregations of abstracts (i.e., replacing functions with relationships), and (ii) a second that replaces abstracts and aggregations of abstracts with aggregations of lexicals and foreign keys (the traditional steps in translating from the ER to the relational model). Essentially, MDM handles a library of elementary transformations and uses them to implement complex transformations.

The major limitation of MDM with respect to our problem is that it considers schema translations only and it does not address data translation at all.

### 1.3 Contribution

This paper proposes *MIDST (Model Independent Data and Schema Translation)* a framework for the development of an effective implementation of a generic (i.e., model independent) platform for schema and data translation. It is among the first approaches that include the latter. (Sec. 6 describes concurrent efforts.) MIDST is based on the following novel ideas:

 – a visible *dictionary* that includes three parts (i) the meta-level that contains the description of models, (ii) the schema-level that contains the description of schemas; (iii) the data-level that contains data for the various schemas. The first two levels are described in detail in Atzeni et al. [2]. Instead, the focus and the novelty here are in the relationship between the second and third levels and in the role of the dictionary in the translation process;
 – the elementary translations are also visible and independent of the engine that executes them. They are implemented by rules in a Datalog variant

with Skolem functions for the invention of identifiers; this enables one to easily modify and personalize rules and reason about their correctness;
- the translations at the data level are also written in Datalog and, more importantly, are generated almost automatically from the rules for schema translation. This is made possible by the close correspondence between the schema-level and the data-level in the dictionary;
- mappings between source and target schemas and data are generated as a by-product, by the materialization of Skolem functions in the dictionary.

A demo description of a preliminary version of the tool considering only the schema level is in Atzeni et al. [1].

### 1.4 Structure of the Paper

The rest of the paper is organized as follows. Sec. 2 explains the schema level of our approach. It describes the dictionary and the Datalog rules we use for the translation. Sec. 3 covers the major contribution: the automatic generation of the rules for the data level translation. Sec. 4 discusses correctness at both schema and data level. Sec. 5 presents experiments and more examples of translations. Sec. 6 discusses related work. Sec. 7 is the conclusion.

## 2 Translation of Schemas

In this section we illustrate our approach to schema translation. We first explain how schemas are described in our dictionary using a relational approach. We then show how translations are specified by Datalog rules, which leverage the relational organization of the dictionary. Two major features of the approach are the unified treatment of schemas within the supermodel and the use of Skolem functors for generating new identifiers in the dictionary. We will comment on each of them while discussing the approach.

### 2.1 Description of Schemas in the Dictionary

A schema is described in the dictionary as a set of schema elements, with references to both its specific model and the supermodel [2]. For example, an entity of an ER schema is described both in a table, say ER_ENTITY, referring to the ER model and in a supermodel table SM_ABSTRACT, corresponding to the abstract metaconstruct to which the entity construct refers. Similarly, a class of a UML diagram gives rise to a tuple in a specific table UML_CLASS and to one in SM_ABSTRACT again, because classes also correspond to abstracts. As we will see in Sec. 2.2, our translation process includes steps ("copy rules") that guarantee the alignment of the two representations.

The supermodel's structure is relatively compact. In our relational implementation, it has a table for each construct. We currently have a dozen constructs, which are sufficient to describe a large variety of models. Translation rules are

| SM_ABSTRACTS | | |
|---|---|---|
| OID | sOID | Name |
| 101 | 1 | Employees |
| 102 | 1 | Departments |
| ... | ... | ... |

| SM_ATTRIBUTEOFABSTRACT | | | | | | |
|---|---|---|---|---|---|---|
| OID | sOID | Name | IsKey | IsNullable | AbsOID | Type |
| 201 | 1 | EmpNo | T | F | 101 | Integer |
| 202 | 1 | Name | F | F | 101 | String |
| 203 | 1 | Name | T | F | 102 | String |
| 204 | 1 | Address | F | F | 102 | String |
| ... | ... | ... | ... | ... | ... | ... |

| SM_REFATTRIBUTEOFABSTRACT | | | | | |
|---|---|---|---|---|---|
| OID | sOID | Name | IsNullable | AbsOID | AbsToOID |
| 301 | 1 | Dept | T | 101 | 102 |
| ... | ... | ... | ... | ... | ... |

Fig. 4. An object-relational schema represented in the dictionary

expressed using supermodel constructs. Therefore, they can translate any construct that corresponds to the same metaconstruct, without having to rewrite rules for each construct of a specific model. Therefore, we concentrate here on the portion of the dictionary that corresponds to the supermodel, as it is the only one really relevant for translations.

In the dictionary, each schema element has (i) a unique identifier (OID), (ii) a reference to the schema it belongs to (sOID), (iii) values of its properties and (iv) references to other elements of the same schema. Each schema element belongs to only one schema.

In the schema of Fig. 1 both EMPLOYEES and DEPARTMENTS are object-tables with identifiers and therefore correspond to the *abstract* metaconstruct. Dept is a reference attribute (its values are system-managed identifiers) and in our terminology corresponds to *reference attribute of abstract*. The other attributes are value based and therefore correspond to the metaconstruct *attribute of abstract*. Fig. 4 shows how the description of the schema in Fig. 1 is organized in the dictionary of MIDST. To illustrate the main points, consider the table SM_REFATTRIBUTEOFABSTRACT. The tuple with OID 301 belongs to schema 1. It has two properties: Name, with value "Dept" and IsNullable with value TRUE (it says that nulls are allowed in the database for this attribute). Finally, it has two references AbsOID and AbsToOID, which denote the element this attribute belongs to and the element it refers to, respectively: this attribute belongs to EMPLOYEES (the abstract with OID 101) and points to DEPARTMENTS (the abstract with OID 102).

## 2.2 Rules for Schema Translation

As in the MDM approach, translations are built by combining elementary translations. The novelty here is that each elementary translation is specified by means of a set of rules written in a Datalog variant with Skolem functors for the generation of new identifiers. Elementary translations can be easily reused because they refer to the constructs in supermodel terms, and so each of them can be applied to all constructs that correspond to the same metaconstruct. The actual translation process includes an initial step for "copying" schemas from the specific source model to the supermodel and a final one for going back from the supermodel to the target model of interest. For the sake of space we omit the discussion of these two steps, as they are straightforward.

We illustrate the major features of our rules by means of an example, which refers to the translation from the OR to the relational models, specifically, mapping the database of Fig.1 to that of Fig.2. The following rule translates object references (attribute Dept in relation EMPLOYEES) into value based references:

SM_ATTRIBUTEOFAGGREGATIONOFLEXICALS(
    OID:#attribute_4(*refAttOid, attOid*), sOID:*target*, Name:*refAttName*,
    IsKey: "FALSE", IsNullable:*isN*, AggOID:#aggregation_2(*absOid*))
← SM_REFATTRIBUTEOFABSTRACT(
    OID:*refAttOid*, sOID:*source*, Name:*refAttName*, IsNullable:*isN*,
    AbsOID:*absOid*, AbsToOID:*absToOid*),
  SM_ATTRIBUTEOFABSTRACT(
    OID:*attOid*, sOID:*source*, Name:*attName*,
    IsKey:"TRUE", AbsOID:*absToOid*)

The rule replaces each reference (SM_REFATTRIBUTEOFABSTRACT) with one column (SM_ATTRIBUTEOFAGGREGATIONOFLEXICALS) for each key attribute of the referenced table. The body unifies with a reference attribute and a key attribute (note the constant TRUE for IsKey in the body) of the abstract that is the target of the reference (note the variable *absToOid* that appears twice in the body). In our example, as DEPARTMENTS has only one key attribute (Name), the rule would generate exactly one new column for the reference.

Skolem functors are used to create new OIDs for the elements the rule produces in the target schema.[1] The head of the rule above has two functors: #attribute_4 for the OID field and #aggregation_2 for the AggOID field. The two play different roles. The former generates a new value, which is distinct for each different tuple of arguments, as the function associated with the functor is injective. This is the case for all the functors appearing in the OID field of the head of a rule. The second functor correlates the element being created with an element created by another rule, namely the rule that generates an aggregation of lexicals (that is, a relation) for each abstract (that is, an object table). The new SM_ATTRIBUTEOFAGGREGATIONOFLEXICALS being generated indeed belongs to the SM_AGGREGATIONOFLEXICALS generated for the SM_ABSTRACT denoted by variable *absOid*.

As another example, consider the rule that, in the second translation mentioned in the Introduction (Fig. 3), produces new key attributes when keys are not defined in the OR-tables in the source schema.

---

[1] A brief comment on notation: functors are denoted by the # sign, include the name of the construct whose OIDs they generate (here often abbreviated for convenience), and have a suffix that distinguishes the various functors associated with a construct.

SM_AttributeOfAggregationOfLexicals(
    OID:#attribute_5(absOid), sOID:target, Name:name+'ID',
    IsNullable:"false", IsKey:"true", AggOID:#aggregation_2(absOid))
← SM_Abstract(
    OID:absOid, sOID:source, Name:name)

The new attribute's name is obtained by concatenating the name of the instance of SM_Abstract with the suffix 'ID'. We obtain EmpID and DeptID as in Fig. 3.

## 3 Data Translation

The main contribution of MIDST is the management of translations of actual data, derived from the translations of schemas. This is made possible by the use of a dictionary for the data level, built in close correspondence with the schema level one. Therefore, we first describe the dictionary and then the rules.

### 3.1 Description of Data

Data are described in a portion of the dictionary whose structure is automatically generated and is similar to the schema portion. The basic idea is that all data elements are represented by means of internal identifiers and also have a value, when appropriate. A portion of the representation of the instance in Fig. 1 is shown in Fig. 5. Let us comment the main points:

- Each table has a dOID (for *database OID*) attribute, instead of the sOID attribute we had at the schema level. Our dictionary can handle various schemas for a model and various instances (or databases) for each schema. In the example, we show only one database, with 1 as the dOID.

| SM_InstOfAbstract | | |
|---|---|---|
| OID | dOID | AbsOID |
| 1001 | 1 | 101 |
| 1002 | 1 | 101 |
| 1003 | 1 | 101 |
| 1004 | 1 | 101 |
| 1005 | 1 | 102 |
| 1006 | 1 | 102 |
| ... | ... | ... |

| SM_InstOfAttributeOfAbstract | | | | |
|---|---|---|---|---|
| OID | dOID | AttOID | i-AbsOID | Value |
| 2001 | 1 | 201 | 1001 | 134 |
| 2002 | 1 | 202 | 1001 | Smith |
| 2003 | 1 | 201 | 1002 | 201 |
| ... | ... | ... | ... | ... |
| 2011 | 1 | 203 | 1005 | A |
| 2012 | 1 | 204 | 1005 | 5, Pine St |
| 2013 | 1 | 203 | 1006 | B |
| ... | ... | ... | ... | ... |

| SM_InstOfRefAttributeOfAbstract | | | | |
|---|---|---|---|---|
| OID | dOID | RefAttOID | i-AbsOID | i-AbsToOID |
| 3001 | 1 | 301 | 1001 | 1005 |
| 3002 | 1 | 301 | 1002 | 1006 |
| ... | ... | ... | ... | ... |

**Fig. 5.** Representation of an object relational instance

- Each data element has a reference to the schema element it instantiates. For example, the first table in Fig. 5 has an AbsOID column, whose values are identifiers for the abstracts in the schema. The first four rows have a value 101 for it, which is, in Fig. 4, the identifier of object-table EMPLOYEES; in fact, the database (see Fig. 1) has four elements in EMPLOYEES.
- "Properties" of schema elements (such as IsKey and IsNullable) do not have a counterpart at the data level: they only are needed as schema information.
- All identifiers appearing at the schema level are replaced by identifiers at the data level. They include both the OID and the references to the OIDs of other tables. In the example, table SM_REFATTRIBUTEOFABSTRACT in Fig. 4 has columns (i) OID, the identifier of the row, (ii) AbsOID, the identifier of the abstract to which the attributes belong, and (iii) AbsToOID, the identifier of the abstract to which the attributes "point". In Fig. 5 each of them is taken one level down: (i) each row is still identified by an OID column, but this is the identifier of the data element; (ii) each value of i-AbsOID indicates the instance of the abstract the attribute is associated with (1001 in the first tuple of SM_INSTOFREFATTRIBUTEOFABSTRACT in Fig. 5 identifies employee Smith); (iii) i-AbsToOID indicates the instance of the abstract the attribute refers to (in the same tuple, 1005 identifies department A);
- If the construct is lexical (that is, has an associated value [18]), then the table has a Value column. In Fig. 5, SM_INSTANCEOFATTRIBUTEOFABSTRACT is the only lexical construct, and Value contains all the values for all the attributes of all the abstracts. Differences in type are not an issue, as we assume the availability of serialization functions that transform values of any type into values of a common one (for example strings).

The above representation for instances is clearly an "internal" one, into which or from which actual database instances or documents have to be transformed. We have developed import/export features that can upload/download instances and schemas of a given model. This representation is somewhat onerous in terms of space, so we are working on a compact version of it that still maintains the close correspondence with the schema level, which is its main advantage.

### 3.2 Rules for Data Translation

The close correspondence between the schema and data levels in the dictionary allows us to automatically generate rules for translating data, with minor refinements in some cases. The technique is based on the DOWN function, which transforms schema translation rules "down to instances." It is defined both on Datalog rules and on literals. If $r$ is a schema level rule with $k$ literals in the body, DOWN($r$) is a rule $r'$, where:

- the head of $r'$ is obtained by applying the DOWN function to the head of $r$ (see below for the definition of DOWN on literals)
- the body of $r'$ has two parts, each with $k$ literals:
    1. literals each obtained by applying DOWN to a literal in the body of $r$;
    2. a copy of the body of $r$.

Let us now define DOWN on literals. A literal is a possibly negated atom. An atom has the form $P(n_1 : a_1, \ldots, n_h : a_h)$, where $P$, the *predicate*, is the name of the table for a supermodel construct (therefore beginning with the prefix SM_), each $n_i$ (a *name*) is a column (property or reference) of $P$ and each $a_i$ is an *argument*, which can be a constant, a variable,[2] or a Skolem functor. In turn, a Skolem functor has the form $F(p_1, \ldots, p_m)$, where $F$ is the name of a Skolem function and each $p_j$ is a constant or a variable.

Given a schema level atom $l_S = P(n_1 : a_1, \ldots, n_h : a_h)$, DOWN produces a data level literal with a predicate name obtained from $P$ by replacing SM_ with SM_INSTANCEOF[3] and arguments as follows.

- Two pairs are built from the OID argument (OID: $a$) of $l_S$:
  - (OID: $a'$) where $a'$ is obtained from $a$ as follows, depending on the form of $a$: if $a$ is a variable, then $a'$ is obtained by prefixing i- to its name; if instead it is a Skolem functor, both the function name and its variable parameters are prefixed with i-;
  - (P-OID: $a$), where P-OID is the reference to the schema element in the dictionary (built as the concatenation of the name of $P$ and the string OID).
- For each pair $(n{:}a)$ in $l_S$ where $n$ is a reference column in table $P$ in the dictionary (that is, one whose values are OIDs), DOWN($l_S$) contains a pair of the form $(n'{:}a')$, where $n'$ is obtained from $n$ by adding a "i-" prefix and $a'$ is obtained from $a$ as above with the additional case that if it is a constant then it is left unchanged.
- If the construct associated with $P$ is lexical (that is, its occurrences at the data level have values), then an additional pair of the form (Value:$e$) is added, where $e$ is an expression that in most cases is just a variable $v$ (we comment on this issue at the end of this section).

Let us consider the first rule presented in Sec. 2.2. At the data level it is as follows:

SM_INSTANCEOFATTRIBUTEOFAGGREGATIONOFLEXICALS(
    OID:#i-attribute_4(*i-refAttOid, i-attOid*),
    AttOfAggOfLexOID:#attribute_4(*refAttOid, attOid*), dOID:*i-target*,
    i-AggOID:#i-aggregation_2(*i-absOid*), Value:*v*)
← SM_INSTANCEOFREFATTRIBUTEOFABSTRACT(
    OID:*i-refAttOid*, RefAttOfAbsOID:*refAttOid*, dOID:*i-source*,
    i-AbsOID:*i-absOid*, i-AbsToOID:*i-absToOid*),
  SM_INSTANCEOFATTRIBUTEOFABSTRACT(
    OID:*i-attOid*, AttOfAbsOID:*attOid*, dOID:*i-source*, i-AbsOID:*i-absToOid*,
    Value:*v*),
  SM_REFATTRIBUTEOFABSTRACT(

---

[2] In general, an argument could also be an expression (for example a string concatenation over constants and variables), but this is not relevant here.
[3] In figures and examples we abbreviate names when needed.

OID:*refAttOid*, sOID:*i-source*, Name:*refAttName*, IsNullable:*isN*,
AbsOID:*absOid*, AbsToOID:*absToOid*),
SM_ATTRIBUTEOFABSTRACT(
OID:*attOid*, sOID:*source*, Name:*attName*,
IsKey:"TRUE", AbsOID:*absToOid*)

Let us comment on some of the main features of the rules generation.

1. schema level identifiers become data level identifiers: OID element;
2. data elements refer to the schema elements they instantiate;
3. references to schemas become references to databases, that is, instances of schemas: both in the head and in the second literal in the body, we have a dOID column instead of the sOID;
4. Skolem functors are replaced by "homologous" functors at the data level, by transforming both the name and the arguments; in this way, they generate new data elements, instead of schema elements;
5. "properties" do not appear in data level literals; they are present in the schema level literals in order to maintain the same selection condition (on schema elements) declared in the body of the schema level translation;
6. lexical constructs have a Value attribute.

The copy of the body of the schema-level rule is needed to maintain the selection condition specified at the schema level. In this way the rule translates only instances of the schema element selected within the schema level rule.

In the rule we just saw, all values in the target instance come from the source. So we only need to copy them, by using a pair (Value:$v$) both in the body and the head. Instead, in the second rule in Sec. 2.2, the values for the new attribute should also be new, and a different value should be generated for each abstract instance. To cover all cases, MIDST allows functions to be associated with the Value field. In most cases, this is just the identity function over values in the source instance (as in the previous rule). In others, the rule designer has to complete the rule by specifying the function. In the example, the rule is as follows:

SM_INSTANCEOFATTRIBUTEOFAGGREGATIONOFLEXICALS(
    OID:#i-attribute_5(*i-absOid*), AttOfAggOfLex:#attribute_5(*absOid*),
    dOID:*i-target*, Value:valueGen(*i-absOid*),
    i-AggOID:#i-aggregation_2(*i-absOid*) )
← SM_INSTANCEOFABSTRACT(
    OID:*i-absOid*, AbsOID:*absOid*, dOID:*i-source*),
    SM_ABSTRACT(
    OID:*absOid*, sOID:*source*, Name:*name*)

## 4 Correctness

In data translation (and integration) frameworks, correctness is usually modelled in terms of information-capacity dominance and equivalence (see Hull [16,17] for the fundamental notions and results and Miller et al. [19, 20] for their role in schema integration and translation). In this context, it turns out that various problems are undecidable if they refer to models that are sufficiently general (see Hull [17, p.53], Miller [20, p.11-13]). Also, a lot of work has been devoted over the years to the correctness of specific translations, with efforts still going on with respect to recently introduced models: see for example the recent contributions by Barbosa et al. [5, 6] on XML-to-relational mappings and by Bohannon et al. [11] on transformations within the XML world. Undecidability results have emerged even in discussions on translations from one specific model to another specific one [5, 11].

Therefore, given the genericity of our approach, it seems hopeless to aim at showing correctness in general. However, this is only a partial limitation, as we are developing a platform to support translations, and some responsibilities can be left to its users (specifically, rule designers, who are expert users), with system support. We briefly elaborate on this issue.

We follow the initial method of Atzeni and Torlone [3] for schema level translations, which uses an "axiomatic" approach. It assumes the basic translations to be correct, a reasonable assumption as they refer to well-known elementary steps developed over the years. It is the responsibility of the rule's designer to specify basic translations that are indeed correct. So given a suitable description of models and rules in terms of the involved constructs, complex translations can be proven correct by induction.

In MIDST, we have the additional benefit of having schema level transformations expressed at a high-level, as Datalog rules. Rather than taking on faith the correctness of the signature of each basic transformation as in [3], we can automatically detect which constructs are used in the body and generated in the head of a Datalog rule and then derive the signature. Since models and rules are expressed in terms of the supermodel's metaconstructs, by induction, the same can be done for the model obtained by applying a complex transformation.

For correctness at the data level, we can reason in a similar way. The main issue is the correctness of the basic transformations, as that of complex ones would follow by induction. Again, it is the responsibility of the designer to verify the correctness of the rules: he/she specifies rules at the schema level, the system generates the corresponding data-level rules, and the designer tunes them if needed and verifies their correctness. It can be seen that our data-level rules generate syntactically correct instances (for example, with only one value for single-valued attributes) if the corresponding schema-level rules generate syntactically correct schemas.

The validity of the approach, given the unavailability of formal results has been evaluated by means of an extensive set of test cases, which have produced positive results. We comment on them in the next section.

## 5 Experimentation

The current MIDST prototype handles a metamodel with a dozen different metaconstructs, each with a number of properties. For example, attributes with nulls and without nulls are just variants of the same construct. These metaconstructs, with their variants, allow for the definition of a huge number of different models (all the major models and many variations of each). For our experiments, we defined a set of significant models, extended-ER, XSD, UML class diagrams, object-relational, object-oriented and relational, each in various versions (with and without nested attributes and generalization hierarchies).

We defined the basic translations needed to handle the set of test models. There are more than twenty of them, the most significant being those for eliminating n-ary aggregations of abstracts, eliminating many-to-many aggregations, eliminating attributes from aggregations of abstracts, introducing an attribute (for example to have a key for an abstract or aggregation of lexicals), replacing aggregations of lexicals with abstracts and vice versa (and introducing or removing foreign keys as needed), unnesting attributes and eliminating generalizations. Each basic transformation required from five to ten Datalog rules.

These basic transformations allow for the definition of translations between each pair of test models. Each of them produced the expected target schemas, according to known standard translations used in database literature and practice.

At the data level, we experimented with the models that handle data, hence object-oriented, object-relational, and nested and flat relational, and families of XML documents. Here we could verify the correctness of the DOWN function, the simplicity of managing the rules at the instance level and the correctness of data translation, which produced the expected results.

In the remainder of this section we illustrate some major points related to two interesting translations. We first show a translation of XML documents

```
...
<employee>
  <name>Cappellari</name>
  <address street="52, Ciclamini St"
    city="Rome"/>
  <company>
    <name>
      University "Roma Tre"
    </name>
    <address street="84, Vasca
      Navale St" city="Rome"/>
  </company>
</employee>
...
```

```
...
<employee>
  <name>Cappellari</name>
  <address>
    <street>52, Ciclamini St</street>
    <city>Rome</city>
  </address>
  <company>
    <name>University "Roma Tre"
    </name>
    <address>
      <street>84, Vasca Navale St</street>
      <city>Rome</city>
    </address>
  </company>
</employee>
...
```

**Fig. 6.** A translation within XML: source and target

between different company standards and then an unnesting case, from XML to the relational model.

For the first example, consider two companies that exchange data as XML documents. Suppose the target company doesn't allow attributes on elements: then, there is the need to translate the source XML conforming a source XSD into another one conforming the target company XSD. Fig. 6 shows a source and a target XML document.

Let us briefly comment on how the XSD model is described by means of our metamodel. XSD-elements are represented with two metaconstructs: abstract for elements declared as complex type and attribute of aggregation of lexicals and abstracts for the others (simple type). XSD-groups are represented by aggregation of lexicals and abstracts and XSD-attributes by attribute of abstract. Abstract also represents XSD-Type.

The translation we are interested in has to generate: (i) a new group (specifically, a sequence group) for each complex-type with attributes, and (ii) a simple-element belonging to such a group for each attribute of the complex-type. Let's see the rule for the second step (with some properties and references omitted in the predicates for the sake of space):

SM_ATTRIBUTEOFAGGREGATIONOFLEXANDABS(
    OID:#attAggLexAbs_6($attOid$), sOID:$target$, Name:$attName$,
    aggLexAbsOID:#aggLexAbs_8($abstractOid$))
← SM_ATTRIBUTEOFABSTACT(
    OID:$attOid$, sOID:$source$, Name:$attName$, abstractOID:$abstractOid$)

Each new element is associated with the group generated by the Skolem functor #aggLexAbs_8($abstractOid$). The same functor is used in the first step of the translation and so here it is used to insert, as reference, OIDs generated in the first step. The data level rule for this step has essentially the same features as the rule we showed in Sec. 3.2: both constructs are lexical, so a Value field is included in both the body and the head. The final result is that values are copied.

As a second example, suppose the target company stores the data in a relational database. This raises the need to translate schema and data. With the relational model as the target, the translation has to generate: (a) a table (aggregation of lexicals) for each complex-type defined in the source schema, (b) a column (attribute of aggregation of lexicals) for each simple-element and (c) a foreign key for each complex element. In our approach we represent foreign keys with two metaconstructs: (i) foreign key to handle the relation between the *from* table and the *to* table and (ii) components of foreign keys to describe columns involved in the foreign key.

Step (i) of the translation can be implemented using the following rule:

SM_FOREIGNKEY(
    OID:#foreignKey_2($abstractOid$), sOID:$target$,
    aggregationToOID:#aggregationOfLexicals_3($abstractTypeOid$),
    aggregationFromOID:#aggregationOfLexicals_3($abstractTypeParentOid$))

← SM_ABSTRACT(
  OID:*abstractTypeOid*, sOID:*source*, isType:"TRUE"),
SM_ABSTRACT(
  OID:*abstractOid*, sOID:*source*, typeAbstractOID:*abstractTypeOid*,
  isType:"FALSE", isTop:"FALSE"),
SM_ABSTRACTCOMPONENTOFAGGREGATIONOFLEXANDABS(
  OID:*absCompAggLexAbsOid*, sOID:*source*,
  aggregationOID:*aggregationOid*, abstractOID:*abstractOid*),
SM_AGGREGATIONOFLEXANDABS(
  OID:*aggregationOid*, sOID:*source*, isTop:"FALSE",
  abstractTypeParentOID:*abstractTypeParentOid*)

In the body of the rule, the first two literals select the non-global complex-element (isTop=FALSE) and its type (isType=TRUE). The other two literals select the group the complex-element belongs to and the parent type through the reference abstractTypeParentOID.

Note that this rule does not involve any lexical construct. As a consequence, the corresponding data-level rule (not shown) does not involve actual values. However, it includes references that are used to maintain connections between values.

Fig. 7 shows the final result of the translation. We assumed that no keys were defined on the document and therefore the translation introduces a new key attribute in each table.

EMPLOYEES

| eID | EmpName | Address | Company |
|---|---|---|---|
| E1 | Cappellari | A1 | C1 |
| E2 | Russo | A2 | C1 |
| E3 | Santarelli | A3 | C2 |

ADDRESS

| aID | Street | City |
|---|---|---|
| A1 | 52, Ciclamini St | Rome |
| A2 | 31, Rose St | Rome |
| A3 | 21, Margherita St | Rome |
| A4 | 84, Vasca Navale St | Rome |

COMPANY

| cID | CompName | Address |
|---|---|---|
| C1 | University "Roma Tre" | A4 |
| C2 | Quadrifoglio s.p.a | A4 |

**Fig. 7.** A relational database for the second document in Fig. 6

## 6 Related Work

Many proposals exist that address schema and data translation. However, most of them only consider specific data models. In this section we present related pieces of work that address the problem of model-independent translations.

The term *ModelGen* was coined in [7] which, along with [8], argues for the development of model management systems consisting of generic operators for solving many schema mapping problems. An example of using *ModelGen* to help solve a schema evolution problem appears in [7].

An early approach to ModelGen was proposed by Atzeni and Torlone [3, 4] who developed the MDM tool, which we have discussed in the introduction. The basic idea behind MDM and the similar approaches (Claypool and Rundensteiner et al. [13, 14] Song et al. [25], and Bézivin et al [10]) is useful but offers only a partial solution to our problem. The main limitation is that they refer only to the schema level. In addition, their representation of the models and transformations is hidden within the tool's imperative source code, not exposed as more declarative, user-comprehensible rules. This leads to several other difficulties. First, only the designers of the tool can extend the models and define the transformations. Thus, instance level transformations would have to be recoded in a similar way. Moreover, correctness of the rules has to be accepted by users as a dogma, since their only expression is in complex imperative code. And any customization would require changes in the tool's source code. The above problems are significant even for a tool that only does schema translation, without instance translation. All of these problems are overcome by our approach.

There are two concurrent projects to develop *ModelGen* with instance translations [9, 22]. The approach of Papotti and Torlone [22] is not rule-based. Rather, their transformations are imperative programs, which have the weaknesses described above. Their instance translation is done by translating the source data into XML, performing an XML-to-XML translation expressed in XQuery to reshape it to be compatible with the target schema, and then translating the XML into the target model. This is similar to our use of a relational database as the "pivot" between the source and target databases.

The approach of Bernstein, Melnik, and Mork [9] is rule-based, like ours. However, unlike ours, it is not driven by a relational dictionary of schemas, models and translation rules. Instead, they focus on flexible mapping of inheritance hierarchies and the incremental regeneration of mappings after the source schema is modified. A detailed description of their approach has not yet appeared.

Bowers and Delcambre [12] present Uni-Level Description (UDL) as a metamodel in which models and translations can be described and managed, with a uniform treatment of models, schemas, and instances. They use it to express specific model-to-model translations of both schemas and instances. Like our approach, their rules are expressed in Datalog. Unlike ours, they are expressed for particular pairs of models.

Data exchange is a different but related problem, the development of user-defined custom translations from a given source schema to a given target, not the automated translation of a source schema to a target model. It is an old database problem, going back at least to the 1970's [24]. Some recent approaches are in Cluet et al. [15], Milo and Zohar [21], and Popa et al. [23].

## 7 Conclusions

In this paper we showed MIDST, an implementation of the ModelGen operator that supports model-generic translations of schemas and their instances within a large family of models. The experiments we conducted confirmed that translations can be effectively performed with our approach.

There are many areas where we believe additional work would be worthwhile. First, as we mentioned earlier, there is a need for more compact and efficient representations of translated instances. Second, despite the obstacles explained in Sec. 4, it would be valuable to produce a practical way to validate the correctness of a set of complex transformations. Third, there is a need to support all of the idiosyncrasies of rich models and exotic models, and to support more complex mappings, such as the many variations of inheritance hierarchies. Fourth, it would be helpful for users to be able to customize the mappings.

## Acknowledgements

We would like to thank Luca Santarelli for his work in the development of the tool and Chiara Russo for contributing to the experimentation and for many helpful discussions.

## References

1. P. Atzeni, P. Cappellari, and P. A. Bernstein. Modelgen: Model independent schema translation. In *ICDE, Tokyo*, pages 1111–1112. IEEE Computer Society, 2005.
2. P. Atzeni, P. Cappellari, and P. A. Bernstein. A multilevel dictionary for model management. In *ER 2005, LNCS 3716*, pages 160–175. Springer, 2005.
3. P. Atzeni and R. Torlone. Management of multiple models in an extensible database design tool. In *EDBT 1996, LNCS 1057*, pages 79–95. Springer, 1996.
4. P. Atzeni and R. Torlone. Mdm: a multiple-data-model tool for the management of heterogeneous database schemes. In *SIGMOD*, pages 528–531. ACM Press, 1997.
5. D. Barbosa, J. Freire, and A. O. Mendelzon. Information preservation in XML-to-relational mappings. In *XSym 2004, LNCS 3186*, pages 66–81. Springer, 2004.
6. D. Barbosa, J. Freire, and A. O. Mendelzon. Designing information-preserving mapping schemes for XML. In *VLDB*, pages 109–120, 2005.
7. P. A. Bernstein. Applying model management to classical meta data problems. *CIDR*, pages 209–220, 2003.
8. P. A. Bernstein, A. Y. Halevy, and R. Pottinger. A vision of management of complex models. *SIGMOD Record*, 29(4):55–63, 2000.
9. P. A. Bernstein, S. Melnik, and P. Mork. Interactive schema translation with instance-level mappings. In *VLDB*, pages 1283–1286, 2005.
10. J. Bézivin, E. Breton, G. Dupé, and P. Valduriez. The ATL transformation-based model management framework. Research Report Report 03.08, IRIN, Université de Nantes, 2003.
11. P. Bohannon, W. Fan, M. Flaster, and P. P. S. Narayan. Information preserving XML schema embedding. In *VLDB*, pages 85–96, 2005.
12. S. Bowers and L. M. L. Delcambre. The Uni-Level Description: A uniform framework for representing information in multiple data models. In *ER 2003, LNCS 2813*, pages 45–58, 2003.

13. K. T. Claypool and E. A. Rundensteiner. Gangam: A transformation modeling framework. In *DASFAA*, pages 47–54, 2003.
14. K. T. Claypool, E. A. Rundensteiner, X. Zhang, H. Su, H. A. Kuno, W.-C. Lee, and G. Mitchell. Sangam - a solution to support multiple data models, their mappings and maintenance. In *SIGMOD Conference*, 2001.
15. S. Cluet, C. Delobel, J. Siméon, and K. Smaga. Your mediators need data conversion! In *SIGMOD Conference*, pages 177–188, 1998.
16. R. Hull. Relative information capacity of simple relational schemata. *SIAM J. Comput.*, 15(3):856–886, 1986.
17. R. Hull. Managing semantic heterogeneity in databases: A theoretical perspective. In *PODS, Tucson, Arizona*, pages 51–61. ACM Press, 1997.
18. R. Hull and R. King. Semantic database modelling: Survey, applications and research issues. *ACM Computing Surveys*, 19(3):201–260, Sept. 1987.
19. R. J. Miller, Y. E. Ioannidis, and R. Ramakrishnan. The use of information capacity in schema integration and translation. In *VLDB*, pages 120–133, 1993.
20. R. J. Miller, Y. E. Ioannidis, and R. Ramakrishnan. Schema equivalence in heterogeneous systems: bridging theory and practice. *Inf. Syst.*, 19(1):3–31, 1994.
21. T. Milo and S. Zohar. Using schema matching to simplify heterogeneous data translation. In *VLDB*, pages 122–133. Morgan Kaufmann Publishers Inc., 1998.
22. P. Papotti and R. Torlone. Heterogeneous data translation through XML conversion. *J. Web Eng.*, 4(3):189–204, 2005.
23. L. Popa, Y. Velegrakis, R. J. Miller, M. A. Hernández, and R. Fagin. Translating Web data. In *VLDB*, pages 598–609, 2002.
24. N. C. Shu, B. C. Housel, R. W. Taylor, S. P. Ghosh, and V. Y. Lum. Express: A data extraction, processing, amd restructuring system. *ACM Trans. Database Syst.*, 2(2):134–174, 1977.
25. G. Song, K. Zhang, and R. Wong. Model management though graph transformations. In *IEEE Symposium on Visual Languages and Human Centric Computing*, pages 75–82, 2004.

# Physical Design Refinement:
# The "Merge-Reduce" Approach

Nicolas Bruno and Surajit Chaudhuri

Microsoft Research, Redmond, WA 98052, USA
{nicolasb, surajitc}@microsoft.com

**Abstract.** Physical database design tools rely on a DBA-provided workload to pick an "optimal" set of indexes and materialized views. Such an approach fails to capture scenarios where DBAs are unable to produce a succinct workload for an automated tool but still able to suggest an ideal physical design based on their broad knowledge of the database usage. Unfortunately, in many cases such an ideal design violates important constraints (e.g., space) and needs to be refined. In this paper, we focus on the important problem of *physical design refinement*, which addresses the above and other related scenarios. We propose to solve the physical refinement problem by using a transformational architecture that is based upon two novel primitive operations, called *merging* and *reduction*. These operators help refine a configuration, treating indexes and materialized views in a unified way, as well as succinctly explain the refinement process to DBAs.

## 1 Introduction

Physical design tuning recently became an important research direction in the database community. In the last decade, several research groups addressed this problem and nowadays database vendors offer automated tools to tune the physical design of a database (e.g., [1, 7, 11]). After DBAs gather a representative workload, these tools recommend indexes and materialized views that fit in the available storage and would make the input workload execute as fast as possible. Unfortunately, the above paradigm of physical database design does not address the following two key scenarios:

- *Significant Manual Design Input:* Many database installations do not have an obviously identifiable workload to drive entirely the physical database design. This is in fact common in database installations of moderate to high complexity. In simpler cases, while a defining workload may exist, the resulting design may be inappropriate due to several reasons: some important query patterns might have been unfortunately ignored by the automated tool, or the proposed design might violate constraints not captured by the automated tool (such as those arising out of replication architectures). In such cases, the DBAs manually design what they believe is a good configuration (even if partially assisted by automated tools), and then try to deploy it. However, due to the complexity of this task, this manual configuration usually has some implicit redundancy, which increases the storage (and update) requirements. DBAs are thus interested in refining this initial configuration into a similar one that is smaller but not significantly less efficient.

— *Responding to Incremental Changes:* Gradual changes in data statistics or usage patterns may make the existing physical design inappropriate. At the same time, physical design changes are disruptive (as query plans can drastically change) and for incremental changes in the data statistics or workload, DBAs desire changes in physical design that are as few as possible and yet meet the constraints on the physical design (such as storage, update cost, or limited degradation with respect to the optimal physical design). Unfortunately, an altogether new design (driven by automated tools) might be very different from the original one as these tools have very limited support for such "incremental tuning". As a consequence, many execution plans would drastically change. In contrast, DBAs are then interested in combining the original and incremental configuration as compactly as possible without sacrificing efficiency.

These examples show the need of additional tools that go beyond statically recommending a configuration for a given workload. Specifically, we believe that it is important to automatically refine a configuration by eliminating implicit redundancy without compromising efficiency (we call this the *Physical Design Refinement* problem). Intuitively, our idea is to start from the initial, possibly redundant configuration, and progressively refine it until some property is satisfied (e.g., the configuration size or its performance degradation meets a pre-specified threshold).

We can think of a refinement session as composed of a series of basic transformations, which locally change the current configuration by trading space and efficiency. In this paper, we identify two atomic operations, *merging* and *reduction*, which provide this basic functionality. Merging and reduction unify different techniques proposed earlier in the literature that apply to indexes and materialized views. Intuitively (see Figure 1), merging combines two views and avoids storing their common information twice, but requires compensating actions to retrieve the original views ($f_1$ and $f_2$ in the figure). Reduction, in turn, keeps a smaller sub-expression of a view, but requires additional work (possibly touching base tables) to recreate the original view. We can see merging and reduction as the analogous to *union* and *subset* operators for sets. It is well known that by applying union and subset operations over a family of sets, we can eventually obtain every possible combination of elements in the family. Analogously, we suggest that merging and reduction are the fundamental building blocks to manipulate designs for indexes and materialized views in a database system. Thus, by using a simple architecture based on merging and reduction transformations, we can easily explain how we obtained the resulting refined configuration. This ensures not only incremental changes but also clear explanations for the recommended refinement, which are crucial for DBAs. We additionally believe that these

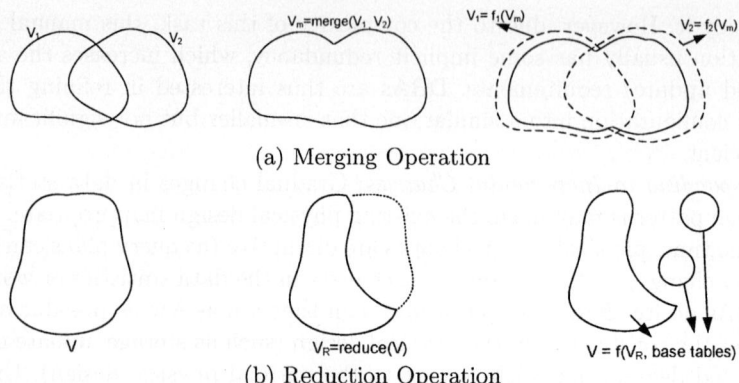

**Fig. 1.** Merging and reduction as primitive operators for physical design tuning

operators have the potential of becoming the foundation of next-generation physical design tuning tools, by unifying seemingly disparate and ad-hoc techniques into a common framework.

The rest of the paper is structured as follows. In Sections 2 and 3 we introduce the primitive operations of merging and reduction. In Section 4 we address the *physical design refinement problem*. In Section 5 we report experimental results and in Section 6 we review related work.

## 2 Merging Operation

In this section we describe the merging operation between materialized views. Merging two materialized views $V_1$ and $V_2$ results in a new materialized view $V_M$ that reduces the amount of redundancy between $V_1$ and $V_2$. The resulting view $V_M$ is usually smaller than the combined sizes of $V_1$ and $V_2$ at the expense of longer execution times for queries that exploit $V_M$ instead of the original ones. As a simple example, consider the following scenario:

$$V_1 = \text{SELECT a,b FROM R WHERE a<10}$$
$$V_2 = \text{SELECT b,c FROM R WHERE b<10}$$

Suppose that the space required to materialize both $V_1$ and $V_2$ is too large. In this case, we can replace both $V_1$ and $V_2$ by the alternative $V_M$ defined as:

$$V_M = \text{SELECT a,b,c FROM R WHERE a<10 OR b<10}$$

The main property of this alternative view is that every query that can be answered using either $V_1$ or $V_2$ can also be answered by $V_M$. The reason is that we can rewrite both $V_1$ and $V_2$ in terms of $V_M$ as follows:

$$V_1 \equiv \text{SELECT a,b FROM } V_M \text{ WHERE a<10}$$
$$V_2 \equiv \text{SELECT b,c FROM } V_M \text{ WHERE b<10}$$

If the tuples that satisfy both $R.a < 10$ and $R.b < 10$ are a significant fraction of $R$, the size of $V_M$ might be much smaller than the sum of the sizes of the original views $V_1$ and $V_2$. Even if no overlap occurs, in this example $V_M$ would still be smaller than the combined sizes of $V_1$ and $V_2$ due to the overlapping column $b$. In fact, $V_M$ is the smallest view that can be used to generate both $V_1$ and $V_2$. It is also important to note that queries that are answered using $V_1$ or $V_2$ are less efficiently answered by $V_M$. The reason is that $V_M$ is a generalization of both $V_1$ and $V_2$ and contains additional, non relevant tuples with respect to the original views. In other words, by merging $V_1$ and $V_2$ into $V_M$ we are effectively trading space for efficiency. We now formally define the merging operation between views.

## 2.1 Formal Model

To formalize the view merging problem, we consider three query languages. Let $\mathcal{L}_I$ be the language that defines input views, $\mathcal{L}_M$ the language that defines merged views, and $\mathcal{L}_C$ the language that defines compensating actions to re-create the original views in terms of the merged view.

**Definition 1.** *Given $V_1$ and $V_2$ from $\mathcal{L}_I$, we denote $V_M = V_1 \oplus V_2$ the merging of $V_1$ and $V_2$ when the following properties hold:*

1. *$V_M$ belongs to $\mathcal{L}_M$.*
2. *$C_1(V_M) \equiv V_1$ and $C_2(V_M) \equiv V_2$ for some $C_1(V_M)$ and $C_2(V_M)$ in $\mathcal{L}_C$.*
3. *If the view matching algorithm matches $V_1$ or $V_2$ for a sub-query $q$, it also matches $V_M$ for $q$ (a view matching algorithm matches a view $V$ for a sub-query $q$ if $q$ can be answered from $V$).*
4. *$V_M$ cannot be further restricted with additional predicates and continue to satisfy the previous properties.*

View merging and view matching are indeed related problems. The idea of view merging is to obtain, for a given pair of views, some sort of *minimal* view that can be matched to a sub-query whenever the original ones do. Although both problems are different, some of the technical details that are introduced below are related to those in the view matching literature.

As an example, suppose that both $\mathcal{L}_I$ and $\mathcal{L}_M$ are the subset of SQL that only allows simple conjunctions over single tables, and $\mathcal{L}_C$ is the full SQL language. Consider the following views:

$$V_1 = \text{SELECT a,b FROM R WHERE 10<d<20}$$
$$V_2 = \text{SELECT b,c FROM R WHERE 30<d<40}$$

In this situation, $V_1 \oplus V_2 =$ SELECT a,b,c FROM R WHERE 10<d<40. The merged $V_1 \oplus V_2$ is not necessarily smaller than the combined sizes of the input views, as this depends on the number of tuples that satisfy $20 \leq d \leq 30$ (and therefore would be additionally included in $V_1 \oplus V_2$). In contrast, suppose that we relax $\mathcal{L}_M$ to also include disjunctions. In this case, $V_1 \oplus V_2 =$ SELECT a,b,c FROM R WHERE 10<d<20 OR 30<d<40. Now $V_1 \oplus V_2$ is always smaller than $V_1$ and $V_2$ put together, because $V_1 \oplus V_2$ contains no additional rows and references only one instance of column $b$. In general, merged views can be larger than their combined inputs even when there is redundancy, as this depends on the expressive power of $\mathcal{L}_M$.

## 2.2 The $\mathcal{L}_{MV}$ Language

In this section we focus on specific query languages and address the view merging operation in detail. Specifically, we set $\mathcal{L}_I$ and $\mathcal{L}_M$ as the subset of SQL that can be used in a database system for materialized view matching (we denote this language as $\mathcal{L}_{MV}$). A view is then given by the following expression:

| | |
|---|---|
| SELECT $S_1, S_2, \ldots$ | – project columns (see below) |
| FROM $T_1, T_2, \ldots$ | – tables in the database |
| WHERE $J_1$ AND $J_2$ AND $\ldots$ | – equi-join predicates |
| $R_1$ AND $R_2$ AND $\ldots$ | – range predicates (see below) |
| $Z_1$ AND $Z_2$ AND $\ldots$ | – residual predicates (see below) |
| GROUP BY $G_1, G_2, \ldots$ | – grouping columns |

where:

- $S_i$ are either base-table columns, column expressions, or aggregates. If the group by clause is present, then every $S_i$ that is not an aggregate must be either equal to one of the $G_j$ columns or be an expression in terms of them.
- $R_i$ are range predicates. The general form of a range predicate is a disjunction of open or closed intervals over the same column (point selections are special cases of intervals). An example of a range predicate is (1<a<10 OR 20<a<30).
- $Z_i$ are residual predicates, that is, the set of predicates in the query definition that cannot be classified as either equi-join or range predicates.

In other words, we can express in $\mathcal{L}_{MV}$ the class of SPJ queries with aggregation. The reason that predicates are split into three disjoint groups (join, range, and residual) is pragmatic. During query optimization, it is easier to perform subsumption tests for view matching if both the view and the candidate subquery are written in this structured way. Specifically, we can then perform simple subsumption tests component by component and fail whenever any of the simple tests fails. For instance, we check that the join predicates in the query are a superset of the join predicates in the view, and the range predicates (column by column) in the query are subsumed by the corresponding ones in the view. Some subsumption tests are more complex than others, notably when group-by clauses are present. We note that this procedure focuses on simplicity and efficiency and therefore can miss some valid matchings due to complex logical rewritings that are not considered by the optimizer. Specifically, consider the case of residual predicates. The problem of determining whether two arbitrary predicates are equivalent can be arbitrarily complex[1]. For that reason, the matching procedure

---

[1] Consider a table with four integer columns $(x, y, z, n)$. Checking that the predicate $x + 1 = x$ is equivalent to $x^n + y^n = z^n \wedge n > 2$ is the same as proving Fermat's last theorem. It took over three hundred years to prove that specific conjecture; expecting such capabilities from a view matching algorithm is unrealistic.

that we consider just checks that every conjunct in the residual predicate of the view appears (syntactically) in the candidate query. Otherwise, although the view can still subsume the query, no match is produced.

We simplify the notation of a view in $\mathcal{L}_{\mathsf{MV}}$ as $(S, T, J, R, Z, G)$ where $S$ is the set of columns in the select clause, $T$ is the set of tables, $J$, $R$, and $Z$ are the sets of join, range, and residual predicates, respectively, and $G$ is the set of grouping columns. In this work we restrict the merging operation so that the input views agree on the set of tables $T$. The reason is twofold. On one hand, many top-down optimizers restrict the view matching operation to queries and views that agree on the input tables (presumably, if a candidate view contains fewer tables than the input query $q$, it should have matched a sub-query of $q$ earlier during optimization). On the other hand, merging views with different input tables can be done by combining the reduce operator of Section 3 and the merging operation as defined in this section. We next define the merging operator in $\mathcal{L}_{\mathsf{MV}}$.

**Case 1: No grouping columns**

Consider merging $V_1 = (S_1, T, J_1, R_1, Z_1, \emptyset)$ and $V_2 = (S_2, T, J_2, R_2, Z_2, \emptyset)$. If the merging language were expressive enough, we could define $V_1 \oplus V_2$ as:

    SELECT $S_1 \cup S_2$
    FROM $T$
    WHERE ($J_1$ AND $R_1$ AND $Z_1$) OR ($J_2$ AND $R_2$ AND $Z_2$)

which satisfies properties 2 and 4 in Definition 1. To satisfy property 1 (i.e., rewriting $V_1 \oplus V_2$ in $\mathcal{L}_{\mathsf{MV}}$), we have no option but consider the whole predicate in the WHERE clause as a single conjunctive residual predicate $Z$. The problem is that now the merged view would not be matched whenever $V_1$ or $V_2$ are matched (property 3) because of the simple procedures used during view matching in general and with respect to residual predicates in particular. We need to obtain the smallest view $V_M$ that is in $\mathcal{L}_{\mathsf{MV}}$ and satisfies property 3. For that purpose, we rewrite the above "minimal" predicate as follows:

$$(\mathsf{J}_1 \wedge \mathsf{R}_1 \wedge \mathsf{Z}_1) \vee (\mathsf{J}_2 \wedge \mathsf{R}_2 \wedge \mathsf{Z}_2) \equiv (\mathsf{J}_1 \vee \mathsf{J}_2) \wedge (\mathsf{R}_1 \vee \mathsf{R}_2) \wedge (\mathsf{Z}_1 \vee \mathsf{Z}_2) \wedge \mathsf{C}$$

where C is the conjunction of all crossed disjuncts $((\mathsf{J}_1 \vee \mathsf{R}_2) \wedge (\mathsf{R}_1 \vee \mathsf{Z}_2) \wedge \ldots)$. Our strategy is to relax this expression until we obtain a predicate that can be written in $\mathcal{L}_{\mathsf{MV}}$ and matches any candidate query that is matched by the original views. Although this procedure seems in general to introduce a lot of redundancy and result in larger views, we experimentally determined that in real-world scenarios this is not the case.

We first relax the expression above by removing the conjunct C. The reason is that it leaves us with three conjuncts ($\mathsf{J}_1 \vee \mathsf{J}_2$, $\mathsf{R}_1 \vee \mathsf{R}_2$, and $\mathsf{Z}_1 \vee \mathsf{Z}_2$), which we next map into the three groups of predicates in $\mathcal{L}_{\mathsf{MV}}$. First consider $\mathsf{J}_1 \vee \mathsf{J}_2$ and recall that each $J_i$ is a conjunct of equi-join predicates. We cannot simply use $\mathsf{J}_1 \vee \mathsf{J}_2$ in the resulting view because the language specifies that this must be a conjunction of simple equi-joins (i.e., no disjunctions are allowed). We rewrite:

$$\mathsf{J}_1 \vee \mathsf{J}_2 \equiv (\mathsf{J}_1^1 \wedge \mathsf{J}_1^2 \wedge \mathsf{J}_1^3 \wedge \ldots) \vee (\mathsf{J}_2^1 \wedge \mathsf{J}_2^2 \wedge \mathsf{J}_2^3 \wedge \ldots) \equiv \bigwedge_{i,j}(\mathsf{J}_1^i \vee \mathsf{J}_2^j)$$

and relax this predicate as follows: we keep each $(i,j)$ conjunct for which $J_1^i \equiv J_2^j$ and discard (i.e., relax) the remaining ones. We obtain then $\bigwedge_{J^k \in J_1 \cap J_2} J^k$ as the set of join predicates in the merged view. Note that this predicate can be much more general than the original $J_1 \vee J_2$, but the view matching procedure would match $V_m$ with respect to the join subsumption test in this case. We use the same idea for $Z_1 \vee Z_2$ and therefore the residual predicate for $V_m$ is $\bigwedge_{Z^k \in Z_1 \cap Z_2} Z^k$.

It turns out that we can do better for range predicates $R_1 \vee R_2$ due to their specific structure. Using the same argument, we first rewrite $R_1 \vee R_2$ as $\bigwedge_{i,j}(R_1^i \vee R_2^j)$ where each $R_1^i$ and $R_2^j$ are disjunctions of open or closed intervals over some column. As before, if $R_1^i$ and $R_2^j$ are defined over different columns, we discard that conjunct. However, if they are defined over the same column, we keep the predicate even when $R_1^i$ and $R_2^j$ are not the same, by taking the union of the corresponding intervals (we denote this operation with the symbol $\bigsqcup$). To avoid missing some predicates, we first add conjuncts $-\infty < x < \infty$ to one of the range predicates if column $x$ is only present in the other range predicate (it does not change the semantics of the input predicates but restricts further the result). Also, if after taking the union the predicate over some column $x$ becomes $-\infty < x < \infty$, we discard this conjunct from the result. As an example, consider:

$$\begin{array}{rl}
R_1 = & (10<a<20 \vee 30<a<40) \wedge (20<b<30) \wedge (c<40) \\
R_2 = & (15<a<35) \wedge (10<b<25) \wedge (c>30) \wedge (10<d<20) \\
\hline
R_1 \bigsqcup R_2 = & (10<a<40) \wedge (10<b<30) \wedge (10<d<20)
\end{array}$$

After obtaining join, range, and residual predicates as described above, we assemble the set of columns in the merged view. At a minimum, this set must contain the union of columns present in both input views. However, this is not enough in general, as illustrated next. Consider for instance:

$$V_1 = \text{SELECT a FROM R WHERE 10<c<20}$$
$$V_2 = \text{SELECT b FROM R WHERE 15<c<30}$$

The candidate merged view $V$=SELECT a,b FROM R WHERE 10<c<30 does not satisfy property 2 in Definition 1 because $V_1$ and $V_2$ cannot be obtained from $V$. The reason is that we need to apply additional predicates to $V$ (c<20 to obtain $V_1$ and 15<c to obtain $V_2$), but $V$ does not expose column c. For that reason, we need to add to the set of columns in the merged view all the columns that are used in join, range, and residual predicates that are eliminated in the merged view. Similarly, if some range predicate changed from the input to the merged view, we need to add the range column as an output column, or otherwise we would not be able to reconstruct the original views. To summarize, the merging of two views as described in this section is as follows:

$$\begin{array}{rl}
V_1 = ( S_1 & , T, J_1 , R_1 , Z_1 , \emptyset ) \\
\oplus V_2 = ( S_2 & , T, J_2 , R_2 , Z_2 , \emptyset ) \\
\hline
V_1 \oplus V_2 = ( S_1 \cup S_2 \cup \text{required columns} & , T, J_1 \cap J_2 , R_1 \bigsqcup R_2 , Z_1 \cap Z_2 , \emptyset )
\end{array}$$

We note that all the transformations mentioned above take into account column equivalence. If both input views contain a join predicate R.x = S.y, then the range predicates R.x < 10 and S.y < 10 are considered to be the same.

*Example 1.* The following example illustrates the ideas described in this section:

| $V_1=$ | $V_2=$ | $V_1 \oplus V_2=$ |
|---|---|---|
| SELECT x,y | SELECT y,z | SELECT x,y,z,a,b,c,d |
| FROM R,S WHERE | FROM R,S WHERE | FROM R,S WHERE |
|   R.x=S.y AND |   R.x=S.y AND |   R.x=S.y AND |
|   10<R.a<20 AND |   15<R.a<50 AND |   10<R.a<50 AND |
|   R.b<10 AND |   R.b>5 AND R.c>5 AND |   R.x+S.d<8 |
|   R.x+S.d<8 |   S.y+S.d<8 AND R.d*R.d=2 | |

## Case 2: Grouping columns

We now consider the case of merging views that involve group-by clauses. Grouping operators partition the input relation into disjoint subsets and return a representative tuple and some aggregates from each group. Conceptually, we see a group-by operator as a post-processing step after the evaluation of the SPJ sub-query. Consider the merged view obtained when the grouping columns are eliminated from the input views. If the group-by columns in the input views are different, each view partitions the input relation in different ways. We then need to partition the merged view in the coarsest way that still allows us to recreate each input view. For that purpose, the set of group-by columns in the merged view must be the union of the group-by columns of the input views. Additionally, each column that is added to the select clause due to predicate relaxation in the input views must also be added as a grouping column. Note that we need to handle a special case properly. If one of the input views contains no group-by clause, the merged view should not contain any group-by clause either, or else we would compromise correctness (i.e., we implicitly define the union of a set of columns and the empty set as the empty set). In these situations, we additionally unfold all original aggregates into base-table columns so that the original aggregates can be computed from the resulting merged view. To summarize, we define $(S_1, T, J_1, R_1, Z_1, G_1) \oplus (S_2, T, J_2, R_2, Z_2, G_2)$ as $(S_M, T, J_1 \cap J_2, R_1 \bigsqcup R_2, Z_1 \cap Z_2, G_M)$ where:

- $S_M$ is the set of columns obtained in the no group-by case, plus the group-by columns if they are not the same as the input views. If the resulting $G_M = \emptyset$, all aggregates are unfolded into base-table columns.
- $G_M = G_1 \cup G_2 \cup$ columns added to $S_M$ (note that $G \cup \emptyset = \emptyset$).

*Example 2.* The following example illustrates the ideas in this section:

| $V_1=$ | $V_2=$ | $V_3=$ |
|---|---|---|
| SELECT R.x,SUM(S.y) | SELECT R.x,R.z | SELECT S.y,SUM(S.z) |
| FROM R,S WHERE | FROM R,S WHERE | FROM R,S WHERE |
|   R.x=S.y AND |   R.x=S.y AND |   R.x=S.z AND |
|   10<R.a<20 |   15<R.a<50 |   10<R.a<25 |
| GROUP BY R.x | | GROUP BY S.y |

$V_1 \oplus V_2 =$
SELECT R.x,R.a,S.y,R.z
FROM R,S WHERE
   R.x=S.y AND
   10<R.a<50

$V_1 \oplus V_3 =$
SELECT R.x,S.y,R.a,SUM(S.y),SUM(S.z) [2]
FROM R,S WHERE
   R.x=S.y AND
   10<R.a<25
GROUP BY R.a,R.x,S.y

## 2.3 Indexes over Materialized Views

So far we have discussed the merging operation applied to materialized views, without paying attention to indexes over those materialized views. In reality, each materialized view is associated with a set of indexes, and those indexes are used during query processing. Previous work in the literature has considered index merging and view merging as separate operations. We know describe how we can handle both structures in a unified manner. For this purpose, we consider all indexes as defined over some view (base tables are also trivial views, so this definition includes regular indexes as well). Specifically, for a sequence of columns $I$ and a view $V$ that contains all $I$ columns in its SELECT clause, we denote $I \mid V$ the index with columns $I$ over the materialized view $V$. For the special case $I = \emptyset$, we define $\emptyset \mid V$ to be the unordered heap containing all the tuples in $V$ (for simplicity, we use $V$ and $\emptyset \mid V$ interchangeably).

### Unified Merging Operator

We now define the merging of two arbitrary indexes over views. Consider the simplest case of merging two indexes defined over the same view. In this case[3]:

$$(I_1 \mid V) \oplus (I_2 \mid V) = (I_1 \oplus I_2) \mid V$$

where $I_1 \oplus I_2$ is the traditional index-merging operation as defined in [4, 6]. That is, $I_1 \oplus I_2 = I_M$ where $I_M$ contains all columns in $I_1$ followed by all columns in $I_2 - I_1$. As an example, we have that $([a, b, c] \mid V) \oplus ([b, a, d] \mid V) = [a, b, c, d] \mid V$.

To address the general case, we need to first introduce the notion of *index promotion*. Consider an index $I \mid V$ and suppose that $V_M = V \oplus V'$ for some view $V'$. Promoting $I$ over $V$ to $V_M$ (denoted $I \uparrow V_M$) results in an index over $V_M$ that can be used (with some compensating action) whenever $I \mid V$ is used. This promoted index contains all columns in the original index followed by every column that was added to the select clause in $V_M$[4]. For instance, consider:

$V_1 =$ SELECT x,y FROM R WHERE 10<a<20
$V_2 =$ SELECT y,z FROM R WHERE 15<a<30
$V_1 \oplus V_2 =$ SELECT a,x,y,z FROM R WHERE 10<a<30

---

[2] To recreate the original views in the presence of general algebraic aggregates, we sometimes need to add additional columns in the merged view, such as SUM(c) and COUNT(*) for an original aggregate AVG(c).

[3] We overload the operator $\oplus$ to operate over indexes, views, or indexes over views. We explicitly state which case we are referring to when this is not clear from the context.

[4] Other column orderings are possible, but we omit these details for simplicity.

We then have that $[x] \uparrow (V_1 \oplus V_2) = [x, a]$. Using index promotion, we now define the merging of two indexes over views as follows:

$$(I_1 \mid V_1) \oplus (I_2 \mid V_2) = ((I_1 \oplus I_2) \uparrow (V_1 \oplus V_2)) \mid (V_1 \oplus V_2)$$

That is, we first obtain the merged index $I_1 \oplus I_2$, then the view $V_1 \oplus V_2$, and finally we promote the merged index to the merged view.

## 3 Reduction Operation

In the previous section we described a mechanism to decrease the amount of redundancy between a pair of indexes over views. The idea was to merge them into a new index that might be smaller than the combined inputs, but at the same time less efficient to answer queries. In this section we present a second operator that follows the same principle, but operates over a single input index.

Specifically, we exploit the fact that associated to each index $I \mid V$ there is a supporting primary index or heap that contains all rows and columns of the view $V$. Therefore, we can transform an index over a view into another one that is smaller but requires a compensating action involving the corresponding supporting structures. Consider for instance an index $I = [a, b, c]$ over a base table $R$. We can transform $I$ into $I' = [a, b]$ which is smaller and requires compensating actions to produce the results that $I$ produces by itself (in this case, fetches to $R$'s primary index or heap to retrieve the missing column $c$). As another example, consider the following view:

$V=$ SELECT R.a,R.b,S.c FROM R,S WHERE R.x=S.y AND R.a=15

and the following *reduced* version of $V$ (which omits table $S$):

$V'=$ SELECT R.a,R.b,R.x FROM R WHERE R.a=15

In this case, we can recreate $V$ from $V'$ by performing a join with the primary index or heap of table $S$. Note that $V'$ must contain column R.x so that the compensating join can be applied. The resulting $V'$ is not necessarily smaller than $V$ because the join predicate can eliminate many tuples from $R$.

The two previous examples illustrate that we can change the definition of an index over a view, possibly reducing its size, and then apply compensating actions to recreate the original structure. We call this operation *reduction* and denote it with the symbol $\rho$. Conceptually, the reduction operation eliminates redundancy just like the merging operation, but it requires a single input structure.

Formally, the reduction operation takes an index $IV$ (we use the language $\mathcal{L}_{MV}$ as in the previous section), a set of tables $T'$ and a set of columns $K'$ as inputs, and returns a new index $\rho(IV, T', K')$. For an index $V = I \mid (S, T, J, R, Z, G)$, the operational semantics of $\rho((I \mid V), T', K')$ are given in three steps as follows:

1. If $T' \not\subseteq T$, the reduction is ill-defined and we stop. Otherwise, we obtain the reduced version of $V$ that only references tables $T'$, defined as $V' = (S', T', J', R', Z', G')$, where:

- $J' \subseteq J$, $R' \subseteq R$, and $Z' \subseteq Z$, where each base-table column referenced in $J'$, $R'$ and $Z'$ refers exclusively to tables in $T'$.
- $S'$ contains the subset of columns in $S$ that belong to tables in $T'$ plus all columns in $T'$ referenced in $J - J'$, $R - R'$ and $Z - Z'$.
- If $G \neq \emptyset$, $G'$ contains all the columns in $G$ that belong to tables in $T'$ plus all columns in $S'$-$S$. Otherwise, $G'=G=\emptyset$.

If $V'$ contains cartesian products we consider the reduction invalid and we stop (a cartesian product does not provide any efficiency advantage and it is always much larger than the input relations).

2. We obtain $I'$ from $I$ by first removing all columns that do not belong to tables in $T'$, and then adding all columns in $S'$ (this step is similar to $I \uparrow V'$).
3. If $K' \not\subseteq I'$, the reduction is ill-defined and we stop. Otherwise, we define $\rho((I \mid V), T', K') = K' \mid V'$.

*Example 3.* The following example illustrates the ideas described in this section:

V = SELECT R.c, S.c         $\rho([R.c, S.c] \mid V, \{R\}, \{R.c, R.x\})$ =
    FROM R, S WHERE             ($\{R.c, R.x\}$, SELECT R.c, R.b, R.x
    R.x=S.y AND                             FROM R
    10<R.a<50 AND                           WHERE 10<R.a<50
    20<S.a<30 AND                           GROUP BY R.c, R.b, R.x )
    R.b+S.b<10
    GROUP BY R.c, S.c

## 4 Physical Design Refinement

We now formally define the physical design refinement problem motivated in the introduction, using merging and reduction as the basic building blocks. Consider a physical database configuration $C = \{I_1 \mid V_1, \ldots, I_n \mid V_n\}$ composed of indexes over views (recall that all base-table indexes are defined over trivial views). We assume that $C$ was obtained by tuning the database system for a typical workload by either a skilled DBA or some automated tool (e.g., [1,7,11]). The size of a configuration $C$ is the combined size of all indexes in $C$ plus the size of heaps for indexes on views that do not have a primary index in $C$ (we need a primary index or heap for each view):

$$size(C) = \sum_{j} size(I_j \mid V_j) + \sum_{V_k \text{ without primary index in } C} size(\emptyset \mid V_k)$$

Now suppose that after some time the database grows –or any other motivating example in the introduction happens– and $size(C)$ becomes larger than the allocated space. We would like to obtain a configuration that fits in the storage constraint without compromising the quality of the original $C$. Instead of considering every possible index for the new configuration, we restrict our search to those that are either in the initial configuration or can be derived from it via a series of merging and reduction operations. The rationale is that every original execution plan can be in principle adapted with local compensating actions so that it uses the views in the new configuration (or, alternatively, we can re-optimize the query and obtain the new optimal plan).

**Comparing Configurations:** During refinement, we need a way to measure the quality of each candidate configuration that we consider. As we stated above, the current configuration resulted from a tuning session either by a DBA or an automated tool. It is then expected that all indexes over views in the current configuration are somehow useful in answering queries in the actual workload. We then propose to infer a hypothetical workload with queries that mimic the functionality of each index present in the current configuration. We assume that if a new configuration can efficiently process such hypothetical workload, the benefits of the original indexes would be preserved. Specifically, we associate each index $IV=I \mid (S,T,R,J,Z,G)$ with a set of queries, called *queries(IV)*, which stress every kind of index usage:

| Scan | Ordered Scan | Seek[5] |
|---|---|---|
| SELECT I | SELECT I | SELECT I |
| FROM T | FROM T | FROM T |
| WHERE R AND J AND Z | WHERE R AND J AND Z | WHERE R AND J AND Z |
| GROUP BY G | GROUP BY G | [ AND "$\sigma$(prefix I)" ] |
|  | ORDER BY I | GROUP BY G |
|  |  | [ HAVING "$\sigma$(prefix I)" ] |

In absence of additional information, we give some predefined weight to each query (to balance different index usages). However, if we tracked the execution of queries in the system, we could have accurate measurements of the relative importance of each index usage and use those relative weights in the refinement process.

### 4.1 Problem Statement

To define the physical design refinement problem, we first introduce the closure of a configuration under the merging and reduction operations:

**Definition 2.** *Let $C$ be a configuration and let $C_i$ ($i \geq 0$) be defined as follows*[6]:

- $C_0 = C$
- $C_{i+1} = C_i \cup \{IV_1 \oplus IV_2 \text{ for each compatible } IV_1, IV_2 \in C_i\}$
  $\cup \{\rho(IV, T, K) \text{ for each } IV \in C_i \text{ and valid choices of } T \text{ and } K\}$

We define closure($C$)=$C_k$, where $k$ is the smallest integer that satisfies $C_k=C_{k+1}$.

**Definition 3 (Physical Design Refinement (PDR) Problem**[7]**).** *Given a configuration $C = \{I_1 \mid V_1, \ldots, I_n \mid V_n\}$ and a storage constraint $B$, we define PDR(C, B) as the refined configuration $C'$ such that:*

---

[5] We use a HAVING clause if $G \neq \emptyset$, and a WHERE clause otherwise. In both cases, the expression "$\sigma$(prefix I)" refers to a sarg-able predicate over a prefix of the index columns.

[6] See Sections 2 and 3 for the formal definition of operators $\oplus$ and $\rho$.

[7] The dual problem can be similarly defined as minimizing the size of a configuration under a given degradation constraint (i.e., $cost(C') \leq \alpha \cdot cost(C)$).

1. $C' \subseteq \text{closure}(C)$.
2. $\text{size}(C') \leq B$.
3. $\sum_{(I \mid V) \in C} \sum_{q_i \in \text{queries } (I \mid V)} (w_i \cdot \text{cost}(q_i, C'))$ is minimized, where $w_i$ is the weight associated with query $q_i$, and $\text{cost}(q, C)$ is the optimizer estimated cost of query $q_i$ under configuration $C$.

**Theorem 1.** *The PDR problem is NP-hard.*

**Proof:** We provide a reduction from knapsack. The knapsack problem takes as inputs an integer capacity $B$ and a set of objects $o_i$, each one with value $a_i$ and volume $b_i$. The output is a subset of $o_i$ whose combined volume fits in $B$ and sum of values is maximized. Consider an arbitrary knapsack problem with capacity $B$ and elements $\{o_1, \ldots, o_n\}$. We create a PDR instance by associating each $o_i$ with a view $V_i$ = SELECT x FROM $T_i$ WHERE x=0, where $T_i$ is a single column table that contains $b_i$ tuples with value zero and $a_i$ tuples with value one. Since all views refer to different tables, there is no possibility of merging views. Additionally, each index is defined over a single column, so no reduction is possible either. The PDR problem then reduces to finding the best subset of the original indexes over views. Now, If $V_i$ is not present in the final configuration, we have to scan the base table $T_i$ to obtain the zero-valued tuples. Base table $T_i$ is $a_i + b_i$ units of size, which is $a_i$ units larger than the view size (there are only $b_i$ tuples in $T_i$ that satisfy $x = 0$). Assuming that scan costs are linear, the value of having $V_i$ in the result (i.e., the time we save by having such an index) is $a_i$ and its size is $b_i$. After solving this PDR problem with storage constraint $B$, we generate the knapsack solution by mapping the subset of views in the result to the original objects $o_i$.

### 4.2 Pruning the Search Space

We now present some properties that are useful in defining heuristics for traversing the search space and approximating PDR. For a configuration $C$ and an index $IV \in \text{closure}(C)$, we define $\text{base}(IV)$ to be the set of original indexes in $C$ which are part of a derivation that uses merging and reduction to produce $IV$.

**Property 1.** *Let $C$ be a configuration, $IV_1$ and $IV_2$ be indexes in $\text{closure}(C)$, and $IV_M = IV_1 \oplus IV_2$. If $IV_M \notin \text{closure}(C - \text{base}(IV1))$, $\text{PDR}(C, B)$ cannot include both $IV_1$ and $IV_M$.*

**Proof [Sketch]:** Suppose that both $IV_1$ and $IV_M$ belong to $\text{PDR}(C, B)$. Consider the indexes in $C$ whose inferred queries are evaluated using $IV_M$ (we call this set $C_M$ in Figure 2). For each index $IV \in C_M$, it must be the case that $IV_M$ matches either $IV$ or some reduction of it. Let us define the set $C'_M$ as composed of the indexes in $C_M$ that are matched by $IV_M$ or their corresponding reductions. Now consider replacing $IV_M$ in $\text{PDR}(C, B)$ by $IV'_M = \oplus_{IV \in C'_M} IV$. We next show that this alternative configuration, denoted $\text{PDR'}(C, B)$, is better than $\text{PDR}(C, B)$. We first show that $\text{PDR'}(C, B)$ is not larger than $\text{PDR}(C, B)$. For that purpose, we note that $IV'_M$ is obtained by merging elements in $C'_M$, which are all subsumed by $IV_M$. Therefore, $IV_M \oplus IV'_M = IV_M$ (the merged

$IV_M$ cannot incorporate anything that is not already captured by $IV_M$). Additionally, by our hypothesis, $IV'_M \neq IV_M$. The reason is that indexes in $base(IV_1)$ do not belong to $C_M$ (the optimizer should have found better execution plans by replacing usages of $IV_M$ with better alternatives that use $IV_1$). Therefore, $IV'_M \in closure(C_M) \subseteq closure(C - base(IV_1))$ and cannot be equal to $IV_M$. We then have that $IV'_M \oplus IV_M = IV_M$ and $IV'_M \neq IV_M$. Consequently, $IV'_M$ is strictly smaller than $IV_M$ and thus PDR'$(C, B)$ is smaller than PDR$(C, B)$. All queries inferred from indexes in $C - C_M$ cannot execute slower in PDR'$(C, B)$ because all supporting indexes are present. Queries inferred from indexes in $C_M$ would execute faster in PDR'$(C, B)$ because the optimizer would replace usages of $IV_M$ in the execution plans with more efficient alternatives that use the smaller $IV'_M$. PDR'$(C, B)$ is also more efficient than PDR$(C, B)$, which proves the property.

Property 1 shows that if we merge two indexes $IV_1$ and $IV_2$, in some cases the optimal solution cannot contain both the merged index and any of its inputs. We next show that sometimes certain indexes cannot be part of the optimal solution.

**Property 2.** Let $C$ be a configuration, let $IV_1$ and $IV_2$ be indexes in $closure(C)$, and let $IV_M = IV_1 \oplus IV_2$. If (i) $size(IV_M) > size(IV_1) + size(IV_2)$, and (ii) for each $IV_k \in closure(C)$ such that $IV_M = IV_M \oplus IV_k$ it holds that $size(IV_M) > size(IV_1) + size(IV_2) + size(IV_k)$, then $IV_M \notin$ PDR$(C, B)$.

**Proof [Sketch]:** Suppose that $IV_M$ belongs to PDR$(C, B)$ configuration but both (i) and (ii) do not hold. Since (i) does not hold, replacing $IV_M$ by both $IV_1$ and $IV_2$ results in a smaller configuration. Additionally, every query inferred from an index in $base(IV_1) \cup base(IV_2)$ can be answered more efficiently by either $IV_1$ or $IV_2$ than it is by $IV_M$. There might be, however, some query inferred from an index $IV_k$ that is not in $base(IV_1) \cup base(IV_2)$, and $IV_k$ might greatly benefit from $IV_M$ (see Figure 2). If that is the case, there is an $IV'_k$ reduced from $IV_k$ such that $IV_M \oplus IV'_k = IV_M$. Since (ii) does not hold, we have that the combined size of $IV_1$, $IV_2$ and $IV_k$ is smaller than that of $IV_M$, so we can

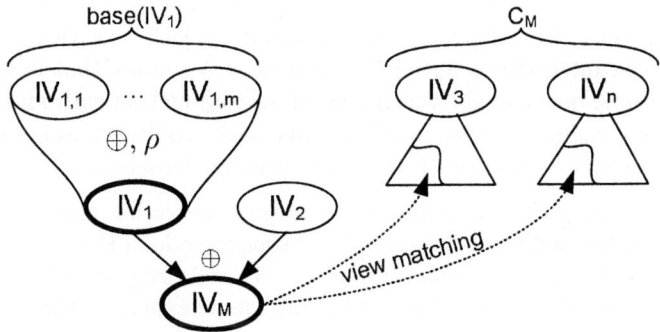

**Fig. 2.** Pruning indexes over views from the PDR search space

replace $IV_M$ by all $IV_i$ and obtain a better configuration. In conclusion, $IV_M$ cannot belong to PDR$(C, B)$ if (i) and (ii) do not hold.

There are analogous properties for the reduction operator, but we omit those due to space constraints.

### 4.3 Heuristic Approach to Approximate PDR

In this section we introduce a heuristic approach to solve PDR that is derived from the greedy solution to the fractional knapsack problem [3]. In the fractional knapsack problem, we first sort the input objects $o_i$ in ascending order by the value-volume ratio $a(o_i)/b(o_i)$ and then remove objects from this sequence until either the remaining objects fill completely the capacity $B$, or the last removed object $o_k$ exceeds $B$. In the latter case, we add back a fraction of $o_k$ so that the total volume is exactly $B$[8]. This assignment is optimal if fractions of objects are allowed in the answer. Even in the 0/1 case (i.e., no fractional objects are allowed), this heuristic performs very well in many practical cases and a very simple refinement guarantees a factor-2 approximation to the optimal solution [3].

A straightforward adaptation of the greedy solution described above would first generate the closure of the input configuration $C$, and then iteratively remove from the current configuration the index with the smallest value-volume ratio until the remaining ones satisfy the storage constraint. This approach has the following problems:

- The size of *closure*($C$) can be in the worst case exponential in the number of original indexes. At the same time, intuitively the *best* views are either the original ones, or obtained via a short sequence of operations (recall that each operation degrades the performance of the workload). Most of the indexes in *closure*($C$) are not present in the optimal configuration.
- The size of an index is not constant but depends on the configuration it belongs to. The reason is that we need to account for a primary index or heap associated with each different view definition. If many indexes share their view definition, we consider a single primary index or heap for them.
- The impact that each index has on the workload cost also depends on the configuration. We cannot assign a constant "value" to each index because of complex interactions inside the optimizer. An index that is not used to answer some query might become useful in conjunction with another index.
- The greedy solution to the fractional knapsack problem does not exploit the domain-specific Properties 1 and 2 for pruning the search space.

To address these issues, we propose a *progressive* variation of the fractional knapsack solution and present its simplified pseudo-code in Figure 3. Essentially, we start with the original configuration (line 1) and progressively refine it into new configurations that are smaller and slightly more expensive (lines 2-4). When

---

[8] In reality, we sort objects in reverse order and keep a prefix of the sequence. This is equivalent to the solution described above, which leads more easily to our adaptation.

```
GreedyPDR (C:configuration, B:storage bound)
01 CF = C
02 while (size(CF) > B)    // or any other ending condition
03    select transformation T with smallest benefit (=largest penalty)
            // T is valid merge or reduction, or deletion of an index
04    CF = CF - "T's antecedents" ∪ "T's consequent"
            // Merge: antecedent are input views, consequent is merged view
            // Reduction: antecedent is input view, consequent is reduced view
            // Deletion: antecedent is view, consequent is empty
05 return CF
```

**Fig. 3.** Progressive knapsack for the physical design refinement problem

we obtain a configuration that is within the storage constraint (or any other stopping criteria), we return it in line 5. One class of transformations in line 3 is the same as in the greedy solution to the fractional knapsack problem (i.e., we remove indexes). However, other transformations explore the augmented search space on demand by replacing one or two indexes with either a merged or reduced index.

In the remainder of this section we discuss some details of the algorithm:

- We consider the following transformations in line 3: (i) deletion of each index in the current configuration $CF$, (ii) merging of each pair of compatible indexes in $CF$, and (iii) reductions of each index in $CF$. Specifically, for (iii) we consider reductions $\rho(IV, T, K)$ so that $K$ are prefixes of the columns in the resulting index, and $T$ are subsets of tables that match another view in $CF$.
- We use a heuristic derived from Property 1 in line 4 by removing the input indexes whenever we introduce a transformed index in $CF$. Note that we do not check whether the transformed index can be generated by other derivations (see Property 1) so there might be some false negatives.
- We use a heuristic derived from Property 2 in line 3 by not considering transformations (merges and reductions) whose result is $(1+\alpha)$ times larger than the combined sizes of their inputs, for a small value of $\alpha$. As before, this heuristic might result in false negatives.
- Rather than assigning a constant "value" and "volume" to each index, we use a dynamic approach that considers the interactions with the optimizer. For a given configuration $C$, we define the *penalty* of a transformation (i.e., deletion, merging, reduction) as $\Delta_{cost}/\Delta_{space}$, where $\Delta_{cost}$ is an estimate of the degradation in cost that we would expect if we applied the transformation, and $\Delta_{space}$ is the amount of space that we would save by applying the transformation. Penalty values are then a measure of units of time that we lose per unit of space that we gain for a given transformation. We obtain $\Delta_{space}$ and $\Delta_{time}$ values as in [4], and use penalties as the dynamic version of the value-volume ratio in the original knapsack formulation.
- To avoid incremental errors in estimation, after each transformation we re-optimize the inferred workload under the new configuration $CF$. We

minimize optimization calls by only re-optimizing the queries in the workload that used an index that got removed from $CF$. The rationale is that we keep replacing indexes with coarser alternatives, so any query that did not use, say, $IV_1$ in a given configuration, should not use $IV_1 \oplus IV_2$ or $\rho(IV_1, T, K)$ if they became additionally available. This heuristic saves significant time and almost never degrades the quality of the final configurations.

## 5 Experimental Results

In this section we report preliminary results obtained with the techniques described in this paper. The goal is to compare our algorithm of Section 4 against state-of-the-art physical design tools regarding the quality of refined configurations and the time it takes to obtain them. We implemented the PDR algorithm of Section 4 as a client application and used Microsoft SQL Server as the database engine. For the experiments in this section, we proceeded using the following setup. First, we took a workload $W$ and tuned it with a physical database design tool for $B$ maximum storage, obtaining a configuration $C_B^{Tool}$. Second, we refined $C_B^{Tool}$ using our PDR implementation with a stricter storage constraint of $B' < B$, obtaining configuration $C_{B'}^{PDR}$. Third, we re-tuned $W$ from scratch using $B'$ as the new storage constraint, obtaining configuration $C_{B'}^{Tool}$. Finally, we evaluated the cost of the original workload $W$ under both $C_{B'}^{PDR}$ and $C_{B'}^{Tool}$, and also the time it took to produce each alternative configuration.

Figure 4 shows the results for a 22-query TPC-H [9] workload $W$ on a $1GB$ database and an initial storage constraint of $B = 2.8$ GB. We used several values of $B'$ ranging from 2.8 GB (no refinement) down to 1.3 GB (very little additional storage). In the figure we measure the cost of $W$ under a given configuration as a fraction of its cost under the initial configuration that only contains primary indexes. We see in Figure 4(a) that in all cases, the refined configuration obtained by PDR is only of slightly less quality than the alternative obtained from scratch with the tuning tool. In fact, the cost difference for the original workload between both configurations is below 10% in all cases. Additionally, Figure 4(b)

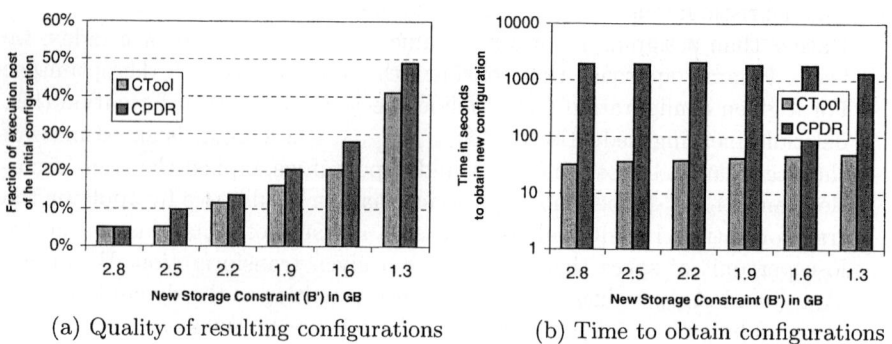

(a) Quality of resulting configurations     (b) Time to obtain configurations

**Fig. 4.** Refining configurations vs. producing new configurations from scratch

shows that the time it takes to refine a configuration can be orders of magnitude smaller than that to produce a new configuration from scratch for a different storage constraint (note the logarithmic scale in Figure 4(b)). We note that when using PDR, the resulting configuration is based on the original one, and we can also explain how we arrived to the refined configuration by presenting the transformations used from the original to the final indexes.

## 6 Related Work

In recent years there has been considerable research on automated physical design in database systems. Several pieces of work (e.g., [2, 5, 6, 10, 12]) detail solutions that consider different physical structures, and some of these ideas were later transferred to commercial products (e.g., [1, 7, 11]). This line of work, while successful, fails to address the common scenarios discussed in the introduction (which we collectively refer to as physical design refinement). In contrast to previous work, this paper presents a new and complementary paradigm that considers the current physical database design and evolves it to meet new requirements.

Previous work in the literature adopted an ad-hoc approach regarding the transformations that can be exploited for physical database design. Reference [6] introduces a concept of index merging that is similar to what we define in this paper, but does not generalize this notion to indexes over views. Similarly, reference [2] exploits a few transformations to combine the information in materialized views without giving a formal and complete framework. Reference [8] presents an overview of related work on view matching, which shares some of the technical details with our work, specifically with respect to view merging. We believe our work is the first to consider a unified approach of primitive operations over indexes and materialized views that can form the basis of physical design tools.

Some of the ideas in this work are inspired by [4], which presents a relaxation-based approach for physical design tuning. This reference introduces the concept of relaxation to transform an optimal configuration obtained by intercepting optimization calls to another one that fits in the available storage. Unlike this work, the main focus in [4] is to obtain an optimal design from scratch for a given workload and therefore the notion of transformations was of secondary importance. Specifically, reference [4] considers transformations for indexes and materialized views as different entities, and does not provide a unifying framework.

## 7 Conclusions

In this paper we introduce the physical design refinement problem, which fills an important gap in the functionality of known physical design tools. Rather than building new configurations from scratch when some requirements change, we enable the progressive transformation of the current configuration into a new one that satisfies the new constraints by means of local transformations. Specifically, we introduce two operators, *merging* and *reduction*, that balance space and efficiency in a database system. The operators are designed to unify previous attempts in the literature that consider indexes, materialized views, and indexes over materialized views as different entities. We believe that this new functionality is an important addition to the repertoire of automated physical design tools.

# References

1. S. Agrawal, S. Chaudhuri, L. Kollar, A. Marathe, V. Narasayya, and M. Syamala. Database Tuning Advisor for Microsoft SQL Server 2005. In *Proceedings of the 30th International Conference on Very Large Databases (VLDB)*, 2004.
2. S. Agrawal, S. Chaudhuri, and V. Narasayya. Automated selection of materialized views and indexes in SQL databases. In *Proceedings of the International Conference on Very Large Databases (VLDB)*, 2000.
3. G. Brassard and P. Bratley. *Fundamental of Algorithmics*. Prentice Hall, 1996.
4. N. Bruno and S. Chaudhuri. Automatic physical database tuning: A relaxation-based approach. In *Proceedings of the ACM International Conference on Management of Data (SIGMOD)*, 05.
5. S. Chaudhuri and V. Narasayya. An efficient cost-driven index selection tool for Microsoft SQL Server. In *Proceedings of the 23rd International Conference on Very Large Databases (VLDB)*, 1997.
6. S. Chaudhuri and V. Narasayya. Index merging. In *Proceedings of the International Conference on Data Engineering (ICDE)*, 1999.
7. B. Dageville, D. Das, K. Dias, K. Yagoub, M. Zait, and M. Ziauddin. Automatic SQL Tuning in Oracle 10g. In *Proceedings of the 30th International Conference on Very Large Databases (VLDB)*, 2004.
8. J. Goldstein and P.-A. Larson. Optimizing queries using materialized views: A practical, scalable solution. In *Proceedings of the ACM International Conference on Management of Data (SIGMOD)*, 2001.
9. TPC Benchmark H. Decision support. *Available at* http://www.tpc.org.
10. G. Valentin, M. Zuliani, D. Zilio, G. Lohman, and A. Skelley. DB2 advisor: An optimizer smart enough to recommend its own indexes. In *Proceedings of the International Conference on Data Engineering (ICDE)*, 2000.
11. D. Zilio et al. DB2 design advisor: Integrated automatic physical database design. In *Proceedings of the 30th International Conference on Very Large Databases (VLDB)*, 2004.
12. D. Zilio, C. Zuzarte, S. Lightstone, W. Ma, G. Lohman, R. Cochrane, H. Pirahesh, L. Colby, J. Gryz, E. Alton, D. Liang, and G. Valentin. Recommending materialized views and indexes with IBM DB2 design advisor. In *International Conference on Autonomic Computing*, 2004.

# Online, Non-blocking Relational Schema Changes

Jørgen Løland and Svein-Olaf Hvasshovd

Dept. of Computer Science, NTNU, Trondheim, Norway
{jorgen.loland, svein-olaf.hvasshovd}@idi.ntnu.no

**Abstract.** A database schema should be able to evolve to reflect changes to the universe it represents. In existing systems, user transactions get blocked during complex schema transformations. Blocking user transactions is not an option in systems with very high availability requirements, like operational telecom databases. A non-blocking transformation framework is therefore needed.

A method for performing non-blocking full outer join and split transformations, suitable for highly available databases, is presented in this paper. Only the log is used for change propagation, and this makes the method easy to integrate into existing DBMSs. Because the involved tables are not locked, the transformation may run as a low priority background process. As a result, the transformation has little impact on concurrent user transactions.

## 1 Introduction

Database schemas are typically designed to model the world as understood at design time. At this point in time, the schema design may be excellent for the intended usage. Many applications change over time, however. In a study of seven applications, Marche [18] reports of significant changes to relational database schemas over time. Only one of the studied schemas had less than 50% of their attributes changed. Furthermore, 16% of all changes were due to changes in the degree of normalization. The evolution of the schemas continued after the development period had ended. A similar study of a health management system [25] came to the same conclusion. This indicates the need for non-trivial schema transformations.

A schema transformation can easily be made if the involved tables can be locked while the transformation is performed. Most databases can do this by issuing an *insert into select* command, where the select statement can be any valid SQL select statement, e.g. join or union.

Databases with very high availability requirements should not be unavailable for long periods of time. For tables with large amounts of data, the *insert into select* method could easily take tens of minutes or more. Such databases, often found in e.g. the telecom industry, would clearly benefit from a mechanism to change the schema without being blocked.

In this paper we suggest schema transformation methods for the full outer join (FOJ) and split relational operators. The methods are non-blocking and are based on log redo. FOJ and split are considered important operators by the authors because they are used to change the normalization degree of the schema.

We assume that both redo and undo log records are produced, and that undo operations produce Compensating Log Records (CLR) [6] as described in the ARIES method [20]. It is also assumed that a log sequence number (LSN) is associated with each record [12].

The paper is organized as follows: Section 2 describes other methods and research areas related to non-blocking transformations. An overview of our transformation framework is presented in 3. Details for how to apply the framework to FOJ and split transformations are presented in Sections 4 and 5, respectively. The framework has been implemented in a prototype and test results from this prototype are discussed in Section 6. Finally, in Section 7, we conclude and suggest further work.

## 2 Related Work

Little research has been published on non-blocking schema transformations in relational databases. Our method does, however, use techniques from both fuzzy copy and materialized views (MVs), as described in the following sections.

### 2.1 Ronströms' Method

Ronström [23] presents a framework that uses both a reorganizer and triggers within user transactions to perform schema transformations. Sagas [7] are used to organize the transformation. New tables, constraints, indices, and triggers are first added to the schema. The reorganizer then scans the old tables, while triggers make sure that updates to the old tables are executed immediately to the transformed table. When the scan is complete, the old and transformed tables are consistent due to the triggered updates.

No implementation or test results have been published on Ronströms method. Triggers are, however, used in a similar way to keep immediate Materialized Views (MVs) up to date. The extra workload incurred with using triggers to update MVs is significant, and deferred MVs are therefore recommended whenever possible (see e.g. [5, 16]).

With our method, there is no need for the transformed table to be consistent with the old table before the very end of the transformation. Updates can therefore be propagated to the transformed tables during low workloads. We also expect our method to be much more efficient in a distributed DBMS where user transactions have to wait for triggers to access other nodes. Finally, our method does not require the use of Sagas.

### 2.2 Fuzzy Copy

Our transformation framework has to make a copy of the source tables without setting locks to satisfy the non-blocking requirement. To do this, we use a modified fuzzy copy technique.

Hvasshovd et al. [4, 13] presents fuzzy copy as a way to copy a table to another node in a cluster without blocking. A *begin-fuzzy mark* is first written to the log. The records in the source table are then read without setting locks, resulting in a *fuzzy copy* where some of the updates that were made during the scan may not be reflected. The log is then redone to the copy in a similar way as ARIES [20] to make it up to date. LSNs on records ensure that the log propagation is idempotent. When all log records have been redone to the copy in ascending order, it is in the same state as the source table. An *end-fuzzy mark* is then written to the log, and the copy process is complete. The method requires CLR to be used for undo processing.

### 2.3 Materialized Views

Materialized views (MVs) store the result of a query. They are used to speed up query processing and must therefore be consistent with the source tables. Methods to propagate changes from the source tables to an MV is an area of extensive research (e.g. [3, 5, 8, 9, 10, 11, 16, 21, 24, 27]). All these propagation methods require the MVs to be consistent with a previous state of the source tables. This incurs that an MV must initially be consistent, i.e. populated with the result of a blocking read.

At first glance, MVs have much in common with our schema transformation framework. Blocking read operations are, however, not allowed in the transformation framework, so fuzzy copies of the source tables are used to create the initial images of transformed tables. Since a fuzzy copy is not consistent with the source table, the MV update methods are not applicable. Further more, schema transformations only require the transformed tables to *converge* to the source tables (i.e. to be consistent when all operations are propagated [27]), whereas MVs require consistency for all intermediate states as well.

### 2.4 Existing Transformations

Existing database systems, including IBM DB2 v8 [14, 15], Microsoft SQL Server 2000 [19], MySQL 4.0 [26] and Oracle 9*i* [1], offer some simple transformation functionality. These include removal of and adding one or more attributes to a table, renaming attributes and the like. Removal of an attribute can be performed by changing the table description only, thus leaving the physical records unchanged for an unspecified period of time. Complex tranformations like join are not supported.

## 3 General Framework

The goal of the transformation framework is to provide methods that transform the schema without blocking other transactions. The transformations are based on relational operators for two reasons: the effect of the transformation is easy to understand for the database administrator (DBA) that initiates it, and it enables us to make use of existing, optimized code (like join algorithms) for parts of the process.

The framework operates in four steps that are common to both the FOJ and split transformations. These steps are briefly explained below.

### 3.1 Preparation Step

Before the transformation starts, the new tables that are to be used after the transformation have to be created. They may include any subset of attributes from the source tables, but must include at least one candidate key from each. The reason for this is that the transformation method needs a way to uniquely identify which records are affected by an operation on a source table record. In the case that the included candidate key attributes are not wanted in the transformed tables, they must be deleted *after* the FOJ or split transformation completes.

Constraints, both new and from the source tables, may be added to the new tables. This should, however, be done with great care since constraint violations may force the transformation to abort.

Any indices that are needed on the new tables should also be created before the transformation starts. These indices will be up to date when the transformation is complete.

## 3.2 Initial Population Step

The newly created transformed tables have to be populated with records from the source tables. The first step of populating the new table is to write a *fuzzy mark* in the log. This log record must include the transaction identifiers of all transactions that are active on the source tables, i.e. a subset of the active transaction table. The source tables are then read fuzzily, returning an inconsistent result since locks are ignored [13]. Once the source tables have been read, the transformation operator is applied and the result, called the *initial image*, is inserted into the transformed tables.

## 3.3 Log Propagation

When the initial image(s) have been inserted into the transformed table(s), another fuzzy mark is written to the log. This log record marks the end of the current log propagation cycle and the beginning of the next one.

Log records of operations that may not be reflected in the transformed tables are now inspected. In the first iteration, the oldest log record that may contain such an operation is the oldest log record of any transaction that was active when the first fuzzy mark was written. Later log propagation iterations only have to read the log after the previous fuzzy mark.

Propagation rules for update, insert and delete of records in a source table differ for each transformation type, and are explained in detail in Sections 4 and 5.

To speed up the synchronization step, locks are maintained on records in the transformed tables during the entire transformation. The locks are likely to conflict during the transformation. Since they are only needed when user transactions access both source and transformed tables, i.e. during synchronization, they are ignored for now.

The synchronization step should not be started if a significant portion of the log remains to be propagated because it involves latching of tables. Each log propagation iteration therefore ends with an analysis of the remaining work. Based on the analysis, either another log propagation iteration or the synchronization step is started. The analysis could be based on, e.g. the time used to complete the current iteration, a count of the remaining log records to be propagated, or an estimated remaining propagation time.

If more log records are produced than the propagator is able to process, the synchronization is never started. If this is the case, the transformation should either be aborted or get higher priority.

The transformed tables of both FOJ and split of consistent data are self-maintainable [22], i.e does not need more information than the log and the transformed tables themselves. This makes them highly suitable for distributed databases as well.

### 3.4 Synchronization

When synchronization is initiated, the state of the transformed tables should be very close to the state of the source tables. This is because the source tables have to be latched during one final log propagation iteration that makes the transformed table consistent with the source tables.

We suggest three ways to synchronize the transformed tables to the source tables and thereby complete the transformation process. These are called blocking commit, non-blocking abort and non-blocking commit synchronization.

*Blocking commit* synchronization starts by blocking all new transactions that try to access any of the tables involved in the transformation. Transactions that already have locks on the source tables are then allowed to complete before a final log propagation iteration is performed. The transformed tables are now consistent with the source tables. New transactions are then given access to the new tables only. This method does not follow the non-blocking requirement.

*The non-blocking abort* strategy begins by placing table latches on the source tables for the duration of one final log propagation. Latching these tables effectively pauses ongoing transactions that work on them, but since there are only a few log records to propagate, the pause should be very brief (less than 1 ms in our current implementation). Once the log propagation is complete, the transformed tables are in the same state as the source tables. Recall from Section 3.3 that locks have been maintained on the transformed tables since the first fuzzy log mark. Records that are locked in the source tables are therefore also locked in the transformed tables. New transactions are now allowed to access the unlocked parts of the transformed table while transactions that were active on the source tables are forced to abort. The log propagation continues as a background process as long as old transactions are alive. Source table locks held in the transformed tables are released as soon as the propagator has processed the abort log record of the lock owner transaction.

*Non-blocking commit* synchronization works much like the previous strategy in that latches are placed on the source tables during one final log propagation. But in contrast to the previous strategy, transactions on the source tables are allowed to continue processing once the tables have been synchronized. This is called a soft transformation in [23]. The drawback of this method is that as long as any of the old transactions are alive, all locks on source tables have to be acquired on the corresponding records in the transformed tables. However, nonconflicting transactions are not aborted due to the transformation.

Finally, the source tables are dropped from the schema, and the transformation is complete.

## 4 Full Outer Join Transformations

The method for FOJ transforms two source tables, $R$ and $S$, into one table $T$ by applying the FOJ operator. An example transformation is shown in Figure 1. The general

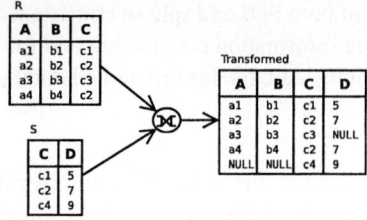

**Fig. 1.** Example full outer join transformation

transformation steps explained in Section 3 are discussed for FOJ below. For readability it is assumed that the join attribute of table $S$ (attribute $c$ in Figure 1) is unique, i.e. there is a one-to-many relation between the source tables. A solution for the many-to-many case is sketched in Section 4.2.

### 4.1 Preparation and Initial Population Steps

In the *preparation* step, the transformed table $T$ is created. As a minimum, $T$ must contain an identifying attribute set from both tables in addition to the join attributes. Constraints may be added, but unique constraints on attributes in $S$ should be avoided since a record in $S$ is likely to occur multiple times in $T$.

Without lack of generality, we assume that the key attributes of $R$ are also the key attributes of $T$. As long as there is a unique way to identify the $T$ records to update, the method will work without this assumption.

To improve transformation performance, an index should be created on the join attributes of $T$. If the join attributes of $S$ are not the same attributes as the primary key, an index should also be created on the primary key attributes of $S$ in the transformed table. These indexes provide fast lookup on all $T$−records that are affected by an operation on an $S$−record.

During the *initial population* step, the source tables are first read fuzzily. The FOJ of the results are then inserted into $T$. Special $R-$ and $S-$ NULL records, denoted $r^{null}$ and $s^{null}$, are joined with records that otherwise would not have a join match, as illustrated in Figure 1.

### 4.2 Log Propagation

The fuzzy copy method of Hvasshovd et al. [13] use a record state identifier, typically the Log Sequence Number (LSN), to make logged operations idempotent. Logged operations are applied to records only if the LSN of the log record is greater than the LSN of the record.

In our framework, there are no valid state identifiers for the records in the newly created $T$. This is because records in $T$ consist of two records, one from each source table. The records from the source tables have an LSN each, while the resulting record may only have one LSN. The LSN of a record in $T$ is therefore not a correct state identifier.

The rest of this section describes how to apply the log to the initial image, i.e. the join of the fuzzy read source tables, without using state identifiers. It works under the assumption that all write operations on the source tables use exclusive locks; i.e. delta updates [17] are not allowed.

When fuzzy read starts, the two source tables are in state 0, denoted $R_0$ and $S_0$. After the initial image has been inserted, $T$ is in an inconsistent state $i$, denoted $T_i$, where all records are in the same or newer state than they had in $R_0$ and $S_0$. All operations on the source tables that happened after state 0 are now applied sequentially to $T$. At some future point in time, during synchronization, all operations in the log have been redone to $T$, making $T$ up to date with $R$ and $S$. The states of the tables at that point in time is called $c$, denoted $R_c$, $S_c$ and $T_c$. $c$ is an action consistent state since both $R$ and $S$ are latched for the final synchronization.

At any point in time during log propagation, $R$ and $S$ have the same or newer state than $T$ for all records. This is a consequence of the fact that all operations reflected in $T$ are simply redoes of operations on $R$ and $S$. In addition, the current state $t$ (denoted $R_t$ and $S_t$) of the source tables precedes the state $c$ for all records. Thus, $0 \leq i \leq t \leq c$, where $a \leq b$ means that $b$ contains at least all operations reflected in $a$, but may also reflect newer operations.

**A Basic Property.** Without valid state identifiers, the log propagator does not know if a log record is already reflected in $T$. The rules are idempotent, i.e., a log record may be redone multiple times. The rules can not handle lost updates, but as shown in the following theorem lost updates never appear:

**Theorem 1.** *(Records in $T_i$ are up to date)*
*Assume that the log propagator is currently processing a log record describing an operation to a source table record. The appropriate records in the transformed tables are then either in the same state as the source table record was in when the operation was originally executed, or in a newer state.*

Assuming that the concurrency controller enforces serializability, the record must have been up to date when the operation was originally executed in the source table [2]. The original sequence of operations on that record is in the same order in the log because the log is sequential and the operations are serializable.

A fuzzy read of a table catches all updates that happened before the read started. As a consequence of the fact that fuzzy read ignores locks, it may also include some updates that happened during the read.

Since all updates that happened before the fuzzy read started are guaranteed to be reflected in the initial image, a lost update must have been introduced after that point in the log. The log propagator starts with the first log record of any active transaction at the time of the first fuzzy mark. This is the first operation that may not be reflected in the initial image of the transformed table.

Assume that the log propagation rules are correct, i.e. all records in the transformed table that should be affected by a logged operation on a source table record, are updated correctly by the propagator. Then, since no lost updates existed in the initial image and because the log is propagated sequentially, no lost updates can exist after the first log record has been applied. By induction, the transformed table has no lost updates when the current log record is encountered.

In other words: as long as the log is applied in sequential order to the initial fuzzy copy, all records in $T_i$ are in the same or a newer state than the source table records were in when the operation was originally executed.

**Insert Operations.** The log propagator may encounter log records describing insert, update and delete operations on records in the base tables. In what follows, rules for how to propagate insert log records are described.

The notation $r_x^y$ means a record from table $R$ where $y$ is the primary key value and $x$ is the join attribute value. By $t_x^y$, we refer to the record in $T$ resulting from the join of $r_x^y$ and $s_x^x$ (abbreviated $s^x$). As previously assumed, the join attribute of $S$ is unique. Records with no join match in the opposite source table are joined with the $R-$ or $S-$ null record ($r^{null}$ and $s^{null}$), as described in Section 4.1. **A** and **B** are the sets of all primary key and join attribute values allowed, respectively.

**Rule 1 (Insert $r_x^y$ into $R$)**
*Check if a record with the key $y$, $t_x^y$, exists in $T_i$. If so, ignore the log record. Otherwise, use the join attribute index of $T$ to find a record with the join attribute value $x$. There are three possible results: If $t_x^{null}$ is found, it is updated with the attribute values of $r_x^y$ to form $t_x^y$. If $t_x^v$ is found ($v \in \mathbf{A}, v \neq y$), a new $t_x^y$–record is inserted after joining $r_x^y$ with the $s^x$–part of $t_x^v$. If no record with this join attribute exists in $T_i$, $t_{null}^y$ is inserted after joining $r_x^y$ with $s^{null}$.*

Theorem 1 states that all records in $T_i$ are up to date with or in a newer state than the log record. For this reason, if $t_x^y$ is found, the log record is already reflected in $T_i$ and can safely be ignored. If this was not the case, two records with the same key $y$ existed in $R$ at the same time.

The other cases are straightforward; by searching the index, the log propagator finds all information necessary to insert $t_x^y$.

Even if $t_w^y$ ($w \in \mathbf{B}$) is not found in $T_i$, it is possible that $T_i$ has a newer state for $t_w^y$ than that of the log. This can only be the case if $t_w^y$ is later deleted, leaving no trace of its existence. If so, the insertion of $t_x^y$ will be corrected when the log record of the delete is encountered later.

**Rule 2 (Insert $s^x$ into $S$)**
*Use the $S$–key index to find all records with the join attribute value $x$ in $T_i$. If any of these records are joined with $s^{null}$, they are updated with the new $s^x$ values. $T$-records joined with an $S$–record other than $s^{null}$ are not updated. Otherwise, if no records have $x$ as the join attribute, $t_x^{null}$ is inserted after joining $r^{null}$ with $s^x$.*

$s^x$–records found in $T_i$ are not modified since Theorem 1 guarantees that they are up to date. For both insert rules, FOJ requires that records with no join match are still present in the result.

**Delete Operations**

**Rule 3 (Delete $r^y$ from $R$)**
*Check if $t^y$ exists in $T_i$, and ignore the log record if not. If $t_{null}^y$ is found, it is simply*

deleted. If $t_x^y$ is found, the index is used to see if $t_x^y$ is the only record in $T_i$ containing $s^x$. If so, $t_x^{null}$ is inserted after joining $s^x$ with $t^{null}$. $t_x^y$ is then deleted.

**Rule 4 (Delete $s^x$ from $S$)**
Use the join attribute index to identify all records with $x$ as join attribute value. If $t_x^{null}$ is found, it is deleted. All other records $t_x^v$ ($v \in \mathbf{A}$) that are found are joined with $s^{null}$.

These rules are simply delete operations that guarantee the continued existence of their joined counterparts.

**Update Operations.** Insert and delete log records contain all the information needed to propagate the log. For insert log records, this information includes all attribute values. For delete log records, the primary key of the record to delete is all the information needed.

Update log records are less informative since they typically contain the primary key and updated attribute values only. The information not found in the log record is, however, available in $T_i$ as described next.

**Rule 5 (Update join attribute of $r_x^y$ to $z$)**
The record with key attribute value $y$, $t_w^y$ ($w \in \mathbf{B}$), is first read from $T_i$. If $t_w^y$ is not found in $T_i$, or if $w \neq x$, the log record is ignored. Assuming that $t_x^y$ is found, the join attribute index of $T_i$ is searched to find if $s^x$ is represented in at least one more record. If not, $t_x^{null}$ is inserted by joining $r^{null}$ with $s^x$.

Next, the join attribute index is searched for a record with $z$ as the join attribute. If $t_z^{null}$ is found, it is updated with the attribute values of $r_z^y$ to form $t_z^y$. If $t_z^v$ ($v \in \mathbf{A}, v \neq y$) is found, a new $t_z^y$–record is inserted after joining $r_z^y$ with the $s^z$– part of $t_z^v$. If no record with this join attribute exists in $T_i$, $t_{null}^y$ is inserted after joining $r_z^y$ with $s^{null}$.

Again, Theorem 1 guarantees that the record $t_w^y$ found in $T_i$ is at least up to date with the log. If $w \neq x$, an operation representing a newer state than that of the log record is already reflected in $t_w^y$. Applying the logged update would not lead to inconsistency in the future state $T_c$ since the log record leading to that newer state will be found in the log before $c$ is reached. Doing so does, however, incur extra work.

Even though the join attribute is guaranteed to be unique in $S$, it is not necessarily the primary key. It may therefore be updated:

**Rule 6 (Update join attribute of $s^x$ to $z$)**
All records in $T_i$ that have $x$ as the join attribute value, are first identified. If no record is found, the log record is ignored. If $t_x^{null}$ is found, it is deleted. If found, all records $t_x^v$ ($v \in \mathbf{A}$) in $T_i$ are joined with $s^{null}$ to form $t_{null}^v$.

Next, all records in $T_i$ that have the new join attribute value, $z$, are identified. If $t_{null}^v$ is found, it is updated with $s^z$ to form $t_z^v$. Any $t_z^v$ record already joined with an $s^z$ record stays unmodified. If no other $T$–record is joined with $s^z$, $r^{null}$ is joined with $s^z$ to form $t_z^{null}$.

This rule operates like delete of $s^x$ followed by insert of $s^z$. Like in propagation rule 5, $s^x$ is used to extract the attribute values of $s^z$ since the log does not include this information.

**Rule 7 (Update other attribute of $r^y$ or $s^x$)**
*If an update of $r^y$ is described, the record $t^y$ with the same primary key is updated with the new attribute values. Similarly, if $s^x$ is updated, the index of $T_i$ is used to identify all records $t_x^v$ ($v \in \mathbf{A}$) with $x$ as the join attribute value. All records found are updated as described in the log. If no records are found, the log record is ignored.*

The rule should be intuitive: all records in $T_i$ that partly consist of the updated record must be updated with the new values. If no records match the key, the log record can safely be ignored since Theorem 1 guarantees that $T_i$ has a newer state for that record when this happens.

**Sketch of Log Propagation for Many-to-Many Relationships.** The described log propagation rules work under the assumption that the join attribute of $S$ is unique. In this section, we sketch what needs to be done when this assumption does not hold.

In many-to-many relationships, each $R$−record can be joined with multiple $S$−records. Because of this, the primary key of $R$ cannot be used as the primary key in $T$ alone. Instead, one or more identifying attributes from both source tables, e.g. their primary keys, should be used together to form the primary key of $T$. In what follows, $t_z^{yx}$ means a record in $T_i$ that consists of a record $r_z^y$ joined on attribute value $z$ with $s_z^x$.

The one-to-many rules for operations on $S$−records does not need modification to work in many-to-many transformations. Operations on $R$−records, however, need to be modified so that all records in $T_i$ that consist of the described $R$−part are affected. An index should be created to speed up the search for these.

For update and deletion of a record $r_z^y$, the modified rules simply has to identify all $T$−records consisting of $r_z^y$ and apply the operation described for the one-to-many case. For every deletion of a $T$−record, the existence of other $S$−records with the same primary key has to be checked to ensure full outer join.

When a log record describes an insert of $r_z^y$, a $t_z^{yv}$−record ($v \in \mathbf{A}$) has to be inserted for every matching record $s_x^v$. When the join attribute of an $r_z^y$ is updated, all existing $T$−records that the $r_z^y$ contributed to must be deleted. The continued existence of the deleted records' $S$−counterparts must be enshured as well. New join-matches are then inserted into $T$.

### 4.3 Synchronization

Synchronization of FOJ transformations are performed as described in Section 3.4. Lock propagation between the old and new tables must, however, be described in more detail for the non-blocking strategies.

Since locks from two source tables $R$ and $S$ are transferred to one new table $T$, the source table locks may conflict in $T$. This is, however, only a consequence of the lock granularity being *record* as opposed to *attribute*. Clearly, operations on $R$ and $S$ do not modify the same attributes. New lock compatibility rules for $T$ are needed to avoid the conflict. Note that this is only needed for the non-blocking strategies.

**Lock Compatibility.** A transaction being aborted cannot acquire new locks, so the *non-blocking abort* strategy only needs lock releases to be transferred from the source tables

|     | R.r | S.r | T.r | R.w | S.w | T.w |
|-----|-----|-----|-----|-----|-----|-----|
| R.r | y   | y   | y   | y   | y   | n   |
| S.r | y   | y   | y   | y   | y   | n   |
| T.r | y   | y   | y   | n   | n   | n   |
| R.w | y   | y   | n   | y   | y   | n   |
| S.w | y   | y   | n   | y   | y   | n   |
| T.w | n   | n   | n   | n   | n   | n   |

**Fig. 2.** Lock compatibility matrix for locks in T for the non-blocking strategies.

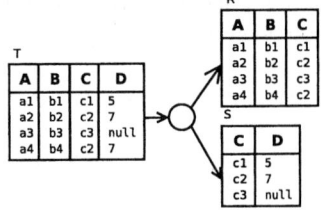

**Fig. 3.** Example Split transformation

to $T$. When a *transaction aborted* log record is encountered in the log, the propagator releases the locks of that transaction in $T$.

With *non-blocking commit*, transactions are active on both the source tables and the transformed table at the same time. All transactions may acquire new locks, but to prevent inconsistencies, locks must be transferred both from $T$ to $R$ and $S$ and vice versa. If a transaction cannot get a lock on all implicated records in all tables, it is not allowed to go forward with the operation.

Because locks from two non-conflicting operations in $R$ and $S$ could conflict in $T$, new lock compatibility rules have been developed for locks that are transferred from the source tables to $T$. As can be seen in Figure 2, the new rules ensure that locks from operations executed by transactions on the source tables do not conflict in $T$, whereas they conflict with operations executed by transactions in $T$. The compatibility matrix can easily be extended to multigranularity locking [2].

As for the non-blocking abort case, locks are released when the propagator encounters a *transaction aborted* or *commited* log record.

## 5 Split Transformation

The (vertical) split transformation takes one source table, $T$, and transforms it into two tables $R$ and $S$. This is the reverse of the FOJ transformation described in the previous section, as illustrated by Figure 3. It follows the four steps described in Section 3.

When a table $T$ is split, multiple records may have equal $S$–parts. These records should be represented by only one record in $S$. Further more, a record in $S$ should only be deleted when there are no more records in $T$ with that $S$–part. To be able to decide if this is the case, a *counter*, similar to that of Gupta et al. [10], is associated with each $S$ record. When an $S$ record is first inserted, it has a counter of 1. After that, the counter is increased every time a record with the same primary key is inserted, and decreased every time one is deleted. If the counter of a record reaches zero, the record is removed from $S$.

The notation is the same as in Section 4: each record $t_x^y$ in $T$ is split into two records, $r_x^y$ and $s^x$ where $y \in A$ and $x \in B$. A and B are the sets of valid primary key values in $R$ and valid values for the attribute used to split, respectively. As for join, the states $R_c$ and $S_c$ is reached at some future point in time when the log propagator has applied the entire log to the transformed tables and the synchronization step is complete.

For readability, we assume that the split attribute is also the primary key in $S$, although this is not required for the method to work. The method does, however, require that the split attribute is a candidate key in $S$, i.e. can be used to identify $S$−records.

### 5.1 Data Consistency

Before the split method is described in detail, we show that inconsistencies that make it impossible to process the transformation may be found in $T$. Consider the following example:

*Example 1.* A company maintains a database of customer contact information, as shown in the table:

| Customer ID | Name | Postal Code | City |
|---|---|---|---|
| 001 | Peter | 7050 | Trondheim |
| 002 | Mark | 5020 | Bergen |
| 003 | Gary | 0050 | Oslo |
| ... | ... | ... | ... |
| 134 | Jen | 7050 | Trnodheim |

Customer ID is used as the primary key of this table. There is also a functional dependency in that postal code determines city.

Notice that there is an inconsistency between customers 001 and 134 since the postal codes are the same, whereas the city names differ. Nothing prevents such inconsistencies from occuring in this table, and the schema transformation framework has no means to decide whether "Trondheim" or "Trnodheim" is correct if we were to split this table on postal code. ♦

If inconsistencies like the one in Example 1 exist in $T$, we are not able to perform a split transformation without fixing them.

The log propagation rules are divided into two parts. Section 5.2 describes rules working under the assumption that inconsistencies does not appear in $T$. Section 5.3 describes additional rules needed when such assumptions are not made.

### 5.2 Split of Consistent Data

In this scenario, it is assumed that the DBMS applies measures that guarantee consistency. The method provides an easy-to-understand basis for the scenario where inconsistencies may occur.

During the *preparation and initial population* steps, $S$ and $R$ are simply created and populated as described in Section 3.

An alternative strategy is to create and populate the $S$−table only. Since all attributes needed in $R$ are already present in $T$, $T$ can be renamed to $R$ during synchronization if attributes that are not part of $R$ are removed first. By utilizing this, the transformation would require less space, and updates that would not affect attributes in $S$ could be ignored. Unfortunately, the log propagator needs information on both the LSN and the split attribute value of each $R$−record in the current intermediate state. A temporary table $P$ would be needed to keep track of this information during propagation.

Although $P$ may potentially be much smaller than $R$, this section describes how the method works when $R$ is created as a separate table. Only minor adjustments are needed for the temporary table method to work.

The *synchronization step* works as described in Section 3.4.

### Insert

After the initial images have been inserted into $R$ and $S$, log propagation can start. When a log record for an insert into $T$ is found in the log, $R$ and $S$ are updated using the following rule:

**Rule 8 (Insert $t_x^y$ into $T$)** *The existence of a record with the primary key value $y$, $r^y$, in $R_i$ is first checked. There are two scenarios: if $r^y$ is found, the log record is ignored. If $r^y$ is not found, the $R$−part of $t_x^y$, $r_x^y$, is inserted into $R_i$.*

*Assuming that $r^y$ did not previously exist in $R_i$, the $S$−part of $t_x^y$, $s^x$, is now inserted into $S_i$. First, the existence of a record with the same primary key $x$ is checked. If found, the counter of that record is increased by one. The LSN is then updated if the LSN of the log record is higher than that of $s^x$. If $s^x$ does not exist in $S_i$, $s^x$ is inserted with a counter of one and the LSN of the log record.*

By Theorem 1, if a record with the key $y$ is found in $R_i$, the log record is guaranteed to be reflected in the transformed tables. Both insertion into $R_i$ and $S_i$ are therefore ignored. With guaranteed consistency, the inserted $s^x$ record is either equal to an existing record in $S_i$, or the transaction that generated this log record also updated all other $T$−records contributing to $s^x$ consistently. Changing nothing but the counter and possibly the LSN is therefore correct.

### Delete

**Rule 9 (Delete $t^y$ from $T$)** *If no record with the primary key value $y$, $r^y$, exists in $R$, or if one exists that has a higher LSN than that of the log record, the log record is ignored.*

*If a record $r_v^y$ ($v \in \mathbf{B}$) exists and has a lower LSN, it is deleted from $R_i$. The counter of $s^v$ is then decreased, and the LSN is changed if the log record has a higher LSN. If the counter reaches zero, the record is completely removed from $S$.*

Using the LSN of the delete operation appears erroneous since it represents the state of a record that does not exist in $T$ anymore. This is not a problem for the transformation framework because the log is propagated sequentially. Changing the LSN of the $S$−record has therefore no consequence on whether future log records will we applied to the table.

We could have chosen not to update the LSN. The same problem would, however, occur in related situations: Assume that the records $t_c^a$ and $t_c^b$ are the only records in $T$ that contribute to the record $s^c$. Also assume that $t_c^a$ is updated and later deleted. Even if the LSN of the $S$−record is not changed by the delete, it still has the LSN value of the update of the record $t_c^a$ that no longer exists.

**Update**

Updating the $R$−part of a record in $T$ is straightforward:

**Rule 10 (Update $t^y$: the $R$−part)** *The existence of a record with the same primary key $y$, $r^y$, in $R_i$ is first checked. If $r^y$ is not found, or if it has a higher LSN than the logged operation, the log record is ignored.*

*Assuming that $r^y$ is found and that it has an LSN lower than the log record, the record and its LSN is simply updated. The LSN is changed even if no attribute values in $r_x^y$ are updated.*

There are two cases of updates propagated to $S_i$ that must be considered: the split attribute is either updated or not. Note that updates are only applied to $S_i$ if $r^y$ was updated in Rule 10. The reason for this is that the LSN values in $R_i$ uniquely identifies which operations in $T$ are already reflected on existing records in the transformed tables. If a logged operation is reflected in $R_i$, it must also be reflected in $S_i$.

**Rule 11 (Update $t_x^y$: the $S$−part)** *The record $s^x$ with the split attribute value $x$, read from $r_x^y$, is first identified. If the LSN of that record is lower than the log record's, the update is propagated as follows: assuming that only non-split attributes are updated, $s^x$ is simply updated with the new attribute values. Otherwise, if the split attribute is updated, the update is treated as a deletion of $s^x$, followed by the insertion of $s^v$ ($v$ being the new split attribute). Following the argument for insert of $S$−records, only the counter and possibly the LSN of the record with the new key is updated.*

## 5.3 Split of Possibly Inconsistent Data

If consistency is not guaranteed by the DBMS, the transformation framework has to make sure that errors like the one in Example 1 are corrected. Performing this check comes with an overhead to the log propagator. The overhead is, however, not present *within* user transactions since the log propagation, and therefore the overhead, runs as a low priority background process.

A flag is associated with each record in $S$. Two values are allowed: Consistent ($C$) and Unknown ($U$). A $C$ flag is used when an $S$−record is known to be consistent, and the $U$ flag is used when an $S$−record is known to be inconsistent or has an unknown consistency state.

Every $S$−record that was consistent in the fuzzy read gets a $C$−flag. All other records get a $U$−flag. During log propagation, inserting a record $s^x$ that is not equal to an existing record with the same split value changes a $C$−flag into $U$. The same happens when an update is applied to an $S$−record with a counter greater than 1. A $U$−flag is changed to $C$ only if the operation updates all non-key attributes of a record with a counter of 1.

A "concistency checker" (CC) is run regularly. A $U$−flagged record, say $s^v$, is first chosen. The CC then writes a "Begin CC on $v$" record to the log. All records in $T$ contributing to $s^v$ are then read without using locks. If they are consistent in $T$, a "CC: $v$ is ok" record is written to the log together with the correct image of $s^v$. The log propagator keeps track of the records being checked: if $s^v$ is not changed in any way between the two log records, $s^v$ is guaranteed to be consistent and is changed accordingly. Note that all records in $S$ should have a $C$−flag before synchronization is started. Because $T$ has to be read during CC, the split of tables with inconsistent data is not self-maintainable.

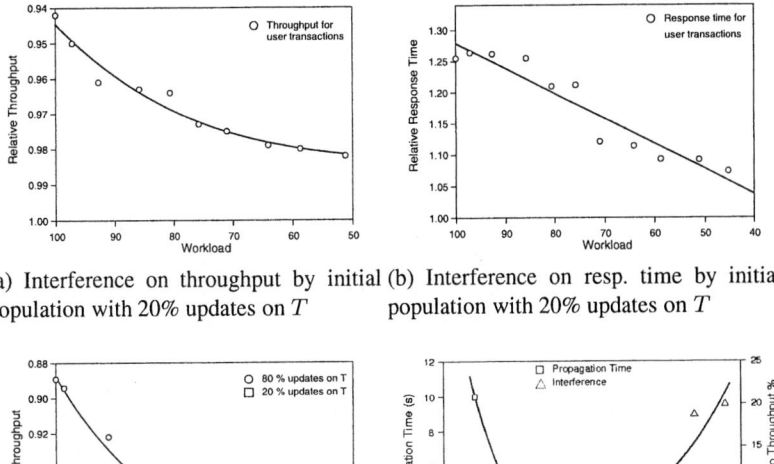

(a) Interference on throughput by initial population with 20% updates on $T$

(b) Interference on resp. time by initial population with 20% updates on $T$

(c) Interference on throughput by log propagation for two update scenarios

(d) Time and interference vs transformation priority at 75% workload

**Fig. 4.** Test results of Split Transformation

## 6 Prototype Implementation

A prototype that performs the described non-blocking transformations has been implemented in Java. It is simplified in that it keeps all data in main memory. This is realistic for databases requiring very fast response time (e.g. [12]), but not for most traditional databases. The costs of the changes are still relevant because we measure *relative* performance, i.e. performance before the change vs. performance during the change.

Four client nodes, one server node and one admin node, all running Linux kernel 2.6, have been used. Each node had 2 AMD Athlon 1600+ CPUs (the prototype has only used one on each node) and 1GB RAM. The nodes were connected with a 100 Mb/s ethernet.

Hundreds of tests have been executed to find the cost of the described schema changes. The cost is measured in reduction in throughput and increased response time of normal transactions run both alone and concurrently with the schema changes.

Each transaction updated 10 records using record locks. 100% workload was defined as the number of concurrent transactions that produced the highest possible throughput. Lower workloads were achieved by reducing the number of concurrent transactions.

The tests for the FOJ transformation were done with 50000 records in $R$ and 20000 records in $S$. For the split transformation, 50000 records were inserted into $T$. These were split into approximately 50000 records in $R$ and 20000 records in $S$.

Some important test results for split transformations are shown in Figure 4. As can be seen in Figures 4(a) and 4(b), the interference incured on user transactions heavily depends on the workload on the server, ranging from approximately 2% to 6% for throughput and 5% to 30% for response time. In these plots, 20% of all updates are on records in the source table. Little variation is observed for throughput tests while the response time tends to vary more with increasing server workload. Tests on concistency checking during split transformations and initial population of FOJ transformations show very similar results to those presented in Figures 4(a) and 4(b).

For log propagation to finish, more log records have to be propagated than generated. Because of this, the propagator needs a higher priority if many log records are generated than it needs if few are generated. Figure 4(c) illustrates this point. Two plots are shown: the lower plot is for tests where 20% of all generated updates are on records in $T$. The upper plot is for 80% updates on $T$, thus 4 times more relevant log records are generated during the same time interval. The operations that are not on $T$ update records in a dummy table to keep the workload constant. The priority of the transformation could be kept lower in the 20% case, resulting in less interference. Again, the same effect is observed on log propagation for FOJ on both throughput and response time.

As discussed, a reduction in the priority of the transformation process reduces interference. Unfortunately, this also increases the completion time of the transformation. Figure 4(d) shows how both the time needed to propagate log and the interference to throughput responds to the same changes in priority. The plot is for log propagation of split transformations with 75% workload on the server. FOJ tests show similar results. The transformation will never finish if the priority is set too low, in this case at about 0.5%. Clearly, the priority of the transformation must be chosen with care.

Transformations should for obvious reasons be executed when the workload on the server is as low as possible. If executed during off-hours, say at 50% workload, the observed interference should be acceptable on both throughput ($< 2\%$) and response time ($< 9\%$). During normal usage, say at 70% workload, the interference on throughput is still acceptable at approximately 2.5%. The interference to response time may, however, be too high. The cost should be carefully considered before the transformation is started. If too much interference is observed, the transformation should be aborted immediately. Aborting the transformation simply means that log propagation is stopped, and that the transformed tables are deleted.

Transactions that operate on the source tables could potentially be long lived. The completion time of the synchronization step is therefore much more predictable if the non-blocking abort strategy is used than if non-blocking commit is used. Synchronization takes less than 1 ms in the prototype tests with non-blocking abort. Interference plots for this step is therefore of little interest.

## 7 Conclusion and Further Work

A method to perform non-blocking full outer join (FOJ) and split schema transformations has been developed for relational databases. A prototype able to perform the transformations with approximately 2% interference on throughput and 5% on response time has also been developed. The results also show that interference increases with increasing workload. Because of this, database schemas should be transformed during periods with as low workload as possible.

FOJ and split are considered the most important nontrivial operators in a transformation framework because the normalization degree can be changed using these. Methods for other relational operators should, however, also be developed.

Even though it is not discussed in this paper, the split framework is able to split one source table into a many-to-many relashionship by repeating splits.

Non-blocking population of tables may have other important usages than schema changes. Using the technique to create other types of derrived tables like Materialized Views is an obvious example.

## References

1. R. Baylis and K. Rich. *Oracle9i Database Administrator's Guide Release 2 (9.2)*. 2002.
2. P. A. Bernstein, V. Hadzilacos, and N. Goodman. *Concurrency Control and Recovery in Database Systems*. Addison-Weslay Publishing Company, 1st edition, 1987.
3. J. A. Blakeley, P.-A. Larson, and F. W. Tompa. Efficiently updating materialized views. In *Proc of the 1986 ACM SIGMOD Intl. Conference on Management of Data*, pages 61–71, 1986.
4. S. E. Bratsberg, S.-O. Hvasshovd, and Ø. Torbjørnsen. Parallel solutions in ClustRa. *IEEE Data Eng. Bull.*, 20(2):13–20, 1997.
5. L. S. Colby, T. Griffin, L. Libkin, I. S. Mumick, and H. Trickey. Algorithms for deferred view maintenance. In *Proc of the 1996 ACM SIGMOD Intl. Conference on Management of Data*, pages 469–480. ACM Press, 1996.
6. R. A. Crus. Data Recovery in IBM Database 2. *IBM Systems Journal*, 23(2):178, 1984.
7. H. Garcia-Molina and K. Salem. Sagas. In *Proc of the 1987 ACM SIGMOD Intl. Conference on Management of Data*, pages 249–259. ACM Press, 1987.
8. T. Griffin and B. Kumar. Algebraic change propagation for semijoin and outerjoin queries. *SIGMOD Rec.*, 27(3):22–27, 1998.
9. A. Gupta, D. Katiyar, and I. S. Mumick. Counting solutions to the view maintenance problem. In *Workshop on Deductive Databases, JICSLP*, pages 185–194, 1992.
10. A. Gupta, I. S. Mumick, and V. S. Subrahmanian. Maintaining views incrementally. In *Proc of the 1993 ACM SIGMOD Intl. conference on Management of data*, pages 157–166. ACM Press, 1993.
11. H. Gupta and I. S. Mumick. Incremental maintenance of aggregate and outerjoin expressions. 2005.
12. S.-O. Hvasshovd. *Recovery in Parallel Database Systems*. Verlag Vieweg, 2nd edition, 1999.
13. S.-O. Hvasshovd, T. Sæter, Ø. Torbjørnsen, P. Moe, and O. Risnes. A continously available and highly scalable transaction server: Design experience from the HypRa project. In *Proc of the 4th International Workshop on High Performance Transaction Systems*, 1991.
14. IBM. *IBM DB2 Universal Database Administration Guide: Implementation, version 8*. IBM.
15. IBM. *IBM DB2 Universal Database SQL Reference, Volume 2*. IBM, 8 edition.
16. A. Kawaguchi, D. F. Lieuwen, I. S. Mumick, D. Quass, and K. A. Ross. Concurrency control theory for deferred materialized views. In *Proc of the International Conference on Database Theory*, pages 306–320, 1997.
17. H. F. Korth. Locking primitives in a database system. *Journal of the ACM*, 30(1):55–79, 1983.

18. S. Marche. Measuring the stability of data. *European Journal of Information Systems*, 2(1):37–47, 1993.
19. Microsoft Corporation. Microsoft sql server 2000 books online, version 8.00.002 (sp3), published 17.01.2003.
20. C. Mohan, D. Haderle, B. Lindsay, H. Pirahesh, and P. Schwarz. Aries: a transaction recovery method supporting fine- granularity locking and partial rollbacks using write-ahead logging. *ACM Transactions on Database Systems*, 17(1):94–162, 1992.
21. X. Qian and G. Wiederhold. Incremental recomputation of active relational expressions. *Knowledge and Data Engineering*, 3(3):337–341, 1991.
22. D. Quass, A. Gupta, I. S. Mumick, and J. Widom. Making views self-maintainable for data warehousing. In *Proc of the 4th International Conference on Parallel and Distributed Information Systems, 1996, USA*, pages 158–169. IEEE Computer Society, 1996.
23. M. Ronström. On-line schema update for a telecom database. *Proc of the 16th International Conference on Data Engineering*, 2000.
24. O. Shmueli and A. Itai. Maintenance of views. In *Proc of the 1984 ACM SIGMOD Intl. Conference on Management of Data*, pages 240–255. ACM Press, 1984.
25. D. Sjøberg. Quantifying schema evolution. *Information and Software Technology*, 35(1):35–44, 1993.
26. M. Widenius and D. Axmark. *MySQL Reference Manual*. O'Reilly & Associates Inc, 1 edition, 2002.
27. Y. Zhuge, H. Garcia-Molina, J. Hammer, and J. Widom. View maintenance in a warehousing environment. In *Proc of the 1995 ACM SIGMOD Intl. conference on Management of data*, pages 316–327. ACM Press, 1995.

# Deferred Maintenance of Disk-Based Random Samples

Rainer Gemulla and Wolfgang Lehner

Dresden University of Technology, 01099 Dresden, Germany
{gemulla, lehner}@inf.tu-dresden.de

**Abstract.** Random sampling is a well-known technique for approximate processing of large datasets. We introduce a set of algorithms for incremental maintenance of large random samples on secondary storage. We show that the sample maintenance cost can be reduced by refreshing the sample in a deferred manner. We introduce a novel type of log file which follows the intuition that only a "sample" of the operations on the base data has to be considered to maintain a random sample in a statistically correct way. Additionally, we develop a deferred refresh algorithm which updates the sample by using fast sequential disk access only, and which does not require any main memory. We conducted an extensive set of experiments and found, that our algorithms reduce maintenance cost by several orders of magnitude.

## 1 Introduction

Random samples are widely used as versatile synopses for large datasets. Such synopses are a must or at least desirable in most real-world scenarios. On the one hand, the complete dataset may not be accessible. For example, the dataset produced by a data stream is unbounded in size, and it is often too expensive to keep track of all the data elements which ever entered the system. Thus, a synopsis with a bounded size, i.e., independent of the dataset size, allows for inference of statistical properties of the dataset at the cost of some precision. On the other hand, the effort to process the complete dataset may be unacceptably high, e.g., when the dataset is very large or when the complexity of the algorithms exceeds the available resources. The latter case is ubiquitous in data warehouse systems which typically contain a huge amount of data subject to complex data mining algorithms.

Within the last decade, random sampling has been proposed as an adequate technique to summarize large datasets. Most applications require uniform samples to derive precise results and error bounds, i.e., each sample of the same size is equally likely to be produced. There exists a variety of alternative synopses for certain scenarios, but uniform random sampling bears the advantage of application neutrality. Whenever it is not known in advance which estimates will be computed on the synopsis, a uniform random sample is a good choice.

Random samples may be computed on-the-fly in certain scenarios. However, this is typically expensive—if not impossible—to perform [1]. Alternatively, one may materialize the sample and update it if the underlying dataset changes. Since synopsis maintenance is no "free" operation, i.e., it has a performance impact on the processing of updates to the dataset, the cost for maintenance should be as small as possible. In the database community, research has shown that it is more efficient to decouple the update of a materialized view from operations on the underlying dataset [2]. This approach is typically referred to as *deferred refresh*.

**Contributions.** In this paper, we propose deferred maintenance strategies for disk-based random samples with a bounded size. Our approach is based on the well-known reservoir sampling scheme. We introduce a novel type of log file and show that it is sufficient to keep track of only a "sample" of the operations on the dataset to maintain a statistically correct random sample. Furthermore, we develop an algorithm for deferred refresh, which performs only fast sequential I/O operations, minimizes the number of reads and writes to the sample, and does not require any main memory. Our experiments indicate, that deferred maintenance reduces the maintenance cost by several orders of magnitude.

**Assumptions.** We assume that the random sample is too large to fit into the main memory and thereby resides on secondary storage. In fact, many estimators based on samples require the sample to be sufficiently large, e.g., even "simple" statistics estimators like the estimation of the number of distinct values do not perform well on undersized samples. The situation gets worse if more complex algorithms are executed on the sample, e.g., association rule mining or clustering algorithms. Moreover, the overall memory consumption increases with the number of samples maintained in-memory.

Concerning the storage system, we assume that sequential access is faster than random access, and that the storage system tries to store data in a sequential sequence of blocks.[1] For example, if the data is stored on a hard disk, sequential access is indeed faster than random access. Most file systems try to arrange data in sequential blocks to make use of this fact, and file system caches allow for "conversion" of random (write) accesses to sequential ones. Again, we assume that the sample is large, and therefore, the effectiveness of the cache is limited.

Throughout the paper, we assume that access to the base data is disallowed at any time. The sample maintenance algorithms "see" only the insertions, updates and deletions executed on the underlying dataset. The internal structure of the dataset is of no interest to the sampling algorithm, so that our approach natively extends to arbitrary settings, e.g., data streams, SQL views or XML repositories. We subsequently assume that the random sample is computed from a dataset $R$.

**Paper Organization.** The remainder of the paper is structured as follows: In Section 2, we discuss related work from the sampling, database and data stream community. Section 3 introduces a novel logging scheme which minimizes storage consumption and logging overhead. In Section 4, we propose efficient algorithms

---

[1] Even if sequential and random access perform similarly, our algorithms reduce the total number of accesses to the storage system. Moreover, if the storage system does not align data in blocks, the performance of our algorithms increases.

to refresh the sample by accessing the log file only. In Section 5 we discuss the applicability of our algorithms in the environment of a DBMS. An extensive set of experiments is presented in Section 6. We conclude the paper with Section 7.

## 2   Related Work

We first present general techniques for bounded-size random sampling, and then discuss specific methods for sampling in a data stream system as well as in a database system.

**Uniform sampling.** Bounded-size sampling schemes produce uniform samples of a given size $M$. *Sequential sampling* [3] is one of the most efficient sampling schemes which fall into this category. It accesses exactly $M$ elements of $R$ to compute the sample. Unfortunately, sequential sampling has to know the dataset size in advance, thus, it is not applicable to sample maintenance. However, the well-known *reservoir sampling* scheme [4] is able to maintain a sample of a dataset of unknown size, as long as there are only insertions. The basic idea is to insert the first $M$ elements into the sample. Afterwards, each newly arriving element replaces a random element of the sample with probability $M/(|R|+1)$, or is rejected otherwise. Vitter [4] developed some techniques to efficiently compute the next element to be inserted into the sample. All the algorithms presented in this paper are based on reservoir sampling.

**Sampling data streams.** Sampling is ubiquitous in data stream management systems for the following two reasons: On the one hand, sampling is used to cope with high system load. If the number of arriving elements is too high to be processed completely, one may "simply" throw away some of the stream elements. This approach often appears in the context of *load shedding* [5, 6]. On the other hand, inference of statistical properties for the whole data stream seen so far is challenging since complete materialization of the stream is not feasible. One solution to this problem is the maintenance of a random sample of the complete data stream, potentially with some bias towards newer elements [7]. The maintenance algorithm has to be efficient, so that it can deal with the high arrival rates found in typical data stream scenarios.

Jermaine et al. introduced the *geometric file* (GF) [7], a technique for disk-based maintenance of samples from a data stream. The technique is based on reservoir sampling and minimizes I/O efforts by decreasing the number of accessed blocks. In fact, the major part of the GF is never read, most updates have block-level granularity and are written sequentially. However, the GF makes use of an in-memory buffer, and its performance depends strongly on the size of this buffer. Since each maintained sample requires its own buffer, the GF does not scale well with the number of samples. The GF is a deferred refresh algorithm since the sample is updated only if the buffer is completely filled. We compare the GF with our algorithms in Section 6.5.

**Sampling in databases.** Database samples are often tailored to their application, e.g., to represent a given workload [8], to handle data skew [9] or to support joins [10] and groupings [11, 12]. Most of these techniques make use of random sampling and extend it by some means or other [7, 8, 9, 10, 11, 12, 13]. In fact, there are lots of sampling schemes which rely on reservoir sampling. These algorithms can be natively extended to support fast deferred refresh using the techniques presented in this paper. We discuss issues specific to database systems in Section 5.

## 3 Logging and Refresh

In this paper, we consider the maintenance of a random sample computed from a dataset $R$. In the following, we assume that a uniform random sample of size $M$ has been computed already (e.g., using reservoir sampling), and that this sample is maintained as the underlying data changes. We distinguish *immediate refresh* strategies, which always keep the sample up-to-date, and *deferred refresh* strategies, which refresh the sample from time to time (e.g., lazily or periodically, see [2]). We say that a maintenance strategy is *incremental* if it never accesses the base data directly, but only the elements which are inserted.[2]

Incremental maintenance strategies consist of two phases: A *log phase* captures the insertions into the dataset, and a *refresh phase* updates the sample using the logged data. This holds for both immediate and deferred refresh strategies. In fact, immediate refresh can be seen as a deferred maintenance strategy which refreshes the sample every time the log has changed. In this section, we introduce several strategies for realizing the log phase in the case of random sampling. We assume that the log file resides on secondary storage, so that no memory is consumed. Additionally, we present naive refresh algorithms which update the sample using the log file.

### 3.1 Full Logging

The most basic logging strategy is to write all the insertions into the log file. We refer to this approach as *full logging*. Probably the simplest way to refresh the sample using the full log is to apply reservoir sampling subsequently to each of its elements. We denote this approach *naive full refresh*. Clearly, this strategy does not make use of the fact that the log file may contain more information than needed to update a sample, since the sample itself reflects only a portion of the underlying dataset. As will become evident in Section 5, there are more efficient refresh strategies with full logs.

The example in Figure 1 depicts a sample consisting of five elements and the full log file after 45 elements have been inserted. The reservoir sampling algorithm decides for every element whether it is included in the sample or not. In the former case, the element is called a *candidate* and replaces a random element of the sample. In the latter case, the element is ignored. As we proceed through the log, there are more and more candidates selected, and each of these

---

[2] We preliminarily assume that the dataset is subject to insertions only, and extend our results to updates and deletions in Section 5.

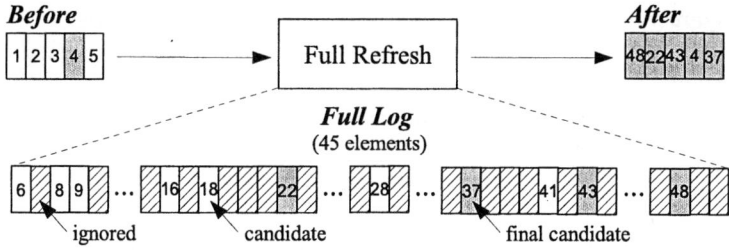

**Fig. 1.** Deferred sample maintenance using a full log

candidates can potentially overwrite a candidate (within the sample) which has been written earlier during the refresh phase. We say that a candidate is *final* if it is not overwritten within the current refresh operation.

Clearly, the above approach has serious disadvantages:

1. Obviously, most of the elements in the full log are not accepted into the sample and therefore logged unnecessarily. In the example, 11 out of 45 elements are made candidates, while only 4 of them remain in the final sample.
2. Updating the sample relies on random I/O (though the logfile is read sequentially). This property is directly inherited from the reservoir sampling algorithm.
3. The algorithm performs unnecessary I/O operations since the non-final candidates are overwritten by later candidates.

We propose an alternative refresh strategy for full logs in Section 5 which eliminates (2) and (3) above.

### 3.2 Candidate Logging

The elimination of (1) above is straightforward. The basic idea is that the elements which are ignored by the refresh operation do not have to be included in the log file. Therefore, we push the acceptance test of the reservoir sampling algorithm to the log phase.[3] Instead of logging every element added to the dataset, we decide on-the-fly whether the element is made a candidate or not. Thus, we write an arriving element to the log file with probability $M/(|R|+1)$ or ignore it otherwise. We refer to this logging strategy as *candidate logging* and denote the log file $C = \{c_1, \ldots, c_l\}$. Note that the order of the elements within the log is important since each candidate has been accepted with a different probability.

For example, instead of writing all 45 elements of Figure 1 to the full log, we only need to log the 11 candidates shown in Figure 2. In fact, the smaller the sample size with respect to the current dataset size, the more elements are skipped between two candidates on average. If we insert $n$ elements into $R$, the expected log file size is given by

---

[3] We are free to use any other acceptance test. For example, the biased reservoir sampling scheme in [7] is more suitable for data stream sampling.

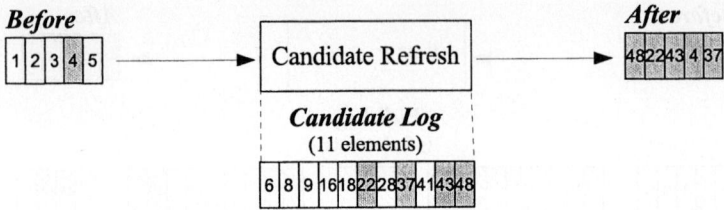

**Fig. 2.** Deferred sample maintenance using a candidate log

$$E(|C|) = \sum_{i=1}^{n} \frac{M}{|R|+i} \approx M \ln \frac{|R|+n}{|R|}.$$

Here, we used the logarithmic approximation for harmonic numbers. Note that $E(|C|)$ decreases as $|R|$ increases. The refresh algorithm has to be modified to make sure that every element of the candidate log is inserted into the sample. We scan the candidate log sequentially and write each candidate to a random position in the sample. We refer to this algorithm as *naive candidate refresh*. It sequentially reads $|C|$ elements of the log file and randomly writes $|C|$ elements to the sample.

Within the next section, we develop algorithms which reduce the number of read and written elements, and access both the log file and the sample sequentially (thereby eliminating (2) and (3) above).

## 4 Algorithms for Candidate Refresh

The naive candidate refresh algorithm has the undesirable property that access to the sample is non-sequential. Additionally, candidates written to the sample may be overwritten by subsequent candidates. This is clearly inefficient since it suffices to write out only the last candidate assigned to each element of the sample. The easiest way to circumvent these drawbacks is to precompute the changes to the sample and to write out the final candidates afterwards. Thus, all the algorithms presented in this section consist of a *precomputation phase* and a *write phase*. Using this approach, we can avoid random I/O completely while at the same time reducing the total number of disk accesses. We will present three different algorithms for precomputation, one using an in-memory array, one using an in-memory LIFO-stack, and one using no memory at all.

### 4.1 Array Refresh

Let $A$ be an integer array of size $M$ with all of its elements set to *empty*. We can use $A$ to determine which elements of the candidate log are going to be included in the final sample. We modify the naive refresh algorithm as follows: Instead of physically reading the candidate log $C = \{c_1, \ldots, c_l\}$, we operate on the indexes $1, \ldots, l$ of the candidates within the log and thereby preliminarily avoid access

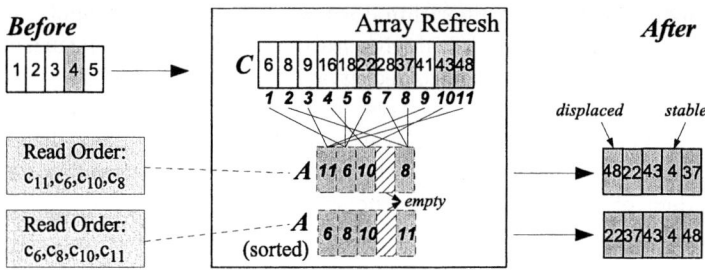

**Fig. 3.** Array Refresh

---

**Algorithm 1.** Array Refresh

**Require:** sample size $M$, candidate log $C$
1: create an in-memory array $A$ with $M$ empty elements
2: **for** $i = 1$ to $|C|$ **do**                                      // indexes of the candidates
3:    write $i$ to a random element of $A$
4: **end for**
5: sort non-empty fields of $A$                                              // optional
6: **for** $j = 1$ to $M$ **do**                                         // indexes of the sample
7:    **if** $A[j]$ is not empty **then**
8:       read candidate $A[j]$
9:       write candidate to the $j$th element of the sample
10:   **end if**
11: **end for**

---

to the log file. Furthermore, instead of writing the candidates to the sample, we store their indexes in the respective element of the in-memory array $A$. This prevents the random I/O of the naive algorithm.

Array $A$ is shown for the example data in Figure 3. For clarity, empty fields are striped and indexes are written in italic and bold letters. The array consists of some empty elements and some elements containing indexes. This information is sufficient to refresh the sample in a sequential scan. Let $j = 1, \ldots, M$ denote the current position within the sample. We look up the $j$th value in $A$ (denoted $A[j]$) and check whether it contains an index or not. In the former case, we write the candidate with the index $A[j]$ to the current element of the sample. We refer to sample elements which are overwritten during the refresh as *displaced elements*. In the latter case, $A[j]$ is empty and we leave the current element of the sample as it is (we do not read it actually). These elements are denoted *stable*. Note that we do not know which elements of the sample are stable and which are displaced until we have finished the precomputation phase.

The *Array Refresh* algorithm is summarized in Algorithm 1, and an example is shown in Figure 3. Access to the sample is now sequential, but access to the log file is not. However, since the order of the elements within the sample is of no interest, we may sort array $A$ right after the preprocessing phase. Care must be taken that the sort algorithm does not move empty elements to another position. These elements are linked with stable elements which in turn should be distributed randomly. Using the sorted array, access to the log file is sequential.

To analyze the I/O effort of the Array Refresh algorithm, we define a random variable $\Psi_j$ which evaluates to 1 if the $j$th element of the sample is displaced and to 0 otherwise $(1 \leq j \leq M)$. Clearly, the probability that an element is displaced is independent of its position within the sample:

$$P(\Psi_j = 1) = 1 - \left(1 - \frac{1}{M}\right)^{|C|}$$

In the example, each element is displaced with a probability of roughly 91%. Let $\Psi = \sum \Psi_j$ describe the total number of displaced elements, which corresponds to the number of elements read from the candidate log and subsequently written to the sample. By linearity of the expected value we get

$$E(\Psi) = M \left(1 - \left(1 - \frac{1}{M}\right)^{|C|}\right)$$

This evaluates to 4.57 in the example ($\Psi$ itself equals 4). The Array Refresh algorithm performs $\Psi$ sequential reads from the log file and $\Psi$ sequential writes to the sample with $\Psi \leq \min(M, |C|)$. Therefore, Array Refresh performs better than the naive refresh algorithm. However, array $A$ consumes a lot of memory and sorting $A$ is an expensive operation. The next algorithm reduces the memory consumption from $M$ to $\Psi$ indexes and does not require a sort operation.

### 4.2 Stack Refresh

The *Stack Refresh* algorithm is based on the observation that the probability of overwriting a candidate by subsequent candidates is decreasing during the processing of the candidate log. For example, the first candidate may be overwritten by all the other candidates, while the last one is never overwritten. Again, we precompute the indexes of the candidates which are going to be written to the sample. A stack is used as internal data structure in order to avoid sorting.

The candidate indexes are processed in reverse order, that is, from $|C|$ to 1. For each index $i$, we decide whether it is part of the sample or overwritten by one of the indexes *already processed*. The latter is the case if $i$ falls onto a position in the sample which is already occupied by one of the candidates. For example, suppose we process the candidate log as shown in Figure 3 but in reverse order. Candidate index 11 occupies sample position 1. Therefore, candidate indexes 9 and 3 – which also try to occupy position 1 – are both overwritten by 11. Therefore, only 11, 10, 8 and 6 are final in the example.

During the precomputation phase, each index $i$ is selected with probability $p_k = (M-k)/M$ with $k$ being the number of indexes selected already. Obviously, $p_k$ remains constant as long as no index selected. The random variable $X_k$

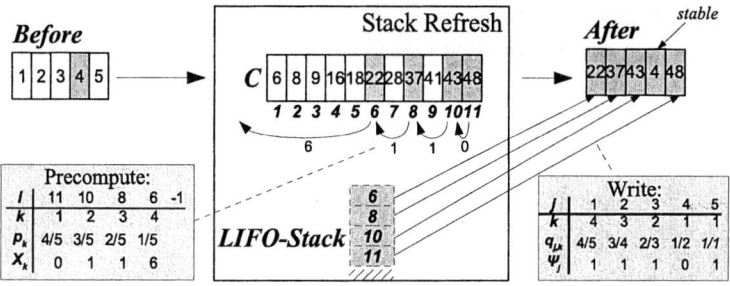

**Fig. 4.** Stack Refresh

describes how many indexes we have to skip until the next one is selected. $X_k$ is geometrically distributed:

$$P(X_k = x) = P(\text{skip } x \text{ elements, select } (x+1)\text{th element})$$
$$= (1-p_k)^x p_k = \left(\frac{k}{M}\right)^x \left(\frac{M-k}{M}\right)$$

To summarize: We select the first index $|C|$. Afterwards, we generate $X_1$, skip $X_1$ indexes, and select the next one. This process is repeated using $X_2$, $X_3$, and so on. The algorithm stops as soon as $M$ indexes have been selected or if there are no more candidates ($i < 1$). As can be seen in Figure 4, the indexes are selected in *descending order*. Therefore, we use a LIFO-stack to keep track of the selected indexes and to reverse their order.

In contrast to the Array Refresh algorithm, we do not maintain the information on which index falls onto which position. In other words, we do not precompute the set of stable and displaced elements. After the precomputation phase has finished, the stack only contains the indexes of the candidates which have to be written to the sample. We have to decide which of the corresponding candidates have to be written to which position of the sample, and which elements of the sample remain stable.

If the stack contains $k$ indexes and the sample has size $M$, there are $M-k$ stable elements. In the example, the 4 selected indexes have to be distributed among the 5 elements of the sample. Therefore, only a single element remains stable. To refresh the sample, we scan it sequentially and decide for each position whether it remains stable or is overwritten by a candidate from the stack.[4] Let $j = 1, ..., M$ be the current position within the sample and $k$ be the current stack size. Then, position $j$ is overwritten with probability:

$$q_{j,k} = \frac{k}{M-j+1} = \frac{\text{remaining indexes}}{\text{remaining sample elements}}$$

In summary, with probability $q_{j,k}$ we pop the uppermost index from the stack, read the corresponding candidate from the log file, and write it to the current

---

[4] This can be done efficiently using the sequential sampling scheme introduced in [3].

---
**Algorithm 2.** Stack Refresh
---
**Require:** sample size $M$, candidate log $C$
1: $k \leftarrow 0;\ i \leftarrow |C|$     // no. of selected indexes; current index
2: **repeat**
3:     PUSH($i$); $k \leftarrow k+1$     // select the current index
4:     $p_k \leftarrow \frac{M-k}{M}$     // selection probability for the next index
5:     $X_k \leftarrow$ NEXTGEOMETRIC($p_k$)     // generate $X_k$
6:     $i \leftarrow i - X_k - 1$     // skip $X_k$ indexes
7: **until** $i < 1 \vee k = M$
8: **for** $j = 1$ **to** $M$ **do**     // indexes of the sample
9:     $q_{j,k} \leftarrow \frac{k}{M-j+1}$     // probability that current element is displaced
10:     **with probability** $q_{j,k}$ **do**
11:         $i \leftarrow$ POP()
12:         read the candidate with index $i$
13:         write the candidate to the $j$th element of the sample
14:         $k \leftarrow k - 1$     // decrease no. of remaining candidates
15:     **end**
16: **end for**
---

position of the sample. In the case of Figure 4, this happens for the first, second, third and fifth element of the sample. The fourth element is stable and therefore not overwritten by a candidate. In this case, we advance to the next position without touching the stack. Algorithm 2 summarizes the complete process.

The Stack Refresh algorithm processes the sample as well as the candidate log sequentially. It needs less memory than Array Refresh since only $\Psi$ indexes are stored in memory. The sort operation is avoided by using a stack as the central data structure. Again, the Stack Refresh algorithm performs $\Psi$ sequential reads from the log file and $\Psi$ sequential writes to the sample. The next algorithm improves Stack Refresh by avoiding any memory consumption.

### 4.3 Nomem Refresh

The Stack Refresh algorithm needs to store the selected indexes in memory for two reasons: First, the order of the generated indexes is descending. If we had not used the stack, access to the candidate log would be in reverse order and therefore less efficient. Second and more important, even if we accepted reverse scanning, we cannot avoid using the stack in general. In order to determine whether the current element of the sample is stable or not, we have to know the number of remaining indexes (see $q_{j,k}$) which is equal to the stack size. Unfortunately, we do not get this information before the precomputation phase has finished, but then we do not know which candidate indexes have been selected unless we store them in memory or are able to compute exactly the same indexes again. We show how to modify the precomputation approach in such a way that in-memory data structures are avoided if a pseudo-random number generator (PRNG) is used.

PRNGs are ubiquitous in current computer systems, e.g., each call to NEXTGEOMETRIC() in Algorithm 2 is implemented by using such a PRNG.

## Algorithm 3. Nomem Refresh

**Require:** sample size $M$, candidate log $C$
1: store state of the geometric PRNG
2: compute $X = \sum(X_k + 1)$ with $k = M - 1, \ldots, 1$
3: restore state of the geometric PRNG
4:   $i \leftarrow |C| - X$      // determine first index
5:   $k \leftarrow M - 1$
6: **while** $i < 1$ **do**      // ignore negative indexes
7:     $i \leftarrow i + X_k + 1$
8:     $k \leftarrow k - 1$
9: **end while**
10: **for** $j = 1$ to $M$ **do**      // indexes of the sample ($k + 1$ candidates left)
11:     **with probability** $q_{j,k+1} = \frac{k+1}{M-j+1}$ **do**      // current element is displaced
12:         read the candidate with index $i$
13:         write the candidate to the $j$th element of the sample
14:         $i \leftarrow i + X_k + 1$
15:         $k \leftarrow k - 1$
16:     **end**
17: **end for**

---

A PRNG computes a sequence of numbers which appears to be random. However, the generated numbers depend only on an internal state. After a random number has been computed, the PRNG advances to the next state by using a certain algorithm. This state transition is deterministic. The central idea of the Nomem Refresh algorithm is to store the state of the PRNG before generating the sequence of selected indexes and to reset it afterwards to allow the generation of the same sequence again. Therefore, there is no need to buffer the indexes in memory. The memory consumption of the PRNG state is negligible ranging from 1 to 1000 words for common generators [14].

Reconsider the random variable $X_k$ of the Stack Refresh algorithm. It denotes how many elements of the candidate log are skipped before the next one is selected. Since the $X_k$ are independent of each other, it does not matter in which order they are generated. The Stack Refresh algorithm selects the candidate indexes in the following order (ignoring indexes smaller than 1):

$$|C|, \quad |C| - \sum_{k=1}^{1}(X_k + 1), \quad |C| - \sum_{k=1}^{2}(X_k + 1), \quad \ldots, \quad |C| - \sum_{k=1}^{M-1}(X_k + 1)$$

To generate this sequence in reverse order, we have to compute the quantity $X = \sum_{k=1}^{M-1}(X_k + 1)$ to determine the first index (with $k = M - 1, \ldots, 1$). Then, we subsequently add $X_k + 1$ to determine the next index. Therefore, each of the $X_k$ is accessed twice. As already stated, we avoid buffering of the $X_k$ by resetting the PRNG after the computation of $X$. The whole procedure is summarized in Algorithm 3. For brevity, we omit details of the generation of $X_k$ since it is identical to Algorithm 2.

As illustrated in Figure 5, the Nomem Refresh algorithm selects the indexes in the following order (ignoring indexes smaller than 1):

$$|C| - X, \ |C| - X + \sum_{k=M-1}^{M-1}(X_k + 1), \ |C| - X + \sum_{k=M-2}^{M-1}(X_k + 1), \ \ldots, |C|$$

Since this sequence is strictly increasing, the candidate log is accessed sequentially. There is no need for any in-memory data structure any longer. The algorithm requires slightly more processing power than Stack Refresh, since twice as many samples from the geometric distribution are computed.

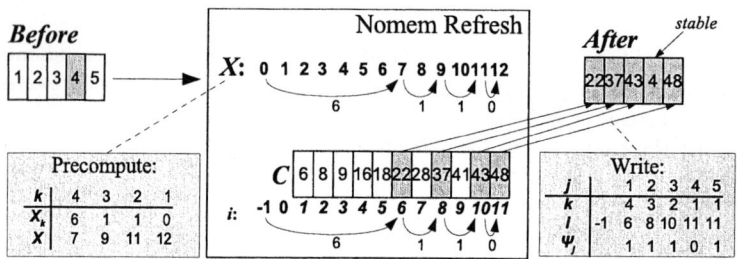

**Fig. 5.** Nomem Refresh

## 5 Deferred Sample Maintenance in a DBMS

Even though the candidate log file is smaller than the full log, there are situations in which full logging is the preferred technique. For example, the transaction log of a database system may already contain all the information we need. Alternatively, if we maintain a materialized view on the very same dataset the sample is built on, and if this view is refreshed using deferred maintenance too, the full log is typically maintained by the database system to incrementally refresh the materialized view, e.g., IBM DB2 makes use of a staging table and the Oracle RDBMS uses a materialized view log. Fortunately, we can apply the candidate refresh algorithms on a full log by using the same idea as used for the Nomem Refresh algorithm.

Each of the candidate refresh algorithms requires the size of the candidate log as its input for precomputing the final sample. If a full log is maintained, one does not know in advance how many tuples will be candidates and how many will be skipped. However, Vitter [4] defined a random variable describing the number of tuples skipped between two subsequent candidates. Thus, we store the state of the PRNG and compute the indexes of the candidates in advance (without actually storing them). Using this procedure, we can precalculate how many tuples of the full log are candidates. Then, we reset the random number generator and run an arbitrary candidate refresh algorithm. Every time the candidate log is accessed, we calculate the index of the respective candidate by computing Vitter's skips again and access the respective tuple of the full log. This procedure is nearly as efficient as if a candidate log were used. The only difference is that the tuples selected for the sample are further apart from each other, so that the number of blocks read from disk increases.

Another problem arising in the context of a DBMS is that there are updates and deletions. We show how our refresh algorithms can be extended to support these operations as well. First, we store all updates in a separate log file and apply all these updates *after* each refresh of the sample. The situation becomes more difficult if some elements are removed from the dataset. In this case, it is not possible to maintain a candidate log since insertions after a deletion are included in the sample with a different probability than assumed during candidate logging. Thus, we use a full log file if there are deletions. If we assume (or make sure) that the insertions and deletions are disjunctive, we first conduct all the deletions and afterwards process the full log using the techniques presented in this paper (using a potentially smaller sample size). We currently investigate how a reservoir sample can be maintained so that deletions are supported as well.

## 6 Experiments

We implemented the various refresh algorithms and conducted a set of experiments to evaluate their performance. We distinguish between online, offline and total cost of maintaining the sample. The online cost is the processing cost of arriving insertions. The offline cost mirrors the cost for refreshing the sample. The total cost is the sum of online and offline cost. This distinction is helpful since it captures different application areas. For example, in a streaming system, the online cost is important since it expresses the processing time for each operation within the sample operator. The refresh may be conducted by an independent system which has access to the log file, thereby not affecting online processing. In a DBMS, both logging and refresh are typically conducted by the very same system, so that the total cost is more important than the online cost. For clarity, we arrange the figures for online and total cost side by side so that they can be compared easily. Note that most of the plots have logarithmic axes.

**Experimental results.** We found that using a candidate log is significantly faster than refreshing the sample immediately or using a full log. When it comes to sample refresh, we found that the refresh algorithms using precomputation outperform the naive ones, and that the computational overhead of Nomem Refresh is negligible. The more operations occur between two consecutive refresh operations, the more is gained by using advanced refresh techniques. Our algorithms scale well, since the sample size has only a linear effect on the refresh costs. In comparison to the geometric file, our techniques are more efficient if the GF is not allowed to consume large amounts of memory for its internal buffer.

### 6.1 Experimental Setup

The experiments were conducted on an Athlon AMD XP 3000+ system running Linux with 2GB of main memory and an IDE hard drive with 7,200 RPM. We first measured the access times per block using a $1.6GB$ on-disk sample (with a cache of $100MB$). Our hard disk is formatted with the ext3 filesystem. It has a block size of 4096 bytes, and we assumed that each element occupies 32 bytes, i.e., each block contains 128 elements. We found that a sequential read/write takes about $0.094ms$ per block, a random read $8.45ms$, and a random write $5.50ms$ (due to asynchronous writes). Now, for each algorithm, we counted the number of sequential/random reads and writes on a block-level basis. We then weighted these numbers with the access times above. This strategy allows for quantifying the cost of the single phases independently, while at the same time enabling us to run a large variety of different experiments.

All the algorithms have been implemented using the Java programming language and Sun's JDK version 1.5.0_03. For full refresh, we used the techniques described in Section 5. Unless stated otherwise, each experiment was run at least one hundred times and results were averaged. We assumed that the sample is refreshed periodically.

## 6.2 Online Cost

We first evaluated the online I/O cost of sample maintenance. We used a sample size of one $1M$ and inserted $100M$ elements into a dataset with initial size $1M$. Figure 6 shows the cumulated cost over time without any intermediate refreshes. Obviously, immediate refresh is far more expensive than writing to a log file. However, if the dataset size gets really large, immediate refresh is cheaper than writing to the full log, since the fraction of the candidate elements decreases over time. Candidate logging is the most efficient technique and is by several orders of magnitude faster than immediate refresh.

Next, we measured the online impact induced by different sample sizes (Figure 8). We used the same setting as in the former experiment, but plotted the cumulated cost after $100M$ operations. Clearly, the maintenance cost of the full log is independent of the actual sample size, while the cost for immediate refresh and candidate logging increases with an increasing sample size, since more candidates are generated if the sample is larger. However, candidate logging is always faster than full logging. In fact, the cost of writing the full log is an upper bound to the cost of writing the candidate log.

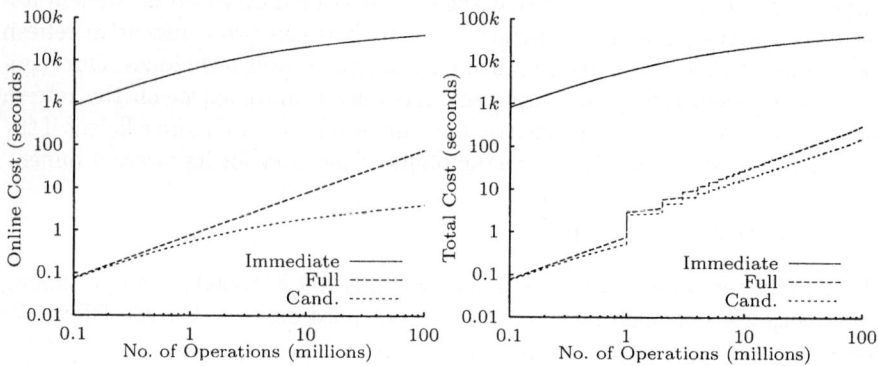

**Fig. 6.** Online cost over time     **Fig. 7.** Total cost over time

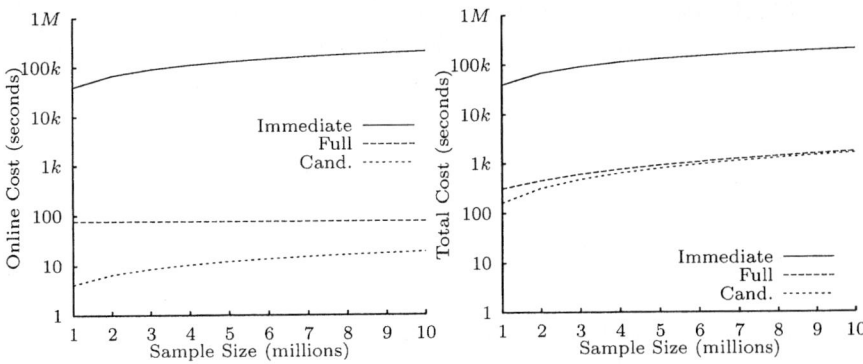

**Fig. 8.** Online cost and sample sizes     **Fig. 9.** Total cost and sample sizes

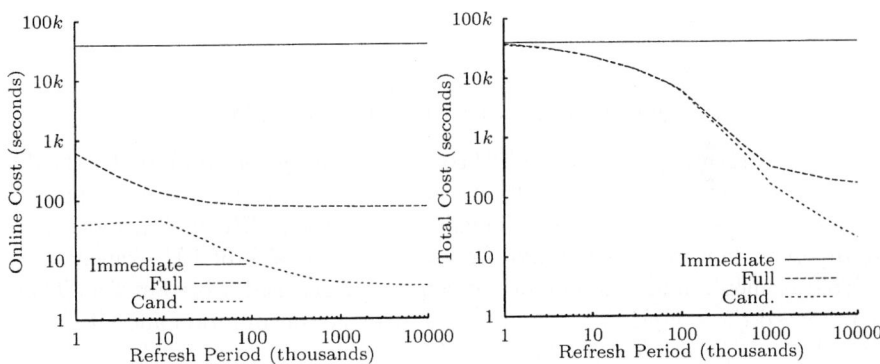

**Fig. 10.** Online cost and refresh period     **Fig. 11.** Total cost and refresh period

Furthermore, we compared the online cost for different refresh periods (Figure 10). We used the same experimental setting as in the former experiments. The cost for maintaining the sample directly is independent of the refresh period (always 1). However, both candidate logging and full logging re-use the log file after a refresh so that one random I/O is performed to move from the current position to the beginning of the log file (otherwise, the costs are independent of the refresh period, too). Thus, with an increasing refresh period, these random I/Os occur less frequently and the cost drops. Again, candidate logging is faster than full logging. Note that if the refresh period is less than $10k$, the candidate log often consists of only a single block, which is the minimum.

### 6.3 Total Cost

We ran the same experiments as above again but now measured the total I/O cost (including refresh). Note that Array, Stack and Nomem Refresh have equal I/O cost. We refreshed the sample after every $1M$ insertions. As can be seen in Figure 7, deferred refresh is significantly faster than immediate refresh. The costs for full and candidate refresh are almost the same since we used the algorithm described in Section 5 for full refresh. However, the costs for writing the log file are different, so that the candidate techniques are faster than the techniques using a full log. The I/O cost of the first few refreshes is magnified due to the log-log-plot.

Figure 9 illustrates that the total costs for maintaining the sample are increasing as the sample size increases. Again, deferred refresh significantly outperforms immediate refresh. The costs of full maintenance and candidate maintenance are almost equal if the sample is really large. However, we performed 100 million operations in every case. If the number of operations were larger, this effect would vanish.

As can be seen in Figure 11, deferred refresh is faster than immediate refresh if refreshes are not extremely frequent. Since the total costs are governed by the refresh cost, full and candidate maintenance strategies perform equally if the refresh period is short. However, the larger the refresh period gets, the more effort is saved by using a candidate log. Thus, the candidate strategies become more efficient than full refresh in this case.

### 6.4 Memory Consumption and Computational Cost

In this experiment, we measured CPU cost and memory consumption for the different implementations of deferred refresh. Even though the disk access pattern is the same for Array, Stack and Nomem Refresh, their CPU and memory costs are different. For the experiments, we used a sample size of $1M$ elements. We inserted elements until the number of candidates reached a certain size. Then, we refreshed the sample and measured the memory consumption and CPU cost. Note that computation and I/O are typically performed in parallel.

Figure 12 plots the consumed memory in dependency of the number of candidates. Array Refresh always maintains an array that has as many elements as the sample. However, the elements of the array are only 4 bytes long (index size), while the sample elements are usually larger. The Stack Refresh algorithm requires more and more memory as the number of candidates in the log file increases. Note that the figure includes extreme cases, e.g., in which the number of candidates is more than twice the sample size. Thus, the memory consumption of Stack Refresh is small in most cases. However, Nomem Refresh does not consume any memory. We plotted the size of the in-memory buffer of the geometric file for expository reasons. The number of candidates in a geometric file can only grow as large as its internal buffer. Thus, if we want to delay the refresh to, say, 100,000 (final) candidates, the buffer of the geometric file has to be as large as 10% of the sample.

In Figure 13, we plot the CPU time for a refresh in the same experimental setting. Clearly, Stack Refresh is the fastest method. For small candidate logs, Array Refresh is more efficient than Nomem Refresh, while the opposite is true for large log files (due to the sort operation of Array Refresh). Nomem Refresh has to compute $2M$ random numbers to select the final candidates. To minimize the total CPU time, we propose the following strategy: If the expected number of final candidates ($E(\Psi)$) is small (say, $< 4k$), we use the Stack Refresh algorithm. Otherwise, we use Nomem Refresh to save main memory.

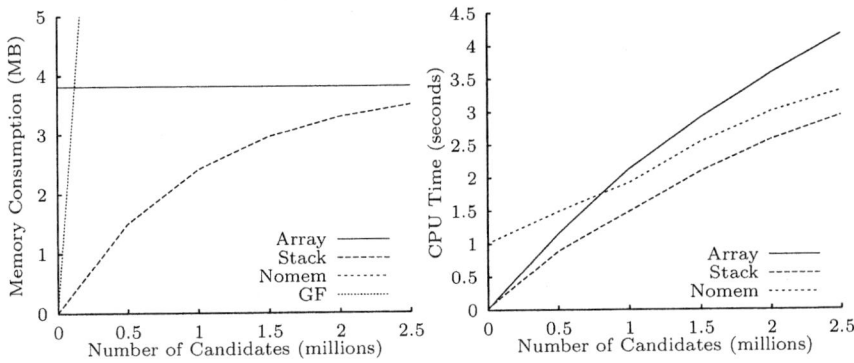

**Fig. 12.** Memory consumption  **Fig. 13.** Computational cost

## 6.5 Comparison to the Geometric File

The GF [7] is the only algorithm known to the authors which targets deferred maintenance of a disk-based sample. In this section, we briefly point out the differences between our algorithms presented and the GF. First, the GF buffers arriving insertions in main memory. In contrast to our algorithms, the buffer is accessed randomly and therefore cannot be serialized to disk without losing performance. Additionally, the GF keeps a part of the sample in memory to optimize the I/O cost, i.e., the on-disk part of the sample is not uniform. This may be problematic in the case of system failures.

Using the GF, one is not able to conduct a refresh at an arbitrary time. In fact, the sample is only refreshed if the buffer reaches its full size. Consequently, one may either control the desired buffer size or the frequency of refresh operations, but not both. To compare our refresh algorithms to the GF,[5] we proceeded as follows: First, we refreshed the sample every time the GF issued a refresh. Thus, the number of refreshes conducted by the GF and by our techniques is equal. Second, we assumed that our algorithms may use the same amount of in-memory buffer as the GF. We used this buffer to store a part of the sample in memory, thereby reducing the number of disk accesses. In fact, if we store 5% of the sample in memory, we expect that the refresh cost drops by 5%.

Again, we set the sample size to $1M$ elements and inserted $100M$ elements. We measured the total cost for different buffer sizes. The results are shown in Figure 14. Clearly, the larger the buffer, the less cost is incurred by the algorithms, since the cumulative number of refreshes is decreasing. If the buffer is less than 3% of the sample size, both full and candidate refresh are faster than the GF. If we increase the buffer to up to 4% of the sample size, the GF is faster than full refresh but slower than candidate refresh. If the buffer is larger than 4% of the sample size, the geometric file is the most efficient algorithm. Thus, the optimal strategy depends on the amount of memory we are willing to sacrifice, and on the desired flexibility of deciding on refresh periods.

---

[5] We used block-aligned segments and set $\beta = 32k$.

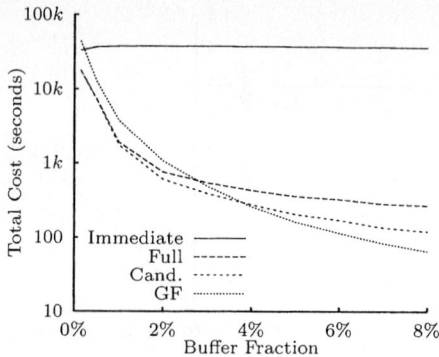

**Fig. 14.** GF buffer size & total cost

## 7 Summary

We developed a set of algorithms which allow for deferred maintenance of random samples of an arbitrary dataset. We introduced a novel type of log file which minimizes the amount of data used to track changes on the underlying dataset. We showed that such a log file imposes far less overhead in processing arriving operations than traditional log files and immediate sample maintenance. Furthermore, we developed different strategies to efficiently process the log file in order to update the sample. We optimized our algorithms so that they rely on fast sequential disk access only, while the number of read and write operations is minimized. Additionally, we showed how main memory consumption can be avoided at the cost of some CPU time. Finally, we conducted a set of experiments indicating that our algorithms are more efficient than any known algorithm using a small amount of in-memory data structures only.

**Acknowledgement.** This work has been supported by the German Research Society (DFG) under LE 1416/3-1. We like to thank the anonymous reviewers, S. Schmidt, and P. Rösch for their helpful comments on a previous version of the paper.

## References

1. Haas, P., König, C.: A Bi-Level Bernoulli Scheme for Database Sampling. In: Proc. ACM SIGMOD. (2004) 275–286
2. Gupta, A., Mumick, I.S., eds.: Materialized Views: Techniques, Implementations, and Applications. MIT Press (1999)
3. Vitter, J.S.: Faster Methods for Random Sampling. Commun. ACM **27** (1984) 703–718
4. Vitter, J.S.: Random Sampling with a Reservoir. ACM TOMS **11** (1985) 37–57
5. Haas, P.J.: Data Stream Sampling: Basic Techniques and Results. In: Data Stream Management: Processing High Speed Data Streams, Springer (2006) (to appear)

6. Tatbul, N., Çetintemel, U., Zdonik, S.B., Cherniack, M., Stonebraker, M.: Load Shedding in a Data Stream Manager. In: Proc. VLDB. (2003) 309–320
7. Jermaine, C., Pol, A., Arumugam, S.: Online Maintenance of Very Large Random Samples. In: Proc. ACM SIGMOD. (2004) 299–310
8. Ganti, V., Lee, M.L., Ramakrishnan, R.: ICICLES: Self-Tuning Samples for Approximate Query Answering. In: The VLDB Journal. (2000) 176–187
9. Chaudhuri, S., Das, G., Datar, M., Narasayya, R.M.V.R.: Overcoming Limitations of Sampling for Aggregation Queries. In: Proc. ICDE. (2001) 534–544
10. Acharya, S., Gibbons, P.B., Poosala, V., Ramaswamy, S.: Join Synopses for Approximate Query Answering. In: Proc. ACM SIGMOD. (1999) 275–286
11. Acharya, S., Gibbons, P.B., Poosala, V.: Congressional Samples for Approximate Answering of Group-By Queries. In: Proc. ACM SIGMOD. (2000) 487–498
12. Babcock, B., Chaudhuri, S., Das, G.: Dynamic Sample Selection for Approximate Query Processing. In: Proc. ACM SIGMOD. (2003) 539–550
13. Olken, F., Rotem, D.: Maintenance of Materialized Views of Sampling Queries. In: Proc. ICDE. (1992)
14. Matsumoto, M., Nishimura, T.: Mersenne Twister: A 623-Dimensionally Equidistributed Uniform Pseudo-Random Number Generator. ACM TOMACS 8 (1998) 3–30

# Exploiting Cluster Analysis for Constructing Multi-dimensional Histograms on Both Static and Evolving Data*

Filippo Furfaro, Giuseppe M. Mazzeo, and Cristina Sirangelo

DEIS, University of Calabria, 87030 Rende, Italy
{furfaro, mazzeo, sirangelo}@si.deis.unical.it

**Abstract.** Density-based clusterization techniques are investigated as a basis for constructing histograms in multi-dimensional scenarios, where traditional techniques fail in providing effective data synopses. The main idea is that locating dense and sparse regions can be exploited to partition the data into homogeneous buckets, preventing dense and sparse regions from being summarized into the same aggregate data. The use of clustering techniques to support the histogram construction is investigated in the context of either static and dynamic data, where the use of incremental clustering strategies is mandatory due to the inefficiency of performing the clusterization task from scratch at each data update.

## 1 Introduction

The need to compress data into synopses of summarized information often arises in many scenarios, where the aim is to retrieve aggregate data efficiently, possibly trading off the computational efficiency with the accuracy of query answers. Selectivity estimation for query optimization in RDBMSs [4, 16], range query answering in OLAP services [17], statistical and scientific data analysis [14], window query answering in spatial databases [1, 15], are examples of application contexts where efficiently aggregating data within specified ranges of the domain is such a crucial issue, that high accuracy in query answers becomes a secondary requirement.

For instance, query optimizers in RDBMSs can build an effective query evaluation plan by estimating the selectivity of intermediate query results: this can be accomplished by retrieving aggregate information on the frequencies of attribute values. In particular, given a relation $R(A_1, \ldots, A_d)$, the selectivity of a query of the form $q = v'_1 < R.A_1 < v''_1 \wedge \ldots \wedge v'_d < R.A_d < v''_d$ (representing the intermediate result of more complex queries) is evaluated by accessing the *joint frequency distribution* [16] associated to $R$. The latter can be viewed as a $d$-dimensional array $\mathcal{F}$ whose dimensions represent the attribute domains, and whose cell with coordinates $< v_1, \ldots, v_d >$ stores the number of tuples of $R$ where $A_1 = v_1, \ldots, A_d = v_d$. The selectivity of the query $q$ defined above is the answer of the range-sum query

---

* This work was supported by a grant from the Italian Research Project FIRB "Grid.it – Enabling ICT Platforms for Distributed High-Performance Computational Grids", funded by MIUR and coordinated by the National Research Council (CNR).

$Q = sum(\langle [v'_1..v''_1], \ldots, [v'_d..v''_d] \rangle)$ posed on $\mathcal{F}$, which returns the sum of the frequencies contained in the multi-dimensional range $\langle [v'_1..v''_1], \ldots, [v'_d..v''_d] \rangle$ of $\mathcal{F}$. As the size of $\mathcal{F}$ is generally very large, evaluating the exact selectivity of $q$ (i.e. the exact answer of $Q$) can be inefficient.

A widely accepted approach to the problem of providing fast estimates of query selectivities consists in compressing $\mathcal{F}$ into a lossy synopsis $\tilde{\mathcal{F}}$, and then evaluating the selectivity of queries by accessing $\tilde{\mathcal{F}}$ rather than $\mathcal{F}$. Histograms [16] are a well-known approach for compressing the joint frequency distribution. A histogram over $\mathcal{F}$ is built by partitioning $\mathcal{F}$ into a number of blocks (called *buckets*), and then storing for each bucket $b$ the number of tuples in $R$ whose attributes have values belonging to the range of $b$. The selectivity of $q$ is estimated on the histogram by summing the values stored in the buckets whose boundaries are completely contained inside the range-sum query $Q$ corresponding to $q$, and then by estimating the "contributions" of the buckets which partially overlap the range of $Q$. These contributions are evaluated by performing linear interpolation, under the assumption that the data distribution inside each bucket is "homogeneous" (that is, the joint distribution of attribute values underlying $b$ is uniform).

As expected, on the one hand, querying the histogram rather than $\mathcal{F}$ reduces the cost of evaluating selectivities (as the histogram size is much less than the original data size); on the other hand, the loss of information due to summarization introduces some approximation. Therefore, a crucial issue when dealing with histograms is finding the partition which provides the "best" accuracy in reconstructing query selectivities.

Existing approaches, such as *MHIST* [16], *MinSkew* [1], *STHoles* [3] and *GENHIST* [12], provide reasonable error rates at low-dimensionality scenarios, but worsen dramatically for higher-dimensionality data. On the one hand, this is somewhat inevitable, since, as dimensionality increases, the size of the data domain grows much more than the number of data points. That is, high-dimensionality data are likely to be much sparser than low-dimensionality ones. This implies that the number of buckets which should be used to effectively approximate data tends to explode as dimensionality increases. For instance, consider two data distributions $D^2$ (of size $n^2$) and $D^{10}$ (of size $n^{10}$), where the same number of data points are distributed, respectively, on a two-dimensional and ten-dimensional domain. If we use the same number of buckets to partition $D^2$ and $D^{10}$, buckets of $D^{10}$ are likely to be much larger in volume than those of $D^2$. Therefore, the aggregate information associated to buckets of $D^{10}$ is less localized than buckets of $D^2$ (as the aggregate value associated to each bucket is spread onto a larger volume), thus providing a poorer description of the actual data distribution.

On the other hand, the low accuracy in query estimates provided by traditional histograms is also due to the ineffectiveness of the adopted heuristics guiding the histogram construction. That is, traditional techniques for constructing histograms often result in partitions where dense and sparse regions are put together in the same bucket which yields poor accuracy in describing data. For instance consider the bucket shown in Fig. 1, where a dense cluster is put together with a sparse region. As the bucket is summarized by the sum of its values, estimating either $Q_1$ and $Q_2$ by performing linear interpolation yields a high error rate, since the total sum is assumed to be homogeneously distributed inside $b$. In fact this assumption is far from being true: most of the sum of $b$ is concentrated in the dense cluster on the right-hand side of $b$.

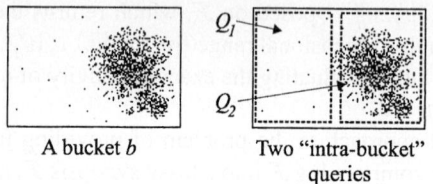

**Fig. 1.** Queries posed into a non-homogeneous bucket

Therefore, it is our belief that improving the ability of distinguishing dense regions can result in more accurate partitions, as this prevents buckets like that of Fig. 1 from being constructed. The problem of searching homogeneous regions is very close to the *data clustering* problem, i.e. the problem of grouping database objects into a set of meaningful classes. This issue has been widely studied in the data mining context, and several algorithms accomplishing data clustering have been proposed. For the sake of brevity we do not provide a classification of existing clustering techniques. The interested reader can find a detailed survey in [13].

This paper stems from our preliminary work [8], where we studied how histogram construction could be supported by density-based cluster analysis. In this work we propose an extension of our clustering-based compression technique to the case that data to be summarized is dynamic. In this context, the issue of maintaining data synopses has received growing attention from the research community in the last few years [5, 10, 11]. In this scenario, re-executing the clustering step at each data update is not feasible, due to the inefficiency of this task. Thus we introduce a strategy for exploiting an incremental clustering approach (where the clusterization is updated at each bulk of updates without re-processing the whole data) to efficiently propagate data updates to the histogram.

## 2 CHist: Clustering-Based Histogram

In this section, we recall our clustering-based technique (namely, *CHist*) for constructing histograms on multi-dimensional static data. Its extension to the case of dynamic data (which is the main contribution of this paper) will be introduced in Section 3.

Our technique works in three steps. At the first step clusters of data and outliers (i.e. points which do not belong to any cluster) are located. At the second step, these clusters and the set of outliers are treated as distinct layers, and each layer is summarized by partitioning it according to a grid-based paradigm. At the last step the histogram is constructed by "assembling" all the buckets obtained at the previous step.

The three phases of our approach are described in detail in the following sections. The description of the algorithm is provided by assuming a $d$-dimensional data distribution $D$. $D$ will be treated as a multi-dimensional array of integers of size $n^d$ (without loss of generality the edges of $D$ are assumed to be of the same size). That is, values of data points of the input distribution are represented into cells of $D$. The cells of $D$ which do not correspond to any data point contain the value 0. A query $Q$ on $D$ is specified by a multi-dimensional range of the domain of $D$ and its answer is the sum of the values of the cells of $D$ inside this range.

Any sub-array of $D$ will be referred to as a *bucket*. The volume of a bucket $b$ (i.e. the number of cells of the sub-array) will be denoted as $vol(b)$, the sum of data point values inside $b$ as $sum(b)$. In order to measure the homogeneity of the data inside a bucket we adopt the SSE (namely *Sum Square Error*), defined as follows:

$$SSE(b) = \sum_{\mathbf{i} \in b} (b[\mathbf{i}] - avg(b))^2,$$

where: $avg(b)$ is the average of cell values inside $b$; the expression $\mathbf{i} \in b$ means that $\mathbf{i}$ denotes the coordinates of a cell inside $b$; $b[\mathbf{i}]$ denotes the value of the cell of $b$ with coordinates $\mathbf{i}$. The amount of available storage space for the representation of the histogram will be denoted as $B$.

## 2.1 Step I: Clustering Data

In our prototype, we have embedded the clustering algorithm DBSCAN [6] in order to group input data into dense clusters. Indeed, our approach can be viewed as orthogonal to any clustering technique: we have chosen DBSCAN as it is representative of density-based clustering algorithms.

The idea underlying DBSCAN is that points belonging to a dense cluster (except those points lying on the border of the cluster) have a dense neighborhood. A point $p$ is said to have a dense neighborhood if there are at least *MinPts* distinct points whose distance from $p$ is less than *Eps* (both *Eps* and *MinPts* are parameters crucial for the definition of clusters). Points with a dense neighborhood are said to be *core points*. DBSCAN scans input data searching for core points. Once a core point $p$ is found, a new cluster $C$ is created, and both $p$ and all of its neighbors are grouped into $C$. Then $C$ is recursively expanded by including the neighbors of all core points put in $C$ at the last step. When $C$ cannot be further expanded, DBSCAN searches for other core points to start new clusters, until no more core points can be found. At the end of the clustering, points which do not belong to any cluster are classified as *outliers*.

## 2.2 Step II: Summarizing Data into Buckets

At this step the input data distribution is viewed as a superposition of layers. Each layer is either a cluster or the set of outliers. In the following we will denote the layer consisting of outliers as $L_0$, and the layers corresponding to dense clusters as $L_1, \ldots, L_c$. $L_0$ will be said to be the *outlier layer*, whereas $L_1, \ldots, L_c$ will be said to be *cluster layers*. Each layer is represented by means of its MBR (*Minimum Bounding Rectangle*, i.e. the minimum hyper-rectangle containing all non-null points of the layer).

The different layers are summarized separately by partitioning their MBRs into buckets. This aims at preventing the construction of buckets where dense and sparse regions are put together, which, as explained before (see Fig. 1), can yield poor accuracy. In more detail, our approach works as follows.

Layers are summarized independently of each other, and the summary of the whole data distribution will be the superimposition of the summaries of all layers. The summarization of layers is accomplished by a multi-step algorithm which, at each step, summarizes a single layer by partitioning it according to a grid and storing, for each bucket defined by this grid, both its MBR and the sum of its values (obviously, the cells of this grid which do not contain any data point result in an empty MBR which is not stored). The MBRs of buckets obtained from the summarization of cluster layers will be said to be *c-buckets*, whereas the MBRs of the buckets constructed by partitioning $L_0$ will be said to be *o-buckets*.

Indeed, layer $L_0$ is processed after the summarization of all the cluster layers. In particular, before summarizing the outlier layer, we scan all outliers to locate those lying onto the range of some c-bucket. Each outlier $o$ which lies onto some c-bucket is removed from $L_0$ and "added" to one c-bucket whose range contains the coordinates of $o$ [1]. This allows us to view c-buckets as "holes" of $L_0$, in the sense that, after performing this task, there are no points lying onto the range of some c-bucket which belong to $L_0$. As it will be clear in the following, this will be exploited in the physical representation of the histogram to improve its accuracy.

We now describe how the available storage space is used to summarize layers. Let $B_i$ be the amount of memory which is left from the $i-1$ previous summarization steps (at the first step, $B_1$ coincides with the initial amount of storage space $B$). The portion of $B_i$ which is invested to summarize $L_i$ is denoted as $B(L_i)$ and is computed by comparing the need of being partitioned of $L_i$ with all remaining layers $L_{i+1}, \ldots, L_c, L_0$. The need of being partitioned of a layer $L$ is estimated by computing its SSE (denoted as $SSE(L)$), thus $B(L_i) = B_i \cdot \frac{SSE(L_i)}{SSE(L_0) + \sum_{j=i}^{c} SSE(L_j)}$.

We now show how $B(L_i)$ is exploited to store a partition of $L_i$ into buckets. The idea is to partition $L_i$ according to a grid and store, for each cell of the grid containing at least one point, the coordinates of its MBR and the sum of the values occurring in it. The grid on a layer $L_i$ is constructed as follows.

If we denote as $W$ the amount of storage space needed to store a bucket[2], the number of buckets produced by the grid on $L_i$ can be no more than $nb = \lfloor \frac{B(L_i)}{W} \rfloor$. Thus, if $t_j$ is the number of divisions of the grid along the $j$-th dimension of $L_i$, it should hold that $\prod_{j=1}^{d} t_j = nb$.

We partition each edge of the MBR of the layer to be summarized into a number of portions which is proportional to the length of the edge itself. See [8] for further details on the technique used for defining such a "uniform" grid for each layer partition. The cells of the grid which correspond to null regions of the data domain are not stored explicitly. In the following, $nb'$ will denote the number of buckets generated by the grid partitioning which are stored explicitly (i.e. the number of buckets containing at least one non-null point). Therefore, after a layer $L_i$ is summarized, the residual amount of storage space which will be available at step $i+1$ is given by $B_{i+1} = B_i - nb' \cdot W$ (that is, if some space which was assigned to the summarization of $L_i$ has not been consumed, it is re-invested at the following steps).

Fig. 2 shows the execution of Step I and Step II on a two-dimensional data distribution.

---

[1] If more than one c-bucket contains $o$, one of these c-buckets is randomly selected to incorporate $o$. Adding an outlier $o$ to a c-bucket $b$ means removing $o$ from $L_0$ and adding the value of $o$ to $sum(b)$.

[2] We use $2 \cdot d$ 32-bit words for storing bucket boundaries, and one 32-bit word for storing the sum-aggregate.

**Remark.** Observe that adopting the grid-based scheme allows us to partition a layer $L$ in linear time (each data point inside $L$ is accessed once and summarized in the cell of the grid where it lies into): this feature will be particularly well-suited for the incremental approach where an efficient partitioning strategy is needed to propagate data changes to the histogram (see Section 3).

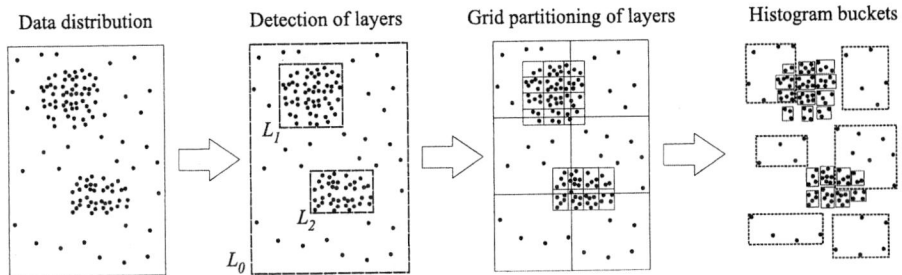

**Fig. 2.** Detection of layers, data partitioning, and bucket definition

### 2.3 Step III: Representation of the Histogram

The strategy adopted to partition layers can yield overlapping buckets. In particular, buckets aggregating points of $L_0$ (the layer consisting of outliers) are likely to be larger than buckets describing clusters. Therefore, several c-buckets $b_1, \ldots, b_k$ can lie onto the range of an o-bucket $b$. In this scenario $b_1, \ldots, b_k$ can be viewed as "holes" of $b$, as the aggregate information associated to $b$ does not refer to points contained inside $b_1, \ldots, b_k$. We now show how this observation can be exploited to make query estimation more accurate. In the following, given an o-bucket $b$, the set of c-buckets completely contained into $b$ will be denoted as $Holes(b)$.

Consider the scenario depicted in Fig. 3(a), where the query $Q_1$ intersects one half of the range associated to the bucket $b$. Adopting linear interpolation to estimate $Q_1$ returns: $\widetilde{Q}_1 = \frac{vol(Q_1 \cap b)}{vol(b)} \cdot sum(b)$, where $Q_1 \cap b$ refers to the intersection between the query range and the range of $b$. In fact points belonging to the ranges of $b_1, \ldots, b_9$ give no contribution to the value of $sum(b)$. Therefore, a more precise estimate for $Q_1$ is: $\widetilde{Q}_1 = \frac{vol(Q_1 \cap b)}{vol(b) - vol(b_1, \ldots, b_9)} \cdot sum(b)$, where $vol(b_1, \ldots, b_9)$ denotes the volume of the range underlying the buckets $b_1, \ldots, b_9$. Likewise, the bucket $b$ should give no contribution to the estimate of the query $Q_2$ in Fig. 3(b), which lies completely on the range underlying the buckets $b_1, \ldots, b_9$.

In the following the number of cells of an o-bucket $b$ which are not contained in any hole of $b$ will be said to be the *actual volume* of $b$. In the case depicted in Fig. 3(a) evaluating the actual volume of $b$ can be accomplished efficiently, as $b_1, \ldots, b_9$ do not overlap. Indeed also c-buckets inside an o-bucket $b$ can intersect one another [3]. For instance, in Fig. 3(c) the three buckets $b_1, b_2, b_3$ inside $b$ overlap. In this case computing

---

[3] Although no pair of clusters $C_1, C_2$ can overlap (otherwise $C_1, C_2$ would be a unique cluster), MBRs of clusters can overlap (see Fig. 3(c)). Thus partitioning overlapping MBRs can result in overlapping c-buckets.

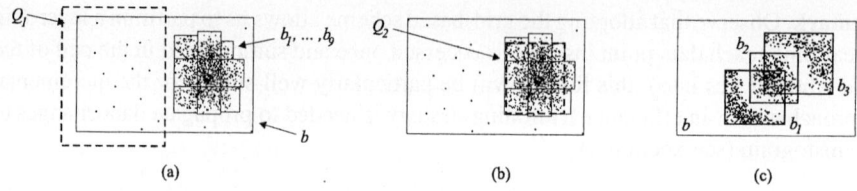

**Fig. 3.** O-buckets with holes

the actual volume of $b$ requires $vol(b_1)$, $vol(b_2)$, $vol(b_3)$, $vol(b_1 \cap b_2)$, $vol(b_2 \cap b_3)$ and $vol(b_1 \cap b_2 \cap b_3)$ to be computed. This computation becomes more and more complex when more buckets intersect in the same region: we need to compute the volumes of all the intersections between 2 holes, 3 holes, and so on. Obviously, this slows down query estimations. Due to this reason, we prefer to estimate the actual volume of an o-bucket $b$ involved in a query instead of evaluating its exact value: To this end we consider only a maximal subset of $Holes(b)$ (denoted as $NOHoles(b)$) consisting of non-overlapping c-buckets, thus avoiding intersections between holes to be computed. For instance, in the case depicted in Fig. 3(c) we can choose $NOHoles(b) = \{b_3\}$, thus we can estimate the actual volume of $b$ as $vol(b) - vol(b_3)$. However we point out that from our experiments on real-life data it turned out that intersections between c-buckets are unlikely to occur.

The adopted representation model partitions buckets into two levels. The buckets at the second level are those belonging to $NOHoles(b)$ for some $b$. The first level consists of all the other buckets. In [8] we present an efficient physical representation scheme, that is based on the possibility to linearize the two bucket levels and allows range query answers to be estimated by accessing each bucket at most once.

## 3 Incremental Maintenance of CHIST on Evolving Data-Sets

The computational complexity of the histogram construction is dominated by the cost of executing DBSCAN. DBSCAN runs in $O(N \cdot \log N)$ if a multi-dimensional indexing technique is adopted to support the efficient location of neighbors. Indeed its complexity degrades to $O(N^2)$ on high-dimensional data sets, where no indexing technique is known to be efficient in searching the neighbors of data points. This is likely to limit the applicability of CHIST to static data sets, such as non-evolving historical data, where the construction of the histogram is performed only once. Otherwise, in the case of evolving data sets, any change of the data would require the re-execution of the algorithm from scratch. In order to reduce the overhead due to this task, the re-computation of the histogram could be scheduled to be run periodically (e.g. every night) or when the system managing data is unloaded. But this could make the histogram out-of-date, thus compromising the estimation accuracy, especially in the case that data change much more frequently w.r.t. histogram re-computation. Observe that the adoption of a clustering technique more efficient than DBSCAN does not suffice to solve this problem, as no technique is known to accomplish the (from-scratch) clusterization fast enough.

A possible solution to this problem is to adopt an incremental clustering technique to propagate efficiently data changes to the clusterization. An incremental clustering algorithm computes the clusterization of the updated data starting from the pre-existing clusterization and modifying it according to the data updates, aiming at reducing as much as possible the amount of data to be accessed. However, replacing the non-incremental clustering step with an incremental one at Step I may not suffice to make the whole technique well-suited for reacting to frequent updates. In fact, Step II requires a linear scanning of data to compute the bucketization of all layers. In order to exploit the advantage of incremental clustering, Step II needs to be changed too, so that layers which are not affected by the data updates are not re-partitioned, thus exploiting as much as possible the pre-existing bucketization.

Motivated by these observations, in this section we propose an incremental algorithm for maintaining the histogram up-to-date w.r.t. data changes. In more detail, our strategy works in three steps, which will be described in the following sections:

I Incremental clustering;
II Storage space distribution among layers and partitioning;
III Re-arrangement of buckets.

Throughout the following sections we assume that each point $p$ of the data distribution is marked with two labels $Flag(p)$ and $Layer(p)$ [4]. The former has a boolean value, specifying whether $p$ is an outlier or belongs to a cluster. $Layer(p)$ is the identifier of the layer where $p$ is summarized: thus, if $p$ is an outlier summarized in a o-bucket then $Layer(p) = 0$, else if $p$ is a point summarized in a c-bucket obtained by partitioning the layer $L_i$ then $Layer(p)$ is the identifier of $L_i$. Basically, the values of $Flag(p)$ and $Layer(p)$ describe the current composition of layers before executing a bulk of updates, and are changed accordingly to the data updates during steps I,II. In particular, during the execution of these steps, $Layer(p)$ can be also assigned $-1$, meaning that $p$ has not been assigned to any layer yet.

### 3.1 Step I: Incremental Clustering

The task performed at this step consists in propagating data updates to the clusterization. There are several techniques in literature which accomplish this task in an incremental fashion, that is they compute the clusterization of updated data without re-executing the clustering algorithm from scratch on all the data. In our prototype we adopted *Incremental DBScan* [7]. According to this technique, data updates may have different effects on the clusterization, and thus on the corresponding layers. When a new point $p$ is added to the data distribution, one of the following cases may occur:

I1- *no new cluster is created, and no old cluster is affected*: this happens if $p$ is an outlier; in this case, the layer of outliers must be augmented, whereas the other layers need no change; $Flag(p)$ is assigned 0 (meaning that $p$ is classified as an outlier) and $Layer(p)$ is assigned $-1$ (meaning that $p$ is an outlier which has not been summarized in any bucket yet);

I2- *a new cluster including $p$ is created, and no old cluster is affected*: in this case, a new layer is created (corresponding to the new cluster), and the layer of outliers may need to be reduced (in the case that some pre-existing outliers are absorbed into

---

[4] Apart from further labels possibly associated to the points by the adopted clustering algorithm.

the new cluster). Layers corresponding to pre-existing clusters need no change. In this case, for each point $p'$ included in the new cluster, $Flag(p')$ is assigned 1 and $Layer(p')$ is assigned the id of the new cluster.

I3- *no new cluster is created, and some old clusters are affected*: this can arise from one of the following cases:
- *p is absorbed by exactly one of the pre-existing clusters*: in this case, the layer of the involved cluster must be augmented; $Flag(p)$ is assigned 1 and $Layer(p)$ is assigned the id of the cluster adsorbing $p$;
- *p is adsorbed by two or more clusters, and these clusters are merged in a single one*: in this case, the layers of the merged clusters must be deleted, and a new layer corresponding to the new cluster must be created. For each point $p'$ adsorbed by the new cluster $Flag(p')$ is assigned 1 and $Layer(p')$ is assigned the id of the new cluster.

Moreover, in both cases the layer of outliers must be reduced if some pre-existing outliers are absorbed into a cluster together with $p$. For each of these points $p'$, $Flag(p')$ changes from 0 to 1 and $Layer(p')$ is assigned the id of the adsorbing cluster.

Analogously, when a point $p$ is deleted from the data distribution it can be one of the following cases:

D1- *no old cluster is affected*: this happens if $p$ was an outlier; in this case, the layer of outliers must be reduced and no other layer need updates;
D2- *exactly one old cluster is affected*: this happens if $p$ belonged to a cluster $C$. In particular, one of the following cases can occur:
  a. $C$ *is reduced*: this happens when after the removal of $p$ some points of $C$ become outliers; in this case the layer of $C$ must be reduced and the outlier layer must be augmented. In particular, for each $p'$ which is no more a cluster point, $Flag(p')$ is assigned 0 and $Layer(p')$ is assigned $-1$;
  b. $C$ *is deleted*: this happens when the removal of $p$ results in making no point of $C$ have a dense neighborhood, thus all points of $C$ become outliers; in this case the layer corresponding to $C$ is deleted and the layer of outliers must be augmented. For each point $p'$ which belonged to $C$ $Flag(p')$ is assigned 0 and $Layer(p')$ are assigned $-1$;
  c. $C$ *is split into two or more clusters*: this happens when, after the removal of $p$, two or more core points are no more density-reachable from one another; thus they define distinct clusters. In this case the layer corresponding to $C$ is split into two layers (i.e. the layer of $C$ is deleted and two new layers are created). Moreover the layer of outliers may need to be augmented (in the case that some points belonging to $C$ become outliers). For each point $p'$ involved in the split, the values of $Flag(p')$ and $Layer(p')$ are changed consistently.

The above-reported list summarizes the operations performed on layers for a single update. Indeed an incremental clustering step consists of processing a bulk of updates, which is processed as a sequence of single updates. See [7] for further details and graphical examples on how inserting/deleting points can change clusterization.

The histogram maintenance is supported by an auxiliary (main-memory resident) data structure consisting of two sets $\mathcal{L}_{new}$ and $\mathcal{L}_{old}$, whose items are of the form $< L, MBR(L), sum(L), sum^2(L), count(L), B(L) >$, where $L$ is a layer identifier and $B(L)$ denotes the amount of storage space which was invested to partition $L$ during the construction of the old histogram (obviously $B(L) = 0$ if $L$ is a newly detected layer). The aggregate data $sum(L)$, $sum^2(L)$ and $count(L)$, as well as $MBR(L)$, will be used at Step 2 to evaluate the SSE of $L$, whereas $B(L)$ will be used to decide whether old layers need to be re-partitioned or not. Basically, at the end of the incremental clustering step, $\mathcal{L}_{new}$ and $\mathcal{L}_{old}$ contain the up-to-date clusterization (w.r.t. the processed bulk of insertions and deletions). In particular, $\mathcal{L}_{old}$ contains the list of the layers which existed before the bulk of updates and which have not been affected by the updates; on the contrary, $\mathcal{L}_{new}$ consists of the layers which were not in the pre-existing clusterization. Neither $\mathcal{L}_{old}$ nor $\mathcal{L}_{new}$ contain any tuple corresponding to the layer of outliers: aggregate data of $L_0$ are stored separately from these lists.

At the beginning of the incremental clustering step, $\mathcal{L}_{new}$ is empty while $\mathcal{L}_{old}$ contains the list of the pre-existing layer identifiers and their aggregate data (except from $L_0$). During the execution of the incremental clustering step, both $\mathcal{L}_{new}$ and $\mathcal{L}_{old}$ are maintained up-to-date as follows. Consider an update operation $u$ (i.e. insertion or deletion) in the processed bulk of updates. Let *Affected*($u$) be the set of layers affected by $u$ and *Created*($u$) the set of layers created after performing $u$. Basically, *Affected*($u$) contains layers in $\mathcal{L}_{old} \cup \mathcal{L}_{new}$ which need either augmentation or reduction or deletion, whereas *Created*($u$) contains layers which need to be created (i.e. layers in *Created*($u$) can result from either splitting clusters, merging clusters, or creating new clusters). For each layer $L$ in *Created*($u$) the tuple $< L, MBR(L), sum(L), sum^2(L), count(L), 0 >$ is inserted into $\mathcal{L}_{new}$. For each layer $L$ in *Affected*($u$) the following operations are performed. If $L$ has to be deleted, then the corresponding tuple is removed from the list it belongs to (either $\mathcal{L}_{new}$ or $\mathcal{L}_{old}$). Otherwise, if $L$ needs either augmentation or reduction, the attributes $MBR(L)$, $sum(L)$, $sum^2(L)$, $count(L)$ in the corresponding tuple are updated. Moreover, if $L$ was in $\mathcal{L}_{old}$ the corresponding tuple is moved to $\mathcal{L}_{new}$ (after assigning 0 to $B(L)$). Finally, for each outlier $p$ which had been summarized into the buckets of some layer in *Affected*($u$) the value of *Layer*($p$) is changed to $-1$.

Therefore, at the end of the incremental clustering, every point $p$ classified as a cluster point is assigned $Flag(p) = 1$ and $Layer(p) = id(L)$, where $L$ is the layer corresponding to the cluster containing $p$. For each outlier $p$, $Flag(p)$ is assigned 0; as regards $Layer(p)$ one of the following cases can occur:

- $Layer(p) = i \geq 0$: this means that $p$ is currently summarized into a bucket associated to the layer $L_i$;
- $Layer(p) = -1$: this means that $p$ is not currently summarized into any bucket (this can be due to two reasons: either $p$ is a newly created outlier, or $p$ was an outlier summarized into a layer affected by the data update).

As we will show in the following section, every outlier whose *Layer* value is $-1$ will be assigned to exactly one layer and summarized into one of its buckets. That is, if the outlier $p$ happens to be summarized into an o-bucket, then $Layer(p)$ will be assigned 0, else if $p$ happens to be adsorbed by a c-bucket $b$, then $Layer(p)$ will be assigned the id of the layer which $b$ refers to.

Lists $\mathcal{L}_{new}$ and $\mathcal{L}_{old}$ will be used at Step II to detect layers which need to be partitioned.

### 3.2 Step II: Storage Space Distribution Among Layers and Partitioning

The incremental clustering step results in a new clusterization, where new layers may be added and some pre-existing layers may be either deleted or modified w.r.t. the previous clusterization. The overall amount of storage space $B$ must be now re-distributed among the layers in $\mathcal{L} = \mathcal{L}_{new} \cup \mathcal{L}_{old} \cup \{L_0\}$. Adopting the same criterion as the non-incremental approach (see Section 2.2) is likely to result in changing the amount of storage space assigned to layers in $\mathcal{L}_{old}$, thus requiring also all layers non-affected by data updates to be re-partitioned. This should be avoided, as it would imply to re-scan all data points. Thus, in the incremental approach, we adopt a different strategy to distribute the available storage space $B$ among layers. This strategy aims at being fair and restricting as much as possible the set of pre-existing layers to be re-partitioned.

Layers in $\mathcal{L}_{old}$ and $\mathcal{L}_{new}$ and the layer of outliers $L_0$ will be considered into three distinct phases, to be executed in the following order.

**Partitioning layers in $\mathcal{L}_{old}$.** We denote as $\widehat{B}(\mathcal{L}_{old})$ the portion of $B$ which we want to assign on the whole to layers in $\mathcal{L}_{old}$. According to a fair distribution of the available storage space $B$ between $\mathcal{L}_{old}$ and $\mathcal{L}_{new}$, we choose:

$$\widehat{B}(\mathcal{L}_{old}) = \frac{SSE(\mathcal{L}_{old})}{SSE(\mathcal{L})} \cdot B,$$

where: $SSE(\mathcal{L}_{old}) = \sum_{L \in \mathcal{L}_{old}} SSE(L)$ is an estimate of the overall inhomogeneity of layers in $\mathcal{L}_{old}$, and: $SSE(\mathcal{L}) = \sum_{L \in \mathcal{L}} SSE(L)$ measures the overall inhomogeneity of all the layers resulting from the clusterization. Notice that the SSE of each layer $L$ is computed by accessing the aggregate data $sum(L)$, $sum^2(L)$, $count(L)$, $MBR(L)$, stored in the tuple in $\mathcal{L}$ corresponding to $L$: $SSE(L) = sum^2(L) - \frac{(sum(L))^2}{Vol(L)}$.

Let $B(\mathcal{L}_{old}) = \sum_{L \in \mathcal{L}_{old}} B(L)$ be the amount of storage space consumed by the summarization of all the layers in $\mathcal{L}_{old}$. First $\widehat{B}(\mathcal{L}_{old})$ is compared to $B(\mathcal{L}_{old})$. The idea is that if $B(\mathcal{L}_{old})$ is pretty "close" to $\widehat{B}(\mathcal{L}_{old})$ we do not re-partition layers in $\mathcal{L}_{old}$. In particular in order to decide whether $B(\mathcal{L}_{old})$ is close to $\widehat{B}(\mathcal{L}_{old})$, we introduce a threshold parameter $t$. Thus if $|\widehat{B}(\mathcal{L}_{old}) - B(\mathcal{L}_{old})| < t \cdot \widehat{B}(\mathcal{L}_{old})$, the pre-existing partition of layers in $\mathcal{L}_{old}$ will not be changed.

Otherwise layers in $\mathcal{L}_{old}$ are re-partitioned depending on which of the following cases occurs:

- $B(\mathcal{L}_{old}) > (1 + t) \cdot \widehat{B}(\mathcal{L}_{old})$: this means that the amount of storage space currently invested to summarize layers in $\mathcal{L}_{old}$ is on the whole too large (according to the adopted fair-distribution criterion); thus we re-partition some layers in $\mathcal{L}_{old}$ by means of a coarser-grain grid in order to release some storage space;
- $B(\mathcal{L}_{old}) < (1 - t) \cdot \widehat{B}(\mathcal{L}_{old})$: in this case we augment the storage space currently invested to summarize $\mathcal{L}_{old}$, by re-partitioning by means of a finer-grain grid the layers in $\mathcal{L}_{old}$ which are the most in need of a finer partition.

In order to choose the layers to be re-partitioned, for each layer $L$ in $\mathcal{L}_{old}$ we evaluate $\widehat{B}(L) = \frac{SSE(L)}{SSE(\mathcal{L})} \cdot B$. The value of $\widehat{B}(L)$ is a fair portion of the available storage space to be assigned to $L$.

A layer $L$ in $\mathcal{L}_{old}$ such that $B(L) > \widehat{B}(L)$ is said to be *indebted*, in the sense that it is assigned an amount of storage space larger than the amount it would be assigned in a fair space distribution based on its relative inhomogeneity. So it is "in debt" of some storage space to other layers. On the contrary, a layer $L$ such that $B(L) < \widehat{B}(L)$ is said to be *creditor*, in the sense that it is assigned an amount of storage space smaller than the one it would need according to its SSE. That is, it is creditor of some storage space.

Consider the case that $B(\mathcal{L}_{old}) > (1+t) \cdot \widehat{B}(\mathcal{L}_{old})$ holds. Then, it is straightforward to see that there is at least one indebted layer in $\mathcal{L}_{old}$ such that $B(L) > (1+t) \cdot \widehat{B}(L)$. Let $L^*$ be the most indebted layer in $\mathcal{L}_{old}$. The idea is to deprive $L^*$ of some storage space in order to make the overall space consumed by layers in $\mathcal{L}_{old}$ closer to $\widehat{B}(\mathcal{L}_{old})$. In particular, we steal from $B(L^*)$ a portion of storage space which makes $L^*$ creditor of $\frac{t}{2} \cdot \widehat{B}(L^*)$. Therefore, the amount of storage space stolen from $L^*$ is:

$$B^-(L^*) = B(L^*) - \left(1 - \frac{t}{2}\right) \cdot \widehat{B}(L^*).$$

Then we re-partition $L^*$ by investing the amount of storage space $B(L^*) - B^-(L^*)$. If at the end of this step $B(\mathcal{L}_{old}) > \widehat{B}(\mathcal{L}_{old})$ still holds, then we choose the layer in $\mathcal{L}_{old}$ which is the most in debt and deprive it of some storage space, using the same strategy as above. This process goes on until $B(\mathcal{L}_{old}) \leq \widehat{B}(\mathcal{L}_{old})$. That is, we take layers which are "very much indebted" and make them "pretty" in credit (we use the threshold value $t/2$ to estimate that a layer is creditor in a small extent): this strategy aims at reaching rapidly the condition $B(\mathcal{L}_{old}) \leq \widehat{B}(\mathcal{L}_{old})$, by reducing the number of layers to be re-partitioned, which is mandatory for the efficiency requirements of the incremental approach.

In the case that $B(\mathcal{L}_{old}) < (1-t) \cdot \widehat{B}(\mathcal{L}_{old})$ an analogous approach is adopted: we choose the layer $L^*$ which is creditor of the largest amount of storage space, and we augment its storage space by adding to it:

$$B^+(L^*) = \left(1 + \frac{t}{2}\right) \cdot \widehat{B}(L^*) - B(L^*),$$

which means making $L^*$ indebted of at most $\frac{t}{2} \cdot B(L^*)$. Then we re-partition $L^*$, and re-iterate this procedure on the other creditors in $\mathcal{L}_{old}$ until $\widehat{B}(\mathcal{L}_{old}) \geq B(\mathcal{L}_{old})$.

By means of experiments, we found that the threshold value $t = 20\%$ preserves the accuracy of the updated histogram and it effectively limits the number of layers to be re-partitioned.

If a layer $L \in \mathcal{L}_{old}$ is chosen to be re-partitioned (as it is creditor or indebted in too large extent), the *Layer* value of the outliers which were summarized in the buckets of $L$ at some previous step is assigned the value $-1$. These outliers will be considered for summarization into some bucket at the following step.

In the following, outliers whose *Layer* value is $-1$ will be said to be *new outliers*, whereas outliers whose *Layer* value is greater than or equal to 0 will be said to be *old outliers*.

***Partitioning layers in*** $\mathcal{L}_{new}$. Layers $L_1, \ldots, L_\alpha$ in $\mathcal{L}_{new}$ are partitioned sequentially according to the same scheme adopted in the non-incremental approach. The amount of storage space invested to partition layers in $\mathcal{L}_{new}$ is $B(\mathcal{L}_{new}) = \frac{SSE(\mathcal{L}_{new})}{SSE(\mathcal{L})} \cdot B$. Then for each $i \in [1..\alpha]$, the layer $L_i$ is summarized according to the grid-partitioning scheme described in Section 2.2 by investing the amount of storage space:
$B(L_i) = B_i \cdot \frac{SSE(L_i)}{SSE(L_0) + \sum_{j=i}^{\alpha} SSE(L_j)}$,
where $B_1 = B(\mathcal{L}_{new})$ and $B_i$ is the portion of $B(\mathcal{L}_{new})$ which is left from the summarization of $L_1, \ldots, L_{i-1}$.

***Partitioning*** $L_0$. Let $B' = B - B(\mathcal{L}_{new}) - B(\mathcal{L}_{old})$ be the amount of storage space which can be invested to summarize $L_0$, i.e. the portion of $B$ which is left from summarizing layers in $\mathcal{L}_{new}$ and $\mathcal{L}_{old}$. $L_0$ is re-partitioned if one of the following cases occurs:

1. $B(L_0) \geq B'$: this means that the current bucketization of $L_0$ makes the overall storage space consumption of the histogram exceed $B$, thus $L_0$ must be re-partitioned using a coarser-grain grid;
2. $B(L_0) \leq (1-t) \cdot B'$: this means that the space currently invested to partition $L_0$ is too small (according to the threshold $t$), thus $L_0$ must be re-partitioned using a finer-grain grid.

If either case 1 or case 2 occurs, $L_0$ must be re-partitioned, thus a new grid is defined on $L_0$ (by investing the amount of storage space $B - B(\mathcal{L}_{new}) - B(\mathcal{L}_{old})$). In this case both new and old outliers are scanned, and each outlier is summarized either into a c-bucket or into an o-bucket, depending on whether it lies into the range of some c-bucket or not.

Otherwise, if neither case 1 nor case 2 occurs, the existing grid-partitioning of $L_0$ is kept and the current summarization is updated as follows. First, the new outliers are scanned and summarized into either a c-bucket or an o-bucket, as for the previous case. Then, the buckets of $L_0$ are deprived of the outliers which lie into the range of some newly created c-bucket.

Details on how these tasks are accomplished in the implementation are given in Section 4.

### 3.3 Step III: Re-arrangement of Buckets

The task accomplished at this step consists of applying the same physical representation scheme as the non-incremental approach to the set of buckets resulting from Step II. The up-to-date histogram consists of buckets of four types: 1) c-buckets resulting from partitioning layers in $\mathcal{L}_{new}$, 2) c-buckets resulting from re-partitioning selected layers in $\mathcal{L}_{old}$, 3) c-buckets inherited from the previous histogram which refer to layers in $\mathcal{L}_{old}$ which have not been re-partitioned, 4) o-buckets partitioning $L_0$ (these buckets can result either from updating the o-buckets of the previous histogram or from re-partitioning $L_0$). The pre-existing arrangement of buckets is not exploited to re-arrange new buckets, as this does not result in a relevant overhead. In fact all the operations needed to accomplish this task are performed in main memory (where the new bucketization is stored), without accessing disk-resident data.

The algorithm implementing steps I to III is shown on the next page.

**Algorithm.** Incremental CHIST
*INPUT*: $D$: a multi-dimensional data distribution; $B$: 32bit words used to store the histogram;
$\quad\quad\quad$ $H$: the histogram currently built on $D$; $u$: the bulk of updates to be propagated to $H$;
*OUTPUT*: $H'$: an up-to-date histogram on $D$ within $B$;

*Step I*
$\quad$ $<\mathcal{L}_{old}, \mathcal{L}_{new}, L_0>:=$ Incremental_DBSCAN$(H, D, u)$;  // the new layerization reflecting updates;

*Step II*
$\quad$ Partitioned=$\emptyset$;  NewBuckets=$\emptyset$;  $\widehat{B}(\mathcal{L}_{old}) = \frac{SSE(\mathcal{L}_{old})}{SSE(\mathcal{L})} \cdot B$;  $\quad$ $B(\mathcal{L}_{old}) = \sum_{L \in \mathcal{L}_{old}} B(L)$;
$\quad$ **if** $B(\mathcal{L}_{old}) \geq (1+t) \cdot \widehat{B}(\mathcal{L}_{old})$ **then**
$\quad\quad$ **while** $B(\mathcal{L}_{old}) \geq (1+t) \cdot \widehat{B}(\mathcal{L}_{old})$ **do**
$\quad\quad\quad$ $L = SelectMostIndebted(\mathcal{L}_{old})$;  Partitioned=Partitioned $\cup$ $L$;  $B(L) = (1-\frac{t}{2}) \cdot \frac{SSE(L)}{SSE(\mathcal{L})} \cdot B$;
$\quad\quad\quad$ NewBuckets= NewBuckets $\cup$ GridPartition$(L, B(L))$;  // $L$ is re-partitioned and all the outliers
$\quad\quad\quad\quad\quad\quad\quad\quad\quad\quad\quad\quad\quad\quad\quad\quad\quad\quad\quad\quad\quad\quad\quad\quad$ // which were summarized in it are
$\quad\quad\quad\quad\quad\quad\quad\quad\quad\quad\quad\quad\quad\quad\quad\quad\quad\quad\quad\quad\quad\quad\quad\quad$ // assigned to $L_0$;
$\quad\quad$ **end_while**
$\quad$ **elsif** $B(\mathcal{L}_{old}) \leq (1-t) \cdot \widehat{B}(\mathcal{L}_{old})$ **then**
$\quad\quad$ **while** $B(\mathcal{L}_{old}) \leq (1-t) \cdot \widehat{B}(\mathcal{L}_{old})$ **do**
$\quad\quad\quad$ $L = SelectMostCreditor(\mathcal{L}_{old})$;  Partitioned=Partitioned $\cup$ $L$;  $B(L) = (1+\frac{t}{2}) \cdot \frac{SSE(L)}{SSE(\mathcal{L})} \cdot B$;
$\quad\quad\quad$ NewBuckets= NewBuckets $\cup$ GridPartition$(L, B(L))$;
$\quad\quad$ **end_while**
$\quad$ **end_if**;
$\quad$ $\mathcal{L}_{old} = \mathcal{L}_{old} \setminus$ Partitioned;  // $\mathcal{L}_{old}$ contains now all the non re-partitioned pre-existing layers;
$\quad$ **for each** $L$ **in** $\mathcal{L}_{new}$ **do**
$\quad\quad$ $B(L) = \frac{L.SSE}{L_0.SSE + SSE(\mathcal{L}_{new})} \cdot (B - size(Partitioned) - size(\mathcal{L}_{old}))$;  // the amount of memory invested
$\quad\quad\quad\quad\quad\quad\quad\quad\quad\quad\quad\quad\quad\quad\quad\quad\quad\quad\quad\quad\quad\quad\quad\quad$ // to summarize $L$;
$\quad\quad$ NewBuckets= NewBuckets $\cup$ GridPartition$(L, B(L))$;  // $L$ is partitioned and resulting buckets
$\quad\quad\quad\quad\quad\quad\quad\quad\quad\quad\quad\quad\quad\quad\quad\quad\quad\quad\quad\quad\quad\quad\quad\quad$ // are added to NewBuckets;
$\quad\quad$ Partitioned=Partitioned $\cup$ $L$;
$\quad$ **end_for**;
$\quad$ $B' = B - size(Partitioned) - size(\mathcal{L}_{old})$;  // function $size$ returns the amount of memory
$\quad\quad\quad\quad\quad\quad\quad\quad\quad\quad\quad\quad\quad\quad\quad\quad\quad\quad\quad\quad$ // needed to store the buckets taken as input;

$\quad$ **if** $B(L_0) \leq B'$ **and** $B(L_0) \geq (1-t) \cdot B'$ **then**
$\quad\quad$ O-Buckets= $H$.O-Buckets;  // $H'$ inherits the set of o-buckets of $H$;
$\quad\quad$ DistributeNewOutliers(NewBuckets, O-Buckets);  // New outliers are distributed among
$\quad\quad\quad\quad\quad\quad\quad\quad\quad\quad\quad\quad\quad\quad\quad\quad\quad\quad\quad\quad$ // new c-buckets and old o-buckets;
$\quad\quad$ MoveOutliers(NewBuckets, O-Buckets);  // O-buckets are deprived of old outliers
$\quad\quad\quad\quad\quad\quad\quad\quad\quad\quad\quad\quad\quad\quad\quad\quad\quad\quad\quad\quad$ // lying into some new c-bucket;
$\quad$ **else**
$\quad\quad$ O-Buckets= PartitionAndDistribute$(L_0, B - size(Partitioned) - size(\mathcal{L}_{old}), NewBuckets)$;
$\quad$ **end**;

*Step III*
$\quad$ $H'$ =Assemble(NewBuckets, UnchangedBuckets$(H, \mathcal{L}_{old})$, O-Buckets);
$\quad$ **return** $H'$;

## 4 Costs of the Non-incremental and Incremental Approaches

The difference in the number of disk accesses between the two approaches is due to two reasons. First, the adoption of the incremental clustering, which is likely to result in much fewer disk accesses w.r.t. the non-incremental one. Secondly, the strategy adopted at Step II, which aims at limiting the number of layers to be re-partitioned, avoiding re-scanning the whole data. As regards the former aspect, the extent of the benefit introduced by the use of an incremental clustering approach strictly depends on the particular clustering algorithm invoked. In the case of DBSCAN, no simple formula is known to provide the speedup factor corresponding to the use of its incremental version, thus the speedup must be determined experimentally.

As regards the second aspect, we can compare the number of disk accesses as follows. In the non incremental approach, after accomplishing the clusterization, a region query must be posed corresponding to the MBR of each detected dense cluster to partition it according to the grid; then, the list of outliers must be scanned to distribute them among c-buckets and o-buckets. Thus, denoting the number of dense clusters as $c$, the number of data points as $N$ and the number of pages containing outliers as $Out$, the number of disk accesses is $O(c \cdot \log N + Out)$ (we assume that a multi-dimensional index enabling region queries to be answered with $\log N$ accesses is maintained, as well as an inverted index of the pages containing outliers). As regards the incremental approach, let $c'$ be the number of clusters which need to be partitioned, $OldOut$ the number of pages containing the old outliers and $NewOut$ the number of pages containing the new outliers. We must pose $c'$ region queries to partition the dense clusters and we have to scan $NewOut$ pages to distribute the new outliers among c-buckets and o-buckets. Moreover, if it is the case that $L_0$ must be re-partitioned, we must also scan $OldOut$ pages to repartition it and possibly adsorb old outliers into new c-buckets. Otherwise, if $L_0$ does not need re-partitioning, we must only pose $b_{new}$ region queries on the set of old outliers to possibly adsorb some of them into new c-buckets ($b_{new}$ denotes the number of the new c-buckets). Therefore, the overall number of disk accesses is $O(c' \cdot \log N + NewOut + X)$, where $X$ is either $b_{new} \cdot \log OldOut$ (if $L_0$ is not re-partitioned) or $OldOut$ (if $L_0$ must be re-partitioned). Observe that in order to support the incremental approach we also maintain an inverted index on the newly detected outliers (which allows us to scan all the new outliers by means of $NewOut$ accesses) as well as a multi-dimensional index to answer region queries on old outliers with $\log Out$ accesses. Notice that in the worst case $NewOut + X = Out$ (in the non-incremental approach there is no distinction between new and old outliers, thus $Out = NewOut + OldOut$), but in the case that the outlier layer is not repartitioned $NewOut + X$ can be reasonably assumed much smaller than $Out$. Moreover we can assume $c'$ much smaller than $c$. Therefore if the number of outliers is "small" w.r.t. the whole data size, then the adoption of the incremental strategy always results in a relevant benefit, otherwise the extent of this benefit depends on the probability that $L_0$ must be repartitioned.

The latter issue cannot be investigated but experimentally, as well as the speedup due to the adoption of the incremental clustering strategy. Therefore in the following section we will provide an experimental analysis of the overall benefit of the incremental approach, which both the incremental clusterization and the partitioning strategy contribute to.

## 5 Experimental Results

Experimental results showing the higher accuracy provided by CHIST w.r.t state-of-the-art techniques on static data have been shown in [8]. Here we present experiments testing the effectiveness of the incremental approach, comparing it with the from-scratch execution of CHIST. Synthetic data sets were generated according to a multi-dimensional zipf distribution law. Basically a data set consists of a number of dense regions randomly distributed in the data domain. Randomly generated points are added to simulate noise (for further details see [8]).

To generate a bulk of insertions on a distribution $D$, we first generated a distribution $D'$ on the same domain and using the same data generator as $D$. Then a bulk of insertions on $D$ is created by randomly extracting some points from $D'$. The idea of extracting points from $D'$ to be inserted into $D$ is that this allows us to simulate both the creation of new dense clusters and new outliers in $D$. Deletions on $D$ consist of randomly selected points of $D$. Thus a bulk of updates is a set of insertions and deletions, generated as explained above. For a bulk of updates $u$, we will denote as $p_u$ the percentage of insertions in $u$.

Diagrams in Fig. 4(a,b,c) refer to a 4D data distribution where $n$ (the edge size of the domain) is 1000, while diagrams in Fig. 4 (d,e,f) refer to an 8D data distribution with $n = 1000$.

Fig. 4 (a,d) show the speedup due to the use of Incremental CHIST versus the size of updates (expressed as percentage of the data size) on a 4D and a 8D synthetic data distribution, respectively. For a bulk of updates $u$, the speedup is the ratio $\frac{N.\ of\ pages\ accessed\ by\ CHIST}{N.\ of\ pages\ accessed\ by\ Incremental\ CHIST}$. Fig. 4 (a,d) show that the benefit of using the incremental approach is very relevant (in both cases we obtained a speedup value of about 200 for update size of 1%). As expected, the speedup decreases as the size of the updates gets larger. Observe that the speedup depends also on the type of updates: the larger the percentage of insertions, the higher the speedup. This is in accordance with [7], where it was observed that deletions on the average result in more complex changes of the clusterization, as they involve a larger number of pre-existing clusters than insertions.

Diagrams in Fig. 4 (b,e) study the accuracy of the incremental approach, compared with that of the non-incremental one. They depict the ratio $e = \frac{e_{ni}}{e_i}$ between the relative errors provided by the non-incremental approach (i.e. $e_{ni}$) and the incremental one (i.e. $e_i$) versus the size of updates. Experiments were conducted investing 2000 buckets to represent the histogram. Two query workloads (one for the 4D case and the other one for the 8D case) were used to evaluate estimation accuracy. Each of them consists of 50000 queries whose selectivity is between 0.4% and 0.5% . Fig. 4 (b,e) show that the ratio $\frac{e_{ni}}{e_i}$ is close to 1 and is almost unaffected by the size of updates. This means that the adoption of the incremental approach does not result in degrading accuracy w.r.t. the non-incremental one.

Observe that the diagrams in Fig. 4 (b,e) do not say that the accuracy provided by the histograms computed after each bulk of updates is constant as data changes. In fact, if the bulk of updates consists mainly of insertions the size of the whole data distribution increases, thus if the size of the histogram is kept constant the accuracy obviously decreases as new data are inserted. Analogously, if the bulk of updates consists mainly of deletions the size of the whole data distribution decreases, a new histogram within

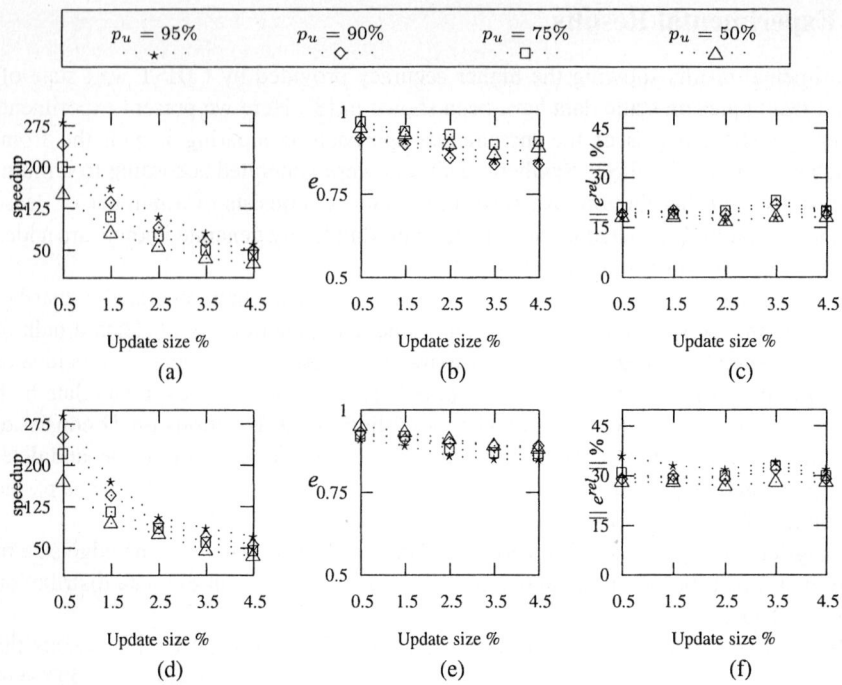

**Fig. 4.** Speedup synthetic data (a,d); ratio $e = \frac{e_{ni}}{e_i}$ for fixed histogram size (b,e); relative error for fixed compression ratio (c,f)

the same storage space bound provides higher accuracy. Thus we performed other experiments keeping the compression ratio constant (i.e. the ratio between the size of the data and that of the histogram): that is, instead of keeping $B$ constant, at each invocation of the incremental algorithm, we re-computed $B$ according to the size of the updated data. Fig. 4(c,f) depict how error rates change w.r.t. update size (compression ratio was kept equal to 50). In these experiments the same query workloads of Fig. 4(b,e) were used. They show that error rates are almost unaffected by changes in update size.

## 6 Conclusions

We have proposed a new technique for constructing multi-dimensional histograms providing high accuracy for selectivity estimation. Our technique invokes a density-based clustering algorithm to partition data into dense and sparse regions which are further partitioned according to a grid-based scheme. We have extended this approach to the case of dynamic data. In this context we have designed a technique exploiting an incremental cluster analysis strategy to propagate data updates to the histogram which aims at limiting the amount of data to be re-processed. We have tested the effectiveness of the incremental approach showing that it yields a relevant speedup factor (w.r.t. the non-incremental one) and that its adoption preserves accuracy as data changes.

Future work will aim at considering different clustering techniques to be embedded into our approach, in order to study how they can be exploited to improve the histogram construction cost while preserving its accuracy. Moreover the effectiveness of combining our approach with techniques for reducing data dimensionality (such as SPARTAN [2]) will be investigated.

**Acknowledgements.** The authors are grateful to Giuseppe Manco for fruitful discussions and valuable comments on several issues related to cluster analysis.

# References

1. Acharya, S., Poosala, V., Ramaswamy, S., Selectivity estimation in spatial databases, *Proc. ACM SIGMOD Conf. 1999.*
2. Babu, S., Garofalakis, M. N., Rastogi, R., SPARTAN: A Model-Based Semantic Compression System for Massive Data Tables, *Proc. ACM SIGMOD Conf. 2001.*
3. Bruno, N., Chaudhuri, S., Gravano, L., STHoles: a multi-dimensional workload aware histogram, *Proc. ACM SIGMOD Conf. 2001*
4. Chaudhuri, S., An Overview of Query Optimization in Relational Systems, *Proc. PODS 1998.*
5. Donjerkovic, D., Ioannidis, Y. E., Ramakrishnan, R., Dynamic Histograms: Capturing Evolving Data Sets, *Proc. ICDE 2000.*
6. Ester, M., Kriegel, H. P., Sander, J., Xu, X., A density-based algorithm for discovering clusters in large spatial databases with noise, *Proc. KDD 1996.*
7. Ester, M., Kriegel, H. P., Wimmer, M., Xu, X., Incremental clustering for mining in a data warehousing environment, *Proc. VLDB 1998.*
8. Furfaro, F., Mazzeo, G., M., Sirangelo, C., Clustering-Based Histograms for Multi-dimensional Data, *Proc. DaWaK 2005.*
9. Garofalakis, M., Gibbons, P.B., Wavelet Synopses with Error Guarantees, *Proc. ACM SIGMOD Conf. 2002.*
10. Gibbons, P. B., Matias, Y., Poosala, V., Fast Incremental Maintenance of Approximate Histograms, *Proc. VLDB 1997.*
11. Guha, S., Indyk, P., Muthukrishnan, M., Strauss, M., Histogramming Data Streams with Fast Per-Item Processing, *Proc. ICALP 2002.*
12. Gunopulos, D., Kollios, G., Tsotras, V. J., Domeniconi, C., Selectivity estimators for multi-dimensional range queries over real attributes, *The VLDB Journal*, Vol. 14(2), April 2005.
13. Kaufman, L., Rousseeuw, P. J., *Finding Groups in Data: An Introduction to Cluster Analysis*, Wiley, 2005.
14. Korn, F., Johnson, T., Jagadish, H. V., Range Selectivity Estimation for Continuous Attributes, *Proc. SSDBM 1999.*
15. Mamoulis, N., Papadias, D., Selectivity Estimation Of Complex Spatial Queries, *Proc. SSTD 2001.*
16. Poosala, V., Ioannidis, Y. E., Selectivity estimation without the attribute value independence assumption, *Proc. VLDB 1997.*
17. Shanmugasundaram, J., Fayyad, U., Bradley, P. S., Compressed data cubes for OLAP aggregate query approximation on continuous dimensions, *Proc. KDD 1999.*

# HASE: A Hybrid Approach to Selectivity Estimation for Conjunctive Predicates

Xiaohui Yu[1], Nick Koudas[1], and Calisto Zuzarte[2]

[1] Department of Computer Science,
University of Toronto,
Toronto, ON, M5S 3G4, Canada
{xhyu, koudas}@cs.toronto.edu

[2] IBM Toronto Lab, 8200 Warden Avenue,
Markham, ON, L6G 1C7, Canada
calisto@ca.ibm.com

**Abstract.** Current methods for selectivity estimation fall into two broad categories, *synopsis-based* and *sampling-based*. Synopsis-based methods, such as histograms, incur minimal overhead at query optimization time and thus are widely used in commercial database systems. Sampling-based methods are more suited for ad-hoc queries, but often involve high I/O cost because of random access to the underlying data. Though both methods serve the same purpose of selectivity estimation, their interaction in the case of selectivity estimation for conjuncts of predicates on multiple attributes is largely unexplored. Our work aims at taking the best of both worlds, by making consistent use of synopses and sample information when they are both present. To achieve this goal, we propose HASE, a novel estimation scheme based on a powerful mechanism called *generalized raking*. We formalize selectivity estimation in the presence of single attribute synopses and sample information as a constrained optimization problem. By solving this problem, we obtain a new set of weights associated with the sampled tuples, which has the nice property of reproducing the known selectivities when applied to individual predicates. We discuss different variants of the optimization problem and provide algorithms for solving it. We also provide asymptotic error bounds on the estimate. Extensive experiments are performed on both synthetic and real data, and the results show that HASE significantly outperforms both synopsis-based and sampling-based methods.

## 1 Introduction

Query optimizers in most relational database systems rely on cost estimation of various candidate query execution plans to select a good one. Accurate plan costing can help avoid intolerably slow plans. A key ingredient in cost estimation is to estimate the selectivity of various predicates. In this paper, we are mainly concerned with selectivity estimation for conjunctive predicates of the form $Q = P_1 \wedge P_2 \ldots P_m$ where each component $P_i$ is a simple predicate on a single attribute, taking the form of (*attribute* op *constant*) with op being one of the comparison operators $<, \leq, =, \neq, \geq,$ or $>$ (e.g., $R.a = 100$ or $R.a \leq 200$).

In terms of methodology, existing work on selectivity estimation takes two fundamentally different approaches: one is based on synopsis data structures and the other is based on sampling. Synopsis-based approaches seek to pre-compute summary data structures which capture statistics on the data (attribute value distributions). Such synopses are stored in the database catalogs, and subsequently used for estimation when required. A prominent example in this class of approaches is histograms, which have received heavy attention; numerous types of histograms [1,2] have been proposed in recent years aiming to improve the accuracy of histogram-based selectivity estimation. Almost all major commercial database management systems (e.g., IBM® DB2® Universal Database™ product(DB2 UDB), Oracle, SQL Server) keep some form of histograms in their catalogs and use them for selectivity estimation.

Sampling-based approaches are more query-driven in nature, in the sense that data is not accessed until optimization time. Given a query, a sample is derived from the database, and selectivities are estimated based on this sample. There exists an extensive literature on sampling-based methods for selectivity estimation; see [3] for a comprehensive survey. In recent years, all of the major commercial database system vendors have incorporated sampling capabilities into their engines [4].

Both approaches have their advantages and disadvantages. Synopsis structures, such as histograms, only need to be computed once and can be used many times while incurring minimal overhead at selectivity estimation time. However, it is difficult to capture all useful information in the limited space. For example, the one-dimensional histograms commonly used in the commercial DBMS's do not provide correlation information between attributes. Although it is possible to compute multi-dimensional histograms for some attribute combinations, it is generally not feasible to compute and store the multi-dimensional histograms for all attribute combinations, because the number of combinations is exponential in the number of attributes [5]. Without knowing of the query workload, deciding which combinations of attributes to choose in order to construct multi-dimensional histograms can be very difficult. Sampling approaches, on the other hand, are able to provide such crucial information through a representative sample of the data. The downside, however, is that sampling at selectivity estimation time incurs non-trivial cost, because in order to obtain a fairly accurate estimate, sometimes a significant portion of the data might have to be accessed. Since sampling requires random access, which is much slower than sequential access, it is possible that the cost of sampling exceeds that of a sequential scan of the data when the sample size is relatively large. (Haas et al. [4] show that under certain assumptions, the cost of sampling is greater than that of sequential scan when the sample rate is greater than 2% and tuple-level sampling is used.)

To the best of our knowledge, there is no previous work exploring the interaction of these two approaches in order to make consistent use of both sources of information. This paper represents a first step in this direction. In particular, we propose HASE (A Hybrid Approach to Selectivity Estimation), a novel method based on the powerful generalized raking procedure originally deployed in the context of survey sampling. Sampling-based methods usually associate with each sampled tuple a *sampling weight* reflecting its inclusion probability (i.e., the probability of being selected to the sample), which is used to produce a selectivity estimate. Given selectivities of individual predicates $P_i$ (which can be easily obtained from attribute synopses) in addition to the sample, we aim to obtain better estimates by adjusting sampling weights, in a way that is consistent with the information on individual selectivities obtained from the synopses. In particular, we adjust the weights of the tuples in the sample, while maintaining the new weights as close as possible to the original weights. We formalize this problem as a constrained optimization problem. Its solution derives the new weights that can then be used to obtain improved selectivity estimates.

We present a general numerical solution to this optimization problem, as well as an iterative solution based on the intrinsic structure of the problem. We consider two different measures of "closeness" between the new weights and the original weights, namely the linear distance function and the multiplicative distance function, and compare them in terms of computational efficiency and interpretability. We also provide asymptotic bounds on the estimation errors.

The rest of this paper is organized as follows. In Section 2, we formally define the problem of selectivity estimation for conjunctive predicates, and describe how selectivity estimates are obtained in existing approaches. Section 3 presents HASE, our proposed approach based on generalized raking. Experimental results on both synthetic and real data sets are presented in Section 4. We briefly review existing approaches to selectivity estimation in Section 5. Section 6 concludes this paper and discusses directions for future work.

## 2 Background

In this section, we formally define the problem of selectivity estimation for conjunctive predicates and discuss two existing ways of conducting the estimation, one based on synopses and one on sampling.

### 2.1 Problem Definition

We are interested in predicates taking the form of $Q = P_1 \wedge P_2 \wedge \cdots \wedge P_m$, where each $P_i (1 \leq i \leq m)$ is a simple predicate of the form (*attribute* op *constant*) with op being one of the comparison operators $<, \leq, =, \neq, \geq,$ or $>$. The selectivity $s_i (\in [0,1])$ is defined as the fraction of tuples on which predicate $P_i$ evaluates to true, i.e., $s_i = N_i/N$, where $N$ is the number of tuples in the table, and $N_i$ is the number of tuples satisfying $P_i$. The selectivity of the conjuncts of predicates $Q$, denoted by $s_Q (\in [0,1])$, is the fraction of tuples satisfying all the $P_i$'s simultaneously. $s_Q$ is the quantity we would like to estimate. When there is no ambiguity, we use $s$ as a shorthand for $s_Q$.

We measure the error of an estimate $\hat{s}$ by the *absolute relative error*

$$E(\hat{s}) = \frac{|\hat{s} - s|}{s}. \tag{1}$$

Throughout the paper, we use the following scenario as a running example. Consider a table $R$ with $N = 10,000$ tuples and three attributes $A_i (i = 1, 2, 3)$. Let $P_1 = (A_1 = 1)$, and $P_2 = (A_2 = 1)$. Suppose we need to estimate the selectivity of the following query: $Q = P_1 \wedge P_2$. If there are 500 tuples satisfying $Q$, then the true selectivity of $Q$ is $s = 500/10000 = 0.05$.

## 2.2 Synopsis-Based Estimation

Assume that we have access to synopsis structures for all individual attributes involved such that selectivity estimates $s_i (1 \leq i \leq m)$ can be obtained. Without any information regarding the correlation between attributes, optimizers in current database systems estimate $s_Q$ based on the assumption that the values in distinct attributes are independently distributed. In other words, knowing that a tuple satisfies a predicate on one attribute does not give any information as to whether it satisfies a predicate on another. Therefore, $s$ is estimated by taking a product of the selectivity estimates of individual predicates, i.e., $\hat{s}_{\text{his}} = \prod_{i=1}^{m} s_i$.

In the running example, suppose we have access to single-attribute histograms on $A_1$ and $A_2$, and therefore we can derive the selectivities of the two predicates, namely $s_1$ and $s_2$, from the histograms. Suppose $s_1 = 0.6$, and $s_2 = 0.3$. If we assume $A_1$ and $A_2$ are independent, then the selectivity of $Q$ is estimated to be $\hat{s}_{\text{his}} = s_1 \cdot s_2 = 0.18$, and the error is $E(\hat{s}_{\text{his}}) = |0.18 - 0.05|/0.05 = 260\%$.

This simple estimation scheme gives accurate estimates when the attributes are indeed independent. Real-life data sets, however, almost always demonstrate a certain degree of correlation between attributes; therefore, making the attribute-value independence assumption often leads to erroneous estimates. In the above example, treating the attributes $A_1$ and $A_2$ as independent incurs a large error (260%). As another example, suppose we have the following query on a CAR table in a vehicle information database: $Q$ = (MAKE = "BMW")$\wedge$(MODEL = "M3"), and we know through one-dimensional histograms that the selectivity of the predicate (MAKE = "BMW") is 0.1, and that the predicate (MODEL = "M3") has a selectivity of 0.01. The optimizer then would estimate the selectivity of $Q$ as $0.1 \times 0.01 = 0.001$, as per the attribute-value independence assumption. Note, however, that there is strong correlation between the attributes MAKE and MODEL. Because M3 is exclusively made by BMW, all tuples satisfying the predicate MODEL="M3" would also satisfy the predicate MAKE="BMW". Therefore, the selectivity of $Q$ is actually 0.01, 10 times that of the estimated selectivity.

## 2.3 Sampling-Based Estimation

Now let us look at how to obtain an estimate of the selectivity based on a sample of the data. Suppose a random sample $S$ of size $n$ is taken from the queried table $R$ of size $N$, where the *inclusion probability* (the probability of being selected into the sample) of the $j$-th tuple is $\pi_j$. The Horvitz-Thompson (HT) estimator [6] for the selectivity of the query $Q$, given the sample $S$, is

$$\hat{s}_{\text{spl}} = \frac{1}{N} \sum_{j \in S} \frac{y_j}{\pi_j} \qquad (2)$$

where $y_j$ is an indicator variable such that $y_j = 1$ if tuple $j$ satisfies $Q$, and $y_j = 0$ otherwise. In the case of simple random sampling (SRS), where the inclusion probabilities are all equal to $n/N$, Eq. (2) simplifies to $\hat{s}_{\text{spl}} = \frac{1}{n} \sum_{j \in S} y_j$.

In our running example, suppose we take an SRS $S$ of size $n = 100$ from table $R$. Clearly, the inclusion probabilities for tuples in $R$ are all equal to $100/10000 = 0.01$. If 9 tuples in the sample satisfy $Q$, then the HT estimator is $\hat{s}_{\text{spl}} = 9/100 = 0.09$, and the error is $E(\hat{s}_{\text{spl}}) = 80\%$.

A major problem with the use of sampling is the I/O overhead incurred. Since sampling requires random access to data, it is often the case that even if a very small sample is taken, the associated I/O cost is comparable to that of a full sequential scan of the data. For example, if each page contains 50 tuples, and the sample rate is higher than 2%, essentially all pages have to be accessed because $50 \times 2\% = 1$ (See [4] and [7] for a detailed analysis of this issue). Recently, there has been work on using page-level sampling in conjunction with tuple-level sampling to reduce the sampling cost [4, 7]. We take a complementary approach to this problem and attempt to decrease the sampling cost by utilizing existing synopsis information on the data. Haas et al. [4] show that the expected fraction $f$ of pages to be accessed for a sample rate of $q$ is given by $f = 1 - (1-q)^c$, where $c$ is the number of tuples on each page. It is evident that $f$ decreases very fast as the sample rate drops, which means that if we can achieve the same level of accuracy with a lower sample rate, the I/O savings can be significant.

## 3 HASE

Our objective is to use the sample information in conjunction with the synopses to obtain better estimates. To this end, we develop a hybrid approach, HASE, by applying *generalized raking* [8, 9], a procedure originally utilized in survey sampling, to the problem of selectivity estimation.

### 3.1 Calibration

Suppose we have obtained a sample of the data, and we also know the selectivities of individual predicates $P_i$. We begin with an estimator constructed based on the sample only, without reference to any additional information, such as the HT estimator (Eq. (2)). For each tuple $j$ in table $R$, in addition to the variable of interest $y_j$, we also associate with it an auxiliary vector $\mathbf{x}_j$ to reflect the results of evaluating $P_i$ on $j$. Suppose each predicate $P_i$ divides tuples in $R$ into two disjoint subsets, $\mathcal{D}_i$ and $\bar{\mathcal{D}}_i$, according to whether they satisfy the predicate or not. We further define $\mathcal{D}_{m+1} = R$, i.e., $j \in \mathcal{D}_{m+1}$ for all $j$. Let $\mathbf{x}_j$ be a column vector of length $m+1$: $\mathbf{x}_j^T = (x_{j1}, \ldots, x_{jm}, x_{j,m+1})$, with the $i$-th ($1 \leq i \leq m+1$) element being 1 if $j \in \mathcal{D}_i$, and 0 otherwise. For instance, in the running example, $\mathbf{x}_j^T = (1,0,1)$ indicates that tuple $j$ satisfies $P_1$, but not $P_2$.

Let $\mathbf{t}_x^T = (t_{x1}, \ldots, t_{xm}, t_{x,m+1}) = \frac{1}{N}\sum_{j \in R} \mathbf{x}_j$. Clearly, $t_{xi} = \frac{1}{N}\sum_{j \in S} x_{ji} = s_i$ ($1 \leq i \leq m$), the selectivity of predicate $P_i$, and $t_{x,m+1} = 1$. Therefore,

$$\mathbf{t}_x^T = (s_1, s_2, \ldots, s_m, 1) \tag{3}$$

Suppose $s_i$ can be obtained based on synopsis structures, and $\mathbf{x}_j$ are observed for each tuple $j \in S$. This allows construction of a new estimator (which we call the *calibration estimator*)

$$\hat{s}_{\text{cal}} = \frac{1}{N} \sum_{j \in S} w_j y_j, \qquad (4)$$

where the weights $w_j$ are as close to the weights $d_j = 1/\pi_j$ as possible according to some distance metric (recall that $\pi_j$ is the inclusion probability of $j$), and where

$$\frac{1}{N} \sum_{j \in S} w_j \mathbf{x}_j = \mathbf{t}_x, \qquad (5)$$

meaning that the weighted average of the observed $\mathbf{x}_j$ has to reproduce the known selectivities $s_i$.

In light of the definition of $\mathbf{x}_j$ and Eq. (3), Eq. (5) can be rewritten as

$$\frac{1}{N} \sum_{j \in S \cap \mathcal{D}_i} w_j = s_i, \quad i = 1, 2, \ldots, m+1. \qquad (6)$$

where $s_{m+1} = s$. Now $w_j$ has a natural representation interpretation: it is the number of tuples "represented" by the sampled tuple $j$.

In our running example, Eq. (6) becomes

$$\frac{1}{10000} \sum_{j \in S \cap \mathcal{D}_1} w_j = 0.6, \ \frac{1}{10000} \sum_{j \in S \cap \mathcal{D}_2} w_j = 0.3, \text{ and } \frac{1}{10000} \sum_{j \in S} w_j = 1. \qquad (7)$$

Although in general, there can be many possible choices for the sets of weights $\{w_j\}$ satisfying the constraints in Eq. (6), our goal is to select a set of new weights that are as close as possible to the original weights $d_i = 1/\pi_i$, which enjoy the desirable property of producing unbiased estimates. By keeping the distance between the new weights and the original weights as small as possible, we expect the new weights to remain nearly unbiased. We formulate this idea as a constrained optimization problem as described below.

### 3.2 The Constrained Optimization Problem

Let $D(x)$ be a distance function (with $x = w_j/d_j$) that measures the distance between the new weights $w_j$ and the original weights $d_j$. We assure that $D(x)$ satisfies the following requirements (for reasons that will become clear later): (i) $D$ is positive and strictly convex, (ii) $D(1) = D'(1) = 0$, and (iii) $D''(1) = 1$. The optimization problem we have to solve is:

Minimize
$$\sum_{j \in S} d_j D(w_j/d_j) \qquad (8)$$

subject to
$$\frac{1}{N} \sum_{j \in S} w_j \mathbf{x}_j = \mathbf{t}_x. \qquad (9)$$

Here, both $\mathbf{x}_j$ and $\mathbf{t}_x$ are defined as in Section 3.1. Since $D(w_j/d_j)$ can have a large response to even a slight change in $w_j$ when $d_j$ is small, we minimize

$\sum_{j \in S} d_j D(w_j/d_j)$ instead of $\sum_{j \in S} D(w_j/d_j)$ in order to dampen this effect. Also note that different distance functions can be used to measure the distance between $\{w_j\}$ and $\{d_j\}$, as long as the distance function complies with conditions (i) to (iii). In this paper, we consider the following two distance functions because of the computational efficiency and interpretability. Both distance functions exhibit properties (i) to (iii). We discuss the choice of distance functions in Section 3.5.

1. The *linear* distance function: $D_{\text{lin}}(w_j/d_j) = \frac{1}{2}(\frac{w_j}{d_j} - 1)^2$, and
2. The *multiplicative* distance function: $D_{\text{mul}}(w_j/d_j) = \frac{w_j}{d_j} \log \frac{w_j}{d_j} - \frac{w_j}{d_j} + 1$

### 3.3 An Algorithm Based on Newton's Method

We now present algorithms to solve the constrained optimization problem. A classical technique for solving constrained optimization problems is the method of Lagrange multipliers [10]. Note that the optimization problem can be rewritten as follows:

Minimize
$$\sum_{j \in S} d_j D(w_j/d_j) - \lambda^T (\sum_{j \in S} w_j \mathbf{x}_j - N\mathbf{t}_x) \quad (10)$$

with respect to $w_j (j \in S)$,
where $\lambda = (\lambda_1, \ldots, \lambda_m, \lambda_{m+1})$ is a Lagrange multiplier. Differentiating Eq. (10) with respect to $w_j$, we have

$$D'(w_j/d_j) - \mathbf{x}_j^T \lambda = 0 \quad (11)$$

Then we can solve the system formed by Eq. (11) and (9) for $w_j$. To do this, we obtain from (11) that

$$w_j = d_j F(\mathbf{x}_j^T \lambda), \quad (12)$$

where $F(x)$ is the inverse function of $D'(x)$. Conditions (i)-(iii) dictate that the inverse function always exists, and $F(0) = F'(0) = 1$. Substituting (12) into Eq. (9), we have the *calibration equations*

$$\sum_{j \in S} d_j F(\mathbf{x}_j^T \lambda) \mathbf{x}_j = N\mathbf{t}_x, \quad (13)$$

which can be solved numerically using Newton's method.
Let $\phi(\lambda) = \sum_{j \in S} d_j F(\mathbf{x}_j^T \lambda) \mathbf{x}_j - N\mathbf{t}_x$. Then

$$\phi'(\lambda) = \partial \phi(\lambda)/\partial \lambda = \sum_{j \in S} d_j F'(\mathbf{x}_j^T \lambda) \mathbf{x}_j \mathbf{x}_j^T.$$

We obtain successive estimates of $\lambda$, denoted by $\lambda_k$ ($k = 0, 1, \ldots$), through the following iteration:

$$\lambda_{k+1} = \lambda_k + [\phi'(\lambda_k)]^{-1} \phi(\lambda_k) \quad (14)$$

We take $\lambda_0 = \mathbf{0}$. Since we have

$$\phi(\mathbf{0}) = \sum_{j \in S} d_j F(\mathbf{0}) \mathbf{x}_j - N \mathbf{t}_x = \sum_{j \in S} d_j \mathbf{x}_j - N \mathbf{t}_x,$$

and

$$\phi'(\mathbf{0}) = \sum_{j \in S} d_j F'(\mathbf{0}) \mathbf{x}_j \mathbf{x}_j^T = \sum_{j \in S} d_j \mathbf{x}_j \mathbf{x}_j^T,$$

the first iteration yields $\lambda_1 = (\sum_{j \in S} d_j \mathbf{x}_j \mathbf{x}_j^T)^{-1}(\sum_{j \in S} d_j \mathbf{x}_j - N \mathbf{t}_x)$. The subsequent values of $\lambda_k$ can be obtained following Eq. (14) until convergence.

In summary, the procedure to estimate the selectivity of $Q$ is presented in Algorithm 1.

---

**Algorithm 1.** An algorithm for computing the calibration estimator based on Newton's method

1: **INPUT:** $Q$, $D$, $S$, $N$, $N_i (i = 1, \ldots, m)$, $d_j (j \in S)$, stopping threshold $\epsilon$.
2: **OUTPUT:** $\hat{s}_{\text{cal}}$
3: **for all** $j \in S$ **do**
4:    Set the values of $y_j$, $\mathbf{x}_j$ according to the rules in Section 3.1;
5: **end for**
6: /*Solving the calibration equations using Newton's method*/
7: $\lambda_0 := \mathbf{0}$; $k := 0$;
8: **repeat**
9:    $\lambda_{k+1} := \lambda_k + [\phi'(\lambda_k)]^{-1} \phi(\lambda_k)$;
10:    $k := k + 1$;
11: **until** $\|\lambda_k - \lambda_{k-1}\| < \epsilon$
12: **for all** $j \in S$ **do**
13:    $w_j := d_j F(\mathbf{x}_j^T \lambda)$;
14: **end for**
15: /*Obtaining the selectivity estimate based on the new weights*/
16: $\hat{s}_{\text{cal}} := \frac{1}{N} \sum_{j \in S} w_j y_j$;

---

Continuing the running example, the true frequencies obtained by evaluating the query $Q$ on table $R$, and the observed frequency information based on a simple random sample $S$ are given in Fig. 1 (both normalized so that all frequencies sum up to 1). The last row and column in each table correspond to the marginal frequencies.

From Fig. 1, we know that the true selectivity of $Q$ is 0.05 (the cell corresponding to $P_1 = true \wedge P_2 = true$ in Fig. 1(a)), and the sampling-based selectivity

|              | $P_2 = true$ | $P_2 = false$ | –    |
|--------------|--------------|---------------|------|
| $P_1 = true$ | 0.05         | 0.55          | 0.60 |
| $P_1 = false$| 0.25         | 0.15          | 0.40 |
| –            | 0.30         | 0.70          |      |

(a) True frequencies

|              | $P_2 = true$ | $P_2 = false$ | –    |
|--------------|--------------|---------------|------|
| $P_1 = true$ | 0.09         | 0.56          | 0.65 |
| $P_1 = false$| 0.24         | 0.11          | 0.35 |
| –            | 0.33         | 0.67          |      |

(b) Observed frequencies

**Fig. 1.** Example: True frequencies and observed frequencies from the sample

estimate is 0.09 (the cell corresponding to $P_1 = true \land P_2 = true$ in Fig. 1(b)). Clearly, the marginal frequencies obtained from the sample do not agree with the true marginal frequencies; therefore, calibration is needed. Applying Algorithm 1 to solve the calibration equations as shown in Eq. (7), we obtain the following calibrated weights (using the multiplicative distance function):

$$w_j \simeq 60 \text{ for } j \in S \cap \mathcal{D}_1 \cap \mathcal{D}_2, w_j \simeq 102 \text{ for } j \in S \cap \mathcal{D}_1 \cap \bar{\mathcal{D}}_2$$
$$w_j \simeq 97 \text{ for } j \in S \cap \bar{\mathcal{D}}_1 \cap \mathcal{D}_2, w_j \simeq 140 \text{ for } j \in S \cap \bar{\mathcal{D}}_1 \cap \bar{\mathcal{D}}_2.$$

The selectivity estimate can then be computed:

$$\hat{s}_{cal} = \frac{1}{N} \sum_{j \in S} w_j y_j = \frac{1}{N} \sum_{j \in S \cap \mathcal{D}_1 \cap \mathcal{D}_2} w_j = 60 \times 9/10000 = 0.054.$$

The estimation error is $E(\hat{s}_{cal}) = |0.054 - 0.05|/0.05 = 8\%$. Compared with the error of the synopsis-based estimate $E(\hat{s}_{his}) = 260\%$ and the error of the sampling-based estimate $E(\hat{s}_{spl}) = 80\%$, this represents a significant improvement in the estimation accuracy.

### 3.4 An Alternative Algorithm

Although Newton's method works well, it is not the only option to conduct the optimization. Now we present an alternative algorithm for solving the calibration equations, which takes advantage of the intrinsic structure of the equations in (6) and does not require matrix inversion.

Since $w_j = d_j F(\mathbf{x}_j^T \lambda)$, Eq. (6) becomes

$$\frac{1}{N} \sum_{j \in S \cap \mathcal{D}_i} d_j F(\mathbf{x}_j^T \lambda) = s_i, \quad i = 1, \ldots, m+1. \tag{15}$$

Observe that the $i$-th Eq. ($2 \leq i \leq m$) can be solved for $\lambda_i$ assuming all other $\lambda_l (l \neq i)$ are known, and the first and last equations can be solved for $\lambda_1$ and $\lambda_{m+1}$ assuming all other $\lambda_l (l \neq 1, l \neq m+1)$ are known. Hence we have the algorithm shown in Algorithm 2. It is well known that such an iterative procedure converges to a proper solution [9], and in the case of multiplicative distance functions, this algorithm yields a variant of the classical iterative proportional fitting algorithm [11].

Replacing lines 6 to 11 in Algorithm 1 with Algorithm 2 results in a complete alternative estimation algorithm.

### 3.5 Distance Measures

We now study the implications of the choice of distance functions $D$. In general, different distance functions result in different calibration estimators. However, it is well known [8] that regardless of the distance functions used (as long as the functions comply with conditions (i)-(iii)), the estimates obtained using the outcome of our specific optimization problem will converge asymptotically. Therefore, for medium to large sized samples (empirically, with sample size greater than 30), the choice of distance function does not have a heavy impact on the properties of the estimator; one can expect only slight difference in the estimates produced by using different functions. The main difference between the distance functions is thus their computational efficiency as well as interpretability.

---

**Algorithm 2.** An alternative algorithm for solving the calibration equations

1: **INPUT**: $D$, $S$, $N_i(i = 1, \ldots, m+1)$, $d_j(j \in S)$, stopping threshold $\epsilon$.
2: **OUTPUT**: $\lambda$
3: $\lambda^{(0)} := \mathbf{0}$;
4: $k := 0$;
5: **repeat**
6:   Solve $\frac{1}{N} \sum_{j \in S \cap \mathcal{D}_1} d_j F(\mathbf{x}_j^T \lambda) = s_1$,
     and $\frac{1}{N} \sum_{j \in S} d_j F(\mathbf{x}_j^T \lambda) = 1$ for $\lambda_1^{(k+1)}$ and $\lambda_{m+1}^{(k+1)}$
     using values of $\lambda_l^{(k)}$ $(l = 2, \ldots, m)$;
7:   **for** $i = 2$ to $m$ **do**
8:     Solve $\sum_{j \in S \cap \mathcal{D}_i} d_j F(\mathbf{x}_j^T \lambda) = s_i$ for $\lambda_i^{(k+1)}$,
       using values of $\lambda_l^{(k)}$ $(l = 1, \ldots, m+1, l \neq i)$;
9:   **end for**
10:  $k := k + 1$;
11:  $MaxChange := \max\{|\lambda_l^{(k)} - \lambda_l^{(k-1)}|\}, l = 1, \ldots, m+1$
12: **until** $MaxChange < \epsilon$

---

For the linear function, $D_{\text{lin}}$, $D'(x) = x - 1$; therefore, the inverse function is $F(z) = z + 1$. In Algorithm 1, it is easy to verify that $\lambda$ converges at $\lambda_1 = (\sum_{j \in S} d_j \mathbf{x}_j \mathbf{x}_j^T)^{-1} (\sum_{j \in S} d_j \mathbf{x}_j - \mathbf{t}_x)$. Therefore, when the linear function is used, only one iteration is required, which makes the linear method the faster of the two distance functions considered here. A major drawback of this function is that the weights can be negative. This can lead to negative selectivity estimates. For instance, in the running example, we take a sample of size 10 from $R$, and the observed frequencies are the following: $P_1 = true \cap P_2 = true$: 2; $P_1 = true, P_2 = false$: 5; $P_1 = false \cap P_2 = true$: 3; $P_1 = false \cap P_2 = false$: 0. Solving the calibration equation, we have $w_j = -500$ for $j \in S \cap \mathcal{D}_1 \cap \mathcal{D}_2$. Therefore, the selectivity estimate $\hat{s}_{\text{cal}} = 2 \times (-500)/10000 = -0.1$. Negative weights and selectivity estimates do not have a natural interpretation and thus are undesirable. Note that, however, this usually only occurs for small-sized samples. When the sample size gets large, all estimators with distance functions satisfying conditions (i)-(iii) are asymptotically equivalent and give positive weights and selectivity estimates.

For the multiplicative function, $D_{\text{mul}}$, $D'(x) = \log x$; the inverse function is therefore $F(z) = e^z$. When the multiplicative function is used, it may require more than one iteration, but our experience indicates that it often converges after only a few iterations (typically two in our experiments). An advantage of using this function is that it always leads to positive weights because $w_j = d_j F(\mathbf{x}_j^T \lambda) = d_j \exp\{\mathbf{x}_j^T \lambda\} > 0$. We will contrast the effects of both functions on the estimation accuracy in Section 4.

## 3.6 Probabilistic Bounds on the Estimation Error

Let $\pi_{jl}$ be the probability that both $j$ and $l$ are included in the sample, and $\pi_{jj} = \pi_j$. We assume that the sampling scheme is such that the $\pi_{jl}$'s are strictly positive. Let $\beta$ be a vector satisfying the equation

$$\sum_{j \in R} d_j \mathbf{x}_j (y_j - \mathbf{x}_j^T \beta) = 0$$

and let $\Delta_{jl} = \pi_{jl} - \pi_j \pi_l$, $\epsilon_j = y_j - \mathbf{x}_j^T \beta$. We have the following result on the error bounds of the estimation error.

**Theorem 1.** *When the sample size is sufficiently large, for a given constant $\alpha \in (0, 1)$, the selectivity $s_Q$ is bounded by $(\hat{s}_{cal} - z_{\alpha/2}\sqrt{V(\hat{s}_{cal})}, \hat{s}_{cal} + z_{\alpha/2}\sqrt{V(\hat{s}_{cal})})$ with probability $1 - \alpha$, where $z_{\alpha/2}$ is the upper $\alpha/2$ point of the standard normal distribution, and $V(\hat{s}_{cal}) = \sum_{j \in R} \sum_{j \in R} (\Delta_{jl}/\pi_{jl})(w_j \epsilon_j)(w_l \epsilon_l)$.*

*Proof Sketch*: When the linear distance function is used, $w_j = d_j(1 + \mathbf{x}_j^T \lambda)$. We know from Section 3.5 that the solution of the calibration equation converges at $\lambda = (\sum_{j \in S} d_j \mathbf{x}_j \mathbf{x}_j^T)^{-1}(\sum_{j \in S} d_j \mathbf{x}_j - \mathbf{t}_x)$. Therefore, $w_j = d_j[1 + \mathbf{x}_j^T (\sum_{j \in S} d_j \mathbf{x}_j \mathbf{x}_j^T)^{-1} (\sum_{j \in S} d_j \mathbf{x}_j - \mathbf{t}_x)]$. Let $\hat{\beta}_S$ be the solution to the equation

$$\sum_{j \in S} d_j \mathbf{x}_j (y_j - \mathbf{x}_j^T \hat{\beta}_S) = 0.$$

Then the estimator $\hat{s}_{cal}$ can be written as

$$\hat{s}_{cal} = \frac{1}{N} \sum_{j \in S} w_j y_j = \hat{s}_{spl} + \frac{1}{N}(\mathbf{t}_x - \sum_{j \in S} d_j \mathbf{x}_j)^T \hat{\beta}_S,$$

which takes the form of a generalized regression estimator (GREG) [12]. Applying results on the asymptotic variance of GREG [12], we obtain the asymptotic variance of the estimator $\hat{s}_{cal}$:

$$V(\hat{s}_{cal}) = \sum_{j \in R} \sum_{j \in R} (\Delta_{jl}/\pi_{jl})(w_j \epsilon_j)(w_l \epsilon_l).$$

Since it has been shown that all estimators with distance functions satisfying conditions (i)-(iii) are asymptotically equivalent [8], all estimators have the same asymptotic variance $V(\hat{s}_{cal})$. When the sample $S$ is large enough, the Central Limit Theorem applies. Therefore, for a given constant $\alpha \in (0, 1)$, $s_Q$ is bounded by $(\hat{s}_{cal} - z_{\alpha/2}\sqrt{V(\hat{s}_{cal})}, \hat{s}_{cal} + z_{\alpha/2}\sqrt{V(\hat{s}_{cal})})$ with probability $1 - \alpha$. □

## 3.7 Utilizing Multi-attribute Synopses

In our discussion, we have assumed that we have knowledge of the selectivities $s_i$ of individual predicates $P_i$ based on single-attribute synopsis structures. In fact, the estimation procedure can be easily extended so that multi-attribute synopsis structures can also be utilized when they are present. Suppose that a multi-dimensional synopsis [13, 2] exists on a set of attributes $\mathcal{A}$. It is relatively easy to derive lower-dimensional synopses from higher-dimensional synopses, i.e., synopses on any subset(s) of $\mathcal{A}$ can be obtained from the synopsis on $\mathcal{A}$. Let $\mathcal{A}_Q$ be the set of attributes involved in query $Q$. If $\mathcal{A} \cap \mathcal{A}_Q \neq \emptyset$, the synopsis on $\mathcal{A}$ can be utilized. Let $\mathcal{U} = \mathcal{A} \cap \mathcal{A}_Q$, and let $P_\mathcal{U}$ be the conjuncts of predicates in which attributes in $\mathcal{U}$ are involved. Then the selectivity $s_\mathcal{U}$ of $P_\mathcal{U}$ can be estimated based on the synopsis on $\mathcal{U}$. We augment the auxiliary vector $\mathbf{x}_j$ by an additional element reflecting whether $j$ satisfies $P_\mathcal{U}$. Changes are also made accordingly to $\mathbf{t}_x$, with the addition of an element with value $s_\mathcal{U}$. The algorithms for solving the calibration equations presented above can then be applied in order to obtain $\hat{s}_{\text{cal}}$.

## 4 Experimental Evaluation

In this section, we report the results of an experimental evaluation of the proposed estimation procedure.

### 4.1 Experiment Setup

We compare the accuracy of HASE with that of the synopsis-based and sampling-based approaches using synthetic as well as a real data set. The real data set we use is the *Census Income* data obtained from the UCI KDD Archive [14].

- Synthetic data are used to study the properties of the HASE in a controlled manner. We generate a large number of synthetic data sets by varying the following parameters:

  **Data skew:** The data in each attribute are generated from a Zipfian distribution with parameter $z$ ranging from 0 (uniform distribution) to 3 (highly-skewed distribution). The number of distinct values in each attribute is fixed to 10.
  **Correlation:** By default, the data are independently generated for each attribute. We introduce correlation between a pair of attributes by transforming the data such that the correlation coefficient between the two attributes is approximately $\rho$. The parameter $\rho$ ranges from 0 to 1, representing an increasing degree of correlation. In particular, $\rho = 0$ corresponds to the case where there is no correlation between the two attributes; $\rho = 1$ indicates that the two attributes are fully dependent, i.e., knowing the value of one attribute enables one to perfectly predict the value of the other attribute. This is achieved by first independently generating the data for both attributes (say, $A_1$ and $A_2$) and then performing the following transformation. For each tuple with $A_1 = a_1$ and $A_2 = a_2$, we replace $a_2$ by $a_1 \times \rho + a_2 \times \sqrt{1 - \rho^2}$, suitably rounded. For three or more attributes, we create data such that the correlation coefficient between any pair of attributes is approximately $\rho$.

  The real data set *Census Income* contains weighted census data extracted from the 1994 and 1995 population surveys conducted by the U.S. Census Bureau. It has 199,523 tuples and 40 attributes representing demographic and employment related information. Out of the 40 attributes, 7 are continuous, and 33 are nominal.

- We evaluate HASE on two different query workloads. The first set of queries consist of 100 range queries where each predicate in the query takes the form of $(attribute <= constant)$ with randomly chosen $constant$. The second set of queries consist of 100 equality queries where each predicate takes the form of $(attribute = constant)$ where $constant$ is randomly chosen.
- We use simple random sampling as the sampling scheme in our experiments for both the sampling-based approach and HASE. All numbers reported are averages of 30 repetitions.
- We use the exact frequency distributions of individual attributes as the synopses.
- The absolute relative error defined in Eq. (1) is used as the error metric.

## 4.2 Results on Synthetic Data

In all experiments, similar trends are observed for both range and equality queries; we only report the results on range queries because of space limitations. We first study the effects of various parameters in the case of two attributes (i.e., only two predicates on two different attributes are involved in the query), and then show the effect of the number of attributes on the estimation accuracy. The individual selectivities are obtained based on the frequencies of values in each attribute. Since our results indicate that the number of tuples $T$ in the table does not have a significant effect on the accuracy of the estimators, only the results for $T = 100,000$ are shown here.

**Correlation.** We study the effect of the correlation between attributes on the estimation accuracy by varying the correlation coefficient $\rho$ from 0 to 1, representing an increasing degree of correlation. Fig. 2(a) presents a typical result.

When the two attributes are totally uncorrelated ($\rho = 0$), the accuracy of the synopsis-based approach is very high, with an error close to zero, better than the other two methods. This is because in such cases, the attribute-value independence assumption holds true, and the selectivity estimate for the query is indeed the product of the individual selectivities of the two predicates. The accuracy of this approach deteriorates when the degree of correlation increases and the actual relationship between the two attributes deviates further from the independence assumption.

The accuracy of the sampling-based approach actually improves when the two attributes become more correlated. The reason is as follows. When the degree of correlation increases, the number of distinct value combinations[1] in the two attributes decreases, as the data become more "concentrated". Therefore, the sample space (containing all distinct value combinations) becomes smaller, and thus sampling becomes more efficient (i.e., for a given sample rate, it is more likely to include in the sample a tuple satisfying the query).

The accuracy of HASE also increases with the degree of correlation. Since HASE utilizes sample information, the preceding argument for the sampling-based approach also applies. Besides, as the degree of correlation increases, the benefit of adjusting the weights in accordance with known single-attribute synopses becomes more evident. In the extreme case where the two attributes are

---

[1] $(a, b)$ is considered a value combination if $\exists j \in R$ such that $A_1 = a$ and $A_2 = b$.

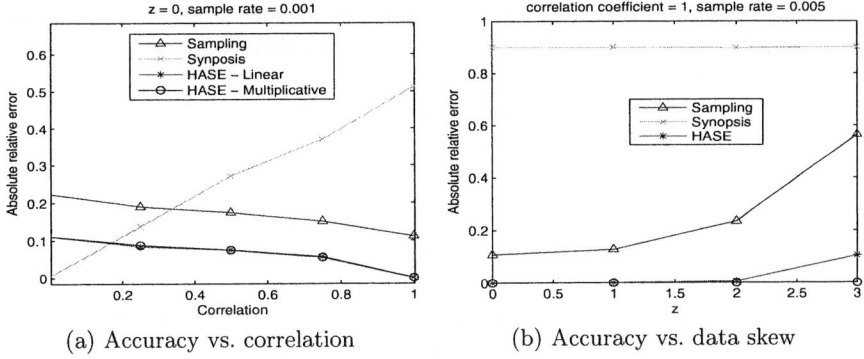

**Fig. 2.** The effects of correlation and data skew

fully dependent ($\rho = 1$), it essentially produces the exact selectivity, provided that there is at least one tuple in the sample satisfying the query. To see why this is the case, consider the following query $Q = P_1 \cap P_2 = (A_1 = a) \cap (A_2 = b)$. Full dependency dictates that if there is at least one tuple in the table satisfying this query, then for any other value $c$ ($c \neq a$) in $A_1$ and $d$ ($d \neq b$) in $A_2$, both $(A_1 = a) \cap (A_2 = d)$ and $(A_1 = c) \cap (A_2 = b)$ evaluate to false. This implies that $s = s_1 = s_2$. Therefore, if in the auxiliary vector $\mathbf{x}_j$ for tuple $j$, we have $x_{j1} = 1$ (which corresponds to $A_1 = a$), then $y_j$ (the variable indicating whether $j$ satisfies $Q$) must also be 1, and vice versa. Since we know $s_1$, we have $\frac{1}{N} \sum_{j \in S} w_j x_{j1} = s_1$ as a constraint in the optimization problem. If we can find a set of $w_j$ that satisfy this constraint, then the calibration estimator $\frac{1}{N} \sum_{j \in S} w_j y_j$ must also yield $s_1$, which means we have a perfect selectivity estimate. One exception to this analysis is that when there is no tuple $j \in S$ satisfying $Q$, we may no longer be able to produce the exact estimate. In such cases, all $y_j (j \in S)$ are 0; therefore, regardless of the weights, the calibration estimator $\frac{1}{N} \sum_{j \in S} w_j y_j$ will also be zero, which may be different from the exact selectivity.

In all cases, HASE produces significantly more accurate estimates than the sampling-based method, with a 50%-100% reduction in error. Both distance functions give very close estimates, verifying the claim that estimators using different distance functions are asymptotically equivalent. In the following discussion, we only show the results for the case of the linear distance function.

**Data skew.** We study the effect of data skew by varying the Zipfian parameter $z$ from 0 (uniform) to 3 (highly-skewed), a typical result is shown in Fig. 2(b). The errors of both HASE and the sampling approach increase as the data becomes increasingly more skewed. The reason is that when the data skew in each attribute increases, the frequencies of some value combinations decrease. As a result, when we query on those value combinations with low occurrence frequencies, it becomes increasingly possible that no sampled tuple can satisfy the query. This gives rise to more errors, because with no sampled tuple satisfying the query, the estimate has to be zero, whereas the actual selectivities are not. Note that this situation is different from the case of increasing correlation as discussed above. The main effect of increasing the skew is a decrease in the frequencies of some value combinations, not necessarily reducing the number of value combinations present in the table. Increasing correlation, on the other hand, generally results in a reduction in the number of value combinations. Therefore, increasing skew and increasing correlation have different effects on the accuracy of HASE as well as the sampling-based approach.

Another interesting observation from Fig. 2(b) is that the accuracy of the synopsis-based approach remains virtually the same regardless of the data skew. The reason is as follows. Assuming independence between attributes, the synopsis-based approach estimates the selectivity by $\hat{s}_{his} = s_1 * s_2$. In Fig. 2(b), the two attributes are fully dependent, which implies that the actual selectivity $s = s_1 = s_2$. Thus, $E(\hat{s}_{his}) = (s - s_1 s_2)/s_1 = 1 - s_1$. The average error over a large number of (uniformly) randomly selected equality queries is therefore $1 - avg(s_1)$. In our case, since there are 10 distinct values in each attribute, $avg(s_1) = 1/10 = 0.1$. the average error of the estimate is thus $1 - 0.1 = 0.9$. Therefore, the accuracy of this approach does not change with data skew in this case.

**Sample rate.** Fig. 3(a) shows a typical result on how the three approaches behave as we increase the sample rate. The number of attributes in the data set is 2. The accuracy of the synopsis-based approach remains unchanged across the range of sample rates, because it does not depend on sampling. The accuracy of both HASE and the sampling-based approach improves with increasing sample rate, as one would expect. For all sample rates, HASE outperforms both the synopsis-based and the sampling-based approaches. It is also worth noting that using HASE, we can achieve the same level of accuracy with a much smaller sample rate than that required by the sampling-based approach. For example, in Fig. 3(a), the sampling-based approach has an error of 0.07 when the sample rate is 0.005. HASE achieves approximately the same level of accuracy with a sample rate of 0.001, resulting in a reduction by a factor of 5. This translates into more significant I/O savings because of the non-linear relationship between the I/O cost and the sample rate as discussed in Section 2.3.

**Number of attributes.** We vary the number of attributes involved in the query from 2 to 5 to study the impact of the number of attributes on the estimation accuracy. A typical result is shown in Fig. 3(b). Clearly, the accuracy of all three

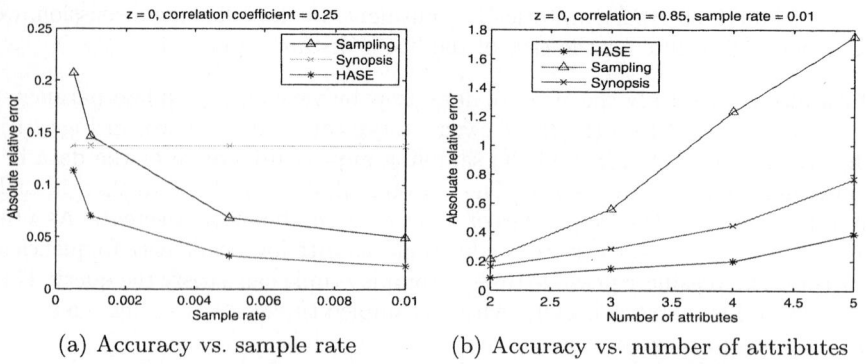

(a) Accuracy vs. sample rate    (b) Accuracy vs. number of attributes

**Fig. 3.** The effects of the sample rate and the number of attributes

approaches decreases as the number of attributes increases. This is not surprising, because having more attributes would introduce more sources of errors. A space of higher dimensionality requires a much larger sample to cover a fixed portion of the space, in comparison with a space of lower dimensionality. Note from Fig. 3(b), however, that HASE outperforms the other two approaches for all number of attributes, and has a lower rate of decrease in accuracy.

### 4.3 Results on Real Data

Since the *Census Income* data has 40 attributes, there are $40 \times 39 = 1560$ attribute pairs. We randomly choose 100 attribute pairs and record the accuracy of the three approaches as the sample rate increases. The result is shown in Fig. 4. The trends are similar to those for the synthetic data, with HASE significantly outperforming both the synopsis-based and the sampling-based approaches. The error response to the number of attributes is also similar to that for the synthetic data, and is therefore omitted here.

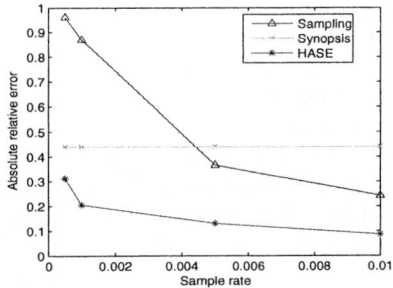

**Fig. 4.** Accuracy vs. sample rate on the *Census Income* data

## 5 Related Work

The issue of selectivity estimation has been extensively studied in the literature and a large variety of methods have been proposed [15, 1, 16, 17].

Histograms are probably the most widely used form of synopses in commercial database systems (e.g., DB2 UDB, Oracle, SQL Server, etc.). See [18] for an excellent survey on this topic. Aside from histograms, other types of synopses have also been proposed in the literature, such as wavelet-based synopses (e.g., [16]) and parametric synopses (e.g., [19]).

Markl et al. [20] propose a method to consistently utilize various multi-dimensional synopsis structures for selectivity estimation of conjunctive predicates. This work is close in spirit to ours in that both of them address the issue of consistent utilization of various sources of information for selectivity estimation. However, their focus is on reconciling the estimates obtained from different synopsis structures, whereas we attack the problem of utilizing both synopses and sample information.

Olken [3] provides a survey of techniques on sampling from databases. Lipton et al. [15] propose an *adaptive sampling* (a.k.a. *sequential sampling*) approach to selectivity estimation. Haas and Swami [21] improve the sequential sampling approach by establishing tighter termination conditions. There has also been work on estimating the number of distinct values via sampling [22, 23, 24]. Recently, Haas et al. [4] and Chaudhuri et al. [7] address the efficiency of sampling and propose techniques to utilize page-level sampling in conjunction with tuple-level sampling. Techniques have also been developed to use sampling to construct synopsis structures [25, 24, 7]. Note that sampling is used here only for fast construction of data synopses, which are then used for selectivity estimation; they do not consider the issue of direct utilization of *both* sampling and synopses for selectivity estimation.

## 6 Conclusions and Future Work

Existing work on selectivity estimation can be classified as either synopsis-based or sampling-based, depending on whether the basis for estimation is the synopsis structures stored in the database or sample information. The presence of both sources of information presents a unique challenge, as it is nontrivial to make consistent use of them in order to obtain better estimation. To the best of our knowledge, we are the first to tackle this challenge. We proposed HASE, a new estimation procedure based on generalized raking, and the problem is formulated as a constrained optimization problem. We then presented two algorithms to solve it. We also discussed the implications of different distance functions, and provided asymptotic error bounds on the selectivity estimate thus obtained. The experiments demonstrated the effectiveness of the proposed approach.

For future work, we would like to consider extending HASE to handle the selectivity estimation of more complex queries, such as joins and aggregations. We also plan to extend HASE to handle the case where multi-attribute synopses (e.g., multi-dimensional histograms) are available. It would also be interesting to study in our framework how to best divide the efforts between constructing histograms and sampling for a given query workload.

## Acknowledgment

The authors would like to thank our friend and mentor Prof. Kenneth C. Sevcik for his comments and encouragement during the course of this work. We miss him dearly.

## Trademarks

IBM, DB2, DB2 Universal Database are trademarks or registered trademarks of International Business Machines Corporation in the United States, other countries, or both. Other company, product, or service names may be trademarks or service marks of others.

# References

1. Poosala, V., Ioannidis, Y.E., Haas, P.J., Shekita, E.J.: Improved histograms for selectivity estimation of range predicates. In: SIGMOD. (1996) 294–305
2. Poosala, V., Ioannidis, Y.E.: Selectivity estimation without the attribute value independence assumption. In: VLDB. (1997) 486–495
3. Olken, F.: Random sampling from databases. PhD thesis, University of California, Berkeley, CA (1993)
4. Haas, P.J., König, C.: A bi-level Bernoulli scheme for database sampling. In: SIGMOD Conference. (2004) 275–286
5. Deshpande, A., Garofalakis, M.N., Rastogi, R.: Independence is good: Dependency-based histogram synopses for high-dimensional data. In: SIGMOD Conference. (2001)
6. Horvitz, D.G., Thompson, D.J.: A generalization of sampling without replacement from a finite universe. Journal of the American Statistical Association **47** (1952) 663–685
7. Chaudhuri, S., Das, G., Srivastava, U.: Effective use of block-level sampling in statistics estimation. In: SIGMOD Conference. (2004) 287–298
8. Deville, J.C., Särndal, C.E.: Calibration estimators in survey sampling. Journal of the American Statistical Association **87** (1992) 376–382
9. Deville, J.C., Särndal, C.E., Sautory, O.: Generalized raking procedures in survey sampling. Journal of the American Statistical Association **88** (1993) 1013–1020
10. Bertsekas, D.P.: Constrained Optimization and Lagrange Multiplier Methods. Athena Scientific (1996)
11. Deming, W.E., Stephan, F.F.: On a least squares adjustment of a sampled frequency table when the expected marginal totals are known. Annals of Mathematical Statistics **11** (1940) 427–444
12. Särndal, C.E., Swensson, B., Wretman, J.: Model Assisted Survey Sampling. Springer-Verlag, New York (1992)
13. Muralikrishna, M., DeWitt, D.J.: Equi-depth histograms for estimating selectivity factors for multi-dimensional queries. In: SIGMOD. (1988) 28–36
14. Hettich, S., Bay, S.D.: The UCI KDD Archive. Irvine, CA: University of California, Department of Information and Computer Science. (1999)
15. Lipton, R.J., Naughton, J.F.: Query size estimation by adaptive sampling. In: PODS. (1990) 40–46
16. Matias, Y., Vitter, J.S., Wang, M.: Wavelet-based histograms for selectivity estimation. In: SIGMOD. (1998) 448–459
17. Aboulnaga, A., Chaudhuri, S.: Self-tuning histograms: building histograms without looking at data. In: SIGMOD, ACM Press (1999) 181–192
18. Ioannidis, Y.E.: The history of histograms (abridged). In: VLDB. (2003) 19–30
19. Fedorowicz, J.: Database evaluation using multiple regression techniques. In: SIGMOD. (1984) 70–76
20. Markl, V., Megiddo, N., Kutsch, M., Tran, T.M., Haas, P.J., Srivastava, U.: Consistently estimating the selectivity of conjuncts of predicates. In: VLDB. (2005) 373–384
21. Haas, P.J., Swami, A.N.: Sequential sampling procedures for query size estimation. In: SIGMOD. (1992) 341–350
22. Naughton, J.F., Seshadri, S.: On estimating the size of projections. In: ICDT. Volume 470. (1990) 499–513
23. Haas, P.J., Naughton, J.F., Seshadri, S., Stokes, L.: Sampling-based estimation of the number of distinct values of an attribute. In: VLDB. (1995) 311–322
24. Chaudhuri, S., Motwani, R., Narasayya, V.R.: Random sampling for histogram construction: How much is enough? In: SIGMOD. (1998) 436–447
25. Gibbons, P.B., Matias, Y., Poosala, V.: Fast incremental maintenance of approximate histograms. In: VLDB. (1997) 466–475

# On High Dimensional Skylines

Chee-Yong Chan, H.V. Jagadish, Kian-Lee Tan,
Anthony K.H. Tung, and Zhenjie Zhang

National University of Singapore & University of Michigan
{chancy, tankl, atung, zhangzh2}@comp.nus.edu.sg,
jag@eecs.umich.edu

**Abstract.** In many decision-making applications, the skyline query is frequently used to find a set of dominating data points (called skyline points) in a multi-dimensional dataset. In a high-dimensional space skyline points no longer offer any interesting insights as there are too many of them. In this paper, we introduce a novel metric, called *skyline frequency* that compares and ranks the interestingness of data points based on how often they are returned in the skyline when different number of dimensions (i.e., subspaces) are considered. Intuitively, a point with a high skyline frequency is more interesting as it can be dominated on fewer combinations of the dimensions. Thus, the problem becomes one of finding top-k frequent skyline points. But the algorithms thus far proposed for skyline computation typically do not scale well with dimensionality. Moreover, frequent skyline computation requires that skylines be computed for each of an exponential number of subsets of the dimensions. We present efficient approximate algorithms to address these twin difficulties. Our extensive performance study shows that our approximate algorithm can run fast and compute the correct result on large data sets in high-dimensional spaces.

## 1 Introduction

Consider a tourist who is looking for hotels, in some city, that are cheap and close to the beach. For this skyline query, a hotel $H$ is in the answer set (i.e., the skyline) if there does not exist any hotel in that city that dominates $H$; i.e., that is both cheaper as well as closer to the beach than $H$. Our tourist can then tradeoff price with distance from the beach from among the points in this answer set (called *skyline points*). Skyline queries are useful as they define an interesting subset of data points with respect to the dimensions considered, and the problem of efficiently computing skylines has attracted a lot of recent interest (e.g., [2, 3, 13, 9, 18]).

A major drawback of skylines is that, in data sets with many dimensions, the number of skyline points becomes large and no longer offer any interesting insights. The reason is that as the number of dimensions increases, for any point $p$, it is more likely there exists another point $q$ where $p$ and $q$ are better than each other over different subsets of dimensions. If our tourist, from the example in the preceding paragraph, cared not just about price and distance to beach, but also about the size of room, the star rating, the friendliness of staff, the availability of restaurants etc., then most hotels in the city may have to be included in the skyline answer set since for each hotel there may be no one hotel that beats it on all criteria, even if it beats it on many. Correlations between

Table 1. Top-10 frequent skyline points in NBA data set

| Top-10 Frequent Skyline Point, p | | Dominating Frequency |
|---|---|---|
| Player Name | Season | d(p) |
| Wilt Chamberlain | 1961 | 1791 |
| Michael Jordan | 1986 | 2266 |
| Michael Jordan | 1987 | 3162 |
| George Mcginnis | 1974 | 4468 |
| Michael Jordan | 1988 | 5854 |
| Bob Mcadoo | 1974 | 6472 |
| Julius Erving | 1975 | 6781 |
| Charles Barkley | 1987 | 8578 |
| Kobe Bryant | 2002 | 9271 |
| Kareem Abdul-Jabbar | 1975 | 9400 |

dimensions ameliorates this problem somewhat, but does not eliminate it. For example, for the NBA statistics data set [1], which is fairly correlated, a skyline query with respect to all 17 dimensions returns over 1000 points.

To deal with this dimensionality curse, one possibility is to reduce the number of dimensions considered. However, which dimensions to retain is not easy to determine, and at the very least requires intimate knowledge of the application domain. In fact, dimensionality reduction of this sort is a desirable goal in many data management and data mining scenarios, and there has been a great deal of effort expended on trying to do this well, with only limited success. Moreover, choosing different subsets of attributes will result in different points being found in the skyline.

In this paper, we introduce a novel metric, called *skyline frequency*, to compare and rank the interestingness of data points based on how often they are returned in the skyline when different subsets of dimensions are considered. Given a set of n-dimensional data points, the skyline frequency of a data point is determined by the $2^n - 1$ distinct skyline queries, one for each possible non-empty subset of the attributes. Intuitively, a point with a high skyline frequency is more interesting since it can be dominated on fewer combinations of the dimensions. Thus, the problem becomes one of finding top-k frequent skyline points.

Referring once more to the 17-dimension NBA statistics data set that records the performance of all players who have played in the NBA from 1946 to 2003. Each dimension represents a certain "skill", e.g., number of 3-pointers, number of rebounds, number of blocks, number of fouls, and so on. There are over 17000 tuples, each reflecting a player's "performance" for a certain year. Note that every player has a tuple for every year he played, so it is possible to have several tuples for one player with different year numbers, like "Michael Jordan in 1986" and "Michael Jordan in 1999". Table 1 lists the top-10 frequent skyline points (represented by a player and season). The skyline frequency of each point $p$ is given by $2^{17} - d(p) - 1$; where $d(p)$, which is the dominating frequency, represents the number of subspaces for which $p$ is dominated by some other point. Readers who follow basketball will agree that this is a very

**Table 2.** Bottom-10 frequent skyline points in NBA data set

| Bottom-10 Frequent Skyline Point, p | | Dominating Frequency |
|---|---|---|
| Player Name | Season | d(p) |
| Terrell Brandon | 2000 | 130559 |
| John Starks | 1991 | 130304 |
| Allen Leavell | 1982 | 130303 |
| Rich Kelley | 1981 | 130047 |
| Rodney Mccray | 1984 | 129823 |
| Reggie Theus | 1990 | 129727 |
| Jamaal Wilkes | 1979 | 129535 |
| John Williams | 1988 | 129151 |
| Purvis Short | 1983 | 129151 |
| Rasheed Wallace | 1999 | 128863 |

reasonable set of top basketball players of all time. Clearly, our top-k frequent skyline query has the notion of picking "the best of the best", and is superior to the simpler skyline points (which in this example will mark as equally interesting all 1051 skyline points!).

To further examine this notion of skyline frequency, we selected the least skyline frequency entries among the 1051 entries in the full skyline. The results are shown in Table 2. These players, particularly in the years specified, can hardly be considered all-time greats. Of course, each is a talented player, as one would expect given that these were all in the top 1051 chosen from among all NBA players by the ordinary skyline algorithm.

Unfortunately, skyline computations are not cheap. Given a data set with $n$ dimensions, skyline frequency computation requires $2^n - 1$ skyline queries to be executed. To address this problem, we propose an efficient approximate algorithm that is based on counting the number of dominating subspaces (i.e., the number of subspaces in which a point is not a skyline point). Our scheme is tunable in that we can tradeoff the accuracy of the top-k answers for speed. We have implemented our scheme, and our extensive performance study shows that our method with approximate counting can run fast in very high dimensional data set without sacrificing much on the accuracy.

We make two key contributions in this paper:

- We introduce skyline frequency as a novel and meaningful measure for comparing and ranking skylines.
- We present efficient approximate algorithms for computing *top-k frequent skylines*, which are the top-k data points whose skyline frequencies are the highest.

The rest of this paper is organized as follows. In Section 2 we formally define the key concepts, including frequent skylines and maximal dominating subspaces. Related work is presented in Section 3. In Section 4, we present our proposed algorithms for computing frequent skylines efficiently. We report on the results of an experimental evaluation in Section 5. Finally, we conclude with a discussion of our findings in Section 6. Due to space limitation, proofs of results are omitted.

## 2 Preliminaries

Given a space $S$ defined by a set of $n$ dimensions $\{d_1, d_2, \ldots, d_n\}$ and a data set $D$ on $S$, a point $p \in D$ can be represented as $p = (p_1, p_2, \ldots, p_n)$ where every $p_i$ is a value on dimension $d_i$. Each non-empty subset of $S$ is referred to as a *subspace*. A point $p \in D$ is said to *dominate* another point $q \in D$ on subspace $S' \subseteq S$ if (1) on every dimension $d_i \in S'$, $p_i \leq q_i$; and (2) on at least one dimension $d_j \in S'$, $p_j < q_j$. The *skyline of a space* $S' \subseteq S$ is a set of points $D' \subseteq D$ which can not be dominated by any other point on space $S'$. That is, $D' = \{p \in D : \nexists q \in D, q \text{ dominates p on space } S'\}$. The points in $D'$ are called *skyline points* on space $S'$.

Based on the definition of skyline points on a subspace, we define the *skyline frequency* of a point $p \in D$, denoted by $f(p)$, as the number of subspaces in which $p$ is a skyline point. Given $S$ and $D$, the *top-k frequent skyline points* are the $k$ points in $D$ that no other point in $D$ can have larger skyline frequency than them. A *top-k frequent skyline query* is a query that computes top-k skyline points for a given data set $D$ and space $S$. A subspace $S' \subseteq S$ is said to be a *dominating subspace* for a data point $p$ if there exists another data point that dominates $p$ on subspace $S'$. We define the *dominating frequency* of $p$, denoted by $d(p)$, as the number of dominating subspaces for $p$. It is easy to see that the skyline frequency $f(p) = 2^n - d(p) - 1$. So, the top-$k$ skyline frequency query can be computed by finding the $k$ points with the smallest dominating frequencies.

Let $DS(q, p)$ denote the set of all subspaces for which a point $q$ dominates another point $p$. We call $DS(q, p)$ the set of *dominating subspaces* of $q$ over $p$. This set can frequently be quite large, and so is unwieldy to enumerate explicitly. Just as a rectangle in cartesian geometry can be represented succinctly by a pair of corner points, we show below in Lemma 1 that the set $DS(q, p)$ can be described succinctly by a pair of subspaces $(U, V)$ where (1) $U \subseteq S$ is the set of dimensions such that $q_i < p_i$ on every dimension $d_i \in U$; and (2) $V \subseteq S$ is the set of dimensions such that $q_i = p_i$ on every dimension $d_i \in V$. It follows that $DS(p, q) = (S - U - V, V)$.

**Lemma 1.** *Let $DS(q, p) = (U, V)$. Then $S' \in DS(q, p)$ if and only if $\exists U' \subseteq U$, $V' \subseteq V$, such that $S' = U' \cup V'$, and $U' \neq \emptyset$.*

It is easy to verify that $|DS(q, p)| = (2^{|U|} - 1)2^{|V|}$.

Given two collections of subspaces $S_1, S_2 \subseteq S$, we say that $S_1$ *covers* $S_2$ if $S_1 \supseteq S_2$. The following result provides a very simple way to determine if $DS(q, p)$ covers $DS(r, p)$ given three points $p$, $q$, and $r$.

**Lemma 2.** *Let $DS(q, p) = (U_q, V_q)$ and $DS(r, p) = (U_r, V_r)$, where $U_q \neq \emptyset$ and $U_r \neq \emptyset$. Then $DS(q, p)$ covers $DS(r, p)$ if and only if (1) $U_r \cup V_r \subseteq U_q \cup V_q$ and (2) $U_r \subseteq U_q$.*

$DS(q, p)$ is said to be a *maximal dominating subspace set* for a point $p$ if there does not exist another point $r$ such that $DS(r, p)$ covers $DS(q, p)$. Therefore, $d(p) = |\bigcup_{M_i \in \mathcal{M}} M_i|$, where $\mathcal{M} = \{DS(q,p) \mid q \in S, DS(q,p)$ is a maximal dominating subspace set for $p\}$.

## 3 Related Work

Computing the skyline of a set of points is also known as the maximum vector problem [10]. Early works on solving the maximum vector problem typically assume that the points fit into the main memory. Algorithms devised include divide-and-conquer paradigm [10], parallel algorithms [17] and those that are specifically designed to target at 2 or very large number of dimensions [12]. Other related problems include top k [4], nearest neighbor search [16], convex hull [16], and multi-objective optimization [14]. These related problems and their relationship to skyline queries have been discussed in [3].

Börzsönyi et al. [3] first introduced the skyline operator into relational database systems by extending the SQL SELECT statement with an optional SKYLINE OF clause. A large number of algorithms have been developed to compute skyline queries. These can be categorized into non-index-based (e.g., *block nested loop* [3], *Sort-Filter-Skyline* [6,7], *divide and conquer* [3]), and index-based (e.g., *B-tree* [3], *bitmap* [18], *index* [18], *nearest neighbor* [9], *BBS* [13]). As expected, the non-index-based strategies are typically inferior to the index-based strategies. It also turns out the index-based schemes can progressively return answers without having to scan the entire data input. The nearest neighbour scheme, which applies the divide and conquer framework on datasets indexed by R-trees, was shown to be superior over earlier schemes in terms of overall performance [9]. There have also been work on processing skyline queries over distributed sources [2], over streaming data [11], and for data with partially-ordered domains [5]. All these algorithms are developed for computing skylines for a specific subspace.

The recent papers on skyline computation in subspaces [19, 15] is more closely related to our work. Yuan et al. [19] proposed two methods to compute skylines in all the subspaces by traversing the lattice of subspaces either in a top-down or bottom-up manner. In the bottom-up approach, the skylines in a subspace are partly derived by merging the skylines from its "child" subspaces at the lower level. In the top-down approach, the sharing-partition-and-merge and sharing-parent property of the DC algorithm [3] is exploited to recursively enumerate the subspaces and compute their skylines from the top to bottom level, which turns out to be much more efficient than the bottom-up approach. Since we can get the skyline frequencies if the skylines in every subspace is available, we compare their top-down approach with our top-k method in the performance study. Another study on computing skylines in subspaces is by Pei et al. [15]. They introduced a new concept called skyline group, every entry of which contains the skyline points sharing the same values in a corresponding subspace collection. They also proposed an algorithm *skyey*, which visits all the subspaces along an enumeration tree, finds the skylines by sorting and creates a new skyline group if some new skyline points are inserted into an old group. The skyline groups found are maintained in a quotient cube structure for queries on subspace skyline. Their study tries to answer where and why a point is part of skyline without any accompanying coincident points. However, their scheme can not help to solve the skyline frequency problem since a point can be in exponential number of skyline groups in high dimensional space.

The approximate counting technique used in our work is related to the problem of counting the number of assignments that satisfies a given disjunctive normal form(DNF). In [8], Karp et. al. proposed a monte-carlo algorithm which takes $2n \ln \frac{2}{\delta} / \epsilon^2$

samples to give an approximate count of the assignments, whose error rate is smaller than $\epsilon$ with probability $1 - \delta$. Since the sample size is irrelevant to the size of the sets, this method is much more efficient than the conventional iteration method, especially when the size of valid assignment set is much larger than sample number.

## 4 Top-k Frequent Skyline Computation

The most straightforward approach to compute top-k frequent skylines is the following two-phase approach. First, compute the skyline points for each subspace by using an existing algorithm (e.g., skycube algorithm [19]). Next, compute the skyline frequency of each point $p$ by summing up the number of subspaces for which $p$ is a skyline. We called this technique a *subspace-based* approach since it essentially enumerates each subspace to compute skylines. A number of recent approaches have been proposed for computing precise skylines for the complete collection of subspaces [19, 15].

However, computing skylines over all subspaces can be costly. In this paper, we propose a novel approach to compute top-k frequent skylines based on computing *maximal dominating subspace sets*. This approach comprises of two key steps. The first step computes the maximal dominating subspace sets for each data point. Based on these, the second step then computes each point's dominating frequency either precisely or approximately. Thus, our approach actually computes the top-k skyline frequencies by computing the bottom-k dominating frequencies.

In the rest of this section, we first give an overview of our approach in Section 4.1, and then present the details of the two phases, maximal dominating subspace set computation and dominating subspace counting, in Sections 4.2 and 4.3, respectively. Finally, we present two optimization techniques to improve the efficiency of our approach in Section 4.4.

### 4.1 Overview

The intuition for our approach is based on the result in Section 2 that each dominating subspace of a point $p$ is covered by some maximal dominating subspace set of $p$. Since the dominating frequency of a point is the dual of its skyline frequency, we can compute the skyline frequency of a point $p$ by computing its dominating frequency in two stages. First, find all the maximal dominating subspace sets of $p$, and then count the number of subspaces covered by them. The top-$k$ frequent skyline points is then obtained by taking the bottom-$k$ points with the lowest dominating frequencies.

The main procedure of our approach is shown in Algorithm 1 which takes a set of data points $D$, a set of dimensions $S$, and an integer value $k$ as inputs and computes the top-$k$ frequent skylines in $D$ w.r.t. $S$. To avoid the complexity of explicitly sorting the points by their dominating frequencies, we maintain a frequency threshold (denoted by $\theta$) that keeps track of the $k^{th}$ smallest dominating frequency among all the processed points. This frequency threshold is initialized in step 1 to $2^{|S|}-1$, which is the maximum possible dominating frequency value. The top-$k$ frequent skylines are maintained in a set $R$ which is initialized to empty in step 2. For each data point $p \in D$ (steps 3-11), the procedure ComputeMaxSubspaceSets is first invoked to compute the set $\mathcal{M}$ of all the maximal dominating subspace sets of point $p$ by comparing every other point with

## Algorithm 1. Top-k Frequent Skyline Algorithm $(D, S, k)$

1: initialize frequency threshold $\theta = 2^{|S|} - 1$
2: initialize $R$, the set of top-$k$ frequent skylines, to be empty
3: **for** every point $p \in D$ **do**
4:     $\mathcal{M}$ = **ComputeMaxSubspaceSets** $(D, S, p, k, \theta, |R|)$
5:     $d(p)$ = **CountDominatingSubspaces** $(\mathcal{M})$
6:     **if** $(|R| < k)$ **or** $(d(p) < \theta)$ **then**
7:         remove the point with the highest dominating frequency in $R$ if $|R| = k$
8:         insert $p$ into $R$
9:         update $\theta$ to be the highest dominating frequency in $R$
10:     **end if**
11: **end for**
12: **return** $R$

point $p$ on all the dimensions. Next, the procedure `CountDominatingSubspaces` is called to compute the dominating frequency $d(p)$ of $p$, which is the total number of subspaces in $S$ that are covered by the maximal dominating subspace sets in $\mathcal{M}$. If $R$ has fewer than $k$ skylines or if the dominating frequency of $p$ (i.e., $d(p)$) is smaller than the frequency threshold $\theta$, then $p$ is inserted into $R$ and the value of $\theta$ updated. Note that if $R$ already has $k$ skylines before a new point is to be inserted, than a point $q$ in $R$ with the largest dominating frequency (i.e., $d(q) = \theta$) is removed from $R$.

*Example 1.* Consider the computation of the top-2 frequent skylines for a set of 4-dimensional data points $D = \{a, b, c, e\}$ shown below:

| Point | $d_1$ | $d_2$ | $d_3$ | $d_4$ |
|---|---|---|---|---|
| $a$ | 2 | 3 | 4 | 5 |
| $b$ | 1 | 5 | 2 | 6 |
| $c$ | 3 | 4 | 4 | 4 |
| $e$ | 4 | 3 | 4 | 3 |

To compute the set of maximal dominating subspace sets of point $a$, we need to determine $DS(q, a)$ for each $q \in D - \{a\}$. We have $DS(b, a) = (\{d_1, d_3\}, \emptyset)$, $DS(c, a) = (\{d_4\}, \{d_3\})$, and $DS(e, a) = (\{d_4\}, \{d_2, d_3\})$. By Lemma 2, $DS(e, a)$ covers $DS(c, a)$, and so $DS(c, a)$ is not a maximal dominating subspace set of $a$. However, since neither $DS(b, a)$ nor $DS(e, a)$ covers each other, they are both maximal dominating subspace sets of $a$. The number of dominating subspaces covered by each of them is given by: $|DS(b, a)| = 3$ and $|DS(e, a)| = 4$. Since there are no common dominating subspaces that are covered by both $DS(b, a)$ and $DS(e, a)$, the number of dominating subspaces of $a$ is $d(a) = |DS(b, a)| + |DS(e, a)| = 7$. Similarly, we have $d(b) = 3$, $d(c) = 11$, and $d(e) = 5$. Thus, the top-2 frequent skylines are $b$ and $e$. □

### 4.2 Maximal Dominating Subspace Computation

Algorithm 2 shows the `ComputeMaxSubspaceSets` procedure to compute the collection of maximal dominating subspace sets of an input point $p \in D$ (w.r.t. a set of

**Algorithm 2.** ComputeMaxSubspaceSets $(D, S, p, k, \theta, r)$

1: initialize $\mathcal{M}$, the set of maximal dominating subspace sets of $p$, to be empty
2: **for** every point $q$ in $D - \{p\}$ **do**
3:    let $U \subseteq S$ such that on every dimension $d_i \in U$, $q_i < p_i$
4:    let $V \subseteq S$ such that on every dimension $d_i \in V$, $q_i = p_i$
5:    **if** $(r = k)$ **and** $((2^{|U|} - 1)2^{|V|} \geq \theta)$ **then**
6:      return $\{(U, V)\}$
7:    **end if**
8:    initialize isMaximal = *true*
9:    **for** every maximal dominating subspace set $(P, Q) \in \mathcal{M}$ **do**
10:      **if** $(U \cup V \subseteq P \cup Q)$ **and** $(U \subseteq P)$ **then**
11:        isMaximal = *false*
12:        break out of for loop
13:      **else if** $(P \cup Q \subseteq U \cup V)$ **and** $(P \subseteq U)$ **then**
14:        remove $(P, Q)$ from $\mathcal{M}$
15:      **end if**
16:    **end for**
17:    **if** isMaximal **then**
18:      insert $(U, V)$ into $\mathcal{M}$
19:    **end if**
20: **end for**
21: **return** $\mathcal{M}$

dimensions $S$). The remaining three input parameters ($k$, $\theta$, and $r$), where $\theta$ is the highest dominating frequency among all the $r$ frequent skylines processed so far, are used to optimize the computation when $p$ is determined to be not among the top-$k$ frequent skylines. The output collection of maximal dominating subspace sets is maintained in a set $M$ which is initialized to be empty in step 1. Each maximal dominating subspace set in $M$ is represented in the form of a subspace pair; i.e., $M = \{(U_1, V_2), (U_2, V_2), \cdots, (U_n, V_n)\}$, where each $(U_i, V_i)$ corresponds to $DS(q_i, p)$ for some point $q_i \in D$.

To compute the maximal dominating subspace sets of $p$, the algorithm compares $p$ against each other point $q$ in $D$ (steps 2-20). First, $DS(q, p) = (U, V)$ is determined in steps 3-4. Steps 5-7 is an optimization (to be explained at the end of the discussion) that can be ignored for now. Steps 8-19 compare $(U, V)$ against each of the maximal dominating subspace sets computed so far in $\mathcal{M}$ to determine if $(U, V)$ is also a maximal dominating subspace set and update $\mathcal{M}$ accordingly. Specifically, if there is some subspace set $(P, Q) \in \mathcal{M}$ that covers $(U, V)$, then by Lemma 2, we can conclude that $(U, V)$ is not a maximal dominating subspace set (steps 11-12). On the other hand, if subspace set $(P, Q) \in \mathcal{M}$ is covered by $(U, V)$, then $(P, Q)$ is not a maximal dominating subspace set and is removed from $\mathcal{M}$ (step 14). Finally, if $(U, V)$ is not covered by any of the maximal dominating subspace sets in $\mathcal{M}$, then $(U, V)$ is a maximal dominating subspace set and it is added to $\mathcal{M}$ (step 18).

We now explain the optimization performed in steps 5-7 that makes use of the additional input parameters $k$, $\theta$, and $r$. The main idea is to avoid computing the precise collection of maximal dominating subspace sets of $p$ if $p$ is determined to be not among

---
**Algorithm 3.** CountDominatingSubspaces ($\mathcal{M}$)
---
1: let $\mathcal{M} = \{M_1, M_2, \cdots, M_n\}$
2: initialize counter $C = 0$
3: **for** $i = 1$ to $n$ **do**
4:     **for** every dominating subspace $(P, Q)$ that is covered by $M_i$ **do**
5:         **if** $(P, Q)$ is not covered by any $M_j, j \in [1, i)$ **then**
6:             $C = C + 1$
7:         **end if**
8:     **end for**
9: **end for**
10: **return** $C$
---

the top-$k$ frequent skylines. Specifically, if there are already $k$ intermediate frequent skylines (i.e., $r = k$) and $|DS(q, p)|$, which is given by $(2^{|U|} - 1)2^{|V|}$, already exceeds $\theta$, then $p$ clearly can not be among the top-$k$ frequent skylines. In this case, it is not necessary to know the precise maximal dominating subspace sets of $p$; instead, the algorithm simply returns the single subspace set $(U, V)$ (in step 6) since this is sufficient for the main algorithm to conclude that $p$ is not a top-$k$ frequent skyline. With this optimization, ComputeMaxSubspaceSets computes the precise collection of maximal dominating subspace sets of $p$ only when $p$ could potentially be a top-$k$ frequent skyline.

Our implementation of ComputeMaxSubspaceSets uses a bitmap representation for subspaces to enable efficient manipulations. If $S$ has $n$ dimensions, then a subspace of $S$ is represented by a $n$-bit bitmap with the $i^{th}$ bit corresponding to dimension $d_i$ such that a bit is set to 1 iff its corresponding dimension is in the subspace. As an example, in an 8-dimensional space $S$, the subspace $\{d_1, d_3, d_5, d_6\}$ is represented by the bitmap "10101100". Given two bitmaps $B_1$ and $B_2$ (corresponding to subspaces $S_1$ and $S_2$, respectively), $S_1$ covers $S_2$ if and only if the logical-AND of $B_1$ and $B_2$ is equal to $B_1$. Furthermore, by exploiting arithmetic bit-operation, $|DS(U, V)|$ for a given subspace set $(U, V)$ can be efficiently computed with a left shift operation in $O(1)$ time.

### 4.3 Dominating Subspace Counting

In this section, we discuss how to derive the number of dominating subspaces for a point $p$ based on the collection $\mathcal{M}$ of maximal dominating subspace sets for $p$ returned by ComputeMaxSubspaceSets for $p$. Since there is usually more than one maximal dominating subspace set in $\mathcal{M}$ and the subspaces covered by them generally overlap, the challenge is to efficiently compute the number of dominating subspace sets taking into account of the overlapping covered subspaces.

As an example, consider $\mathcal{M} = \{M_1, M_2\}$, where $M_1 = (\{d_1, d_2\}, \{d_3\})$ and $M_2 = (\{d_1, d_3\}, \{d_4\})$. Note that there are a total of eight dominating subspaces covered by $\mathcal{M}$: $\{d_2\}, \{d_2, d_3\}, \{d_1, d_2\}, \{d_1, d_2, d_3\}, \{d_1\}, \{d_1, d_3\}, \{d_1, d_4\}$ and $\{d_1, d_3, d_4\}$. Among these, the first six are covered by $M_1$ while the last four are covered by $M_2$; hence, there are two dominating subspaces (i.e., $\{d_1\}$ and $\{d_1, d_3\}$) that are covered by both $M_1$ and $M_2$.

One direct approach to derive the number of dominating subspaces is to apply the *Inclusion-Exclusion* principle to obtain the union of all the subspaces covered by the maximal dominating subspaces. However, this method is non-trivial as it requires enumerating all the subspaces covered by each maximal dominating subspace and checking if the enumerated subspace has already been previously generated. In the following, we propose two alternative methods based on precise counting and approximate counting, respectively, for counting the number of dominating subspaces covered by $\mathcal{M}$.

**Precise Counting.** Our improved approach for computing the exact number of dominating subspaces is shown in Algorithm 3. For each maximal dominating subspace set $M_i \in \mathcal{M}$, let $S_i$ denote the collection of dominating subspaces that are covered by $M_i$. We define for each $S_i$, a new subspace collection (denoted by $S'_i$) as follows: $S'_i = S_i - \bigcup_{j \in [1,i)} S_j$. It is easy to verify that (1) $\bigcup_{M_i \in \mathcal{M}} S_i = \bigcup_{M_i \in \mathcal{M}} S'_i$; and (2) $S'_i \cap S'_j = \emptyset$ for any distinct pair $S'_i$ and $S'_j$. In this way, we transform the problem of counting the union of a collection of sets to a subset counting problem without any intersection among the subsets. For every maximal dominating subspace set $M_i \in \mathcal{M}$, we enumerate over each of the subspaces covered by $M_i$ and check whether it is also covered by an earlier maximal dominating subspace set $M_j, j \in [1, i)$. Referring to the preceding example with $\mathcal{M} = \{M_1, M_2\}$, we have $S'_1 = \{\{d_1\}, \{d_1, d_3\}, \{d_2\}, \{d_2, d_3\}, \{d_1, d_2\}, \{d_1, d_2, d_3\}\}$, and $S'_2 = \{\{d_1, d_4\}, \{d_1, d_3, d_4\}\}$.

However, the simple precise counting method can not scale efficiently to handle high-dimensional spaces because we still need to enumerate all the $(2^{|U|} - 1)2^{|V|}$ subspaces for a maximal dominating subspace $(U, V)$. For example, with $|U| = 20$, over one million of subspaces need to be compared against with every previous maximal dominating subspace.

**Approximate Counting.** To avoid the high complexity of the precise counting approach, we present an effective approximate counting method that is based on extending a Monte-Carlo counting algorithm [8] originally proposed for counting the number of assignments that satisfy a specified DNF formula, which is a #P-complete problem.

Our approach is shown in Algorithm 4 which takes three input parameters ($\mathcal{M}$, $\epsilon$, and $\delta$) and returns an approximate count of the number of dominating subspaces covered by a collection $\mathcal{M}$ of maximal dominating subspace sets for some point. The approximate answer is within an error of $\epsilon$ with a confidence level of at least $1 - \delta$. Steps 1-6 first compute the number of subspaces (denoted by $N_i$) covered by each maximal dominating subspace set $M_i \in \mathcal{M}$, and the total number of these (possibly overlapping) subspaces denoted by $N$. To obtain the desired error bound, a random repeatable sample of $T = 2n \ln(2/\delta)/\epsilon^2$ number of maximal dominating subspace sets is selected from $\mathcal{M}$, where the probability of sampling $M_i$ is proportional to the number of subspaces covered by $M_i$. For each generated maximal dominating subspace set $M_i$, a dominating subspace set $(U, V)$ that is covered by $M_i$ is randomly selected and checked if it is also covered by any maximal dominating subspace sets $M_j, j \in [1, i)$. A counter, denoted by $C$, is used to keep track of the number of distinct dominating subspaces determined from this sampling process. The approximate count output by the algorithm is given $(N \times C)/T$; the proof of the error bound follows from [8].

**Algorithm 4. ApproxCountDominatingSubspaces** ($\mathcal{M}, \epsilon, \delta$)
1: let $\mathcal{M} = \{M_1, M_2, \cdots, M_n\}$
2: **for** $i = 1$ to $n$ **do**
3:    let $M_i = (U_i, V_i)$
4:    $N_i = (2^{|U_i|} - 1)2^{|V_i|}$
5: **end for**
6: $N = \sum_{M_i \in \mathcal{M}} N_i$
7: $T = 2n \ln(2/\delta)/\epsilon^2$
8: initialize $C = 0$
9: **for** $i = 1$ to $T$ **do**
10:    choose a maximal dominating subspace set $M_i$ with probability $N_i/N$
11:    choose a subspace set $(U, V)$ that is covered by $M_i$ with equal probability
12:    **if** $(U, V)$ is not covered by any $M_j, j \in [1, i)$ **then**
13:       $C = C + 1$
14:    **end if**
15: **end for**
16: **return** $N \cdot C/T$

**Complexity Analysis.** Let $\mathcal{M} = \{(U_1, V_1), (U_2, V_2), \ldots, (U_n, V_n))\}$. We use $U_m$, $V_m$, $U_a$ and $V_a$ to denote $\max_{1 \leq i \leq n}\{|U_i|\}$, $\max_{1 \leq i \leq n}\{|V_i|\}$, $\sum_{i=1}^{n}|U_i|/n$, and $\sum_{i=1}^{n}|V_i|/n$, respectively.

In the exact counting algorithm, since each covered subspace for a maximal dominating subspace set $(U_i, V_i)$ must be compared with the previous maximal dominating subspace sets, the computation complexity for $(U_i, V_i)$ is $(i-1)(2^{|U_i|-1})2^{|V_i|}$. Therefore, the total time complexity of the exact counting algorithm is $\sum(i-1)(2^{|U_i|-1})2^{|V_i|}$ $= O(n^2 2^{U_m + V_m})$. Note that by Jensen's Inequality, $\sum(i-1)(2^{|U_i|-1})2^{|V_i|} = \Omega(n^2 2^{U_a + V_a - 1})$.

In the approximate counting algorithm, the sampling process is independent of $|U_i|$ and $|V_i|$. Since there are a total of $2n \ln(2/\delta)/\epsilon^2$ subspace sets sampled, the upper and lower bounds on the computation complexity of the approximate counting approach are $O(2n^2 \ln(2/\delta)/\epsilon^2)$ and $\Omega(2n \ln(2/\delta)/\epsilon^2)$, respectively.

With the above analysis, it is not difficult to verify that the exact counting method can not be slower than approximate counting method in constant factor when $U_m + V_m \leq \ln \ln(2/\delta) + 2\ln(1/\epsilon) - \ln n + 1$, while the approximate counting method can not be slower than exact counting method when $U_a + V_a \geq \ln \ln(2/\delta) + 2\ln(1/\epsilon) + \ln n + 2$.

### 4.4 Optimizations

In this section, we present two optimizations to further improve the performance of the ComputeMaxSubspaceSets algorithm presented in Section 4.2. In the current ComputeMaxSubspaceSets algorithm, the main optimization relies on using the frequency threshold $\theta$ (steps 5-7) as a quick filtering test to check whether a point is guaranteed to be not among the top-$k$ frequent skylines. Clearly, it is desirable to prune out points that are not top-k frequent skylines as early as possible using this efficient checking to reduce the unnecessary elaborate enumeration and comparison performed in steps 8-19.

**Pre-Sorting.** Our first optimization is based on the observation that the effectiveness of the pruning test is dependent on the order in which the data points are processed. For example, no early pruning would be possible if the points are processed in non-descending order of their skyline frequencies. One idea to maximize the pruning effectiveness is to first sort the data points based on some simple criterion such that points that have higher potential to be top-k frequent skylines appear earlier. Our optimization simply sorts the points in non-descending order of the sum of their dimension values. The intuition behind this heuristic is that a point with a smaller sum is likely to have smaller values on more dimensions and is therefore likely to have a higher skyline frequency. A similar idea was previously used in [6, 15, 19].

**Checkpoint.** Our second optimization aims to generalize the pruning test to improve its effectiveness. Currently, the pruning test for a point $p$ is applied in the context of a single maximal dominating subspace set (i.e., $DS(q,p)$ for some $q \in D$). However, when the number of maximal dominating subspace sets is large, it is possible that each maximal dominating subspace set in $\mathcal{M}$ on its own does not cover too many dominating subspaces (to cause $p$ to be pruned) even though the collection of dominating subspaces covered by $\mathcal{M}$ as a whole is large.

To overcome this limitation, we extend the pruning test to be done at several "checkpoints" by invoking CountDominatingSubspaces to count the number of dominating subspaces at intermediate stages and performing the pruning tests using intermediate collections of $\mathcal{M}$ each of which generally consists of more than one maximal dominating subspace set. Thus, by counting the coverage for multiple maximal dominating subspace sets rather than a single maximal dominating subspace set, the opportunity for pruning is increased.

In the implementation of this optimization, we set checkpoints at exponential sizes; i.e., when the number of maximal dominating subspace sets reaches $2^t$ (for some $t > 0$), the counting process is invoked to check whether the current number of subspaces covered has already exceeded the threshold. This exponential checkpoint setup turns out to perform better than any "linear" checkpoint setup since the number of subspaces covered is usually proportional to the number of maximal dominating subspace sets.

## 5 Performance Study

In this section, we present an experimental evaluation of our proposed algorithms for computing top-$k$ frequent skylines using both synthetic as well as real data sets.

### 5.1 Experimental Setup

We generated synthetic data sets by varying the number of dimensions, the size of the data set and the distributions of the data set; in particular, we considered the three commonly used types of data distributions: independent, correlated, and anti-correlated. In addition, we also conducted experiments on the NBA real data set [1] that is mentioned throughout this paper. The characteristics of this real data set most closely resembles a correlated data distribution.

We compare the performance of the following four algorithm variants:

1. **Exact Count (EC):** This scheme adopts exact counting, and employs the Pre-Sorting and Checkpoint optimizations.
2. **Approx Count without Sorting (ACWS):** This scheme uses approximate counting and only the Checkpoint optimization.
3. **Approx Count without Checkpoint (ACWC):** This scheme employs approximate counting with only the Pre-Sorting optimization.
4. **Approx Count(AC):** This scheme adopts approximate counting together with both Pre-Sorting and Checkpoint optimizations.

All experiments were carried out on a PC with a 2 GHz AMD Athlon processor and 2 GB of main memory running the Linux operating system. Unless otherwise stated, we use the following default setting in our study: 15-dimensional data set with 100K records, $\epsilon = 0.2$, $k = 10$, and $\delta = 0.05$. The default algorithm for all experiments is AC, which we expect to show is the algorithm of choice.

### 5.2 Tuning the Approximate Counting Scheme

There are several tunable parameters in the approximate counting scheme: $\epsilon$, $\delta$ and $k$. We study the relationship between the effect of these parameters on efficiency and precision. The efficiency result is shown in Fig. 1, while the precison result is shown in Fig. 2.

We first discuss the efficiency results which compare the computation time as a function of different parameters. When we vary $\epsilon$ from 0.1 to 0.4 in AC, the processing time decreases greatly since the number of samples is quadratic to $1/\epsilon$ in approximate counting. When we vary $\delta$ from 0.025 to 0.1 in AC, the processing time is very stable since the number of samples in approximate counting is linear to $\ln(2/\delta)$, which does not change much with $\delta$. From Fig. 1(c), which shows the result when $k$ is varied from 10 to 70, we can see that the increase trend of the processing time is almost linear to the result size $k$, which indicates that AC is scalable to various values of $k$.

The effectiveness of the method is measured by precision, which is the ratio between the number of true top-k frequent skylines and the result size k. Looking at Fig. 2, we note that the precision on correlated data set is always close to 1. Even on independent and anti-correlated data sets, the AC algorithm can achieve precision over 90% with a large range of different parameters. The figure also indicates that $\epsilon$ is the most important

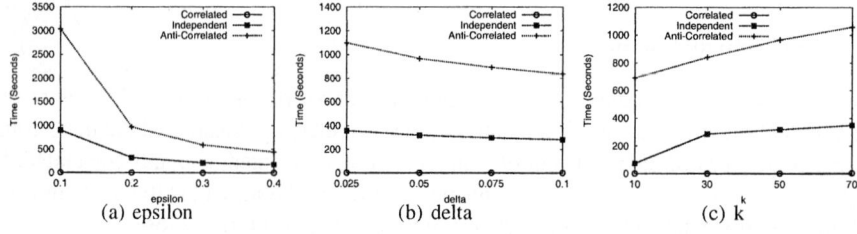

**Fig. 1.** Efficiency comparison as a function of different parameters

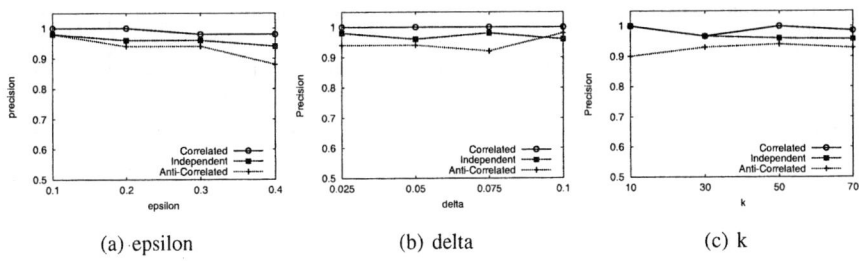

**Fig. 2.** Precision comparison as a function of different parameters

factor affecting the precision of the result. The precision decreases monotonically with the increase of $\epsilon$, while the other two parameters, $\delta$ and $k$, do not have too much impact on the precision.

From this experiment, we can conclude that even setting $\epsilon = 0.2$ and $\delta = 0.05$ is enough to provide very good results for top-k frequent skyline queries. As such, we use these as the default setting.

### 5.3 Effect of Number of Dimensions

We study the impact of dimensionality on the efficiency of the algorithms. We compare all the four algorithms EC, AC, ACWS and ACWC on data sets ranging from 10-25 dimensions. The results on the three synthetic data sets are shown in Fig. 3.

First, we look at the three approximate counting schemes. In the figure, the "bars" that are beyond the maximum time plotted are truncated (in other words, all "bars" with the maximum value have much larger value than the maximum value plotted). From the poor performance of ACWS and ACWC, we can see the effect of the pre-sorting and checkpoint optimizations. It is clear that pre-sorting is an important optimization. Without pre-sorting, the efficiency decreases by at least one order of magnitude. The checkpoint optimization is useful when the dimensions are independent or anti-correlated since it can prune many points. The combined effect of both optimizations contributes to the superior performance of AC.

Now, comparing AC and EC, we observe that EC slightly outperforms AC at low dimensionality ($< 15$). This is because when the dimensionality is low, the subspaces covered by those maximal subspace sets are fewer than the number of samples needed by AC. However, when the dimensionality is high, AC shows its strength since the number of samples is irrelevant to the dimensionality, while EC must enumerate all the covered subspaces whose number is exponential to the dimensionality.

Third, looking at the figure, we see that the relative performance of the schemes remain largely unchanged under different distributions. As expected, the computation time is higher for all schemes when the data becomes more anti-correlated.

Since ACWS and ACWC perform poorly relative to AC, we shall not discuss them further.

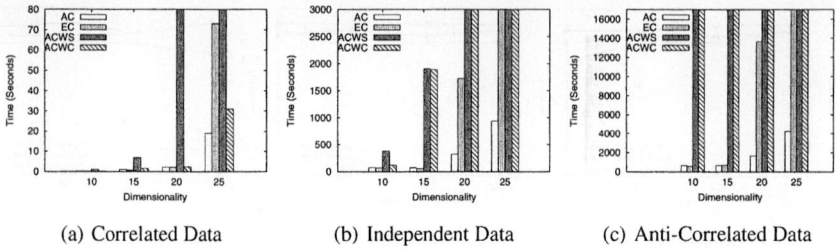

(a) Correlated Data   (b) Independent Data   (c) Anti-Correlated Data

**Fig. 3.** Efficiency comparison on varying dimensionality

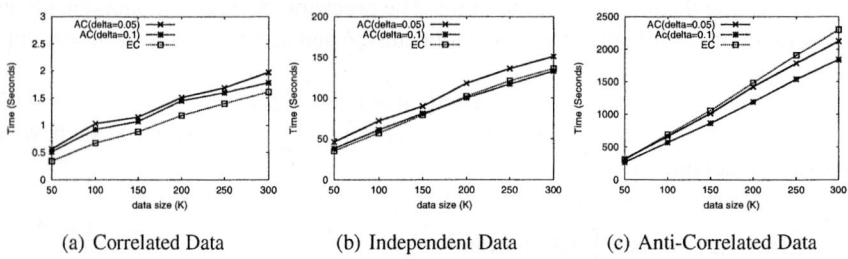

(a) Correlated Data   (b) Independent Data   (c) Anti-Correlated Data

**Fig. 4.** Efficiency comparison on varying data size

### 5.4 Effect of Data Set Cardinality

In this experiment, we evaluate the impact of data size on the computation efficiency for 15-dimensional data. The data size is varied from 50K to 300K. We study two variants of AC: $\delta = 0.05$ and $\delta = 0.1$. The results in Fig. 4 show that although the time complexity of Algorithm 1 is theoretically quadratic to the data size in the worst case, the actual efficiency of these methods is almost linear in the data size. On the correlated data set, EC always outperforms the algorithms with approximate counting. This is because the dominating frequencies of the top-k points are all very small when the data is correlated. For the data set with independent dimensions, EC outperforms AC ($\delta = 0.05$) but only outperforms AC ($\delta = 0.1$) when the data size is smaller than 200K. For the anti-correlated data set, both AC ($\delta = 0.05$) and AC ($\delta = 0.1$) are faster than EC since the dominating frequency is large enough.

### 5.5 Results on Real Data Set

We use the NBA player statistics data set as our real data set for this experiment. As noted, there are 17266 tuples over 17 dimensions.

Fig. 5 compares the efficiency of the four algorithms, AC, EC, ACWS and ACWC. From the figure, we can see that ACWC outperforms all the other methods on the real data set; this is due to the fact that the NBA data set is fairly correlated. Although AC is slower than ACWC by a little (due to the cost of the unnecessary checkpoints), its performance is still much better than that of the exact counting algorithm.

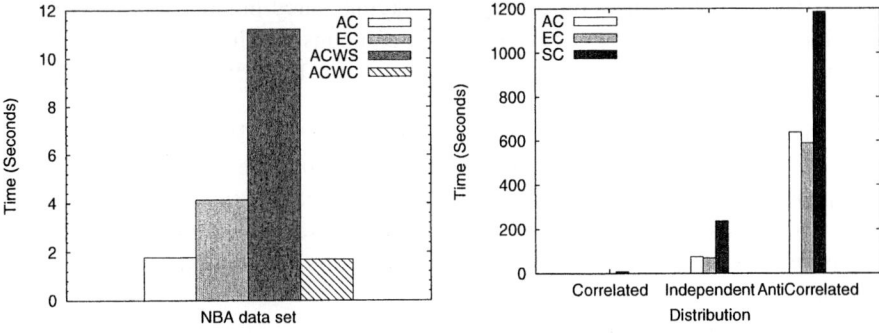

**Fig. 5.** Efficiency comparison on NBA data set   **Fig. 6.** Efficiency comparison with Skycube algorithm

### 5.6 Comparison of Number of Maximal Dominating Subspaces

Table 3 compares the number of maximal dominating subspaces that are maintained by the various algorithms for different number of data dimensions and data distributions (i.e., correlated, independent, and anti-correlated). The last column in the table lists the upper bounds on the number of maximal dominating subspace sets. Note that for a data set with $D$ dimensions, the upper bound is given by $\binom{D}{\lceil D/2 \rceil}$, where each maximal dominating subspace consists of $\lceil D/2 \rceil$ dimensions.

As expected, the points in the anti-correlated data set has the maximum number of maximal dominating subspaces. However, the number of maximal dominating subspace is still much smaller than the theoretical upper bound listed in the last column. This indicates that our method does not suffer from the exponential increase of dimensionality in practice.

**Table 3.** Comparison of number of maximal dominating subspaces

| Dimensionality | Correlated | Independent | Anti-Correlated | Upper Bound |
|:---:|:---:|:---:|:---:|:---:|
| 10 | 17 | 64 | 62 | 252 |
| 15 | 72 | 483 | 565 | 6435 |
| 20 | 188 | 1897 | 2477 | 184756 |
| 25 | 587 | 5119 | 7617 | 5200300 |

### 5.7 Comparative Study

We also compared our EC and AC schemes against the Skycube algorithm [19]. Although the Skycube algorithm (denoted as SC) can find the precise top-k frequent skylines, it does not scale beyond 15 dimensions. Our results show that it takes more than 10 hours for SC to run on the independent data set with 100K 15-dimensional points.

This is because SC focuses on conventional skyline query in any specified subspace, and thus spends most of its computation time on points which cannot be top frequent skyline points. As such, we only present the results for 100K 10-dimensional data sets in Fig. 7.

From the figure, it is clear that both EC and AC are superior to SC in all the three types of data sets. SC is not scalable as it may need to compute all the subspaces which is exponential in the number of dimensions. We note that for small number of dimensions (10 in this case), our AC scheme returns the exact answers, i.e., it has 100% precision. That is, we do not give up any precision loss to obtain performance gain in this case.

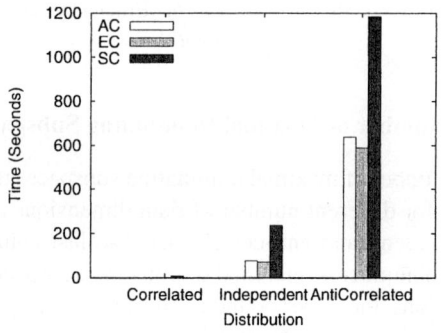

**Fig. 7.** Efficiency Comparison on 10D

## 6 Conclusions

Skyline queries have been lauded for their ability to find the most interesting points in a data set. However, in high dimensional data sets, there are too many skyline points for them to be of practical value. In this paper, we introduced skyline frequency as a measure of interestingness for points in the data set. The skyline frequency of a point measures the number of subspaces in which the point is a skyline. We developed an efficient approximation algorithm to compute the top-k frequent skyline query. Our experimental study demonstrated the performance and the effectiveness of the proposed algorithm.

We plan to extend this work in several directions. First, we would like to explore precomputation techniques (e.g., indexes) to further speed up the computation of top-k frequent skyline query. Second, our current work assumes a static data set. We would like to study techniques to facilitate incremental updates. Finally, exploring other interestingness measures of skyline points is also part of our future work.

**Acknowledgement.** We thank the authors of [19] for sharing their implementation of the Skycube algorithm.

# References

1. NBA basketball statistics. http://databasebasketball.com/stats.download.
2. W. Balke, U. Güntzer, and X. Zheng. Efficient distributed skylining for web information systems. In *EDBT'04*.
3. S. Börzsönyi, D. Kossmann, and K. Stocker. The skyline operator. In *ICDE'01*.
4. M. Carey and D. Kossmann. On saying "enough already!" in SQL. In *SIGMOD'97*.
5. C.-Y. Chan, P.-K. Eng, and K.-L. Tan. Stratified computation of skylines with partially-ordered domains. In *SIGMOD'05*.
6. J. Chomicki, P. Godfrey, J. Gryz, and D. Liang. Skyline with presorting. In *ICDE'03*.
7. P. Godfrey, R. Shipley, and J. Gryz. Maximal vector computation in large data sets. In *VLDB'05*.
8. R. M. Kapp, M. Luby, and N. Madras. Monte-Carlo approximation algorithms for enumeration problems. *J. Algorithms*, 10(3):429–448, 1989.
9. D. Kossmann, F. Ramsak, and S. Rost. Shooting stars in the sky: an online algorithm for skyline queries. In *VLDB'02*.
10. H.T. Kung, F. Luccio, and F.P. Preparata. On finding the maxima of a set of vectors. *JACM*, 22(4), 1975.
11. X. Lin, Y. Yuan, W. Wang, and H. Lu. Stabbing the sky: efficient skyline computation over sliding windows. In *ICDE'05*.
12. J. Matousek. Computing dominances in $E^n$. *Information Processing Letters*, 38(5):277–278, 1991.
13. D. Papadias, Y. Tao, G. Fu, and B. Seeger. An optimal and progressive algorithm for skyline queries. In *SIGMOD'03*.
14. C. H. Papadimitriou and M. Yannakakis. Multiobjective query optimization. In *PODS'01*.
15. J. Pei, W. Jin, M. Ester, and Y. Tao. Catching the best views of skyline: a semantic approach based on decisive subspaces. In *VLDB'05*.
16. F. P. Preparata and M. I. Shamos. *Computational Geometry: An Introduction*. Springer-Verlag, 1985.
17. I. Stojmenovic and M. Miyakawa. An optimal parallel algorithm for solving the maximal elements problem in the plane. *Parallel Computing*, 7(2), June 1988.
18. K.-L. Tan, P.-K. Eng, and B.C. Ooi. Efficient progressive skyline computation. In *VLDB'01*.
19. Y. Yuan, X. Lin, Q. Liu, W. Wang, J.X. Yu, and Q. Zhang. Efficient computation of skyline cube. In *VLDB'05*.

# From Analysis to Interactive Exploration: Building Visual Hierarchies from OLAP Cubes

Svetlana Vinnik and Florian Mansmann

University of Konstanz, P.O.Box D188, 78457 Konstanz, Germany
{vinnik, mansmann}@inf.uni-konstanz.de

**Abstract.** We present a novel framework for comprehensive exploration of OLAP data by means of user-defined dynamic hierarchical visualizations. The multidimensional data model behind the OLAP architecture is particularly suitable for sophisticated analysis of large data volumes. However, the ultimate benefit of applying OLAP technology depends on the "intelligence" and usability of visual tools available to end-users.

The explorative framework of our proposed interface consists of the navigation structure, a selection of hierarchical visualization techniques, and a set of interaction features. The navigation interface allows users to pursue arbitrary disaggregation paths within single data cubes and, more importantly, across multiple cubes. In the course of interaction, the navigation view adapts itself to display the chosen path and the options valid in the current context. Special effort has been invested in handling non-trivial relationships (e.g., mixed granularity) within hierarchical dimensions in a way transparent to the user.

We propose a visual structure called *Enhanced Decomposition Tree* to to be used along with popular "state-of-the-art" hierarchical visualization techniques. Each level of the tree is produced by a disaggregation step, whereas the nodes display the specified subset of measures, either as plain numbers or as an embedded chart. The proposed technique enables a stepwise descent towards the desired level of detail while preserving the history of the interaction. Aesthetic hierarchical layout of the node-link tree ensures clear structural separation between the analyzed values embedded in the nodes and their dimensional characteristics which label the links. Our framework provides an intuitive and powerful interface for exploring complex multidimensional data sets.

## 1 Introduction

With rapid evolvement of *data warehouse* technology in the last decade huge volumes of data have become available for analysis and exploration. Data warehouses integrate data from heterogeneous sources into a single repository for comprehensive analytical processing. Apart from generating standard reports, the users are able to gain deeper insights into the data by means of dynamically formulating and verifying their hypotheses about it. Arranging the data into a multidimensional space is especially beneficial for decision support due to the potential of retrieving the data subsets of interest in the form exactly satisfying the users' information needs. Furthermore, multiple coordinated views of the same data set help to dynamically explore it and uncover the "hidden gems", such as outliers, peculiar patterns, trends or clusters.

Data warehouses increasingly adopt the *multidimensional data model* which was designed to meet the challenges of the online analytical processing (OLAP) [5] by providing efficient execution of queries that aggregate over large amounts of detailed data [14]. This model uses numerical *measures* as its analytical objects, with each measure uniquely determined by its *dimensions* and therefore treated as a point in a multidimensional space [3]. Depending on the expected type of queries the data can be organized into *hypercubes* with a measure (or multiple measures) as the value under analysis stored in the cube's cells, the measure's determining dimensions as the cube's axes and the dimensions' values as the coordinates of respective measure cells.

The desired data view can be retrieved from the cubes by applying OLAP operations, such as *slice-and-dice* to reduce the cube, *drill-down* and *roll-up* to perform aggregation and disaggregation, respectively, along a hierarchical dimension, *drill-across* to combine multiple cubes, *ranking* to find the outlier values, and *rotating* to see the data grouped by other dimensions [14].

The standard interface for exploring OLAP data is a *Pivot Table*, or *Cross Tab* [10], which is a 2-dimensional spreadsheet with associated totals and subtotals. Pivot Tables allow nesting of multiple dimensions within the same axis. This technique is adequate for displaying the query results in a straightforward fashion but it fails to show the selected values in a larger context and is thus a rather poor option for complex data exploration. Advanced OLAP tools overcome the limits of the cross tab interface by offering a multitude of powerful visual alternatives for retrieving, displaying, and interactively exploring the data. Continuous efforts are put into providing new approaches to visual exploration of the hypercube data, such as hierarchical visualizations (decomposition trees, chart trees, treemaps etc.), multiscale views, interactive scatter-plots, etc. described in the next section.

## 2 Related Work

The work related to ours in one way or another can be sub-divided into three major groups, namely, multidimensional data modeling, visualization techniques, and explorative interfaces.

### 2.1 Multidimensional Modeling and Data Warehouse Design

Modeling challenges arise whenever dimensional hierarchies contain irregularities preventing their straightforward mapping to balanced dimensional trees as required for OLAP operations. A proposal to transforming such data into summarizable structures, transparent to the user, can be found in [15]. Implications of unbalanced hierarchies on the logical data warehouse design are explained in [12]. Most of the data warehouse research, however, is concerned with performance issues and is orthogonal to the scope of this paper.

## 2.2 Visualizing OLAP Data

Besides the classical visualization techniques, such as Pivot Tables [10] and 2-dimensional plots and charts, familiar to any OLAP analyst, a wide variety of more comprehensive visual frameworks for incremental exploration and navigation in large multidimensional data volumes have emerged. Hierarchy-aware visualization techniques applicable in the OLAP context can be grouped into the following categories:

- *Geometric* (Scatterplots, Landscapes, Hyperslice, Parallel Coordinates)
- *Icon-based* (Chernoff Faces, Stick Figures, Color Icons, TileBars)
- *Pixel-oriented* (Recursive Pattern, Circle Segments)
- *Hierarchical* (Dimensional Stacking, Worlds-within-Worlds, Treemap, Cone Trees, InfoCube)
- *Graph-Based* (Straight-, Poly- and Curved-Line, DAG, Symmetric, Cluster)
- *Hybrid* techniques which arbitrarily combine any of the above.

Applicability of any particular technique or their combination depends largely on the analysis needs and the level of user expertise. An overview of the above techniques with respect to OLAP data can be found in [13].

Conventional node-link trees in a classical aesthetical view [17] and in a variety of more compact layouts (*hyperbolic, balloon, radial,* etc. presented in [8]) which are rather familiar and intuitive to interpret can be used to increase the user's awareness of the hierarchical relationships within the data or allow users to define their own hierarchies. More comprehensive and specialized techniques are appreciated for complex analysis, scientific visualization and data mining. [18] presents some advances in hierarchy visualization and its use for exploring user-defined hierarchies. A well structured classification of the "state-of-the-art" visualization and interaction techniques with respect to the type and the dimensionality of the data is produced in [9].

## 2.3 Exploration Tools

There is an abundance of tools and interfaces for exploring multidimensional data. We limit ourselves to naming a few products which offer distinguished features relevant for our work. One developed system called Polaris [20] extends the Pivot Table interface by offering a combination of a variety of displays and tools for visual specification of analysis tasks. Polaris is a predecessor of a recently released business intelligence product called Tableau Software [2]. ProClarity was the first to enhance business intelligence with *Decomposition Trees* [16] for visual node-by-node disaggregation of data cubes. XMLA enriches the idea of hierarchical disaggregation by arranging the decomposed subtotals of each parent value into a nested chart (Bar- and Pie-Chart Trees) in its Report Portal OLAP client [21]. Visual Insights has developed a family of tools, called ADVIZOR, with an intuitive framework for parallel exploration of multiple measures [7].

Our interface differs from the standard OLAP tools in the way data navigation is built (attribute hierarchies with data on-demand) and the way the data is presented (hierarchical visualizations instead of spreadsheets and charts).

## 3 Handling Complex Multidimensional Data

OLAP architecture performs well on the facts that are summarizable along each dimension, i.e. where all dimensions are balanced hierarchies, however, it fails to adequately support irregular dimension hierarchies [14]. Our ambition is to tackle some of the frequently observed irregularity patterns in complex dimensions.

Throughout the remainder of the paper we will refer to the following fragment of a (simplified) university data warehouse consisting of two OLAP cubes:

1. **Orders** with the facts about the university's expenditures.
   Measure: *total amount in €*. Dimensions: *Interval, Category, Institution, Project*, and *Funds*.
2. **Students** with the facts about the number of enrolled students.
   Measures: *number of cases, number of heads*[1]. Dimensions: *Semester, Term, Nationality, TeachingUnit, Degree, Gender, Eligibility* (certificate type).

The logical design of the above database roughly corresponds to the *snowflake schema* [3] which explicitly decomposes hierarchical dimensions into per-level subdimensional tables. Fact tables contain measure attribute(s) and their dimensional characteristics. The latter are the foreign keys referencing the respective dimension table. In case of a hierarchical dimension, each subdimensional table is connected to the next level table(s) by means of foreign keys. Thereby, a snowflake shape is produced by the fact table in the center, surrounded by the directly referenced bottom-level dimensions with all their referenced upper levels at periphery. The data schema described above is depicted in Fig. 1.

We have deliberately chosen a rather complex data warehouse fragment in order to examine various patterns in hierarchical dimensions as well as the ability of our navigational framework to handle them in a way intuitive for the user.

### 3.1 Classification of Dimensional Hierarchies

The OLAP cube has a relation schema $D_1 \cup D_2 \cup ... D_n$, where each $D_i$ is a dimensional attribute with its corresponding relation $d_i$ referred to as a *dimension*. Hierarchical dimensions consist of subdimensions, or nodes, for each of its levels. The tuples in a relation are the members, or *entities*, of the respective dimension, a tuple of $d_i$ is denoted $t[d_i]$.

We extend the notion of dimension to include *abstract* nodes, i.e. without associated relations and entities. Abstract nodes are used simply as an upper class for uniting multiple child categories or as a root node at the top of the entire underlying hierarchy: $D_i$ is abstract if its $d_i = \emptyset$. The next-level subdimension $D_k$ of any $D_i$ is called its *child*, $D_k = child(D_i)$, and the set of all children of node $D_i$ is given by the function $children(D_i)$. The cardinality of node $D_i$ equals the number of its children: $|D_i| = |children(D_i)|$.

---

[1] Head statistics counts physical persons, assigning each "head" to the supervising faculty of his/her major. Case statistics splits single enrollment into separate cases, one for each major/minor, to register a student as a "case" at each involved faculty.

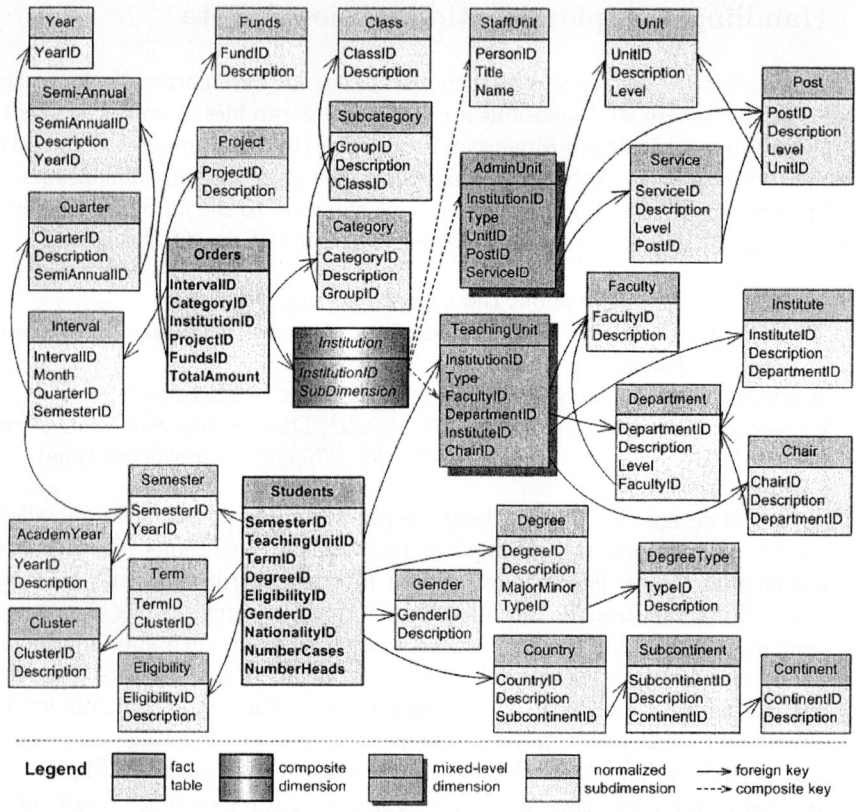

**Fig. 1.** Logical schema of the university data warehouse fragment

The hierarchical behavior of a dimensional node can be described based on 1) its relation (or members), 2) cardinality, and 3) its relationship w.r.t. its children. Notice, that the type characterizes solely the node itself, and not its entire subtree (the descendants may be of various types). Based on the logical schema in Fig. 1, one can identify at least the following five distinct behaviors:

- **Simple:** a non-hierarchical dimension (e.g., *Gender, Project*);
  $D_i$ is *simple* $\rightarrow |D_i| = 0 \land d_i \neq \emptyset$.
- **Single Hierarchy:** a strict hierarchy (e.g., *Interval, Category*) has just a single decomposition path; $D_i$ is *single* $\rightarrow |D_i| = 1 \land d_i \neq \emptyset$.
- **Multiple Hierarchy:** a dimension is subdivided in multiple ways. For instance, *Intervals* can be aggregated along semester $\rightarrow$ academic year, or along quarter $\rightarrow$ semi-annual $\rightarrow$ calendar year. Multiple paths are placed into the same abstract parent node; $D_i$ is *multiple* $\rightarrow |D_i| > 1 \land d_i = \emptyset$.
- **Composite Hierarchy:** an "umbrella" dimension uniting heterogeneous members from multiple relations in a single superclass (e.g., the members of *Institution* may refer to *StaffUnit, AdminUnit,* or *TeachingUnit*):

$D_i$ is composite $\rightarrow |D_i| > 1 \land d_i \neq \emptyset \land \forall\, D_k \in children(D_i) : d_k \subset d_i$. Since *InstituionID* in *Orders* may point to the entry from any of the three tables, a composite *Institution* dimension is built by extracting the primary keys of original dimensional tables, along with the table's name, into a new table.

- **Mixed-Level Hierarchy:** the entities from upper hierarchy levels do not merely serve for aggregating (as in single hierarchy), but also participate as end-entities in the fact table. Therefore, an additional relation is built on the top of the respective hierarchy by denormalizing the latter into a single table (as in *AdminUnit* or *TeachingUnit*). To separate its twofold role, the dimension's node has to contain its own level's relation as a *simple* child subdimension (see section 5 for further details);
$D_i$ is mixed-level $\rightarrow |D_i| \geq 1 \land d_i \neq \emptyset \land \exists D_k \in children(D_i) : d_k = d_i$

The two cubes do not have any directly shared dimensions within their schemata, and, therefore, cannot be drilled-across for parallel exploration by means of a natural join. However, a closer inspection reveals two linking options:

- *Semester* in *Students* and *Intervals* in *Orders* are summarizable by semester,
- *TeachingUnit* in *Students* is a subclass of *Institution* in *Orders*.

These linkages encourage the anticipation that both fact tables can be joined for cross-cube exploration at their shared aggregation levels.

## 4  OLAP Cube as a Decomposition Tree

OLAP operations, such as *drill-down*, *roll-up*, and *cube*, transform the data from a fact table into a hierarchy by aggregating or disaggregating the measure along specified dimensions. A series of successive disaggregation steps can be presented as a *Decomposition Tree*. Notice that decomposition is a process contrary to aggregation. The measure's total, aggregated along all selected attributes, forms the root node of the tree. The next level emerges by computing the subtotals of a disaggregation along any specified dimension. Each subsequent $k$-th level will contain the subtotals disaggregated by $k$ specified dimensions[2]. Back to our example, the measures of cube *Students* may be decomposed along the following sequence of dimensional attributes (see Fig. 2):

$$AcademYear \rightarrow Semester \rightarrow Gender \rightarrow Degree \rightarrow \ldots$$

Unlike standard spreadsheet views, the hierarchical presentation in Fig. 2 by its very nature has an advantage of supporting arbitrary number of split dimensions in arbitrary order while preserving this order in its levels. All nodes at the same level correspond to the same granularity whereas nested charts accelerate identification of interesting values and directions for further expansion. Interactive filtering can be applied to eliminate or temporarily hide irrelevant subtrees.

---

[2] In terms of a SQL statement, decomposition adds the chosen dimension's attribute to the GROUP BY clause.

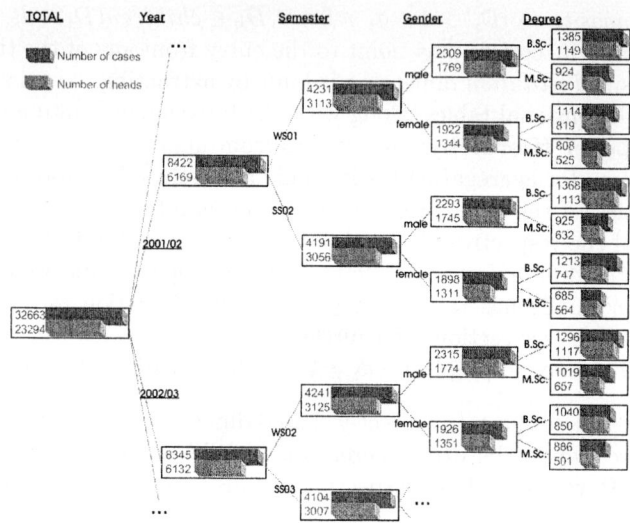

**Fig. 2.** A user-driven hierarchical decomposition of cube *Students*

Further perceptional improvement is achieved by clearly separating the structural information from the actual data: the split dimensions are used as titles for their respective tree levels, the dimension entities label the edges and the measure values are displayed within the nodes. The contents of the nodes can be heterogeneous, such as text, numbers, charts or a combination thereof.

Since there are as many disaggregation operations possible within a cube as the total number of its dimensions including all subdimensions, and since the order of splitting can be arbitrary, OLAP cubes offer a huge exploration potential ($n!$ disaggregation paths in case of $n$ dimensions) by means of hierarchical decompositions. However, it is rather challenging to incorporate the required framework for interactive construction of user-defined hierarchical visualizations into OLAP interfaces in a fast, intuitive and user-friendly way. In the remaining sections we describe our proposed solution to empowering an OLAP tool with the above exploration technique.

## 5 Designing the Navigational Framework

Probably the most popular paradigm underlying the OLAP navigation structure is that of a file browser, with each cube as a folder containing the list of top-level dimensions and the list of available measures, as found in Cognos PowerPlay [6], BusinessObjects [1], CNS DataWarehouse Explorer [4], and many other commercial OLAP tools. Each hierarchical dimension is itself a folder containing its child entities. Hierarchical entities can be recursively expanded to show the subtrees of their descendants. The entities of the highest granularity (i.e. the leaf nodes) are represented as files and are non-expandable.

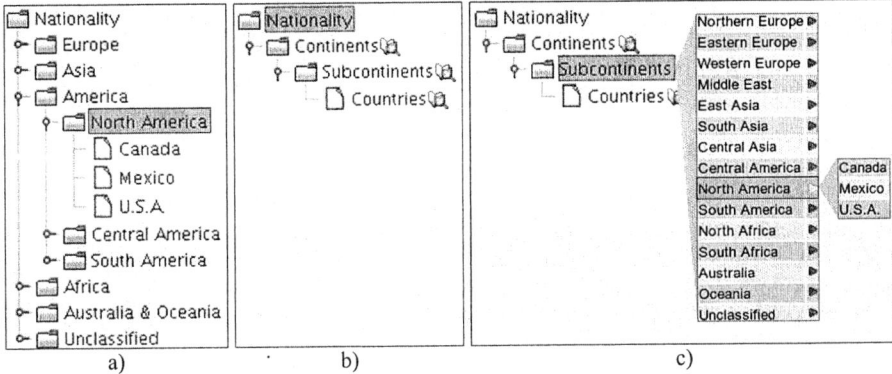

**Fig. 3.** Navigating in the hierarchical dimension *Nationality*. a) "show-data"-approach b) "show-structure"-approach c) on-demand preview in the "show-structure"-approach.

Standard OLAP interfaces allow users to navigate directly in the dimensional data rather than in a dimensional hierarchy. Our approach, however, pursues a clear distinction between the dimension's structure and its instances. Therefore, expansion of a dimension folder reveals solely the nested folders of its subdimensions, contrary to the standard OLAP navigation displaying the child-level data. The instances of any subdimension can be retrieved on-demand. Fig. 3 a)-b) demonstrates the differences between the standard "show-data" and our proposed "show-structure" interfaces, respectively, at the example of a hierarchical dimension *Nationality*. Notice that expanding the top-level dimension *Nationality* in Fig. 3 b) reveals its entire descendant hierarchy, enabling the user to "jump over" right to the desired granularity level. The data view is available on explicit demand by clicking the preview button of the respective category. Fig. 3 c) shows the activated preview of *Subcontinents* with the option to drill-down into any subcontinent's descendant subtree. The advantages of our proposed navigation structure for building hierarchies can be summarized as follows:

- clear distinction between the dimension's structure and its contents
- immediate overview of all granularity levels in a hierarchical dimension
- the ability to drill-through directly to any descendant subdimension
- on-demand preview of the data as well as any data node's descendant entities
- compactness on the display due to moderate expansion at most steps
- the entire navigation is built from a single meta table of the kind

| title | table | parent | root | hierarchy |
|---|---|---|---|---|
| *Nationality* | NULL | NULL | NULL | *single* |
| *Subcontinents* | *dim_subcontinent* | *Continents* | *Nationality* | *single* |
| *Countries* | *dim_country* | *Subcontinents* | *Nationality* | *simple* |
| ... | ... | ... | ... | ... |

containing, for each dimension entry, its title and table, references to its parent (NULL for top-level) and root[3] dimensions, and its hierarchy type (as classified in section 3)
- the actual data is retrieved only if explicitly requested
- it is easier to find the entries of interest even somewhere deep in the hierarchy without knowing the data (e.g. any country can be accessed directly through the preview of *Countries* without searching for and drilling through its ancestors in *Continents* and *Subcontinents*).

As for various hierarchy types defined in section 3, our approach can handle each of them accordingly, using solely the above meta table[4], as pseudo-coded in Algorithm 1. The basic rule is to discontinue recursive expansion whenever mutually exclusive child paths arise since at those points the user is called upon to stick to just one of them. The case of a mixed-level hierarchy deserves a closer inspection. To reflect the twofold role of its subdimensions (i.e. both as leaf nodes and as aggregation levels), each of such subdimension contains, apart from its child

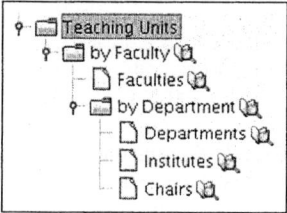

**Fig. 4.** A mixed-level hierarchy navigation node

level, its own self as a simple, i.e. non-hierarchical, subdimension, as can be seen in Fig. 4 at the example of expanding *TeachingUnit* in the cube *Orders*. Decomposing along *by Faculty* computes the subtotals for each faculty including all its subordinate institutions, whereas choosing its child *Faculties* computes the subtotal only for the faculties themselves as end-entities.

### 5.1 Parallel Exploration of Multiple Cubes

*OLAP Join*, or drill-across, allows linking multiple OLAP cubes to compare their measures or derive new ones under the condition that the cubes share at least one dimension. We define a dimension to be *partially shared* if the cubes impose different hierarchies upon it which share at least one aggregation level. Apparently, the cubes can also be joined on partially shared dimensions, as long as each cube is pre-aggregated to the shared level. Let us extend the proposed navigation framework to support parallel exploration of multiple cubes for each shared subdimension. For any number of cubes, pre-selected for a drill-across, the navigation structure can be built in the following steps:

1. Unnest the *top-level dimensions* and the *measures* from their respective fact table folders into a common navigational hierarchy.
2. Identify all partially or fully shared dimensions and the actually shared subdimensions therein (this phase is critical since sharing is not always obvious, e.g. implied by foreign key or other constraints).

---

[3] *Root* reference helps to identify top-level nodes and to avoid recursive SQL queries when retrieving descendant dimensions.
[4] Implementation of the data display routines behind the *Preview* buttons involves more complicated algorithms and is not considered at this stage.

**Algorithm 1.** Expanding a Dimension's Navigation Node

**input** : dimension name $D$, nesting counter $level$, recursion $propagate$
**result**: the dimension's sub-tree is displayed

**procedure** expandNode (Node $D$, int $level$)
**begin**
    $type \leftarrow$ SQL: SELECT type FROM meta WHERE title='$D$';
    **if** $type = simple$ **then return**; // cannot be expanded, so no action
    **else**
        Array $children \leftarrow$ SQL: SELECT title FROM meta WHERE parent='$D$';
        **switch** $type$ **do**
            **case** *single hierarchy*
                drawNode ($children[0]$, ++$level$, TRUE);// expand recursively
                break;
            **case** *mixed-level hierarchy*
                **foreach** $child$ $in$ $children$ **do**
                    drawNode ($child$, ++$level$, TRUE);// expand recursively
                break;
            **case** *composite*
            **case** *multiple hierarchy*
                **foreach** $child$ $in$ $children$ **do**
                    drawNode ($child$, ++$level$, FALSE);// no recursion
                break;
            **case** ... // define further cases
**end**

**procedure** drawNode (Node $D$, int $level$, boolean $propagate$)
**begin**
    Array $info \leftarrow$ SQL: SELECT type, table FROM meta WHERE title='$D$';
    $icon \leftarrow$ getIcon ( $info[type]$);
    indent according to $level$, display $icon$ and $D$'s title
    **if** $info[table]$ is not NULL **then**
        display preview icon // there is data to preview
    **if** $propagate$ **then**
        expandNode ($D$, $level$); // propagate expansion
**end**

3. For each group of partially shared dimensions, create a new upper-level dimension to serve as their parent and place the former ones underneath the new parent as a multiple hierarchy.
4. Single paths within the created multiple hierarchy might need to be adjusted to contain newly enabled additional aggregation opportunities.

The process of merging the *Interval* dimension of *Orders* and the *Semester* dimension of *Students* is shown in Fig. 5, with their shared levels highlighted.

Visual distinction between shared and non-shared navigation paths can be done by assigning each cube a unique color. The same colors are then used for

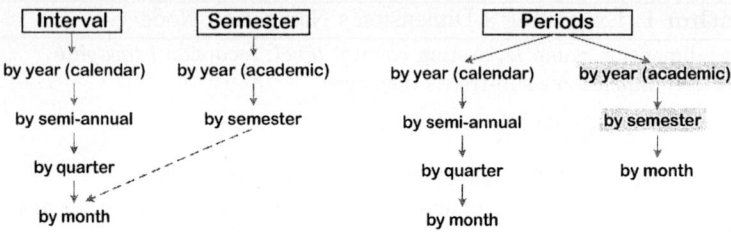

**Fig. 5.** Unifying partially shared dimensions

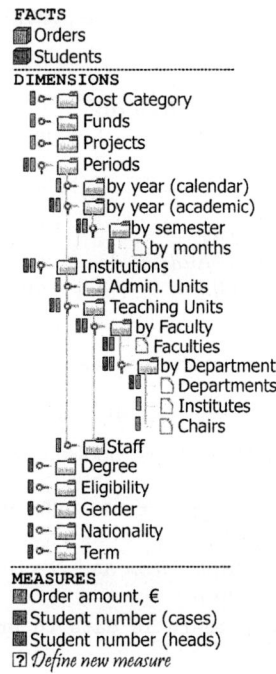

**Fig. 6.** Navigating in multiple cubes

marking each cube's measures and dimensions. All partially and fully shared top-level dimensions have the color marks of all involved cubes thus giving user a hint about the linking potential. Subdimensions, on the contrary, carry the marks of exclusively those cubes actually sharing that aggregation level. Fig. 6 demonstrates the above idea of using color marks.

## 6 Interactive Generation of Visual Hierarchies

The purpose of the navigational framework is to enable interactive retrieval of the data to be displayed in the visualization window according to the specified layout (e.g., Pivot Table, Decomposition Tree, etc.). In case of a hierarchical visualization the only supported direction of retrieval is disaggregation: each level of the hierarchy is produced by adding a new dimension or drilling down any already added hierarchical dimension. In what follows we explain the basic steps of generating a tree-like visualization at the example of a bar-chart tree built from the *Orders* cube:

- *Measure selection*: Selecting / de-selecting measures in the navigation panel causes them to be added to / removed from the visualization, whereas the following modalities can be distinguished:
  - *Displaying multiple measures per node*: when more than one measure is dragged, a dialog window will pop up prompting the user to specify the measures' display options (plain numbers, nested charts, or both)
  - *Specifying no measure*: with no measure chosen, one can display the structure of a hierarchical dimension without associated subtotals
  - *Adjusting the measure's format*: via the *Options* menu, the measure's display options, such as rounding, range, units etc., can be specified
  - *Defining a new measure*: advanced users can use this option (see bottom of Fig. 6) to define a new measure by combining existing ones through arithmetic operations or functions.

  Back to our scenario, dragging the measure *Order Amount*, € into an empty plane displays its total value as a root node, as shown in Fig. 7 a).

- *Decomposition*: Dragging any dimension into the visualization window is interpreted as *disaggregation* along that dimension. The dragged dimension along with all its ancestor hierarchy up to the root are added to the list of *split dimensions* and are made undraggable in order to disable upward steps (roll-up) invalid in this context. Decomposition causes the new level with decomposed subtotals to be added to the visual hierarchy, except in the case of a nested-chart-tree where the following options need to be distinguished:

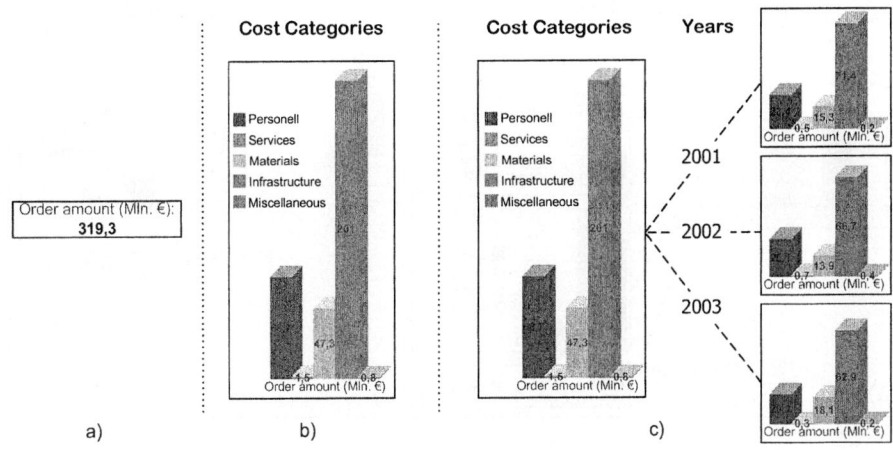

**Fig. 7.** Generating a bar-chart tree visualization a) initialization b) creating the root node c) adding a new level

- *Initializing*: the first chosen dimension is used for decomposing the root node value into a nested chart, thus defining the chart's granularity within the node, and is denoted $Dim_{inner}$. Fig. 7 b) shows the results of choosing *Cost Category* to be $Dim_{inner}$.
- *Outer Decomposition*: Splitting along any dimension which is not a descendant of $Dim_{inner}$ produces a new level with unchanged entities in the nested charts but with the respectively decomposed values in them, as depicted in Fig. 7 c) where the root node was split along *Year*.
- *Inner Decomposition / Drill-down*: Drilling down into a descendant of $Dim_{inner}$ turns the split dimension to be the new $Dim_{inner}$ changing the nested chart's granularity to the new level. The entities of the previous $Dim_{inner}$ serve as the outer split dimension, as shown in Fig. 8 a).

– *Global Filtering*: Any dimension can be applied as a global filter if dragged into the filter panel. Filtering results in the measure being aggregated only for the explicitly selected entities of the filter dimension. Filtering along an *unsplit* dimension does not reduce the number of nodes, but rather influences the measure values in the nodes. For example, filtering the tree in Fig. 7 c) by *Project* would simply recompute the subtotals in the nested charts based on the selected projects. Filtering along an already split dimension will not only recompute the subtotals at each level, but will actually remove the subtrees of deselected entities (or, in case of $Dim_{inner}$ or its ancestor, the

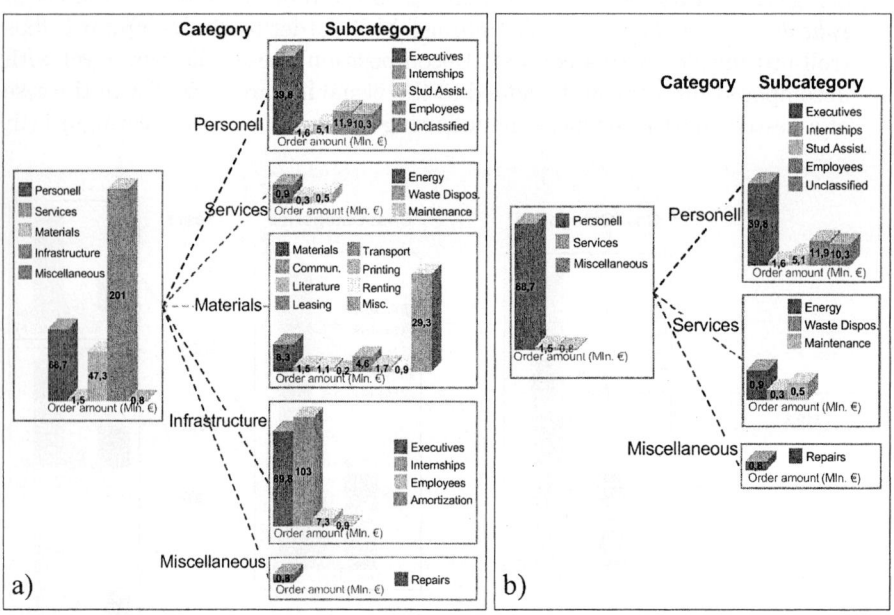

**Fig. 8.** Interacting with a bar-chart tree a) Performing an inner decomposition b) Applying global filtering

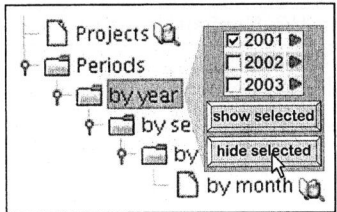

**Fig. 9.** Inline filtering of the nodes to display

entries within the charts) from the visualization. Fig. 8 b) shows the effect of eliminating two entities in the filter dimension *Cost Categories*.
– *Local Filtering*: By default, dragging a dimension into the visualization would create a child node for each of its entities. Alternatively, the user can explicitly specify the subset of entities in the current to-be-split dimension directly in the dimension's preview. Such inline filtering is interpreted as local, i.e. it affects only the current tree level leaving the upper levels unchanged. For example, inline elimination of the entry *2001* when performing a decomposition shown in Fig. 9 would cause that year's node in Fig. 7 c) to be withdrawn. Local filtering is equivalent to simply deleting irrelevant nodes from the visualization.

## 6.1 Interaction-Preserving Navigation

In the process of constructing complex hierarchies the user may lose the orientation as more navigational nodes at various levels become expanded and used as inline or global filters. Manageability of the navigation can be improved by forcing the displayed navigational hierarchy to adapt to the course of interaction. The core idea is to visually separate the expired paths (i.e. those already used as decomposition axes) from the still available ones. This is achieved by partitioning the background behind the list of dimensions vertically into the *expired* (dark background) and the *active* areas. Initially, all dimensions are placed into the active area. Two lists are managed in the course of interaction:

- *ActiveList*: contains the top-level nodes of all unsplit paths
- *ExpiredList*: contains the nodes of all dimensions already split

Each time a decomposition step is performed, the split dimension along with all its ancestors are shifted into the expired area. The entire navigation gets adjusted according to the rules described in Algorithm 2.

Fig. 10 demonstrates the presented adaptation procedure at the example of decomposing the *Orders* cube, with the navigation structure prior to the first split operation, its adjustment after performing it, and its state after multiple interactions, as subfigures a), b), and c), respectively. Furthermore, we suggest that the entire expired area should be hidden from the display by putting the navigation structure into a horizontally scrollable window, as shown in Fig. 10 c). The advantages of the adaptive display can be summarized as follows:

**Algorithm 2.** Adjusting the Navigation after a Decomposition Step

**input** : Split dimension $D$
**result**: re-arranged display of the navigation hierarchy

**procedure** shiftDimension (Node $D$)
**begin**
    $offsets = 1$; // offset = horizontal space between 2 adjacent nodes
    **if** $D$ in $ActiveList$ **then**
        $activeRoot \leftarrow D$ // only this node must be re-displayed
    **else**
        $activeRoot \leftarrow$ find $D$'s ancestor in $ActiveList$;
        $offsets$ += number of $D$'s ancestors up to $activeRoot$; // the number
            of shifts must correspond to the length of the expired path
    **foreach** *node* in *ExpiredList* **do**
        // shift all previously expired entities
        shift *node*'s segment backwards by 1 offset;
    Redisplay the segment $[ActiveRoot, D]$ moved backwards by $offsets$ shifts;
    Change $D$'s icon to *split*, its ancestors to *expired*;
    $ExpiredList \rightarrow$ add($D$);
    $ActiveList \rightarrow$ remove($activeRoot$);
    expandNode $(D, 0)$; // replace the expired node with its subtree
    **Array** *children* $\leftarrow$ SQL: SELECT title FROM meta WHERE parent='$D$';
    **foreach** *child* in *children* **do**
        $ActiveList \rightarrow$ add($child$);
**end**

- the expired segments are removed from the active area thus preventing the user from erroneous attempts to access them
- all valid decomposition paths and their still available granularity levels are clearly displayed in the active area
- the split dimensions in the expired area are horizontally ordered to preserve the order of splitting, with more recent steps being closer to the active area
- any expired split step can be undone, causing the corresponding tree level to be removed from the visualization. The navigation structure accounts for the undone split by re-activating the respective path.

# 7 Enhanced Decomposition Trees

Any particular visualization technique has its pros and cons depending on the type of task to be solved. In case of a dynamic disaggregation of OLAP cubes, the most common tasks are to "drill" into an aggregate in order to trace its behavior along certain dimensional axes and to compare the subtotals within the same granularity level against each other. Standard decomposition tree patented by Proclarity [16] are used to decompose an aggregate along multiple dimension axes. The measure's subtotals as numbers and percentage, as well as the corresponding split dimension's entity are placed inside the nodes. Only one node per interaction can be expandable. Our proposed enhancement of the standard decomposition tree technique is multi-directional and comprises the categories presented below.

***Layout.*** Decomposition trees adopt the classical aesthetic layout due to its visual support of both vertical (parent - children) and horizontal (same level nodes) comparison: children are placed below their parent and each tree level is aligned. Both the top-down and the left-to-right layouts are supported. Directing the nested bar-charts orthogonal to the tree layout (i.e., horizontal bars in case of a top-down tree) puts the charts in each

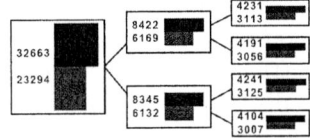

**Fig. 11.** Using area-aware chart bars

level onto the same axis and is therefore optimal for perceiving the entire level as a single chart (as in Fig. 2). The inherent wastefulness in terms of display area (scarcely populated upper levels consume as much area the bottom ones) can be minimized by adding space awareness to its nodes, as exemplified in Fig. 11. Feasibility of distinct display optimization measures depends on the type and behavior of the value(s) in the nodes. For instance, when decomposing a single measure, the children of each parent can be arranged into "Slice&Dice" treemaps [19], as shown in Fig. 12.

***Node contents.*** The node contents may be heterogeneous, such as a single value or a set of values with their dimensional characteristics. Multiple values per node arise whenever the user has chosen multiple measures to display or a nested-chart technique for a single measure. Our intention in this respect is to migrate from a plain value display towards a value visualization within and across the nodes. Nested bar-charts appear to be a rather suitable way of presenting nested decomposition or comparing multiple measures by putting them onto the same scale (see Fig. 2). Visual enhancements in part of parent-child or child-

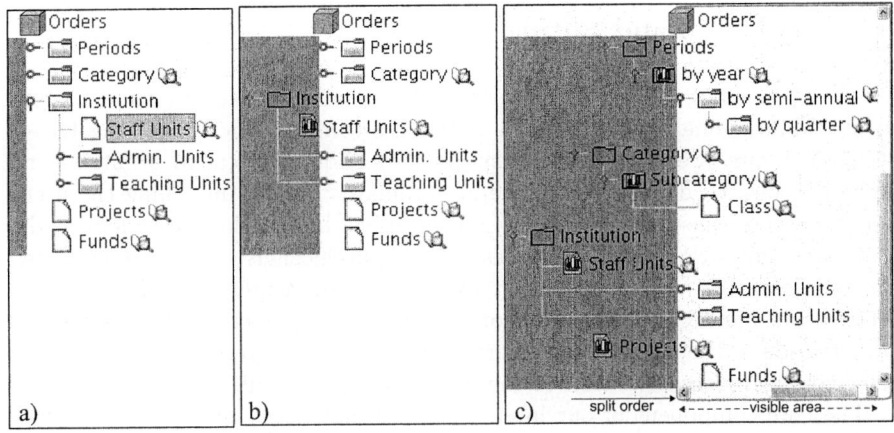

**Fig. 10.** Adaptive navigation structure a) initial state b) after the first decomposition c) after multiple decompositions

child relationships are best achieved by applying enclosure mechanisms, such as bounding boxes, subtree area division [11], or recursive partitioning of the node region as in treemaps [19].

***Visual elements.*** We suggest that the dimensional characteristics are used for labeling the node's links instead of putting them inside the nodes. This approach contributes to display optimization by reducing the node's inner area and filling the sparsely filled link areas. Another benefit is an improved logical structuring of the data: the aggregate is inside the node whereas its dimensional coordinate is attached to the link, connecting the node to its parent.

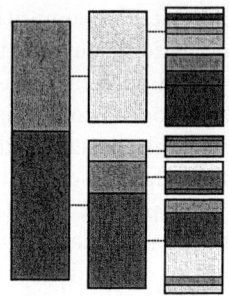

Fig. 12. "Slice&Dice" treemaps as nodes

***Generating the visualization.*** Unlike with the standard node-by-node expansion approach, our navigational framework empowers fast generation of arbitrarily large trees. A single *drag&drop* interaction is required for generating the entire tree level. The navigational hierarchy adapts itself every time the visualization is re-rendered to hide no longer valid navigation paths from the display and thus leaving the user very little space to lose the orientation or attempt an erroneous operation.

***Interaction Features.*** Interaction serves for exploring the visual hierarchy as well as for its dynamic modification. *Dragging* the nodes is straightforward and is used to deliberately re-arrange the nodes on the dispay. Single nodes can be minimized to icons (*temporary elimination*) by closing them to be reopened later. Deleting marked nodes or regions is equivalent to *local filtering*. *Zooming* is available in a form of a slider for resizing the entire visualization and as a dynamic zoom cursor for zooming on a single node. Power options, such as sorting, changing the display options, re-scaling the inner charts, etc. are accessed via an *"Options"* box placed next to each tree level.

## 8 Conclusion and Future Work

We have presented a navigation framework for advanced exploration and analysis of multidimensional data in a data warehouse context. The underlying OLAP technology empowers the decision support by allowing users to intuitively retrieve the desired data in a layout and granularity exactly matching the user's needs. We enhanced a standard OLAP interface by enabling user-defined dynamic decompositions of OLAP cubes using hierarchical visualization techniques. Since explorative analysis is driven by the insights acquired in the course of interaction, hierarchical visualization is especially appreciated for its natural preservation of the interaction history and for enabling gradual "descent" from a heavily aggregated overview to the desired level of detail.

The core component of our interface is the introduced navigation structure optimized for fast and easy generation of hierarchical visualizations from OLAP cube data by exploiting the logical data warehouse design. Our framework enables convenient navigation within a single OLAP cube as well as pursuing any valid drill-across paths for joined exploration of multiple facts. The visualization toolkit consists of the popular "state-of-the-art" hierarchical layouts. We also extended the classical node-link tree technique into an OLAP-aware *Enhanced Decomposition Tree*. The displayed data can be clearly structured by placing the aggregates inside the nodes, using their dimensional characteristics for labeling the nodes and the dimension titles for naming the tree levels. The values within the nodes can be arranged into nested charts to facilitate their visual perception.

The directions of our future activities are manifold: 1) to further explore challenging data patterns and new application domains with respect to their adequate mapping in the OLAP model, 2) to examine various visualization techniques as to what extent they qualify or can be adjusted for exploring OLAP data, 3) to refine our implementation to make it more generic and extendable to incorporate new data patterns and visualization techniques, and, 4) to obtain user feedback in order to evaluate and to revise our framework accordingly.

# References

1. Business Objects SA, "BusinessObjects OLAP Intelligence," 2005. [Online]. Available: http://www.businessobjects.com/products/queryanalysis/olapi.asp
2. C. Chabot, P. Hanrahan, C. Stolte, K. Brown, T. Walker, E. Johnson, and J. Mackinlay, "Tableau software," 2005. [Online]. Available: http://www.tableausoftware.com
3. S. Chaudhuri, U. Dayal, and V. Ganti, "Database technology for decision support systems," *Computer*, vol. 34, no. 12, pp. 48–55, 2001.
4. CNS International, "DataWarehouse Explorer," 2005. [Online]. Available: http://www.dwexplorer.com/products/producttour
5. E. F. Codd, S. B. Codd, and C. T. Salley, "Providing OLAP (on-line analytical processing) to user-analysts: An IT mandate," *Technical report, E.F.Codd & Associates*, 1993.
6. Cognos Software Corporation, "Cognos PowerPlay: Overview–OLAP Software," 2005. [Online]. Available: http://www.cognos.com/powerplay
7. S. G. Eick, "Visualizing multi-dimensional data," *SIGGRAPH Comput. Graph.*, vol. 34, no. 1, pp. 61–67, 2000.
8. I. Herman, G. Melançon, and M. S. Marshall, "Graph visualization and navigation in information visualization: A survey," *IEEE Transactions on Visualization and Computer Graphics*, vol. 6, no. 1, pp. 24–43, 2000.
9. D. A. Keim, "Information visualization and visual data mining," *IEEE Transactions on Visualization and Computer Graphics*, vol. 8, no. 1, pp. 1–8, 2002.
10. Microsoft, "Microsoft Excel –User's Guide," *Redmond, Wash.*, 1995.
11. Q. V. Nguyen and M. L. Huang, "Space-optimized tree: a connection+enclosure approach for the visualization of large hierarchies," *Information Visualization*, vol. 2, no. 1, pp. 3–15, 2003.
12. T. Niemi, J. Nummenmaa, and P. Thanisch, "Logical multidimensional database design for ragged and unbalanced aggregation," in *Design and Management of Data Warehouses*, 2001, p. 7.
13. V. K. Pang-Ning Tan, Michael Steinbach, *Introduction to Data Mining: Concepts and Techniques*. Addison Wesley, 2006.

14. T. B. Pedersen and C. S. Jensen, "Multidimensional database technology," *IEEE Computer*, vol. 34, no. 12, pp. 40–46, 2001.
15. T. B. Pedersen, C. S. Jensen, and C. E. Dyreson, "Extending practical pre-aggregation in on-line analytical processing," in *The VLDB Journal*, 1999, pp. 663–674.
16. ProClarity, "Business management software overview," 2005. [Online]. Available: http://www.proclarity.com/products
17. E. Reingold and J. Tilford, "Tidier drawing of trees," *IEEE Transactions on Software Engineering*, vol. 7, pp. 223–228, 1981.
18. R. D. B. Richard M. Wilson, "Dynamic hierarchy specification and visualization," in *Proceedings of the 1999 IEEE Symposium on Information Visualization*, 1999, p. 65.
19. B. Shneiderman, "Tree visualization with tree-maps: 2-d space-filling approach," *ACM Trans. Graph.*, vol. 11, no. 1, pp. 92–99, 1992.
20. C. Stolte, D. Tang, and P. Hanrahan, "Polaris: A system for query, analysis, and visualization of multidimensional relational databases," *IEEE Transactions on Visualization and Computer Graphics*, vol. 8, no. 1, pp. 52–65, 2002.
21. XMLA, "Report Portal: Zero-footprint olap web client solution," 2005. [Online]. Available: http://www.reportportal.com

# DPTree: A Distributed Pattern Tree Index for Partial-Match Queries in Peer-to-Peer Networks

Dyce Jing Zhao, Dik Lun Lee, and Qiong Luo

Department of Computer Science,
Hong Kong University of Science & Technology, Hong Kong
{zhaojing, dlee, luo}@cs.ust.hk

**Abstract.** Partial-match queries return data items that contain a subset of the query keywords and order the results based on the statistical properties of the matched keywords. They are essential for information retrieval on large document repositories. However, most current peer-to-peer networks for information retrieval are based on distributed hashing and as such cannot support partial-match queries efficiently. In this paper, we describe an efficient and scalable technique to support partial-match queries on peer-to-peer networks. We observe that the combinations of keywords in the queries are only a small subset of all possible combinations of the keywords in the documents. Therefore, we propose a distributed index structure, called a distributed pattern tree (DPTree), to record frequent query patterns, i.e., combinations of keywords, learnt from the query history at each node in the network. Using this index, a query can identify its best matching patterns quickly and data lookup can be done in logarithmic time with respect to the network size. Our simulation studies on the TREC data sets have shown promising results in comparison with other previous approaches.

## 1 Introduction

While the decentralized nature of peer-to-peer file sharing systems enables robustness and scalability, it also poses great challenges for resource lookup in these systems. Most existing peer-to-peer approaches do not support complex queries efficiently. Unstructured peer-to-peer systems maintain no forward knowledge for remote computers. As a result they are essentially in the dilemma between network coverage and bandwidth cost while searching, whether using simple or complex queries. Structured peer-to-peer systems, such as Chord [6] and Pastry [2], are mostly based on distributed hash tables (DHT). They determine the hosting peer(s) of a data item by applying hash functions on the descriptors (e.g., the keys) of the data item. Therefore, they can quickly route a query to the destination where matching data items can be found, but they only allow exact match, i.e., the query and the descriptors of the data items must be identical. Exact match does not meet the needs of full-text keyword queries. It is difficult for such structured peer-to-peer systems to support more complex queries such as partial-match queries efficiently.

Generally speaking, a partial-match query returns data items that contain the query keywords and ranks the results according to the matched keywords. For example, a full-text retrieval system accepts keywords as the query, and retrieves and ranks documents containing the keywords. There are many ranking functions. In this paper, we adopt the inner product similarity because it ranks documents purely based on the matched keywords without considering other non-matching keywords in the documents. Inner product is not only simple but also suitable for users who are looking for some relevant documents (i.e., most web search users). For example, assessors for TREC relevance judgments consider a document to be relevant to a query if any slice of the document is relevant to the query [21].

We note that most existing peer-to-peer networks for information retrieval are based on distributed hashing and as such cannot support partial-match queries efficiently. In this paper, we propose to develop a distributed index called *DPTree* which supports full-text partial-match queries efficiently on peer-to-peer networks. The idea is that each node manages a list of relevant documents for popular queries, and organizes the document lists to be searchable within $O(\log N)$ time where $N$ is the total number of participating nodes. In this paper, we use the term *pattern* to represent the (unordered) set of keywords that a query contains. While the number of possible patterns is astronomical, given the large and ever-growing document repositories nowadays, we observe that only a small portion of the patterns are frequently used in the queries. This observation motivates us to focus on frequent patterns mined from the query history. In fact, query history has been utilized successfully in many peer-to-peer search systems to improve the performance [8, 11, 22].

To support the organization of patterns and pattern mining, we developed the distributed pattern trees (DPTree). By definition, a DPTree is a tree structure that can be implemented on one or more computers: a node can be implemented on more than one computer, or alternatively, the whole tree can be implemented on one computer. Each DPTree node corresponds to a pattern. In particular, the root of a DPTree represents a single-word pattern, its children are responsible for 2-word patterns, and its grand children correspond to 3-word patterns, etc. Each node maintains an index to the list of documents matching the pattern that the node maintains. For clarity, we hereafter use the terms *DPTree node* to refer to the node itself, the *pattern* it maintains or the machine (or machines) that implement the node when no ambiguity arise.

A DPTree node is capable of initiating, forwarding and responding to queries. During the search procedure, a DPTree node selectively records a query history, from which frequent patterns can be mined periodically. A DPTree starts with a single-word pattern (i.e., the root node) and is expanded and adapted dynamically based on the frequent patterns found. The roots of the DPTree's form an addressable network using distributed hash tables. By applying mining technique on query history, our approach is able to answer most queries quickly and precisely by managing a suitable number of frequent patterns. In addition, we employ *random access sequence* on patterns to establish strict mapping between a pattern and the DPTree that it resides. This eliminates redundant patterns across DPTree's without breaking the storage and network load balance among the peers. Another data structure called *sub-tree summary* enables a DPTree node to estimate its entire sub-tree in an economical way, which spares overlay maintenance cost.

We conducted simulation over TREC data and compared our system with other two systems [3, 17] which are to be introduced in the next section. The experimental results show that our approach achieves significant gain on search effectiveness and efficiency.

The remainder of this paper is organized as follows: Section 2 introduces some related works. Section 3 describes the basic DPTree approach in detail. We discuss some improvements for the basic approach in section 4 concerning redundancy and maintenance. Section 5 presents our experimental results and Section 6 summarizes our work.

## 2 Related Work

To our current knowledge, no authoritative peer-to-peer approaches were found for partial-match full-text queries. However, concerning the larger domain of similarity search, there are some impressive works [3, 4, 13].

pSearch [3][4] and SSW [13] use Latent Semantic Indexing (LSI) to map documents into a semantic vector space and perform search based on the Euclidian distance between the query point and the document points. In especial, pSearch is developed on top of CAN. In addition to the use of LSI, pSearch applies rolling index and register a document to $p$ places in the CAN using $p$ separate partial semantic spaces. This reduces the dimensionality and therefore enables CAN to manage full-text documents. In SSW, computers form clusters, each of which manages non-overlapping regions of the semantic vector space. A cluster is split into two at a certain cluster size when new nodes join the network. Every computer in a cluster knows its region and splitting history, which are used to compute a unique ID for the cluster. All the clusters form a circle with clockwise ascending cluster ID's. A query message computes a partial cluster ID using available splitting history and hops along the circle in a greedy manner until it reaches the cluster with the complete ID. Query routing is efficient in both pSearch and SSW. pSearch and SSW split successively the vector space into cells and position data points according to the cells that they reside in. These approaches work well with similarity metrics such as cosine or Euclidian distance. They are, however, inherently not applicable to partial match. This is because although various document ranking metrics (e.g., inner product) can be applied to process partial-match queries, none of the metrics follow the triangle rule (i.e., $d_{AC} \leq d_{AB} + d_{BC}$ for any three points $A, B,$ and $C$, where $d_{XY}$ is the distance between point $X$ and point $Y$.). This indicates that documents relevant to a query are not guaranteed to be similar to each other. As a result, the basic assumption of pSearch and SSW does not hold that data points relevant to a query reside in a small number of adjacent cells.

Efforts were made to address the particular issue of partial-match query [5, 10, 15, 17, 18]. One approach [15] assigns every keyword set that appears in the network a computer which indexes a list of relevant documents for the keyword set. A document is said to be relevant to a keyword set if all of its keywords co-exist in at least one slice (or a window) of the document. While this method does partial-match search quickly, it bears large storage and maintenance overhead since, with no selectivity, it will possibly supervise a huge number of keyword sets.

Another approach [17] applies joins in distributed database to work with partial-match search. It maintains a list of documents for each single keyword. To compute the result set for a multi-keyword query consisting of more than one keywords, it starts with the first keyword and locates quickly a list of relevant documents. A bloom filter is computed based on the document list retrieved which is much smaller in size compared to the list of relevant documents. The bloom filter is sent to the next keyword along with the query. Upon receiving the query and the bloom filter, the computer responsible for the next keyword will integrate the bloom filter and its document indices into a new relevant list. This method is efficient for small data sets. However, it is shown [9] that the bloom filter consumes significant bandwidth cost in large-scale networks.

## 3  Partial-Match Search Using Distributed Pattern Trees

Our observation is that compared to the huge number of possible keyword sets, only a very small portion of them are frequently used as queries. Therefore, it is unnecessary as well as infeasible to create a document list for every possible pattern. This motivates us to use distributed pattern trees that extend themselves from query history. The DPTree's manage a tree hierarchy of popular query patterns. Every node for a DPTree is associated with a pattern and is represented by a cluster of strongly connected computers responsible for a pattern. The parent-child relationship between two DPTree nodes indicates the containment relationship between their patterns. A pattern $P_2$ is said to contain another pattern $P_1$ if and only if all keywords that appear in $P_1$ also exist in $P_2$. The root of a DPTree is a pattern of a single keyword. The root nodes are positioned using distributed hash table while the single-word patterns that they manage serve as the key. Among a few applicable DHT's [1, 2, 6], we choose Chord [6] for placement of pattern tree roots.

During a series of query sessions, every DPTree node selectively collects its query history and mines the frequent patterns periodically. The DPTree's, initially consisting of only roots, are then expanded dynamically as new frequent patterns are discovered. A keyword based search starts from one single word clusters and is propagated along the pattern trees until the patterns that best match the query are reached.

### 3.1  Overlay Formation

We now discuss the construction of the overlay network. In essence, our approach uses distributed pattern trees on top of the Chord protocol. Figure 1 displays a

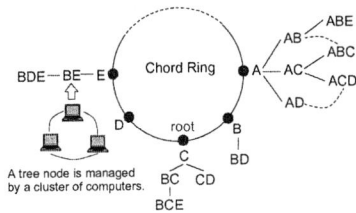

**Fig. 1.** Distributed pattern trees positioned along a Chord ring

simple example of the network containing five DPTree's, rooted at $A$, $B$, $C$, $D$, and $E$, respectively. Each node is labelled with the pattern that it manages.

In the initial state, a DPTree contains only the root, which corresponds to a single-word pattern. The DPTree's are generated dynamically. When a DPTree node $N_i$ receives a query, it checks if it fully matches the query. If so, it answers the query. If not, it checks if any of its child nodes matches the query. If a match is found, the query is forwarded to the corresponding child node for processing. Otherwise, $N_i$ is considered the best matching node and the answers are returned from $N_i$. Since $N_i$ does not fully match the query, it records the query in its query history. Algorithm 1. describes this query logging procedure.

---

**Algorithm 1.** Query logging during a search session

**Input:**
    $N$ is a node of a DPTree
    $Q$ is a query message
    $P$ is the peer that initiates a query
Procedure:  $query(N, Q, P)$
1: **if** $N$ fully matches $Q$ **then**
2:    $retrieve(N, Q, P)$
3: **else**
4:    **if** $\exists N'$, $N'$ is a child of $N$ **and** $N'$ matches $Q$ **then**
5:      $query(N', Q, P)$;
6:    **else**
7:      $retrieve(N, Q, P)$;
8:      log $Q$ in the local query history
Procedure:  $retrieve(N, Q, P)$
9: flood $Q$ within the cluster of computers for $N$;
10: return the highest-ranked documents to $P$;

---

A DPTree node, say node $N_0$, monitors its own query history. It mines periodically the frequent query patterns using any pattern mining methods such as Apriori [19] and Eclat [14]. If $N_0$ contains $t$ words, the pattern mining process mines all frequent patterns containing $t + 1$. A new node is created for each of the mined frequent patterns and becomes the child of $N_0$.

In the DPTree, the parent and child nodes can communicate with each other and know each other's patterns. Suppose $N_0$ manages pattern $P_0$. To create a child node, $N_1$, whose pattern is $P_1$ ($P_0 \subset P_1$), the list of documents maintained by $N_0$ is split such that documents that match $N_1$ are moved to $N_1$. In addition, queries in $N_0$'s query history that are longer than $P_0$ are moved $N_1$.

Recall that DPTree nodes are distributed on a set of machines and that a DPTree node can be implemented on more than one machine. To minimize the network cost for DPTree node splitting and to balance the overlay maintenance overhead among the peers, we use a splitting strategy as follows,

1. for every machine involved, count the number of its indexed documents that match $P_1$ and rank the machines using their counts;
2. assign machines to the new node $N_1$ in descending order of the machines' ranks;
3. stop splitting when the storage for the document indices are roughly balanced between the machines managing node $N_0$ and those managing node $N_1$.

Node $N_0$ notifies the creation of the new node $N_1$ to its parent. The parent is responsible for two tasks:

1. it checks if the same pattern exists by polling all of its children with pattern $P_1$; if the same pattern is found, it asks the two corresponding tree nodes to merge into one;
2. if $P_1$ does not exist in the children, the parent continues to look for children that match a sub-pattern of $P_1$ and build unidirectional links from the matching children to $N_1$.

The unidirectional links (shown as dotted curves in Figure 1) are used to ensure that every pattern of the pattern tree can be reached from the root in a greedy manner. These links lower the search cost by relaxing the strict tree structure of DPTree.

At the initial stage, there may be insufficient query history available for pattern tree generation. As an alternative, a pattern tree can extend itself by mining the frequent patterns based on the label of its indexed documents.

### 3.2 Maintenance and Search

A machine or a peer in our peer-to-peer network is capable of initiating two classes of operations: the maintenance operation when a peer joins or leaves the network and the search operation when a peer submits a query. In this section, we discuss how these operations are performed in the order that they appear during the lifetime of a peer.

The maintenance and search operations involve four types of messages. Table 1 lists the information that the four types of messages carry, where *foreign index* means the index for a document on a remote peer.

Among these messages, peer join and document registration messages are for the peer joining operation; query and peer leave messages are for search and peer leaving operations, respectively.

**Table 1.** Description of messages used in the system

| Message Name | Message Information |
|---|---|
| peer join | peer label, peer address |
| document registration | document label, registration key, peer address |
| query | keyword list, peer address |
| peer leave | foreign indices, query history, peer address |

**Peer Joining.** When a peer $P_{new}$ joins a network, it first computes the label for itself and generates a peer join message. While a peer label can be defined in various ways, we use the centroid of the peer's local document set as the peer's label. This method takes advantage of data locality and query locality, and hence helps to reduce maintenance and search costs.

$P_{new}$ sends its peer join message to an existing peer $P_0$ randomly selected in the network. The message is then directed to a DPTree root $N_r$ which matches the most frequent word in $P_{new}$'s local repository. $N_r$ can be located by following the tree edges from $P_0$ to $P_0$'s tree root, $N_{r0}$, and along the Chord ring from $N_{r0}$ to $N_r$. This operation is efficient because:

1. the height of a DPTree is small, since DPTree height is bounded by the lengths of the user queries which are typically short [23];
2. searching on the Chord ring takes only logarithmic time with respect to the number of pattern trees, and only the tree roots are positioned along the Chord ring.

Upon receiving $P_{new}$'s join message, $N_r$ computes its *recruiting priority* with respect to $P_{new}$. The recruiting priority of all of $N_r$'s child nodes are also computed. The recruiting priority between a tree node $N$ and $P_{new}$ indicates how likely $P_{new}$ is going to join $N$. Formally, $N$'s recruiting priority is defined as follows.

$$rp(P_{new}, N) = L_N * Sim(P_{new}, N), \qquad L_N = AR_N * (FI_N/Cap_N),$$

where $Sim(P_{new}, N)$ denotes the similarity between $P_{new}$ and $C$. The label of a DPTree node is the pattern that it manages. The factor $L_N$ in the equation evaluates $N$'s workload for maintaining foreign indices and for processing query requests. To compute $L_N$ we use $N$'s recent access rate $AR_N$ (i.e., the number of messages received/forwarded/returned during a time unit) and the *consumption ratio* (i.e., the percentage of storage that's already consumed) of $N$'s local storage which is represented by $N$'s current storage for foreign indices, $FI_N$, over $N$'s capacity, $Cap_N$. This indicates that the possibility of a new peer joining a DPTree node is subject to two factors: the peer's relevance to the tree node and the maintenance overhead of the node. Therefore, the use of recruiting priority helps balance the load among the tree nodes.

If $N_r$ gets the highest recruiting priority, $P_{new}$ joins the cluster responsible for $N_r$. Otherwise, the peer join message is forwarded to the child of $N_r$ which has the highest recruiting priority and the join process continues in a similar way. After the peer joins a tree node, it prepares the document registration messages for each of its local documents. The registration key in a document registration message is a word appearing in the document and is used to find a pattern tree root. $P_{new}$'s documents are then published to all of the relevant tree nodes using the document registration messages.

**Search.** The search consists of two steps. In the first step, when a peer $P$ initiates a query, the query message is propagated to the DPTree roots that match one of the query keywords. A query is routed from the starting peer to the relevant roots in the same way as a peer join message is routed. Note that it is possible that a query word does not match any of the DPTree's on the Chord ring. In this case, a failure message is returned since the query word is obviously beyond the global vocabulary.

In the second step, a separate search process is executed on each of the relevant DPTree's. Upon receiving a query message, a DPTree node (or, more precisely, a peer responsible for the DPTree node) first checks whether it is the most similar node to the query, and responds to the query if it is. Otherwise, the query is propagated to a randomly selected child node that is more similar to the query. The detailed procedure is described in Algorithm 1. in Section 3.1.

When the second step completes, we are able to identify the tree nodes that best satisfy the query, although they may not be perfect matches. When a tree node decides to answer a query, it uses the document labels of its foreign indices to compute the relevance score and returns the top $M$ results, where $M$ is a pre-defined number. If multiple DPTree's are contacted during a search process, the query initiator will do a local re-ranking after all query results are returned.

**Peer Leaving.** When a peer leaves the network, it hands its foreign indices and query history to one of its neighbors in the cluster. If a leaving peer is the last peer in the cluster, it contacts a neighboring cluster which bears the lowest maintenance overhead and asks the neighbor to take over its task.

In addition to the activities mentioned previously, a peer may fail unexpectedly. Our system is insensitive to single peer failure due to the use of clusters. As an alternative, the foreign indices can be replicated within a cluster. Should a peer fail, the peers within the same cluster will seamlessly take over its job.

## 4 Improvements

After we describe the basic model, we are now able to estimate theoretically the performance of our DPTree approach. The network costs can be formulated as follows.

$$CSearch = O(\log N' + QLength + 2 * M); \qquad (1)$$
$$CJoin = O(\log N' + (\log N' + TSize) * D * W). \qquad (2)$$

We use $N'$ to denote the number of clusters that manage DPTree roots, and use $N$ to denote the number of peers in the overlay network. $N'/N$ is about $1/3$ in our experiments. Equation (1) summarizes the search cost for a query with $QLength$ query words if $M$ query results are to be returned. Equation (2) shows the join cost for a new peer with $D$ documents and on average $W$ words per document. $TSize$ is the average number of nodes contained in a DPTree. The first item in the equation is the overlay maintenance cost, while the second item is the document registration cost.

The above equations for cost estimation suggest DPTree's superiority in searching. However, they also reveal the non-trivial cost for peer joining or leaving. In this section, we propose two methods, *random access sequence* and *sub-tree summary*, to cope with the considerable maintenance cost.

### 4.1 Random Access Sequence

The DPTree-based network contains a certain degree of redundancy. For example, a query with three words $A$, $B$ and $D$ may be directed to DPTree($A$) as well as DPTree($B$). In a network as shown in Figure 1, both node $AD$ under DPTree($A$) and node $BD$ under DPTree($B$) will have query $ABD$ in their query history. Therefore, it is possible that the pattern $ABD$ will appear in more than one DPTree, as shown in blue in Figure 2.

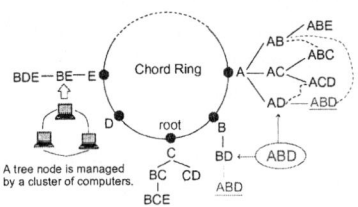

**Fig. 2.** Redundancy in the network

To eliminate redundant patterns, we generate a random access sequence (RAS) for every multi-keyword query. RAS determines the order that the query keywords are processed. When a query is initiated, the search process generates the random access sequence of the query, and contact DPTree's according to the order of the single keywords listed in RAS. Similarly, when a new frequent pattern is mined, RAS is used to determine which DPTree is going to create a node for the new pattern. Given a multi-keyword query $Q$, the random access sequence is generated as described in Algorithm 2.

The use of random access sequence avoids redundant patterns across DPTree's. As a result, the cost for document registration and search is decreased. In addition, applying RAS does not break the balance of the storage and network workload because the access sequence of a query is random. Therefore, although the search process favors some DPTree's over others with respect to

**Algorithm 2.** Random access sequence

**Input:**
  $Q$ is a query message
**Output:**
  $Q$ whose keywords are re-ordered
*Procedure:* $RAS(Q)$
1: order the keywords in $Q$ alphabetically;
2: $srandom(Q)$
3: $s = $ number of keywords in $Q$;
4: **for** $i=s$ to 2 **do**
5:   $p = [random()\ mod\ (i-1)] + 1$;
6:   swap the $i$ th keyword and the $(i-p)$th keyword in $Q$;
7: **return** $Q$;

---

a single query, globally the storage and network overheads of the DPTree's are not biased.

### 4.2 Sub-tree Summary

It is shown that the bulk of the peer joining cost comes from document registration. The reason is that in the document registration procedure, when a document tries to find relevant patterns in a DPTree, it has to explore every node of the DPTree, which involves a large amount of data transmission among the peers. We use a data structure called *sub-tree summary* to avoid unnecessary DPTree node access and as such to reduce the document registration cost by avoiding unnecessary DPTree node access.

In essential, every DPTree node keeps a summary of the sub-tree under it. The summary of a sub-tree contains the following information:

- the location of the sub-tree root;
- for every node N in the sub-tree, a $< P_N, R_N >$ pair, where $P_N$ is the pattern for node N and $R_N$ is the minimum relevance score that N permits.

A document is forwarded to node N if the relevance score between the document and $P_N$ is greater than $R_N$. Using the sub-tree summaries, a new document will have to access only the DPTree nodes along the path to a relevant node.

To estimate the relevance score threshold $R_N$ for a pattern tree node $N$, the following information is used:

- The relevance score of every foreign index that $N$ contains.
- The maximum number of foreign indices that $N$ will maintain, denoted as $M'_N$. $N$ is set to be proportional to the number of queries that $N$ does not perfectly match but answered.
- An amplification factor $\gamma(\gamma > 1)$ which is universal for all nodes.

We assume that with respect to a pattern $P_N$, the relevance score distribution of all its relevant documents follows the Zipf's law. We use the current set of foreign index to approximate the distribution curve. We set the maximum foreign index number with two values: $M'_N$ and $M_N = \gamma * M'_N$. We use $M'_N$ and $M_N$ to compute two relevance score thresholds, $R'_N$ and $R_N$, respectively ($R'_N > R_N$). $R_N$ is sent to $N$'s parent node for sub-tree summarizing. We will explain later in this section why we use two thresholds.

The sub-tree summaries are built as follows:

- **DPTree node creation.** When a DPTree node $N_0$ creates a new child $N$, it creates a summary for the resulting sub-tree containing only $N$. The summary contains the location of node $N$ and $< P_N, 0 >$. When the sub-tree summary for any DPTree is updated, the node propagates the update to its parent, whose sub-tree summary is updated consequently.
- **Foreign index update.** A node $N$ knows its relevance score threshold $R_N$ which is used for sub-tree summarizing.
  - When a foreign index is deleted from node $N$, $N$ uses the resulting new list of foreign indices to compute the new values for its two relevance score thresholds $R'_{N\_new}$ and $R_{N\_new}$ ($R'_{N\_new} > R_{N\_new}, R_N > R_{N\_new}$). If $R'_{N\_new} < R_N$, we update the pair $< P_N, R_N >$ with $< P_N, R_{N\_new} >$ for all nodes along the path from N to the pattern tree root.
  - When a foreign index is inserted into node $N$, nothing is done. However, when a document reaches a node $N$ but is rejected, $N$ will compute the updated value for its relevance score thresholds $R_{N\_new}$ and replace $< P_N, R_N >$ with $< P_N, R_{N\_new} >$ if $R_{N\_new} > R_N$.

This method greatly reduces the number of peers accessed for document registration, and thus reducing the registration cost. However, it introduces overheads for sub-tree summary update. We minimize the sub-tree summary update cost by setting a looser relevance score threshold than the actual estimation. This allows the sub-tree summaries to be updated only after a number of successive index deletions have been done. It should be noted that the value of the amplifying factor $\gamma$ is a trade off between the redundant peer access cost and sub-tree summary update cost.

## 5 Experiments

To evaluate the proposed distributed index, we compare our method to the Bloom filter approach [17] which is specifically for partial-match queries and pSearch [3] which is a well-studied peer-to-peer search method.

We apply the vector space model and label a document as a term vector. "Term frequency inverse document frequency" (TFIDF) is used to compute the weight of a term in a document. Since it is impractical to obtain the global document frequency in a dynamic peer-to-peer system, we use the local document frequency instead. Both our DPTree and the bloom filter method are built on top of the Chord protocol.

Given a keyword based query, the goal of search is to find a specified number of documents that are most relevant to the query.

## 5.1 Simulation Setup

The document set consists of about 500,000 documents taken from Volumes 4[1] and 5[2] of the TREC collection, consisting of about 500,000 documents. The query keywords were generated from the global keyword database according to their document frequencies in the Web repository maintained by the UC Berkeley and Stanford Dig- ital Library projects (See http://elib.cs.berkeley.edu/docfreq/), which consists of 49,602,191 pages.

All programs were written in Java (JDK 1.2.0) and run on a PC with 2.5G Pentium 4 processor and 512M memory.

We used the following metrics in the simulation:

1. **Effectiveness** is measured by the average precision and recall. We define the *hit list* for a query as a list of all available documents on the network that match the query. Let the hit list be $H$ and the returned result list be $R$ for any query. Precision is defined as $\frac{|R \cap H|}{|R|}$, and recall is defined as $\frac{|R \cap H|}{|H|}$.
2. **Search Path Length** is defined as the average number of logical hops traversed by a query message before it reaches the destination.
3. **Search cost** is defined as the average number of messages that a query incurs in the search process.
4. **Maintenance cost** is defined as the average number of messages used to handle peer activities including peer joining and leaving.
5. **Storage cost** is defined as the average number of foreign indices that a peer maintains.

The simulation parameters, their range of values and default settings are specified in Table 2.

**Table 2.** Simulation parameters

|   | Description | Range | Default |
|---|---|---|---|
| N | Number of peers in the network | 1k - 20k | 10k |
| n | Number of document per peer | 1 - 20 | 5 |
| L | Length of queries | 1 - 5 | |
| M | Number of document returned | | 20 |
| $\lambda$ | Number of operations per round | | 100 |
| w | Number of warm-up queries used | 0 - 5k | 1k |

We used a large number of peers in the simulation to evaluate the scalability of the three methods. The number of keywords in a query ranges from 1 to 5 with a

---

[1] TREC Volume 4, May 1996 Collection includes material from the Financial Times Limited (1991, 1992, 1993, 1994), the Congressional Record of the 103rd Congress (1993), and the Federal Register (1994).
[2] TREC Volume 5, April 1997 Collection includes material from the Foreign Broadcast Information Service (1996) and the Los Angeles Times (1989, 1990).

uniform distribution. This was to approximate the real-word query lengths [16]. We set the number of returned documents to 20, which is the typical number of documents that most web users are willing to examine. To generate a new peer, we varied the number of documents per peer from 1 to 20 and assigned documents randomly selected from the TREC collection. As a result, duplicated documents may exist in our simulation. Since our method applies mining techniques in building up the distributed index, a longer warm-up period would likely yield better search performance. To examine the effect of the mining techniques, experiments with no warm-up queries and with a rich query history were run.

## 5.2 Comparison

We conducted extensive experiments to compare our work with two other approaches: the Bloom filter approach and pSearch. According to the configuration in [3], we let pSearch take 4 partial semantic spaces, and the dimension of each partial semantic space was $2.3 log_N$ where $N$ was the network size. Considering the unavailability of a global document set, we randomly picked a subset of 5,000 documents from the TREC collection and LSI via singular value decomposition (SVD) was applied to to the subset to generate the semantic space. For simplicity, we denote our DPTree method by *DPTree* and the Bloom filter approach by *BLF* (BLF for bloom filter) in the later experiments.

First, we compared the search effectiveness of the three methods. Figure 3 presents the precision-recall curve for networks with 1,000 to 20,000 nodes. Our method (DPTree) yields a much higher search quality especially when the number of peers in the network is large. Its retrieval precision is about 35% better than both of the other methods when the network size $N = 20k$. This was due to the use of the distributed pattern trees. By mining the frequent patterns dynamically, our approach adapts user needs and is insensitive to network size. It should be noted, however, that inner-product was used as the similarity measure

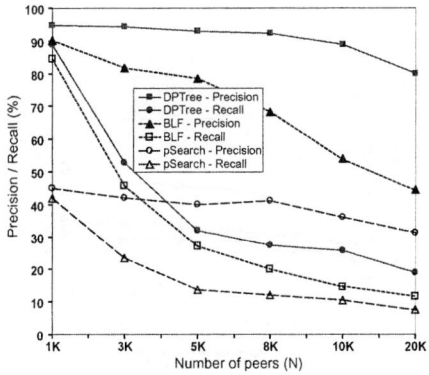

**Fig. 3.** Precision-recall curve

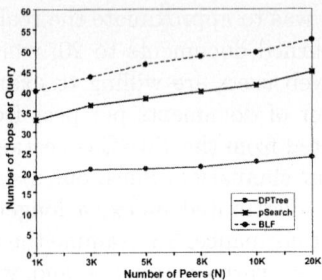

**Fig. 4.** Search Path Length

in the experiments and that since pSearch was not designed for partial-match, it is expected to yield poor performance.

In Figures 4, 5, and 6 we examined the scalability of the three methods in terms of the search cost, search path length and system maintenance cost, respectively.

Search path length is an important performance measure since it affects the query response time. shows that the search path in our method is shortest. To identify the destination for a query, our system takes almost only half of the number of hops compared to the other two approaches. The search path length was logarithmic with respect to the network size for all of the three methods, but our method carried a smaller constant term since DHT was applied to the tree roots instead of the entire set of peer computers in our system.

Figure 5 depicts the search cost in terms of the total number of messages transferred for a query. Our methods outperformed the other two especially when sufficient query history was available. With our default setting (N = 10k,

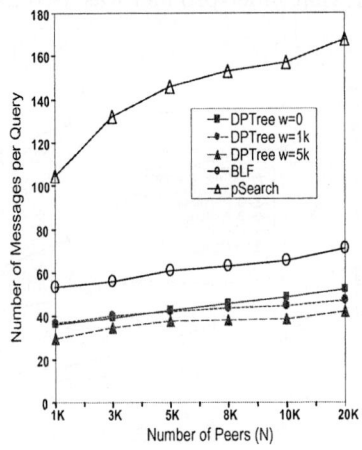

**Fig. 5.** Search cost

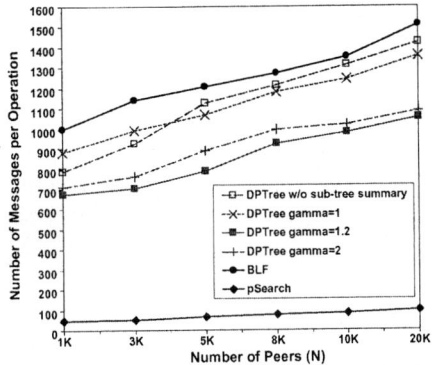

**Fig. 6.** Maintenance for various number of peers

$w = 1k$), DPTree on average spent about 70% less messages than pSearch and about 12% less than BLF. pSearch incurred a much higher cost during search since it performed four separate searches over the entire network for every query.

We evaluate the average maintenance cost of each method by setting the rates that peers joined and left the network to be the same and varying the network size from 1k to 20k nodes. No query was performed during this round of experiments so that the system maintenance cost was isolated from the search cost. Figure 6 presents the maintenance cost of the three methods. The effect of sub-tree summary for DPTree was also measured, with the amplification factor $\gamma$ set to 1, 1.2 and 2. It can be observed that when the $\gamma$ is at 1.2, applying sub-tree summary can reduce the maintenance cost by 25% compared to our basic approach (see Figure 6). Thus the effectiveness of sub-tree summary is justified. However, Figure 6 also shows that except for pSearch, both our approach and the bloom filter approach incur a considerable maintenance overhead when peer membership changes very frequently.

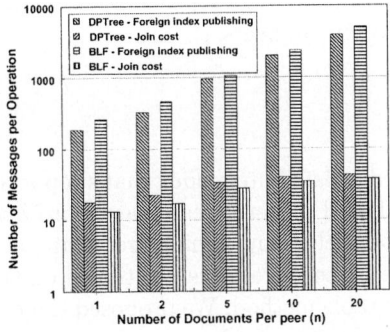

**Fig. 7.** Maintenance for various number of documents per peer

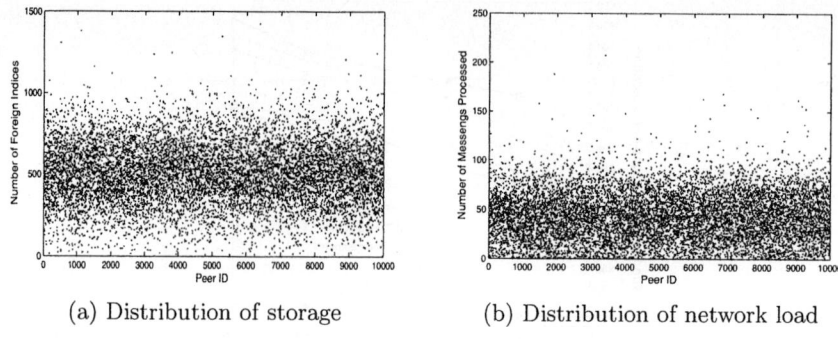

(a) Distribution of storage   (b) Distribution of network load

**Fig. 8.** Distribution of storage and network load among peers

To further analyze the network maintenance cost, we varied the number of documents that a peer held from 1 to 20, and displayed in Figure 7 the overlay maintenance cost and the document registration cost separately. The y-axis of Figure 7 is displayed in logarithmic scale. The experimental result indicates that the vast majority of the maintenance cost for peer membership changes comes from foreign document registration. Therefore, although our method incurs non-trivial network cost in a highly dynamic environment, we can apply various techniques to reduce the cost. For example, lazy update can greatly reduce document registration cost when some peers keep joining and leaving the network frequently. Moreover, document registration can even be suspended during a period of heavy network traffic since it does not affect the correctness of the overlay. As a result, we believe that our approach could scale in terms of query efficiency, search cost as well as maintenance cost.

To estimate the workload distribution among all the peers, we plotted the network and storage loads with respect to the peer ID's in Figure 8. Figure 8(a) displays the number of foreign indices that each peer maintains, and it shows that the storage load for most peers was close to the average load. In addition, the maximum number of foreign indices per peer does not exceed 1,500 while the average number is 514. Figure 8(b) displays the number of messages processed during a certain time period for 10,000 peers. It shows that the distribution of network load is balanced among peers.

## 6  Conclusion

In this paper we proposed a distributed index that supports partial-match search. We developed the distributed pattern trees that record query history in a selective way and extend themselves by mining frequent patterns from the query history. The roots of the pattern trees are positioned on the overlay network using any distributed hash table method. We proposed the random access sequence and sub-tree summary techniques to decrease the maintenance cost.

Experiments showed that our approach yields high precision for keyword-based partial-match queries. Our method was also proven to be efficient in query routing. The performance of data look-up improves after a certain warm-up period. It was also shown that our approach achieves good load balance. Although peer membership changes incur a considerable maintenance overhead, the majority of the costs comes from foreign-index publishing, and the network cost for the peer join operation was small. We argue that foreign-index publishing can be suspended in a heavy traffic period and that peer join and data lookup are not affected by this suspended operation. Moreover, applying lazy update can further reduce the maintenance cost. As a result, our approach is scalable.

# References

1. B.Y. Zhao and J.D. Kubiatowicz, A.D. Joseph, *Tapestry: An Infrastructure for Fault-tolerant Wide-area Location and Routing*, Technical Report UCB/CSD-01-1141, U. C. Berkeley, April 2001.
2. A. Rowstron, P. Druschel, *Pastry: Scalable, distributed object location and routing for large-scale peer-to-peer systems*, IFIP/ACM International Conference on Distributed Systems Platforms (Middleware), Heidelberg, Germany, pages 329-350, November, 2001
3. C. Tang, Z. Xu, S. Dwarkadas, *Peer-to-Peer Information Retrieval Using Self-Organizing Semantic Overlay Networks*, ACM SIGCOMM 2003, Karlsruhe, Germany, August 2003.
4. C. Tang, S. Dwarkadas, Z. Xu, *On Scaling Latent Semantic Indexing for Large Peer-to-Peer Systems*, Proc. 27th Annual International ACM SIGIR Conference, Sheffield, UK, July, 2004.
5. E. Cohen, A. Fiat, H. Kaplan, *A case for associative peer to peer overlays*, ACM SIGCOMM Computer Communication Review, Volume 33, Issue 1 (January 2003).
6. I. Stoica, R. Morris, D. Karger, M.F. Kaashoek, H. Balakrishnan, *Chord: A scalable peer-to-peer lookup service for internet applications*, In Proc. ACM SIGCOMM 2001, August 2001.
7. D. Karger, E. Lehman, F.T. Leighton, M. Levine, D. Lewin, R. Panigrahy. *Consistent hashing and random trees: Distributed caching protocols for relieving hot spots on the World Wide Web*. In Proc. 29th Annual ACM Symposium on Theory of Computing, pages 654-663, May 1997.
8. H. Cai, J. Wang, *Peer-to-peer computing: Foreseer: a novel, locality-aware peer-to-peer system architecture for keyword searches*, Proc. the 5th ACM/IFIP/USENIX international conference on Middleware, Oct 2004.
9. J. Li, B. T. Loo, J. M. Hellerstein, M. F. Kaashoek, D. Karger, R. Morris, *On the feasibility of peer-to-peer web indexing and search*. In 2nd International Workshop on Peer-to-Peer Systems (IPTPS), 2003.
10. J. Lu, J. Callan. *Content-based retrieval in hybrid peer-to-peer networks*, Proc. the 12th international conference on Information and knowledge management (CIKM), Pages: 199 - 206.
11. M. Aneiros, V. Estivill-Castro, C. Sun, *Social browsing: Group unified histories an instrument for productive unconstrained co-browsing*, Proc. 2003 International ACM SIGGROUP Conference on Supporting Group Work, Nov 2003.
12. M.W. Berry, Z. Drmac, E.R. Jessup, *Matrices, Vector Spaces, and Information Retrieval*, SIAM Review, pages 335-362, June 1999.

13. M. Li, W.C. Lee, A. Sivasubramaniam, D.L. Lee, *A Small World Overlay Network for Semantic Based Search in P2P*, 2nd Workshop on Semantics in Peer-to-Peer and Grid Computing.
14. M. Zaki, S. Parthasarathy, M. Ogihara, W. Li. *New algorithms for fast discovery of association rules*. Proc. the 3rd Int'l Conf. Knowledge Discovery and Data Mining (KDD), 1997.
15. O. Gnawali, *A keyword-set search system for peer-to-peer networks*. Master's thesis, Massachusetts Institute of Technology, 2002.
16. Onestat.com, *Most People Use 2 Word Phrases in Search Engines According to OneStat.com*, available at http://www.onestat.com/html/aboutus_pressbox27.html
17. P. Reynolds, A. Vahdat, *Efficient peer-to-peer keyword searching*. In Proceedings of ACM/IFIP/USENIX Middleware Conference, volume 2672, pages 21-40, Rio de Janeiro, Brazil, June 2003.
18. P. Francis, T. Kambayashi, S. Sato, S. Shimizu, *Ingrid: A Self-Configuring Information Navigation Infrastructure*, 4th International World Wide Web Conference, December 11-14, 1995.
19. R. Agrawal, R. Srikant, *Fast algorithms for mining association rules*, Proc. 20th International Conference on Very Large Data Bases (VLDB), pages 487-499, Morgan Kaufmann, 1994.
20. S. Ratnasamy, P. Francis, M. Handley, R. Karp, S. Shenker, *A scalable content-addressable network*, In Proc. ACM SIGCOMM 2001, August 2001.
21. *TREC relevance judgments*, http://trec.nist.gov/data/reljudge_eng.html.
22. Y. Shao, R.Y. Wang, *BuddyNet: History-Based P2P Search*, 23-37, ECIR, 2005.
23. Z. Wu, W. Meng, C.T. Yu, Z. Li, *Towards a Highly-scalable and Effective Metasearch Engine*, Proc. 10th International World Wide Web Conference, 2001.

# A Decomposition-Based Probabilistic Framework for Estimating the Selectivity of XML Twig Queries

Chao Wang, Srinivasan Parthasarathy, and Ruoming Jin

Department of Computer Science and Engineering,
The Ohio State University
srini@cse.ohio-state.edu

**Abstract.** In this paper we present a novel approach for estimating the selectivity of XML twig queries. Such a technique is useful for answering approximate queries as well as for determining an optimal query plan for complex queries based on said estimates. Our approach relies on a summary structure that contains the occurrence statistics of small twigs. We rely on a novel probabilistic approach for decomposing larger twig queries into smaller ones. We then show how it can be used to estimate the selectivity of the larger query in conjunction with the summary information. We present and evaluate different strategies for decomposition and compare this work against a state-of-the-art selectivity estimation approach on synthetic and real datasets. The experimental results show that our proposed approach is very effective in estimating the selectivity of XML twig queries.

## 1 Introduction

XML is gaining acceptance as a standard for data representation and exchange over the World Wide Web. However, for wide-spread deployment and use it is becoming increasingly clear that the design of an efficient high-level querying mechanism is necessary. Since XML documents may be represented as a rooted and labeled tree, this necessity has led to the development of tree-based (twig) querying mechanisms. Twig queries describe a complex traversal of the document graph and retrieve document elements through an intertwined (i.e., joint) evaluation of multiple path expressions.

Given the importance of twig queries as a basic selection mechanism in XML [1, 2, 3], efficient support for accurately estimating their selectivity is crucial for the optimization of complex queries. This is analogous to selectivity estimation in relational databases [4, 5, 6, 7]. Accurate selectivity estimation is also desirable in interactive settings and for approximate queries. For instance, an end-user can interactively refine their query if they know it will return an overwhelmingly large result set. Similarly, the estimated value can be returned as an approximate answer to aggregate queries using the COUNT primitive.

The early work in this area has focused on determining the selectivity of path expressions (a special case of twig queries) [8, 9, 10, 11, 12, 13]. The Lore system [8] adopts a Markov model-based approach for this purpose. The Markov table method [10] improves on the Lore system through the use of intelligent pruning and aggregation to reduce space requirements. Recently, Lim and Wang proposed XPathLearner [9], an on-line, tunable Markov table method which has been shown to be effective for path expression selectivity. A key limitation of these methods is that they do not adapt well to twig queries because they do not account for path correlations.

More recently, researchers have focused on selectivity estimation for twig queries [14, 3, 15, 2, 1]. Examples include Correlated Sub-Trees [3], XSketches [15, 1] and Tree- Sketches [2]. Among these it has been shown that TreeSketches is the most accurate and efficient method [2]. TreeSketches [2], a successor of XSketches, clusters the similar fragments of XML data together to generate its synopsis. The granularity of the clustering depends on the memory budget.

To estimate the selectivity of XML twig queries, the above approaches, as well as the approach presented in this paper, define a summary data structure that houses important statistics about the data from which the selectivity may be estimated. Important issues at hand include: the quality of estimation from the given summary; the time to construct the summary; and finally, the time to estimate the selectivity of queries from the summary. To address these issues we present a new approach to selectivity estimation. The key contributions of our approach are highlighted below.

First, we present a framework under which the selectivity of a query (represented as a rooted tree) can be estimated from its subtrees. We present and evaluate different strategies for decomposing the query into subtrees. These subtrees can then be used to arrive at a selectivity estimate. We present a theoretical basis for this approach and furthermore show that it subsumes the Markov model-based XML path selectivity estimation as a special case.

Second, to summarize an XML dataset we leverage the use of frequent tree mining. A dynamically-determined subset[1] of all the discovered subtrees up to a certain size (number of nodes), coupled with associated occurrence statistics, forms the basis of our summary structure. More specifically, the dynamic subset we store is based on the notion of *(non)-derivable* patterns. We also rely on fast searching mechanisms to locate the subtrees of a given twig query within our summary structure.

Third, we conducted an extensive experimental study to examine the benefits of our approach and compare it against TreeSketches[2]. Empirical results show that our approach takes less time to construct the summary, and is usually much faster when computing the selectivity estimates. In our qualitative assessment we also find that our approach compares favorably with TreeSketches. We also offer a detailed explanation as to why the new approach (called *TreeLattice*) outperforms TreeSketches [2] under certain conditions.

The rest of the paper is organized as follows. We formally define our problem and give an overview of TreeLattice in Section 2. In Section 3, we detail our proposed summary structure and twig decomposition-based XML twig selectivity estimation framework. We present experimental results in Section 4 and related work in Section 5. Finally we discuss the future work and conclude in Section 6.

---

[1] Due to storage costs, the complete lattice (all frequent patterns) cannot be held in memory, thus we only store a portion of it, which is dynamic and data dependent.

[2] We are grateful to Neoklis Polyzotis for providing us with the TreeSketches executable and also for helping us tune the algorithm for a fair comparison.

## 2 Problem Definition and TreeLattice Overview

In the following section, we formally define the problem of estimating XML twig selectivity (Subsection 2.1). We follow with a discussion of the basic ideas and key challenges in our new approach, TreeLattice (Subsection 2.2).

### 2.1 Problem Definition

An XML document can be structurally modeled as a tree where each node is typically associated with a tag or a value. In practice, values are almost always associated with leaf nodes and tags with interior nodes. As with prior work by Polyzotis and Garofalakis [16], we do not model value elements.

A twig query $T_Q$ is defined as a node-labeled tree $T_Q(V_Q, E_Q)$, where each node $t_i \in V_Q$ is labeled with a path expression $P_i$. At an abstract level, each node $t_i$ corresponds to a subset of elements, while the path $P_i$ describes the structural relationship that must be satisfied between the elements in $t_i$ and the elements in its parent node. In particular, we only consider the parent/child relationship between different elements. Research on the more general ancestor/descendant relationship is underway. We next present the definition of a twig match as given by Chen et al. [3].

**Definition 1.** *A match of a twig query* $T_Q = (V_Q, E_Q)$ *in a node-labeled data tree* $T = (V_T, E_T)$ *is defined by a* $1-1$ *mapping:* $f : V_Q \mapsto V_T$ *such that if* $f(u) = v$ *for* $u \in V_Q$ *and* $v \in V_T$, *then (i) Label(u) = Label(v) and (ii) if* $(u, u') \in E_Q$, *then* $(f(u), f(u')) \in E_T$.

The selectivity $\sigma(T_Q)$ of twig query $T_Q$ is defined as the number of matches of $T_Q$ in the data tree. Our objective is to accurately estimate the selectivity of an XML twig query $T_Q$ as efficiently as possible given constraints in space (summary storage) and time (summary construction and estimation time).

### 2.2 Basic Ideas and Key Challenges of TreeLattice

The first basic idea in TreeLattice comes from the observation that in many cases, the selectivity of a given twig query $\sigma(T_Q)$ can be reasonably estimated from the selectivity information of its sub-twig queries. For example, suppose twig $T_Q$ is the union of two sub-twigs $T_1$ and $T_2$, which differ by only one edge and share a common part $T$ (Figure 1a). We can expect $\sigma(T_1)$, $\sigma(T_2)$ and $\sigma(T)$ to provide good clues for estimating $\sigma(T_Q)$ in many real datasets. Furthermore, if the twig $T_Q$ is the union of a set of sub-twigs, the selectivity of all these sub-twigs can be used to estimate $\sigma(T_Q)$. Therefore, the first problem we face is *can we develop a reasonable selectivity estimate for a given twig query $T_Q$ by utilizing the selectivity of its sub-twigs*? This problem is answered in Subsection 3.1, where we construct such an estimator based on the *conditional independence assumption for growing a tree*. Note that in order to systematically estimate the selectivity of twig queries with this approach, we need to pre-compute a group of small twigs as the basis.

However, we can also expect that our assumption will likely be violated for some twig queries on a given XML dataset. To deal with this issue, we use another basic idea from the observation that the selectivity information of different twigs can be of differing importance in terms of capturing the underlying twig distribution. For example, if the selectivity of $T_1, T_2$, and $T$ are available and $T_Q$ can be *precisely* estimated from them, then the selectivity of $T_Q$ should not be pre-computed. Here, we face another key challenge in TreeLattice: *how can we select a group of twigs as the basis for selectivity estimation in order to minimize the estimation error?* In particular, such selection needs to be performed under the budget of user-defined memory cost. Another problem closely related to this challenge is *how can we decompose a large twig query into basic twigs and perform estimations if different decompositions exist?* The solution to the latter actually helps us determine a solution for the former. In Subsection 3.2, we discuss the decomposition problem and in Subsection 3.3, we introduce our method to select basis for selectivity estimation.

Given the above discussion, we can see that our TreeLattice has three basic components: *Basis Building, Twig Decomposition, Augmenting Estimation*. The basis building is off-line and the other two components are computed at runtime while processing a query. When a new query arrives, we first decompose it into the small twigs in the basis and use the pre-computed selectivity of these basic twigs to infer the selectivity of the complex (larger) one.

## 3 An Estimation Framework Based on Twig Decomposition

In this section, we will answer the three questions posed in the previous section. The twig decomposition-based selectivity estimation framework will be formulated during the course of this discussion.

### 3.1 Augmenting Twigs

Suppose we have two basic twigs $T_1$ and $T_2$, and they differ by only one edge (Figure 1(a)). If $T$ is common to both, then we can express $T_1$ as $T \cup \{e_1\}$ and $T_2$ as $T \cup \{e_2\}$, where $e_1$ and $e_2$ are two *distinct* edges. The edges are distinct in that they either attach to different nodes of $T$, or the two additional nodes $x$ and $y$ introduced by these two edges are different. The two twigs can be augmented together to generate a

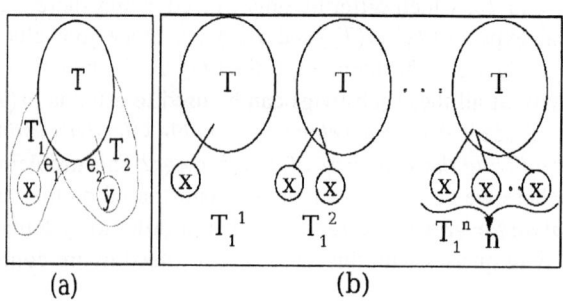

**Fig. 1.** (a) Augmented twigs $T_1 \cup T_2$; (b) Growing $T_1$ from $T$

larger twig, denoted as $T_1 \cup T_2 = T \cup \{e_1\} \cup \{e_2\}$. Assuming the counts of $T_1, T_2$ and their common part $T$ are available and denoted as $\sigma(T_1), \sigma(T_2)$ and $\sigma(T)$, respectively, we are interested in estimating the count of the augmented twig, $T_1 \cup T_2$, based on this information.

A complication arises when the occurrence of $T$ is coupled with one or more instances of edge $e_1$, as shown in Figure 1(b). Let $T_1^i$ denote the occurrence of $T$ with $i$ edges of type $e_1$. Then it is easy to see that the selectivity of $T_1$ is given by the decomposition formula[3]:

$$\sigma(T_1) = \sigma(T_1^1) + 2 \times \sigma(T_1^2) + \cdots n \times \sigma(T_1^n)$$

and similarly the selectivity of $T_2$ is given by:

$$\sigma(T_2) = \sigma(T_2^1) + 2 \times \sigma(T_2^2) + \cdots m \times \sigma(T_2^m)$$

In order to derive our formula for estimating the augmented twig $T_1 \cup T_2$, we assume that the event of growing $T_1$ from $T$ is conditionally independent from the event of growing $T_2$ from $T$ (called the *tree-growing independence assumption*). More formally we have:

$$Pr(T_1^i \cup T_2^j | T) = Pr(T_1^i | T) \times Pr(T_2^j | T)$$

where:

$$Pr(T_1^i | T) = \sigma(T_1^i) / \sigma(T)$$

and:

$$Pr(T_2^i | T) = \sigma(T_2^i) / \sigma(T)$$

**Theorem 1.** *Given two non-trivial rooted and labeled twigs $T_1$ and $T_2$, which differ by only one edge, let $T$ be the common part between $T_1$ and $T_2$. Under the tree-growing independence assumption, the expected count of $T_1 \cup T_2$ is given by $\sigma(T_1) \times \sigma(T_2) / \sigma(T)$.*

**Proof:** Given the tree-growing independence assumption, we can treat the count of $T_1 \cup T_2$ as a random variable. The expected value of this random variable, $E(\sigma(T_1 \cup T_2))$, is as follows: □

(From the decomposition formula)

$$E(\sigma(T_1 \cup T_2)) = \sum_{i=1}^{n} \sum_{j=1}^{m} E(\sigma(T_1^i \cup T_2^j))$$

$$= \sum_{i=1}^{n} \sum_{j=1}^{m} (i \times j \times Pr(T_1^i \cup T_2^j | T) \times \sigma(T))$$

(By the conditional independence assumption)

$$= \sum_{i=1}^{n} \sum_{j=1}^{m} i \times j \times Pr(T_1^i | T) \times Pr(T_2^j | T) \times \sigma(T)$$

---

[3] The coefficients in front of each term represents the number of choices one has to grow from $T$ to $T_1$. $n$ is the maximal number of $e_1$ edges under $T$. Similarly, $m$ is the maximal number of $e_2$ edges under $T$.

$$= \sigma(T) \times \sum_{i=1}^{n} i \times Pr(T_1^i|T) \times (\sum_{j=1}^{m} j \times Pr(T_2^j|T))$$

$$= \sigma(T) \times \sum_{i=1}^{n} i \times Pr(T_1^i|T) \times (\sum_{j=1}^{m} j \times \frac{\sigma(T_2^j)}{\sigma(T)})$$

$$= \sigma(T) \times \sum_{i=1}^{n} i \times Pr(T_1^i|T) \times \frac{1}{\sigma(T)} \times (\sum_{j=1}^{m} j \times \sigma(T_2^j))$$

(The decomposition of count of $\mathbf{T_2}$, $\sigma(\mathbf{T_2})$)

$$= \sigma(T) \times \sum_{i=1}^{n} i \times Pr(T_1^i|T) \times \frac{\sigma(T_2)}{\sigma(T)}$$

(The decomposition of count of $\mathbf{T_1}$, $\sigma(\mathbf{T_1})$)

$$= \sigma(T) \times \frac{\sigma(T_1)}{\sigma(T)} \times \frac{\sigma(T_2)}{\sigma(T)}$$

$$= \sigma(T_1) \times \sigma(T_2)/\sigma(T) \qquad \square$$

In our approach, we will use the expected count of $T_1 \cup T_2$ as the estimate of the true count of $T_1 \cup T_2$, denoted as $\hat{\sigma}(T_1 \cup T_2) = \sigma(T_1) \times \sigma(T_2)/\sigma(T)$.

An important lemma that follows from this theorem is stated next and its proof can be found in the full version of this paper [17].

**Lemma 1.** *Given two subtrees $T_1$ and $T_2$ that share a common subtree $T$, where*

$$|T| = min(|T_1|, |T_2|) - 1$$

*then $\sigma(T_1 \cup T_2)$ can be estimated as follows:*

$$\sigma(T_1 \cup T_2) = \frac{\sigma(T_1) \times \sigma(T_2)}{\sigma(T)}$$

### 3.2 Twig Decomposition

In this section, we discuss how to decompose a large twig query into basic twigs and also how to estimate its selectivity.

**Recursive Decomposition Scheme.** This decomposition is obtained directly from Lemma 1. Since each tree has at least two leaf nodes(if the root node has degree 1, it can also be considered a leaf node for our purposes), we can always obtain two subtrees of the original tree by removing one leaf node or the other. These subtrees are labeled $T_1$ and $T_2$, respectively. If the size of $T$ is $k$, then the size of $T_1$ and $T_2$ will be $(k-1)$. Suppose the common part between $T_1$ and $T_2$ is $T_3$, then we can apply the above formula to estimate the selectivity of $T$, given the selectivity of $T_1$, $T_2$ and $T_3$.

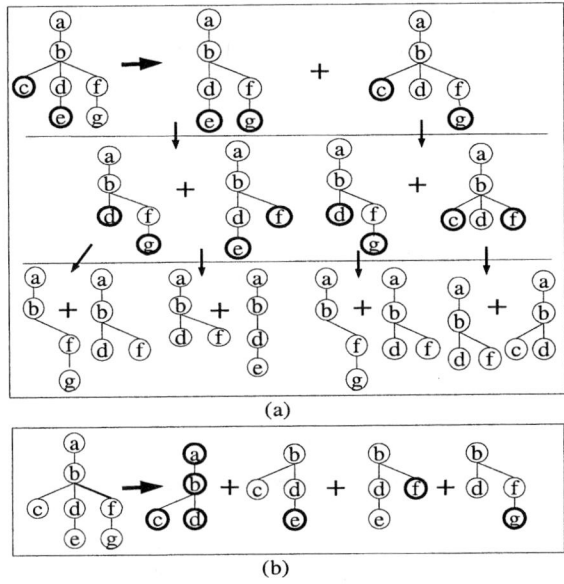

**Fig. 2.** (a) Recursive decomposition scheme; (b) Fixed-sized decomposition scheme

This decomposition scheme ensures that the overlap between $T_1$ and $T_2$ is maximal and thus ensures that the correlation of occurrence is well captured. If $T_1$ and $T_2$ are too large to fit in the lattice summary, then we execute the above decomposition process recursively, until we reach the brim of the lattice summary. We present an example of this recursive decomposition in Figure 2a. Here a twig of size 7 is decomposed into a set of sub-twigs of size 4. The bold nodes are chosen to be eliminated at each step in the recursion. Figure 3 presents the formal algorithm of the estimator.

**Voting Scheme Extension.** We note that a twig may have more than two leaves. In this case the choice of leaf nodes for decomposition may result in different estimates.

---

Algorithm: Estimate $(T, L)$
Input: $T$, an XML twig;
    $L$, the lattice summary;
Output: $\hat{\sigma}$, selectivity estimation for $T$;
1. **if** $T$ is in $L$
    return the associated count;
2. **else**
    pick a pair of $T$'s nodes$(v_1, v_2)$ having degree of 1;
    remove $v_1$ from $T$ to get $T_1$;
    remove $v_2$ from $T$ to get $T_2$;
    evaluate $T_3 = T_1 \cap T_2$;
    $\hat{\sigma} = \frac{Estimate(T_1,L)*Estimate(T_2,L)}{Estimate(T_3,L)}$

---

**Fig. 3.** Algorithm for recursive decomposition estimator

```
Algorithm: FSD(T, k)
Input: T, an XML twig of size n; k, a fixed size;
Output: D, a set of k-subtrees satisfying the condition
        in Theorem 2;
1. Order all nodes of T according to pre-order:
     i.e., v_1, v_2, v_3, ..., v_n;
2. Choose the subtree t_1 consisting of the first k nodes
   from the node list and label them as covered;
   //t_1 must be a valid subtree;
   Initialize T_c by t_1, add t_1 to D;
3. for each remaining uncovered node v_i:
4.    pick a subtree t_i containing v_i as the
      rightmost node, all other nodes are from T_c;
5.    add v_i to T_c, label v_i as covered
      and add t_i to D;
6. return D;
```

**Fig. 4.** Fixed-sized decomposition algorithm

Correspondingly, we can have multiple estimations at each recursive step. As an optimization, we record all the estimations at a given level and average them to obtain a resulting estimate to be used in the next step. Intuitively, we expect to avoid skewed estimates resulting from poor initial choices and that this optimization will prevent the propagation of errors during the course of the decomposition. Different voting schemes can be applied here. We will demonstrate the effect of this optimization in Section 4.

**Fast Fixed-Sized Decomposition Scheme.** Assuming we can keep the information of all subtrees no larger than $k$ in the lattice summary, we can decompose a large query $T$ in the following way: We use small fixed-sized subtrees to progressively cover $T$. First, we sort all nodes in the twig in pre-order fashion. Then we choose a $k$-subtree of $T$ to cover the first $k$ nodes. Let the covered portion of $T$ be denoted as $T_c$. At each following step we cover a new node $v$ using $T_{new}$, where all the nodes of $T_{new}$ is a subset of $T_c$ except $v$. Correspondingly, we update $T_c$ as the union of the previous $T_c$ and $T_{new}$. Thus, $T_c$ will progressively grow until it covers all the nodes in $T$. Also, it holds that the part common between $T_c$ and $T_{new}$ is a $(k-1)$-subtree. Clearly, $T$ can be covered by exactly $(size(T) - k + 1)$ $k$-subtrees. The correlation between two subtree patterns is captured by their common part. In Figure 2b, we present an example of this decomposition. Newly covered nodes are highlighted at each step. Figure 4 presents the formal algorithm of the fixed-sized decomposition scheme.

The correctness of the above algorithm is formally stated as Lemma 2. Furthermore, Lemma 3 describes the corresponding selectivity estimator using such a decomposition scheme. Again, the detailed proofs of Lemma 2 and 3 can be found in the full version of this paper.

**Lemma 2.** *Given a rooted ordered labeled tree $T$ of size $n$, it can be covered by $n - k + 1$ of its subtrees of size $k$ ($n > k$), i.e., $T_1, T_2, \ldots, T_i, \ldots, T_{n-k+1}$, such that $T_i \cap (\bigcup_{j=1}^{i-1} T_j)$ is a $(k-1)$-subtree.*

**Lemma 3.** *Assume we have a twig query $T$ decomposed into $k$-subtrees, i.e., $T_1, T_2, \ldots, T_i, \ldots, T_{n-k+1}$, and, $C_{i-1} = T_i \cap (\bigcup_{j=1}^{i-1} T_j)$, $2 < i \leq n - k + 1$. Then the selectivity of $T$ may be estimated as follows:*

$$\hat{\sigma}(T) = \frac{\prod_{i=1}^{n-k+1} \sigma(T_i)}{\prod_{j=1}^{n-k} \sigma(C_j)}$$

The advantage of this scheme is that it is very simple and the decomposition is very fast. In reality however, the lattice summary does not necessarily store all patterns up to some size. Thus, the above decomposition can not be applied directly. To overcome this problem, we devise a hybrid version of this scheme and the recursive decomposition scheme with voting. The hybrid scheme works as follows: For a large twig, we first decompose it into fixed-sized sub-twigs and then use the recursive decomposition scheme with voting to estimate the selectivity of all of these sub-twigs. Finally, we use Lemma 3 to obtain the estimation for the original query. The advantage of this scheme is that it is much faster than the recursive decomposition scheme with voting. Additionally, it utilizes the summary information more effectively through voting, compared to the recursive decomposition scheme without voting. We call this hybrid version the *fast fixed-sized decomposition scheme* and refer it as *fast decomposition* in Section 4.

### 3.3 Building Basis Statistics

The summary records the occurrence statistics of basic twigs. There exists redundancy in the summary that can be pruned to reduce its size. With this in mind, we formally define the notion of a $\delta$-derivable pattern.

**Definition 2.** *A twig pattern is $\delta$-derivable if and only if its true selectivity is within an error tolerance of $\delta$ to its expected selectivity (according to TreeLattice).*

By Definition 2, 0-derivable ($\delta$-derivable with $\delta = 0$) patterns have the exact true selectivity as their expected selectivity. It is therefore safe to prune away the 0-derivable patterns from the lattice summary without sacrificing the quality of the estimations. This observation is formally stated as Lemma 4. As a result, we have more space to store more non-derivable patterns in the lattice summary.

**Lemma 4.** *The estimation given by TreeLattice with a lattice summary $L$ is exactly the same as that when 0-derivable patterns are removed from $L$.*

**Proof:** The proof is trivial and is omitted. □

The above idea can be generalized by varying $\delta$, thereby controlling the trade-off between accuracy and memory utilization. We build the basis statistics in a bottom-up fashion. We collect the selectivity information of small twigs first, followed by the larger twigs. Essentially, we give more priority to smaller twigs, since they are more basic building blocks. Furthermore, at each level, we give priority to the more frequent twigs, as they are more important in capturing the overall twig distribution. Note that we only keep the information of non-derivable patterns in the lattice summary. Figure 5 presents the formal algorithm of building the basis statistics.

```
Algorithm: TreeLattice-Build (D, S, δ)
Input: XML document D; space budget S; error tolerance δ;
Output: TreeLattice summary L of size ≤ S;
1. Obtain all 1-subtree and 2-subtree patterns in D
   and their counts; Use them to initialize L;
2. k = 3;
3. While k < MAX_LEVEL
4.   Obtain all k-subtree patterns in D and their counts;
5.   Sort these patterns in decreasing order of their counts;
6.   For each k-subtree pattern p:
7.     Estimate σ(p) and compute the estimation
       error e;
8.     if e > δ then add p to L;
9.     if size(L) ≥ S exit;
7.   k++;
8. return L;
```

**Fig. 5.** Algorithm TreeLattice-Build

## 4 Experiments

In this section, we examine the performance of our proposed approach for XML twig selectivity estimation on synthetic and real-life datasets. We compare our approach with TreeSketches, a state-of-the-art scheme [2].

### 4.1 Experimental Setup

All the experiments were conducted on a Pentium 4 2.66GHz machine with 1GB RAM running Linux 2.6.8. Below we detail the datasets, workloads and error metric considered in our evaluation.

**Datasets.** We use four publicly available datasets in our experiments: *Nasa*, a real-life dataset converted from legacy flat-file format into XML and made available to the public; *PSD* (Protein Sequence Database), a real-life dataset of integrated collection of functionally annotated protein sequences; *XMark*, a synthetic dataset that models transactions in an on-line auction site and *IMDB*, a real-life dataset from the Internet Movie Database Project. We would like to note that for the PSD dataset, both algorithms take a long time to process, so we present results on a sample. The main characteristics of the datasets are summarized in Table 1.

**Query Workloads.** In our experiments, we consider three different kinds of workloads: random, frequent-twig and negative-query. Regardless of workload, the first step is to enumerate all possible queries for a given dataset. This set of queries is further partitioned, where each partition corresponds to twig queries of a certain size. For the *random* workload, we sample a fixed amount from each partition under a uniform random distribution to yield a total of 1000 queries. This level-wise partitioning and sampling

**Table 1.** Dataset characteristics

| Dataset | Elements | File Size(MB) |
|---|---|---|
| Nasa | 476646 | 24 |
| PSD | 335193 | 12 |
| XMark | 167864 | 12 |
| IMDB | 155898 | 7 |

**Table 2.** Workload characteristics (average no. of binding tuples)

| Dataset | Nasa | | PSD | | XMark | | IMDB | |
|---|---|---|---|---|---|---|---|---|
| Query Size | Frequent | Random | Frequent | Random | Frequent | Random | Frequent | Random |
| 4 | 5377 | 4073 | 6601 | 3321 | 2774 | 1722 | 3519 | 784 |
| 5 | 8282 | 3742 | 11563 | 2827 | 5995 | 2058 | 40703 | 985 |
| 6 | 21334 | 3978 | 28160 | 2398 | 6347 | 3251 | 11815 | 1982 |
| 7 | 58920 | 4004 | 68877 | 2383 | 169993 | 6641 | 17193 | 2937 |
| 8 | 29558 | 2855 | 129892 | 2920 | 288944 | 10394 | 29962 | 3559 |
| 9 | 18814 | 2608 | 148993 | 2464 | 281808 | 5748 | 37963 | 5825 |

also enables us to evaluate the performance of our strategies, in particular their error propagation, in a controlled manner.

For the *frequent-twig* workload, we pick the most frequent 1000 twig queries as the workload. An alternative strategy would be to sample twigs as a function of the frequency of occurrence (a stratified sampling model). However, we observed little difference in the performance of these two frequency-based strategies and thus limit our discussion to the frequent-twig workload. Twig queries in the frequent-twig workload will have large selectivity rates, as expected.

We also generate and evaluate various *negative-query* workloads (workloads exclusively consisting of queries with zero selectivity). To generate these workloads, we followed the initial step of enumerating all possible queries. For each twig we then replaced node labels in accordance with their frequency of occurrence. More frequent labels are used for replacement more often so there is a greater chance for erroneous predictions (since sub-twigs are more likely to occur frequently). We then filter those queries whose selectivity is above 0. Once again we limit the workloads to be of size 1000. Experimental results show that TreeSketches is always accurate (100% of the time), and that TreeLattice is almost always as accurate (99% of the time), and returns the correct answer (zero). There is little difference between these two strategies for negative workloads, so we do not consider this workload further.

**Error Metric.** We quantify the accuracy of estimations using the average absolute relative error over all queries in the workload. The absolute relative error is defined as $|\sigma - \hat{\sigma}| / \max(s, \sigma)$, where the sanity bound $s$ is used to avoid the artificially high percentages of low selectivity queries. Following common practice [2, 1], we set $s$ to be the 10-percentile of true query counts. We use a lower bound of 10 if $s$ should fall below that value.

## 4.2 Accuracy of Estimators

Here we examine the accuracy of the estimators on our workloads. For both TreeLattice and TreeSketches, we limit the summary size to 50KB. Figures 6a-d show the average selectivity estimation error on various frequent-twig workloads for all four datasets.

An obvious trend that stands out is that as the size of the twig query increases, the quality of the estimation decreases. This is not surprising, since the estimation errors grow for larger-sized queries for both strategies. Specifically for TreeLattice, the smaller sized queries are closer to the lattice boundary (exact information maintained in the summary) and thus subject to less estimation error. In contrast, for larger queries, depending on the number of decomposition and estimation steps, the error will accumulate, finally affecting the quality of the estimations. On the Nasa dataset, for example, the recursive decomposition estimator yields very accurate estimations on frequent-twig workloads of size 5 and 6, with error 0.0% and 4.2%, respectively. In contrast, on the frequent-twig workloads of size 8 and 9, the error increases to 11.6% and 17.8%, respectively. The effect of error accumulation can be clearly seen from the results. The other two estimators have a similar trend when working on various workloads for all datasets.

We would like to note that the voting scheme refines the estimations effectively by mitigating the error propagation. The recursive decomposition estimator with voting usually yields the most accurate estimations. Additionally, one should note that the estimations returned by the fast decomposition estimator is very similar to that returned by recursive decomposition estimator with voting.

When comparing the two strategies, it can be observed that TreeLattice significantly outperforms TreeSketches for both the Nasa and PSD workload on all query sizes. On the XMark dataset, TreeLattice is near perfect and TreeSketches is marginally worse (note the Y-axis scale). On the IMDB workload, TreeSketches outperforms TreeLattice significantly on larger query sizes. On smaller query sizes, the difference is not as significant. Note that on Nasa, PSD and XMark, in most cases, even the weakest estimation strategy in TreeLattice, recursive decomposition estimator without voting, does better than TreeSketches.

Figures 7a-d show the average selectivity estimation error on the random workloads for all four datasets. The trends are very similar to the ones observed for the frequent-twig workloads. Two differences are that TreeLattice is closer in performance

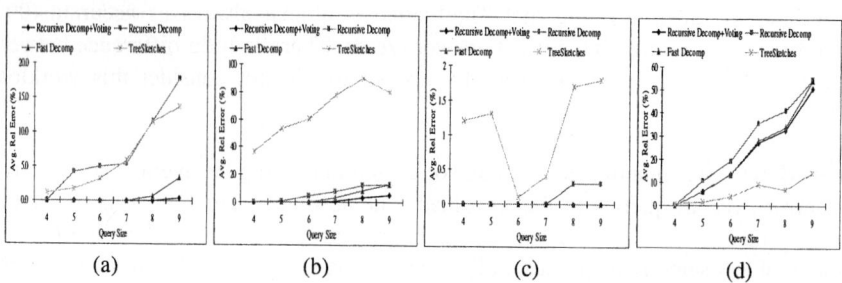

**Fig. 6.** Average estimation error on frequent-twig workload: (a)Nasa (b)PSD (c)XMark (d)IMDB

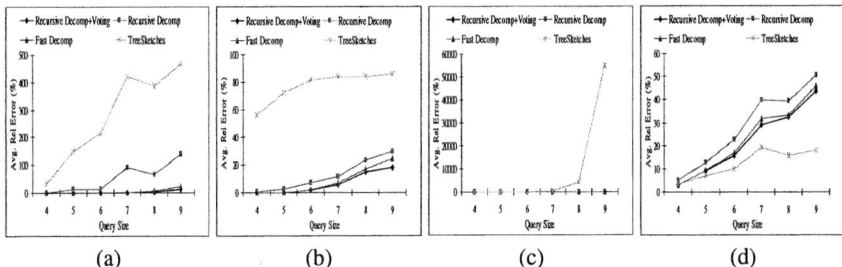

**Fig. 7.** Average estimation error on random workload: (a)Nasa (b)PSD (c)XMark (d)IMDB

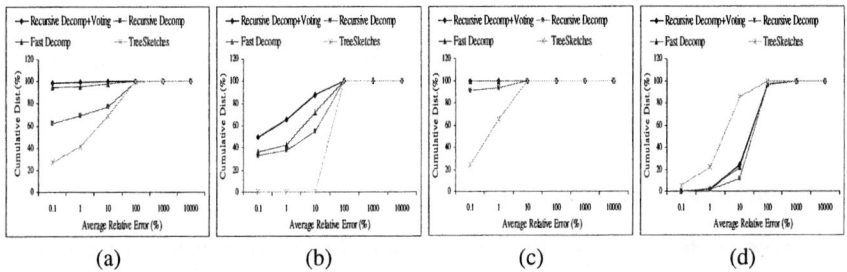

**Fig. 8.** Average estimation error distribution on frequent-twig workload: (a)Nasa (b)PSD (c)XMark (d)IMDB

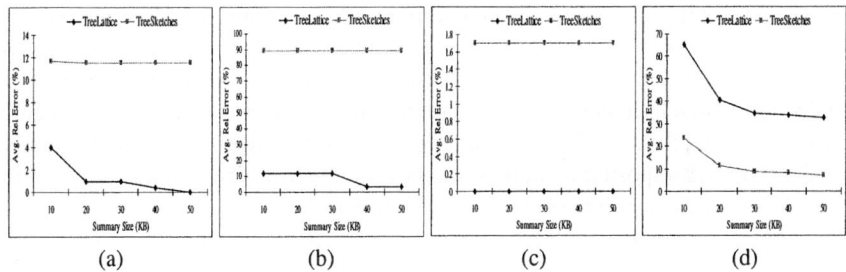

**Fig. 9.** Average estimation error when varying summary size: (a)Nasa (b)PSD (c)XMark (d)IMDB

to TreeSketches on the IMDB dataset and on the XMark dataset TreeSketches performs poorly (the errors are well above 100% in some cases).

To examine a possible outlier effect, we plotted the cumulative distribution function of the errors. Figures 8a-d present the results for frequent-twig workloads. The results are consistent with Figure 6, showing that TreeLattice outperforms TreeSketches consistently on all datasets except IMDB. The results on random workloads are similar and are omitted in the interest of space. The complete results can be found in the full version of this paper [17].

In conclusion, these results demonstrate that TreeLattice is effective in summarizing the distribution of the underlying twigs. Furthermore, we show that TreeLattice is effective in processing both frequent and infrequent twig queries. When the query size is increased, the quality of the estimation is reduced (due to the error propagation). Specifically among the strategies evaluated, the recursive decomposition with voting estimator usually yields the best estimations. Finally, the fast decomposition estimator yields close estimations to the recursive decomposition estimator with voting.

### 4.3 Impact of Varying Summary Size

In this experiment, we measure the estimation error while varying the summary size. We use a frequent-twig workload containing frequent 8-twig queries. Figures 9a-d show the average selectivity estimation error when varying the summary size for Nasa, PSD, XMark and IMDB, respectively. As expected, we observe that an increase in the size of the summary yields more accurate estimations. As before, TreeLattice works extremely well for Nasa, PSD and XMark. An important point here is that the estimation error for these datasets is well below 10% when we use at least a 40KB summary. For the IMDB dataset, TreeSketches is better than TreeLattice.

### 4.4 Implications on Estimation Time

In this experiment, we compare TreeLattice against TreeSketches in terms of selectivity-estimation time. Figures 10a-d present the response times of the different approaches on frequent-twig workloads for Nasa, IMDB, PSD and XMark, respectively. The results on random workloads are similar and are omitted in the interest of space, though the complete results can be found in the full version of the paper. As seen in the figures, in most cases, all TreeLattice estimators are much more efficient than TreeSketches. Specifically, TreeLattice runs extremely fast when processing relatively small twig queries. As we increase the query size of the workload, the recursive decomposition estimator with voting becomes much slower. The degradation of response time becomes more significant as we increase the size of the twig queries. This is not surprising, since the number of all possible decompositions increases exponentially with the number of recursion levels. The recursive decomposition without voting is fastest. However in terms of accuracy, this strategy is the weakest among the three. *The overall performance of the fast decomposition estimator is clearly the best since it is close to recursive decomposition estimator in terms of response time, and it is close to the recursive decomposition estimator with voting in terms of estimation quality.*

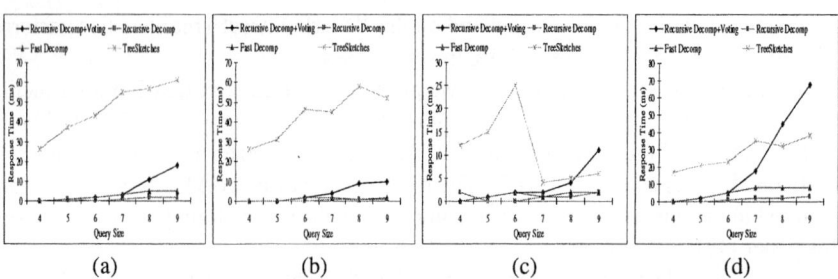

**Fig. 10.** Average response time on frequent-twig workload: (a)Nasa (b)PSD (c)XMark (d)IMDB

## 4.5 Impact of δ-Derivable Pruning

The pruning strategy we describe earlier allows us to replace $\delta$-derivable patterns with non-derivable patterns in the lattice summary. Here we examine the potential benefits of this strategy on the IMDB dataset. We use the frequent-twig workload for this experiment. Figure 11 presents the estimation quality at the different $\delta$-levels. All summary sizes are fixed at 50KB. As can be seen in the figure, when we increase $\delta$, the estimations become more accurate for large twig queries. This comes at a small sacrifice in the estimation accuracy for small twig queries. If the estimation error for the small twig queries is tolerable, we can continue to increase $\delta$ for the benefit of improved estimations for large twig queries. If we consider a single large workload consisting of a uniform number of different-sized queries (4 to 9), $\delta = 20\%$ gives the lowest average error (17.9%).

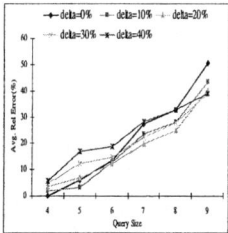

**Fig. 11.** Average selectivity estimation error when varying delta (IMDB)

## 4.6 Comparison of Summary Construction Times

In this experiment, we evaluate the cost of constructing the summary. In TreeSketches, this is a very expensive operation as it involves a bottom-up clustering of similar substructures in the XML data tree. In contrast, our approach relies on fast off-the-shelf efficient tree-mining algorithms to build the summary. Table 3 presents the time required by both approaches to construct a 50KB summary on each of the four datasets. The advantage of our approach over TreeSketches is quite telling–with an improvement of about one order of magnitude.

## 4.7 Result Summary and Rationale

The experimental results have shown that TreeLattice is very effective and efficient in estimating selectivity of the XML twig queries. In most cases, TreeLattice outperforms TreeSketches in terms of both accuracy and response time. In addition, pruning $\delta$-derivable patterns can further refine the selectivity estimation for large queries. We also notice that TreeLattice is outperformed by TreeSketches on IMDB, though it still yields reasonable estimations. Here we attempt to explain the rationale behind these results.

We know that TreeLattice is based on the conditional independence assumption of twig growing. If real XML data satisfy this assumption well, then TreeLattice will perform well. On the other hand, if the assumption does not hold, it will not. From the

**Table 3.** Summary construction time (in minutes)

| Dataset | TreeLattice | TreeSketches |
|---|---|---|
| Nasa | 10 | 80 |
| PSD | 21 | 102 |
| XMark | 15 | 78 |
| IMDB | 1 | 8 |

experimental results, it would appear that Nasa, PSD and XMark satisfy the assumption well and IMDB does not. Our expectation is supported by Table 4, which lists the number of patterns satisfying the assumption at different lattice levels on the four datasets. From the table, we see for the Nasa, PSD and XMark datasets, the ratio of 0-derivable patterns to total patterns is quite high, meaning they satisfy the assumption well. In contrast, the ratio on IMDB is much lower, which is reflected in the results.

Now let us take a closer look at TreeSketches. The TreeSketches synopsis is constructed by a bottom-up clustering of the similar substructures in the XML data tree. In it, an edge $(x, y)$ with weight $\alpha$ represents that on *average*, each node in set $x$ has $\alpha$ children in set $y$. Assume we have $n$ nodes in set $x$, and the nodes have $\alpha_1, \cdots, \alpha_n$, children in set $y$, respectively. If there are many similar substructures in the XML data tree found by bottom-up clustering, then TreeSketches should work very well (e.g., IMDB). On a detailed examination of IMDB, we find this to be the case. However, if this does not hold, then one is forced to cluster substructures that are not very similar in order to compress the XML data tree. This results in a large variance of $\alpha_i$ which leads to larger errors that propagate rapidly. We believe this explains the poor performance of TreeSketches on the other three datasets.

**Table 4.** Number of total and 0-derivable patterns on four datasets

| Dataset | Nasa | | PSD | | XMark | | IMDB | |
|---|---|---|---|---|---|---|---|---|
| Lattice Level | # total | # 0-derivable | # total | # 0-derivable | # total | # 0-derivable | # total | # 0-derivable |
| 3 | 213 | 174 | 282 | 201 | 365 | 302 | 877 | 156 |
| 4 | 668 | 434 | 1284 | 1016 | 1283 | 1138 | 9839 | 3625 |
| 5 | 2296 | 1866 | 6728 | 5778 | 4378 | 3948 | - | - |
| 6 | 8274 | 7768 | 34976 | 31580 | 14492 | 13251 | - | - |
| 7 | 30492 | 29232 | - | - | 46628 | 43373 | - | - |

## 5 Related Work

Chen et al. [3] were among the first to study the problem of estimating twig counts. They propose the Correlated Sub-path Tree (CST) method for estimating the selectivity of XML twig queries. A CST is a suffix tree-based data structure used to store all the paths up to certain length. To estimate the selectivity of a given twig query, this approach needs to decompose a twig into a set of paths stored in the CST. Note that even though both the CST and our TreeLattice approach depend on decomposing a large twig into basic twigs, they are quite different in several respects. First, our approach utilizes the *subtrees* instead of paths as the summary of an XML document. Our results have shown that these subtrees capture the structure of an XML document very effectively. In contrast, in order to perform selectivity estimation, CST has to store additional information, called *set hashing signature*, in order to capture the correlation among paths. Our approach is essentially a generalization of the Markov model-based approach for XML path selectivity estimation. When dealing with XML path queries, TreeLattice yields the same selectivity estimation as the Markov model-based approaches, which have been shown to be more effective than the CST-based approach [10].

XSketches [16] exploits localized graph stability in a graph-synopsis model to approximate path and branching distribution in an XML data graph. Its successor integrates support for value constraints as well, by using a multidimensional synopsis to capture value correlations [15]. They augment the XSketches model with new distribution information [1] to estimate the selectivity of XML twig queries and show that XSketches performs better than CST, yielding estimates with significantly lower estimation error.

TreeSketches [2], a successor of XSketches, clusters similar fragments of XML data together to generate its synopsis. The granularity of the clustering depends on the memory budget. Also, it outperforms its predecessors in terms of both accuracy and construction time. We note that the scope of TreeSketches is much broader than that of TreeLattice, since they are able to handle more general twigs (containing // operator).

A particular case of the twig query is the XML path query. The wide use of XML path queries has motivated many researches on estimating their selectivity. The Lore system [8] is one of the earliest works in this direction. It stores statistics of all distinct paths up to length $m$, with $m$ being a tunable parameter. Selectivity of paths longer than $m$ are estimated assuming the Markov property. Aboulnaga *et al.* [10], extends the idea used by Lore system in their Markov table method. It consists of a set of pruning and aggregation techniques on the statistics used in the Lore system and therefore offers an improvement by reducing the space requirements. Aboulnaga *et al.* [10], also propose a tree-based method known as the *path tree*, for estimating the selectivity of XML paths without data values. A path tree is a summarized form of the XML data tree. Compared with the Markov table method, this approach is inferior in terms of estimation accuracy for real datasets [10].

XPathLearner [9], is an on-line, self-tuning, Markov table-based approach used to estimate the selectivity of XML paths. The statistics of the data are collected in an on-line fashion, thus it is workload-aware. By design, our approach is also incremental in nature and can maintain summaries on-line, though we do not evaluate this aspect here. Our method is a generalization of these Markov model-based approaches for more complex twig queries. Recently, Wang *et al.* [12] propose the use of Bloom Histograms to estimate XML path selectivity. It is the first approach that gives a theoretical bound on the estimation error. However, it does not handle twig queries.

## 6 Conclusions and Future Work

In this paper, we have described a new approach, TreeLattice, to estimate the selectivity of XML twig queries with branching predicates. TreeLattice is shown to be comparable or better than TreeSketches in terms of estimation accuracy. Moreover, our technique is significantly faster both in terms of summary construction and in terms of selectivity estimation. Furthermore, we have provided theoretical foundations for the estimation process and have shown that TreeLattice subsumes the successful Markov model-based XML path selectivity estimation approach as a special case.

In the future, we will study the following issues: First, we would like to extend TreeLattice to handle more complex twig queries with recursion predicates (// operator). In this case, we are allowed to grow the twig in a more relaxed fashion. We conjecture that the conditional independence assumption of tree growing will still hold even for this case. Second, an error bound associated with the estimation would be very useful and we have made some initial progress towards this end. Third, we would like to adapt TreeLattice in a manner similar to XPathLearner, where information learned from an on-line workload can dynamically guide what is to be maintained in the summary structure.

## References

1. Polyzotis, N., Garofalakis, M., Ioannidis, Y.: Selectivity estimation for xml twigs. In: Proceedings of the International Conference on Data Engineering. (2004)
2. Polyzotis, N., Garofalakis, M., Ioannidis, Y.: Approximate xml query answers. In: Proceedings of the ACM SIGMOD International Conference on Management of Data. (2004)
3. Chen, Z., H.V.Jagadish, *et al.*: Counting twig matches in a tree. In: Proceedings of the International Conference on Data Engineering. (2001)
4. Chen, Z., Korn, F., *et al.*: Selectivity estimation for boolean queries. In: Proceedings of the ACM SIGMOD-SIGACT-SIGART Symposium on Principles of Database Systems. (2000)
5. Jagadish, H., Kapitskaia, O., *et al.*: Multi-dimensional substring selectivity estimation. In: Proceedings of the International Conference on Very Large Data Bases. (1999)
6. Jagadish, H., T.Ng, R., *et al.*: Substring selectivity estimation. In: Proceedings of the ACM SIGACT-SIGMOD-SIGART Symposium on Principles of Database Systems. (1999)
7. P.Krishnan, Vitter, J.S., Iyer, B.: Estimating alphanumeric selectivity in the presence of wildcards. In: Proceedings of the ACM SIGMOD International Conference on Management of Data. (1996)
8. McHugh, J., Widom, J.: Query optimization for xml. In: Proceedings of the International Conference on Very Large Data Bases. (1999)
9. Lim, L., Wang, M., *et al.*: Xpathlearner: An on-line self-tuning markov histogram for xml path selectivity estimation. In: Proceedings of the International Conference on Very Large Data Bases. (2002)
10. Aboulnaga, A., Alameldeen, A.R., Naughton, J.F.: Estimating the selectivity of xml path expressions for internet scale applications. In: Proceedings of the International Conference on Very Large Data Bases. (2001)
11. Wu, Y., Patel, J.M., Jagadish, H.: Estimating answer sizes for xml queries. In: Proceedings of the International Conference on Extending Database Technology (EDBT). (2002)
12. Wang, W., Jiang, H., Lu, H., Yu, J.X.: Bloom histogram: Path selectivity estimation for xml data with updates. In: Proceedings of the International Conference on Very Large Data Bases. (2004)
13. Jiang,W., Jiang, H., Lu, H., Yu, J.X.: Containment join size estimation: Models and methods. In: Proceedings of the ACM SIGMOD International Conference on Management of Data. (2003)

14. Freire, J., Haritsa, J.R., *et al.*: Statix: Making xml count. In: Proceedings of the ACM SIGMOD International Conference on Management of Data. (2002)
15. Polyzotis, N., Garofalakis, M.: Structure and value synopses for xml data graphs. In: Proceedings of the International Conference on Very Large Data Bases. (2002)
16. Polyzotis, N., Garofalakis, M.: Statistical synopses for graph-structured xml databases. In: Proceedings of the ACM SIGMOD International Conference on Management of Data. (2002)
17. Wang, C., Parthasarathy, S., Jin, R.: A decomposition-based probabilistic framework for estimating the selectivity of xml twig queries. In: The Ohio State University, Technical Report. (2005)

# Conflicting XML Updates

Mukund Raghavachari[1] and Oded Shmueli[2,*]

[1] IBM T.J. Watson Research Center
raghavac@us.ibm.com
[2] Technion — Israel Institute of Technology
oshmu@cs.technion.ac.il

**Abstract.** There has been growing interest in the addition of update operations to languages that operate on XML data, for example, XQuery and XJ. These update operations support efficient and declarative specification of transformations of XML data. The presence of update operations raises the question of detecting data dependencies between reads and updates of XML documents. The ability to optimize the execution of update operations depends on the ability to detect such conflicts. In this paper, we formalize the notions of updates on XML data and conflicts between update operations. We show that conflict detection is NP-complete when the update operations are specified using XPath expressions that support the use of the child and descendant axis, wildcard symbols, and branching. We also provide efficient polynomial algorithms for update conflict detection when the patterns do not use branching.

## 1 Introduction

The proliferation of XML data in domains such as databases, messaging systems, Web Services, etc. has led to an increased interest in the support of updates on XML data. For example, efforts are underway [9, 12] to extend XQuery [11] with update operations, and programming languages for operating on XML data, such as XJ [5] and C$\omega$ [3], offer mechanisms for specifying updates on XML data.

When a query language supports update operations, a classical and fundamental problem is the detection of conflicts between operations, that is, when reads and writes may operate on the same data. This question has relevance in many situations:

- *Query optimization:* The ability to detect that reads and writes do not conflict allows a query compiler to reorder operations to improve efficiency. Consider the following program fragment written in a language that supports elementary updates (such a language could be the target language for an XQuery compiler):

```
1 x = ...
2 y = read $x//A
3 z = read $x//C
4 insert $x/B, <C/>
```

* O. Shmueli was funded in part by ISF grant 890015 and by the P. and E. Nathan Research fund.

The first assignment to y returns all A descendants of the tree referred to by x. A "read" operation returns references to nodes in x that are in the result of the evaluation of the XPath expression on x. The "insert" operation adds a C child to all nodes labeled B that are children of the root of the tree referred to by x (if there are no B children in the tree, then no nodes are added). x is changed in place. Clearly, the read of Line 2 cannot be interchanged with the insertion of Line 4. If they were to be interchanged, then if x has a B child, the read $x//C$ would "see" the C children added by the insertion operation. Suppose, however, the read operation of Line 3 were z = read $x//D$. Then, it could safely be interchanged with the insertion of Line 4. This could enable many optimizations. For example, in searching the tree referred to by x for A descendants in Line 2, the query compiler could perform the insertions and retrieve all the D descendants as well.

- *Concurrency:* The ability to detect whether reads and writes conflict is useful in determining whether two or more concurrent operations may execute in parallel, without explicit synchronization.
- *XML Processing Languages:* In languages such as XJ and C$\omega$ that are designed to process XML robustly and efficiently, the ability to detect conflicts between operations is essential for compiler optimizations. For example, it can be used to unify loops so as to avoid extraneous tree traversals.

The subject of this paper is the detection of conflicts between update operations on XML data. We consider three operations — read, insertion, and deletion — the semantics of which are formalized in Section 3. A read $R$ and an insert operation $I$ conflict if the result of executing $R(I(t))$ is different from that of executing $R(t)$ for some XML tree $t$. We focus on a reference-based semantics based on that proposed by the XQuery update standard [9, 12] and XJ [5]. We discuss alternate semantics as well and how results can be applied in a straightforward manner to these semantics. The operations we define use a restricted subset of XPath expressions — only the child and descendant axes will be allowed (along with wildcards and branching). We show that even for this simple subset (and even when the inserted tree is constant), all conflict detection problems are NP-complete. We provide polynomial-time algorithms for the subset that does not allow the use of branching. The contributions of this paper are the following:

- A formalization of the update conflict problem for XML data. We present formalizations of two different reference-based semantics (*node conflicts* and *tree conflicts*). To the best of our knowledge, this paper is the first to draw the distinction between these forms of conflicts. We focus on node conflict semantics, but discuss how to modify results to apply them to the other semantics.
- We show that the read-insert conflict problem and the read-delete conflict problem are NP-complete for XPath expressions that use only the child and descendant axes, and have branching and wildcard symbols. Read-Insert conflict detection is NP-complete even if the inserted tree is constant and is known statically.

– We provide polynomial-time algorithms for the read-insert conflict problem and the read-delete conflict problem for XPath expressions that use only the child and descendant axes, and wildcard symbols (no branching). We consider both the case where an insertion operation inserts a constant tree that is known statically as well as when the inserted tree is variable (no information about the inserted tree is available statically).

Section 2 formalizes the abstractions we use for XML and XPath expressions. Section 3 defines the semantics of reads, insertions, and deletions and provides the formal statement of update conflict detection. Section 4 provides polynomial time algorithms for read-insert and read-delete detection, when the XPath expressions used do not contain branching. Section 5 demonstrates that the detection problem is NP-complete for the general XPath expressions we consider in the paper. In Section 6, we discuss extending our results to other domains (for example, schema-based conflict detection). In Section 7, we review related work, and we conclude in Section 8.

## 2 Preliminaries

We present mostly conventional abstractions for XML documents and XPath expressions (adapted from Miklau and Suciu [6]). In the next section, we define the syntax and semantics of *reads*, *insertions*, and *deletions* which will lead to the formal statement of the *conflict* problem.

**XML Trees.** An XML document is modeled as a labeled tree, where each node of a tree is labeled with a symbol from an infinite alphabet $\Sigma$. The set of all trees over $\Sigma$ will be denoted $T_\Sigma$. Since the fragment of XPath expressions we consider in this paper does not depend on the order between children, the trees in $T_\Sigma$ are unordered, and as is standard with XML, unranked (that is, the symbols in $\Sigma$ do not specify an arity). The subset of $\Sigma$ that is used as labels of nodes of a tree $t \in T_\Sigma$ will be denoted $\Sigma_t$.

For a tree $t \in T_\Sigma$, we will use NODES$_t$ and EDGES$_t$ to refer to the sets of nodes and edges of the tree, respectively; ROOT$(t)$ will refer to the root node of the tree $t$, and for a node $n \in$ NODES$_t$, LABEL$_t(n)$ will refer to the label on $n$ (LABEL$_t(n) \in \Sigma$). The size of a tree, $|t|$, is the number of nodes in NODES$_t$. We assume relations CHILD$(t) \subseteq$ NODES$_t \times$ NODES$_t$ and DESC$(t) \subseteq$ NODES$_t \times$ NODES$_t$ that are defined in the obvious manner.

A *path* from $n_1$ to $n_k$ in a tree is a sequence of edges $(n_1, n_2), (n_2, n_3), \ldots, (n_{k-1}, n_k)$ such that $(n_i, n_{i+1}) \in$ EDGES$_p, 1 \le i \le k-1$.

A subtree $t'$ of a tree $t$ rooted at a node $n \in$ NODES$_t$, SUBTREE$_n(t)$, is defined as the tree where NODES$_{t'}$ is the set of nodes consisting of $n$ and all descendants of $n$ in $t$. The edges of $t'$ are all edges $(u, v) \in$ EDGES$_t$ such that $u$ and $v$ are both in NODES$_{t'}$.

**Tree Patterns.** Rather than working with XPath expressions directly, we use a more convenient formalism, *tree pattern* [6], that corresponds (roughly) to the

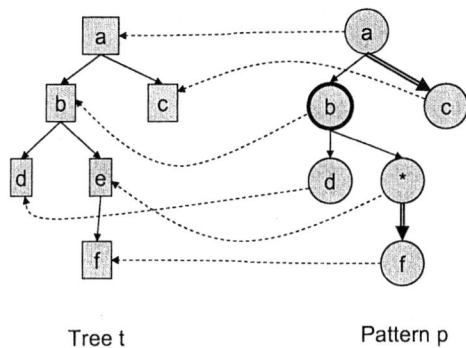

**Fig. 1.** Example of an XML tree $t$, a tree pattern $p$, and an embedding from $p$ into $t$. Double-lined edges in the figure depict edges in $\text{EDGES}_{//}(p)$. The node corresponding to $\mathscr{O}(p)$ is marked with a thick border.

XPath grammar below. The symbol $* \notin \Sigma$ denotes a wildcard label (it will match any label), and $\sigma \in \Sigma$:

$$e \to e/e \mid e//e \mid e[e] \mid e[.//e] \mid \sigma \mid *$$

A tree pattern $p$ is a tree over the alphabet $\Sigma \cup \{*\}$. The set of edges of $p$ is partitioned into two disjoint sets, $\text{EDGES}_/(p)$ and $\text{EDGES}_{//}(p)$, which represent *child constraints* and *descendant constraints*, respectively. We will depict descendant edges with double lines, and child edges with single lines in figures. Each pattern contains a distinguished node $\mathscr{O}(p) \in \text{NODES}_p$. We depict output nodes by using a thicker border for them than for other nodes. The size of a pattern, $|p|$, is defined as the number of nodes in $\text{NODES}_p$. The subset of $\Sigma$ that is used as labels of nodes of a pattern $p$ will be denoted $\Sigma_p$.

The set of all tree patterns will be denoted $P^{//,[],*}$. We will also be interested in the class of *linear patterns*, $P^{//,*}$, which is defined as the subset of $P^{//,[],*}$ where each node has a single outgoing edge, and the output node is the leaf node of the tree. The translation of XPath expressions into tree patterns is straightforward, and is omitted. In Figure 1, the tree pattern $p$ is derived from the XPath expression $a[.//c]/b[d][*//f]$.

The subpattern $p'$ of a pattern $p$ rooted at a node $n \in \text{NODES}_p$, $\text{SUBPATTERN}_n(p)$, is defined as the subtree of $p$ rooted at $n$. For our purposes, it will be sufficient to assume that an arbitrary node in $p'$ is marked as the output node. Given a pattern $p$ and $n, n' \in \text{NODES}_p$, $\text{SEQ}_n^{n'}$ is the linear pattern $p'$ derived from $p$, where $\text{NODES}_{p'} = \{\omega \in \text{NODES}_p | \omega$ is in the path from $n$ to $n'\}$, and $\text{EDGES}_{p'}$ consists of the edges used in the path from $n$ to $n'$.

**Embeddings.** The semantics of the evaluation of an XPath expression is given in terms of embeddings [6] of a tree pattern $p$ into a tree $t$. An *embedding* is a function $\mathcal{E} : \text{NODES}_p \to \text{NODES}_t$ such that all of the following conditions are satisfied (Figure 1 depicts the embedding of a tree pattern $p$ into a tree $t$) :

- (ROOT-PRESERVING) $\mathcal{E}(\text{ROOT}(p)) = \text{ROOT}(t)$
- (LABEL-PRESERVING) $\forall n \in \text{NODES}_p, \text{LABEL}_p(n) = * \vee \text{LABEL}_p(n) = \text{LABEL}_t(\mathcal{E}(n))$
- (EDGES$_/$($p$)-SATISFIED) $\forall (u,v) \in \text{EDGES}_/(p), (\mathcal{E}(u), \mathcal{E}(v)) \in \text{CHILD}(t)$
- (EDGES$_{//}$($p$)-SATISFIED) $\forall (u,v) \in \text{EDGES}_{//}(p), (\mathcal{E}(u), \mathcal{E}(v)) \in \text{DESC}(t)$

Given the definition of embeddings, the *evaluation* of a tree pattern $p$ on a tree $t$, $[\![p]\!](t)$, is defined as the subset of NODES$_t$ such that:

$$[\![p]\!](t) = \{\mathcal{E}(\mathcal{O}(p)) | \mathcal{E} \text{ is an embedding from } p \text{ into } t\}$$

We will sometimes use an alternative (non-standard) semantics of XPath expressions, $[\![p]\!]_T(t)$, that returns a set of trees rather than a set of nodes:

$$[\![p]\!]_T(t) = \{t' \in T_\Sigma | t' = \text{SUBTREE}_n(t), n \in [\![p]\!](t)\}$$

The tree patterns in $P^{//,[],*}$ are always *satisfiable*, that is, there is always at least one tree $t \in T_\Sigma$ such that $[\![p]\!](t) \neq \emptyset$. For any pattern $p$, consider the tree $W$, where NODES$_W$ = NODES$_p$ and EDGES$_W$ = EDGES$_p$. If LABEL$_p(n) \neq *$, LABEL$_W(n)$ = LABEL$_p(n)$; otherwise, LABEL$_W(n) = \sigma$, for some arbitrary $\sigma \in \Sigma$. It is straightforward to see that there is an embedding of $p$ into $W$. We shall refer to $W$ as a *model* for $p$, denoted $\mathcal{M}_p$. For example, the tree $t$ in Figure 1 is a model for the tree pattern $p$ in the figure.

## 3 Defining Conflicts

We present the semantics for read, insertion, and deletion operations and two different reference-based semantics for determining when conflicts occur.

**Definition 1.** *Trees $t, t'$ are* equivalent *if* NODES$_t$ = NODES$_{t'}$ *and* EDGES$_t$ = EDGES$_{t'}$. *Equivalence of sets of trees is based on this notion of equivalence.*

We now define the operations supported on trees:

- READ$_p(t)$ where $p \in P^{//,[],*}$ and $t \in T_\Sigma$ projects a set of nodes from a tree. It is defined as $[\![p]\!](t)$.
- INSERT$_{p,X}(t)$, where $p \in P^{//,[],*}$ and $t, X \in T_\Sigma$: The insertion operation evaluates $p$ on $t$ and inserts a fresh copy of $X$ as a subtree of each node in the result of the evaluation.
  Let $\mathcal{R} = [\![p]\!](t)$. Let $X_1, X_2, \ldots, X_{|\mathcal{R}|}$ be a set of trees such that each $X_i$ is a copy of $X$ and NODES$_{X_i}$ $\cap$ NODES$_{X_j} = \emptyset, 1 \leq i, j \leq |\mathcal{R}|$. Furthermore, the set of nodes of each $X_i$ is disjoint from NODES$_t$. For each $n_i \in \mathcal{R}, 1 \leq i \leq |\mathcal{R}|$ add $X_i$ as a child of $n_i$. In other words, construct a tree $t'$, such that NODES$_{t'}$ = NODES$_t \cup \bigcup_{i=1}^{|\mathcal{R}|}$ NODES$_{X_i}$ and EDGES$_{t'}$ = EDGES$_t \cup \bigcup_{i=1}^{|\mathcal{R}|}$(EDGES$_{X_i} \cup \{(n_i, \text{ROOT}(X_i))\}$).
  We will refer to the nodes in $\mathcal{R}$ as *insertion points*. Observe that if the result of evaluation of $p$ on $t$ is the empty set, $t$ is unchanged.
  In the definition of an insertion, $X$ is a constant tree that is specified statically. We will also consider the case where $X$ is variable (that is, the value of $X$ is not known until the execution of the statement).

- DELETE$_p(t)$, where $p \in P^{//,[],*}, t \in T_\Sigma$: The delete operation evaluates $p$ on $t$ and deletes the subtree rooted at any node in the result of the evaluation. Let $\mathcal{R} = [\![p]\!](t)$. Let $\mathcal{D}$ be the set consisting of all $n$ and descendants of $n$ in $t$, where $n \in \mathcal{R}$. The result of the delete operation is a tree $t'$, where NODES$_{t'}$ = NODES$_t - \mathcal{D}$, and EDGES$_{t'}$ consists of the edges $(u, v)$ in EDGES$_t$ where both $u$ and $v$ are in NODES$_{t'}$.

  We will refer to the nodes in $\mathcal{R}$ as *deletion points*. We require that $\mathcal{O}(p) \neq$ ROOT$(p)$, which ensures that the result of the deletion is a tree.

For notational convenience, we will often conflate the tree pattern associated with an operation with the tree pattern itself. For example, $\mathcal{O}(R)$ will stand for $\mathcal{O}(p)$ in the read operation $R = \text{READ}_p(t)$.

The read, insertion, and deletion operations can be executed on a tree $t$ in time polynomial in the size of their inputs (that is, $|t|, |p|$, and $|X|$). The patterns we consider are a subset of *Core XPath*, which can be evaluated in time linear in the size of the tree and the pattern [4]. Given the result of the evaluation of a pattern, the insertion and deletion operations can be executed easily in time linear in the size of $t$ (technically, the insertion operation can be performed in time $|t| \cdot |X|$, since copies of $X$ must be made) in standard tree representations. We now define what it means for two operations to *conflict*.

**Definition 2 (read-insert conflict).** *A read $R = \text{READ}_p(t)$ has a node conflict with an insertion $I = \text{INSERT}_{p',X}(t)$ if there exists $t \in T_\Sigma$, $R(I(t)) \neq R(t)$. If such a t exists, we call $t$ a witness to the conflict.*

*A read $R = \text{READ}_p(t)$ has a tree conflict with an insertion $I = \text{INSERT}_{p',X}(t)$ if there exists $t \in T_\Sigma$, $[\![p]\!]_T(I(t)) \neq [\![p]\!]_T(t)$.*

*If $X$ is not constant (that is, it is variable), $R$ and $I$ have a node (tree) conflict if there exists an assignment of a tree in $T_\Sigma$ to $X$ that would cause a read-insert node (tree)conflict.*

Intuitively, the difference between node and tree conflicts is that the node conflict definition only verifies that the nodes returned by $R(t)$ and $R(I(t))$ are the same. The tree conflict definition verifies that no node conflict exists *and* none of the trees rooted at a node in $R(I(t))$ contains a modified subtree. For example, consider the read operation $R$ that returns the root node of a tree, and an insertion operation $I$ that adds a subtree $X$ to a child labeled B of the root node. According to the node conflict definition, the two operations do not conflict — $R(t)$ and $R(I(t))$ both return the root node of the document. The tree conflict definition, however, would signal a conflict since the subtree of $I(t)$ rooted at ROOT$(I(t))$ is not the same as the subtree of $t$ rooted at ROOT$(t)$. Observe that the absence of a tree conflict implies that no node conflict exists, but the converse is not true.

Both definitions are useful in practice. Suppose one had a query of the form $I; \ldots;$ R (where $I$ is executed before $R$), and $I$ and $R$ have a node conflict. A query compiler could choose to perform the read $R$ before the insert $I$ as long it ensures that any operation that depends on the result of $R$, and that observes the modification made by $I$, executes after $I$. The tree semantics of conflict is useful to determine when the subtree of a node accessed by $R$ may conflict with an insertion or deletion, which may be useful in concurrency applications. We now present a parallel definition for read-delete conflicts.

**Definition 3 (read-delete conflict).** *A read $R = \text{READ}_p(t)$ has a node conflict with a deletion $D = \text{DELETE}_{p'}(t)$ if there exists $t \in T_\Sigma$, $R(D(t)) \neq R(t)$.*

*A read $R = \text{READ}_p(t)$ has a tree conflict with a deletion $D = \text{DELETE}_{p'}(t)$ if there exists $t \in T_\Sigma$, $[\![p]\!]_T(D(t)) \neq [\![p]\!]_T(t)$.*

Evidently, other kinds of conflicts can arise, for example, delete-insert conflicts. In this paper, we mostly focus on read-insert and read-delete conflicts and defer discussion of other update conflicts to Section 6.

Given a tree $t$, whether $t$ is a witness to a read-insert or read-delete conflict can be decided in polynomial time for both semantics of conflicts.

**Lemma 1.** *Given a tree $t \in T_\Sigma$, a read $R$ and an insertion $I$ (resp. a deletion $D$), it can be determined in polynomial time whether $t$ is a witness to a node or tree conflict between $R$ and $I$ (resp. $R$ and $D$).*

*Proof.* The case for node conflict is trivial since it involves evaluating $R(t)$ and $R(I(t))$ (which can be performed in polynomial time, as stated previously) and verifying that the resulting sets are identical.

For tree conflicts, one can associate with each node in $t$ a flag marking whether the subtree under it has been modified. In an appropriate tree representation, an insertion or deletion operation can update this information in time linear in the size of $t$. Checking for a conflict requires verifying set equality of the results of $R(t)$ and $R(I(t))$ and ensuring that none of the nodes in $R(I(t))$ have been marked.

The proof for read-delete conflicts is similar. ∎

In this paper, based on the proposed semantics for XQuery and XJ, we focus mainly on *node conflicts* with reference-based semantics (all future references to "conflict" should be interpreted as such, unless stated otherwise explicitly). All results can be extended to tree conflicts as well, and where appropriate, we will discuss the modifications necessary.

## 4 Efficient Algorithms for $P^{//,*}$

We provide polynomial-time algorithms for detecting read-delete and read-insert conflicts when the patterns are linear. What is perhaps surprising is that only the read pattern need be linear — the pattern for the insert and delete can be any pattern in $P^{//,[],*}$. This is surprising because as we show in the next section, when both patterns are in $P^{//,[],*}$, read-insert and read-delete conflict detection is NP-complete.

### 4.1 Read-Delete Node Conflicts

We start with examining the read-delete case, because it is more straightforward than the read-insert case. Consider an example of a conflict when the deletion

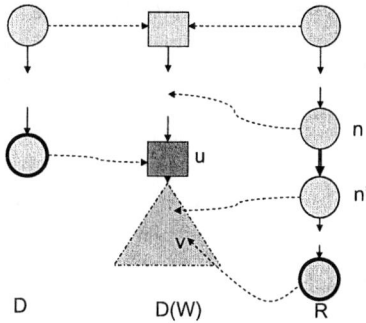

**Fig. 2.** Structure of a read-delete node conflict

and the read are linear patterns. Figure 2 shows the structure that any conflict must have. The figure depicts a deletion $D$ and a read $R$ and the tree that is the result of applying $D$ to a tree $W$ (the shaded subtree rooted at $u$ is deleted from $W$).

The existence of a node conflict implies that there is an embedding of $R$ into $W$ that maps $\mathscr{O}(R)$ to some node $v$ that is deleted in $D(W)$. There is a node $u$ in NODES$_W$ that is either an ancestor of $v$ or $v$ itself (there must be at least one for $v$ to have been deleted), where $u$ is a node in $[\![D]\!](W)$.

Consider the edge $(n, n')$ in Figure 2. The nodes in the path from ROOT($R$) to $n$ are mapped to nodes in $W$ in the path from ROOT($W$) to node $u$. The nodes in $D$ from ROOT($D$) to $\mathscr{O}(D)$ can be embedded into nodes in $W$ in the path from ROOT($W$) to $u$ as well (since $u \in [\![D]\!](W)$). Since portions of both $R$ and $D$ are mapped to the nodes in the path ROOT($W$) to $u$, the nodes in $R$ from ROOT($R$) to the node $n$ must "match" the nodes in $D$ from ROOT($D$) to $\mathscr{O}(D)$. In other words, the sequence of nodes in $W$ from ROOT($W$) to $u$ supports embeddings $\mathcal{E}_1$ from $D$, and $\mathcal{E}_2$ from SEQ$^n_{\text{ROOT}(R)}$. We formalize this notion of matching and show how we can use it to detect read-delete node conflicts.

**Definition 4.** *Linear patterns $l$ and $l'$ match weakly if there exists a tree $t \in T_\Sigma$ such that there is an embedding $\mathcal{E}_1$ from $l$ into $t$ and an embedding $\mathcal{E}_2$ from $l'$ into $t$, and $\mathcal{E}_1(\mathscr{O}(l)) = \mathcal{E}_2(\mathscr{O}(l'))$ or $\mathcal{E}_1(\mathscr{O}(l))$ is a descendant of $\mathcal{E}_2(\mathscr{O}(l'))$.*

*Two linear patterns $l$ and $l'$ match strongly if they match weakly and $\mathcal{E}_1(\mathscr{O}(l)) = \mathcal{E}_2(\mathscr{O}(l'))$.*

We will use this notion of matching as the basis of our algorithm for read-delete conflict detection. The following theorem is useful for this purpose.

**Theorem 1.** *Consider a read $R = $ READ$_p$ and a deletion $D = $ DELETE$_{p'}$. There is a read-delete node conflict between $R$ and $D$ if and only if there exists an edge $(n, n')$ in EDGES$_R$ such that:*

- *$(n, n') \in$ EDGES$_{//}(p)$, $D$ and SEQ$^n_{\text{ROOT}(R)}$ match weakly, or*
- *$(n, n') \in$ EDGES$_{/}(p)$, $D$ and SEQ$^{n'}_{\text{ROOT}(R)}$ match strongly.* ∎

Theorem 1 suggests a mechanism for detecting read-delete conflicts — find an edge $(n, n') \in \text{EDGES}_R$ such that $D$ matches the subpattern of $R$ induced by the edge strongly or weakly as appropriate. We sketch an algorithm for determining whether two patterns match.

Given linear patterns $l$ and $l'$, we construct regular expressions from the patterns and use language intersection to check whether $l$ and $l'$ match strongly or weakly. First, some technicalities. Since $\Sigma$ is infinite, we assert that we can restrict the alphabet to the symbols used in $l$ and $l'$, that is $\Sigma_l \cup \Sigma_{l'}$. Let $\Sigma_{l,l'} = \Sigma_l \cup \Sigma_{l'}$. If there is a witness tree $W$ to a matching that uses symbols other than those in $\Sigma_{l,l'}$, observe that we can replace those symbols with ones from $\Sigma_{l,l'}$; only nodes labeled $*$ in $l$ and $l'$ could have mapped to them. Secondly, note that the size of $\Sigma_{l,l'}$ depends solely on the sizes of $l$ and $l'$.

We now describe the construction of regular expressions from linear patterns. Let (.) be stand for any symbol in $\Sigma_{l,l'}$, that is, it is equivalent to $\sigma_1|\sigma_2|\ldots$ for each $\sigma_i \in \Sigma_{l,l'}$. For a node $n$ in a pattern $l$, let $sym(n)$ be defined as $\text{LABEL}_l(n)$ if $\text{LABEL}_l(n) \neq *$, and (.), otherwise.

We define a function $\mathscr{R}$ : NODES $\to$ $regexp$ as follows (for a pattern $l$):

- $\mathscr{R}(\text{ROOT}(l)) = sym(n)$,
- $\mathscr{R}(n \neq \text{ROOT}(l))$: Let $n'$ be the parent of $n$ in $l$. If $(n', n)$ is a descendant edge, $\mathscr{R}(n) = \mathscr{R}(n') \cdot (.)^* \cdot sym(n)$. If $(n', n)$ is a child edge, $\mathscr{R}(n) = \mathscr{R}(n') \cdot sym(n)$.

Let $r_1 = \mathscr{R}(\mathcal{O}(l))$ and $r_2 = \mathscr{R}(\mathcal{O}(l'))$. We state (the proof is omitted for space) that the linear patterns $l$ and $l'$ match strongly if and only if $L(r_1) \cap L(r_2) \neq \emptyset$, where $L(r_1)$ and $L(r_2)$ are the languages denoted by $r_1$ and $r_2$, respectively. $l$ and $l'$ match weakly if and only if $L(r_1) \cap L(r_2 \cdot (.)^*) \neq \emptyset$. As is customary, we can construct non-deterministic finite state automata from the regular expressions, and verify in time polynomial in the size of $l$ and $l'$ whether the intersection is non-empty.

Since we can detect whether a linear pattern matches another (weakly or strongly) in polynomial time, for each edge $(n, n')$ in $\text{EDGES}_R$ in a read $R$, we can verify whether a deletion $D$ matches $\text{SEQ}^n_{\text{ROOT}(R)}$ or $\text{SEQ}^{n'}_{\text{ROOT}(R)}$ (as appropriate). By Theorem 1, if we find any such $(n, n')$, a read-delete conflict exists. In practice, rather than verifying each edge in $R$ separately, one can use an algorithm based on dynamic programming to determine whether a match exists. With respect to alternate semantics of updates, observe that a tree conflict occurs if and only if either there is a node conflict or $D$ is weakly matched by $R$. Therefore, we can use a slight modification of the mechanism for node conflicts to handle tree conflicts.

We show now that the deletion operation need not be linear. As long as the read operation is in $P^{//,*}$, we can detect read-delete conflicts in polynomial time.

**Theorem 2.** *A read* $R = \text{READ}_p$ *and a deletion* $D = \text{DELETE}_{p'}$*, where* $p$ *is a linear pattern and* $p' \in P^{//,[],*}$*, have a node conflict if and only if* $R$ *and* $D' = \text{SEQ}^{\mathcal{O}(D)}_{\text{ROOT}(D)}$ *have a node conflict. Note* $D$ *is not necessarily a linear pattern.*

*Proof.* (Only if) If $R$ and $D$ have a conflict, there is a tree $W$ that is a witness to the conflict. $W$ is also a witness to a read-delete conflict between $D'$ and $R$.

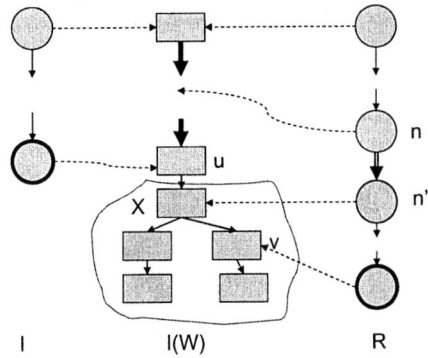

**Fig. 3.** Structure of a read-insert node conflict

$[\![D]\!](W) \subseteq [\![D']\!](W)$, because any embedding of $D$ into $W$ defines an embedding of $D'$ into $W$. Since the set of deletion points in the evaluation of $D'$ on $W$ contains all the deletion points of $D$ on $W$, any node whose deletion is necessary to show the conflict in $R(D(W))$ will also be deleted in $R(D'(W))$.

(If) If $D'$ and $R$ have a conflict, let $W$ be a witness to the conflict. We construct a tree $W'$ from $W$ as follows. Consider any node $n \in \text{NODES}_{D'}$. Let $c$ be a child of $n$ in $D$ that is not in $D'$, and let $\mathcal{M}_c$ be a model for $\text{SUBPATTERN}_c(D)$. Add $\mathcal{M}_c$ as a child of each node in $W$. This will ensure that any embedding of $D'$ into $W$ can be extended easily into an embedding of $D$ into $W'$.

Given an embedding $\mathcal{E}$ of $D'$ into $W$, let $n$ be a node in $\text{NODES}_{D'}$ and let $c \notin \text{NODES}_{D'}$ be a child of $n$ in $D$. The extension of $\mathcal{E}$ maps the subpattern of $D$ rooted at $c$ to the child of $\mathcal{E}(n)$ in $W'$ that corresponds to $\mathcal{M}_c$. Since any embedding of $D'$ into $W$ can be extended into one of $D$ into $W'$, $[\![D']\!](W) \subseteq [\![D]\!](W')$. Moreover, since $W'$ only adds nodes to $W$, $[\![R]\!](W) \subseteq [\![R]\!](W')$. Let $v$ be a node in $R(W)$ that is deleted in $R(D'(W))$. $v$ will be a node in $R(W')$ and the deletion point that causes $v$ to be deleted will be present in $[\![D]\!](W')$. Therefore, there is a read-delete conflict between $R$ and $D$. ∎

**Corollary 1.** *For a read $R = \text{READ}_p$ and a deletion $D = \text{DELETE}_{p'}$, where $p \in P^{//,*}$ and $p' \in P^{//,[],*}$, a read-delete node conflict can be detected in polynomial time.*

### 4.2 Read-Insert Node Conflicts

Consider an example of a node conflict when the insert $I$ and the read $R$ are linear patterns. Figure 3 shows the structure that any such node conflict must have. The figure depicts $I$ and $R$ and the tree that is the result of applying $I$ to a tree $W$ (a subtree $X$ is inserted as a child of a node $u$).

While the structure is similar to the read-delete case, the read-insert case is somewhat more complicated. Unlike the read-delete case, where the subtree rooted at $u$ can be any tree, in the read-insert case, the nodes in $R$ from $n'$ to $\mathcal{O}(R)$ should be mappable to $X$ for a conflict to occur. The existence of a conflict implies that there is an embedding that maps $\mathcal{O}(R)$ to some node $v$ in $X$ and maps the nodes in $R$ in the path from $\text{ROOT}(R)$ to $\mathcal{O}(R)$ to nodes in the path from $\text{ROOT}(W)$ to $v$ in $I(W)$. Since $v$ is in $X$, it must be the descendant of an insertion point $u \in \text{NODES}_W$ (the insertion point where $X$ is inserted). For $u$ to have been selected as an insertion point, there must have been an embedding of $I$ to the nodes in the path from $\text{ROOT}(W)$ to $u$.

We consider two cases for read-insert conflicts. First, the tree $X$ that is inserted is variable and not known statically, that is, it can be bound to *any* tree at runtime. A conservative compiler must ensure that for all trees $t$ that can be bound to $X$, a read-insert conflict would not occur. In the second case, the tree $X$ is a constant tree $C$ and the compiler can use this information to detect whether a read-insert conflict would occur.

We show that if $X$ is variable, read-insert conflict detection reduces to the problem of read-delete conflict detection. A query compiler could use the techniques described previously for the read-delete case to efficiently detect conflicts.

**Theorem 3.** *Consider a read $R$ and an insertion $I = \text{INSERT}_{p,X}$, where both $R$ and $I$ use linear patterns and $X$ is a variable that can be bound to any tree in $T_\Sigma$. There is a read-insert conflict between $R$ and $I$ if and only if there is a read-delete conflict between $R$ and $D = \text{DELETE}_{p'}$, where $p'$ is derived from $p$ by adding a node labeled $*$ as a child of the output node of $p$ (connected by a child edge), and marking this node labeled $*$ as the output node of $p'$.*

*Proof.* [Sketch] Let $t$ be a witness to a read-delete conflict between $R$ and $D$. Let $n$ be a node in $t$ that is not deleted in $D(t)$ and has a child $u$ that is deleted in $D(t)$ such that $R(t)$ contains a node in the subtree of $t$ rooted at $u$. By the definition of read-delete conflicts, there must be such a node $n$. Let $t'$ be the subtree of $t$ rooted at $u$. We claim that $W = D(t)$ is a witness to a read-insert conflict between $R$ and $I$, when $X$ is bound to $t'$. Observe that if the pattern $p'$ used in $D$ selects $u$ as a deletion point, the pattern $p$ used in $I$ would select $n$ in $W$, and the insertion of $t'$ as a child of $n$ would cause $R(I(W))$ to contain a node in $t'$, which would not be in $R(W)$. The case of proving that a read-insert conflict implies a read-delete conflict is similar and is omitted. ∎

In the other case, where $X$ is a constant tree $C$, a query compiler has more information about the insertion operation. We show how this information may be used to detect read-insert conflicts. Consider the edge $(n, n')$ in Figure 3. It is the edge in $R$ in the path from $\text{ROOT}(R)$ to $\mathcal{O}(R)$ that straddles $W$ and $X$ in the sense that $n$ is mapped to a node in $W$ and $n'$ is mapped to a node in $X$. In any witness to a conflict, there must always be such an edge because $\text{ROOT}(R)$ is always mapped to $\text{ROOT}(W)$ and $\mathcal{O}(R)$ is mapped to $v$ which is a node in $X$.

**Definition 5.** *Given a read $R$ and an insert $I$, let $(n, n')$ be an edge in $\text{EDGES}_R$. $(n, n')$ is the* cut edge *for $R$ and $I$ if there exists a tree $W \in T_\Sigma$ and an embedding $\mathcal{E}$ of $R$ into $I(W)$ such that $\mathcal{E}(n) \in \text{NODES}_W$ and $\mathcal{E}(n') \notin \text{NODES}_W$.*

**Lemma 2.** *There is a read-insert conflict between $R$ and $I$ if and only if there is a cut edge for $R$ and $I$.* ∎

Since any embedding of $R$ into $I(W)$ that causes a conflict must have a cut edge $(n, n')$, we can use a similar strategy as for the read-delete case to detect conflicts:

- Choose an edge $(n, n')$ in $\text{EDGES}_R$.
- Construct a witness tree $W$ such that $(n, n')$ is a cut edge for an embedding of $R$ into $I(W)$. If such a tree can be constructed, a conflict exists.
- If no such tree can be constructed, choose another edge until all edges have been tried.
- If no edge can be found, $R$ and $I$ do not have a read-insert conflict.

From Figure 3, it should be clear that for an edge $(n, n') \in \text{EDGES}_R$ to be a cut edge, it must satisfy two constraints. The insert $I$ must match $\text{SEQ}_{\text{ROOT}(R)}^n$, and there should be an embedding of $\text{SEQ}_{\text{ROOT}(n')}^{\mathscr{O}(R)}$ into $X$. We formalize these requirements below.

**Lemma 3.** *Consider a read $R = \text{READ}_p$ and an insert $I = \text{INSERT}_{p', X}$. Let $(n, n')$ be an edge in $\text{EDGES}_p$. $(n, n')$ is a cut edge for $R$ and $I$ if and only if:*

- *If $(n, n') \in \text{EDGES}_/(p)$, $I$ and $\text{SEQ}_{\text{ROOT}(R)}^n$ match strongly. If $(n, n') \in \text{EDGES}_{//}(p)$, $I$ and $\text{SEQ}_{\text{ROOT}(R)}^n$ match weakly, and*
- *If $(n, n') \in \text{EDGES}_/(p)$, there is an embedding from $\text{SEQ}_{n'}^{\mathscr{O}(R)}$ to $X$. If $(n, n') \in \text{EDGES}_{//}(p)$, there is an embedding from $\text{SEQ}_{n'}^{\mathscr{O}(R)}$ to $X$ or some subtree of $X$.* ∎

Using the mechanisms described in the previous section for detecting matches, we can identify cut edges in polynomial time. As a result, we can conclude that read-insert conflicts can be detected in polynomial time.

**Theorem 4.** *For a read $R$ and an insertion $I$, a read-insert node conflict can be detected in polynomial time if $R$ and $I$ use patterns in $P^{//,*}$, and the tree $X$ inserted by $I$ is constant.*

*Proof.* Given $R$ and $(n, n')$, we can verify whether $I$ and $\text{SEQ}_{\text{ROOT}(R)}^n$ match weakly or strongly as appropriate in polynomial time. We can also verify whether there is an embedding of $\text{SEQ}_{n'}^{\mathscr{O}(R)}$ into $X$ or a subtree of $X$ as appropriate. By Lemma 3, these facts are sufficient to determine whether $(n, n')$ is a cut edge for $R$ and $I$. By Lemma 2, identification of cut edges is necessary and sufficient for read-insert conflict detection. ∎

REMARKS: As in the read-delete case, $I$ and $R$ have a tree conflict if and only if $I$ and $R$ have a node conflict or $I$ and $R$ match weakly. We conclude, therefore, that the theorem above applies to tree conflicts as well.

Similar to the read-delete case, even when the insert is not a linear pattern, conflict detection is in polynomial time as long as the read pattern is linear.

**Theorem 5.** *A read $R = \text{READ}_p$ and an insertion $I = \text{INSERT}_{p',X}$, where $p$ is a linear pattern and $p' \in P^{//,[],*}$ and $X$ is a constant tree, have a node conflict if and only if $R$ and $I' = \text{SEQ}_{\text{ROOT}(I)}^{\mathscr{O}(I)}$ have a node conflict. Note $I$ is not necessarily a linear pattern.*

**Corollary 2.** *For a read $R = \text{READ}_p$ and an insertion $I = \text{INSERT}_{p',X}$, where $p \in P^{//,*}$ and $p' \in P^{//,[],*}$, a read-insert node conflict can be detected in polynomial time.*

## 5  NP-Completeness of $P^{//,[],*}$

We show that the read-insert and read-delete node conflict problems are NP-complete when the patterns used are from $P^{//,[],*}$. In fact, in the read-insert case, conflict detection is NP-complete even when the tree $X$ in the insertion is constant and consists of a single node.

### 5.1  Read-Insert Node Conflicts

Suppose a read operation $R = \text{READ}_p(t)$ conflicts with an insertion $I = \text{INSERT}_{p',X}(t)$, there is an XML tree $W$ that witnesses the conflict, where the size of $W$ is polynomial in the size of $R$ and $I$. This fact allows one to present a non-deterministic polynomial time algorithm for deciding whether a read-insert conflict exists. One can guess a tree $W$ of size polynomial in the inputs, and execute $R(W)$ and $R(I(W))$ to verify whether $W$ acts as a witness. For the NP-hardness result, we reduce the problem of containment of XPath expressions [6] to the read-insert conflict problem (actually, we reduce the dual non-containment problem).

**Theorem 6.** *Read-insert node conflict detection for $P^{//,[],*}$ is in NP.*

*Proof.* [Sketch] The proof depends on non-deterministically guessing a tree of size polynomial in the inputs and verifying that the tree is a witness to the conflict. It relies on the fact that if a witness exists, "inessential" nodes can be pruned away so that a tree polynomial in the size of the inputs can be constructed. By Lemma 1, we can verify in polynomial time whether a tree $t$ is a witness to the read-insert conflict. ∎

For the NP-hardness result, we reduce the non-containment problem for XPath expressions:

**Definition 6.** *A pattern $p$ is contained in another pattern $p'$, denoted $p \subseteq p'$, if $\forall t \in T_\Sigma, [\![p]\!](t) \neq \emptyset \implies [\![p']\!](t) \neq \emptyset$. In other words, the existence of an embedding of $p$ into $t$ implies the existence of an embedding of $p'$ into $t$.*

Let $p, p'$ be two patterns in $P^{//,[],*}$. Miklau and Suciu [6] have shown that the decision problem of whether $p \not\subseteq p'$ is NP-hard. We reduce the non-containment problem to that of determining whether a read-insert conflict exists.

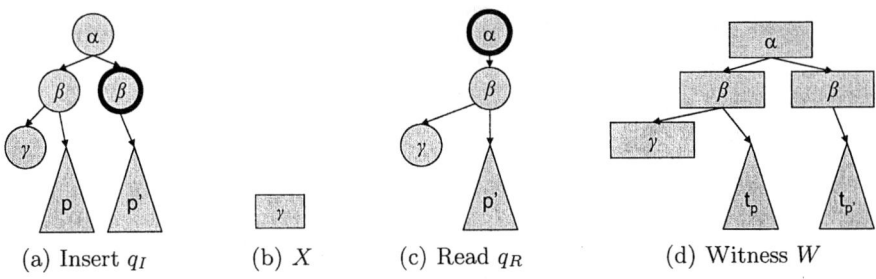

**Fig. 4.** (a) Query $q_I$ used in insertion operation (b) Tree added in insertion operation (c) query $q_R$ used in read operation (d) Structure of witness tree

**Theorem 7.** *Read-insert node conflict detection for $P^{//,[],*}$ is NP-hard.*

*Proof.* Given an instance of the non-containment problem, that is, two patterns $p, p' \in P^{//,[],*}$, we construct an instance of the read-insert conflict problem. We construct an insertion operation $I = \text{INSERT}_{q_I, X}$ and a read operation, $R = \text{READ}_{q_R}$, where $q_I$, $X$, and $q_R$ are constructed from $p$ and $p'$ as depicted in Figure 4a-c; $q_I$ is the pattern equivalent to the XPath expression $\alpha[\beta[p][\gamma]]/\beta[p']$, $q_R$ is equivalent to $\alpha[\beta[p'][\gamma]]$, and $X$ is the tree consisting of a single node labeled $\gamma$, where $\alpha, \beta, \gamma$ are symbols not used in $p$ and $p'$. Observe that the construction can be performed in polynomial time.

There is a read-insert node conflict between $R$ and $I$ if and only if $p \not\sqsubseteq p'$. if $p \not\sqsubseteq p'$, then there is a witness tree $W$ as shown in Figure 4d, where the root node, which is labeled $\alpha$, has two distinct children labeled $\beta$. One $\beta$ child contains a subtree $t_p$ for which there is an embedding of $p$ into $t$, but no embedding of $p'$ into $t_p$. Since $p \not\sqsubseteq p'$, the existence of such a $t_p$ is guaranteed. This $\beta$ child also contains a node labeled $\gamma$. The other $\beta$ child contains a tree $t_{p'}$ for which there is an embedding of $p'$ into $t_{p'}$, but no $\gamma$ child. $R$ has no embedding in $W$ because the $\beta$ child of $\text{ROOT}(W)$ that matches $p'$ does not have a $\gamma$ child. $R$ does have an embedding after the execution of the insertion operation, which inserts a $\gamma$ node into the appropriate point. As a result, $R(W) = \emptyset$, but $R(I(W)) = \{\text{ROOT}(W)\}$, which implies a read-insert conflict.

If there is a read-insert conflict, there is a tree $W$ that is a witness to the conflict. Observe that for all $t \in T_\Sigma$, $R(t)$ returns at the most a single node ($\text{ROOT}(t)$). Since $R(W) \neq R(I(W))$, $R(W)$ must be empty and $R(I(W))$ must be $\{\text{ROOT}(W)\}$. Since $R(I(W))$ and $R(W)$ are different, the insert operation modifies the tree $W$. There must be, therefore, an embedding of $I$ into $W$. Consider the subtree of $W$, $t_p$, to which an embedding maps the subpattern of $I$ corresponding to $p$. There can be no embedding from $p'$ into this subtree; this would imply that there is an embedding of $R$ into $W$ where the subpattern corresponding to $p'$ is mapped to $t_p$. As a result, $t_p$ is a tree that has an embedding from $p$ but not from $p'$, proving the assertion that $p \not\sqsubseteq p'$.

Since $R$ and $I$ conflict if and only if $p \not\sqsubseteq p'$, the read-insert node conflict problem is NP-hard. ∎

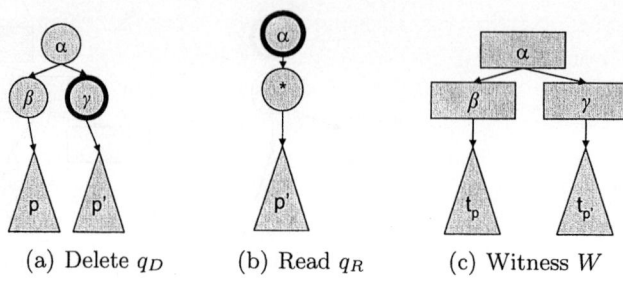

**Fig. 5.** (a) Query $q_D$ used in deletion operation (b) query $q_R$ used in read operation (c) Witness $W$ to read-delete conflict

**Corollary 3.** *Read-insert node conflict detection for patterns in $P^{//,[],*}$ is NP-complete.*

REMARKS: Observe that the reduction shown for node conflicts cannot be used directly to show NP-hardness of tree conflict detection. The patterns in Figure 4 are such that every tree that causes an insertion to occur would be a witness to a tree conflict. We modify $R$ slightly, where we add a child node labeled $\delta$ to ROOT($R$) and mark this child node as the output node. Since the subtree under a node matching $\delta$ is never modified by $I$, there will be a tree conflict between the modified $R$ and $I$ if and only if there is a node conflict between the modified $R$ and $I$.

## 5.2 Read-Delete Node Conflicts

The characteristics of the read-delete conflict detection problem for $P^{//,[],*}$ are similar to that of the read-insert problem. We, therefore, omit the proof of membership in NP and only sketch the proof of NP-hardness.

**Theorem 8.** *Read-delete node conflict detection for $P^{//,[],*}$ is in NP.*

**Theorem 9.** *Read-delete node conflict detection for $P^{//,[],*}$ is NP-hard.*

*Proof.* As in the read-insert case, we provide a reduction from the non-containment problem. Given an instance of the non-containment problem, that is, two patterns $p, p' \in P^{//,[],*}$, we construct an instance of the read-delete conflict problem. We construct a deletion operation $D = \text{DELETE}_{q_D}$ and a read operation, $R = \text{READ}_{q_R}$, where $q_D, q_R$ are constructed from $p$ and $p'$ as depicted in Figure 5a-b; $q$ is the pattern equivalent (roughly) to the XPath expression $q_D = \alpha[\beta[p]]/\gamma[p']$, and $q_R$ is equivalent to $\alpha[*[p']]$, where $\alpha, \beta, \gamma$ are arbitrary symbols. Observe that the construction can be performed in polynomial time.

We show that $p \not\sqsubseteq p'$ if and only if $D$ and $R$ have a read-delete conflict. If $p \not\sqsubseteq p'$, there must be a tree $t_p$ such that there is no embedding from $p'$ into $t_p$, but for which there is an embedding from $p$. We use the witness tree in Figure 5c to show a read-delete node conflict. In $W$, $t_{p'}$ is some tree for which there is an embedding of $p'$ into $t_{p'}$. Clearly $[\![R]\!](W)$ contains ROOT($W$) since ROOT($W$)

contains a grandchild that has an embedding from $p'$. The delete operation, $D$, will remove the subtree of $W$ rooted at the node labeled $\gamma$. Therefore, $R(D(W))$ will not contain ROOT($W$) since $D(W)$ does not contain any child of ROOT($W$) into which $p'$ can be embedded (by assumption, $p'$ cannot be embedded into $t_p$). As a result $W$ is a witness to a read-delete conflict.

If there is a read-delete conflict, let $W$ be a witness to the conflict. Since $R(D(W)) \neq R(W)$ and $R(t)$ for any tree in $T_\Sigma$ contains at most one node (the root of $t$), $R(D(W)) = \emptyset$. Suppose $p \subseteq p'$. Since the deletion operation modifies $W$, there must be an embedding of $D$ into $W$. Therefore, ROOT($W$) must contain a child $u$ labeled $\beta$ such that there is an embedding of $p$ into a subtree under $u$, $t_p$, where the root of $p$ is mapped to the root of $t_p$. This tree is not deleted by $D$ — only children of ROOT($W$) labeled $\gamma$ are affected by the delete operation. As a result, since $p \subseteq p'$, there must be an embedding of $R$ into $D(W)$, where the node labeled $*$ in $R$ is mapped to $u$ and $p'$ in $R$ is mapped to $t_p$. The existence of an embedding contradicts the fact that $R(D(W)) = \emptyset$. Therefore, $p \not\subseteq p'$.

Since $p \not\subseteq p'$ if and only if $D$ and $R$ have a read-delete conflict, we conclude that the read-delete problem for patterns in $P^{//,[],*}$ is NP-hard. ∎

**Corollary 4.** *Read-delete conflict detection for patterns in $P^{//,[],*}$ is NP-complete.*

REMARKS: As in the read-insert case, a slight modification to $R$ (adding a child labeled $\delta$ of ROOT($R$) as the output node) will ensure that $p \not\subseteq p'$ if and only if the modified $R$ and $D$ do not have a tree conflict. The details are omitted.

## 6 Discussion

**Complex Updates.** While we have focused on read-delete and read-insert conflicts, the other conflicts (delete-insert, delete-delete, and insert-insert) are of interest as well. Informally, we can define conflicts in these situations as two operations $o_1, o_2$ conflict if there is a tree $t \in T_\Sigma$ such that $o_1(o_2(t))$ is not equal to $o_2(o_1(t))$, where $o_1$ and $o_2$ can be either an insert or a delete.

In the reference-based semantics, the definition of these conflicts is not completely straightforward. Two insertions $I_1$ and $I_2$ ought not to have an insert-insert conflict if $I_1$ and $I_2$ are identical; in this case, for any $t \in T_\Sigma$, $I_1(I_2(t))$ ought to be considered equivalent to $I_2(I_1(t))$. In the reference semantics, the problem is with the clones of $X$ (in INSERT$_{p,X}$) that are inserted into any tree — they do not preserve node equality. A suitable reference-based semantics of conflicts would have to distinguish these nodes appropriately.

The reductions from XPath containment provided in Section 5 can be modified in a straightforward manner to show that each of these conflicts is NP-hard.

**Schema Information.** The complexity of conflicts when schema information (for example, DTDs) is available is an open problem. In general, the addition of DTDs appears to raise the complexity of problems related to XPath. For example, as mentioned before, containment of $P^{//,[]}$ in in PTIME. When the problem of containment is constrained to detect whether for all trees conforming to a DTD, one XPath is contained in another, the problem is coNP-complete [7].

## 7 Related Work

The subject of updates in XML has only recently started getting attention. Efforts have been focused on the syntax and semantics of update operations [9, 10, 12] and incremental validation of XML [1, 8]. Benedikt et al [2] consider the snapshot semantics for XQuery and two optimizations — (1) reordering updates and, (2) mixing evaluation of XQuery sub-expressions and concrete updates. They state that the determination of whether mixing updates and evaluation is safe is undecidable when a schema (represented as an automaton) is present.

In their system, a program is non-interfering if none of its generated concrete updates can affect the result of any of its query evaluations. Interference of programs is similar to our notion of conflicts. In order to detect when this reordering optimization is safe, Benedikt et al provide a conservative, approximate algorithm for generating a system of equations from an update program such that the unsatisfiability of the set of equations allows one to conclude that the program is non-interfering [2]. Unsatisfiability detection for their system of equations is claimed to be coNP-complete. Only a reduction from an update program to a system of equations is provided and no reduction from the unsatisfiability problem to the non-interference problem. Therefore, only an upper bound of the complexity of non-interference is obtained.

We address the more focused problem of conflicts between two operations, a read and an insertion (or deletion), and show that exact conflict detection is NP-complete (thus providing a tight classification). We show that even when the inserted tree is a constant tree of a single node (and there is no schema information, which typically raises the general complexity of such problems), conflict detection is NP-complete. Furthermore, we provide efficient polynomial algorithms for conflict detection for linear patterns, which are common in practice.

## 8 Conclusion

We believe that update operations will be an important component of XML query and processing languages. The presence of update operations leads to the natural question of when modifications to data cause two operations to conflict. We have provided two formulations of semantics for conflicts. For linear XPath expressions that do not support branching, but allow child and descendant axes, and the wildcard operator, we have shown that polynomial-time algorithms exist. For read-insert conflicts, we have provide polynomial algorithms for detecting conflicts when the tree that is inserted in constant and known statically, and for detecting potential conflicts when the inserted tree is variable. If the branching operator is also allowed, the problem becomes NP-complete. The development of an understanding of updates can lead to more efficient compilers for languages such as XQuery and XJ.

# References

1. A. Balmin, Y. Papakonstantinou, and V. Vianu. Incremental validation of XML documents. *ACM Transactions on Database Systems (TODS)*, 29(4):710–751, 2004.
2. M. Benedikt, A. Bonifati, S. Flesca, and A. Vyas. Verification of tree updates for optimization. In *17th International Conference on Computer Aided Verification (CAV)*, July 2005.
3. G. Bierman, E. Meijer, and W. Schulte. The essence of data access in Cω. http://research.microsoft.com/~emeijer.
4. G. Gottlob, C. Koch, and R. Pichler. Efficient algorithms for processing XPath queries. In *Proceedings of the 28th International Conference on Very Large Data Bases (VLDB)*, Hong Kong, 2002.
5. M. Harren, M. Raghavachari, O. Shmueli, M. Burke, R. Bordawekar, I. Pechtchanski, and V. Sarkar. XJ: Facilitating XML processing in Java. In *Proceedings of World Wide Web (WWW)*, pages 278–287, May 2005.
6. G. Miklau and D. Suciu. Containment and equivalence for a fragment of XPath. *J. ACM*, 51(1):2–45, 2004.
7. F. Neven and T. Schwentick. XPath containment in the presence of disjunction, DTDs, and variables. In *Proceedings of the 9th International Conference on Database Theory*, pages 315–329. Springer-Verlag, 2002.
8. M. Raghavachari and O. Shmueli. Efficient schema-based revalidation of XML. In *Proceedings of Extending Database Technology (EDBT)*, volume 2992 of *LNCS*, March 2004.
9. G. Sur, J. Hammer, and J. Siméon. UpdateX - an XQuery-based language for processing updates. In *PLAN-X*, January 2004.
10. I. Tatarinov, Z. Ives, A. Halevy, and D. Weld. Updating XML. In *Proc. ACM SIGMOD Int. Conf. on Management of Data*, June 2001.
11. World Wide Web Consortium. *XQuery 1.0: An XML Query Language*, April 2005. W3C Working draft.
12. World Wide Web Consortium. *XQuery Update Facility Requirements*, June 2005.

# Improving the Efficiency of XPath Execution on Relational Systems

Haris Georgiadis and Vasilis Vassalos

Department of Informatics,
Athens University of Economics and Business Athens, Greece
{harisgeo, vassalos}@aueb.gr

**Abstract.** This work describes a method for processing XPath on a relational back-end that significantly limits the number of SQL joins required, takes advantage of the strengths of modern SQL query processors, exploits XML schema information and has low implementation complexity. The method is based on the splitting of XPath expressions into Primary Path Fragments (PPFs) and their subsequent combination using an efficient structural join method, and is applicable to all XPath axes. A detailed description of the method is followed by an experimental study that shows our technique yields significant efficiency improvements over other XPath processing techniques and systems.

## 1 Introduction

In the past few years the adoption of XML for a variety of roles in e-business applications has increased significantly and continues to increase. XML is increasingly used as a data exchange/messaging format between applications or Web services [22], as a data model for middleware-based data integration [23] and as a data model for storing and querying application data [24]. Given the growing importance and presence of XML data, the need to query and maintain them arises in most of the above cases. At the same time, business applications as always rely heavily on agreed-upon schemas and descriptions for data modeling (in the case of XML, XML Schema [25] or DTD). XML storage and query systems fall into three main categories:

- Native XML systems [29,30] that use storage models indexing and querying mechanisms specially designed for XML data. Storage models are based on path sequences, flat files [31], tree-based node clustering [29] or other techniques.
- XML-shredding systems [2,3,4,5,18] that decompose XML documents into relations, store them in RDBMSs and process them using RDBMS machinery.
- Hybrid approaches that store XML as CLOBs/BLOBs into relational tables, either exclusively or in combination with shredding [26].

XML shredding techniques can be schema-oblivious, where the relations into which XML is translated are fixed irrespective of the XML document structure, as in the Edge mapping [1]. There, all element nodes are stored as tuples in a single central relation. Alternatively, shredding can be schema-aware [4,5], where the relational schema constructed is adapted to the XML schema information available.

Because of the wide availability, robustness and manageability of RDBMSs, the shredding and hybrid solutions have received a lot of attention. Several techniques and systems have been proposed [2,3,11,12] for SQL-based XML processing, supporting large subsets of well-known XML query languages, namely XQuery[7] or XPath[6]. These systems and techniques translate expressions of these languages into SQL equivalents and execute them on relational back ends. In earlier attempts, e.g., [4], the SQL translations had a large number of foreign-key joins, usually proportional to the number of steps in paths. This technique was unable or inefficient to handle a series of XPath features, such as the descendant '//' and several other axes, recursion and wildcards ('*'). Several techniques have been proposed to tackle the above problems. For schema-oblivious mappings, efficient methods such as region encoding [2] and dewey encoding [9] have been proposed to encode both structural relationships among elements and ordering information, and to transform structural relationships such as "descendant" into range comparisons. These techniques, by themselves, do not accelerate simple path traversals: again the number of joins is proportional to the number of steps. Regarding schema-aware mapping, for example, schema information can has been used to eliminate redundant joins [11], whereas recursive queries can be handled using the recursion capabilities of SQL99 [12].

This work describes a novel XPath processing approach that yields significant performance benefits while being quite easy to implement and combine with existing techniques. A key novel concept of our approach is the Primitive Path Fragment (PPF), which is a syntactic unit of an XPath expression. PPFs can be efficiently evaluated in a holistic fashion using a root-to-node path index and regular expression matching, to eliminate the need for structural joins. We describe Primitive Path Fragments and their processing in Section 4.3. The second important part of our approach is a method based on the properties of Dewey encoding [9] for efficiently performing the necessary structural joins between PPFs. Our implementation of Dewey encoding, its properties and its use for joining PPFs are described in Section 4.2. The complete XPath to SQL translation algorithm is presented in Section 4.3.

PPF-based XPath processing can be applied both to schema-oblivious and schema aware XML shredding. In schema-aware shredding, data are apportioned into several relations. The existence of schema information and its utilization in the translation, allows for optimizations, such as avoiding redundant root-to-node path filtering, as discussed in Section 4.5. The experimental evaluation in Section 5.1 confirms the benefits of applying the PPF-based processing in conjunction with schema-aware XML shredding. Hence this work focuses on such a translation scheme, describing it briefly in Section 3. Our implementation of PPF-based processing is built on top of an Oracle 10g-based XML management system using schema-aware XML shredding. In our experimental study, which is in Section 5, we are comparing our technique to the latest version of MonetDB/XQuery, our implementation of XPath accelerator on top of Oracle 10g, and the built-in XPath processor of a major commercial RDBMS, on a large number of representative XPath queries on different data sets. We discuss related work in Section 6 and present our conclusions in Section 7.

In summary, we show how PPF-based XPath processing can handle efficiently a large subset of XPath 2.0 that includes all XPath axes, path union, nested expressions, and logical, arithmetic and position predicates. PPF-based XPath processing offers a comprehensive solution to the problem of XPath processing that exploits the strengths of relational query processing and optimization with minimal tuning and gives significant performance gains over existing techniques with much less implementation complexity.

## 2 Background

### 2.1 XML Data Model, XML Schema and XPath

An XML document can be represented as a rooted, ordered, labeled tree, where each node corresponds to an element or a text value. The edges represent (direct) element-subelement or element-value relationships. Tags, IDs, IDREFs and other attributes are modeled by node labels consisting of a set of attribute-value pairs. The ordering of sibling nodes implicitly defines a total order on the nodes in a tree, obtained by a preorder traversal of the tree nodes. Figure 1(b) shows the tree representation of an XML document, where the numbers outside the nodes represent node identifiers.

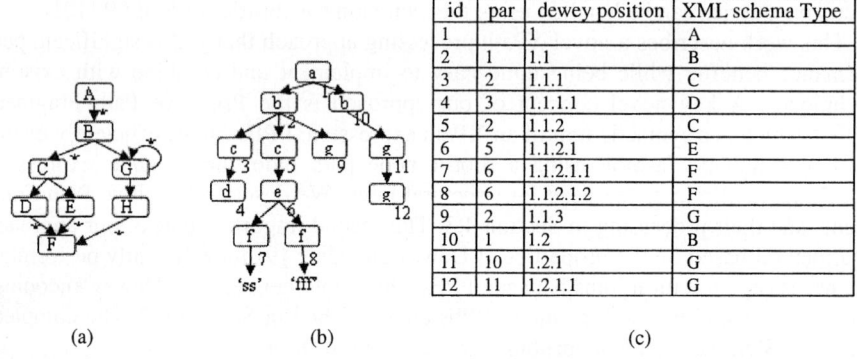

(a) Graph representation of an XML Schema
(b) Sample XML document conforming to Schema
(c) XML element descriptors

**Fig. 1.**

The structure of an XML document can be described by an XML Schema. An XML Schema can be represented as a directed graph [12], where vertices correspond to element definitions and edges represent nesting relationships. A simple XML Schema graph is illustrated in Figure 1(a). An element node in a document described by an XML Schema instantiates a particular type defined in the schema.

XPath [6] is a language for locating XML nodes. The main construct of XPath is the path expression which consists of a sequence of steps, separated with the '/' character, to address nodes within the tree representation of an XML document. Each step has three parts: an *axis*, such as *child*, *parent* and *descendant*, which defines the structural relationship of nodes to be selected with respect to those selected by the preceding step, a *node test* which defines the name or the kind of nodes to be selected and, optionally, one or more *predicates* which set further restrictions to the nodes to be selected. Wildcards ('*') can be used as node tests that select nodes regardless of their name. For example, the XPath expression '/A/*[C//F=2]' returns elements that are children of element 'A', and have at least a child element 'C', which has at least one descendant element named 'F' with text value equal to 2.

## 2.2 XML Element Position Representation

A key issue for efficient XML processing is an appropriate representation of the positions of XML elements. In order to preserve the document order of elements and also to test more directly the structural relationship among nodes, we use dewey encoding [9]. Dewey encoding assigns to each node a vector that represents the path from the document's root to the node. Each component of the path represents the local order of an ancestor node. The dewey encoding for each element of Figure 1(a) is shown in Figure 1(c). Dewey encoding, like other positional encodings such as region encoding [9] and ORDPATH [19], allows the transformation of structural relationships, such as *descendant* or *sibling*, into a number or string comparisons of the encodings. For example, a tree node $n$ encoded as $n_1.n_2....n_k$ is a descendant of tree node $m$ encoded as $m_1.m_2...m_f$ iff $k > f$ and $n1. n_1.n_2....n_f = m_1.m_2...m_f$.

## 3 XML Schema-to-Relational Mapping

In order to represent XML elements in relational structures, we have defined 4 descriptors that characterize all element nodes, as shown in Figure 1(c). Apart from node id and Dewey position, mentioned earlier, we also keep a node's parent id. Moreover, we associate with each element a root-to-node path id. Path ids and their use as an index are described in the next Section. We describe below how these descriptors as well as text and attribute values are stored in relational structures.

Even though PPF-based processing can be used effectively with schema-oblivious XML shredding, as we will see in Section 5, it yields greater benefits used on top of a schema-aware XML to relational translation, and this is what we focus on.

Our system takes as input the XML Schema's graph representation and creates the respective relational structures according to a fixed set of mapping rules, where:

- each complex type is mapped into a separate relation,
- each element definition is also mapped into a separate relation, unless it is of a globally defined, already mapped complex type,
- text and attribute nodes of an element are mapped into columns of the appropriate type in the element's corresponding relation

Each relation has a primary key 'id' column that stores the element id, and one or more foreign key columns referring to all possible parent relations, for storing element nesting relationships. Note that, in case of recursive schemata where a complex type contains elements of the same complex type, the corresponding relation maintains a foreign key relationship to itself. Relations that correspond to document elements have an additional column, named 'doc_id', to distinguish documents from one another. Finally, Dewey position is stored in the 'dewey_pos' column as a binary string. The specific encoding and its properties are discussed in Section 4.2.

Note that our mapping scheme does not use inlining [5], namely, the mapping of certain element definitions into columns instead of separate relations. This technique is mainly used to reduce the total number of relations and, subsequently, the number of structural joins in the SQL translations. As we discuss in section 4, PPF-based processing eliminates many of these joins in a different effective fashion.

### 3.1 Root-to-Node Path Index and Other Relational Indices

We store for each element node its root-to-node path and use it as an index. Since, for a typical set of XML documents conforming to an XML schema, the total number of distinct paths is expected to be much smaller than the total number of nodes, all paths are stored in a separate relation, named 'Paths'. All mapping relations maintain a foreign key reference to this relation, in a column named 'path_id'. The 'Paths' relation is filled gradually during insertions: when an element is to be inserted, its path will be inserted in the 'Paths' relation, as long as it hasn't been already inserted during a previous element insertion. As we discuss further in Section 4.1, *Primitive Path Fragments* of an XPath query can be handled by applying simple regular expression filtering over root-to-node paths, which significantly reduces the number of structural joins in the final SQL statement.

For each relation, the following relational indexes are also created and maintained: an index for the 'id' column, one index for each parent foreign-key column and one concatenated (composite) index on columns dewey_pos and path_id. In our current implementation, all indices are created as standard B-trees.

## 4 XPath-to-SQL Translation

This section describes PPF-based XPath processing. A key novel concept of our approach is the *Primitive Path Fragment* (PPF), which is a syntactic unit of an XPath expression. PPFs can be efficiently evaluated in a holistic fashion using a root-to-node *path index* and *regular expression matching,* to eliminate the need for structural joins. In particular, a PPF can be handled by a natural join of a single relation with the 'Paths' relation, followed by an appropriate restriction in the 'where' clause of the SQL statement. This restriction filters the root-to-node paths against a regular expression derived from the step sequence of the fragment. We describe Primitive Path Fragments and their processing in the next section.

The hierarchical relationship of each consecutive pair of such fragments is handled by theta-joining the two relations with appropriate lexicographic comparison between their dewey_pos columns. We describe the method for combining PPFs in Section 4.2. The complete XPath to SQL translation algorithm is presented in Section 4.3, while additional optimizations are described in Sections 4.4 and 4.5.

### 4.1 Identifying and Processing Primitive Path Fragments

Let's suppose we want to translate the XPath expression '/A/B/C/*/F' into an equivalent SQL statement for documents conforming to the XML schema shown in Figure 1(a). Taking into account the graph representation of the schema and its relational mapping, it is easy to conclude that F is the only relation that could potentially store the 'F' elements defined by the given XPath expression. Each tuple in 'F' is assigned a path-id number referring to a certain root-to-node path in the 'Paths' relation.

Therefore, the tuples corresponding to the required 'F' elements can be retrieved with a single SQL select statement that joins relations 'F' and 'Paths' and adds a restriction to the 'path' column of the 'Paths' relation so as to match the path '/A/B/C/*/F'. SQL's *LIKE* operator, in combination with string manipulation functions, could handle such simple pattern matching. To deal with more complex patterns, as are many XPath expressions, we translate the path into a simple regular expression and then use a regular expression filtering function, within the SQL statement, to perform the matching. Several commercial RDBMSs (e.g., mySQL, Oracle 10g) have incorporated such functions into their function library. We use the *REGEXP_LIKE* function of Oracle 10g which follows the exact Extended Regular Expression (ERE) syntax and semantics defined in the POSIX [17].

Path id filtering helps us handle certain sequences of steps in an XPath expression. The steps of such a sequence must

- all have only forward axes or only backward axes and,
- they must not have predicates, except for the last step.

We call such paths *Forward Simple Paths* and *Backward Simple Paths* respectively. Table 1 illustrates several forward and backward simple paths and their corresponding regular expression equivalents.

**Table 1.** Examples of mapping forward or backward paths into regular expressions

| Forward or Backward Path | Regular expression |
|---|---|
| //B/C | '^.*/B/C$' |
| /A/B//F | '^A/B/(.+/ )?F$' |
| //C/*/F | '^.*/C/[^/]+/F$' |
| /parent::F/ancestror::B/parent::A | '^.*/A/B/(.+/ )?F$' |

More specifically, we divide the main path of an XPath expression which we call '*Backbone Path*', as well as the paths included in predicates, into fragments, named '*Primitive Path Fragments*' (PPFs).

**Definition:** We call '*Primitive Path Fragment*', a sequence of one or more consecutive steps of an XPath expression for which one of the following is true:

a) It is a *forward simple path*
b) It is a *backward simple path*
c) It is a single step whose axis is one of the following: *following, following-sibling, preceding or preceding-sibling*

Recall that a forward or backward simple path can have predicate(s) only in the last step, thus a predicate in an intermediate step of a forward or backward path always separates the path into two PPFs. Our PPF-processing system parses the XPath expression and creates a corresponding syntax tree. It navigates through the tree representation of the XPath expression, by traversing the Backbone Path. During this traversal, the system identifies PPFs and assigns a schema relation to the last step of each PPF (using the graph representation of the schema). We call the last step of a PPF the *Prominent Step* and the respective relation *Prominent Relation* of the PPF.

The detailed algorithm for gradually building the SQL equivalent of the XPath expression is presented in Section 4.3 and examples are shown in Table 3. The case where we need to assign multiple relations to the last step of a PPF (e.g., if the last step has a wildcard) is addressed in Section 4.4.

## 4.2 Joining PPFs

Let's suppose that we want to translate the XPath expression '/A[@x=4]//C'. It is obvious that, in addition to 'C', the 'A' relation must also be involved in the SQL statement, since we need to set a restriction on the 'x' column of this relation (x=4). Dewey encoding is used in order to join the two relations in such a way so as to satisfy the '//' axis. In particular, in order for two elements to have an ancestor-descendant relationship, the Dewey vector of the former must be a prefix of the Dewey vector of the later [9], and similar conditions hold for the structural relationships corresponding to the other XPath axes.

We implement the Dewey position of a node as a binary string consisting of one or more components of 3 bytes each. So, if $d(n)$ denotes the Dewey position of node $n$ and $k$ is its level, we have $d(n) = C_1 || C_2 || ... || C_k$, where '||' is the binary string concatenation operator and $C_i$ a component of the dewey vector.

Each component has its first bit equal to zero, thus ranging from 0 up to 7FFFFF (in hex notation). Using this representation, we can use simple *lexicographical* comparisons between the Dewey positions of two nodes in order to perform a structural join over any XPath axis, as shown by the lemmas below.

Let '≻', '≺' be the operators for lexicographically 'greater' and 'smaller' respectively. In what follows, we use the hexadecimal notation for Dewey positions.

*Lemma 1:* Node $n_2$ is a descendant of node $n_1$ if and only if
$$d(n_2) \succ d(n_1) \land d(n_2) \prec d(n_1) || \text{'F'}$$

*Lemma 2:* Node $n_2$ is a following node of $n_1$ if and only if: $d(n_2) \succ d(n_1) || \text{'F'}$

Proofs of the two lemmas can be found in the extended version of the paper in [32]. In a similar manner, we can use lexicographical comparisons over dewey positions to handle all XPath axes. Table 2 (1-6) lists the XPath axes and the respective conditions in SQL, assuming that relations R2 and R1 correspond to two consecutive steps of a path, the second of which having the axis shown in the left column.

**Table 2.** Axes handled using Dewey encoding

| Axis | SQL Condition | |
|---|---|---|
| descendant/ descendant-or-self | R2.dewey_pos BETWEEN R1.dewey_pos AND R1.dewey_pos||'F' | (1) |
| ancestor/ ancestor-or-self | R1.dewey_pos BETWEEN R2.dewey_pos AND R2.dewey_pos||'F' | (2) |
| following | R2.dewey_pos > R1.dewey_pos || 'f' | (3) |
| following-sibling | R2.dewey_pos > R1.dewey_pos AND R1.par_id = R2.par_id | (4) |
| preceding | R1.dewey_pos > R2.dewey_pos || 'f' | (5) |
| preceding-sibling | R1.dewey_pos > R2.dewey_pos AND R1.par_id = R2.par_id | (6) |

Notice that parent and child axes can be handled either with Dewey order comparison or with foreign key referencing, with a join between the same two relations in both cases, but on different columns. In particular, the join conditions for these two axes (following the notation of Table 2) are: for child, R2.par_id = R1.id, and for parent, R2.id = R1.par_id. Our algorithm uses the second way, because it is expected to be faster: foreign key and primary key columns, which are integers, are much smaller than dewey_pos columns, which are binary strings of variable length, and moreover equijoins perform generally better than theta-joins on an RDBMS. For examples, see Table 3 (2) in the next Section.

### 4.3 PPF-Based XPath Processing Algorithm

Each time a *Primitive Path Fragment* is parsed, the procedure presented in Algorithm 1 is executed to gradually build the SQL equivalent of the XPath expression.

The algorithm adds the name of the prominent relation in the 'from' clause (line 1) and the appropriate restrictions in the 'where' clause of the SQL statement (lines 2-14). The restrictions depend on the type of the PPF and whether it is the first in the backbone path or not. If the last step of the PPF has predicate(s), then one or more sub-selects are created and added in the main SQL statement (lines 15-16).

If it is a forward PPF, the prominent relation is joined with the 'Paths' relation, to which, in turn, a restriction is set filtering the root-to-node path column (lines 2-3) so as to match the regular expression derived from the PPF. If there are one or more consecutive forward PPFs just before the current PPF, then the regular expression includes the entire forward path.

For a backward PPF, the prominent relation of the *previous* PPF is joined with the 'Paths' relation with the restriction that the path column matches the regular expression derived from the path of the current PPF (lines 4-5). For a single-step PPF whose axis is one of the subsequent: *following-sibling, following, preceding-sibling* or *proceeding*, the prominent relation is joined with the 'Paths' relation, with the restriction that the path column ends with the step's *name test* (lines 6-7). Table 4 shows 2 examples with PPFs that have the *following-sibling* and *preceding* axes.

If the PPF is not the first of the backbone path, then its prominent relation is also joined (structural join, using Dewey encoding) with the prominent relation of the previous PPF (lines 8-14). Particularly, if the current PPF is a multiple-step PPF or a single-step PPF whose axis is not *child* or *parent*, like those shown in Table 3 (1) and (3) (grey parts of SQL statements) and Table 5, then this join occurs over the dewey_pos columns of the two relations (lines 13-14), according to Table 1. Otherwise, if the PPF has only one step with the *child* or *parent* axes, the join is a natural join on the foreign-key reference (lines 9-12), as illustrated in Table 3 (2).

Logical predicates are handled as follows: We assume that a predicate consists of one or more predicate clauses, combined with logical operators (or, and, not()). Each predicate clause can be a path, a comparison between a path and an atomic value, or a comparison between paths (predicate join-clause). The logical structure of an XPath predicate is translated into a corresponding logical structure in the 'where' clause of the SQL statement (with the same combination of logical operators and parentheses), where each predicate clause is translated into an 'exists()' clause, incorporating a sub-select statement. In what follows, a step of the XPath expression on which a predicate is attached is called a *predicated step*.

## Algorithm 1 SQL Gradual Building per PPF parsing

```
parsePPF(PPF curPPF) {
1    SQLStmt.getFromClause().AddRelation(
        curPPF.getPromintentRelation());
2    if (curPPF.isForward()) {
3      SQLStmt.JoinWithPaths(curPPF.getProminentRelation(),
        curPPF.getMaxFarwardPath().createRegularExpr());
     }
4    else if (currentPPF.isBackward() {
5      SQLStmt.JoinWithPaths(
        curPPF.getPrevPPF().getProminentRelation(),
        curPPF.getBackwardPath().createRegularExpr());
     }
6    else{
7      SQLStmt.JoinWithPaths(curPPF.getProminentRelation(),
        "^./" + curPPF.getLastStepName() + "$")
     }
8    if (PPF.notFirst()){
9      if (PPF.isSingleStep() &&
        PPF.getLastStep().getAxis() == "parent")
10       SQLStmt.FKStructuralJoin(
          curPPF.getProminentRelation(),
          curPPF.getPrevPPF().getProminentRelation());
11     else if (PPF.isSingleStep() &&
        PPF.getLastStep().getAxis() == "child")
12       SQLStmt.FKStructuralJoin(
          curPPF.getPrevPPF().getProminentRelation(),
          curPPF.getProminentRelation());
13     else
14       SQLStmt.DeweyStructuralJoin(
          curPPF.getPrevPPF().getProminentRelation(),
          curPPF.getProminentRelation(),
          curPPF.getStructuralRelationship());
     }
15   if (curPPF.getPredicates()!=NULL)
16     SQLStmt.getWhereClause().AddPredicates(
        curPPF.getPredicates());
}
```

If the predicate clause is a (relative) path or a comparison between a path and an atomic value, the respective sub-select statement is created similarly to the main SQL statement for a given backbone path (as in lines 1-14). The difference is that the prominent relation of the first PPF of the path *inside* the predicate clause, (which is included in the 'from' clause of the sub-select statement) is joined appropriately in the outer SQL select statement to the relation corresponding to the predicated step. An example is shown in Table 5 (1).

If a predicate clause consists only of a Backward Simple Path, instead of joining the prominent relation of this path to the relation corresponding to the predicated step, we can once again exploit path id filtering. Particularly, we add an additional restriction to the root-to-node path of the predicated step so as to match the regular expression equivalent of the backward path within the predicate clause. Table 5 (2) shows an example with a predicate which consists of two backward path predicate clauses.

**Table 3.** Forward (1,2) and Backward (3) PPFs translation examples

| XPath | SQL Translation | |
|---|---|---|
| /A[@x=3]/B/C//F | select distinct F.id, F.dewey_pos, F.text<br>from A, F, Paths F_Paths<br>where F.path_id = F_paths.id<br>and REGEXP_LIKE(F_Paths.path, '/A/B/C/.*/F')<br>and C.dewey_pos between A.dewey_pos and A.dewey_pos∥'f'<br>and A.x=3 order by F.dewey_pos | (1) |
| /A[@x=3]/B ... | select ... from A, B, Paths B_Paths<br>where B.path_id = B_Paths.id and B_paths.path = '/A/B'<br>and B.A_id = A.id and A.x=3 ... | (2) |
| //F/parent::D/<br>ancestor::B... | select ... from F, Paths F_Paths, B, ...<br>where F.dewey_pos between B.dewey_pos and B.dewey_pos ∥'f'<br>and F.path_id = F_Paths.id and REGEXP_LIKE(F_Paths.path,<br>'.*/B/.*/D/F') | (3) |

**Table 4.** Translation examples of steps with following-sibling (1) and preceding axes (2)

| XPath | SQL Translation | |
|---|---|---|
| //D[@x=4]/<br>following-sibling::E ... | select ... from ...D, E, ...<br>where E.dewey_pos > D.dewey_pos<br>and D.C_id = E.C_id and D.x=4 ... | (1) |
| //D[@x=4]/<br>preceding::H... | select ... from ...D, H, ...<br>where D.dewey_pos > H.dewey_pos ∥ 'f' and D.x=4 ... | (2) |

**Table 5.** Translation examples of XPath expressions containing predicates

| Axis | SQL Condition | |
|---|---|---|
| /A/B[C/*/F=2].. | select ... from B, Paths B_paths, ...<br>where B.path_id = B_paths.id and B_paths.path = '/A/B'<br>and exists (<br>select null from F, Paths F_paths<br>where F.path_id = F_paths.id and REGEXP_LIKE(F_Paths.path,<br>'/A/B/C/.*(/)?F')<br>and F.dewey_pos between B.dewey_pos and B.dewey_pos ∥ 'f' and<br>F.text = 2) ... | (1) |
| //F[parent::D or<br>ancestor::G] ... | select ... from F, Paths F_paths, ...where F.path_id = F_paths.id and<br>REGEXP_LIKE(F_Paths.path, '^.*/G/.*(/)?F')<br>or REGEXP_LIKE(F_Paths.path, '^.*/D/F$'') ... | (2) |

Finally, if the predicate clause is a comparison between two relative paths, the respective sub-select includes all the prominent relations of the PPFs of the first path, joined properly, all the prominent relations of the PPFs of the second path, also joined properly, and an additional theta-join between the relations corresponding to the last PPF of each path.[1]

---

[1] The condition of the theta-join is a comparison between the appropriate columns. The SQL comparison operator is derived from the XPath comparison operator of the predicate clause.

After all PPFs have been parsed, the SQL statement is completed by adding the 'distinct' SQL keyword before the projection, so as to avoid duplicates in results, and also the 'order by' clause, at the end of the statement, applied on the dewey_pos column of the prominent relation of the last PPF, so that the tuples of the results are retrieved in document order.

### 4.4 Eliminating SQL Splitting

As we saw in the previous sections, the prominent step of each PPF causes a relation to be added in the final SQL statement. If the prominent step of a PPF corresponds to more than one relation, the SQL statement needs to be split into multiple statements combined by UNION. For example, the XPath expression 'A/B/*[//F]' contains two PPFs: the 'A/B/*' and '//F', the first of which, evaluated over the XML Schema of Figure 1(a), corresponds to two relations. The SQL translation of the expression has two SQL statements, with different FROM clauses. We call this *SQL splitting*.

Prominent steps of PPFs that appear in predicates do not cause SQL splitting. If such a PPF corresponds to multiple relations, then, instead of splitting the entire SQL statement, only the sub-select corresponding to the predicate clause is split into multiple sub-selects, one for each relation, separated with the 'OR' operator. An example is illustrated in Table 6.

**Table 6.** SQL translation of XPath query which contains a predicate with an ambiguous path

| Axis | SQL Condition |
|---|---|
| /A/B[C/*]… | select … from B, Paths B_paths, … |
| | where B.path_id = B_paths.id and B_paths.path = '/A/B' |
| | and exists ( select null from D, Paths D_paths where D.path_id = D_paths.id |
| | and REGEXP_LIKE(D_Paths.path, '/A/B/C/.*(/)?') |
| | and D.dewey_pos between D.dewey_pos and D.dewey_pos‖ 'f') |
| | or exists ( select null from E, Paths E_paths where E.path_id = E_paths.id |
| | and REGEXP_LIKE(E_Paths.path, '/A/B/C/.*(/)?') |
| | and E.dewey_pos between E.dewey_pos and E.dewey_pos ‖ 'f') … |

SQL splitting is a significant issue for existing schema-aware XPath to SQL translateon techniques [11]. Consider the XPath expression '/A/B[@x=4]/C/*/F'. If we use existing methods for schema-aware SQL translation, we must first find all possible relation sequences corresponding to the path '/A/B/C/*/F', which are A-B-C-D-F and A-B-C-E-F, and then create a separate SQL statement for each such sequence, where the relations would be joined (natural joins) per consecutive pair. A more advanced algorithm, such as the one presented in [11], detects that elements B can be nested only to elements A, which means that the join between relations A and B is redundant and could be omitted. In contrast, using PPF-based processing, only relations B and F need to be joined, whereas the wildcard is incorporated into an appropriate regular expression filtering on the root-to-node path values, without the need of using two SQL statements.

The combination of root-to-node path filtering, Dewey encoding and schema-aware mapping can reduce the incidence of SQL splitting, and the concomitant problems of multiple query optimization faced in that case by an RDBMS.

## 4.5 Omitting Unnecessary Root-to-Node Path Filtering

Combining schema knowledge with root-to-node path ids gives an optimization opportunity not present in schema-oblivious systems: under certain circumstances path id filtering is redundant and can be omitted. For example, consider the XPath query '/A/B/C/D'. According to the XML Schema (Figure 1), the only possible root-to-node path of elements 'D' coincides with the path of the XPath query. Therefore, there is no need to join relations 'D' and 'Paths'.

We avoid the unnecessary path index lookup (which results in an SQL join) in the following way: After the corresponding graph for an XML Schema has been created, we mark all nodes of the graph that have a unique path towards the root node of the graph with a 'U-P' (Unique Path) tag, all nodes of the graph that have at least one cycle in a path towards the root with a 'I-P' (Infinite Paths) tag and, finally, the remaining graph nodes with a 'F-P' (Finite Paths) tag. 'F-P' nodes are also assigned a list of all possible root-to-node paths. An example is shown in Figure 2.

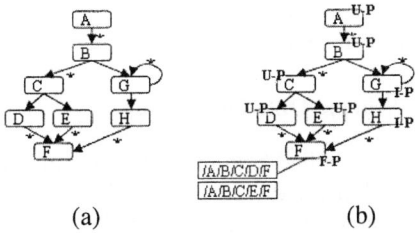

**Fig. 2.** Marking the XML Schema graph

Relations corresponding to 'U-P' graph nodes are never joined to the Path relation. When an 'F-P' relation is involved in an SQL statement, after translating the PPF path into a regular expression, we test the root-to-node paths of the respective node graph against the regular expression. The relation is joined to the Paths relation and the regular expression restriction is added only if there is at least one such path that doesn't match. Finally, a 'I-P' relation is always joined to the Paths relation with the 'path' column filtered by the regular expression.

## 5 Experimental Evaluation

In this section we present the results of the experimental testing of the performance of PPF-based processing. We use Oracle 10g (release 10.1 for Windows) as our RDBMS backend. First, we compare PPF-based processing on a schema-aware XML-to-relational system against a schema-oblivious version of same. Moreover, we compare the performance of PPF-based processing with the MonetDB/XQuery [18], which is an XQuery implementation on the MonetDB server backend, the XPath Accelerator mapping scheme [2], which we implemented over Oracle 10g, and a major commercial RDMS with a built-in XML shredding mechanism.

We experiment with both synthetic and real data. For synthetic data we use the XMark [20] benchmark variation for XPath, called XPathMark [21]. Using the

**Table 7.** The XPath queries used for DBLP XML document

| | |
|---|---|
| QD1 | //inproceedings/title[preceding-sibling::author = 'Harold G. Longbotham'] |
| QD2 | /dblp/inproceedings[year>=1994]//sup |
| QD3 | /dblp/inproceedings/title/sup |
| QD4 | //i[parent::*/parent::sub/ancestor::article] |
| QD5 | /dblp/inproceedings[author=/dblp/book/author]/title |

XMark XML generator, we created two XML documents of 12 and 113 MBs. From the query set of the benchmark we chose a subset of 16 queries (Q1- Q7, Q9-Q13, Q21-Q24), that are compatible with the XPath subset supported by our system. The list of queries can be found in the full version of the paper [32] as well as in [21]. We also added query **Q-A**: /site/open_auctions/open_auction[bidder/date = interval/start] which contains a join predicate clause. We also use the 130MB DBLP XML database.[2] The query set for this database is shown in Table 7.

Experiments were performed on a Pentium 4 PC at 3GHz with 1 GB RAM, running Windows XP. All the queries were executed against a cold cache. For each query we recorded the average time for 5 repetitions.

## 5.1 Schema-Aware vs. Schema Oblivious Storage

PPF-based processing can be applied both in a schema-aware and a schema-oblivious setting. Moreover, some of the individual techniques we use, notably exploiting Dewey encoding for structural join, have been employed in the context of schema-oblivious systems. We implemented a variation of PPF-based processing tailored to an Edge-like mapping and compared its performance with the PPF-based processing algorithm described in the previous Section. The results confirm our intuition, that apportioning XML content into several relations leads to better query execution performance, and support our decision to focus on implementing and improving PPF-based processing on a schema-aware system (our schema-based optimizations are described in Section 4.5).

The results of the experiments are shown in figure 3. The most remarkable differences are observed in queries involving structural joins, such as Q6, Q7, Q-A, DQ2 and DQ5. This is due to the fact that, in the schema-oblivious version, these joins are self-joins that join a large relation to itself, in contrast with schema-aware structural joins that join much smaller relations. Even when a concatenated (composite) index is used in the dewey_pos and path_id columns, which is the case, this is larger in the schema-oblivious mapping, compared to all such indices for each mapping relation in the schema-aware mapping, thus the number of I/O is much bigger. Q12 and Q13 also perform remarkably worse in the schema-oblivious version of PPF-based processing. Another factor is that an extra join must take place, since in Edge-like mapping schemes attributes cannot be inlined as columns in the central element relation. Therefore, they are mapped either as separate tuples in the central relation or as tuples in a separate relation exclusively dedicated for attribute storage[3].

---

[2] Available from http://www.cs.washington.edu/research/xmldatasets/
[3] We used the second option.

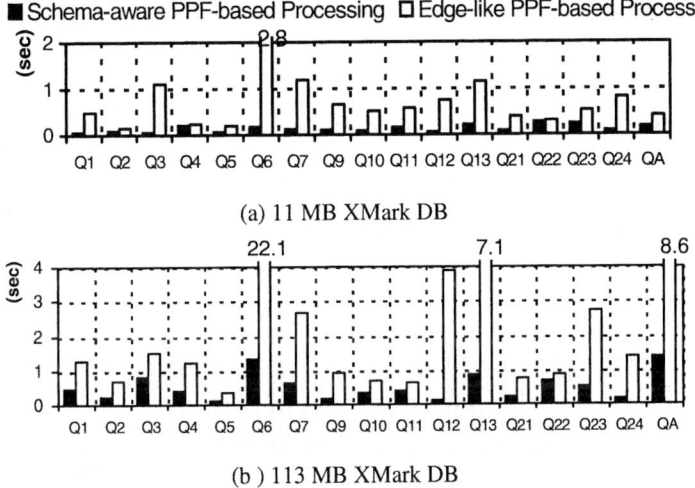

**Fig. 3.** Schema-aware vs schema-oblivious PPF-based Processing performance

## 5.2 Performance Evaluation of PPF-Based Processing

The comparison among PPF-based processing, MonetDB/XQuery and XPath Accelerator scheme is indicative and does not allow us to draw absolute conclusions. We should take into account that the two systems are implemented over different DBMS back-ends, the comparison of which is beyond of the scope of this paper. Moreover, MonetDB/XQuery employs a number of optimizations, most notably the use of staircase joins for structural join. Combining PPF-based processing with join techniques specifically designed for XML data, such as staircase join, is the topic of future work. The comparison between PPF-based processing and our implementation of XPath Accelerator is more direct and allows us to draw more concrete conclusions about the benefits of PPF-based processing. Notice that the translation of the test queries into SQL was made manually following strictly the '*Staked Out Query Window Sizes*' algorithm presented in [2]. As for the commercial RDBMS, the built-in shredding/XPath processing mechanism supports only three of the XPathMark queries, and hence it is not shown in the Figures below (the numbers are available in [32]).

The two major reasons why PPF-based processing outperforms the other systems in almost all queries are the following:

- the joins performed in PPF-based processing occur between much smaller relations, and
- the number of joins in an average SQL translation is much smaller due to the handling of PPFs using regular expression filtering.

These two factors do not affect all queries. For example, queries Q6, Q7 and QD2 involve structural joins that cannot be removed with root-to-node path filtering. Q6 on the large XMark document and DQ2 are faster in MonetDB possibly because of other optimizations applied by MonetDB, the staircase join being one of these. We will

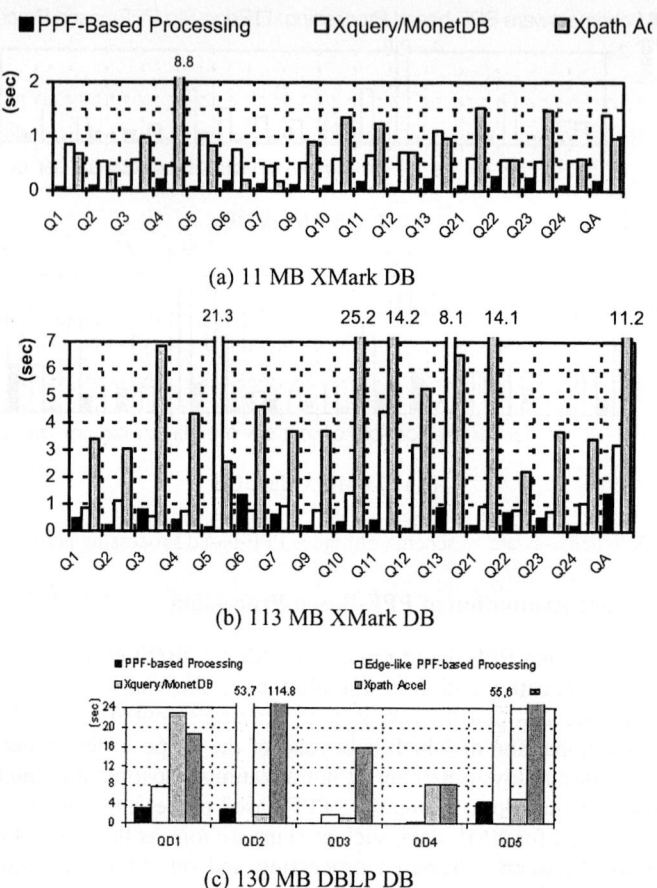

**Fig. 4.** Comparison of PPF-based processing to other systems/techniques

explore combining such optimizations with our techniques as part of future work. Notice especially the performance gains of PPF-based processing on Q5 and QD4. Our technique achieves this level of performance because these queries involve predicate clauses consisting only of backward simple paths, a case which our algorithm handles completely by exploiting path id filtering (see Table 5-2) instead of using structural joins.

## 6 Related Work

Numerous systems and techniques have been developed in the last few years [4,5] that map XML structures to relations using schema information. Shrex [4] is a system for shredding, loading and querying XML documents using relational systems. The mapping mechanism is flexible, allowing the user to define mapping practices. The XPath-To-XML translation mechanism is rather conventional, since it handles paths with sequential foreign key joins, in contrast to our proposal which involves root-to-node path filtering. Shrex also suffers from the problem of SQL splitting, which we tackle, as described in section 3.4. In [11] an algorithm is presented which, under certain circumstances, alleviates the SQL splitting problem removing at the same time joins which are implied by the schema as redundant. Our proposal alleviates the SQL splitting problem and reduces the number of joins by using PPF-based processing, and uses schema information in order to reduce redundant root-to-node path filtering, as described in Section 3.5. The evaluation of recursive paths is handled in [12], where an algorithm is presented exploiting recursion capabilities of SQL99. In our approach, recursive queries are not considered as a separate problem: a recursive path will be translated into an appropriate regular expression which will be used to detect all matching root-to-node paths.

For schema-oblivious mappings, one of the most comprehensive proposals is XPath Accelerator [2], based on region encoding. XQuery/MonetDB [18] is an XQuery implementation based on the XPath Accelerator on top of the MonetDB DBMS. It supports a large portion of the XQuery recommendation achieving, at the same time, remarkably good performances due to several optimizations and advanced query processing techniques, such as the staircase joins. A detailed comparison of PPF-based encoding to XPath Accelarator and MonetDB/XQuery can be found in Section 5.2. Other Edge-oriented proposals exploit also region encoding, such as [8] and XRel[3]. In [3], region encoding is combined with root-to-node path storage in order to reduce the number of structural joins. Instead of region encoding, [16] uses an update-friendly variation of dewey encoding, called ORDPATH [19], in combination to root-to-node path storage. However both [3] and [16] support only forward axes and moreover their root-to-node path testing cannot discriminate between wildcards and '//'. In particular, XRel does not handle wildcards, whereas [16] handles '//' with structural join.

## 7 Conclusions and Future Work

In this paper, we describe a framework based on identifying, processing and combining *Primitive Path Fragments* for processing XPath expressions on a relational back-end. Our technique significantly limits the number of SQL joins required, takes advantage of the strengths of modern SQL query processors and exploits XML schema information to achieve big performance gains with low implementation complexity. Based on our work and the experimental results so far, we can conclude that PPF-based processing is an efficient and easy to implement technique for handling a large XPath subset, including all axes, on top of a relational back end. Root-to-node path indexing is very beneficial for PPF processing when combined with regular expression matching, and is used to holistically process a PPF without any structural joins. We believe that PPF-based processing can be easily adapted to native XML processing systems, and can be combined with native XML join techniques such as twig join [28], yielding performance benefits simply by reducing the number of joins required for a specific XPath expression. We are currently exploring this issue.

Schema-aware mapping can benefit query performance as long as it is combined with proper XML structural encoding techniques, such as presented in this paper.

Furthermore, by exploiting XML Schema information, in some cases even root-to-node path filtering is redundant and, thus can be omitted.

Our PPF-based XPath to SQL translation algorithm leads to SQL queries that involve only the necessary relations, with the minimum number of structural joins and the maximum exploitation of root-to-node path ids. Our technique also deals with the problem of SQL splitting, which is common for schema aware mapping systems.

We are currently investigating techniques for increasing the efficiency of XPath processing by exploiting special features of commercial RDBMSs. An interesting question for our technique, explored also in [27] (though with a focus on XML publishing), is how to teach the RDBMS optimizer to produce more efficient query plans.

## References

1. D.Florescu, D.Kossmann: Storing and Querying XML Data using an RDMBS. Data Engineering Bulletin, 22(3), 1999.
2. T.Grust, M. V.Keulen, J.Teubner: Accelerating XPath Evaluation in Any RDBMS. ACM Transactions on Database Systems, Vol. 29, No. 1, 2004.
3. M.Yoshikawa, T.Amagasa, T.Shimura, S.Uemura: XRel: A Path-Based Approach to Storage and Retrieval of XML Documents Using Relational Databases. ACM Transactions on Internet Technology, Vol. 1, No. 1, 2001.
4. S.Amer Yahia, F.Du, J.Freire: A Comprehensive Solution to the XML-to-Relational Mapping Problem. WIDM'04, 12–13, 2004.
5. J.Shanmugasundaram, K.Tufte, et al.: Relational Databases for Querying XML Documents:Limitations and Opportunities. Proc. of the 25th VLDB Conf., 1999
6. J.Clark, S.DeRose: XML Path Language (XPath) Version 1.0. W3C Recommendation 16 November 1999. http://www.w3.org/TR/xpath.
7. S.Boag, D.Chamberlin, et al. : Query 1.0: An XML Query Language. W3C Working Draft 04 April 2005. http://www.w3.org/TR/xquery/.
8. D.DeHaan, D.Toman, M.P.Consens, M. T. Ozsu: A Comprehensive XQuery to SQL Translation using Dynamic Interval Encoding, SIGMOD 2003
9. I. Tatarinov, S. Viglas, K. Beyer, J. Shanmugasundaram, E.Shekita, and C. Zhang: Storing and querying ordered XML using a relational database system. SIGMOD 2002
10. A.Virmani, S.Agarwal, R.Thathoo, S.Suman, S. Sanyal: A Fast XPATH Evaluation Technique with the Facility of Updates. CIKM '03 ACM, 2003
11. R.Krishnamurthy, R.Kaushik, J.F.Naughton: Efficient XML-to-SQL Query Translation: Where to Add the Intelligence? Proc. of the 30th VLDB Conf., 2004.
12. R.Krishnamurthy, V.T.Chakaravarthy, R. Kaushik, J.F.Naughton: Recursive XML Schemas, Recursive XML Queries, and Relational Storage: XML-to-SQL Query Translation. Proc. of the 20th ICDE, 2004.
13. A.Berglund, S.Boag, et al.: XML Path Language (XPath) 2.0. W3C Working Draft 2005. http://www.w3.org/TR/xpath20/.
14. G.M.Sur, J.Hammer, J.Siméon, UpdateX - An XQuery-Based Language for Processing Updates in XML. PLAN-X 2004 In. Proc., BRICS Notes Series NS-03-4, 2004
15. K.Deschler, E.Rundensteiner: MASS: A Multi-Axis Storage Structure for Large XML Documents. CIKM '03, 2003.
16. S.Pal, I.Cseri, O.Seeliger, G.Schaller, L.Giakoumakis, V.Zolotov: Indexing XML Data Stored in a Relational Database. Proc. of the 30th VLDB Conference, 2004.
17. IEEE Std 1003.1, Open Group Technical Standard

18. P.Boncz, T.Grust, M.Keulen et al.: PathFinder/MonetDB: XQuery-The Relational Way. Proc. of the 31st VLDB Conference, 2005
19. P. O'Neil, E. O'Neill, S.Pal, I.Cseri, G.Schalle, N.Westbury: ORDPATHs: Insert-Friendly XML Node Labels. SIGMOD 2004
20. A. Schmidt, F. Waas, M. Kersten, et al..: XMark: A Benchmark for XML Data Management. In Proc. of the 28th VLDB Conference, 2002
21. M. Franceschet.: an XPath benchmark for the XMark generated data. XSym '05: 129-143, 2005
22. D. Florescu et al. The BEA streaming XQuery processor. VLDB Journal 13(3), 2004.
23. Y. Papakonstantinou, V. Vassalos. Architecture and Implementation of an XQuery-based Information Integration Platform. IEEE Data Eng. Bull. 25(1): 18-26 , 2002
24. H. Schöning, J. Wäsch. Tamino - An Internet Database System. In Proc. EDBT 2000
25. XML Schema. http://www.w3.org/XML/Schema
26. A.Balmin, Y.Papakonstantinou: Storing and querying XML data using denormalized relational databases. Springer-Verlag 2004.
27. S. Amer-Yahia, Y. Kotidis, D. Srivastava: Teaching Relational Optimizers About XML Processing. XSym 2004
28. N. Bruno, N. Koudas, D. Srivastava: Holistic twig joins: optimal XML pattern matching. SIGMOD Conference 2002
29. T. Fiebig, S. Helmer, et al.: Anatomy of a native XML base management system. VLDB J. 11(4): 292-314, 2002
30. S. Paparizos, S. Al-Khalifa, et al.: TIMBER: A Native System for Querying XML. SIGMOD Conference 2003
31. S. Abiteboul, S. Cluet, and T. Milo: Querying and Updating the File. In Proc. VLDB Conf. 1993
32. H. Georgiadis, V. Vassalos: Improving the Efficiency of XPath Execution on Relational Systems, Extended version. Available from wim.aueb.gr/papers/PPFProcessingfull.pdf

# Bridging Physical and Virtual Worlds: Complex Event Processing for RFID Data Streams

Fusheng Wang[1], Shaorong Liu[2,*], Peiya Liu[1], and Yijian Bai[2]

[1] Integrated Data Systems Department,
Siemens Corporate Research,
Princeton, NJ 08540, USA
{fusheng.wang, peiya.liu}@siemens.com
[2] Computer Science Department,
University of California, Los Angeles,
Los Angeles, CA 90095, USA
{sliu, bai}@cs.ucla.edu

**Abstract.** Advances of sensor and RFID technology provide significant new power for humans to sense, understand and manage the world. RFID provides fast data collection with precise identification of objects with unique IDs without line of sight, thus it can be used for identifying, locating, tracking and monitoring physical objects. Despite these benefits, RFID poses many challenges for data processing and management: i) RFID observations contain duplicates, which have to be filtered; ii) RFID observations have implicit meanings, which have to be transformed and aggregated into semantic data represented in their data models; and iii) RFID data are temporal, streaming, and in high volume, and have to be processed on the fly. Thus, a general RFID data processing framework is needed to automate the transformation of physical RFID observations into the virtual counterparts in the virtual world linked to business applications. In this paper, we take an event-oriented approach to process RFID data, by devising RFID application logic into complex events. We then formalize the specification and semantics of RFID events and rules. We demonstrate that traditional ECA event engine cannot be used to support highly temporally constrained RFID events, and develop an RFID event detection engine that can effectively process complex RFID events. The declarative event-based approach greatly simplifies the work of RFID data processing, and significantly reduces the cost of RFID data integration.

## 1 Introduction and Motivation

**Background**

An RFID (radio frequency identification) system consists of a host computer, RFID reader, antenna (which is often integrated into readers), transponders or RF tags. An RFID tag is always uniquely identified by a tag ID stored in its memory, and can be attached to almost anything. The EPC (electronic product code) standard [1] defines such unique IDs around the world. Readers can be mounted at entrance/exit, point of

---

* Work done while visiting Siemens Corporate Research.

sale, warehouse, and so on. When a tag is in the vicinity of a reader, the reader sends energy through RF signal to the tag for power, and the tag sends back modulated signal with ID and data. The reader then decodes and sends the data to the host computer.

With RFID technology, it is possible to create a physically linked world in which every object is numbered, identified, cataloged, and tracked. RFID is automatic and fast, and does not require line of sight or contact between readers and tagged objects. With the significant advantages of RFID technology, RFID is being gradually adopted and deployed in a wide area of applications, such as access control, library checkin and checkout, document tracking, smart box, highway tolls, logistics and supply chain, security and healthcare.

To achieve these, the first task for RFID applications is to map objects and their behaviors in the physical world into the virtual counterparts and their virtual behaviors in the applications by semantically interpreting and transforming RFID data.

## RFID Data Transformation and Aggregation

There are generally two types of RFID applications: i) history-oriented object tracking and ii) real-time oriented monitoring. Both need to transform RFID observations into logic data.

*History-oriented object tracking.* In this type of RFID applications, RFID data streams are collected from multiple RFID readers at distributed locations, and transformed into semantic data stored in RFID data store. The semantics of the data include:

- *Location*, which can be either a geographic location or a symbolic location such as a warehouse, a shipping route, a surgery room, or a smart box. A change of location of an EPC-tagged object is often signaled by certain RFID readers. The location histories of RFID objects are then transformed automatically from these RFID readings, and stored in a location history relation in an RFID data store [2];
- *Aggregation*, i.e., formation of relationship among objects. A common case is the containment relationship, e.g., containment relationship as shown next in Example 1. How to associate relationship among RFID objects in an Auto-ID environment has been identified as a difficult issue for RFID applications [3]. To our best knowledge, no work has been published on solving this problem.
  *Example 1: Data Aggregation. In Fig. 1a, on a packing conveyer, a sequence of tagged items move through Reader A and are observed by the reader as a sequence of observations, and then a tagged case is read by Reader B as another observation. After that, all items of this sequence are packed into the case.*
- *Temporal.* RFID observations and their collected data are highly temporal, as studied in [2]. The RFID data store essentially preserves the history of the movement and behaviors of objects.

*Real-time Monitoring.* RFID is also widely used for real-time applications, where patterns of RFID observations implying special application logic can trigger real-time response. An example is discussed as follows.

*Example 2. A company uses RFID tags to identify asset items and employees in the building, and only authorized users (superusers) can move the asset items out of the*

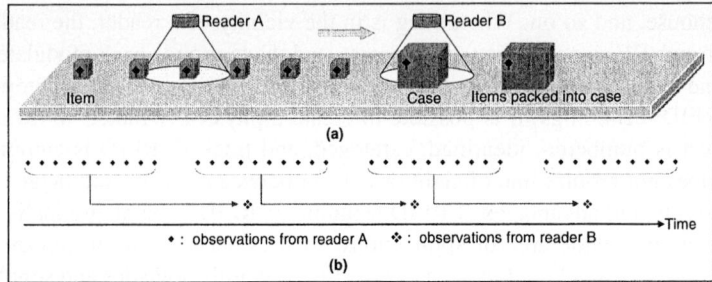

**Fig. 1.** Sample aggregation in RFID. a) Packing of items into its container case; b) Complex events used for aggregation.

*building. When an unauthorized employee or a criminal takes a laptop (with an embedded RFID tag) out of the building, the system will send an alert to the security personnel for response.*

**Event-Oriented Processing of RFID Data Streams**

Indeed, automatic RFID data transformation can be achieved by first devising application logic as complex events, and then detecting such complex events (Fig. 2). After the detection of these complex events, the semantics are interpreted and can be easily integrated into business applications. RFID reader observations are the only primitive events, which then form complex events. Next we show how to devise complex events for data transformation.

- *Data Aggregation Event.* For Example 1, indeed, the items in the conveyer can be arranged as a sequence of events $TSEQ_A$ with certain temporal constraint (Fig. 1). Then the packing step becomes a sequence event from Reader A, followed by a primitive event $O_B$, an observation of case B from Reader B. Then, the containment relationship is detected and transformed into a containment relation inside the RFID data store.
- *Real-time Monitoring Event.* Example 2 can be simplified by a complex event: the system detects an event A – observation of an object of type "laptop", and within certain interval $\tau$, e.g., 5 seconds, it does not detect any occurrence of event B – observation of a superuser, i.e., a negated event, then the event triggers an alert action.

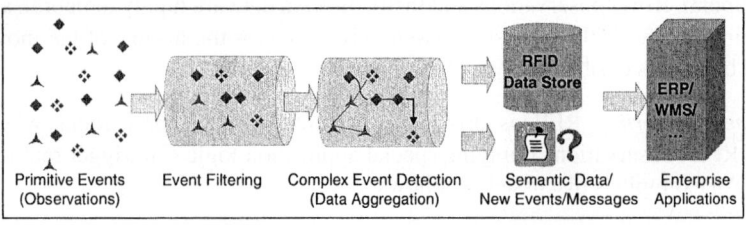

**Fig. 2.** RFID Events Processing

RFID events, however, have their own characteristics and cannot be supported by traditional event systems. The two examples above show that RFID events are temporal constrained: both the temporal distance between two events and the interval of a single event are critical for event detection. Such temporal constraints, however, are not well supported by traditional ECA rules detection systems. In addition, non-spontaneous events, including negated events and temporal constrained events, are important for many RFID applications but difficult to support in past event detection engines. Moreover, the actions from RFID events are quite different: they neither trigger new primitive events for the system, nor lead to a cascade of rule firings as in active databases. Thus, there is an opportunity to build a scalable rule-based system to process complex RFID events.

**Our Contribution**

In this paper, we formulate a declarative rule based approach to provide powerful support of automatic RFID data transformation between the physical world and the virtual world. We develop a graph-based RFID complex event detection engine – RCEDA, where temporal constraint is taken as a first class object in event detection. We introduce pseudo events in event detection to process non-spontaneous events, which are difficult to support in traditional event detection systems. We show that our approach can support RFID applications effectively, and the performance of our event detection engine is quite scalable as well.

The paper is organized as follows. We first give a formal definition of RFID events in Section 2, and then discuss the declarative RFID rules language in Section 3. Event detection engine is discussed in Section 4, and performance is studied in Section 5. Related work is discussed in Section 6, followed by conclusions.

## 2  RFID Events

In this section, we will formalize the semantics and specification for RFID events. In particular, we will discuss temporal RFID events, which are highly temporally constrained and cannot be well supported by traditional ECA (Event-Condition-Action) rule systems.

An *event* is defined to be an occurrence of interest in time, which could be either a *primitive* event or a *complex* event. Primitive events occur at a point in time, while complex events are patterns of primitive events and happen over a period of time.

In the following discussion, we use E to represent an event type, and e to represent an event instance.

We first define several functions used in our event expressions (Fig. 3). t_begin(e) returns the starting time of an event instance e, and t_end(e) returns the ending time. interval(e) returns the interval of an event instance: t_end(e) - t_begin(e); dist($e_1$, $e_2$) returns the distance between two event instances $e_1$ and $e_2$, which is equal to t_end($e_2$) - t_end($e_1$); interval($e_1$, $e_2$) returns the interval between two event instances $e_1$ and $e_2$, which is equal to max{t_end($e_2$), t_end($e_1$)} - min{t_begin($e_2$), t_begin($e_1$)}.

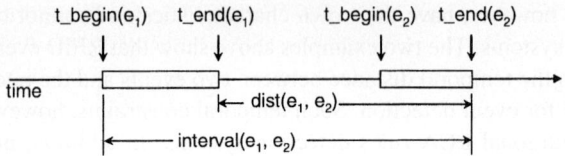

**Fig. 3.** An illustration of functions used in event expressions

## 2.1 Primitive Event

Primitive events in RFID applications are events generated during the interaction between readers and tagged objects. That is, a primitive event is a reader observation, in the format of observation(r, o, t), where r represents the reader EPC, o represents the object EPC and t represents the timestamp when the observation is made. For example, observation('$r_1$', o, t) represents events generated from a reader with EPC '$r_1$'. Primitive events are instantaneous. That is, given any primitive event instance e, t_begin(e) = t_end(e). Primitive events are also atomic: a primitive event either happens completely or does not happen at all.

*Definition of Primitive Event Types.* While primitive events are all from observations, they can be of different types, according to the reader EPC, or tag EPC. We first present two user-defined functions on primitive event attributes used to define primitive event types.

- group(r) – the group which the reader r belongs to. Readers are often deployed into groups in which readers perform the same functionality.
- type(o) – the type of the object with EPC o. The type can be extracted from its EPC value with a user-defined extraction function, or specified by a user with a mapping function. For example, type('8E5YUK691I0J60KDN')='laptop' while type('UH7JEFU63MAW6I610') = 'pallet'.

With above functions, we can define primitive event types. For example, the primitive event type E is defined as:
E = observation(r, o, t), group(r)='$g_1$', type(o) ='case'
That is, observations of 'case' by readers in group '$g_1$' are of type E.

If group() and type() functions are not explicitly specified, the default primitive event type is a group with the reader itself.
E = observation('r', o, t) ⟺
E = observation('r', o, t), group(r)='r'

## 2.2 Complex Event

A complex event is usually defined by applying event *constructors* to its constituent events, which are either primitive events or other complex events. There are two types of RFID event constructors: *non-temporal* and *temporal*, and the latter contains order, temporal constraints, or both. While complex events defined with non-temporal event constructors can be detected without considering the orders among constituent events, complex events defined with temporal event constructors cannot be detected without checking the orders and/or other temporal constraints (e.g., distance or interval) among constituent events.

**Basic Non-Temporal Complex Event Constructors**

- OR ($\vee$): Disjunction of two events $E_1$ and $E_2$, $E_1 \vee E_2$, occurs when either $E_1$ or $E_2$ occurs.
- AND ($\wedge$): Conjunction of two events $E_1$ and $E_2$, $E_1 \wedge E_2$, occurs when both $E_1$ and $E_2$ occur disregarding their occurrence orders.
- NOT($\neg$): Negation of an event E, $\neg$E, occurs if no instance of E ever occurs. Negated events themselves are non-spontaneous and they are usually combined with other events and/or with some temporal constraints.

In this paper, we only consider the above three basic non-temporal complex event constructors, which are in fact sufficient for expressing any complex event patterns without temporal constraints. For example, a complex event E = ALL($E_1$, $E_2$, ..., $E_n$), which occurs if all $E_1$, $E_2$, ..., $E_n$ occur irrespective of their orders, is equivalent to E = $E_1 \wedge E_2 \wedge ... \wedge E_n$.

**Temporal Complex Event Constructors**

- SEQ(;): Sequence of two events $E_1$ and $E_2$, denoted by $E_1$;$E_2$, occurs when $E_2$ occurs given that $E_1$ has already occurred. (Here we assume that $E_1$ ends before $E_2$ starts.)
- TSEQ(:): Distance-constrained sequence of two events $E_1$ and $E_2$, TSEQ($E_1$;$E_2$, $\tau_l$, $\tau_u$), occurs when $E_2$ occurs given that $E_1$ has already occurred and that the temporal distance between the occurrences of $E_1$ and $E_2$ is bounded by [$\tau_l$, $\tau_u$]. That is, $\tau_l \leq$ dist(T$E_1$, $E_2$) $\leq \tau_u$.
- SEQ$^+$(;$^+$): The aperiodic sequence operator, SEQ$^+$(E), allows one to express one or more occurrences of an event E.
- TSEQ$^+$(:$^+$): The distance-constrained aperiodic sequence operator, TSEQ$^+$(E, $\tau_l$, $\tau_u$), allows one to express one or more occurrences of an event E such that the temporal distance between any two adjacent occurrences of E are bounded by [$\tau_l$, $\tau_u$].
- WITHIN: An interval-constrained event, WITHIN(E, $\tau$), occurs if an instance of E, e.g., e, occurs and interval(e) $\leq \tau$.

*Temporal Constraints.* While non-temporal event constructors above were discussed in the past [4,5], the new temporal event constructors that we propose are essential for RFID applications. As shown above, most temporal event constructors use temporal constraints to specify temporal complex events. These include *distance constraint*: minimal distance ($\tau_l$) between two events in a temporal sequence TSEQ and maximal distance ($\tau_u$) between two events in a temporal sequence TSEQ; and *interval constraint*: maximal interval size ($\tau$) of a complex event as in the WITHIN constructor. These temporal constraints are not supported in past event systems.

*Examples of Complex Events.* In Example 1, the complex event is:
$$\text{TSEQ}(\ \text{TSEQ}^+(E_1,\ \tau_{l1},\ \tau_{u2})\ ;\ E_2,\ \tau_{l2},\ \tau_{u2}\ ),$$
where event types $E_1$ = observation($r_1$, $o_1$, $t_1$), group($r_1$) = '$r_1$' and $E_2$ = observation($r_2$, $o_2$, $t_2$), group($r_2$) = '$r_2$'.

In Example 2, the complex event is:
$$\text{WITHIN}(E_1 \land \neg\ E_2,\ 5\text{sec}),$$
where $E_1$ = observation('$r_2$', $o_1$, $t_1$), type($o_1$) = 'laptop' and $E_2$ = observation('$r_2$', $o_2$, $t_2$), type($o_2$) = 'superuser'.

## 3 RFID Rules

Based on event specification described above, we now define RFID rules. We first introduce the syntax of RFID rules as follows:

> CREATE RULE rule_id, rule_name
> ON event
> IF condition
> DO action$_1$; action$_2$; ...; action$_n$

where rule_id and rule_name stand for the unique id and name for a rule; event is the event part of the rule, condition is a boolean combination of user-defined boolean functions and SQL queries; and action$_1$; action$_2$; ...; action$_n$ is an ordered list of actions, where each action is either a SQL statement or a user-defined procedure, e.g., to send out alarms.

An alias of an event can be defined for reuse in the following form:

> DEFINE event_name = event specification

Next, we show that with declarative RFID rules, we can provide powerful support for RFID data processing, including data filtering, data transformation and aggregation, and real-time monitoring.

### 3.1 RFID Data Filtering

Before RFID data are further processed, they need to be filtered first. There are two types of data filtering for RFID data: *low level data filtering*, and *semantic data filtering*. The low level data filtering cleans raw RFID data, and semantic data filtering extracts data on demand or interprets semantics from RFID data.

**Low Level Data Filtering: Duplicate Detection**
Duplicate observations are common in RFID applications. This can be caused by several reasons: i) tags in the scope of a reader for a long time (in multiple reading frames) are read by the reader multiple times; ii) multiple readers are installed to cover larger area or distance, and tags in the overlapped areas are read by multiple readers; and iii) to enhance reading accuracy, multiple tags with same EPCs are attached to the same object.

*Rule 1.* If the same reader observes the same object multiple times within a short interval, e.g., 5 seconds, then mark the previous event as a duplicate.

```
CREATE RULE r2, duplicate_detection_rule
ON WITHIN(observation(r, o, t1); observation(r, o, t2), 5sec)
IF true
DO
   send_duplicate_msg(observation(r, o, t1))
```

Similarly, we can filter duplicates from multiple readers (e.g., r1 and r2), by defining a reader group containing these readers.

### Semantic Data Filtering: Infield/Outfield Filtering

RFID rules can also be used to perform effective semantical data filtering. For example, *infield* and *outfield* events are used in smart shelf applications [6]. Although tagged objects on a smart shelf are read all the times, applications may only be interested in when an object is put on the shelf (infield) and when an object is taken off the shelf (outfield) in order to update inventory automatically. The following example illustrates how to use an RFID rule to express infield events and perform the corresponding actions.

*Rule 2.* If an object is observed by a reader r on a smart shelf for the first time, then the rule will insert the observation into the OBSERVATION table. (We assume that the reader is scheduled to bulk-read all objects every 30 seconds in the following example.)

```
CREATE RULE r2, infield_filtering
ON WITHIN(¬observation(r, o, t1); observation(r, o, t2), 30sec)
IF true
DO
   INSERT INTO OBSERVATION
   VALUES (r, o, t2)
```

Outfield filtering can be defined similarly by switching the order of the negated event.

### 3.2 Data Transformation and Aggregation

One significant benefit of RFID rules is that data transformation and aggregation is simplified in a declarative way. With a set of data transformation and aggregation rules, RFID observations are automatically interpreted and mapped into their data models and stored in RFID data store.

In the following, we show two examples of how to devise data transformation and aggregation rules, and detect such rules to generate semantic data in a fully automatic environment. We assume that object containment relationships are stored in table OBJECTCONTAINMENT(object_epc, parent_epc, tstart, tend), where object_epc stands for the EPC of the object being contained, parent_epc stands for the EPC of the container object, and [tstart, tend] stands for the period of the containment relationship.

### Location Transformation

RFID observations may imply location changes and business movements. For example, an observation by a reader r of an object o at time t implies that the object has entered the location where the reader resides in starting from time t.

In the following, we assume that object location information is stored in table OBJECTLOCATION (object_epc, loc_id, tstart, tend), with the EPC of an object, location ID of the object, and the period during which the object stayed.

*Rule 3.* Any observation by a reader $r$ will change the location of the observed object $o$: updating the object's current location by changing its tend from "Until Changed" (UC) to t and inserting a new location for this object, i.e., the reader's new location with its starting timestamp t and ending timestamp "UC."

```
CREATE RULE r3, location_change_rule
ON observation(r, o, t)
IF true
DO
     UPDATE OBJECTLOCATION
     SET tend = t
     WHERE object_epc = o and tend = "UC";
     INSERT INTO OBJECTLOCATION VALUES(o, "loc2", t, "UC");
```

**Containment Relationship Aggregation**

Automatic data aggregation, a difficult task for RFID applications [3], can now be greatly simplified with RFID rules. (RFID applications need to be engineered accordingly to generate proper patterns.)

*Rule 4.* If a distance-constrained aperiodic sequence of readings from reader "$r_1$" is observed followed by a distinct reading from a reader "$r_2$," it implies that objects observed by "$r_1$" are being packed in the object observed by "$r_2$." Then the rule will insert new containment relationships into the OBJECTCONTAINMENT table (Fig. 1).

```
DEFINE E1 = observation("r1", o1, t1)
DEFINE E2 = observation("r2", o2, t2)
CREATE RULE r4, containment_rule
ON TSEQ(TSEQ⁺(E1, 0.1sec, 1sec); E2, 10sec, 20sec)
IF true
DO
     BULK INSERT INTO CONTAINMENT
     VALUES (o2, o1, t2, "UC")
```

The keyword "BULK" will enforce a bulk insertion of all contained objects into the container.

### 3.3 Real-Time Monitoring

RFID rules can also provide effective support of real-time monitoring, as shown in the following asset monitoring example.

*Rule 5.* As shown in Example 2, if the reader mounted at a building exit, "$r_4$," detects a tagged laptop but does not detect any tagged superuser (who is authorized to move asset items out of the building) within certain time threshold, e.g., 5 seconds, then it implies that the laptop is being taken out illegally, and an alert is sent to a security personnel.

```
DEFINE E4 = observation("r4", o4, t4), type(o4) = "laptop"
DEFINE E5 = observation("r4", o5, t5), type(o5) = "superuser"
CREATE RULE r5, asset_monitoring_rule
ON WITHIN(E4 ∧ ¬E5, 5sec)
IF true
DO send_alarm
```

## 4 RCEDA: RFID Complex Event Detection

While RFID rules provide powerful support for data transformation and monitoring, the detection of complex RFID events is quite challenging. We next discuss the differences between RFID event detection and traditional ECA event detection.

### 4.1 RFID Event Detection Versus Traditional ECA Event Detection

First, many RFID events (e.g., events containing constructors of TSEQ, TSEQ⁺ and WITHIN) contain temporal constraints at instance level, which are not supported by traditional ECA rules. In traditional ECA rule systems [7,8,4,9], event detection is performed at type level, but instance level constraints (such as temporal constraints) are not supported. (Snoop supports interval for periodic events, which have to be between two events.) Thus, in such systems, instance-level constraint checking has to be performed as condition checking. In RFID events, temporal constraints, however, are inherent to the events and highly essential to the correctness of event detection. Thus, RFID temporal constraints cannot be simply taken as conditions. Next we show an example that traditional ECA event detection will not work properly for temporal RFID events. Suppose that we have the following complex event to detect the packing of items into cases in an assembly line (Fig. 1):

```
E = TSEQ(TSEQ⁺(E₁, 0sec, 1sec); E₂, 5sec, 10sec)
```

where $E_1$ represents an observation of an item and $E_2$ represents an observation of a case.

If the event detection is done through ECA systems, where instance level temporal constraints are checked as conditions, we will first detect the following instances for complex event E, given the event history in Fig. 4.

$$\{e_1^1,\ e_1^2,\ e_1^3,\ e_1^5,\ e_1^6,\ e_1^7\};\ e_2^{12}$$

where $e_i^j$ denotes an instance of event type $E_i$ at time j. The instances $\{e_1^1,\ e_1^2,\ e_1^3,\ e_1^5,\ e_1^6,\ e_1^7\}$, however, do not satisfy the temporal constraints in TSEQ⁺(E₁, 0sec, 1sec) because the distance between $e_1^3$ and $e_1^5$ is larger than the upper bound, 1sec. With such an event processing approach, no instances for complex event E will be generated, which, however, is not correct. Therefore, for proper processing of RFID events, we must consider temporal constraints as an integral part of the event detection step. Thus, existing ECA-based event systems cannot be used for detecting RFID events.

Second, RFID events by constructors such as SEQ⁺ and NOT are non-spontaneous or induced: they cannot detect their occurrences by themselves unless they either get

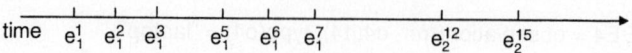

**Fig. 4.** Sample event history for complex event E = TSEQ(TSEQ$^+$(E$_1$, 0sec, 1sec); E$_2$, 5sec, 10sec)

expired or are explicitly queried. Most existing event systems, however, only detect spontaneous events, i.e., events that can detect their occurrences by themselves. For example, while Snoop [4] supports aperiodic sequence and negation constructors, these constructors, however, must always start with an initiator event and end with a terminator event, which is not general enough. The non-spontaneous nature of many RFID event constructors demands a new approach for RFID event processing and detection.

To this end, in this paper, we develop a general <u>R</u>FID <u>C</u>omplex <u>E</u>vent <u>D</u>etection <u>A</u>lgorithm (RCEDA). In our approach, temporal constraints become the first class objects in the event detection phase. To support detection of non-spontaneous events, the system automatically generates *pseudo events* to actively trigger the querying of the occurrences of these non-spontaneous events.

Next, we first discuss the parameter context applicable to RFID applications, then present in detail how to effectively detect RFID complex events under such parameter context.

### 4.2 Parameter Context for RFID Event Detection

Parameter contexts define which instances of a complex event are actually pulled out of a history of multiple constituent events. Events can always be detected using unrestricted (or general) context, in which all combinations of instances of constituent events are returned as instances of a complex event. The unrestricted parameter context usually produces a large number of event instances. Only some of these combinations, however, are meaningful for an application. Thus, four different restricted parameter contexts have been proposed in [4], including *recent, continuous, cumulative and chronicle*.

Among the four types of contexts, only the *chronicle* context will work for RFID events. This is because that complex RFID events often overlap with each other (e.g., Fig. 1b), since multiple readers (often deployed in a sequence of locations) produce observations simultaneously and these observations are collected and processed together. Under the other three types of contexts, there are often events matched from overlapped events which lead to incorrect detection. The *chronicle* context detects complex events in chronicle order of occurrence: the oldest initiator is paired with the oldest terminator. Thus it works properly even when instances for a complex event overlaps. For example, instances for event E in Fig. 4 under chronicle context will include $\{e_1^1, e_1^2, e_1^3, e_2^{12}\}$, $\{e_1^5, e_1^6, e_1^7, e_2^{15}\}$, which are as intended. Thus, we use chronicle context for detecting complex events in RFID applications.

### 4.3 Graphical Representation of Complex Events

Our event detection uses a graph-based computation model. We first introduce the graphical representation for each complex event constructor and then present how to construct event graphs for complex events in RFID rules.

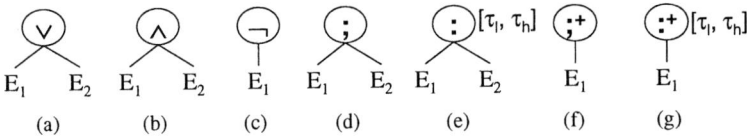

**Fig. 5.** Graphical representations of complex event constructors: (a) E = $E_1 \vee E_2$, (b) E = $E_1 \wedge E_2$, (c) E = $\neg E_1$, (d) E = $E_1; E_2$, (e) E = TSEQ($E_1; E_2$, $\tau_l$, $\tau_u$), (f) E = SEQ$^+$($E_1$) and (g) E = TSEQ$^+$($E_1$, $\tau_l$, $\tau_u$)

Fig. 5 illustrates the graphical representation of each event constructor discussed in Section 2.2, where constituent events are represented as child nodes, and the constructed events are represented as parent nodes. We denote a node that represents an event E as $v_E$. Note that the temporal sequence events are also associated with their distance constraints.

An exception is the WITHIN constructor, which is represented as an interval constraint of the constituent node. For example, Fig. 6a shows the graphical representation of an interval-constrained event E = WITHIN($E_1 \wedge E_2$, 10sec). As another example, Fig. 6b shows the graphical representation of a complex event with both interval-constraint and distance-constraint: E = WITHIN(TSEQ$^+$($E_1$, 0.1sec, 1sec), 100sec).

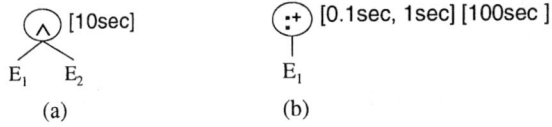

**Fig. 6.** Graphical representations of interval-constrained complex events: (a) WITHIN($E_1 \wedge E_2$, 10sec) and (b) WITHIN( TSEQ$^+$($E_1$, 0.1sec, 1sec), 100sec)

Given a set of RFID rules R = $\{r_1, r_2, \ldots, r_n\}$, we construct a graph representing the events for these rules in the following steps.

- *First, build an event graph for each rule's event.* For each rule $r_i$ in R, we build an event graph $T_i$ with leaf nodes representing primitive events, internal nodes representing complex events and edges linking constituent events with parent complex events. The root node of $T_i$ represents the event part of the rule $r_i$.
- *Second, propagate interval constraints.* For each event graph $T_i$, if there is any interval constraint defined on an event node $v_E \in T_i$, propagate $v_E$'s interval constraint to all the descendant nodes of $v_E$. This is because that a complex event always has a longer interval than its constituent events. Interval constraints are propagated top-down in the event graph: given any event node $v_E$, its interval constraint is set to be the minimum of the current interval constraint of E (if any) and that of its parent event node, if any. For example, Fig. 7b illustrates the graphical representation of a complex event E = WITHIN(TSEQ$^+$($E_1 \vee E_2$, 0.1sec, 1sec)

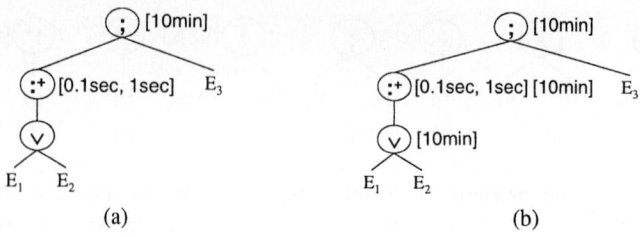

**Fig. 7.** Graphical representations of an interval-constrained complex event E = WITHIN(TSEQ⁺(E₁ ∨ E₂, 0.1sec, 1sec) ; E₃, 10min): (a) before propagating the interval constraint; and (b) after propagating the interval constraint.

; $E_3$, 10min) after interval propagating from Fig. 7a. We use $v_E$.within to represent the interval constraint on event E.
– *Finally, merge common sub-graphs.* We can combine any common sub-graphs in $\{T_1, T_2, \ldots, T_n\}$ to form an event graph G, thus avoid detecting common sub-events multiple times to improve efficiency and reduce space requirements. For convenience, we use $p(v_E)$ to represent the set of nodes that are parents of $v_E$ in G; and we use $r(v_E)$ to represent a rule whose event part is represented by $v_E$.

By integrating temporal constraints into event graphs, temporal constraints become first class constructs in event detection, and are checked during the detection process, as discussed later.

### 4.4 RFID Event Detection Mode

Traditional graph-based event processing systems detect complex events in a bottom-up fashion: occurrences of primitive events are injected at the leaves and flow upwards to trigger parent complex events. Such a bottom-up event detection approach, however, is inapplicable to detecting RFID events. In fact, many RFID events (such as those generated from SEQ⁺ and NOT constructors) are non-spontaneous: they cannot detect their occurrences by themselves unless they either get expired – if they are associated with interval constraints – or are explicitly queried about their occurrences from their parent nodes.

Next, we generalize three RFID event detection modes for each node $v_E$ in G.

– *Push(↑)*: An event node $v_E$'s detection mode is push if E is a spontaneous event such that any occurrence of E will trigger $v_E$ to automatically detect the occurrences and propagate them to their parents. For example, primitive events will always automatically propagate their instances to their parents, thus are always in push mode.
– *Pull(↓)*: An event node $v_E$'s detection mode is pull if E is a non-spontaneous event such that $v_E$ cannot determine whether instances of E have occurred or not unless being explicitly queried by $v_E$'s parent node. For example, the detection mode for a NOT event is always pull.

- *Mixed*($\updownarrow$): An event node $v_E$'s detection mode is mixed if its detection mode is neither *push* nor *pull*. Such event nodes are usually associated with temporal constraints. For example, the detection mode for a complex event E = TSEQ$^+$(E$_1$, $\tau_l$, $\tau_u$) is mixed if E$_1$ is a spontaneous event. When an instance of E$_1$ arrives at time timestamp, $v_E$ cannot determine whether the sequence has ended or not unless there is no arrival of other instance of E$_1$ during the period of [timestamp, timestamp + $\tau_u$].

We can compute the event detection modes for the nodes in an event graph G recursively by starting from primitive event nodes on the leaf level. While the detection mode for a primitive event node is always push, the detection mode for a complex event depends on the event constructor type and the modes of its constituent sub-events.

An RFID rule r is *valid* only if the detection mode for its event E is in either push mode or mixed mode. In this paper, we propose a method to detect mixed mode events by the introduction of *pseudo events*. (If the detection mode for r's event E is pull, then occurrences of E can never be detected and thus r will never be triggered. We call such events invalid events, and corresponding rules invalid rules.)

### 4.5 Pseudo Events

Existence of non-spontaneous RFID events causes mixed detection mode. Mixed mode RFID event nodes cannot be supported in traditional graph-based event detection systems, which propagate event occurrences bottom up. To address this challenge, we propose to generate *pseudo events* when necessary to trigger explicit queries about the occurrences of these non-spontaneous events, i.e., in a top-down way.

A pseudo event is a special artificial event used for querying the occurrences of non-spontaneous events during a specific period, and is scheduled to happen at an event node's expiration time. We represent a pseudo event instance as $e_i'^{[t_c, t_e]}$, with its target event id i, creation time $t_c$ and execution time $t_e$. A pseudo event $e_i'^{[t_c, t_e]}$ will query the occurrences of event i during the period [$t_c$, $t_e$], or non-occurrences of event i during the period [$t_c$, $t_e$] if the constructor for event i is NOT.

For a rule r with a push mode event r.E, there is no need to generate pseudo events even though r.E contains non-spontaneous sub-events.

For example, suppose that the event of rule r is WITHIN($\neg$E$_1$; E$_2$, $\tau$) where E$_1$ and E$_2$ are primitive events, any occurrence of E$_2$ ( e.g., e$_2$) will trigger the querying about the non-occurrences of E$_1$ during the period [t_end(e$_2$) - $\tau$, t_end(e$_2$)]. Thus, there is no need to generate pseudo events in this case.

For a mixed mode event r.E, however, we need to generate pseudo events to trigger the querying about the occurrences of non-spontaneous sub-events. For example, for an interval-constrained complex event E = WITHIN(E$_1$ $\wedge$ $\neg$E$_2$, $\tau$) where E$_1$ and E$_2$ are primitive events; if E$_1$ happens first, we need to make sure that there is no occurrence of E$_2$ within $\tau$. Therefore, if there is no occurrence of E$_2$ during the interval of E$_1$'s instance, occurrence of an E$_1$ instance e$_1$ will create a pseudo event with the target event $\neg$E$_2$, creation time t_end(e$_1$) and execution time t_begin(e$_1$) + $\tau$. This pseudo event will query about the non-occurrence of event E$_2$ during the period [t_end(e$_1$), t_begin(e$_1$) + $\tau$].

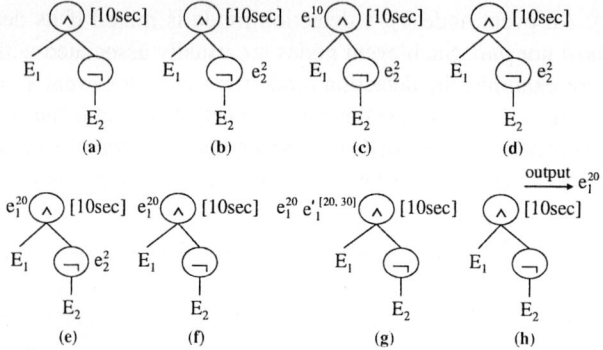

**Fig. 8.** An example of detecting a complex event E = WITHIN(E$_1$ ∧ ¬ E$_2$, 10sec) with event history $\{e_2^2,\ e_1^{10},\ e_1^{20}\}$: (a) graphical representation for E; (b) on arrival of $e_2^2$; (c) on arrival of $e_1^{10}$; (d) after processing of (c); (e) on arrival of $e_1^{20}$; (f) after processing of (e); (g) after arrival of pseudo event $e_3^{\prime[20,30]}$, where the event id for ¬ E$_2$ is 3; and (h) after processing of (g).

For a mixed mode event, we can determine whether a node v in the event graph G needs to generate pseudo events in a top-down way.

The notations used here include: i) v$_E$.mode: the detection mode for v$_E$; ii) v$_E$.pseudo: v$_E$'s pseudo event generation flag; and iii) v$_E$.pseudo_target: the target event of a pseudo event from v$_E$.

*Implementation of Pseudo Events.* When pseudo events are created, they are put into a sorted pseudo queue (pseudo_queue) according to their scheduled execution timestamps. The incoming RFID event queue (event_queue) is ordered by their observation timestamps. When the event engine fetches an event, it always fetches the earliest event from the two queues.

## An Example of Detecting Complex Events Using Pseudo Events

Fig. 8 illustrates an example of detecting a complex event E = WITHIN(E$_1$ ∧ ¬E$_2$, 10sec) with pseudo events. We assume an event history $\{e_2^2,\ e_1^{10},\ e_1^{20}\}$, where $e_i^j$ represents an occurrence of event E$_i$ at time j. The steps are described as follows:

1. On arrival of $e_2^2$, v$_{E_2}$ propagates $e_2^2$ to its parent node. Since the parent node is non-spontaneous, it will not further propagate the occurrence (Fig. 8b);
2. On the arrival of $e_1^{10}$, v$_{E_1}$ propagates its occurrence to v$_E$, which triggers the querying about the non-occurrence of E$_2$ during the period [t_end($e_1^{10}$) - 10sec, t_end($e_1^{10}$)], i.e., [0sec, 10sec] (Fig. 8c);
3. Since there is an occurrence $e_2^2$ of E$_2$ during the period of [0sec, 10sec], $e_1^{10}$ cannot be a constituent instance of an E's occurrence. Thus, $e_1^{10}$ is deleted (Fig. 8d);
4. Similarly, on the arrival of $e_1^{20}$, v$_{E_1}$ propagates its occurrence to v$_E$, which triggers the querying about the non-occurrence of E$_2$ during the period [t_end($e_1^{20}$) - 10sec, t_end($e_1^{20}$)], i.e., [10sec, 20sec] (Fig. 8e);
5. Since there is no occurrence of E$_2$, v$_E$ cannot detect its occurrence unless there is no occurrence of E$_2$ during the period [t_end($e_1^{20}$), t_begin($e_1^{20}$) +

10sec]), i.e., [20sec, 30sec] (Fig. 8f). Thus, a pseudo event $e_3'^{[20,30]}$ is scheduled to be generated at time 30sec to query the event node $v_{\neg E_2}$. We assume that the event id for $\neg E_2$ is 3;

6. The arrival of $e_3'^{[20,30]}$ will trigger the querying about the non-occurrence of event $E_2$ during the period [20sec, 30sec] (Fig. 8g). Since there is no occurrence of $E_2$ during that period, occurrence of E is detected (Fig. 8h).

### 4.6 RFID Complex Event Detection Algorithm (RCEDA)

In this subsection, we discuss how to efficiently detect RFID complex events under chronicle parameter context (Algorithm RFID_COMPLEX_EVENT_DETECTION).

RFID_COMPLEX_EVENT_DETECTION(R = $\{r_1, r_2, ..., r_n\}$)
1    Construct an event graph G representing the rules in R (Section 4.3)
2    //begin of initializing event graph
3    Propagate interval constraints starting from the root node of G
4    Assign an event detection mode for each node in G
5    Assign pseudo event flag and target for each node in G
6    //end of initializing event graph
7    **for** each incoming event $e_1$
8      **do if** $e_1$ is an instance of a primitive event $E_1$
9        **then for** each parent node $v_E$ of $v_{E_1}$
10          **do** ACTIVATE_PARENT_NODE($v_E, e_1$)
11            **if** $v_{E_1}$.pseudo
12              **then** GENERATE_PSEUDO_EVENT($v_{E_1}, v_E, e_1$)
13          **for** each rule $r$ whose event part is represented by $v_{E_1}$
14            **do** trigger the rule $r$
15      **if** $e_1$ is a pseudo event
16        **then** let E be the target event of $e_1$
17          let tstart be the creation timestamp of $e_1$
18          let tend be the execution timestamp of $e_1$
19          EList ← QUERY_INTERVAL_NODE($v_E$, tstart, tend)
20          **for** each event instance e in EList
21            **do for** each parent node, v, of $v_E$
22              **do** ACTIVATE_PARENT_NODE($v, e$)

Given an event graph G, we first initialize G by: i) propagating interval constraints in a top-down way (Algorithm PROPAGATE_INTERVAL_CONSTRAINT); ii) assigning event detection modes bottom-up based on event constructors and interval constraints (Section 4.4); and iii) assigning pseudo event generation flags top-down based on the event detection modes (Algorithm ASSIGN_PSEUDO_EVENT_FLAG). Then, we can use this event graph to monitor the occurrences of events based on the algorithm RCEDA. The algorithm has three main functions:

- ACTIVATE_PARENT_NODE($v_E, e_1$): This recursive function propagates an event instance $e_1$ from one sub-event $E_1$ of E to $v_E$ and detects whether any instance of E has occurred or not. If yes, $v_E$ will recursively propagate its occurrence to its parent node (if any), i.e. call the ACTIVATE_PARENT_NODE function again, or

trigger a rule $r$ whose event part is represented by $v_E$. If the pseudo flag of $v_{E1}$ is set to true during the event graph initialization, this function will also generate a pseudo event from $v_{E1}$, $e_i'^{[t_s,t_e]}$, where $i$ is the id of $v_E$'s pseudo event target, i.e., $v_E$.pseudo_target, $t_s$ and $t_e$ are set based on t_begin($e_1$), t_end($e_1$) and the temporal constraints on E.
- QUERY_INTERVAL_NODE($v_E$, tstart, tend): This function queries about occurrences of the event E during the period [tstart, tend] and outputs such occurrences if any.
- GENERATE_PSEUDO_EVENT($v_{E_1}$, $v_E$, $e_2$): This function will generate a pseudo event for the target event $v_{E_1}$ on the occurrence of an event instance $e_2$, where $e_2$ is an instance of one of $v_E$'s sub-events; $v_{E_1}$ is either the same as $v_E$ or a child node of $v_E$. The creation time and execution time for the pseudo event will depend on the temporal constraints on $v_E$, t_begin($e_2$) and t_end($e_2$).

The algorithm RCEDA works as follows:

- On each occurrence of a primitive event $e_1$ (of type $E_1$) attached to a leaf node $v_{E1}$, the algorithm will propagate $e_1$ to all the internal event nodes $v_E$ where $E_1$ is a sub-event of E. That is, the occurrence of $e_1$ will call the function ACTIVATE_PARENT_NODE($v_E$, $e_1$). Also, the occurrence of $e_1$ will also trigger all the rules whose events are represented by $v_{E_1}$.
- On each occurrence of a pseudo event $e_i'^{[t_s,t_e]}$, the algorithm will query about the occurrences of the target event with id $i$ during the period [$t_s$, $t_e$], with the function query_internal_node($v_{E_i}$, $t_s$, $t_e$). The algorithm will recursively propagate each occurrence, $e_i$, in the query results to event $i$'s parent node $v$, with the function ACTIVATE_PARENT_NODE($v$, $e_i$).
- On each occurrence $e$ of an event E, either primitive or complex, if the pseudo flag of $v_E$ is set to true during the event graph initialization, the algorithm will generate a pseudo event for $v_E$.pseudo_target. The creation and execution timestamps of the pseudo event are set based on the t_begin(e), t_end(e) and the temporal constraints between E and the target event. This is done with the function generate_pseudo_event($v_E$, $v$, $e$), where $v$ is the common parent node between $v_E$ and $v_E$'s pseudo target event node.

## 5 Performance Study

To evaluate the performance of our approach, we developed a simulator of an RFID-enabled supply chain system with warehouses, shipping, retail stores and sale to customers. Rules are defined for the system to automatically transform and aggregate data. The machine used is a Dell Latitude D610, with 2GHz Pentium M CPU and 1GB memory, installed with Windows XP. We implemented our event detection algorithm RCEDA in C#.

We tested the total event processing time versus the number of primitive events and versus the number of rules, with event arrival rate of 1000 events per second. (To simplify the test, action cost such as database update cost is not counted in the processing time.) The experiment result shown in Fig. 9 demonstrates that the cost increases almost

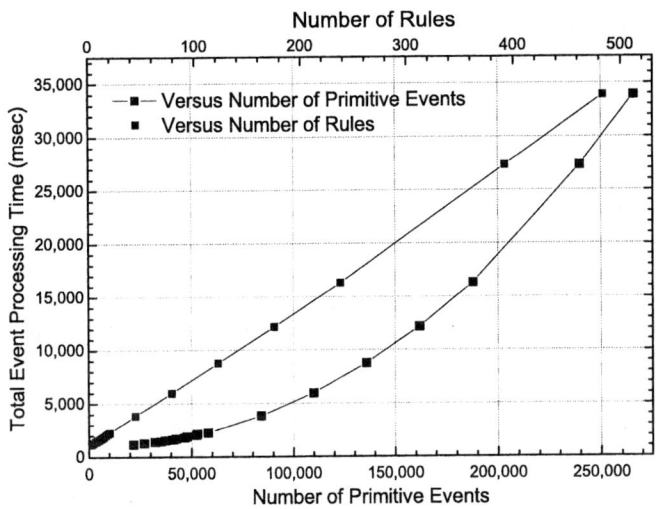

**Fig. 9.** Event processing time versus number of events and number of rules

linearly versus the number of events, and that the performance versus number of rules is also quite scalable.

## 6 Related Work

RFID technology has emerged for years and poses new challenges for data processing and management. The importance of event processing is pointed out in [10], but methodology is not provided. In [2], a temporal-based data model is developed for RFID data, and how to use rules to transform RFID data from observations into the data model is also discussed; however, it lacks a complete framework and implementation.

Recently, major IT vendors are providing sophisticated RFID platforms, including the Sun EPC Network [11], SAP Auto-ID Infrastructure [12], Oracle Sensor Edge Server [13], IBM WebSphere RFID Premises Server [14], Sybase RFID Solutions [15], and UCLA's WinRFID Middleware[16]. These platforms provide a general interface to collect RFID data from readers, and then forward the data to applications. These systems, however, only support limited RFID rules: in fact they only support primitive events or their simple combinations. Thus it is up to users' applications to detect complex events. RFID event processing is also discussed in [17, 18], where no formal method is proposed.

Event processing has been studied extensively in the past [19, 9, 7], in the context of active databases. These systems normally use Event-Condition-Action (ECA) rules for event processing. RFID events differ from traditional events in several ways, including the high temporal nature and existence of non-spontaneous events. Thus it is difficult for traditional event detection systems to support RFID event detection.

Temporal constraints are considered in [20, 21], which, however, cannot be used to support the special RFID events such as temporal sequence and temporal negation.

Event negation is discussed in [7], where a negated event must have an initiator event and a terminate event. Motakis et al [5] provide a formal discussion of active rules including negated events, but the implementation approach is not provided.

## 7 Conclusions

One of the major challenges for RFID applications is to bridge the physical world represented with EPC tags, and the virtual world represented with application logic. To address this challenge, we develop an event-oriented framework that can effectively transform and aggregate raw RFID data into semantic data, by i) declarative event specification with temporal constraints; ii) declarative rules definition to support data transformation and real-time monitoring; and iii) an RFID complex event detection engine that supports temporal constraints by integrating instance level constraint checking into the detection process, and uses pseudo events to actively detect non-spontaneous events. The event framework provides comprehensive support of RFID applications, including object tracking and real-time monitoring. For the latter, the difficulty of data aggregation can now be solved soundly through complex event generation and detection. The performance study shows that our system is efficient and scalable. The technology developed in this paper is now integrated into Siemens RFID Middleware [2] to provide integrated RFID solutions for RFID-enabled business applications.

## References

1. EPC Tag Data Standards Version 1.1. Technical report, EPCGlobal Inc, April 2004.
2. F. Wang and P. Liu. Temporal Management of RFID Data. In *VLDB*, 2005.
3. RFID 2004 FORUM Report. http://www.wireless.ucla.edu/techreports2/RFID-2004-Forum.pdf.
4. S. Chakravarthy and D. Mishra. Snoop: an Expressive Event Specification Language for Active Databases. *Data Knowl. Eng.*, 14(1):1–26, 1994.
5. I. Motakis and C. Zaniolo. Formal Semantics for Composite Temporal Events in Active Database Rules. *Journal of Systems Integration*, 7(3/4):291–325, 1997.
6. The METRO Group Future Store Initiative. http://www.future-store.org.
7. S. Chakravarthy, V. Krishnaprasad, E. Anwar, and S.-K. Kim. Composite Events for Active Databases: Semantics, Contexts and Detection. In *VLDB*, pages 606–617, 1994.
8. Jennifer Widom and Stefano Ceri. *Active Database Systems: Triggers and Rules For Advanced Database Processing*. Morgan Kaufmann, 1996.
9. N. H. Gehani, H. V. Jagadish, , and O. Shmueli. Composite Event Specification in Active Databases: Model & Implementation. In *VLDB*, 1992.
10. M. Palmer. Seven Principles of Effective RFID Data Management. www.objectstore.com/docs/ articles/7principles_rfid_mgmnt.pdf, Aug. 2004.
11. A. Gupta and M. Srivastava. Developing Auto-ID Solutions using Sun Java System RFID Software. http://java.sun.com/developer/technicalArticles/Ecommerce/rfid/sjsrfid/RFID.html, Oct 2004.
12. C. Bornhoevd, T. Lin, S. Haller, and J. Schaper. Integrating Automatic Data Acquisition with Business Processes - Experiences with SAP's Auto-ID Infrastructure. In *VLDB*, pages 1182–1188, 2004.
13. Oracle Sensor Edge Server. http://www.oracle.com /technology/products/iaswe/edge_server.

14. WebSphere RFID Premises Server. http://www-306.ibm.com/software/pervasive/ws_rfid_premises_server/, December 2004.
15. Sybase RFID Solutions. http://www.sybase.com/rfid, 2005.
16. UCLA WinRFID Middleware. http://www.wireless.ucla.edu/rfid/winrfid/.
17. M. J. Franklin, S. R. Jeffery, S. Krishnamurthy, F. Reiss, S. Rizvi, E. Wu, O. Cooper, A. Edakkunni, and W. Hong. Design Considerations for High Fan-In Systems: The HiFi Approach. In *CIDR*, pages 290–304, 2005.
18. S. Rizvi, S. R. Jeffery, S. Krishnamurthy, M. J. Franklin, N. Burkhart, A. Edakkunni, and L. Liang. Events on the Edge. In *SIGMOD*, pages 885–887, 2005.
19. S. Gatziu and K. R. Dirtrich. Detecting Composite Events in Active Databases Using Petri Nets. In *Workshop on Research Issues in Data Engineering: Active Database Systems*, 1994.
20. M. Mansouri-Samani and M. Sloman. GEM: a Generalized Event Monitoring Language for Distributed Systems. *Distributed Systems Engineering*, 4(2):96–108, 1997.
21. G. Liu, A. Mok, and P. Konana. A Unified Approach for Specifying Timing Constraints and Composite Events in Active Real-Time Database Systems. In *RTAS*, 1998.

# On Concurrency Control in Sliding Window Queries over Data Streams[*]

Lukasz Golab[1], Kumar Gaurav Bijay[2], and M. Tamer Özsu[1]

[1] School of Computer Science, University of Waterloo, Canada
{lgolab, tozsu}@uwaterloo.ca
[2] Department of Computer Science and Engineering, IIT Bombay, India
gauravk@cse.iitb.ac.in

**Abstract.** Data stream systems execute a dynamic workload of long-running and one-time queries, with the streaming inputs typically bounded by sliding windows. For efficiency, windows may be advanced periodically by replacing the oldest part of the window with a batch of new data. Existing work on stream processing assumes that a window cannot be advanced while it is being accessed by a query. In this paper, we argue that concurrent processing of queries (reads) and window-slides (writes) is required by data stream systems in order to allow prioritized query scheduling and improve the freshness of answers. We prove that the traditional notion of conflict serializability is insufficient in this context and define stronger isolation levels that restrict the allowed serialization orders. We also design and experimentally evaluate a transaction scheduler that efficiently enforces the new isolation levels.

## 1 Introduction

A Data Stream Management System (DSMS) executes two types of queries—*long-running* and *snapshot*—whose input streams are typically bounded by sliding windows. Long-running queries return updated answers periodically and often involve complex aggregation for monitoring purposes. Snapshot queries are analogous to traditional database queries in that they can be submitted to the DSMS at any time, are executed once, and return an answer over the current state of the inputs. Snapshot queries may be used to obtain further details in response to a change in the result of a long-running query.

Previous work on sliding window query processing [1-5] and stream query languages [6-8] assumes that windows slide periodically by replacing the oldest part of the window with a batch of fresh data. A periodically-sliding window can be modeled as a circular array of sub-windows, each spanning an equal time interval for time-based windows (e.g., a ten-minute window that slides every minute) or an equal number of tuples for tuple-based windows (e.g., a 100-tuple

---

[*] This research is partially supported by the Natural Sciences and Engineering Research Council of Canada (NSERC) and Communications and Information Technology Ontario (CITO).

window that slides every ten tuples). We define a *window update* as the process of replacing the oldest sub-window with newly arrived data, thereby sliding the window forward by one sub-window. We will use the terms window update, window movement, and window-slide interchangeably.

As the windows slide forward, a DSMS executes a dynamic workload of long-running and snapshot queries. Suppose that query execution involves accessing a window, one sub-window at a time (we will discuss this in more detail in Sect. 2). Combined with periodic window movements, we can model DSMS data access in terms of two atomic operations: sub-window scan (read) and replacement of the oldest sub-window with new data (write). Thus, a window update is a single write operation, whereas a query is a sequence of sub-window read operations such that each sub-window is read exactly once.

A window may slide while being accessed by a query, resulting in a *read-write conflict*. Consider a sequence of operations illustrated in Fig. 1 (a), where the processing times of window updates ($U$) and queries ($Q_1$, $Q_2$, and $Q_3$) are shown on a time axis. This represents an ideal scenario, where it is possible to execute all three queries between every pair of window updates, thereby avoiding read-write conflicts. However, the system environment, such as the query workload, stream arrival rates, and availability of system resources, can change greatly during the lifetime of a long-running query. Thus, a more realistic sequence is shown in Fig. 1 (b), where $Q_2$ takes longer to execute than expected. $Q_3$ is still running when the second update is ready to be applied, causing a delay in performing the update, and, in turn, causing another read-write conflict when $Q_3$ is re-executed and the third update is about to take place.

It may appear that read-write conflicts can be prevented by increasing the time interval between window updates, i.e., the sub-window size. However, all sub-windows must have the same size so that the overall window size is fixed at all times. Therefore, either the system must be taken off-line to re-partition the entire window, or two sets of sub-windows must be maintained during the transition period until the window "rolls over" and all the sub-windows have the

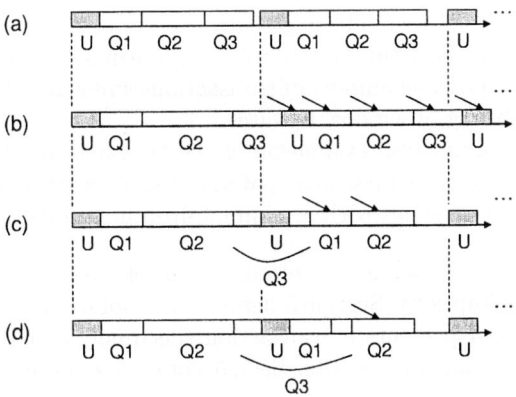

**Fig. 1.** Examples of query and window update sequences in a DSMS

new size. The first case is inappropriate for an on-line DSMS, whereas the second solution does not immediately eliminate read-write conflicts until the transition period is over.

Existing data stream solutions avoid read-write conflicts by serially executing queries and window movements. In other words, a query locks the window that it is scanning in order to prevent concurrent window movements. Interleaved execution of updates while a window is being scanned by a query is advantageous, provided that the following issue is resolved. Consider suspending the processing of $Q_3$ in order to perform a window update, as in Fig. 1 (c). Recall that each query is assumed to perform a sequence of atomic sub-window reads, therefore it may be interrupted after it has read one or more sub-windows. It must be ensured that when resumed, $Q_3$ can correctly read the updated window state. If so, then the answer of $Q_3$ is slightly delayed (by the time taken to perform the update), but it is more up-to-date because it reflects the second update as well as the first. Otherwise, we are worse off than in Fig. 1 (b), because the answer of $Q_3$ is delayed, but it is still not up-to-date. Another example is illustrated in Fig. 1 (d), where $Q_3$ is suspended not only to perform a window update, but also to run $Q_1$ immediately afterwards. This is desirable if $Q_1$ is an important query that requires an immediate and up-to-date answer.

This paper studies concurrency control issues in a DSMS with periodic window movements, periodic executions of long-running queries, and on-demand snapshot querying. Our goal is to provide query scheduling flexibility and guarantee up-to-date results. The particular contributions of this paper are as follows.

- By modeling window movements and queries as transactions consisting of atomic sub-window reads and writes, we extend concurrency theory to cover queries over periodically-advancing windows. We show that conflict serializability is not sufficient in the presence of interleaved queries and window movements because some serialization orders produce incorrect answers.
- We propose two isolation levels that are stronger than conflict serializability in that they restrict the permissible serialization orders.
- We design a transaction scheduler that efficiently enforces the desired isolation levels. The main idea is to exploit the access patterns of queries and window updates. The scheduler is proven to be optimal in the sense that it aborts the smallest possible number of transactions while allowing immediate (optimistic) scheduling of window updates.
- We perform an experimental evaluation of the transaction scheduler under various query workloads and system parameters, showing improved query freshness and response times with a minimal drop in throughput.

The remainder of this paper is organized as follows. Section 2 explains our system model and assumptions. Section 3 defines new isolation levels for DSMS transactions, and Sect. 4 presents a transaction scheduler for enforcing them. Section 5 presents experimental results, Sect. 6 compares the contributions of this paper to previous work, and Sect. 7 concludes the paper.

## 2 System Model and Assumptions

### 2.1 Data and Query Model

A data stream is assumed to consist of relational tuples with a fixed schema. Without loss of generality, we assume that each stream is bounded by a time-based window. A window of time-length $nt$ is stored as a circular array of $n$ sub-windows, each spanning a time-length of $t$ (each window may have different values for $n$ and $t$). Every $t$ time units, the oldest sub-window is replaced with a buffer containing incoming tuples that have arrived in the last $t$ time units. Additionally, the DSMS may materialize intermediate results of selected queries or sub-queries, e.g., sliding window joins [2], which may also be stored as arrays of sub-windows [9]. We assume that $t$ is significantly larger than the time taken to perform a window update (otherwise, the system would spend all of its time advancing the windows rather than executing queries).

Given that long-running queries are used for monitoring purposes, they typically compute aggregates over a single window or a join of several windows; a selection predicate may precede the aggregate and a group-by condition may follow it. Each long-running query $Q$ also specifies its desired re-execution frequency. The frequency must be a multiple of $t$, i.e., $Q$ will be scheduled for re-execution every $m$ window updates, where $1 \leq m < n$. The DSMS attempts to execute all the queries with the desired frequencies, but it cannot guarantee that this will be the case at all times due to unpredictable system conditions.

Queries are executed using one of two techniques (a discussion of other possible evaluation methods and justification of our choice may be found in the extended version of this paper [10]). First, a default access plan scans the entire window (or windows), one sub-window at a time, and computes the query from scratch. Second, aggregates may be computed by accessing a summary, which contains pre-aggregated values for each sub-window. An example is illustrated in Fig. 2, showing a summary that stores the maximum of all the values in each sub-window. A single scan of the summary, from youngest sub-window to oldest, may be used to compute the maximum over windows of different lengths. As illustrated, $max1$ is the maximum over a window of size $6t$, which is re-used to compute the maximum over a window of size $10t$ ($max2$). The size of a summary depends on the type of aggregate. Associative aggregates, such as MAX and MIN, require one value per sub-window (in case of group-by, a separate value is stored for each group). Non-associative aggregates, such as median, top-$k$, and COUNT DISTINCT, need access to the frequency counts of all the distinct values

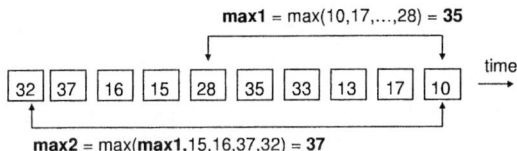

**Fig. 2.** Window summary for computing the maximum

on each sub-window. Alternatively, approximate answers to complex aggregates may be computed by storing summaries that contain estimates of the distribution of values in each sub-window. Examples include Count-Min sketch [11] and Flajolet-Martin sketch [12]. In all cases, query evaluation involves scanning and merging each sub-window summary, from youngest sub-window to oldest.

## 2.2 System Architecture

The assumed system architecture is illustrated in Fig. 3. Let $w[i]$ denote the replacement of the $i$th sub-window with newly arrived data, for $0 \leq i \leq n-1$. Each data stream generates periodic write-only transactions $T_j$ in subscript order, defined as $T_j = \{w_j[j \bmod n]\}$. They are processed by the transaction manager, which immediately propagates updates to all the summaries and materialized results that reference this window (e.g., new tuples are passed to the join operator, which probes the other window and generates new join results). For each stream, the transaction manager initially executes $T_0$ through $T_{n-1}$ to fill up the windows. Thereafter, each $T_j$ has the effect of moving the window forward by one sub-window. In order to ensure that queries have access to the latest data, the transaction scheduler executes each $T_j$ as soon as a buffer is full.

Snapshot queries are executed by scanning a suitable summary, if available, or accessing the underlying window(s). Answers are returned in the form of a table. Long-running queries are re-executed periodically throughout their *lifetimes* and generate a stream of updated answers. A new long-running query is inserted into the query manager, or may be rejected if the system is overloaded. The query manager then determines an appropriate execution strategy for the new query, e.g., whether an existing summary may be used or a new summary should be built, and whether the new query may be merged into a group of similar queries for shared processing. The design of the query manager is an orthogonal topic, which we pursue in separate work. In this paper, we define an interface between the query manager and the transaction scheduler, which consists of read-only transactions corresponding to re-execution of one or several similar

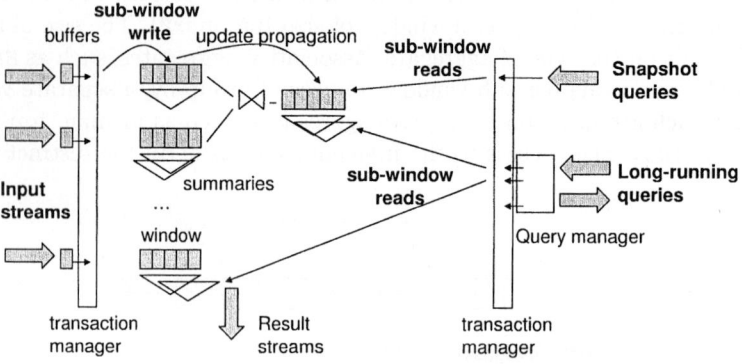

**Fig. 3.** Assumed system architecture

queries. We define $r[i]$ be a scan (read) of the $i$th sub-window, or its summary, for $0 \leq i \leq n - 1$ (without loss of generality, in the rest of the paper, we will refer to either of these as a sub-window). A snapshot query or a particular re-execution of one or more long-running queries is a read-only transaction $T_{Qk}$, defined as $T_{Qk} = \{r_{Qk}[0], r_{Qk}[1], \ldots, r_{Qk}[n-1]\}$. That is, each $T_{Qk}$ performs a scan of a window, sub-result, or summary, by reading each sub-window exactly once (queries over windows shorter than $nt$ may be defined similarly). We assume that sub-windows may be read in arbitrary order.

## 3 Conflict Serializability in the Context of Sliding Window Queries

### 3.1 Serializability and Serialization Orders

We begin by analyzing the isolation level requirements of queries over periodically-sliding windows. Due to space constraints, we assume that queries access a single window and deal with materialized sub-results in the extended version of this paper [10]. First, we define the possible types of conflicts arising from concurrent execution of transactions. A conflict occurs when two interleaved transactions operate on the same sub-window and at least one of the operations is a write. Clearly, a read-write conflict occurs whenever $T_j$ interrupts $T_{Qk}$, as in Fig. 1 (c) and (d). This is because each $T_{Qk}$ reads every sub-window, including the sub-window overwritten by $T_j$. Since we assumed that window movements are executed immediately, we can ignore write-write conflicts. The traditional method for dealing with conflicts requires an execution history $H$ to be serializable. We show that serializability is insufficient in our context using the following example.

Assume a sliding window partitioned into five sub-windows, numbered zero through four, with sub-window zero being the oldest at the current time. Consider the following four histories—$H_a$, $H_b$, $H_c$, and $H_d$—with $c_j$ or $c_{Qk}$ denoting that transaction $T_j$ or $T_{Qk}$, respectively, has committed (we omit the initial transactions $T_0$ through $T_4$ that fill up the window).

$H_a = r_{Q1}[0]\ w_5[0]\ c_5\ w_6[1]\ c_6\ r_{Q1}[1]\ r_{Q1}[2]\ r_{Q1}[3]\ r_{Q1}[4]\ c_{Q1}$
$H_b = r_{Q1}[0]\ w_5[0]\ c_5\ r_{Q1}[1]\ w_6[1]\ c_6\ r_{Q1}[2]\ r_{Q1}[3]\ r_{Q1}[4]\ c_{Q1}$
$H_c = r_{Q1}[4]\ w_5[0]\ c_5\ r_{Q1}[3]\ r_{Q1}[2]\ r_{Q1}[1]\ w_6[1]\ c_6\ r_{Q1}[0]\ c_{Q1}$
$H_d = r_{Q1}[4]\ w_5[0]\ c_5\ r_{Q1}[0]\ r_{Q1}[3]\ r_{Q1}[2]\ w_6[1]\ c_6\ r_{Q1}[1]\ c_{Q1}$

Each history represents interleaved execution of a read-only transaction $T_{Q1}$ and two window movements, $T_5$ and $T_6$. Note that $H_c$ and $H_d$ reorder the read operations within $T_{Q1}$; we will say more about ordering atomic operations in Sect. 4. The associated serialization graphs are drawn in Fig. 4. The direction of the edges corresponds to the order in which conflicting operations are serialized. In particular, there are two pairs of conflicting operations in each schedule: $r_{Q1}[0]$ and $w_5[0]$, and $r_{Q1}[1]$ and $w_6[1]$. Note that all four graphs are acyclic, therefore all four histories are serializable, but their serialization orders are different.

Let us analyze the data read by $T_{Q1}$. For each history, consider the state of the sliding window shown in Fig. 5, where the first sub-windows on the left

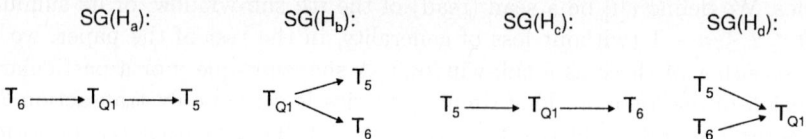

**Fig. 4.** Serialization graphs for $H_a$, $H_b$, $H_c$, and $H_d$

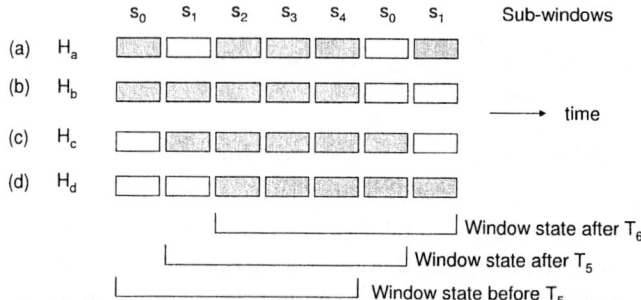

**Fig. 5.** Differences in the results returned by $T_{Q1}$ in $H_a$, $H_b$, $H_c$, and $H_d$

($s_0$ through $s_4$) correspond to the initial state of the window after $T_0$ through $T_4$ were executed. Next, $T_5$ advances the window forward by one sub-window, which may be thought of as overwriting the old copy of sub-window $s_0$ (on the far left) with a new copy, appended after $s_4$. Thus, the state of the window after $T_5$ commits is represented by the contiguous sequence of sub-windows $\{s_1, s_2, s_3, s_4, s_0\}$. Then, $T_6$ advances the window again by appending a new copy of $s_1$ on the far right and implicitly deleting the old copy of $s_1$ on the left. Hence, the state of the window after $T_6$ commits is equivalent to the contiguous sequence of sub-windows $\{s_2, s_3, s_4, s_0, s_1\}$. Shaded sub-windows represent those which were read by $T_{Q1}$ in each of the four histories, as explained next.

First, consider $SG(H_a)$ and note that $H_a$ serializes $T_6$ before $T_{Q1}$, meaning that the window movement caused by $T_6$ (creation of a new version of sub-window $s_1$) is reflected in the query. However, $H_a$ serializes an earlier window update $T_5$ after $T_{Q1}$, therefore the prior window movement caused by $T_5$ (creation of a new version of $s_0$) is hidden from the query. Hence, $H_a$ causes $T_{Q1}$ to read an old copy of $s_0$ and a new copy of $s_1$, as illustrated in Fig. 5 (a), which does not correspond to a window state at any point in time. This is because the shaded rectangles do not form a contiguous sequence of five sub-windows. Next, recall that $H_b$ serializes both window movements after $T_{Q1}$, therefore the query reads old versions of $s_0$ and $s_1$, as illustrated in Fig. 5 (b). This corresponds to the state of the window after $T_4$ commits. By similar reasoning, $H_c$ allows $T_{Q1}$ to read the state of the window after $T_5$ commits (Fig. 5 (c)), and only $H_d$ ensures that $T_{Q1}$ reads the most up-to-date state of the window that reflects both $T_5$ and $T_6$ (Fig. 5 (d)). Again, this is because only $SG(H_d)$ serializes both window movements before $T_{Qk}$, meaning that $T_{Qk}$ sees both updates.

## 3.2 Isolation Levels for Sliding Window Queries

Having shown that the serialization order affects the semantics of read-only transactions, we propose two stronger isolation levels that restrict the allowed serialization orders.

**Definition 1.** A serializable history $H$ is said to be *window-serializable (WS)* if all of its committed $T_{Qk}$ transactions read a true state of the sliding window as of some point in the past or present (i.e., a contiguous sequence of sub-windows is read, as in Fig. 5 (b), (c), and (d)).

**Definition 2.** A window-serializable history $H$ is said to be *latest-window-serializable (LWS)* if all of its committed $T_{Qk}$ transactions read the state of the sliding window that reflects all the window update transactions that have committed before $T_{Qk}$ commits.

Note that only *LWS* guarantees that queries read the most up-to-date state of the window Motivated by Fig. 4, we prove the following results.

**Theorem 1.** A history $H$ is window-serializable iff $SG(H)$ has the following property: for any $T_{Qk}$, if any $T_i$ is serialized before $T_{Qk}$, then for all $T_j$ serialized after $T_{Qk}$, $i < j$.

**Proof.** Suppose that $H$ is *WS*. If all transactions $T_{Qk}$ contained in $H$ incur at most one concurrent window movement, then clearly, $SG(H)$ satisfies the desired property. Otherwise, note that for $T_{Qk}$ to read a sliding window state from some point in the past or present, it must be the case that either $T_{Qk}$ is isolated from all the concurrent window updates, or it only reads the least recent update, or it only reads the two oldest updates, and so on. In all cases, $SG(H)$ contains less recent updates serialized before the query and more recent updates serialized after the query, as wanted. Now suppose that $SG(H)$ satisfies the property that all $T_j$ serialized after any $T_{Qk}$ have higher subscripts than those serialized before $T_{Qk}$. Let $m$ be the maximum subscript of any transaction $T_i$ serialized before $T_{Qk}$. It follows that $T_{Qk}$ reads a sliding window state that resulted from applying all the updates up to $T_m$ and therefore $H$ is *WS*. □

**Theorem 2.** A history $H$ is latest-window-serializable iff $SG(H)$ has the following property: for any $T_{Qk}$, all concurrent $T_i$ transactions must be serialized before $T_{Qk}$.

**Proof.** Suppose that $H$ is *LWS* and let $T_{Qk}$ be any query that incurs at least one concurrent window movement. It follows that $T_{Qk}$ reads a state of the window that results from applying all the concurrent updates. Hence, concurrent window updates must be serialized before queries, as wanted. Now suppose that $SG(H)$ does not contain any links pointing from any $T_{Qk}$ to any $T_i$. This means that there are no queries that have been interrupted by window updates which the queries then did not see. Hence, $H$ is *LWS*. □

## 4 Transaction Scheduler Design

### 4.1 Producing *LWS* Histories

We now present the design of a DSMS transaction scheduler that produces *LWS* histories. Recall from Sect. 2 that write-only transactions $T_j$ must be executed with highest priority so that queries have access to an up-to-date version of the window. Given this assumption, our scheduler executes window movements optimistically and uses *serialization graph testing (SGT)* to abort any read-only transaction that causes a read-write conflict. In general, *SGT* may suffer from high space usage and long running time if many conflicts among many transactions must be tracked over time [13]. Fortunately, in our context, the serialization graph is simple and can be pruned dynamically. In particular, for each currently running $T_{Qk}$, it suffices to monitor concurrent window movements $T_j$ and ensure that all interleaved $T_j$ are serialized before $T_{Qk}$ (recall Fig. 4). Once $T_{Qk}$ commits, it is guaranteed not to cause *LWS* violations at any point in the future, and therefore its node can be safely deleted from the serialization graph.

The scheduler is summarized as Algorithm 1. Lines 3 and 4 serially execute window movements immediately (technically, line 4 must wait for an acknowledgement that the write operation has been performed). Lines 8 through 11 initialize a bit array $B_{Qk}$ for each newly arrived $T_{Qk}$, where bit $i$ is set if $T_{Qk}$ has already read sub-window $i$. Lines 12 through 18 execute read-only transactions, one sub-window scan at a time, and set the corresponding bit in $B_{Qk}$ to true. Again, before committing $T_{Ql}$ in line 17, the algorithm must wait for an acknowledgement of performing the read operation from line 14. Note that Algorithm 1 allows multiple read-only transactions to be executed at the same time in any order (line 13) because they do not conflict with one another. Lines 5 through 7 resolve *LWS* conflicts, as proven below.

**Theorem 3.** *Algorithm 1 produces LWS histories.*

**Proof.** As per Definition 2, we need to show that all committed read-only transactions $T_{Qk}$ have the property that any window movements $T_j$ that were executed at the same time as $T_{Qk}$ are serialized before $T_{Qk}$. First, note that the only time that a new *LWS* violation may possibly appear is after a window update $T_j$ commits while one or more $T_{Qk}$ transactions are still running. Furthermore, a *LWS* conflict appears only if any $T_j$ has updated a sub-window (an older copy of) which has already been read by any of the currently running $T_{Qk}$ transactions, in which case $T_j$ would be serialized before $T_{Qk}$. This occurs if $B_{Qk}[j \bmod n]$ is set for any currently running $T_{Qk}$. In this case, Algorithm 1 aborts $T_{Qk}$ (line 7), ensuring that all $T_{Qk}$ committed in line 17 satisfy Definition 2. □

Algorithm 1 supports read-only transactions with different priorities, such as snapshot queries or "important" long-running queries (as in $Q_1$ from Fig. 1 (d)). To do this, we assume that the query manager embeds a priority $p$ within each $T_{Qk}$ and we change line 13 in Algorithm 1 to read: "let $T_{Ql}$ be the transaction in $L$ with the highest value of $p$". Consequently, if a low-priority $T_{Qk}$ is currently being

## Algorithm 1. DSMS Transaction Scheduler

```
1   let L be the list of currently running T_Qk transactions
2   loop
3       if new transaction T_j arrives for scheduling then
4           execute w_j[j mod n], c_j
5           for each T_Qk in L
6               if B_Qk[j mod n] = true then
7                   execute a_Qk (abort T_Qk)
8       elseif new transaction T_Qk arrives for scheduling then
9           add T_Qk to L
10          for i = 0 to n − 1
11              set B_Qk[i] = false
12      if L is not empty then
13          choose any T_Ql from L
14          execute next operation of T_Ql, call it r_Ql[m]
15          set B_Ql[m] = true
16          if no more read operations left in T_Ql then
17              execute c_Ql
18              remove T_Ql and B_Ql from L
```

executed, then a higher-priority $T_{Qm}$ transaction has the effect of suspending $T_{Qk}$. This extension does not impact the correctness of Algorithm 1 as it does not introduce any new *LWS* conflicts.

### 4.2 Optimal Ordering of Read Operations

Given that Algorithm 1 may abort read-only transactions in order to guarantee *LWS*, we want to minimize the required number of aborts. The idea is to shuffle the read operations within $T_{Qk}$ given the following insight. Since aborts occur when a sub-window is being updated but an older version of it has already been read by a concurrent $T_{Qk}$ transaction, we should execute $T_{Qk}$ by first reading the sub-window which is scheduled to be updated the farthest out into the future. More precisely, we define the *time-to-update (TTU)* of a sub-window as the number of window-movement transactions $T_j$ that must be applied until this sub-window is updated. When the scheduler chooses a read-only transaction $T_{Qk}$ to process, it always executes the remaining read operation of $T_{Qk}$ whose sub-window has the highest *TTU* value at the given time. The revised scheduler is shown below as Algorithm 2 (again, adding support for multiple priority levels can be done by changing line 17 to process the highest-priority transaction). There are two main changes. First, lines 6 through 8 update the *TTU* values of each sub-window after every window movement. The newly updated sub-window receives a value of $n$ (it will take $n$ write-only transaction until this sub-window is updated again), whereas the *TTU* values of the remaining sub-windows are decremented. Furthermore, line 18 selects $m$ to be the index of the sub-window which has the highest *TTU* value and has not been read by $T_{Ql}$.

**Algorithm 2.** DSMS Transaction Scheduler with TTU

```
1   let L be the list of currently running T_{Qk} transactions
2   let TTU[n] be an array of sub-window TTU values
3   loop
4       if new transaction T_j arrives for scheduling then
5           execute w_j[j mod n], c_j
6           for i = 0 to n − 1
7               set TTU[i] = TTU[i] − 1
8           set TTU[j mod n] = n
9           for each T_{Qk} in L
10              if B_{Qk}[j mod n] = true then
11                  execute a_{Qk} (abort T_{Qk})
12      elseif new transaction T_{Qk} arrives for scheduling then
13          add T_{Qk} to L
14          for i = 0 to n − 1
15              set B_{Qk}[i] = false
16      if L is not empty then
17          choose any T_{Ql} from L
18          let m = argmax_{B_{Ql}[i]=false} TTU[i]
19          execute r_{Ql}[m]
20          set B_{Ql}[m] = true
21          if no more read operations left in T_{Ql} then
22              execute c_{Ql}
23              remove T_{Ql} and B_{Ql} from L
```

The idea in Algorithm 2 is similar to the Longest Forward Distance (LFD) cache replacement algorithm [14], which always evicts the page whose next access is latest. LFD is optimal in the off-line case in terms of the number of page faults, given that the system knows the entire page request sequence and that all page faults have the same cost.

**Theorem 4.** Algorithm 2 is optimal for ensuring LWS in the sense that it performs the fewest possible aborts for any history $H$.

**Proof.** Let $A$ be the scheduler in Algorithm 2 and let $S$ be any other transaction scheduler that serializes transactions in the same way as $A$, but only differs in the ordering of read operations inside one or more read-only transactions. That is, $S$ corresponds to Algorithm 1 with some arbitrary implementation of the meaning of "next operation" in line 14. We need to prove that $S$ performs no fewer aborts than $A$ for any history $H$. Let $H_i$ be the prefix of $H$ containing the first $i$ read operations (interleaved with zero or more write operations, and zero or more commit or abort operations). The proof proceeds by inductively transforming the sequence of read operations produced by $S$ into that produced by $A$, one read operation at a time. To accomplish this, we let $S_0 = S$ and define a transaction scheduler $S_{i+1}$ that, given $S_i$, has the following two properties.

1. Both $S_i$ and $S_{i+1}$ order all the read operations in $H_i$ in the same way as $A$.
2. $S_{i+1}$ orders all the read operations in $H_{i+1}$ in the same way as $A$ and performs no more aborts than $S_i$ in $H_{i+1}$.

Let $r_k[y]$ be the $(i+1)$st read operation executed by $S_i$ and $r_k[z]$ be the $(i+1)$st read operation executed by $S_{i+1}$. Due to our assumption that $A$ and $S$ only differ in the ordering of read operations inside read-only transactions, the $(i+1)$st read operations done by $S_i$ and $S_{i+1}$ both belong to the same transaction, call it $T_{Qk}$. Thus, sub-window $z \pmod{n}$ has the highest $TTU$ value at this time. Now, if $z = y$ then $S_{i+1} = S_i$ and we are done (property 2 holds). Otherwise, $S_{i+1}$ and $S_i$ differ in the $(i+1)$st read operation. First, suppose that $T_{Qk}$ is not interrupted by any write-only transactions before the next read operation. Then, $T_{Qk}$ is not aborted by $S_i$ or by $S_{i+1}$ in $H_{i+1}$ and we are done (property 2 holds). Next, suppose that $T_{Qk}$ is interrupted by at least one write-only transaction before the next read operation. The remainder of the proof is broken into the following three cases, which collectively prove property 2.

In the first case, suppose that the set of interrupting transactions contains $T_y$, but not $T_z$. Given that sub-window $z \pmod{n}$ has the highest $TTU$ value at this time, and that write-only transactions are generated and serially executed in increasing order of their subscripts, the most recent write-only transaction can have a subscript no higher than $z - 1$. Then, $S_i$ aborts $T_{Qk}$ in $H_{i+1}$. This is because $T_{Qk}$ has already read an old version of sub-window $y \pmod{n}$ and therefore $T_y$ would have been serialized after $T_{Qk}$. However, $S_{i+1}$ does not abort $T_{Qk}$ in $H_{i+1}$. To see this, observe that $T_{Qk}$ could not have possibly read any of the sub-windows that have just been updated. This is due to the fact that those sub-windows must have lower $TTU$ values than sub-window $z \pmod{n}$ and must necessarily be scheduled after sub-window $z \pmod{n}$ by $S_{i+1}$.

In the second case, suppose that the set of interrupting transactions does not contain $T_y$ or $T_z$. By the same reasoning, the most recent write-only transaction can have a subscript no higher than $y - 1$. Again, $S_{i+1}$ does not abort $T_{Qk}$ in $H_{i+1}$ because $T_{Qk}$ could not have possibly read any of the sub-windows updated by or before $T_{y-1}$ (they all have lower $TTU$ values than sub-window $z \pmod{n}$). In terms of satisfying property 2, it does not matter what $S_i$ does in this case.

Finally, in the third case, suppose that the set of interrupting transactions contains both $T_y$ and $T_z$. Then, both $S_i$ and $S_{i+1}$ abort $T_{Qk}$ in $H_{i+1}$ because both schedulers allow $T_{Qk}$ to read a sub-window that has now been updated. □

## 5 Experiments

### 5.1 Implementation Details and Experimental Procedure

We implemented the following transaction schedulers: Algorithm 2 (abbreviated *TTU*), Algorithm 1 (which does not re-order the read operations within transactions, abbreviated *LWS*), a scheduler similar to Algorithm 2 that only enforces window-serializability (abbreviated *WS*), and a scheduler that executes transactions serially (as in current DSMSs, abbreviated *Serial*). The implementation was done in Java 1.4.2, while the experiments were performed on a Pentium-IV PC with a 3 GHz CPU and 1 Gb of RAM, running Linux. The input stream is a sequence of simulated IP packet headers with randomly generated values, e.g., the source and destination addresses have one of one thousand random values, whereas the packet length is a random integer between one and 100. The average data rate is one packet per millisecond, but the specific rate over a particular sub-window is allowed to deviate from the average rate by a factor of up to ten.

We use a long-running query workload representative of an on-line network traffic analysis application (see, e.g., [15, 16]), consisting of top-$k$ queries over the source or destination IP addresses, and percentiles over the total bandwidth consumed by (or directed to) distinct IP addresses. The window sizes referenced by queries are generated randomly between one and $n$, where $n$ is the total number of sub-windows. Similar aggregates over different window sizes are evaluated together. For simplicity of implementation, long-running queries are executed by scanning the window and building a hash table on the required attribute. Snapshot queries are chosen from a set of simple aggregates over a random subset of the source and destination IP addresses. Each query references the same time-based window, which is stored in main memory.

After initializing the sliding window using a randomly generated input stream, we test each of the four transaction schedulers over an identical query workload. The tests proceed for a time equal to the window length. We then repeat each test five times using different input streams and calculate the average of each measurement being reported. The parameters being varied in (and across) the experiments are the query workload, the window size (controlled via the number of sub-windows), and the length of each sub-window (which controls the frequency of window movements). The following performance metrics are used to evaluate the four transaction schedulers (as illustrated on a time line in Fig. 6).

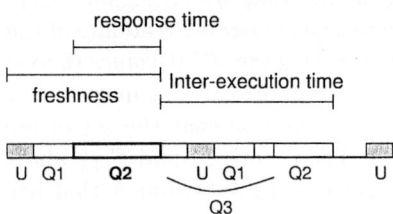

**Fig. 6.** Freshness, response time, and inter-execution time of query $Q_2$

- *Query freshness* is the difference between the time that a query reports an answer and the time of the last window update reflected in the answer.
- *Response time* is the difference between the query execution start time and end time. This metric is particularly important for snapshot queries, which are usually time-sensitive.
- *Inter-execution time* of a long-running query is the length of the interval between its re-executions. A DSMS is expected to tolerate slightly longer

inter-execution times if the returned answers are more up-to-date. The motivation for this is that even if we return an older answer earlier, we would have to re-execute the query soon in order to produce an answer that reflects the new state of the window.

## 5.2 Experiments with Long-Running Queries

We begin by executing *Serial*, *WS*, *LWS*, and *TTU* on a workload consisting of long-running queries and interleaved window movements. We test two sub-window sizes: $t = 1$ sec. and $t = 5$ sec., with the number of sub-windows varied from ten to 100. The number of queries is set to 40 for $t = 1$ sec. and 100 for $t = 5$ sec. For now, we assume that snapshot queries are not posed. We measure the average freshness, inter-execution time, and throughput.

The average query freshness is shown in Fig. 7 (the lower the value, the better). *TTU* and *LWS* clearly outperform *WS* and *Serial* because the first two guarantee latest-window-serializable schedules, where queries have access to an up-to-date state of the window. Freshness deteriorates for all four schedulers as the sub-window size grows to $t = 5$ sec. and window movements become less frequent. Moreover, increasing the number of sub-windows (or equivalently, increasing the window length) generally has an adverse effect on freshness because the query execution times increase. Note that *Serial* performs slightly better than *WS* because *WS* adds to the query execution time by performing concurrent window movements, yet the answer does not reflect any of the updates. Overall, *TTU* provides the best query freshness in all tested scenarios.

The average query inter-execution times are illustrated in Fig. 8. Each cluster of eight bars corresponds, in order, to *Serial*, *WS*, *LWS*, and *TTU* for $t = 1$ sec., followed by *Serial*, *WS*, *LWS*, and *TTU* for $t = 5$ sec. Serial has the best (lowest) inter-execution times because it does not incur the overhead of serialization graph testing, therefore its total query execution time is slightly lower. Notably, *LWS* (corresponding to the third and seventh bars in each cluster) performs the worst because it aborts a significant percentage of transactions (see [10] for full details).

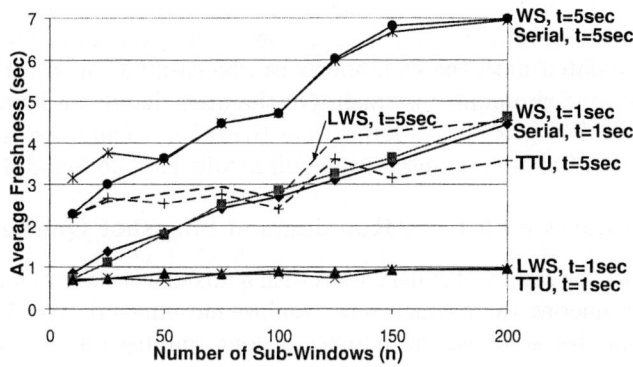

**Fig. 7.** Comparison of query freshness for Serial, WS, LWS, and TTU

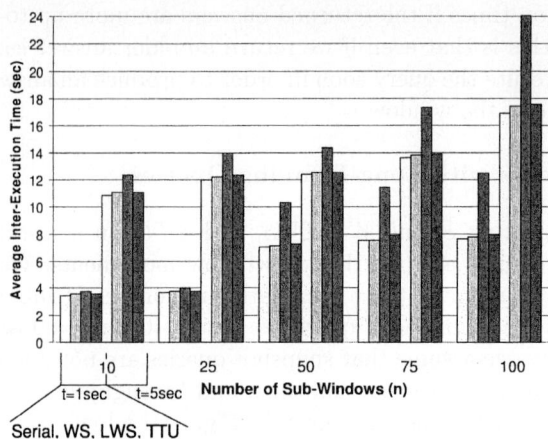

**Fig. 8.** Comparison of query inter-execution times for Serial, WS, LWS, and TTU

For instance, aborting every second re-execution of a long-running query means that its inter-execution time doubles. In general, increasing the sub-window size to $t = 5$ sec. (and hence, increasing the total window size) leads to longer inter-execution times for all four schedulers as the queries take longer to process. Similarly, increasing the number of sub-windows increases the query evaluation times and therefore negatively affects the inter-execution times. Overall, *Serial* yields the best query inter-execution times, with *WS* and *TTU* following closely behind, whereas *LWS* performs badly due to aborted transactions.

We briefly mention that throughput measurements revealed a very small penalty incurred by *TTU* versus *Serial*—typically below two percent and at most four percent. This is because the serialization graph testing done by *TTU* consists of simple bit operations after each window movement and causes negligible overhead. Furthermore, *TTU* did not abort any transactions in any of the tests. This is because during normal execution, a long-running query does not incur more than one concurrent window update, unless suspended for a long time in order to run a heavy workload of snapshot queries. Since Algorithm 2 ensures that read-only transactions postpone reading the sub-window that is about to be updated until the end, aborts can be easily avoided if the number of concurrent window updates is small. On the other hand, we found that the throughput of *LWS* was always lower than the other techniques because of a high proportion of aborted transactions. Full details may be found in [10].

### 5.3 Experiments with Long-Running and Snapshot Queries

Next, we report the results of experiments with a mixed workload of long-running and snapshot queries (and concurrent window movements). We fix the sub-window size at five seconds, the number of long-running queries at 100, and the number of snapshot queries per sub-window length at five. Snapshot queries are scheduled at random times with an average time between requests set to one

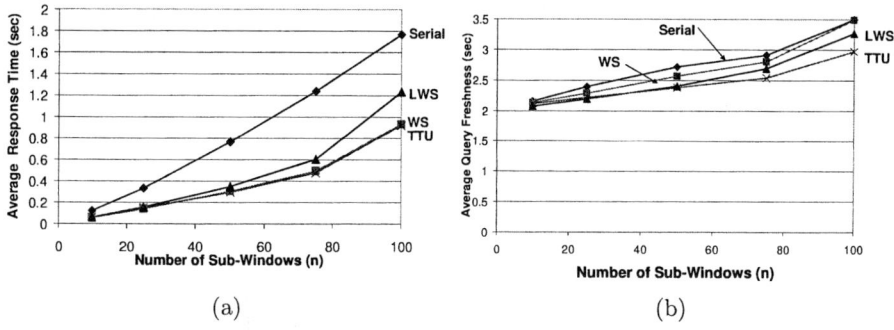

**Fig. 9.** Comparison of snapshot query response time (a) and freshness (b) for Serial, WS, LWS, and TTU

second. We report the average snapshot query response time, and we separately measure the average freshness of snapshot and long-running queries.

Average snapshot query response times are illustrated in Fig. 9 (a). *TTU* and *WS* perform best and yield nearly identical response times. The response times of *LWS* are noticeably longer because it is forced to abort and restart some queries. *Serial* exhibits the worst results because it is unable to suspend a long-running query and execute a snapshot query immediately; in general, *Serial* is inappropriate for any situation involving prioritized scheduling. As the number of sub-windows increases, the response time achieved by each of the four schedulers worsens because it is now more costly to execute each query.

Figure 9 (b) plots the average snapshot query freshness. *TTU* outperforms the other schedulers because it guarantees latest-window serializability and did not abort any read transactions. The performance of *LWS* is somewhat worse because some of the transactions corresponding to snapshot queries are aborted and restarted at a later time. *WS* and *Serial* do not guarantee latest-window serializability and therefore exhibit the worst performance. Overall, *TTU* yields the best results in terms of snapshot query freshness and is tied for best in terms of the response time.

Finally, we separately examine the average freshness of long-running queries in order to verify that the performance edge of *TTU* in the context of snapshot query freshness does not come at a cost of poor long-running query freshness. We found that *TTU* maintains its superiority in producing the most up-to-date results of long-running queries (see [10] for full details).

## 6 Comparison with Related Work

The concurrency control mechanisms presented in this paper are compatible with any DSMS that employs periodic updates of sliding windows and query results, e.g., [2-8]. Our techniques are also applicable to a system such as PSoup [17], where mobile users connect to a DSMS intermittently and retrieve the latest results of sliding window queries. In our context, these asynchronous requests may be modeled as snapshot queries posed at various times. Given that mobile users may have low connectivity with the system (e.g., via a wireless channel), it is particularly important to guarantee low response times and up-to-date query answers. Our transaction scheduler fulfills both of these requirements.

As discussed in Sect. 2, we assumed an evaluation model in which queries are re-executed by scanning one or more windows or summaries, or a materialized sub-result. Similar techniques were used in [1,3,5]. Our procedure for incremental maintenance of materialized join results—using a batch of newly arrived tuples from one window to probe the other window and generate new results—is similar to the lazy multi-way join from [18]. In general, our query model of a final aggregation function applied on a window or materialized sub-result is similar to NiagaraCQ [2], but less expressive than, e.g., Aurora [6] and STREAM [7]. However, we believe that our model is sufficiently expressive for many applications that require long-running queries for monitoring purposes, while at the same time being simple enough to allow straightforward solutions of concurrency control issues.

Our transaction model resembles multi-level concurrency control and multi-granularity locking as it considers a sub-window, rather than an entire window, to be an atomic data object. The novelty of our solution is that the order in which read operations are performed is chosen in such a way as to minimize the number of aborted transactions.

Our transaction scheduler employed serialization graph testing. Other scheduling techniques include two-phase locking and timestamping [13]. However, two-phase locking may not be appropriate in our context because it is not clear how to force a particular serialization order using locks. Moreover, the possible problem with using timestamping for DSMS concurrency control is the difficulty of ensuring latest-window serializability. Suppose that each transaction receives a timestamp when it is passed to the transaction scheduler and that serialization order is determined by timestamps. In this case, any concurrent window update transaction is assigned a higher timestamp than a read-only transaction and is therefore serialized before the read-only transaction. Hence, Algorithm 2 would be forced to abort every read-only transaction that is interrupted by a window movement. A similar issue appears if we want to adapt multi-versioning concurrency control techniques to enforce latest-window serializability, among them snapshot isolation and commit-order preserving serializability [19].

## 7 Conclusions and Future Work

This paper presented DSMS concurrency control mechanisms that allow a window to slide forward while it, or an associated summary structure, is being scanned by a query. Our solution is based upon a model that views DSMS data access as a mix of concurrent read-only and write-only transactions. We proved that conflict serializability is insufficiently strong to guarantee correct and up-to-date query results, and defined more appropriate isolation levels. We also implemented a transaction scheduler for enforcing the new isolation levels that is provably optimal in reducing the number of aborted transactions. Our scheduler was experimentally shown to improve query freshness and response times while maintaining high transaction throughput.

We are interested in the following two directions for future work. First, we want to extend our query execution model and investigate concurrency control issues in query plans containing an arbitrary number of pipelined window operators. One issue in this context is synchronization among the levels in the pipeline, e.g., updates to the individual windows may take some time as they are propagated up the pipeline to the final query operator. Another problem appears when the same sub-query occurs more than once within a query, in which case our current assumption of queries scanning each window once may not hold (unless the sub-query can be flattened). Second, we want to extend our treatment of DSMS concurrency control to include the semantics of data loss and crash recovery, e.g., loss of data for a particular time interval, which might make it impossible for queries to read a full window.

# References

1. Arasu, A., Widom, J.: Resource sharing in continuous sliding-window aggregates. In: Proc. VLDB Conference (2004) 336–347
2. Chen, J., DeWitt, D., Tian, F., Wang, Y.: NiagaraCQ: A scalable continuous query system for Internet databases. In: Proc. SIGMOD Conference (2000) 379–390
3. Golab, L., Garg, S., Özsu, M.T.: On indexing sliding windows over on-line data streams. In: Proc. EDBT Conference (2004) 712–729
4. Shivakumar, N., García-Molina, H.: Wave-indices: indexing evolving databases. In: Proc. SIGMOD Conference (1997) 381–392
5. Zhu, Y., Shasha, D.: StatStream: Statistical monitoring of thousands of data streams in real time. In: Proc. VLDB Conference (2002) 358–369
6. Abadi, D., et al.: Aurora: A new model and architecture for data stream management. VLDB Journal **12** (2003) 120–139
7. Arasu, A., Babu, S., Widom, J.: The CQL continuous query language: Semantic foundations and query execution. VLDB Journal **14** (2005) to appear
8. Chandrasekaran, S., et al.: TelegraphCQ: Continuous dataflow processing for an uncertain world. In: Proc. CIDR Conference (2003) 269–280
9. Golab, L., Özsu, M.T.: Update-pattern aware modeling and processing of continuous queries. In: Proc. SIGMOD Conference (2005) 658–669
10. Golab, L., Bijay, K.G., Özsu, M.T.: On concurrency control in sliding window queries over data streams. University of Waterloo Technical Report CS-2005-28. Available at http://www.cs.uwaterloo.ca/research/tr/cs-2005-28.pdf.
11. Cormode, G., Muthukrishnan, S.: An improved data stream summary: The count-min sketch and its applications. In: Proc. Latin American Theoretical Informatics Conference (LATIN) (2004) 29–38
12. Flajolet, P., Martin, G.N.: Probabilistic counting. In: Proc. FOCS Conference. (1983) 76–82
13. Bernstein, P., Hadzilacos, V., Goodman, N.: Concurrency Control and Recovery in Database Systems. Addison-Wesley (1987)
14. Belady, L.: A study of replacement algorithms for virtual storage computers. IBM Syst. J. **5** (1966) 78–101

15. Cormode, G., et al.: Holistic UDAFs at streaming speeds. In: Proc. SIGMOD Conference (2004) 35–46
16. Cranor, C., Johnson, T., Spatscheck, O., Shkapenyuk, V.: Gigascope: High performance network monitoring with an SQL interface. In: Proc. SIGMOD Conference (2003) 647–651
17. Chandrasekaran, S., Franklin, M.: PSoup: a system for streaming queries over streaming data. VLDB Journal **12** (2003) 140–156
18. Golab, L., Özsu, M.T.: Processing sliding window multi-joins in continuous queries over data streams. In: Proc. VLDB Conference (2003) 500–511
19. Weikum, G., Vossen, G.: Transactional Information Systems. Theory, Algorithms, and the Practice of Concurrency Control and Recovery. Morgan Kauffman (2002)

# Towards Expressive Publish/Subscribe Systems

Alan Demers, Johannes Gehrke, Mingsheng Hong,
Mirek Riedewald, and Walker White

Cornell University, Department of Computer Science
{ademers, johannes, mshong, mirek, wmwhite}@cs.cornell.edu

**Abstract.** Traditional content based publish/subscribe (pub/sub) systems allow users to express stateless subscriptions evaluated on individual events. However, many applications such as monitoring RSS streams, stock tickers, or management of RFID data streams require the ability to handle *stateful* subscriptions. In this paper, we introduce Cayuga, a stateful pub/sub system based on non-deterministic finite state automata (NFA). Cayuga allows users to express subscriptions that span multiple events, and it supports powerful language features such as parameterization and aggregation, which significantly extend the expressive power of standard pub/sub systems. Based on a set of formally defined language operators, the subscription language of Cayuga provides non-ambiguous subscription semantics as well as unique opportunities for optimizations. We experimentally demonstrate that common optimization techniques used in NFA-based systems such as state merging have only limited effectiveness, and we propose novel efficient indexing methods to speed up subscription processing. In a thorough experimental evaluation we show the efficacy of our approach.

## 1 Introduction

Publish/Subscribe is a popular paradigm for users to express their interests ("subscriptions") in certain kinds of events ("publications"). Traditional publish/subscribe (pub/sub) systems such as topic-based and content-based pub/sub systems allow users to express stateless subscriptions that are evaluated over each event that arrives at the system; and there has been much work on efficient implementations [14]. However, many applications require the ability to handle *stateful* subscriptions that involve more than a single event, and users want to be notified with customized witness events as soon as one of their stateful subscriptions is satisfied. Let us give two example applications that motivate the types of stateful subscriptions that a *stateful* pub/sub system needs to handle.

**Example 1: Stock Ticker Event Monitoring.** Consider a system that permits financial analysts to compose subscriptions over a stream of stock ticks [1]. Some sample subscriptions are shown in Table 1. Subscription S1 is a traditional pub/sub subscription, and it can be evaluated on each incoming event individually. However, an important capability of event processing systems is to detect specific *sequences* of events, as shown in the next four subscriptions. To detect sequences, the system has to maintain *state* about events that have previously entered the system. For example, to process Subscription S2, the system has to "remember" whether an event with a stock price of IBM

**Table 1.** Sample Subscriptions

| Subscription | Description |
|---|---|
| S1 | Notify me when the price of IBM is above $100. |
| S2 | Notify me when the price of IBM is above $100, and the *first* MSFT price afterwards is below $25. |
| S3 | Notify me when there is a sale of some stock at some price (say $p$), and the next transaction is a sale of the same stock at a price above $1.05 \cdot p$. |
| S4 | Notify me when the price of any stock increases monotonically for $\geq 30$ minutes. |
| S5 | Notify me when the next IBM stock is above its 52-week average. |
| S6 | Once military.blog.com posts an article on US troop morale, send me the first post referencing (i.e., containing a link to) this article from the blogs to which I subscribe. |
| S7 | Send postings from all blogs to which I subscribe, in which the first posting is a reference to a sensitive site XYZ, and each later posting is a reference to the previous. |

above $100 has happened since the most recent MSFT event; only then are we interested in learning about future MSFT prices. Subscriptions S3 and S4 illustrate another important component: We need to support parameterized subscriptions, i.e., subscriptions that contain parameters that are bound at run-time to values seen in events. As an example, in Subscription S3, we are looking for *some* stock that exhibits a 5% jump in price; instead of having to register a subscription for each possible stock symbol, we register a single subscription with a *parameter* that is set at run time. Subscription S4 requires support for *aggregation*, and Subscription S5 is an example that combines both parameterization and aggregation.

**Example 2: RSS Feed Monitoring.** Our second motivating application is online RSS Feed Message Brokering. RSS feeds have become increasingly important for online exchange of news and opinions. With a stateful pub/sub system, users can monitor RSS Feeds and register complex subscriptions that notify the users as soon as their requested RSS message sequences have occured. Subscriptions S6 and S7 in Figure 1 are examples in this domain.

To reiterate: Traditional pub/sub systems scale to millions of registered subscriptions and very high event rates, but have limited expressive power. In these systems, users can only submit subscriptions that are predicates to be evaluated on single events. Any operation across multiple events must be handled externally. In our proposed stateful pub/sub system, however, subscriptions can span multiple events, involving parameterization and aggregation, while maintaining scalability in the number of subscriptions and event rate. In comparison, full-fledged Data Stream Management Systems (DSMS) [2, 25, 11] have powerful query languages that allow them to express much more powerful subscriptions than stateful pub/sub systems; however, this limits their scalability with the number of subscriptions, and existing DSMSs only do limited query optimization. Figure 1 illustrates these tradeoffs.

Another area very closely related to stateful pub/sub is work on *event systems*. Event systems can be programmed in languages (called *event algebras*) that can compose complex events from either basic or complex events arriving online. However, we have observed an unfortunate dichotomy between theoretical and systems-oriented approaches in this area. Theoretical approaches, based on formal languages and well-defined semantics, generally lack efficient, scalable implementations. Systems approaches usually lack a precise formal specification, limiting the opportunities for query optimization and query rewrites. Indeed, previous work has shown that the lack of clean operator semantics can lead to unexpected and undesirable behavior of complex algebra expressions [15, 31]. Our approach was informed by this dichotomy, and we have taken great care to define a language that can express very powerful subscriptions, has a precise formal semantics, and can be implemented efficiently.

**Our Contributions.** In this paper, we propose Cayuga, a stateful publish/subscribe system based on a nondeterministic finite state automata (NFA) model. We start by introducing the Cayuga event algebra, which can express all example subscriptions shown in Table 1, and we illustrate how algebra expressions map to linear finite sate automata with self-loops and buffers (Section 2). To the best of our knowledge, this is the first work that combines a formal event language definition with a methodology to efficiently implement the language. We then overview the implementation of our system which leverages techniques from traditional pub/sub systems as well as novel Multi-Query Optimization (MQO) techniques to achieve scalability (Section 3). In a thorough experimental study, we evaluate the scalability of our system both with the number of subscriptions and their complexity, we evaluate the efficacy of our MQO techniques, and we show the performance of our system with real data from our two example application domains (Section 4). We discuss related work in Section 5, and conclude in Section 6.

In closing this introduction, we would like to emphasize two important aspects of our approach. First, instead of adding features to a pub/sub system in an ad-hoc fashion, our system is based on formal language operators and therefore provides unambiguous query semantics that are necessary for query optimization. Second, compared to similar approaches that use NFAs for scalability such as YFilter [13], Cayuga supports novel powerful language features such as parameterization and aggregation. One interesting result from our experimental study is that common optimization techniques used in NFA-based systems, such as state merging, have only limited effectiveness for the workloads that we consider. On the other hand, some of our novel MQO techniques can potentially be applied to other NFA-based systems.

## 2 Cayuga Algebra and Automaton

### 2.1 Data Model

Our event algebra consists of a data model for event streams plus operators for producing new events from existing events. An event stream, denoted as $S$ or $S_i$, is a (possibly infinite) set of event tuples $\langle \bar{a}; t_0, t_1 \rangle$. As in the relational model, $\bar{a} = (a_1, \ldots, a_n)$ are data values with corresponding attributes (symbolic names). The $t_i$'s are temporal values representing the start ($t_0$) and end timestamps ($t_1$) of the event. For example, in the stock monitoring application, assume the stream of stock sales published by the data source has fields (name, price, vol; timestamp). An event from that stream then could be the tuple $\langle \text{IBM}, 90, 15000; 9{:}10, 9{:}10 \rangle$. The timestamps are identical, because each sale is an instantaneous event. We assume each event stream has a fixed

Table 2. Algebraic Expressions

| Algebraic Expressions |
|---|
| S1: $\sigma_\theta(S_1)$, where $\theta = S_1.\text{name} = \text{IBM} \wedge S_1.\text{price} > 100$ |
| S2: $\sigma_{\theta_2}(\sigma_\theta(S_1);_{\theta_1} S_2)$, where $\theta$ same as in Subscription S1, $\theta_1 = S_2.\text{name} = \text{MSFT}, \theta_2 = S_2.\text{price} < 25$ |
| S3: $\sigma_{\theta_2}(S_1;_{\theta_1} S_2)$, where $\theta_1 = S_2.\text{name} = S_1.\text{name}, \theta_2 = S_2.\text{price} > 1.05 * S_1.\text{price}$ |
| S4: $\sigma_{\theta_3}(\mu_{\sigma_{\theta_2},\theta_1}(S_1,S_2))$, where<br>$\theta_1 = S_2.\text{name} = S_1.\text{name}, \theta_2 = S_2.\text{price} \mathrel{>}= S_2.\text{price.last}, \theta_3 = \text{DUR} \mathrel{>}= 30min$ |
| S5: $\sigma_{\theta_2}(\mathcal{E};_{\theta_1} S_3)$, where $\mathcal{E} = \sigma_{\text{DUR}=52\text{ weeks}}(\mu_{\alpha_{g_2},\text{TRUE}}(\alpha_{g_1} \circ \sigma_\theta(S_1),\sigma_\theta(S_2)))$,<br>$\theta = \text{name} = \text{IBM}, \theta_1 = S_3.\text{name} = \text{IBM}, \theta_2 = S_3.\text{price} > \text{AVG}$ |
| S6: $\sigma_{\theta_1}(S_1);_{\theta_2} \sigma_{\theta_3}(S_2))$, where<br>$\theta_1 = S_1.\text{website} = \text{'military.blog.com'} \wedge S_1.\text{category} = \text{'US troop morale'}$,<br>$\theta_2 = contains(S_2.\text{description}, S_1.\text{link}), \theta_3 = (S_2.\text{website} = site_1 \vee \ldots S_2.\text{website} = site_n)$ |
| S7: $\mu_{\text{ID},\theta_1}(\sigma_{\theta_3 \wedge \theta_2}(S_1),\sigma_{\theta_3}(S_2))$, where $\theta_1 = contains(S_2.\text{description}, S_2.\text{link.last})$,<br>$\theta_2 = contains(S_1.\text{description},\text{'}XYZ\text{'}), \theta_3$ same as in Subscription S6 |

schema, and events arrive in temporal order. That is, event $e_1$ is processed before $e_2$ iff $e_1.t_1 \leq e_2.t_1$. However, a stream may contain events with non-zero duration, overlapping events and simultaneous events (events with identical time stamp values). Our operator definitions depend on the timestamp values, so we do not allow users to query or modify them directly. However, we do allow constraints on the *duration* of an event, defined as $t_1 - t_0 + 1$ (we treat time as discrete, so the duration of an event is the number of clock ticks it spans). We store starting as well as ending timestamps and use interval-based semantics to avoid well-known problems involving concatenation of complex events [15].

### 2.2 Operators

Our algebra has four unary and three binary operators. Due to space constraints, we give here only a brief description of them here; a formal definition and more examples can be found in our technical report [12].

The first three unary operators, the **projection** operator $\pi_X$, the **selection** operator $\sigma_\theta$, and the **renaming** operator $\rho_f$ are well known from relational algebra. Projection and renaming can only affect data values; temporal values are always preserved. As the renaming operator only affects the schema of a stream and not its contents, we will often ignore this operator for ease of exposition. Instead, we will denote attributes of an event using the input stream and a dot notation, making renaming implicit. For example, the name attribute of events from stream $S_1$ will be referred to as $S_1.\text{name}$. A selection formula is any boolean combination of atomic predicates of the form $\tau_1$ relop $\tau_2$, where the $\tau_i$ are arithmetic combinations of attributes and constants, and relop can be one of $=, \leq, <, \geq, >$, or string matching. We also allow predicates of the form DUR relop $c$ where the special attribute DUR denotes event duration and $c$ is a constant. The unary operators above enable filtering of single events and attributes, equivalent to a classical pub/sub system. Subscription S1 is an example of such a stateless subscription.

The added expressive power of our algebra lies in the binary operators, which support subscriptions over multiple events. All of these operators are motivated by a corresponding operator in regular expressions. The first binary operator is the standard

**union** operator $\cup$, where $S_1 \cup S_2$ is defined as $\{\,e \mid e \in S_1 \text{ or } e \in S_2\,\}$. Our second operator is the **conditional sequence** operator $S_1 ;_\theta S_2$. For streams $S_1$ and $S_2$, and selection formula $\theta$ (a predicate), $S_1 ;_\theta S_2$ computes sequences of two consecutive and non-overlapping events, filtering out those events from $S_2$ that do not satisfy $\theta$. Adding this feature is essential for parameterization, because $\theta$ can refer to attributes of both $S_1$ and $S_2$. This enables us to express "group-by" operations, e.g., to group stock quotes by name via $S_1 ;_\theta S_2$, with $\theta$ being $S_1.\text{name} = S_2.\text{name}$. $S_1 ;_\theta S_2$ essentially works as a join, combining each event in $S_1$ with the event immediately after it in $S_2$. However, $\theta$ works as a filter, removing uninteresting intervening events. Subscriptions S2 and S3 are examples of such subscriptions.

Our third binary operator is the **iteration** operator $\mu_{\mathfrak{F},\theta}(S_1, S_2)$, motivated by the Kleene-+ operator. Informally, we can think of $\mu_{\mathfrak{F},\theta}(S_1, S_2)$ as a repeated application of conditional sequencing: $(S_1 ;_\theta S_2) \cup (S_1 ;_\theta S_2 ;_\theta S_2) \cup \cdots$. Each clause separated by the $\cup$ operator corresponds to an iteration of processing an event from $S_2$ which satisfies $\theta$. The additional parameter $\mathfrak{F}$, a composition of selection, projection and renaming operators, enables us to modify the result of each iteration. Thus $\mu$ acts as a fixed point operator, applying the operator $;_\theta$ on each incoming event repeatedly until it produces an empty result. To avoid unbounded storage, at each interation, it will only remember the attribute values from stream $S_1$ and the values from the most recent iteration of $S_2$. For any attribute $\text{ATT}_i$ in $S_2$, we refer to the value from the most recent iteration via $\text{ATT}_i.\texttt{last}$. Initially, this value is equivalent to the corresponding attribute in $S_1$, but it will be overwritten by each iteration.

At first it might seem surprising that our algebra needs $\mu_{\mathfrak{F},\theta}(S_1, S_2)$ to express the equivalent of something as simple as $(S_2)^+$ in regular languages. The reason, like for the $;_\theta$ operator, is that we want to support parameterization efficiently. In fact, $\theta$ serves the same purpose as in $;_\theta$: during each iteration it filters irrelevant events from $S_2$ when the *next* event from $S_2$ is selected. In Subscription S5, it was used to make sure that no quotes for other companies would be selected for a sequence of IBM prices, and vice versa. Similarly, $\mathfrak{F}$ removes irrelevant events during each iteration, like non-increasing sequences in the example. Another interesting feature is that $\mu$ is a binary operator, while Kleene-+ is unary. One reason, as can be seen in the definition of $\mu$, is that we need a way to initialize our attributes $\text{ATT}_i.\texttt{last}$. The other reason is that, by adding $S_1$ to $\mu$, both $\mathfrak{F}$ and $\theta$ can refer to $S_1$'s attributes. This enables us to support powerful parameterized subscriptions such as S4.

Aggregates fit naturally into our algebra, where aggregation occurs over a sequence of events. Our **aggregate** operator is $\alpha_g$, where $g$ is a function used to introduce a new attribute to the output. Together with $\mu$, we get a natural aggregate of the form $\alpha_{g_3}\big(\mu_{\alpha_{g_2} \circ \mathcal{F},\theta}(\alpha_{g_1}(\mathcal{E}_1), \mathcal{E}_2)\big)$. In this expression, $\alpha_{g_1}$ functions as an initializer, $\alpha_{g_2}$ is an accumulator, and $\alpha_{g_3}$ is a finalizer. For example, suppose we want the average of IBM stock over the past 52 weeks, as referenced in Subscription S5. If we let $S_1, S_2, S_3$ all refer to our stream of stock quotes, $S$, this is expressed as $\mathcal{E} = \sigma_{\text{DUR}=52\,\text{weeks}}\big(\mu_{\alpha_{g_2},\text{TRUE}}(\alpha_{g_1} \circ \sigma_\theta(S_1), \sigma_\theta(S_2))\big)$, where $\theta$ is name $=$ IBM, $g_1$ is defined as AVG $\mapsto$ price, COUNT $\mapsto$ 1, and $g_2$ is defined as AVG $\mapsto \frac{\text{COUNT.last} \times \text{AVG.last} + \text{price}}{\text{COUNT.last}+1}$, COUNT $\mapsto$ COUNT.last$+1$. Notice that we use the $\texttt{last}$ feature of $\mu$ to compute our aggregate recursively. The average is now a value attached to an attribute and can be used by the remaining part of Subscription S5. Therefore Subscription S5 can be expressed as $\sigma_{\theta_2}(\mathcal{E};_{\theta_1} S_3)$ where $\mathcal{E}$ is defined above, $\theta_1$ is $S_3\text{.name} = \text{IBM}$, and $\theta_2$ is $S_3\text{.price} > \text{AVG}$.

For completeness, Table 2 also contains the two RSS subscriptions listed in Table 1. Here we assume all the blogs the user subscribes to consist of $site_1, \cdots, site_n$, and $contains(T, P)$ is the substring match operator that tries to find substring pattern $P$ in text $T$; ID is the identity function that has no effect on the input.

## 2.3 Automaton Description

Given the algebra's similarity to regular expressions, finite automata would appear to be a natural implementation choice. Similar to the classic NFA model, for an incoming event, an automaton instance in one state can explore all the out-going edges, and non-deterministically traverse any number of them. If it cannot traverse any edge, however, this instance will be *dropped*.

We extend standard finite automata [19] in two ways. First, attributes of events can have infinite domains, e.g., text attributes, and therefore the input alphabet of our automaton, which is the set of all possible events, can be infinite as well. To handle this case, we associate each automaton edge with a *predicate*, and for an incoming event, this edge is traversed iff the predicate is satisfied by this event. Second, to be able to generate customized notification and to handle parameterized predicates over infinite domains, we need to store in each automaton instance the attributes and values of those events that have contributed to the state transition of this instance. These attributes and values are called *bindings*. To avoid overwriting the bindings of earlier events with that of latter events, we also need an attribute renaming function for each edge so that when an event makes an automaton instance traverse that edge, the bindings in that event are properly renamed before being stored in the instance.

We have developed a mechanical way to translate algebra expressions into automata. Details of this mechanism as well as the proof of correctness can be found in our technical report [12]. Intuitively, for a given algebra expression, we first construct a parse tree, and then translate each tree node corresponding to a binary operator into an automaton node. In our mechanism any left-deep parse tree can be translated into a single automaton, referred to as a *left-deep* automaton. In the following sections, we focus only on left-deep expressions and automata, and we leave general algebra expressions to future work.

We use an example to illustrate a left-deep automaton. Let subscription AutQ be "Notify me when for any stock $s$, there is a monotonic decrease in price for at least 10 minutes, which starts at a large trade ($\text{vol} > 10,000$). The immediately next quote on the same stock after this monotonic sequence should have a price 5% above the previously seen (bottom) price." Its algebra expression is $\sigma_{\theta_5}(\sigma_{\theta_4}(\mu_{\sigma_{\theta_3},\theta_2}(S_1, S_2));_{\theta_2} S_3)$. The $S_i$ are shorthand notation for appropriately renamed and projected versions of $S$: $S_1 \equiv \rho_{f_1} \circ \pi_{\text{name,price}} \circ \sigma_{\theta_1}(S)$, $S_2 \equiv \rho_{f_2} \circ \pi_{\text{name,price}}(S)$, $S_3 \equiv \rho_{f_3} \circ \pi_{\text{name,price}}(S)$. The corresponding predicates and renaming functions are: $\theta_1 \equiv \text{vol} > 10,000$, $\theta_2 \equiv \text{company} = \text{company.last}$, $\theta_3 \equiv \theta_2 \wedge \text{minP} < \text{minP.last}$, $\theta_4 \equiv \theta_3 \wedge \text{DUR} \geq 10\,\text{min}$, $\theta_5 \equiv \theta_2 \wedge \text{price} > 1.05\,\text{minP}$, $f_1 \equiv (\text{name}, \text{price}) \mapsto (\text{company}, \text{maxP})$, $f_2 \equiv (\text{name}, \text{price}) \mapsto (\text{company}, \text{minP})$, $f_3 \equiv (\text{name}, \text{price}) \mapsto (\text{company}, \text{finalP})$. The explicit use of renaming is necessary for this example to make the schemas of the intermediate results at the different automaton nodes clear. The corresponding automaton is shown in Figure 2.

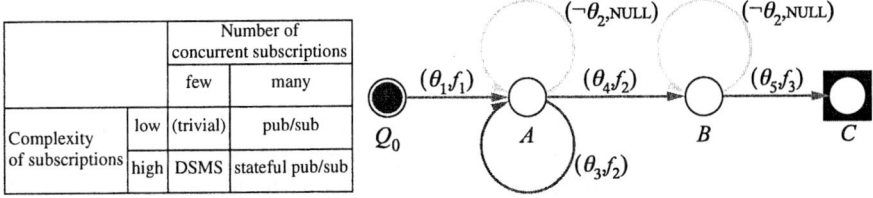

**Fig. 1.** Tradeoffs between pub/sub and Data Stream Management Systems

**Fig. 2.** Automaton for query AutQ

As opposed to NFA's with arbitrary structures, certain regularity is enforced by the translation from Cayuga algebra expressions. Now we describe some important properties of the structure of a left-deep automaton. Note that our MQO techniques described in Section 3 have a crucial dependence on these properties.

Each left-deep automaton is acyclic, except for self-loops. There are three types of edges, described as follows. *Forward* edges are those edges whose destination node is different from the source node, e.g., the edge from $A$ to $B$ in the example. Each node has at least one forward edge, except for the end node. Also on each node other than the start node, there will be two self-loop edges called *filter* and *rebind* edge, respectively. We draw a filter edge on top of the node, a rebind edge below the node (see node $A$ in Fig. 2). The predicate on a filter edge (or *filter predicate*) corresponds to the negation of the filter formula $\theta$ in $;_\theta$ or $\mu_{\mathfrak{F},\theta}$. Nodes $A$ and $B$ in Figure 2 are two examples of nodes containing filter edges that are translated from operators $\mu_{\mathfrak{F},\theta}$ and $;_\theta$ respectively. Also, by construction $\theta$ will appear in the forward and rebind edges of the same node as a conjunction to the remaining predicate there. Predicate $\theta_4$ on the forward edge between node $A$ and $B$ in Figure 2 illustrates this. The reason for this automaton construction from algebra operators is that on the algebra side, an event is filtered when $\theta$ is not satisfied (or $\neg\theta$ is satisfied), and on the automaton side, this happens if it traverses the filter edge (and therefore cannot traverse any forward/rebind edge). Filter edges are unique among the three types of edges in that the traversal of a filter edge does not modify the bindings of the instance. If a node is not translated from $;_\theta$ or $\mu_{\mathfrak{F},\theta}$, the filter predicate will be FALSE, and we omit drawing the edge. A rebind predicate corresponds to the selection formula in $\mathfrak{F}$ of $\mu_{\mathfrak{F},\theta}$. Similarly, if a node is not translated from $\mu_{\mathfrak{F},\theta}$, the rebind predicate is FALSE, and we omit drawing the edge. The construction of rebind edge is illustrated in Figure 2 by node $A$, translated from $\mu_{\sigma\theta_3,\theta_2}$. Node $B$ is shown without rebind edge since it is translated from operator $;_{\theta_2}$.

## 3  Implementation and MQO Techniques

Our algebra and automaton model are designed to be amenable to multi-query optimization. An obvious optimization is to merge equivalent states that occur in several automata. This is the approach taken by YFilter; details can be found in the paper by Diao et al. [13]. The result of the merging process is a DAG with a single start node. In the following we focus on implementation challenges that are unique to Cayuga. For this discussion we need some additional notation.

### 3.1 Notation

A *static predicate* is a conjunction of atomic predicates that compare attribute values of the incoming event to constants, e.g., name = IBM ∧ price > 10. A *dynamic predicate* (or *parameterized* predicate) is a conjunction of atomic predicates of the form $ATT_1$ relop $ATT_2$, which compares an attribute value of the incoming event with an attribute of an earlier event. An example is $\theta_2$ in Subscription S3.

For ease of exposition, in the following discussion we assume that each predicate is a conjunction of atomic predicates. Our techniques can be easily generalized to arbitrary boolean combinations of atomic predicates by requiring that predicates be supplied in disjunctive normal form (DNF), a disjunction of conjunctions of atomic predicates. Each conjunction $P$ can be rewritten as $P = \bigwedge_i ATT_i$ relop $CONST_i \wedge \bigwedge_j ATT_j$ relop $ATT_{k_j}$. We refer to $\bigwedge_i ATT_i$ relop $CONST_i$ and $\bigwedge_j ATT_j$ relop $ATT_{k_j}$ as the *static* and *dynamic* parts of $P$, respectively. If either part is empty, it is equivalent to TRUE.

A node of an automaton is *active* if there are automaton instances at the node. For each incoming event, an automaton instance is *unaffected* if that event makes the instance traverse its *filter* edge; otherwise it is *affected*. For example, in Subscription S2 the filter condition $\theta_1$ ensures that after matching the high-price IBM quote, the corresponding instance of the automaton will be affected only by MSFT quotes and can safely ignore quotes for other companies.

### 3.2 Design Challenges

Effective multi-query optimization for Cayuga's stateful parameterized subscriptions must meet three crucial challenges. **Evaluating Static Predicates.** Evaluation of Cayuga's subscriptions is driven by edge predicates being satisfied (or not) for an incoming event. The number of active automaton instances and the number of edges that each instance could potentially traverse can be very large. Hence, evaluating all these edge predicates for each incoming event is not feasible. So we need to index the predicates, which is the classic pub/sub matching problem. **Evaluating Dynamic Predicates.** Besides the static predicates handled by traditional pub/sub systems, Cayuga also needs to deal with dynamic predicates. This problem has not been studied in traditional pub/sub systems. **Identifying Affected Instances.** Although the *total* number of automaton instances can be very large at any time, the number of instances *affected* by an event is typically orders of magnitude lower. In the stock monitoring application, for example, a subscription that matches a sequence of IBM prices can ignore events for any other company. So we need an index that enables us to identify the affected instances quickly.

Observe that an instance is affected iff it cannot traverse the filter edge of its state (i.e., its filter predicate is satisfied). Therefore the problem of identifying affected instances is the same as the problem of efficiently evaluating predicates.

While we can use standard data structures from the pub/sub literature for indexing static predicates, it is not obvious how to index dynamic predicates. We propose two general approaches: (1) dynamic predicates are handled like static predicates once the parameter values are known, and (2) dynamic predicates are not indexed. The first approach is based on the observation that for an instance in automaton state $X$, all the parameters on the outgoing edges of state $X$ are already bound by that instance. For example, in Subscription S3, assume the automaton advances to the first state on an incoming stock quote for IBM. Now the name parameter ($S_1$.name in $\theta_1$) is bound to IBM, and hence $\theta_1$ will check if the name attribute of later stock quotes is equal to IBM. At this time the corresponding predicate $S_2$.name = IBM can be inserted into a (pub/sub) index. There is an obvious tradeoff with this approach: if we index the dynamic predicates, index maintenance becomes much more expensive compared to not indexing dynamic predicates. On the other hand, if we index only the static predicates, the index will be less selective and require evaluating the dynamic parts of those predicates whose static part is satisfied.

In the following sections, we describe our solutions to handling dynamic predicates for the case of indexing filter predicates and FR predicates (predicates on forward or rebind edges) respectively.

### 3.3 AN-Index and AI-Index

The goal of these indexes is to efficiently identify the instances that are affected by an incoming event. To do so, we index each instance by the filter predicate of its current state. More precisely, the index takes the filter predicate as the key and the corresponding instance as the value. We implement this index with a two-level scheme. The first level index only works on the static part of filter predicates. We refer to it as the *Active Node Index* (AN-Index), since it essentially returns all the automaton instances of those active nodes on which the static parts of filter predicates are satisfied. Then, for each such node, the second level index, called the *Active Instance Index* (AI-Index), is used to further prune the candidate set of affected instances by indexing the dynamic part of the filter predicates.

One reason for this separation is that it enables us to leverage existing data structures. For the fairly static AN-index, we can use a pub/sub index like Le Subscribe [14]. However, to keep index maintenance costs in the second level low, the AI-indexes are simple hash tables. Hence only equality predicates are indexed. This nevertheless proves to be a very useful feature for supporting parameterized atomic predicates like name = $S_i$.name, which simulates a grouping by name and essentially has the same effect as the frequently-used "partition-by" window feature in CQL [25]. The two-level approach also simplifies data structure optimizations. If the system determines that for one of the AI-indexes the maintenance overhead exceeds the savings from improved selectivity, this AI-index can be disabled without affecting the use of the first level index.

### 3.4 FR-Index

Knowing the instances affected by an incoming event is not sufficient. We also have to determine, which forward and rebind edges these instances will traverse. Traversing an FR edge modifies instance bindings, affecting the instance content; if no edge can be traversed, the instance is affected by being deleted. A second pub/sub-style index, called the *FR-Index*, is used in Cayuga to index the static part of the FR predicates. Since all FR predicates are conjunctions, after using the FR-Index, we still need to eliminate false hits by post-processing those instances whose static predicates are satisfied by evaluating their dynamic predicates.

Here we do not index the dynamic part of each FR predicate, because for each incoming event, only the affected instances will need to have their FR predicates further evaluated. This leads to a much lower benefit-cost ratio compared to the problem of finding affected instances.

Figure 3 illustrates the relationship between the different indices with respect to how the search space of instances is pruned. The AN-Index and AI-Index identify affected instances efficiently, while the FR-Index evaluates the static part of FR predicates of each instance so that a decision of whether to advance or drop the instance can be made quickly.

### 3.5 System Architecture and Data Flow

The overall system architecture of Cayuga is shown in Figure 4. Its core component is the *State Machine Manager*, which manages the merged query DAG and the automaton instances at the nodes. It also maintains the AN-Index and AI-Index. Outside the State Machine Manager, there is the FR-Index.

Cayuga needs to handle two types of updates—insertion/deletion of subscriptions and arrival of input events. A new query is inserted by first merging it into the query DAG in the State Machine Manager. Then, for each forward and each rebind edge, an entry is added into the FR-index for the static part of the edge predicate. When the query is deleted, the insertion process is simply reversed.

The diagram in Figure 5 summarizes the Cayuga event processing steps. On arrival of an event, the following happens. First, the FR-index generates the set of IDs of the satisfied static predicates on FR edges, and the AN-index returns the set of AI-Index instances. Then, for each AI-Index instance in the set, we do the following. We first obtain from this AI-index the set of relevant instances for which the dynamic equality predicate of the filter condition is satisfied. For each of these instances the remaining dynamic atomic predicates of the filter edge are evaluated. This gives us the set of affected

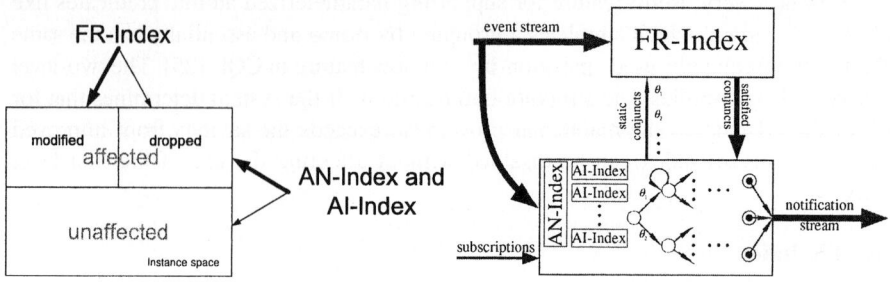

**Fig. 3.** InstanceSearchSpace       **Fig. 4.** Cayuga architecture

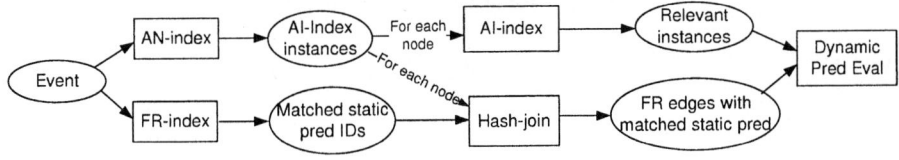

**Fig. 5.** Event Processing Diagram

instances. Then we determine for each affected instance the candidates of satisfied FR edges by intersecting the output of FR-index with the set of IDs of the static FR predicates associated with the current node, followed by an evaluation of the dynamic parts of FR predicates whose static parts are satisfied.

Simultaneous event arrivals pose no serious problems for our implementation. We compute new instances for each arriving event as discussed above, but do not install them into the NFA. When we see an incoming event with end timestamp strictly greater than all previous events, we install all new instances atomically.

We use a garbage collection mechanism to manage the memory resource consumed by storing bindings in events and automaton instances. Details are omitted due to space constraint.

## 4 Performance Evaluation

We built an initial prototype of Cayuga in C++. All experiments were run on a 3 GHz Pentium 4 PC with 1 GB of RAM and 512 KB cache. The operating system is Red Hat Linux 9. We loaded the input stream into memory before starting the experiment to make sure that the input tuples are delivered as fast as our system can process them. We measured the *total* runtime for matching all incoming events with all subscriptions in the system. For each experiment we perform several runs. The standard deviation in all experimental runs was well below 1%; we therefore only report averages and omit error bars from the graphs.

### 4.1 Technical Benchmark

To test the overall efficiency of Cayuga and measure the evaluation cost of the different operators of our algebra, we designed a synthetic technical benchmark motivated by the stock application, but more complex to provide flexibility in subjecting our system to a stress test.

**Event and Subscription Generation.** We use an event stream with eight data attributes: four discrete attributes (e.g., company name) and four continuous attributes (e.g., stock price). The parameters for generating the stream and the associated subscriptions are shown in Table 3.

We generated subscriptions according to five different templates: LinearStat, LinearDyn, Filter, NonDeterministic, and NonDeterministicAgg. All subscriptions are over a single input stream $S$. We use $S_i$ to refer to an appropriately renamed occurrence of $S$ in the algebraic expression.

**Table 3.** Parameters (default values)

| Variable | Value | Variable | Value |
|---|---|---|---|
| Number of events | 100,000 | Number of attributes per event | 8 |
| Number of discrete attributes | 4 | Number of continuous attributes | 4 |
| Number of subscriptions | 200,000 | Domain size of discrete attribute | 100 |
| Number of atomic predicates (discrete + continuous) | 2 + 2 | Number of distinct ranges that can be selected for inequality predicates | 25 |
| Selectivity of atomic inequality predicate | 0.7 | Number of steps per sequence query | 3 |
| Zipf parameter, first step ($zipf_1$) | 1 | Zipf parameter, second step ($zipf_2$) | 1 |
| Zipf parameter, third step ($zipf_3$) | 0.8 | Duration constant ($t$) | 20 |

LinearStat subscriptions define simple sequential patterns of three consecutive events, expressed as $\sigma_{\theta_3}(\sigma_{\theta_2}(\sigma_{\theta_1}(S_1); S_2); S_3)$ in our algebra. Essentially, this query looks at any three consecutive events in the stream, and outputs the concatenated result if all of the three selections are satisfied. If such a template were applied to our stock stream example, then our template might generate the following subscription Q: "Notify me when there are three consecutive stock quotes representing IBM below $10, followed by IBM above $15, and finally IBM below $15." The $\theta_i$ are conjuncts of four *static* atomic predicates: two equality predicates on two of the discrete attributes, and two inequality predicates on two of the continuous attributes. One of the discrete attributes, ATT, is designated as the *primary attribute* of the query. This attribute is guaranteed to appear in all three of the $\theta_i$, and to select exactly the same value for each formula. The name attribute in Subscription Q is an example of such an attribute, as it is assigned to IBM in each case. As all of the formula select the same value, we refer to the predicate ATT = CONST as the *primary predicate* of the query.

Attributes and their values are selected independently, using $zipf_1$ to select attributes and $zipf_i$ to select the value for $\theta_i$. This setup is motivated by practical scenarios where user preferences typically follow a skewed (often Zipf) distribution. By adjusting the Zipf parameter, we can control the similarity of the different subscriptions.

To test the overhead of evaluating *parameterized* predicates in Cayuga, we designed the LinearDyn based on LinearStat. The difference between it and LinearStat is that $\theta_2$ and $\theta_3$ now have an additional *parameterized* atomic predicate. An example of such a predicate from our stock stream would be the requirement that the stock price from the second quote is 1% above the price of the original quote.

The overhead of evaluating filter predicates is measured with the Filter template $\sigma_{\theta_3}(\sigma_{\theta_2}(\sigma_{\theta_1}(S_1); \theta_4 S_2); \theta_5 S_3)$. In this template, $\theta_1, \theta_2, \theta_3$ are all selected in the same way as for LinearStat. On the other hand, $\theta_4$ is a filter formula of the form DUR $\leq t \wedge S_2$.ATT = CONST, where the default value of $t$ is shown in Table 3 and $S_2$.ATT = CONST is the primary predicate of the query in LinearStat. $\theta_4$ relaxes the selectivity of the original LinearStat query by allowing intermediate non-matching events to be filtered out. The second filter formula $\theta_5$ is similar to $\theta_4$; we merely replace $S_2$.ATT with $S_3$.ATT. To illustrate this idea with our stock stream example, suppose we took Subscription Q and made $\theta_4$ the filter predicate DUR $\leq$ 10min $\wedge S_2$.name = IBM. In this case, stock quotes of other companies that arrive between the first two IBM quotes would not lead to a failure of the pattern, as long as consecutive IBM quotes arrive within 10 minutes of each other.

The effect of non-determinism in our automata is measured by the NonDeterministic template $\sigma_{\theta_3} \circ \mu_{\text{ID},\theta_5}(\sigma_{\theta_2} \circ \mu_{\text{ID},\theta_4}(\sigma_{\theta_1}(S_1), S_2), S_3)$. This query is much more powerful than the previous queries. An analogy based on Subscription Q would be a query that not only searches for patterns of *consecutive* IBM stock quotes, but one that finds *any n-tuple* of IBM stock quotes ($n \geq 3$) that satisfies the duration constraints and selection criteria $\theta_4$ and $\theta_5$, ignoring all stock quotes in between. Hence the output of this query will be a superset of the Filter query with exactly the same formulas $\theta_i$.

Finally, template NonDeterministicAgg implements aggregation. It extends NonDeterministic by computing the sum of the values of the continuous attributes, for the $n$ events that satisfy the query pattern.

In processing these subscriptions, events were generated by uniformly selecting values for each of the eight attributes of the stream schema. We also examined skewed event distributions, but observed the same trends.

**Experimental Results.** Figure 6 illustrates the results of various throughput experiments. Figure 6(a) shows how the system throughput changes with the number of subscriptions. Even for 400K concurrently active subscriptions, throughput is well above 1000 events per second. As expected, the more complex the query workload, the lower the throughput, except for LinearStat and LinearDyn, which are almost identical because the cost of checking parameterized predicates is negligible compared to the other matching costs and the cost of maintaining the index structures.

Cayuga's high throughput is achieved for a challenging workload. Each event on average matches about 100 static predicates in the FR index. Furthermore, at any time, an average of 6000 to 16,000 nodes are active in the State Machine Manager, indicating that events satisfied a high percentage of the edge predicates. The high throughput was achieved because the index structures ensured that only about 40 to 120 of these active nodes had to be accessed per incoming event.

Note also that, despite the skewed query distribution, the merged query DAG is very large. For instance, before merging states the DAG for 100K subscriptions would have 300K nodes and edges. Our merged DAG still has about 215K nodes: 48K at level 1, 71K at level 2, and 96K at level 3.

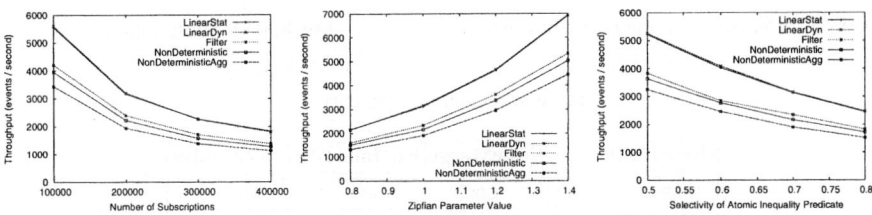

(a) Throughput vs. number of subscriptions  (b) Throughput vs. Zipf skew  (c) Throughput vs. inequality selectivity

**Fig. 6.** Throughput Measurements

In Figure 6(b), we compare the effect of parameter $zipf_1$ on system performance. Less skew makes the subscriptions less similar, hence reduces the possibilities for state merging. This can be observed in the graph. Most of the performance difference is caused by the number of level 1 nodes in the query DAG, because that is where most activity takes place. For Zipf parameter 0.8, there are 101K nodes, while for Zipf parameter 1.4, there are 36K nodes. The overall number of matched subscriptions is virtually unaffected by the Zipf parameter, because there is no correlation between event values and query constants. This shows that state merging is effective when subscriptions follow a very skew distribution. However, by looking at the trend of curves in Figure 6(b), state merging becomes less important when the query distribution is less skew (e.g. zipfian value no greater than 1).

Finally, we examined the effect of edge predicate selectivity on the performance. Figure 6(c) shows how the throughput decreases when the inequality predicates on the continuous attributes select more values. Notice that the curve's slope is inverse quadratic, which is to be expected, as we are varying the selectivity of two predicates simultaneously.

**Multi-query Optimization.** In order to see the benefits of our MQO techniques, we run our system with different optimizations being turned on/off against the technical benchmark. Due to limited space, we report only the result on Filter workload. Other results are similar.

Figure 7 shows the performance of Cayuga compared to four other system modes explained in Table 4. "Instance Index" corresponds to AN-Index + AI-Index. To keep the runtime of the naive system manageable, we reduced the number of concurrently active

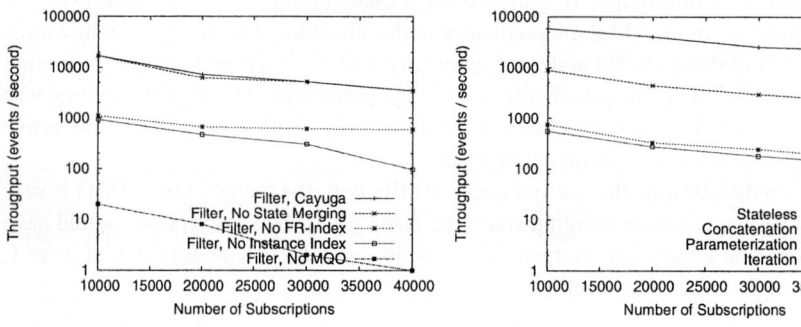

**Fig. 7.** Effect of multi-query optimization      **Fig. 8.** RSS Subscription

**Table 4.** Meaning of the curves

| Mode Name | StateMerge | FR-Index | Instance Index |
|---|---|---|---|
| Cayuga | on | on | on |
| No State Merging | off | on | on |
| No FR-Index | on | off | on |
| No Instance Index | on | on | off |
| No MQO | off | off | off |

subscriptions to 10K-40K, compared to 100K-400K in other experiments. Note that the y-axis is a *log scale*; hence with multi-query optimization the system is faster by a few orders of magnitude compared to that of a system without any of our MQO techniques.

It is clear from the graph that most of the performance gain comes from the indexing of FR predicates and instances, and not from merging automata states. This is true especially when the query workload is generated with a medium zipfian value, such as the default value 1.0 in our setup.

### 4.2 Experiments with Real Data

Full-fledged DSMSs are expressive enough to support extended pub/sub subscriptions, although the have only limited support for MQO and the query language based on SQL is not suitable for online event detection, as will be elaborated in Section 5. We used real stock data to compare Cayuga with the Stanford STREAM system, a general stream processing system with a relatively mature implementation. The result confirms our expectation that Cayuga is more suitable to extended pub/sub applications. Due to space constraints, we refer to the interested readers to our technical report for a full description of this experiment [12].

**Subscriptions on RSS Feeds.** We obtained RSS V2.0 feeds from 415 websites. Since our current prototype cannot handle string comparison, we preprocessed the feeds by converting each RSS feed item into a Cayuga event by hashing the string values of the RSS fields to integers. Some RSS fields such as <title> and <link> occur in each item, while others such as <author> are optional. To be able to pose interesting subscriptions, we augment the event schema with three additional attributes: website, channel, and popularity. The information of the first two attributes can be obtained directly from the feeds, while that of the last attribute is obtained through an external source that maintains the hit counts of these feeds. We sort the feed items by their publication date (<pubDate> field) and form an event stream of 26,623 events. The number of attribute/value pairs in each event varies from 6 to 11.

We composed four query templates shown in Table 5. To generate 10K to 40K subscriptions for each template, we randomly pick integer values to instantiate $W$ and $X$. The domain sizes of $W$ and $X$ are respectively 415 and 100. The duration constraint of each query is fixed to be no more than 100 events.

The result is shown in Figure 8. The trade-off between query expressiveness and system throughput is well exhibited. However, even when processing 40K subscriptions of Iteration template, where thousands of witnesses are found and output, the system can still maintain a throughput of more than 100 events per second.

**Table 5.** Template Name and Description

| |
|---|
| Stateless: return all articles from website $W$ with popularity $> X$. |
| Concatenation: return a series of 3 articles from website $W$ with popularity $> X$. |
| Parameterization: return a series of 3 articles from website $W$ on the same channel with increasing popularity. |
| Iteration: return a series of $N$ articles from website $W$ on the same channel with increasing popularity. $N$ unbounded. |

## 5   Related Work

There has been much interest in event processing systems with a wide variety of expressiveness of the subscriptio language. At one end of the spectrum lie pub/sub systems [4, 30, 14]. These systems sacrifice expressiveness to achieve high performance. Work on large-scale filtering of streaming XML documents handles query languages that are fragments of XPath, which is more expressive than pub/sub [13, 10, 18, 17]. However, XML filtering systems do not address parameterization, and they cannot handle subscriptions across multiple XML documents. Automata are also a popular choice for many systems in this category [13, 18]. Our FR-Index can be potentially useful to YFilter, given that currently YFilter will have to sequentially evaluate all the structure predicates (usually equality comparison on string tags) on out-going edges for each active node to make non-deterministic state transitions [13].

Somewhat higher in the expressiveness spectrum is work from the Active Database community [29] on languages for specifying more complex event-condition-action rules. The composite event definition languages of SNOOP [9, 3] and ODE [16] are important representatives of this class. Both systems describe composite events in a formalism related to regular expressions, allowing events to be recognized using a nondeterministic finite automaton model. The automaton construction of [16] supports a limited form of parameterized composite events defined by equality constraints between attributes of primitive events. However, the semantics of some of the more expressive event languages is not well-defined [15, 31], and it is not clear how the different languages compare to each other in terms of expressiveness. In addition, the performance of event processing systems with very expressive query languages has not been explored in depth, especially in terms of scalability with the number of subscriptions. Our work can be viewed as extending this style of system with full support for parameterized composite events and support for aggregate subscriptions, focusing on multi-query optimization using a combination of state merging and indexing techniques.

Still higher in the spectrum, several groups are building systems with very expressive query languages [8, 25, 11, 2]. Sistla and Wolfson [27] describe an event definition and aggregation language based on Past Temporal Logic. The TREPLE language [24] is a Datalog-based system with a precise formal specification; it extends the parameterized composite event specification language of EPL [23] with a powerful aggregation mechanism that is capable of explicit recursion. Perhaps the most powerful formal approach is STREAM's CQL query language [25], which extends SQL with support for window queries. Like SQL itself, CQL is declarative and admits of a formal specification [6]; and there are some initial results characterizing a sub-class of queries that can be computed with bounded memory [28, 5]. However, as we pointed out in the introduction, it is not clear whether SQL based languages with set semantics are suitable for real-time event detection and composition. Similar to SQL, the data model underlying these stream query languages is unordered, and so in order to pin-point the $i$-th tuple (in terms of temporal order) within a set of $N$ tuples returned by a window operator, an $N$-way self-join with temporal constraints on these $N$ tuples is required. A similarly powerful approach is represented by Aurora and Borealis [8, 2]. These two systems, however, use a procedural boxes-and-arrows paradigm which is much less amenable to formal specification in our style. Without formal semantics, it is hard to prove the correctness of query formulations, and opportunities for query rewrite/optimization in such systems are limited since many operator boxes are treated as black boxes.

There has also been some work in extending the expressiveness of pub/sub systems [22, 21]. However, [22] focuses on a distributed setting, and the degree of expressive power achieved by its query language is not as high as our algebra (e.g. no parameterization), and its implementation does not have MQO techniques other than state merging. There is no query language defined in [21], and the notion of a "stateful" subscription there is based on "state transition"; that is, when a regular (stateless) pub/sub subscription starts to be satisfied, or ceases to be satisfied.

Related to our implementation, Sellis [26] is one of the first to address general multi-query optimization in databases. Traditionally this is performed by sharing operators and query results [7, 8, 11, 20]. Our multi-query optimization is fundamentally different and aggressively exploits the relationship of our event algebra to automata.

## 6 Conclusions and Future Work

We presented Cayuga, a novel solution for extended pub/sub applications. Cayuga extends previous work on event processing by adding built-in support for parameterization, aggregatation, and it supports simultaneous events and events with non-trivial duration. We plan to extend this work by developing a complete optimization framework, including query rewrite rules and more effective MQO strategies. It would also be interesting to investigate how to adapt Cayuga to a distributed setting.

**Acknowledgments.** This work was supported in part by the DARPA SRS Program, by the KDD Program, and by NSF Grants IIS-0121175, IIS-0133481, and IIS-0330201. Any opinions, findings, conclusions or recommendations expressed in this material are those of the author(s) and do not necessarily reflect the views of the sponsors.

## References

1. Traderbot financial search engine. http://www.traderbot.com/.
2. D. J. Abadi, Y. Ahmad, M. Balazinska, U. Çetintemel, M. Cherniack, J.-H. Hwang, W. Lindner, A. Maskey, A. Rasin, E. Ryvkina, N. Tatbul, Y. Xing, and S. B. Zdonik. The design of the borealis stream processing engine. In *Proc. CIDR*, pages 277–289, 2005.
3. R. Adaikkalavan and S. Chakravarthy. Snoopib: Interval-based event specification and detection for active databases. In *Proc. ADBIS*, pages 190–204, 2003.
4. M. K. Aguilera, R. E. Strom, D. C. Sturman, M. Astley, and T. D. Chandra. Matching events in a content-based subscription system. In *Proc. PODC*, pages 53–61, 1999.
5. A. Arasu, B. Babcock, S. Babu, J. McAlister, and J. Widom. Characterizing memory requirements for queries over continuous data streams. In *Proc. PODS*, pages 221–232, 2002.
6. A. Arasu, S. Babu, and J. Widom. The CQL continuous query language: Semantic foundations and query execution. Technical report, Stanford University, 2003.
7. B. Babcock, S. Babu, M. Datar, R. Motwani, and J. Widom. Models and issues in data stream systems. In *Proc. PODS*, pages 1–16, 2002.
8. D. Carney, U. Çetintemel, M. Cherniack, C. Convey, S. Lee, G. Seidman, M. Stonebraker, N. Tatbul, and S. Zdonik. Monitoring streams — a new class of data management applications. In *Proc. VLDB*, 2002.

9. S. Chakravarthy, V. Krishnaprasad, E. Anwar, and S.-K. Kim. Composite events for active databases: Semantics, contexts and detection. In *Proc. VLDB*, pages 606–617, 1994.
10. C. Y. Chan, P. Felber, M. N. Garofalakis, and R. Rastogi. Efficient filtering of XML documents with XPath expressions. In *Proc. ICDE*, pages 235–244, 2002.
11. S. Chandrasekaran, O. Cooper, A. Deshpande, M. J. Franklin, J. M. Hellerstein, W. Hong, S. Krishnamurthy, S. R. Madden, V. Raman, F. Reiss, and M. A. Shah. TelegraphCQ: Continuous dataflow processing for an uncertain world. In *Proc. CIDR*, 2003.
12. A. Demers, J. Gehrke, M. Hong, M. Riedewald, and W. White. A general algebra and implementation for monitoring event streams. Technical report, Cornell University, 2005. http://techreports.library.cornell.edu.
13. Y. Diao, M. Altinel, M. J. Franklin, H. Zhang, and P. M. Fischer. Path sharing and predicate evaluation for high-performance XML filtering. *ACM TODS*, 28(4):467–516, 2003.
14. F. Fabret, H.-A. Jacobsen, F. Llirbat, J. Pereira, K. A. Ross, and D. Shasha. Filtering algorithms and implementation for very fast publish/subscribe. In *Proc. SIGMOD*, pages 115–126, 2001.
15. A. Galton and J. C. Augusto. Two approaches to event definition. In *Proc. DEXA*, pages 547–556, 2002.
16. N. H. Gehani, H. V. Jagadish, and O. Shmueli. Composite event specification in active databases: Model and implementation. In *Proc. VLDB*, pages 327–338, 1992.
17. T. J. Green, G. Miklau, M. Onizuka, and D. Suciu. Processing XML streams with deterministic automata. In *Proc. ICDT*, pages 173–189, 2003.
18. A. K. Gupta and D. Suciu. Stream processing of XPath queries with predicates. In *Proc. SIGMOD*, pages 419–430, 2003.
19. J. E. Hopcroft, R. Motwani, and J. D. Ullman. *Introduction to Automata Theory, Languages, and Computation*. Addison Wesley, 2nd edition, 2000.
20. S. Krishnamurthy, M. J. Franklin, J. M. Hellerstein, and G. Jacobson. The case for precision sharing. In *Proc. VLDB*, pages 972–986, 2004.
21. H. Leung and H. Jacobsen. Efficient matching for state-persistent publish/subscribe systems. In *CASCON '03: Proceedings of the 2003 conference of the Centre for Advanced Studies on Collaborative research*, pages 182–196. IBM Press, 2003.
22. G. Li and H. Jacobsen. Composite subscriptions in content-based publish/subscribe systems. In *Proc. ACM/IFIP/USENIX International Middleware Conference*, 2005.
23. I. Motakis and C. Zaniolo. Formal semantics for composite temporal events in active database rules. *Journal of Systems Integration*, 7(3-4):291–325, 1997.
24. I. Motakis and C. Zaniolo. Temporal aggregation in active database rules. In *Proc. SIGMOD*, pages 440–451, 1997.
25. R. Motwani, J. Widom, A. Arasu, B. Babcock, S. Babu, M. Datar, G. S. Manku, C. Olston, J. Rosenstein, and R. Varma. Query processing, approximation, and resource management in a data stream management system. In *Proc. CIDR*, 2003.
26. T. K. Sellis. Multiple-query optimization. *ACM TODS*, 13(1):23–52, 1988.
27. A. P. Sistla and O. Wolfson. Temporal conditions and integrity constraints in active database systems. In *Proc. SIGMOD*, pages 269–280, 1995.
28. U. Srivastava and J. Widom. Memory-limited execution of windowed stream joins. In *Proc. VLDB*, pages 324–335, 2004.
29. J. Widom and S. Ceri, editors. *Active Database Systems: Triggers and Rules For Advanced Database Processing*. Morgan Kaufmann Publishers, 1996.
30. A. Yalamanchi, J. Srinivasan, and D. Gawlick. Managing expressions as data in relational database systems. In *Proc. CIDR*, 2003.
31. D. Zimmer and R. Unland. On the semantics of complex events in active database management systems. In *Proc. ICDE*, pages 392–399, 1999.

# Finding Data Broadness Via Generalized Nearest Neighbors

Jayendra Venkateswaran[1], Tamer Kahveci[1], and Orhan Camoglu[2]

[1] CISE Department University of Florida Gainesville, FL 32611
{jgvenkat, tamer}@cise.ufl.edu
[2] University of California, Santa Barbara, CA 93106
orhan@cs.ucsb.edu

**Abstract.** A data object is broad if it is one of the $k$-Nearest Neighbors ($k$-NN) of many data objects. We introduce a new database primitive called Generalized Nearest Neighbor (GNN) to express data broadness. We also develop three strategies to answer GNN queries efficiently for large datasets of multidimensional objects. The R*-Tree based search algorithm generates candidate pages and ranks them based on their distances. Our first algorithm, Fetch All (FA), fetches as many candidate pages as possible. Our second algorithm, Fetch One (FO), fetches one candidate page at a time. Our third algorithm, Fetch Dynamic (FD), dynamically decides on the number of pages that needs to be fetched. We also propose three optimizations, Column Filter, Row Filter and Adaptive Filter, to eliminate pages from each dataset. Column Filter prunes the pages that are guaranteed to be non-broad. Row Filter prunes the pages whose removal do not change the broadness of any data point. Adaptive Filter prunes the search space dynamically along each dimension to eliminate unpromising objects. Our experiments show that FA is the fastest when the buffer size is large and FO is the fastest when the buffer size is small. FD is always either fastest or very close to the faster of FA and FO. FD is significantly faster than the existing methods adapted to the GNN problem.

## 1 Motivation

Given two datasets $R$ and $S$, an object in $S$ is called *broad* if it is one of the $k$ Nearest Neighbors ($k$-NN) of many objects in $R$. A $k$-NN query seeks the $k$ closest objects in a dataset $S$ to a given query object $q$ with respect to a predefined distance function, where $k$ is a given positive integer. Finding the broadness of data is needed in many applications such as life sciences (e.g., detecting repeat regions in biological sequences [10] or protein classification [6]), distributed systems (e.g., resource allocation), Spatial databases (e.g.,Decision Support Systems or Continuous Referral Systems [12]), profile-based marketing, etc.

In this paper, we define a new database primitive, called the *Generalized Nearest Neighbor (GNN)* which naturally detects data broadness. Given two datasets $R$ and $S$, the GNN query finds all the objects in $S' \subseteq S$ that appear in the $k$-NN set of at least $t$ objects of $R$, where $t$ is a cutoff threshold. The objects in the result set of a GNN query are broad. Here, $S'$ is the set of objects that the user focuses on for broadness property. If $R = S$, then it is called *mono-chromatic* query. Otherwise, it is called *bi-chromatic* query. Following examples present GNN queries in two different problem domains.

*Example 1.* (*Bioinformatics*) Functional relations among families of genes are usually found through similarity of their features (e.g., sequences, structures). If a gene from family $S$ is one of the top closest genes to many of the genes from family $R$, then that gene is considered too broad (or useless) for classification. Such genes are filtered to obtain better efficiency and classification quality since they mask the results from other genes [8]. In this example, $R = $ first family of genes, $S = S' = $ second family of genes. □

*Example 2.* (*Spatial databases*) Suppose that people usually dine at one of the three closest restaurants to their houses. An entrepreneur who wants to invest in Mexican restaurant business would want to know the Mexican restaurants that potentially have many customers. In this example $R = $ set of houses, $S = $ set of restaurants, and $S' = $ set of Mexican restaurants. □

The trivial solution to a GNN query is to run a $k$-NN query for each object in $R$ one by one, and accumulate the results for each object in $S$. Currently, biologists are using this approach for the queries in Example 1. However, this approach suffers from both excessive amount of disk I/Os and CPU computations. When the datasets do not fit into the available buffer, a page that will be needed again might be removed from buffer while processing a single $k$-NN query. CPU cost also accounts for a significant portion of the total cost.

In this paper, we assume datasets to be larger than the available buffer. We propose three solutions. Our methods arrange the data objects into pages. Each page contains a set of objects and is represented by their minimum bounding rectangle (MBR). Two R*-trees [2] are built on objects in $R$ and $S$. The candidate pages from $S$ that may contain $k$-NNs for the MBRs of $R$ are predicted. Each candidate page $s \in S$ is assigned a priority based on its proximity to a MBR $r \in R$ and is stored in a Priority Table (PT). Our first algorithm, pessimistic approach, fetches as many candidate pages as possible from $S$ for each $r$. Our second algorithm, optimistic approach, fetches one $s$ at a time for each $r$. Our third algorithm dynamically decides the number of pages that needs to be fetched for each $r$ by analyzing query history. We reduce the CPU and I/O cost significantly through three optimizations by dynamically pruning 1) pages of $S$ that are not in the $k$-NN set of sufficiently many objects in $R$, and 2) pages of $R$ whose nearest neighbors do not contribute to the result 3) objects in candidate MBRs of $S$ that are too far from the MBRs of $R$. We further reduce these costs by pre-processing the input datasets using a packing technique called Sort-Tile-Recursive (STR) [16].

Experiments show that our optimistic strategy works best when the buffer size is small and pessimistic strategy when the buffer size is large. On the other hand, dynamic strategy is always either the best of the three or very close to the better of the two other strategies. Our methods are significantly faster than sequential scan, R-tree–based branch-and-bound method [15], GORDER [21], MuX index [5] and RkNN [20].

Data broadness is a new problem that requires new approaches. To our best knowledge, all of the following ideas are introduced first time in this paper and has not been discussed elsewhere before:

- The GNN problem.
- Use of PT to obtain global-coarse-grain view.
- Three search strategies: FA, FO and FD.
- Column, Row and Adaptive Filters.

The rest of the paper is organized as follows. Section 2 presents background on well known NN query types. Section 3 introduces the problem. Section 4 explains how the candidate pages are determined. Section 5 discusses our pessimistic and optimistic strategies. Section 6 discusses our dynamic strategy. Section 7 presents an optimization strategy for reducing the CPU and I/O costs. Section 8 presents our experimental results. We end with a brief discussion in Section 9.

## 2 Related Work

A number of index-based methods have been developed for $k$-NN queries. Hjaltson and Samet [9] used PMR quadtree to index the search space. They search this tree in a depth-first manner until the $k$ nearest neighbors are found. Roussopoulos et. al., [15] employed a branch-and-bound R-Tree traversal algorithm. The two-phase method [13] determines $k$ closest objects based on feature distance. It then runs a range query using the actual distance to the $k$th closest object found in the first phase as the query range. Seidl and Kriegel [18] proposed a method that runs in multiple phases iteratively updating the upper and lower bounds of $k$th NN. It stops when these bounds coincide. Berchtold et. al., [3] divide the search space using Voronoi cells. Beyer et. al., [4] show that for a broad set of data distributions most of the known $k$-NN algorithms run slower than sequential scan. Thus, despite its simplicity, sequential scan still remains a formidable competitor to index-based $k$-NN methods.

Korn et. al., [12] introduced the *Reverse Nearest Neighbor (RNN)* problem. They precompute the NN of all the objects in the dataset. Yang and Lin introduced the Rdnn-tree for RNN queries [22]. Stanoi et. al., proposed to compute a region of influence with the help of a Voronoi Diagram [19]. It then performs a range search with radius equal to the radius of the influence region. Tao et. al., [20] generalize the RNN problem to arbitrary number of NNs using a filter-and-refine approach.

Despite its wide use in many areas, *All Nearest Neighbor (ANN)* is the least studied NN query type. MuX uses a two-level index structure called MuX index [5]. At the top level, MuX index contains large pages (or MBRs). At the next level, these pages contain much smaller buckets. For each bucket from $R$, it computes a pruning distance as it scans the candidate points from $S$. It prunes the pages, buckets, and points of $S$ beyond this distance for each bucket of $R$. GORDER [21] is a block nested loop join method. It first reduces the dimensionality of $R$ and $S$ by using Principal Component Analysis (PCA). It then places a grid on the space defined by PCA and hashes data objects into grid cells. Later, it reads blocks of data objects from grid cells by traversing the cells in grid order and compares all the objects in pairs of grid cells whose MINDIST is less than the pruning distance defined by the $k$th NN.

## 3 Problem Definition

Let $R$ and $S$ be two datasets. The GNN query is defined by a 5-tuple GNN($R$, $S$, $S'$, $k$, $t$), where $S' \subseteq S$, and $k$ and $t$ are positive integers. This query returns the set of tuples $(s, R_s)$, where $s \in S'$, $R_s \subseteq R$ is the set of objects that have $s$ as one of their $k$-NN, and $|R_s| \geq t$. We use the Euclidean distance as the distance measure in this paper unless otherwise stated.

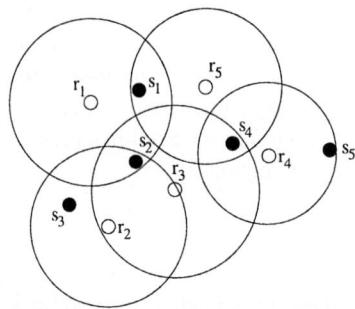

**Fig. 1.** The white and black points are the locations of the 2-D objects in datasets $R = \{r_1, \cdots, r_5\}$ and $S = \{s_1, \cdots, s_5\}$ respectively. The circles show the 2-NNs of the objects of $R$ in $S$.

Assume that the white and black points in Figure 1 show the layout of 2-D datasets $R = \{r_1, \cdots, r_5\}$ and $S = \{s_1, \cdots, s_5\}$ respectively. Consider the following query:

$$\text{GNN}(R, S, S' = \{s_1, s_2, s_5\}, 2, 3).$$

This translates as: "Find the objects in $S'$ that are in the 2-NN set of at least three objects in $R$". In Figure 1, the circles centered at each $r_i \in R$ covers the 2-NN of $r_i$, $\forall i$. Only $s_2$ and $s_4$ are covered by at least three circles. We ignore $s_4$ since $s_4 \notin S'$. The set $\{r_1, r_2, r_3\}$ has $s_2$ in their 2-NN. Therefore, the output of this query is $\{(s_2, \{r_1, r_2, r_3\})\}$. Note that we cannot ignore the data points in $S - S'$ prior to GNN query. In other words GNN($R$, $S$, $S'$, $k$, $t$) $\neq$ GNN($R$, $S'$, $S'$, $k$, $t$). For example, in Figure 1, removal of $s_3$ and $s_4$ prior to GNN query changes the 2-NNs of $r_2$, $r_3$ and $r_4$. As a result $s_1$ becomes one of the 2NNs of $r_2$ and $r_3$. Hence $s_1$ is incorrectly classified as broad.

A nice property of the GNN query is that both mono-chromatic and bi-chromatic versions of the standard $k$-NN, ANN and RNN queries are its special cases. Following observations state these cases. One can prove these from the definition of the GNN query. Note that the goal of this paper is not to find different solutions to each of these special cases. Our goal is to solve a broader problem which can not be solved trivially using these special cases.

**Observation 1.** *GNN($\{r\}$, $S$, $S$, $k$, 1) returns the k-NN of the object $r$ in $S$. If $r \in S$, then it corresponds to the mono-chromatic k-NN query. Otherwise, it corresponds to the bi-chromatic k-NN query.*

**Observation 2.** *GNN($R$, $S$, $S$, 1, 1) returns the ANN of $R$ in $S$. If $R = S$, then it is the mono-chromatic case, otherwise bi-chromatic case.*

**Observation 3.** *GNN(R, S, {s}, 1, 1), where $s \in S$, returns the RNN of the object s in R. If $R = S$, then it is the mono-chromatic case, otherwise bi-chromatic case.*

## 4 Predicting the Solution: Priority Table Construction

Let $R$ and $S$ be two given datasets, and $\mathcal{A}$ and $\mathcal{B}$ be the sets of MBRs that contain the objects in these datasets. We discuss the computation of the candidate set of MBR pairs one from $\mathcal{A}$ and the other from $\mathcal{B}$ that needs to be inspected to calculate a given GNN query. We assume that the datasets are packed and indexed prior to the GNN query. We discuss packing of the dataset in more detail in Section 7. This is a one time cost per dataset; the same index will be used for all the queries. We use STR [16] for a total ordering of the data. Throughout this paper R*-Tree is used to index the datasets. Other index structures can be used to replace the R*-tree. For simplicity, we choose the capacity of each MBR of the R*-tree as one disk page and use leaf level MBRs to prune the solution space.

Given two MBRs $B_1$ and $B_2$, we define MAXDIST($B_1$, $B_2$) and MINDIST($B_1$, $B_2$) as the maximum and minimum distance between $B_1$ and $B_2$. The following lemma establishes an upper bound to the $k$-NN distance to the objects in a set of MBRs.

**Lemma 1.** *Let $A$ be the MBR of a set of objects and $a \in A$ be an object. Let $\mathcal{B} = \{B_1, \cdots, B_{|\mathcal{B}|}\}$ be the set of leaf level MBRs of an index structure built on a dataset. Assume that the MBRs in $\mathcal{B}'$, where $\mathcal{B}' \subseteq \mathcal{B}$, contain at least $K$ objects. Let $\varepsilon$ denote the distance of object $a$ to its kth NN in $\mathcal{B}$, then*

$$\varepsilon \leq \max_{B \in \mathcal{B}'}\{\text{MAXDIST}(A, B)\}, \forall k, 1 \leq k \leq K.$$

Proof follows from the observation that all objects in $\mathcal{B}'$ appear in $\mathcal{B}$ too. For a given positive integer $k$, let $m$ be the integer, $1 \leq m < |\mathcal{B}|$, for which

$$\sum_{i=1}^{m-1} |B_i| < k \leq \sum_{i=1}^{m} |B_i|,$$

where $|B_i|$ is the number of objects in $B_i$. Let MAXDIST($A$, $B_i$) $\leq$ MAXDIST($A$, $B_{i+1}$), $\forall i$ $1 \leq i < |\mathcal{B}|$, where $|\mathcal{B}|$ is the cardinality of $\mathcal{B}$.

From Lemma 1, we know that the $k$-NN distance of the objects in $A$ to the objects in $\mathcal{B}$ is at most MAXDIST($A$, $B_m$). Hence, if MAXDIST($A$, $B_m$) < MINDIST($A$, $B$), $B \in \mathcal{B}$, then $B$ does not contain any object from the $k$-NN set of any object in $A$. Therefore, $B$ can be pruned away from $\mathcal{B}$ without any false dismissals during the computation of the $k$-NNs of the objects in $A$. From these observations, given a GNN query, GNN($R$, $S$, $S' \subseteq S$, $k$, $t$), for each $A \in \mathcal{A}$, we compute a priority list of the candidate boxes in $\mathcal{B}$ as follows:

- For each $A \in \mathcal{A}$,
  **Step 1:** Compute MAXDIST($A$, $B_m$) for the given value of $k$ as discussed above.
  **Step 2:** Find the MBRs, $B \in \mathcal{B}$ for which MINDIST($A$, $B$) $\leq$ MAXDIST($A$, $B_m$).
  **Step 3:** Assign priorities to these MBRs in increasing MINDIST($A$, $B$) order.

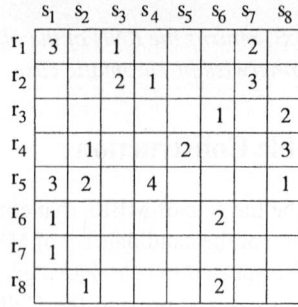
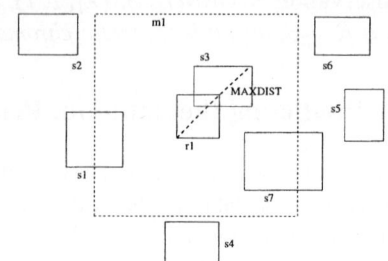

**Fig. 2.** A sample Priority Table for two datasets $R$ and $S$. Each row/column corresponds to a page of $R$/$S$ on disk. Numbers in cells show the priority of pages in $S$ for that row.

**Fig. 3.** First row of the Priority Table. Here $r_1 \in R$ and $S = \{s_1, \cdots, s_7\}$. Objects in $m_1$ are within MAXDIST distance from $r_1$.

The algorithm for Step 1 takes an MBR $A$, the root node of an R*-tree, and an integer $k$ as input. The root node is stored using a min-heap. The node with the smallest MAXDIST to $A$ is extracted from this heap. If the MINDIST of this node to $A$ is more than the threshold, then it is omitted. Otherwise it is inspected. If it is an internal node, then its children are inserted into the min-heap. Otherwise, it is inserted into the candidate set, which is maintained using a max-heap. If the candidate set contains more objects than necessary, then the MBR with the largest MINDIST value is removed from the candidate set. Although the worst case time complexity of this step is $O(|\mathcal{B}|)$ (i.e., the entire index is traversed) with an amortized complexity of $O(\log(|\mathcal{B}|))$. Step 2 is computed using the classic range search algorithm on R-trees having a complexity of $O(\log(|\mathcal{B}|))$. This step eliminates all the leaf level MBRs that only contain irrelevant points. Naturally, if an MBR contains at least one relevant point, it will be processed by the strategies proposed in Section 5. Step 3 takes $O(C \log C)$ time where $C$ is number of candidate MBRs found at Step 2.

The candidates for all MBRs in $\mathcal{A}$ are stored in a *Priority Table (PT)*. Figure 2 depicts the PT constructed for the GNN($R$, $S$, $S'$, $k$, $t$) query. Here, $r_i$ and $s_i$ correspond to MBRs for $R$ and $S$. We assume that $S' = \{s_1, s_3, s_4, s_5, s_7\}$ in this example. In this figure, each row and column corresponds to $r_i$ and $s_i$ respectively. For simplicity, we make two assumptions without affecting the generality: 1) The objects in $R$ and $S$ are located sequentially on disk. 2) Each row and column of the PT (i.e., each MBR) corresponds to one disk page. The numbers at each row show the priority of the candidate MBRs in $S$ for the corresponding MBR in $R$. For example in row 1, the MBRs $s_1$, $s_3$ and $s_7$ are in the candidate set of $r_1$, such that $s_3$ has the highest priority and $s_1$ has the lowest priority. This is depicted in Figure 3. If an MBR of $S$ is not in the candidate set of an MBR in $R$, then the corresponding cell is unnumbered.

Given a query, GNN($R$, $S$, $S' \subseteq S$, $k$, $t$), our search methods reduce the solution space by pruning the PT. Following two optimizations can be made to reduce search space by inspecting the PT:

**Optimization 1.** (Column Filter) *Let $s_i$ correspond to an MBR in $S'$. If the total number of objects in the MBRs in $R$ which have $s_i$ in their candidate set is less than $t$, then that column can be removed from $S'$.*

For example, in Figure 2, $s_5$ is in the candidate set of only $r_4$. If the total number of objects in $r_4$ is less than $t$, then $s_5$ can be removed from $S'$ safely. The correctness of *Column Filter* can be proven from the fact that an object in a column, $s_i$ can be in the $k$-NN set of the objects in the rows only that have $s_i$ in the candidate set.

**Optimization 2.** (Row Filter) *If a row does not contain any candidate MBRs in $S'$, then it can be removed from PT.*

For example, in Figure 2, rows $r_3$ and $r_8$ do not have any candidates in $S'$. Therefore, these rows can be omitted safely. If $s_5$ is pruned from $S'$ due to Column Filter, then the row, $r_4$, can also be ignored.

## 5 Static Search Strategies

PT defines the MBR pairs that (potentially) need to be compared to answer a given GNN query. In this section, we develop two methods to compute a GNN query, GNN($R$, $S$, $S' \subseteq S$, $k$, $t$), given the PT of the datasets $R$ and $S$. We name these methods *Fetch All (FA)* and *Fetch One (FO)*. We assume a limited buffer space $B$ throughout this section. That is, the sizes of both $R$ and $S$ are larger than $B$.

### 5.1 Fetch All

Our first method uses a pessimistic strategy: to process each page (i.e., MBR) of $R$, (i.e., one row in PT), it reads as many candidate pages from $S$ as possible into buffer at once starting from the one with the highest priority. For example, for $r_1$, FA reads $s_1$, $s_3$, and $s_7$. FA runs in 3 phases: (1) find maximal clusters that fit into buffer, (2) reorder the clusters to maximize the overlap and (3) read the pages for each cluster and process the contents. Next, we elaborate on each phase.

**Phase 1.** We create clusters by iteratively adding rows into the current cluster, starting from the first row, until its size becomes $B$. When the cluster becomes large enough, we start a new cluster. For example, if $B = 6$ pages, then the clusters for the PT in Figure 2 are $C_1 = \{r_1, r_2, s_1, s_3, s_4, s_7\}$, $C_2 = \{r_3, r_4, s_2, s_5, s_6, s_8\}$, $C_3 = \{r_5, s_1, s_2, s_4, s_8\}$, and $C_4 = \{r_6, r_7, r_8, s_1, s_2, s_6\}$. The total cost of this step is linear in the number of candidate pages since each candidate page is visited only once.

**Phase 2.** The order for reading the clusters affects the total amount of disk I/O. This is because, if consecutive clusters have common pages, these pages will be reused and they do not need to be read again. For example, if $C_3$ is read after $C_1$, then $s_1$ and $s_4$ will be reused, saving two disk reads. Given a read schedule of clusters, the total amount of disk reads saved by reusing buffer is equal to the sum of the common pages between consecutive clusters. For example, if the clusters are read in the order of $C_1$, $C_3$, $C_2$, $C_4$, then total savings adds up to 6 pages (i.e., $|C_1 \cap C_3| + |C_3 \cap C_2| + |C_2 \cap C_4| = 6$).

One can show that the Traveling Salesman Problem (TSP) can be reduced to the problem of finding the best schedule for reading clusters. Intuitively, the proof is as follows.

**Procedure ProcessBuffer($k$)**  /* Let k be a positive integer. */
**For** each row $r_i$ in the buffer **do**
- **while** row $r_i$ has more uninspected candidate MBRs in the buffer **do**
    1. Let $s_{r_i}$ be the next unprocessed candidate MBR with the highest priority.
    2. Find the $k$-NN of each object in $r_i$ in $s_{r_i}$. Store the maximum of these $k$-NN distances in $d_{max}$.
    3. Remove all candidates, $s$, of $r$ in PT for which MINDIST($r, s$) > $d_{max}$.

**Fig. 4.** The procedure to process a Buffer

Each vertex of TSP maps to a cluster. Each edge weight $w_{i,j}$ between clusters $C_i$ and $C_j$ is computed as the number of overlapping pages between $C_i$ and $C_j$. The best schedule on this graph is the Hamiltonian Path that maximizes the sum of edge weights. Since TSP minimizes the sum of edge weights, we update the weight of each edge $w_{i,j}$ as $w'_{i,j} = w_{max} - w_{i,j}$, where $w_{max}$ is the largest edge weight. This guarantees that the new edge weights are non-negative. Then we create a new node $v$ and is connected to all nodes by zero-weight edges. The optimal schedule is the path with the smallest sum of edge weights which begins at vertex $v$ and visits all nodes once. We use a greedy heuristic to find a good schedule as follows: We start with an empty path. While there are unvisited vertices, we insert the next edge with the smallest weight into the path if it does not destroy the path. Finally, we attach the disconnected paths randomly if there are any.

**Phase 3.** Once the cluster schedule is determined, the contents of each cluster are iteratively read into buffer using optimal disk scheduling [17]. Figure 4 shows the procedure used to process each cluster after it is fetched into buffer. For each row in the cluster, the algorithm searches the $k$-NN of each object starting from the box with the highest priority (Steps 1 and 2). The results obtained at this step are used to prune the candidate set (Step 3). After the candidate set is pruned, Optimizations 1 and 2 are applied to PT in order to further reduce the solution space.

### 5.2 Fetch One

FA reads many redundant pages if only a small percentage of the candidate pages contain actual $k$-NNs. FO uses optimistic approach to avoid this problem. FO iteratively reads one page per row as long as there are more candidates.

Figure 5 presents the pseudocode for FO. The algorithm splits buffer equally for each of the datasets. This is because, one candidate page is read per row starting from the highest priority (Step 1). Therefore, the number of pages from each dataset in the buffer will be equal at all times if all the candidate pages are distinct. After searching each candidate page (Step 2), PT is further pruned by eliminating the pages that are farther than the $k$th NN found so fa (Step 3)r, and using Optimizations 1 and 2 (Step 4).

For example, for the PT in Figure 2, let buffer size be 6 pages, then FO reads $\{r_1, r_2, r_3\}$ and $\{s_3, s_4, s_6\}$ into buffer. Assume that the third candidate of $r_1$ is pruned at the end of this step. Next, $\{s_7, s_8\}$ are read to replace $\{s_4, s_6\}$. Although it is the second

```
/*Let k be a integer.*/

Procedure FO(k)
While there are unprocessed rows do

  1. Fill half of buffer with the MBRs, $r_i$,
     from R and one page from S ($s_{r_i}$) for
     each $r_i$.
  2. ProcessBuffer(k).
  3. Remove all the rows, $r_i$, from the
     buffer that has no other uninspected
     candidate MBRs.
  4. Apply Optimizations 1 and 2 on PT.
```

**Fig. 5.** The Fetch One procedure

```
/*Let k be an integer.*/
/*Let B be buffer size.*/

Procedure FD(k)

  1. Initialize f.
  2. while there are unprocessed rows do
    (a) Fill buffer with $\lfloor \frac{B}{f+1} \rfloor$ pages ($r_i$)
        from R and f pages from S ($s_{r_i}$)
        for each $r_i$.
    (b) ProcessBuffer(k).
    (c) Remove all rows $r_i$, from buffer
        that has no other uninspected can-
        didate MBRs.
    (d) Apply Optimization 1 and 2 on
        PT.
    (e) Update value of f.
```

**Fig. 6.** The Fetch Dynamic procedure

candidate of $r_2$, we do not read $s_3$ at this step since it is already in buffer. Assume that the third candidate of $r_2$ is pruned at the end of this step. Since none of the rows $\{r_1, r_2, r_3\}$ have any remaining candidates FO does not need to read any more pages for these rows. Therefore, $\{r_1, r_2, r_3\}$ is replaced with $\{r_4, r_5, r_6\}$, and the search continues recursively.

## 6 Dynamic Strategy

FO reads only the necessary pages (i.e., MBRs) to compute a given GNN(R, S, S', k, t) query since it reads one page at a time starting from the highest priority and stops when the distance to the next MBR is more than the distance to the kth NN found so far. However, this does not guarantee that the total I/O cost is minimized. This is because FO incurs a random seek cost every time a new page is fetched from disk. Since a random seek is significantly more costly than a page transfer, reading a few redundant pages sequentially at once may be faster than FO. Thus, neither FO nor FA ensures the optimal I/O cost. The number of pages read at each iteration, $f$, that minimizes the I/O cost depends on the query parameters and the distribution of the database. A good approximation to this number can be obtained by sampling the MBRs of R.

Our third method, *Fetch Dynamic (FD)* adaptively determines the value of $f$ as follows. It starts by guessing the value of $f$. It then reads the first cluster using this value. As it finds the $k$-NNs of all the objects in the first cluster, it computes the optimal value of $f$ for that cluster. It then uses this value of $f$ to choose the next cluster. After processing each cluster, it iteratively updates $f$ as the median of the number of pages needed for all of the rows processed so far. Note that, the choice of the initial value of $f$ has no impact in the performance after the first step, since $f$ is updated immediately after every iteration. As more rows are processed in each iteration, $f$ adapts to the query parameters and data distribution.

Figure 6 presents the pseudocode of FD. The algorithm first assigns an initial value for $f$ ($1 \leq f \leq$ candidate size). We use 20 % of the average number of candidates of $R$ as our initial guess. Let $B$ denote the buffer size. While there are unprocessed rows, FD reads $\lfloor \frac{B}{f+1} \rfloor$ pages ($r_i$) from $R$ and $f$ pages ($s_{r_i}$) from $S$ with the highest priority for each $R$ page in buffer (Step 2.a). Thus, if all the candidates are distinct, buffer is filled with pages from $R$ and $S$. Steps 2.b processes each candidate page $s_{r_i}$. The processed pages ($r_i$s) are removed from buffer at Step 2.c. The algorithm continues with Steps 2.a to 2.c until all the rows in buffer are exhausted. Then Optimizations 1 and 2 are applied (Step 2.d). The value of $f$ is updated at Step 2.e as the median of the number of candidates of the processed pages in $R$.

## 7 Further Improvements for GNN Queries

So far we have discussed two optimizations, row filter and column filter to trim both I/O and CPU costs. In this section, we will discuss further optimizations to cut down both CPU and I/O costs of FA, FO, and FD.

**Adaptive Filter.** Our third optimization follows from the following observation. For a given MBR $r$ we expand it by $d_{\max}$ in all dimensions. If a candidate MBR $s$ overlaps with this expanded MBR, then we compute the distance between all pairs of points from $r$ and $s$. (Steps 2 and 3 of Figure 4) This incurs $O(t^2)$ comparisons if each MBR contain $O(t)$ points. We reduce this cost in two ways. First, instead of expanding by $d_{\max}$, we can adaptively expand by different amounts along different dimensions. Second, we avoid $t^2$ comparisons by pruning unpromising points from S in a single pass. More formally, we first find all points in a candidate MBR $s$ that are contained in the expanded MBR of $r$. Next, we compute the distances between all those points and all points of $r$. Let $t'$, $t' \leq t$, be the number of points in $s$ that are contained in the expanded MBR of $r$. The CPU cost for the comparison of MBR pairs drops from $O(t^2)$ to $O(t + t \cdot t')$. This is summarized as our third optimization, *Adaptive Filter*.

**Optimization 3.** (Adaptive Filter) *Let $p$ be a point in MBR $r$. Let $d$ be the kNN distance of $p$ to the points in MBR $s$. Let kNN-sphere of $p$ denote the sphere with radius $d$, centered at $p$. Let $M$ denote the MBR that tightly covers the kNN-spheres of all the points in $r$. A point can not be a kNN of a point in $r$ if it is not contained in $M$.*

In Figure 7, the expanded MBR of $r$ in the worst case is given by $m_1$. When adaptive bounds are used, the expanded MBR $m_2$ is obtained. In the former case, two MBRs $s_1$ and $s_2$ intersect with $m_1$. Thus, 3 disk I/Os ($r, s_1, s_2$) and 32 comparisons are made. However, only $s_1$ intersects with $m_2$ in the latter case. Hence MBR $s_2$, which do not have any point inside $m_2$, can be pruned. This reduces the I/O cost to 2 page reads ($r, s_1$) and the CPU cost to 16 comparisons. However, Optimization 3 states that a point in S is considered only if it is inside $m_2$. Therefore, we scan each point in $s_1$ once to find such points. These points are then compared to the points in $r$ to update $k$-NNs. Thus the CPU cost reduces to 12 comparisons (4 for scanning $s$ and 8 for comparison of the points in $r$ with $q_1$ and $q_2$).

**Partitioning.** Optimization 3 is improved further by partitioning the MBR $r$ along selected dimensions. Dimensions with high variances are selected for the partitioning. We start from the dimension with the highest variance. We split the MBR along this dimension into two MBRs, such that each resulting MBR contains the same number of objects. Each of these MBRs are then recursively partitioned along the dimension with the next highest variance recursively.

Partitioning improves the performance in two ways. First, since each of the partitions is smaller than the original MBR, the pruning distance ($d_{\max}$) along each dimension is reduced. This reduces the I/O cost. Second, without partitioning, an object in MBR $s$ is compared to all the objects in $r$ if the extended MBR of $r$ contains it. However, with partitioning, an object in $s$ is not compared to the objects in partitions whose extended MBR does not contain it. Thus, CPU cost is reduced by avoiding unnecessary comparisons. Note that as the number of partitions increases, the number of point-MBR comparisons increases. When the number of partitions becomes $O(t)$ (i.e., the number of objects per MBR), the number of such comparisons becomes $O(t^2)$. Thus, partitioning becomes useless. In our experiments, we partitioned along at most eight dimensions for the best performance.

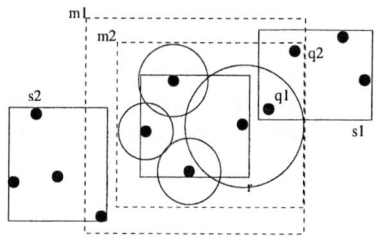 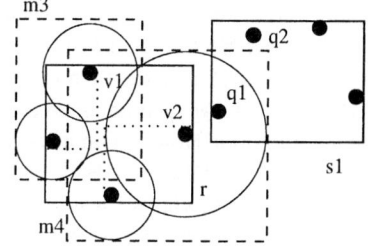

**Fig. 7.** $m_1$, $m_2$ are the expanded MBRs for the $r$ without using and using the *Adaptive Filter* respectively. $s_1, s_2 \subseteq S$, $s_1$ is the MBR of the points $\{q_1, q_2, q_3, q_4\}$.

**Fig. 8.** $v_1$ and $v_2$ are two partitions of MBR $r$ and $m_3$ and $m_4$ are their extended MBRs. $s_1 \subseteq S$ is the MBR of the points $\{q_1, q_2, q_3, q_4\}$.

In Figure 8, horizontal dimension is used to partition the MBR $r$ into two partitions. $v_1$ and $v_2$ are the MBRs of these partitions having $m_3$ and $m_4$ as extended MBRs. MBR $s_2$, which do not have any points inside $m_2$, can be pruned. We scan each point in $s_1$ once to find the candidate points for the partitions $v_1$ and $v_2$. Only $q_1$ is present in the extended MBR of $v_2$, reducing the CPU cost to 10 (8 for comparing points in $s_1$ with $v_1$ and $v_2$ and 2 for comparing the points in $v_2$ with $q_1$).

**Packing.** The performance of R-Tree based methods can be improved by using *packing* algorithms which group similar objects (objects within a close neighborhood) together. we employ the Sort-Tile-Recursive (STR) method [16] for packing the R*-Tree, built on the datasets. Let $N$ be the number of $d$-dimensional objects in a dataset, $B$ be the capacity of a node in R-Tree and let $P = \lceil \frac{N}{B} \rceil$. STR sorts objects according to the first dimension. Then the data is divided into $S = \lceil P^{\frac{1}{d}} \rceil$ slabs, where a slab consists of a run of $n.\lceil P^{\frac{d-1}{d}} \rceil$ consecutive objects from the sorted list. Now each slab is processed recursively using the remaining $d-1$ coordinates. It has been shown in [16] that for most types of data distributions STR-Ordering performs better than space-filling-curve based Hilbert-Ordering [11].

## 8 Experimental Evaluation

We use two classes of datasets in our experiments.

**Image datasets.** Each of *Image1* and *Image2* contains 60-dimensional feature vectors of 34,433 satellite images. We have created two datasets from Image1 and Image2 by splitting each 60-dimensional vector into 30 two-dimensional vectors. Each of the resulting datasets contains 1,032,990 data points.

**Protein structure datasets.** Each of *Protein1* and *Protein2* contains 288,156 three-dimensional feature vectors for secondary structures of proteins from Protein Data Bank (ftp://ftp.rcsb.org/pub/pdb) as discussed in [6].

In addition to FA, FO, and FD, we have implemented three existing methods: sequential search (SS) and the R-tree-based NN method of Roussopoulos et. al., (RT) [15] and Mux-Join [5]. To implement the buffer restrictions into RT, we use half of the available buffer for $R$ and the other half for $S$. In order to adapt these methods GNN($R$, $S$, $S'$, $k$, $t$), we performed a $k$-NN search for each object in $R$. We included SS in our experiments, as SS is better than many complicated NN methods for a broad set of data distributions [4]. We also obtained the source codes of GORDER [21] and RkNN [20], from their authors. However, at its current state, we found it impossible to restrict memory usage of GORDER to a desired amount. Therefore, we used GORDER in only one of our experiments where it was possible.

In all our experiments, we use $S' = S$ unless otherwise stated. We use 4 kB as the page size in all our experiments. We ran our experiments on an Intel Pentium 4 processor with 2.8 GHz clock speed.

### 8.1 Evaluation of Optimizations

In this section, we inspect the performance gain due to Optimizations 1, 2 and 3 and the improvements in Section 7. We perform GNN query by varying the size of $S'$ from 0.5 % to 8 % of $S$, by selecting pages of $S$ randomly. In this experiment, we use FD for $k = 10$, $t = 3,000$, and buffer size = 10 % of the dataset size. The queries are run on the two dimensional image dataset.

Figure 9 displays the I/O and the running times for Optimizations 1, 2 and 3 on an unpacked dataset. According to our results, the main performance gain is obtained from Optimizations 2 and 3, yet there is a slight performance gain from Optimization 1. The reason that the Optimization 1 has a smaller impact can be explained as follows. $t$ is only 0.3 % of the total number of objects in $R$. Thus, Optimization 1 can eliminate a page of $S$ only if it is in the candidate set of less than 3 pages of $R$. The impact of Optimization 1 is larger when the ratio of the average number of candidate pages to $t$ is lower. This happens when $t$ is large or $k$ is small. Optimization 2 has a high impact when $S'$ is smaller. This is because fewer rows in PT have candidates in $S'$ for small $S'$. Another way to obtain high filtering rate from Optimization 2 is to

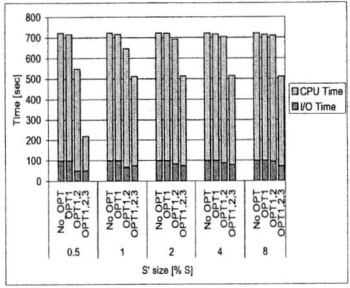 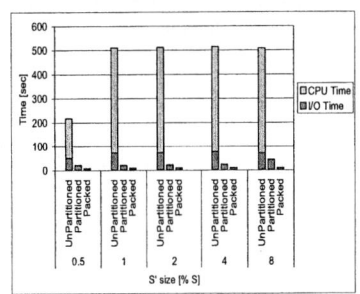

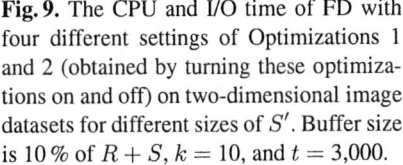

**Fig. 9.** The CPU and I/O time of FD with four different settings of Optimizations 1 and 2 (obtained by turning these optimizations on and off) on two-dimensional image datasets for different sizes of $S'$. Buffer size is 10 % of $R + S$, $k = 10$, and $t = 3{,}000$.

**Fig. 10.** The CPU and I/O time of FD with three different settings Unpartitioned, Partitioned, and Packed (along with partition) on two-dimensional image datasets for different sizes of $S'$. Buffer size is 10 % of $R+S$, $k = 10$, and $t = 3{,}000$.

reduce the average number of candidate pages per row by choosing a small value for $k$. Optimization 3 effectively reduces the CPU and I/O cost for different sizes of $S'$. We can also see that for higher percentages of $S$, the impact of this optimization remains constant and is independent of the size of $S'$. This can be understood from the fact that for a fixed value of $k$ and at higher percentages of $S$, every MBR $r \in R$ has same number of candidate MBRs from $S$. This results in constant reduction in CPU and I/O costs.

Figure 10 compares the performance gains on top of Optimizations 1, 2, and 3 (Unpartitioned algorithm) by partitioning the MBRs and by using the STR-method based packing algorithm. Here, packing is applied along with partitioning. Partitioning reduces the I/O cost up to factor of 3 and CPU costs by orders of magnitude. The tighter bounds of the extended MBRs of the partitions resulted in a reduction of the pruning distance. This explains the I/O and CPU performance gains from the partitioned algorithm. Packing utilizes the distribution of data and groups similar objects in MBRs that have common parent and a better organization of the R*-Tree index structure. This results in a lower value for the parameter $f$ in FD and hence has better performance gains. Packing reduces the I/O cost up to 10 times and CPU cost by orders of magnitude faster than an unpartitioned algorithm. It outperforms partitioned algorithm by up to a factor of 2 and 6 in I/O and CPU costs respectively. From here on we will use all the optimizations in all of our methods.

Scheduling pages is known as paging problem [14]. Chan [7] proposed heuristic based $O((R_p + S_p)^2)$ algorithms ($R_p$ and $S_p$ are the number of pages in two datasets) for Index-based Joins. For large datasets, however, these heuristics are not efficient. An online scheduling algorithm is evaluated using *competitive analysis* [1]. In competitive analysis, an online algorithm is compared with an optimal off-line algorithm which knows all candidate pages in advance. An algorithm is *c-Competitive* if for all sequences of page requests, $C_A \leq c.\bar{C} + b$, where $C_A$ is the cost of the given algorithm, $\bar{C}$ is the cost of the off-line algorithm, $b$ is a constant, and $c$ is the *competitive ratio*.

**Table 1.** Number of Page Reads from FA, FD and FO and Optimal Page Reads on two-dimensional image datasets. $k = 10$, and $t = 100$

| Buffer Size (%) | 5 | 10 | 20 | 40 |
|---:|---:|---:|---:|---:|
| Oracle | 11245 | 10980 | 10244 | 10252 |
| FO | 14601 | 13425 | 12710 | 12393 |
| FD | 16706 | 13825 | 11702 | 10789 |
| FA | 155727 | 73238 | 23885 | 10328 |

We compared the performance of our online methods with its off-line version, named *Oracle*. For each MBR $r \in R$, we provide *Oracle*, the set of MBRs from S such that every MBR in this set contains at least one $k$-NN of at least one object in $r$. We then optimize the number of I/Os of *Oracle* using the heuristic discussed in Section 5. We also compute a lower bound to the optimal number of I/Os as the total number of pages in R and S. The purpose of this experiment is to observe how the I/O cost of our online methods compare to that of an off-line method and the minimum possible I/O cost. Table 1 compares the performance of Oracle with our methods.

Since each dataset has 5064 pages, we compute the lower bound to the number of disk I/Os as 10128 (5064+5064). The *competitive ratio* of FA is smallest for large buffer sizes (1.008 for 40% buffer) and for FO it is smallest for small buffer sizes (1.3 for 5% buffer). FD has a smaller *competitive ratio* (1.5 for 5% buffer to 1.05 for 40% buffer). We conclude that our methods perform very close to the off-line method.

### 8.2 Comparison of Our Methods

In this section, we compare FA, FO, and FD to each other for different parameter settings.

**Evaluation of buffer size.** Here, we compare the performance of FA, FO, and FD when the buffer size varies from 5 to 40 % of the total size of $R$ and $S$. We use two-dimensional image dataset with $k = 10$ and $t = 500$.

Figure 11 shows the I/O time and the running time of our methods. For lower buffer sizes, FA retrieves all the candidate MBRs for every row and hence I/O cost takes up most of the total time. We can observe this from the performance of FA at buffer size

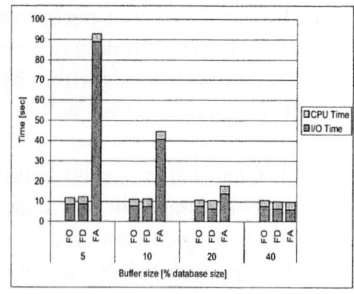
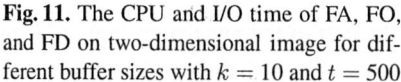
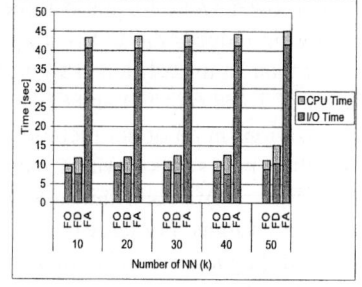

**Fig. 11.** The CPU and I/O time of FA, FO, and FD on two-dimensional image for different buffer sizes with $k = 10$ and $t = 500$

**Fig. 12.** The CPU and I/O time of FA, FO, and FD on the two-dimensional image, dataset for different values of $k$

5 % and is dominated by the I/O cost. As buffer size increases, the cost of all three strategies drop since more pages can be kept in buffer at a time. For small buffer sizes FO has the lowest cost since it does not load unnecessary candidates. As buffer size increases, FA has the lowest cost since it keeps almost entire $S$ in buffer. However, in all these experiments, the cost of FD is either the lowest or very close to the lower of FA and FO. This means that FD can adapt to the available buffer size.

**Evaluation of the number of NN.** Our next experiment compares the performance of FA, FO, and FD for different values of $k$. We use 10 % buffer size and $t = 500$ for the two-dimensional image dataset.

Figure 12 presents the I/O and the running times. The costs of all these methods increase as $k$ increases. For different values of $k$ FO has the lowest cost and FA has the highest cost, since we use a small buffer size (10%). Even when it does not have the lowest cost, FD is very close to FO. This means that FD can adapt to the parameter $k$.

### 8.3 Comparison to Existing Methods

In this section, we compared FD to five existing methods SS, RT, Mux-Index, RkNN, and GORDER for different parameter settings. We used two-dimensional image and protein datasets in our experiments. Due to space limitations, we do not include theoretical comparison of FD to existing $k$-NN, RNN and ANN methods as the main intent of this paper is not to solve these problems. We present experimental results comparing FD with well known methods for these special cases.

**Evaluation of buffer size.** In this experiment set, we fixed the values of $k$ and $t$, and vary the buffer size. We used the two-dimensional image dataset and $k = 10$. The running times of GORDER with different amounts of memory usage and that of FD with 1.6 MB memory were computed. We measured the actual memory usage of the methods using the *top* command of Linux. Although we set the buffer size (an input parameter to GORDER) to 20 % of the total dataset size, we observed that GORDER uses significant amount of memory (up to 175 % of the dataset size) for additional book keeping. In order to reduce the actual memory usage we ran GORDER with grid numbers 1000, 500, 200, and 100. However the actual memory usage of GORDER was always much larger than 20 % of the total dataset size (i.e., 8 MB). For different memory settings, the running time of GORDER varied from 300 to 4000 seconds while for the same query, FD running times varied from 10 to 13 seconds (see Table 2. According to these experiments, FD runs an order of magnitude faster than GORDER even when it uses much smaller buffer. We found it impossible to reduce the actual memory usage of GORDER

**Table 2.** Memory Usage and Running times (seconds) of GORDER on image dataset with varying grid sizes. FD runs in only 11.03 seconds for the same dataset using 20% buffer.

| Grid Size | 1000 | 500 | 200 | 100 |
|---|---|---|---|---|
| Buffer Size (%) | 175 | 108 | 88 | 85 |
| Time (seconds) | 305 | 535 | 1519 | 4259 |

**Table 3.** Running times (seconds) of FD and RkNn on image dataset with $k = 10$, 20, 30, 40 and 50 using 10% buffer for 100 queries

| $k$ | 10 | 20 | 30 | 40 |
|---|---|---|---|---|
| RkNN | 2620 | 11750 | 84145 | 175495 |
| FD | 101 | 101.76 | 101.3 | 101.83 |

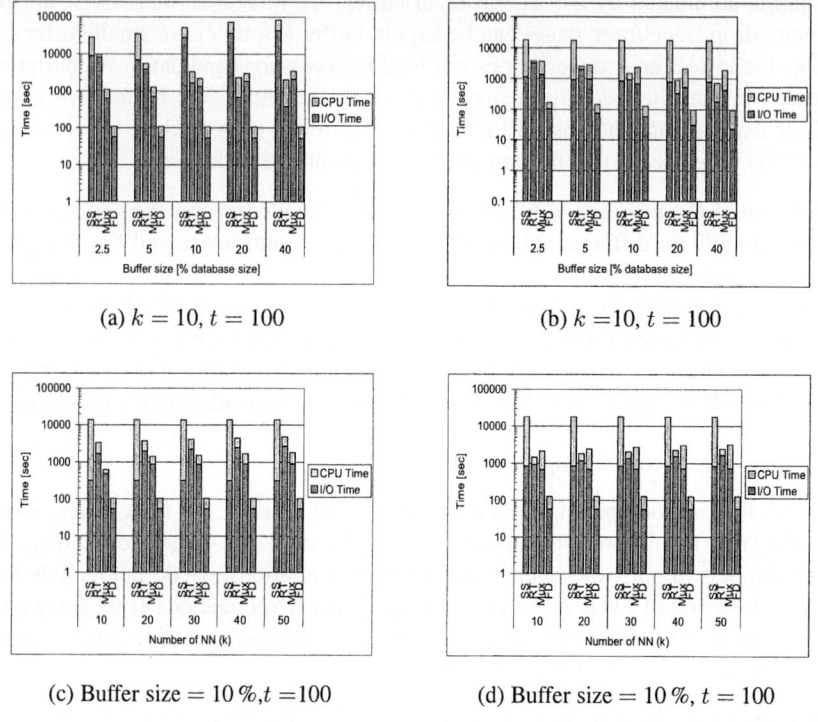

**Fig. 13.** The CPU and I/O time of SS, RT, Mux and FD on (a) two-dimensional image, and (b) protein datasets for different buffer sizes. The CPU and I/O time of SS, RT, and Mux FD on (c) two-dimensional image and (d) protein datasets for different values of $k$.

to 20 % at its current implementation. Therefore, in order to be fair, we do not include it in our remaining experiments.

Figures 13(a) and 13(b) show the I/O and the running times of SS, RT, Mux-index [5] and FD for different buffer sizes on two-dimensional image and protein datasets. We use $k = 10$ and $t = 100$. FD is the fastest of the three methods in all settings. We can see that for small buffer sizes RT is dominated by I/O cost. As buffer size increases, CPU cost of RT dominates. Sequential scan is dominated by the CPU cost in all the experiments. The I/O cost of FD is a fraction of that of RT. FD also reduces CPU cost aggressively through Optimizations 1 to 3 and partitioning. In all the experiments, the total time of FD is less than the I/O time of RT or SS alone. Mux-Index is dominated by I/O costs in all experiments. This is because for each block in $R$ it fills the buffer with blocks from $S$. Because of the nature of GNN queries, one needs to load pages multiple times while working with limited amount of memory, independent of the method used, naive (sequential scan) or more sophisticated (RT and Mux-Index). FD performs only the necessary leaf comparisons and uses the near optimal buffering schedule, thus reduces both the CPU and I/O cost effectively.

**Evaluation of the number NN.** Here, we compare the performance of FD, SS, Mux, RkNN and RT for different values of $k$. We use 10 % buffer size and $t = 500$ for two-

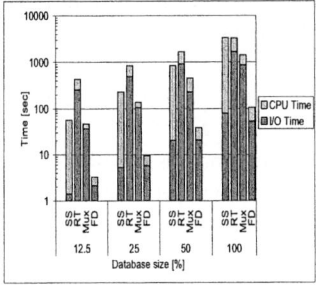 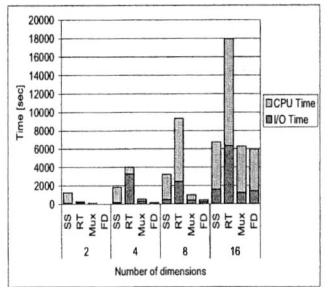

**Fig. 14.** The CPU and I/O time of SS, RT, Mux and FD on two-dimensional image datasets for varying database sizes. Buffer size is 10 % of the original image database, $k = 10$, and $t = 500$.

**Fig. 15.** The CPU and I/O time of SS, RT, and FD on two-dimensional image datasets for varying dimensionalities. Buffer size is 10 % of the database, $k = 10$, and $t = 500$.

dimensional image and protein datasets. We evaluated the RkNN by querying for 100 random query points for different values of $k$.

Figures 13(c) and 13(d) present the I/O and the running times. The cost of SS is almost the same for all values of $k$. It increases slightly as $k$ increases due to maintaining cost of the top $k$ closest objects. The costs of RT, Mux and FD increase as $k$ increases since their pruning power drops for large values of $k$. The running times of RT, Mux and FD do not exceed SS as $k$ increases. FD runs significantly faster than others. Depending on the value of $k$, FD runs orders of magnitude faster than RT, SS and Mux. The I/O cost increases much slower for FD. This is because FD adapts to different parameter settings quickly to minimize the amount of disk reads. Table 3 present the running times of FD and RkNN for 100 query points. While the running time of RkNN increases at faster rate and is not scalable for higher values of $k$, the running times of FD, including the time taken for the creation of priority table for each $k$, for the same query set is almost constant and is order of magnitude faster than RkNN.

**Evaluation of dataset size.** In this experiment, we observe the performance of FD, SS, Mux, and RT for increasing dataset sizes. We create smaller datasets from the original two-dimensional image datasets by randomly choosing 50, 25, and 12.5 % of all the vectors. We fix the buffer size to 10 % of the original image dataset, $k = 10$, and $t = 500$.

Figure 14 shows the I/O and the running times. As $R$ and $S$ grows, the running time of FD increases almost linearly. This is because when both datasets are doubled, the average number of candidate pages per row in the PT stays almost the same. On the other hand, the total running time of SS increases quadratically since it has to compare all pairs of data points. The running time of RT is dominated by I/O cost and increases faster than that of FD and slower than that of SS. Like SS, the running time Mux increases quadratically since it fills the buffer with blocks from $S$ and is dominated by I/O costs. Thus, the speedup of FD over SS, Mux and RT increases as dataset size increases. This means that our method scales better with increasing dataset size.

**Evaluation of the number of dimensions.** In this experiment, we observe the performance of FD, SS, Mux, and RT for increasing number of dimensions. We create datasets of $d = 2, 4, 8, 16$ dimensions by choosing the first $d$ values of the feature vectors from the original 60-dimensional image datasets. We fix the buffer size to 10% of the total size of $R$ and $S$, $k = 10$, and $t = 500$. Figure 15 shows the I/O and the running times. As the number of dimensions increases, the running time of SS increases linearly. On the other hand, the running times of RT and Mux increases faster. This is also known as the *dimensionality curse*. For all the methods CPU time increases with the increase in dimension and is significantly larger for 16 dimensions. However even at 16 dimensions FD is 1.3 times faster than the sequential scan, up to 3.5 times faster than RT and up to 1.2 times faster than Mux-Index.

## 9 Discussion

We considered the problem of detecting data broadness. We introduced a new database primitive called Generalized Nearest Neighbor (GNN) that expresses data broadness. We showed that the GNN queries can answer a much broader range of problems than the $k$-Nearest Neighbor query and its variants Reverse Nearest Neighbor query and All Nearest Neighbor query. Based on the available memory and the number of nearest-neighbors, either CPU or I/O time can dominate the computations. Thus, one has to optimize both I/O and CPU cost for this problem.

We proposed three methods to solve GNN queries. Our methods arrange two datasets into pages and compute a Priority Table for each page. Priority Table ranks the candidate pages based on their distance. Our first algorithm, FA, uses pessimistic approach. It fetches as many candidate pages as possible into available buffer. Our second algorithm, FO, uses optimistic approach. It fetches one candidate page at a time. Our third algorithm, FD, dynamically computes the number of pages that needs to be fetched by analyzing past experience. We also proposed three optimizations, Column Filter, Row Filter and Adaptive Filter to reduce the solution space of the priority table. We used packing and partitioning strategies which provided significant performance gains. These optimizations reduce the CPU cost of the $k$-NN searches and eliminates additional I/O costs by pruning the MBRs which do not have a $k$-NN.

According to our experiments, FA is best when the buffer size is large and FO is best when the buffer size is small. FD is the fastest method in most of the parameter settings. Even when it is not the fastest, the running time of FD is very close to that of the faster of FA and FO. FD is significantly faster compared to sequential scan and the standard R-tree based branch-and-bound $k$-NN solution to the GNN problem.

## References

1. Susanne Albers. Competitive Online Algorithms. Technical Report LS-96-2, brics, September 1996.
2. N. Beckmann, H.-P. Kriegel, R. Schneider, and B. Seeger. The R*-tree: An Efficient and Robust Access Method for Points and Rectangles. In *International Conference on Management of Data (SIGMOD)*, pages 322–331, 1990.
3. S. Berchtold, B. Ertl, D.A. Keim, H.-P. Kriegel, and T. Seidl. Fast Nearest Neighbor Search in High-dimensional Space. In *International Conference on Data Engineering (ICDE)*, pages 209–218, 1998.

4. K. S. Beyer, J. Goldstein, R. Ramakrishnan, and U. Shaft. When Is "Nearest Neighbor" Meaningful? In *International Conference on Database Theory (ICDT)*, pages 217–235, 1999.
5. C. Böhm and F. Krebs. The k-Nearest Neighbour Join: Turbo Charging the KDD Process. *Knowledge and Information Systems (KAIS)*, 6(6), 2004.
6. O. Çamoğlu, T. Kahveci, and A. K. Singh. Towards Index-based Similarity Search for Protein Structure Databases. *Journal of Bioinformatics and Computational Biology (JBCB)*, 2(1):99–126, 2004.
7. Chee Yong Chan and Beng Chin Ooi. Efficient Scheduling of Page Access in Index-Based Join Processing. *IEEE Transactions on Knowledge and Data Engineering (TKDE)*, 9(6):1005–1011, November/December 1997.
8. C. Ding and H. Peng. Minimum redundancy feature selection from microarray gene expression data. In *Computational Systems Bioinformatics Conference (CSB)*, pages 523–528, 2003.
9. G.R. Hjaltason and H. Samet. Ranking in Spatial Databases. In *Symposium on Spatial Databases*, pages 83–95, Portland, Maine, August 1995.
10. X. Huang and A. Madan. CAP3: A DNA Sequence Assembly Program. *Genome Research*, 9(9):868–877, 1999.
11. Ibrahim Kamel and Christos Faloutsos. Hilbert R-tree: An Improved R-tree using Fractals. In *International Conference on Very Large Databases (VLDB)*, pages 500–509, 1994.
12. F. Korn and S. Muthukrishnan. Influence sets based on reverse nearest neighbor queries. In *International Conference on Management of Data (SIGMOD)*, pages 201–212, 2000.
13. F. Korn, N. Sidiropoulos, C. Faloutsos, E. Siegel, and Z. Protopapas. Fast Nearest Neighbor Search in Medical Databases. In *International Conference on Very Large Databases (VLDB)*, pages 215–226, India, 1996.
14. T. H. Merrett, Yahiko Kambayashi, and H. Yasuura. Scheduling of Page-Fetches in Join Operations. In *International Conference on Very Large Databases (VLDB)*, pages 488–498, 1981.
15. N. Roussopoulos, S. Kelley, and F. Vincent. Nearest Neighbor Queries. In *International Conference on Management of Data (SIGMOD)*, San Jose, CA, 1995.
16. Mario Lopez Scott Leutenegger and Jeffrey Edgington. STR: A Simple and Efficient Algorithm for R-Tree Packing. In *International Conference on Data Engineering (ICDE)*, pages 497–506, 1997.
17. B. Seeger. An analysis of schedules for performing multi-page requests. *Information Systems*, 21(5):387–407, 1996.
18. T. Seidl and H.P. Kriegel. Optimal Multi-Step $k$-Nearest Neighbor Search. In *International Conference on Management of Data (SIGMOD)*, 1998.
19. I. Stanoi, M. Riedewald, D. Agrawal, and A.E. Abbadi. Discovery of Influence Sets in Frequently Updated Databases. In *International Conference on Very Large Databases (VLDB)*, pages 99–108, 2001.
20. Y. Tao, D. Papadias, and X. Lian. Reverse kNN Search in Arbitrary Dimensionality. In *International Conference on Very Large Databases (VLDB)*, 2004.
21. C. Xia, H. Lu, B.C. Ooi, and J. Hu. GORDER: An Efficient Method for KNN Join Processing. In *International Conference on Very Large Databases (VLDB)*, 2004.
22. C. Yang and K.-I. Lin. An Index Structure for Efficient Reverse Nearest Neighbor Queries. In *International Conference on Data Engineering (ICDE)*, pages 485–492, 2001.

# TrajPattern: Mining Sequential Patterns from Imprecise Trajectories of Mobile Objects

Jiong Yang and Meng Hu

EECS, Case Western Reserve University
jiong.yang@case.edu, meng.hu@case.edu

**Abstract.** Mobile objects have become ubiquitous in our everyday lives, ranging from cellular phones to sensors, therefore, analyzing and mining mobile data becomes an interesting problem with great practical importance. For instance, by finding trajectory patterns of the mobile clients, the mobile communication network can allocate resources more efficiently. However, due to the limited power of the mobile devices, we are only able to obtain the imprecise location of a mobile object at a given time. Sequential patterns are a popular data mining model. By applying the sequential pattern model on the set of imprecise trajectories of the mobile objects, we may uncover important information or further our understanding of the inherent characteristics of the mobile objects, e.g., constructing a classifier based on the discovered patterns or using the patterns to improve the accuracy of location prediction. Since the input data is highly imprecise, it may not be possible to directly apply any existing sequential pattern discovery algorithm to the problem in this paper. Thus, we propose the model of the trajectory patterns and a novel measure to represent the expected occurrences of a pattern in a set of imprecise trajectories. The concept of pattern groups is introduced to present the trajectory patterns in a concise manner. Since the Apriori property no longer holds on the trajectory patterns, a new **min-max** property is identified and a novel TrajPattern algorithm is devised based on the newly discovered property. Last but not least, we apply the TrajPattern algorithm on a wide range of real and synthetic data sets to demonstrate the usefulness, efficiency, and scalability of this approach.

## 1 Introduction

Mobile devices have been widely used in our everyday life, from handheld devices, e.g., PDA, to embedded devices, e.g., sensors. The trend is expected to intensify in the coming years. It is projected that in the next few years, all Hertz rental cars will be equipped with global positioning systems (GPS). One may infer important information from the trajectories of mobile objects. Most of the recent research effort has been concentrated in modeling the trajectory of mobile objects [2, 10, 11, 12] and indexing mobile objects [7, 9]. However, mining mobile data has received little attention so far. In this paper, we investigate the problem of mining and analyzing trajectories of moving objects. The following is a list of applications of analyzing the mobile trajectory data.

- Due to the limited power on the mobile devices and the unreliable communication links, we may want to infer the location of a mobile object based on its previous

locations. If we can find some moving patterns that are common to a large set of mobile objects, then these moving patterns may be useful for predicting the locations of an object in the future.
- In location-based commerce advertisement, if customers are willing to receive advertisements, retail stores will distribute e-Flyers to potential customers' mobile devices based on their locations. In this setting, finding common moving patterns of mobile devices is valuable for inferring potential movement of mobile device users, and thus helps to efficiently distribute the advertisement.
- Using a remote sensing system, the animals in a large farming area can be tracked. The sensors are limited in power and may fail from time to time. By mining the imprecise trajectories of animals, it is possible to determine migration patterns of certain animal or groups of animals. These patterns could be useful to analyze the migration behavior of different species of animals.

The energy in a mobile device is very limited, so it is impossible for a mobile object to continuously send out its location information. To reduce the energy consumption, many methods [2, 11, 12] are developed for obtaining (predicting) the approximate location of a mobile object. At a high level, all of these methods share the same principle. These methods first use some predictive model, e.g., Kalman Filter, linear model, etc., to predict an expected location of a mobile object at a given time $t$. If the actual location of the mobile object differs too much from the predicted location, then the mobile object reports the new location. Otherwise, it does not report the new location.

In this paper, our aim is not to develop a data mining approach which depends on a particular prediction model, but rather develop a general data mining framework that can be applied to a large number of existing location prediction methods. In the data mining field, there exist a large number of different models, from association to classification. Among these models, frequent patterns are one of the most basic and widely employed models. In addition, most of the previous proposed location prediction models for mobile objects assume one type of movement, e.g., linear, quadratic, etc. However, the type of movement for a mobile object may not be known ahead. Moreover, a mobile object may change the type of movement at any time. Therefore, the accuracy of these models might not be high. The frequent patterns may help to improve the accuracy of the prediction module. If an object follows some moving patterns, e.g., an object always changes its velocity or directions after it moves in a certain manner, then this knowledge can be integrated into the location prediction module and the location prediction can be adjusted accordingly. Looking ahead, we will show the usefulness of the frequent patterns of the imprecise trajectories on real data sets via the location prediction.

The traditional frequent pattern models and approaches could not be directly applied to the trajectories due to their imprecise nature. In the traditional frequent sequential pattern setting, the sequences are synchronized and we know exactly the occurrences of the symbol or values at every synchronized point. In this paper, a series of synchronization points can be superimposed on the trajectories. The interpolated values (at synchronization points) can be taken as the input for the frequent pattern mining process. In many applications, it is more useful to find patterns on the velocities rather than the locations. In such a case, we can transform the location trajectories (sequences) into velocity trajectories (sequences). Thus, our frequent pattern model can be constructed on a set of either location or velocity trajectories.

A sequential pattern is an ordered list of symbols. It is intuitive and easy for a user to comprehend, thus we also use the sequential pattern model in this paper. A trajectory pattern is an ordered list of positions. For instance, a pattern $(p_1, p_2, \ldots, p_m)$ can be considered as the possible positions of an object at $m$ consecutive snapshots. The support model is usually used to measure the importance of a pattern, i.e., if a pattern occurs a large number of times, then it is an important pattern. However, in the context of the imprecise trajectories, at any given moment, the location of an object in a trajectory is not precise, but rather a distribution of possible locations. Thus, we do not know for sure whether a pattern occurs or not. This could be a very challenging issue for formulating the frequent sequential pattern model. In this paper, we propose the normalized match (NM) measure to capture the importance of a trajectory pattern. We show the benefits of the NM measure over other measures in the experimental results section.

Most previous frequent sequential pattern algorithms utilize the Apriori property. However, the Apriori property does not hold for our NM measure. Fortunately, we are able to identify another property, called **min-max** property, which is weaker than the Apriori property. Thus it is necessary for us to devise a new algorithm for mining the NM patterns. Based on the min-max property, we develop a trajectory pattern mining algorithm called **TrajPattern**. The user will specify $k$, the number of trajectory patterns that he wants. Our goal is to mine the $k$ patterns with the most NM. Due to the presence of noise in the trajectories, many similar patterns may be found in the mining process. The concept of **pattern groups** is introduced to compactly represent a large number of similar trajectory patterns via a small number of groups. The TrajPattern algorithm mines the patterns by a *growing* process. We first identify short patterns with high NM value, and then try to extend these short patterns to find longer patterns with high NM via the min-max property. With the min-max property, a novel pruning method is devised to reduce the number of candidate patterns, thus the efficiency of the mining algorithm can be greatly improved. In addition, the TrajPattern algorithm can be used for mining any type of patterns satisfying the min-max property.

The remainder of this paper is organized as follows. We briefly describe some related work at Section 2. The problem model is presented in Section 3. The TrajPattern algorithm is discussed in Section 4. Additional issues of the trajectory pattern model and algorithm are discussed in Section 5. The experimental results are shown in Section 6. Finally, we draw our conclusions in Section 7.

## 2 Related Work

There is a large amount of work in location modeling and prediction. In [2] the Kalman Filter is used to predict the location of a mobile object at a given time while in [11], the authors used not only a single previous location, but rather multiple locations to predict the current location. Authors in [12] assumed that the object moves in a piece-wise linear manner. Thus the location of an object can be predicted by its previous locations and velocities.

Data mining has been an active research area in the past decade. Many data mining models and approaches have been proposed. However, there is limited work on spatiotemporal data mining. In [5], the proposed algorithm treated spatiotemporal data as a generalization of pattern mining in time-series data to capture the frequent moving patterns of users from a set of log data in a mobile environment. Authors in [6] processed moving nearest-neighbor queries in R-trees by employing sampling. In [9] the TPR-tree is presented as an extension of the R-tree to answer prediction queries on dynamic objects. Very recently, researchers began to study the problem of mining the trajectories of mobile objects. In [3] the authors proposed a method on clustering the locations of mobile objects continuously. It groups nearby objects into small microclusters and each micro-cluster is treated as an entity so that the computation time can be saved. The authors of [4] proposed a method to find periodic patterns for trajectories of mobile objects. This work aims to find the periodic moving patterns in the history of one object. In addition, all above works also assume that the input data is a sequence of precise locations, which is quite different from our assumption that the locations of objects are imprecise. Therefore the support measure can be used to qualify the importance of patterns in [4], but it could not be applied to our problem. To the best of our knowledge, we are the first to tackle the problem of mining imprecise trajectories.

Sequential patterns has been an active research topic in recent years, and many sequential pattern mining models and approaches have been proposed. One category of sequential patterns is the periodic patterns [1, 4] which repeat themselves over the time. Another category is the frequent sequential patterns [8, 13, 14, 15], which is more related to the problem in this paper. A frequent sequential pattern is a pattern which occurs at a large number of sequences. Several models and approaches have been proposed for this problem. In [8] the authors used the prefix-tree to maintain the set of prefixes of frequent patterns and later grow the set of patterns. The author of [15] designed an efficient algorithm for mining frequent subsequences in a long sequence. Both above approaches assume that the symbol in each position is accurate and the Apriori Property is used for devising efficient algorithms.

In [14] the authors studied the problem that symbols in a set of sequences are not accurate and may mutate due to noise. There is a mutation matrix which shows the probability that a symbol $a$ may mutate to $b$ in the input data sequence. The match model is invented for representing the true (or expected) occurrences of a pattern. The match of a pattern within a sequence is the joint probability of the occurrence of the symbols in the pattern. The match value of a pattern is not normalized according to its length. As a result, the non-normalized match of a longer pattern is smaller. This property is not desirable in many applications where longer patterns are needed since longer patterns usually consist of more information. Since the Apriori property holds for the match measure, the authors in [14] devised an algorithm based on the Apriori property, which could not be directly applied to the problem in this paper.

## 3 Preliminaries and Problem Statement

In this paper, we study the problem of identifying sequential patterns of imprecise trajectories of mobile devices. We assume that there is a server and a set of mobile devices. The mobile devices have the capability to know their own locations (e.g. via GPS) and they asynchronously report their locations to the server via some wireless network.

## 3.1 Location Reporting Scheme

A mobile object may choose not to notify the server its current location for a long time when the location can be derived from its previous locations, speed, directions, etc. There are many methods (e.g., [2, 11, 12], etc.) for a server to predict the location of a mobile device. Our aim is to develop a general pattern mining framework that can be used with various different location inference models, so we only require that the location prediction method has the following property. At any given time $t$, each mobile object has a predicted location. The actual location of the mobile object follows a certain distribution around the predicted location.

Most of the proposed location inference techniques satisfy the above property. Without loss of generality, we choose the method proposed in [12] as an example to demonstrate our problem model and solution. For a given device $o$, let $last\_loc$ be the last known location of the object and $v$ be the velocity vector of the object. The predicted position of $o$ ($predict\_loc$) is defined as follows:

$$predict\_loc = last\_loc + v \times t \tag{1}$$

Here, $t$ is the number of time units that have elapsed since the last known position of $o$. Since this is only a prediction, the actual position of $o$ may vary from the predicted position. It is assumed that the actual position of $o$ follows the $k$-dimensional multivariate normal distribution $N_k(\mu, \Sigma)$ where $k$ is equal to the dimension of the space, the mean $\mu = predict\_loc$, and $\Sigma$ is the variance-covariance matrix. The variance-covariance matrix is a symmetric $k \times k$ matrix with diagonal elements $\sigma^2$ equal to the variance of the marginal distributions. $\sigma$ is defined as $\frac{1}{c}U$ where $U$ is the tolerable uncertainty distance of the object and $c$ is a constant. A mobile object may choose to report its actual location only if it is more than $U$ away from the predicted position $\mu$. There are several ways to assess the parameters $U$ and $c$. $U$ can be either a constant, a function of the elapse time $t$, or the expected traversed distance $d$. In this paper, we assume that $U$ is a constant so that all objects in the database have the same uncertainty. This assumption has been practically used since it is difficult to find the uncertainty for each object. $c$ is a constant which may depend on the network reliability, etc. With the greater $c$, the probability that the actual location close to the predicted location is higher. For instance, a mobile device is within $U$ distance from $\mu$ with probability 0.68, 0.95 and 0.997 for $c = 1, 2, 3$, respectively. Since there may be an error during the communication between the mobile object and the server, the location information may be lost during the transmission. If there exists a 5% chance that the message will be lost during the location notification, then $c$ should be set to 2 so that the probability that the actual location is more than $U$ away from $\mu$ is equal to 5%.

## 3.2 Location and Velocity Trajectories

To provide a consistent view of all objects, a set of synchronous snapshots are generated on the server. A series of synchronization points can be superimposed on the asynchronous data. The interpolated values (at synchronization points) can be taken as the input to the data mining modules. Let's assume that we generate a snapshot at time point $t$. For every object we could calculate its locations at $t$ via some prediction method.

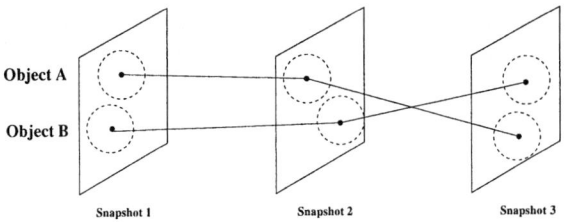

**Fig. 1.** Location Trajectories

For instance, we can apply Equation 1 to compute the expected location of an object based on the last reported location before $t$. Based on this model, at each snapshot, every object will have an expected location and a distribution of errors. The frequency of the snapshots may vary in different applications. We will discuss how to choose this parameter in a later section.

The locations of a mobile object $o$ at each snapshot can form a sequence $T$. We call $T$ the *location trajectory* of object $o$. Here $T = (l_1, \sigma_1), (l_2, \sigma_2), \ldots$ where $l_i$ and $\sigma_i$ are the mean and standard deviation of the distribution of the true location of $o$ at $i$th snapshot, respectively. $l_i$ and $\sigma_i$ can be calculated via Equation 1. Figure 1 shows two location trajectories.

In many applications, two mobile objects may travel in different regions of space. Thus these two location trajectories could not be compared directly. On the other hand, the velocities may be more important. In these applications, we need to transform the location trajectories to a sequence of velocities, or *velocity trajectories*. This can be achieved by taking the difference between two consecutive snapshots. For example, let $T = (l_1, \sigma_1), (l_2, \sigma_2), (l_3, \sigma_3), \ldots$ be a location trajectory where $l_i$ and $\sigma_i$ are the expected location and the standard deviation of the mobile object at the $i$th snapshot. The velocity trajectory is generated as follows. We consider the location of a mobile object at $i$th and $i+1$th snapshot as two random variables of normal distribution with mean $l_i$ and $l_{i+1}$ and standard deviation $\sigma_i$ and $\sigma_{i+1}$. The difference of these two random variables can be considered as the velocity of the mobile object at $i$th snapshot. The difference is also a normal distribution random variable where the mean is $l_{i+1} - l_i$ and the standard deviation is $\sqrt{\sigma_i^2 + \sigma_{i+1}^2}$. (A slightly more complicated formula can be used to compute the standard deviation if the two random variables are not independent.) Thus the new velocity trajectory $T'$ is in the following form: $T' = (l'_1, \sigma'_1), (l'_2, \sigma'_2), (l'_3, \sigma'_3), \ldots$ where $l'_i = l_{i+1} - l_i$ and $\sigma'_i = \sqrt{\sigma_i^2 + \sigma_{i+1}^2}$. It is obvious that the transformed velocity trajectories are in the same form as the original location trajectories. Thus, we call both the velocity trajectories and location trajectories as *trajectories*. In this paper, we assume that the input data is a set of trajectories, each of which is in the form of $T$.

### 3.3 Model of Trajectory Pattern

A trajectory pattern $P$ can be represented as $P = (p_1, p_2, \ldots, p_m)$ where $p_i$ is a location. $P$ can be interpreted as the following: the mobile object is located at $p_1$, $p_2$, ..., and $p_m$ at $m$ consecutive snapshots. The **length** of a pattern $P$ is the number of positions in $P$, which is $m$ in this example. We call a pattern of length 1 as a *singular* *pattern*. In theory, the space in which the objects travel is continuous, which means that there are infinite possible choices for a position in a pattern. To expedite the mining process, we discretize the space into small regions and only the centers of these regions may serve as the positions in a pattern. Let $G_x, G_y$ be the grid size on a 2-dimensional space. As long as $G_x, G_y$ are sufficiently small, our model will provide a very good approximation.

The support model has been used to measure the importance of a pattern in many applications [8, 15]. According to the traditional support model, we may define the support of a trajectory pattern as follows. A trajectory sequence $T$ supports a pattern if there exists a consecutive segment $((l_k, \sigma_k), (l_{k+1}, \sigma_{k+1}), \ldots, (l_{k+m-1}, \sigma_{k+m-1}))$ such that $l_{k+i-1}$ is equal to $p_i$ for $1 \leq i \leq m$. However, in the context of this problem, the support model may not work well due to the presence of noises. The degradation of quality of the data may conceal the real frequent patterns. The spirit of the support model is to find frequently occurred patterns. Due to the uncertainty (which is described as a probabilistic function), we have to find expected frequently occurred patterns instead. In [14] the match model is proposed to measure the expected number of occurrences of a pattern. Intuitively, the match model computes the expectation on how likely a pattern occurs in a trajectory or the degree that a trajectory confirms (supports) a trajectory pattern.

Let $\delta$ be the indifferent parameter such that for any coordinate (x, y), if an object $o$ is at most $\delta$ away from $(x, y)$, then the location of $o$ is considered indifferent from $(x, y)$. With the indifferent parameter, we can define the match of a trajectory pattern as the following. If at a snapshot the expected location of an object is $l$ with standard deviation $\sigma$, the probability that the true location of the object is within $\delta$ away from another location $p$ is denoted as $Prob(l, \sigma, p, \delta)$, which represents how likely the object is truly very close to a position $p$. Let $T' = ((l_k, \sigma_k), (l_{k+1}, \sigma_{k+1}), \ldots, (l_{k+m-1}, \sigma_{k+m-1}))$ be a contiguous segment of a trajectory sequence and $P = (p_1, p_2, \ldots, p_m)$ be a trajectory pattern, the probability that for every $1 \leq i \leq m$, the true location of the mobile object is located within at most $\delta$ away from $p_i$ is[1]

$$M(P, T') = Prob(P, T') = \Pi_{i=1}^{m} Prob(l_{k+i-1}, \sigma_{k+i-1}, p_i, \delta) \quad (2)$$

We call $M(P, T')$ the *match* between a pattern $P$ and a trajectory $T'$ of the same length. This is essentially the same measure as in [14].

Based on the definition of *match*, the value of *match* monotonously decreases with the growth of pattern length $m$. For example, if the probabilities of observing symbol $a$, $b$, and $c$ at position 1, 2, and 3 are all 0.9, then the joint probability of $(a, b)$ is 0.81 while the joint probability of $(a, b, c)$ is 0.729. In this case, only short patterns can be found and the measurement can not be compared between patterns of different lengths. To normalize this effect, we choose the geometric mean to denote the match between $T'$ and $P$, which is $(M(P, T'))^{\frac{1}{m}}$. To speed up the computation we use the logarithmic value to present the match between a trajectory and a pattern with the same length, i.e.,

$$NM(P, T') = \log M^{1/m}(P, T') = \frac{\log M(P, T')}{m}. \quad (3)$$

---

[1] We assume that the error in location prediction in $T'$ is independent, but the locations of the mobile objects in $T'$ are not assumed independent.

We call $NM(P,T')$ the *normalized match* (NM) of a pattern $P$ with a trajectory $T'$ of the same length. In reality, the length of a trajectory $T$ is usually much longer than that of a pattern $P$ (with $m$ locations). Thus, we use the maximum NM between any continuous segment of $m$ locations in $T$ and $P$ as the NM between $T$ and $P$. Formally, the NM between $T$ and $P$ is defined as follows.

$$NM(P,T) = \max_{\forall T' \subseteq T, |T'|=|P|} NM(P,T') \qquad (4)$$

In a data set $\mathcal{D}$, the NM of a pattern $P$ is equal to $\sum_{T \in \mathcal{D}} NM(T,P)$, i.e., the sum of NM between $P$ and each trajectory in $\mathcal{D}$. Here, the NM between $P$ and a trajectory actually represents how likely the pattern occurs in the trajectory. The sum of NM measures the expected occurrence of the pattern in a trajectory set. This is essentially based on the same intuition that, in traditional frequent patterns, the support of a pattern is defined as the total number of exact occurrences in a data set. The match measure can be defined similarly. The Apriori property holds on the match measure, but not on the NM measure, because the NM is normalized according to the pattern length. Thus, the algorithm proposed in [14] can only be applied for mining patterns according to the match measure. We need to develop algorithms to mine the patterns according to the NM measure.

### 3.4 Definition of Pattern Group

Since the trajectories are imprecise, many mined trajectory patterns are very similar. At each snapshot of trajectory, the true location of the moving object follows a normal distribution where the mean is the expected location of the object. Therefore, due to the bell shape of the normal distribution, the probabilities that the true location of the object falls into two adjacent grids could be similar. As a result, the NM of two patterns consisting of nearby grids could be similar.

The pattern group is a concept which helps to compactly present the results of imprecise trajectory mining, in which many patterns are similar to each other. The similar patterns can be clustered into a small number of groups. Intuitively, similar patterns should be close to each other at any snapshot. The similar relation of patterns and the concept of pattern group are formally defined as below:

**Definition 1.** *Given two patterns of the same length, if at every snapshot of the patterns, the distance between the two patterns is no larger than a pre-defined value $\gamma$, we say that these two patterns are* **similar patterns**.

$\gamma$ is called the maximum similar pattern distance. How to set this parameter is discussed in a later section.

**Definition 2.** *A* **pattern group** *is a set of patterns, which contains the maximum number of patterns that are similar to each other.*

### Problem Statement

In this paper, we try to solve the following problem. For a given set of imprecise trajectories, we want to find $k$ patterns with the most normalized match. These qualified patterns are represented via the concept of pattern groups.

## 3.5 Properties of Trajectory Patterns

As discussed above, the NM measure does not possess the Apriori property. As a result, many algorithms that utilize the Apriori property could not be applied here. However, the NM of trajectory patterns exhibit the following property which can be used to facilitate the mining process. Before stating the property, we first define some terms that will be used in the remainder of this paper.

**Definition 3.** *Let $P = (p_1, p_2, \ldots, p_m)$ and $P' = (p'_1, p'_2, \ldots, p'_n)$ be two trajectory patterns. $P$ is a **super-pattern** of $P'$ iff there exists an integer $i \geq 0$ such that for all $1 \leq j \leq n$, $p_{i+j} = p'_j$. In addition, $P$ is called a **proper super-pattern** of $P'$ if $m > n$.*

For example, let $P = (p_1, p_2, p_3)$ and $P' = (p_2, p_3)$. We call $P$ a super-pattern or proper super-pattern of $P'$. On the other hand, we also call $P'$ a sub-pattern or proper sub-pattern of $P$.

**Definition 4.** *A trajectory pattern $P$ is called an i-trajectory pattern (or $i - $ pattern for short) if there are i positions specified in $P$, i.e., $P = (p_1, p_2, \ldots, p_i)$.*

**Property 1.** *Given two trajectory patterns $P' = (p'_1, p'_2, \ldots, p'_i)$ and $P'' = (p''_1, p''_2, \ldots, p''_j)$. Let $P = (p'_1, p'_2, \ldots, p'_i, p''_1, \ldots, p''_j)$ be the trajectory pattern by appending $P''$ to the end of $P'$. Within a given set of trajectories $\mathcal{D}$, $NM(P) \leq \max(NM(P'), NM(P''))$. We call it the **min-max** property.*

*Proof.* For each trajectory $T \in \mathcal{D}$, there exists a sub-trajectory $T'$, where $|T'| = |P|$ and $NM(P, T) = NM(P, T')$. By definition, we have $(i + j) \times NM(P, T') \leq i \times NM(P', T') + j \times NM(P'', T') \leq i \times NM(P', T) + j \times NM(P'', T)$. Thus, $(i + j) \times NM(P) = \sum_{T \in \mathcal{D}}(i + j) \times NM(P, T) \leq \sum_{T \in \mathcal{D}} i \times NM(P', T) + \sum_{T \in \mathcal{D}} j \times NM(P'', T) = i \times NM(P') + j \times NM(P'')$. As a result, $NM(P) \leq \max(NM(P'), NM(P''))$.

Note that the above min-max property is very different from the Apriori property. The Apriori property states that the support of a pattern is less than or equal to any of its sub-patterns, while the min-max property is much looser. For each partition of a pattern $P$, we have two portions (sub-patterns) $P_{left}$ and $P_{right}$. The min-max property requires that the NM of $P$ is less than or equal to either $P_{left}$ or $P_{right}$. The algorithms developed for mining the patterns satisfying the Apriori property may not be directly applied to the trajectory patterns with NM. As a result, it is necessary to develop a new algorithm for mining NM patterns.

## 4 TrajPattern Algorithm

In this section, we present the TrajPattern algorithm to mine the $k$ trajectory patterns with the most normalized match (NM), and cluster these patterns into pattern groups. The following observations are used for the mining process.

1. The length of the discovered trajectory patterns is usually much shorter than the length of the trajectory. A trajectory could contain thousands of snapshots while a

qualified trajectory pattern often has much less positions, e.g., tens. Based on this observation, it is reasonable to start the search process from the short patterns, and grow to longer patterns.

2. Our goal is to find the $k$ patterns with the most NM. If we know the NM threshold $\omega$, then this threshold can be used for pruning the search space. Unfortunately, we do not know $\omega$. However, if we find a set of patterns $Q$, then the NM threshold $\omega$ should be greater than or equal to the $k$th maximum NM of the patterns in $Q$. Based on this observation, we can dynamically maintain a set of patterns $Q$, and the NM threshold $\omega$ should be the $k$th maximum NM of the patterns in $Q$. With more patterns discovered, we can update the threshold $\omega$, which could increase the pruning power.

3. Based on the min-max property, if a pattern $P_1$ is below a NM threshold $\omega$, then in order to find a super-pattern $P = (P_1, P_2)$ such that $NM(P) \geq \omega$, the NM of the pattern $P_2$ has to be greater than or equal to $\omega$. As a result, if the NM of a pattern $P$ is below $\omega$, then $P$ will only be combined with patterns whose NM is at least $\omega$ to generate the candidate patterns. Thus, we may consider the set of patterns with NM at least $\omega$ as the seeds for generating the candidate patterns.

Based on the previous observations, we devise an algorithm called *TrajPattern* to mine the set of $k$ trajectories with the most NM. We first partition the space into grids, and the grid centers serve as the singular patterns. Then we initialize the set $Q$ to include all these singular patterns and set the NM threshold $\omega$ to be the $k$th maximum NM of patterns in $Q$. The set of patterns in $Q$ with NM lower than $\omega$ is marked as *low* patterns and denoted as $\mathcal{L}$ while the set of patterns in Q with NM greater than or equal to $\omega$ is labeled as *high* patterns and denoted as $\mathcal{H}$. We can generate the candidate patterns from the set of high patterns as follows. For each high pattern $P \in \mathcal{H}$, we extend $P$ by adding each pattern $P' \in Q$. Note that $P'$ may be a high pattern or a low pattern. Let $P = (p_1, p_2, \ldots, p_m)$ and $P' = (p'_1, p'_2, \ldots, p'_l)$. Two candidate patterns $(p_1, \ldots, p_m, p'_1, \ldots, p'_l)$ and $(p'_1, \ldots, p'_l, p_1, \ldots, p_m)$ will be generated. The NM of these candidate patterns are computed and these newly generated patterns are inserted into $Q$. Based on these patterns, we can update the threshold $\omega$ and mark all patterns as high or low according to the new threshold $\omega$. Then, patterns in $Q$ are pruned to reduce the cardinality and improve the efficiency (The detail is explain of the pruning step later.) The mining process terminates when the set of high patterns does not change during the last iteration. Lastly, pattern groups are discovered from the set of high patterns. The formal description of the TrajPattern algorithm can be found in [17].

### 4.1 Pruning

In the TrajPattern algorithm, the main problem is the size of $Q$. If it is too large, then the algorithm would be very inefficient. During an iteration, the size of $Q$ increases by $2k$ fold. Without any pruning, $Q$ would grow to $2k^iG$ after $i$th iteration where $G$ is the number of grids in the space. This could be too large. In order to provide an efficient algorithm, it is necessary to reduce the size of $Q$. Fortunately, we can prune $Q$ based on the following observation. We only need to keep the set of low patterns satisfying the following *1-extension* property.

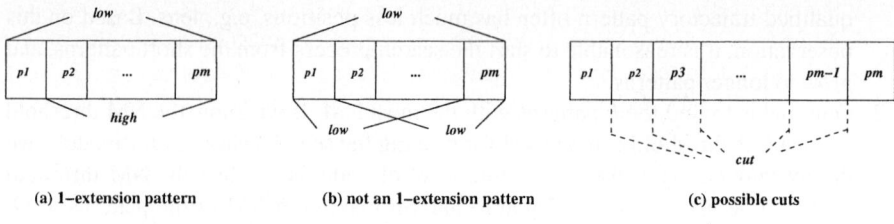

**Fig. 2.** 1-extension patterns

**Definition 5.** *(1) For a j-pattern(j > 1) P, if there exists a (j − 1)-pattern P′ which is the proper sub-pattern of P and P′ is a high pattern, then we say that P satisfies the 1-extension property. (2) Any 1-pattern satisfies the 1-extension property.*

For example, the pattern in Figure 2(a) can be viewed as a pattern satisfying the 1-extension property while the pattern in Figure 2(b) does not satisfy the 1-extension property. The reason that we only need to retain the set of low patterns satisfying the 1-extension property is due to the following lemma.

**Lemma 1.** *Any high pattern P can be obtained by extending a high pattern P′ with either a high pattern or a low pattern P″ satisfying the 1-extension property.*

*Proof.* Let's consider the high pattern $P = (p_1, p_2, \ldots, p_m)$ shown in Figure 2(c). A "cut" partitions $P$ into two non-overlapping complementary patterns $P_{left}$ and $P_{right}$ where $P_{left}$ and $P_{right}$ contains the sub-patterns left and right to the cut respectively. Assume the cut is made at the end of the first position of $P$, then $P_{left} = (p_1)$ and $P_{right} = (p_2, \ldots, p_m)$. There are three cases. (1) Both $P_{left}$ and $P_{right}$ are high patterns, then the lemma holds. (2) $P_{left}$ is low while $P_{right}$ is high. Since $P_{left}$ is a 1-pattern (i.e., 1-extension pattern), then the lemma also holds. (3) $P_{left}$ is high and $P_{right}$ is low. In this case, we move the cut from the left to the right one position at a time. If $P_{left}$ is always high with respect to all cuts, then this lemma also holds because when the cut is at the $(m − 1)$th position, $P_{right}$ is of length 1 (a 1-extension pattern). Let's assume that there exists a position $1 < i \leq m − 1$, such that $(p_1, p_2, \ldots, p_i)$ is high and $(p_1, p_2, \ldots, p_i, p_{i+1})$ is low. This means that $(p_{i+2}, \ldots, p_m)$ is a high pattern by the min-max property. In addition, $(p_1, p_2, \ldots, p_{i+1})$ is a 1-extension pattern by the definition. Thus the lemma holds.

Armed with the above lemma, we can remove all low patterns that do not satisfy the 1-extension property. In the *Prune* procedure, for each low pattern $P$, we examine whether $P$ is an 1-extension pattern. This can be achieved by removing either the first or the last position in $P$ and search whether the resulting pattern exists in $H_{new}$. If it exists, then $P$ is an 1-extension pattern and it will remain in $Q$, otherwise, it is removed.

### 4.2 Pattern Groups Discovery

After obtaining the top $k$ patterns, we first group these qualified patterns by their lengths, then cluster the patterns of the same length into pattern groups. The clustering process can be conducted in the following way. First, the patterns are clustered at each snapshot based on their distances. We refer to these clusters as snapshot groups. If any pattern is clustered into a single snapshot group at certain snapshot, according to the definition of pattern group, this pattern should be in a single pattern group. Then this pattern is removed from all remaining snapshot groups. Next, we start from the smallest snapshot group at all snapshots, denoted as $G$, to check whether $G$ exists at other snapshots. If so, patterns in $G$ are qualified as a pattern group at all snapshots, and should be removed from all remaining snapshot groups. If $G$ does not exist at other snapshots, we find the snapshot group at other snapshots $G'$, which makes $G \cap G'$ has the minimum number of patterns. We continue to check whether $G \cap G'$ exists at other snapshots, until we find a proper pattern group. This process continues until all patterns are grouped.

For example, assume we have six patterns of length two: $P_1 = (p_1, p'_1)$, $P_2 = (p_2, p'_2)$, $P_3 = (p_3, p'_3)$, $P_4 = (p_4, p'_4)$, $P_5 = (p_5, p'_5)$ and $P_6 = (p_6, p'_6)$. We cluster these six patterns according to their locations at the two snapshots. Assume that at the first snapshot we have snapshot groups $(p_1, p_3, p_4, p_5)$ and $(p_2, p_6)$; at the second snapshot we have snapshot groups $(p'_1, p'_3, p'_6)$, $(p'_2, p'_4)$ and $(p'_5)$. We start with the snapshot group containing only one pattern, which is $(p'_5)$ at the second snapshot. Then $P_5$ is assigned into a single pattern group and we remove $P_5$ from all remaining snapshot groups. After this step, $(p_1, p_3, p_4)$ and $(p_2, p_6)$ remain for the first snapshot, while $(p'_1, p'_3, p'_6)$ and $(p'_2, p'_4)$ remain for the second snapshot. Now the smallest snapshot group is $(p_2, p_6)$. Since this snapshot group does not exist at the second snapshot, we find the smallest subset of $(p_2, p_6)$ contained in any snapshot groups at the second snapshot, which is either $P_2$ or $P_6$. For the same reason as $P_5$, $P_2$ and $P_6$ are assigned into single pattern groups separately. After removing $P_2$ and $P_6$, $P_4$ is also assigned into a single pattern group. Now $(p_1, p_3)$ and $(p'_1, p'_3)$ remain for both snapshots, and $(P_1, P_3)$ is qualified as a pattern group. Thus the final pattern groups are $(P_2)$, $(P_4)$, $(P_5)$, $(P_6)$, and $(P_1, P_3)$.

### 4.3 Correctness Analysis

In this subsection we show the correctness of the TrajPattern algorithm.

**Theorem 1.** *Let $\mathcal{H}_{new}$ be the set of high patterns in $\mathcal{Q}$ when the TrajPattern algorithm terminates and $\mathcal{K}$ be the set of $k$ patterns with the highest NM. Then $\mathcal{Q} = \mathcal{K}$.*

*Proof.* Since the cardinality of $\mathcal{H}_{new}$ and $\mathcal{K}$ is the same, ie., $k$, we only need to prove $\mathcal{K} \subseteq \mathcal{H}_{new}$. Let $P_i \in \mathcal{K}$ be the pattern of length $i$. We prove via induction that $P_i$ is also in $\mathcal{H}_{new}$. First, when $i = 1$, $P_i$ is a singular pattern. This pattern will be generated in $\mathcal{Q}$ at the beginning and thus $P_1 \in \mathcal{H}_{new}$. Assume that for each $i \leq m$, any pattern $P_i$ is in $\mathcal{H}_{new}$ where $m$ is a positive integer. For a pattern $P_{m+1}$ there exists a proper subpattern $P_m$ of $P_{m+1}$ and $M(P_m) \geq M(P_{m+1})$ by the min-max property. $P_{m+1}$ can be obtained via extending the high pattern $P_m$ by adding an 1-extension pattern (a singular pattern). Thus at the latest $P_{m+1}$ will be inserted into $\mathcal{H}_{new}$ after $P_m$ is inserted into $\mathcal{H}_{new}$. Therefore $P_{m+1}$ will be in $\mathcal{H}_{new}$ by the end of the TrajPattern algorithm.

### 4.4 Complexity Analysis

To analyze the complexity of the algorithm we need to determine the number of iterations executed by TrajPattern. For the same reason as in the previous proof, by the $i$th iteration, all high patterns with length less than or equal to $i$ is inserted in $\mathcal{H}$. Therefore the max number of iterations is $O(M)$ where $M$ is the maximum length of the pattern with top $k$ NM.

Second, we need to analyze the number of patterns in $\mathcal{Q}$. $\mathcal{Q}$ consists of two types of patterns: high patterns and low patterns. The low patterns are the 1-extension patterns. Let $G$ be the number of grids in the space. Each high pattern $P$ can generate at most $2G$ low 1-extension patterns by extending one position before the first or after the last position. Therefore, we have at most $(2G|\mathcal{H}| + G)$ low patterns, which is $O(kG)$. During the candidate pattern generation phase there are a total of $O(k^2G)$ candidate patterns. The time complexity to compute the NM of a pattern is $O(MN)$ where $M$ is the maximum length of a pattern and $N$ is the size of the input trajectory data set, i.e., $|\mathcal{D}|$. Thus, during one iteration, the total time spent in computing the NM of all candidate patterns is $O(k^2MNG)$. All other operations, e.g., choosing top $k$ patterns, extending high patterns, pruning, etc. have lower complexity than the computation of NM. As a result, the total time complexity of the TrajPattern algorithm is $O(k^2M^2NG)$.

The largest data structure to maintain is $\mathcal{Q}$, which has the space complexity $O(kMG)$. Although the input data set size $N$ could be larger than that of $\mathcal{Q}$, it is not necessary to load the entire input data set at once since we only need a portion of the data set at a time for computing the NM. Thus the space complexity of our algorithm can be considered as $O(kMG)$.

## 5 Discussion

In this section we will further discuss some additional issues in the TrajPattern approach. First, in the context of the problem studied in this paper, it is desirable to find patterns with some wild card positions or gaps. A wild card position represented by the "*" symbol can be considered as a "don't care" position and any location can match this position. An additional parameter $d$ can be used to limit the number of consecutive "don't care" symbols in a pattern. For each pattern $P$ in $\mathcal{Q}$, we can add between 0 and $d$ "*" symbols either in the left side or right side of $P$. A gap can be viewed as a variant number of consecutive "*"s. When computing the NM of a pattern, the dynamic programming technique can be used in this case.

In our current problem statement, the discovered pattern may contain any number of positions. In many applications, it may be desirable to find longer patterns, i.e., patterns longer than a certain threshold $d$, since longer patterns usually contain more information. This additional constraint poses a significant challenge due to the fact that we no longer know how large of a set of $\mathcal{Q}$ we need to track. To adapt the TrajPattern algorithm to this new problem, we only need to perform the following modification. The NM threshold $\omega$ is set to the minimum NM of the set of $k$ patterns with the most NM of length at least $d$. In $\mathcal{Q}$, the set of patterns with NM more than $\omega$ are labeled as high patterns. The set of high patterns may be more than $k$. When more patterns of at least length $d$ are inserted into $\mathcal{H}$, $\omega$ will be updated. This modification enables us to find patterns with the highest NM and at least length $d$.

In the TrajPattern algorithm, there are several parameters: the time interval between two consecutive snapshots $t$, the indifference threshold $\delta$, the size of a grid $g_x$ and $g_y$, and the maximum similar pattern distance $\gamma$. For the snapshot interval, we can use a small time unit, e.g., seconds or minutes. It can be specified by a domain expert. $\delta$ can be set to a small distance unit, which can be considered as ignorable by the domain experts. The unit length of a grid along the x and y directions $g_x$ and $g_y$ can be set to $\delta$. The larger grid will reduce the computation complexity but provide inaccurate results, while the finer grid would increase the computation complexity but provide more accurate results. The sensitivity of our algorithm to $\delta$ and the computation cost of various grid size are analyzed in the experimental results section. For the maximum similar pattern distance $\gamma$, we can decide its value based on the probabilistic distribution of the location prediction model. Here due to the property of normal distribution, that is, the probability within the range between $-3 \times \sigma$ and $3 \times \sigma$ is approximately 0.97, we can set $\gamma$ equal to $3 \times \sigma$.

## 6 Experimental Results

In this paper we implemented the TrajPattern algorithm in the C++ programming language. All experiments are running on a PC with a 3.2 GHz Pentium-4 processor and 1GB main memory. The PC is running Windows XP. It is also equipped with 160 GB disk of 7200 RPM rotation speed. We use both real and synthetical data to analyze the performance of the TrajPattern algorithm.

To illustrate the usefulness of the NM model, we compare it with the match model. The border collapsing algorithm in [14] is used to mine patterns according to match (since the Apriori property holds on the match). In addition, to show the scalability of the TrajPattern algorithm, we compare it with the PB approach [13] (used for mining the same set of NM patterns).

### 6.1 Effectiveness of the NM Model

We use two real data sets for demonstrating the usefulness of the trajectory patterns. One is a bus route data set, and the other is a human posture data set. Due to the space limitations, we only present the first one in this paper. The second has similar results.

In the bus data set, we have the locations of 50 buses belonging to 5 routes. Each bus is equipped with a small sensor and is able to obtain its locations via GPS. It transmits its location reading every minute. We obtain the traces of these 50 buses for 10 weekdays. Thus we have a total number of 500 traces. Each reading consists of the longitude and latitude of the bus' location. Although this data set does not use any predictive model, we can transform it to the predictive model $\mathcal{M}$ as follows. For a location reading at time $t$, if the location can be predicted with sufficient accuracy by the previous location(s) according to $\mathcal{M}$, then the location reading is omitted. As a result, we only retain these readings that can not be predicted by $\mathcal{M}$ accurately, which is the same as using the predictive model $\mathcal{M}$. Next we transform the location trajectories into velocity trajectories and align all 500 trajectories on a set of 100 snapshots.

For mining the trajectory patterns, we assume that the objects are traveling in a square, $g_x$, $g_y$, and $\delta$ are set to $\frac{1}{1000}$ of the side of the space. In the bus route data set, it takes TrajPattern a couple minutes to mine 1000 NM patterns. The average length of top-1000 match patterns with length at least 3 is about 3.18, while the average length of top-1000 NM patterns with length at least 3 is 4.2, which is much longer than that of match patterns.

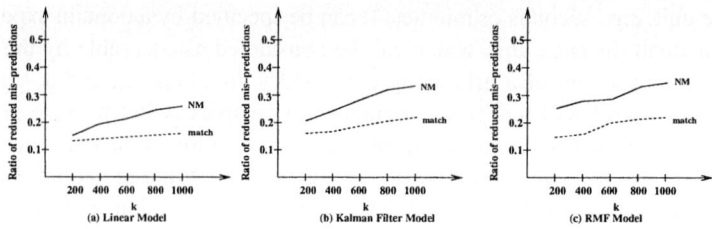

**Fig. 3.** Location Predictions for Bus Traces

To analyze the usefulness of the trajectory pattern model, we study the effects of employing trajectory patterns in the location prediction module. We assume that a particular module is used to predict the locations and integrate the trajectory patterns into the location prediction module. We first mine a set of $k$ patterns of length at least 4 with the most match on the 450 velocity trajectories. Then we apply the discovered patterns to the location prediction module for the remaining 50 trajectories. When an object needs to decide whether to report a location, it first checks whether the previous portion of the trajectory confirms[2] with a discovered pattern. If so, we will use the pattern for the prediction. Otherwise, the location calculated according to the prediction module will be used. We chose three prediction modules, i.e., the linear model (LM) [12], linear Kalman Filter (LMF) [2], and the recursive motion function (RMF) [11] for the comparison. If the predicted location is too far away from the actual location such that a message has to be sent from the mobile object to the server, this is called a mis-prediction. Figure 3 shows the ratio of reduced mis-predictions by each approach. By employing the top-$k$ NM patterns, the mis-predictions can be reduced by 20% to 40% for the three prediction methods, while with the top-$k$ match patterns we only can reduce the mis-predictions by around 10% to 20%. This also demonstrates the effectiveness of the NM model and the trajectory patterns.

## 6.2 Scalability and Sensitivity

To further analyze the performance and sensitivity of our TrajPattern algorithm, we utilize a large set of synthetic data. A projection based (PB) approach [13] to mine the normalized match is presented as a baseline algorithm. We apply the TrajPattern algorithm and the PB algorithm on the synthetic data and analyze their scalability with respect to the growth of the number of patterns wanted, the number of grids in the space, the number of trajectories and the average length of the trajectories.

Synthetic data is generated according to the following parameters: the average length of a trajectory $L$, the number of trajectories $S$ and the number of grids $G$. We generate the synthetic data in two different ways. The first data set is generated based on a similar data generation method as in [9]. The second data set is generated based on the ZebraNet data [16]. In the ZebraNet project, traces of wild zebras are recorded by deploying wireless devices on zebras in Kenya. We first extract the movement of zebras from the real traces, including the moving distance in a unit time and moving directions. There

---

[2] Here, we assume that a segment of trajectory confirms with a pattern if the probability that the trajectory segment is generated by the pattern (based on Equation 2) is above 90%.

are a certain number of zebra groups, within which zebras move together. For each time snapshot, each group is randomly assigned a moving distance and a moving direction that are extracted from the real traces. A randomness is added to every individual zebra to simulate noise in trajectories. Meanwhile, at each time snapshot, a certain small number of zebras will leave the group and move individually. In this paper, we only present the experimental results of the ZebraNet data set.

The projection based (PB) algorithm [13] suffers from the fact that a large set of prefixes need to be maintained. At each unspecified position, the maximum match of a position $p$ is used as the up-bound of the possible match. However, this bound could be very loose. As a result, it could be true that every prefix up to length $c$ could be extensible where $c$ is a small positive integer. In this case, we need to keep $G^c$ prefixes, which may be too large when $c$ is larger than 3 or 4. This could render the projection based algorithm inefficient.

We compare the performance (efficiency) of the TrajPattern algorithm against the baseline projection based (PB) approach. The experimental results show that the Traj-Pattern algorithms outperforms the PB approach with a wide margin.

First we evaluate the performance with respect to the number of patterns needed, $k$. Figure 4(a) shows the average execution time of two algorithms with respect to $k$. Although the response time of the TrajPattern algorithm and the PB algorithm grow super-linearly with the increase of $k$, the response time of the TrajPattern algorithm grows at a much slower pace than that of the PB approach due to the following reason. In the previous section, we have shown that the time complexity of TrajPattern is quadratical to $k$, while in the PB approach the thresholds $\omega$ is lower and $M$ is larger with larger $k$. As a result, the number of extensible prefixes in PB approach could increase at an exponential pace. Thus the TrajPattern is much more scalable than the PB algorithm as $k$ increases.

The second aspect that we investigate is the scalability with the number of sequences $S$. The empirical results from Figure 4(b) have confirmed that the time complexity of the TrajPattern algorithm is linearly proportional to $S$. On the other hand, the response

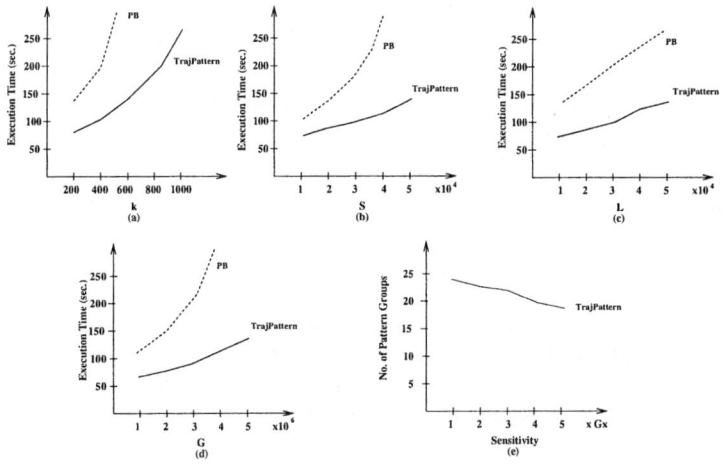

**Fig. 4.** Scalability and Sensitivity

time of the PB approach increases super-linearly with respect to $S$ due to the following reason. When the number of trajectories increases, the NM of singular patterns increases and in turn the number of extendible prefixes increases exponentially. As a result, the response time of the PB algorithm increases at a much faster pace than those of the two TrajPattern algorithms.

Third, we study the effects of the average length of a sequence $L$. From Figure 4(c), $L$ has similar effects on two algorithms since the time to scan a data set increases linearly with $L$.

Lastly, we examine the response time with various number of grids $G$. The TrajPattern algorithm is more scalable than the PB algorithm since the time complexity of the TrajPattern algorithm is linear with respect to $G$. On the other hand, in the PB approach, there are more candidate locations for each unspecified position, and in turn the number of extensible prefixes increases exponentially. Our empirical results in Figure 4(d) also confirm the theoretical analysis. The response time of the PB approach grows exponentially while the response time of the TrajPattern algorithm increases linearly.

The last experiment is performed to study the effect of the indifferent threshold $\delta$ on the mining results. Figure 4(e) shows that the number of discovered pattern groups decreases with the growth of the indifferent threshold $\delta$. As analyzed in Section 3, the larger the indifferent threshold $\delta$, the more grids will be considered indifferent from the expected location of the object, thus the more similar patterns will be found from the same set of trajectories. Because the number of patterns to mine is determined, the number of pattern groups becomes smaller when $\delta$ becomes larger, thus the discovered patterns represent a smaller amount of "useful information".

# 7 Conclusion

In this paper, we study a new problem, mining trajectory patterns from a set of imprecise trajectories. A novel measure is devised to represent the importance of a trajectory pattern. The min-max property is identified for the trajectory patterns. Based on this property, we develop the TrajPattern algorithm to mine the trajectory patterns, which first finds short patterns and then extends them in a systematic manner. The concept of pattern group is defined to present the trajectory patterns. Both real and synthetic data sets are used to demonstrate the usefulness of the trajectory patterns and the efficiency of the TrajPattern algorithm.

## References

1. J. Han, G. Dong, and Y. Yin. Efficient mining partial periodic patterns in time series database. *Proc. of ICDE*, 1999.
2. A. Jain, E. Chang, Y. Wang. Adaptive stream resource management using Kalman filters. *Proc. of SIGMOD*, 2004.
3. Y. Li, J. Han, and J. Yang. Clustering mobile objects. *Proc. of KDD*, 2004.
4. N. Mamoulis, H. Cao. G. Kollios, M. Hadjieleftheriou, Y. Tao, D. Cheung. Mining, indexing, and querying historical spatiotemporal data. *Proc. of KDD*, 2004.
5. W.-C. Peng and M.-S. Chen. Developing data allocation schemes by incremental mining of user moving patterns in a mobile computing system. *IEEE TKDE*, 2003.

6. Song, Z., Roussopoulos, N. K-Nearest neighbor search for moving query point. *SSTD*, 2001.
7. J. Patel, Y. Chen, V. Chakka STRIPES: an efficient index for predicted trajectories. In *Proc. of SIGMOD*, 2004.
8. J. Pei, J. Han, H. Pinto, Q. Chen, U. Dayal, and M. Hsu. PrefixSpan: mining sequential patterns efficiently by prefix-projected pattern growth. *Proc. of ICDE*, 2001.
9. S. Saltenis, C.S. Jensen, S.T. Leutenegger, and M.A. Lopez. Indexing the positions of continuously moving objects, In *Proc. of SIGMOD*, 2000.
10. Y. Tao, J. Sun, and D. Papadias. Selectivity estimation for predictive spatio-temporal queries. In *Proc. of ICDE*, pp. 417–428, Bangalore, India, Mar. 2003.
11. Y. Tao, C. Faloutsos, and D. Papadias. Prediction and indexing of moving objects with unknown motion patterns. In *Proc. of SIGMOD*, 2004.
12. O. Wolfson, P. Sistla, S. Chamberlain, and Y. Yesha. Updating and query databases that track mobile unites. *Distributed and Parallel Databases*, 7(3), 1999.
13. J. Yang, W. Wang, and P. Yu. Infominer: mining surprising periodic patterns. *Proc. of (KDD)*. pp. 395-400, 2001.
14. J. Yang, W. Wang, P. Yu, and J. Han. Mining long sequential patterns in a noisy environment. *Proc. of SIGMOD*, 2002.
15. M. Zaki. SPADE: an efficient algorithm for mining frequent sequences. *Machine Learning*, 42(1/2):31-60, 2001.
16. Y. Wang, M. Martonosi, L.S. Peh, P. Zhang, C. Sadler, T. Liu, D. Rubenstein, S.A. Lyon. ZebraNet mobility data. unpublished, Princeton University 2004
17. J. Yang and M. Hu. TrajPattern: Mining sequential patterns from imprecise trajectories of mobile objects. *Technical Report*, EECS, Case Western Reserve University, 2005

# On Exploring the Power-Law Relationship in the Itemset Support Distribution

Kun-Ta Chuang[1], Jiun-Long Huang[2], and Ming-Syan Chen[1]

[1] Graduate Institute of Communication Engineering,
National Taiwan University, Taipei, Taiwan, ROC
doug@arbor.ee.ntu.edu.tw, mschen@cc.ee.ntu.edu.tw
[2] Department of Computer Science,
National Chiao Tung University, Hsinchu, Taiwan, ROC
jlhuang@csie.nctu.edu.tw

**Abstract.** We identify and explore in this paper an important phenomenon which points out that the power-law relationship appears in the distribution of itemset supports. Characterizing such a relationship will benefit many applications such as providing the direction of tuning the performance of the frequent-itemset mining. Nevertheless, due to the explosive number of itemsets, it will be prohibitively expensive to retrieve characteristics of the power-law relationship in the distribution of itemset supports. As such, we also propose in this paper a valid and cost-effective algorithm, called algorithm *PPL*, to extract characteristics of the distribution without the need of discovering all itemsets in advance. Experimental results demonstrate that algorithm *PPL* is able to efficiently extract the characteristics of the power-law relationship with high accuracy.

## 1 Introduction

The importance of mining frequent itemsets has been recognized in various applications, including web log mining, DNA sequence mining, frequent episodes mining, periodic patterns, to name a few [8]. Due to the data-driven nature of mining algorithms, it is believed in the literature that the parameter tuning of the designed algorithm is usually requested in order to achieve the better result on the targeted applications. It is beyond dispute that the deeper knowledge about the characteristics of your data will lead to the better execution efficiency and the better interpretation of the mining result. As such, a mechanism to precisely estimate the data characteristics is usually deemed as an important pre-processing means for mining applications.

Recent research advances in frequent-itemset mining algorithms are thus in the direction of discovering characteristics of real datasets. For example, the works in [7] and [11] both seek the relationship between different itemset lengths in the targeted dataset. Such relationships can be further utilized to control the mining process [7], or to generate the realistic synthetic datasets for the system parameter tuning [11].

To provide better understanding on real datasets, we in this paper investigate the more important characteristic in real datasets, named the *itemset support* distribution. The *itemset support distribution* refers to the distribution of the count of itemsets versus the itemset support, where an itemset complies with the definition in [1]. Explicitly, we shall study the relationship between the value of support, say 0.01, and the number of itemsets having the support 0.01 in the dataset. The *itemset support distribution*, which is indeed a kind of the probability density function, will state the degree of the cohesion between different items in the dataset. To the best of our knowledge, this fundamental question has not been formally addressed.

Inspired by the power-law relationship observed in many distributions of single words (users, web pages) [3][17], it is important to examine whether the *itemset support distribution* also follows the power-law relationship. From observations on various retail datasets and as validated by our empirical studies later, it is amazingly found that the power-law relationship indeed also appears in the *itemset support distribution* and we can characterize that by the Zipf distribution [17].

However, to find the parameters characterizing the *itemset support distribution* will be more challenging than to find the parameters in the distribution of single items since all itemsets need to be retrieved. The extremely large time and memory consumption cannot be avoided due to the itemset combinational explosion. Note that the costly process will drastically decrease the practicability of knowing the characteristics of the *itemset support distribution*. To remedy this, we also propose in this paper a valid and cost-effective algorithm, called algorithm *PPL* (standing for **P**redict the **P**ower-**L**aw relationship), to correctly estimate the parameters of the *itemset support distribution* from a sample dataset while avoiding the need of generating all itemsets. As shown in our empirical studies, algorithm *PPL* is able to efficiently and precisely extract the characteristics of the power-law relationship. Hence algorithm *PPL* can be utilized as an excellent pre-processing step for extensive applications of mining frequent patterns.

Our contributions are to solidly study issues related to the power-law relationship in the *itemset support distribution*. More precisely:

(1) We first formalize the problem of the *itemset support distribution* and explore the important phenomenon that the distribution follows the Zipf distribution.
(2) We present a valid and cost-effective algorithm, called algorithm *PPL*, to identify characteristics of the *itemset support distribution* without the need of discovering all itemsets in advance.
(3) We complement our analytical and algorithmic results by a thorough empirical study on real data and demonstrate that the *PPL* algorithm is able to accurately the characterization of the *itemset support distribution*.

We then individually present these issues in the following sections.

## 2 Identify the Power-Law Relationship in the Itemset Support Distribution

### 2.1 Review of the Power-Law Relationship

Since the first observation of the power-law relationship in [17], which discovered the frequency of the $n^{th}$ most-frequently-used word in the natural language is approximately inversely proportional to $n$, the power-law relationship has been successively discovered in many real world data, including WWW characteristics, Internet topology, to name a few[1]. Specifically, the power-law relationship can be characterized by several mathematical models, including the well-known Zipf distribution and its variations such as the DGX distribution [2]. Among them, the Zipf distribution is the most widely used form due to its simplicity, as shown by $f_i \propto \left(1/r_i^\phi\right)$, where $f_i$ denotes the frequency of words (users, events, ...) that are ranked as the $r_i^{th}$ most frequent words (users, events, ...) in the dataset, and $\phi$ is the parameter characterizing the skewness of the distribution. In practice, the Zipf distribution can be further extended to characterize the "count-frequency" relationship, which is stated as $f_i \propto \left(1/c_i^\phi\right)$, where $f_i$ is the count of distinct words that appear $c_i$ times in the dataset [2]. Without loss of generality, we will discuss the "count-frequency" relationship in the sequel because the "count-frequency" relationship can be deemed as a kind of the probability density function, which is more desirable.

In essence, the Zipf distribution is often demonstrated by scatterplotting the data with the x axis being $\log(c_i)$ and the y axis being $\log(f_i)$. The distribution will be deemed following the power-law relationship if the points in the log-log plot are close to a single straight line, as shown by

$$\log(f_i) = \theta \log(c_i) + \Omega. \qquad (1)$$

In particular, the slope $\theta$ and the $Y$-intercept $\Omega$ in Eq. 1 can be estimated by the linear regression[2]:

$$\theta = \frac{\sum_{i=1}^{k}\log(c_i)\log(f_i) - \frac{\left(\sum_{i=1}^{k}\log(c_i)\right)\times\left(\sum_{i=1}^{k}\log(f_i)\right)}{k}}{\sum_{i=1}^{k}\log^2(c_i) - \frac{\left(\sum_{i=1}^{k}\log(c_i)\right)^2}{k}}, \qquad (2)$$

$$\Omega = \frac{\sum_{i=1}^{k}\log(f_i)}{k} - \theta \times \frac{\sum_{i=1}^{k}\log(c_i)}{k}, \qquad (3)$$

where $k$ denotes the number of points in the log-log plot. Note that the linear regression technique is a method based on the least-square errors. The correlation coefficient[3] (or said the *goodness of fit* of the regression line) can be utilized to examine whether those points in the log-log plot exactly lie in the line $\log(f_i) = \theta \log(c_i) + \Omega$ or not [12]. Due to space limitations, we only describe the Zipf

---

[1] See http://www.nslij-genetics.org/wli/zipf/ for the power-law references from different domains.
[2] Other measurements to estimate the parameters of the power-law distribution include the non-linear regression and the maximum likelihood estimation. Among them, the linear regression is the most widely utilized approach due to its feasibility and simplicity.
[3] For convenience of discussion, we will postpone the formula of the correlation coefficient to Eq. 5 in Section 3.3.

distribution here. For details of the regression technique, which will be out of scope for this paper, the reader is asked to follow the pointers in some well-known materials such as [12].

Note that previous observations mostly concentrate on the power-law relationship in the distribution consisting of single events, e.g., single words or single items [3][17]. Naturally, it is important to investigate whether the prevalent power-law relationship also appears in the support distribution of units consisting of a set of words or items. Such cases were first investigated in the computational linguistics literature [6], where the power-law relationship of N-grams had been demonstrated (N-grams denote phrases consisting of N consecutive words). Their studies show that the "count-frequency" relationship of N-grams (with a fixed $N$) follows the Zipf distribution.

## 2.2 Observations on the Itemset Support Distribution

In this paper, our first goal is to investigate whether the power-law relationship appears in the distribution of itemset supports in real datasets, where an itemset complies with the definition in [1]. Specifically, let $\mathcal{I} = \{x_1, x_2, ..., x_m\}$ be a set of distinct items in the dataset. A set $X \subseteq \mathcal{I}$ with $k = |X|$ is called a $k$-itemset or simply an itemset. Let the support of an itemset $X$ in the database $D$ be the fraction of transactions in $D$ that contain $X$[4]. We would like to investigate whether the support distribution of itemsets follows the Zipf distribution, as the form shown by

$$\log(f_i) = \theta \log(s_i) + \Omega, \qquad (4)$$

where $s_i$ denotes the support of itemsets and $f_i$ denotes the frequency of itemsets whose supports are $s_i$. Note that the "support-frequency" relationship in Eq. 4 is physically equivalent to the "count-frequency" relationship since the "count" presents the absolute support count. For interest of space, we in this paper concentrate on the investigation of retail datasets, which are skewed and sparse, and most association-rule discovery algorithms were designed for such types of data [16] (interested readers can find observations on other types of real datasets in http://arbor.ee.ntu.edu.tw/~doug/paper/PPL/index.html).

Table 1. Parameters of real datasets

| Dataset | $I_s$ | $|D|$ | $T_{max}$ | $T_{avg}$ |
|---|---|---|---|---|
| BMS-POS | 1,657 | 515,596 | 164 | 6.5 |
| Retail | 16,470 | 88,162 | 76 | 10.3 |
| 3C_chain | 130,108 | 8,000,000 | 87 | 5.4 |
| Book | 12,082 | 100,000 | 13 | 2.3 |

To examine whether the support distribution of itemsets in retail datasets follows the Zipf distribution, four real datasets are investigated in this paper, in-

---

[4] The support is considered as the *relative* occurrence frequency. Note that it is defined in some literature as the *absolute* one, i.e., the occurrence frequency in the database.

cluding two well-known retail benchmark datasets[5], and two transaction datasets from a 3C chain store and a large book store in Taiwan. Those datasets are summarized in Table 1, where $I_s$ denotes the distinct items in the dataset, $|D|$ denotes the number of transactions, $T_{\max}$ denotes the maximum itemset length and $T_{avg}$ denotes the average itemset length. Furthermore, we execute algorithm FP-growth downloaded from Christian Borgelt's website[6] to obtain itemsets with their supports. Since the number of all itemsets is extremely large (there are $2^{I_s} - 1$ possible itemsets at most), it is very difficult to discover all itemsets in a reasonable execution time. For efficiency reasons, we did not retrieve all itemsets in the BMS-POS and the 3C_chain datasets, but instead retrieve itemsets whose support counts exceed 30, where 30 is a sufficient number in the statistical sense [12].

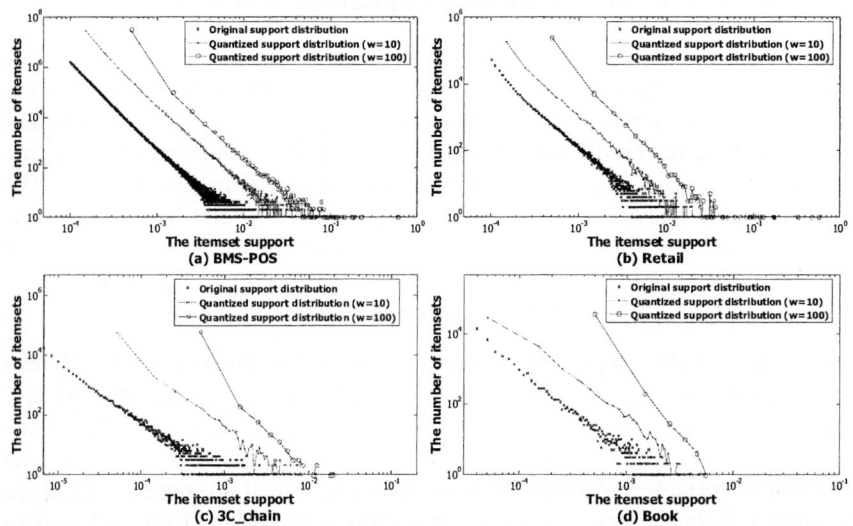

**Fig. 1.** The support distribution of four real datasets

The observations are shown in Figure 1, where the curve of the *original support distribution* presents the log-log relationship of the itemset support versus the number of itemsets with the corresponding support (the curve of the *quantized support distribution* will be discussed in the next section). As can be seen, the log-log plot is very Zipf-like, meaning that the power-law relationship indeed appears in the distribution of the itemset support. In addition, the "top-concavity"[7] phenomenon, which is prevalent in the distribution of single items [2][17], is

---

[5] Downloaded from the website, http://fimi.cs.helsinki.fi/data/, of the ICDM workshop on Frequent Itemset Mining, 2003.
[6] The URL is http://fuzzy.cs.uni-magdeburg.de/~borgelt/fpgrowth.html
[7] The "top concavity" phenomenon refers to that the top part of the log-log curve tilts vertically (with relatively concave shapes).

insignificant in the distribution of itemset supports. As such, the Zipf distribution is enough to correctly characterize the power-law relationship in the itemset support distribution. We accordingly demonstrate the fact that the power-law relationship appears in the itemset support distribution.

## 3 Design of Algorithm PPL

As mentioned above, recognizing characteristics of the support distribution will benefit the proper mining system design. However, although we have demonstrated in Section 2 that the power-law relationship appears in the support distribution, it is prohibitively expensive to find all itemsets and further estimate the characteristics of the Zipf distribution, i.e., the slope $\theta$ and the $Y$-intercept $\Omega$ in Eqs. 2 and 3. The extremely large time consumption results from the expensive process to retrieve all itemsets without the support pruning. An efficient approach is still demanded to correctly estimate those parameters.

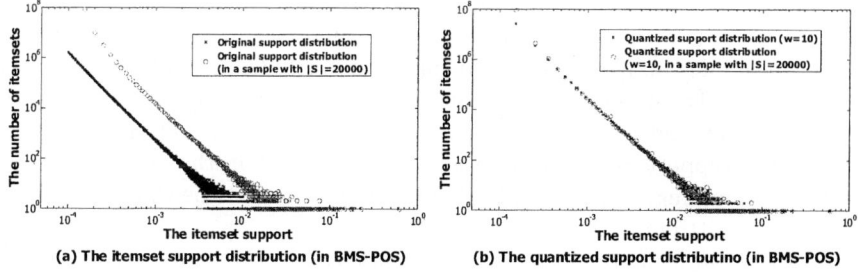

**Fig. 2.** The support distribution after sampling (the BMS-POS dataset)

As a consequence, we propose in this paper a valid and cost-effective solution, named *PPL* (standing for **P**redict the **P**ower-**L**aw relationship), to estimate the parameters of the power-law relationship in the *itemset support distribution*. Since the time consumption is dominated by the process of retrieving all itemsets in the large database, algorithm *PPL* utilizes two approaches to improve the efficiency. The first one is to utilize *sampling* techniques to retrieve itemsets [13]. The other approach is to retrieve *only the set of high-support itemsets* with the help of the support pruning techniques [10] so as to efficiently discover the parameters of the power-law relationship from the partial set of itemsets. Specifically, to fully utilize the capability of these two approaches, algorithm *PPL* is devised as a three-phase approach: (1) sampling; (2) obtaining high-support itemsets; (3) estimating the parameters of the power-law relationship by the linear regression from the high-support itemsets discovered in the sample.

However, while pursuing the efficiency, algorithm *PPL* will face three challenges:

(1) *The support distribution obtained in a sample will deviate from the support distribution in the original database.* Note that after sampling, the supports

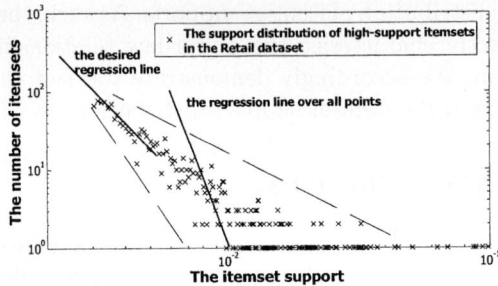

**Fig. 3.** Estimating the power-law relationship from high-support itemsets

of many low-support itemsets will become higher, and vice versa [15]. Unfortunately, as pointed out in [15], the number of itemsets with a specified support is likely to *increase* after sampling due to the large amount of transfers from low-support itemsets (the number of low-support itemsets is larger than the number of high-support itemsets). As shown in our empirical studies in Figure 2(a), where the support distributions obtained in the original dataset and in a random sample with 20,000 tuples are included, it can be apparently observed that the support distribution in the sample deviates from that in the original dataset. Indeed, due to randomness, we cannot estimate the deviation between the support distribution in a sample and that in the original dataset. Thus after sampling, it will be difficult to correctly predict the characteristics of the support distribution in the original dataset.

(2) *It is very difficult to determine the appropriate minimum support without prior knowledge.* Note that *PPL* will only discover high-support itemsets. However, we will not know how to determine the subtle minimum support. A large minimum support will result in too few itemsets to provide the sufficient information to correctly estimate the parameters of the Zipf distribution. Oppositely, the small minimum support will generate a lot of itemsets, thus resulting in inefficiency.

(3) *It is difficult to obtain the desired regression line due to the support fluctuation on high-support itemsets.* Note that the Zipf distribution can be characterized by the regression line. However, consider the observation in Figure 3, where a solid straight line represents the regression line over all points with respect to high supports, and the dotted lines show the envelope of the support fluctuation. As can be seen, points with respect to high supports do not exactly follow the Zipf distribution, and the support distribution of these points has the large support fluctuation. It will incur the large least-square errors, and the regression line over points with respect to high supports may deviate from the desired regression line[8].

---

[8] In [3], the slope of the log-log plot is obtained by using the linear regression, excluding the rightmost 100 points to avoid the serious effect of the fluctuation. However, such an approach will fail in our cases since we may only have the rightmost 100 points which are summarized from high support itemsets.

To overcome those challenges, several novel mechanisms will be devised in algorithm *PPL*. In the following, we perform step-by-step analysis to discuss the details.

### 3.1 Phase I: Sampling

The goal of Phase I is to select a sample from the original dataset. Note that as mentioned in the first challenge described above, the support distribution in a sample will deviate from that in the original dataset, and the deviation is unpredictable. In fact, this phenomenon can be significantly reduced in the *quantized support distribution*, which will be obtained by the *histogram* technique [9]. Explicitly, all itemsets can be aggregated by means of the traditional equi-width *histogram* and then obtain the *quantized support distribution*. We give the formal definition of the *quantized support distribution* below.

**Definition 1 (The Quantized Support Distribution).** *Given all points $(s_i, f_i)$ in the original support distribution, where $s_i$ denotes the support of itemsets and $f_i$ denotes the count of itemsets whose supports are $s_i$. After aggregating those points by means of the equi-width histogram, a set of new points $(\widehat{s}_j, \widehat{f}_j)$ will be obtained, where $\widehat{s}_j$ denotes the representative value (the default is the median value) of the support range corresponding to the $j^{th}$ bucket of the histogram, and $\widehat{f}_j$ denotes the count of itemsets with supports falling in the $j^{th}$ bucket. The quantized support distribution is the distribution consisting of all points $(\widehat{s}_j, \widehat{f}_j)$.*

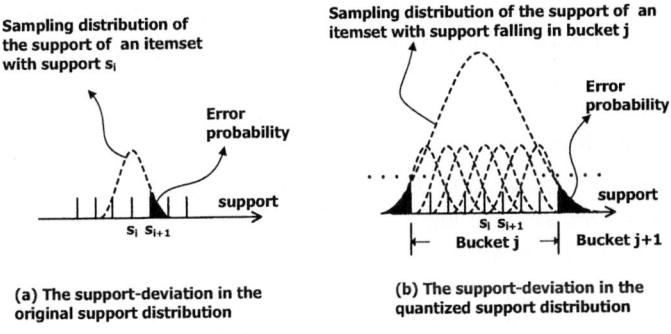

**Fig. 4.** Influence of the support-deviation

The argument that the *quantized support distribution* is able to reduce the influence of support-deviation follows the observation below:

**Observation.** Suppose that we repeatedly generate a lot of samples of the same sample size. The distribution of the *support* of $X$ among these samples, i.e., the *sampling distribution* of the support of $X$, will approximately follow a *normal* distribution with *mean* equal to the support of $X$ in the entire dataset [5]. In addition, the variance of the *sampling distribution* depends on the sample size [13]. As shown in Figure 4(a), the *sampling distribution* of an itemset with support equal to $s_i$ in the entire database indicates that the support will be likely larger than $s_i$ with the probability equal to the shadow region. As a result, a percentage of itemsets in the sample will have supports inconsistent with the corresponding support in the entire dataset. Accordingly, the *itemset support distribution* after sampling will deviate from the *itemset support distribution* in the entire dataset. This argument is demonstrated in Figure 2(a).

On the other hand, consider the case of the *quantized support distribution*. As shown in Figure 4(b), the error probability, i.e., the probability of itemsets with supports in bucket $j$ changing to bucket $j+1$ after sampling, will be relatively small as compared to the error probability illustrated in Figure 4(a). The reason lies in that the supports of most itemsets are likely to remain in the same support bucket after sampling. In other words, only itemsets with supports in the margin of a bucket are likely to have the support not falling in the same bucket after sampling. This argument is demonstrated in Figure 2(b), where the *quantized support distributions* obtained in the original dataset and in the sample with 20,000 tuples are shown and the parameter $w$ denotes the number of aggregated points. It is clear to see that the *quantized support distribution* in a sample will be close to the *quantized support distribution* in the original dataset. ∎

Following the observation, we comment that the *quantized support distribution* will be insensitive to the support-deviation, meaning that *the quantized support distribution in the sample will be close to the quantized support distribution in the entire dataset*. As a result, we will aim to obtain the *quantized support distribution* in the sample.

Another problem, as shown in Figure 1, is that the *quantized support distribution* still deviates from the original support distribution. Importantly, assuming that the original support distribution approximately follows the Zipf distribution, Proposition 1 below indicates that the *quantized support distribution* also has the same slope as the slope in the original support distribution and has a "predictable" drift of the Y-intercept.

**Proposition 1.** *Suppose that the itemset support distribution follows the Zipf distribution so that we have $\log(f_i) \approx \theta \log(s_i) + \Omega$. Assuming that there are $w$ distinct points in the original support distribution being aggregated as a point in the quantized support distribution, we will have an approximate Zipf distribution as the form*

$$\log(\widehat{f}_k) \approx \theta \log(\widehat{s}_k) + \Omega + \log(w),$$

*in the quantized support distribution, where $\widehat{s}_k$ denotes the representative of the quantized support in the $k^{th}$ bucket and $\widehat{f}_k$ denotes the count of itemsets whose supports fall in the $k^{th}$ bucket. As such, the log-log plot in the quantized support distribution has the slop $\theta$ and the Y-intercept $\Omega + \log(w)$.*

**Proof.** Note that we have $e^{\Omega} \times s_{i,j}^{\theta} \approx f_{i,j}$ for the point $(s_{i,j}, f_{i,j})$ in the original support distribution since it follows the Zipf distribution. Suppose that $|D|$ is the database size. Let points $(s_{k,1}, f_{k,1})$, $(s_{k,2}, f_{k,2})$, ..., $(s_{k,w}, f_{k,w})$ be summarized as the $k^{th}$ point $(\widehat{s}_k, \widehat{f}_k)$ in the *quantized support distribution*. We have $\widehat{f}_k = \sum_{j=1}^{w} f_{k,j}$, and

$$\widehat{s}_k = \frac{s_{k,1} + s_{k,w}}{2} = \frac{s_{k,1} + \left(s_{k,1} + \frac{w}{|D|}\right)}{2} = s_{k,1} + \frac{w}{2 \times |D|}.$$

Since $\frac{w}{|D|}$ is in general much weak as compared to $s_{k,1}$, we have

$$\frac{s_{k,j}^\theta}{\widehat{s}_k^\theta} = \left(\frac{s_{k,1} + \frac{j}{|D|}}{s_{k,1} + \frac{w}{2\times|D|}}\right)^\theta \approx 1.$$

Therefore $s_{k,j}^\theta$, for $1 \leq j \leq w$, will be approximately equal to $\widehat{s}_k^\theta$, which yields that

$$\widehat{f}_k = \sum_{j=1}^{w} f_{k,j} \approx e^\Omega \times \sum_{j=1}^{w} \widehat{s}_k^\theta = e^\Omega \times w \times \widehat{s}_k^\theta,$$

$$\log(\widehat{f}_k) \approx \theta \log(\widehat{s}_k) + \Omega + \log(w). \blacksquare$$

Proposition 1 indicates that the slope $\theta$ remains in the *quantized support distribution*, and the Y-intercept will be changed to $\Omega + \log(w)$. Figure 1 demonstrates Proposition 1, where we can see that, for high-support points, the slope of the *quantized support distribution* ($w = 10$ or $100$) is equal to that of the *quantized support distribution* without sampling. As a result, the side-effect of sampling is overcome.

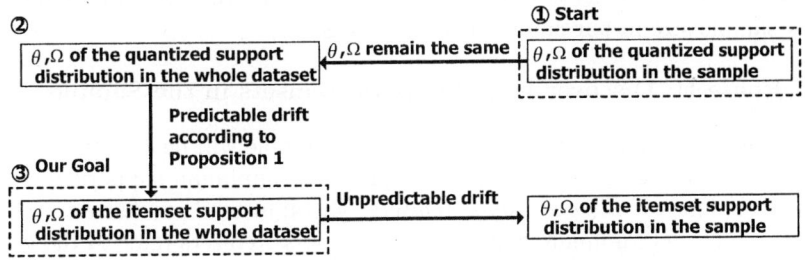

**Fig. 5.** The flow to overcome problems incurred by sampling

Based on the foregoing, the process to overcome problems incurred by sampling, as shown in Figure 5, will be summarized as:

(1) Obtain the characteristics of the *quantized support distribution* in the sample.
(2) The characteristics of the *quantized support distribution* in the whole dataset are expected equal to that in the sample.
(3) In light of Proposition 1, obtain the characteristics of the original *itemset support distribution*.

Note that while step 1 is completed, steps 2 and 3 can be straightforwardly executed with the mathematical manipulation mentioned above. How to precisely achieve step 1 will be discussed in Section 3.2 and Section 3.3.

The remaining issue in this phase is, what is the appropriate sample size to obtain the *quantized support distribution* in the sample which is consistent with that in the entire database. Formally, the level of consistency depends on the variance of the *sampling distribution* of the support, and the variance relies on the sample size [13]. A small sample size will lead to a large variance as compared to the variance in a large sample size. As pointed out in previous works of sampling for mining association rules, a sample size equal to 20,000 [13] or a sample rate equal to 10% [15], will be sufficient to generate the accurate set of frequent itemsets. We argue that the sample size 20,000 or 10% is also sufficient to generate the accurate *quantized support distribution* by following several points: (1) the complexity to generate the accurate *quantized support distribution* is analogous to the complexity to generate accurate frequent itemsets; (2) in Phase II only high-support itemsets will be generated, whose supports, as indicated in [13], can be easily preserved in samples as compared to supports of low-support itemsets; (3) the discrepancy between counts of itemsets within a bucket in the sample and in the entire dataset will be unapparent in the log-log scale (the characteristics of the power-law relationship is estimated in the log-log scale); (4) the technique in Phase III is specifically designed to be robust to the inconsistency between *quantized support distributions* in the sample and in the entire dataset.

As simultaneously considering execution efficiency and above points, we therefore set the sample size as 20,000 in default since the sample can be easily executed and maintained in main memory. The discreet users can set the size as 10% of the entire size, as the suggestion in [15]. We will also investigate the issue of the sample size in our empirical studies later.

### 3.2 Phase II: Discover High-Support Itemsets in the Sample

In this phase, the high-support itemsets in the sample will be discovered. Without prior knowledge to determine the appropriate minimum support, we resort to the technique of "*discover top-k itemsets*" [4][14] instead of "discover itemsets with the specified minimum support," where *top-k* itemsets refer to the $k$ most frequent itemsets in the dataset. In practice, the size of $k$ can be easily specified a priori. As will be shown in our experimental results, $k$ equal to 5,000 will suffice to correctly estimate the parameters of the power-law relationship in most cases. As such we set $k$ as 5,000 in default, where top 5,000 itemsets can be efficiently retrieved by the state-of-the-art algorithm for mining *top-k* frequent itemsets.

### 3.3 Phase III: Characterize the Power-Law Relationship

The parameters of the Zipf distribution will be estimated in this phase. Suppose that $\{X_1, ..., X_k\}$ is the set of *top-k* itemsets which are obtained in Phase II. At the beginning of this phase, we will aggregate these itemsets by means of *histogram* with the support bucket width equal to $\frac{w}{|S|}$, where $|S|$ is the size of the sample dataset and $w$ is the number of distinct and consecutive support counts which will be aggregated into the same bucket. Note that the default of $w$ is 10 in this paper since empirically $w = 10$ is able to preserve the slope of the *itemset support distribution*, as shown in Figure 1. As such, *top-k* itemsets will be aggregated into a set of points $H_k = \{(\widehat{s}_1, \widehat{f}_1), (\widehat{s}_2, \widehat{f}_2), ..., (\widehat{s}_z, \widehat{f}_z)\}$

sorted by $\widehat{s}_i$, where $\widehat{s}_i < \widehat{s}_j$ iff $i < j$. We therefore can characterize the power-law relationship by performing the regression analysis over the partial *quantized support distribution* which is summarized from *top-k* itemsets discovered in the sample.

However, as pointed out as the third challenge described in the beginning of Section 3, directly executing the regression analysis over all points in $H_k$ will result in the incorrect estimation due to the support fluctuation on high support itemsets. Therefore the problem arises: *"how to select an appropriate subset of points from $H_k$ to correctly estimate the parameters of the Zipf distribution?"* Recall the observation in Figure 3. Points with respect to very high-supports usually do not accurately follow the Zipf distribution. On the other hand, without loss of generality, points with respect to low supports usually follow the Zipf distribution. As such, one may intuitively claim a naive approach as follows.

**Naive Approach.** It is intuitive to suggest the regression line over first several points in $H_k$ since they are sufficient to correctly fit the power-law relationship. For example, we may estimate the power-law relationship by performing the regression analysis over the first five points in $H_k$, i.e., $\{(\widehat{s}_1, \widehat{f}_1), ..., (\widehat{s}_5, \widehat{f}_5)\}$. Nevertheless, we indeed did not know how many points are sufficient to obtain the desired regression line. Thus we have to examine all possible regression lines, and then select the one with the best correlation coefficient since it will have the best power to explain the log-log relationship in the Zipf distribution. ∎

However, such an approach suffers from the problem that the best correlation coefficient does not imply the best fit of the Zipf distribution. In particular, sometimes few points will result in the best correlation coefficient, but the regression line could be bias to outlier points [12]. In addition, sampling in Phase I may incur noise, which will also affect the result of the linear regression. As a result, we devise a novel solution, which is inspired from the training and testing scenario in supervised learning [8], to correctly estimate the parameters of the Zipf distribution from $H_k$.

**Minimizing Testing Error Approach.** Suppose that $H_k$ is divided into two distinct and consecutive subsets of points, i.e., the training set $T_r$ and the testing set $T_e$, where $T_e = \{(\widehat{s}_1, \widehat{f}_1), ..., (\widehat{s}_m, \widehat{f}_m)\}$ and $T_r = \{(\widehat{s}_{m+1}, \widehat{f}_{m+1}), ..., (\widehat{s}_z, \widehat{f}_z)\}$. Here $m$ is the parameter to adjust the size of the testing set and $m < z$. Consider the illustration in Figure 6, where each point in $T_e$ is called a testing point. Our goal is to find the *best fit regression line* from $T_r$ so that all testing points in $T_e$ can well lie in the line. Formally, we give the definition of the *best fit regression line* in the following.

**Definition 2 (Best Fit Regression Line).** Given the training set $T_r$ and the testing set $T_e$. The best fit regression line, denoted by $\mathbb{R}_g(\widehat{s}_i) = \widehat{\theta}_g \log(\widehat{s}_i) + \widehat{\Omega}_g$, will satisfy:

(1) $\mathbb{R}_g(\widehat{s}_i) = \widehat{\theta}_g \log(\widehat{s}_i) + \widehat{\Omega}_g$ is the regression line over the first $g$ points in $T_r$, i.e., $\{(\widehat{s}_{m+1}, \widehat{f}_{m+1}), ..., (\widehat{s}_g, \widehat{f}_g)\}$, where $m + 1 \leq g \leq z$.

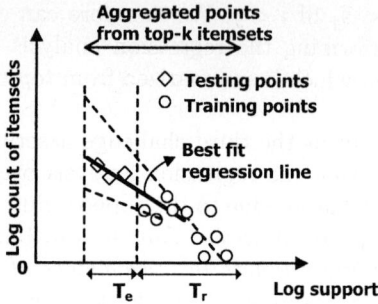

**Fig. 6.** The illustration of the best fit regression line

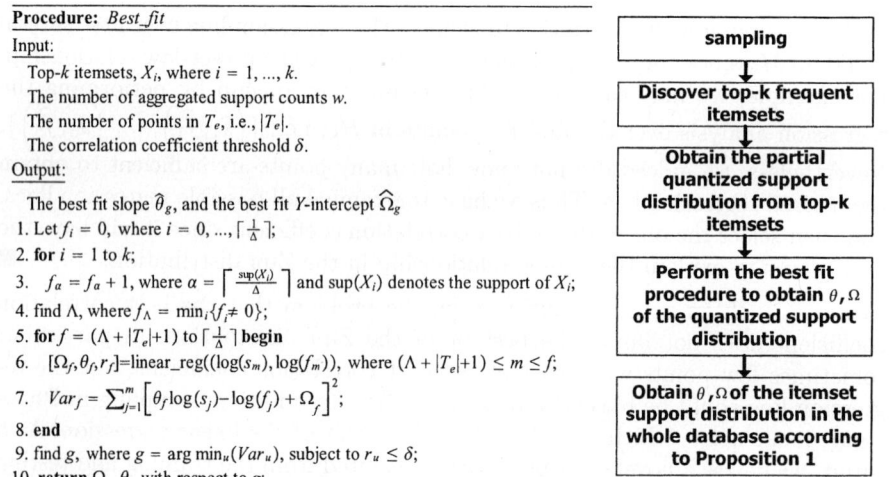

(a) Procedure Best_fit    (b) Overall flow of algorithm PPL

**Fig. 7.** The implementation of algorithm *PPL*

(2) The correlation coefficient, $r_g$, over the data points $\left\{\left(\widehat{s}_{m+1}, \widehat{f}_{m+1}\right), ..., \left(\widehat{s}_g, \widehat{f}_g\right)\right\}$ is smaller than a pre-defined threshold $\delta$. Note that,

$$r_g = \frac{\sum_{i=m+1}^{g}\sum_{j=m+1}^{g}(\log(\widehat{s}_i) - u_s)\left(\log(\widehat{f}_j) - u_f\right)}{\sqrt{\sum_{i=m+1}^{g}(\log(\widehat{s}_i) - u_s)^2}\sqrt{\sum_{j=m+1}^{g}\left(\log(\widehat{f}_j) - u_f\right)^2}}, \quad (5)$$

where $u_s$ and $u_f$ are the mean of $\log(\widehat{s}_i)$ and $\log(\widehat{f}_j)$, respectively.

(3) $g = \arg\min_u \left\{\sum_{j=1}^{m}\left(\mathbb{R}_u(\widehat{s}_j) - \log(\widehat{f}_j)\right)^2\right\}$, subject to the correlation coefficient $r_f \leq \delta$ and $m+1 \leq u \leq z$.

The whole procedure to find the best fit regression line is outlined in Procedure *Best_fit* in Figure 7(a), where the function linear_reg() will return three parameters, the intercept $\Omega$ (see Eq. 3), the slope $\theta$ (see Eq. 2) and the *correlation coefficient r*. Specifically, the correlation coefficient $r_g$ (a value between -1 and 1) can represent the level how those points are explained by the regression line. The regression line will fit points better when $r_g \to -1$ since without loss of generality, $\hat{f}_i$ and $\hat{s}_i$ are negatively correlated. Statistically, it is believed that $r_g \leq -0.8$ is sufficient to claim the regression line can explain these points [12]. Thus $\delta$ is set as $-0.8$ in default. Note that criterion 3 in Definition 2 states that we desire the regression line with the minimum testing error. It is worth mentioning that, algorithm *PPL* will degenerate to the naive approach if there is no testing point in $T_e$ and simply choose the regression line with the best correlation coefficient. For comparison purposes, we will also show the result of the naive approach in our experimental results. Note that the best fit regression line will be discovered in the *quantized support distribution* generated from top-k itemsets in the sample. In light of Proposition 1, the slope and the Y-intercept in the original *itemset support distribution* will be equal to $\hat{\theta}_g$ and $\hat{\Omega}_g - \log(w)$, respectively.

We finally summarize the overall flow of algorithm *PPL*, as shown in Figure 7(b): (1) sampling; (2) discover *top-k* frequent itemsets in the sample; (3) aggregate the support of *top-k* itemsets by means of the equi-width histogram so as to obtain the partial *quantized support distribution*; (4) perform Procedure *Best_fit* to obtain the characteristics of the *quantized support distribution* in the sample; (5) identify the characteristics of the power-law relationship in the *itemset support distribution* in the entire database according to Proposition 1.

## 4 Experimental Studies

The four real skewed datasets described in Table 1 are utilized in our experimental studies. Since the goal to show the support distribution follows the Zipf distribution has been demonstrated in Section 2, we in this section investigate whether algorithm *PPL* can efficiently and correctly estimate the parameters of the power-law relationship in the itemset support distribution. The simulation is coded by C++ and performed on Windows XP in a 1.7GHz IBM compatible PC with 512MB of memory. The default parameters in the experiments are: (1) $k = 5,000$ (*top-k* itemsets); (2) the number of aggregated support counts $w = 10$; (3) the number of points in the training set $|T_e| = 5$; (4) the correlation coefficient threshold $\delta = -0.8$; (5) the sample size $|S| = 20,000$.

We investigate whether algorithm *PPL* with the default parameters is able to correctly characterize the power-law relationship in four real datasets. The results are presented in Figure 8(a)~Figure 8(d), where the original support distributions and the *best fit regression lines* obtained by algorithm *PPL* (with their slopes $\theta$ and Y-intercepts $\Omega$) are shown. Note that the *best fit regression line* is discovered in the quantized support distribution in the sample. As can be seen, the *best fit regression line* can perfectly characterize the Zipf distribution in the four real datasets, showing the effectiveness of *PPL*.

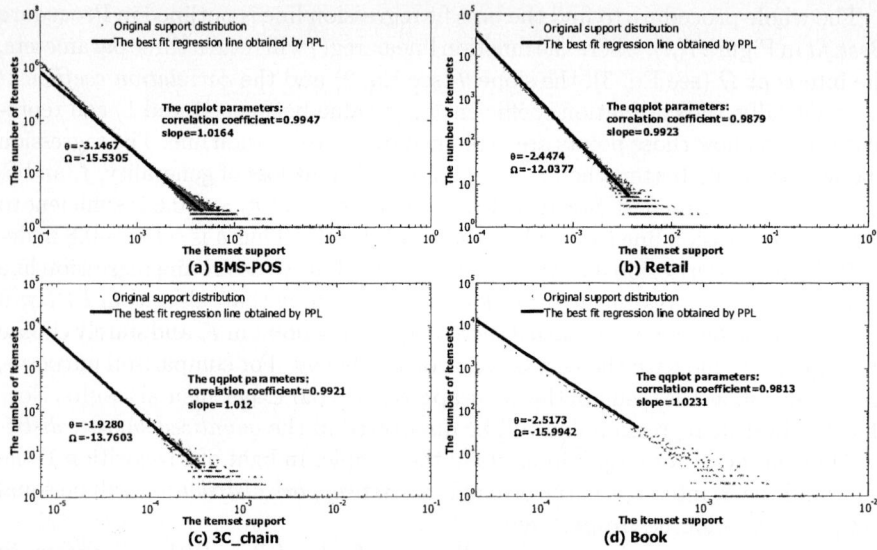

**Fig. 8.** The results of algorithm *PPL*

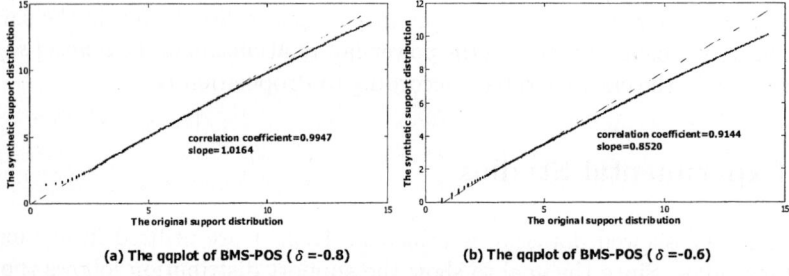

**Fig. 9.** The qqplot results in BMS-POS with various $\delta$

Furthermore, the execution time is shown in Figure 10, where the execution time of "Brute force approach" indicates the time to retrieve the original support distribution in Figure 1 by algorithm FP-growth. Indeed, the brute force approach can correctly determine the parameters of the Zipf distribution by finding most of itemsets, but it will pay for the extremely large time consumption. On the other hand, *PPL* can efficiently estimate the parameters of the power-law relationship by avoiding the expensive process to obtain all itemsets. It is worth mentioning that the efficiency gain in Figure 10, which is calculated as the execution time of the brute force approach divided by the execution time of algorithm *PPL*, shows that algorithm *PPL* is in orders of magnitude faster than the brute force approach.

Same as the experiments in [2], the quantitative analysis of algorithm *PPL* will be evaluated by the traditional method of quantile-quantile plot (qqplot), as

| Dataset | Brute force approach | Algorithm PPL | Efficiency Gain |
|---|---|---|---|
| BMS-POS | 632 sec | 8 sec | 79 |
| Retail | 1248 sec | 5 sec | 249.6 |
| 3C_chain | 2547 sec | 10 sec | 254.7 |
| Book | 492 sec | 3 sec | 164 |

**Fig. 10.** The execution time of different approaches

| Variant Parameters | BMS-POS Corr. Coef. | BMS-POS Slope | Retail Corr. Coef. | Retail Slope | 3C_chain Corr. Coef. | 3C_chain Slope | Book Corr. Coef. | Book Slope |
|---|---|---|---|---|---|---|---|---|
| Default | 0.99 | 1.02 | 0.99 | 0.99 | 0.99 | 1.01 | 0.98 | 1.02 |
| $|T_e|=0$ (naive) | 0.89 | 0.73 | 0.83 | 0.82 | 0.91 | 0.83 | 0.87 | 0.93 |
| $|T_e|=10$ | 0.99 | 0.98 | 0.98 | 0.96 | 0.98 | 1.01 | 0.99 | 1.02 |
| $\delta=-0.5$ | 0.84 | 0.86 | 0.91 | 1.08 | 0.92 | 0.94 | 0.87 | 1.11 |
| $\delta=-0.9$ | 0.99 | 1.01 | 0.99 | 1.02 | 0.97 | 1.06 | 0.98 | 1.03 |
| $|T_e|=0; \delta=-0.5$ | 0.81 | 1.21 | 0.77 | 1.11 | 0.73 | 1.18 | 0.84 | 1.13 |
| k=10,000 | 0.98 | 1.02 | 0.99 | 0.97 | 0.97 | 1.08 | 0.98 | 1.07 |
| k=50,000 | 0.99 | 0.99 | 0.99 | 1.02 | 0.98 | 0.97 | 0.98 | 0.94 |
| $|S|$=10,000 | 0.93 | 1.09 | 0.98 | 0.97 | 0.95 | 1.09 | 0.98 | 0.97 |
| $|S|$=50,000 | 0.99 | 0.99 | 0.99 | 1.03 | 0.98 | 0.99 | 0.99 | 1.03 |
| $|S|$=0.1$|D|$ | 0.99 | 1.03 | 0.93 | 1.13 | 0.99 | 0.98 | 0.91 | 0.94 |
| $|S|$=0.2$|D|$ | 0.99 | 1.01 | 0.94 | 1.04 | 0.98 | 0.96 | 0.94 | 1.03 |
| w=50 | 0.98 | 1.03 | 0.91 | 0.94 | 0.94 | 1.02 | 0.96 | 1.08 |
| w=100 | 0.93 | 1.14 | 0.88 | 1.13 | 0.98 | 1.01 | 0.92 | 0.94 |

**Fig. 11.** The qqplot results of four real datasets

the one shown in Figure 9. The qqplot is used to compare the quantiles of two datasets. If the distributions of these two datasets are similar, the qqplot will be linear and the slope will be close to one. As such, we generate a synthetic support distribution according to the parameters estimated by algorithm *PPL*, and then make a qqplot between the original support distribution and the synthetic support distribution. Afterward, two important factors can be calculated: (1) the slope of the qqplot; (2) the correlation coefficient of points in the qqplot. If both are close to one, we can claim that the real distribution and the synthetic distribution are from the same distribution [2], meaning that the regression line can perfectly represent the data distribution.

The qqplots on various correlation coefficient thresholds $\delta$ are shown in Figure 9, where Figure 9(a) is the qqplot corresponding to the result of Figure 8(a). We can find that the qqplot in Figure 9(a) is close to linear, except points with respect to very low supports and very high supports. Note that points with respect to high supports have been observed not exactly following the power-law relationship and points with respect to low supports in the BMS-POS dataset upwardly vary from the Zipf distribution, thus causing the deviation of a few points. However, the slope and the correlation coefficient are very close to unity, indicating that the synthetic distribution can mostly correctly fit the real distribution. Furthermore, when we increase the threshold $\delta$, as shown in Figure 9(b), the estimated quality degrades, showing the importance of the criterion 2 of the *best fit regression line*. Indeed, a regression line with the low correlation coefficient loses its effectiveness to estimate the power-law relationship, even though it satisfies criterion 3, i.e., having the minimum testing error.

Due to space limitations, other qqplot results of four real datasets are summarized in Figure 11. At first, we observe results with various $|T_e|$. Note that the case $|T_e| = 0$ can be deemed as the naive approach discussed in Section 3.3. As can be seen, the naive approach cannot correctly model the distribution since the correlation coefficient and the slope deviate a lot from unity. On the other hand, $|T_e| = 5$ (default cases) and $|T_e| = 10$ both lead to the desirable result. Moreover, the studies of various $\delta$ are also shown, and we can find that $\delta = -0.8$ (default cases) or $-0.9$ will result in the correlation coefficient and the slope close to one. Note that without loss of generality, the results of $|T_e| = 0$ and $\delta = -0.5$ can be deemed as the case to obtain the regression line over all points from top-$k$ itemsets. It can be seen that the regression line over all points loses of its power to explain the real data distribution. The above observations all demonstrate the effectiveness of algorithm PPL.

In addition, with the result of various $k$, we can conclude that the default $k = 5,000$ is sufficient to obtain high quality results. Note that top-5000 itemsets can be efficiently retrieved in the sample, indicating the efficiency and effectiveness of algorithm PPL. We also investigate the influence of the sample size. Clearly, the result obtained in the sample with the default size 20,000 is close to the result obtained in the large sample with size equal to $0.2 \times |D|$, showing that the resulting quality is insensitive to the sample size if the sample size is not arbitrarily small. Finally, we observe the result of various $w$. Note that Proposition 1 will not hold when $w$ is large. Thus it can be seen that $w = 100$ slightly degrades the estimated quality of algorithm PPL. Since the goal of *histogram* in this paper is to diminish the side-effect of sampling, we conclude that $w = 10$ is sufficient to achieve this, and will give the excellent fit of the itemset support distribution.

## 5  Conclusions

In this paper, we demonstrated that the power-law relationship appears in the distribution of itemset supports in the real datasets. Discovering such a relationship is useful for many applications. To avoid the costly process of retrieving all itemsets, we proposed algorithm PPL to efficiently extract characteristics of the power-law relationship. As shown in the experimental results, algorithm PPL is able to efficiently extract the characteristics of the power-law relationship with high accuracy.

## References

1. R. Agrawal and R. Srikant. Fast algorithms for mining association rules. In *Proc. of VLDB*, 1994.
2. Z. Bi, C. Faloutsos, and F. Korn. The "DGX" Distribution for Mining Massive, Skewed Data. In *Proc. of SIGKDD*, 2000.
3. L. Breslau, P. Cao, L. Fan, G. Phillips, and S. Shenker. Web caching and zipf-like distributions: Evidence and implications. In *Proc. of IEEE INFOCOM*, 1999.

4. Y.L. Cheung and A.W. Fu. Mining Association Rules without Support Threshold: with and without Item Constraints. In *TKDE*, 2004.
5. W. G. Cochran. *Sampling Techniques*. John Wiley and Sons, 1977.
6. L. Egghe. The distribution of n-grams. *Scientometrics*, 2000.
7. F. Geerts, B. Goethals, and J. V. d. Bussche. A tight upper bound on the number of candidate patterns. In *Proc. of IEEE ICDM*, 2001.
8. J. Han and M. Kamber. *Data Mining: Concepts and Techniques*. Morgan Kaufmann, 2000.
9. Y. Ioannidis. The history of histograms. In *Proc. of VLDB*, 2003.
10. J.-S. Park, M.-S. Chen, and P. S. Yu. An effective hash based algorithm for mining association rules. In *Proc. of SIGMOD*, 1995.
11. G. Ramesh, W. A. Maniatty, and M. J. Zaki. Feasible itemset distributions in data mining: Theory and application. In *Proc. of ACM PODS*, 2003.
12. J. A. Rice. *Mathematical statistics and data analysis*. Duxbury Press, 1995.
13. H. Toivonen. Sampling large databases for association rules. In *Proc. of VLDB*, 1996.
14. J. Wang, J. Han, Y. Lu, and P. Tzvetkov. TFP: An Efficient Algorithm for Mining Top-K Frequent Closed Itemsets. In *TKDE*, 2005.
15. M.J. Zaki, S. Parthasarathy, Wei Li, and M. Ogihara. Evaluation of sampling for data mining of association rules. In *Int. Workshop on Research Issues in Data Engineering*, 1997.
16. Z. Zheng, R. Kohavi, and L. Mason. Real world performance of association rule algorithms. In *Proc. of SIGKDD*, 2001.
17. G.K. Zipf. *Human Behavior and the Principle of Least Effort*. Addison-Wesley Press, 1949.

# Fast Query Point Movement Techniques with Relevance Feedback for Content-Based Image Retrieval

Danzhou Liu, Kien A. Hua, Khanh Vu, and Ning Yu

School of Computer Science,
University of Central Florida,
Orlando, Florida 32816, USA
{dzliu, kienhua, khanh, nyu}@cs.ucf.edu
http://www.cs.ucf.edu/~dzliu

**Abstract.** Target search in content-based image retrieval (CBIR) systems refers to finding a specific (target) image such as a particular registered logo or a specific historical photograph. Existing techniques were designed around query refinement based on relevance feedback, suffer from slow convergence, and do not even guarantee to find intended targets. To address those limitations, we propose several efficient query point movement methods. We theoretically prove that our approach is able to reach any given target image with fewer iterations in the worst and average cases. Extensive experiments in simulated and realistic environments show that our approach significantly reduces the number of iterations and improves overall retrieval performance. The experiments also confirm that our approach can always retrieve intended targets even with poor selection of initial query points and can be employed to improve the effectiveness and efficiency of existing CBIR systems.

## 1 Introduction

Content-based image retrieval (CBIR) has received much research attention in the last decade, motivated by the immensely growing amount of multimedia data. Many CBIR systems have recently been developed, including QBIC [5], MARS [11, 14], Blobworld [2], PicHunter [4], and others [15, 18, 20, 21]. In a typical CBIR system, low-level visual image features (e.g., color, texture and shape) are automatically extracted for image descriptions and indexing purposes. To search for desirable images, a user presents an image as an example of similarity. The system then returns a set of similar images based on the extracted features. In CBIR systems with relevance feedback, the user can mark returned images as positive or negative, which are fed back into the system as a new, refined query for the next round of retrieval. The process is repeated until the user is satisfied with the query result. Relevance feedback helps bridge the semantic gap between the descriptive limitations of low-level features and human perception of similarity [16]. Such systems achieve high effectiveness for many practical applications [6].

There are two general types of search: *target search* and *category search* [4, 6]. The goal of target search is to find a specific (target) image (e.g., a registered logo, a historical photograph or a painting), which can be determined based on low-level features. The goal of category search is to retrieve a particular semantic class or genre of images (e.g. scenery images or skyscrapers). Target search corresponds to *known-item search* in information retrieval; category search corresponds to *high-precision search*. Due to semantic gaps, images in a semantic category might scatter in several clusters in low-level feature space. To retrieve a semantic class, category search is normally decomposed into several target searches, in which representatives of the clusters are located. The representatives are then used to retrieve the members of the clusters. Efficient target search techniques are therefore essential for both target search and category search. Hence, we focus on target search in this paper.

Existing target search techniques allow the re-retrieval of checked images when they fall in the search range. This leads to a host of major disadvantages:

 – Local maximum traps. Since query points in relevance feedback systems have to move through many regions before reaching a target, it is possible that they get trapped in one of these regions. Figure 1 illustrates a possible scenario. As a result of a 3-NN search at $p_s$, the system returns points $p_1$ and $p_2$, in addition to query point $p_s$ ($s$ and $t$ respectively denote the starting query point $p_s$ and the target point $p_t$). Since both $p_1$ and $p_2$ are relevant, the refined query point $p_r$ is their centroid and the anchor of the next 3-NN search. However, the system will retrieve exactly the same set, from which points $p_1$ and $p_2$ are again selected. In other words, the system can never get out because the retrieval set is saturated with the $k$ checked images. Although, the system can escape with a larger $k$, it is difficult to guess a proper threshold (up to $k = 14$ in this example). Consequently, we might not even know a local maximum trap is occurring.
 – No guarantee that returned images are the most relevant. This is due to local maximum traps and thereby no guarantee to find the target image.
 – Slow convergence. The centroid of the relevant points is typically selected as the anchor of refined queries. This, coupling with possible retrieval of already visited images, prevents aggressive movement of search (see Figure 2, where $k = 3$). Slow convergence also implies that users must spend more time with the system, refining intermediate queries.
 – High resource requirements. These overheads are the results of slow convergence, local maximum traps and larger intermediate results.

To address the above limitations, we propose four target search methods: naïve random scan (NRS), local neighboring movement (LNM), neighboring divide and conquer (NDC), and global divide and conquer (GDC) methods. All these methods are built around a common strategy: they do not retrieve checked images (i.e., shrink the search space). Furthermore, NDC and GDC exploit Voronoi diagrams to aggressively prune the search space and move towards target images. We theoretically prove that the convergence speeds of GDC and

NDC are much faster than those of NRS and recent methods. Results of extensive experiments confirm our complexity analysis and show the superiority of our techniques in both the simulated and realistic environments. A preliminary design based on heuristics was presented in [10]. This paper introduces theories and formal proofs to support the proposed techniques, and presents more extensive experiments.

The remaining of the paper is organized as follows. In Section 2, we survey recent works on target search. Section 3 presents in detail our proposed methods for target search. Section 4 describes our performance experiments and discusses the results. Finally, we conclude the paper and highlight our future research directions in Section 5.

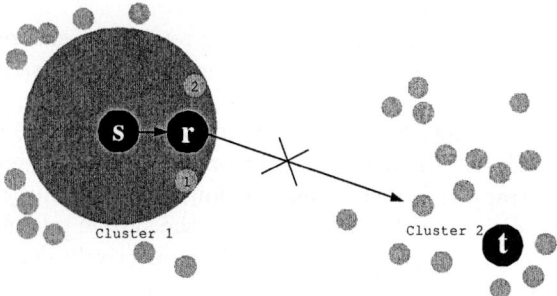

**Fig. 1.** Local maximum trap

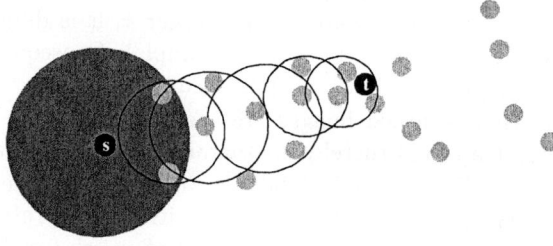

**Fig. 2.** Slow convergence

## 2 Related Work

In this section, we survey existing techniques for target search. We also review category search techniques because they are closely related. Category search techniques can be used for target search if we assume the desired category has only one target image.

Two well-known techniques for target search were proposed in QBIC [5] and PicHunter [4]. IBM's QBIC system allows users to compose queries based on visual image features such as color percentage, color layout, and texture present in the target image, and ranks retrieved images according to those criteria. To achieve good results, users are required to compose queries with an adequate knowledge of the targets' properties, which is normally a difficult and time-consuming process for unskilled users. To lessen the burden on users, PicHunter proposes to predict query's intents using a Bayesian-based relevance feedback technique to guide query refinement and target search. PicHunter's performance, however, depends on the consistency of users' behavior and the accuracy of the prediction algorithm. In addition, both QBIC and PicHunter do not guarantee to find target images and suffer local maximum traps.

Techniques for category search can be divided into two groups: single-point and multipoint movement techniques. A technique is classified as a single-point movement technique if the refined query $Q_r$ at each iteration consists of only one query point. Otherwise, it is a multi-point movement technique. Typical query shapes of single-point movement and multi-point movement techniques are shown in Figures 3 and 4 where the contours represent equi-similarity surfaces. Single-point movement techniques, such as MARS [11, 14] and MindReader [8], construct a single query point, which is close to relevant images and away from irrelevant ones. MARS uses a weighted distance (producing shapes as shown in Figure 3.2), where each dimension weight is inversely proportional to the standard deviation of the relevant images' feature values in that dimension. The rationale is that a small variation among the values is more likely to express restrictions on the feature, and thereby should carry a higher weight. On the other hand, a large variation indicates this dimension is not significant in the query, thus should assume a low weight. MindReader achieves better results by using a generalized weighted distance, see Figure 3.3 for its shape.

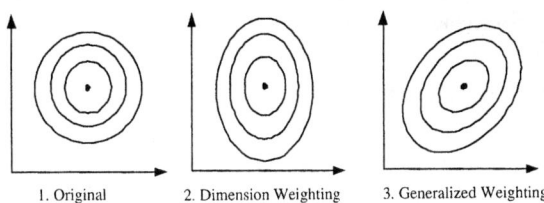

1. Original    2. Dimension Weighting    3. Generalized Weighting

**Fig. 3.** Single-points movement query shapes

In multipoint movement techniques such as Query expansion [3], Qcluster [9], and Query Decomposition [7], multiple query points are used to define the ideal space that is most likely to contain relevant results. Query expansion groups query points into clusters and chooses their centroids as $Q_r$'s representatives, see Figure 4.1. The distance of a point to $Q_r$ is defined as a weighted sum of individual distances to those representatives. The weights are proportional to the number of relevant objects in the clusters. Thus, Query expansion treats local clusters differently, compared to the equal treatment in single-points movement techniques.

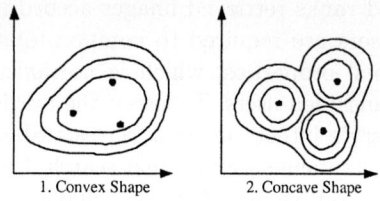

**Fig. 4.** Multiple point movement query shapes

In some queries, clusters are too far apart for a unified, all-encompassing contour to be effective; separate contours can yield more selective retrieval. This observation motivated Qcluster to employ an adaptive classification and cluster-merging method to determine optimal contour shapes for complex queries. Qcluster supports disjunctive queries, where similarity to any of the query points is considered as good, see Figure 4.2. To handle disjunctive queries both in vector space and in arbitrary metric space, a technique was proposed in FALCON [22]. It uses an aggregate distance function to estimate the (dis)similarity of an object to a set of desirable images. To handle semantic gaps better, we recently proposed a query decomposition technique [7]. In general, the above category search techniques do not guarantee to find target images and still suffer slow convergence, local maximum traps and high computation overhead.

To avoid local maximum traps and their problems, our methods will ignore all checked images. They will be discussed in the order of their sophistication in the next section. The most complex, GDC, is based on the single-point movement method, which proves to converge faster than multipoint movement mehthods. It employs Voronoi diagrams to prune irrelevant images, assisting users in query refinement and enabling fast convergence.

## 3  Target Search Methods

In this section, we present the four proposed target search methods. Again, the goals of our target search methods are avoiding local maximum traps, achieving fast convergence, reducing resource requirements, and guaranteeing to find target images. Reconsidering already checked images is one of the several shortcomings of existing techniques that causes local maximum trap and slow convergence. The idea of leaving out checked images is our motivation for a new design principle. We assume that users are able to accurately identify the most relevant image out of the returned images, and the most relevant image is the closest image to the target image among the returned ones. We will also discuss the steps to ensure our target search system less sensitive to users' inaccurate relevance feedback in Section 4.

The ultimate goal of target search is to find target images. Thus if target images were not found, the final precision and recall would be zero. In CBIR with relevance feedback, the traditional recall and precision can be computed for individual iteration. For target search, we can use the so-called 'aggregate' recall and precision: if after several, say $i$, iterations the target image is found, the average precision and recall are $1/(i \cdot k)$ and $1/i$, where $k$ is the number of images retrieved at each iteration. In short, the number of iterations to find target images is not only the most significant measure of efficiency but also the most significant indicator of precision and recall. Therefore, we use the number of iterations as the major measure for theoretical analysis and experimental evaluation of the four proposed target search methods.

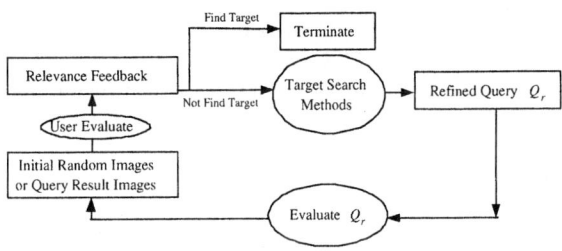

**Fig. 5.** Overview of the target search systems

A query is defined as $Q = \langle n_Q, P_Q, W_Q, D_Q, \mathbb{S}, k \rangle$, where $n_Q$ denotes the number of query points in $Q$, $P_Q$ the set of $n_Q$ query points in the search space $\mathbb{S}$, $W_Q$ the set of weights associated with $P_Q$, $D_Q$ the distance function, and $k$ the number of points to be retrieved in each iteration (see Figure 5). For single point movement techniques, $n_Q = 1$; for multipoint movement techniques, $n_Q > 1$; and $n_Q = 0$ signifies that the query is to randomly retrieve $k$ points in $\mathbb{S}$. This definition is a generalized version of $Q = \langle n_Q, P_Q, W_Q, D_Q \rangle$ defined in [3], where the search space is assumed to be the whole database for every search. In our generalized definition, $\mathbb{S}$ is included to account for the dynamic change of search space, which is usually reduced after each iteration. Let $Q_s$ denote the starting query, $Q_r$ a refined query at a feedback iteration, $Q_t$ a target query which results in the retrieval of the intended target, and $\mathbb{S}_k$ the query result set.

### 3.1 Naïve Random Scan Method

The NRS method randomly retrieves $k$ different images at a time until the user finds the target image or the remaining set is exhausted, see Figure 6. Specifically, at each iteration, a set of $k$ random images are retrieved from the candidate (i.e. unchecked) set $\mathbb{S}'$ for relevance feedback (lines 2 and 6), and $\mathbb{S}'$ is then reduced by $k$ (lines 3 and 7). Clearly, the naïve scan algorithm does not suffer local maximum traps and is able to locate the target image after some finite number of iterations. In the best case, NRS takes one iteration, while the worst case requires $\lceil \frac{|\mathbb{S}|}{k} \rceil$. On average NRS can find the target in $\left\lceil \sum_{i=1}^{\lceil \frac{|\mathbb{S}|}{k} \rceil} i / \lceil \frac{|\mathbb{S}|}{k} \rceil \right\rceil = \left\lceil (\lceil \frac{|\mathbb{S}|}{k} \rceil + 1)/2 \right\rceil$ iterations. In other words, NRS takes $\mathcal{O}(|\mathbb{S}|)$ to reach the target point. Therefore, NRS is only suitable for a small database set.

NAIVERANDOMSCAN(S, $k$)

**Input:**
set of images                                        S
number of retrieved images at each iteration $k$
**Output:**
target image $p_t$

```
01   Q_s ← ⟨0, P_Q, W_Q, D_Q, S, k⟩
02   S_k ← EVALUATEQUERY(Q_s)   /* randomly retrieve k points in S */
03   S' ← S − S_k
04   while user does not find p_t in S_k do
05       Q_r ← ⟨0, P_Q, W_Q, D_Q, S', k⟩
06       S_k ← EVALUATEQUERY(Q_r)  /* randomly retrieve k points in S' */
07       S' ← S' − S_k
08   enddo
09   return p_t
```

**Fig. 6.** Naïve Random Scan Method

### 3.2 Local Neighboring Movement Method

Existing techniques allow already checked images to be reconsidered, which leads to several major drawbacks as mentioned in Section 1. We apply our non-re-retrieval strategy to one such method, such as MindReader [8], to produce the LNM method. LNM is similar to NRS except lines 5 and 6 as follows:

```
05       Q_r ← ⟨n_Q, P_Q, W_Q, D_Q, S', k⟩  based on the user's relevance feedback
06       S_k ← EVALUATEQUERY(Q_r)    /* perform a k-NN query in S' */
```

Specifically, $Q_r$ is constructed such that it moves towards neighboring relevant points and away from irrelevant ones, and $k$-NN query is now evaluated against S' instead of S (lines 5 and 6). When LNM encounters a local maximum trap, it enumerates neighboring points of the query, and selects the one closest to the target. Therefore, LNM can overcome local maximum traps, although it could take many iterations to do so.

Again, one iteration is required in the best case. To simplify the following worst-case and average-case complexity analysis, we assume that S is uniformly distributed in the $n$-dimensional hypercube and the distance between two nearest points is a unit.

**Theorem 1.** *For LNM, the worst and average cases are* $\left\lceil \sqrt{n} \sqrt[n]{|S|} / \lceil \log_{2^n} k \rceil \right\rceil$ *and* $\left\lceil (\frac{\sqrt{n} \sqrt[n]{|S|}}{\lceil \log_{2^n} k \rceil} + 1)/2 \right\rceil$, *respectively, assuming* S *is uniformly distributed.*

*Proof.* The hypercube's edge length is $\sqrt[n]{|S|}-1$, and the diagonal's $\sqrt{n}(\sqrt[n]{|S|}-1)$. Let the distance between the initial query point and the target point be $l$, then $l \leq \sqrt{n}(\sqrt[n]{|S|} - 1) < \sqrt{n}\sqrt[n]{|S|}$. Note that the expected radius for $k$-NN search in $\mathbb{S}$ is $r = \lceil \log_{2^n} k \rceil$. Since $\mathbb{S}' \subset \mathbb{S}$, $k$-NN search in LNM requires a radius larger than $r$, but less than $2r$. In other words, at each iteration, LNM moves towards the target image at an average speed of $cr$ where $1 \le c < 2$. It follows that the number of iterations needed to reach the target is $\lceil l/(c\lceil \log_{2^n} k \rceil) \rceil$, which is bounded by $\left\lceil \sqrt{n} \sqrt[n]{|\mathbb{S}|}/\lceil \log_{2^n} k \rceil \right\rceil$. Then, the worst and average cases are $\left\lceil \sqrt{n} \sqrt[n]{|\mathbb{S}|}/\lceil \log_{2^n} k \rceil \right\rceil$ and $\left\lceil (\frac{\sqrt{n} \sqrt[n]{|\mathbb{S}|}}{\lceil \log_{2^n} k \rceil} + 1)/2 \right\rceil$, respectively. ∎

If data were arbitrarily distributed, then the worst case could be as high as NRS's, i.e. $\left\lceil \frac{|\mathbb{S}|}{k} \right\rceil$ iterations (e.g., when all points are on a line). In summary, in the worst case LNM could take anywhere from $\mathcal{O}(\sqrt[n]{|\mathbb{S}|})$ to $\mathcal{O}(|\mathbb{S}|)$.

### 3.3 Neighboring Divide and Conquer Method

Although LNM can overcome local maximum traps, it does so inefficiently, taking many iterations and in the process returning numerous false hits. To speed up convergence, we propose to use Voronoi diagrams [13] in NDC to reduce search space. The Voronoi diagram approach finds the nearest neighbors of a given query point by locating the Voronoi cell containing the query point. Specifically, NDC searches for the target as follows, see Figure 7. From the starting query $Q_s$, $k$ points are randomly retrieved (line 2). Then the Voronoi region $VR_i$ is initially set to the minimum bounding box of $\mathbb{S}$ (line 3). In the **while** loop, NDC first determines the Voronoi seed set $\mathbb{S}_{k+1}$ (lines 6 to 10) and $p_i$, the most relevant point in $\mathbb{S}_{k+1}$ according to the user's relevance feedback (line 11). Next, it constructs a Voronoi diagram $VD$ inside $VR_i$ using $\mathbb{S}_{k+1}$ (line 12). The Voronoi cell region containing $p_i$ in $VD$ is now the new $VR_i$ (line 13). Because only $VR_i$ can contain the target (as proved in Theorem 2), we can safely prune out the other Voronoi cell regions. To continue the search in $VR_i$, NDC constructs a $k$-NN query using $p_i$ as the anchor point (line 15), and evaluates it (line 16). The procedure is repeated until the target $p_t$ is found. When NDC encounters a local maximum trap, it employs Voronoi diagrams to aggressively prune the search space and move towards the target image, thus significantly speeding up the convergence. Therefore, NDC can overcome local maximum traps and achieve fast convergence. We prove the following invariant.

**Theorem 2.** *The target point is always contained inside or on an edge (surface) of $VR_i$, the Voronoi cell region enclosing the most relevant point $p_i$.*

*Proof.* Theorem 2 can be proved by contradiction. First, note that according to the properties of the Voronoi cell construction, if $VR_i$ contains the most relevant point (i.e. the closest point) $p_i$ to the target point $p_t$, its seed $p_i$ is the nearest neighbor of $p_t$ among $\mathbb{S}_{k+1}$. Suppose $p_t$ is inside $VR_j$, $i \ne j$. Then there exits another point in $\mathbb{S}_{k+1}$ closer to $p_t$ than $p_i$, a contradiction. ∎

NEIGHBORINGDIVIDECONQUER(S, k)

**Input:**
set of images S
number of retrieved images at each iteration k
**Output:**
target image $p_t$

```
01    Q_s ← ⟨0, P_Q, W_Q, D_Q, S, k⟩
02    S_k ← EVALUATEQUERY(Q_s)  /* randomly retrieve k points in S */
03    VR_i ← the minimum bounding box of S
04    iter ← 1
05    while user does not find p_t in S_k do
06        if iter ≠ 1 then
07            S_{k+1} ← S_k + {p_i}
08        else
09            S_{k+1} ← S_k
10        endif
11        p_i ← the most relevant point ∈ S_{k+1}
12        construct a Voronoi diagram VD inside VR_i using points in S_{k+1} as
              Voronoi seeds
13        VR_i ← the Voronoi cell region associated with the Voronoi seed p_i
              in VD
14        S' ← such points ∈ S that are inside VR_i except p_i
15        Q_r ← ⟨1, {p_i}, W_Q, D_Q, S', k⟩
16        S_k ← EVALUATEQUERY(Q_r)  /* perform a k-NN query in S' */
17        iter ← iter + 1
18    enddo
19    return p_t
```

**Fig. 7.** Neighboring Divide and Conquer Method

Figure 8 explains how NDC approaches the target. In the first iteration, $S_k = \{p_1, p_2, p_s\}$ is randomly picked by the system, assuming $k = 3$. The user identifies $p_s$ as $p_i$ (the most relevant point in $S_k$). NDC then constructs a Voronoi diagram based on those three points in $S_{k+1} = S_k$, partitioning the search space into three regions. According to Theorem 2, the target must be in $VR_i$. NDC thus ignoring the other two regions, performs a $k$-NN query anchored at $p_s$ and retrieves $S_k = \{p_3, p_4, p_5\}$, the three closest points inside $VR_i$. Again, the user correctly identifies $p_5$ as the most relevant point in $S_{k+1} = \{p_s, p_3, p_4, p_5\}$. The system constructs a Voronoi diagram and searches only the Voronoi cell associated with $p_5$. The search continues and, finally, at the fourth iteration, the target point is reached as the result of a $k$-NN query of $p_6$, the most relevant point in $\{p_5, p_6, p_7, p_8\}$ retrieved in the third iteration. We now determine the worst-case complexity for NDC, assuming that S is uniformly distributed.

**Theorem 3.** *Starting from any point in S, NDC can reach any target point in $\mathcal{O}(\log_k |S|)$ iterations.*

*Proof.* At the first iteration, $\mathbb{S}$ is divided into $k$ Voronoi cells. Since the points are uniformly distributed from which $k$ points are randomly sampled, each $VR$ is expected to contain $\lceil \frac{|\mathbb{S}|}{k} \rceil$ points. According to Theorem 2, we only need to search one $VR$, which contains about $\lceil \frac{|\mathbb{S}|}{k} \rceil$ points. In the second iteration, the searched $VR$ contains $\lceil (\frac{|\mathbb{S}|}{k} - 1)/k \rceil \simeq \lceil |\mathbb{S}|/k^2 \rceil$ points. In the $i^{th}$ iteration, each $VR$ contains about $\lceil \frac{|\mathbb{S}|}{k^i} \rceil$ points. Since $\frac{|\mathbb{S}|}{k^i} \geq 1$, NDC will stop by $i \leq \log_k |\mathbb{S}|$. Hence, NDC reaches the target point in no more than $\mathcal{O}(\log_k |\mathbb{S}|)$ iterations. ∎

When $\mathbb{S}$ is arbitrarily distributed, the worst case could take up to $\lceil \frac{\mathbb{S}}{k} \rceil$ iterations (e.g., all points are on a line), the same as that of NRS. In other words, NDC could still require $\mathcal{O}(|\mathbb{S}|)$ iterations to reach the target point in the worst case.

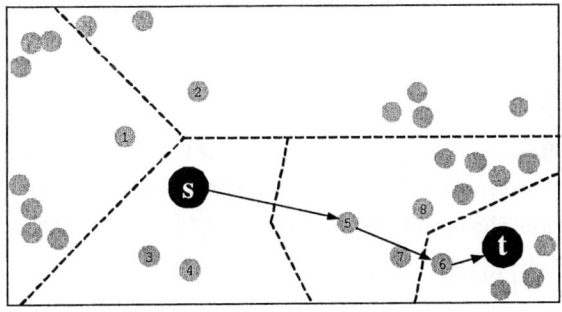

**Fig. 8.** Example of NDC

### 3.4 Global Divide and Conquer Method

To reduce the number of iterations in the worst case in NDC, we propose the GDC method. Instead of using a query point and its neighboring points to construct a Voronoi diagram, GDC uses the query point and $k$ points randomly sampled from $VR_i$. Specifically, GDC replaces lines 15 and 16 in NDC with:

15      $Q_r \leftarrow \langle 0, P_Q, W_Q, D_Q, \mathbb{S}', k \rangle$
16      $\mathbb{S}_k \leftarrow \text{EVALUATEQUERY}(Q_r)$ /* randomly retrieve $k$ points in $\mathbb{S}'$ */

Similar to NDC, when encountering a local maximum trap, GDC employs Voronoi diagrams as well to aggressively prune the search space and move towards the target image, thus significantly speeding up the convergence. Therefore, GDC can overcome local maximum traps and achieve fast convergence.

Figure 9 shows how the target could be located according to GDC. In the first iteration, $\mathbb{S}_k = \{p_1, p_2, p_s\}$ is the result of $k = 3$ randomly sampled points, of which $p_s$ is picked as $p_i$. Next, GDC constructs a Voronoi diagram and searches the $VR$ enclosing $p_s$. At the second iteration, $\mathbb{S}_{k+1} = \{p_s, p_4, p_5, p_6\}$ and $p_5$ is the most relevant point $p_i$. In the third and final iteration, the target point is

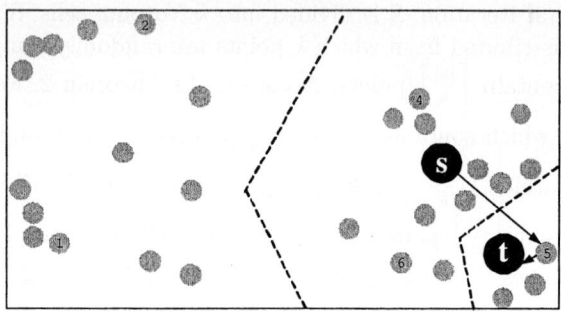

**Fig. 9.** Example of GDC

located; GDC takes 3 iterations to reach the target point. We prove that the worst case for GDC is bounded by $\mathcal{O}(\log_k |\mathbb{S}|)$.

**Theorem 4.** *Starting from an initial point in $\mathbb{S}$, GDC can reach any target point in $\mathcal{O}(\log_k |\mathbb{S}|)$ iterations.*

*Proof.* We will focus our attention on the size of $VR$ at each iteration, keeping in mind that points are randomly sampled for Voronoi diagram construction. Thus, at the first iteration, the searched $VR$ contains $\left\lceil \frac{|\mathbb{S}|}{k} \right\rceil$ points; at the second iteration, it contains $\left\lceil \frac{|\mathbb{S}|}{k \cdot (k+1)} \right\rceil$ points; and so on. At the $i^{th}$ iteration, it contains $\left\lceil \frac{|\mathbb{S}|}{k \cdot (k+1)^{i-1}} \right\rceil$ points. Because $\frac{|\mathbb{S}|}{k \cdot (k+1)^{i-1}} > 1$, that is, it requires that $i < \log_k |\mathbb{S}|$. In other words, GDC can reach any target point in no more than $\mathcal{O}(\log_k |\mathbb{S}|)$ iterations. ∎

Theorem 4 implies that for arbitrarily distributed datasets, GDC converges faster than NDC in general, although NDC might be as fast as GDC in certain queries, e.g., if the starting query point is close to the target point. In the previous example (Figure 8), NDC could also take three iterations, instead of four, to reach the target point if the initial $k$ points were the same as in Figure 9, as opposed to Figure 8.

For simplicity, we assume that users accurately pick the most relevant image out of the returned images for each iteration in the above discussion. In practice, however, this cannot be easily achieved by users, and typically users can pick several relevant images instead of one in target search systems. Therefore, we can construct, in each iteration, a single query point that is the weighted centroid of all the picked relevant images as in MARS and MindReader.

## 4 Experiments

In this section, we present the experimental results in both simulated and realistic environments. Our dataset consists of more than 68,040 images from the COREL library. There are a total of 37 visual image features in three main groups: colors

(9 features) [19], texture (10 features) [17], and edge structure (18 features) [23]. Our experiments were run on Sun UltraSPARC with 2GB memory. All the data resided in memory.

### 4.1 Simulated Experiments

In these experiments, we evaluated the performances of MARS [11, 14], MindReader [8], and Qcluster [9] against our techniques (NRS's results are omitted since its performance can be statistically predicted). The performance metrics of interest are average total visited images, precision, recall, computation time and the number of iterations (average, maximum, minimum, and their variance) needed for each method to retrieve an intended target. These were measured as $k$ takes different values in $\{5, 15, 30, 50, 75, 100\}$. There were 100 pairs of starting points-target points selected randomly for the experiments.

In order to avoid the effects of user's subjective and inconsistent behaviors, relevance feedback was simulated; the point in the retrieval set that is closest to the target point is automatically selected as the most relevant point. To save computation overhead for NDC and GDC, we constructed the Voronoi region $VR_i$ containing the most relevant point instead of the whole Voronoi diagram, and approximated $VR_i$ by its minimum boundary box if $VR_i$ contains too many surfaces.

To illustrate common problems (slow convergence, local maximum traps, etc.) with existing approaches, we demonstrate that MARS, MindReader and Qcluster have poor false hit ratios for small $k$. Figure 10 shows that when $k$ is small, their performance is affected by local maximum traps, i.e., their false hit ratios are very high. Even for a fairly large $k$, false hits remain very high. For example, when $k = 100$, MARS's false hit ratio is about 20% and Qcluster's exceeds 40%, while the best performer MindReader is just below the 20% mark. As a result, users of these techniques have to examine a large number of returned images, but might not find their intended targets.

In the experiments that produced the number of iterations, we had to make sure that the compared techniques could successfully reach the intended targets. We thus used LNM in place of MindReader (LNM is an improved version of MindReader, see Section 3). The experimental results for LNM, NDC and GDC are shown in Figures 11 to 18. They show that NDC and GDC perform more efficiently when $k$ is small, with GDC being slightly better than NDC. Specifically, when $k = 5$, the average numbers of iterations for LNM, NDC and GDC (see Figure 11) are roughly 21, 10 and 7, respectively (compared to $\frac{68040}{5} = 13608$ iterations in NRS); the maximum numbers are 58, 20 and 11, respectively (see Figure 12); and the minimum numbers are 7, 4 and 4, respectively (see Figure 13). The results also confirm our analysis of GDC complexity (see Figure 11): GDC can reach the target point in $\mathcal{O}(\log_k |\mathbb{S}|) = (\log_5 68040) = 6.9141 \simeq 7$ iterations.

The standard deviations of the iterations are shown in Figure 14. GDC and NDC are much more stable than LNM, with GDC's slightly more uniform than

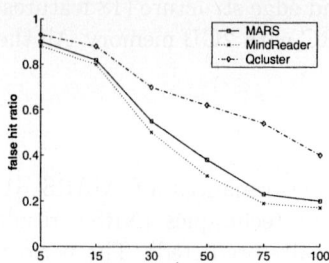

**Fig. 10.** False Hit Ratio

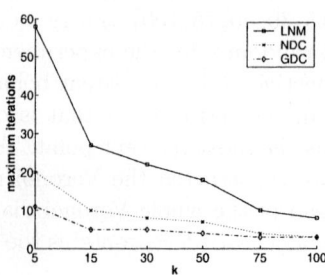

**Fig. 12.** Maximum Iterations

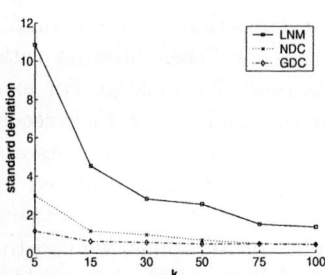

**Fig. 14.** Standard Deviation of Iterations

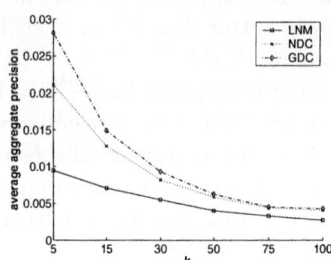

**Fig. 16.** Average Aggregate Precision

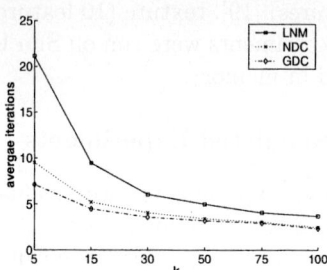

**Fig. 11.** Average Iterations

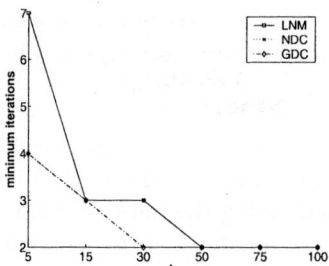

**Fig. 13.** Minimum Iterations

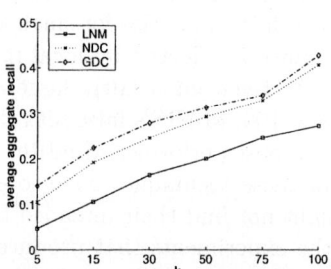

**Fig. 15.** Average Aggregate Recall

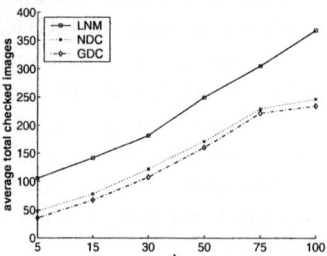

**Fig. 17.** Average Total Checked Images

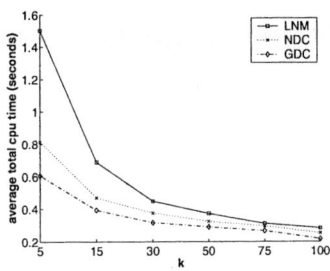

**Fig. 18.** CPU Time

NDC's. This indicates that GDC and NDC can achieve fast convergence even with a poor selection of initial query points.

The average 'aggregate' recalls and precisions, defined in Section 3, are shown in Figures 15 and 16 respectively. Again, experimental results show that NDC and GDC achieve better retrieval effectiveness (precision and recall) when $k$ is small compared to LNM, with GDC being slightly better than NDC.

The average total checked images for LNM, NDC, and GDC in the experiments are plotted in Figure 17. The figure shows that GDC and NDC examine fewer than half of the total checked images of LNM (compared to $\frac{68040}{2} = 34020$ images need to be checked in NRS). In terms of CPU time, GDC is the most efficient, although the difference is smaller as $k$ increases (see Figure 18). This is because NDC and GDC take some computation overhead to construct $VR_i$, while LNM requires more iterations and associated computation time for adjusting the generalized distance function. Overall, GDC and NDC significantly outperform LNM, with GDC slightly outdoing NDC.

### 4.2 Realistic Experiments

In simulated experiments, the most relevant points were assumed to be accurately selected among the returned points. In practice, however, this cannot be easily achieved by human evaluators, unless the most relevant images are distinctly stood out. To evaluate our methods' performance in realistic environments, we have developed an image retrieval system based on ImageGrouper [12]. Our prototype, shown in Figure 19, allows users to pose queries by dragging and grouping multiple relevant images on the work space, choose discriminative visual features, and select one of the three retrieval methods (LNM, NDC and GDC). It also allows users to rollback inaccurate relevance feedback in the previous iteration. Thus, for instance, if there are several relevant images, the user can group them together to form a query, and if he reaches a dead-end without finding the target image, he can rollback.

We trained 20 graduate students how to use the target search system and asked them to find 36 given target images from different semantic categories. In Figure 20, we show the results for the given 36 target images with $k = 50$. Two images, race cars and an ancient building, averagely took more iterations

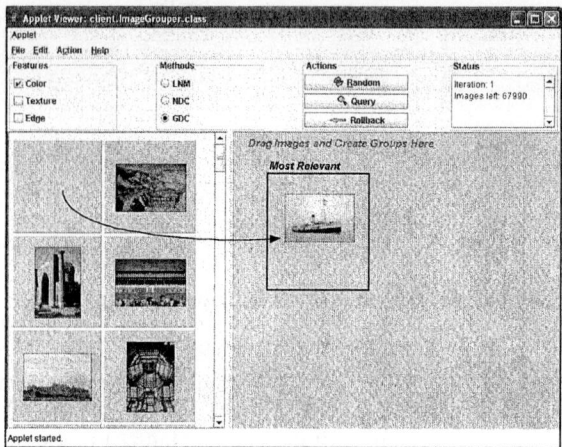

**Fig. 19.** Target Search GUI Interface

than the others to retrieve, mainly because many similar images exist in the collection. Even so, only 7 iterations on average were needed to locate them.

Users' inaccurate relevance feedback is a major issue for almost all CBIR systems with relevant feedback. We have taken steps to ensure our system is less sensitive to users' inaccurate relevance feedback, in design and in implementation. In the experimental study, our system monitored users' feedback and was capable of detecting inconsistent behavior (in the NDC and GDC algorithms, query points are selected following a general direction toward the target, i.e. in the active Vonoroi cell). Our prototype (see Figure 19) allows users to backtrack their selections if missteps are made. The results were excellent overall, indicated by the successful finding of the intended targets. Of course users' inaccurate relevance feedback is a difficult problem but our results are encouraging.

## 5 Conclusions

In this paper, we proposed four target search methods using relevance feedback for content-based image retrieval systems. Our research was motivated by the observation that revisiting of checked images can cause many drawbacks including local maximum traps and slow convergence. Our methods outperform existing techniques including MARS (employing feature weighting), MindReader (employing better feature weighting), and Qcluster (employing probabilistic models). All our methods are able to find the target images, with NDC and GDC converging faster than NRS and LNM (which represents an improved version of MindReader). Again, the number of iterations to find target images is not only the most significant measure of efficiency but also the most significant indicator of precision and recall. Simulated experiments have shown that NDC and GDC work more efficiently and effectively when $k$ is smaller, and GDC achieving $\mathcal{O}(\log_k |\mathbb{S}|)$ iterations

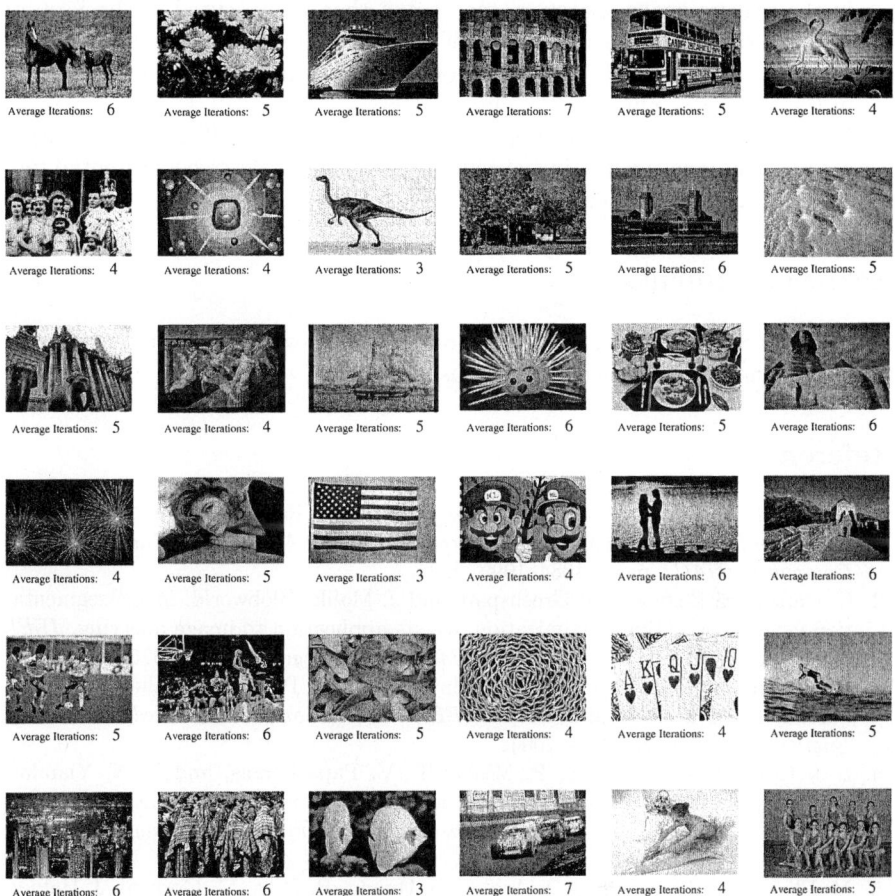

**Fig. 20.** GUI results with $k=50$

is slightly better than NDC. Experiments with our prototype show that our approach can achieve fast convergence (i.e. $\mathcal{O}(\log_k |\mathbb{S}|)$ iterations) even in the realistic environments.

We outline below some ongoing research to improve the system's performance:

- Evaluating different visual features and deducting rules for identifying the most discriminative features of image queries so that higher accuracy of relevance feedback can be achieved.
- Adopting the idea of ostensive relevance feedback [1], where the checked images are used to refine the query, and the length of time since an image was checked is used in a decay function to modulate the impact of those already checked images.
- Extending our methods to support category search. Recall that, due to semantic gaps, images in a semantic class might scatter in several clusters

in the feature space. Category search can then be executed in the form of multiple target searches. Each target search is to find a representative image of a cluster, which will be the anchor of a $k$-NN query to find other images in the respective cluster.
- Extending our methods to support video target search. Efficient video target search technique (i.e. finding specific scenes in videos) is also an essential tool for video retrieval applications.

## Acknowledgments

The authors would like to thank the anonymous reviewers for their constructive comments and suggestions on a previous draft.

## References

1. P. Browne and A. F. Smeaton. Video Information Retrieval Using Objects and Ostensive Relevance Feedback. In *Proceedings of the ACM Symposium on Applied Computing (SAC)*, pages 1084–1090, 2004.
2. C. Carson, S. Belongie, H. Greenspan, and J. Malik. Blobworld: image segmentation using expectation-maximization and its application to image querying. *IEEE Transactions on Pattern Analysis and Machine Intelligence*, 24(8):1026–1038, 2002.
3. K. Chakrabarti, O.-B. Michael, S. Mehrotra, and K. Porkaew. Evaluating refined queries in top-k retrieval systems. *IEEE Transactions on Knowledge and Data Engineering*, 16(2):256–270, 2004.
4. I. J. Cox, M. L. Miller, T. P. Minka, T. V. Papathomas, and P. N. Yianilos. The Bayesian image retrieval system, PicHunter: theory, implementation, and psychophysical experiments. *IEEE Transactions on Image Processing*, 9(1):20–37, 2000.
5. M. Flickner, H. S. Sawhney, J. Ashley, Q. Huang, B. Dom, M. Gorkani, J. Hafner, D. Lee, D. Petkovic, D. Steele, and P. Yanker. Query by image and video content: The QBIC system. *IEEE Computer*, 28(9):23–32, 1995.
6. T. Gevers and A. Smeulders. Content-based image retrieval: An overview. In G. Medioni and S. B. Kang, editors, *Emerging Topics in Computer Vision*. Prentice Hall, 2004.
7. K. A. Hua, N. Yu, and D. Liu. Query Decomposition: A Multiple Neighborhood Approach to Relevance Feedback Processing in Content-based Image Retrieval. In *Proceedings of the IEEE ICDE Conference*, 2006.
8. Y. Ishikawa, R. Subramanya, and C. Faloutsos. MindReader: Querying databases through multiple examples. In *Proceedings of the 24th VLDB Conference*, pages 218–227, 1998.
9. D.-H. Kim and C.-W. Chung. Qcluster: relevance feedback using adaptive clustering for content-based image retrieval. In *Proceedings of the ACM SIGMOD Conference*, pages 599–610, 2003.
10. D. Liu, K. A. Hua, K. Vu, and N. Yu. Efficient Target Search with Relevance Feedback for Large CBIR Systems. In *Proceedings of the 21st Annual ACM Symposium on Applied Computing*, 2006.
11. O.-B. Michael and S. Mehrotra. Relevance feedback techniques in the MARS image retrieval systems. *Multimedia Systems*, (9):535–547, 2004.

12. M. Nakazato, L. Manola, and T. S. Huang. ImageGrouper: a group-oriented user interface for content-based image retrieval and digital image arrangement. *Journal of Visual Languages and Computing*, 14(4):363–386, 2003.
13. F. P. Preparata and M. I. Shamos. *Computational Geometry: An Introduction.* Springer-Verlag, New York Inc., 1985.
14. Y. Rui, T. Huang, M. Ortega, and S. Mehrotra. Relevance feedback: A power tool for interactive content-based image retrieval. *IEEE Transactions on Circuits and Systems for Video Technology*, 8(5):644–655, 1998.
15. H. T. Shen, B. C. Ooi, and X. Zhou. Towards effective indexing for very large video sequence database. In *Proceedings of the ACM SIGMOD Conference*, pages 730–741, 2005.
16. A. W. M. Smeulders, M. Worring, A. G. S. Santini, and R. Jain. Content-based image retrieval at the end of the early years. *IEEE Transactions on Pattern Analysis and Machine Intelligence*, 22(12):1349–1380, 2000.
17. J. R. Smith and S.-F. Chang. Transform features for texture classification and discrimination in large image databases. In *Proceedings of the International Conference on Image Processing*, pages 407–411, 1994.
18. J. R. Smith and S.-F. Chang. VisualSEEk: A fully automated content-based image query system. In *Proceedings of the 4th ACM Multimedia Conference*, pages 87–98, 1996.
19. M. A. Stricker and M. Orengo. Similarity of color images. In *Proceedings of Storage and Retrieval for Image and Video Databases (SPIE)*, pages 381–392, 1995.
20. K. Vu, K. A. Hua, and W. Tavanapong. Image retrieval based on regions of interest. *IEEE Transactions on Knowledge and Data Engineering*, 15(4):1045–1049, 2003.
21. J. Z. Wang, J. Li, and G. Wiederhold. SIMPLIcity: Semantics-sensitive integrated matching for picture libraries. *IEEE Transactions on Pattern Analysis and Machine Intelligence*, 23(9):947–963, 2001.
22. L. Wu, C. Faloutsos, K. Sycara, and T. R. Payne. FALCON: feedback adaptive loop for content-based retrieval. In *Proceedings of the 26th VLDB Conference*, pages 297–306, 2000.
23. X. S. Zhou and T. S. Huang. Edge-based structural features for content-based image retrieval. *Pattern Recognition Letters*, 22(5):457–468, 2001.

# On Fast Non-metric Similarity Search by Metric Access Methods

Tomáš Skopal

Charles University in Prague, FMP, Department of Software Engineering,
Malostranské nám. 25, 118 00 Prague 1, Czech Republic
tomas@skopal.net

**Abstract.** The retrieval of objects from a multimedia database employs a measure which defines a similarity score for every pair of objects. The measure should *effectively* follow the nature of similarity, hence, it should not be limited by the triangular inequality, regarded as a restriction in similarity modeling. On the other hand, the retrieval should be as *efficient* (or fast) as possible. The measure is thus often restricted to a *metric*, because then the search can be handled by *metric access methods* (MAMs). In this paper we propose a general method of non-metric search by MAMs. We show the triangular inequality can be enforced for any *semimetric* (reflexive, non-negative and symmetric measure), resulting in a metric that preserves the original similarity orderings (retrieval effectiveness). We propose the *TriGen* algorithm for turning any black-box semimetric into (approximated) metric, just by use of distance distribution in a fraction of the database. The algorithm finds such a metric for which the retrieval efficiency is maximized, considering any MAM.

## 1 Introduction

In multimedia databases the semantics of data objects is defined loosely, while for querying such objects we usually need a similarity measure standing for a judging mechanism of how much are two objects similar. We can observe two particular research directions in the area of content-based multimedia retrieval, however, both are essential. The first one follows the subject of retrieval *effectiveness*, where the goal is to achieve query results complying with the user's expectations (measured by the *precision* and *recall* scores). As the effectiveness is obviously dependent on the semantics of similarity measure, we require the possibilities of similarity measuring as rich as possible, thus, the measure should not be limited by properties regarded as restrictive for similarity modeling.

Following the second direction, the retrieval should be as *efficient* (or fast) as possible, because the number of objects in a database can be large and the similarity scores are often expensive to compute. Therefore, the similarity measure is often restricted by metric properties, so that retrieval can be realized by metric access methods. Here we have reached the point. The "effectiveness researchers" claim the metric properties, especially the triangular inequality, are too restrictive. However, the "efficiency researchers" reply the triangular inequality is the most powerful tool to keep the search in a database efficient.

In this paper we show the triangular inequality is not restrictive for similarity search, since every semimetric can be modified into a suitable metric and used for the search instead. Such a metric can be constructed even automatically, just with a partial information about distance distribution in the database.

## 1.1 Preliminaries

Let a multimedia object $\mathcal{O}$ be modeled by a *model object* $O \in \mathbb{U}$, where $\mathbb{U}$ is a model universe. A multimedia database is then represented by a dataset $\mathbb{S} \subset \mathbb{U}$.

**Definition 1** (similarity & dissimilarity measure)

Let $s : \mathbb{U} \times \mathbb{U} \mapsto \mathbb{R}$ be a *similarity measure*, where $s(O_i, O_j)$ is considered as a similarity score of objects $\mathcal{O}_i$ and $\mathcal{O}_j$. In many cases it is more suitable to use a *dissimilarity measure* $d : \mathbb{U} \times \mathbb{U} \mapsto \mathbb{R}$ equivalent to a similarity measure $s$ as $s(Q, O_i) > s(Q, O_j) \Leftrightarrow d(Q, O_i) < d(Q, O_j)$. A dissimilarity measure assigns a higher score (or *distance*) to less similar objects, and vice versa.

The measures often satisfy some of the metric properties. The *reflexivity* ($d(O_i, O_j) = 0 \Leftrightarrow O_i = O_j$) permits the zero distance just for identical objects. Both reflexivity and *non-negativity* ($d(O_i, O_j) \geq 0$) guarantee every two distinct objects are somehow positively dissimilar. If $d$ satisfies reflexivity, non-negativity and *symmetry* ($d(O_i, O_j) = d(O_j, O_i)$), we call $d$ a *semimetric*. Finally, if a semimetric $d$ satisfies also the *triangular inequality* ($d(O_i, O_j) + d(O_j, O_k) \geq d(O_i, O_k)$), we call $d$ a *metric* (or metric distance). This inequality is a kind of transitivity property; it says if $O_i, O_j$ and $O_j, O_k$ are similar, then also $O_i, O_k$ are similar. If there is an upper bound $d^+$ such that $d : \mathbb{U} \times \mathbb{U} \mapsto \langle 0, d^+ \rangle$, we call $d$ a *bounded metric*. The pair $\mathcal{M} = (\mathbb{U}, d)$ is called a (bounded) *metric space*. □

**Definition 2** (triangular triplet)

A triplet $(a, b, c)$, $a, b, c \geq 0$, $a + b \geq c$, $b + c \geq a$, $a + c \geq b$, is called a *triangular triplet*. Let $(a, b, c)$ be ordered as $a \leq b \leq c$, then $(a, b, c)$ is an *ordered triplet*. If $a \leq b \leq c$ and $a + b \geq c$, then $(a, b, c)$ is called an *ordered triangular triplet*. □

A metric $d$ generates just the (ordered) triangular triplets, i.e. $\forall O_i, O_j, O_k \in \mathbb{U}$, $(d(O_i, O_j), d(O_j, O_k), d(O_i, O_k))$ is triangular triplet. Conversely, if a measure generates just the triangular triplets, then it satisfies the triangular inequality.

## 1.2 Similarity Queries

In the following we consider the *query-by-example* concept; we look for objects similar to a query object $Q \in \mathbb{U}$ ($Q$ is derived from an example object). Necessary to the query-by-example retrieval is a notion of *similarity ordering*, where the objects $O_i \in \mathbb{S}$ are ordered according to the distances to $Q$. For a particular query there is specified a portion of the ordering returned as the query result. The *range query* and the $k$ *nearest neighbors* ($k$-NN) *query* are the most popular ones. A range query $(Q, r_Q)$ selects objects from the similarity ordering for which $d(Q, O_i) \leq r_Q$, where $r_Q \geq 0$ is a distance threshold (or query radius). A $k$-NN query $(Q, k)$ selects the $k$ most similar objects (first $k$ objects in the ordering).

### 1.3 Metric Access Methods

Once we have to search according to a metric $d$, we can use the *metric access methods* (MAMs) [5], which organize (or index) a given dataset $\mathbb{S}$ in a way that similarity queries can be processed efficiently by use of a *metric index*, hence, without the need of searching the entire dataset $\mathbb{S}$. The main principle behind all MAMs is a utilization of the triangular inequality (satisfied by any metric), due to which MAMs can organize the objects of $\mathbb{S}$ in distinct classes. When a query is processed, only the candidate classes are searched (such classes which overlap the query), so the searching becomes more efficient (see Figure 1a).

In addition to the number of distance computations $d(\cdot, \cdot)$ needed (the *computation costs*), the retrieval efficiency is affected also by the *I/O costs*. To minimize the search costs, i.e. to increase the retrieval efficiency, there were developed many MAMs for different scenarios (e.g. designed to secondary storage or main memory management). Besides others we name *M-tree*, *vp-tree*, *LAESA* (we refer to a survey [5]), or more recent ones, *D-index* [9] and *PM-tree* [27].

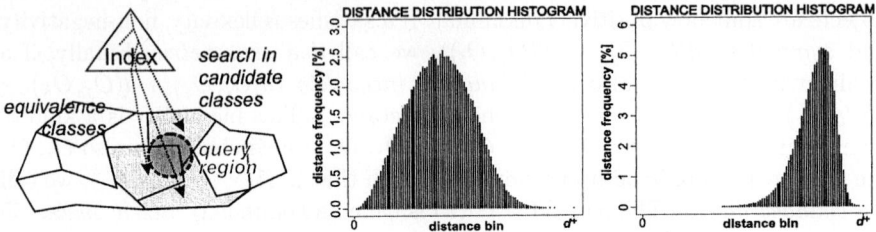

**Fig. 1.** Search by MAMs (a), DDHs indicating low (b) and high (c) intrinsic dim

### 1.4 Intrinsic Dimensionality

The metric access methods are not successful for all datasets and all metrics; the retrieval efficiency is heavily affected by *distance distribution* in the dataset. Given a dataset $\mathbb{S}$ and a metric $d$, the efficiency limits of any MAM are indicated by the *intrinsic dimensionality*, defined as $\rho(\mathbb{S}, d) = \frac{\mu^2}{2\sigma^2}$, where $\mu$ and $\sigma^2$ are the mean and the variance of the distance distribution in $\mathbb{S}$ (proposed in [4]). In Figures 1b,c see an example of distance distribution histograms (DDHs) indicating low ($\rho = 3.61$) and high ($\rho = 42.35$) intrinsic dimensionalities.

The intrinsic dimensionality is low if there exist tight clusters of objects. Conversely, if all the indexed objects are almost equally distant, then intrinsic dimensionality is high, which means the dataset is poorly intrinsically structured. A high $\rho$ value says that many (even all) of MAM's classes created on $\mathbb{S}$ are overlapped by every possible query, so that processing deteriorates to sequential search in all the classes. The problem of high intrinsic dimensionality is, in fact, a generalization of the *curse of dimensionality* [31, 4] into metric spaces.

## 1.5 Theories of Similarity Modeling

The metric properties have been argued against as restrictive in similarity modeling [25, 28]. In particular, the reflexivity and non-negativity have been refuted [21, 28] by claiming that different objects could be differently self-similar. Nevertheless, these are the less problematic properties. The symmetry was questioned by showing that a prototypical object can be less similar to an indistinct one than vice versa [23, 24]. The triangular inequality is the most attacked property [2, 29]. Some theories point out the similarity has not to be transitive. Demonstrated by the well-known example, a man is similar to a centaur, the centaur is similar to a horse, but the man is completely dissimilar to the horse.

## 1.6 Examples of Non-metric Measures

In the following we name several dissimilarity measures of two kinds, proved to be effective in similarity search, but which violate the triangular inequality.

**Robust Measures.** A *robust* measure is resistant to outliers – anomalous or "noisy" objects. For example, various *k-median distances* measure the $k$th most similar portion of the compared objects. Generally, a $k$-median distance $d$ is of form $d(O_1, O_2) = k\text{-}med(\delta_1(O_1, O_2), \delta_2(O_1, O_2), \ldots, \delta_n(O_1, O_2))$, where $\delta_i(O_1, O_2)$ is a distance between $O_1$ and $O_2$, considering the $i$th portion of the objects. Among the partial distances $\delta_i$ the *k-med* operator returns the $k$th smallest value. As a special $k$-median distance derived from the Hausdorff metric, the *partial Hausdorff distance (pHD)* has been proposed for shape-based image retrieval [17]. Given two sets $S_1, S_2$ of points (e.g. two polygons), the partial Hausdorff distance uses $\delta_i(S_1, S_2) = dNP(S_1^i, S_2)$, where $dNP$ is the Euclidean ($L_2$) distance of the $i$th point in $S_1$ to the nearest point in $S_2$. To keep the distance symmetric, $pHD$ is the maximum, i.e. $pHD(S_1, S_2) = max(d(S_1, S_2), d(S_2, S_1))$. Similar to $pHD$ is another modification of Hausdorff metric, used for face detection [20], where the average of $dNP$ distances is considered, instead of $k$-median.

The *time warping distance* for sequence aligning has been used in time series retrieval [33], and even in shape retrieval [3]. The *fractional $L_p$ distances* [1] have been suggested for robust image matching [10] and retrieval [16]. Unlike classic $L_p$ metrics ($L_p(u, v) = (\sum_{i=1}^{n} |u_i - v_i|^p)^{\frac{1}{p}}, p \geq 1$), the fractional $L_p$ distances use $0 < p < 1$, which allows us to inhibit extreme differences in coordinate values.

**Complex Measures.** In the real world, the algorithms for similarity measuring are often complex, even adaptive or learning. Moreover, they are often implemented by heuristic algorithms which combine several measuring strategies. Obviously, an analytic enforcement of triangular inequality for such measures can be simply too difficult. The COSIMIR method [22] uses a back-propagation neural network for supervised similarity modeling and retrieval. Given two vectors $u, v \in \mathbb{S}$, the distance between $u$ and $v$ is computed by activation of three-layer network. This approach allows to train the similarity measure by means of user-assessed pairs of objects. Another example of complex measure can be the *matching by deformable templates* [19], utilized in handwritten digits recognition. Two digits are compared by deforming the contour of one to fit the edges of the other. The distance is derived from the amount of deformation needed, the goodness of edges fit, and the interior overlap between the deformed shapes.

### 1.7 Paper Contributions

In this paper we present a general approach to efficient and effective non-metric search by metric access methods. First, we show that every semimetric can be non-trivially turned into metric and used for similarity search by MAMs. To achieve this goal, we modify the semimetric by a suitable *triangle-generating modifier*. In consequence, we also claim the triangular inequality is completely unrestrictive with respect to the effectiveness of similarity search. Second, we propose the *TriGen* algorithm for automatic conversion of any "black-box" semimetric (i.e. semimetric given in a non-analytic form) into (approximated) metric, such that intrinsic dimensionality of the indexed dataset is kept as low as possible. The optimal triangle-generating modifier is found by use of predefined base modifiers and by use of distance distribution in a (small) portion of the dataset.

## 2 Related Work

The simplest approach to non-metric similarity search is the *sequential search* of the entire dataset. The query object is compared against every object in the dataset, resulting in a similarity ordering which is used for the query evaluation. The sequential search often provides a baseline for other retrieval methods.

### 2.1 Mapping Methods

The non-metric search can be indirectly carried out by various *mapping methods* [11, 15] (e.g. MDS, FastMap, MetricMap, SparseMap). The dataset $\mathbb{S}$ is embedded into a vector space $(\mathbb{R}^k, \delta)$ by a mapping $F: \mathbb{S} \mapsto \mathbb{R}^k$, where the distances $d(\cdot, \cdot)$ are (approximately) preserved by a cheap vector metric $\delta$ (often the $L_2$ distance). Sometimes the mapping $F$ is required to be *contractive*, i.e. $\delta(F(O_i), F(O_j)) \leq d(O_i, O_j)$, which allows to filter out some irrelevant objects using $\delta$, but some other irrelevant objects, called *false hits*, must be re-filtered by $d$ (see e.g. [12]). The mapped vectors can be indexed/retrieved by any MAM.

To say the drawbacks, the mapping methods are expensive, while the distances are preserved only approximately, which leads to *false dismissals* (i.e. to relevant objects being not retrieved). The contractive methods eliminate the false dismissals but suffer from a great number of false hits (especially when $k$ is low), which leads to lower retrieval efficiency. In most cases the methods need to process the dataset in a batch, so they are suitable for static MAMs only.

### 2.2 Lower-Bounding Metrics

To support similarity search by a non-metric distance $d_Q$, the QIC-M-tree [6] has been proposed as an extension of the M-tree (the key idea is applicable also to other MAMs). The M-tree index is built by use of an index distance $d_I$, which is a metric *lower-bounding* the query distance $d_Q$ (up to a scaling constant $S_{I \to Q}$), i.e. $d_I(O_i, O_j) \leq S_{I \to Q}\, d_Q(O_i, O_j), \forall O_i, O_j \in \mathbb{U}$. As $d_I$ lower-bounds $d_Q$, a query can be partially processed by $d_I$ (which, moreover, could be much cheaper than $d_Q$), such that many irrelevant classes of objects (subtrees in M-tree) are filtered out. All objects in the non-filtered classes are compared against $Q$ using $d_Q$. Actually, this approach is similar to the usage of contractive mapping methods ($d_I$ is an analogy to $\delta$), but here the objects generally need not to be mapped into a vector space. However, this approach has two major limitations. First, for a given non-metric distance $d_Q$ there was not proposed a general way how to find the metric $d_I$. Although $d_I$ could be found "manually" for a particular $d_Q$ (as in [3]), this is not easy for $d_Q$ given as a black box (an algorithmically described one). Second, the lower-bounding metric should be as tight approximation of $d_Q$ as possible, because this "tightness" heavily affects the intrinsic dimensionality, the number of MAMs' filtered classes, and so the retrieval efficiency.

### 2.3 Classification

Quite many attempts to non-metric nearest neighbor (NN) search have been tried out in the classification area. Let us recall the basic three steps of classification. First, the dataset is organized in classes of similar objects (by user annotation or clustering). Then, for each class a description consisting of the most representative object(s) is created; this is achieved by *condensing* [14] or *editing* [32] algorithms. Third, the NN search is accomplished as a classification of the query object. Such a class is searched, to which the query object is "nearest", since there is an assumption the nearest neighbor is located in the "nearest class". For non-metric classification there have been proposed methods enhancing the description of classes (step 2). In particular, condensing algorithms producing *atypical points* [13] or *correlated points* [18] have been successfully applied.

The drawbacks of classification-based methods reside in static indexing and limited scalability, while the querying is restricted just to approximate ($k$-)NN.

## 3 Turning Semimetric into Metric

In our approach, a given dissimilarity measure is turned into a metric, so that MAMs can be directly used for the search. This idea could seem to disclaim the results of similarity theories (mentioned in Section 1.5), however, we must realize the task of **similarity search** employs only a limited modality of **similarity modeling**. In fact, in similarity search we just need to order the dataset objects according to a single query object and pick the most similar ones. Clearly, if we find a metric for which such similarity orderings are the same as for the original dissimilarity measure, we can safely use the metric instead of the measure.

### 3.1 Assumptions

We assume $d$ satisfies reflexivity and non-negativity but, as we have mentioned in Section 1.5, these are the less restrictive properties and can be handled easily; e.g. the *non-negativity* is satisfied by a shift of the distances, while for the *reflexivity* property we require every two non-identical objects are at least $d^-$-distant ($d^-$ is some positive distance lower bound). Furthermore, searching by an *asymmetric measure* $\delta$ could be partially provided by a symmetric measure $d$, e.g. $d(O_i, O_j) = min\{\delta(O_i, O_j), \delta(O_j, O_i)\}$. Using the symmetric measure some irrelevant objects can be filtered out, while the original asymmetric measure $\delta$ is then used to rank the remaining non-filtered objects. In the following we assume the measure $d$ is a bounded semimetric, nevertheless, this assumption is introduced just for clarity of the following presentation. Finally, as $d$ is bounded by $d^+$, we can further simplify the semimetric such that it assigns distances from $\langle 0, 1 \rangle$. This can be achieved simply by scaling the original value $d(O_i, O_j)$ to $d(O_i, O_j)/d^+$. The same way a range query radius $r_Q$ must be scaled to $r_Q/d^+$, when searching.

## 3.2 Similarity-Preserving Modifications

Based on the assumptions, the only property we have to solve is the triangular inequality. To do so, we apply some special modifying function on the semimetric, such that the original similarity orderings are preserved.

**Definition 3** (similarity-preserving modification)

Given a measure $d$, we call $d^f(O_i, O_j) = f(d(O_i, O_j))$ a *similarity-preserving modification of $d$* (or *SP-modification*), where $f$, called the *similarity-preserving modifier* (or *SP-modifier*), is a strictly increasing function for which $f(0) = 0$. Again, for clarity reasons we assume $f$ is bounded, i.e. $f : \langle 0, 1 \rangle \mapsto \langle 0, 1 \rangle$. □

**Definition 4** (similarity ordering)

We define $SimOrder_d: \mathbb{U} \mapsto 2^{\mathbb{U} \times \mathbb{U}}, \forall O_i, O_j, Q \in \mathbb{U}$ as $\langle O_i, O_j \rangle \in SimOrder_d(Q) \Leftrightarrow d(Q, O_i) < d(Q, O_j)$, i.e. $SimOrder_d$ orders objects by their distances to $Q$. □

**Lemma 1**

Given a metric $d$ and any $d^f$, then $SimOrder_d(Q) = SimOrder_{d^f}(Q), \forall Q \in \mathbb{U}$.

**Proof.** As $f$ is increasing, then $\forall Q, O_i, O_j \in \mathbb{U}$ it follows that $d(Q, O_i) > d(Q, O_j) \Leftrightarrow f(d(Q, O_i)) > f(d(Q, O_j))$. ∎

In other words, every SP-modification $d^f$ preserves the similarity orderings generated by $d$. Consequently, if a query is processed sequentially (by comparing all objects in $\mathbb{S}$ to the query object $Q$), then it does not matter if we use either $d$ or any $d^f$, because both ways induce the same similarity orderings. Naturally, the radius $r_Q$ of a range query must be modified to $f(r_Q)$, when searching by $d^f$.

## 3.3 Triangle-Generating Modifiers

To obtain a modification forcing a semimetric to satisfy the triangular inequality, we have to use some special SP-modifiers based on metric-preserving functions.

**Definition 5** (metric-preserving SP-modifier)

A SP-modifier $f$ is *metric-preserving* if for every metric $d$ the SP-modification $d^f$ preserves the triangular inequality, i.e. $d^f$ is also metric. Such a SP-modifier must be additionally *subadditive* ($f(x) + f(y) \geq f(x + y), \forall x, y$). □

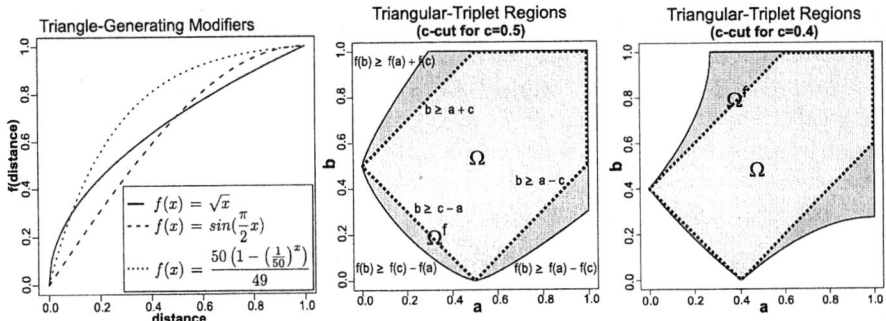

**Fig. 2.** (a) Several TG-modifiers. Regions $\Omega$, $\Omega^f$; (b) $f(x) = x^{\frac{3}{4}}$ (c) $f(x) = sin(\frac{\pi}{2}x)$.

**Lemma 2**
(a) Every concave SP-modifier $f$ is metric-preserving.
(b) Let $(a, b, c)$ be a triangular triplet and $f$ be metric-preserving, then $(f(a), f(b), f(c))$ is a triangular triplet as well.

**Proof.** For the proof and for more about metric-preserving functions see [8]. ∎

To modify a semimetric into metric, we have utilized a class of metric-preserving SP-modifiers, denoted as the triangle-generating modifiers.

**Definition 6** (triangle-generating modifier)
Let a strictly concave SP-modifier $f$ be called a *triangle-generating modifier* (or *TG-modifier*). Having a TG-modifier $f$, let a $d^f$ be called a *TG-modification*. □

The TG-modifiers (see examples in Figure 2a) not only preserve the triangular inequality, they can even enforce it, as follows.

**Theorem 1**
Given a semimetric $d$, then there always exists a TG-modifier $f$, such that the SP-modification $d^f$ is a metric.

**Proof.** We show that every ordered triplet $(a, b, c)$ generated by $d$ can be turned by a single TG-modifier $f$ into an ordered triangular triplet.
1. As every semimetric is reflexive and non-negative, it generates ordered triplets just of forms $(0, 0, 0)$, $(0, c, c)$, and $(a, b, c)$, where $a, b, c > 0$. Among these, just the triplets $(a, b, c)$, $0 < a \leq b < c$, can be non-triangular. Hence, it is sufficient to show how to turn such triplets by a TG-modifier into triangular ones.
2. Suppose an arbitrary TG-modifier $f_1$. From TG-modifiers' properties it follows that $\frac{f_1(a)}{f_1(c)} > \frac{a}{c}$, $\frac{f_1(b)}{f_1(c)} > \frac{b}{c}$, hence $\frac{f_1(a)+f_1(b)}{f_1(c)} > \frac{a+b}{c}$ (theory of concave functions). If $(f_1(a) + f_1(b))/f_1(c) \geq 1$, the triplet $(f_1(a), f_1(b), f_1(c))$ becomes triangular (i.e. $f_1(a) + f_1(b) \geq f_1(c)$ is true). In case there still exist triplets which have not become triangular after application of $f_1$, we take another TG-modifier $f_2$ and compose $f_1$ and $f_2$ into $f^*(x) = f_2(f_1(x))$. The compositions (or nestings) $f^*(x) = f_i(\ldots f_2(f_1(x))\ldots)$ are repeated until $f^*$ turns all triplets generated by $d$ into triangular ones – then $f^*$ is the single TG-modifier $f$ we are looking for. ∎

The proof shows the more concave TG-modifier we apply, the more triplets become triangular. This effect can be visualized by 3D regions in the space $\langle 0, 1\rangle^3$ of all possible distance triplets, where the three dimensions represent the distance values a,b,c, respectively. In Figures 2b,c see examples of region[1] $\Omega$ of all triangular triplets as the dotted-line area. The super-region $\Omega^f$ (the solid-line area) represents all the triplets which become (or remain) triangular after the application of TG-modifier $f(x) = x^{\frac{3}{4}}$ and $f(x) = sin(\frac{\pi}{2}x)$, respectively.

## 3.4 TG-Modifiers Suitable for Metric Search

Although there exist infinitely many TG-modifiers which turn a semimetric $d$ into a metric $d^f$, their properties can be quite different with respect to the efficiency of search by MAMs. For example, $f(x) = \begin{cases} 0 & \text{(for } x = 0) \\ \frac{x+d^+}{2} & \text{(otherwise)} \end{cases}$ turns every $d^+$-bounded semimetric $d$ into a metric $d^f$. However, such a metric is useless for searching, since all classes of objects maintained by a MAM are overlapped by every query, so the retrieval deteriorates to sequential search. This behavior is also reflected in high intrinsic dimensionality of $\mathbb{S}$ with respect to $d^f$.

In fact, we look for an *optimal* TG-modifier, i.e. a TG-modifier which turns only such non-triangular triplets into triangular ones, which are generated by $d$. The non-triangular triplets which are not generated by $d$ should remain non-triangular (the white areas in Figures 2b,c), since such triplets represent the "decisions" used by MAMs for filtering of irrelevant objects or classes. The more often such decisions occur, the more efficient the search is (and the lower the intrinsic dimensionality of $\mathbb{S}$ is). As an example, given two vectors $u, v$ of dimensionality $n$, the optimal TG-modifier for semimetric $d(u,v) = \sum_{i=1}^n |u_i - v_i|^2$ is $f(x) = \sqrt{x}$, turning $d$ into the Euclidean ($L_2$) distance.

From another point of view, the concavity of $f$ determines how much the object clusters (MAMs' classes respectively) become indistinct (overlapped by other clusters/classes). This can be observed indirectly in Figure 2a, where the concave modifiers make the small distances greater, while the great distances remain great; i.e. the mean of distances increases, whereas the variance decreases. To illustrate this fact, we can reuse the example back in Figures 1b,c, where the first DDH was sampled for $d_1 = L_2$, while the second one was sampled for a modification $d_2 = L_2^f$, $f(x) = x^{\frac{1}{4}}$.

In summary, given a dataset $\mathbb{S}$, a semimetric $d$, and a TG-modifier $f$, the intrinsic dimensionality is always higher for the modification $d^f$ than for $d$, i.e. $\rho(\mathbb{S}, d^f) > \rho(\mathbb{S}, d)$. Therefore, an optimal TG-modifier should minimize the increase of intrinsic dimensionality, yet generate the necessary triangular triplets.

## 4 The TriGen Algorithm

The question is how to find the optimal TG-modifier $f$. Had we known an analytical form of $d$, we could find the TG-modifier "manually". However, if $d$ is

---
[1] The 2D representations of $\Omega$ and $\Omega^f$ regions are c-cuts of the real 3D regions.

implemented by an algorithm, or if the analytical form of $d$ is too complex (e.g. the neural network representation used by COSIMIR), it could be very hard to determine $f$ analytically. Instead, our intention is to find $f$ automatically, regardless of analytical form of $d$. In other words, we consider a given semimetric $d$ generally as a black box that returns a distance value from a two-object input.

The idea of automatic determination of $f$ makes use of the distance distribution in a sample $\mathbb{S}^*$ of the dataset $\mathbb{S}$. We take $m$ ordered triplets, where each triplet $(a,b,c)$ stores distances between some objects $O_i, O_j, O_k \in \mathbb{S}^* \subseteq \mathbb{S}$, i.e. $(a=d(O_i,O_j), b=d(O_j,O_k), c=d(O_i,O_k))$. Some predefined *base TG-modifiers* $f_i$ (or *TG-bases*) are then applied on the triplets; for each triplet $(a,b,c)$ a modified triplet $(f_i(a), f_i(b), f_i(c))$ is obtained. The *triangle-generating error* $\varepsilon_\Delta$ (or *TG-error*) is computed as the fraction of triplets remaining non-triangular, $\varepsilon_\Delta = \frac{m_{nt}}{m}$, where $m_{nt}$ is the number of modified triplets remaining non-triangular. Finally, such $f_i$ are selected as *candidates* for the optimal TG-modifier, for which $\varepsilon_\Delta = 0$ or, possibly, $\varepsilon_\Delta \leq \theta$ (where $\theta$ is a *TG-error tolerance*). To control the degree of concavity, the TG-bases $f_i$ are parameterizable by a *concavity weight* $w \geq 0$, where $w = 0$ makes every $f_i$ the identity, i.e. $f_i(x, 0) = x$, while with increasing $w$ the concavity of $f_i$ increases as well (a more concave $f_i$ decreases $m_{nt}$; it turns more triplets into triangular ones). In such a way any TG-base can be forced by an increase of $w$ to minimize the TG-error $\varepsilon_\Delta$ (possibly to zero).

Among the TG-base candidates the optimal TG-modifier $(f_i, w)$ is chosen such that $\rho(\mathbb{S}^*, d^{f^*(x, w^*)})$ is as low as possible. The TriGen algorithm (see Listing 1) takes advantage of halving the concavity interval $\langle w_{\text{LB}}, w_{\text{UB}} \rangle$ or doubling the upper bound $w_{\text{UB}}$, in order to quickly find the optimal concavity weight $w$ for a TG-base $f^*$. To keep the computation scalable, the number of iterations (in each iteration $w$ is improved) is limited to e.g. 24 (the iterLimit constant).

**Listing 1.** (The TriGen algorithm)

---

*Input:* semimetric $d$, set $\mathcal{F}$ of TG-bases, sample $\mathbb{S}^*$, TG-error tolerance $\theta$, iteration limit iterLimit
*Output:* optimal $f$, $w$

```
f = w = null; minIDim = ∞                                                    1
sample m distance triplets into a set T (from S* using d)                    2
for each f* in F                                                             3
    wLB = 0; wUB = ∞; w* = 1; wbest = -1; i = 0                              4
    while i < iterLimit                                                      5
        if TGError(f*,w*,T) ≤ θ then wUB = wbest = w* else wLB = w*          6
        if wUB ≠ ∞ then w* = (wLB + wUB)/2 else w* = 2 * w*                  7
        i = i + 1;                                                           8
    end while                                                                9
    if wbest ≥ 0 then                                                        10
        idim = IDim(f*,wbest,T)                                              11
        if idim < minIDim then f = f*; w = wbest; minIDim = idim             12
    end if                                                                   13
end for                                                                      14
```

---

In Listing 2 the TGError function is described. The TG-error $\varepsilon_\Delta$ is computed by taking $m$ distance triplets from the dataset sample $\mathbb{S}^*$ onto which the examined TG-base $f^*$ together with the current weight $w^*$ is applied. The distance triplets are sampled only once – at the beginning of the TriGen's run – whereas the modified triplets are recomputed for each particular $f^*, w^*$.

The not-listed function IDim (computing $\rho(\mathbb{S}^*, d^{f^*(x,w^*)})$) makes use of the previously obtained modified triplets as well, however, the values in the triplets are used independently; just for evaluation of the intrinsic dimensionality.

**Listing 2.** (The TGError function)

---
*Input:* TG-base $f^*$, concavity weight $w^*$, set $\mathcal{T}$ of $m$ sampled distance triplets
*Output:* TG-error $\varepsilon_\Delta$

```
m_nt = 0                                                                    1
for each ot in T  // "ot" stands for "ordered triplet"                      2
    if f*(ot.a, w*) + f*(ot.b, w*) < f*(ot.c, w*) then m_nt = m_nt + 1      3
end for                                                                     4
ε_Δ = m_nt / m                                                              5
```
---

### 4.1 Sampling the Distance Triplets

Initially, we have $n$ objects in the dataset sample $\mathbb{S}^*$. Then we create an $n \times n$ distance matrix for storage of pairwise distances $d_{ij} = d(O_i, O_j)$ between the sampled objects. In such a way we are able to obtain up to $m = \binom{n}{3}$ distance triplets for at most $\frac{n(n-1)}{2}$ distance computations. Thus, to obtain a sufficiently large number of distance triplets, the dataset sample $\mathbb{S}^*$ needs to be quite small. Each of the $m$ distance triplets is sampled by a random choice of three among the $n$ objects, while the respective distances are retrieved from the matrix. Naturally, the values in the matrix could be computed "on-demand", just in the moment a distance retrieval is requested. Since $d$ is symmetric, the sub-diagonal half of the matrix can be used for storage of the modified distances $d^f_{ji} = f^*(d_{ij}, w^*)$, however, these are recomputed for each particular $f^*, w^*$. As in case of distances, also the modified distances can be computed "on-demand".

### 4.2 Time Complexity Analysis (Simplified)

Let $|\mathbb{S}^*|$ be the number of objects in the sample $\mathbb{S}^*$, $m$ be the number of sampled triplets, and $O(d)$ be the complexity of single distance computation. The complexity of $f(\cdot)$ computation is supposed $O(1)$. The overall complexity of TriGen is then $O(|\mathbb{S}^*|^2 * O(d) + \text{iterLimit} * |\mathcal{F}| * m)$, i.e. the distance matrix computation plus the main algorithm. The number of TG-bases $|\mathcal{F}|$ as well as the number of iterations (variable iterLimit) are assumed as (small) constants, hence we get $O(|\mathbb{S}^*|^2 * O(d) + m)$. The size of $\mathbb{S}^*$ and the number $m$ affect the precision of TGError and IDim values, so we can trade off the TriGen's complexity and the precision by choosing $|\mathbb{S}^*| = O(1), O(|\mathbb{S}|)$ and $m = O(1), O(|\mathbb{S}^*|)$, or e.g. $O(|\mathbb{S}^*|^2)$.

### 4.3 Default TG-Bases

We propose two general-purpose TG-bases for the TriGen algorithm. The simpler one, the *Fractional-Power TG-base* (or *FP-base*), is defined as $\text{FP}(x, w) = x^{\frac{1}{1+w}}$, see Figure 3a. The advantage of FP-base is there always exists a concavity weight $w$ for which the modified semimetric becomes metric, i.e. the TriGen will always find a solution (after a number of iterations). Furthermore, when using the

FP-base, the semimetric $d$ needs not to be bounded. A particular disadvantage of the FP-base is that its concavity is controlled globally, just by the weight $w$.

As a more flexible TG-base, we have utilized the Rational Bézier Quadratic curve. To derive a proper TG-base from the curve, the three Bézier points are specified as $(0,0), (a,b), (1,1)$, where $0 \leq a < b \leq 1$, see Figure 3b. The *Rational Bézier Quadratic TG-base* (simply RBQ-base) is defined as $\text{RBQ}_{(a,b)}(x,w) = -(\Psi - x + wx - aw) \cdot (-2bwx + 2bw^2x - 2abw^2 + 2bw - x + wx - aw + \Psi(1 - 2bw))/(-1 + 2aw - 4awx - 4a^2w^2 + 2aw^2 + 4aw^2x + 2wx - 2w^2x + 2\Psi(1-w))$, where $\Psi = \sqrt{-x^2 + x^2w^2 - 2aw^2x + a^2w^2 + x}$. The additional RBQ parameters $a, b$ (the second Bézier point) are treated as constants, i.e. for various $a, b$ values (see the dots in Figure 3b) we get multiple RBQ-bases, which are all individually inserted into the set $\mathcal{F}$ of TriGen's input. To keep the RBQ evaluation correct, a possible division by zero or $\Psi^2 < 0$ is prevented by a slight shift of $a$ or $w$. The advantage of RBQ-bases is the place of maximal concavity can be controlled locally by a choice of $(a,b)$, hence, for a given concavity weight $w^*$ we can achieve lower value of either $\rho(\mathbb{S}^*, d^{f^*(x,w^*)})$ or $\varepsilon_\Delta$ just by choosing different $a, b$.

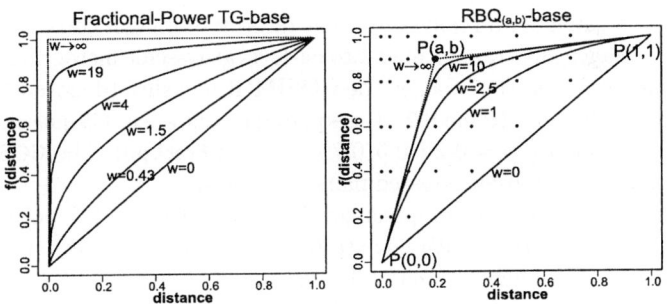

**Fig. 3.** (a) FP-base (b) $\text{RBQ}_{(a,b)}$-base

As a particular limitation, for usage of RBQ-bases the semimetric $d$ must be bounded (due to the third Bézier point $(1,1)$). Furthermore, for an RBQ-base with $(a,b) \neq (0,1)$ the TG-error $\varepsilon_\Delta$ could be generally greater than the TG-error tolerance $\theta$, even in case $w \to \infty$. Nevertheless, having the FP-base or the $\text{RBQ}_{(0,1)}$-base in $\mathcal{F}$, the TriGen will always find a TG-modifier such that $\varepsilon_\Delta \leq \theta$.

### 4.4 Notes on the Triangular Inequality

As we have shown, the TriGen algorithm produces a TG-modifier which generates the triangular inequality property for a particular semimetric $d$. However, we have to realize the triangular inequality is generated just according to the dataset sample $\mathbb{S}^*$ (to the sampled distance triplets, actually). A TG-modification $d^f$ being metric according to $\mathbb{S}^*$ has not to be a "full metric" according to the entire dataset $\mathbb{S}$ (or even to $\mathbb{U}$), so that searching in $\mathbb{S}$ by a MAM could become only approximate, even in case $\theta = 0$. Nevertheless, in most applications a (random) dataset sample $\mathbb{S}^*$ is supposed to have the distance distribution similar to that of $\mathbb{S} \cup \{Q\}$, and also the sampled distance triplets are expected to be representative.

Moreover, the construction of such a TG-modifier $f$, for which $(\mathbb{S}, d^f)$ is metric space but $(\mathbb{U}, d^f)$ is not, can be beneficial for the efficiency of search, since the intrinsic dimensionality of $(\mathbb{S}, d^f)$ can be significantly lower than that of $(\mathbb{U}, d^f)$. The above claims are verified experimentally in the following section, where the retrieval error (besides pure $\varepsilon_\Delta$) and the retrieval efficiency (besides pure $\rho(\mathbb{S}, d^f)$) are evaluated. Nonetheless, to keep the terminology correct let us read a metric $d^f$ created by the TriGen as a *TriGen-approximated metric*.

## 5 Experimental Results

To examine the proposed method, we have performed extensive testing of the TriGen algorithm as well as evaluation of the generated distances with respect to the effectiveness and efficiency of retrieval by two MAMs (M-tree and PM-tree).

### 5.1 The Testbed

We have examined 10 non-metric distance measures (all described in Section 1.6) on two datasets (images and polygons). The dataset of images consisted of 10,000 web-crawled images [30] transformed into 64-level gray-scale histograms. We have tested 6 semimetrics on the images: the COSIMIR measure (denoted **COSIMIR**), the 5-median $L_2$ distance (**5-medL2**), the squared $L_2$ distance (**L2square**), and three fractional $L_p$ distances ($p = 0.25, 0.5, 0.75$, denoted **FracLp$p$**). The **COSIMIR** network was trained by 28 user-assessed pairs of images.

The synthetic dataset of polygons consisted of 1,000,000 2D polygons, each consisting of 5 to 10 vertices. We have tested 4 semimetrics on the polygons: the 3-median and 5-median Hausdorff distances (denoted **3-medHausdorff**, **5-medHausdorff**), and the time warping distance with $\delta$ chosen as $L_2$ and $L_\infty$, respectively (denoted **TimeWarpL2, TimeWarpLmax**). The **COSIMIR**, **5-medL2** and $k$-**medHausdorff** measures were adjusted to be semimetrics, as described in Section 3.1. All the semimetrics were normed to return distances from $\langle 0, 1 \rangle$.

### 5.2 The TriGen Setup

The TriGen algorithm was used to generate the optimal TG-modifier for each semimetric (considering the respective dataset). To examine the relation between retrieval error of MAMs and the TG-error, we have constructed several TG-modifiers for each semimetric, considering different values of TG-error tolerance $\theta \geq 0$. The TriGen's set of bases $\mathcal{F}$ was populated by the FP-base and 116 RBQ-bases parametrized by all such pairs $(a, b)$ that $a \in \{0, 0.005, 0.015, 0.035, 0.075, 0.155\}$, where for a value of $a$ the values of $b$ were multiples of 0.05 limited by $a < b \leq 1$. The dataset sample $\mathbb{S}^*$ used by TriGen consisted of $n = 1000$ randomly selected objects in case of images (10% of the dataset), and $n = 5000$ in case of polygons (0.5% of the dataset). The distance matrix built from the respective dataset sample $\mathbb{S}^*$ was used to form $m = 10^6$ distance triplets.

In Table 1 see the optimal TG-modifiers found for the semimetrics by TriGen, considering $\theta = 0$ and $\theta = 0.05$, respectively. In the first column, best RBQ

**Table 1.** TG-modifiers found by TriGen

|  | $\theta = 0.00$ | | | | $\theta = 0.05$ | | | |
|---|---|---|---|---|---|---|---|---|
|  | best RBQ-base | | FP-base | | best RBQ-base | | FP-base | |
| semimetric | $(a, b)$ | $\rho$ | $\rho$ | $w$ | $(a, b)$ | $\rho$ | $\rho$ | $w$ |
| L2square | (0, 0.15) | 3.74 | 4.22 | 0.99 | (0, 0.05) | 2.82 | 3.02 | 0.59 |
| COSIMIR | (0, 0.45) | 12.2 | 27.2 | 4.33 | (0.005, 0.15) | 3.19 | 3.80 | 0.63 |
| 5-medL2 | (0, 0.1) | 37.7 | 19.8 | 16.5 | (0, 0.05) | 4.28 | 3.17 | 3.88 |
| FracLp0.25 | (0, 0.45) | 12.7 | 15.2 | 2.29 | (0.035, 0.05) | 3.50 | 3.30 | 0.30 |
| FracLp0.5 | (0, 0.05) | 7.57 | 8.37 | 0.87 | (0, 0.2) | 3.28 | 3.34 | 0.06 |
| FracLp0.75 | (0, 0.75) | 5.13 | 5.69 | 0.30 | any | 3.77 | 3.77 | 0 |
| 3-medHausdorff | (0, 0.05) | 3.77 | 5.11 | 0.60 | any | 2.28 | 2.28 | 0 |
| 5-medHausdorff | (0, 0.05) | 3.42 | 4.12 | 0.35 | any | 2.45 | 2.45 | 0 |
| TimeWarpL2 | (0, 0.55) | 10.0 | 9.48 | 1.48 | (0.035, 0.1) | 2.72 | 2.76 | 0.23 |
| TimeWarpLmax | (0.005, 0.3) | 8.75 | 9.69 | 1.52 | (0, 0.1) | 2.83 | 2.86 | 0.26 |

modifier parameters (best in sense of lowest $\rho$ depending on $a, b$) are presented. In the second column, the achieved $\rho$ for a concavity weight $w$ of the FP-base is presented, in order to make a comparison with the best RBQ modifier. Among RBQ- and FP-bases, the winning modifier (with respect to lowest $\rho$) is printed in bold. When considering $\theta = 0.05$, **FracLp0.5**, **3-medHausdorff**, **5-medHausdorff** even need not to be modified (see the zero weights by the FP-base), since the TG-error is already below $\theta$. Also note that for **L2square** and $\theta = 0$ the weight of FP-base modifier is $w = 0.99$, instead of $w = 1.0$ (which would turn **L2square** into $L_2$ distance). That is because the intrinsic dimensionality of the dataset sample $\mathbb{S}^*$ is lower than that of the universe $\mathbb{U}$ (64-dimensional vector space).

In Figure 4 see the intrinsic dimensionalities $\rho(\mathbb{S}^*, d^f)$ with respect to the growing TG-error tolerance $\theta$ ($f$ is the optimal TG-modifier found by TriGen).

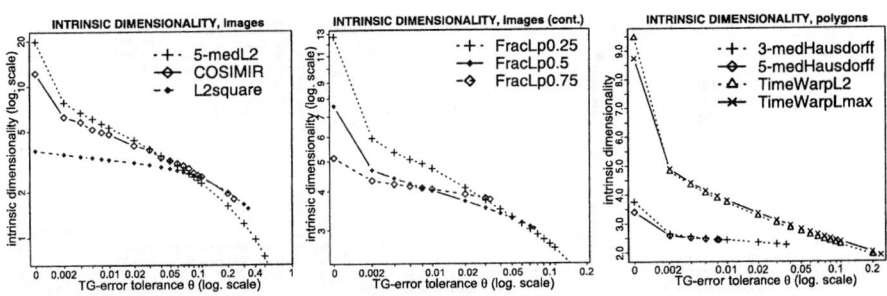

**Fig. 4.** Intrinsic dimensionality of images and polygons

The rightmost point $[\theta, \rho]$ of a particular curve in each figure means $\theta$ is the maximum $\varepsilon_\Delta$ value that can be reached; for such a value (and all greater) the concavity weight $w$ becomes zero. Similar "endpoints" on curves appear also in other following curves that depend on the TG-error tolerance.

The Figure 5a shows the impact of $m$ sampled triplets (used by TGError) on the intrinsic dimensionality, considering $\theta = 0$ and only the FP-base in $\mathcal{F}$. The more triplets, the more accurate value of $\varepsilon_\Delta$ and the more concave TG-modifier is needed to keep $\varepsilon_\Delta = 0$, so the concavity weight and the intrinsic dimensionality grow. However, except for **5-medHausdorff**, the growth of intrinsic dimensionality is quite slow for $m > 10^6$ (and even slower if we set $\theta > 0$).

For the future we plan to improve the simple random selection of triplets from the distance matrix, in order to obtain more representative triplets, and thus more accurate values of $\varepsilon_\Delta$ together with keeping $m$ low.

### 5.3 Indexing and Querying

In order to evaluate the efficiency and effectiveness of search when using TriGen-approximated metrics, we have utilized the M-tree [7] and the PM-tree [27].

For either of the datasets several M-tree and PM-tree indices were built, differed in the metric $d^f$ employed – for each semimetric and each $\theta$ value a $d^f$ was found by TriGen, and an index created. The setup of (P)M-tree indices is summarized in Table 2 (for technical details see [7, 26, 27]).

Table 2. M-tree and PM-tree setup

| | |
|---|---|
| disk page size: | 4 kB  avg. page utilization: 41%–68% |
| PM-tree pivots: | 64 inner node pivots, 0 leaf pivots |
| image indices size: | 1–2 MB (M-tree) 1.2–2.2 MB (PM-tree) |
| polygon indices size: | 140–150 MB (both M-tree and PM-tree) |
| construction method: | MinMax + SingleWay (+ slim-down) |

To achieve more compact MAM classes, the indices (both M-tree and PM-tree) built on the image dataset were post-processed by the *generalized slim-down algorithm* [26]. The 64 global pivot objects used by PM-tree indices were sampled among the $n$ objects already used for the TriGen's distance matrix construction.

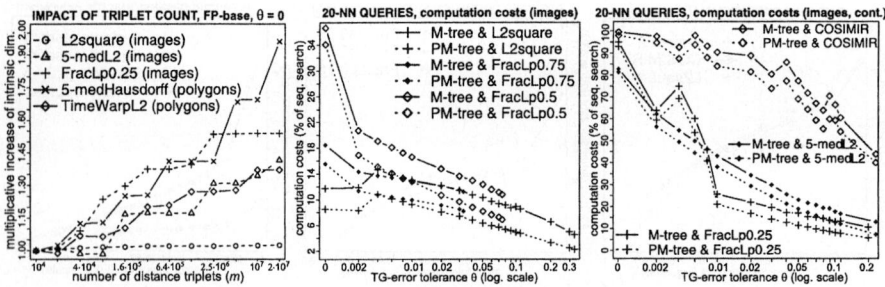

**Fig. 5.** Impact of triplet count; 20-NN queries on images (costs)

All the (P)M-tree indices were used to process $k$-NN queries. Since the TriGen-generated modifications are generally metric approximations (especially when $\theta > 0$), the filtration of (P)M-tree branches was affected by a *retrieval error* (the relative error in precision and recall). The retrieval error was computed as the *Jaccard distance* $E_{NO}$ (or normed overlap distance) between the query result $QR_{MAM}$ returned by a (P)M-tree index and the correct query result $QR_{SEQ}$ (obtained by sequential search of the dataset), i.e. $E_{NO} = 1 - \frac{|QR_{MAM} \cap QR_{SEQ}|}{|QR_{MAM} \cup QR_{SEQ}|}$.

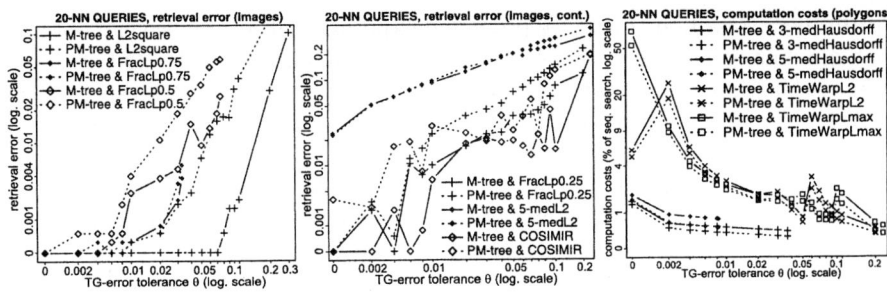

**Fig. 6.** 20-NN queries on images and polygons (retrieval error, costs)

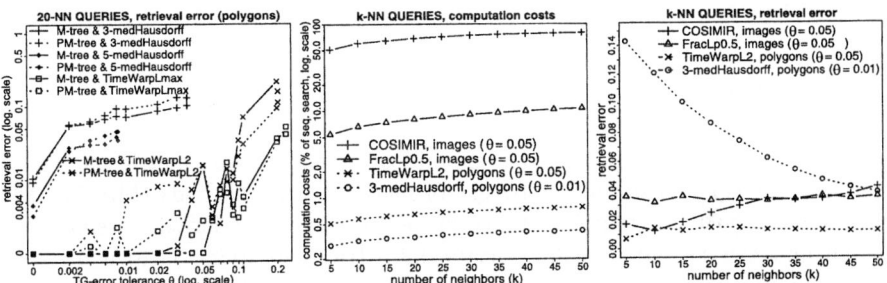

**Fig. 7.** 20-NN queries on polygons (retrieval error); $k$-NN queries (costs, retrieval error)

To examine retrieval efficiency, the computation costs needed for query evaluation were compared to the costs spent by sequential search. Every query was repeated for 200 randomly selected query objects, and the results were averaged.

In Figures 5b,c see the costs of 20-NN queries processed on image indices, depending on growing $\theta$. The intrinsic dimensionalities decrease, and so the searching becomes more efficient (e.g. down to 2% of costs spent by sequential search for $\theta = 0.4$ and the TG-modification of **L2square**). On the other hand, for $\theta = 0$ the TG-modifications of **COSIMIR** and **FracLp0.25** imply high intrinsic dimensionality, so the retrieval deteriorates to almost sequential search.

In Figures 6a,b the retrieval error $E_{NO}$ is presented for growing $\theta$. In Figures 6c and 7a see the retrieval efficiency and error for 20-NN querying on the polygon indices. As supposed, the error grows with growing TG-error tolerance $\theta$. Interestingly, the values of $\theta$ tend to be the upper bounds to the values of $E_{NO}$, so we could utilize $\theta$ in an *error model* for prediction of $E_{NO}$.

In case of **5-medL2, 3-medHausdorff** (and partly **COSIMIR, 5-medHausdorff**) indices, the retrieval error was non-zero even for $\theta = 0$. This was caused by neglecting some "pathological" distance triplets when computing the TGError function (see Section 4), so the triangular inequality was not preserved for all triplets, and the filtering performed by (P)M-tree was sometimes (but rarely) incorrect. In other cases (where $\theta = 0$) the retrieval error was zero.

The costs and the error for $k$-NN querying are presented in Figures 7b,c – with respect to the increasing number of nearest neighbors $k$.

**Summary.** Based on the above presented experimental results, we can observe that non-metric searching by MAMs, together with usage of the TriGen algorithm as the first step of the indexing, can successfully merge both aspects, the retrieval efficiency as well as the effectiveness. The efficiency achieved is by far higher than simple sequential search (even for $\theta = 0$), whereas the retrieval error is kept very low for reasonable values of $\theta$. Moreover, by choosing different values of $\theta$ we get a trade-off between the effectiveness and efficiency thus, the TriGen algorithm provides a scalability mechanism for non-metric search by MAMs.

On the other hand, some non-metric measures are very hard to use for efficient *exact* search by MAMs (i.e. keeping $E_{NO} = 0$), in particular the **COSIMIR** and the **FracLp0.25** measures. Nevertheless, for *approximate* search ($E_{NO} > 0$) also these measures can be utilized efficiently.

## 6 Conclusions

In this paper we have proposed a general approach to non-metric similarity search in multimedia databases by use of metric access methods (MAMs). We have shown the triangular inequality property is not restrictive for similarity search and can be enforced for every semimetric (modifying it to a metric). Furthermore, we have introduced the TriGen algorithm for automatic turning of any black-box semimetric into metric (or at least approximation of a metric) just by use of distance distribution in a fraction of the database. Such a "TriGen-approximated metric" can be safely used to search the database by any MAM, while the similarity orderings with respect to a query object (the retrieval effectiveness) are correctly preserved. The main result of the paper is a fact that we can quickly search a multimedia database when using unknown non-metric similarity measures, while the retrieval error achieved can be very low.

**Acknowledgements.** This research has been supported by grants 201/05/P036 of the Czech Science Foundation (GAČR) and "Information Society" 1ET100300419 – National Research Programme of the Czech Republic. I also thank Július Štroffek for his implementation of backpropagation network (used for the COSIMIR experiments).

## References

1. C. C. Aggarwal, A. Hinneburg, and D. A. Keim. On the surprising behavior of distance metrics in high dimensional spaces. In *ICDT*. LNCS, Springer, 2001.
2. F. Ashby and N. Perrin. Toward a unified theory of similarity and recognition. *Psychological Review*, 95(1):124–150, 1988.
3. I. Bartolini, P. Ciaccia, and M. Patella. WARP: Accurate Retrieval of Shapes Using Phase of Fourier Descriptors and Time Warping Distance. *IEEE Pattern Analysis and Machine Intelligence*, 27(1):142–147, 2005.

4. E. Chávez and G. Navarro. A Probabilistic Spell for the Curse of Dimensionality. In *ALENEX'01, LNCS 2153*, pages 147–160. Springer, 2001.
5. E. Chávez, G. Navarro, R. Baeza-Yates, and J. L. Marroquín. Searching in metric spaces. *ACM Computing Surveys*, 33(3):273–321, 2001.
6. P. Ciaccia and M. Patella. Searching in metric spaces with user-defined and approximate distances. *ACM Database Systems*, 27(4):398–437, 2002.
7. P. Ciaccia, M. Patella, and P. Zezula. M-tree: An Efficient Access Method for Similarity Search in Metric Spaces. In *VLDB'97*, pages 426–435, 1997.
8. P. Corazza. Introduction to metric-preserving functions. *American Mathematical Monthly*, 104(4):309–23, 1999.
9. V. Dohnal, C. Gennaro, P. Savino, and P. Zezula. D-index: Distance searching index for metric data sets. *Multimedia Tools and Applications*, 21(1):9–33, 2003.
10. M. Donahue, D. Geiger, T. Liu, and R. Hummel. Sparse representations for image decomposition with occlusions. In *CVPR*, pages 7–12, 1996.
11. C. Faloutsos and K. Lin. Fastmap: A Fast Algorithm for Indexing, Data-Mining and Visualization of Traditional and Multimedia Datasets. In *SIGMOD*, 1995.
12. R. F. S. Filho, A. J. M. Traina, C. Traina, and C. Faloutsos. Similarity search without tears: The OMNI family of all-purpose access methods. In *ICDE*, 2001.
13. K.-S. Goh, B. Li, and E. Chang. DynDex: a dynamic and non-metric space indexer. In *ACM Multimedia*, 2002.
14. P. Hart. The condensed nearest neighbour rule. *IEEE Transactions on Information Theory*, 14(3):515–516, 1968.
15. G. R. Hjaltason and H. Samet. Properties of embedding methods for similarity searching in metric spaces. *IEEE Patt.Anal. and Mach.Intell.*, 25(5):530–549, 2003.
16. P. Howarth and S. Ruger. Fractional distance measures for content-based image retrieval. In *ECIR 2005*, pages 447–456. LNCS 3408, Springer-Verlag, 2005.
17. D. Huttenlocher, G. Klanderman, and W. Rucklidge. Comparing images using the hausdorff distance. *IEEE Patt. Anal. and Mach. Intell.*, 15(9):850–863, 1993.
18. D. Jacobs, D. Weinshall, and Y. Gdalyahu. Classification with nonmetric distances: Image retrieval and class representation. *IEEE Pattern Analysis and Machine Intelligence*, 22(6):583–600, 2000.
19. A. K. Jain and D. E. Zongker. Representation and recognition of handwritten digits using deformable templates. *IEEE Patt.Anal.Mach.Intell.*, 19(12):1386–1391, 1997.
20. O. Jesorsky, K. J. Kirchberg, and R. Frischholz. Robust face detection using the hausdorff distance. In *AVBPA*, pages 90–95. LNCS 2091, Springer-Verlag, 2001.
21. C. L. Krumhansl. Concerning the applicability of geometric models to similar data: The interrelationship between similarity and spatial density. *Psychological Review*, 85(5):445–463, 1978.
22. T. Mandl. Learning similarity functions in information retrieval. In *EUFIT*, 1998.
23. E. Rosch. Cognitive reference points. *Cognitive Psychology*, 7:532–47, 1975.
24. E. Rothkopf. A measure of stimulus similarity and errors in some paired-associate learning tasks. *J. of Experimental Psychology*, 53(2):94–101, 1957.
25. S. Santini and R. Jain. Similarity measures. *IEEE Pattern Analysis and Machine Intelligence*, 21(9):871–883, 1999.
26. T. Skopal, J. Pokorný, M. Krátký, and V. Snášel. Revisiting M-tree Building Principles. In *ADBIS, Dresden*, pages 148–162. LNCS 2798, Springer, 2003.
27. T. Skopal, J. Pokorný, and V. Snášel. Nearest Neighbours Search using the PM-tree. In *DASFAA '05, Beijing, China*, pages 803–815. LNCS 3453, Springer, 2005.
28. A. Tversky. Features of similarity. *Psychological review*, 84(4):327–352, 1977.

29. A. Tversky and I. Gati. Similarity, separability, and the triangle inequality. *Psychological Review*, 89(2):123–154, 1982.
30. Wavelet-based Image Indexing and Searching, Stanford University, wang.ist.psu.edu.
31. R. Weber, H.-J. Schek, and S. Blott. A quantitative analysis and performance study for similarity-search methods in high-dimensional spaces. In *VLDB*, 1998.
32. D. L. Wilson. Asymptotic properties of nearest neighbor rules using edited data. *IEEE Transactions on Systems, Man, and Cybernetics*, 2(3):408–421, 1972.
33. B.-K. Yi, H. V. Jagadish, and C. Faloutsos. Efficient retrieval of similar time sequences under time warping. In *ICDE '98*, pages 201–208, 1998.

# Constructing a Generic Natural Language Interface for an XML Database*

Yunyao Li[1], Huahai Yang[2], and H.V. Jagadish[1]

[1] University of Michigan, Ann Arbor, MI 48109, USA
(yunyaol, jag)@eecs.umich.edu
[2] University at Albany, SUNY, Albany, NY 12222, USA
hyang@albany.edu

**Abstract.** We describe the construction of a generic natural language query interface to an XML database. Our interface can accept an arbitrary English sentence as a query, which can be quite complex and include aggregation, nesting, and value joins, among other things. This query is translated, potentially after reformulation, into an XQuery expression. The translation is based on mapping grammatical proximity of natural language parsed tokens in the parse tree of the query sentence to proximity of corresponding elements in the XML data to be retrieved. Our experimental assessment, through a user study, demonstrates that this type of natural language interface is good enough to be usable now, with no restrictions on the application domain.

## 1 Introduction

In the real world we obtain information by asking questions in a natural language, such as English. Supporting arbitrary natural language queries is regarded by many as the ultimate goal for a database query interface, and there have been numerous attempts towards this goal. However, two major obstacles lie in the way of reaching the ultimate goal of support for arbitrary natural language queries: first, automatically understanding natural language is itself still an open research problem, not just semantically but even syntactically; second, even if we could fully understand any arbitrary natural language query, translating this parsed natural language query into a correct formal query remains an issue since this translation requires mapping the understanding of intent into a specific database schema.

In this paper, we propose a framework for building a generic interactive natural language interface to database systems. Our focus is on the second challenge: given a parsed natural language query, how to translate it into a correct structured query against the database. The issues we deal with include those of attribute name confusion (e.g. asked "Who is the president of YMCA," we do not know whether YMCA is a country, a corporation, or a club) and of query structure confusion (e.g. the query "Return the lowest price for each book" is totally different from the query "Return the book with the lowest price," even though the words used in the two are almost the same). We address these issues in this paper through the introduction of the notions of *token attachment* and *token relationship* in natural language parse trees. We also propose the concept of *core token* as an effective mechanism to perform semantic grouping and hence determine both query nesting and structural relationships between result elements when mapping tokens to queries. Details of these notions can be found in Sec. 3.

---

* Supported in part by NSF 0219513 and 0438909, and NIH 1-U54-DA021519-01A1.

Of course, the first challenge of understanding arbitrary natural language cannot be ignored. But a novel solution to this problem per se is out of the scope of this paper. Instead, we leverage existing natural language processing techniques, and use an off-the-shelf natural language parser in our system. We then extract semantics expressible by XQuery from the output of the parser, and whenever needed, interactively guide the user to pose queries that our system can understand by providing meaningful feedback and helpful rephrasing suggestions. Sec. 4 discusses how the system interacts with a user and facilitates query formulation during the query translation process.

We have incorporated our ideas into a working software system called NaLIX[1], which we evaluated by means of a user study. Our experimental results in Sec. 5 demonstrate the feasibility of such an interactive natural language interface to database systems. In most cases no more than two iterations appears to suffice for the user to submit a natural language query that the system can parse. Previous studies [4, 25] show that even casual users frequently revise queries to meet their information needs. Therefore, our system can be considered to be usable in practice. In NaLIX, a correctly parsed query is almost always translated into a structured query that correctly retrieves the desired answer (average precision = 95.1%, average recall = 97.6%).

Finally, we discuss related work in Sec. 6 and conclude in Sec. 7. We begin with some necessary background material in Sec. 2.

In summary, we have been able to produce a natural language query interface for a database that, while far from being able to pass the Turing test, is perfectly usable in practice, and able to handle even quite complex queries, e.g. involving nesting and aggregation, in a variety of application domains.

## 2 Background

Keyword search interfaces to databases have begun to receive increasing attention [6, 10, 11, 12, 16, 18], and can be considered a first step towards addressing the challenge of natural language querying. Our work builds upon this stream of research, so we present some essential background material here. Additional efforts at constructing natural language interfaces are described in Sec. 6.

There are two main ideas in using keyword search for databases. First, sets of keywords expressed together in a query must match objects that are "close together" in the database (using some appropriate notions of "close together"). Second, there is a recognition that pure keyword queries are rather blunt – too many things of interest are hard to specify. So somewhat richer query mechanisms are folded in along with the basic keyword search. A recent effort in this stream of work is Schema-Free XQuery [16, 18].

The central idea in Schema-Free XQuery is that of a *meaningful query focus* (MQF) of a set of nodes. Beginning with a given collection of keywords, each of which identifies a candidate XML element to relate to, the MQF of these elements, if one exists, automatically finds relationships between these elements, if any, including additional related elements as appropriate. For example, for the query "Find the director of Gone with the Wind," there may be *title* of *movie*, and *title* of *book* with value "Gone with the Wind" in the database. However, we do not need advanced semantic reasoning capability to know that only movies can have a director and hence "Gone with the Wind" should be the *title* of a *movie* instead of a *book*. Rather, the computation of $\underline{\text{mqf}}(director, title)$ will automatically choose only *title* of *movie*, as this *title* has a structurally meaningful relationship with *director*. Furthermore, it does not matter whether the schema

---

[1] NaLIX was demonstrated at SIGMOD 2005, and voted the Best Demo [17].

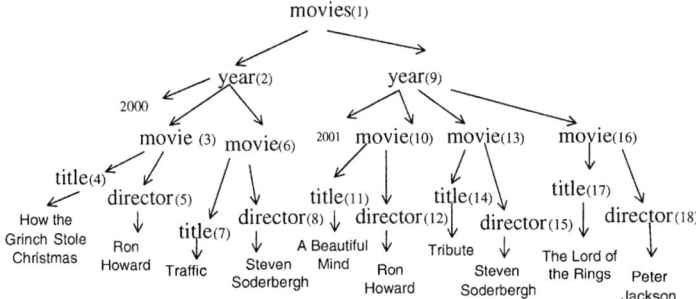

**Query 1:** *Return every director who has directed as many movies as has Ron Howard.*
**Query 2:** *Return every director, where the number of movies directed by the director is the same as the number of movies directed by Ron Howard.*
**Query 3:** *Return the directors of movies, where the title of each movie is the same as the title of a book.*

**Fig. 1.** Querying XML database with natural language queries

has *director* under *movie* or vice versa (for example, movies could have been classified based on their directors). In either case, the correct structural relationships will be found, with the correct *director* elements be returned.

Schema-Free XQuery greatly eases our burden in translating natural language queries in that it is no longer necessary to map the query to the precise underlying schema. We will use it as the target language of our translation process. From now on, we will refer to Schema-Free XQuery as XQuery for simplicity, unless noted otherwise.

## 3 From Natural Language Query to XQuery

The relationships between words in the natural language query must decide how the corresponding components in XQuery will be related to each other and thus the semantic meaning of the resulting query. We obtain such relationship information between parsed tokens from a dependency parser, which is based on the relationship between words rather than hierarchical constituents (group of words) [20, 28]. The parser currently used in NaLIX is Minipar [19]. The reason we chose Minipar is two-fold: (i) it is a state-of-art dependency parser; (ii) it is free off-the-shelf software, and thus allows easier replication of our system.

There are three main steps in translating queries from natural language queries into corresponding XQuery expressions. Sec. 3.1 presents the method to identify and classify terms in a parse tree output of a natural language parser. This parse tree is then validated, but we defer the discussion of this second step until Sec. 4. Sec. 3.2 demonstrates how a validated parse tree is translated into an XQuery expression. These three key steps are independent of one another; improvements can be made to any one without impacting the other two. The software architecture of NaLIX has been described in [17], but not the query transformation algorithms. Figure 1 is used as our running example to illustrate the query transformation process.

### 3.1 Token Classification

To translate a natural language query into an XQuery expression, we first need to identify words/phrases in the original sentence that can be mapped into corresponding

**Table 1.** Different Types of Tokens

| Type of Token | Query Component | Description |
|---|---|---|
| Command Token(CMT) | Return Clause | Top main verb or wh-phrase [24] of parse tree, from an enum set of words and phrases |
| Order by Token(OBT) | Order By Clause | A phrase from an enum set of phrases |
| Function token(FT) | Function | A word or phrase from an enum set of adjectives and noun phrases |
| Operator Token(OT) | Operator | A phrase from an enum set of preposition phrases |
| Value Token(VT) | Value | A noun or noun phrase in quotation marks, a proper noun or noun phrase, or a number |
| Name token(NT) | Basic Variable | A non-VT noun or noun phrase |
| Negation (NEG) | function not() | Adjective "not" |
| Quantifier Token(QT) | Quantifier | A word from an enum set of adjectives serving as determiners |

**Table 2.** Different Types of Markers

| Type of Marker | Semantic Contribution | Description |
|---|---|---|
| Connection Marker(CM) | Connect two related tokens | A preposition from an enumerated set, or non-token main verb |
| Modifier Marker(MM) | Distinguish two NTs | An adjective as determiner or a numeral as predeterminer or postdeterminer |
| Pronoun Marker(PM) | None due to parser's limitation | Pronouns |
| General Marker(GM) | None | Auxiliary verbs, articles |

components of XQuery. We call each such word/phrase a *token*, and one that does not match any component of XQuery a *marker*. Tokens can be further divided into different types shown in Table 1 according to the type of query components they match.[2] Enumerated sets of phrases (enum sets) are the real-world "knowledge base" for the system. In NaLIX, we have kept these small - each set has about a dozen elements. Markers can be divided into different types depending on their semantic contribution to the translation. A unique id is assigned to each token or marker. The parse tree after token identification for Query 2 in Figure 1 is shown in Figure 2. Note that node **11** is not in the query, nor in the output of the parser. Rather, it is an *implicit* node (formally defined in Sec. 4) that has been inserted by the token validation process.

Note that because of the vocabulary restriction of the system, some terms in a query may not be classified into one of the categories of token or marker. Obviously, such unclassified terms cannot be properly mapped into XQuery. Sec. 4 describes how these are reported to the user during parse tree validation, when the relationship of the "unknown" terms with other tokens (markers) can be better identified.

### 3.2 Translation into XQuery

Given a valid parse tree (discussion on parse tree validation is deferred until Sec. 4), we show here how to translate it into XQuery. XML documents are designed with the goal to be "human-legible and reasonably clear." [32] Therefore, any reasonably designed XML document should reflect certain semantic structure isomorphous to human conceptual structure, and hence expressible by human natural language. The challenge is to utilize the structure of the natural language constructions, as reflected in the parse tree, to generate appropriate structure in the XQuery expression (If we do not establish this structure, then we may as well just issue a simple keyword query!!). For simplicity of presentation, we use the symbol for each type of token (resp. marker) to refer to tokens (markers) of that type, and use subscripts to distinguish different tokens (markers) of the same type if needed. For instance, we will write, "Given $NT_1$, $NT_2$, ..." as a short hand for "Given name tokens $u$ and $v$, ..."

---

[2] When a noun/noun phrase matches certain XQuery keywords, such as "string", special handling is required. Such special cases are not listed in the table, and will not be discussed in the paper due to space limitation.

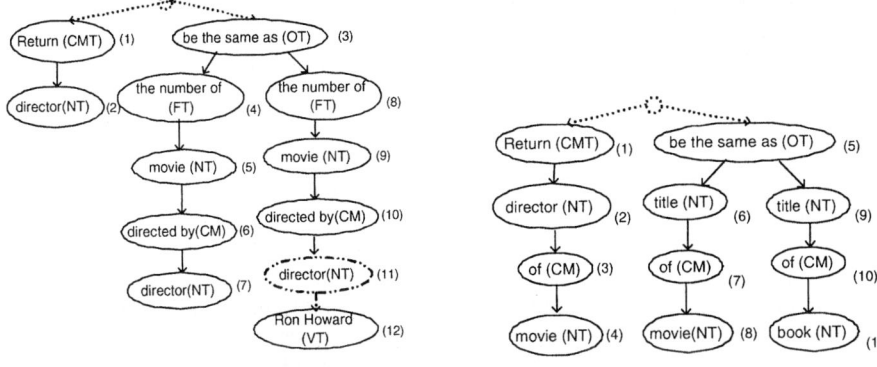

**Fig. 2.** Parse tree for Query 2 in Figure 1    **Fig. 3.** Parse tree for Query 3 in Figure 1

### 3.2.1 Concepts and Definitions

A natural language query may contain multiple name tokens (NTs), each corresponding to an element or attribute in the database. NTs "related" to each other should be mapped into the same **mqf** function in Schema-Free XQuery and hence found in structurally related elements in the database. However, this relationship among the NTs is not straightforward. Consider the example in Figure 3, nodes **2** (*director*) and **4** (*movie*) should be considered as related to nodes **6** (*title*) and **8** (*movie*), since the two *movie* nodes (**4, 8**) are semantically equivalent. However, they are not related to nodes **9** (*title*) or **11** (*book*), although the structural relationship between nodes **9, 11** and nodes **2, 4** is exactly the same as that between nodes **6, 8** and nodes **2, 4**. An intuitive explanation for this distinction is that the two sets of NTs (*director, movie*) and (*title, movie*) are related to each other semantically because they share NTs representing the same *movie* elements in the database, whereas the (*title, book*) pair does not. We now capture this intuition formally.

**Definition 1 (Name Token Equivalence).** $NT_1$ and $NT_2$ are said to be equivalent if they are (i) both not implicit [3] and composed of the same noun phrase with equivalent modifiers[4]; OR (ii) both implicit and correspond to VTs of the same value.

In consequence of the above definition, if a query has two occurrences of *book*, the corresponding name tokens will be considered equivalent, if they are not qualified in any way. However, we distinguish *first book* from *second book*: even though both correspond to *book* nodes, the corresponding name tokens are not equivalent, since they have different modifiers.

**Definition 2 (Sub-Parse Tree).** *A subtree rooted at an operator token node that has at least two children is called a sub-parse tree.*

**Definition 3 (Core Token).** *A name token is called a core token if (i) it occurs in a sub-parse tree and has no descendant name tokens; OR (ii) it is equivalent to a core token.*

---

[3] An implicit NT is a NT not explicitly included in the query. It is formally defined in Definition 11, Sec. 4.

[4] Two modifiers are obviously equivalent if they are the same. But some pairs of distinct modifiers may also be equivalent. We do not discuss modifier equivalence further in this paper for lack of space.

**Definition 4 (Directly Related Name Tokens).** *$NT_1$ and $NT_2$ are said to be directly related to each other, if and only if they have a parent-child relationship (ignoring any intervening markers, and FT and OT nodes with a single child).*

**Definition 5 (Related by Core Token).** *$NT_1$ and $NT_2$ are said to be related by core token, if and only if they are directly related to the same or equivalent core tokens.*

**Definition 6 (Related Name Tokens).** *$NT_1$ and $NT_2$ are said to be related, if they are directly related, or related by core token, or related to the same NT.*

For Query 3 in Figure 3, only one operator token (OT), node **5** exists in the parse tree. The lowest NTs of the OT's sub-parse trees, nodes **8** (*movie*) and **11** (*book*), are the core tokens in the query. Nodes **2**, **6** and **9** are directly related to nodes **4**, **8** and **11** respectively, by Definition 4. Node **4** is equivalent to node **8**. Hence, according to Definition 6, two sets of related nodes {**2, 4, 6, 8**} and {**9, 11**} can be obtained.

All NTs related to each other should be mapped to the same **mqf** function since we seek elements (and attributes) matching these NTs in the database that are structurally related.

Additional relationships between tokens (not just name tokens) needed for query translation are captured by the following definition of *attachment*.

**Definition 7 (Attachment).** *Given any two tokens $T_a$ and $T_b$, where $T_a$ is the parent of $T_b$ in the parse tree (ignoring all intervening markers), if $T_b$ follows $T_a$ in the original sentence, then $T_a$ is said to attach to $T_b$; otherwise, $T_b$ is said to attach to $T_a$.*

### 3.2.2 Token Translation.
Given the conceptual framework established above, we describe in this section how each token in the parse tree is mapped into an XQuery fragment. The mapping process has several steps. We illustrate each step with our running example.

**Identify Core Token.** Core tokens in the parse tree are identified according to Definition 3. Two different core tokens can be found in Query 2 in Figure 1. One is *director*, represented by nodes **2** and **7**. The other is a different *director*, represented by node **11**. Note although node **11** and nodes **2, 7** are composed of the same word, they are regarded as different core tokens, as node **11** is an implicit NT, while nodes **2, 7** are not.

**Variable Binding.** Each NT in the parse tree should be bound to a basic variable in Schema-Free XQuery. We denote such variable binding as: $\langle var \rangle \to NT$

Two name tokens should be bound to different basic variables, unless they are regarded as the same core token, or identical by the following definition:

**Definition 8 (Identical Name Tokens).** *$NT_1$ and $NT_2$ are identical, if and only if (i) they are equivalent, and indirectly related; AND (ii) the NTs directly related with them, if any are identical; AND (iii) no FT or QT attaching to either of them.*

We then define the relationships between two basic variables based on the relationships of their corresponding NTs as follows:

**Definition 9 (Directly Related Variables).** *Two basic variables $\langle var_1 \rangle$ and $\langle var_2 \rangle$ are said to be directly related, if and only if for any $NT_1$ corresponding to $\langle var_1 \rangle$, there exists a $NT_2$ corresponding to $\langle var_2 \rangle$ such that $NT_1$ and $NT_2$ are directly related, and vice versa.*

**Definition 10 (Related Variables).** *Two basic variables $\langle var_1 \rangle$ and $\langle var_2 \rangle$ are said to be related, if and only if any NTs corresponding to them are related or there is no core token in the query parse tree.*

**Table 3.** Variable Bindings for Query 2

| Variable | Associated Content | Nodes | Related To |
|---|---|---|---|
| $v_1^*$ | director | 2,7 | $v_2$ |
| $v_2$ | movie | 5 | $v_1$ |
| $v_3$ | movie | 9 | $v_4$ |
| $v_4^*$ | director | 11 | $v_3$ |
| $cv_1$ | count($v_2$) | 4+5 | N/A |
| $cv_2$ | count($v_4$) | 8+9 | N/A |

**Table 4.** Direct Mapping for Query 2

| Pattern | Query Fragment |
|---|---|
| $v_1$ | for $v_1$ in ⟨doc⟩//director |
| $v_2$ | for $v_2$ in ⟨doc⟩//movie |
| $v_3$ | for $v_3$ in ⟨doc⟩//movie |
| $v_4$ | for $v_4$ in ⟨doc⟩//director |
| $cv_1$+⟨eq⟩+$cv_2$ | where $cv_1$ = $cv_2$ |
| $v_4$+⟨constant⟩ | where $v_4$ = "Ron Howard" |
| ⟨return⟩ + $v_1$ | return $v_1$ |

- **FOR clause:**
  Let basic() be the function that returns the name token corresponding to basic variable in ⟨var⟩ or ⟨cmpvar⟩
  ⟨var⟩ ⤳ for ⟨var⟩ in ⟨doc⟩//basic(⟨var⟩)
- **WHERE clause:**
  ⟨variable⟩ → ⟨var⟩|⟨cmpvar⟩
  ⟨constant⟩ → VT
  ⟨arg⟩ → ⟨variable⟩|⟨constant⟩
  ⟨opr⟩ → OT
  ⟨neg⟩ → NEG
  ⟨quantifier⟩ → QT
  ⟨var⟩+⟨constant⟩ ⤳ where ⟨var⟩ = ⟨constant⟩
  (⟨variable⟩+⟨opr⟩+⟨arg⟩)|(⟨opr⟩+⟨var⟩+⟨constant⟩) ⤳ where ⟨variable⟩+⟨opr⟩+⟨arg⟩
  ⟨variable⟩+⟨neg⟩+⟨opr⟩+⟨arg⟩ ⤳ where not (⟨variable⟩+⟨opr⟩+⟨arg⟩)
  ⟨opr⟩+⟨constant⟩+⟨variable⟩ ⤳ ⟨cmpvar⟩ → count(⟨variable⟩)
  where ⟨cmpvar⟩ + ⟨opr⟩ + ⟨constant⟩
  ⟨neg⟩+⟨opr⟩+⟨constant⟩+⟨variable⟩ ⤳ ⟨cmpvar⟩ → count(⟨variable⟩)
  where not (⟨cmpvar⟩ + ⟨opr⟩ + ⟨constant⟩)
- **ORDERBY clause:**
  ⟨sort⟩ → OBT
  ⟨sort⟩ + ⟨variable⟩ ⤳ orderby ⟨variable⟩
- **RETURN clause:**
  ⟨cmd⟩ → CMT
  ⟨cmd⟩ + ⟨variable⟩ ⤳ return ⟨variable⟩

**Fig. 4.** Mapping from token patterns to query fragments

Patterns ⟨FT + NT⟩|⟨FT₁ + FT₂ + NT⟩ should also be bound to variables. Variables bound with such patterns are called *composed variables*, denoted as ⟨cmpvar⟩, to distinguish them from the basic variables bound to NTs. We denote such variable binding as:

⟨function⟩ → FT
⟨cmpvar⟩ → (⟨function⟩ + ⟨var⟩)|(⟨function⟩ + ⟨cmpvar⟩)

Table 3 shows the variable bindings[5] for Query 2 in Figure 1. The nodes referred to in the table are from the parse tree of Query 2 in Figure 2.

**Mapping.** Certain patterns of tokens can be mapped directly into clauses in XQuery. A complete list of patterns and their corresponding clauses in XQuery can be found in Figure 4. Table 4 shows a list of direct mappings from token patterns to query fragments for Query 2 in Figure 1 (⤳ is used to abbreviate 'translates into').

### 3.2.3 Grouping and Nesting

The grouping and nesting of the XQuery fragments obtained in the mapping process has to be considered when there are function tokens in the natural language query, which correspond to aggregate functions in XQuery, or when there are quantifier tokens, which correspond to quantifiers in XQuery. Determining grouping and nesting for aggregate functions is difficult, because the scope of the aggregate function is not always obvious

---

[5] The * mark next to $v_1$, $v_4$ indicates that the corresponding NTs are core tokens.

Let innerFT() be function returning innermost FT in $\langle cmpvar \rangle$

$\langle connector \rangle \rightarrow CM$
$\langle cmpvar \rangle \rightarrow FT + \langle var_2 \rangle$
$\langle var_1 \rangle + \langle connector \rangle + \langle cmpvar \rangle \rightsquigarrow \quad \langle var_2 \rangle_{new} \rightarrow \text{basic}(\langle cmpvar \rangle)$
$\qquad \qquad \qquad \qquad \qquad \text{if innerFT}(\langle cmpvar \rangle) \neq \text{null, then}$
$\qquad \qquad \qquad \qquad \qquad \quad \underline{\text{where}} \; \langle \text{innerFT}(\langle cmpvar \rangle) \rangle + \langle var_2 \rangle_{new} = \langle cmpvar \rangle$
$\qquad \qquad \qquad \qquad \qquad \textbf{else}$
$\qquad \qquad \qquad \qquad \qquad \quad \underline{\text{where}} \; \langle var_2 \rangle_{new} = \langle cmpvar \rangle$
Record $\langle var_2 \rangle_{new}$ as related to $\langle var_1 \rangle$, $\langle var_2 \rangle$ as unrelated to $\langle var_1 \rangle$

**Fig. 5.** Semantic contribution of connection marker in query translation

from the token it directly attaches to. Determining grouping and nesting for quantifiers is comparatively easier.

Consider the following two queries: "Return the lowest price for each book," and "Return each book with the lowest price." For the first query, the scope of function min() corresponding to "lowest" is within each book, but for the second query, the scope of function min() corresponding to "lowest" is among all the books. We observe that *price*, the NT the aggregate function attaching to, is related to *book* in different ways in the two queries. We also notice that the CM "with" in the second query implies that a *price* node related to *book* has the same value as the lowest price of all the *book*s. Based on the above observation, we propose the transformation rules shown in Figure 5 to take the semantic contribution of connection markers into consideration.

We then propose the mapping rules shown in Figure 6 to determine the nesting scope for aggregate functions. Specifically, we identify two different nesting scopes that result from using an aggregate function - *inner* and *outer*, with respect to the basic variable $\langle var \rangle$ that the function directly attaches to. The nesting scope of the LET clause corresponding to an aggregate function depends on the basic variable that it attaches to. The idea is that if an aggregate function attaches to a basic variable that represents a core token, then all the clauses containing variables related to the core token should be put inside the LET clause of this function; otherwise, the relationships between name tokens (represented by variables) via the core token will be lost. For example, given the query "Return the total number of movies, where the director of each movie is Ron Howard," the only core token is *movie*. Clearly, the condition clause "<u>where</u> $dir = 'Ron Howard'" should be bound with each *movie* inside the LET clause. Therefore, the nesting scope of a LET clause corresponding to the core token is marked as *inner* with respect to $\langle var \rangle$ (in this case $movie). On the other hand, if an aggregate function attaches to a basic variable $\langle var \rangle$ representing non-core token, only clauses containing variables directly related to $\langle var \rangle$ should be put inside of the LET clause, since $\langle var \rangle$ is only associated with other variables related to it via a core token. The nesting scope of the LET clause should be marked as *outer*, with respect to $\langle var \rangle$. Similarly, when there is no core token, $\langle var \rangle$ may only be associated with other variables indirectly related to it via value joins. The nesting scope of the LET clause should also be marked as *outer* with respect to $\langle var \rangle$. In such a case, the nesting scope determination for Query 2 can be found in Figure 8. The updated variable bindings and relationships between basic variables for the query can be found in Table 5.

The nesting scope determination for a quantifier (Figure 7) is similar to that for an aggregate function, except that the nesting scope is now associated with a quantifier inside a WHERE clause. The nesting scope of a quantifier is marked as *inner* with respect to $\langle var \rangle$ the quantifier attaching to, when the variable $\langle var \rangle$ is a core token. Otherwise, it is marked as *outer* with respect to $\langle var \rangle$. The meanings of *inner* and *outer* are the

```
Denote ⟨core⟩ as the core token related to ⟨var⟩, if any; else as a variable ⟨var⟩
attaching to and directly related to, if any; else as a randomly chosen variable
indirectly related to ⟨var⟩.
Denote ⟨v⟩ as variables directly related to ⟨var⟩.
if ⟨cmpvar⟩ → ⟨function⟩+⟨var⟩
   then ⟨cmpvar⟩ ⤳
   - if ⟨var⟩ is not a core token itself, or there is no core token, then
              let ⟨vars⟩ := {
                 for    ⟨core₁⟩ in  ⟨doc⟩//basic(⟨core⟩)
                 where  ⟨core₁⟩ = ⟨core⟩
                 return  ⟨var⟩}
       Replace ⟨cmpvar⟩ with ⟨function⟩ + ⟨vars⟩.
       Mark ⟨var⟩ and ⟨core⟩, ⟨v⟩ and ⟨core⟩ as unrelated.
       Mark ⟨var⟩ and ⟨core₁⟩, ⟨v⟩ and ⟨core₁⟩ as related.
       Mark nesting scope for the LET clause as outer with respect to ⟨var⟩.
   - else if ⟨var⟩ is a core token itself, or no ⟨core⟩ exists, then
              let ⟨vars⟩ := { return    ⟨var⟩}
       Replace ⟨cmpvar⟩ with ⟨function⟩ + ⟨vars⟩.
       Mark nesting scope for the LET clause as inner with respect to ⟨var⟩.
else if ⟨cmpvar⟩ → ⟨function⟩+⟨cmpvar₁⟩
   then ⟨function⟩+⟨cmpvar₁⟩ ⤳
           let ⟨vars⟩ := {⟨cmpvar₁⟩}
   Recursively rewrite ⟨cmpvar₁⟩.
   Replace ⟨cmpvar⟩ with ⟨function⟩ + ⟨vars⟩.
```

**Fig. 6.** Grouping and nesting scope determination for aggregate functions

```
/*⟨core⟩ is the same as that defined in Figure 6*/
if ⟨cmpvar⟩ → ⟨quantifier⟩+⟨var⟩
   then ⟨cmpvar⟩ ⤳
   - if ⟨var⟩ is not a core token itself, or there is no core token, then
                let ⟨vars⟩ := {
                   for    ⟨core₁⟩ in  ⟨doc⟩//basic(⟨core⟩)
                   where  ⟨core₁⟩ = ⟨core⟩
                   return  ⟨var⟩}
                where ⟨quantifier⟩ ⟨var₁⟩ in ⟨vars⟩ satisfies { }
       Mark ⟨var⟩ and ⟨core,⟩, ⟨core₁⟩ as unrelated.
       Replace ⟨var⟩ elsewhere with ⟨var₁⟩, except in FOR clause.
       Mark nesting scope for the WHERE clause with the quantifier as outer with
       respect to ⟨var⟩.
   - else if ⟨var⟩ is a core token itself, or no ⟨core⟩ exists, then
                let ⟨vars⟩ := { return    ⟨var⟩}
                where ⟨quantifier⟩ ⟨var₁⟩ in ⟨vars⟩ satisfies { }
       Mark nesting scope for the WHERE clause with the quantifier as inner with
       respect to ⟨var⟩.
       Replace ⟨var⟩ elsewhere with ⟨var₁⟩, except in FOR clause.
```

**Fig. 7.** Grouping and nesting scope determination for quantifier

same as those for aggregate functions, except that now only WHERE clauses may be put inside of a quantifier.

**MQF Function.** As we have previously discussed in Sec. 3.2, all name tokens related to each other should be mapped into the same **mqf** function. Hence, basic variables corresponding to such name tokens should be put into the same **mqf** function. One WHERE clause containing **mqf** function can be obtained for each set of related basic variables:

⟨vars⟩ → the union of all ⟨var⟩s related to each other
⟨vars⟩ ⤳ where mqf(⟨vars⟩)

(1) $cv_1 \rightarrow$ count($v_2$)
$v_2$ is not a core token, and the core token related to it is $v_1$, therefore $cv_1 \rightsquigarrow$

    let $vars_1$ := {
      for $v_5$ in $\langle doc \rangle$//director
      where  mqf($v_2$, $v_5$)
      and  $\overline{v_5}$ = $v_1$
      return  $v_2$}

Replace all $cv_1$ with count($vars_1$).
Mark $v_2$, $v_1$ as unrelated.
Mark $v_2$, $v_5$ as related.
Mark nesting scope for the LET clause as *outer* with respect to $v_2$.

(2) $cv_2 \rightarrow$ count($v_3$)
$v_3$ is not a core token, and the core token related to it is $v_4$, therefore $cv_1 \rightsquigarrow$

    let $vars_2$ := {
      for $v_6$ in $\langle doc \rangle$//director
      where  mqf($v_3$, $v_6$)
      and  $\overline{v_6}$ = $v_4$
      return  $v_3$}

Replace all $cv_2$ with count($vars_2$).
Mark $v_3$, $v_4$ as unrelated.
Mark $v_3$, $v_6$ as related.
Mark nesting scope for the LET clause as *outer* with respect to $v_3$.

**Fig. 8.** Grouping and nesting scope determination in Query 2

for $v_1$ in doc("movie.xml")//director,
    $v_4$ in doc("movie.xml")//director
let $vars_1$ := {
    for $v_5$ in doc("movie.xml")//director,
      $v_2$ in doc("movie.xml")//movie
    where  mqf($v_2$,$v_5$)
    and  $\overline{v_5}$ = $v_1$
    return  $v_2$}
let $vars_2$ := {
    for $v_6$ in doc("movie.xml")//director,
      $v_3$ in doc("movie.xml")//movie
    where  mqf($v_3$,$v_6$)
    and  $\overline{v_6}$ = $v_4$
    return  $v_3$}
where  count($vars_1$) = count($vars_2$)
    and  $v_4$ = "Ron Howard"
return  $v_1$

**Fig. 9.** Full translation for Query 2

**Table 5.** Updated variable bindings for Query 2

| Variable | Associated Content | Nodes | Related To |
|---|---|---|---|
| $v_1^*$ | director | 2,7 | null |
| $v_2$ | movie | 5 | $v_5$ |
| $v_3$ | movie | 9 | $v_6$ |
| $v_4^*$ | director | 11 | null |
| $v_5^*$ | director | N/A | $v_2$ |
| $v_6^*$ | director | N/A | $v_3$ |
| $cv_1$ | count($vars_1$) | 4+5 | N/A |
| $cv_2$ | count($vars_2$) | 8+9 | N/A |

**Table 6.** Grammar supported by NaLIX*

1. Q → RETURN PREDICATE* ORDER_BY?
2. RETURN → CMT+(RNP|GVT|PREDICATE)
3. PREDICATE → QT?+((RNP$_1$|GVT$_1$)+GOT+(RNP$_2$|GVT$_2$)
4.     |(GOT?+RNP+GVT)
5.     |(GOT?+GVT+RNP)
6.     |(GOT?+[NT]+GVT)
7.     |RNP
8. ORDER_BY → OBT+RNP
9. RNP → NT |(QT+RNP)|(FT+RNP)|(RNP∧RNP)
10. GOT → OT|(NEG+OT)|(GOT∧GOT)
11. GVT → VT |(GVT∧GVT)
12. CM → (CM+CM)

*Symbol "+" represents attachment relation between two tokens; "[]" indicates implicit token, as defined in Def. 11.

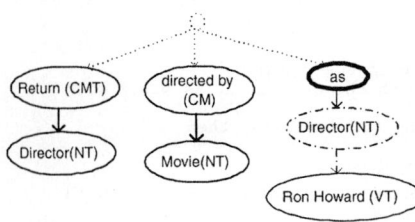

**Fig. 10.** Parse tree for Query 1 in Figure 1

As can be seen from Table 5, two sets of related variables can be found for Query 2 in Figure 1: {$v_5$,$v_2$} and {$v_3$,$v_6$}. The corresponding WHERE clauses containing **mqf** function are: where mqf($v_5$,$v_2$) and where mqf($v_3$,$v_6$).

### 3.2.4 Full Query Construction

Multiple XQuery fragments may be obtained from token translation. These fragments alone do not constitute a meaningful query. We need to construct a semantically meaningful Schema-Free XQuery by putting these fragments together with appropriate nestings and groupings.

Following the defined nesting scopes (Figure 6,7), we construct the query starting from innermost clauses and work outwards. If the scope defined is *inner* with respect to $\langle var \rangle$, then all the other query fragments containing $\langle var \rangle$ or basic variables related to $\langle var \rangle$ are put within an inner query following the FLOWR convention (e.g., conditions in WHERE clauses are connected by <u>and</u>) as part of the query at outer level. If the scope defined is *outer* with respect to $\langle var \rangle$, then only queries fragments containing $\langle var \rangle$, and clauses (in case of quantifier, only WHERE clauses) containing basic variables directly related to $\langle var \rangle$ are put inside the inner query, while query fragments of other basic variables indirectly related to $\langle var \rangle$ are put outside of the clause at the same level of nesting. The remaining clauses are put in the appropriate places at the outmost level of the query following the FLOWR convention. Full translation for Query 2 in Figure 1 can be found in Figure 9.

## 4 Interactive Query Formulation

The mapping process from natural language to XQuery requires our system to be able to map words to query components based on token classification. Due to the limited vocabulary understood by the system, certain terms cannot be properly classified. Clever natural language understanding systems attempt to apply reasoning to interpret these terms, with partial success. We make no attempt at superior understanding of natural language. Rather, our approach is to get the user to rephrase the query into terms that we can understand. By doing so, we shift some burden of semantic disambiguation from the system to the user, to whom such task is usually trivial. In return, the user obtains better accessibility to information via precise querying.

To ensure that this process proceeds smoothly for the user, we provide the user with specific feedback on how to rephrase. In this section we describe the validation process we use to determine whether we can translate a user specified query. We also discuss the informative error messages we produce when validation fails.

NaLIX is designed to be a query interface for XML by translating natural language queries into Schema-Free XQuery. As such, the linguistic capability of our system is essentially restricted by the expressiveness of XQuery. This is to say, a natural language query that may be understood and thus meaningfully mapped into XQuery by NaLIX is one whose semantics is expressible in XQuery. Furthermore, for the purpose of evaluating the query, only the semantics that can be expressed by XQuery need to be extracted and mapped into XQuery.

Consider the following query: "Find all the movies directed by director Ron Howard." The meaning of "directed by" cannot be directly expressed in XQuery. It is neither possible nor necessary for NaLIX to understand such semantics. Instead based on the dependency parse tree, we can determine that "movie" and "director" are related and should be mapped into the same **mqf** function. Then the structural relationship between *movie* and *director* nodes in the database, which corresponds to "directed by," will be properly captured by Schema-Free XQuery. Generally, the semantics extracted by NaLIX from a given natural langauge query comprise two parts: (i) tokens that can be directly mapped into XQuery; (ii) semantic relationships between tokens, which are inexpressible in XQuery, but are reflected by database schema, such as the attachment relation between "movie" and "director" via "directed by" in the above example.

The grammar for natural language corresponding to the XQuery grammar supported by NaLIX is shown in Table 6 (ignoring all markers).We call a normalized parse tree that satisfies the above grammar a *valid* parse tree.

A valid parse tree can be translated to an XQuery expression as described in Sec 3.2. An invalid parse tree, however, will be rejected by the system, with error message(s).[6] Each error message is dynamically generated, tailored to the actual query causing the error. Inside each message, possible ways to revise the query are also suggested. For example, Query 1 in Figure 1 is found to be an invalid query, since it contains an unknown term "as" as highlighted in the parse tree in Figure 10. An error message will be returned to the user, and suggest "the same as" as a possible replacement for "as." Query 3 in Figure 3 is likely to be the new query written by the user by using the suggested term "the same as." Screenshots of the above iteration can be found in [17]. By providing such meaningful feedback tailored to each particular query instance, we eliminate the need to require users to study and remember tedious instructions on the system's linguistic coverage. Instead, through such interactive query formulation process, a user will gradually learn the linguistic coverage of the system. Note that we assume user queries are written in correct English, and thus do not specify any rules to deal with incorrect English.

For some queries, the system successfully parses and translates the queries, yet may not be able to correctly interpret the user's intent. These queries will be accepted by the system, but with warnings. For example, determining pronoun references (the "anaphora" resolution problem) remains an issue in natural language processing. Whenever there exists a pronoun in a user query, we include a warning message in the feedback and let the user be aware of the potential misunderstanding.

During the validation process, we also perform the following additional tasks concerned with database specific situations.

**Term Expansion.** A user may not be familiar with the specific attributes and element names in the database. Therefore, a name token specified in the user query may be different from the actual name(s) of element or attribute in the database matching this particular name token. The task of finding the name(s) of element or attribute in the database that matches with a given name token is accomplished by ontology-based term expansion using generic thesaurus WordNet [36] and domain-specific ontology whenever one is available.

**Implicit Name Token.** In a natural language query, we may find value tokens where the name tokens attaching to them are implicit in the query. For example, in Query 1 of Figure 10, element *director* in the database is related to value token "Ron Howard," but is not explicitly included in the query. We call such name tokens *implicit name token* as defined below. See Table 6 for the definitions of GVT, GOT and RNP.

**Definition 11 (Implicit Name Token).** *For any GVT, if it is not attached by a CMT, nor adjacent to a RNP, nor attached by a GOT that is attached by a RNP or GVT, then each VT within the GVT is said to be related to an implicit NT (denoted as [NT]). An implicit NT related to a VT is the name(s) of element or attribute with the value of VT in the database.*

If no name matching a name token or the value of a value token can be found in the database, an error message will be returned. If multiple element or attribute with different names matching the name token or value token are found in the database, the disjunctive form of the names is regarded as the corresponding name for the given name token, or implicit name token for the given value token. Users may also change the query by choosing one or more of the actual names.

---

[6] More details on the generation of error and warning messages in NaLIX can be found on the Web at http://www.umich.edu/ yunyao/NaLIX/index.html

## 5 Experimental Evaluation

We implemented NaLIX as a stand-alone interface to the Timber native XML database [13, 33] that supports Schema-Free XQuery. We used Minipar [19] as our natural language parser. To evaluate the relative strength of NaLIX, we experimentally compared it with a keyword search interface that supports search over XML documents based on Meet [26]. We would have liked to compare NaLIX with an existing NLP system. Unfortunately, existing NLP systems are mainly designed for textual content, not for structured data. As such, NLP question answering system cannot handle queries as complex as NaLIX and we believe no meaningful comparison is possible.

### 5.1 Methods

Participants were recruited with flyers posted on a university campus. Eighteen of them completed the full experiment. Their age ranged from 19 to 55 with an average of 27. A questionnaire indicated that all participants were familiar with some form of keyword search (e.g. Google) but had little knowledge of any formal query language.

**Procedures.** The experiment was a within-subject design, with each participant using either NaLIX or keyword search interface in one experimental block. The order of the two blocks was randomly assigned for each participant. Within each block, each participant was asked to accomplish 9 search tasks in a random order determined by a pair of orthogonal 9 by 9 Latin Squares.

The search tasks were adapted from the "XMP" set in the XQuery Use Cases [31]. Each search task was described with the elaborated form of an "XMP" query[7] taken from XQuery Use Cases [31]. Participants received no training at all on how to formulate a query, except being instructed to use either an English sentence or some keywords as the query depending on which experiment block the participant was in.

We noted that in an experimental setting, a participant could be easily satisfied with poor search quality and go on to the next search task. In order to obtain objective measurement of interactive query performance, a search quality criteria was adopted. Specifically, the results of a participant's query were compared against a standard results set, upon which precision and recall were automatically calculated. A harmonic mean of precision and recall [27] greater than 0.5 was set as passing criteria, beyond which the participant may move on to the next task. To alleviate participants' frustration and fatigue from repeated passing failures, a time limit of 5 minutes was set for each task. If a participant reached the criteria before the time limit, he or she was given the choice to move on or to revise the query to get better results.

**Measurement.** We evaluated our system on two objective metrics: how hard it was for the users to specify a query (*ease of use*); and how good was the query produced in terms of retrieving correct results (*search quality*).

**Ease of Use.** For each search task, we recorded the number of iterations and the actual time (from the moment the participant started a search task by clicking on a button) it took for a participant to formulate a system-acceptable query that returned the best

---

[7] Q12 is not included, as set comparison is not yet supported in Timber. Q5 is not included, as NaLIX current only supports queries over a single document. Q11 contains two separate search tasks: the second task was used as Q11 in our experiment; the first task, along with Q2, is the same as Q3, and thus is not included, as they only differ in the form of result display, which is not the focus of NaLIX.

results (i.e., highest harmonic mean of precision and recall) within the time limit for the task. We also evaluated NaLIX subjectively by asking each participant to fill out a post-experiment questionnaire.

**Search Quality.** The quality of a query was measured in terms of accuracy and comprehensiveness using standard precision and recall metrics. The correct results for each search task is easy to obtain given the corresponding correct schema-aware XQuery. Since the expected results were sometimes complex, with multiple elements (attributes) of interest, we considered each element and attribute value as an independent value for the purposes of precision and recall computation. Thus, a query that returned all the right elements, but only 3 out of 4 attributes requested for each element, would have a recall score of 75%. Ordering of results was not considered when computing precision and recall, unless the task specifically asked the results be sorted.

Finally, we measured the time NaLIX took for query translation and the time Timber took for query evaluation for each query. Both numbers were consistently very small (less than one second), and so not of sufficient interest to be worth reporting here. The fast query translation is expected, given that query sentences were themselves not very large. The fast evaluation time is an artifact of the miniscule data set that was used. The data set we used was a sub-collection of DBLP, which included all the elements on books in DBLP and twice as many elements on articles. The total size of the data set is 1.44MB, with 73142 nodes when loaded into Timber. We chose DBLP because it is semantically close to the data set for the XMP use case such that the "XMP" queries can be applied with only minor changes (e.g., tag name *year* is used to replace *price*, which is not in the data set but has similar characteristics). A pilot study showed that slow system response times (likely with very large data sets) resulted in frustration and fatigue for the participants. Since query evaluation time is not a focus of this paper, we felt that it is most appropriate to use this data set to balance the trade-off between performance and realism: we minimized the overhead resulting from the use of a larger data set both in terms of query evaluation and precision/recall computation time; at the same time, the correct results obtained for any "XMP" query from our data set were the same as those would have been obtained by using the whole DBLP, as correct answers for each query included elements related to *book* elements only.

### 5.2 Results and Discussion

**Ease of Use.** The time and the number of iterations needed for participants to formulate a valid natural language query with the best search results is shown in Figure 11. As can be seen, the average total time needed for each search task is usually less than 90 seconds, including the time used to read, understand the task description, mentally formulate a query, type in the query, read the feedback message, revise the query, browse the results and decide to accept the results. In consequence, there seems to be a floor of about 50 seconds, which is the average minimum time required for any query. The average number of iterations needed for formulating a query acceptable by NaLIX is less than 2, with an average of 3.8 iterations needed for the worst query. For about half of the search tasks (not the same tasks for each participant), all the participants were able to formulate a natural language query acceptable by NaLIX on the first attempt (i.e., with zero iterations). Also, for each task, there was at least one user (not the same one each time) who had an acceptable phrasing right off the bat (i.e. the minimum number of iterations was zero for each task).

It is worth noting that there was no instance where a participant became frustrated with the natural language interface and abandoned his/her query attempt. However, two

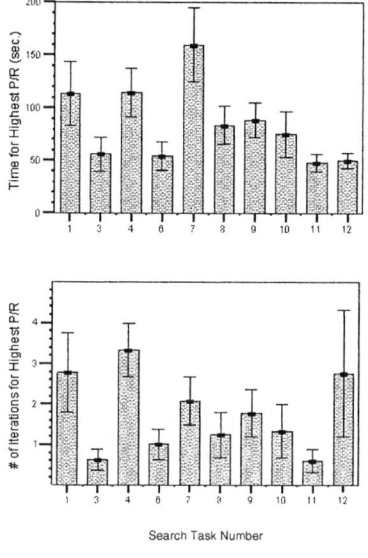
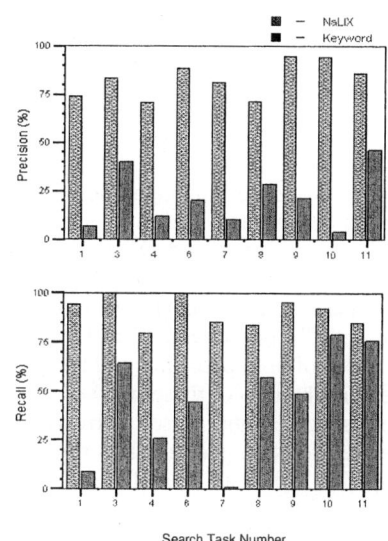

**Fig. 11.** Average time (in *sec.*) and average number of iterations needed for each "XMP" search task. Error bars show standard errors of means.

**Fig. 12.** Average precision and recall for each "XMP" search task

participants decided to stop the experiment due to frustration during the keyword search block.

According to the questionnaire results, the users felt that simple keyword search would not have sufficed for the query tasks they had to do. They welcomed the idea of a natural language query interface, and found NaLIX easy to use. The average participants' levels of satisfaction with NaLIX was 4.11 on a scale of 1 to 5, where 5 denotes "extremely easy to use."

**Search quality.** Figure 12 compares the average precision and recall of NaLIX with that of a keyword search interface in the experiment. As can be seen, the search quality of natural language queries was consistently better than that of keyword search queries. The precision of NaLIX is 83.0% on average, with an average precision of 70.9% for the worst query; for 2 out of the 9 search tasks, NaLIX achieved perfect recall, with an average recall of 90.1% for all the queries and an average recall of 79.4% for the worst query. In contrast, keyword search performed poorly on most of the search tasks[8], especially on those requiring complex manipulations such as aggregation or sorting (e.g. Q7, Q10). Even for queries with simple constant search conditions and requiring no further manipulation (e.g. Q4, Q11), keyword searches produced results that were less than desirable.

In our experiments, we found two major factors contributing to search quality loss for NaLIX. First, the participants sometimes failed to write a natural language query that matched the exact task description. For instance, one of the users expressed Q6 as "List books with title and authors" (rather than only list the title and authors of the book), resulting in a loss of precision. The second had to do with parsing error. Given

---

[8] Each search task corresponds to an "XMP" query in [31] with the same task number.

**Table 7.** Average Precision and Recall

|  | avg.precision | avg.recall | total queries |
|---|---|---|---|
| all queries | 83.0% | 90.1% | 162 |
| all queries specified correctly | 91.4% | 97.8% | 120 |
| all queries specified parsed correctly | 95.1% | 97.6% | 112 |

a generic natural language query, it is sometimes difficult to determine what exactly should be returned, and the parse tree obtained may be incorrect.[9] For example, one of the users formulated Q1 as "List books published by Addison-Wesley after 1991, including their year and title." Minipar wrongly determined that only "book" and "title" depended on "List," and failed to recognize the conjunctive relationship between "year" and "title." Consequently, NaLIX failed to return *year* elements in the result, resulting in a loss of both precision and recall. Table 7 presents summary statistics to tease out the contributions of these two factors. If one considers only the 112 of 162 queries that were specified and parsed correctly, then the error rate (how much less than perfect are the precision and recall) is roughly reduced by 75%, and NaLIX achieved average precision and recall of 95.1% and 97.6%, respectively, in the experiments.

## 6 Related Work

In the information retrieval field, research efforts have long been made on natural language interfaces that take keyword search query as the target language [5, 8]. In recent years, keyword search interfaces to databases have begun to receive increasing attention [6, 10, 11, 12, 16, 18], and have been considered a first step towards addressing the challenge of natural language querying. Our work builds upon this stream of research. However, our system is not a simple imitation of those in information retrieval field in that it supports a richer query mechanism that allow us to convey much more complex semantic meaning than pure keyword search.

Extensive research has been done on developing natural language interfaces to databases (NLIDB), especially during the 1980's [2]. The architecture of our system bears most similarity to syntax-based NLIDBs, where the resulting parse tree of a user query is directly mapped into a database query expression. However, previous syntax-based NLIDBs, such as LUNAR [35], interface to application-specific database systems, and depend on the database query languages specially designed to facilitate the mapping from the parse tree to the database query [2]. Our system, in contrast, uses a generic query language, XQuery, as our target language. In addition, unlike previous systems such as the one reported in [29], our system does not rely on extensive domain-specific knowledge.

The idea of interactive NLIDB has been discussed in some early NLIDB literature [2, 15]. The majority of these focus on generating cooperative responses using query results obtained from a database with respect to a user's task(s). In contrast, the focus of the interactive process of our system is purely query formulation: only one query is actually evaluated against the database. There has also been work to build interactive query interfaces to facilitate query formulation [14, 34]. These works depend on domain-specific knowledge. Also, they assist the construction of structured queries rather than natural language queries.

---

[9] Minipar achieves about 88% precision and 80% recall with respect to dependency relations with the SUSANNE Corpus [19].

There are a few notable recent works on NLIDB ([21, 22, 23, 30]). A learning approach as a combination of learning methods is presented in [30]. We view such learning approaches and our approach as complimentary to each other - while learning techniques may help NaLIX to expand its linguistic coverage, NaLIX can provide training sources for a learning system. A NLIDB based on a query formulator is described in [21]. A statistical approach is applied to determine the meaning of a keyword. The keywords can then be categorized into query topics, selection list, and query constraints as the input of query formulator. No experimental evaluation on the effectiveness of the system has been reported. PRECISION [22, 23] is a NLIDB that translates *semantically tractable* NL questions into corresponding SQL queries. While PRECISION extensively depends on database schema for query mapping, NaLIX does not rely on the availability of a schema for query translation. In addition, PRECISION requires each database attribute be manually assigned with a compatible *wh-value*, while NaLIX does not. Finally, NaLIX covers a much broader range of natural language questions than PRECISION with promising quality.

In NaLIX, we obtain the semantic relationships between words via a dependency parser. Recent work in question answering [3, 7, 9] has pointed out the value of utilizing the dependency relation between words in English sentence to improve the precision of question answering. Such dependency relations are obtained either from dependency parsers such as Minipar [3, 7] or through statistic training [9]. These works all focus on full text retrieval, and thus cannot directly apply to XML databases. Nevertheless, they inspired us to use a dependency parser to obtain semantic relationship between words, as we have done in NaLIX.

## 7 Conclusion and Future Work

We have described a natural language query interface for a database. A large class of natural language queries can be translated into XQuery expressions that can then be evaluated against an XML database. Where natural language queries outside this class are posed, an interactive feedback mechanism is described to lead the user to pose an acceptable query. The ideas described in this paper have been implemented, and actual user experience gathered. Our system as it stands supports comparison predicates, conjunctions, simple negation, quantification, nesting, aggregation, value joins, and sorting. In the future, we plan to add support for disjunction, for multi-sentence queries, for complex negation, and for composite result construction. Our current system is oriented at structured XML databases: we intend to incorporate support for phrase matching by incorporating full-text techniques in XQuery such as TeXQuery [1], thereby extending our applicability to databases primarily comprising text stored as XML.

The system as we have it, even without all these planned extensions, is already very useful in practice. We already have a request for production deployment by a group outside computer science. We expect the work described in this paper to lead to a whole new generation of query interfaces for databases.

## References

1. S. Amer-Yahia et al. TeXQuery: A full-text search extension to XQuery. In *WWW*, 2004.
2. I. Androutsopoulos et al. Natural language interfaces to databases - an introduction. *Journal of Language Engineering*, 1(1):29–81, 1995.
3. G. Attardi et al. PiQASso: Pisa question answering system. In *TREC*, 2001.

4. M. J. Bates. The design of browsing and berrypicking techniques for the on-line search interface. *Online Review*, 13(5):407–431, 1989.
5. J. Chu-carroll et al. A hybrid approach to natural language Web search. In *EMNLP*, 2002.
6. S. Cohen et al. XSEarch: A semantic search engine for XML. In *VLDB*, 2003.
7. H. Cui et al. Question answering passage retrieval using dependency relations. In *SIGIR*, 2005.
8. S. V. Delden and F. Gomez. Retrieving NASA problem reports: a case study in natural language information retrieval. *Data & Knowledge Engineering*, 48(2):231–246, 2004.
9. J. Gao et al. Dependency language model for information retrieval. In *SIGIR*, 2004.
10. L. Guo et al. XRANK: Ranked keyword search over XML documents. In *SIGMOD*, 2003.
11. V. Hristidis et al. Keyword proximity search on XML graphs. In *ICDE*, 2003.
12. A. Hulgeri et al. Keyword search in databases. *IEEE Data Engineering Bulletin*, 24:22–32, 2001.
13. H. V. Jagadish et al. Timber: A native xml database. *The VLDB Journa*, 11(4):274–291, 2002.
14. E. Kapetanios and P. Groenewoud. Query construction through meaningful suggestions of terms. In *FQAS*, 2002.
15. D. Kupper et al. NAUDA: A cooperative natural language interface to relational databases. *SIGMOD Record*, 22(2):529–533, 1993.
16. Y. Li et al. Schema-Free XQuery. In *VLDB*, 2004.
17. Y. Li et al. NaLIX: an interactive natural language interface for querying XML. In *SIGMOD*, 2005.
18. Y. Li et al. Enabling Schema-Free XQuery with Meaningful Query Focus. *To appear in VLDB Journal*, 2006.
19. D. Lin. Dependency-based evaluation of MINIPAR. In *Workshop on the Evaluation of Parsing Systems*, 1998.
20. I. A. Mel'čuk. *Studies in dependency syntax*. Karoma Publishers, Ann Arbor, MI, 1979.
21. F. Meng and W. Chu. Database query formation from natural language using semantic modeling and statistical keyword meaning disambiguation. Technical Report 16, UCLA, 1999.
22. A.-M. Popescu et al. Towards a theory of natural language interfaces to databases. In *IUI*, 2003.
23. A.-M. Popescu et al. Modern natural language interfaces to databases: Composing statistical parsing with semantic tractability. In *COLING*, 2004.
24. R. Quirk et al. *A Comprehensive Grammar of the English Language*. Longman, London, 1985.
25. J. R. Remde et al. Superbook: an automatic tool for information exploration - hypertext? In *Hypertext*, pages 175–188. ACM Press, 1987.
26. A. Schmidt et al. Querying XML documents made easy: Nearest concept queries. *ICDE*, 2001.
27. W. Shaw Jr. et al. Performance standards and evaluations in IR test collections: Cluster-based retrieval modles. *Information Processing and Management*, 33(1):1–14, 1997.
28. D. Sleator and D. Temperley. Parsing English with a link grammar. In *International Workshop on Parsing Technologies*, 1993.
29. D. Stallard. A terminological transformation for natural language question-answering systems. In *ANLP*, 1986.
30. L. R. Tang and R. J. Mooney. Using multiple clause constructors in inductive logic programming for semantic parsing. In *ECML*, 2001.
31. The World Wide Web Consortium. XML Query Use Cases. W3C Working Draft. Available at http://www.w3.org/TR/xquery-use-cases, 2003.
32. The World Wide Web Consortium. Extensible Markup Language (XML) 1.0 (Third Edition). W3C Recommendation. Available at http://www.w3.org/TR/REC-xml, 2004.
33. Timber: http://www.eecs.umich.edu/db/timber.
34. A. Trigoni. Interactive query formulation in semistructured databases. In *FQAS*, 2002.
35. W. Woods et al. *The Lunar Sciences Natural Language Information System: Final Report*. Bolt Beranek and Newman Inc., Cambridge, MA, 1972.
36. WordNet: http://www.cogsci.princeton.edu/~wn.

# A New Design for a Native XML Storage and Indexing Manager

Jihad Boulos and Shant Karakashian

Department of Computer Science,
American University of Beirut,
P.O.Box 11-0236 Riad El-Solh,
Beirut, Lebanon.
{boulos, smk09}@aub.edu.lb

**Abstract.** This paper describes the design and implementation of an XML storage manager for fast and interactive XPath expressions evaluation. This storage manager has two main parts: the XML data storage structure and the index over this data. The system is designed in such a way that it minimizes the number of page reads for retrieving any XPath expression results while avoiding the shortcomings of previous work on storing XML data where the index must adapt to the most frequent queries. Hence, the main advantage of our index is that it can handle any new XPath expression without any need for adaptation. We show comparable performance of our design by presenting path evaluation results of our index against those of the currently most known index on documents of different sizes.

## 1 Introduction

This paper presents a new storage manager and its indexing scheme for XML data. XML is becoming widely used for data exchange and manipulation in local but mostly distributed environments. It is becoming the foundation of the semi-structured and labeled graph data model where this data can be irregular and/or incomplete and consisting of atomic or composite elements that are nested in a hierarchical manner. This storage manager is part of the Al𝒳emist [1] project that we are designing and implementing for processing XQuery queries on stored and streaming XML data.

There have been many proposals for native XML storage managers and indexing schemes (*e.g.* [2,3]). Contrary to the widely used approach in these systems where the storage keeps subtree nodes physically close to each other, our scheme only considers the depth and the element name for physical proximity. The logical structure information is preserved by a now classic element numbering scheme. We store XML elements through a breadth-first data layout instead of depth-first; this last approach is mostly adopted for storing and retrieving document subtrees in the same data pages, and this is probably the main reason for its adoption by most previous data layouts. However, we show that our breadth-first design does not have the subtree reconstruction performance hit that one may imagine for the most typical queries. We use a layered approach for storing XML documents and building indexes on them, and this approach demonstrates comparable performances to those of the currently most known approaches for retrieving both document subtrees and elements only as results for XPath expressions. Our approach, however, does not need to force an adaptation of the index to the most frequent XPath expressions, but is most general and can handle any new expression.

XQuery is fast becoming the de-facto querying language for XML data. It is based on XPath querying and matching. A path expression matches a node in the XML tree if the path from the root to the node has the same sequence of labels as the path expression. Paths also might have ancestor-descendant (*i.e.* //), wildcard elements (*i.e.* /*) and branches. A naive evaluation of path expressions may require a complete scan of the document; this is too expensive for large documents where these documents do not fit in memory (the same also can be said about memory-resident documents). For this reason, we propose a structural summary index that has a tree structure, summarizing the nodes of the indexed XML document. The size of the index tree remains much smaller than the size of the document (more on that to come). Evaluating an XPath expression on the index and retrieving the resultant elements from the data pages prevent the scan of the whole document tree. Unlike other structural summary indexes (*e.g.* [4–7]) that require being adapted to the most frequent path expressions (FUP's), our index is a general one that can be used to evaluate any path expression without any pre-processing.

The rest of the paper is organized as follows: In Section 2 we mention some related work. We then describe in Section 3 our data layout design for XML documents and then in Section 4 the design of our index. In Section 5, our XPath expression matching algorithm is presented and then in Section 6 the results of some experiments are presented. We conclude in Section 7.

## 2 Related Work

Several mapping techniques have been proposed [8–11] for storing XML documents in flat tables of relational databases. [8–10] consider XML documents as graphs, and store these graph nodes with their edges in relational database tables. [11] presents a mapping that explores the XML data and creates a mapping to a relational database, separating the objects by their types. The rationale behind this mapping is to use the mature RDBMS technology in indexing and querying XML documents. For this purpose, [9] proposes algorithms for translating XPath expressions to SQL. [8] also proposes a similar conversion from Quilt to SQL.

XML database systems like [2, 3] store XML documents in native storage managers. These systems relieve the processing from additional layers for mapping the logical data to the physical layout, which eventually slows down query processing [12]. [2] stores subtrees in clustered physical pages, and [3] stores XML documents in pre-order traversal in order to cluster sub-elements together.

We also store the XML documents natively, but we store them in breadth-first order, without clustering the elements with their subelements. We cluster only elements of the same name and depth together.

A number of structural indexes for XML have been proposed (*e.g.* [4–7, 13]). These indexes are structural summaries of the target XML documents and are based on the notion of bisimilarity. Two nodes are bisimilar if they have identical label paths. Bisimilar nodes are grouped together in one index node. The 1-Index [14] was the first to propose the idea of bisimilarity. It can answer path expressions of any size without referring to the data nodes. The drawback of the 1-Index is that the size of the index depends upon the regularity of the data graph. For irregular data graphs, the size may become quite large, and the path evaluation time, being proportional to the size of the index node, may also become too high. In many cases where long path expressions are not used, the 1-index may not be necessary. The A($k$)-Index was proposed to overcome these shortcomings and is based on the notion of $k$-bisimilarity. A($k$)-Index can answer, without referring to the data graph, path expressions of lengths at most $k$, where this last value controls the resolution of the index and influences its size in a proportional manner. For large $k$ values, the size of the index may grow to large sizes, and have the same problem as the 1-Index. For small values of $k$, the size of the index can be substantially smaller, but cannot handle long path expressions.

To accommodate path expressions of various lengths, without unnecessarily increasing the size of the whole index, D($k$)-Index [5] was proposed. This index can assign different $k$ values for different index nodes. These $k$ values are assigned to be in conformance with a given set of frequently used path expressions (FUP's). For parts of the index corresponding to parts of the data graph targeted by long path expressions, large values of $k$ are assigned, and small values of $k$ are assigned for parts corresponding to data targeted by short path expressions. To facilitate the evaluation of path expressions with branching, UD($k, l$)-Index [6] was proposed. It is similar to A($k$)-Index, but also imposes downwards similarity.

A D($k$)-Index builds a coarser index than an A($k$)-Index, but has the problem of over-refinement. [7] identifies four types of over-refinements, and proposes the M($k$)-Index as a solution for all of them. M*($k$)-Index (again in [7]) is an extension to the M($k$)-Index and is in fact the combination of several M($k$)-Indexes in such a way that each one of these has a different resolution. This design solves the problem of large scan space in the index, while the path coverage is not affected. The drawback of this design is inherited from the D($k$)-Index and is the requirement to adapt to a given list of FUP's.

Our proposed U($*$)-Index (for Universal-generic) also uses the notion of bisimilarity in a relatively similar way to the 1-Index. However, and in order to overcome the problem of large search space for XPath evaluation on the index, we use a special labeling scheme of index nodes that enables the pruning of the search space. More importantly, our index does not need to be adapted to any particular list of FUP's; it has a uniform resolution and hence is more generic.

## 3 Data Layout

We describe in this section how an XML document is shredded in stored data pages. As we mentioned earlier, and contrary to previous approaches, we store XML elements (and their related attributes and text) according to their depths and names. We came in fact to this design after designing, implementing and testing several other approaches. We show in the experimental results section, and contrary to previously believed common sense, that the reconstruction of a result subtree is not as expensive as it was thought to be for the most common queries. This is mainly justified by the relatively few levels in most XML schemas (and hence documents). Moreover, as XPath expressions get longer, the height of their resulting trees get smaller, which reduces even more the cost of subtree reconstruction. For queries with large result sizes, subtree reconstruction is always quite expensive.

### 3.1 Data Shredding

To store an XML document in disk pages, we partition it by element depth and name. All elements named $e$ at depth $i$ belong to the same partition (called "extent" on the storage device). All elements belonging to the same extent are stored in a chain of contiguously clustered pages. With this scheme, all elements in a chain have the same depth and element name. The algorithm that builds these chains is not mentioned here due to space limits but is simple to explain. While scanning an original XML document, pages in memory are created and filled according to the conditions mentioned above (*i.e.* names and levels). When a page is filled, it is saved at its designated disk page in the extent dedicated to that chain of pages.

### 3.2 Enumeration

In order to preserve the structural information of the XML document in the stored pages, two position numbers are assigned to and stored with each element in the data pages: the start index ($sIndex$) and the end index ($eIndex$) [15]. The $sIndex$ of element $e$ is the depth-first order of $e$ in the document tree (starting with 0 for the root). An $sIndex$ is unique in a document. The $eIndex$ of element $e$ is the greatest $sIndex$ in the subtree of $e$. If $e$ is a leaf, then $sIndex = eIndex$. More than one element can have the same $eIndex$. The $eIndex$, $sIndex$ and the depth of an element are necessary and sufficient to reconstruct the XML document tree from the stored structure. The depth of an element does not need to be stored with an element since it is retrieved from the storage structure. Fig. 1 shows how a sample XMark [16] XML document fragment is numbered.

### 3.3 Internal Representation

Fig. 2 shows the internal page representation of the document shown in Fig. 1. A page holds variable sized elements, and is filled until the next element does not fit in. Each rectangle in Fig. 2 represents a disk page (other details of this

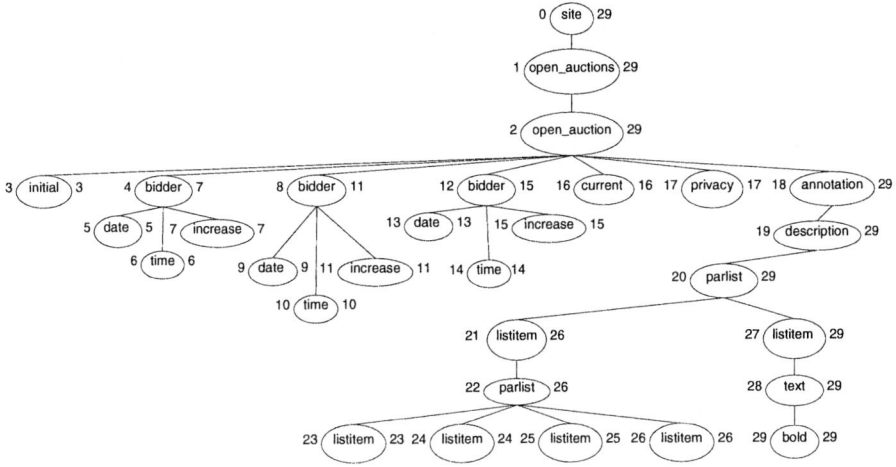

**Fig. 1.** A sample XMark-fragment document tree

| Depth | | | |
|---|---|---|---|
| 0 | site | : | 0(0) |
| 1 | open_auctions | : | 1(1) |
| 2 | open_auction | : | 2(2) |
| 3 | initial | : | 3(3) |
|   | bidder | : | 4(4) 8(4) 12(4) |
|   | current | : | 16(8) |
|   | privacy | : | 17(9) |
|   | annotation | : | 18(10) |

| | | | | |
|---|---|---|---|---|
| 4 | date | : | 5(5) 9(5) 13(5) | |
|   | time | : | 6(6) 10(6) 14(6) | |
|   | increase | : | 7(7) 11(7) 15(7) | |
|   | description | : | 19(11) | |
| 5 | parlist | : | 20(12) | |
| 6 | listitem | : | 21(13) 27(16) | |
| 7 | parlist | : | 22(14) | |
|   | text | : | 28(17) | |
| 8 | listitem | : | 23(15) 24(15) 25(15) | 26(15) |
|   | bold | : | 29(18) | |

**Fig. 2.** The stored pages of the data in Fig. 1

figure are presented in the following section). For clarity, it is assumed that each page can hold a maximum of 3 elements. An element is stored with its name, *sIndex*, *eIndex* (these are the numbers to the left and to the right of nodes in Fig. 1), and eventually its attribute names and values, and its *text()* value. A crucial point to notice here is that elements are stored in page chains ordered by *sIndex*. The index tree for our running example is shown in Fig. 3 and is explained in the next Section.

## 4 Structural Index

Our main contribution in this paper is a disk resident structural summary index for XML documents that we call U(∗)-Index. This index is constructed on an XML document independent of path expressions and how the XML data is stored in data pages. Hence, it evaluates path expressions without requiring any

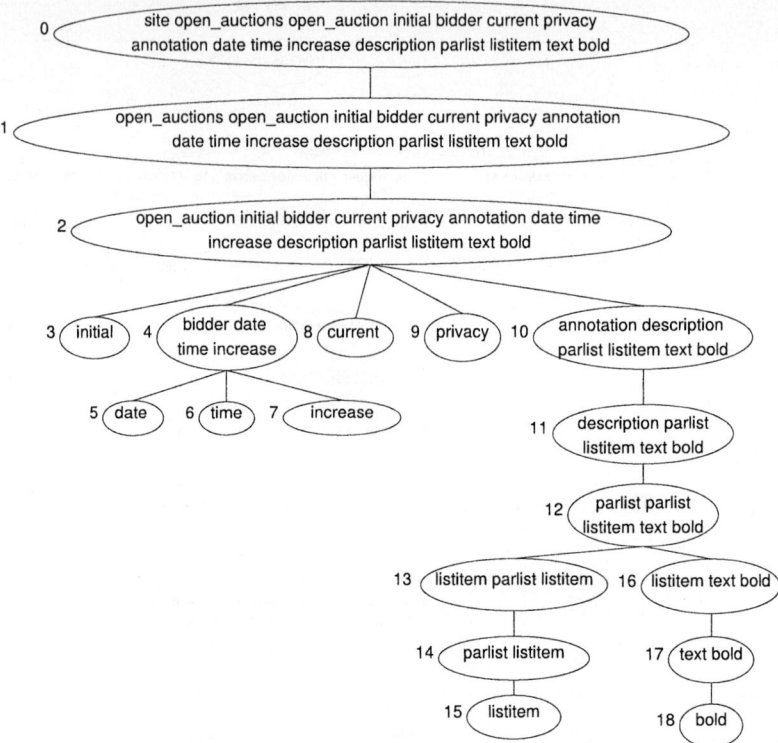

**Fig. 3.** The structure index of the document in Fig. 1

adaptation or index structure modification to specific path expressions and is detached from how the XML data is clustered in data pages.

Each index node points to a group of elements in data pages. All elements pointed to by an index node $i$ have the same name, depth, *subtree label (SL)* and path label sequence from the document root. The depth of $i$ is equal to the depth of the elements pointed to by $i$.

**Definition 1 (Subtree Label ($SL$)).** *The Subtree Label of a node $i$ is the sorted list of all distinct element names in the subtree of $i$. E.g. the SL of index node corresponding to root "a" in document: $<a><c><b/><b/><a/><$ $/c><$ /a $>$ is "abc". The SL of a leaf node is the empty string $\varepsilon$.*

For an index node $i$, the path label sequence from the root of the index tree to $i$ is the same as the path label sequence of all elements pointed to by $i$ from the root of the XML document. The parent of an element $e$ pointed to by index node $i$ is pointed to by the parent node of $i$. Similarly, the children of $e$ are pointed to by index node(s) that are the children of $i$ in the index tree. Algorithm 1. is a trivial algorithm that shows how the skeleton of an index is constructed and Algorithm 2. shows how an index node is labeled. These two algorithms are quite simple and clear. Algorithm 3. compresses the index by grouping the nodes

### Algorithm 1. Index Construction

ConstructIndex ($DocumentRoot, indexRoot$)
1:   $indexRoot.elementName = DocumentRoot.elementName$
2:   $indexRoot.SL = \epsilon$
3:   **for all** $child \in indexRoot.children$ **do**
4:     $indexRoot$.addChild($e$)
5:     ConstructIndex ($child, e$)
6:   **end for**
7:   LabelIndex ($indexRoot$)
8:   Compress ($indexRoot$)


### Algorithm 2. Index Labeling

LabelIndex ($root$)
1:   **for all** $child \in root.children$ **do**
2:     LabelIndex ($child$)
3:     $root.SL = child.elementName \cup root.SL$
4:     $root.SL = child.SL \cup root.SL$
5:   **end for**


### Algorithm 3. Index Compression

Compress ($root$)
1:   **for all** $e \in root.children$ **do**
2:     **for all** $e' \in root.children$ **do**
3:       **if** $e.elementName == e'.elementName$ & $e.SL == e'.SL$ **then**
4:         $e.extent = e.extent \cup e'.extent$
5:         $e.children = e.children \cup e'.children$
6:         Delete $e'$
7:       **end if**
8:     **end for**
9:   **end for**
10: **for all** $child \in root.children$ **do**
11:     Compress ($child$)
12: **end for**


based on the criteria mentioned above (*i.e.* element name, depth, $SL$, and path label from root).

Fig. 3 shows the index tree for the XML document in Fig. 1. The names in the ovals are the name of the index node, followed by the $SL$. The numbers to the left of the nodes in Fig. 3 are fictitious and added only for clarity. These are the same numbers between parenthesis in Fig. 2 and are shown in this paper for the reader to make the connection between the index nodes and the data pages. *E.g.* the elements pointed to by the index node 4 have $sIndex$ 4, 8, and 12.

## 4.1 Index Node

An index node $i$ in U(*)-Index is identified by its name, depth and $SL$. The name of an index node is the name $e$ of the elements it points to (they all have the same name $e$). The depth is equal to the depth of these element(s), and the $SL$ of that index node corresponds to the $SL$ of the data nodes pointed to by $i$. No more than one index node can exist having the same name, $SL$ and parent. Every index node has at least one pointer to an element in the data pages. With every pointer, $i$ also contains the $sIndex$ and $eIndex$ of the pointed element. E.g. the node 4 of the index in Fig. 3 is of depth 3 and of name "bidder"; All elements pointed to by it are also necessarily and exclusively in the pages of elements of depth 3 and name "bidder" (Fig. 2). However, it is not necessarily true that all elements in element pages of the same depth and the same name be pointed to by the same index node (e.g. elements "listitem" of depth 6 in Fig 2). Fig. 4 shows in a more visual manner how the nodes of an XML document are mapped to the nodes of their index.

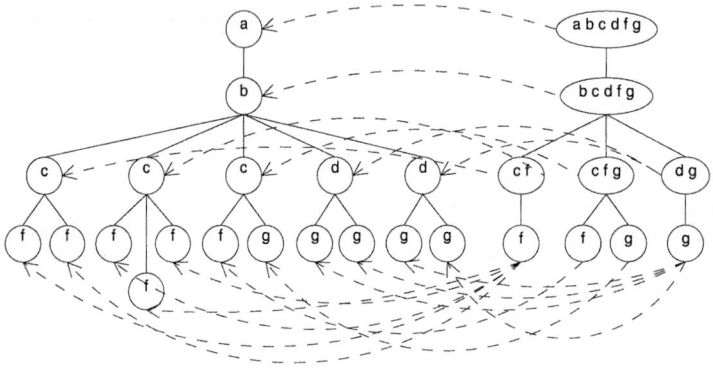

**Fig. 4.** Sample XML document mapping to its index

## 4.2 Index Disk Pages

At the implementation level, there are two different internal page structures that make an index. Each one of these page types makes a chain of contiguously clustered disk pages. These two page types are respectively shown on the left and right in Fig. 5. The first chain contains for each index node the name, $SL$, the pointers to its children index nodes, a count of the number of instances for that element, and a pointer to the location in the second chain holding the pointers to the element(s) in the XML document storage. The order of index nodes stored in this chain is the depth-first ordering of the index tree. In the second chain, we store the pointers to elements in the XML document storage (i.e. data pages). With each pointer $P$, we store the $sIndex$ and $eIndex$ of the element pointed to by $P$.

| CI | Name | SL | Children | PC | SPL |
|---|---|---|---|---|---|
| 0 | site | open_auctions ... | 1 | 1 | 0 |
| 1 | open_auctions | open_auction initial ... | 2 | 1 | 1 |
| 2 | open_auction | initial bidder current ... | 3, 4, 8, 9, 10 | 1 | 2 |
| 3 | initial | | | 1 | 3 |
| 4 | bidder | date time increase | 5, 6, 7 | 3 | 4 |
| 5 | date | | | 3 | 7 |
| 6 | time | | | 3 | 10 |
| 7 | increase | | | 3 | 13 |
| 8 | current | | | 1 | 16 |
| 9 | privacy | | | 1 | 17 |
| 10 | annotation | description parlist ... | 11 | 1 | 18 |
| 11 | description | parlist listitem text ... | 12 | 1 | 19 |
| 12 | parlist | parlist listitem text ... | 13, 16 | 1 | 20 |
| 13 | listitem | parlist listitem | 14 | 1 | 21 |
| 14 | parlist | listitem | 15 | 1 | 22 |
| 15 | listitem | | | 3 | 23 |
| 16 | listitem | text bold | 17 | 1 | 27 |
| 17 | text | bold | 18 | 1 | 28 |
| 18 | bold | | | 1 | 29 |

| CI | sIndex | eIndex | P |
|---|---|---|---|
| 0 | 0 | 29 | |
| 1 | 1 | 29 | |
| 2 | 2 | 29 | |
| 3 | 3 | 3 | |
| 4 | 12 | 15 | |
| 5 | 4 | 7 | |
| 6 | 8 | 11 | |
| 7 | 5 | 5 | |
| 8 | 9 | 9 | |
| 9 | 13 | 13 | |

| CI | sIndex | eIndex | P |
|---|---|---|---|
| 10 | 14 | 14 | |
| 11 | 10 | 10 | |
| 12 | 6 | 6 | |
| 13 | 15 | 15 | |
| 14 | 11 | 11 | |
| 15 | 7 | 7 | |
| 16 | 16 | 16 | |
| 17 | 17 | 17 | |
| 18 | 18 | 29 | |
| 19 | 19 | 29 | |

| CI | sIndex | eIndex | P |
|---|---|---|---|
| 20 | 20 | 29 | |
| 21 | 21 | 26 | |
| 22 | 22 | 26 | |
| 23 | 24 | 24 | |
| 24 | 25 | 25 | |
| 25 | 26 | 26 | |
| 26 | 23 | 23 | |
| 27 | 27 | 29 | |
| 28 | 28 | 29 | |
| 29 | 29 | 29 | |

**Fig. 5.** Sample index layout

Within this second chain of pages, entries are logically grouped together according to the pointers from the first type of pages and their counters; each group belongs to an index node. Physically the pages in the second chain contain entries where each one of these makes a sequence of four integers. Fig. 5 shows in fact how the conceptual index tree is stored in disk pages. Each block represents a physical disk page. The three wide blocks belong to the first chain, and the three other blocks belong to the second chain. Columns "CI" in both page types denote a logical address for that tuple. Column "Children" shows the "CI's" of the children nodes, "PC" the number of pointers in the group associated with the index node in the second chain. "SPL" shows the position of the group of pointers in the second chain. The small arrows in the last column of the second chain stand for the pointers pointing to the XML data. The groups are ordered in the same order as the index nodes in the first chain. Each group constitutes the *extent* of its index node.

### 4.3 Index Size

The cost of path expression evaluation is directly proportional to the size of the index tree. The limit size of the index tree depends upon the number of distinct element names and the maximum depth of a specific XML document. An index node $i$ can have a maximum of $n2^n$ children ($n$ if children are leafs), where $n$ is the number of distinct element names in the subtree rooted by $i$. This limit is reached when for every distinct element name "$m$" in the subtree of $i$, there are $2^n$ subtrees, rooted by $2^n$ "$m$"'s, all children of $i$, with each "$m$" having a distinct $SL$. This limit is unlikely to be reached for the following reasons: first, it is unlikely for a node to have a big number of children with distinct names; and second, it is unlikely for elements, with parents of the same name and of the same depth, to have a big number of distinct $SL$.

## 5 Path Expression Evaluation

The semantics of XPath makes it necessary to fetch as the result of an XPath expression the subtree rooted at the target element from the queried XML document. However, for XQuery several XPath expressions may exist in the *"For-Let-Where"* parts of the query and only predicates on the target elements (and/or on their attributes and *text()*) in these expressions are applied; hence, there is no need to fetch the whole subtrees for these expressions. Only expressions in the *"Return"* clause of an XQuery need the resulting subtrees if what is required is not explicitly stated as an element name and/or its *text()* value, or attributes for some elements. Our storage manager and U(*)-Index return both types of required results.

Path expressions requiring only target elements are evaluated using the index only, without accessing the document data pages. Attributes and *text()*'s of these target elements are fetched from data pages. U(*)-Index returns pointers to the locations of these elements in data pages and, for an element, it costs an average of one disk access to fetch its attributes and *text()*. Since elements at the same document level and with the same name are clustered together in data pages, we have here a high cache hit ratio. This is the main advantage of our data shredding layout.

The result of a path expression evaluation on the index contains exactly all the matches in the document. Consider an XML document $D$. Let $I$ be the U(*)-Index built on $D$. For any index node $i \in I$, the path label sequence from the root of $I$ to $i$ is the same as the path label sequence of all elements $e$ in $D$ that are pointed to by $i$. Also, all elements $e \in D$ satisfying a path expression $p$ are pointed to by index nodes $i$'s that satisfy $p$. Thus all $i$'s with path label sequence from root of $I$ to $i$ satisfying a path expression $p$ contain exactly all the matches of $p$ in $D$ (the statement is made in both directions to stress the point that it is equivalent to the *if and only if* condition). We explain next how our U(*)-Index is used in matching simple and branching expressions.

### 5.1 Evaluating Simple Expressions

Algorithm 4. is called recursively to evaluate an XPath expression. We next explain how this matching process is done on a sample XPath expression. Consider the *path* expression */site//open_auction/*/time* to be evaluated on the index in Fig. 3. Line 1 of the algorithm parses the *path* to get *separator1*="/", *label*="site", *separator2*="//" and *remainingPath*= "*open_auction/*/time*".

First, the algorithm checks if the index node under consideration (*indexRoot* in Algorithm 4.) has the same label as the head of *path* (line 3). After the check passes for *"site"*, it proceeds to check for branches in *path* (lines 4–10). If no branches are found in the path expression, it proceeds to line 11; otherwise, it pushes these branches on a stack. If the *label* is the leaf of *path*, it adds the extent (calling Algorithm 5.) of the node *indexRoot* to the results (lines 11–12). While the *remainingPath* is not empty, it prepares to evaluate *remainingPath* on *indexRoot*'s children.

## Algorithm 4. XPath Evaluation

Evaluate $(path, indexRoot)$
1:  $separator1.label.separator2.remainingPath = path$
2:  $branchAdded = 0$
3:  **if** $indexRoot.elementName == label$ **then**
4:    **while** $separator2 = $ '[' **do**
5:      branch=getBranch($remainingPath$)
6:      '['...']'.$remainingPath = remainingPath$
7:      pushBranchToStack($branch, indexRoot$)
8:      $branchAdded = branchAdded + 1$
9:      $separator2.remainingPath = remainingPath$
10:    **end while**
11:    **if** $remainingPath = \epsilon$ **then**
12:      $result = result \cup$ returnExtent($indexRoot$)
13:    **else**
14:      **if** subtreeContains($indexRoot, remainingPath$) **then**
15:        **for all** $child \in indexRoot.children$ **do**
16:          $result = result \cup$ Evaluate ($separator2.remainingPath, child$)
17:        **end for**
18:      **end if**
19:    **end if**
20:  **end if**
21:  **if** $separator1 == $ '//' **then**
22:    **if** subtreeContains($indexRoot, path$) **then**
23:      **for all** $child \in indexRoot.children$ **do**
24:        $result = result \cup$ Evaluate ($path, child$)
25:      **end for**
26:    **end if**
27:  **end if**
28:  **while** $branchAdded \geq 0$ **do**
29:    popBranchFromStack()
30:    $branchAdded = branchAdded - 1$
31:  **end while**
32:  **return** $result$

Since every index node has a list of element names in its subtree ($SL$), Algorithm 6. is called in line 14 to check for any possibility of matches for the *remaining Path* in the subtree of *indexRoot*. Algorithm 6. checks for every *label* in *path* its availability in the index subtree rooted by *indexRoot*. This check is done by simply scanning the *SL* of *indexRoot*. This algorithm helps in pruning unpromising branches in the index and hence speeds up a lot the matching process.

On our running example, the *remainingPath* has labels "*open_auction*" and "*time*", and both are found in the *SL* "*open_auctions...*" of node 0 in Fig. 3, so we recursively call *Evaluate* on the children of *indexRoot* with *separator2. remainingPath* which is currently "*//open_auction/*/time*". In this recursive call, *separator1*= "*//*", *label*= "*open_auction*", *separator2*= "*/*" and *remaining − Path*= "**/time*". The condition in line 3 fails, because *indexRoot.element*

**Algorithm 5.** Return Extent

returnExtent $(indexNode)$
1: **for all** $(branch, stackIndexNode)$ in stack **do**
2:    **if** $\neg$ Evaluated$(branchExtent[branch])$ **then**
3:       $branchExtent[branch]$=Evaluate $(branch, stackIndexNode)$
4:    **end if**
5: **end for**
6: **for all** $e \in indexNode.extent$ **do**
7:    $matched = true$
8:    **for all** $(branch, stackIndexNode)$ in stack **do**
9:       **if** $\nexists\ b \in branchExtent[branch]\ |\ \exists\ p \in stackIndexNode.extent$ and $e.sIndex \geq p.sIndex$ and $e.eIndex \leq p.eIndex$ and $b.sIndex \geq p.sIndex$ and $b.eIndex \leq p.eIndex$ **then**
10:          $matched = false$
11:       **end if**
12:    **end for**
13:    **if** $matched = true$ **then**
14:       $result = result \cup e$
15:    **end if**
16: **end for**
17: **return** $result$

**Algorithm 6.** Subtree Contains Elements

subtreeContains $(indexRoot, path)$
1: **for all** $label \in path$ **do**
2:    **if** $label \notin indexRoot.SL$ **then**
3:       **return** $false$
4:    **end if**
5: **end for**
6: **return** $true$

$Name =$ "$open\_auctions$" and $label =$ "$open\_auction$". Since $separator1=$"$//$", the $label$ "$open\_auction$" is to be evaluated for all descendants of $indexRoot$. Line 24 recursively calls $Evaluate$ on the children of $indexRoot$ to evaluate "$//open\_auction/*/time$" after checking for the possible availability of "$open\_auction$" and "$time$" in $SL$ of $indexRoot$ which is "$open\_auction\ldots$" (node 1 in Fig. 3) in line 22. $indexRoot$ "$open\_auctions$" has only one child "$open\_auction$" that matches the $label$ in the following recursive call. The condition in line 14 is satisfied, and $Evaluate$ is called with $separator2.remainingPath$ "$/*/time$" for the children of index node named "$open\_auction$". For all calls of $Evaluate$ on the children of "$open\_auction$" with $path =$ "$/*/time$", the condition in line 3 would evaluate to $true$, since $label$ is a wildcard, but the condition in line 14 will fail for all but "$bidder$", since only index node "$bidder$" has "$time$" in its $SL$. The recursive call of $Evaluate$ will continue for index nodes "$date$", "$time$" and "$increase$" with path expression "$/time$". The condition in line 3 will fail for *"date"* and *"increase"* and only *"time"* will jump to line 12 because $remainingPath = \epsilon$. Algorithm 5. is then called and it simply returns the extents of *"time"*.

## 5.2 Evaluating Branching Expressions

Evaluating branches in an XPath expression happens only when the target index node for that expression (*i.e.* the index node corresponding to the leaf element in the expression) has been reached. This evaluation is cached until the depth-first scan of the index tree backtracks the branching index node. Again, running an example here may be the most appropriate way to explain how branches are evaluated. Let's consider a simpler version of our previous example and add a branching expression to it so it becomes /site//open_auction/bidder[./date]/time.

After encountering the *"/date"* branching in line 4 of Algorithm 4., it is pushed onto a global stack along with the branching index node *"bidder"*. The matching process proceeds as it was explained in the previous section, up until a *"time"* element matches. At that time, and while fetching the extent of *"time"* in Algorithm 5., the *"/date"* branching is evaluated on the subtree rooted by *"bidder"*, if it hasn't been evaluated previously. For each extent of *"time"*, Algorithm 5. checks in line 9 if it matches a *"date"* extent with the same parent *"bidder"*; if so, it adds that *"time"* extent to the results. When the recursive call that pushed that branch onto the stack reaches line 28 (*i.e.* backtracks the branching node), it pops up that branch from the stack and deletes it.

## 5.3 Analysis

We present in this subsection some analysis on the average size of a U(*)-Index for a certain XML document and on the average evaluation cost for an XPath expression relative to its characteristics.

*Index Size:* Consider a schema for an XML document of depth $d$ and let $\mu$ be the average schema child count, and $\nu$ be the average schema optional descendant count. Let $\alpha \in [0..1]$ be a parameter associated with the presence of the optional descendants; when $\alpha = 1$ then the appearance of the optional elements in subtrees makes all possible combinations (*i.e.* $2^\nu$), and when $\alpha = 0$ then the appearance of optional elements in subtrees makes a single combination. $\alpha$ is almost always very close to 0. Let $\mathcal{X}$ be the average number of nodes in the index tree; then

$$\mathcal{X} = \sum_{i=0}^{d}(\mu 2^{\alpha\nu})^i \qquad (1)$$

*Evaluation Cost:* Let $\beta$ be the number of nodes visited to evaluate a sub-path expression $p_j$ of the format *"separator label"* from an expression $p = p_1 p_2 \ldots p_n$ on an index node $i$, where *separator* can be "/" or "//", and *"label"* can be an element name or a wildcard. Let $d_i$ be the depth of that index node $i$ and $d_e$ be the depth of the deepest occurrence of element named *label*; then

$$\beta(p_j) = \begin{cases} 2^{\alpha\nu} & \text{if } label \neq * \text{ AND } separator = / \\ \mu 2^{\alpha\nu} & \text{if } label = * \text{ AND } separator = / \\ \sum_{x=d_i}^{d_e} (2^{\alpha\nu})^{x-d_i} & \text{if } label \neq * \text{ AND } separator = // \\ \sum_{x=d_i}^{d_e} (\mu 2^{\alpha\nu})^{x-d_i} & \text{if } label = * \text{ AND } separator = // \end{cases}$$

The overall cost of evaluating a path expression of depth $d_e$ is:

$$\prod_{j=1}^{n} \beta(p_j) \qquad (2)$$

For path expressions with branching, the additional cost for a branch is:

$$\sum_{\forall x} \beta(p_j)\beta(p_b) \qquad (3)$$

where $p_j$ is the separator and branching node label, $p_b$ is the separator and the branch leaf label and $x$ is the number of index nodes matching the branching node.

Although one can see that these formulae have exponential complexities, they are rarely exponential in reality because in most cases $\alpha \to 0$ and both $\mu$ and $\nu$ tend to 1 as the processing goes down the index tree.

## 6 Experimental Results

We present in this Section the performance results of our proposed data shredding scheme and its U(∗)-Index. The implementation of these two components went through several refinements, and we also implemented the D(k)-Index in order to compare its execution times against those of U(∗)-Index and to cross-check the correctness of our implementation by making sure that both indexes returned the same results for about 70 queries. The codes for the data page manager, U(∗)-Index and D(k)-Index were all implemented in Java and made about 15,000 lines of code. Both data loading and index building were performed from and into normal disk files. We conducted our experiments on a Pentium 4 machine with 3.2GHz processor and 512MB RAM, running Linux Fedora. The set of path expressions that were used in our experiments were always evaluated with an initially empty buffer. We ran in fact a large set of experiments where different parameters were varied. For lack of space, we only show here some representative results, but we would like to mention that with all the variations in the experiments, most results went in the same direction. For all performance results, the average of 5 runs for a query is reported here.

*Datasets:* We used as our data and path expressions the XMark benchmark [16] that is becoming widely used for its typical and representative data and queries. We generated documents of sizes 200, 400, 600, 800 and 1000 MB and loaded them into the storage manager and then built their indexes. The D(k) index was also built on the same data layout as U(∗), so that this data layout does not affect the performance comparison of the two indexes. For both U(∗)-Index and D(k)-Index, their sizes were about 25% of the XML document sizes.

*Path expressions:* We extracted a list of path expressions from XMark [16], and modified some of them to have path expressions with single, double and triple // along with their normal /; we also introduced path queries with wildcards and branches. The list of these expressions is shown in the technical report of this paper [1]. We also divided these expressions into six different classes according to the count of //, ∗, and branching present in an expression. Although we ran our experiments with about 70 XPath expressions, we report the results here of only 22 expressions for lack of space and similarity in the results.

*Performance comparison of U(∗) versus D(k):* Fig. 6 shows the results of both D(k) and U(∗) when evaluating the different queries on the five different data sizes. From this figure we can state that when the expressions are relatively simple (*e.g.* query classes 1, 2, and 3) the performance of both D(k) and U(∗) are comparable, with a slight advantage for U(∗). However, when the queries become complex (*e.g.* query classes 4, 5, and 6) U(∗) largely beats D(K) up to an order of magnitude on some queries. The technical report shows next to each XPath expression the number of elements returned by that expression on the 200 MB data size; these numbers justify some high execution times for some expressions. We must mention here that we ran all the reported queries on D(k) in advance and it took several minutes of processing every time to adapt to a query. The results reported here for D(k) are those after the adaptation pre-processing took place. For U(∗), and as we mentioned earlier, no adaptation is needed.

*Subtree reconstruction:* Fig. 7(a) shows a comparison for the execution times of sample queries from the six different classes when the required results are only the target elements in the XPath expressions versus the subtree reconstruction for these elements. The figure plots the execution times for only two data sizes since for higher sizes an extrapolation can easily be made by the reader. For these expressions, the subtree reconstruction times are quite high, but when the sizes of these subtrees are carefully looked at (see Table 1), one can understand these costs. These result sizes are very large and not typical, and are to a certain extent extreme cases. For Q18, for example, where the returned element is a leaf element in the original XML document and hence does not have a subtree, the cost of accessing the data pages is almost negligible.

*Top 500 results:* Another set of results that we show here are related to the cost of fetching the first 500 matching elements for different expressions from the six query classes. Fig. 7(b) compares for six different expressions the execution times

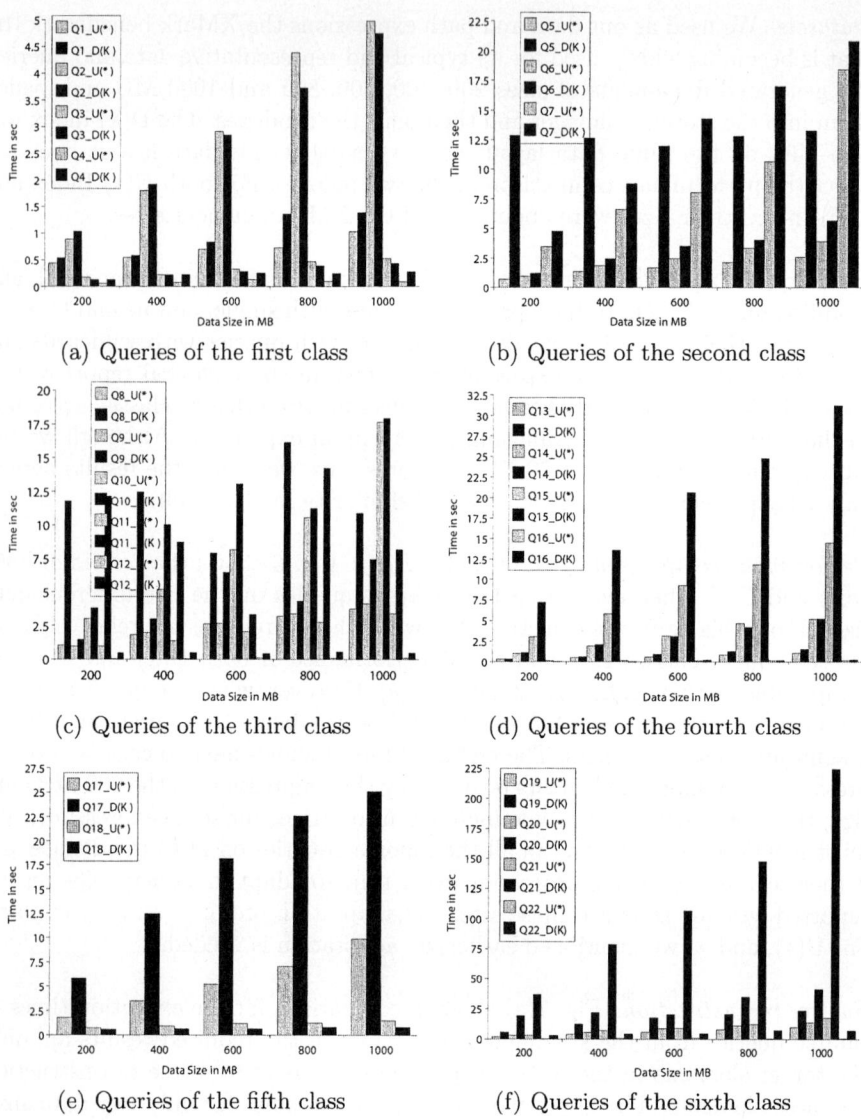

**Fig. 6.** Performance of both D(k) and U(∗) on the different data sizes of XMark

when the whole results are returned versus the times needed to return the first 500 matching elements for each expression. From that graph, we can observe how the response times remained within the realm of few tens to few hundreds of milliseconds when only the top 500 elements for all the queries were returned and when the data set was scaled up to 1GB. This shows that the scalability of U(∗)-Index is not greatly affected by the size of the XML data, but mostly by its number of levels and the variations in element names and their relative positions.

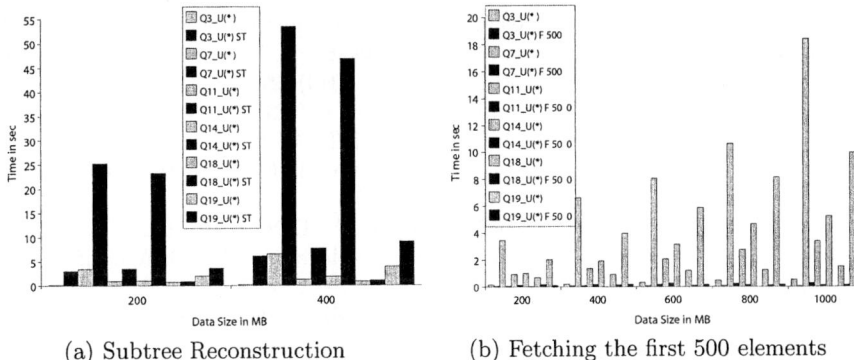

**Fig. 7.** Performance of U(∗) for subtree reconstruction and top 500 results

**Table 1.** Number of Returned Elements on 200 MB

|  | Elements Only | Element with Subtree |
|---|---|---|
| Q3 | 4400 | 113768 |
| Q7 | 121537 | 635919 |
| Q11 | 33287 | 100243 |
| Q14 | 51000 | 662212 |
| Q18 | 3600 | 3600 |
| Q19 | 26401 | 21596140 |

## 7 Conclusion

We presented in this paper the design, implementation and performance results of a native storage manager for XML data. A tightly coupled structural index to that layout was also presented. Our experimental results validate this design and show the comparable performances of U(∗)-Index relative to the D($k$)-index. The major advantage of U(∗)-Index relative to the D($k$)-index is its generality and non-need for adaptation to frequent queries.

Although not mentioned in this paper, we already augmented our structural index with an inverted index—that is quite similar to a B-tree—to fetch results of XPath expressions having value predicates on element texts and attribute values. We intend in a coming paper to publish results on the performance of this inverted index when used with our structural index. We are currently in the process of implementing another structural index that has been recently published and plan to compare its performance against our U(∗)-Index.

## References

1. Boulos, J., Awada, R., Abdel-Kader, R., Hashem, A., Karakashian, S., El-Sebaaly, J.: The AlXemist project, (http://www.cs.aub.edu.lb/boulos/AlXemist.htm)
2. Fiebig, T., Helmer, S., Kanne, C.C., Moerkotte, G., Neumann, N., Schele, R., Westmann, T.: Anatomy of a native XML base management system, The VLDB Journal, 11(4), 292-314 (2002)

3. Jagadish, H.V., Al-Kalifa, S., Chapman, A., Lashmanan, L.V.S., Nierman, A., Paparizos, S., Patel, J.M., Srivastava, D., Wiwatwattana, N., Wu, Y., Yu, C.: Timber: A native XML database, The VLDB Journal, 11(4), 274-291 (2002)
4. Kaushik, R., Shenoy, P., Bohannon, P., Gudes, E.: Exploiting local similarity for indexing paths in graph-structured data, IEEE ICDE (2002)
5. Chen, Q., Lim, A., Ong, K.W.: D(k)-index: An adaptive structural summary for graph-structured data, ACM SIGMOD (2003)
6. Wu, H., Wang, Q., Yu, J.X., Zhou, A., Zhou, S.: UD(k and l)-index: An efficient approximate index for XML data, China, Fourth Int. Conf. Web-Age Information Management, WAIM, Springer-Verlag LNCS 2762 (2003)
7. He, H., Yang, J.: Multiresolution indexing of XMl for frequent queries, IEEE ICDE (2004)
8. Manolescu, I., Florescu, D., Kossmann, D., Xhumari, F., Olteanu, D.: Agora: Living with XML and relational, 26th VLDB Conference (2000)
9. Tatarinov, I., Viglas, S.D., Beyer, K., Shanmugasundaram, J., Shekita, E., Zhang, C.: Storing and querying ordered xml data using a relational database system, ACM SIGMOD (2002)
10. Florescu, D., Kossmann, D.: Storing and querying XML data using an rdbms, IEEE Data Eng. Bull., 22(3), pp. 27-34 (1999)
11. Deutsch, A., Fernandez, M., Suciu, D.: Storing semistructured data with stored, ACM SIGMOD (1999)
12. Kanne, C.C., Moerkotte, G.: Efficient storage of XML data, IEEE ICDE (2000)
13. Chung, C.W., Min, J.K., Shim, K.: APEX: An adaptive path index for XML data, ACM SIGMOD (2002)
14. Milo, T., Suciu, D.: Index structures for path expressions, Proceeding of the 7th International Conference on Database Theory (1999)
15. Al-Khalifa, S., Jagadish, H.V., Koudas, N., Patel, J.M., Srivastava, D., Wu, Y.: Structural joins: A primitive for efficient XML query pattern matching, IEEE ICDE (2002)
16. Schmidt, A., Waas, F., Kersten, M., Carey, M.J.: Xmark: A benchmark for XML data management, 28th VLDB Conference (2002)

# XML Duplicate Detection Using Sorted Neighborhoods

Sven Puhlmann, Melanie Weis, and Felix Naumann

Humboldt-Universität zu Berlin,
Unter den Linden 6, 10099 Berlin, Germany
sven.puhlmann@alumni.hu-berlin.de,
{mweis, naumann}@informatik.hu-berlin.de

**Abstract.** Detecting duplicates is a problem with a long tradition in many domains, such as customer relationship management and data warehousing. The problem is twofold: First define a suitable similarity measure, and second efficiently apply the measure to all pairs of objects. With the advent and pervasion of the XML data model, it is necessary to find new similarity measures and to develop efficient methods to detect duplicate elements in nested XML data.

A classical approach to duplicate detection in flat relational data is the sorted neighborhood method, which draws its efficiency from sliding a window over the relation and comparing only tuples within that window. We extend the algorithm to cover not only a single relation but nested XML elements. To compare objects we make use of XML parent and child relationships. For efficiency, we apply the windowing technique in a bottom-up fashion, detecting duplicates at each level of the XML hierarchy. Experiments show a speedup comparable to the original method data and they show the high effectiveness of our algorithm in detecting XML duplicates.

## 1 Introduction

The problem of duplicate detection has been considered under many different names, such as record linkage[1], merge/purge[2], entity identification [3], and object matching [4]. It generally addresses the problem of finding different representations of a same real-world object, which we refer to as duplicates. Various representations are due to errors, such as typographical errors, inconsistent representations, synonyms, and missing data. Examples for applications where data cleansing and hence duplicate detection are a necessary (pre)processing step are data mining, data warehouses, and customer relationship management. Another scenario where duplicates naturally occur and need to be identified is data integration, where data from distributed and heterogeneous data sources are combined into a unique, complete, and correct representation for every real-world object.

Most approaches address the problem for data stored in a single relation, where a tuple represents an object and duplicate detection is performed by comparing tuples. In most cases however, data is stored in more complex schemas, e.g., in a relational database tables are related through foreign key constraints, or, in the case of XML data, elements are related through nesting. Only recently has duplicate detection been considered for data other than data stored in a single relation [5, 6, 7, 8].

The work presented in this paper focuses on duplicate detection in XML. More specifically, we present an approach that adapts the sorted neighborhood method (SNM), a very efficient approach for duplicate detection in a single relation, to complex XML data consisting of several types of objects related to each other through nesting. We compare XML elements describing the same type of object similarly to the relational SNM. First, our XML adaptation to SNM, called SXNM, generates a key for every element subject to comparisons in the XML data source. This phase is referred to as *key generation*. In the second phase, namely the *duplicate detection* phase, the elements are sorted using these keys and a sliding window is applied over the sorted elements. Assuming that the order sorts duplicates close to each other, we drastically improve efficiency while maintaining good effectiveness by comparing elements within the window. Relationships between different types of objects are exploited by our similarity measure, which considers duplicates among descendants, in addition to the information defined manually to describe the particular object (a so called *object description*). Therefore, we compare XML elements in a bottom-up fashion. Experiments show that SXNM is an effective and efficient algorithm for duplicate detection in XML data.

The remainder of this paper is structured as follows. In Sec. 2, we describe related work with a special focus on the relational sorted neighborhood method. Sec. 3 describes how sorted neighborhoods are used in XML. In Sec. 4, we show results of evaluating our algorithm. To conclude, we provide a summary of the paper and directions for further research in Sec. 5.

## 2 Related Work

### 2.1 Duplicate Detection

The problem of duplicate detection, originally defined by Newcombe [9] and and formalized in the Fellegi-Sunter ][10] model for record linkage has received much attention in the relational world and has concentrated on efficiently and effectively finding duplicate records. Some approaches are specifically geared towards a particular domain, including census, medical, and genealogical data [1, 11, 12], and require the help of a human expert for calibration [13]. Other algorithms are domain-independent, e.g., those presented in [3, 14].

Recent projects consider detecting duplicates in hierarchical and XML data. This includes DELPHI [5], which identifies duplicates in hierarchically organized tables of a data warehouse using a top-down approach along a single data warehouse dimension. The algorithm is efficient because it compares only children with same or similar ancestors. This top-down approach, however, is not well-suited for 1:N parent-child relationships. As an example, let us consider <movie> elements nesting <actor> elements. The top-down approach prunes comparisons of children not having the same ancestors, an assumption that misses duplicates for an M:N relationship between parent and child such as movie and actor, because an actor can play in several different movies. Our bottom-up approach overcomes these issues. In the example of movies nesting actors, we first compare actors independently of movies, and then compare movies also considering duplicates found in actors. Consequently, duplicate actors can play in different movies whereas duplicate movies are detected through co-occurring actors. We compensate the additional comparisons by using sorted neighborhoods.

Work presented in [6, 15] describes efficient identification of similar hierarchical data, but it does not describe how effective the approaches are for XML duplicate detection. At the other end of the spectrum, we have approaches that consider effectiveness (in terms of recall and precision) [16, 7, 17]. For example, Dong et al. present duplicate detection for complex data in the context of personal information management [7], where different kinds of entities such as conferences, authors, and publications are related to each other, giving a graph-like structure. The algorithm propagates similarities of entity pairs through the graph. Any similarity score above a given threshold can trigger a new propagation of similarities, meaning that similarities for pairs of entities may be computed more than once. Although this improves effectiveness, efficiency is compromised. In [8], we presented the domain-independent DogmatiX algorithm, which considers both effectiveness by defining a suited domain-independent similarity measure using information in ancestors and descendants of an XML element, and efficiency by defining a filter to prune comparisons. However, in the worst case, all pairs of elements need to be compared, unlike the sorted neighborhood method that has a lower complexity.

## 2.2 The Sorted Neighborhood Method

The Sorted Neighborhood Method (SNM) is a well known algorithm for the efficient detection of duplicates in relational data [13]. We describe it in detail, as the method introduced in this paper is based on SNM. Given a relation with duplicate tuples, the algorithm consists of three main steps:

1. *Key Generation*: For each tuple in the relation a key is extracted according to a given key definition specified by an expert. Normally a generated key is a string consisting of concatenated parts of the tuple's contents. Each key is linked with a reference to its tuple. Consider a relation MOVIE(TITLE, YEAR) and let a tuple of the relation be M<u>ask</u> o<u>f</u> Zorro, 1998. The key is defined as the first four consonants of the title and the third and fourth digit of the year. Then, the key value for the sample tuple movie is MSKF98 (underlined characters).
2. *Sorting*: The keys generated in Step 1 are sorted lexicographically.
3. *Duplicate Detection*: A window of fixed size slides over the sorted keys and searches duplicates only in the tuples referenced in the window, thus limiting the number of comparisons. The size of the window is crucial for the effectiveness of the algorithm and the quality of the result. With a small window only a small set of elements are compared, leading to a relatively

fast duplicate detection, though with possibly poor recall. A large window results in a slower algorithm, but the chance to find duplicates is better as more comparisons are performed.

To compare tuples referenced by keys in the window SNM uses an equational theory combined with a similarity measure. The equational theory defines under which circumstances two tuples are considered duplicates (e.g., if a person's name and address are sufficiently similar).

Using the transitive closure on the duplicates detected increases the number of duplicates found. Moreover the multi-pass method, which executes SNM several times using different keys each time, significantly increases the recall [13]. For large amounts of data as well as for repeatedly updated data there exists an incremental version of the method dealing with how to combine data that have already been deduplicated with new data packets. The basic SNM is very effective for duplicate detection in relational data and achieves high recall and precision values. We adapt the method to XML as described next.

## 3 SXNM – The Sorted XML Neighborhood Method

We apply the idea of the SNM to nested XML data and call our algorithm the Sorted XML Neighborhood Method (SXNM). SXNM consists of two independent phases: The *key generation* and the *duplicate detection* phase. Figure 1 shows the basic workflow of SXNM with its two phases. The key generation algorithm uses the XML data source and some configuration as its input and returns the generated keys. Note that our algorithm assumes that the XML data has a common schema. That is, elements having the same XPath represent the same type of object, and elements with different XPath have different object types and are not compared. This assumption can be satisfied by applying schema matching and data integration into a target schema prior to SXNM. During the duplicate detection phase, elements are sorted according to their generated keys and a sliding window is applied over the elements, possibly using multiple passes if multiple keys have been defined. To detect duplicates for every element in the document—that is traversed in a bottom-up fashion—information about previously detected duplicates, i.e., duplicates in descendants, is used. Details about each step are provided in separate subsections as indicated in Fig. 1, but first, we illustrate our approach with an example.

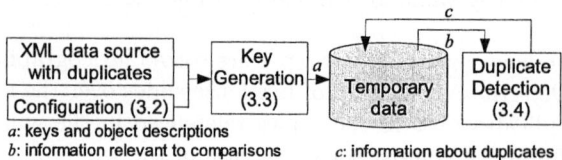

**Fig. 1.** The SXNM workflow

## 3.1 Example

As input, SXNM requires some configuration in addition to the XML data on which duplicate detection is applied. The configuration includes (i) the definition of what object types are subject to deduplication, so called *candidates*, (ii) the definition of what data describes an object, that is, its *object description (OD)*, and (iii) the definition of keys. To illustrate the configuration, we consider the <movie> element in Fig. 2(a). The ellipses, rectangles, and dashed ellipses depict XML elements, text nodes, and attributes respectively. Matrix, the <title> content of the <movie> element, is referenced by the relative path title/text(), the text node of the <title> child. Further relative paths might include people/person[1]/text() and @year.

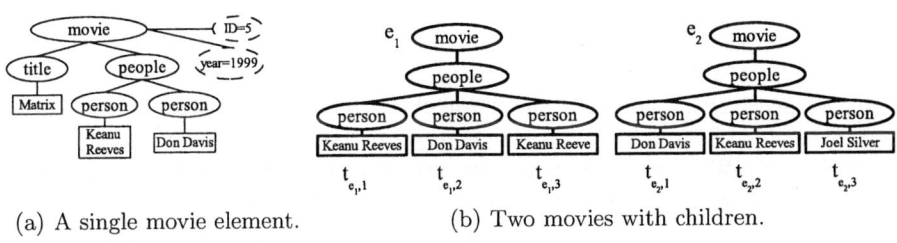

(a) A single movie element.    (b) Two movies with children.

**Fig. 2.** Two examples for XML data

In the configuration, which is provided itself as an XML document, we define all candidates using relative paths. For the bottom-up traversal, the algorithm considers only the subtrees consisting of candidates. Consider a simplified structure of an XML data source depicted in Fig. 3(a). Candidates are shaded, and for these keys and ODs are defined, as we will see shortly. The numbers and ranges at the elements indicate the possible number of children. Note that for the XML elements <actor>, <title>, and <person> only the object descriptions can be used for comparisons, whereas for the XML elements <screenplay> and <movie> information about duplicates in descendants can be used additionally.

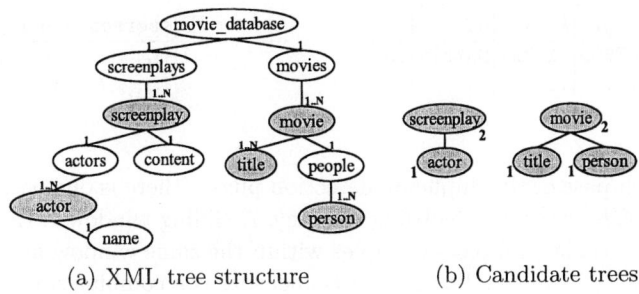

(a) XML tree structure    (b) Candidate trees

**Fig. 3.** XML candidates in an XML data source (a) and extracted subtrees (b)

**Table 1.** Relations defining the keys and object descriptions for `<movie>` elements

(a) $PATH_{movie}$

| id | relPath |
|---|---|
| 1 | title/text() |
| 2 | @ID |
| 3 | @year |

(b) $OD_{movie}$

| pid | relevance |
|---|---|
| 1 | 0.8 |
| 3 | 0.2 |

(c) $KEY_{movie,1}$

| pid | order | pattern |
|---|---|---|
| 1 | 1 | K1,K2 |
| 3 | 2 | D3,D4 |

(d) $KEY_{movie,2}$

| pid | order | pattern |
|---|---|---|
| 2 | 1 | D1 |
| 1 | 2 | C1,C2 |

Fig. 3(b) shows the subtrees consisting of candidates extracted only from the XML structure in Fig. 3(a). The numbers at the elements indicate the order in which the duplicate detection is executed.

For every candidate, the object description and key are defined as shown in Tab. 1 for the particular candidate `<movie>`. The tables hold the definition for two keys for `<movie>` elements (relations $KEY_{movie,1}$ and $KEY_{movie,2}$) and the object descriptions definition (in $OD_{movie}$). In the *pattern* attribute of the key relations, K, C, and D stand for the character types consonants, characters, and digits respectively. The number after the character type indicates its position in the text value of the relative path referenced by the *pid* attribute and stored in *relPath*. For example, the first key for `<movie>` elements uses relative paths 1 and 3, which are `title/text()` and `@year`. From the text value of path 1, the key definition defines a key consisting of the first two consonants from path 1 concatenated with the third and fourth digit from path 3. Applying both key definitions to the `<movie>` element of Fig. 2(a), we obtain the keys MT99 and 5MA.

Using all these definitions provided in the configuration, we begin key generation. To save an extra pass of the XML data, we extract the object descriptions that are necessary for the second phase from the XML document simultaneously. The result of the first phase is a temporary relation $GK$ for every candidate storing the generated keys as well as the corresponding object descriptions. For example, using the definitions for the movie candidate in Tab. 1, we obtain $GK_{movie}$ shown in Tab. 2(a). The sample tuple describes the movie of Fig. 2(a). Further tuples represent other movies stored in the XML document.

**Table 2.** Temporary tables used by SXNM

(a) Subset of the $GK_{movie}$ relation

| elID | $key_1$ | $key_2$ | $od_1$ | $od_2$ |
|---|---|---|---|---|
| 1 | MTR99 | KNRMAT | Matrix | 1999 |
| ... | ... | ... | ... | ... |

(b) Several clusters in $CS_{person}$

| cluster ID | `<person>` elements |
|---|---|
| 1 | $\{t_{e_1,1}, t_{e_1,3}, t_{e_2,2}\}$ |
| 4 | $\{t_{e_1,2}, t_{e_2,1}\}$ |
| 8 | $\{t_{e_2,3}\}$ |

During each pass of the duplicate detection phase (there is one pass for every defined key), $GK$ is sorted according to a key. A sliding window is then applied over the sorted table, and pairs of tuples within the same window are compared using a similarity measure. The similarity measure is a combination of the similarity of object descriptions and the similarity of children sets, if applicable. The similarity measure is defined in Sec. 3.4. By applying the transitive closure over duplicate pairs over all passes, we obtain clusters of duplicates. For every candidate, cluster sets are stored in a temporary table $CS$ together with information that can be used for computing similarities of ancestors. As an example, consider the <movie> elements $e_1$ and $e_2$ in Fig. 2(b). Information about duplicates in <person> elements helps to detect duplicates in <movie> elements. As the result of duplicate detection in <person> elements, Tab. 2(b) shows clusters in $CS_{person}$. We observe that $e_1$ and $e_2$ have two actors in common, namely Keanu Reeves and Don Davis. Consequently, we conclude that $e_1$ and $e_2$ are similar enough based on children data to be duplicates.

For every candidate, the result of duplicate detection can be retrieved from the corresponding $CS$ table for further processing. The following sections provide formal definitions and descriptions for every phase of Fig. 1.

## 3.2 Configuration

In addition to the XML data to be deduplicated, our algorithm requires some configuration. The configuration contains information about

- *Candidates*: the XML elements for which duplicates should be detected, and which therefore need a generated key.
- *Object description*: which information (text elements) of candidates is used for comparisons.
- *Key definition*: which information (text elements) of candidates is used to generate keys.
- *Key patterns*: which parts of this information comprise the keys.

As we need to distinguish specific XML elements and their corresponding XML schema elements in the following, we use $s$ as an element in an XML schema and $e$ as an instance of $s$.

Candidates are specified by their absolute XPath and are given a unique name, which is required to associate configuration tables with temporary tables. For example, the <movie> candidate of Fig. 3(a) is specified with the XPath movie_database/movies/movie and is assigned the name *name* =*movie*. To specify information necessary for key generation and duplicate detection for a single candidate, we use *relative paths (relPath)*, i.e., XPath structures relative to the candidate. Relative paths identify text nodes or attribute values that belong to either the key or the object description of the candidate.

We construct separate relations for paths, keys, and object descriptions relevant for comparisons of instances of an XML schema element $s$. We show examples in Tables 1.

- $PATH_s(id, relPath)$ is the *path relation* containing all relative paths that refer to information of an XML element, used for key definitions and object descriptions. The *id* attribute contains a unique id of the relative path.
- The relation $KEY_{s,i}(pid, order, pattern)$ defines the $i^{th}$ key of $s$. The *pid* attribute is a foreign key to *id* in $PATH_s$ and refers to the relative path of the information that build parts of the key. The *order* attribute indicates the

position of the information in the key, and *pattern* describes what characters to extract from a description referenced by the relative path. Note that we allow an arbitrary number of keys for each relevant XML element, enabling the use of the multi-pass variant of SNM [13].
- $OD_s(pid, relevance)$ is the *object description relation (OD relation)* indicating the information that is compared between two instances of $s$. The *relevance* attribute constitutes the relevancy (weighting) of the information, which is used by our similarity measure, and $pid$ references the $id$ of $PATH_s$.

Parameters are needed in conjunction with the XML data source to provide input for the key generation algorithm. For an XML schema element $s$, its parameters $P_s = \{PATH_s, OD_s, KEY_{s,1}, \ldots, KEY_{s,n}\}$ (where $n$ is the number of keys defined for $s$) contain all relations needed for the key generation algorithm. For the set $S$ of all XML schema elements for which definitions are made, the *parameter set* $P = \bigcup_{s \in S} \{P_s\}$ denotes the complete set of parameters.

### 3.3 Key Generation

$P$ provides the input for the key generation algorithm. Whilst this task for the original SNM was to extract only the keys, the key generation algorithm of SXNM extracts the keys as well as the object descriptions needed for comparisons, reading the given XML data in a single pass. The result of the key generation algorithm is $GK$, the set of generated keys, again stored in a relation. Let $S$ be the set of all XML schema elements, for whose instances duplicates should be detected, and $s \in S$. The relation $GK_s = (eid, key_1, \ldots, key_n, od_1, \ldots, od_n)$ denotes the result of the key generation. The attribute $eid$ contains the ID of the respective XML element—for instance the position of the element in the data source; $key_1, \ldots, key_n$ and $od_1, \ldots, od_n$ contain the keys generated for this XML element and the extracted object descriptions respectively. $GK = \bigcup_{s \in S} \{GK_s\}$ denotes the combination of all generated keys.

### 3.4 Duplicate Detection

In the duplicate detection step the generated keys in $GK$ are processed. Along with $GK$, the duplicate detection process takes several parameters:

- The parameter set $P$ containing object description and their relevancies,
- the window sizes to use for the XML elements,
- thresholds needed to classify XML elements as duplicates and non-duplicates,
- information about when not to use descendants for duplicate detection.

As the main idea of SXNM is to use information about duplicates in descendants, the order in which candidates are processed hast to be defined accordingly. In the following, we start with a description of how duplicates for a single candidate are detected. Thereafter we describe the order in which candidates are processed.

**The general duplicate detection process.** For each key attribute in $GK_s$, e.g., $key_1$, the $GK_s$ relation is sorted according to the appropriate key attribute. A sliding window of a specified size $w_s$ slides over the tuples in the sorted relation, in analogy to the window in the relational SNM. For each pair of tuples in the window, a similarity is computed based on their object description and descendants, if available. If the similarity exceeds a given threshold, the corresponding XML elements are classified as duplicates. The result of this multi-pass method executed for $s$ is a set of element ID pairs that represent duplicates. A transitive closure algorithm is applied to the duplicates, resulting in the cluster set $CS_s$.

**Definition 1 (Cluster Set).** *Let $s$ be an element of an XML schema. $CS_s = \{C_1, \ldots, C_m\}$, $m \leq n$ is a cluster set where each cluster represents a real-world object $o$, holds a unique cluster ID, and contains references to all XML data instances of $s$ represented by $o$. Each instance of $s$ belongs to exactly one cluster of the cluster set.*

A cluster set is created for every candidate XML schema element. The cluster sets can then be used to create a de-duplicated version of the XML data source. Moreover, cluster sets help to detect and verify duplicates in other XML elements, using a bottom-up duplicate detection process.

**Bottom-up duplicate detection.** In SXNM, the similarity of two XML elements can consist of (i) the similarity of their object descriptions (Def. 2) and (ii) the similarity of their descendants (Def. 3).

Using information about key elements stored in $P$, the tree structure of the entire XML document can be split into a set of trees by extracting all elements $s$ ($P_s \in P$) from the XML document and preserving the ancestor-descendant relationships. This was demonstrated in Figure 3. We need this tree set structure to execute duplicate detection in a bottom-up fashion. The duplicate detection process as described above can be executed on an extracted tree independently from other extracted trees. For each tree, the process starts with the nodes having the largest distance $\delta$ to the root node. It continues with the nodes having distance $\delta - 1$ etc. up to the root node.

Lacking descendants of their own, the similarity of elements that are instances of the XML schema elements (represented by the leaf nodes of the extracted tree structures) is based on the similarity of their object descriptions alone. This is true also for other schema elements, for which the expert decided that descendants should not be taken into account during duplicate detection.

**Definition 2 (OD Similarity).** *Let $e_1$ and $e_2$ be two instances of schema element $s$ occurring together in a sliding window. Let $OD_s$ contain $n$ entries $od_{e_j,1}, \ldots, od_{e_j,n}$; $r_i$ indicates the relevancy of path $i$ as defined in the $OD_s$ relation. With $\phi_i^{OD}$ being a similarity function for the $i^{th}$ entry in $OD_s$, the similarity of the object descriptions of $e_1$ and $e_2$ is $sim_{e_1,e_2}^{OD} = \sum_{i=1}^{n} r_i \phi_i^{OD}(od_{e_1,i}, od_{e_2,i})$.*

An example for a $\phi^{OD}$ function is the edit distance [18], with computes the minimum number of operations needed to convert one string into another. Using domain-knowledge, more accurate $\phi^{OD}$ functions can be used, e.g., a numeric distance function for numerical values.

Except for XML elements that are leaf nodes where only the object description is available, duplicate detection for XML elements can be performed using the similarity of their object descriptions and their descendants. As an XML element can have descendants of several types, we start with the similarity of individual descendants and combine the similarities of all descendants of this XML element thereafter.

For two instances $e_1$ and $e_2$ of an XML schema element $s$ having a descendant schema element $t$, $t_{e_j,i}$ denotes the $i$-th instance of $t$ descendant of $e_j$ ($j \in \{1,2\}$). As our duplicate detection is a bottom-up process, duplicates in the instances of $t$ have already been detected, leading to the cluster set $CS_t$, which helps to detect whether $e_1$ and $e_2$ are duplicates. The function cid returns the unique cluster ID of a cluster in a cluster set (cf. Def. 1), given a cluster set and an instance of an element in the cluster set. Using cid we define lists of cluster IDs for $e_1$ and $e_2$ and with them the descendant-based similarity of two elements:

$$l_{e_1} = (\text{cid}(t_{e_1,1}, CS_t), \ldots, \text{cid}(t_{e_1,i}, CS_t)) = (id_1, \ldots, id_i)$$
$$l_{e_2} = (\text{cid}(t_{e_2,1}, CS_t), \ldots, \text{cid}(t_{e_2,j}, CS_t)) = (id_1, \ldots, id_j)$$

**Definition 3 (Descendants Similarity).** *The similarity of two instances $e_1$ and $e_2$ of an XML schema element $s$ regarding a single descendant schema element $t$ is calculated using the $\phi_t^{desc}$ function: $sim_{e_1,e_2,t}^{desc} = \phi_t^{desc}(l_{e_1}, l_{e_2})$.*

*Let $t_1, \ldots, t_n$ be the $n$ descendant schema elements of $s$. We use agg() to obtain the combined similarity $sim_{e_1,e_2}^{Desc}$ for all instances of the descendants of $e_1$ and $e_2$: $sim_{e_1,e_2}^{Desc} = agg(sim_{e_1,e_2,t_1}^{desc}, \ldots, sim_{e_1,e_2,t_n}^{desc})$*

There are numerous possibilities for the $\phi^{desc}$ and $agg()$ functions. One example for the first would be to calculate the ratio between the cardinalities of the intersection and the union of $l_{e_1}$ and $l_{e_2}$—this is implemented in our current implementation. The $agg()$ function could simply calculate the average of its arguments, or it could weigh the importance of different descendants. Currently, we calculate the average; future implementations will have declarations of different weights in the configuration.

Consider the <movie> elements $e_1$ and $e_2$ in Fig. 2(b). Information about duplicates in <person> elements helps to detect duplicates in <movie> elements. As the result of duplicate detection in <person> elements, Tab. 2(b) shows clusters in $CS_t$, $t = person$. This leads to $l_{e_1} = (\text{cid}(t_{e_1,1}, CS_t), \text{cid}(t_{e_1,2}, CS_t), \text{cid}(t_{e_1,3}, CS_t)) = (1, 4, 1)$ and $l_{e_2} = (4, 1, 8)$. Using the similarity function proposed above we have $sim_{e_1,e_2,t}^{desc} = \frac{|l_{e_1} \cap l_{e_2}|}{|l_{e_1} \cup l_{e_2}|} = \frac{2}{3}$.

Finally, to gain the resulting similarity for the XML elements $e_1$ and $e_2$ of the same schema element $s$ we combine $sim_{e_1,e_2}^{OD}$ and $sim_{e_1,e_2}^{Desc}$. The result is $sim_{e_1,e_2}^{comb}$, reflecting the final combined similarity of both XML elements. An example for calculating the combined similarity is to weigh $sim_{e_1,e_2}^{OD}$ and $sim_{e_1,e_2}^{Desc}$ to gain $sim_{e_1,e_2}^{comb}$. Our current implementation calculates the average of the two values.

Having executed the duplicate detection process for all instances of the defined XML schema elements, we have a resulting cluster set for each of these schema elements. What to do with this information remains up to the domain specific application. A typical approach selects a *prime representative* for each cluster and discards the others. More sophisticated approaches perform data fusion by resolving conflicts among the different representations.

## 4 Evaluation

In this section we present various experimental results of SXNM and show that this method is ready to detect duplicates in complex, large, and nested XML data structures.

### 4.1 Data Sets

We use three different data sets for our experiments—both artificial and real-world XML data. To generate artificial data, we use two tools consecutively: The first is ToXGene[1], which, using a template similar to an XML schema, generates clean XML data sets. We assign an unique ID to the data objects for identification. The second tool is the Dirty XML Data Generator[2]. It uses the clean XML data and some parameters, e.g., the duplication probability, the number of duplicates, and the errors to introduce into the duplicates, as its input and generates dirty XML data according to the parameters. To observe the recall, precision, and f-measure values the unique IDs of the clean data objects are used. Of course these IDs are not made available to SXNM. The data sets are further described below. When not specified, the OD of a candidate is its text node with relative path text() and relevance 1. Key definitions used in our experiments are provided in Tab. 3.

**Dataset 1: Artificial movie data.** We generate various data sets of different sizes consisting of artificially generated <movie> data using ToXGene and the Dirty XML Data Generator. The resulting <movie> elements in the data sets contain several <title>, <person>, and <review> descendants. The <person> elements can contain one <lastname> and several <firstname> elements. A <movie> element has two attributes, namely year and length. As a candidate, we consider the movie schema element only. As its object description, we use title/text() and @length with respective relevancies 0.8 and 0.2.

**Dataset 2: Real-world CD data, artificially polluted.** Here we use real-world CD data consisting of 500 clean CD objects extracted from the FreeDB dataset[3] and 500 artificially generated duplicates (one duplicate for each CD; using the Dirty XML Data Generator) as a test data set. Each <disc>

---

[1] http://www.cs.toronto.edu/tox/toxgene/
[2] http://www.informatik.hu-berlin.de/mac/dirtyxml/
[3] http://www.freedb.de

element contains several <title> descendants nested under a <tracks> element and at least one <artist> and <dtitle>. Optional children of <disc> are <year>, <did>, a disc id that FreeDB provides and <genre>. As candidates, we use disc schema elements and their descendant /tracks/title. The object description of a disc consists of did/text(), artist/text() and dtitle/text() with respective relevancies of 0.4, 0.3, and 0.3.

**Dataset 3: Real-world movie data.** For precision tests of larger bodies of XML data we use real-world movie data consisting of 10,000 CDs selected from FreeDB. Having the same schema as Dataset 2, the candidates are disc, disc/title, disc/artist and disc/tracks/title.

**Table 3.** Configuration

(a) Dataset 1

| candidate | key relPath | pattern |
|---|---|---|
| movie | title/text() | K1-K5 |
|  | @year | D3,D4 |
|  | @length | D1,D2 |
|  | title/text() | K1,K2 |
|  | @genre | C1,C2 |
|  | title/text() | K1-K4 |

(b) Dataset 2

| candidate | key relPath | pattern |
|---|---|---|
| disc | artist[1]/text() | K1-K4 |
|  | year/text() | D3,D4 |
|  | did/text() | C1-C4 |
|  | dtitle[1]/text() | C1-C4 |
|  | genre/text() | C1,C2 |
|  | year/text() | D3,D4 |
|  | artist[1]/text() | K1,K2 |
|  | did/text() | C1,C2 |
| disc/tracks/title | text() | C1-C6 |

(c) Dataset 3

| candidate | key relPath | pattern |
|---|---|---|
| disc | dtitle[1]/text() | K1-K6 |
|  | artist[1]/text() | K1-K4 |
|  | did/text() | C1-C4 |
|  | dtitle[1]/text() | C1-C4 |
| disc/dtitle | text() | C1-C6 |
| disc/artist | text() | C1-C6 |
| disc/tracks/title | text() | C1-C6 |

### 4.2 Experimental Results

We now show the results of a variety of experiments. In the first set of experiments we examine SXNM in terms of recall, precision, and f-measure. The second set of experiments deals with the scalability of our duplicate detection method. Finally, in the third set of experiments we show how and when duplicates in descendants help to detect duplicates in higher levels of the hierarchy. For all experiments we only show a selection of the result graphs.

**Experiment set 1: Single- vs. Multi-Pass with varying window sizes**
PURPOSE: In these experiments we show the overall effectiveness of our method by examining recall, precision, and f-measure results on different data sets. We use varying window sizes and different keys. Moreover, the advantage of the multi-pass vs. the single-pass method is shown.

METHODOLOGY: We use Datasets 1, 2, and 3 for this experiment. For Datasets 1 and 2, we can evaluate recall and precision and therefore calculate the f-measure, because we know the true duplicates in these data sets. This is not the case for Dataset 3, which we can evaluate only in terms of precision. For all experiments in this subsection, we used threshold values that we consider sensible based on our experience. Results are shown in Figure 4. Each line represents the use of a different key in single-pass SXNM (SP), or the combination of all keys for the multi-pass SXNM (MP).

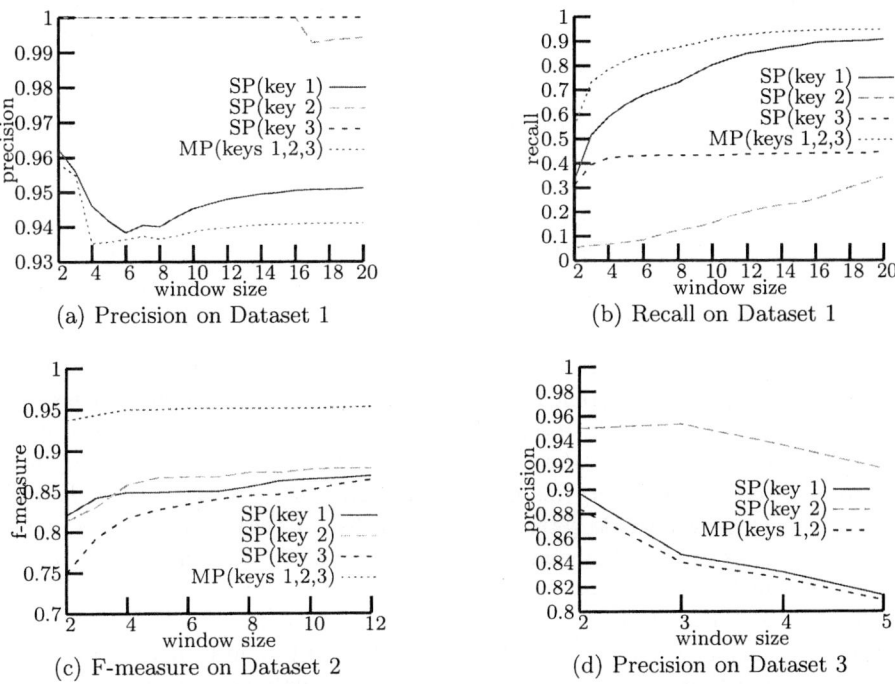

**Fig. 4.** Results for Experiment set 1 on effectiveness

DISCUSSION DATASET 1: The results for this experiment on artificial movies can be seen in Fig. 4 (top). We used the three different keys shown in Tab. 3(a). As an example of how to read the table, consider the first key defined for the relative path "title/text()" as "K1-K5". The relative path of the key definition points to the movie's title, from which the first five consonants are used as key.

We can see in Fig. 4(b) that for the single keys as well as for the multi-pass method the recall increases with increasing window size after a certain point. The single keys lead to very different results. In terms of recall, Key 2 leads to the worst results. This is explained by the fact that the first part of this key consists of the year of the movie, which results in poorly sorted keys when the year is missing or contains severe errors. With increasing window size, more pairs are compared and more duplicates are found, which increases the recall of Key 2, while precision is not considerably compromised. The same argument can be used to explain the results of Key 3, however, the development with increasing window size is not as pronounced as for Key 2.

Key 1 performs best and almost as good as the multi-pass method which uses all keys. This is because the first five consonants of a movie's title are very distinguishing and lead to a very good order after sorting. The precision curve of Key 1 (and consequently of MP) shows an at first surprising decrease in precision for small window-sizes (2-6) and increases afterwards to converge to a precision around 0.95. This can be explained as follows: Because we introduced artificial errors in titles that constitute the key, the good order is compromised. Indeed, 5% of the titles were polluted in such a way that their keys are sorted far apart. These duplicates are not detected for small window sizes but can be found with larger windows. The convergence to a precision of 0.95 is due to the fact that the similarity measure limits the number of false duplicates. In terms of recall, the multi-pass method performs best (as already shown in [13]) but not much better SP for Key 1, because Keys 2 and 3 do not increase the number of detected duplicates much (low recall values). However, in terms of precision the multi-pass method performs worst (although overall the values are still high between 0.93 and 0.96). This is because the multi-pass method executes the largest number of comparisons and there is an increased probability of false positives.

DISCUSSION DATASET 2: We discuss the results on Dataset 2 for the disc candidate only, using three different keys shown in Tab. 3(b). Figure 4(c) shows the result of this experiment in terms of f-measure. The single keys perform in a similar range between 0.75 and 0.87. Key 3 leads to the worst results because genre and year are not very distinctive attributes (same reason as for Key 2 in Dataset 1). Key 1 yields better results than Key 3 because an artist's name is more distinctive than the genre. Key 2 consists of the first characters of the CD's ID, which in only some cases is incorrect and missing and therefore leads altogether to the best results. The multi-pass method results show that even the smallest window size (2) leads to much better results in terms of f-measure than the largest tested window size of 12 for the single keys. Larger windows give only slight improvement, so in this case window size 4 is sufficient. For all keys (single-pass and multi-pass) we observe that the f-measure increases with increasing window size and converges to an f-measure. This is explained by the fact that with increasing window size, the recall increases because more pairs are compared. At the same time, the precision settles at large window sizes because its degradation is limited by the similarity measure.

DISCUSSION DATASET 3: In Fig. 4(d), we show the f-measure for different window sizes obtained using SXNM on 10,000 disc candidates and the keys of Tab. 3(c). Recall could not be measured, because we do not know all duplicates in this data set. We observe that Key 2, which is the same as Key 2 used on Dataset 2 again yields the highest precision. At window size 5, we detect 48 duplicates. Key 1 results in a lower precision but detects far more duplicates, e.g., at window size 5, it finds 289 duplicates. Using multi-pass SXNM with both Key 1 and Key 2 results in the worst precision, because the false positives of both keys are cumulated. In this real-world data set, we observe that most duplicate clusters consist of two elements only, and that our algorithm detects false duplicates mainly due to two reasons. Between 54% and 77% (decreasing with increasing window size) of false duplicates are pairs of CDs that are part of a series and differ in a single number only, e.g., Christmas Songs (CD1) and Christmas Songs (CD2) or that feature various artists (the two cases being often correlated). Between 19% and 36% (increasing with increasing window size) of false duplicates are CDs whose text is provided in a format that failed to enter the database (e.g., Japanese or Russian). Comparisons were then only performed on "readable" attributes (year and genre). For any window size, less that 10% of false duplicates are due to other reasons.

To summarize the experiments for all three datasets, SXNM achieves overall high precision and recall, comparable or exceeding related approaches. Also as expected, the multipass method outperforms the single-pass method. Finally, the choice of good keys is of course very decisive to achieve good results.

**Experiment set 2: Scalability**

PURPOSE: In the second series of experiments, we show how the individual phases of SXNM scale with the amount of data and the number of duplicates. The distinguished phases are key generation (KG), sliding window (SW), transitive closure (TC) as currently provided in our implementation, and overall duplicate detection (DD), which is the sum of the SW and TC.

METHODOLOGY: We use artificially generated movie data so we can generate data sets with different sizes and numbers of duplicates. With ToXgene we generated 9 XML files containing from 100 to 2000 movies. Each movie has one to three title- and three to ten person-descendants. Using the Dirty XML Data Generator, we polluted the clean movie data using two configurations with different duplication probabilities (dupProb) and different numbers of duplicates for <movie> and <person> elements to obtain two different pollution degrees:

- *few duplicates*: 20% dupProb for <movie>, <title>, and <person> elements each producing exactly one duplicate
- *many duplicates*: 100% dupProb for <movie> and <person>, each generating up to two duplicates, and 20% dupProb for <title> elements each generating exactly one duplicate object.

We polluted the text nodes of the duplicate elements by deleting, inserting, or swapping characters as described for the Dirty XML Data Generator. The window size used in these experiments is 3.

DISCUSSION: Figure 5 shows the results for this series of experiments. To enable a comparison to the clean XML data resulting from ToXGene, we executed SXNM over the set of clean movie data to show the difference to the least possible time needed to detect duplicates in a specific data set (Fig. 5(a)). In all graphs, the *duplicate detection* time DD is the sum of the *transitive closure* TC and the *sliding window* SW time. SXNM's comparisons are made in the sliding window.

The overall time (duplicate detection) needed for the largest clean data set is 129 s. Although there are no duplicates and the transitive closure algorithm is expected to need almost no time, there is an increasing possibility for false

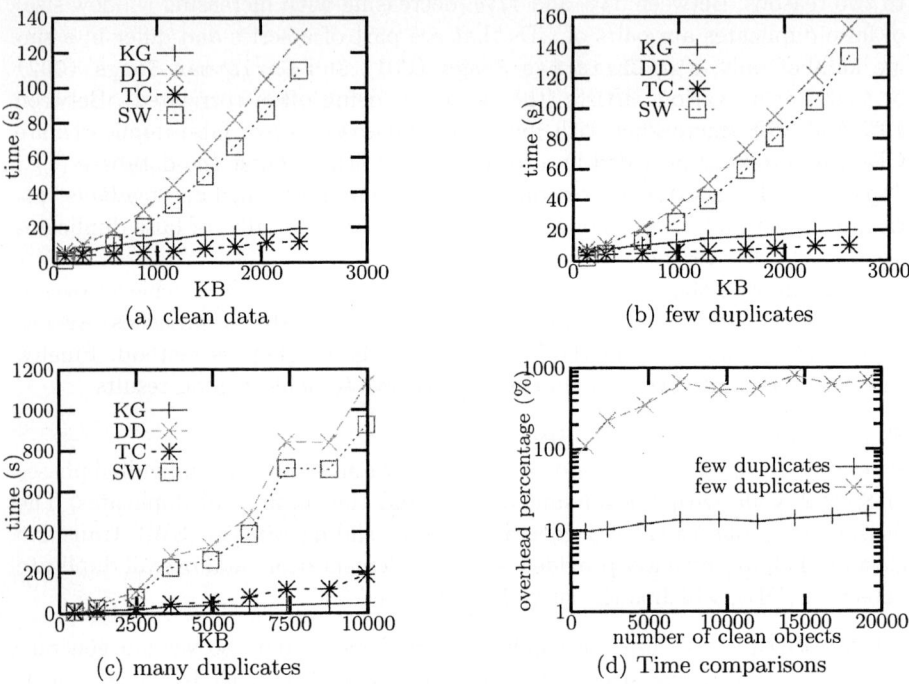

**Fig. 5.** Results for experiment set 2 on scalability

duplicates when the file size increases, leading to some pairs of duplicates for which the transitive closure algorithm is executed. Altogether, the key generation is a linear process, compared to the comparisons in the sliding window, which is polynomial.

We can also see from both figures that the duplicate detection for the file with "few duplicates" performs almost as well as for the clean data. Looking on Fig. 5(d), which shows the time overhead of the sum of key generation and sliding window for both few and many duplicates, compared to the time needed on clean data, we observe a time overhead of below 20% for few duplicates. For the file with "many duplicates" the time needed for the transitive closure exceeds the time needed for key generation, as the transitive closure algorithm has to process many duplicate pairs. Additionally, for the largest file size, this file needs almost 20 minutes for duplicate detection (the dirty data is about four times the size of the clean data) and represents a considerable time overhead compared on clean data.

**Experiment set 3: Threshold impact**

PURPOSE: In our third experiment we evaluate the effect of different thresholds on recall, precision and f-measure. The two thresholds are the OD threshold that is used for comparisons of two element's object description, and the descendants threshold that is used for the similarity measurement of children. It shows how descendants help duplicate detection, depending on thresholds.

METHODOLOGY: We use Dataset 2 for this experiment. First, we detect duplicates in <disc> elements using only the object descriptions of the CDs, namely the disc ID, the artist and the CD title. We vary the OD threshold from 0.5 to 1. Afterwards, we use a fixed threshold for the OD and take the descendants <title> elements of the <disc> elements into account for duplicate detection. For these, we vary the descendants threshold from 0.1 to 0.9. Figure 6 shows the results of our experiments.

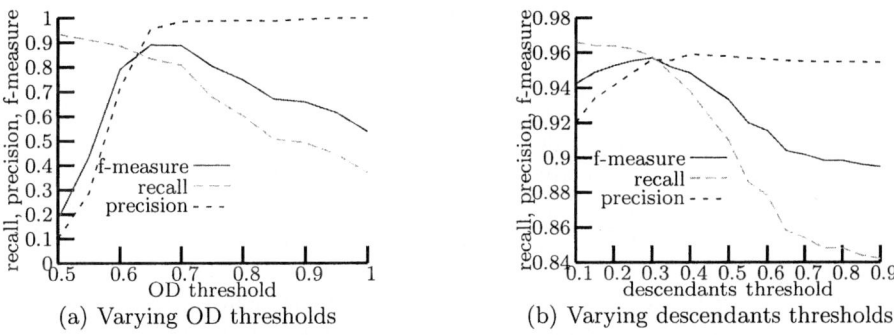

(a) Varying OD thresholds          (b) Varying descendants thresholds

**Fig. 6.** Results for experiment set 3 on threshold impact

DISCUSSION: Figure 6(a) shows the results for different object description thresholds. Using a low threshold of 0.5 results in a large amount of detected duplicates, leading to high recall but also to low precision, as many false positives occur. When the threshold increases, precision increases and recall decreases as expected. The f-measure peaks at a threshold of 0.65.

For the varying descendants threshold we use the OD threshold of 0.65 determined as optimal from the last experiment. We vary the descendants threshold from 0.1 to 0.9 and observe two things. First, Figure 6(b) shows that the best f-measure obtained using descendants is higher than the best f-measure obtained when only considering the object description. Thus, we can conclude that it is worthwhile to take into account descendant information when detecting duplicates. Second, we observe that a very high descendants threshold downgrades the results, whereas the low descendants threshold of 0.3 leads to the best result of almost 0.96 in terms of f-measure. Choosing a low descendants threshold yields better results because it implies that a small overlap in children is already sufficient to consider children sets as similar. This compensates the effect of non-overlapping children, which drastically reduces similarity in our similarity measure (Def. 3).

## 5 Conclusions and Outlook

The Sorted Neighborhood Method is a very efficient method to detect duplicates in relational data. We have shown that our extension of this method to XML data, combined with new approaches in duplicate detection, is a reasonable alternative for XML duplicate detection for large amounts of data. However, there remain several open issues to further improve our method both in efficiency and in effectiveness.

**Efficiency.** In previous work we have shown that filters are quite effective to avoid comparisons, especially with the edit distance operations [17]. The work presented in the paper at hand also performs filtering but based on the generated keys and the sliding window. It will be interesting to see how the two filters interact. Moreover it could be useful to include the ideas of the Duplicate Elimination Sorted Neighborhood Method (DE-SNM) of [19] in our algorithm.

**Effectiveness.** In our current algorithm we use a simple approach of similarity function and threshold to determine whether two elements are duplicates. However, our algorithm is ready for the usage of equational theory, which was used for the relational SNM. We believe that the domain knowledge considered using the equational theory will yield even better results. Also, the choice of the thresholds yet remains an open issue. In [5] the authors propose a corresponding learning technique, which we plan to adapt to our problem of more than one type of descendant. Another knob to turn is the window size. In [20], a method to dynamically adapt the window size using distance measures on the keys is proposed. We plan to examine how sampling techniques can help determine an appropriate window size for each data set.

**Acknowledgment.** This research was supported by the German Research Society (DFG grant no. NA 432).

# References

1. Winkler, W.E.: Advanced methods for record linkage. Technical report, Statistical Research Division, U.S. Census Bureau, Washington, DC (1994)
2. Hernández, M.A., Stolfo, S.J.: The merge/purge problem for large databases. In: SIGMOD Conference, San Jose, CA (1995) 127–138
3. Lim, E.P., Srivastava, J., Prabhakar, S., Richardson, J.: Entity identification in database integration. In: ICDE Conference, Vienna, Austria (1993) 294–301
4. Doan, A., Lu, Y., Lee, Y., Han, J.: Object matching for information integration: A profiler-based approach. IEEE Intelligent Systems, pages 54-59 (2003)
5. Ananthakrishna, R., Chaudhuri, S., Ganti, V.: Eliminating fuzzy duplicates in data warehouses. In: International Conference on VLDB, Hong Kong, China (2002)
6. Guha, S., Jagadish, H.V., Koudas, N., Srivastava, D., Yu, T.: Approximate XML joins. In: SIGMOD Conference, Madison, Wisconsin, USA (2002) 287–298
7. Dong, X., Halevy, A., Madhavan, J.: Reference reconciliation in complex information spaces. In: SIGMOD Conference, Baltimore, MD (2005) 85–96
8. Weis, M., Naumann, F.: DogmatiX Tracks down Duplicates in XML. In: SIGMOD Conference, Baltimore, MD (2005)
9. Newcombe, H., Kennedy, J., Axford, S., James, A.: Automatic linkage of vital records. Science 130 (1959) no. 3381 (1959) 954–959

10. Fellegi, I.P., Sunter, A.B.: A theory for record linkage. Journal of the American Statistical Association (1969)
11. Jaro, M.A.: Probabilistic linkage of large public health data files. Statistics in Medicine **14** (1995) 491–498
12. Quass, D., Starkey, P.: Record linkage for genealogical databases. In: KDD Workshop on Data Cleaning, Record Linkage, and Object Consolidation, Washington, DC (2003) 40–42
13. Hernández, M.A., Stolfo, S.J.: Real-world data is dirty: Data cleansing and the merge/purge problem. Data Mining and Knowledge Discovery **2(1)** (1998) 9–37
14. Monge, A.E., Elkan, C.P.: An efficient domain-independent algorithm for detecting approximately duplicate database records. In: SIGMOD Workshop on Research Issues on Data Mining and Knowledge Discovery, Tuscon, AZ (1997) 23–29
15. Kailing, K., Kriegel, H.P., Schnauer, S., Seidl, T.: Efficient similarity search for hierarchical data in large databases. International Conference on EDBT (2002) 676–693
16. Carvalho, J.C., da Silva, A.S.: Finding similar identities among objects from multiple web sources. In: CIKM Workshop on Web Information and Data Management, New Orleans, Louisiana, USA (2003) 90–93
17. Weis, M., Naumann, F.: Duplicate detection in XML. In: SIGMOD Workshop on Information Quality in Information Systems, Paris, France (2004) 10–19
18. Smith, T.F., Waterman, M.S.: Identification of common molecular subsequences. In: Journal of Molecular Biology. Volume 147. (1981) 195–197
19. Hernández, M.A.: A Generalization of Band Joins and The Merge/Purge Problem. PhD thesis, Columbia University, Department of Computer Science, New York (1996)
20. Lehti, P., Fankhauser, P.: A precise blocking method for record linkage. In: International Conference on Data Warehousing and Knowledge Discovery (DaWaK, Copenhagen, Denmark (2005) 210–220

# Handling Interlinked XML Instances on the Web

Erik Behrends, Oliver Fritzen, and Wolfgang May

Institut für Informatik, Universität Göttingen, Germany
{behrends, fritzen, may}@informatik.uni-goettingen.de

**Abstract.** XML instances are not necessarily self-contained but may have links to remote XML data residing on other servers. Links between (autonomous) XML instances can be expressed by the XLink language; although, querying such interlinked sources is not yet actually supported.

We describe a model of such linked XML instances where the links are not seen as explicit links (where the users must be aware of the links and traverse them explicitly in their queries), but where the links define views that combine into a logical, transparent (XML) model that then can be queried by XPath/XQuery. We motivate the underlying modeling and give a concise and declarative specification as an XML-to-XML mapping. We also describe the implementation of the model as an extension of the eXist [exi] XML database system and point out some perspectives and combinations with related research aspects.

## 1 Introduction

XML is increasingly used for providing data sources on the Web and for exchanging data. XML instances are not necessarily self-contained but rather may refer to information on other, autonomous servers. Such references can be expressed by the XLink language [XLi01], based on the XPointer Framework [XPt03] and the XPointer addressing scheme [XPt02]: An XPointer expression of the form *url*#xpointer(*xpointer-expr*) identifies a *document fragment* inside the XML document located at *url*. In the following, we consider only XPath expressions in place of the *xpointer-expr*. We use excerpts of the distributed MONDIAL XML database [Mon] for illustration: the document countries.xml in Figure 1 contains basic data about all countries, and for each country, cities-XX.xml (where XX is the country's car code) contains information about the cities in this country. The XPointer http://www.foo.de/countries.xml#xpointer(/countries/country[@car_code="D"]) addresses the node that represents Germany in http://www.foo.de/countries.xml. XPointer in turn provides the foundation for XLink [XLi01] that allows to define XML elements that express links to other XML documents. In this paper, the focus of our interest is on *simple XLinks*, where one XLink element with one XPointer references one or more nodes in a remote document. XLink extends HTML's <a href="*url*#*anchor*"> referencing mechanism from using simple anchors to use full XPointer expressions as fragment identifiers.

*Query Support for References.* How can data that is linked in this way be queried – e.g., for finding out how many inhabitants the capital of Belgium

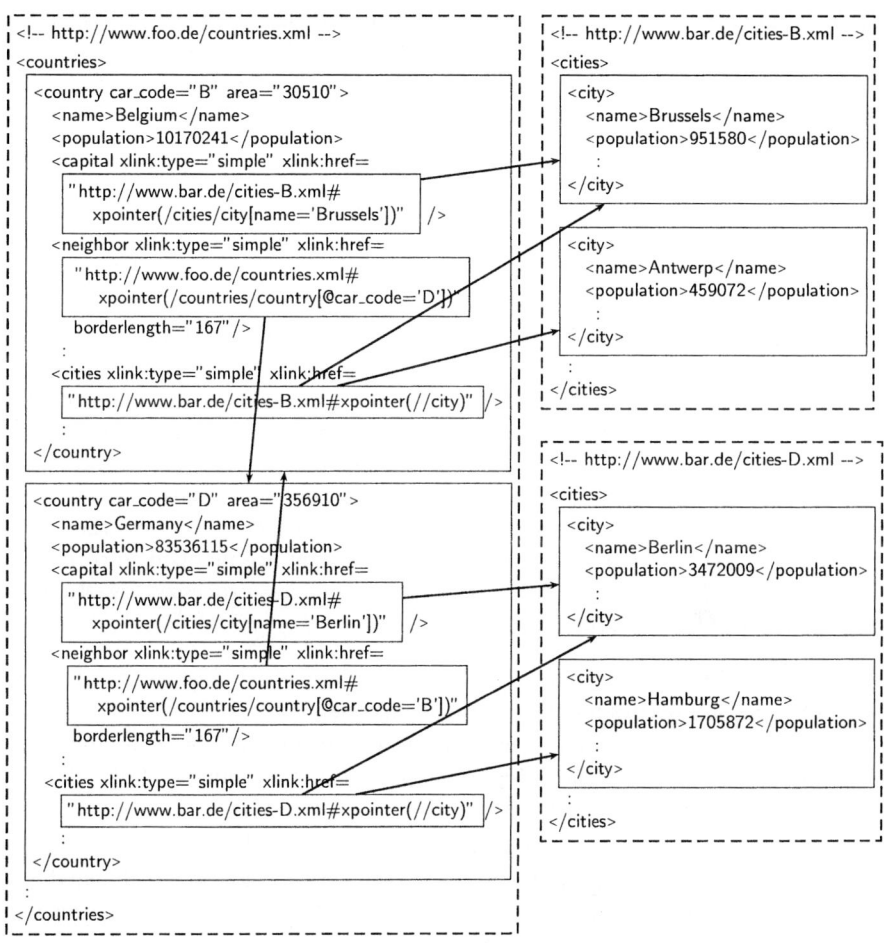

**Fig. 1.** Excerpt of the Distributed MONDIAL XML Database [Mon]

has? Although the *XML Query Requirements* [XMQ03, Sec. 3.3.4] explicitly state that querying along references, both within an XML document and between documents, must be supported, there is currently no way to query inter-document links in the general case. While for intra-document references, the id(...) function does this task, and the doc(...) function allows for accessing remote documents, there is not yet complete support for XPointer in XPath/XQuery: even if the user knows about the schema and the semantics of XLink, he can select the pointer with let $pointer := doc("http://www.foo.de/countries.xml")//country[@car_code="B"]/capital/@href but XQuery cannot be told to resolve it. Simple XPointers ("shorthand pointers" in [XPt03]), actually consisting of ID references, e.g., http://.../country.xml#D or *url*#xpointer(id(*id*)) can be resolved by combining the doc() and id() functions.

The general case following the xpointer scheme [XPt02] like http://www.bar.de/cities-B.xml#xpointer(/cities/city[name="Brussels"]) that includes an XPath expression to specify the referenced node(s) cannot be resolved in this way: resolving such pointers requires to read a data item (the XPointer given in the href attribute of the XLink element), and then to evaluate it. Such functionality is not yet available in XQuery (and can also not be programmed by the current *XQuery 1.0 and XPath 2.0 Functions and Operators* [XPQ01]), but is e.g. proposed in Saxon [Kay99] as an XSLT extension function saxon:evaluate(), or recently in [RBHS04] as an extension of XQuery as "execute at *url* xquery { *xquery* }".

Still, the above proposals for querying in the presence of XLink elements require that the query expressions *explicitly* include the dereferencing operation. Going one step further, we follow an approach for handling distributed XML data where the links are *transparent*, i.e., we define a logical, transparent model for mapping distributed, XLinked XML documents to *one* virtual, integrated XML instance: The XLink elements are seen as view definitions that integrate the referenced XML data within the referencing XML instance (where the XLink element specifies the referenced nodes, and how they are mapped into the surrounding instance). This virtual instance can then be processed by standard languages like XPath, XQuery, or XSLT.

*Applications: Data Integration and Splitting Documents.* The usage of linked XML information occurs mainly in two situations:
– Data integration: building (virtual) XML documents by combining autonomous sources. In the integrated view, the "combining" links may be desired as subelement or IDREF attribute relationships.
– Building a distributed database by splitting an XML document over different servers. In this case, it is intended to keep the external schema unchanged, i.e., the *virtual* model of the linked documents should be valid wrt. the *original* DTD, and all queries against the root document still yield the same answers as before. This requires that the "cutting edges" – that can be between elements and their subtrees, or at (reference) attributes – can be reassembled flexibly.

For providing flexibility in fine-tuning the logical model of the linked data, we propose to extend XLink elements with *modeling switches* for designing an external schema by combining fragments of the documents in different ways.

*Structure of the Paper.* An early sketch of the *virtual* model has been presented in [May02]. The model has now been refined into a formal specification, and an implementation as an extension to the XML database system "eXist" [exi] has been done. In this paper, we focus on *simple links*. We start with an abstract and intuitive analysis of transparently querying distributed data sources in Section 2, and give the formal specification of the logical model as an XML-to-XML transformation in Section 3. Section 4 discusses the evaluation of queries in this model. The implementation based on the eXist XML database system and some special issues are described in Section 5. A comparison with related work is given in Section 6, and Section 7 concludes the paper.

## 2 A Model for Querying Along XLinks

In [May02], we proposed to use a *logical* model that transparently resolves XLinks into one virtual XML instance by extending the XLink specification with attributes in the dbxlink namespace for specifying the database-specific semantics and the behavior of XLink elements wrt. querying:

- dbxlink:transparent: mapping of the linked resources to a logical model,
- dbxlink:actuate: timepoint when the XLinks are evaluated to generate the view (materialization at parse time, or on-demand for answering a query),
- dbxlink:eval: location where the XPointers and query expressions are evaluated (locally at the referencing server, or remotely at the referenced one),
- dbxlink:cache: caching strategies for views and intermediate results.

We first consider the dbxlink:transparent attribute and extend the non-formal description given in [May02] in a precise way as an XML-to-XML mapping. The other dbxlink attributes are dealt with in Section 4 when discussing query evaluation. In our approach, linked XML resources are seen as one virtual XML instance where for all link elements, the result set defined by the XPointers in their xlink:href attributes is silently mapped into the referencing XML structure. In order to get an intuition of this model, see Figure 2.

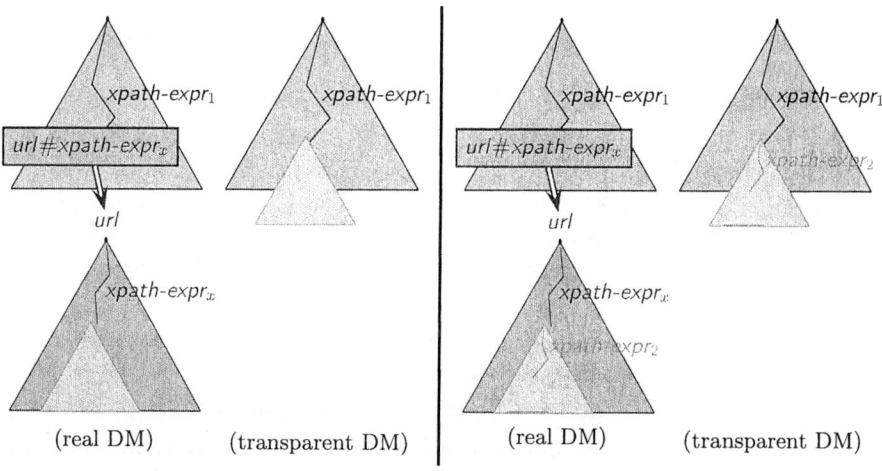

**Fig. 2.** Left: Data Model with XLink Elements; Right: Query

Although the first intuition of the above idea would be simply to "copy" the target of the XPointer into the XLink element (as XInclude [XIn04] does), there are several possibilities *how* the mapping exactly takes place – e.g., to "plug in" the referenced fragments as subelements or via reference attributes, depending on the intended target DTD. A possible mapping from the fragments shown in Figure 1 could e.g. result in a model that allows for the following XPath queries:

- model the capital as an attribute: doc("http://.../countries.xml")// country[@car_code="B"]/id(@capital)/population
- model cities as subelements, dropping the "auxiliary" cities element: doc("http://www.foo.de/countries.xml")//country[@car_code="B"]/city/name
- model neighbors as subelements that contain the referenced country data and the link's borderlength attribute: doc("...")// country[@car_code="B"]/neighbor[name="Germany"]/@borderlength (note that the virtual substructure that matches the latter part is obtained from combining the country element with its name subelement "Germany", and the neighbor subelement of Belgium with its attribute borderlength).

*Modeling Parameters.* We first identify the components of the modeling, and present the formal specification in Section 3. Consider the following abstract XML/XLink fragment:

&lt;linkelement xlink:href="*xpointer*" dbxlink:transparent="*to be described*" *non-xlink-attributes*&gt; *content* &lt;/linkelement&gt;

The virtual model of this fragment is defined as a combination of parts of the *linkelement* (its "hull" – i.e., its tags; and its "body", i.e., its attributes and contents), and of parts of the nodes referenced by *xpointer* (which consist also of a "hull" and a "body"). This fine-tuning of the mapping is declaratively specified by the dbxlink:transparent directive that describes (i) the mapping of the result set of *xpointer*, and (ii) the mapping of the XLink element itself. The directives have been chosen under consideration of application for data integration and document splitting.

i) Consider a result set containing (for simplicity only) one element (and implicitly its child elements, text and attribute nodes). The result element can be inserted "as a whole" ("insert-nodes"), or only its body ("insert-bodies"), namely its element and text children and attributes are used (for text and attribute nodes, "body" is considered empty). Analogously, if the result set contains multiple nodes.

ii) The treatment of the XLink element itself influences the structure of the virtual instance. Here, the following options exist:
  - drop the XLink element and replace it with the result set ("drop-element"),
  - drop its hull and use only the information of its body (non-XLink attributes and content) for enriching the referenced nodes ("keep-body"),
  - keep it and "wrap it around" the referenced nodes (around all of them; "group-in-element"), or duplicate it and wrap it around each of them ("duplicate-element"), or
  - replace it with an IDREF attribute with the same name as the link element ("make-attribute").

To put it all together, mapping an XLink element consists of three steps that determine the formal specification given in Section 3: (i) mapping the result set (yielding a set of nodes ("insert-nodes"), or a set of bodies ("insert-bodies")),

(ii) mapping the XLink element itself, and (iii) mapping the result to a nodeset which is then added to the parent element as new children and/or attributes. The mapping in the two first steps is chosen by the user amongst the above alternatives; the step (iii) is then solely a transformation into well-formed XML.

The dbxlink:transparency directive thus consists of two keywords: (i) one determining the mapping of the result set ("right-hand directive"; duplicate-element, group-in-element, drop-element, keep-body, or make-attribute), and (ii) one determining the mapping of the link element itself ("left-hand directive"; insert-nodes or insert-bodies).

*Example.* Figure 3 shows an excerpt of doc("http://www.foo.de/countries.xml") where the cities XLink element has been extended with a dbxlink:transparent specification. The logical model of the fragment is obtained by dropping the cities link elements and inserting the referenced nodes instead.

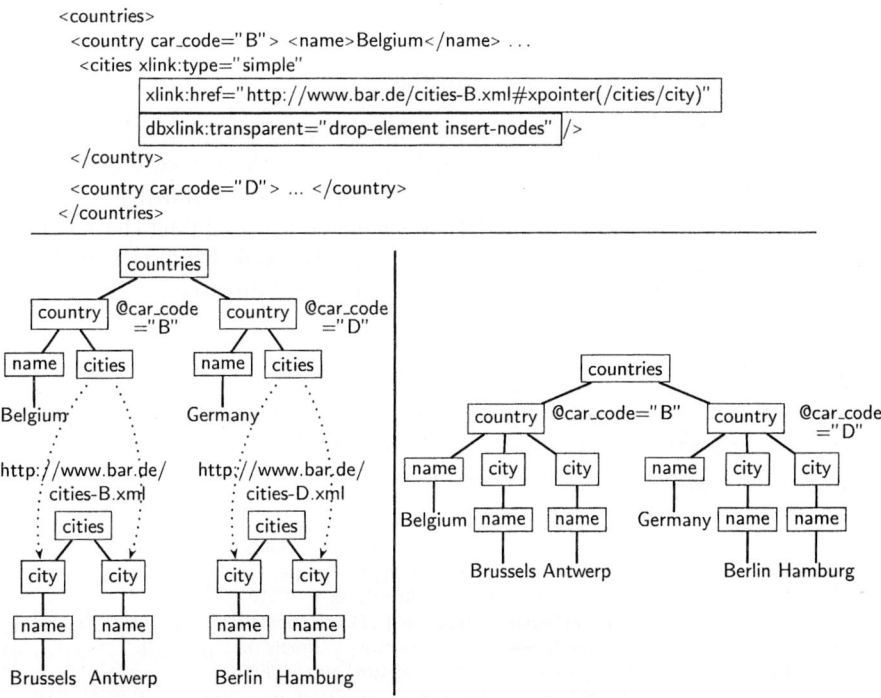

**Fig. 3.** Illustration of the Semantics: Above: Fragment Extended with dbxlink:transparent – Left: Document Trees with XLink References – Right: Induced Logical Model

*Default Mapping.* In case that no dbxlink:transparent directive is given (i.e., for XML documents on the Web that have been created without using dbxlink), dbxlink:transparent="drop-element insert-nodes" is used as default directive. This is compliant with the specification of XInclude [XIn04] (see Section 6).

## 3 Formal Specification

For the scope of this specification, we use an abstract XML data model, only distinguishing the notions of *nodes* (text, attribute and element nodes), *nodelists*, and *fragments*. A fragment is a node or a nodelist. Lists are written as usual as $[a, b, c]$ where concatenation is denoted by the "∘" operator. The following constructors and accessors for XML fragments are used, similar to the DOM and XQuery Data Model:

- Elem : QNAME × NODELIST → ELEM  constructs an element with name, attributes and children, similar to the XQuery element {*name*} {*expr**} constructor. Note: the result of *expr** contains element, attribute and text nodes.
- Attr : QNAME × STRING → ATTR  constructs a new attribute node.
- Name : NODE → QNAME  returns the name of an element or attribute node.
- Attrs, Children: NODE → NODELIST  return the list of attributes or children.
- Attrs$_X$ : NODE → NODELIST  returns the list of the non-XLink attributes.

### 3.1 Phi: The XML-to-XML Mapping

The definition of the logical model as an XML-to-XML mapping is based on an operator $\phi$ that recursively traverses an XML tree, with an auxiliary operator $\phi^*$ (for lists). Each occurrence of an XLink element is expanded by $\gamma$, using the sub-operators $\gamma_L$ (mapping the XLink element), $\gamma_R$ (mapping the XPointer result set) and $\gamma_{LR}$ (combining both $\gamma_L$ and $\gamma_R$; $L$ stands for "Link" or "Left-hand-directive", $R$ stands for "Result" or "Right-hand-directive".

---

$\phi(countries) = \phi(\mathsf{Elem}("countries", [country\_B, country\_D, \ldots])) =$
$\qquad = [\mathsf{Elem}("countries", \phi^*([country\_B, country\_D, \ldots])] =$
$\qquad = [\mathsf{Elem}("countries", \boxed{\phi(country\_B)} \circ \phi(country\_D) \circ \ldots)]$

where $\phi(country\_B) =$
$= [\phi(\mathsf{Elem}("country", [\mathsf{Attr}("car\_code", "B"), \mathsf{Attr}("area", "30510"),$
$\qquad\qquad \mathsf{Elem}("name", ["Belgium"]), \mathsf{Elem}("population", ["10170241"]),$
$\qquad\qquad \mathsf{Elem}("cities", [\mathsf{Attr}("xlink:type", "simple"), \ldots]), \ldots]))]$
$= [\mathsf{Elem}("country", \phi^*([\mathsf{Attr}("car\_code", "B"), \mathsf{Attr}("area", "30510"),$
$\qquad\qquad \mathsf{Elem}("name", ["Belgium"]), \mathsf{Elem}("population", ["10170241"]),$
$\qquad\qquad \mathsf{Elem}("cities", [\mathsf{Attr}("xlink:type", "simple"), \ldots]), \ldots])]$
$= [\mathsf{Elem}("country", \phi(\mathsf{Attr}("car\_code", "B")) \circ \phi(\mathsf{Attr}("area", "30510")) \circ$
$\qquad\qquad \phi(\mathsf{Elem}("name", ["Belgium"])) \circ \phi(\mathsf{Elem}("population", ["10170241"])) \circ$
$\qquad\qquad \phi(\mathsf{Elem}("cities", [\mathsf{Attr}("xlink:type", "simple"), \ldots])) \circ \ldots)]$
$= [\mathsf{Elem}("country", [\mathsf{Attr}("car\_code", "B")] \circ [\mathsf{Attr}("area", "30510")] \circ$
$\qquad\qquad [\mathsf{Elem}("name", ["Belgium"])] \circ [\mathsf{Elem}("population", ["10170241"])] \circ$
$\qquad\qquad \phi^*( \boxed{\gamma(\mathsf{Elem}("cities", [\mathsf{Attr}("xlink:type", "simple"), \ldots]))}), \ldots)]$
where the cities XLink element is mapped/expanded by the $\gamma$ operator, see Sec. 3.2
$= \ldots$

**Fig. 4.** Expansion by $\phi$

*Signature and Definition of $\phi$.*
Signature: $\phi$ : NODE $\rightarrow$ NODELIST ; $\phi^*$ : NODELIST $\rightarrow$ NODELIST

For non-XLink elements, the list $\phi(X)$ will contain a single element; in case that a document does not contain any XLink elements, for its root element $R$, $\phi(R) = [R]$ holds.

Definition:

- application of $\phi$ to a **non-XLink element** contains the recursion together with $\phi^*$: $\phi(elem) = [\mathsf{Elem}(\mathsf{Name}(elem), \phi^*(\mathsf{Attrs}(elem) \circ \mathsf{Children}(elem)))]$ ,
  $\phi^*([n_1, \ldots, n_k]) = \phi(n_1) \circ \ldots \circ \phi(n_k)$ ,
- for **text nodes** and **attribute nodes**, $\phi$ maps the nodes into a unary list:
  $\phi(text\text{-}node) = [text\text{-}node]$ and $\phi(attr\text{-}node) = [attr\text{-}node]$ ,
- application of $\phi$ to an **XLink element** means to expand the XLink element with $\gamma$ (see Section 3.2) and mapping the result recursively by $\phi$:
  $\phi(xlink\text{-}element) = \phi^*(\gamma(xlink\text{-}element))$.

For the example depicted in Figure 3, the transformation starts with applying $\phi$ to the countries element, which means to apply $\phi$ recursively to the countries element's attributes and children as shown in Figure 4. The $\phi$ expansion of *country_B* (shown in the inner box) applies $\phi$ again recursively to *country_B*'s attributes and children. The attributes and the name and population subelements remain unmodified. The cities subelement is an XLink element and is therefore mapped by the $\gamma$ operator as depicted in Figure 5.

### 3.2 Gamma: Expanding Individual XLink Elements

The $\gamma$ operator describes the XLink expansion itself according to the XLink element's xlink:href pointer and its dbxlink:transparent transparency directives. The operator $\gamma_R$ returns a fragment list obtained by mapping the nodes referenced by the XPointer according to the right-hand directive. The operator $\gamma_L$ (left-hand directive) modifies the returned fragment list by mapping the XLink itself. The main part of $\gamma$ then maps this fragment list into a nodelist, using auxiliary operators attr_union : NODELIST $\times$ NODELIST $\rightarrow$ NODELIST and accessors Attrs and Children that are defined as expected. Consider an XLink element

```
<linkelement xlink:href=" xpointer"
    dbxlink:transparent=" left-hand-directive right-hand-directive" attributes>
    content
</linkelement>
```

or, in our example, as shown in Figure 5, *cities_B* :=
```
<cities xlink:type="simple"  dbxlink:transparent="drop-element insert-nodes"
    xlink:href=" http://www.bar.de/cities-B.xml#xpointer(/cities/city)" >
```

*Signature and Definition of $\gamma_R$.* The arguments of the operator $\gamma_R$ (right-hand directive) are an XLink element *xlink* and the nodes that are addressed by the pure XPointer. In our example, we have $\gamma_R(cities\_B, referenced)$ where *referenced* is the result from evaluating http://www.bar.de/cities-B.xml#xpointer(/cities/city).

```
φ(countries) = φ(Elem("countries", [country_B, country_D, ...]))
             = [Elem("countries", φ(country_B) ∘ φ(country_D) ∘ ...)]

  where φ(country_B) = ... see Figure 4 ...
  = [Elem("country", [Attr("car_code", "B")] ∘ [Attr("area", "30510")] ∘
    [Elem("name", ["Belgium"])] ∘ [Elem("population", ["10170241"])] ∘
    φ*( γ(Elem("cities", [Attr("xlink:type", "simple"), ...])) ) ∘ ...)]

    //   let cities_B denote the "cities" link element of Belgium
    where γ(cities_B) = flatten(γ_{LR}(cities_B)) =
    = flatten( γ_L(cities_B, γ_R(cities_B, Eval("http://www.bar.de/cities-B.xml#xpointer(/cities/city)")) ) )

      where γ_R(cities_B, Eval("http://www.bar.de/cities-B.xml#xpointer(/cities/city)")) =
      = <city> <name>Brussels</name> <population>951580</population> ... </city>
        <city> <name>Antwerp</name> <population>459072</population> ... </city>

        //  let Γ_R denote  γ_R(cities_B, Eval(...))
        γ_L(cities_B, Γ_R) = Γ_R
      = <city> <name>Brussels</name> <population>951580</population> ... </city>
        <city> <name>Antwerp</name> <population>459072</population> ... </city>

    ... this nodelist does not contain XLink elements, thus φ*(this_list) = this_list and we obtain
    φ(country_B) = [ <country car_code="B" area="30510">
                     <name>Belgium</name><population>10170241</population>
                     <city> <name>Brussels</name> <population>951580</population> ... </city>
                     <city> <name>Antwerp</name> <population>459072</population> ... </city>
                     </country> ]   as depicted in Figure 3.

  = ...
```

**Fig. 5.** Expansion by $\gamma$

Signature: $\gamma_R$ : ELEM × NODELIST → FRAGMENTLIST
$(xlink, result) \mapsto fragment\_list$

Definition:
- if the R-directive specifies insert-nodes: $\gamma_R(xlink, result) = result$.
- if the R-directive specifies insert-bodies: $\gamma_R(xlink, [u_1, \ldots, u_n]) = [fr_1, \ldots, fr_n]$ where $fr_i$ is Attrs$(u_i)$ ∘ Children$(u_i)$ (intention: this content is later "packed" into the XLink element's "hull" by $\gamma_L$ or added to a surrounding element).

Note that in either case, there is no recursive mapping of the nodes with $\phi$ – the result of $\gamma$ is expanded afterwards (see the definition of $\phi$).

In our example, the right-hand-side directive of $cities\_B$ is insert-nodes, thus the complete nodes in $referenced$ are selected: $\gamma_R(cities\_B, referenced) = referenced$.

*Signature and Definition of $\gamma_L$.* The operator $\gamma_L$ combines the list of fragments returned by $\gamma_R$ with the information of the XLink element according to the left-hand-directive.

Signature: $\gamma_L$ : ELEM × FRAGMENTLIST → FRAGMENTLIST
$(xlink, frags) \mapsto fragment\_list$

**Definition:**
- if the L-directive specifies **drop-element**, then the XLink element is actually replaced by *frags*: $\gamma_L(xlink, frags) = frags$
- if the L-directive specifies **group-in-element**, then the XLink element is basically kept (note that the original XLink element may also have non-XLink attributes and children elements that are also kept in the result), all attribute nodes and element nodes of all of the *frags* is added to the XLink element: $\gamma_L(xlink, frags) =$ Elem(Name($xlink$), attr_union(Attrs$_X$($xlink$), Attrs($frags$))) ∘ Children($xlink$) ∘ Children($frags$))
- if the L-directive specifies **duplicate-element**, then fragment $fr_i$ in *frags* is mapped to a separate instance of the XLink element where all attribute nodes and element nodes of $fr_i$ are added: $\gamma_L(xlink, [fr_1, \ldots, fr_n]) = [e_1, \ldots, e_n]$ where $e_i =$ Elem(Name($xlink$), attr_union(Attrs$_X$($xlink$), Attrs($fr_i$))) ∘ Children($xlink$) ∘ Children($fr_i$))
- if the L-directive specifies **keep-body**, then the XLink element "hull" is dropped, but its "information", i.e., non-XLink attributes and children, are added to each element node in *frags* (all other nodes in *frags* are dropped in this case):
$\gamma_L(xlink, frags) = [n_1, \ldots, n_k]$ where for each $e_i$ which is an element node in one of the *frags*, $n_i =$ Elem(Name($e_i$), attr_union(Attrs$_X$($xlink$), Attrs($e_i$)) ∘ Children($xlink$) ∘ Children($e_i$))
- if the L-directive specifies **make-attribute**, then a single attribute node is created as $\gamma_L(xlink, frags) =$ Attr(Name($xlink$), $u_1 \circ \ldots \circ u_n$), with the name of the link element where for each node $n$ in *frags*,
  - if $n$ is an attribute or text node then $u_i =$ value($n$),
  - if $n$ is an element node, extend $n$ with an attribute node Attr(dbxlink:ID, $id$) where $id$ is a new id and put it in a bucket, and set $u_i = id$.
  The content of the bucket is a separate part of the virtual instance which is reachable by the id() function.
  
  In any meaningful application for **make-attribute**, *frags* will be either a set of elements (e.g., **capital** in our example), a set of attribute and/or text nodes, or a single attribute or text node.

Returning to the running example, $\gamma_L(cities\_B, referenced) = referenced$ since **drop-element** is specified.

*Signature and Definition of $\gamma_{LR}$.* The operator $\gamma_{LR}$ combines the application of the functions $\gamma_L$ and $\gamma_R$, yielding a fragment as result:

$\gamma_{LR}$ : NODE → FRAGMENTLIST : $xlink \mapsto \gamma_L(xlink, \gamma_R(xlink, \text{Eval}(xpointer)))$

where *xpointer* is the value of the href attribute of *xlink* and Eval(*xpointer*) is the set of nodes addressed by *xpointer*.

For the running example, not surprisingly, $\gamma_{LR}(cities\_B) = referenced$ – which mirrors the fact that (i) the XLink element is dropped, and (ii) the referenced nodes are inserted instead.

Note that in case that make-attribute is specified, $\gamma_{LR}$ may yield an attribute node which is then inserted into the surrounding element. The insertion of the result from calling $\gamma_{LR}$ is finally done by $\gamma$, as shown below.

*Signature and Definition of $\gamma$.* We now get back to the outer operator $\gamma$. It maps the result from $\gamma_{LR}$ (that is formally a fragment) to a nodelist (in all cases of reasonable applications, the fragment is not nested):

$$\gamma : \mathsf{NODE} \rightarrow \mathsf{NODELIST} \; ; \; xlink \mapsto \mathsf{flatten}(\gamma_{LR}(xlink))$$

where flatten flattens a possibly nested fragment list into a nodelist.

Note again that the resolving of XLinks can not only result in nodes that just replace the XLink element, but can also add attribute nodes to the surrounding element. According to the semantics of XQuery's computed element constructor, the resulting attribute nodes are seamlessly appended to the surrounding element. In our semantics, this happens in the recursive application of the $\phi$ operator (first item) where the result is constructed as

$$\phi(elem) = \mathsf{Elem}(\mathsf{Name}(elem), \phi^*(\mathsf{Attrs}(elem) \circ \mathsf{Children}(elem)))$$

and all elements, text, and attribute nodes in $\phi^*(...)$ are added to the surrounding element.

*Summary.* The logical model is defined as the result of mapping an XML tree by $\phi$ and $\gamma$ as described above. Note that the *logical* model is a possibly infinite tree (e.g. for the neighbor relationship in our example in Figure 1 – Belgium is a neighbor of France which is a neighbor of Germany which is again a neighbor of Belgium ...), but as long as only a finite set of Web sources is involved, it has a finite representation as a graph. For the abstract definition of the logical model, this is no problem – only the actual query evaluation wrt. this (abstract) model must then care for detecting cycles.

## 4  Query Evaluation

Given the above formal definition and a query $Q$ whose entry point to a linked network of XML documents is the document at $url$, the answer to $Q$ is defined as the answer to $Q$ against $\phi(\mathsf{doc}(url))$. For *evaluation* of a query, it is in general not necessary to create the whole virtual model, but to expand links *on demand*, inducing a simple, "naive" evaluation strategy. In contrast to Active XML, e.g., [ABC+04], where the *potentially* relevant links are identified and evaluated before the actual query evaluation, the strategy evaluates only those views that are actually needed (we assume views in general to be larger than the mostly small Web Service answers that are considered in the Active XML framework).

### 4.1  Example: Naive Evaluation

The following simple XPath expression that returns all names of Belgian cities illustrates how a query against the virtual instance of the above example is evaluated: doc("countries.xml")/countries/country[@car_code="B"]/city/name. When starting with the first two location steps, doc("countries.xml") and its countries root element are accessed. The subsequent step, country[@car_code="B"], actually consists of (i) an axis step country and (ii) the evaluation of the predicate. For (i), all subelements of the countries element have to be considered. These are only the country elements, and there are no direct XLink subelements whose evaluation results in additional subelements.

Thus, the axis step results in all country elements (here, Belgium and Germany). For evaluation of the predicate, all attributes of these elements *in the virtual model* have to be checked, searching for an attribute with name car_code and value "B". From this step, only the country element for Belgium qualifies. The next step, city, now searches for city subelements of Belgium. Here, all subelements of Belgium that are city elements (none), and additionally, the cities subelement is resolved – according to its dbxlink:transparent specification as "drop-element insert-nodes". Its XPointer points to the city elements in http://www.bar.de/cities-B.xml that are inserted as they are; the cities XLink element is replaced by them as shown in Fig. 3. The city step then results in the two city elements. The next step (name) then results in "Brussels" and "Antwerp".

### 4.2 Evaluation Strategies

For evaluating queries that navigate through link elements, there are several possibilities, concerning the issues, *when* and *where* parts of the query are evaluated. Any XPath expression that "passes" through an XLink element can be decomposed into three parts (cf. the right part of Figure 2): (i) the "upper" part xpath-expr$_1$ that traverses the local data, (ii) the XPointer expression xpath-expr$_x$ that defines the view, and (iii) the remaining part xpath-expr$_2$ of the query that is evaluated against the view. The dbxlink:eval attribute specifies where the evaluation of these parts actually takes place, according to the classification in [FJK96]:

- dblink:eval="local": access the whole contents of *url* and evaluate xpath-expr$_x$/xpath-expr$_2$ locally (*data-shipping*).
- dblink:eval="distributed": submit the query xpath-expr$_x$ to the server at *url* and receive the result. Then, evaluate xpath-expr$_2$ against it (*hybrid shipping*).
- dblink:eval="remote": submit the query xpath-expr$_x$/xpath-expr$_2$ (in an adapted rewriting that encodes the "inverse" of the dbxlink:transparent mapping) to the server at *url*. In this case, the views defined by the link remain completely virtual also during evaluation (complete *query-shipping*). Note that this requires the remote service to be XML/XPath-aware which is e.g. not the case in Active XML where the remote service can be any kind of Web Service.

Links that do not have a dbxlink:eval directive are by default evaluated according to the dbxlink:eval="distributed" strategy. If the target of the link resides on a remote server, the actually applicable strategies depend on the provided services (i.e., whether the whole XML document is accessible, and/or what queries can be answered). If the remote server returns an error message (e.g., because it is not capable of answering XPath queries), then dbxlink:eval="local" is used as fallback, trying to access the whole referenced document and evaluating the query locally.

### 4.3 Evaluation Timepoints/Activating Event

XLink defines several attributes for link elements that specify the *behavior* of the link element, i.e., *when* it should become "activated" and *what* happens then. This behavior is tailored to the use of links when browsing; it does not cover the requirements of querying XML instances. The activating event of links is considered in XLink with the dbxlink:actuate attribute: In the browsing context, auto means that the XPointer is evaluated when the node containing it is parsed (i.e., when the HTML page is accessed, or when XML content is processed by a stylesheet), whereas user states that it is activated by the user (HTML: clicking). In the database context, dbxlink:actuate="parse" means that the XLink is evaluated when the document is added to the database (or when the XLink element is created) – thus, the view is materialized in this case. The keyword "user" denotes that it is evaluated on-demand when it is used by a query, which guarantees that always the current state of the referenced resource is queried. The default setting is dbxlink:actuate="user".

Whereas for browsing, the difference between "parse" and "user" is rather small, in the context of persistent data in databases and queries against it, there is a wide area of materializing, i.e., *caching*, and reusing intermediate results.

### 4.4 Caching Strategies

As stated above, when accessing a remote server and answering queries, the obtained data may be cached for reuse in subsequent queries. Caching can be specified by the dbxlink:cache attribute of XLink elements:

- dbxlink:cache="complete" (in combination with dbxlink:eval="local", where the referenced document is accessed completely) stores the referenced document in the local XML database. When later another query traverses the link, it can be evaluated against the cached document;
- dbxlink:cache="pointer" (in combination with dbxlink:eval="local" and dbxlink:eval="distributed") caches the result of evaluating the XPointer;
- dbxlink:cache="answer" caches the answer to a query against an XLink view;
- dbxlink:cache="none" caches nothing (which is also the default setting, since then always the current state of resources is accessed).

## 5  Implementation

As a proof-of-concept, the approach has been implemented as an extension of the open source XML database *eXist* [exi], a native XML database system. For enabling navigation along XLinks according to the proposed semantics, the XPath evaluation engine has been modified. Link elements are replaced on-demand during query evaluation.

Starting with the root element of an XML document (or with an element bound to a variable), XPath steps are evaluated recursively. Each step defines a new set of nodes, the *context* to which the next step is applied. In order to implicitly replace all relevant link elements during navigation in an XML tree, thus making the navigation transparent, all subelements of every node belonging to the *context* have to be analyzed: any XLink subelement of the current context node can potentially be replaced by one or more nodes that are relevant for the next step. Note that XLink elements with left-hand-directives "duplicate-element", "group-in-element", and "make-attribute" are only relevant if their name matches the next step. Thus, a kind of forward evaluation in order to make the required nodes available for the next step has been implemented according to the specification presented in Section 3, temporarily materializing fragments of the virtual instance on-demand. Basically, $\gamma_R$ and $\gamma_L$ are implemented as two independent modules, dealing with the right-hand-directive and the left-hand-directive, respectively.

*Distributed Evaluation.* For illustration, consider the dbxlink:eval="distributed" strategy (whose evaluation is closest to the formal definition of the operators) when answering a query as discussed in Section 4.2:

1. For applying the right-hand directive, the XPath expression xlink:href="*xpath-expr$_x$*" of the current XLink element is sent to the remote server by using the *XML-RPC* protocol,
2. $\gamma_R$: The returned result is mapped by $\gamma_R$ according to the right-hand-directive,
3. $\gamma_L$: The intermediate fragments are then temporarily added to the virtual instance by $\gamma_L$ according to the left-hand-directive,
4. the remaining query is then evaluated against the temporarily extended virtual instance.

Caching is –according to dbxlink:cache– optionally applied to the returned result after step (1) and to the result of step (4). Analogously, cache-lookup is applied first for the result of the query, and then for the result of the XPointer.

*Local Evaluation.* Alternatively, if dbxlink:eval="local" is specified, or the remote source does not support XPath queries (including XLink resolving), the whole remote document is accessed, and the referenced nodes are computed locally; then it continues as above. Caching and cache-lookup can be applied for the referenced document, and for the answer to the query.

*Remote Evaluation: Query Shipping.* In case that dbxlink:eval="remote" is specified, the remaining query expression *xpath-expr$_x$*/*xpath-expr$_2$* that will be shipped to the remote server must be adapted according to the (inverse of the) mappings $\gamma_L$ and $\gamma_R$, concerning the final step of *xpath-expr$_x$* and the first step of *xpath-expr$_2$*; depending on the left-hand-directive, one more step is done locally.

*Example.* Consider the query "population of the city 'Antwerp' in Belgium" against the example shown in Figure 3,

//country[name="Belgium"]/city[name="Antwerp"]/population.

After navigating to Belgium, the database engine must resolve its XLink subelements in order to check if there are some city elements in the virtual model. The remaining query part is *xpath-expr$_2$* = city[name="Antwerp"]/population. In this situation, there is only the cities XLink element with an XPointer *xpath-expr$_x$* = #xpointer(/cities/city) and the directives "drop-element insert-nodes". Since "drop-element" is specified, we do not have to care for the XLink element itself. The city step occurs twice: once in the XPointer *xpath-expr$_x$* for *selecting* the nodes, and once at the beginning of *xpath-expr$_2$* for traversing them. Thus, the last step of *xpath-expr$_x$* and the first step of *xpath-expr$_2$* must be merged, keeping the stricter nodetest and the predicates. This leads to shipping the combined query /cities/city[name="Antwerp"]/population to the remote node.

In the general case, the inverse mappings of $\gamma_L$ and $\gamma_R$ combine as follows:

- XLink elements with (L) "duplicate-element", "group-in-element", and "make-attribute" are only relevant if their name and resulting axis matches the next step in *xpath-expr$_2$*, which is then removed from *xpath-expr$_2$*.
- for (L) "drop-element", and "keep-body", *xpath-expr$_2$* is not changed.
- for (L) "keep-body", *xpath-expr$_2$* must also be evaluated locally against the contents and attributes of the XLink element,
- for (R) "insert-nodes", the last step of *xpath-expr$_x$* and the first step of *xpath-expr$_2$* are merged as described in the above example.
- for (R) "insert-bodies", *xpath-expr$_x$*/*xpath-expr$_2$* are just concatenated.

*Remote evaluation: Non-downward Axes.* The user's queries are stated against the virtual model. Thus, if the *xpath-expr$_2$* part uses an absolute path in a filter (semijoin) or a non-downward axis like ancestor, siblings, or preceding/following that potentially leaves the embedded view part, the query must not be shipped. In this case, only local and distributed evaluation lead to correct results.

## Search Space and Cycles

*Descendant Axis: Search Space.* For evaluating queries that use the descendant axis, in general all XLink elements (except those with "make-attribute") must (recursively) be resolved (which can lead to searching the whole Web). Since this *is* necessarily the case for guaranteeing completeness, this problem is not special to our approach, but applies to any approach that allows for including views on distributed XML resources. We propose the following handling:

- Design: use (L) "make-attribute" in all cases where the resulting structure is not inherently nested – here, the descendant axis ends.
- Metadata about the element and attribute names and paths contained in a document (including recursive views) can help not only for detecting cycles, but also for pruning the search space (see Related Work).

*Descendant Axis: Cycles.* As discussed at the end of Section 3, even with only a finite set of Web sources involved, there can be infinite chains in the descendant axis due to cyclic links. Depending on the chosen shipping strategies, appropriate auxiliary information must be generated or provided for controlling the evaluation process:

- remote evaluation: in case of a cycle, the same query is shipped around this cycle. Keeping a "shipping history" allows for detecting such cycles and returning an empty answer.
- local and distributed: in case of a cycle, the same remaining query (in the above terminology, *xpath-expr*$_2$) is evaluated twice against the result of the same XPointer (*xpath-expr*$_x$). Here, bookkeeping which pairs (*xpath-expr*$_x$, *xpath-expr*$_2$) have already been processed allows to detect cycles and to return an empty answer.

**Testbed and Demonstrator.** For testing the functionality and experimenting with different strategies, a network of dbxlink-enabled eXist servers on different hosts is used. The main demonstrator is based on a distributed version of the MONDIAL database [Mon]. The "central" server contains all countries (countries.xml) and serves usually as the entry point for queries. The remaining servers host documents concerning geographic information, organizations and memberships, as well as cities and provinces (by country):

- countries.xml (all countries)
- cities-XX.xml (cities for each country, where XX is the car code of the respective country)
- organizations.xml (organizations)
- memberships.xml (countries ↔ organizations)
- geo.xml (mountains, waters etc.)

The distributed scenario can be queried via a public XPath/XQuery interface at [Lin].

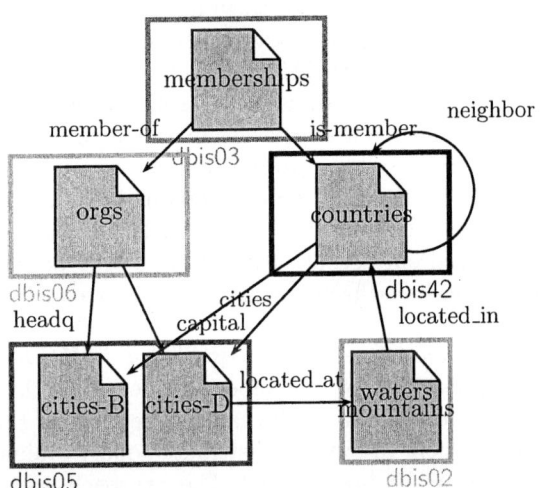

## 6 Related Approaches

*XLink Browsing and XInclude.* Up to now, the XLink approach is primarily interpreted for browsing, as it is mirrored by the W3C XLink Recommendation [XLi01] where several attributes for link elements are defined that specify the *behavior* of the link element during browsing. The show="embed" behavior of XLink can be seen as one special case of our approach, featuring dbxlink:transparent="group-by-element insert-nodes".

XInclude [XIn04] is a restricted approach for including documents: it defines a fixed XML-to-XML transformation where the <xi:include href="*xpointer*"> elements are *replaced* by the corresponding included items (cf. dbxlink:transparent= "drop-element insert-nodes"), evaluating the references at parse time.

In contrast to the XLink and XInclude models, our approach allows for fine-tuning the logical model, e.g., adhering to a common, integrating target DTD.

The XInclude handling of references is also not suitable for database environments: The XInclude parse-time evaluation in fact materializes the referenced contents which is reasonable for lightweight tools such as Saxon; whereas in a database environment, this would mean to evaluate the references once when storing the document. In contrast to that, dbxlink allows to keep the links in the database, only evaluating them on-demand, always using the current contents of the referenced sources.

*Active XML.* A general approach for integrating remote access functionality into XML documents is proposed by *Active XML* [ABM+02]: <axml:call> elements allow for embedding *service calls* into XML documents. Active XML and dbxlink differ significantly wrt. generality (Active XML) and specialization (dbxlink) and in the degree of integration with the database functionality. While the dbxlink approach is an incremental extension to the existing concepts of XLink and XPointer, targeting to provide a transparent data model and support XPath/XQuery for them from the database point of view, Active XML is a generic extension of functionality towards Web Services. Instantiating a dbxlink service with Active XML could only provide the "remote" $\gamma_R$ part of the model (which would e.g. be sufficient for implementing XInclude). Tasks that need close interaction with the query evaluation algorithms, like integrating the result into the model according to $\gamma_L$ (in case of data or hybrid shipping) or accessing *xpath-expr*$_2$ (in case of query shipping) cannot be supported in Active XML. On the other hand, since arbitrary URLs can be used in XPointers (where we here considered only XPath expressions), Web Service calls can also be handled by an XLink-based framework, here also extended with dbxlink flexibility.

*Decomposing Queries on Distributed XML Data.* Several approaches dealing with strategies for decomposing queries on distributed XML data have been investigated whose results can also be used for the implementation of the dbxlink specification. In [Suc02], distributed query evaluation for general semistructured data graphs is investigated. The approach assumes that a fixed community of sites agrees on sharing their data and answering queries. They split the query into a *decomposed query*, evaluate its parts independently at each site, and assemble the result fragments. In contrast to this, the scenario of our approach considers XLink references between *arbitrary* sources, and the specification for mapping the linked fragments to a virtual instance and querying it. The logical modeling of [Suc02] is similar to XInclude. In [BG03], the distribution of XML repositories is investigated, focussing on index structures. The above approaches are orthogonal to ours (where the focus is on the modeling and handling of the interplay of links seen as views) and could probably be applied for a more efficient implementation.

## 7 Conclusion and Perspectives

We have presented an approach that allows for querying networks of XLink-ed XML documents, using a *logical* model for such documents. With this, XPath (and thus also XQuery, XSLT etc.) constructs can be used to operate transparently on linked documents. The reference implementation is done as a modification of eXist [exi]. In general, the approach can be implemented as an extension to any XPath/XQuery engine.

The contribution of the paper is to provide a database-oriented interpretation of XLink, together with a proof-of-concept implementation. The implementation does not deal with the evaluation of distributed queries in the most elaborate and efficient way. These issues pose a lot of questions that call for combinations with results of other work, e.g., parallel evaluation of remote queries and strategies for the case that a remote source does not answer, refined caching strategies, query containment and rewriting, optimization strategies for local evaluation of XPath queries and stream processing of the results of XPointers, as well as strategies based on metadata, schema reasoning, and path indexes for finding which XLinks will contribute to the result of a given query. In a global scale, such strategies require a sophisticated P2P-based infrastructure with appropriate communication. In these aspects, more specialized research results, some of which are mentioned above, can be applied.

*Acknowledgements.* This work is supported by the German Research Foundation (DFG) within the LinXIS project.

## References

[ABM+02]   S. Abiteboul, O. Benjelloun, I. Manolescu, T. Milo, and R. Weber. Active XML: Peer-to-Peer Data and Web Services Integration. *VLDB*, 2002.

[ABC+04]   S. Abiteboul, O. Benjelloun, B. Cautis, I. Manolescu, T. Milo, N. Preda. Lazy Query Evaluation for Active XML *SIGMOD*, 2004.

[BG03]   J. Bremer and M. Gertz. On Distributing XML Repositories. *WebDB*, 2003.

[exi]   eXist: an Open Source Native XML Database. http://exist-db.org/.

[FJK96]   M. J. Franklin, B. T. Jonsson, and D. Kossmann. Performance Tradeoffs for Client-Server Query Processing. *SIGMOD*, 1996.

[Kay99]   M. Kay. SAXON. http://saxon.sourceforge.net/, 1999.

[Lin]   The LinXIS Project. http://dbis.informatik.uni-goettingen.de/LinXIS/.

[May02]   W. May. Querying Linked XML Document Networks in the Web. *11th. WWW Conference*, 2002. http://www2002.org/CDROM/alternate/166/.

[Mon]   MONDIAL Database. http://dbis.informatik.uni-goettingen.de/Mondial.

[RBHS04]   C. Re, J. Brinkley, K. Hinshaw, and D. Suciu. Distributed XQuery. *Workshop on Information Integration on the Web (IIWEB)*, 2004.

[Suc02] D. Suciu. Distributed Query Evaluation on Semistructured Data. *ACM Transactions on Database Systems (TODS)*, 27(1):1–62, 2002.
[XIn04] XML Inclusions (XInclude). http://www.w3.org/TR/xinclude/, 2004.
[XLi01] XML Linking Language (XLink). http://www.w3.org/TR/xlink, 2001.
[XMQ03] XML Query Requirements. http://www.w3.org/TR/xmlquery-req, 2003.
[XPQ01] XQuery 1.0 and XPath 2.0 Functions and Operators. http://www.w3.org/TR/xquery-operators, 2001.
[XPt02] XPointer xpointer() Scheme. http://www.w3.org/TR/xptr-xpointer, 2002.
[XPt03] XPointer Framework. http://www.w3.org/TR/xptr-framework, 2003.

# Query Planning in the Presence of Overlapping Sources

Jens Bleiholder[1], Samir Khuller[2], Felix Naumann[1],
Louiqa Raschid[2], and Yao Wu[2]

[1] Humboldt-Universität zu Berlin, Germany
{naumann, bleiho}@informatik.hu-berlin.de
[2] University of Maryland, College Park, Maryland, USA
{samir, yaowu}@cs.umd.edu, louiqa@umiacs.umd.edu

**Abstract.** Navigational queries on Web-accessible life science sources pose unique query optimization challenges. The objects in these sources are interconnected to objects in other sources, forming a large and complex graph, and there is an overlap of objects in the sources. Answering a query requires the traversal of multiple alternate paths through these sources. Each path can be associated with the benefit or the cardinality of the target object set (TOS) of objects reached in the result. There is also an evaluation cost of reaching the TOS.

We present dual problems in selecting the best set of paths. The first problem is to select a set of paths that satisfy a constraint on the evaluation cost while maximizing the benefit (number of distinct objects in the TOS). The dual problem is to select a set of paths that satisfies a threshold of the TOS benefit with minimal evaluation cost. The two problems can be mapped to the budgeted maximum coverage problem and the maximal set cover with a threshold. To solve these problems, we explore several solutions including greedy heuristics, a randomized search, and a traditional IP/LP formulation with bounds. We perform experiments on a real-world graph of life sciences objects from NCBI and report on the computational overhead of our solutions and their performance compared to the optimal solution.

## 1 Introduction

The last few years have seen an explosion in the number of public life science data sources, as well as the volume of data entries about scientific entities, such as genes, proteins, sequences, etc. Consequently, biologists spend a considerable amount of time navigating through the contents of these sources to obtain useful information. Life sciences sources, and the navigational queries that are of interest to scientists, pose some unique challenges. First, information about a certain scientific entity, e.g., a protein, may be available in a large number of autonomous sources, each possibly providing a different characterization of the entity. While the contents of these sources *overlap*, they are not replicas. Second, the *links* between scientific entities (links between data objects) in the different sources are unique in this domain in that they capture significant knowledge about the relationship and interactions between these entities. These links are uncovered in the process of navigation. Third, users are usually interested in navigational queries.

We consider a given set of sources and assume that the data objects in any of these sources have links to data objects in the other sources. We further assume that a (simple) navigational query identifies an origin class, e.g., protein, and possibly a (set of) origin sources that are of interest, e.g., UniProt. The query also identifies a target class of interest, e.g., publications, as well as an optional list of intermediate sources. Answering such queries involves exploring the data sources and classes, and the links between data sources. Our goal is to find paths at the logical level (among classes) and paths at the physical level (among sources implementing these classes). While we note that the query language can be extended to other query types, for our study we use a simple query.

Each path is associated with a *benefit*, namely the number of distinct objects reached in the target object set (TOS) in the target class. Each path is also associated with a *cost* of evaluating the query on the sources to compute the TOS. Given the overlap between sources and the highly interconnected nature of the object graph, each m-way combination of TOSs of paths is also associated with a *TOS overlap*. This overlap represents same objects reached in the TOS using different paths, and reduces the combined benefit of this path combination.

We present dual problems in this context of selecting the best set of paths. The first problem is to select a set of paths that satisfy a constraint on the evaluation cost while maximizing the benefit or the number of distinct objects in the TOS of these paths. This problem maps to the budgeted maximum coverage (BMC) problem [1]. We expect that in many cases, a user is more interested in reaching some desired minimal number of objects and may not set a constraint on the budget. To explore this situation, we consider the dual problem, which selects a set of paths that satisfies a threshold of the TOS benefit with minimal evaluation cost. The dual can be mapped to the maximal set cover with a threshold (MSCT).

The problems we address apply to many other scenarios. Consider a general problem - find a best set of paths to the data sources - and a simpler subproblem - find the best set of sources, ignoring that there might be multiple heterogeneous paths to reach these sources. This subproblem arises in many data integration situations, namely whenever (i) the integrated system has access to multiple sources that overlap in the data they store, (ii) it is not necessarily required to retrieve *all* answers to a query (some are enough), and (iii) some per-source cost is incurred to find and retrieve answers. Applications include metasearch engines and search engines for intranets, stock information systems (queries cost money), shopping agents, and digital libraries. For each of these systems it is worthwhile to access only some data sources and still find satisfying results.

Life science data sources are distributed web accessible sources. Consider the NCBI that is a portal providing access to all public NIH funded sources. For our research we created a warehouse of a subset of the links between 5 sources. We note that creating a warehouse of links for all web access sources á la Google and providing the statistics needed to solve our problems is a difficult problem and is discussed in the experiment section.

**Contributions.** We identify a path overlap problem faced by life scientists in navigating paths among multiple interconnected and overlapping sources and we model it as a BMC problem and a dual MSCT problem. We propose an exact solution (IP), a randomized approximate solution with bounds (LP), unbounded greedy heuristics, and unbounded randomized solutions. Finally, we present empirical results of our strategies on a sampled real world data graph from the NCBI. The graph is stored in a database and we discuss the computational overhead supporting our solutions.

**Outline.** Sec. 2 first introduces our model of sources, objects, links, queries, and paths, and next formally states the two optimization problems. To solve the problems, Sec. 3 presents algorithms to compute exact solutions, an algorithm with known optimality bounds, and efficient but unbounded algorithms. Sec. 4 describes our experimental data of linked NCBI sources and their source-metrics, such as cardinality and overlap. In Sec. 5 we report on our experimental results showing good performance and solution quality for both problems. Finally, Sec. 6 reviews related work and Sec. 7 concludes.

## 2 Modeling Life Science Data Sources

We introduce a model for life science data sources and queries, and then define the problem of selecting sources and source paths to answer queries. Further and more detailed definitions are in [2].

### 2.1 Data Model and Queries

A scientific entity or class represents instances of a *logical class* of objects, e.g., Disease, Sequence, etc. A *logical link* is a directed relationship between two logical classes. The set of logical classes and logical links between them form the directed *logical graph LG*. A logical graph $LG$ is an abstraction (or schema) of the source graph $SG$ with data sources as nodes. A source $S$ is a real-world accessible data source. Each logical class can be implemented by several sources. In turn, the object graph $OG$ is an instance of $SG$ containing representations of real-world objects and links between them. Finally, a result graph $RG$ is a subset of $OG$ and contains the data objects and links specific to a particular query. $LG$, $OG$, and $RG$ are analogous to the schema, database instance, and result of a query.

Figure 1 shows an example of a world with four logical classes, Disease, Protein, Sequence, and Publication, and five sources. OMIM is the source that stores data on genetic knowledge on *Disease*, and Publications are stored in two sources PUBMED and BOOKS. Each source has some objects stored within, each having zero or more links to objects in other sources.

A source path $p$ is a path from an *origin source* in the source graph $SG$ to a *target source* of $SG$. Figure 2 lists the five source paths connecting origin source OMIM and target source PUBMED or BOOKS in our example $SG$.

An *object link* is a directed edge between two data objects in two different sources. Given a source graph, the *object graph* $OG$ is a directed graph in which the set $O$ of all data objects stored by the sources are the nodes, and the set $L$ of object links between these objects are the edges. The object graph represents our world model of all the objects and links that we consider. We note that object t in the $OG$ of Fig. 1 occurs in the path overlap of two paths from OMIM to PUBMED, and in the path overlap of two paths from OMIM to BOOKS.

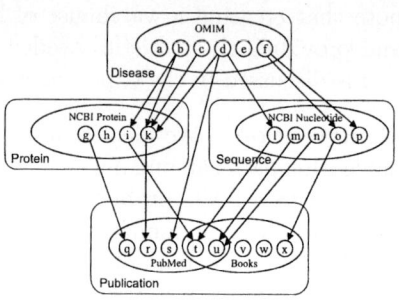

**Fig. 1.** A simple model with classes, sources, objects, and links

Consider the following query: *"Return all Publications of PUBMED that are linked to an OMIM entry about Diseases related to the keyword tumor."* To answer this query, a set of source paths in $SG$ from OMIM to PUBMED are identified. A keyword search on tumor is used to retrieve relevant entries from OMIM. Then, for each source path, starting from the selected OMIM objects, all paths in $OG$ that reach PUBMED entries are traversed. We define a result graph as representing

(P1) OMIM → PUBMED
(P2) OMIM → NCBI_Protein → PUBMED
(P3) OMIM → NCBI_Nucleotide → PUBMED
(P4) OMIM → NCBI_Protein → BOOKS
(P5) OMIM → NCBI_Nucleotide → BOOKS

**Fig. 2.** Five paths from OMIM to PUBMED or BOOKS through the source graph of Fig. 1

the answers of a query against the $OG$. A result graph is a subset of the object graph. The *target object set (TOS)* is the set of objects in the $RG$ reached in the target source of a particular source path. In the example the objects reached in PUBMED. Either the RG or the TOS for each of the source paths can be considered to be answers to the query. For the purposes of this paper, we consider simple queries that start with a set of objects in an origin source and traverse paths in $OG$ to reach a set of objects (TOS) in each target source. More complex navigational queries are described in [3].

A source path $p$ in $SG$ can be characterized by a number of metrics, including the following:

- Length of the path
- Cardinality of attributes of all sources visited by $p$
- Cardinality of objects in the target source (TOS) - also called the benefit
- Cost of evaluating this source path on $OG$
- User's preference for objects in the TOS reached by traversing $p$

In related work we consider a multi-criteria optimization problem to generate the best K source paths or skyline paths [4].

## 2.2 Problem Statement

We formulate dual problems with respect to maximizing benefit given some starting object(s) and a cost constraint. The dual is to find a set of paths with benefit above a threshold that has the least cost.

Consider the TOSs of two paths. We assume that the benefit of an object is 1. An important observation when counting target objects is that there is no additional benefit when the same object occurs in both TOS. We describe this as *TOS overlap*. TOS overlap can occur at different degrees, i.e., it can be disjoint, contained, equivalent, or have some concrete value. A discussion of overlap and methods to estimate overlap under certain assumptions is given in [2]. We note that while our problem definition assumes that there is no benefit of finding objects multiple times in overlapping paths, there are other contexts in which semantic knowledge is associated with overlap. For example, the fact that an object was reached by traversing two specific alternate paths may convey some knowledge about the characteristics of this object, or the sources involved in the paths.

We assume that there is a cost (or delay) associated with traversing the paths. This is realistic since accessing multiple sources may both delay the scientists as they wait for answers to be computed and delivered. It may also have a negative impact on all other users of these sources. Finally, the commercialization of certain data products means that actual payments may also be involved. A simple cost model would be to assign each path a unit cost (1). This turns the problem into choosing a combination of the best $k$ paths among all possible paths. A more realistic way of assigning costs to the paths is to follow a cost model for query evaluation. In a later section, we discuss computing the metrics of paths in detail.

Assuming non-uniform costs, benefits, and TOS overlap, the problem is formally defined as follows:

**Problem 1 (BMC).** Consider a collection of paths $\mathcal{P} = \{p_1, p_2, \ldots p_m\}$, a world of objects $Z = \{z_1, z_2, \ldots z_n\}$ and a mapping to indicate if element $z_j$ occurs in the TOS of path $p_i$. There is an associated cost for picking each path and an associated benefit for covering each element. Consider a collection of paths $\mathcal{P}' \subseteq \mathcal{P}$; the distinct objects in the corresponding union of the TOS for $\mathcal{P}'$ is labeled UnionTOS. The goal of our first problem is to find a set $\mathcal{P}'$ such that the total (adjusted) benefit of UnionTOS gained by picking $\mathcal{P}'$ is maximized, and the total cost of $\mathcal{P}'$ does not exceed a given budget $B$. The problem is known as the Budgeted Maximum Coverage (BMC) problem in the literature and is NP-hard [1]. Note that while the overall cost is the sum of the individual costs, the overall benefit is not the sum of individual benefits but must be adjusted (reduced) by any existing overlap.

**Problem 2 (MSCT).** The dual of this problem is the Maximal Set Coverage (with Threshold) or MSCT problem. The goal is to find a collection of paths

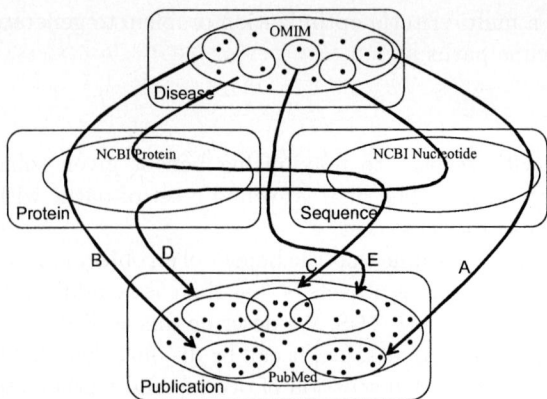

**Fig. 3.** An example graph with five overlapping paths from OMIM to PUBMED and their benefit and cost

$\mathcal{P}' \subseteq \mathcal{P}$ such that the (adjusted) benefit of UnionTOS gained by picking $\mathcal{P}'$ is at least $T$ while minimizing the total cost of $\mathcal{P}'$.

### 2.3 An Example

To illustrate how to choose combinations of paths we present an example. Figure 3 shows four data sources OMIM, PUBMED, NCBI_PROTEIN, and NCBI_SEQUENCE. There are five possible paths from OMIM to PUBMED (labeled A to E). Each path starts with a set of OMIM objects and terminates in a set of PUBMED objects. This results in the path benefit is also shown. The intermediate objects are not shown in Fig. 3 to not confuse the reader. The table of Fig. 3 shows cost and benefit/cost ratio.

Assume a cost limit of 20, which must be met and overlap as given in Fig. 3 (overlap(CD)=1 and overlap(CE)=2). We cannot follow all paths given the cost limit. We use this example in the following section to explain the different algorithms of finding the best subset of paths.

## 3 Algorithms

To solve BMC and MSCT, we implemented several algorithms to find a combination of best paths. After stating how to determine exact solutions for comparison purposes, we model the problem as an IP/LP, and then present some unbounded solutions including greedy algorithms and a random search algorithm. While the algorithms are applied to our small example here, we show how they perform on real-world data sets in Sec. 5.

### 3.1 Computing Exact Solutions

**BMC:** Determining an exact solution for BMC requires looking at all combinations of paths and their TOS, and choosing the one with the highest overlap-adjusted benefit. The overlap-adjusted benefit simply eliminates duplicate objects in UnionTOS and then determines the cardinality. As the number of paths is exponential in the number of sources and the number of possible combinations is also exponential ($2^n$, $n$ being the number of paths) we are dealing with a "doubly exponential" problem in the number of sources. However, due to the given cost limit, we may not need to consider all combinations. In our example only the combinations A, BE, CD, CE, and DE are below the cost limit of 20, the adjusted benefit results are 11, 14, 13, 10, and 10 respectively. We can see that the solution BE provides the best adjusted benefit of 14.

**MSCT:** Determining an exact solution for MSCT requires looking at all possible combinations of paths and their combined cost. The combination with the least cost is chosen, given that the overlap-adjusted benefit exceeds some threshold. In the example the maximum benefit one can gain is 36. If we want to find the cheapest solution with a guaranteed benefit of 29 (roughly 80%) only the combinations ABCDE (36), ABCD (34), ABCE (31), ABDE (31), and ABC (29) need to be considered (overlap adjusted benefit in parentheses). Among these ABC is cheapest with a cost of 43, still meeting the threshold.

Both problems can be modeled as Integer Programming to get an exact solution.

In summary, in both cases (BMC and MSCT) we are able to apply some pruning technique so that we do not need to consider all combinations and are able to speed up computation.

### 3.2 Formulation as an IP/LP

We solve BMC and MSCT using a standard LP relaxation and rounding approach. We show that the expected cost does not exceed the budget in BMC, and the expected benefit is within a factor of the optimal solution. We show that the expected benefit meets the threshold of the MSCT problem and the expected cost is at least within some factor of optimal. Interestingly, an almost identical randomized rounding approach is suitable for both problems as we show in [5].

**BMC Problem:** Let $\mathcal{S}$ be a family of sets (paths). Let $\mathcal{S} = \{S_1, S_2, \ldots S_m\}$ and let $Z$ be the set of all objects, $Z = \{z_1, z_2, \ldots z_n\}$. Let $B$ be the budget allowed to choose the subset of paths. We set integer variables $x_i = 1$ iff set $S_i$ is picked and $y_j = 1$ iff $z_j$ is covered. Let $c(S_i)$ be the cost of picking set $S_i$. $w_j$ is the benefit of covering element $z_j$. In our problem, we consider a uniform benefit for all objects; that is, $w_j = 1$ for each object $z_j$. The IP formulation is as follows:

maximize $\sum_{j=1}^{n} y_j \cdot w_j$ subject to $\sum_{i=1}^{m} c(S_i) \cdot x_i \leq B$

$\qquad\qquad\qquad\qquad\qquad\quad y_j \leq \sum_{\{l | z_j \in S_l\}} x_l$ for all $j$

$\qquad\qquad\qquad\qquad\qquad\quad x_i \in \{0,1\}$ for all $i$

$\qquad\qquad\qquad\qquad\qquad\quad y_j \in \{0,1\}$ for all $j$

Although the IP gives an optimal solution to the problem, it is impractical to compute exact solutions; the IP problem is NP-complete. By relaxing the constraints that $x_i$ and $y_j$ must be integers, we have the following Linear Program (LP) formulation. Note that only the two last constraints of the IP formulation have been modified as follows: $x_i \leq 1$, $y_j \leq 1$.

We solve the LP (using the LP solver CPLEX) thus obtaining an optimal fractional solution, $(x^*, y^*)$. We then choose a collection of sets $S'$ such that $Pr[$ Set $S_i$ is chosen in the set $S'] = x_i^*$ by using a standard technique known as *randomized rounding* [6].

**Algorithm. BMC_LP**
 – Solve the LP relaxation.
 – Obtain fractional solution $(x^*, y^*)$.
 – Round $x^*$ values to pick a subset of paths $S'$.

This algorithm produces solutions whose expected costs do not exceed $B$ and have an expected weight of the covered elements (TOS benefit) at least $(1 - \frac{1}{e})$ times the LP benefit [5]. Since the LP benefit is an upper bound on the optimal integral solution, this would be another way of deriving the bound developed earlier using a greedy algorithm combined with an enumeration approach [1].

**MSCT Problem:** The notation is the same as in the BMC problem, except that we want to choose a subset of paths that meet the threshold $T$ while minimizing the cost. The IP formulation is as follows:

$$\text{minimize } \sum_{i=1}^{m} c(S_i) \cdot x_i \text{ subject to } \sum_{j=1}^{n} y_j \cdot w_j \geq T$$
$$y_j \leq \sum_{\{l|z_j \in S_l\}} x_l \text{ for all } j$$
$$x_i \in \{0, 1\} \text{ for all } i$$
$$y_j \in \{0, 1\} \text{ for all } j$$

We relax the last two constraints in IP to obtain the LP formulation: $x_i \geq 0$, $y_j \geq 0$.

Let $(x^*, y^*)$ be the fractional solution obtained by CPLEX. We choose a collection of sets $S'$ such that $Pr[$ Set $S_i$ is chosen in $S'] = \min(1, \alpha x_i^*)$, where $\alpha$ is a boosting factor to ensure that we reach the threshold. This algorithm produces solutions with expected benefit at least $(1 - \frac{1}{e^\alpha}) \cdot T$ and expected cost at most $\alpha \cdot$ OPT [5].

## 3.3 Greedy Algorithms

We implemented several variants of a greedy heuristic and describe their evaluation in our experiments. Tab. 1 summarizes the results of all greedy algorithms for the example of Fig. 3. The choice of paths of each algorithm is indicated with a ∗ in Tab. 1.

**Overlap-adjusted Greedy for BMC:** Simple greedy variants (choosing paths in descending order of benefit or benefit/cost ratio) are not optimal, because the benefit considered does not take into account the overlap. In our example C and

E overlap by 2 so choosing C and E would give a benefit of only 10 instead of a benefit of 12. So the overlap-adjusted benefit should be taken into account in computing benefit to cost ratio. This strategy has been suggested in [1]. This requires some more computation as all benefits need to be adjusted in each step.

**Algorithm.** BMC_GREEDY
- Rank paths by benefit/cost ratio, in descending order.
- Pick paths with largest benefit/cost ratio, adjust benefit/cost ratio of the remaining paths.
- Continue as long as the cost constraint (budget) is not exceeded.

In our example, path C is chosen first, as the benefit/cost ratio is highest. After choosing C the benefit/cost ratios are adjusted. As A and B cannot be chosen, because of exceeding cost limit, the algorithm chooses D next. This results in a solution of 93% (13/14) of the optimal solution.

**Overlap-adjusted Greedy for MSCT:** Similar to BMC_Greedy the greedy algorithm for MSCT also ranks the paths, but now by their cost/benefit ratio and the lowest ranked path at a time is chosen. The cost/benefit ratios of the other paths are adjusted. A solution is found as soon as the adjusted benefit of the combination meets the threshold. This threshold is equivalent to some fraction (e.g., 90%) of the maximum benefit possible, i.e., the overlap adjusted benefit if one chooses all possible paths. The algorithm finds a low cost solution guaranteeing a certain benefit (e.g., 90% of maximum benefit possible).

**Algorithm.** MSCT_GREEDY
- Rank paths by cost/benefit ratio, in ascending order.
- Pick paths with smallest cost/benefit ratio, adjust cost/benefit ratio of the remaining paths.
- Continue as long as the benefit constraint is not met.

Assuming a benefit threshold of 29 (roughly 80%), path C is chosen first, as the cost/benefit ratio is lowest. Next, the ratios are adjusted and B and D are chosen, resulting in a partial solution with a cost of 33 and an adjusted benefit of 23. In a last step, the algorithm chooses A and reaches an adjusted benefit of 34 at a cost of 53. As the threshold of 29 is met, the algorithm stops with a solution of 123% (53/43) of the optimal.

**Overlap-adjusted Greedy for MSCT with pruning:** As one looks closer at the solution of MSCT_Greedy one finds that having chosen path D was a bad choice as even without it the benefit threshold also would have been met. Therefore we devised an improved version of the greedy algorithm, MSCT_Pruning, which, having chosen a combination of paths, reexamines all paths chosen and deletes one single redundant path, if one exists. If there is more than one redundant path, the path with the highest cost is deleted.

**Table 1.** Results of all greedy algorithms compared to the optimal solutions

| path | benefit/cost ratio | BMC_-optimal | BMC_-Greedy | cost/benefit ratio | MSCT_-optimal | MSCT_Greedy | MSCT_Pruning |
|---|---|---|---|---|---|---|---|
| A | 0.55 |   | (0.55) | 1.81 | * | *(1.81) | * |
| B | 0.77 | * | (0.62) | 1.3 | * | *(1.3) | * |
| C | 0.8 |   | * (n/a) | 1.25 | * | * | * |
| D | 0.6 |   | * (0.5) | 1.67 |   | * (1.43) | (*) |
| E | 0.67 | * | (0.33) | 1.5 |   | (3) |   |
| achieved benefit |   | 14 | 13 |   | 29 | 34 | 29 |
| achieved cost |   | 19 | 20 |   | 43 | 53 | 43 |

**Algorithm.** MSCT_PRUNING
- Perform MSCT_Greedy.
- Pick each path of the combination, delete it; determine cost and benefit.
- Choose among these combinations the one with the smallest cost which also meets the threshold.

In our example, after having found the combination **CBDA** with a benefit of 34 and a cost of 53, the four combinations **BDA** (benefit 27, cost 43), **CDA** (benefit 24, cost 40), **CBA** (benefit 29, cost 43) and **CBD** (benefit 23, cost 33) are examined additionally. Combination CBA is chosen, as it meets the threshold at lowest cost.

### 3.4 Applying Randomized Optimization

We also applied a randomized technique to the BMC problem. Randomized approaches find solutions by searching guided by an utility function. The search through the search space involves random steps, in most cases resulting in faster convergence to a solution by leaving out unpromising parts of the search space.

**Base algorithm.** Goos describes different approaches to randomized optimization [7]. We use one specific specialization of the base algorithm, which is known as *Simulated Annealing*. Starting from an initial configuration $K_0$, new configurations are created involving the old configuration and some random decision. A new configuration is accepted if it is better than the old one, but it is also accepted with a certain probability if it is worse. The acceptance probability depends on the current *temperature*, lower temperature meaning lower acceptance probability. This enables the algorithm to escape local minima; escaping is likely in the beginning and becomes more and more unlikely. The temperature decreases over time, and the algorithm ends if the temperature drops below a predefined temperature, when it has "cooled down".

**Modeling and implementation.** We applied this random algorithm by modeling and changing configurations and minimizing an utility function. A configuration $K$ to our problem consists of a set of paths, new configurations are created as follows:

1. Choose randomly among all available paths and combine them to a path set. This is done when initializing the start configuration $K_0$.
2. Add or delete a path. First, a path is chosen with a fixed probability out of all available paths and added to the set of paths if it is not already part of the set. Second, a path is randomly chosen out of all paths in the set and deleted from the set. This allows for inserting, deleting, and changing paths in the set. Creating a new configuration given an old one is done this way.

When changing a configuration (adding, deleting path), updating cost and benefit information could be done in $O(1)$, when using a bitset representation. When designing the utility function for BMC, overlap-adjusted benefit plays an important role, but also cost and other information could be used. Already a simple utility function consisting only of the overlap-adjusted benefit ($OAB$) and a penalty term for not complying with the cost limit yielded good results. The penalty term ($MAX\_COST$) is set to a fixed number, exceeding the highest single path cost. The chosen utility function for BMC is shown in Equation 1.

$$UF_{BMC}(K) = \begin{cases} -OAB + MAX\_COST & \text{limit exceeded,} \\ -OAB & \text{otherwise} \end{cases} \quad (1)$$

### 3.5 Computational Complexity

**LP:** LP problem can be solved by Simplex algorithm in linear time "in practice". That is, the number of iterations is linear in the number of constraints, which is the total number of paths and objects. LP can also be solved in polynomial time by using Karmarkar's interior point method.

**Greedy Algorithms:** Given $n$ paths and bitset representations of the paths and their objects, adjusting the benefit/cost ratio of a remaining path after having chosen a path could be done in constant time. Then all greedy variants have a computational complexity of $O(n^2)$.

**Randomized Algorithm:** The random approach has a computational complexity of $c*O(1)$. Here, $c$ is a constant given by $c \leq a*b$ where $a$ is the maximum number of configurations tested for acceptability per temperature and $b$ is the number of distinct temperatures tried.

## 4 NCBI Data

### 4.1 NCBI Data Sources

NCBI/NIH is the gatekeeper for all biological data produced using federal funds in the US[1]. For the purpose of our experiments, we consider a source graph $SG$ of five NCBI data sources (OMIM, PUBMED, NCBI_PROTEIN, NCBI_NUCLEOTIDE, and SNP), and the 10 links between these sources. We used the EFetch utility to sample all objects from these five sources that matched against

---
[1] www.ncbi.nlm.nih.gov

a set of several hundred keywords of interest. We then used the ELink utility to obtain all the links from these objects, along the 10 links, to the four other sources. We obtained an $OG$ of approx. 28 million objects and 10 million links.

For simplicity, a query identified an origin source and a target source, and an optional keyword. A query is satisfied by up to sixteen source paths in the $SG$ and is evaluated against the database of the sampled $OG$. For each of the source paths (and optional keyword), we determine the TOS; this is the set of objects reached in the target source. We also determine the cost of evaluating the TOS and the benefit (cardinality of the TOS).

## 4.2 Metrics for the NCBI Graph

We use a *bitset* data structure to store the TOS for each path and to compute the overlap of a set of TOS, and to store UnionTOS. UnionTOS is the union of a set of TOS(without duplicates). If an object (some position in the UnionTOS) is present in the path, the corresponding bit in the bitset vector for that path is set to 1. The bitset is used to efficiently compute the overlap adjusted benefit of a set of paths. We use DB2 union operator to help us to compute UnionTOS.

The IP/LP requires that the bitset for all paths must be computed a priori in order to set up the constraints of the IP/LP formulation. The greedy algorithm requires that some of the overlap adjusted benefits be pre-computed. While it does not require that the bitset be computed a priori, computing the bitset assists the algorithm. The random algorithm also computes the overlap adjusted benefit in an incremental manner and can benefit from the a priori computation of the bitset.

In general, the overhead of maintaining the desired metrics can be expensive. We briefly discuss some of the challenges. Consider computing the TOS or computing the benefit (cardinality of the TOS). Since we created a local database (warehouse) of all the objects that matched the keywords of interest, we could directly compute the TOS or its benefit. If the objects corresponding to the keyword were not sampled and stored in the relational database, we would have to *estimate* the TOS and its benefit. In prior work we have developed a model to make such estimations [2]. That model has the strong assumption of link independence, which may not hold for real sources.

Determining the cost associated with evaluating each search path on $OG$ to compute the TOS is also straightforward in our case, because we consider only simple queries with a keyword of interest and we assume that the links of $OG$ are stored in our relational database. In general, determining the cost of evaluating each source path involves estimating the cost of submitting EFetch queries to the NCBI servers to determine the objects that satisfied some complex search criterion, and possibly calls to ELink to find all objects that have links to an object of interest. It may also include some local join processing costs. The EFetch and ELink access cost depends on the workload on the NCBI servers and the network workload between the client and the NCBI servers. In our experiments, the cost associated with a path is the cost of computing the TOS of the path on the locally stored $OG$.

Consider for instance a query where the start source is PUBMED and the target source is NCBI_PROTEIN. As mentioned there are 16 source paths P0 through P15 between these two sources in this NCBI source graph; they visit the intermediate nodes NCBI_NUCLEOTIDE, SNP, or OMIM. Note that the source paths do not have cycles and we do not visit a node or an edge more than once.

**Table 2.** Benefit of TOS and pair-wise overlap of 6 paths from PUBMED to NCBI_PROTEIN

|    | P0    | P1    | P2   | P3 | P4   | P5  |
|----|-------|-------|------|----|------|-----|
| P0 | 30735 | 22729 | 2876 | 26 | 1560 | 166 |
| P1 |       | 23916 | 1857 | 25 | 1573 | 108 |
| P2 |       |       | 3261 | 24 | 1046 | 175 |
| P3 |       |       |      | 40 | 37   | 21  |
| P4 |       |       |      |    | 2848 | 80  |
| P5 |       |       |      |    |      | 175 |

Table 2 reports on the TOS benefit for each path in the diagonal as well as the pair-wise TOS overlap between pairs of paths. For lack of space we report on only 6 of the 16 paths. As can be seen in Tab. 2, the TOS benefit for each individual path varies widely from 40 to 30735. We also note that the pair-wise TOS overlap between pairs of source paths has a wide variance of values and ranges from a low of 21 to a high of 22729.

We also illustrate the time to compute the Union-TOS and the time to compute the bitsets for a set of paths. We study 5 different queries, which induce different size

**Table 3.** Running Time to Compute Metrics for a Large Object Graph and Result Graph

| Query    | size of UnionTOS | Time to Compute UnionTOS(msec) | Time to Compute bitset (msec) |
|----------|------------------|--------------------------------|-------------------------------|
| NU to OM | 8047             | 258095                         | 609                           |
| NU to PU | 122615           | 217412                         | 7993                          |
| NU to PR | 561358           | 164905                         | 34689                         |
| PU to NU | 1484403          | 282613                         | 92329                         |
| NU to SN | 1995918          | 502012                         | 130765                        |

of result graph. Thanks to DB2's union operator, we are able to compute Union-TOS for result graph of size hundreds of millions efficiently. Note that the time to compute UnionTOS is not proportional to the cardinality of the union, but depends on the inherent join complexity, that is cardinality of intermediate sources involved in the join. For example, consider the query from the origin source NCBI_NUCLEOTIDE to the target source OMIM, even the cardinality of Union-TOS is relatively small, the join complexity is still comparable to rest queries.

The time to create bitsets for result graph is proportional to cardinality of UnionTOS as we expected. In the source graph we are interested in, where there are 5 sources and 10 links, the result graph can be computed efficiently. Computing these metrics for a large source graph could introduce scalability challenges and in the future work we will consider both specialized data structures and methods to estimate these metrics.

## 5 Experiments on NCBI Data

To demonstrate the effectiveness and efficiency of the different algorithms for the dual problems, we performed extensive experiments on different sampled real-world datasets. These are characterized by different start/end sources. For both BMC and MSCT we used a variety of budgets for cost and thresholds for benefit and compared the greedy, the random, and the LP solution to the exact solution. We first describe results for BMC, then for MSCT, and conclude with some remarks on their runtime.

We used a total of 20 different start/end source combinations, but show results for only 2 characteristic ones; values are averaged over 10 samples. First we describe the experimental results, then we analyze them. The following figures all show relative solution quality compared to the optimal solution at varying budgets (BMC) and varying benefit thresholds (MSCT). Because BMC maximizes benefit, the algorithms do not reach 100% whereas MSCT minimizes cost and therefore the values are above 100%.

**Results for BMC:** Figure 4(a) shows results of experiments with all paths between sources SNP and PubMed with different cost limits. Algorithm Greedy is between 75% and 97% of the optimal solution, being worse at small budgets but with better relative results at higher budgets. The LP solution also lies between 75% and 95%, not showing improved performance with higher budgets, whereas the Random algorithm performs well for all budgets. The chosen path combinations (not shown here) consists of only a few paths. This leads to the difference in solution quality, as benefit may differ substantially if one single path is added/removed to/from the optimal solution.

The results of experiments with all paths between source NCBI_Protein and PubMed are shown in Fig. 4(b). Here, all approaches perform exceptionally well, occasionally not finding the optimal solution but one at approximately 99.9% of it. Regarding the same path with smaller budgets in Fig. 4(c) shows something different: The same algorithms perform worse than with larger budgets (except Random). The reason for this behavior is that the budgets in the former case are so large that (almost) all paths are part of the solution. So the solution quality is influenced by the given budget.

**Results for MSCT:** Figure 4(d) shows results of experiments with all paths between source SNP and PubMed, with different benefit thresholds (0.7 meaning that the benefit of the solution is guaranteed to be at least 70% of the maximum possible benefit). Both algorithms perform well, Pruning being at least equal, but in most cases better than Greedy. At a threshold of 1.0 all paths must be chosen, except redundant paths. Greedy sometimes chooses these redundant paths and Pruning does not remove all, but only one. Therefore, both variants do not always find the optimal solution.

**Discussion:** Greedy seems to be the most unreliable algorithm among all. If the optimal solution is unambiguous (one path, all paths) it mostly finds it, but it has weaknesses in between. There is also a difference in solution quality, if two

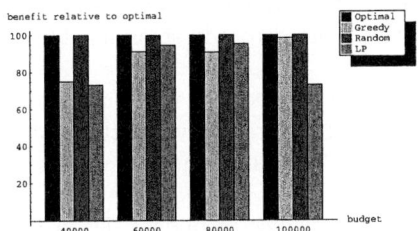
(a) BMC Algorithm Results for datasets from SNP to PUBMED, large budgets.

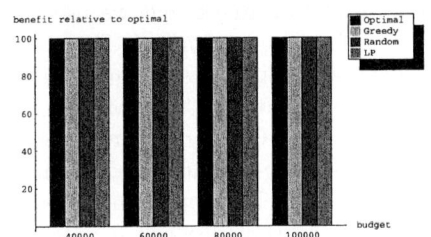
(b) BMC Algorithm Results for datasets from NCBI_PROTEIN to PUBMED, large budgets.

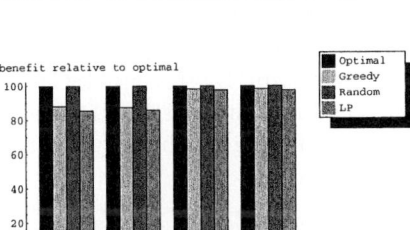
(c) BMC Algorithm Results for datasets from NCBI_PROTEIN to PUBMED, small budgets.

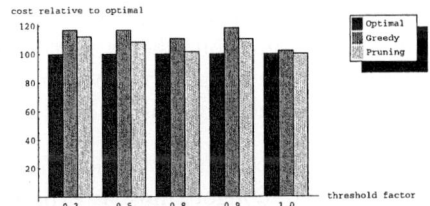
(d) MSCT Algorithm Results for datasets from SNP to PUBMED with different threshold.

**Fig. 4.** Selected experimental results

different datasets are compared. This seems to be accountable to the particular characteristics of the datasets. Comparing the solution quality of Greedy on the datasets SNP → PUBMED (Fig. 4(a)) and NCBI_PROTEIN → PUBMED (Fig. 4(b)), Greedy performs better on the former. The difference in these two datasets lies in the cardinality and the spread of the overlap. In the sets where Greedy performs better, there is much more variation in the amount of overlap, ranging from just a few objects to paths that consist of 80% of all objects, including several fully contained other paths.

LP performance is comparable to that of Greedy. The differences in solution quality in different budgets may be explained by the randomized rounding approach: If LP happens to choose paths with a fractional value close to 1, and we set the budget as cut-off line, we have a good solution; but if LP chooses several paths with more or less equal probability around 0.5 (e.g., p1 with 0.51 and p2 with 0.52), then rounding favors p2 to p1. This may not be good in general.

In all tested samples Random performed very well. This is due to the inherent nature of randomized optimization: the randomness in considering different combinations of paths. Whereas Greedy deterministically determines a combination of paths, and may be misguided, Random chooses randomly, keeps good combinations and throws away poor ones. Performance also depends on a good utility function, which is very simple in our case but does a good job. It is important to remark that we use one more or less straight forward parameter setting for all experiments. There is currently no need to adjust parameters to the characteristics of different data sets.

The fact that BMC and MSCT are coupled can also be seen in the results. In settings where Greedy performs better on BMC, it generally gives better results on MSCT, too. In that sense, characteristics of the data set in question influence the solution of both problems in a similar way.

One important decision in solving BMC is the choice of budget. From Figures 4(a) and 4(b) one can see that equal budgets result in different solution qualities, given different data sets. As different data sets result from different queries, we do not know in advance what quality the solution will preserve. In this sense, the MSCT problem is in fact the more interesting problem, as we can require a certain solution quality, as desired by scientists. By solving MSCT we gain information about the datasets, then we could make use of this knowledge and determine a budget for BMC if we have limited budget. This way the two problems interact and assist each other.

**Runtime:** Concerning average running time, the Greedy algorithms are the fastest among all algorithms, as expected. For all samples and all different budgets a solution is found within a few milliseconds on a state-of-the-art desktop computer. The runtime of Random is a few seconds on average whereas computing an optimal solution depends on the number of paths present in the data. In the real-world samples we tested, there are only 16 paths leading to an average runtime of a little less than a second, using the pruning technique mentioned in Sec. 3.1. However, determining exact solutions for worlds with more paths soon becomes infeasible. LP usually takes half a minute. However, since LP was run on a different platform, the runtimes are not directly comparable.

All algorithms would have longer running time if the computation of UnionTOS and the bitset were not completed a priori. The most significant performance impact is the LP formulation, which requires the complete computation of the bitset since it is needed to set up the constraints.

In summary, when an optimal solution is infeasible to compute, Greedy is the fastest while still returning good results. If one is able to invest some time, one should employ Random, as it gives nearly optimal objective values at reasonable runtimes. The advantage of LP is the guarantee (bounds) on the solution quality, albeit at a higher cost (higher runtime).

## 6 Related Work

Research in [8] and for Bibfinder [9] addresses the task of learning and maintaining statistics for distributed wide area applications. Bibfinder learns statistics for a variety of popular bibliographic data sources. Using a combination of machine learning and data mining techniques, it learns both coverage statistics of a source with respect to a query term (keyword) as well as the overlap among sources. We note that our task is more difficult, because we must consider the overlap of source paths, and the contents of all the sources occurring in the source path may be associated (indexed) based on some query terms or keywords. Properties of links and paths have been studied in the context of XML document processing in the XSketch project [10], but the authors also do not consider overlap as a part of their framework.

While the optimization goal of conventional DBMS optimizers—find the complete and correct query result with minimal cost—is certainly different from the goal of this paper—find the most complete answer within a fixed budget—there are several aspects that carry over to our problem.

The first is *selectivity estimation* of query predicates, for instance as introduced in [11]. In our case, predicates are query keywords, which amounts to "="-predicates, and links between sources, which amounts to foreign key predicates. Based on certain assumptions, such as independence and uniform distribution of data values, selectivity estimators use table cardinalities and selectivity factors to estimate the result of joins and other operations. In our case, even the cardinality of base tables is difficult to assess. Currently we assume to simply have that information. Compounding the problem is the overlap of sources, which in effect reduces the cardinality-contribution of sources in some unknown way. The basics of selectivity estimation are used in our system, and future work will extend the metadata with histograms and will drop many of the underlying assumptions. Also, the advanced technique of learning statistics [12] is particularly useful in our scenario, as we are not merely dealing with approximate statistics but often with wholly unknown statistics of foreign sources.

A second similarity of conventional optimization lies in the *cost model*. Conventional optimizers usually model cost as processing time or throughput. In our scenario, the dominant cost is network traffic and the fetching of objects in other sources. Currently, we do not support different access paths, thus modeling the cost for us is straightforward. Again, future work can adopt a more sophisticated cost model making use of different ways to access data in sources, such as Web Services, JDBC, HTML forms, etc.

Finally, there is of course much to learn from distributed query processing [13]. As the query model presented in this paper is fairly simple and we focus on the logical aspects rather than the physical aspects of query execution, we do not discuss the relevance here. Our first priority is to provide functionality to biologists, our second is to provide it efficiently.

## 7 Conclusions and Future Work

Originally motivated by the problem of finding good paths and sets of paths through NCBI life sciences sources we have generalized the problem to data integration in the presence of overlapping sources, which applies to many different kinds of information systems. We presented a broad range of algorithms to solve this problem, from exact algorithms to bounded algorithms to greedy algorithms and simulated annealing. Each of these algorithms has different properties that we analyze and verify experimentally. To summarize, life sciences data sources are an excellent field to test new query models (paths through sources) and optimization problems (overlap-adjusted benefit), all the while solving problems that are relevant to biologists.

Possible future work is abundant. In a direct continuation of the work presented here we plan to expand on the types of queries to find out how our algorithms fare under different applications. Further strands of research are in the field of path query languages, efficient enumeration of all possible paths, and finally optimization techniques on the actual web-accessible NCBI sources rather than on large sampled sets stored in a local database.

**Acknowledgment.** This research was supported in part by the German Research Society (DFG grant no. NA 432) and NSF Grants IIS0205489, IIS0219909 and EIA0130422. We thank Maria Esther Vidal for helpful discussions.

# References

1. Khuller, S., Moss, A., Naor, J.S.: The budgeted maximum coverage problem. Inf. Process. Lett. **70** (1999) 39–45
2. Lacroix, Z., Murthy, H., Naumann, F., Raschid, L.: Links and paths through life sciences data sources. In: Proceedings of the International Workshop on Data Integration for the Life Sciences (DILS), Springer (2004) 203–211
3. Mihaila, G., Naumann, F., Raschid, L., Vidal, M.E.: A data model and query language to explore enhanced links and paths in life science sources. In: Proceedings of the ACM SIGMOD Workshop on The Web and Databases (WebDB). (2005)
4. Raschid, L., Vidal, M.E., Cardenas, M., Marquez, N., Wu, Y.: Challenges of navigational queries: Finding best paths in graphs. Technical report, University of Maryland (2005)
5. Khuller, S., Raschid, L., Wu, Y.: LP randomized rounding for maximum coverage problem and minimum set cover with threshold problem. Technical report, University of Maryland (2005)
6. Motwani, R., Raghavan, P.: Randomized algorithms. Cambridge University Press (1995)
7. Goos, G.: Vorlesungen über Informatik - Paralleles Rechnen und nicht-analytische Lösungsverfahren. Volume 4. Springer Verlag, Berlin, Germany (1998)
8. Gruser, J.R., Raschid, L., Zadorozhny, V., Zhan, T.: Learning response time for websources using query feedback and application in query optimization. VLDB Journal **9** (2000) 18–37
9. Nie, Z., Kambhampati, S.: A frequency-based approach for mining coverage statistics in data integration. In: Proceedings of the International Conference on Data Engineering (ICDE). (2004) 387–398
10. Polyzotis, N., Garofalakis, M.: Structure and value synopses for XML data graphs. In: Proc. of the Int. Conf. on Very Large Databases (VLDB). (2002)
11. Selinger, P., Astrahan, M., Chamberlin, D., Lorie, R., Price, T.: Access path selection in a relational database management system. In: Proce. of the ACM Int. Conf. on Management of Data (SIGMOD), Boston, MA (1979) 23–34
12. Stillger, M., Lohman, G.M., Markl, V., Kandil, M.: LEO - DB2's LEarning Optimizer. In: Proc. of the Int. Conf. on Very Large Databases (VLDB), Rome, Italy (2001) 19–28
13. Kossmann, D.: The state of the art in distributed query processing. ACM Computing Surveys **32** (2000) 422–469

# Optimizing Monitoring Queries over Distributed Data

Frank Neven and Dieter Van de Craen*

Hasselt University and Transnational University of Limburg,
Agoralaan, 3590 Diepenbeek, Belgium
{frank.neven, dieter.vandecraen}@uhasselt.be

**Abstract.** Scientific data in the life sciences is distributed over various independent multi-format databases and is constantly expanding. We discuss a scenario where a life science research lab monitors over time the results of queries to remote databases beyond their control. Queries are registered at a local system and get executed on a daily basis in batch mode. The goal of the paper is to study evaluation strategies minimizing the total number of accesses to databases when evaluating all queries in bulk. We use an abstraction based on the relational model with fan-out constraints and conjunctive queries. We show that the above problem remains NP-hard in two restricted settings: queries of bounded depth and the scenario with a fixed schema. We further show that both restrictions taken together results in a tractable problem. As the constant for the latter algorithm is too high to be feasible in practice, we present four heuristic methods that are experimentally compared on randomly generated and biologically motivated schemas. Our algorithms are based on a greedy method and approximations for the shortest common super sequence problem.

## 1 Introduction

In the field of the life sciences, scientific data is distributed over various web sites and data is mostly accessible via browsers or in some cases through primitive web services [13]. A characteristic of biological data is that it is abundantly available and rapidly growing. For instance, the daily updates to Genbank [5] alone range in size from 40 till 200 Megabytes. Therefore, the answers to searches may vary over time as more data becomes available. However, due to the limited access to the distributed sources it is cumbersome to repeat searches over time especially if they combine information from several web sites. In this paper, we consider the setting of a light-weight monitoring system that runs at a research lab where users can register queries which are executed periodically. Users are then notified when new answers to their queries arrive.

We give an example of the kind of queries biologists would like to monitor over time: a certain biological experiment on a rare organism results in a set of genes.

---

* Contact author.

A search of the available data reveals a set of related genes in other organisms. However, only for a very small fraction of those genes their function is known. The researcher therefore would like to be notified when more information on the function of these genes becomes available. As shown in Example 2, such a query combines information from three sites: Genbank [5] containing gene related info and references to corresponding proteins, SwissProt [3] containing protein related info and some links to GO-entries, and GO [2] containing functional descriptions of proteins.

Although most popular biological websites and web services can be freely accessed, there are restrictions on the number of accesses and the amount of data that can be transferred per request. Furthermore, most data is transmitted using the HTTP-protocol, which makes the connection setup cost much higher than the data transfer cost. One single connection that transfers a lot of data is preferable to several smaller connections each transferring small amounts of data [18]. It is therefore of prime concern to combine queries and minimize the number of different communications. The goal of the paper is to study the latter problem.

We model a situation where a limited number of sites is available: rather twenty than hundreds or thousands as for instance is the case for peer-to-peer computing. Further, we consider a light-weight system and assume at most a few thousands of registered queries. Queries also have to be re-executed from scratch as there usually is no access to the updates the web sites receive. Although in practice most data is stored as flat files, we assume a relational view on this data and use conjunctive queries as a query language. This means that the actual queries should then be translated to appropriate calls to the web services or into HTTP-requests. We choose for this kind of abstraction rather than, for instance, going through an XML query language, as the focus of the paper is on minimizing communication not on the actual form of queries. Furthermore, the formalism of the relational model and conjunctive queries is sufficiently general to capture large parts of the available data and path-like search queries as described in the above scenario. On the other hand, the approach is specific enough to be translated into any reasonable query language or model.

We only allow an evaluation protocol for a set of queries to send a constant number of messages, where every message is a query or the transfer of a bounded number of tuples. We refer to these as bounded protocols. In Section 3, we require that messages are of size logarithmic in the size of the data which amounts to the same requirement. To allow queries to satisfy this requirement, schemas impose fan-out constraints which are for instance determined by domain experts (cf. Section 2).

We summarize the main results of the paper:

1. Not every conjunctive query can be evaluated by a bounded protocol. We show in Section 3 that deciding whether a set of queries can be evaluated by a bounded protocol is in polynomial time.
2. Minimizing the number of communications to simultaneously evaluate a set of queries is NP-complete. In Section 4, we show hardness for two restricted cases: (1) queries of bounded depth (cf. Section 3); and, (2), queries over

a fixed database schema. We use reductions from the Feedback Vertex Set (FVS) [8] and the Shortest Common supersequence problem (SCS) [15] which are known to be NP-hard. Furthermore, we show that both restrictions taken together results in a tractable problem which, unfortunately, is not practically useful due to the large constant.
3. We present four heuristic methods in Section 5. The first method is greedy-based. The other methods are based on approximations for SCS. Our experiments show that over random database schemas the Pairwise SCS performs best, while over a concrete biologically motivated database schema the greedy-method outperforms the rest in finding the best evaluation strategy. Finally, we remark that our experiments show that using our heuristics for 1000 random queries (consisting of 10 atoms each) on average only around 50 accesses to websites are necessary.

Due to space constraints, some proofs are omitted.

*Related Work.* The above described monitoring system is different from the usual publish/subscribe systems where users can specify by means of patterns what type of messages they are interested in. Such systems usually focus on new data only and can account for millions of subscribers [1]. A well known publish/subscribe system for biological researchers is PubCrawler [9] which scans daily updates to PubMed and Genbank, it keeps researchers informed on the current contents of PubMed and Genbank. Our setting allows for more advanced querying rather than keyword searching. A distributed database system consists of a single distributed DBMS. This DBMS manages multiple databases. A number of classes of distributed query optimization problems are known to be NP-complete [22]. They do not consider the setting of bounded communication. Heuristic methods were therefore developed to deal with these problems. An example of such an heuristic method is the query optimizer of SDD-1, which uses a greedy approach to find the semijoin order [4]. A multi database system supports operations on multiple heterogeneous local databases [17]. The most distinctive features of multi database systems are site autonomy and heterogeneity [14]. Distributed query optimization and multi database query optimization are distinctively different problems [14]. Our problem shows the strongest resemblance to the multi database query optimization. However, in our situation we have to evaluate multiple queries while using a minimal number of communications and a bounded number of tuples. In multi-query optimization the aim is to optimize in parallel a set of queries [16]. In contrast with our setting they do not consider minimizing the number of communications, also the number of considered queries is small (e.g., 5).

## 2 Definitions

In this section, we present the necessary background and definitions. To keep our exposition simple, we model every biological website or source by one relation (as opposed to several relations which would be more realistic). It is straightforward to adapt our results to that setting. The distributed sources are hence modeled by a set of relation names in the understanding that every relation resides at a different site.

We assume an infinite set of relation names $\mathcal{R}$ and attribute names $\mathcal{A}$ with $\mathcal{R} \cap \mathcal{A} = \emptyset$. Every relation name has an associated finite set of attributes, denoted by $\text{Att}(R)$. Let $\mathbf{D} = \{\mathbf{d_1}, \mathbf{d_2}, \ldots\}$ be an infinite domain of data values. An $R$-tuple $t$ is a function from $\text{Att}(R)$ to $\mathbf{D}$. An $R$-relation $R^\mathbf{D}$ is a finite set of $R$-tuples. The cardinality of a relation $R$, denoted by $|R|$, is the number of tuples in $R$. The size of a relation, denoted by $||R||$, is $k \times |R|$ where $k$ is the number of attributes of $R$.

A *distributed schema* $(\mathcal{S}, \Delta)$ is a set of relation names $\mathcal{S}$ with associated attributes together with a set of fan-out constraints $\Delta$ defined below. A *database* $\mathcal{D}$ over $\mathcal{S}$ assigns an $R$-relation to every relation name $R$ in $\mathcal{S}$. In the sequel we do not distinguish between the relation name $R$ and the $R$-relation itself: we denote both of them by $R$. Denote by $\text{DB}(\mathcal{S})$ the class of all databases over $\mathcal{S}$. To emphasize that the various relations in $\mathcal{S}$ are distributed we refer to them as *sites* or *sources*.

A *fan-out constraint* is a rule of the form $R : X \to_k Y$, where $X, Y \subseteq \text{Att}(R)$. A database $\mathcal{D}$ satisfies a set of fan-out constraints $\Delta$, denoted $\mathcal{D} \models \Delta$, iff for every rule $R : X \to_k Y \in \Delta$ and every tuple $t$, $|\pi_Y(\sigma_{X=t(X)}(R))| \leq k$. Here, $\pi$ and $\sigma$ are the relational operators denoting projection and selection. By $X = t(X)$, we abuse notation and mean $\bigwedge_{i=1}^{\ell} A_i = t(A_i)$ for $X = \{A_1, \ldots, A_\ell\}$. Intuitively, the constraint says that in $R$ for every fixed value for the attributes in $X$ there are at most $k$ different values for the attributes in $Y$. In the sequel, we do not care about the actual value of $k$ and simply write $R : X \to Y$ rather than $R : X \to_k Y$ to denote that there is some bound.

*Example 1.* Consider the following relational schema constituting four sites:

> Genbank(gene_id, protein_id, organism),
> SwissProt(protein_id, go_id, organism),
> Go(go_id, name), and
> Kegg(pathway_id, protein_id).

A tuple in Genbank contains a gene_id representing the id of the gene at hand. Every gene corresponds to one or more proteins which are listed in the SwissProt database by protein_id. The third component is the organism from which the gene originates, e.g., human, mouse, rat, .... Go is a database/ontology that contains function descriptions of proteins, e.g., serine protease. Only for a very limited number of proteins a functional description is actually known. Kegg contains information on pathways where special proteins are involved. We have the following fan-out constraints:

> Genbank : gene_id $\to$ protein_id, organism
> Genbank : protein_id $\to$ gene_id
> SwissProt : protein_id $\to$ go_id, organism
> Go : go_id $\to$ name
> Kegg : pathway_id $\to$ protein_id

Note that these are not necessarily keys. For instance, a gene_id can correspond to several protein_ids. The above relations are crude abstractions of existing sites [5, 3, 2, 11]. In [20] a more elaborate abstraction is given which we used for our experiments. □

As a query language, we employ the well-known formalism of *conjunctive queries*. An atom $L$ is an expression $R(A_1 : x_1, \ldots, A_n : x_n)$, where $R$ is a relation symbol, $A_i \in \text{Att}(R)$ and $x_i$ is a variable or a data value for $i = 1, \ldots, n$. We require that $A_i \neq A_j$ for all $i \neq j$. Note that $\{A_1, \ldots, A_n\}$ need not be equal to $\text{Att}(R)$. A *variable assignment* $\rho$ for $L$ is a mapping that assigns to each variable in $L$ a data value in $\mathbf{D}$. The atom $L = R(A_1 : x_1, \ldots, A_n : x_n)$ holds in $\mathcal{D}$ under $\rho$, denoted $\mathcal{D} \models L[\rho]$, iff there is a tuple $t \in R$ such that for every $i$, $t(A_i) = \rho(x_i)$.

A *conjunctive query* is then an expressions of the form

$$Q(X_1 : x_1, \ldots, X_k : x_k) \leftarrow L_1, \ldots, L_n,$$

where each $L_i$ is an atom and each $x_i$ occurs in at least one atom. The semantics is the usual one: $Q$ defines the relation $Q(\mathcal{D}) = \{(X_1 : \rho(x_1), \ldots, X_n : \rho(x_n)) \mid \rho \text{ is an assignment s.t. } \forall i, \mathcal{D} \models L_i(\rho)\}$. The relational schema associated to $Q(\mathcal{D})$ consists of the single relation symbol $Q$ where $\text{Att}(Q) := \{X_1, \ldots, X_n\}$.

The *size of an atom* is equal to the number of variables appearing in the atom. The *size of a query* is the sum of the sizes of its atoms.

*Example 2.* Consider the query

$$Q \leftarrow \text{Genbank}(\text{gene\_id} : \text{'AC04654'}, \text{protein\_id} : x),$$
$$\text{SwissProt}(\text{protein\_id} : x, \text{go\_id} : y),$$
$$\text{Go}(\text{go\_id} : y, \text{name} : z).$$

which is Boolean and asks whether the function of the gene AC04654 is known. As there is no direct link from Genbank to Go, the query has to access SwissProt in between.

The following query asks for all the gene_ids from proteins wich are involved in pathway 0052 and have as function "catalytic activity":

$$Q'(y) \leftarrow \text{Kegg}(\text{pathway\_id} : \text{'0052'}, \text{protein\_id} : x),$$
$$\text{SwissProt}(\text{protein\_id} : x, \text{go\_id} : z),$$
$$\text{Go}(\text{go\_id} : z, \text{name} : \text{'catalytic activity'}),$$
$$\text{Genbank}(\text{gene\_id} : y, \text{protein\_id} : x). \qquad \square$$

We conclude this section, by introducing the Shortest Common Supersequence (SCS) problem which is used in Section 4 and 5. For a finite alphabet $\Sigma$, a string $s = a_1 \cdots a_n$ is a finite sequence of $\Sigma$-symbols. We denote the empty string by $\varepsilon$ and the set of all strings by $\Sigma^*$. A string $s'$ is a supersequence of $s$ iff $s'$ is of the form $w_1 a_1 w_2 a_2 \cdots w_n a_n w_{n+1}$ where each $w_i \in \Sigma^*$. A string $s = a_1 \cdots a_n$ is non-repeating when for all $i < n$, $a_i \neq a_{i+1}$.

The Shortest Common Supersequence problem (SCS) is defined as follows. Given strings $s_1, \ldots, s_n$ and a natural number $K$. Is there a string of length at most $K$ that is a supersequence of every $s_i$? SCS is known to be NP-complete for strings over a binary alphabet [15].

## 3 Distributed Evaluation

In the following, a communication is the sending of a set of queries to a specific source together with the receiving of the query results. We adapt the approach of Suciu [18] to our setting in defining what constitutes an efficient distributed evaluation algorithm:

(*) In evaluating a query on a distributed database, only a constant number of messages (independent of the data at the sources) should be send and received, and the size of each message is at most logarithmic in the size of the data.

The above means that for every set of queries a fixed number of communications should suffice and that every communication transfers a constant number of tuples.[1] This constant is independent of the distributed database, but depends on the actual queries and the distributed schema. The constant will be determined by the fan-out constraints. However, in the present paper we are not interested in the actual size of this constant: only in the knowledge that a certain constant exists.

Rather than discussing general evaluation algorithms, we employ a scheme where conjunctive queries and answers to those are transmitted. In brief, the source sends out queries and builds up a local database. Here the transmitted values can depend on received values. In the following definitions, fix a distributed schema $\mathcal{S} = (\{R_1, \ldots, R_\ell\}, \Delta)$.

**Definition 1.** An *evaluation protocol* is a pair $P = (\overline{\mathcal{Q}}; \bar{\xi})$ where $\overline{\mathcal{Q}} := Q_1, \ldots, Q_n$ is a finite sequence of conjunctive queries such that each query $Q_i$ is over the relational schema $\{R_k\} \cup \bigcup_{j<i} Q_j$ for some $k$; $\bar{\xi}$ is a finite sequence of conjunctive queries over the relational schema $\overline{\mathcal{Q}}$.

Intuitively, a protocol issues queries one at a time to a source ($R_k$) thereby possibly reusing results of previous queries ($\bigcup_{j \leq i} Q_j$). We refer to the latter as the local repository. Finally, the answer to every query $Q_i$ is computed locally by evaluating the query $\xi_i$ on the local repository. The *size* of a protocol is the sum of the sizes of the queries.

*Remark 1.* Apart from in the examples, we assume in the following that all attributes at the various sites are disjoint. We further assume that all variables occurring in different queries are disjoint.

We denote by $\overline{\mathcal{Q}}(\mathcal{D})$ the relational database $\bigcup_{i \leq n} Q_i(\mathcal{D})$.

---

[1] We assume a reasonable binary encoding here.

**Definition 2.** An evaluation protocol $P = (\overline{Q}; \bar{\xi})$ is *bounded* if there is a natural number $N$, such that for every database $\mathcal{D}$ over $(\mathcal{S}, \Delta)$, $|Q_i(\mathcal{D} \cup \bigcup_{j \leq i} Q_j)| \leq N$.

**Definition 3.** An evaluation protocol $(\overline{Q}; \bar{\xi})$ *evaluates* a sequence of conjunctive queries $\gamma_1, \ldots, \gamma_n$ iff for every database $\mathcal{D}$, $\gamma_i(\mathcal{D}) = \xi_i(\overline{Q}(\mathcal{D}))$ for all $i \leq n$.

*Example 3.* We refer to the conjunctive queries $Q$ and $Q'$ of Example 2. A protocol that evaluates $Q$ is the following: $P_1 = (Q_1, Q_2, Q_3; \xi)$ where

$Q_1(\text{protein\_id}: x_1) \leftarrow \text{Genbank}(\text{gene\_id}: \text{'AC04654'}, \text{protein\_id}: x_1)$
$Q_2(\text{go\_id}: y_1) \leftarrow \text{SwissProt}(\text{protein\_id}: x_1, \text{go\_id}: y_1),$
$\qquad\qquad\qquad\quad Q_1(\text{protein\_id}: x_1)$
$Q_3 \leftarrow \text{Go}(\text{go\_id}: y_1, \text{name}: z_1), Q_2(\text{go\_id}: y_1)$
$\xi \leftarrow Q_3$

The intuition of the above protocol is as follows:

1. first we fetch all protein\_ids related to AC04654 in Genbank.
2. Next, for every such protein\_id, we fetch all related go\_ids.
3. Finally, we check whether the function of any of these go\_ids is known.

Note that every query $Q_i$ only uses atoms that refer to one site or to the local repository. Further, the protocol is bounded as we have the constraints Genbank : gene\_id $\rightarrow$ protein\_id, organism and SwissProt : protein\_id $\rightarrow$ go\_id, organism.

An evaluation protocol for $Q'$ is given next. Formally, we have $P_2 = (Q_4, Q_5, Q_6, Q_7; \xi')$ with

$Q_4(\text{protein\_id}: x_2) \leftarrow \text{Kegg}(\text{pathway\_id}: \text{'0052'}, \text{protein\_id}: x_2),$
$Q_5(\text{protein\_id}: x_2, \text{go\_id}: z_2) \leftarrow \text{SwissProt}(\text{protein\_id}: x_2, \text{go\_id}: z_2),$
$\qquad\qquad\qquad\quad Q_4(\text{protein\_id}: x_2)$
$Q_6(\text{go\_id}: z_2) \leftarrow \text{Go}(\text{go\_id}: z_2, \text{name}: \text{'catalytic activity'}),$
$\qquad\qquad\qquad\quad Q_5(\text{go\_id}: z_2)$
$Q_7(\text{gene\_id}: y_2, \text{protein\_id}: x_2) \leftarrow \text{Genbank}(\text{gene\_id}: y_2, \text{protein\_id}: x_2),$
$\qquad\qquad\qquad\quad Q_4(\text{protein\_id}: x_2)$
$\xi'(\text{gene\_id}: y_2) \leftarrow Q_5(\text{protein\_id}: x_2, \text{go\_id}: z_2),$
$\qquad\qquad\qquad\quad Q_6(\text{go\_id}: z_2),$
$\qquad\qquad\qquad\quad Q_7(\text{gene\_id}: y_2, \text{protein\_id}: x_2)$

An evaluation protocol for the sequence of queries $(Q, Q')$ is $P_3 = (Q_1, Q_4, Q_2, Q_5, Q_7, Q_3, Q_6; \xi, \xi')$. Note that the two last evaluation protocols are bounded and that the protocol for $(Q, Q')$ evaluates $(Q, Q')$. □

Note that the notion of bounded evaluation protocol corresponds to the requirements presented in (*) at the beginning of this section. Of course, queries of the form

$Q_5(\text{protein\_id}: x_2, \text{go\_id}: z_2) \leftarrow$
$\quad \text{SwissProt}(\text{protein\_id}: x_2, \text{go\_id}: z_2), Q_4(\text{protein\_id}: x_2)$

as in the above example use atoms referring both to a distributed site and the local repository. However, as the size of the local repository will always be bounded, the local relation can be shipped together with the query to the remote site or can be hard coded in the query.

It remains to discuss how to decide that for a given query a bounded protocol exists. The previous two examples are rather simple as for every separate query only one communication is needed for every atom to determine the tuples that make this atom true. In general, there can be atoms

$$R(A_1 : c, A_2 : x_2, A_3 : x_3, A_4 : x_4), S(B_2 : x_2, B_3 : x_3, B_3 : x_4)$$

with a constant $c$ and fan-out constraints $R : A_1 \to A_2$, $R : A_3 \to A_4$, and $S : B_2 \to B_3$. A protocol then first needs to access $R$ to get all possible values for $x_2$. We refer to the latter set as the domain of $x_2$. Then $S$ can be accessed to determine the domain of $x_3$. Finally, $R$ should be accessed again to compute the domain of $x_4$. At the same time, the set of tuples that hold in $R$ can be obtained. One final communication is then needed to determine the tuples that hold in $S$. In the next proposition, we show that this strategy of limiting the domain of variables suffices to check whether a query can be evaluated by a bounded protocol.

First, we introduce the following notion.

**Definition 4.** Given a sequence of queries $\bar{Q}$. Let $T_{\bar{Q}}$ be the set of pairs $(A, x)$, where $A$ is an attribute and $x$ is a variable such that $A : x$ occurs in some atom of a query in $\bar{Q}$. Define the following sets: $\text{Bound}_0$ contains all pairs $(A, x) \in T_{\bar{Q}}$ where $x$ is a constant. Further, $\text{Bound}_{i+1}$ contains all pairs $(A, x) \in T_{\bar{Q}}$ such that

1. $(A, x) \in \text{Bound}_i$,
2. there is a $(B, x) \in \text{Bound}_i$ for some $B \neq A$; or,
3. there is an atom $R(\ldots, A_1 : x_1, \ldots, A_n : x_n, A : x, \ldots)$ such that each $(A_j, x_j) \in \text{Bound}_i$ and there is a constraint $R : \{A_1, \ldots, A_n\} \to Y$ where $A \in Y$.

Since $\text{Bound}_i \subseteq T_{\bar{Q}}$ for every $i$, there is an $n$ such that $\text{Bound}_n = \text{Bound}_{n+1}$. Let Bound equal $\text{Bound}_n$ for the smallest such $n$. We refer to $n$ as the *depth* of $\bar{Q}$. We call all pairs in Bound *bounded*.

Note that the above definition induces a polynomial time algorithm to decide whether a pair is bounded.

A variable $x$ is *local* if it only occurs in atoms that correspond to the same site and it does not occur in any of the heads.

**Theorem 1.** Given a sequence $\bar{Q}$ of queries over $(\mathcal{S}, \Delta)$. There is a bounded protocol $P$ that evaluates $\bar{Q}$ iff every pair $(A, x)$ in $T_{\bar{Q}}$ where $x$ is not local is bounded. Moreover, the size of $P$ is at most linear in the size of $\bar{Q}$ and $(\mathcal{S}, \Delta)$.

*Proof.* Suppose that every pair $(A, x)$ in $\bar{Q}$ where $x$ is not local is bounded. The protocol that evaluates $\bar{Q}$ proceeds by computing for every such variable its domain. In the worst case, it needs one communication for every pair in $T_{\bar{Q}}$. Then it needs to check which assignments of values to the variables makes each of the queries true. To this end, it needs to contact each site at most once. In this last step, the local variables can be evaluated. Hence, the size of the protocol is at most linear in the size of $\bar{Q}$ and $(\mathcal{S}, \Delta)$. The protocol is described more formally in the appendix.

For the other direction, suppose there is a non-local variable $x$ such that no pair $(A, x)$ is bounded. Let $(A, x)$ and $(A', x)$ be two pairs in $T_{\bar{Q}}$ occurring in two atoms $L$ and $L'$, respectively. Then it is easy to show by a fooling set technique from communication complexity that no protocol sending a logarithmic number of bits can check whether there is an assignment to the variables of $L$ and $L'$ that satisfies them both [12]. □

**Corollary 1.** *For a sequence of queries, it is decidable in polynomial time whether there is a bounded protocol that evaluates it.*

As we are interested in minimizing the number of different communications to the various sites, we define the following notion. Let $P = (Q_1, \ldots, Q_n; \bar{\xi})$ be an evaluation protocol. An *ordered partition of* $P$ is an ordered sequence $1 = i_0 < \cdots < i_k = n$ of integers such that all $Q_{i_j}, \ldots, Q_{i_{j+1}-1}$ are queries over the same relational schema. The size of the partition is $k$.

**Definition 5.** *The* communication size *of an evaluation protocol $P$, denoted by* $\mathrm{cs}(P)$, *is the minimal size of all its ordered partitions.*

*Example 4.* We refer to the protocols of Example 3. The communication sizes of $P_1$ and $P_2$ are 3 and 4, respectively, while that of $P_3$ is 5. For the latter, the ordered partition is $\{1\}, \{4\}, \{2, 5\}, \{7\}, \{3, 6\}$. Here, the queries are to the sites Genbank, Kegg, SwissProt, Genbank, and Go, respectively. □

**Definition 6.** *A bounded protocol is* minimal for a sequence of conjunctive queries *if there is no bounded protocol with a smaller communication size.*

**Proposition 1.** *Given a sequence of queries $\bar{Q}$. If there is a bounded protocol that evaluates $\bar{Q}$, then its communication size is always less than or equal to the sum of the sizes of the queries in $\bar{Q}$.*

*Proof.* It suffices to note that the bounded protocol sketched in the proof of Theorem 1 has the required size. □

## 4 Decision Problems

We define the decision problem central to the paper:

**Definition 7.** *Given a natural number $K$, a distributed schema $(\mathcal{S}, \Delta)$, and a sequence of conjunctive queries $\bar{Q}$ over $(\mathcal{S}, \Delta)$,* MIN-COM *is the problem to decide whether there is a bounded evaluation protocol for $\bar{Q}$ of communication size at most $K$.*

By Proposition 1 it does not matter whether $K$ is given in unary or binary as the size of a minimal protocol is at most linear in the size of the input. It is easy to see that MIN-COM is in NP.

**Proposition 2.** MIN-COM *is in* NP.

### 4.1 Lower Bounds

It is hardly surprising that MIN-COM is in fact NP-complete. However, we prove the latter for two restricted cases. In the following, a fan-out constraint $R : X \to Y$ is *unary*, when $|X| = |Y| = 1$.

Consider the following decision problems:

1. MIN-COM$^{\text{depth } k}$ is the problem MIN-COM where in addition all fan-out constraints are unary and every input sequence of queries has depth at most $k$;
2. MIN-COM$_{\mathcal{S},\Delta}$ is the problem MIN-COM where in addition all fan-out constraints are unary and the queries are over the fixed distributed schema $(\mathcal{S}, \Delta)$.

The first problem gravely restricts the way in which the domain of every variable can be determined: in a constant number of steps. Intractability can then be encoded by allowing an unbounded number of relations. The second problem corresponds to the more realistic situation where the database schema is fixed in advance. In this case, intractability can be encoded by allowing arbitrarily entangled input queries. In Section 4.2, we show that when both restrictions are enforced, we get a tractable problem. Our results, hence, provide a complete picture of the worst-case complexity of the problem.

**Theorem 2**

1. MIN-COM$^{\text{depth } 2}$ *is* NP-*hard*.
2. MIN-COM$_{\mathcal{S},\Delta}$ *is* NP-*hard*.

*Proof.* (1) We use a reduction from Feedback Vertex Set (FVS) [8] which is known to be NP-complete. The problem is defined as follows. Given a directed graph $G = (V, E)$, with $V$ a set of vertices and $E \subseteq V \times V$ a set of edges, and a natural number $K$. Is there a feedback vertex set of size at most $K$, i.e., a subset $V' \subseteq V$ such that $V'$ contains at least one vertex from every directed cycle in $G$? Here, only cycles of length greater than one are considered.

Let $G = (V = \{v_1, \ldots, v_n\}, E)$ be a graph and $K$ a natural number. Then define $\mathcal{S} = \{R_1, \ldots, R_n\}$, where each relation $R_i$ corresponds to the node $v_i$. The relation $R_i$ has the attributes $A^i$, $A^i_i$, and for every $j$ such that $(v_j, v_i) \in E$, an attribute $A^i_j$. We have the following fan-out constraints, for every $i$, $R_i : \{A^i\} \to \{A^i_i\}$. Let $c$ be a constant. Then $\bar{Q}$ consists of the single query containing the following atoms: for all $i$,

$$R_i(A^i : c, A^i_i : v_i, A^i_{i_1} : v_{i_1}, \ldots, A^i_{i_n} : v_{i_n})$$

where $v_{i_1}, \ldots, v_{i_n}$ are all nodes for which $(v_{i_j}, v_i) \in E$. Note that the depth of $\bar{Q}$ is two. Indeed, every $A^i : c$ is of depth zero, every $A^i_i : v_i$ is of depth one and all other pairs are of depth two.

It can be argued that $G$ has a feedback vertex set of size at most $K$ iff there is a bounded evaluation protocol for $\bar{Q}$ of communication size at most $K + |V|$.

(2) Define SCS-NR as the problem SCS where every input string is non-repeating (cf. Section 2).

**Lemma 1.** *For a fixed alphabet of arity at least four, SCS-NR is NP-complete.*

Fix the alphabet $\Sigma = \{\sigma_1, \ldots, \sigma_k\}$. We now reduce SCS-NR to MIN-COM. Let $s_1, \ldots, s_n$ be a sequence of non-repeating strings and $K$ be a natural number. Define the binary relations $\sigma_i$ with attributes $A$ and $B$. For every $i$, we have the fan-out constraint $\sigma_i : \{A\} \to \{B\}$.

Let $s_i = s_{i1} \cdots s_{in_i}$. For $i \leq n$ and $2 \leq j \leq n_i$, let $L_{ij}$ be the atom $s_{ij}(A : x_{ij}, B : x_{i(j+1)})$. Define $L_{i1}$ as the atom $s_{i1}(A : c, B : x_{i2})$ for a constant $c$. Then define $Q$ as the query consisting of all atoms $L_{ij}$.

We show that $s_1, \ldots, s_n$ has a supersequence of length at most $K$ iff there is a bounded protocol of communication size at most $K$ that evaluates $Q$.

Let $s$ be a supersequence of length at most $K$. Clearly, the protocol that accesses the relations in the order induced by $s$ is bounded and determines the domain of all variables. A query over the local repository then evaluates $Q$.

Conversely, let $P$ be a protocol of communication size at most $K$ that evaluates $Q$. Let $s = s_{i_1 1} \cdots s_{i_\ell \ell}$ be the order in which the different sites are addressed. As the $s_i$'s are non-repeating, $P$ cannot evaluate two successive $s_{ij}, s_{i(j+1)}$ with a single communication. Hence, $\ell \leq K$. As $P$ evaluates $Q$ and hence determines all the variables, every string $s_i$ has to be a subsequence of $s$. □

### 4.2 A Tractable Case

Define MIN-COM$_\mathcal{S}^{\text{depth } k}$ as the problem MIN-COM where every input sequence of queries has depth at most $k$ and the queries are over the distributed schema $\mathcal{S}$. So, $\mathcal{S}$ is given but not $\Delta$.

**Theorem 3.** MIN-COM$_\mathcal{S}^{\text{depth } k}$ *is in P.*

*Proof.* Let $\mathcal{S} = \{R_1, \ldots, R_m\}$. We first argue that the minimal protocol is at most of communication size $m^k + m$. Indeed, following the construction in the proof of Proposition 1, the protocol first determines the domain of all variables. As the depth of every input sequence of queries $\bar{Q}$ is $k$, for every pair $(A, x) \in T_{\bar{Q}}$, $k$ communications suffice to bound the value of $x$ in the atom it appears in. So, when executing all communication sequences of length $k$ one after another, the domain of every variable is known. This needs $m^k$ communications in total. Then, at every site it needs to be checked which assignments of variables make the atoms true. This needs another $m$ communications as there are $m$ sites. So, $m^k + m$ is an upper bound for the communication size of the minimal protocol evaluating $\bar{Q}$.

To find the minimal protocol, we only need to consider protocols of communication size at most $m^k + m$. The minimal one can be found by exploring a search tree of depth $m^k + m$ and width $m$. At every step there is the choice to access one of the $m$ sites. An access to relation $R_i$ determines as many values of variables as possible in atoms referring to $R_i$ or when all variables are known for an atom, fetches all tuples that make that atom true. In the end, the protocol with the least communication size is taken. □

## 5 Heuristics

Although the algorithm described in the proof of Theorem 3 is in polynomial time, the degree of the polynomial is too high to be useful in practice. Therefore, we present in this section four heuristic algorithms to approximate MIN-COM. They are experimentally evaluated in the next section.

### 5.1 Greedy

The Greedy method proceeds by bounding the domains of variables. When for a certain site, only one more access is necessary to bound the domain of every variable in every atom that refers to that site, we call that site *fully determined*. We can then bound the domain of these last variables together with evaluating every such atom by one communication to the site. The latter is also the final access to that site. Therefore, the algorithm gives priority in accessing fully determined relations. If no site is fully determined, the protocol chooses to access that site which maximizes the number of variables that become bounded. This is the greedy step. We formally describe the algorithm and illustrate it by means of an example.

We introduce some terminology. Assume given a sequence of queries $\bar{Q} = Q_1, \ldots, Q_\ell$. Let $\{R_1, \ldots, R_n\}$ be the relational schema. We define the set of bound variables w.r.t. to the sequence of accesses to the different sites. Therefore, let $s \in \{1, \ldots, n\}^*$, where $s = 123$ means that we first access site $R_1$, then $R_2$ and finally $R_3$. Define $\text{Bound}_\varepsilon$ as the set containing all pairs $(A, x) \in T_{\bar{Q}}$ for $x$ a constant. Further, $\text{Bound}_{s \cdot i}$ contains $\text{Bound}_s$ and all pairs $(A, x)$ such that

- $x$ is non-local,
- no $(B, x) \in \text{Bound}_{s \cdot i}$ with $B \neq A$; and
- there is an atom $R_i(\ldots, A_1 : x_1, \ldots, A_n : x_n, A : x, \ldots)$ such that each $(A_j, x_j) \in \text{Bound}_s$ and there is a constraint $R_i : \{A_1, \ldots, A_n\} \to Y$ where $A \in Y$.

A relation $R$ is *fully determined* at step $s$ when every pair $(A, x)$ in every atom in $\bar{Q}$ referring to $R$ is in $\text{Bound}_s$.

We describe the Greedy method. To start let $s = \varepsilon$.

1. Let $j$ be such that $R_j$ is fully determined at step $s \cdot j$ and $R_j$ is unmarked. Otherwise choose $j$ be such that $|\text{Bound}_{s \cdot j}| \geq |\text{Bound}_{s \cdot i}|$, for all $i \neq j$ and $R_j$ is unmarked. Otherwise if all relations are marked stop.

2. We first add for every pair $(A, x) \in \text{Bound}_{s \cdot j} \setminus \text{Bound}_s$ the query $Q_x$ that defines the set of possible values of $x$ to the protocol: $Q_x(A_x : x) \leftarrow R(A_1 : x_1, \ldots, A_n : x_n, A : x), Q_{x_{i_1}}(A_{x_{i_1}} : x_{i_1}), \ldots, Q_{x_{i_m}}(A_{x_{i_m}} : x_{i_m})$. Here, $\{x_{i_1}, \ldots, x_{i_m}\}$ are the variables in $\{x_1, \ldots, x_n\}$. The remainder are constants.
3. If $R_j$ is fully determined, mark $R_j$ and add $Q_{i,R_j}$ for every $i \leq \ell$, defined as follows. For every query $Q_i$ and site $R$, let $L_1, \ldots, L_k$ be the atoms in $Q_i$ referring to $R$. Let $x_1, \ldots, x_n$ be the set of non-local variables that appear in $Q_i$. Define the query $Q_{i,R}(A_{x_1} : x_1, \ldots, A_{x_n} : x_n) \leftarrow L_1, \ldots, L_k, Q_{x_1}(A_{x_1} : x_1), \ldots, Q_{x_n}(A_{x_n} : x_n)$. The latter query evaluates the part of every query in $Q$ that refers to $R$.
4. Set $s$ to $s \cdot j$. Go to (1).

For every $i \leq \ell$, define $\xi_i$ as the conjunction of all $Q_{i,R}$.

*Example 5.* We illustrate the approach by means of an example. Consider the distributed schema $R_1(A_1, A_2, A_3, A_4)$, $R_2(A_5, A_6, A_7, A_8)$, and $R_3(A_9, A_{10}, A_{11})$, with fan-out constraints $R_1 : A_1 \to A_2, A_3$, $R_2 : A_5 \to A_6$, and $R_3 : A_9 \to A_{10}, A_{11}$. We evaluate the following two queries:

$$Q_1 \leftarrow R_1(A_1 : \text{'a'}, A_2 : x_1, A_3 : x_2, A_4 : x_3),$$
$$R_2(A_5 : \text{'a'}, A_6 : x_4, A_7 : x_2, A_8 : x_3),$$
$$R_3(A_9 : x_4, A_{10} : x_1, A_{11} : x_3).$$
$$Q_2 \leftarrow R_1(A_1 : \text{'b'}, A_2 : x'_1, A_3 : x'_2, A_4 : x'_3),$$
$$R_2(A_5 : \text{'b'}, A_6 : x'_4, A_7 : x'_2, A_8 : x'_5),$$

Denote by $\text{Bound}'_{s \cdot i}$ the set $\text{Bound}_{s \cdot i} \setminus \text{Bound}_s$. Now, $\text{Bound}'_1 = \{A_2 : x_1, A_3 : x_2, A_3 : x'_2\}$, $\text{Bound}'_2 = \{A_6 : x_4\}$, and $\text{Bound}'_3 = \emptyset$. Note that $x'_1$ and $x'_4$ are excluded as they are local. Further, none of the relations are fully determined at this point. Set $s = 1$ and add the queries

$$Q_{x_1}(A_{x_1} : x_1) \leftarrow R_1(A_1 : \text{'a'}, A_2 : x_1)$$
$$Q_{x_2}(A_{x_2} : x_2) \leftarrow R_1(A_1 : \text{'a'}, A_3 : x_2)$$
$$Q_{x'_2}(A_{x'_2} : x'_2) \leftarrow R_1(A_1 : \text{'b'}, A_3 : x'_2)$$

computing the domain of the variables $x_1, x_2, x'_2$. Then, $\text{Bound}'_{12} = \{A_6 : x_4\}$ and $\text{Bound}'_{11} = \text{Bound}'_{13} = \emptyset$. Furthermore, $R_2$ is not fully determined as $x_3$ is an unbounded non-local variable. Set $s = 12$ and add

$$Q_{x_4}(A_{x_4} : x_4) \leftarrow R_2(A_5 : \text{'a'}, A_6 : x_4)$$

Note that $\text{Bound}'_{123} = \{A_{11} : x_3\}$ and that $R_3$ is fully determined. Therefore, set $s = 123$, mark $R_3$ and add[2]

$$Q_{x_3}(A_{x_3} : x_3) \leftarrow R_3(A_9 : x_4, A_{11} : x_3), Q_{x_4}(A_{x_4} : x_4)$$
$$Q_{1,R_3}(x_1, x_3, x_4) \leftarrow R_3(A_9 : x_4, A_{10} : x_1, A_{11} : x_3), Q_{x_1}(A_{x_1} : x_1),$$
$$Q_{x_3}(A_{x_3} : x_3), Q_{x_4}(A_{x_4} : x_4)$$

---
[2] To keep queries readable we omit the attributes in the heads of each $Q_{i,R_j}$.

At this point, all non-local variables are bounded and thus all sites are fully determined. Now set $s = 1231$, mark $R_1$, and add

$$Q_{1,R_1}(x_1, x_2, x_3) \leftarrow R_1(A_1 : \text{'a'}, A_2 : x_1, A_3 : x_2, A_4 : x_3),$$
$$Q_{x_1}(A_{x_1} : x_1), Q_{x_2}(A_{x_2} : x_2), Q_{x_3}(A_{x_3} : x_3)$$
$$Q_{2,R_1}(x_2') \leftarrow R_1(A_1 : \text{'b'}, A_2 : x_1', A_3 : x_2', A_4 : x_3'), Q_{x_2'}(A_{x_2'} : x_2')$$

Next, set $s = 12312$, mark $R_2$, and add

$$Q_{1,R_2}(x_4, x_2, x_3) \leftarrow R_2(A_5 : \text{'a'}, A_6 : x_4, A_7 : x_2, A_8 : x_3), Q_{x_4}(A_{x_4} : x_4),$$
$$, Q_{x_2}(A_{x_2} : x_2), Q_{x_3}(A_{x_3} : x_3)$$
$$Q_{2,R_2}(x_2') \leftarrow R_2(A_5 : \text{'b'}, A_6 : x_4', A_7 : x_2', A_8 : x_5'), Q_{x_2'}(A_{x_2'} : x_2')$$

Finally, add to $\xi$

$$\xi_1 \leftarrow Q_{1,R_1}(x_1, x_2, x_3), Q_{1,R_2}(x_2, x_3), Q_{1,R_3}(x_1, x_3, x_4)$$
$$\xi_2 \leftarrow Q_{2,R_1}(x_2'), Q_{2,R_2}(x_2')$$

Note that the constructed protocol is not minimal. The minimal protocol can be constructed from the sequence 2312. □

### 5.2 SCS Majority-Merge (MM)

We now compute for every separate query in $\bar{Q}$ a minimal protocol by exhaustive search. All the obtained minimal protocols for the separate queries are then combined in an overall protocol by using the Majority-Merge algorithm [7, 10] which is an approximation of SCS. The latter is illustrated in Example 6.

First, we explain how a minimal protocol is computed for every query. We consider all possible sequences of accesses to the sites. At every access we determine the domains of as many variables as possible. Whenever the domain of every variable in an atom is determined, that atom is evaluated. For simplicity, in the sequel, we only talk about the order in which we access the sites and do not give the concrete queries. It should be understood that they follow the strategy outlined above. The latter brute-force approach is feasible as the size of each separate query is expected to be small, say consisting of around 10 atoms.

*Example 6.* Assume we have three queries $Q_1, Q_2$ and $Q_3$ whose respective minimal protocols access the sites in the following order: $R_1 R_2 R_3 R_2 R_1$, $R_1 R_3 R_1 R_2$ and $R_2 R_3 R_1$. The next step is to find an overall protocol which is a supersequence of every single protocol. The Majority-Merge algorithm iteratively adds the symbol that occurs the most among the leftmost symbols of the remaining sequences and removes it from those sequences. The following overview shows the respective iterations for the given sequences:

| 1 | 2 | 3 | 4 | 5 | 6 |
|---|---|---|---|---|---|
| $R_1$ | $R_2$ | $R_3$ |   | $R_2$ | $R_1$ |
| $R_1$ |   | $R_3$ | $R_1$ | $R_2$ |   |
|   | $R_2$ | $R_3$ | $R_1$ |   |   |

The obtained supersequence then is $R_1 R_2 R_3 R_1 R_2 R_1$.

**Improvement.** As explained above, every generated protocol has two kind of queries: those that get the domain of bounded variables and those that evaluate atoms. At a certain point, a protocol only contains queries of the second kind. We refer to this as phase two. Clearly, the order of the calls in the second phase is irrelevant. This means that every permutation of the sites in the second phase leads to another minimal protocol. We exploit this fact by aligning only the first phases of the protocols and then checking which sites still have to be added to the protocol. We denote this heuristic method with iMM.

*Example 7.* We take the same queries as in Example 6. Suppose the first phases for the three queries are $R_1R_2R_3R_2$, $R_1R_3$ and $R_2R_3$. The Majority-Merge algorithm returns the sequence $R_1R_2R_3R_2$. The next step is to check for every query which of the relations in the second phase still have to be added to the sequence. For the first query $R_1$ has to be added and the sequence now becomes $R_1R_2R_3R_2R_1$. For the second and third query nothing has to be added, as the sequence formed by their first phase and a permutation of their second phase is a subsequence of the overall protocol. We, hence, obtain a shorter overall protocol. □

### 5.3 Pairwise SCS (PSCS)

Even excluding permutations of calls in the second phase, some queries have more than one minimal protocol. The choice of which minimal protocol to use to construct the overall protocol can therefore strongly affect the overall protocol. In the PSCS-approach we consider all minimal protocols for every separate query (rather than just one), but construct the overall protocol by pairwise alignment as it is known that the SCS problem for two sequences is solvable in polynomial time [21].

We outline the PSCS algorithm:

1. Compute for every separate query the set of all minimal protocols by exhaustive search. For a query $Q$, denote by $S_Q$ the set of sequences corresponding to the first phases of the minimal protocols.
2. Take two arbitrary queries $Q_1$ and $Q_2$ in $\bar{Q}$. Compute for every pair of sequences in $S_{Q_1} \times S_{Q_2}$ its shortest common supersequence. Let $s$ be the shortest among all of these.
3. For every remaining query $Q$, compute the shortest common supersequence of $s$ and each $s_Q \in S_Q$. Set $s$ to be the shortest among them.
4. Add second phases to $s$ as long as necessary like in the iMM-approach.

## 6 Experiments

Next, we experimentally validate our four algorithms. We randomly generate 1000 queries of varying length. To be precise, the number of atoms for each query is drawn from a Poisson-distribution with average size 10. Relations for atoms are randomly selected. Variables and data values are randomly assigned to

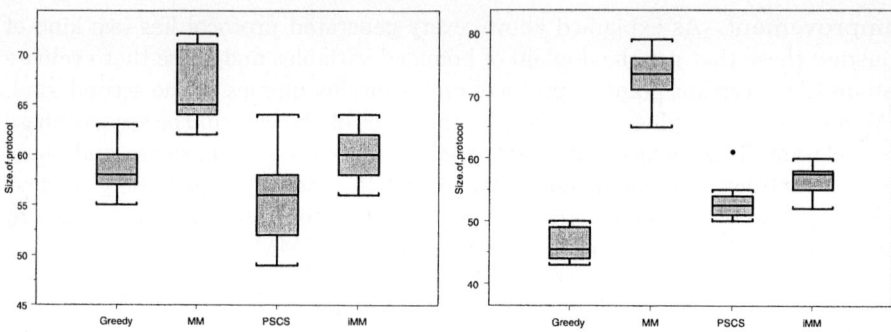

**Fig. 1.** Box plot of protocol size for 20 experiments with 1000 queries over a random schema

**Fig. 2.** Box plot of protocol size for 10 experiments with 1000 queries over the biological schema

the attributes of these relations. The experiments were performed on a Pentium IV (3.0 GHz) architecture with 1 GB of internal memory running under Linux 2.6. All programs are written in Java.

We considered two kinds of schemas: (1) randomly generated schemas with 10 relations and random fan-out constraints allowing for queries of at least depth five; (2) a fixed biologically motivated schema given in [20] created by examining popular life science web sites.

Figures 1 and 2 present a box plot of the sizes of the protocols produced by the four algorithms over random schemas and the biological schema, respectively. In brief, the lower and upper ends of the box indicate the 25th and 75th percentiles, respectively, while the line inside the box indicates the 50th percentile. The top and bottom lines of the tails indicate the 10th and 90th percentile (cf., e.g., [19].). A circle indicates an outlier. The box plots visualize data from 20 and 10 experiments, respectively. It is immediate that iMM provides a serious improvement over MM. In the case of random schemas, Figure 1 already indicates that PSCS performs better than the other methods. Further, a T-test on the data generated by the experiments establishes that the average length of protocols generated by PSCS is significantly smaller than those generated by the other methods. In the case of the biological schema, the visualization in Figure 2 alone already shows that the Greedy method outperforms all the others. The reason is that the complexity of the structure of the fan-out constraints for the biological schema is far less complicated than those of the randomly generated schemas. It appears that the Greedy method has a better performance in such a situation. Furthermore, PSCS performs better than iMM.

Figure 3 shows that for small numbers of queries, our three heuristics Greedy, iMM, and PSCS, generate a protocol whose length is close to the length of the optimal protocol (computed by exhaustive search). For larger numbers of queries it was not possible to obtain a solution by brute-force search.

Finally, we compare running times in Figure 4. While the SCS-based methods iMM and PSCS are very fast, the Greedy method is several orders of magnitude

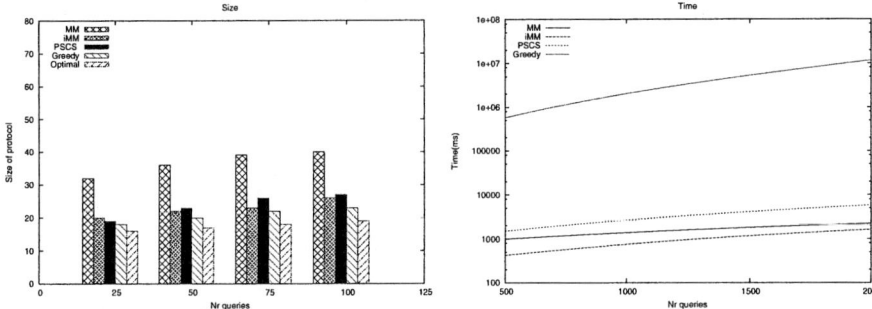

**Fig. 3.** Comparison of protocol size with optimal solution for a small number of queries

**Fig. 4.** Average logarithmic time

slower. The bottleneck of the algorithm is in the computation of the sets $\text{Bound}_{s \cdot j}$ for which every atom in every query has to be accessed in every iteration of the algorithm.

## 7 Conclusion

We proved MIN-COM to be an intractable problem (even under severe restrictions) and provided four heuristics. When to use which heuristic depends on the setting. Our experiments show that in a setting with a schema with a low complexity structure of fan-out constraints, as is the case in our biological scenario, the Greedy method performs best. In a random scenario PSCS outperforms the other methods. The latter method has the additional advantage that it is much faster than the Greedy method: 2.7 hours (Greedy) versus 10 seconds (PSCS) for 2000 random queries. The main drawback of the present approach is that only the number of accesses to sites is minimized, the overall amount of transmitted data remains the same. In future work we plan to address that issue.

*Acknowledgments.* We thank Ivy Jansen for her suggestion to use and the creation of the box plots in Figures 1 and 2, Kerstin Koch for her help in constructing the biological schema, and, Stijn Vansummeren and Dan Suciu for their helpful comments on a previous draft of this paper.

## References

1. M. Altinel and M. J. Franklin. Efficient filtering of XML documents for selective dissemination of information. In *Proc. of the 26th International Conference on Very Large Data Bases (VLDB 2000)*, pages 53–64. Morgan Kaufmann, 2000.
2. M. Ashburner et al. Gene Ontology: tool for the unification of biology. *Nature Genetics*, 25(1):25–29, 2000.
3. A. Bairoch and R. Apweiler. The SWISS-PROT protein sequence data bank and its new supplement TREMBL. *Nucleic Acids Research*, 24(1):21–25, 1996.

4. P. A. Bernstein, N. Goodman, E. Wong, C. L. Reeve, and Jr. J. B. Rothnie. Query processing in a system for distributed databases (SDD-1). *ACM Transactions on Database Systems*, 6(4):602–625, 1981.
5. H.S. Bilofsky et al. The GenBank Genetic Sequence Databank. *Nucleic Acids Research*, 14:1–4, 1986.
6. A. Chandra and P. Merlin. Optimal implementation of conjunctive queries in relational data bases. In *Proceedings 9th ACM Symposium on Theory of Computing (STOC 1977)*, pages 77–90. ACM Press, 1977.
7. D. E. Foulser, M. Li, and Q. Yang. Theory and algorithms for plan merging. *Artificial Intelligence*, 57(2-3):143–181, 1992.
8. M.R. Garey and D.S. Johnson. *Computers and Intractability: A Guide to the Theory of NP-Completeness*. Freeman, 1979.
9. K. Hokamp and K. Wolfe. What's new in the library? What's new in GenBank? Let PubCrawler tell you. *Trends in Genetics*, 15(11):471–472, 1999.
10. T. Jiang and M. Li. On the approximation of shortest common supersequences and longest common subsequences. *SIAM Journal on Computing*, 24(5):1122–1139, 1995.
11. M. Kanehisa and S. Goto. KEGG: kyoto encyclopedia of genes and genomes. *Nucleic Acids Research*, 28(1):27–30, 2000.
12. E. Kushilevitz and N. Nisan. *Communication complexity*. Cambridge University Press, 1997.
13. Z. Lacroix and T. Critchlow. *Bioinformatics: Managing Scientific Data*. Morgan Kaufmann, 2003.
14. H. Lu, B. Ooi, and C. Goh. On global multidatabase query optimization. *SIGMOD Record*, 21(4):6–11, 1992.
15. K.J. Raeiha and E. Ukkonen. Shortest common supersequence problem over binary alphabet is NP-complete. *Theoretical Computer Science*, 16(2):187–198, 1981.
16. P. Roy, S. Seshadri, S. Sudarshan, and S. Bhobe. Efficient and extensible algorithms for multi query optimization. In *Proceedings of the 2000 ACM SIGMOD international conference on Management of data (SIGMOD 2000)*, pages 249–260. ACM Press, 2000.
17. A. P. Sheth and J. A. Larson. Federated database systems for managing distributed, heterogeneous, and autonomous databases. *ACM Computing Surveys*, 22(3):183–236, 1990.
18. D. Suciu. Distributed query evaluation on semistructured data. *ACM Transactions on Database Systems*, 27(1):1–62, 2002.
19. P.-N. Tan, M. Steinbach, and V. Kumar. *Introduction to data mining*. Addison-Wesley, 2005.
20. D. Van de Craen. Biologically motivated schema. http://alpha.uhasselt.be/~lucp1631/files/biodbschema.pdf
21. R. A. Wagner and M. J. Fischer. The string-to-string correction problem. *Journal of the ACM*, 21(1):168–173, 1974.
22. C. Wang and M. Chen. On the complexity of distributed query optimization. *IEEE Transactions on Knowledge and Data Engineering*, 8(4):650–662, 1996.

# Progressive Query Optimization for Federated Queries

Stephan Ewen[1], Holger Kache[2], Volker Markl[3], and Vijayshankar Raman[3]

[1] IBM Germany, Am Fichtenberg 1, 71083 Herrenberg, Germany
ewens@de.ibm.com
[2] IBM Silicon Valley Laboratory, 555 Bailey Avenue, San José, CA, USA
kache@us.ibm.com
[3] IBM Almaden Research Center, 650 Harry Road, San José, CA, USA
{markelv, ravijay}@us.ibm.com

**Abstract.** Database Management Systems (DBMS) perform query plan selection by mathematically modeling the execution cost of candidate execution plans and choosing the cheapest query execution plan (QEP) according to that cost model. The cost model requires accurate estimates of the sizes of intermediate results of all steps in the QEP. Outdated or incomplete statistics, parameter markers and complex skewed data frequently cause the selection of a suboptimal query plan, which in turn results in bad query performance. Federated queries are regular relational queries accessing data on one or more remote relational or non-relational data sources, possibly combining them with tables stored in the federated DBMS server. Their execution is typically divided between the federated server and the remote data sources. Outdated and incomplete statistics have a bigger impact on federated DBMS than on regular DBMS, as maintenance of federated statistics is unequally more complicated and expensive than the maintenance of the local statistics; consequently bad performance commonly occurs for federated queries due to the selection of a suboptimal query plan. We present an extension of the mid-query reoptimization technique "Progressive Query Optimization" (POP), which adds robustness to query processing by dynamically detecting if an access plan is suboptimal and by triggering a reoptimization in that case. Our extensions enable efficient reoptimization of federated queries. Our contributions are (a) an opportunistic, but risk controlled, reoptimization technique for federated DBMS (b) a technique for multiple reoptimizations during federated query processing, with a strategy to discover redundant and eliminate partial results and (c) a mechanism to eagerly procure statistics in a federated environment. We have implemented these techniques in a prototype version of WebSphere Information Integrator for DB2. Our enhancements enable robust and acceptable performance for federated queries, even if the remote data sources provided almost no statistical information about the data. An extensive case study on real world data shows POP has negligible runtime overhead and improves the performance of complex federated queries by up to a full order of magnitude.

## 1 Introduction

Traditionally, modern Database Management Systems (DBMSs) translate declarative SQL statements into an executable plan prior to the actual execution of the query, hence strictly separating the plan selection and execution phases. To achieve optimal performance, the translation phase employs an optimizer component, which searches the space of all possible *query execution plans* (QEPs) for the optimal plan with respect to expected query execution cost [8, 18]. This cost model requires the accurate estimation of the intermediate result sizes (*cardinalities*) of each processing step. The estimation error in these intermediate cardinalities usually increases exponentially in the plan [5], as estimates are computed by multiplication of selectivities obtained from statistics in the system catalog [1, 9, 21].

For complex queries with a high number of tables and predicates, this can easily lead to a situation, where the estimation is very far off and the optimizer picks a highly suboptimal execution plan, resulting in unnecessarily long query execution time. Even for only moderately complex queries, this situation occurs frequently when either parameter markers are used, or the optimizer's estimation process makes assumptions about the underlying data that do not hold. Prominent examples are the independence- and uniformity assumption that the optimizer employs, as long as no statistics are available that indicate the contrary.

Cost based optimization of federated queries transparently extends optimization across data sources [11], by introducing communication cost, but otherwise treating remote tables similar to local tables and by introducing a *source-* or *server* property that describes where the processing of the current plan operator happens. A special operator (SHIP) describes the point in the QEP where intermediate results are communicated between a remote datasource and the federated DBMS. The statistics that are used to estimate cardinalities for remote base tables are in most cases obtained from the remote datasource, since the gathering of statistics on remote data is very expensive for the federated DBMS. The variety of relational DBMSs, which can be a remote source, employ different optimizers and utilize different forms of statistics. Often, the federated server can only exploit very basic statistics about the number of rows in a table. The federated DBMS's optimizer is hence not able to model data distribution and correlation in detail, as this would require distribution and multivariate statistics. The worst cases are federated queries that access non-relational remote datasources or remote DBMSs that do not employ a cost based optimizer. In those cases, there are no statistics on the remote data available at all and the optimizer is forced to derive its cardinality estimates from default values.

Federated queries therefore quite frequently execute using a suboptimal QEP. For local parts of a federated query, the overall model of the data is in most cases fairly accurate and the cardinality misestimates are caused by isolated predicates. For the federated part of the worst case queries, however, misestimates occur at virtually every point in the plan. In comparison to purely local queries, the performance degradation, by means of absolute execution time, through a suboptimal QEP is higher for federated queries, because the remote data cannot be accessed natively, but only through a declarative relational interface, which adds its own overhead.

In this paper, we describe how the technique of Progressive Optimization [15] (POP) can be extended for federated queries to recover from suboptimal QEPs. POP is a mid query reoptimization technique that introduces special checkpoint operators (CHECK) that detect plan suboptimality during execution and trigger a repeated optimization to improve the plan. POP ensures that when a plan is determined to be suboptimal, it is not executed to the end; instead, a different plan to continue from the point where the query execution was aborted, is developed and executed. That way, it acts like an insurance against suboptimally performing queries. We employ POP to check federated queries at the SHIP operator, which is a very suitable spot, as here the quality of the cardinality estimates and the cost regime change gravely and it marks the lowest possible point of intervention by the federated DBMS. Beyond the changes that are done for local plans, federated queries gain performance by changing the remote query represented by a SHIP operator and hence pushing work to the remote datasource or pulling processing to the local side. This way, performance cannot only be gained on the federated DBMS, but also on the remote datasource. Further more, we perform a reordering of the subplan executions in a way that does not influence the overall execution time, but does expose critical knowledge earlier and allows for faster detection of plan suboptimality and more effective reoptimization.

The contributions of this paper are strategies to increase opportunity for reoptimization of federated queries, considerations about multiple reoptimizations and a method to reorder subplans to reoptimize more efficiently. The reordering provides knowledge for efficient reoptimization earlier, without impacting the query performance. We give a detailed analysis of POP's behavior and examine opportunity, risk and behavioral stability in different federated environments.

The remainder of this section describes the prototype of POP for local queries in serial processing and performs a survey on related work. Section 2 describes the optimization and processing of federated queries with different strategies to access remote data, and section 3 discusses how POP can be extended to add robustness to those queries. The necessity for multiple reoptimizations and special issues associated with this are discussed in section 4, whereas section 5 discusses the subplan reordering for more efficient reoptimization. Section 6 performs a detailed analysis of the performance benefits and the behavior of POP in different environments. We give our conclusions in section 7.

## 1.1 POP for Serial Local Queries

Progressive Optimization (POP) [15] is a compromise between static optimization and continuous dynamic optimization. It acts as an insurance policy against bad performance degradation. POP combines a plan optimality criterion with checkpoints, runtime monitoring and a sophisticated matching of intermediate results. It can this way catch badly performing queries and improve them, while still imposing only a negligible overhead on well performing queries.

During access plan selection, POP determines criteria for estimated parameters that are required to hold if the plan is to be the optimal one. The current prototype uses only the estimated cardinality, which is the most important parameter and also the one subject to the gravest estimation error. It computes the *validity range* around it, an interval that describes for which cardinality range the current plan is truly the optimal one. It then places CHECK operators at strategic points, which in turn validate during plan execution that the actual cardinality, obtained from the runtime monitor, is within the validity range. If this is not the case, all intermediate results from fully materialized points are retained and the optimizer is called again. The actual cardinalities from the aborted query execution are made available to the optimizer so that it is able to develop a better plan, which is not subject to the estimation error that caused the reoptimization. Note that this makes POP suitable for any source of cardinality estimation error, be it bad statistics, wrong assumptions, or parameter markers. The retained intermediate results are treated as *materialized views*, also called *materialized query tables (MQT)* or *automatic summary tables* in DB2 [23]. The optimizer has the cost-based choice to match them back into the plan, enabling the query to basically continue from the point it was aborted for reoptimization, avoiding the re-execution of previously executed parts.

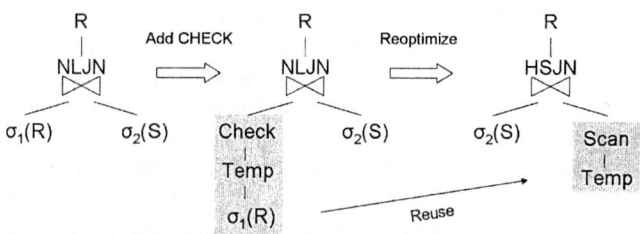

**Fig. 1.** POP reoptimizing a suboptimal nested-loop-join QEP. The intermediate result after scanning the car table and applying its local predicates is reused as a temporary table in the re-optimized plan (note that the build side of the hash-join is considered the right leg).

Figure 1 shows an example of this process. The left side shows a simple initial plan that uses a nested-loop-join. During optimization, POP computes the validity ranges around the edges of the plan and places CHECK operators at places that are suitable or performance critical. The CHECK operator, in this case with artificial materialization, takes the validity range of its child edge as parameter. During runtime, it identifies whether the actual cardinality is within validity ranges, and triggers reoptimization if not. The optimizer uses knowledge about the actual cardinality to develop the new plan; the intermediate result is matched into the plan as a temporary table (right side).

[15] introduces different flavors of check operators for eager checking (tuple pipelines) and lazy checking (full materialization points in a QEP). The extremely high communication and mediation costs for federated queries strongly suggest using the lazy variants, as they solely support the re-use of intermediate results. Our heuristics ensure that pipelines are not wildly broken, but in a very risk-controlled manner.. In addition, so far no research has proposed a good way to determine the validity range for eager checkpoints, which has to consider the cost inherent to partial re-execution; this implies a high risk of unnecessary reoptimization and -execution.

### 1.2 Related Work

The inadequacy of traditional query optimization for federated systems has been recognized for a long time. In Mariposa [20], sites were autonomous and could move data fragments independently, hence no site has good global knowledge of data sizes or layouts. So Mariposa adopted a hierarchical query optimization approach where sites sub-contract out query fragments to other sites via a bidding process that is done just before query execution begins. Other Federated DBMSs (e.g., [6, 7, 11, 24]) also provide calibration functions to help wrappers update their statistics periodically.

However all of these approaches are compile-time or just-before-execution approaches, and are hence vulnerable to bad cardinality estimates.

More run-time solutions to adaptive query processing have been proposed for traditional (non-federated) DBMSs. Among the earliest was the work on choose-plan operators [10] which pick one among multiple pre-chosen plans during query execution based on the value of run-time parameters. The disadvantage of this approach is that pre-choosing all possibly optimal plans leads to combinatorial explosion; whereas in POP we only need to maintain one optimal plan at any given time. In the DEC RDB system [2], multiple access methods are run competitively before one is picked. The Redbrick DBMS from IBM/Informix performs star-joins by first computing the intermediate results of all dimension table accesses, and uses the cardinality of these intermediate results to decide the join method for the star-join. Such intra-operator adaptation is complementary to POP.

POP and extensions ([15, 4]) belongs to a family of mid-query re-optimization techniques beginning with the work of [13]. [13] re-optimizes after hash join operators by materializing their result, rewriting the SQL query to use this result, and invoking the optimizer again. The Query Scrambling project [22] also re-optimizes queries, but its focus was on handling delayed sources as opposed to incorrect cardinalities. POP is a more general solution that can re-optimize at a much larger number of points during query execution (for example, above federated SHIP operators), and is more careful about cost-based reuse of intermediate results. In Adaptive Data Partitioning [12] each re-optimization phase works on a separate partition of the input and a final cleanup phase combines results from previous phases.

To the best of our knowledge, the early materialization idea (reordering plans so that wildly uncertain cardinalities are resolved with actual values early during execution) has not been proposed or implemented before.

The LEO project at IBM Almaden [19] uses query feedback to optimize future queries based on cardinality estimation errors observed during previous query executions. POP complements LEO by providing a methodology for fixing the currently running query.

A completely different approach to adaptive query processing is to view query processing as tuple routing, and optimize routing of each tuple separately. In Telegraph, a separate Eddy operator is used to continually adapt the tuple routing between other operators [3]. As shown in [3, 16, 17] this mechanism is powerful and can be used to adapt join orders, access paths and join algorithms, especially for wide area and Internet data sources. However per-tuple routing does impose an overhead which can lead to performance regression when the initial plan does not change. Moreover, currently proposed Eddy routing policies are greedy policies – these are fine for Telegraph's interactive and continuous processing metrics, but it is not clear if any policy simpler than regular dynamic programming optimization would work for completion time or total work metrics.

## 2 Federated Query Processing

Federated query compilation and execution is invoked by WebSphere Information Integrator whenever a query references at least one view over a remote table. Federated processing techniques are various; we will deal with the techniques of WebSphere

Information Integrator, which are based on the work of [11]. Here, the optimizer is augmented by a component called *pushdown analyzer*, which ensures that no plan candidates are generated containing an operation that the remote source is not capable of performing. A SHIP operator is placed during candidate plan generation whenever one of the following circumstances is met: An operation is required to be local (such as RETURN); the pushdown analysis determines that the remote datasource is not capable of this operation; an n-ary operator has data streams from different remote sources and needs to bring them to the same server before processing them. An example for the latter one is a join of data from two different servers, which need to be carried out locally. In addition to this, different operations generate alternatives where the operation is done locally and remotely.

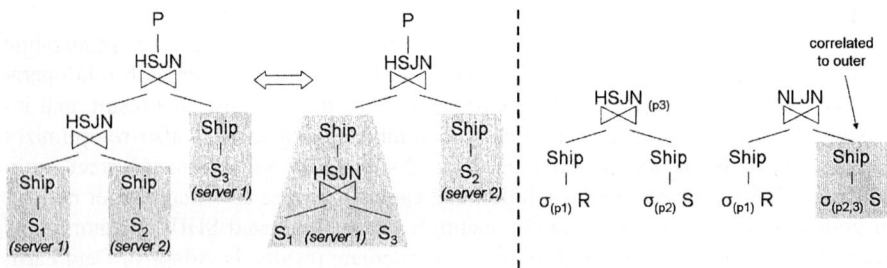

**Fig. 2.** Alternative strategies for federated queries. On the left side, local joining vs. a *pushed down* join; on the right side, uncorrelated SHIP vs. correlated SHIP (right legs).

The placement of a SHIP for the latest of the three mentioned reasons has the implication that for different join orders, the amount of processing done on the remote and local sever changes. Figure 2 shows how that happens. If tables from the same remote server are neighbors during joining, the join is performed on the remote server, otherwise it is performed locally. Further more, for nested-loop-joins (NLJNs) or subqueries, a SHIP can become correlated to another stream (Figure 2, right). In this case, the remote datasource is queried multiple times for the rows that match the current join- or subquery predicate. Again, the portion of work performed by the remote source as well as the number of tuples that are communicated between the data sources vary greatly.

After completion of the optimizer phase, a component called statement generator translates the remote parts of the plan below a SHIP operator back into an SQL statement in the dialect of the targeted remote datasource. When runtime encounters a SHIP, it invokes the SHIP's translated statement on the remote datasource through a custom wrapper, which acts as a client to the datasource and mediates the request with respect to formats and commands. In the case of a correlated SHIP, the statement is prepared once with a parameter marker and then invoked repeatedly, having the parameter marker bound to the current value of the correlated predicate.

## 3 Reoptimizing Federated Queries

Performance degradation is mainly caused by incorrectly chosen table access strategies (index scan instead of table scan) and wrong join considerations. Since table access strategies fall into the remote query part and can hence not be targeted, we restrain our effort to SHIPs below joins. Other locations of SHIPs, such as below UNION or RETURN offer little opportunity for performance gain through POP. Further more, we target only SHIPs that bring data from a remote source to the local side.

As outlined earlier, reoptimization with the possibility to reuse all of the aborted execution phase can only occur at full materialization points in the QEP, such as the construction of a temporary table (TEMP), sorting (SORT), or when building hash tables for a hash-join (HSJN). Eager reoptimization is unattractive for federated queries, because it is highly desirable to spare the remote datasources the overhead of repeated executions. Consequently, to effectively enable reoptimization at SHIP operators, we need to make sure that materialization occurs above them. For SHIPs below joins, materialization occurs naturally at the SORTs for a merge-join and at the build side of a hash-join. All other ones are artificially materialized in our prototype by inserting a TEMP operator above them, which creates a temporary table at this point. Correlated SHIPs have to be excluded from this strategy, as they are repeatedly executed and their correlated results allow hardly any conclusion about cardinality estimation errors and cannot be reused after reoptimization. While this approach is very opportunistic and allows for reoptimization at every SHIP, it implies a significant risk, because materialization, especially of larger intermediate results, imposes commonly an overhead on the execution compared to the pipelined plan. Reduction of this risk is done by employing three heuristics to exclude certain points.

The first heuristic excludes SHIPs where the intermediate result is already expected to be large and the current plan to be a robust candidate and perform well even in case of underestimation. A simple, yet confident means of prediction for this is POP's validity range, which defines the cardinality range for an edge $e$ for which the operator $o$ that this edge flows into, roots the optimal subplan $p$ with respect to the optimizer's cost model. If $e$ has a validity range with an undetermined upper bound $u$, then an underestimation of the intermediate cardinality at $e$ can never contribute to the suboptimality of $o$, and we can exclude $e$ it from being checked and materialized. The case of overestimation is not caught by this heuristic, but is commonly considered rather uncritical. This heuristic reduces risk greatly while still maintaining high opportunity.

The second heuristic performs materialization based on the sensitivity of the SHIP operators plan context. This heuristic excludes robust locations in the QEP from materialization to reduce overhead. Let $e$ be an edge and $o$ the operator this edge flows into. Then $e$ is considered to be robust if the performance of $o$ is largely independent of the cardinality of $e$. Examples are presorted streams feeding into a merge-join or the stream into the probe side of the hash-join. In the later case, the build side, which largely determines the optimality of the join, has already been processed by the time the probe stream is produced. Taking into account the naturally occurring materialization and excluding the robust spots, materialization becomes in most cases limited to nested-loop-join outer legs. This second heuristic runs practically risk free and still with considerable opportunity.

A third, complementary heuristic considers GROUP BY operations that are pushed through join operators and occur directly adjacent to a SHIP. In the case of aggregation through sorting, the SORT already provides the opportunity for reoptimization. For aggregation on pre-sorted streams or hashed group-by, the aggregation result can be materialized risk free, as it is expected to be very small when an aggregation occurs below a join. If it is in fact large and the materialization imposes significant overhead, we will most likely have a reoptimization, which justifies the imposed overhead.

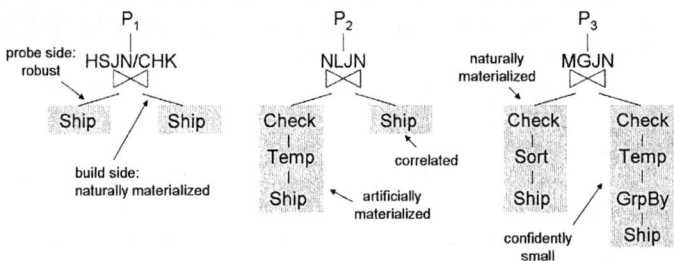

**Fig. 3.** Materialization of SHIP operators depending on their plan context. The GROUP-BY (GrpBy) on the right is risk free materialized, even though its context is robust.

Additional suitable points for checking would be RID lists or key lists for semijoins, as both mark small, but significant intermediate results. Since WebSphere II supports currently only the shipping of scalar values to remote datasources, we cannot target these cases.

## 4 Multiple Reoptimizations

A reoptimization is able to compensate for a single point of cardinality misestimation in a plan. For local queries, this yields astonishing performance speedups, because their optimization happens commonly with good overall statistics and cardinality estimation. Hence, estimation errors, caused by a small set of predicates on correlated or non uniform data columns, occur isolated and can be perfectly compensated for by POP. For the set of federated queries that are optimized in a comparable environment of knowledge, this naturally holds as well. However, for federated queries that are optimized with virtually no available statistics and consequently use default values for table cardinalities and predicate selectivities, virtually every point marks a grave cardinality misestimation. The plans are however in many cases acceptable, especially on databases that are centered on one or two fact tables. This is due to the fact that the number of applied predicates becomes implicitly a heuristic for the join order of the tables and bushy join trees become favored, resulting not in optimal plans but acceptably robust plans.

A single reoptimization results mostly in a worse access plan and performance regression. Reoptimization occurs for these plans basically at the very first CHECK at the lowest join. Perfect actual knowledge about the single remote result (SHIP operator) causes it in many cases to become part of a later join, because the actual cardinality is often higher than the comparatively low default estimates. This problem is caused by the fact that the optimizer cannot treat perfect actual knowledge with different confidence than the default estimate values. In the cases where actual cardinalities are a lot higher than the estimates derived from the sparse statistics or default values, the optimizer will favor plans where the actual cardinalities affect the plan at the latest possible point. We call this phenomenon of heavy bias *"fleeing from knowledge to ignorance"*. It is discussed in more detail in [14].

Consider the example from figure 4 and let $|\sigma_{(p6)}T| > |\sigma_{(p4,5)}S| > |\sigma_{(p1,2,3)}R|$. The initial plan chooses wrong physical join operators, but a correct join order. Assuming that $|\sigma_{(p1,2,3)}R|$ is larger than the default estimates for the accesses to $S$ and $T$, a reoptimization would place the partial result from the access to table R in the last join. Even though the reoptimized plan uses a more efficient join operator for the second join, the order becomes highly suboptimal, resulting in many cases in a worse overall query performance. Compensation for this is possible by introducing several rounds of reoptimization. Here, each round adds knowledge about additional parts of the plan until finally the whole plan is covered with actual knowledge and a good final access plan is developed (Figure 4). The number of reoptimizations is commonly as high as the number of uncorrelated SHIP operators in the federated query plan, possibly higher if correlation on join predicates that span several SHIPs occurs.

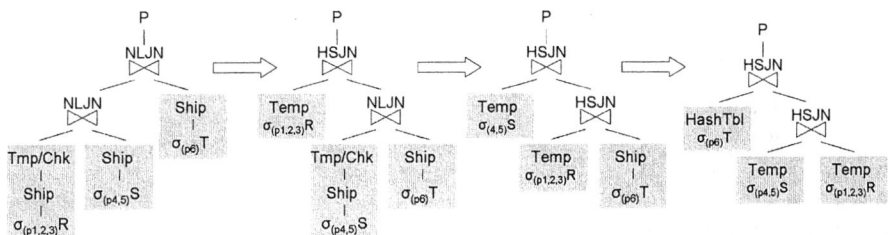

**Fig. 4.** Multiple reoptimizations of a query with little initial knowledge about the data. Each reoptimization adds actual knowledge about a single table only.

A problem associated with multiple rounds of reoptimization is the stockpiling of partial results, as each iteration introduces new temporary tables. POP is not forced to reuse partial results but rather performs the decision to reuse them on a cost base. Through this mechanism, it occurs that POP ignores partial results but reconsiders them after another round of reoptimization or decides to fall back to another partial result; this happens especially when new knowledge that was added in the course of another reoptimization compensated for correlation on join predicates. It is consequently dangerous and regressive to throw away partial results as soon as POP does not consider them during a reoptimization. A more commonly occurring situation is however that the query continues from a partial result and creates another partial result. An example for this is when during a reoptimization, the general join order remains constant and only the physical join operator is changed (see Fig. 5), or a join becomes pushed down to the remote datasource. In those cases, the prior partial results are redundant and need to be dropped in order to free temporary storage space from the DBMS.

The rule after which to decide whether to declare a partial result redundant can be formulated the following way: Let $o_1$ and $o_2$ be operators producing the partial results $t_1$ and $t_2$ respectively. Further more let $R$ be a subplan rooting at $o_2$ and taking $o_1$ as an input. The partial result $t_2$ is then considered to subsume $t_1$. In means of relational properties this implies that the properties of $o_1$ are a subset of the properties of $o_2$. Further more, $t_2$ has to be matched in the reoptimized QEP and $t_1$ has to be discarded.

In this case, $t_1$ can be declared redundant and be dropped without risk. The intuitive sense behind this is that when $t_2$ is derived from $t_1$ by processing $R$ and during reoptimization the optimizer matches $t_2$ knowing its actual cardinality, then it declares the decision to process $R$ correct and will not fall back to a state prior to processing $R$, such as $t_1$. The ideal point to perform this analysis and the dropping of the temporary results is in the transition between the query compiler and the plan execution. At this point, the QEP has been developed and it is known which partial results have been picked to be reused, but the query has not begun to be processed. Dropping redundant partial results here ensures that the DBMS processes the query, and also other concurrently running queries, with the maximum possible temporary storage space.

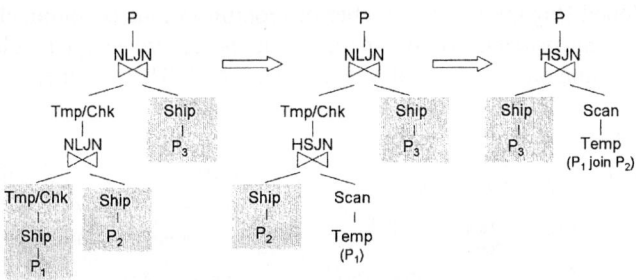

**Fig. 5.** Iteratively changing the physical join operator. The partial result *Temp ($P_1$)* is redundant after the first reoptimization.

## 5 Early Materialization

Running a reoptimization for every remote access imposes a high optimization overhead on the query, and can in some cases cause so many oscillations between bad plans that the overall performance has already degraded before finally picking the correct plan. The reason for this is that a single reoptimization adds knowledge only to the point where it was triggered. As outlined earlier, comparing unreliable estimates with hard facts leads the optimizer into a heavy plan bias. To our best knowledge, the problem of optimizing for a best plan with knowledge of different quality has not yet been solved. We therefore suggest an approach that gathers more knowledge per reoptimization, also more evenly distributed over the plan, by materializing the partial results from the SHIP operators a priori. After this, reoptimization is considered based on the violation of at least one validity range.

Through this mechanism, the first reoptimization is aware of the actual cardinalities of all uncorrelated SHIP operators and can directly come up with a very good plan, reducing the required reoptimizations due to missing statistics a single one. As in figure 6, traditional reoptimization requires three reoptimizations to add the knowledge about the gray shaded remote accesses; early materialization reduces this to a single one. Subsequent reoptimizations occur to compensate for correlations that involve a join predicate for a local join. As an additional impact, this approach adds the knowledge evenly to multiple parts of the plan rather than to an isolated point only, consequently preventing the optimizer to fall into a plan bias, because comparison between result sizes is done for all SHIP operators equally on base of either estimates or actual knowledge. The only side effect of performing the materialization up front is that the temporary storage space, which is used for temporary tables, sorted results and hash-tables, is occupied for a longer time.

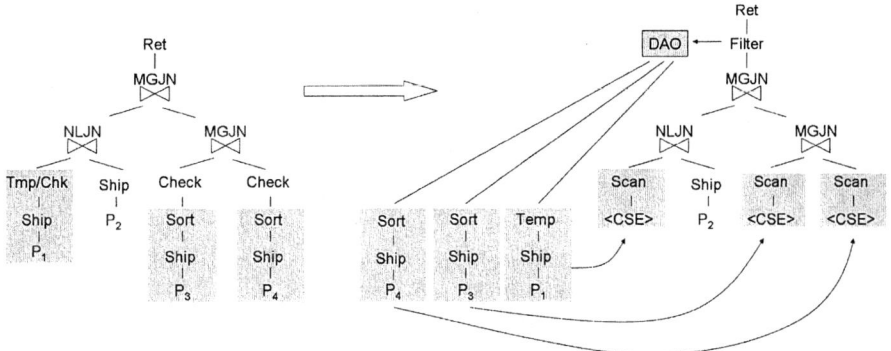

**Fig. 6.** Early Materialization realized through Do-At-Open (DAO) plan maps. The SHIPs are materialized in the plan map of the dummy FILTER and accessed like common-sub-expression (CSE) clients. Correlated SHIPs are excluded from the materialization.

Realizing early materialization is straightforward using Do-At-Open (DAO) plans. DAO plans map to an operator with a special predicate and are evaluated prior to the subplan that roots at this operator. If the DAO plan evaluates to true, the subplan of the operator that it maps to is executed, otherwise it is skipped. Ships are early materialized by inserting a dummy operator (e.g. a FILTER) with a dummy predicate, which always evaluates to true, at the top of the QEP and creating a DAO map for every SHIP operator. The materialized result is then accessed in the same way as the client of a common sub expression. Figure 6 illustrates this principle.

A second strategy for realizing early materialization is to directly modify the executable plan, if it is available in the form of executable or interpretable code. The code consists of a series of threads, each of which describes a pipeline. Reordering the series in which the threads are invoked, such that the threads that read from the SHIPs and write into the next TEMP, SORT or Hash Table are executed first, would model the reordering of the subplans very naturally, can however cause problems with the complex environment of code optimization and processing. The reordering is conceptually transferable to nested iterators.

For gravely underestimated cardinalities, commonly left deep join trees of nested-loop-joins are chosen, resulting in all except one SHIP operator to be correlated. This scenario voids the benefits of the early materialization strategy, as only a single uncorrelated SHIP remains. Materialization of correlated SHIP operators is very expensive and impracticable. In practice however, the majority of the correlated SHIPs contain a series of uncorrelated predicates, so that their uncorrelated part can be practically materialized. This is applicable, when the reoptimization is expected to turn the correlated SHIP operators into uncorrelated ones, which frequently occurs when the uncorrelated SHIPs were underestimated and exceed their upper validity range. Therefore violation of all upper validity range bounds can be employed as a trigger to materialize partially correlated SHIPs, as indicated in figure 7.

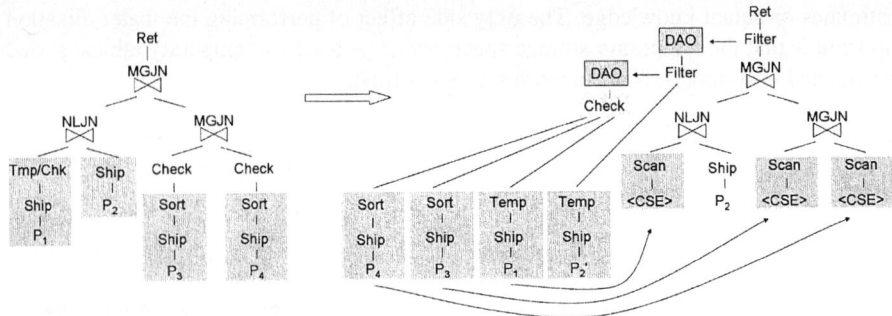

**Fig. 7.** Materializing partly correlated SHIP operators dependent on violation of the uncorrelated SHIPs' validity range. The Check causes the DAO plan to evaluate to true, if the SHIPs' validity ranges are violated. The subplan of the DAO-Filer is then invoked and materializes the uncorrelated portion of the partially correlated SHIP. The right NLJN does not access the materialized result, because if it is materialized, we are guaranteed to have a reoptimization.

Please note that early materialization does not directly imply any additional materialization, only performing the materialization that POP performs anyways a priori. To reduce overhead, a staging between sensitive and robust spots (see section 3) is easily introduced in a similar fashion as for correlated SHIPs (figure 7).

In the presence of certain constructs, early materialization runs the risk of executing overeagerly accessing rows. *Do-At-Open* plans, *Early Out* conditions and *Fetch-First-N-Rows* clauses need to be treated wih special care to prevent early materialization from voiding the benefits of these constructs.

The concept of early materialization is not limited to federated query plans, but can as well be applied to local queries to obtain actual knowledge about cardinalities earlier, and support more efficient reoptimization. Eager materialization, as is beneficial for federated queries, might not be desirable for local queries, but any naturally occurring materialization can be executed a priori. For local queries, this would result in early hash-table building, early sorting, etc. Because the cost for obtaining the knowledge earlier is only a longer occupation of the DBMS's temporary storage space and not impacting the query's performance, we believe this is a useful piece for any mid-query reoptimization technique.

## 6 Case Study

We study the performance and behavior of POP in several environments using a prototype implementation in a leading commercial federated DBMS. We perform test workloads on a large real world database, a smaller synthetic database derived from the large database, and the TPC-H standard benchmark. The data was in all cases held completely in remote relational databases and accessed through two different virtual servers in the same instance. This setup ensures that the tests require some local processing and are not biased by differences in the performance of the remote backends.

All experiments were conducted with the federated instance on a P615 server, 2-way Power4 1.4 GHz CPU with 1.5MB L2 cache, 4GB real memory, and 8 GB swapping space running a 64 bit AIX 5.2. The standard TPC-H benchmark test uses a

4GB database backend hosted on a 6-way 32 bit AIX 5.1 system. The real world database is from a department of motor vehicles (DMV) and is hosted on an 8-way 64 bit AIX 5.2 system and is about 8GB in size. The major tables are the CAR and OWNER table storing 8 million and 6 million records respectively. Both tables contain major local correlation (e.g. car.make and car.model); correlation occurs also across columns from both tables (owner.age and car.model). The synthetic database is a small model of the DMV database with 4 tables and 2 million owners and 2.2 cars. It is co-located with the federated instance. The workload used to test POP on these databases contains the actual queries used by the DMV.

The first section analyzes the performance impact of POP in different scenarios, whereas the second section deals with the qualitative behavior and describes which changes are prevalently occurring.

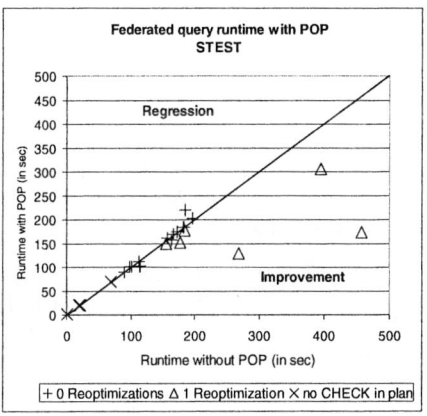

**Fig. 8.** Execution time plot for a workload on a synthetic database, comparing execution time without POP and with POP respectively. Only a single reoptimization is permitted.

## 6.1 Performance

We use the smaller synthetic database to evaluate the opportunity of POP with a single round of reoptimization. Our current prototype implementation does not support reusing Hash-Tables. The statistics about the remote data that are available to the federated instance for optimization are as good as federated statistics get; they comprise complete table, column and index statistics, lack however distribution and multivariate statistics. Data correlation and non-uniform distribution can consequently not be modeled. Figure 8 compares the query execution times of the workload with the query runtime of the same queries using the POP prototype. Speedup of up to a factor of two is achieved in this workload with a single round of reoptimization. The rather low complexity of the queries and further choice narrowing conditions, such as table co-locations, offer only small opportunity for POP, especially when only a single reoptimization is permitted. This workload illustrates, however, the stability of POP for skewed data. Only one slight regression occurs, caused by an inconsistent plan choice by the optimizer.

Having understood the opportunity for a single reoptimization, we studied a far more complex workload on the real world (DMV) database, allowing for an arbitrary number of reoptimizations. The workload has again correct federated statistics, so that cardinality misestimation occurs only based on missing correlation statistics and not through lack of knowledge about base table cardinalities. Figure 9 shows the results from this workload, impressively illustrating how POP adds robustness to this complex federated workload. The speedup factor increases with the number of reoptimizations to a maximum of an order of magnitude. The absolute query runtime improvements for the queries were in the range of several hours.

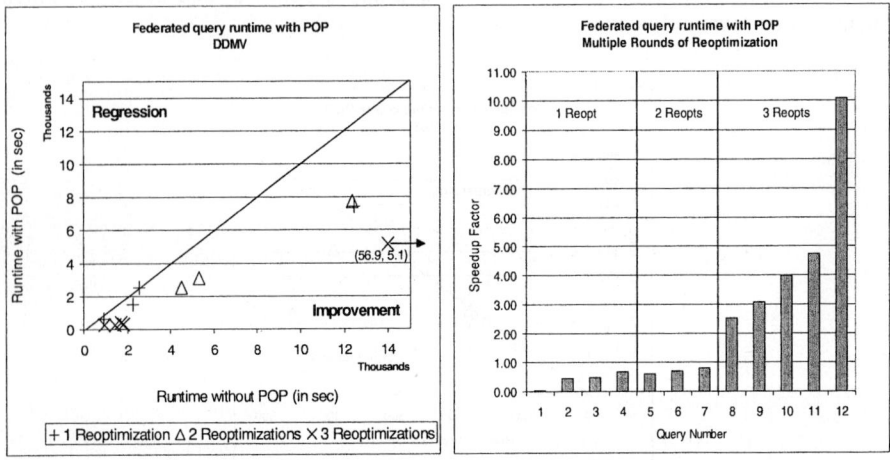

**Fig. 9.** Query performance for a large real world workload with multiple reoptimizations. The left shows a comparison of query execution time with POP disabled and enabled, the right the speedup factor of the individual queries, associated with their number of reoptimizations.

Note that we have virtually no regression in the query execution for this workload. This indicates that POP is very stable in this environment, also for multiple reoptimizations, and is in this environment not subject to the phenomenon of thrashing, which is described in [3]. Whenever a reoptimization is done over-aggressively, the sophisticated matching of partial results enables POP to continue the query right were it was aborted. The overhead of calling the optimizer again is absolutely negligible for long running queries like these.

It is interesting to observe where the savings in execution time take place. For this reason, we study local and remote processing time separately. Figure 10 breaks the normalized query execution time down into the portions processed on the federated instance and on the remote datasources for regular query processing and query processing with POP. The graph shows that POP is able to reduce the processing on the federated instance to a minimum by picking the best possible local strategies. Note that POP also reduces in some cases the work performed by the remote datasources considerably. This happens primarily through changing correlated SHIP operators into uncorrelated ones and is in more detail described in section 6.2.

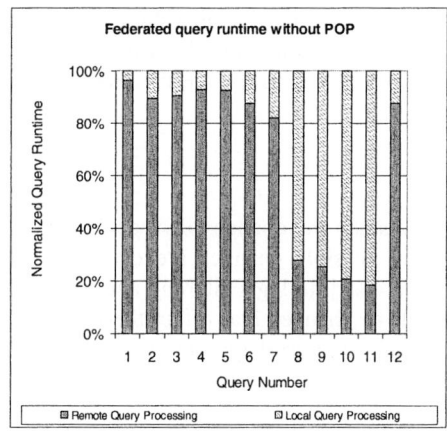 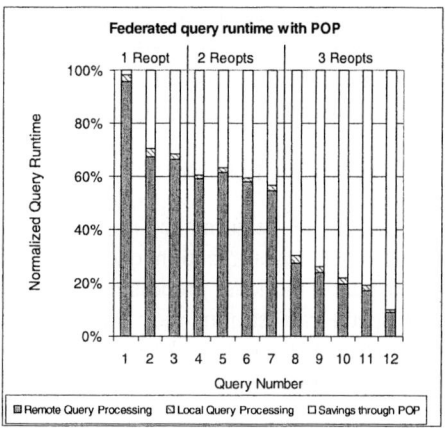

**Fig. 10.** Normalized query execution times, divided by local and remote query processing. Original execution times (left) and execution times and savings with POP (right).

Finally, we studied the impact of the early materialization technique. We set up the standard TPC-H workload and erased all statistics to simulate federated query processing against non-relational datasources or other datasources with no exploitable statistics. The optimization of the queries happened purely on the basis of default values for base table cardinalities and predicate selectivities. The tests were realized through automatic generation of materialized views from the query plan and recompilation of the query. For the workload, all uncorrelated SHIPs were materialized up front and then a single reoptimization was triggered, exploiting these partial results. This very conservative application of early materialization is already providing good results, as can be concluded from the execution times plotted in figure 11.

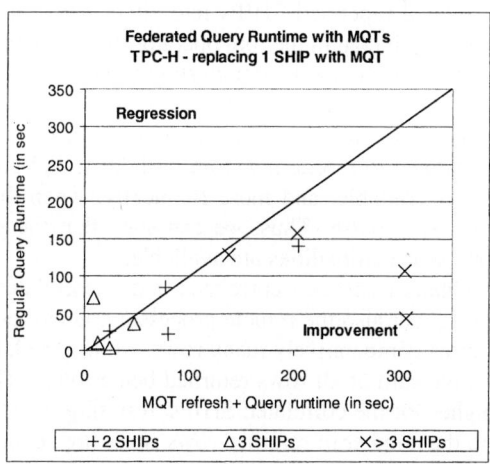

**Fig. 11.** Performance comparison between regular query processing and reoptimization with early materialization. The optimizer had no statistics about the underlying data.

A single regression can be observed, which is due to the inconsistency described by the *"fleeing from knowledge to ignorance"* phenomenon. Note that this conservative usage of early materialization still leaves default values for the cardinality estimates of the correlated and partially correlated SHIP operators.

### 6.2 Qualitative Behavior

Besides the net performance impact of POP, we study the changes POP actually performs when reoptimization occurs. Among the possible changes are changes that affect purely the local processing, such as join order, join leg switching and physical join operator (hash-join vs. merge-join), as well as changes that affect the access to the remote datasources, like join pushdown or pull-up, correlating and un-correlating SHIP operators.

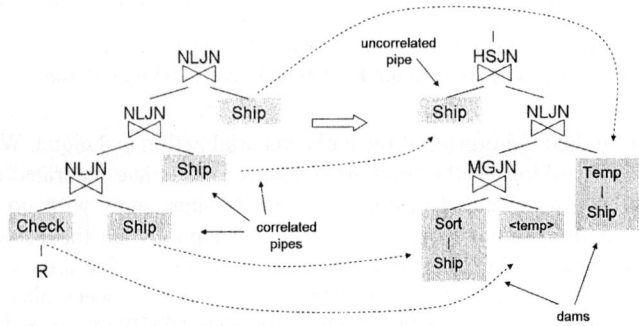

**Fig. 12.** Typical plan change for a federated QEP through reoptimization. All correlated SHIPs are turned into uncorrelated SHIPs.

Analyzing queries from the workload shows, how performance is gained mainly through changing correlated pipelined SHIPs into either dams or uncorrelated pipelines. This usually causes a change in the join operator, but does not necessarily imply avoiding nested-loop-joins, as figure 12 demonstrates. Reverse change, from an uncorrelated SHIP to a correlated happens rarely, which is due to the fact that most estimation errors are underestimates. The lowest join stays in most cases the same, the order of later joins is subject to reordering. Join pushdown and pull-up occur rarely, when most statistics are available, and more frequently, when the knowledge used during optimization is very sparse. Thus, we can state that the pushdown analysis works accurately when basic cardinalities are available.

It is obvious how changes between correlated and uncorrelated SHIPs affect not only the local processing, but also the remote processing. Uncorrelated SHIPs submit a single query that returns comparatively many rows, while correlates SHIPs submit a series of queries, with the sum of all rows returned being lower. The remote processing cost per row is higher for the correlated SHIPs, resulting in more remote processing if the difference in the number of returned rows is not high enough.

For early materialization, observations like these are possible only in a limited way, because the first optimizer plan is mainly used to discover the uncorrelated and partly SHIPs and materialize them. The actual optimization happens after the materialization. An obvious tendency is however again the avoidance of correlated SHIPs and long pipelines.

## 7 Conclusions

POP is a powerful technique to add robustness to queries, based on optimality checks during runtime and possible reoptimization with rematching of partial results. We have pointed out that federated queries have generally more problems to come up with the optimal QEP due to the different environment and the frequently bad statistics with which they are optimized. POP makes federated query processing very robust by judiciously materializing remote results and verifying their cardinality estimates, triggering a reoptimization upon violation of their validity range. Savings in processing time occur both on the federated instance and on the remote datasources. POP reoptimizes queries for an arbitrary number of times and avoids wasting storage space by analyzing partial results for redundancy and cleaning up after each reoptimization.

For federated queries that were optimized with little knowledge, early materialization reorders the subplans in a way that data access, in the federated case access to the remote results, is done prior to the actual plan execution. It provides knowledge about actual cardinalities earlier and reduces number of reoptimizations. Through a more evenly provided knowledge, the optimizer runs less risk of getting into a plan bias.

In a case study, performed with an implementation into a leading commercial federated DBMS, we verify that for well running federated queries the overhead is negligible, while for complex queries with estimation errors, POP speeds up query execution time, increasing with the number of reoptimizations, up to an order of magnitude. Early materialization is able to greatly improve the execution time of federated queries that were optimized without statistics.

## References

1. R. Ahad, K.V.B. Rao, D. McLeod - On Estimating the Cardinality of the Projection of a Database Relation, Proc. TODS 1989
2. G. Antoshenkov, M. Ziauddin - Query Processing and Optimization in Oracle Rdb, VLDB Journal, 5(4) 1996.
3. R. Avnur, J.M. Hellerstein - Eddies: Continuously Adaptive Query Processing, Proc. ACM SIGMOD 2000
4. S. Babu, P. Bizarro, D. DeWitt - Proactive Re-Optimization, Proc. ACM SIGMOD 2005
5. S. Christodoulakis - Implications of Certain Assumptions in Database Performance Evaluation, Proc. ACM Trans. on Database Systems, 1984
6. W. Du, R. Krishnamurthy, M.-C. Shan - Query optimization in heterogeneous DBMS, VLDB 1992.
7. G. Gardarin, F. Sha, Z.-H. Tang - Calibrating the query optimizer cost model of IRO-DB, an object-oriented federated database system, VLDB 1996.
8. P. Gassner, G. M. Lohman, K. B. Schiefer, Y. Wang - Query Optimization in the IBM DB2 Family, IEEE Data Engineering Bulletin 1994
9. A. Van Gelder - Multiple Join Size Estimation by Virtual Domains, Proc. PODS 1993
10. G. Graefe, K. Ward - Dynamic query evaluation plans, Proc. ACM SIGMOD 1989

11. L. M. Haas, D. Kossmann, E. L. Wimmers, Jun Yang – Optimizing Queries across Diverse Data Sources, Proc. VLDB 1997
12. Z. Ives, A. Halevy, D. Weld. - Adapting to Source Properties in Processing Data Integration Queries, Proc. ACM SIGMOD 2004
13. N. Kabra, D. DeWitt - Efficient Mid-Query Re-Optimization of Suboptimal Query Execution Plans, Proc. ACM SIGMOD 1998
14. V. Markl, N. Megiddo, M. Kutsch, T. M. Tran, P. Haas, U. Srivastava - Consistently Estimating the Selectivity of Conjuncts of Predicates, Proc. VLDB 2005
15. V. Markl, V. Raman, D. Simmen, G. Lohman, H. Pirahesh, M. Cilimdzic - Robust Query Processing through Progressive Optimization, Proc. ACM SIGMOD 2004
16. V. Raman, J. Hellerstein - Partial Results for Online Query Processing, Proc. ACM SIGMOD 2002
17. V. Raman, A. Deshpande, J. Hellerstein - Using State Modules for Adaptive Query Processing, ICDE 2003.
18. P. G. Selinger, M. M. Astrahan, D. D. Chamberlain, R. A. Lorie, T. G. Price - Access Path Selection in a Relational Database, Proc. ACM SIGMOD 1979
19. M. Stillger, G. Lohman, V. Markl, and M. Kandil – LEO: DB2's Learning Optimizer, Proc. VLDB 2001
20. M. Stonebraker, P. M. Aoki, R. Devine, W. Litwin, M. Olson - Mariposa: A New Architecture for Distributed Data, ICDE 1994. Also Sequoia 2000 TR 93/31, UC Berkeley, 1993.
21. A. N. Swami and K. B. Schiefer - On the Estimation of Join Result Sizes, Proc. EDBT 1994
22. T. Urhan, M. J. Franklin, L. Amsaleg - Cost Based Query Scrambling for Initial Delays, Proc. ACM SIGMOD 1998
23. M. Zaharioudakis, R. Cochrane, G. Lapis, H. Pirahesh, M. Urata - Answering Complex SQL Queries Using Automatic Summary Tables, Proc. ACM SIGMOD 2000
24. Q. Zhu, P. Larson - Solving local cost estimation for global query optimization in multidatabase systems, Distributed and Parallel Databases, 6:1–51, 1998

# Indexing Spatially Sensitive Distance Measures Using Multi-resolution Lower Bounds

Vebjorn Ljosa, Arnab Bhattacharya, and Ambuj K. Singh

University of California, Santa Barbara, CA 93106-5010, USA
{ljosa, arnab, ambuj}@cs.ucsb.edu

**Abstract.** Comparison of images requires a distance metric that is sensitive to the spatial location of objects and features. Such sensitive distance measures can, however, be computationally infeasible due to the high dimensionality of feature spaces coupled with the need to model the spatial structure of the images.

We present a novel multi-resolution approach to indexing spatially sensitive distance measures. We derive practical lower bounds for the earth mover's distance (EMD). Multiple levels of lower bounds, one for each resolution of the index structure, are incorporated into algorithms for answering range queries and $k$-NN queries, both by sequential scan and using an M-tree index structure. Experiments show that using the lower bounds reduces the running time of similarity queries by a factor of up to 36 compared to a sequential scan without lower bounds. Computing separately for each dimension of the feature vector yields a speedup of ∼14. By combining the two techniques, similarity queries can be answered more than 500 times faster.

## 1 Introduction

Any image database, whether a newspaper photo archive, a repository for biomedical images, or a surveillance system, must be able to compare images in order to be more than an expensive file cabinet. Content-based access is key to making use of large image databases, such as a collection of decades' worth of diverse photographs or the torrent of images from new, high-throughput microscopes [1]. Having a notion of distance is also necessary for global analyses of image collections, ranging from general-purpose techniques such as clustering and outlier detection to specialized machine learning applications that attempt to model biological processes.

Comparing two images requires a *feature extraction method* and a *distance metric*. A feature is a compact representation of the contents of an image. The MPEG-7 standard [2] specifies a number of image features for visual browsing. A distance metric computes a scalar distance between two features: examples are the Euclidean ($L_2$) distance, the Manhattan ($L_1$) distance, and the Mahalanobis distance [3]. The choice of image feature and distance metric depends on the nature of the images, as well as the kind of similarity one hopes to capture.

For many classes of images, the spatial location is important for whether two images should be considered similar. For instance, two photographs with a large

 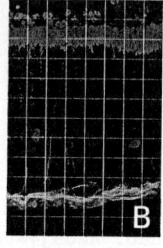 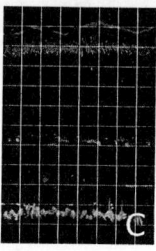

**Fig. 1.** Biologists consider images A and B more similar than images A and C, so if image A is a query on a database consisting of images B and C, a 1-NN query should return image B, not image C. To capture this, a distance metric must take the spatial location into account.

blue region (the sky) in the upper half and a large green region (a field) in the lower half might be similar to each other, but different from an image with a large green region (a tree) in the upper half and a large blue region (a lake) in the lower half. As a second example, Figure 1 contains three fluorescent confocal microscopy images of retinas, collected for studying how the mammalian retina responds to injury.[1] The isolectin B4-labeled objects (shown in blue) in the subretinal space (near the top of the image) are macrophages and the basement membrane of the RPE, whereas the isolectin B4-labeled tissue in the inner retina (lower half of the image) consists of microglial cells and blood vessels [4]. Other examples can be constructed from photographs or surveillance images where one wishes to discount small rotations or translations in defining image similarity.

The earth mover's distance (EMD),[2] first proposed by Werman et al. [6], captures the spatial aspect of the different features extracted from the images. The distance between two images measures both the distance in the feature space and the spatial distance. As an example, suppose we extract a very simple feature, the number of blue pixels, from each tile of the images in Figure 1. The EMD considers each feature a mass located at the position of the tile it came from, and measures the distance between two images by computing the amount of work required to transform one image into the other. In the example, the EMD from query image A to database images B and C are 23 and 37, respectively, so A is more similar to B than to C. In contrast, the $L_2$-norm yields a distance of 8.7 from A to B and 7.5 from A to C. A biologist would agree with the EMD: The retina in image C is normal, whereas the two others have been detached (lifted from their normal position in the eye) for 1 day.

Rubner et al. [5] successfully use the EMD for image retrieval by similarity from large databases and show that it generally outperforms other distance measures like the $L_p$-norm, Jeffrey divergence, $\chi^2$ statistics, and quadratic-form distance in terms of precision and recall. Stricker and Orengo [9] show that for

---

[1] See color images in the electronic version of the paper. More images can be found in the UCSB Bioimage database, http://www.bioimage.ucsb.edu.

[2] The name was first used by Rubner et al. [5]. Earlier works (e.g., [6,7]) call it the *match distance*, and statistics literature uses *Mallows* or *Wasserstein* distance [8].

image retrieval, the $L_1$ distance results in many false negatives because neighboring bins are not considered. The EMD has strong theoretical foundations [7] and is robust to small translations and rotations in an image. It is general and flexible, and can be tuned to behave like any $L_p$-norm with appropriate parameters. The EMD has also been successfully applied to image retrieval based on contours [10] and texture [11], as well as similarity search on melodies [12], graphs [13], and vector fields [14].

Computing the EMD is a linear programming (LP) problem, and therefore computationally expensive. For instance, computing the EMD for 12-dimensional features extracted from images partitioned into 8 × 12 tiles takes 41 s, so a similarity search on a database of 4,000 images can take 46 h. (See Section 5.)

In this paper, we propose the *LB-index*, a multi-resolution approach to indexing the EMD. The representation of an image in feature space is condensed into progressively coarser summaries. We develop lower bounds for the EMD that can be computed from the summaries at various resolutions, and apply these lower bounds to the problem of similarity search in an image database. This paper makes the following contributions:

- We formulate the EMD to work directly with feature vectors of any dimensionality without requiring the feature values of the images to add up to the same number. The formulation extends to concatenation of different feature vectors, as weights can be added to each dimension of the feature vector.
- We show that the distance can be computed separately for each dimension of the feature vector. This leads to a speedup of ~14.
- We derive a lower bound for the EMD. The bound is reasonably tight, much faster to compute than the actual distance, and can be computed from a low-resolution summary of the features representing an image. Different levels of lower bounds can be computed: Higher-level bounds are less tight, but less expensive to compute.
- We show how sequential scan and variants of the M-tree algorithms can use the lower bounds to speed up similarity search. Experiments show that the lower bounds increase the speed of range and $k$-NN queries by factors of ~36 and ~7, respectively. With the two techniques (decomposition and lower bounds) combined, similarity queries can be answered ~500 times faster.

The rest of the paper is organized as follows. Section 2 formally defines our distance measure and shows that it can be computed separately for each dimension of the feature vector. Section 3 introduces our multi-resolution lower-bound approach. Section 4 explains how the lower bounds can be used for similarity search, both by sequential scan and using an M-tree. Section 5 evaluates the multi-resolution approach experimentally. Finally, Section 6 discusses related work, before Section 7 concludes the paper.

## 2  The Earth Mover's Distance

In this section, we formally define the EMD between images, extending Werman et al.'s [6] formulation for grayscale images. The definition applies to feature vectors extracted from image regions. The image feature can be of any dimensionality; in Section 2.1, we show that the distance can be computed independently for each dimension of the feature vector and added up to get the total distance. All feature values must be non-negative, but this is not an important restriction, as they can be made positive by adding the same large number to all feature values of all images. This will not affect the value of the EMD.

Suppose that the images $A$ and $B$ are composed of $n$ and $m$ regions, respectively. For any two regions $i \in A$ and $j \in B$, the *ground distance* $c_{ij}$ is the spatial distance between the two regions. A common choice is to use the $L_2$-distance between the centroids of the two regions as the ground distance.

Feature vectors are extracted from each region of each image. The feature vectors of image $A$ are $\{a_0, \ldots, a_{n-1}\}$, and those of $B$ are $\{b_0, \ldots, b_{m-1}\}$. If the feature vectors are $d$-dimensional, then each $a_i$ and $b_i$ is a column vector of $d$ values. A weight vector $w = [w_1 \ldots w_d]^T$ specifies a weight for each dimension of the feature vector. For simple features, $w = [1 \ldots 1]^T$. However, a different $w$ may be useful, for instance when several different features are concatenated into one vector and one would like to assign them different weights.

Computing the EMD involves finding a *flow matrix* $F = \{f_{ij}\}$, where each flow $f_{ij}$ denotes mass to be moved from each region $i$ in image $A$ to each region $j$ in image $B$ such that image $A$ is transformed into image $B$. Note that each $f_{ij}$ is a column vector of $d$ elements. Also note that both $F$ and $C = \{c_{ij}\}$ are matrices of size $n \times m$.

The cost of moving mass $f_{ij}$ from region $i$ to region $j$ is the ground distance from $i$ to $j$ multiplied by the mass to be moved, or $c_{ij} w^T f_{ij}$, where the weight vector $w$ is used to combine the $d$ elements of $f_{ij}$ into a scalar. The EMD, which is the minimum cost of transforming $A$ into $B$, can then be defined as

$$\min_F \sum_{i=0}^{n-1} \sum_{j=0}^{m-1} c_{ij} w^T f_{ij} \qquad (1)$$

subject to $\quad f_{ij} \geq 0, \quad \sum_{j=0}^{m-1} f_{ij} = a_i, \quad \text{and} \quad \sum_{i=0}^{n-1} f_{ij} = b_j,$

element-wise and $\forall i \in \{0, \ldots, n-1\}, \forall j \in \{0, \ldots, m-1\}$.

Finding the optimal flow matrix $F$ is a linear programming problem. It can be solved with the simplex method [15], but in the worst case, its running time is exponential in the number of regions [16].

An important assumption so far is that $\sum_{i=0}^{n-1} a_i = \sum_{j=0}^{m-1} b_j$, i.e., the images have the same total mass. This is not generally the case. For instance, if the image feature is the intensity, a generally dark image will have a total mass that is lower than that of a generally light image. Werman et al. [6] suggest normalizing the images so that their intensities add up to the same value, but this causes problems, as the distinction between a dark image and a light image will be lost. Instead, we introduce flows to and from a special "region" called the *bank*. The effect of these flows is to allow the total mass of one image to be

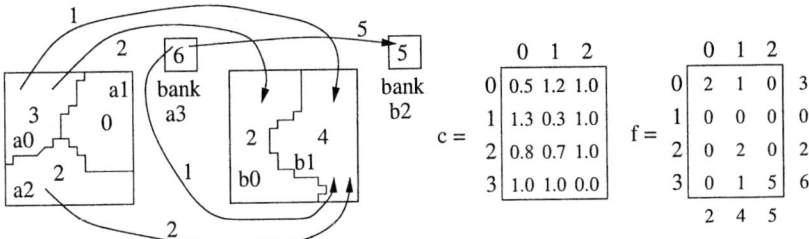

**Fig. 2.** An example computation of the EMD between two images A and B with arbitrary regions. The "banks" are initialized with values such that the sum of the feature values for A and B become equal. The ground distance matrix $c$ is shown on the left while the optimal flow matrix $\boldsymbol{F}$ is shown on the right. The cost to the bank, $\alpha = 1.0$. The flows are shown by arrows with the corresponding mass. The EMD is 4.6.

increased in order to match the total mass of the other, but at a cost proportional to the increase. We add this extra bank region to each image. The bank region has the same ground distance to all other regions, denoted by the parameter $\alpha$. The ground distance from the bank to itself is, of course, 0. The banks of the images $A$ and $B$ are initialized with element-wise non-negative feature values $a_n = \sum_{j=0}^{m-1} b_j$ and $b_m = \sum_{i=0}^{n-1} a_i$. The EMD can now be reformulated to include flows to and from the banks (the $n$-th and $m$-th region of the two images, respectively):

$$\rho_{AB} = \min_F \sum_{i=0}^{n} \sum_{j=0}^{m} c_{ij} \boldsymbol{w}^\mathrm{T} \boldsymbol{f}_{ij} \qquad (2)$$

$$\text{subject to} \quad \boldsymbol{f}_{ij} \geq \boldsymbol{0}, \quad \sum_{j=0}^{m} \boldsymbol{f}_{ij} = \boldsymbol{a}_i, \quad \text{and} \quad \sum_{i=0}^{n} \boldsymbol{f}_{ij} = \boldsymbol{b}_j,$$

element-wise and $\forall i \in \{0, \ldots, n\}, \forall j \in \{0, \ldots, m\}$.

Notice that when $\alpha$ is no more than half the minimum ground distance, the EMD is the same as the $L_1$ distance (scaled by $2\alpha$) because a flow from region $i$ to the bank and back to region $j$ is never more expensive than a flow directly from $i$ to $j$. The EMD is a metric, provided the ground distance is a metric [6]. Introducing the banks can make the ground distance non-metric, but the EMD remains metric as the solution to the LP problem never uses the ground distances that violate the triangle inequality. (Proof omitted due to lack of space.)

An example EMD computation is shown in Figure 2. Image $A$ is composed of regions $a_0, a_1, a_2$ (and bank $a_3$). Image $B$ is composed of regions $b_0, b_1$ (and bank $b_2$). The example assumes $\alpha = 1.0$. The EMD is $\sum_{i=0}^{3} \sum_{j=0}^{2} c_{ij} \mathbf{1}^\mathrm{T} \boldsymbol{f}_{ij} = 4.6$.

## 2.1 Decomposing the EMD for Quicker Computation

The EMD, as defined in Eq. (2), is a large linear programming problem because the flows are vectors of the same dimensionality as the image features. Notice, however, that there is no "cross-talk" among the dimensions of the feature vectors, i.e., there are no direct flows from one dimension to another. Thus, the flows can be decomposed by considering only one dimension at a time, and we can solve $d$ smaller LP problems (where $d$ is the dimensionality of the feature vector) and combine the solutions. Eq. (2) can be written as

$$\rho_{AB} = \min_{F} \sum_{i=0}^{n} \sum_{j=0}^{m} c_{ij} \boldsymbol{w}^T \boldsymbol{f}_{ij} = \min_{F} \sum_{i=0}^{n} \sum_{j=0}^{m} c_{ij} \sum_{k=1}^{d} w_k f_{ijk}. \qquad (3)$$

Theorem 1 shows that Eq. (3) reduces to

$$\rho_{AB} = \sum_{k=1}^{d} \min_{F_k} \sum_{i=0}^{n} \sum_{j=0}^{m} c_{ij} w_k f_{ijk}. \qquad (4)$$

**Theorem 1 (decomposition).** *The minimum cost when all dimensions of the feature vector are considered simultaneously is the same as the sum of minimum costs when each dimension of the feature vector is considered separately, i.e.,*

$$\min_{F} \sum_{i=0}^{n} \sum_{j=0}^{m} c_{ij} \sum_{k=1}^{d} w_k f_{ijk} = \sum_{k=1}^{d} \min_{F_k} \sum_{i=0}^{n} \sum_{j=0}^{m} c_{ij} w_k f_{ijk}. \qquad (5)$$

*Proof (sketch).* Since the constraints in the definition of the EMD in Eq. (2) are all element-wise, they can be separated and solved as separate problems and then added up to get the actual solution. (Full proof omitted.) □

The EMD formulation in Eq. (2) is directly applicable when the dimensions of the feature vectors are independent. This is the case, for instance, for the Color Layout Descriptor (CLD) [2]. Other feature vectors, like the Color Structure Descriptor or the Homogeneous Texture Descriptor, can be subjected to principal component analysis (PCA) in order to find their orthogonal bases. The LP problems for these independent bases can then be solved separately. Another way to deal with dependence between dimensions is to cluster the dimensions so that there is no crosstalk between clusters, and then compute separately for each cluster. This approach is applicable, for instance, to biomedical images showing protein localization, where features are extracted independently for each protein.

Experiments (see Section 5) show that Theorem 1 can reduce the running time and main memory requirements of EMD computations by factors of up to 14 and 7,600, respectively.

## 3  Multi-resolution Lower Bounds for the EMD

Theorem 1 makes the time complexity of computing the earth mover's distance (EMD) linear in the dimensionality of the feature vector, but the running time is still high for large number of regions because the number of variables in the LP problem increases quadratically with the number of regions. Unfortunately, a relatively large number of regions is necessary in order to capture the essential traits of some classes of images, so working with a small number of regions is not always an option. We found that increasing the number of regions from 6 to 24 increased the accuracy of classification of confocal images of feline retinas from 90 % to 96 %. This, however, increased the running time for each distance computation from 4 ms to 62 ms. With 96 regions, the accuracy was 98 %, but the running time went up to 2.9 s.

In this section, we show how a lower bound for the distance using a large number of regions can be computed using a smaller number of regions. This allows us to combine the high accuracy of many regions with the high speed of few regions. As we will see in Section 4, this is key to indexing the EMD.

Suppose image $A$ is divided into $n$ non-bank regions $\mathbb{Z}_n = \{0, 1, \ldots, n-1\}$, and $a_i$ is the feature vector of region $i$. Given an integer $n' < n$, we partition $\mathbb{Z}_n$ into $n'$ non-empty sets $A'_0, \ldots, A'_{n'-1}$. We write $A'$ for the set of sets thus obtained, and add to it a special set $A'_{n'}$ containing only the bank region, $n$. Given $m' < m$, $B'$ is defined for image $B$ in the same way.

Recall that the ground distance $c$ is defined on $\mathbb{Z}_{n+1} \times \mathbb{Z}_{m+1}$. A new distance function $c'$ is defined on $\mathbb{Z}_{n'+1} \times \mathbb{Z}_{m'+1}$. The distance between partitions is the minimum pairwise ground distance between the partitions' respective members:

$$c'_{ij} = \min_{r \in A'_i, s \in B'_j} c_{rs} \qquad (6)$$

The feature vector $a'_i$ of a partition $A'_i$ is the sum of feature vectors of the partition's member regions:

$$a'_i = \sum_{j \in A'_i} a_j \qquad (7)$$

We can now solve the linear programming problem

$$\rho'_{AB} = \min_{F'} \sum_{i=0}^{n'} \sum_{j=0}^{m'} c'_{ij} \boldsymbol{w}^{\mathrm{T}} \boldsymbol{f}'_{ij} \qquad (8)$$

subject to $\quad f'_{ij} \geq 0, \quad \sum_{j=0}^{m'} f'_{ij} = a'_i, \quad$ and $\quad \sum_{i=0}^{n'} f'_{ij} = b'_j,$

element-wise and $\forall i \in \{0, \ldots, n'\}, \forall j \in \{0, \ldots, m'\}$.

This is less computationally demanding because the number of variables in the LP problem is reduced by a factor of $(n/n')(m/m')$. For instance, if 4 and 4 regions are combined in both images, the number of variables is reduced by a factor of 16. The following theorem proves that $\rho'_{AB}$ is a lower bound for $\rho_{AB}$.

**Theorem 2 (lower bound).** *The distance $\rho'_{AB}$, defined in Eq. (8), computed from the coarse representations $A'$ and $B'$ using the modified ground distance $c'$ of Eq. (6), is a lower bound for the EMD $\rho_{AB}$, defined in Eq. (2).*

*Proof.* We construct a flow matrix $\boldsymbol{F'}$ for the coarse representations $A'$ and $B'$ from the corresponding optimal flow matrix $\boldsymbol{F}$ for $A$ and $B$ as follows:

$$f'_{ij} = \sum_{r \in A'_i} \sum_{s \in B'_j} f_{rs}. \tag{9}$$

Note that $\boldsymbol{F'}$ may not be the optimal flow matrix for $A'$ and $B'$.

Eq. (2) can be expressed as sums over the partitions $A'$ and $B'$ of the images and then over the regions $r$ and $s$ in each partition, i.e.,

$$\rho_{AB} = \min_{\boldsymbol{F}} \sum_{i=0}^{n} \sum_{j=0}^{m} c_{ij} \boldsymbol{w}^{\mathrm{T}} \boldsymbol{f}_{ij} = \min_{\boldsymbol{F}} \sum_{i=0}^{n'} \sum_{r \in A'_i} \sum_{j=0}^{m'} \sum_{s \in B'_j} c_{rs} \boldsymbol{w}^{\mathrm{T}} \boldsymbol{f}_{rs} \tag{10}$$

By Eq. (6), this is at least

$$\min_{\boldsymbol{F}} \sum_{i=0}^{n'} \sum_{r \in A'_i} \sum_{j=0}^{m'} \sum_{s \in B'_j} c'_{ij} \boldsymbol{w}^{\mathrm{T}} \boldsymbol{f}_{rs}.$$

Therefore,

$$\rho_{AB} \geq \min_{\boldsymbol{F}} \sum_{i=0}^{n'} \sum_{r \in A'_i} \sum_{j=0}^{m'} \sum_{s \in B'_j} c'_{ij} \boldsymbol{w}^{\mathrm{T}} \boldsymbol{f}_{rs} = \min_{\boldsymbol{F}} \sum_{i=0}^{n'} \sum_{j=0}^{m'} c'_{ij} \boldsymbol{w}^{\mathrm{T}} \left( \sum_{r \in A'_i} \sum_{s \in B'_j} \boldsymbol{f}_{rs} \right),$$

which, by Eq. (9), is equal to

$$\min_{\boldsymbol{F'}} \sum_{i=0}^{n'} \sum_{j=0}^{m'} c'_{ij} \boldsymbol{w}^{\mathrm{T}} \boldsymbol{f}'_{ij} = \rho'_{AB}. \tag{11}$$

Finally, by Eq. (7), the constraints of $\rho_{AB}$ and $\rho'_{AB}$ are equivalent. □

Theorem 2 can easily be generalized to apply even when there is crosstalk between different dimensions of the feature vector, i.e., when there are flows directly from one dimension of one region to another dimension in another region. (The definition in Eq. (2) allows for such flows only indirectly, through the bank.) The generalized proof has been omitted because of space constraints.

Although Theorem 2 is formulated in terms of the EMD definition in Eq. (2), with feature values as mass, it can easily be adapted to work with an alternative definition of EMD, used by Rubner et al. [5], where the image is clustered into regions of similar feature values and the mass is the number of pixels in each region. The only changes needed are: (1) remove the bank region, (2) make the ground distance the distance between centroids of the sets (i.e., the weighted mean of the members' centroids), and (3) combine the weights of each set's members rather than their feature values.

**Multi-resolution Lower Bounds.** So far, we have obtained a coarser summary of an image by combining $n$ *level-0* regions into $n'$ *level-1* regions. It is possible to repeat this process, combining the $n'$ level-1 regions into even fewer $n''$ *level-2* regions, and so on. The ground distance between regions at level $i$ ($i > 0$) is the minimum pairwise distance between the corresponding regions at level ($i - 1$). Multiple levels of lower bounds are key to building efficient index structures for computationally costly distances such as the EMD: Large numbers of higher-level distances can be computed quickly while searching a tree or scanning a list of objects. Most objects can be disregarded based on the lower bound, and the time-consuming lower-level distances need only be computed for the remaining objects. This is the principle behind the search algorithms in Section 4.

## 4 Using Lower Bounds to Speed Up Similarity Search

This section presents *LB-index* algorithms that use the lower bounds derived in Section 3 to search a large database quickly. We consider range queries and $k$-NN queries. In the context of image similarity search, a range query $(A, \tau)$ asks for all images that have a distance of no more than $\tau$ from a query image $A$. (Rather than give the threshold $\tau$ explicitly, a user may derive it from a third image $B$ as $\tau = \rho_{AB}$.) A $k$-NN query $(A, k)$ asks for the $k$ images that have the lowest distance from a query image $A$.

For each class of queries, two algorithms are presented: sequential scan and M-tree. The algorithms are applicable not only to the EMD, but to any distance measure for which a reasonable lower bound can be computed much more quickly than the actual distance. For clarity, we present the algorithms with exactly two levels of lower bounds. It should be obvious how to extend them to work with any number of lower-bound levels.

### 4.1 Sequential-Scan Algorithms

Weber et al. [17] showed that for high-dimensional vector spaces, sequential scan outperforms any index structure. It has the additional benefits of being simple and not requiring a priori construction of any index structure. Hence, making sequential scan faster is important. In this section, we describe sequential-scan algorithms for range and $k$-NN queries. For further reference and for brevity, we name the algorithms SEQ-RANGE-LB2 and SEQ-KNN-LB2, respectively.

The range-query algorithm SEQ-RANGE-LB2 takes two arguments, a query object $O_q$ and a query radius $r(O_q)$, and returns all objects in the database whose distance to $O_q$ is less than or equal to $r(O_q)$. For each object $O_j$ in the database, SEQ-RANGE-LB2 computes $d_{\mathrm{LB2}}(O_q, O_j)$, the second-level lower bound on the distance from the query object to the database object. If $d_{\mathrm{LB2}}(O_q, O_j)$ exceeds $r(O_q)$, then the actual distance $d(O_q, O_j)$ must also exceed $r(O_q)$, so $O_j$ can be safely pruned. Otherwise, the first-level lower bound, $d_{\mathrm{LB}}(O_q, O_j)$, is computed and the same test repeated: if $d_{\mathrm{LB}}(O_q, O_j)$ exceeds $r(O_q)$, then the object can be pruned. Finally, if both $d_{\mathrm{LB2}}(O_q, O_j)$ and $d_{\mathrm{LB}}(O_q, O_j)$ were within the query radius, then the exact distance, $d(O_q, O_j)$, is computed, and if $d(O_q, O_j) \leq r(Q)$, $O_j$ is added to the answer set.

The $k$-NN-query algorithm SEQ-KNN-LB2 takes as arguments a query object $O_q$ and the number of nearest neighbors to retrieve $k$, and returns the $k$ objects in the database that are nearest to $O_q$ (ranked according to their distances). A list $L$ (initially empty) of up to $k$ nearest neighbors seen so far is maintained, sorted by actual distance to the query. The variable $d_k$ keeps track of the actual distance to the $k$-th nearest object seen so far, and is $\infty$ if fewer than $k$ actual distances have been computed.

The algorithm starts by computing $d_{\text{LB2}}$ to all objects in the database and sorting them by $d_{\text{LB2}}$. The sorted list $L$ is then traversed in order. For each object $O_j$, the second-level lower bound on its distance to the query is compared to $d_k$. If $d_{\text{LB2}}(O_j, O_q) > d_k$, the algorithm halts and returns $L$. If not, the first-level lower bound, $d_{\text{LB}}(O_j, O_q)$, is computed. If $d_{\text{LB}}(O_j, O_q) > d_k$, the object $O_j$ is not considered any more. Otherwise, the object could be one of $O_q$'s $k$ nearest neighbors, so the actual distance $d(O_j, O_q)$ is computed. If $d(O_j, O_q) \leq d_k$, $O_j$ is inserted at the proper place in $L$, $d_k$ is updated, and objects in $L$ whose actual distance to $O_q$ exceeds $d_k$ are removed.

### 4.2 Algorithm for Range Queries Using M-Tree

Ciaccia et al.'s M-tree [18] is perhaps the most well-known metric tree, and organizes objects in a metric space into a tree structure so that the triangle inequality can be used to prune subtrees during search. We present the algorithm M-RANGE-LB2, which performs a range search in an M-tree using lower bounds. The algorithm is based on Ciaccia et al.'s original M-tree range query algorithm [18], which we refer to as M-RANGE.

Let $N$ be a node, $O_p$ the parent node of $N$, $Q$ the query object, $O_r$ a child node of $N$ (if $N$ is an internal node), and $O_j$ an object of $N$ (if $N$ is a leaf node).

If $N$ is an internal node, M-RANGE decides not to search the subtree rooted at $O_r$ if $|d(O_p, Q) - d(O_r, O_p)| > r(Q) + r(O_r)$. In M-RANGE-LB2, we replace the condition with one that will prune fewer subtrees, but which can be calculated much more quickly from $d_{\text{LB2}}(O_p, Q)$:

$$d_{\text{LB2}}(O_p, Q) - d(O_r, O_p) > r(Q) + r(O_r) \qquad (12)$$

Note that the modulus (absolute value) sign cannot be applied as it violates the correctness of the algorithm: if $d_{\text{LB2}}(O_p, Q) - d(O_r, O_p) > r(Q) + r(O_r)$, then $d(O_p, Q) - d(O_r, O_p) > r(Q) + r(O_r)$, so we can prune; but, if $d(O_r, O_p) - d_{\text{LB2}}(O_p, Q) > r(Q) + r(O_r)$, then it is not necessary that $d(O_r, O_p) - d(O_p, Q) > r(Q) + r(O_r)$, so pruning the subtree would be incorrect.

If $N$ is a leaf node, M-RANGE discards $O_j$ without computing $d(O_j, Q)$ if $|d(O_p, Q) - d(O_j, O_p)| > r(Q)$. In M-RANGE-LB2, we replace the condition with

$$d_{\text{LB2}}(O_p, Q) - d(O_j, O_p) > r(Q), \qquad (13)$$

which again prunes fewer subtrees but is faster to calculate. Once more, we cannot consider the absolute value as that would violate the correctness of the algorithm. If condition (13) fails to prune an object $O_j$, approximations to the distance from $O_j$ to the query $Q$ are computed—first the second-level lower bound, then the first-level lower bound, and finally the exact distance. The algorithm proceeds to the next level only if the object cannot be pruned based on the previous level. The rest of the algorithm and the data structures remain unchanged from M-RANGE.

### 4.3 Algorithm for $k$-NN Queries Using M-Tree

Our algorithm for answering $k$-NN queries, which uses the lower bounds, is called M-KNN-LB2. It is based on the original $k$-NN algorithm for M-trees [18], which we refer to as M-KNN. We only describe the procedure M-KNN-NODESEARCH-LB2, since the rest of the algorithm and the data structures are identical.

Let $N$ be a node, $O_p$ the parent node of $N$, $Q$ the query object, $O_r$ a child node of $N$ (if $N$ is an internal node), and $O_j$ an object of $N$ (if $N$ is a leaf node). We maintain $d_{\min}$ for the tree $T(O_r)$ rooted at $O_r$ as

$$d_{\min}(T(O_r)) = \max\{d_{LB2}(O_r, Q) - r(O_r), 0\}. \tag{14}$$

If $N$ is an internal node, M-KNN decides not to search the subtree rooted at $O_r$ if $|d(O_p, Q) - d(O_r, O_p)| > d_k + r(O_r)$ where $d_k$ is maintained as the actual distance to the $k$th nearest object. In M-KNN-LB2, we replace this condition with one that is faster to calculate but has less pruning power:

$$d_{LB2}(O_p, Q) - d(O_r, O_p) > d_k + r(O_r) \tag{15}$$

If $N$ is a leaf node, M-KNN prunes $O_j$ without computing $d(O_j, Q)$ if $|d(O_p, Q) - d(O_j, O_p)| > d_k$. In M-KNN-LB2, we replace this condition with

$$d_{LB2}(O_p, Q) - d(O_j, O_p) > d_k, \tag{16}$$

which again has less pruning capacity, but can be calculated much faster. If an object cannot be pruned based on condition (16), the second-level lower bound $d_{LB2}(O_j, Q)$ is computed and compared to $d_k$. If this test fails to prune the object, the first-level lower bound $d_{LB}(O_j, Q)$ is computed. The actual distance $d(O_j, Q)$ is computed only if the first-level lower bound fails to prune the object.

Finally, we have removed the part of the algorithm that computes an upper bound $d_{\max}(T(O_r))$ on the distance from $Q$ to any object in the tree rooted at $O_r$. This is because the upper bound would require the computation of $d(O_r, Q)$; using $d_{LB2}(O_r, Q)$ would invalidate the bound.

### 4.4 Discussion

The M-tree range query algorithm never computes more actual distances than does the sequential scan. It may, however, compute more lower bounds and therefore take more time. To see this, recollect that the actual distances are never computed for internal nodes. For child nodes, the actual distance is computed

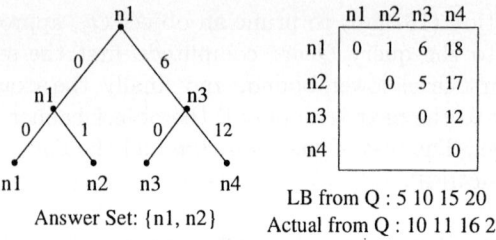

**Fig. 3.** Example where the M-tree performs worse than sequential scan for $k$-NN query. The M-tree shown on the left is built on the database $\{n_1, n_2, n_3, n_4\}$. The distance matrix of the objects is shown on the right together with the actual and lower bound distances from the query Q to all database objects. A 2-NN query for Q returns $\{n_1, n_2\}$. Sequential scan performs 2 actual computations while M-tree performs 4 actual computations. For details, see text.

only if the lower bound is within the range of the query, in which case the sequential-scan algorithm must compute it as well. The number of lower bound computations may be higher, as that depends on the order of traversal.

The M-tree $k$-NN query algorithm can end up computing more actual distances than the sequential scan (leading to higher running time) when using the lower bounds. Figure 3 gives an example. There are 4 objects in the database: $n_1$, $n_2$, $n_3$ and $n_4$. The actual distances among them are shown in the distance matrix on the right. The M-tree on the left is built on these objects. For the 2-NN query of an object $Q$, the actual distances and the lower bound distances are (10, 11, 16, 28) and (5, 10, 15, 20), respectively. Sequential scan computes actual distances to $n_1$ and $n_2$, and since the lower bound to $n_3$ is greater than the actual distance to $n_2$, it stops. The M-tree, on the other hand, first tries to search the right subtree rooted at $n_3$ instead of the left subtree rooted at $n_1$ since $d_{\text{LB}}(n_3, q) - r(n_3) < d_{\text{LB}}(n_1, q) - r(n_1)$. As a result, it computes the actual distances to $n_3$ and $n_4$. Finally, when the left subtree is searched, it computes actual distances for $n_1$ and $n_2$ and ends up with 4 actual distance computations.

We chose to use the M-tree because it is the most well-known metric index structure; other index structures could also have been used. We do not focus on the dynamic aspects of the index structure, and merely note that good insert and split decisions can usually be made based on the lower bounds.

## 5 Experimental Results

We used two sets of confocal micrographs of cat retinas: (1) a set of 218 images of retinal tissue labeled with anti-rhodopsin, anti-glial fibrillary acidic protein (anti-GFAP), and isolectin B4; and (2) a set of 3932 images of retinal tissue labeled with various antibodies and other labels. Querying a dataset of only a few thousand images is challenging because of the EMD's high computational cost, so even though the second dataset may appear small, its size is sufficient to demonstrate the benefits of our techniques. The experiments were run on computers with Intel Xeon 3 GHz CPUs, Linux 2.6.9, and GLPK 4.8.

Except where noted, images were partitioned into $8 \times 12 = 96$ tiles. All images were $512 \times 768$ pixels, so each tile was 64 pixels square. We used the 12-dimensional MPEG-7 color layout descriptor (CLD) [2] as our image feature.

In order to assess the tightness of our lower bounds, we compared the actual EMD with the first- and second-level lower bounds. We also compared to a lower bound proposed by Rubner et al. [5], using the $L_1$ ground distance. One image was chosen at random from the 218 dataset, and the exact distances from that image to each of the 217 other images were computed, along with the three lower bounds. Figure 4 shows the result, ordered by the actual distance. We see that all three lower bounds are tight enough to be of use, but our first- and second-level lower bounds are tighter than that of Rubner et al. This is not surprising, since the latter uses the center of mass for all regions, and therefore loses all spatial information. Using random images as queries, on average, the first-level, second-level, and Rubner et al. lower bounds were 25%, 44%, and 68% below the actual distances, respectively. Also, none of the three lower bounds were monotonic with respect to the actual distance.

Our second experiment measures the impact of Theorem 1 (decomposition). All pairs of distances were computed between the color layout descriptors of 10 random images. The CLD has 12 dimensions, and computing for all dimensions at once (i.e., without applying Theorem 1), took 41 s and used 37 MB of main memory. Applying the theorem and computing the distances by solving 12 smaller LP problems reduced this to 2.9 s and 5 kB, respectively.

Our third experiment measures how the time to compute the EMD increases with the number of regions. Ten images were chosen at random from the 218 data set and tiled with four different tile sizes: 256, 128, 64, and 32 pixels square. This corresponds to 6, 24, 96, and 384 tiles per image, respectively. All 100 distances between the 10 images were computed for the four tile sizes using the simplex method. The running times were 4 ms, 62 ms, 2.89 s, and 319 s, respectively. In comparison, the Rubner et al. lower bound took 1.4 ms to compute. We see that reducing the number of tiles from 96 to 24 reduces the running time by a factor of 47, so our lower bound has a great potential for speeding up queries, provided that it is tight enough. As pointed out in Section 2.1, the distance is computed independently for each dimension of the feature vector, so the running time is linear in the number of dimensions. Thus, speedup achieved by computing for a lower number of bins is independent of the dimensionality of the feature vector.

## 5.1 Sequential-Scan Experiments

The next set of experiments measures how lower bounds reduce the cost of answering range and $k$-NN queries on the 3932 dataset using sequential-scan algorithms. All results are averages over 50 queries. Each query is a random image from the dataset. We measure range query running times with a range of 3.7% of the maximum distance between any two images in the database. On average, this returns 25 images. For $k$-NN queries, we measure times for $k = 25$.

Figure 5 compares the impacts of decomposition (Theorem 1) and lower bounds (Theorem 2). We see that the two techniques separately reduce the

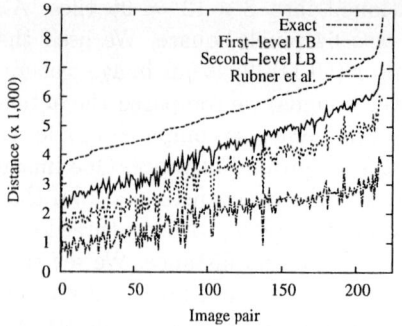
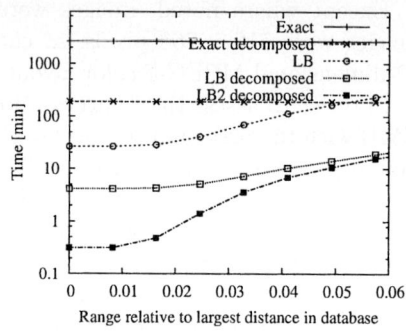

**Fig. 4.** The first-level and second-level lower bounds are tighter than Rubner et al.'s lower bound. They are tight enough to be of practical use.

**Fig. 5.** For sequential-scan range queries, decomposition leads to a speedup of 14. One and two levels of lower bounds lead to additional speedups of 22 and 36, respectively. Total speedup is more than 500.

running time from over 40 h to 3.2 h and 1.5 h, respectively. Together, they answer the query in 9 min. Adding a second level of lower bounds reduces this further to 5 min, for a total speedup of more than 500.

The running times for range queries are shown in Figure 6. (The figure also contains M-tree results, which will be discussed in Section 5.2.) The first-level lower bounds result in a speedup of 22. Using both the first- and second-level lower bounds increases the speedup to 36. In comparison, the Rubner et al. lower bound led to a speedup of 5.7. For large ranges, the speedup diminishes, and the algorithm computes all lower bounds as well as all exact distances.

The running times for $k$-NN queries are shown in Figure 7. For $k = 25$, the first-level lower bound achieves a speedup of 6, and adding the second-level lower bound makes 25-NN queries run 7 times faster than a sequential scan without lower bounds. The Rubner et al. lower bound led to a speedup of 1.6.

Figure 8 shows how the total computation time for queries is divided between actual distances, first-level lower bounds, and second-level lower bounds. Without lower bounds, the average query takes 3.2 h (not shown). With the first-level lower bound, this is reduced to 9 min. The first bar in the figure shows that about 50 % of this time is spent computing first-level lower bounds. Introducing a second-level lower bound reduces the number of first-level computations. It adds 3932 second-level computations, but these are comparatively cheap, so the running time is reduced by another factor of two. We see from the second bar that only a small portion of the total time is spent computing second-level lower bounds, so adding another level (or the Rubner et al. lower bound) would not reduce the total time much. Obviously, if the first-level lower bound cannot prune an object, the second-level lower bound cannot prune it either, so adding the second level does not impact the time spent computing exact distances.

For 25-NN queries, the first-level lower bounds reduce the running time from 3.2 h to 30 min. Adding the second-level lower bounds increases the number of actual computations slightly because pruning based on second-level bounds is

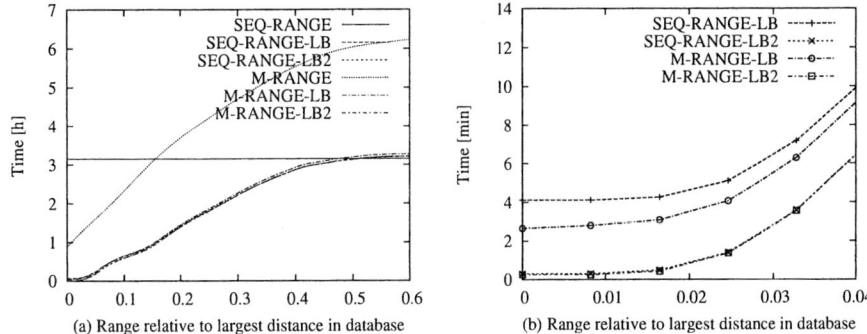

**Fig. 6.** Running time for range queries. Figure (b) is a magnified view of the portion of Figure (a) near the origin. For queries with a range of 3.7% (returning on average 25 images), sequential scan runs 22 times faster when the first-level lower bound is used and 36 times faster when both the first- and second-level lower bounds are used. The M-tree by itself speeds up the search for small ranges, but very quickly becomes worse than sequential scan. M-tree using the first level of lower bound achieves a speedup of 24. When using 2 levels, M-tree is not much better than sequential scan.

less effective than pruning based on first-level bounds. It saves many first-level distance computations, however, yielding a net reduction in running time.

### 5.2 M-Tree Experiments

An M-tree index structure [18] was constructed on the 3932 dataset using the bulk-loading algorithm of Ciaccia and Patella [19]. Color layout feature vectors are 12 bytes for each tile, which amounts to 1.1 kB for each image. Because the distance computations are so expensive, disk access times are negligible: With a recent-model 15,000 rpm disk drive, a seek takes 3.6 ms, transfer of 1.1 kB takes 0.02 ms, and the latency of the disk drive is 2 ms. This adds up to 5.6 ms, compared to 4 ms for computing a single second-level lower bound. As shown in Figure 8, computing second-level lower bounds is only a small part of the total running time, so disk access times are also low. Consequently, saving distance computations is much more important than saving disk accesses, and we choose a page size of 2.5 kB, which yields a branching factor of two. The M-tree had 1968 internal nodes (each with one centroid) and 1966 leaf nodes (each with two objects). Therefore, the total size of the M-tree index structure was $(1968 + 1966 \times 2) \times 1.1$ kB = 6.3 MB. In comparison, each image is about 1.1 MB, and so the index structure was only 0.15% of the database size. For each query, we counted the number of distance computations of each type and computed total running times using the times reported in Section 5.

Figure 6 shows that the M-tree range search always outperforms sequential scan with the same lower bounds. With a query range of 3.7%, the speedup is 9% over sequential scan with the first-level lower bound. Adding the second level yields only a negligible improvement, however. M-tree range search with Rubner et al.'s lower bound is 7 times slower than that with our lower bounds.

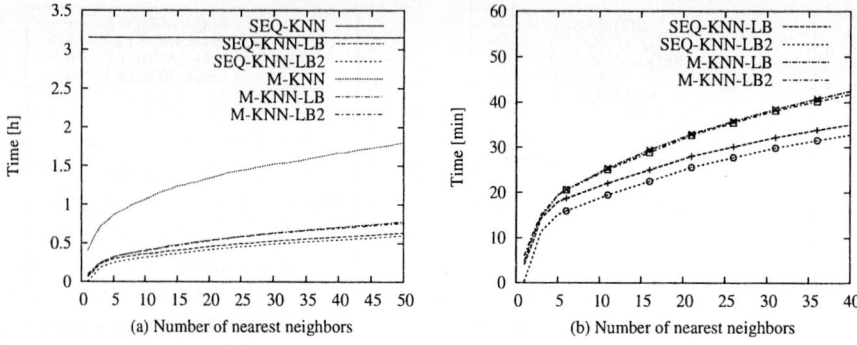

**Fig. 7.** Running time for $k$-NN queries. Figure (b) is a magnified view of the portion of Figure (a) near the origin. For 25-NN queries, sequential scan runs 6 times faster when the first-level lower bound is used and 7 times faster when both lower bounds are used. The M-tree, by itself, speeds up the search 2.2 times. M-tree using the first level of lower bound achieves a speedup of 5.3, which is less than the corresponding speedup of the sequential scan. When using 2 levels, it accelerates the query 5.4 times.

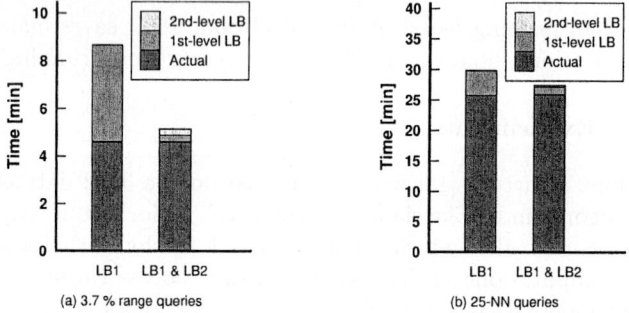

**Fig. 8.** The first-level lower bound reduces the running time of a range query from 3.2 h (not shown) to 9 min. Introducing a second-level lower bound reduces the total running time to 5 min. The time to answer a 25-NN query is reduced from 3.2 h (not shown) to 30 min, and further to 27 min.

Without lower bounds, the cost of an M-tree is extremely high because an exact distance must be computed for every internal node considered in the search. The pruning achieved by the index structure was not enough to offset this huge cost. Caching of distances might help, as the centroid of an internal node will reappear at least once in its subtree, but this is outside the scope of this paper.

We see from Figure 7 that the M-tree $k$-NN algorithm with lower bounds does not perform as well as its sequential scan counterpart. The reason is that the algorithm must decide on an order in which to search the subtrees without full knowledge of their contents. In contrast, sequential scan has full access to all the lower bounds. An exact distance computation is more than 700 times costlier than a second-level lower bound computation, so the sequential scan algorithm's strategy to compute 3932 lower bounds up front pays off if it saves 6 or more exact distance computations. For comparison, M-tree $k$-NN search performs 3 times slower with Rubner et al.'s lower bound than that with ours.

## 6 Related Work

Werman et al. [6] define the *match distance* for multidimensional histograms and suggest its application to texture features, shape matching, and image comparison. For the latter, the intensity of pixels is used as the mass. Peleg et al. [7] formulate the match distance as an LP problem. Rubner et al. [5] introduce the name *earth mover's distance*, and study image retrieval using color distributions and texture features. Their LP problem is substantially the same, but the input slightly different: Pixels with similar feature values are clustered, and the number of pixels in each cluster is used as the mass. We are not aware of any study that compares the two definitions experimentally. Our lower bounds and index structures can be used with either definition. We use the name EMD for both.

Rubner et al. [5] also derive a lower bound—the distance between the centers of mass (in feature space) of the two images—for the EMD. Their bound disregards position information, as the center of mass of each image lies at the physical center of the image and contributes zero to the bound. We implemented their lower bound, compared it with ours, and found (Section 5) that our lower bounds were consistently tighter. As a consequence, our lower bounds resulted in significantly faster querying, even though they were not as quick to compute.

Indyk and Thaper [20] embed the EMD in Euclidean space, and then use locality-sensitive hashing to find nearest neighbors. VA-files [17] use a notion of approximation similar to ours, and use lower and upper bounds on distances to speed up searches.

The MPEG-7 color layout descriptor (CLD) [2] is resolution invariant and uses the YCbCr color space. The image is divided into 64 blocks, and one representative color is chosen from each block. The discrete cosine transform (DCT) of each color component is then computed, resulting in three sets of 64 coefficients. The coefficients are finally zigzag scanned and non-linearly quantized to retain 12 coefficients: 6 for luminance and 3 for each chrominance.

## 7 Conclusion

This article considered the problem of speeding up the computation of spatially-sensitive distance measures between images. Adopting the earth mover's distance, we showed how it can be decomposed, leading to a 14-fold speedup. We then developed a novel multi-resolution index structure, *LB-index*, which consists of progressively coarser summaries of the representation of an image. We derived lower bounds that can be computed at multiple levels, corresponding to the various resolutions of the index structure.

We developed a suite of similarity search algorithms that use the multiple levels of lower bounds to speed up queries. The sequential scan algorithms achieved speedups of up to 36 and 7 for range queries and $k$-NN queries, respectively.

We also incorporated the lower bounds into the range search and $k$-NN search algorithms for the M-tree index structure. These algorithms reduced the running times of range queries and $k$-NN queries by factors of up to 36 and 5, respectively.

Possible avenues of future work are considering other spatially sensitive distance measures and extending our approach to other tasks, such as classification and data mining.

**Acknowledgements.** We would like to thank Geoffrey P. Lewis from the laboratory of Steven K. Fisher at UCSB for providing the retinal images. This work was supported in part by grants ITR-0331697 and EIA-0080134 from the National Science Foundation.

# References

1. Swedlow, J.R., Goldberg, I., Brauner, E., Sorger, P.K.: Informatics and quantitative analysis in biological imaging. Science **300** (2003) 100–102
2. Manjunath, B.S., Salembier, P., Sikora, T., eds.: Introduction to MPEG 7: Multimedia Content Description Language. Wiley (2002)
3. Mahalanobis, P.: On the generalised distance in statistics. Proc. Nat. Inst. Sci. India **12** (1936) 49–55
4. Lewis, G.P., Guerin, C.J., Anderson, D.H., to, B.M., Fisher, S.K.: Rapid changes in the expression of glial cell proteins caused by experimental retinal detachment. Am. J. of Ophtalmol. **118** (1994) 368–376
5. Rubner, Y., Tomasi, C., Guibas, L.J.: The earth mover's distance as a metric for image retrieval. International Journal of Computer Vision **40** (2000) 99–121
6. Werman, M., Peleg, S., Rosenfeld, A.: A distance metric for multi-dimensional histograms. Computer, Vision, Graphics, and Image Proc. **32** (1985) 328–336
7. Peleg, S., Werman, M., Rom, H.: A unified approach to the change of resolution: Space and gray-level. IEEE Trans. PAMI **11** (1989) 739–742
8. Levina, E., Bickel, P.: The earth mover's distance is the Mallows distance: Some insights from statistics. In: Proc. ICCV. Volume 2. (2001) 251–256
9. Stricker, M.A., Orengo, M.: Similarity of color images. In Niblack, C.W., Jain, R.C., eds.: Storage and Retrieval for Image and Video Databases III. Volume 2420 of Proceedings of SPIE. (1995) 381–392
10. Grauman, K., Darrell, T.: Fast contour matching using approximate earth mover's distance. In: Proc. CVPR. (2004)
11. Lazebnik, S., Schmid, C., Ponce, J.: Sparse texture representation using affine-invariant neighborhoods. In: Proc. CVPR. (2003)
12. Typke, R., Veltkamp, R., Wiering, F.: Searching notated polyphonic music using transportation distances. In: Proc. Int. Conf. Multimedia. (2004) 128–135
13. Demirci, M.F., Shokoufandeh, A., Dickinson, S., Keselman, Y., Bretzner, L.: Many-to-many feature matching using spherical coding of directed graphs. In: Proc. European Conf. Computer Vision (ECCV). (2004)
14. Lavin, Y., Batra, R., Hesselink, L.: Feature comparisons of vector fields using earth mover's distance. In: Proc. of the Conference on Visualization. (1998) 103–109
15. Hillier, F.S., Lieberman, G.J.: Introduction to Mathematical Programming. 1st edn. McGraw-Hill, New York (1990)
16. Klee, V., Minty, G.: How good is the simplex algorithm. In Shisha, O., ed.: Inequalities. Volume III., New York, NY, Academic Press (1972) 159–175

17. Weber, R., Schek, H.J., Blott, S.: A quantitative analysis and performance study for similarity-search methods in high-dimensional spaces. In: Proc. VLDB. (1998) 194–205
18. Ciaccia, P., Patella, M., Zezula, P.: M-tree: An efficient access method for similarity search in metric spaces. In: Proc. VLDB. (1997) 426–435
19. Ciaccia, P., Patella, M.: Bulk loading the M-tree. In: Proc. ADC. (1998)
20. Indyk, P., Thaper, N.: Fast image retrieval via embeddings. In: Proc. Internat. Workshop on Statistical and Computational Theories of Vision. (2003)

# Indexing Incomplete Databases

Guadalupe Canahuate, Michael Gibas, and Hakan Ferhatosmanoglu

Department of Computer Science and Engineering,
The Ohio State University
{canahuat, gibas, hakan}@cse.ohio-state.edu

**Abstract.** Incomplete databases, that is, databases that are missing data, are present in many research domains. It is important to derive techniques to access these databases efficiently. We first show that known indexing techniques for multi-dimensional data search break down in terms of performance when indexed attributes contain missing data. This paper utilizes two popularly employed indexing techniques, bitmaps and quantization, to correctly and efficiently answer queries in the presence of missing data. Query execution and interval evaluation are formalized for the indexing structures based on whether missing data is considered to be a query match or not. The performance of Bitmap indexes and quantization based indexes is evaluated and compared over a variety of analysis parameters for real and synthetic data sets. Insights into the conditions for which to use each technique are provided.

## 1 Introduction

Real world applications using databases with missing data are common. Databases with missing data occur in a wide range of research and industry domains. Some examples of these are:

1. A census database that allow null values for some attributes
2. A survey database where answers to one question cause other questions to be skipped
3. A medical database that relates human body analyte (a substance that can be measured in the blood or urine) measurements to a number of diseases, or patient risk factors to a specific disease

The goal of this paper is to provide techniques that access databases efficiently in the presence of missing data.

There are a variety of reasons why databases may be missing data. The data may not be available at the time the record was populated or it was not recorded because of equipment malfunction or adverse conditions. Data may have been unintentionally omitted or the data is not relevant to the record at hand. The allowance for and use of missing data may be intentionally designed into the database. In some cases, the missingness of data is random, i.e. the missingness of some value does not depend on the value of another variable. In that case, the missingness is ignorable and the way of dealing with it is to "complete" the value using regression or other statistical model and treat the data as if it was never missing. However, if the data are missing as a function of some other variable, a complete treatment of missing data would have to include a model that accounts for missing data. Consider the example of the analyte-disease database where diseases are the records and analyte ranges are the attributes. This database would contain values for analyte ranges if they are relevant for a specific disease, or null values if the analyte readings are not important in the diagnosis of that disease. We may query such a database with a patient's analyte readings to get a list of potential diagnoses. We do not want to discount diseases that do not have a value for an analyte included in the query, because the act of taking an analyte's measurement has no bearing on if a patient has a disease that is not relevant to that particular analyte. So in this case, missing data should be interpreted as a query match for that attribute. Alternatively, the intent of a query may not be to return records that *could* match query criteria, but to only return records that definitely match query criteria. In this case any missing data for a record that occurs in an attribute specified by the query search key means that the record does *not* match the query. An example of this could be a survey results query where the query asks for a count of respondents that answered question 5 with answer "A" and question 8 with answer "C".

This paper deals with data where missingness is not ignorable, in other words whether a data value is missing or not is important and we want to be able to distinguish between the real values and the absence of such values. In order to achieve this, we could assign a specific value for missing fields that is not in the domain of that particular attribute. For example, if the domain of an attribute is the positive integers, a value of -1 may be used to denote missing data. Then the transformed, complete multi-dimensional database could be indexed using traditional hierarchical multi-dimensional indexing techniques. However, this solution for indexing databases with missing data experiences significant performance issues when applied to hierarchical indexing techniques. To illustrate this point, we performed a set of experiments on two-dimensional data sets that are identical except that they vary with respect to their percentage of missing data. We built an R-tree index on the different datasets and executed 2-dimensional queries with a global selectivity of 25%. Figure 1 shows the effect on query execution time as missing data probability varies.

The graph shows time performance of a query using an R-tree built on the different data sets, normalized to the time to perform the query on a complete data set. This graph shows that even for a data set and index that is only two dimensions, we get far worse performance when the database contains missing data. Even when there is only 10% missing data for each attribute, the time performance is 23 times worse than if the data set were complete.

Multi-dimensional indexing techniques work best when records are mapped to non-overlapping hypercubes. When missing data are mapped to a single value, the overlaps associated with the index structure increase.

One technique to deal with this issue is to somehow randomize the values assigned to missing data so pruning potential results when traversing the index

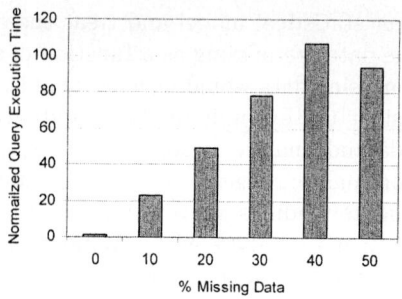

**Fig. 1.** Normalized Query Execution Time versus Percent Missing Data, Query Selectivity = 25%, 2-D Data Set

structure is not compromised. However, it becomes necessary to transform the initial query involving $k$ attributes into $2^k$ subqueries. This is because there are $2^k$ possible combinations of missing and non-missing values among the $k$ attributes in the search key. Therefore there are $2^k$ subspaces where query matching data can reside, and all of them must be searched. This fact causes query execution performance to become exponentially worse with respect to query dimensionality. Lastly, as described in [15] all hierarchical multi-dimensional index structures break down after a certain number of dimensions indexed.

Space partitioning multi-dimensional indexing techniques would also suffer from the same weaknesses in the presence of missing data. Records with missing data values would get mapped to lesser-dimensioned spaces, and the full benefit of data space partitioning would not be realized. Again, partitioning the data space beyond a certain number of dimensions has limitations as discussed in [15].

Data repositories need techniques for indexing multi-dimensional data that work well in the presence of missing data. Further benefit is derived if the techniques also work for databases with higher dimensionality than can be achieved effectively using hierarchical or data partitioning indexes. The objective of this paper is to facilitate efficient access to and define query execution for databases with missing data in a way that even works well when the database dimensionality is high. The techniques introduced are evaluated in terms of performance against a number of parameters including database dimensionality, missing data frequency, query selectivity, and query semantics (whether missing data indicates a query match or not).

Contributions of this paper include the following:

1. Efficiently indexing databases with missing data using variations of bitmaps and VA-Files.
2. Demonstrating that missing data not only causes semantic problems but also degradation in the performance of queries.
3. Formalization of query processing operations for the proposed techniques in the presence of missing data.

4. Insights into the environments appropriate for each technique. Although bitmaps and quantization (VA-Files) have been extensively studied, and their applications are similar, we know of no work that compares and contrasts them.
5. Empirical study and evaluation of results over several analysis parameters.

The rest of this paper is organized as follows: Section 2 discusses related work, Section 3 defines the problem addressed in this paper, Section 4 describes the proposed solutions and Section 5 presents the experimental results. Finally, we conclude in Section 6 and provide directions for future work.

## 2 Related Work

**Missing Data.** Although databases commonly deal with or contain missing data, relatively little work has been performed for this topic. Formal definitions for imperfect databases, of which databases with missing data is a subset, and database operations are provided in [21]. Two techniques for indexing databases with missing data are introduced and evaluated in [12]. This is the only paper we are aware of that focuses on indexing missing data. These are the bitstring augmented method and the multiple one-dimensional one-attribute indexes technique, called MOSAIC.

For the bitstring-augmented index, the average of the non-missing values is used as a mapping function for the missing values. The goal is to avoid skewing the data by assigning missing values to several distinct values. However, by applying this method it becomes necessary to transform the initial query involving k attributes into $2^k$ subqueries, making the technique infeasible for large k. MOSAIC is a set of B+-Trees where missing data is mapped to a distinguished value. Similarly to the previous method, it becomes necessary to transform the initial query involving k attributes into $2k$ subqueries, one for each attribute.

What makes MOSAIC perform better than the Bitstring-Augmented index for point queries is that it uses independent indices for each dimension. However, by using several B+-Trees the query has to be decomposed and intersection and union operations need to be performed to obtain the final result. Queries that could gain a greater performance benefit by utilizing multiple-dimension indexes would not achieve it using this technique. Therefore, this method may not be useful for multiple-dimension range queries, or other queries where the number of matches associated with a single dimension is high.

Our work differs from [12] in that we introduce and evaluate techniques that do not suffer the same weaknesses as their techniques. In our approach the query need not be transformed into exponential number of queries and no extra expensive computation, such as set operations, needs to be performed in order to obtain the final result set. Moreover, even though VA-File is not a hierarchical index it benefits from pruning multiple dimensions in one pass through the structure. In addition, our solution using bitmaps and VA-Files is also scalable with respect to the data dimensionality.

**Bitmaps.** The topic of bitmap indexes was introduced in [10]. Several bitmap encoding schemes have been developed, such as equality [10], range [5], interval [5], and workload and attribute distribution oriented [9]. Several commercial database management systems use bitmaps [11, 3, 7]. Numerous performance evaluations and improvements have been performed over bitmaps [4, 17, 13, 8, 18, 19, 5, 20]. While the fast bitwise operations afforded by bitmaps are perhaps their biggest advantage, a limitation of bitmaps is the index size. Several compression techniques have been proposed [2, 16, 1, 13] to reduce the bitmap index size. Some of the most popular compression techniques such as Byte-Aligned Bitmap Code (BBC) [2] and Word Aligned Hybrid (WAH) code [16], use a hybrid between the run-length encoding and the literal scheme to compress the bitmap.

**VA-Files.** The motivation for VA-files is introduced in [15]. This paper showed theoretical limitations for the classes of data and space partitioning indexing techniques with respect to dimensionality. Since reading all database pages becomes unavoidable when the number of indexed dimensions is high, the authors suggest reading a much smaller approximate version, or vector approximation (VA), of each record in the database. An initial read approximately answers queries, and actual database pages are read to determine the exact query answer. VA-files are more thoroughly described in [14].

To the best of our knowledge this is the first paper that compares and contrasts bitmaps and VA-files and discusses them together and the first paper in which these techniques are used to index incomplete databases.

## 3 Problem Definition

Let D be a database with a schema of the form $(A_1, A_2, \ldots, A_d)$. D is said to be incomplete if tuples in it are allowed to have missing attribute values. Without loss of generality, assume the domain of the attribute values is the integers from 1 to $C_i$, where $C_i$ is the cardinality of attribute $A_i$. We assume that data retrieval is based on a k-dimensional search key, where k is less than or equal to d.

In range queries, a lower- and upper-bound is specified for each attribute in the search key. Each interval in the query is represented as $v_1 \leq A_i \leq v_2$, where $v_1$ and $v_2$ are between 1 and $C_i$. The query is said to be a point query if all lower bounds are equal to the corresponding upper bound for each attribute in the search key.

Given a range query Q with a k-dimensional search key, we have two ways to compute the results for Q. When missing data is considered to be a query match, a tuple t in the database is said to be an answer for Q if every attribute of t which appears in the search key that is not a missing value falls in the corresponding range defined in the query or is a missing value. When missing is not a match, a tuple t in the database is said to be an answer for Q if every attribute of t which appears in the search key is not missing and falls in the corresponding range defined in the query.

The performance of a query can be characterized by the time it takes to perform the query and the accuracy of the result. For this work we only consider techniques that provide accurate query results. The time it takes to perform a query when an index is used is made up of the time to read the index (if the index does not already reside in memory), the time to execute the query over the index, and the time to read the database pages indicated by the index. The goal of this work is to propose indexing techniques that exhibit better performance than existing techniques and sequential scan when the database attributes that are specified in a search key have missing data.

When measuring query performance we consider two metrics: index size and query execution time. Index size is simply measured as the size of the requisite index files on disk. It is indicative of the time required to initially load the index structures. Although this metric is not as critical for static read-only databases with ample disk-space available, it becomes important as database updates become more frequent or available disk space becomes limited. Query execution time is measured in milliseconds for a query set. Given that the indexes are in memory, this measurement indicates the time required to process a set of queries and arrive at a set of pointers to records in the database that *could* match the query criteria.

## 4 Proposed Solutions

Our proposed solutions are to apply the techniques of bitmap indexes and vector-approximation (VA) files modified appropriately to account for missing data and to execute the query according to the query's semantics. The reason is that we want to independently index each dimension and execute queries efficiently without needing to perform expensive operations to obtain the final result. Bit operations for bitmaps provide fast computation and VA-Files provide pruning in multiple dimensions at the same time using cheap comparisons.

### 4.1 Bitmap Indexes

We base one solution for the efficient access of incomplete databases on bitmap indexes. In the bitmap index context, records are represented by a bit string. Each attribute $A_i$ would be represented by at most $C_i$ bits of the string where $C_i$ is the cardinality of $A_i$, i.e. the number of distinct non-null values among all records for attribute $A_i$. A bitmap is a column wise representation of each position of the bit string. Each bitmap would have n bits where n is the number of records in the dataset. Given a dataset D = $(A_1, A_2, ..., A_d)$ for each $A_i$ attribute we build a certain number of bitmaps depending on $C_i$. To handle missing data using bitmaps, we map missing values to a distinct value, i.e. 0. By doing this we are increasing the number of bitmaps for each attribute with missing data by 1. While mapping missing data to a distinct value fails for multi-dimensional indexes, it is acceptable for bitmaps because the attributes are indexed independently and we are not creating an exponential number of subspaces that must be searched to answer a query.

Let's denote the bitvectors or bitmap vectors for attribute $A_i$ by $B_{i,j}$ where $0 \leq j \leq C_i$ if $A_i$ has missing values and $1 \leq j \leq C_i$ otherwise. $B_{i,0}$ represents the bitvector for missing values.

Let's denote by $B_{i,j}[x]$ where $1 \leq x \leq n$ the bit value for record x in the bitmap for attribute $A_i$ and value $j$.

Using bitmap indices, queries are executed by performing bit operations over the relevant bitmaps. OR, XOR, AND and NOT are commonly used.

An important aspect of a bitmap index is the type of encoding of the records. We explore two alternatives: equality and range encoding.

## 4.2 Bitmap Equality Encoding (BEE)

Using equality encoded bitmaps, bit $B_{i,j}[x]$ is 1 if record x has value $j$ for attribute $A_i$ and 0 otherwise. Using this encoding, if $B_{i,j}[x] = 1$ then $B_{i,k}[x] = 0$ for all $k \neq j$. If attribute $A_i$ has missing values, we add the bitmap $B_{i,0}$ that behaves in the same manner explained above.

Adding an extra bitmap for each attribute with missing data is not a major burden with few records or few dimensions, but when we consider 1,000,000 records with 100 dimensions we are effectively adding 100,000,000 bits to our index which correspond to approximately 12 MB in size.

An intuitive solution that could be used to encode missing data without adding an extra bitmap would be to use different encodings depending on whether missing data is a match or not. In this alternative, when missing is a match we make $B_{i,j}[x] = 1$ for all j if record x has missing data in attribute $A_i$; and when missing is not a match, we make $B_{i,j}[x] = 0$ for all j if record x has missing data in attribute $A_i$.

However, there are some problems with this approach. We will need to perform more bitmap operations when we use the NOT operator. The reason is that when we negate a bitmap when missing data is considered to be a query match, the resulting bitmap would have 0's for the missing records. In order to recover the records with missing data we will need to AND together two bit columns. We then need to OR that result with the original negated bitmap to arrive at a correct final result. When missing data does not imply a query match, we would need to OR together two bit columns to ensure we are eliminating the records with missing values and then AND this result with the negated bitmap to get correct results. Using this approach, it would also be impossible to distinguish between missing values and a real value when the cardinality of the attribute is 1. In addition, by making all bits 1 for the attribute when missing is a match we interrupt the runs of 0s and compression decreases dramatically for the attribute bitmaps.

Empirically, we realized that after compression using WAH, the addition of an extra bitmap to handle missing data did not introduce much overhead. For the same example of 1,000,000 records with 100 dimensions, and assuming 10,000 records with missing data, each bitmap for missing values would have approximately a compression ratio of 0.47 and overall the compression ratio for the dataset would also improve.

**Table 1.** Equality encoded with missing data

| Record | Value | $B_{1,0}$ | $B_{1,1}$ | $B_{1,2}$ | $B_{1,3}$ | $B_{1,4}$ | $B_{1,5}$ |
|---|---|---|---|---|---|---|---|
| 1 | 5 | 0 | 0 | 0 | 0 | 0 | 1 |
| 2 | 2 | 0 | 0 | 1 | 0 | 0 | 0 |
| 3 | 3 | 0 | 0 | 0 | 1 | 0 | 0 |
| 4 | missing | 1 | 0 | 0 | 0 | 0 | 0 |
| 5 | 4 | 0 | 0 | 0 | 0 | 1 | 0 |
| 6 | 5 | 0 | 0 | 0 | 0 | 0 | 1 |
| 7 | 1 | 0 | 1 | 0 | 0 | 0 | 0 |
| 8 | 3 | 0 | 0 | 0 | 1 | 0 | 0 |
| 9 | missing | 1 | 0 | 0 | 0 | 0 | 0 |
| 10 | 2 | 0 | 0 | 1 | 0 | 0 | 0 |

**Table 2.** Bitmap indices

| Bitmap Vector | Value |
|---|---|
| $B_{1,0}$ | 0001000010 |
| $B_{1,1}$ | 0000001000 |
| $B_{1,2}$ | 0100000001 |
| $B_{1,3}$ | 0010000100 |
| $B_{1,4}$ | 0000100000 |
| $B_{1,5}$ | 1000010000 |

$v_1 \leq A_i \leq v_2 =$

$$\begin{cases} (\bigcup_{j=v_1}^{v_2} B_{i,j}) \vee B_{i,0} & \text{if } v_2 - v_1 \leq \lfloor C_i/2 \rfloor \\ \bigcup_{j=1}^{v_1-1} B_{i,j} \vee \bigcup_{j=v_2+1}^{C_i} B_{i,j} & \text{otherwise} \end{cases}$$

(a) Missing Data is a Match

$$\begin{cases} (\bigcup_{j=v_1}^{v_2} B_{i,j}) & \text{if } v_2 - v_1 \leq \lfloor C_i/2 \rfloor \\ \bigcup_{j=1}^{v_1-1} B_{i,j} \vee \bigcup_{j=v_2+1}^{C_i} B_{i,j} \oplus B_{i,0} & \text{otherwise} \end{cases}$$

(b) Missing Data is not a Match

**Fig. 2.** Interval Evaluation for Bitmap Equality Encoding

**Query Execution** With equality encoded bitmaps a point query is executed by ANDing together the bit vectors corresponding to the values specified in the search key. Bitmap Equality Encoded are optimal for point queries [5]. However, with missing data when missing data means a query match we need to use two bitmaps instead of one to answer the query, i.e. the bitmap corresponding to the value queried and the one for missing values.

Range queries are executed by first ORing together all bit vectors specified by each range in the search key and then ANDing the answers together. If the query range for an attribute queried includes more than half of the cardinality then we execute the query by taking the complement of the ORed bitmaps that are not included in the range query.

With our approach we execute the query differently depending on whether missing data is a query match or not. Figure 2(a) shows how a query interval for one attribute is evaluated when missing data implies a query match. Figure 2(b) shows the same evaluation when missing data is not a match. The query execution time is a function of the number of bitvectors used to answer the query. The number of bitvectors used in the worst case to evaluate a single interval in the query is equal to $\min(AS_i, 1 - AS_i) * C_i + 1$ where $AS_i$ is the attribute selectivity of attribute $A_i$ for this query.

## 4.3 Bitmap Range Encoding (BRE)

For range encoded bitmaps, bit $B_{i,j}[x]$ is 1 if record x has a value that is less than or equal to $j$ for attribute $A_i$ and 0 otherwise. Using this encoding if $B_{i,j}[x] = 1$ then $B_{i,k}[x] = 1$ for all $k > j$. In this case the last bitmap $B_{i,C_i}$ for each attribute $A_i$ is all 1s. Thus, we drop this bitmap and only keep $C_i - 1$ bitmaps to represent each attribute. If attribute $A_i$ has missing values we add the bitmap $B_{i,0}$ which has $B_{i,0}[x] = 1$ if record x has a missing value for attribute $A_i$. Also in this case $B_{i,j}[x] = 1$ for all j. We are treating missing data as the next smallest possible value outside the lower bound of the domain, in our case, the value 0. In total the set of bitmaps required to represent attribute $A_i$ with missing values is $C_i$.

We also tried another kind of encoding in which instead of making missing data the smallest value we consider the extra bitmap to be a flag indicating whether the data is missing. In this alternative, if record x has a missing value for attribute $A_i$, $B_{i,0}[x] = 1$ and $B_{i,j}[x] = 0$ for all $j > 0$. However, by making $B_{i,C_i}[x] = 0$ when $x$ has a missing value for attribute $A_i$, we can no longer drop it. This will effectively increase the number of bitmaps for attribute $A_i$ to $C_i+1$, and will not provide any advantage to the query evaluation logic.

**Query Execution.** With range encoded bitmaps the bitmaps used and the operations performed to execute a query depend on the range being queried. We identify three scenarios, depending on whether the range includes the minimum

$$v_1 \leq A_i \leq v_2 = \begin{cases} B_{i,1} & \text{if } v_2 = v_1 = 1 \\ B_{i,v_1} \oplus B_{i,v_1-1} \vee B_{i,0} & \text{if } 1 < v_1 = v_2 < C_i \\ \overline{B_{i,C_i-1}} \vee B_{i,0} & \text{if } 1 < v_1 = v_2 = C_i \\ \overline{B_{i,v_1-1}} \vee B_{i,0} & \text{if } 1 < v_1 < C_i, \; v_2 = C_i \\ B_{i,v_2} & \text{if } v_1 = 1, \; 1 < v_2 < C_i \\ B_{i,v_2} \oplus B_{i,v_1-1} \vee B_{i,0} & \text{otherwise} \end{cases}$$

(a) Missing Data is a Match

$$\begin{cases} B_{i,1} \oplus B_{i,0} & \text{if } v_2 = v_1 = 1 \\ B_{i,v_1} \oplus B_{i,v_1-1} & \text{if } 1 < v_1 = v_2 < C_i \\ \overline{B_{i,C_i-1}} & \text{if } 1 < v_1 = v_2 = C_i \\ \overline{B_{i,v_1-1}} & \text{if } 1 < v_1 < C_i, \; v_2 = C_i \\ B_{i,v_2} \oplus B_{i,0} & \text{if } v_1 = 1, \; 1 < v_2 < C_i \\ B_{i,v_2} \oplus B_{i,v_1-1} & \text{otherwise} \end{cases}$$

(b) Missing Data is not a Match

**Fig. 3.** Interval Evaluation for Bitmap Range Encoding

**Table 3.** Sample data using Range encoding

| Record | Value | $B_{1,0}$ | $B_{1,1}$ | $B_{1,2}$ | $B_{1,3}$ | $B_{1,4}$ | $B_{1,5}$ |
|---|---|---|---|---|---|---|---|
| 1 | 5 | 0 | 0 | 0 | 0 | 0 | 1 |
| 2 | 2 | 0 | 0 | 1 | 1 | 1 | 1 |
| 3 | 3 | 0 | 0 | 0 | 1 | 1 | 1 |
| 4 | missing | 1 | 1 | 1 | 1 | 1 | 1 |
| 5 | 4 | 0 | 0 | 0 | 0 | 1 | 1 |
| 6 | 5 | 0 | 0 | 0 | 0 | 0 | 1 |
| 7 | 1 | 0 | 1 | 1 | 1 | 1 | 1 |
| 8 | 3 | 0 | 0 | 0 | 1 | 1 | 1 |
| 9 | missing | 1 | 1 | 1 | 1 | 1 | 1 |
| 10 | 2 | 0 | 0 | 1 | 1 | 1 | 1 |

**Table 4.** Range Encoded Bitmap indices

| Bitmap Vector | Value |
|---|---|
| $B_{1,0}$ | 0001000010 |
| $B_{1,1}$ | 0001001010 |
| $B_{1,2}$ | 0101001011 |
| $B_{1,3}$ | 0111001111 |
| $B_{1,4}$ | 0111101111 |

value, or includes the maximum value, or is within the domain and includes neither the minimum or maximum.

Figures 3(a) and 3(b) show how the interval is evaluated for a single query attribute when missing data implies a match or does not imply a match respectively.

The first three conditions in Figures 3(a) and 3(b) refer to point queries. The other three refer to range queries.

In the presence of missing data, range encoded bitmaps are more efficient for range queries than equality encoded bitmaps in all but extreme cases.

In the case where missing data is a query match, we will need to access between 1 and 3 bitvectors per query dimension. In databases without missing data, we would need to access between 1 and 2 bitvectors per query dimension. We introduce some overhead to deal with the missing data case.

In the case where missing data is not a match, we need to access between 1 and 2 bitvectors per query dimension. This is also true for databases without missing data, but there are two conditions, specifically the conditions where the query range includes the minimum domain value, that require 1 extra bitvector access. This is due to the fact that missing values are encoded as 1's in all bitmaps and a XOR operation is required to eliminate missing data from the result set.

## 4.4 Bitmap Compression

One of the biggest disadvantages of bitmap indices is the amount of space they require. Several compression techniques have been developed in order to reduce bitmap size and at the same time maintain the advantage of fast operations [2, 16, 1, 13].

The two most popular compression techniques are the Byte-aligned Bitmap Code (BBC) [2] and the Word-Aligned Hybrid (WAH) code [16]. BBC stores the compressed data in Bytes while WAH stores it in words. WAH is simpler because it only has two types of words: literal words and fill words. In our implementation it is the most significant bit that indicates the type of word we are dealing with. Let w denote the number of bits in a word, the lower (w-1) bits of a literal word contain the bit values from the bitmap. If the word is a fill, then the second most significant bit is the fill bit, and the remaining (w-2) bits store the fill length. WAH imposes the word-alignment requirement on the fills. This requirement is key to ensure that logical operations only access words.

We chose WAH over BBC because the bit operations over the compressed WAH bitmap file are faster than BBC (2-20 times) [16]. However, we do sacrifice space since BBC gives better compression ratio.

Logical operations are performed over the compressed bitmaps resulting in another compressed bitmap.

## 4.5 VA-Files

For traditional VA-files, data values are approximated by one of $2^b$ strings of length b bits. A lookup table provides value ranges for each of the $2^b$ possible representations. For each attribute $A_i$ in the database we use $b_i$ bits to represent $2^{b_i}$ bins that enclose the entire attribute domain. In general $b_i \ll \lg C_i$ when the cardinality is high. We made $b_i = \lceil \lg(C_i + 1) \rceil$. For our purposes, we use $2^b - 1$ possible representations for data values and we use a string of b 0's to represent missing data values. A VA-file lookup table relates attribute values to the appropriate bin number. For VA-files we make a modification to the query based on the query semantics. For a range query where missing data is not a query match, we look for matches over the range of bins returned by the lookup table. In the case where missing data means a query match, we also include those records in the all 0's bin as a query match.

Tables 5 and 6 show a simple example of a VA-file using our missing data modification. If we perform a query "return all records where value is 4 or 5",

**Table 5.** Database and VA-File representations

| Record Number | Data Value | VA-File Representation |
|---|---|---|
| 1 | 6 | 11 |
| 2 | 1 | 01 |
| 3 | 3 | 10 |
| 4 | missing | 00 |

**Table 6.** VA-file representations and data ranges

| VA-File Representation | Range |
|---|---|
| 00 | missing |
| 01 | 1-2 |
| 10 | 3-4 |
| 11 | 5-6 |

**Table 7.** Synthetic and Census Datasets Distribution

| Synthetic Dataset | | | | | | |
|---|---|---|---|---|---|---|
| | % of Missing Data | | | | | Total |
| Card | 10 | 20 | 30 | 40 | 50 | Columns |
| 2 | 10 | 10 | 10 | 10 | 10 | 50 |
| 5 | 10 | 10 | 10 | 10 | 10 | 50 |
| 10 | 20 | 20 | 20 | 20 | 20 | 100 |
| 20 | 20 | 20 | 20 | 20 | 20 | 100 |
| 50 | 20 | 20 | 20 | 20 | 20 | 100 |
| 100 | 10 | 10 | 10 | 10 | 10 | 50 |
| Total | 90 | 90 | 90 | 90 | 90 | 450 |

| Census Dataset | | | | | | |
|---|---|---|---|---|---|---|
| | % of Missing Data | | | | | Total |
| Card | 0 | ≤10 | ≤50 | ≤90 | >90 | Columns |
| <10 | 11 | 0 | 2 | 2 | 0 | 15 |
| 10-50 | 7 | 2 | 3 | 5 | 4 | 21 |
| 51-100 | 2 | 0 | 1 | 2 | 2 | 7 |
| >100 | 0 | 0 | 1 | 2 | 2 | 5 |
| Total | 20 | 2 | 7 | 11 | 8 | 48 |

our VA-file technique will return the records in bins 00, 10, 11 as approximate answers in the case where missing data is a match. A filtering step would verify that record 1 does not answer the query. In the case where missing data is not a match, only the records in bins 10 and 11 would be returned in the first step.

Query translation is simple. When missing data implies a match, a range query in the form $v_1 \leq A_i \leq v_2$ is converted to $(VA(v_1) \leq VA(A_i) \leq VA(v_2)) \vee (VA(A_i) = 0^b)$, where $VA(x)$ is a function that converts values to their representative VA-file bit representation and $b$ is the number of bits used to define an attribute.

These techniques are easy to apply and require little or no modification of the queries or query processing. As shown using empirical experiments, they are also scalable in terms of the number of data dimensions.

## 5 Experiments and Results

### 5.1 Experimental Framework

We performed experiments using both synthetic and real datasets. By using the synthetic data set we could control analysis parameters individually and gain insights into the behavior of the indexing techniques. We applied the techniques to a real data set to verify the effectiveness of the techniques on real scenarios.

For the synthetic data, we generated a uniformly distributed random dataset set with 450 attributes and 100,000 records. For the set of attributes we varied the cardinality and percent of missing data. Cardinality varied among 2, 5, 10, 20, 50, and 100 values and percent of missing data among 10, 20, 30, 40, and 50 percent.

The real data is census data with 48 attributes and 463,733 records. The attribute cardinalities widely vary from 2 to 165 (average of 37) and percent of missing data varies from 0% to 98.5% (average of 41%). Table 7 details the distribution for the synthetic and the real dataset.

We implemented query executors for both bitmaps and VA-Files in Java. We ran 100 queries for each type of experiment. Queries were executed in both scenarios when missing data is a query match and when missing data is not a query match. Since the graphs look very similar in both scenarios we present only results for queries executed where missing data is a match.

Given that we used the same precision (100%) for our implementations we compared bitmap indices and VA-Files in terms of:

- **Index Size.** Index Size is an important factor in any indexing technique. We are interested in indices that can fit into memory to ensure fast query execution without the overhead introduced when reading from disk.
- **Query Execution Time.** Query Execution Time is the time required to produce a query result set.

## 5.2 Index Size

In this section we evaluate how the attribute cardinality and the percentage of missing data affects index size.

**Attribute Cardinality.** For cardinality less than 10 there is not much room for compression and the index size is equal for both types of bitmap encoding and is not sensitive to the percent of missing data. For equality encoded bitmaps, as the attribute cardinality increases the compression ratio improves considerably, however, at the same time, bitmaps index size increases linearly with cardinality. For VA-Files the index grows very slowly with cardinality given our current quantization strategy. Index sizes are presented for attributes with 10% missing data in Figure 4(a). As can be seen, BRE does not benefit from WAH compression.

With real data, compression rate is highly variable with respect to attribute cardinality. Since real data can be far from uniform, an attribute that has low cardinality but frequently has one value can acheive high compression ratios. With our set of real data, those attributes which have cardinalities of between 1 and 10 and are not missing any data have a compression ratio between 0.002 and 1.03 using equality encoding and between 0.001 and 0.82 using bitmap range encoding. The wide range is attributable to the bit density (ratio of 1's) in the bit columns. As the bit density approaches 1 or 0, the compression ratio improves. Therefore, if one particular value is frequent, then the bit density for that value's column is close to 1 yielding good compression ratio for that column and the bit density for all other bit columns is close to 0, which results in good compression ratio for them.

**Percent of Missing Data.** For equality encoded bitmaps, as the percent of missing data increases the compression ratio decreases making the index smaller.

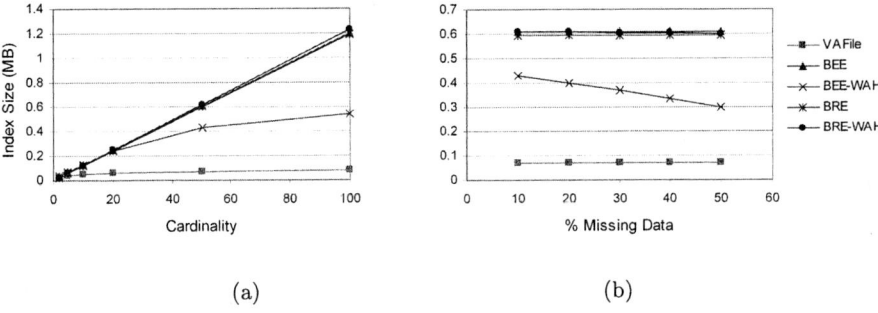

**Fig. 4.** Index Size Versus (a) Cardinality and (b) Percent of Missing Data

Range encoding does not get significant compression using WAH code. VA-File is not sensitive to the presence of missing data and its size is independent of it. In any case the index size for VA-Files is much smaller than bitmaps. Index sizes are presented for cardinality 50 in Figure 4(b).

Good compression is also obtained on the real dataset when an attribute has a high occurrence of missing data. The missing data bit column has a bit density close to 1 and all other columns are close to 0. This leads to very good compression ratios for equality encoded bitmaps (between 0.01 and 0.09 for each of the 8 attributes in our real data set which have more than 90% missing data) and decent compresison ratios for range encoded bitmaps (between 0.11 and 0.44). Overall, this real data set had an equality encoded bitmap compression ratio of 0.17 and a range encoded bitmap compression ratio of 0.70.

### 5.3 Query Execution Time

To measure the effect of the various parameters over the query execution time of the 100 queries we needed to have control over the global query selectivity, i.e. the number of records that match the given query. The following formula relates Global Selectivity (GS), Attribute Selectivity ($AS = (v_2 - v_1 + 1)/C_i$) and Percent of Missing Data ($P_{m_i}$) of all the attributes involved in the queries:

$$GS = \prod_{i=1}^{k}((1 - P_{m_i})AS_i + P_{m_i}),$$

where $k$ is the number of dimensions involved in the query. In order to simplify this formula we assume equal attribute selectivity on all the attributes in the query. By doing this, individual attribute selectivities are easy to compute but we lose some precision on the global query selectivity. To measure query execution time we fixed the global query selectivity to 1 percent. Plugging in different values for the parameters into $GS = [(1 - P_m)AS + P_m]^k$ we compute the attribute selectivity for each attribute in the query. Note that the granularity of attribute selectivity is limited by $C_i$. In general, our estimate was very close to 1 percent but sometimes the actual global query selectivity went up to 3

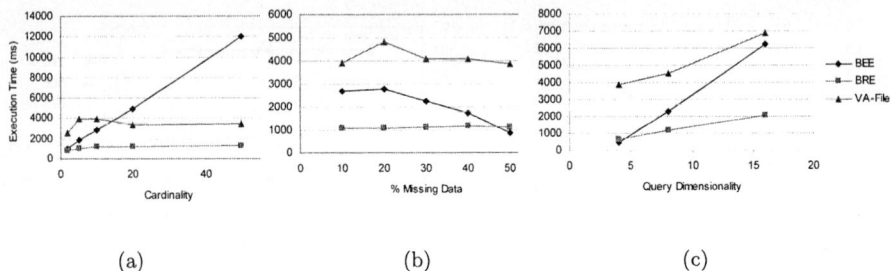

(a)                    (b)                   (c)

**Fig. 5.** Query Execution Time Versus (a) Cardinality, (b) Percent of Missing Data, and (c) Query Dimensionality

percent. Note that when we make the global selectivity constant and increase the percent of missing data, the attribute selectivity decreases. We tested the effect of attribute selectivity, percent of missing data, and query dimensionality against query execution time.

**Attribute Cardinality.** Figure 5(a) shows the query execution time of 100 queries over attributes with 10 percent missing data and various cardinalities. Also in this case the execution time for BRE and VA-Files remains somewhat constant with BRE being faster than VA-Files. For BEE, the execution time is linear since the number of bitmaps used to answer the queries depends on the cardinality of the attribute and its selectivity.

**Percent of Missing Data.** Figure 5(b) shows the results of these experiments for attributes with cardinality 10. For equality encoded bitmaps, the execution time decreases when the percent of missing data increases. This is because when we make the global selectivity constant and increase the percent of missing data, the attribute selectivity decreases and the number of bitmaps used in the query execution depends on the attribute selectivity for this kind of encoding. For range encoded bitmaps, the execution time remains somewhat constant. The small variations are due to the possibility of using between 1 and 3 bitmaps per dimension over the query execution. It turns out that as the percent of missing data increases the number of bitmaps used per dimension gets closer to 3. For VA-Files, the execution time is also somewhat constant. The variations are due to the actual global selectivity for cardinality 10 and 8 dimensions in the query. For cardinality 10 and 50 % missing data the global selectivity is 0.84%, for 30 and 40 is 1.28%, but for 20 is 1.7%. In general, BRE executes range queries faster than the other two. The only case in which BEE performs better than BRE is at 50% missing when the attribute selectivity is 10% and the range query becomes a point query.

**Query Dimensionality.** Figure 5(c) shows the query execution of 100 queries over attributes with cardinality 10 and 30 percent of missing data. For all indices the execution is linear in the number of query dimensions. BRE grows very slowly since we are only using between 1 and 3 bitmaps per query dimension. BEE grows much faster since as we increase the number of dimensions with this percent of missing data the attribute selectivity get closer to 50 %. For smaller percents of missing data and same cardinality the attribute selectivity is greater than 50 %, around 70 % so effectively we only access the 30 % of the bitmaps and therefore the execution time does not increase linearly. For VA-Files the execution time also increases with the query dimensionality.

**Results on Real Data.** Experiments using this real data set yielded several conclusions. For this data set, the bitmap solutions were significantly faster than the VA-File solution (3 to 10 times faster). This was because the skewness of this particular data set allowed for very good compression of the bitmaps and while the VA-file implementation had to operate over about 500,000 vector approximations of the records, the bitmap implementations performed bit operations over substantially fewer words. The average compression ratio for the equality encoding bitmaps was 0.17 (with 23 attributes compressing to less than 0.1 times their original size). The average compression ratio for the range encoding bitmaps was 0.7 (with 18 attributes compressing to less than 0.5 times their original size and only 3 attributes not compressing at all).

Also of note is that whereas the presence of missing data can introduce a degradation of a couple of orders of magnitude in hierachical multiple-dimension indexes as shown in the motivating example, there is not a large degradation asociated with the presence of missing data using these techniques. Performance can be as high as two times slower with our techniques, and this is attributable to extra bit operations required to handle the missing data.

In our experiments with real data, the range encoded bitmaps performed faster than the equality encoded bitmaps. In these experiments we used range queries over 20% of the queried attribute possible values and would expect this result since range encoded bitmaps are tailored for range queries.

## 6 Conclusions

The techniques presented in this paper are easy to apply and allow the effective indexing of missing data. As opposed to traditional hierarchical indexing structures and previously proposed missing data indexing techniques, these techniques exhibit linear performance for query execution time with respect to database and query dimensionality. This is done by essentially indexing attributes independently. Our solutions take advantage of this independence by handling missing data for each attribute, and still maintain the linear performance associated with respect to dimensionality that bitmaps and VA-files have been known for.

These techniques exhibit a tradeoff between execution time and indexing space. The bit operations used to evaluate queries for bitmaps are fast, but the space required to represent an exact bitmap can be much higher than a corresponding exact VA-file.

The range encoded bitmaps typically offer the best time performance but, at least using the techniques we used, can not be compressed as much as equality encoded bitmaps. They typically perform faster because there is a limit on the number of bit operations that must be performed to evaluate a query for each dimension.

Equality encoded bitmaps perform a maximum of $C/2+1$ bit operations per query dimension and can perform faster than range encoded bitmaps for point queries or range queries with small ranges. Equality encoded bitmaps can be compressed much more than range encoded bitmaps.

VA-files offer the least size to represent the same information offered by bitmaps, but the operations performed are not bit operations, they usually do not operate as fast as the range encoded bitmaps.

There are several areas in which the techniques proposed here could be improved. The biggest weakness of the range encoded bitmaps is the inability to compress them. We would like to explore techniques such as BBC compression and row reordering in order to achieve more compression of these bitmaps. The same modifications made to the basic VA-file to account for missing data could also be applied to the VA-plus file, a technique to quantize skewed data sets described in [6].

**Acknowledgement.** This research was supported by Department of Energy (DOE) grant DE-FG02-03ER25573 and National Science Foundation (NSF) grant CNS-0403342.

# References

1. S. Amer-Yahia and T. Johnson. Optimizing queries on compressed bitmaps. In *The VLDB Journal*, pages 329–338, 2000.
2. G. Antoshenkov. Byte-aligned bitmap compression. In *Data Compression Conference*, Nashua, NH, 1995. Oracle Corp.
3. G. Antoshenkov and M. Ziauddin. Query processing and optimization in oracle rdb. *The VLDB Journal*, 1996.
4. C.-Y. Chan and Y. E. Ioannidis. Bitmap index design and evaluation. In *Proceedings of the 1998 ACM SIGMOD international conference on Management of data*, pages 355–366. ACM Press, 1998.
5. C.-Y. Chan and Y. E. Ioannidis. An efficient bitmap encoding scheme for selection queries. *SIGMOD Rec.*, 28(2):215–226, 1999.
6. H. Ferhatosmanoglu, E. Tuncel, D. Agrawal, and A. E. Abbadi. Vector approximation based indexing for non-uniform high dimensional data sets. In *Proceedings of the ninth international conference on Information and knowledge management*, pages 202–209. ACM Press, 2000.
7. S. Inc. *Sybase IQ Indexes.*, chapter Sybase IQ Release 11.2 Collection, chapter 5. Sybase Inc., March 1997.
8. T. Johnson. Performance measurements of compressed bitmap indices. In *Proceedings of the 25th International Conference on Very Large Data Bases*, pages 278–289. Morgan Kaufmann Publishers Inc., 1999.
9. N. Koudas. Space efficient bitmap indexing. In *Proceedings of the ninth international conference on Information and knowledge management*, pages 194–201. ACM Press, 2000.

10. P. O'Neil and D. Quass. Improved query performance with variant indexes. In *Proceedings of the 1997 ACM SIGMOD international conference on Management of data*, pages 38–49. ACM Press, 1997.
11. P. E. O'Neil. Model 204 architecture and performance. In *Proceedings of the 2nd International Workshop on High Performance Transaction Systems*, pages 40–59. Springer-Verlag, 1989.
12. B. C. Ooi, C. H. Goh, and K.-L. Tan. Fast high-dimensional data search in incomplete databases. In *Proceedings of the 24rd International Conference on Very Large Data Bases*, pages 357–367. Morgan Kaufmann Publishers Inc., 1998.
13. K. Stockinger. Bitmap indices for speeding up high-dimensional data analysis. In *Proceedings of the 13th International Conference on Database and Expert Systems Applications*, pages 881–890. Springer-Verlag, 2002.
14. R. Weber and S. Blott. An approximation based data structure for similarity search, 1997.
15. R. Weber, H.-J. Schek, and S. Blott. A quantitative analysis and performance study for similarity-search methods in high-dimensional spaces. In *Proceedings of the 24th International Conference on Very Large Databases*, pages 194–205, 1998.
16. K. Wu, E. Otoo, and A. Shoshani. Compressing bitmap indexes for faster search operations. In *SSDBM*, 2002.
17. K. Wu, E. Otoo, and A. Shoshani. On the performance of bitmap indices for high cardinality attributes. Technical Report LBNL-54673, Lawrence Berkeley National Laboratory, March 2004.
18. K. Wu, E. J. Otoo, and A. Shoshani. A performance comparison of bitmap indexes. In *Proceedings of the tenth international conference on Information and knowledge management*, pages 559–561. ACM Press, 2001.
19. K. Wu, E. J. Otoo, A. Shoshani, and H. Nordberg. Notes on design and implementation of compressed bit vectors. Technical Report LBNL PUB-3161, Lawrence Berkeley National Laboratory, 2001.
20. M.-C. Wu. Query optimization for selections using bitmaps. In *Proceedings of the 1999 ACM SIGMOD international conference on Management of data*, pages 227–238. ACM Press, 1999.
21. E. Zimanyi. *Incomplete and Uncertain Information in Relational Databases*. PhD thesis, Université Libre de Bruxelles, 1992.

# FlexInd: A Flexible and Parameterizable Air-Indexing Scheme for Data Broadcast Systems

André Seifert[1] and Jen-Jou Hung[2]

[1] University of Konstanz, Database Research Group,
P.O. BOX D188, 78457 Konstanz, Germany
andre.seifert@uni-konstanz.de
[2] National Taiwan University of Science and Technology,
Department of Information Management,
No. 43, Section 4, Keelung Road, 10672 Taipei, Taiwan R.O.C
jjhung@juno.cs.ntust.edu.tw

**Abstract.** In wireless data broadcast systems, popular information is repetitively disseminated through possibly multiple communication channels to mobile clients using various types of battery-operated devices. Access latency and tuning time are two conflicting performance metrics used in such systems to measure their efficiency. In practice, different application and usage scenarios may require different performance trade-offs between the two metrics: some may tolerate slightly longer access latencies to benefit from lower energy requirements, while others may favor shorter access latencies at the cost of higher energy expenditures. To provide data broadcast service providers with the freedom to trade-off between both metrics in an adjustable way, we propose a new flexible and parameterizable air-indexing scheme, called FlexInd. FlexInd is a hybrid indexing method that takes advantage of three separate air-indexing approaches, namely (a) no-indexing, (b) exponential indexing, and (c) flexible distributed indexing, to optimize either access latency or tuning time with certain performance guarantees on the other metric. Based on the access latency or energy conservation requirements imposed on the system, FlexInd chooses among the three indexing schemes the one which yields the best performance results with the access latency or tuning time bounded by a given limit. A performance study confirms that FlexInd is able to achieve lower average access latencies and tuning times than existing indexing schemes since it provides greater flexibility in trading-off access efficiency for power expenditure and vice versa.

## 1 Introduction

Wireless data broadcasting is a powerful and efficient way to deliver popular information to a large number of clients, anytime, anywhere, and anyhow. Wireless data broadcast service providers such as Ambient [1], Microsoft [11], or SkyTel [15] try to benefit from the widespread deployment of wireless networks and the proliferation of feature-rich mobile devices by continuously disseminating interesting private and public information to mobile clients subscribed to their broadcast channels. Since available mobile client and network bandwidth resources are scarce and network service subscribers expect the best possible service, the broadcast service providers need to be concerned with two critical issues when generating broadcast programs, namely (a) *access latency* and (b) *power expenditure*. Unfortunately, none of the two performance metrics can be optimized without adversely impacting the other one, i.e., data broadcast service providers are doomed to trade-off between minimum access latency and minimum power expenditure. This adversarial relationship between both metrics is straightforward to explain: To access a desired data item in the broadcast channel, the mobile client has to stay tuned to it until the data arrives. Obviously, this approach will maximize the energy consumption of the mobile client since it has to remain active monitoring the broadcast channel in order not to miss any requested data item when it passes by. A solution to the energy problem is to interleave *indexes* with the data broadcast to the mobile clients. The basic idea of air-indexing is to include index information about the arrival times of the data items into the broadcast program. Then, by accessing the air-index, mobile clients are able to predict the arrival times of the data items disseminated, which, in turn, allows them to switch their devices into doze mode during waiting time and eventually helps them to reduce their devices' power expenditure [17]. The major drawback of this solution, however, is that the length of the broadcast program increases due to the additional index information. This clearly illustrates that we cannot optimize either of the two performance metrics without adversely affecting the other metric.

The existing trade-off between access and energy efficiency emphasizes the benefit and necessity of providing system builders and designers with a *tunable air-indexing scheme* that is adjustable in a flexible manner such that a variety of performance guarantees are possible. More specifically, a good tunable air-index should be able to cater for different application scenarios by facilitating both *latency bounded* and *tuning time bounded* performance tuning. In order to provide system architects with the necessary flexibility in tuning the performance along the latency and tuning time dimensions, we propose a new hybrid air-indexing method, called FlexInd, that takes advantage of the virtues of the *no-indexing* or NoInd, *exponential indexing* or ExpInd [18] and *flexible distributed indexing* or FlexDistInd schemes. We opted to build FlexInd upon these three indexing methods since (a) we are not aware of any existing air-indexing method which is able to outperform the others for every realistically conceivable latency bounded and tuning time bounded tuning problem and (b) any of these three indexing schemes may be superior to the others given some performance requirements.

**Contributions.** In particular, the paper makes the following contributions:

- We address the issue of designing a highly adjustable air-indexing scheme that provides great flexibility in trading-off among access latency and tuning time. While the idea of making air-indexes flexible in adjusting access latency and tuning time is not new to the database community [7, 18], the approach to combine various (parameterizable) indexing methods into a hybrid scheme to benefit from the merits of each of them and to achieve a much higher degree of tuning flexibility than any of them alone is capable of, is one of the paper's main contributions.
- We propose a new tree-structured parameterizable indexing method, called FlexDistInd, which is one of the three cornerstones of FlexInd. FlexDistInd is able to cut down on the long tuning times of the NoInd and ExpInd schemes, while also being straightforward to implement and efficient in terms of access latency.

- We analyze FlexInd's access efficiency and energy conservation in terms of two performance metrics, namely average access latency and worst case tuning time, and derive formulae upon which FlexInd is able to select the indexing method that achieves the best solution for a given access latency bounded or tuning time bounded tuning problem.
- We perform an extensive experimental evaluation of FlexInd and show its inherent flexibility in trading-off among access latency and tuning time by judiciously selecting and parameterizing its underlying indexing methods.

**Organization.** The remainder of the paper is organized as follows: In the next section related work will be reviewed, followed by the definition of some notations and terminologies used throughout the paper in Section 3. Section 4 describes the three indexing schemes upon which FlexInd is built with particular emphasis on the newly proposed FlexDistInd scheme. This section also analyzes the access latency and tuning time of the three indexing methods and explains how FlexInd finds the best indexing scheme for a given latency bounded or tuning time bounded optimization problem. Experimental results are presented in Section 5 and the paper is concluded in Section 6.

## 2 Related Work

The issue of air-indexing has received much attention lately and was first discussed in the seminal papers by Imielinski et al. [6, 7, 8]. Existing indexing methods can roughly to categorized into the following four classes: (a) signature-based [10], (b) hashing-based [7], (c) tree-based [3, 6, 8, 14, 16], and (d) table-based indexing techniques [7, 16, 18]. *Signature* and *hashing schemes* have been proposed to support exact-match queries [7, 10] and the signature method has been identified as particular attractive for multi-attribute indexing [4, 5]. The majority of the proposed indexing methods, however, adopts a tree-based structure based on that of the $B^+$-tree.

The most prominent *tree-based indexing techniques* for flat broadcast schedules, defined as those in which each data item is broadcast only once per broadcast cycle or, as we call it, m̲ajor b̲roadcast c̲ycle (MBC), are the $(1, m)$ indexing and the distributed indexing schemes [6, 8]. The $(1, m)$ indexing method generates a "full" index of the broadcast program, i.e., the index contains entries for each scheduled data item, and it broadcasts the full index $m$ times during an MBC. The distributed indexing scheme improves on the access efficiency of the $(1, m)$ indexing method by generating several distinct "partial" indexes with each of them indexing a different portion of the broadcast program. Tan et al. [16] addressed the issue of indexing skewed broadcast schedules, defined as those in which some data items are broadcast multiple times per MBC, by adapting and extending the $(1, m)$ and flexible indexing schemes [6, 7, 8]. In the same vein, Chen et al. and Shivakumar et al. proposed to use unbalanced tree structures to optimize the tuning time for non-uniform distributions of index accesses [3, 14].

What all the above indexing techniques have in common is that they are not flexible in trading-off between access latency and tuning time. To resolve this problem, two parameterized *table-based indexing schemes* were proposed. One of them is the flexible indexing method [7] which provides the tuning parameters $p$ and $m$ in order to achieve either a good access latency or a good tuning time. By the tuning parameter $p$, the flexible indexing scheme splits a sorted list of data items into $p$ equal-sized segments. At the beginning of each segment, there is a two-columned control index consisting of a global index that maps key values to the respective segment containing that key, and a local index (being an $m$-entry index) that maps key values to the bucket in the current data segment where the respective key resides. The other one is the ExpInd method [18], which enhances the flexible indexing scheme by (a) allowing the indexing space to be exponentially partitioned at any base value, (b) allowing each data segment to index into the next data segment, and (c) providing the mathematical foundations behind exhibiting different trade-offs between access latency and tuning time.

Despite all of these enhancements, the tuning flexibility of the ExpInd method is still quite limited and depends largely on the data organization of the broadcast program. Like the flexible indexing method, ExpInd requires the data items to be sorted on the indexed attribute. While such a requirement does not constrain its tuning flexibility for flat broadcast schedules, it, however, does so for skewed ones. In non-uniform broadcast schedules, the broadcast program is partitioned into a number of segments, called minor broadcast cycles (MIBC), each of which consists of a sequence of data items which are ordered according to the indexed attribute. As the values of the search keys may overlap between MIBCs, multiple MIBCs may need to be searched in order to find the data item to be accessed. As a result, the tuning time of ExpInd is directly proportional to the number of MIBCs of the broadcast program, and thus cannot be freely adjusted to suit all application and usage scenarios. To compensate for this shortfall, we propose to use the FlexDistInd scheme in at least those cases where the given limit on the tuning time cannot be achieved by ExpInd.

## 3 Preliminaries: Assumptions and Notations

Apart from indexing, data scheduling is a major factor impacting the access latency and tuning time of mobile clients. The broadcast scheduling policy determines the contents of the broadcast program and the broadcast frequency of the data items. We assume that the *FlexSched* scheduling scheme is used to construct the broadcast schedule [13]. We opted for the FlexSched algorithm since it produces perfectly periodic schedules which are cost-efficient to generate and allow mobile clients to save significantly on energy. On top of that, it is able to outperform other state-of-the-art scheduling algorithms [2, 9, 12], and is therefore preferable to them.

In order to become more technically, let an ordered set $D = \{d_1, d_2, \ldots, d_n\}$ of $N$ data items represent (a pre-selected subset of) a database to be broadcast over some broadcast channel $c$. Each data item $d_i$ has a demand probability $p_i$ to be accessed by mobile clients and the demand probability of the data items is used as sorting criterion for $D$. More precisely, let $d_i$ and $d_j$ be two data items with $d_i, d_j \in D$. Then, if $d_i < d_j$, then $p_i \geq p_j$. Clearly, $\sum_{i=1}^{N} p_i = 1$. In order to generate the broadcast schedule for broadcast channel $c$, FlexSched partitions the ordered set $D$ of data items into an ordered set $G = \{g_1, g_2, \ldots, g_m\}$ of $M$ data groups and assigns each data group $g_k \in G$ an integer-valued broadcast frequency $bf_k$ representing the number of instances of data items belonging to group $g_k$ that are broadcast per MIBC. The scheduled data items themselves are collected in and transferred as buckets with each split up into a fixed number of packets — the basic unit of message transfer in wireless networks. We distinguish between three types of buckets: (a) *data buckets* which hold data items only, (b) *index buckets* which contain index information only, and (c) *hybrid buckets* which include both data and index information. To allow mobile clients to interpret the data instantly as they fly by and to enable them to orientate themselves in the broadcast program, buckets are designed to be self-explanatory by including header information in each bucket similar to [8].

## 4 The FlexInd Indexing Scheme

In what follows, we will show, by means of a running example, the fundamental characteristics and general structure of the three index schemes upon which FlexInd is built and also present a performance analysis of each of them. The description of the running example is as follows:

*Example 1.* Consider a broadcast server that maintains 33 data items which were partitioned by the FlexSched scheduling algorithm into a set $G = \{g_1, g_2, g_3, \text{ and } g_4\}$ of 4 data groups, where groups $g_1 = \{1-2\}$, $g_2 = \{3-8\}$, $g_3 = \{9-17\}$, and $g_4 = \{18-33\}$ comprise 2, 6, 9, and 16 data items, respectively. Suppose that the data items of data groups $g_1, g_2, g_3$, and $g_4$ are broadcast with frequencies 2, 3, 3, and 4, respectively, i.e., it takes $max_{\forall g_j \in G} |g_j|/bf_j = 16/4 = 4$ MIBCs until all data items belonging to the data groups of $G$ are disseminated at least once. Each data bucket, index bucket, and hybrid bucket is assumed to accommodate up to 3 data items, an index table with up to 18 entries (rows), and 2 data items and an index table with up to 6 entries (rows), respectively.

### 4.1 No-Indexing Scheme

The first indexing method contained under the "umbrella" of the FlexInd indexing method is the *NoInd* scheme. As its name implies, the NoInd scheme does not interleave any index information with the data broadcast and as such, it generates broadcast schedules that ensure the lowest possible access time, while at the same time incurring the longest tuning time among the three indexing schemes.

*Example 2.* Figure 1 shows the broadcast program produced by FlexSched/NoInd according to the specifications of the running example. It is easy to see that it consists of a sequence of 16 buckets which are partitioned into 4 MIBCs, each containing 4 data buckets. Obviously, the worst case tuning time of the broadcast program is 16 buckets and the average access time for data item 1, for example, is 2 buckets, which is half of its average inter-arrival time.

To facilitate a quantitative comparison of the three indexing schemes, in what follows, we will analyze the *average access time* and *worst case tuning time* of each of them once their main properties have been explained. We opted for the worst case tuning time, rather than its average, as a means for comparison since we believe that the former metric is more appropriate for this purpose and it also eases the process of specifying tuning time boundaries. To start with, we analyze the performance of the NoInd scheme.

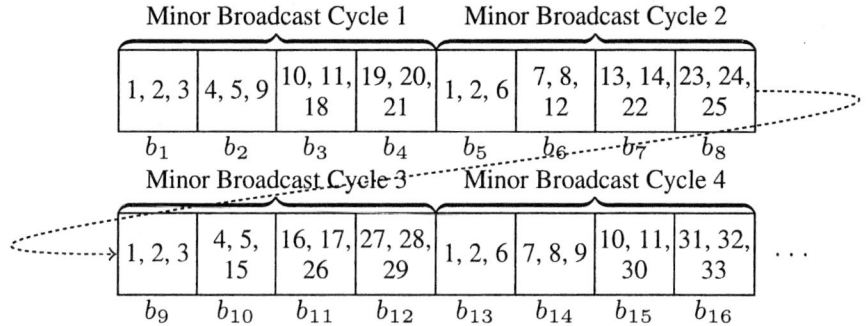

**Fig. 1.** Illustration of the no-indexing scheme

**Average Access Time.** The overall average access time of a broadcast schedule when using NoInd for "air-indexing", denoted $AT_{no-ind}$, is defined as the average waiting time encountered by a client averaged over all data items. More precisely,

$$AT_{no-ind} = \sum_{i=1}^{N} p_i \cdot w_i, \qquad (1)$$

where $N$ denotes the number of distinct data items disseminated in the broadcast channel, $p_i$ represents the probability of a data item $d_i \in D$ being requested by a client, and $w_i$ denotes the average wait time encountered by a client needing to inspect $d_i$. The average wait time $w_i$ for a data item $d_i$ is half the average inter-arrival time $t_i$ between two consecutive instances of $d_i$. Since FlexSched enforces the equal-spacing assumption for each data item in $D$ [13] and its average wait time is given by $w_i = t_i/2$, the overall average access time can be computed by:

$$AT_{no-ind} = \frac{1}{2} \cdot \sum_{i=1}^{N} p_i \cdot t_i. \qquad (2)$$

**Worst Case Tuning Time.** Next, we derive the worst case tuning time. As no index information is provided with the broadcast program, the worst case tuning time is the maximum value of the set of spacings between two consecutive instances of the same data item of all data items transmitted in the broadcast channel. More formally, the worst case tuning time to locate and download a data item from the broadcast channel, denoted $TT_{no-ind}$, is given by:

$$TT_{no-ind} = \max_{\forall d_i \in D} t_i. \qquad (3)$$

### 4.2 Exponential Indexing Scheme

The second indexing method supported by FlexInd is the *ExpInd* scheme [18]. To cut down on the long tuning times of NoInd, the ExpInd scheme splits the broadcast program into equal-sized data chunks and disseminates at the beginning of each data chunk an exponential index. In brief, the ExpInd scheme provides system designers with two tuning knobs, namely (a) *data chunk size* $I$ and (b) *index base* $r$, to trade-off access latency against tuning time and vice versa.

To enable system designers to reduce the indexing overhead and tuning time, ExpInd allows to group $I$ consecutive data buckets together into a data chunk and to build the exponential index on a per data chunk rather than per bucket basis. Each data chunk itself begins with a hybrid bucket which contains, besides a set of data items, the exponential index. The exponential index is organized as an index table consisting of two components: (a) a *global index* and (b) a *local index*. While the global index is used to determine the range of data chunks in which the desired data item may be located, the local index provides the offset to the bucket of the local data chunk where the data item may be found.

To allow system designers to specify the number of index entries contained in the global index, ExpInd provides the index base $r$ which can be set to any value $r \geq 1$ (with $r \in \mathbb{R}$) and causes the size of the indexed sequence of data chunks to grow exponentially. While the first entry of any global index describes the next data chunk, each following $i$-th index entry indexes a sequence of data chunks that are $\lfloor \sum_{j=0}^{i-2} r^j + 1 \rfloor$ to $\lfloor \sum_{j=0}^{i-1} r^j \rfloor$ away from the current data chunk. In the global index, entries are ordered pairs of the form $(indRange, mKey)$, where $indRange$ represents the distance range (in units of data chunks) from the current data chunk to the beginning and to the end of the sequence of data chunks indexed by this entry and $mKey$ is the maximum key value of this sequence. An exception to this rule occurs when an entry indexes into the next MIBC. In such a case, $mKey$ represents the maximum key value of the bucket of the next MIBC that is the farthest bucket in this sequence of buckets whose attribute value is less than that of the current bucket. Local index entries are of the same type as those of the global index, but with a slightly different meaning. Here $indRange$ denotes the distance of the indexed bucket from the current bucket and $mKey$ is the maximum key value of this bucket.

*Example 3.* Figure 2 illustrates the basic working principle of the ExpInd scheme for our running example. In the broadcast program shown in Figure 2, the data chunk size $I$ and the index base $r$ are both set to 2. As a result of $I = 2$, each data chuck consists of two buckets: (a) a hybrid bucket at the beginning and (b) a data bucket at the end of it. Since the broadcast program is skewed, the exponential index is built upon a per MIBC rather than per MBC basis. Consider the index entries of hybrid bucket $b_{11}$ of data chunk 6 as an example of an exponential index. There are 2 entries in the global index of $b_{11}$. The first entry, (1–1 chunk, 29), implies that data items that are larger than 4, but equal to or less than 29 can be found in data chunk 7. The second entry, (2–3 chunks, 2), means that data items that are larger than 29 and equal to or less than 33 can be found in data chunks 8–9. It also indicates that data items whose values fall within the interval [1, 2] can be found here. The local index of $b_{11}$ contains 1 entry. The entry, (1 bucket, 16), implies that data items that are larger than 4 and equal to or less than 16 can be found 1 bucket away from bucket $b_{11}$, i.e., in bucket $b_{12}$.

**Average Access Time.** Let $B_d$ and $B_h$ denote the number of data items that a data bucket and hybrid bucket, respectively, can hold and let $n_{items}^{MIBC}$ represent the total

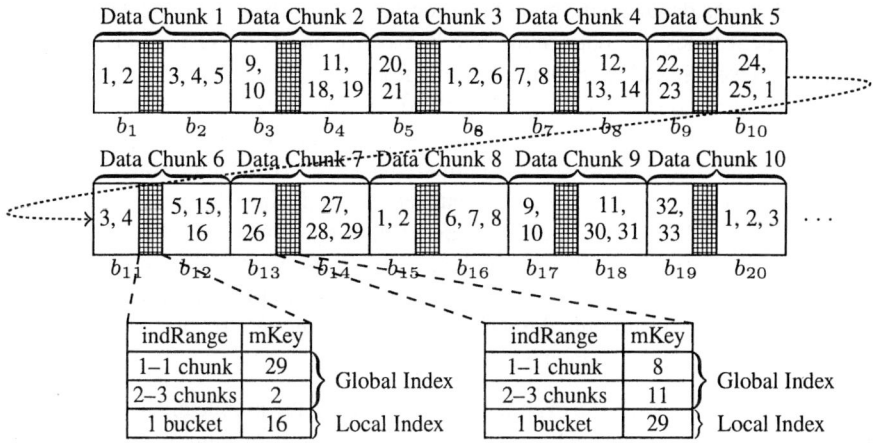

**Fig. 2.** Illustration of the exponential indexing scheme

number of data items broadcast per MIBC, i.e., $n_{items}^{MIBC} = \sum_{k=1}^{|G|} bf_k$. Given the data chunk size $I$, the number of data buckets and hybrid buckets of an MIBC, denoted by $n_{data}^{MIBC}$ and $n_{hybrid}^{MIBC}$, respectively, is given by

$$n_{data}^{MIBC} = (I-1) \lceil n_{items}^{MIBC} / (B_d(I-1) + B_h) \rceil \qquad (4)$$

and

$$n_{hybrid}^{MIBC} = \lceil n_{items}^{MIBC} / (B_d(I-1) + B_h) \rceil, \qquad (5)$$

respectively. The overall average access time of a broadcast program when using the ExpInd method for air-indexing, denoted $AT_{exp}$, can then simply be obtained by adding half the length of an MBC ($\equiv$ avg. broadcast wait time) to the average amount of time between the initial probe of the broadcast channel and the dissemination of the nearest exponential index ($\equiv$ avg. index probe wait time), i.e.,

$$AT_{exp} = \underbrace{\frac{I}{2}}_{\text{avg. index probe wait time}} + \underbrace{\frac{1}{2} \sum_{k=1}^{|G|} p_k \cdot s_k \cdot (n_{data}^{MIBC} + n_{hybrid}^{MIBC})}_{\text{avg. broadcast wait time}}, \qquad (6)$$

where $p_k$ denotes the sum of the demand access probabilities of the data items belonging to data group $g_k$ and $s_k$ represents the spacing (in the unit of MIBCs) between two consecutive instances of a data item belonging to data group $g_k$, i.e., $s_k = |g_k|/bf_k$.

**Worst Case Tuning Time.** To derive the worst case tuning time of the ExpInd scheme, additional notations are required. Similar to [18], let $C$ denote the number of data chunks in an MIBC which is given by $C = (n_{data}^{MIBC} + n_{hybrid}^{MIBC})/I$ and let $n_c$ denote the number of global index entries in an index table of a hybrid bucket. To get more insight into the matter of deriving the worst case tuning time, the following example is provided.

*Example 4.* Consider again the broadcast program as illustrated in Figure 2 and suppose a mobile client tunes into data chunk 5 at bucket $b_{10}$ and is interested in data item 32 located in bucket $b_{19}$ (what is obviously not known yet). Since the first bucket accessed is not a hybrid bucket, it obviously takes the client one bucket to probe the first index bucket $b_{11}$. After examining the information in the index table of bucket $b_{11}$, the client is then guided to data chunks 8–9 to continue the search. The client examines the first bucket of the refined search space (i.e., bucket $b_{15}$) and trims the search space again. Since data item 32 obviously falls into the value range covered by bucket $b_{15}$, there is no need to examine other buckets indexed by the current MIBC. However, as data item 32 is not found in bucket $b_{15}$, the client needs to continue the refinement-based search procedure by examining the index tables of the next MIBC. By doing so, it will eventually find the desired data item in bucket $b_{19}$.

As this example shows, the exponential index directs the mobile client to a consecutive sequence of data chunks whose size is at most $r^{n_c-1}$ data chunks. Since the initial search space is $C$ or about $(r^{n_c} - 1)/(r - 1)$ data chunks, the search space is reduced by approx. $r/(r-1)$ in each refinement step. Thus, the worst case tuning time amounts to $\lceil \log_{r/(r-1)}(C-1) \rceil + 1$ buckets per MIBC. If the number of buckets per data chunk is larger than 1, i.e., $I > 1$, the mobile client might need one more bucket access to probe the first hybrid bucket and another one to get to the candidate bucket in which the desired data item may be located. Thus, the worst case tuning time is bounded by:

$$TT_{exp} = \begin{cases} n_{MIBC}^{MBC} \cdot (\lceil \log_{\frac{r}{r-1}}(C-1) \rceil + 1) & , \text{if } I = 1 \\ n_{MIBC}^{MBC} \cdot (\lceil \log_{\frac{r}{r-1}}(C-1) \rceil + 2) + 1, & \text{if } I > 1, \end{cases} \quad (7)$$

where $n_{MIBC}^{MBC}$ denotes the total number of MIBCs in an MBC.

### 4.3 Flexible Distributed Indexing Scheme

The *FlexDistInd* scheme is the third and last indexing method considered by FlexInd when searching for an indexing method that best meets the specified performance requirements of the broadcast system. The inclusion of an additional, yet novel, indexing method into FlexInd is motivated by the observation that NoInd and ExpInd alone cannot achieve the highest possible degree of flexibility in adjusting the trade-off between access latency and tuning time. Their greatest drawback by far is their limitation in tuning the system performance along the tuning time dimension. While NoInd provides no means to cut down on the tuning time at all, the trade-off potential of ExpInd is quite limited here too (see Section 2). To remedy this problem, we propose the FlexDistInd scheme which significantly enhances FlexInd's flexibility in adjusting the tuning time, at the expense of slightly higher access time. This gain in flexibility is achieved by (a) partitioning the broadcast program into a number of equal-sized *data segments* such that a given limit on the tuning time will not be exceeded and (b) building a *dense* rather than a sparse *index* on the data broadcast.

Similar to (1, m) indexing [6], FlexDistInd adopts a tree structure based on the $B^+$-tree for air-indexing and it uses an index allocation method in which index information is broadcast multiple times during an MBC. However, and contrary to (1, m) indexing,

FlexDistInd does not necessarily index the whole broadcast program. Rather, it partitions the broadcast program into a set $P = \{p_1, p_2, \ldots, p_t\}$ of $T$ data segments and each index tree describes the data of the data segment which immediately follows it. The only exception to this rule may occur when an index tree needs to be replicated multiple times in the broadcast program so as to minimize the access latency of it with the tuning time bounded by a given limit (see the example below). Then, index tree entries may also refer to data items which are contained in subsequent data segments of the immediately following data segment.

Entries of index buckets which represent a leaf node of the index tree are arranged as a sequence of $([key\_values], dist)$ pairs, where $dist$ specifies the distance from the current bucket to the data bucket that contains the data items identified by the attribute values included in the sorted list $[key\_values]$. Entries of index buckets representing non-leaf index nodes of a (multi-level) index tree are organized as a sequence of $(sep\_value, dist)$ pairs. Here, however, $dist$ does not represent the offset to a data bucket, but rather the distance to another index bucket which itself either guides the user to another (lower) node in the index tree or to the data bucket containing the requested data item and $sep\_value$ is the separation value that splits the tree into two subtrees.

*Example 5.* Figure 3 illustrates the application of the FlexDistInd scheme to our running example where both the limit of the worst case tuning time, denoted $L_{tun}$, and the tuning parameter $T$ are set to 4 (see Equation 11 on how to compute the optimal value of $T$). As $L_{tun} = 4$ and a client typically needs an initial bucket probe to get to the nearest index bucket and another probe to eventually download the desired data item, only 2 index bucket probes remain to find out about the position of the desired data item in the program. In order not to exceed the limit $L_{tun} = 4$ while still being able to partition the data schedule into 4 data segments and to disseminate 4 index trees per MBC, FlexDistInd departs from the general rule that an index tree may only describe the data of an immediately following data segment. Since each index bucket is assumed to maintain up to 18 index entries and those index slots are sufficient to represent half of the broadcast program, each flexible distributed index needs to cover two consecutive data segments, i.e., 2 rather than 4 index trees (consisting of one node only) are used in Figure 3 to describe the entire broadcast program. Besides, each flexible distributed index $Ind_i$ is replicated once within the broadcast program to satisfy the constraint of broadcasting 4 index trees per MBC.

In this respect it is important to note that a replica $Rep_i$ of a flexible distributed index $Ind_i$ is not a one-to-one copy of the latter, but rather a modify version of it with the offset values associated to the original key values being adjusted to the actual broadcast position of the replica in the broadcast program.

*Example 6.* As an example illustrating how index entries of a replicated index may deviate from their original entries, consider the index entry $([1, 2, 3], 1)$ of the index tree $Ind_2$ in Figure 3. Since the replica $Rep_2$ of the index $Ind_2$ is disseminated after bucket $b_{12}$ and data item 3 is not contained in data bucket $b_{17}$, it is obvious that the index entry's content needs to be modified in $Rep_2$. Therefore, $Rep_2$ contains the index entries $([1, 2], 1)$ and $([3], 6)$ rather than $([1, 2, 3], 1)$.

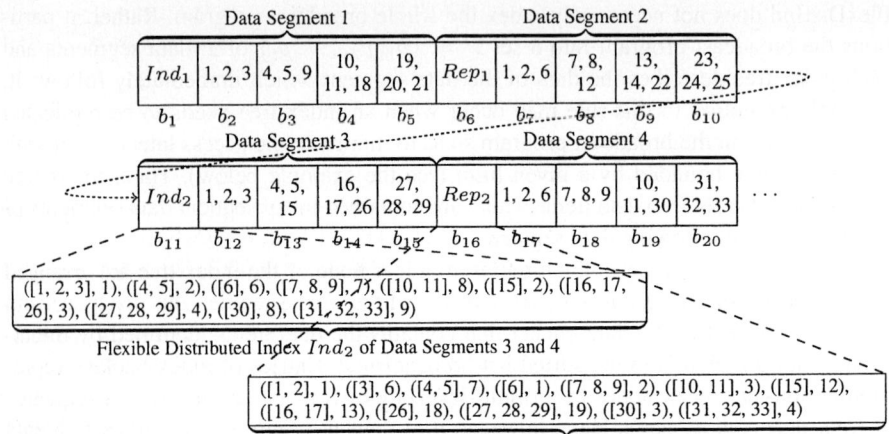

**Fig. 3.** Illustration of the flexible distributed indexing scheme

**Average Access Time.** Let $t$ represent the number of distinct index trees interleaved with the data in an MBC and let $r$ denote the number of times each distinct flexible distributed index tree is replicated per MBC. Given $t$ and $n_{MIBC}^{MBC}$, i.e., the number of MIBCs in an MBC, the number of data items upon which a distinct index tree is built, denoted by $n_{items}^{tree}$, is given by:

$$n_{items}^{tree} = \sum_{k=1}^{|G|} \min\left(\frac{n_{MIBC}^{MBC} \cdot bf_k}{t}, |g_k|\right). \qquad (8)$$

An upper bound on the number of levels in a distinct flexible distributed index tree, denoted by $n_{levels}^{tree}$, can be computed by $n_{levels}^{tree} = \lceil \log_{B_i}(n_{items}^{tree}) \rceil$, where $B_i$ denotes the maximum number of index entries that an index bucket can hold. Given $n_{levels}^{tree}$, the maximum number of index buckets required to hold the respective tree, denoted by $n_{index}^{tree}$, can be derived as follows:

$$n_{index}^{tree} = \sum_{k=1}^{n_{levels}^{tree}} \left\lceil \frac{n_{items}^{tree}}{(B_i)^k} \right\rceil. \qquad (9)$$

An upper bound on the average access time, denoted $AT_{flex}$, is thus given by:

$$AT_{flex} = \underbrace{\frac{1}{2}\left(\frac{n_{data}^{MBC}}{t \cdot r} + n_{index}^{tree}\right)}_{\text{avg. index probe wait time}} +$$

$$\underbrace{n_{index}^{tree} + \frac{1}{2}\sum_{k=1}^{|G|}\left(((t \cdot r - 1) \cdot n_{index}^{tree} + n_{data}^{MBC}) \cdot \frac{p_k \cdot s_k}{n_{MIBC}^{MBC}}\right)}_{\text{avg. broadcast wait time}}, \qquad (10)$$

where $p_k$ denotes the sum of the access probabilities of the data items belonging to data group $g_k$, $s_k$ represents the spacing between two consecutive instances of a data item belonging to data group $g_k$, and $n_{data}^{MBC}$ denotes the number of data buckets accommodated in an MBC, i.e., $n_{data}^{MBC} = n_{MIBC}^{MBC} \cdot \lceil n_{items}^{MIBC}/B_d \rceil$.

Given Equation 10 and knowing the optimal number $t^*$ of distinct flexible distributed index trees to be disseminated per MBC (see Equation 14 on how to compute $t^*$), we are able to derive a formula by which the optimal *index tree replication factor*, denoted by $r^*$, can be computed so as to minimize the access latency of the broadcast schedule. To do so, we differentiate Equation 10 w.r.t. $r$, equate it to zero and solve the equation for $r$. The optimal index tree replication factor is thus given by:

$$r^* = round\left(\frac{1}{t^*}\sqrt{\frac{n_{data}^{MBC}}{n_{index}^{tree} \cdot \sum_{k=1}^{|G|} \frac{p_k \cdot s_k}{n_{MIBC}^{MBC}}}}\right). \quad (11)$$

In order to achieve the minimal average expected access latency of a broadcast program which contains $t^*$ distinct index trees, we need to divide the broadcast program into a set $P = \{p_1, p_2, \ldots, p_{t^*}\}$ of $T$ equal-sized data segments, where $T$ is given by $T = r^* \cdot t^*$ and broadcast every $r^*$-th data segment preceded by a distinct index tree; all other $r^* \cdot t^* - t^*$ data segments are prefixed by a replica of the nearest preceding distinct index tree and the first data segment is always prepended with a distinct index tree.

**Worst Case Tuning Time.** Similar to NoInd, the worst case tuning time is straightforward to calculate. In the worst possible scenario, a mobile client would need to traverse all $t$ distinct index trees of an MBC in order to locate the desired data item. In addition to the tuning time required for inspecting the $t$ index trees, a mobile client might need one more bucket access to find the nearest index tree and another one to retrieve the desired data item after locating the target bucket. Therefore, the worst case tuning time of FlexDistInd, denoted $TT_{flex}$, is bounded by:

$$TT_{flex} = t \cdot n_{levels}^{tree} + 2. \quad (12)$$

### 4.4 Selection of the Appropriate Indexing Method

To enable system designers to effectively trade-off access latency for tuning time and vice versa, FlexInd allows them to specify an upper boundary on either the average access latency or the worst case tuning time. As a result, two separate optimization problems arise, which will be briefly discussed next:

- **Tuning time bounded tuning:** Given a limit $L_{tun}$ on the worst case tuning time, which indexing scheme should be used, and how to set the parameters of the indexing scheme to obtain the shortest average access time?
- **Access time bounded tuning:** Given a limit $L_{acc}$ on the average access time, which indexing scheme should be used, and how to set the tuning parameters of the particular indexing scheme to obtain the shortest worst case tuning time?

**Case 1: Tuning time bounded tuning.** Since the NoInd scheme does not interleave index information with the data disseminated, it is easy to see that it generates broadcast schedules that ensure the lowest access latency and the longest worst case tuning time among all three indexing schemes. The NoInd scheme will therefore only be applied by FlexInd when the specified value for $L_{tun}$ is larger than the method's worst case tuning time, i.e., the number of data buckets belonging to an MBC; otherwise, either ExpInd or FlexDistInd is to be used since both methods are able to cut down on the tuning time (in contrast to NoInd). Based on the results of the performance analysis presented in Sections 4.2 and 4.3, the optimal solution to the tuning time bounded tuning problem can be obtained by first searching for the optimal values of the tuning parameters of both methods and then comparing the average access times that are achieved by setting the tuning parameters to their optimal values.

For the ExpInd scheme, the tuning time bounded tuning problem is an issue of finding optimal values for $B_h$ and $I$, denoted by $B_h^*$ and $I^*$, respectively, and these values can be obtained as follows:

$$AT_{exp}(I^*, B_h^*) = \min_{\substack{I=\{1,2,\ldots,\lceil n_{items}^{MIBC}/B_d \rceil+1\}, \\ B_h=\{0,1,\ldots,\lfloor B_d-((I-1)\cdot s_i)/s_d \rfloor\}}} AT_{exp}(I, B_h)$$

$$s.\,t.\ TT_{exp}(I, B_h) \leq L_{tun}, \tag{13}$$

where $s_i$ and $s_d$ are the sizes of an index entry and a data item, respectively. It is easy to observe that the time complexity of the search problem is bounded by $\mathcal{O}(n_{items}^{MIBC})$, i.e., it is proportional to the number of data items disseminated per MIBC.

For the FlexDistInd scheme, the limit $L_{tun}$ on the worst case tuning time is related to the tuning parameter $t$ according to the inequality $n_{levels}^{tree} \cdot t \leq L_{tun} - 2$. Since the smallest possible value of the number of levels in a flexible distributed index tree is 1, the maximum possible value of $t$ is $L_{tun} - 2$. Thus, the tuning time bounded optimization problem can be stated as follows:

$$AT_{flex}(t^*) = \min_{t=\{1,2,\ldots,L_{tun}-2\}} AT_{flex}(t)$$

$$s.\,t.\ n_{levels}^{tree} \cdot t \leq L_{tun} - 2, \tag{14}$$

where $t^*$ denotes the optimal number of distinct index trees to be included in an MBC so as to minimize the average access time. Again, it is easy to see that the time complexity for solving the tuning time bounded tuning problem is $\mathcal{O}(L_{tun})$. Since multiple indexing methods may be able to remain itself within a given limit $L_{tun}$, FlexInd obviously chooses among those schemes (that are able to satisfy $L_{tun}$) the one which achieves the lowest average access latency.

**Case 2: Access time bounded tuning.** The access time bounded tuning problem can be defined analogous to the tuning time bounded optimization problem. Since the NoInd scheme provides the shortest access time along with the longest worst case tuning time, FlexInd deploys it only when the value of $L_{acc}$ is smaller than the lowest average access time that ExpInd and FlexDistInd are able to achieve; otherwise, either ExpInd or FlexDistInd will be adopted.

For the ExpInd scheme, the access time bounded tuning problem involves the search for the optimal values of the tuning parameters $I$ and $B_h$. This time, however, their values need to be chosen such that the access time limit is not exceeded and the tuning time is minimized. More specifically, the access time bounded optimization problem can be stated as follows:

$$TT_{exp}(I^*, B_h^*) = \min_{\substack{I=\{1,2,...,\lceil n_{items}^{MIBC}/B_d\rceil+1\}, \\ B_h=\{0,1,...,\lfloor B_d-((I-1)\cdot s_i)/s_d\rfloor\}}} TT_{exp}(I, B_h)$$

$$s.\,t.\ AT_{exp}(I, B_h) \leq L_{acc}. \tag{15}$$

Again, the time complexity for finding the optimal values of $I$ and $B_h$ is bounded by $\mathcal{O}(n_{items}^{MIBC})$.

Analogous to the above definition, we can define the access time bounded tuning problem of the FlexDistInd method as follows:

$$TT_{flex}(t^*) = \min_{t=\{1,2,...,n_{data}^{MBC}\}} TT_{flex}(t)$$

$$s.\,t.\ AT_{flex}(t) \leq L_{acc}. \tag{16}$$

It is again straightforward to observe that the worst case time complexity of the search problem is bounded by $\mathcal{O}(n_{data}^{MBC})$, i.e., the complexity of finding the optimal solution is proportional to the number of data buckets in an MBC. As for the previous tuning problem, once we have determined the optimal solutions for the access time bounded tuning problem for each of the three indexing methods, FlexInd selects among the indexing methods (that are able to satisfy $L_{acc}$) the one which achieves the lowest tuning time.

## 5 Performance Evaluation

This section presents results of a simulation study conducted to evaluate the performance of FlexInd and to show its flexibility in trading-off between access latency and tuning time. In order to investigate FlexInd's performance in comparison to the state-of-the-art indexes (including its own underlying indexing schemes), we also examined the following indexing schemes: (a) (1, m) indexing [6], (b) ExpInd [18], (c) FlexDistInd, and (d) NoInd. We compare the indexing schemes in terms of the access latency and tuning time metrics which are measured in the unit of buckets. If not otherwise stated, in each simulation run the number of data items disseminated by the broadcast server amounts to 100,000. Similar to other researchers [3, 14, 16], we assume that the demand probability of data items follows a Zipf distribution [19] with the parameter $\theta$ set to 0.8, meaning that approximately 75% of all requests apply to 25% of the data items. For the ExpInd scheme, an index entry contains only a key value (as $indRange$ values can be inferred from the position of the entry in the index table) and its size $s_i$ is set to 4 bytes. For the (1, m) indexing and FlexDistInd schemes, the index entry size $s_i$ is set to a lower bound of 8 bytes since each entry contains at least one key value of 4 bytes as well as the offset of 4 bytes to the data bucket containing the key value. We have run experiments with different combinations of data item sizes $s_d$ and data bucket capacities $B_d$. In what follows, we report results for one informative setting only, i.e., $s_d = 100$ bytes and $B_d = 40$.

## 5.1 Experiment 1. Effectiveness in Optimizing the Access Latency

In the first experiment, we studied the effectiveness of the investigated indexing schemes in optimizing the access latency when the tuning time is bounded. To do this, we varied the value of the worst case tuning time $L_{tun}$ in the range of 4 to 10,000. Note that $L_{tun} = 4$ is the lowest worst case tuning time that any of the examined indexing schemes can achieve and has therefore been chosen as lower boundary for $L_{tun}$. Figure 4(a) summarizes the results of the experiment. From the figure, we observe that, with the exception of the (1, m) indexing and NoInd schemes, the average access time of the indexing methods decreases as $L_{tun}$ increases. It can also be seen that both ExpInd and FlexDistInd are able to significantly cut down on the average access time in contrast to the (1, m) indexing scheme. The average access time of FlexDistInd and ExpInd is, on average, about 40% and 50%, respectively, lower than that of the (1, m) indexing scheme. We also observe from the figure that the performance behavior of FlexInd is exactly what we would have expected. FlexInd always performs as well as the best air-indexing method available. It achieves this by adopting the indexing method which yields the best performance results given the respective constraint on the worst case tuning time. For example, if $L_{tun}$ is restricted to a value smaller than 60, FlexInd chooses FlexDistInd for air-indexing, whereas for a value of $L_{tun}$ in the range between 60 and 6,177, it applies the ExpInd scheme. If even larger values for $L_{tun}$ were allowed, FlexInd would adopt the NoInd scheme.

## 5.2 Experiment 2. Effectiveness in Optimizing the Tuning Time

Next, we examined the effectiveness of the indexing schemes in optimizing the tuning time when the average access time is bounded. To obtained the results, we varied the value of $L_{acc}$ in the range of 790 to 2,000. Note that the average access latency of the broadcast program amounts to 790 if no index information is interleaved with the data broadcast and has therefore been selected as a lower boundary for $L_{acc}$. Note further that the average access latency of any of the investigate indexing schemes is upper-bounded by 1,700. So setting the upper boundary of $L_{acc}$ to 2,000 is completely sufficient to fully evaluate the indexes' ability to optimize the tuning time. Figure 4(b) shows the worst case tuning time of the investigated indexing schemes as a function of $L_{acc}$. According to the figure, we observe that if $L_{acc}$ is smaller than 980, the worst case tuning time of ExpInd is lower than that of FlexDistInd. However, if $L_{acc}$ is assigned a larger value, the situation reverses and FlexDistInd becomes superior to ExpInd. The reason why FlexDistInd performs better than ExpInd when allowing longer access times is that ExpInd is not as flexible as FlexDistInd in trading-off tuning time for access time. More specifically, in this particular experiment, it is impossible for ExpInd to achieve a worst case tuning time shorter than 60. As a result, if $L_{acc}$ is set to a value larger than 880, the worst case tuning time remains constant. The FlexDistInd scheme, however, is

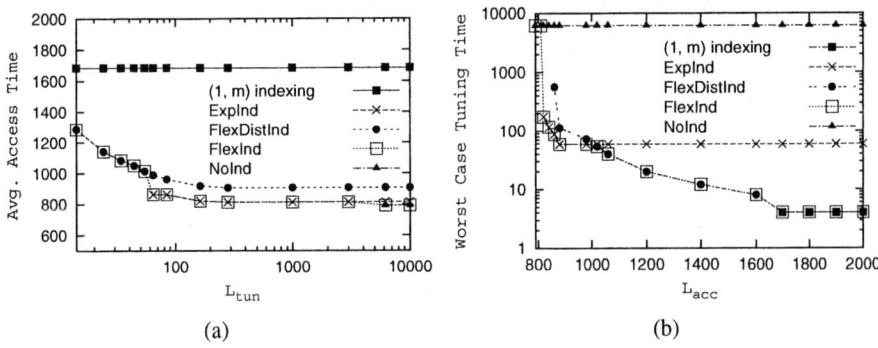

**Fig. 4.** Average access time (a) and worst case tuning time (b) of various indexing methods as a function of $L_{tun}$ and $L_{acc}$, respectively

more flexible in this respect and is able to achieve a worst case tuning time of only 4 bucket probes if $L_{acc}$ is set to 1700 or a larger value. In this situation, FlexDistInd disseminates only one index tree per MBC and achieves the same performance results as the $(1, m)$ indexing scheme. Again, Figure 4(b) confirms FlexInd's ability to choose among its underlying indexing schemes exactly the right one which provides the lowest worst case tuning time with the average access time bounded by the specified limit.

### 5.3 Experiment 3. The Effect of the Access Skew Coefficient $\theta$

In order to investigate the effect of the skewness in the distribution of the demand probabilities of the data items on the performance characteristics of the indexing schemes, we varied the value of the access skew coefficient $\theta$ from 0.1 to 1.0. First, we look at the tuning time bounded tuning problem. Figure 5(a) shows the average access time of the investigated indexing schemes given that $L_{tun}$ is set to a value equal to 5 times the worst case tuning time of the $(1, m)$ indexing scheme. Notice that the NoInd scheme fails to meet this limit on the worst case tuning time; however, we nevertheless included the results of the NoInd scheme into Figure 5(a) so as to provide information on the lower bound of the average access time in this experiment. As shown by Figure 5(a), as $\theta$ increases, the average access time of the indexing schemes decreases, because more and more data requests are directed towards a relatively small group of data items that are broadcast relatively frequently. As a result, a large portion of the issued data requests can be answered relatively quickly and the average access time decreases. A second observation from Figure 5(a) is that ExpInd can only generate valid broadcast schedules in the sense that they fulfill the specified tuning time requirement if $\theta \leq 0.5$. The reason is that the worst case tuning time of ExpInd is proportional to the number of MIBCs in an MBC. As $\theta$ increases, the number of MIBCs in an MBC increases too, leading (at the point of $\theta \leq 0.5$) to the problem that ExpInd fails to meet $L_{tun}$.

Finally, the access latency bounded tuning problem is examined. Figure 5(b) shows the worst case tuning time of the indexing schemes with $L_{acc}$ set to 1.5 times the average access time of the NoInd scheme. This time, the $(1, m)$ indexing scheme fails to meet the specified limit on the average access time; but, again, its performance results are included in Figure 5(b) for reasons of comparison. According to the figure, the worst case tuning time of the NoInd, ExpInd, and FlexDistInd schemes increases as the degree of skewness in the data access distribution increases. However, the reason for the increase is different in each of the three cases. By knowing that the worst case tuning time of the NoInd scheme is equal to the length of the broadcast program and its length increases as the data access skewness increases (as data items with higher access probabilities will be broadcast more frequently), the observed performance behavior of the NoInd scheme should become plausible. The reason for the increase in the worst case tuning time of the ExpInd scheme is again related to the fact that its tuning time grows in proportion to the number of MIBCs in an MBC. When $\theta$ gets larger, the number of MIBCs per MBC enlarges too, resulting in an increase in the worst case tuning time of ExpInd. The increase in the worst case tuning time of FlexDistInd can best be explained by looking back at Figure 5(a). Here, we observe that as $\theta$ increases, the performance gap between NoInd and FlexDistInd increases too. For example, if $\theta$ is equal to 0.5, the relative performance difference between both schemes is only 23%, but if $\theta$ is increased to 1, the relative performance disadvantage of FlexDistInd increases to as much as 77%. In order to counteract the performance degradation of FlexDistInd as $\theta$ increases, FlexDistInd tends to interleave more index trees with the data disseminated to the mobile clients, and thus the worst case tuning time increases.

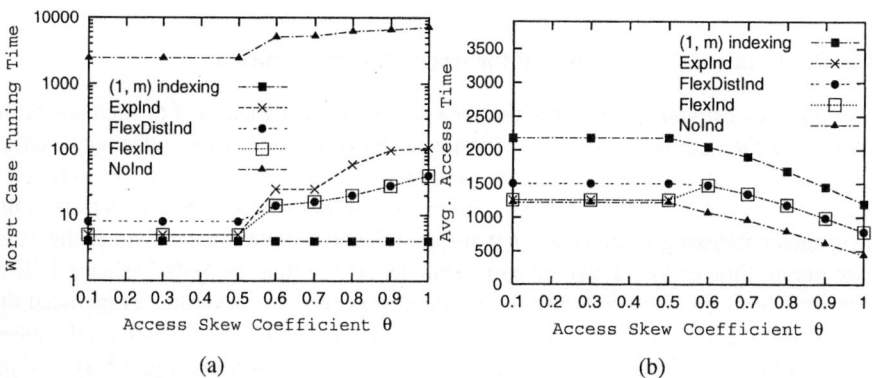

**Fig. 5.** Average access time (a) and worst case tuning time (b) of various indexing methods under different values of the access skew coefficient $\theta$

## 6 Summary

Access latency and tuning time are the most critical issues for mobile users in wireless data broadcast systems. Unfortunately, optimizing one of these two metrics always conflicts with optimizing the other one. To be able to meet different performance requirements of different applications, we need a flexible and tunable air-indexing scheme that is able to optimize the system performance with certain guarantees on either of the two performance metrics. In this paper, we proposed a new hybrid indexing scheme which incorporates and builds upon three different air-indexing schemes, namely (a) the NoInd, (b) ExpInd, and (c) FlexDistInd schemes. We presented the reasons for integrating each of the three indexing methods into FlexInd, discussed their main characteristics, exemplified their key concepts through a running example, provided formulae to determine their access latency and tuning time, and analyzed how to optimize the access latency (tuning time) with a bounded tuning time (access time) by searching the optimal values of the tuning parameters of the schemes. Through extensive experiments, we demonstrated that:

- Each of the three indexing methods of FlexInd has its performance limitations that render it inappropriate to be used alone,
- FlexInd is able to determine among its three indexing schemes the one which achieves the best performance with the access latency or tuning time bounded by a given limit, and
- FlexInd achieves a much greater flexibility in trading-off between access latency and tuning time than state-of-the-art indexing schemes.

## References

1. Ambient Devices Inc. Ambient Information Network and Device Design, 2005, http://www.ambientdevices.com.
2. E. Ardizzoni, A. A. Bertossi, M. C. Pinotti, S. Ramaprasad, R. Rizzi, and M. V. S. Shashanka. Optimal Skewed Data Allocation on Multiple Channels with Flat Broadcast per Channel. *IEEE Trans. on Computers* 54(5):558–572, 2005.
3. M. S. Chen, K. L. Wu, and P. S. Yu. Optimizing Index Allocation for Sequential Data Broadcasting in Wireless Mobile Computing. *IEEE TKDE* 15(1):161–173, 2003.
4. Q. L. Hu, W. C. Lee, and D. L. Lee. Power Conservative Multi-Attribute Queries on Data Broadcast. *ICDE 2000*, pp. 157–166, 2000.
5. Q. L. Hu, W. C. Lee, and D. L. Lee. A Hybrid Index Technique for Power Efficient Data Broadcast. *DPDB* 9(2):151–177, 2001.
6. T. Imielinski, S. Viswanathan, and B. R. Badrinath. Energy Efficient Indexing on Air. *Proc. ACM SIGMOD Conf. 1994*, pp. 25–36. ACM Press, 1994.
7. T. Imielinski, S. Viswanathan, and B. R. Badrinath. Power Efficient Filtering of Data an Air. *EDBT 1994*, pp. 245–258, 1994.
8. T. Imielinski, S. Viswanathan, and B. R. Badrinath. Data on Air: Organization and Access. *IEEE Transactions on Knowledge and Data Engineering* 9(3):353–372, 1997.
9. D. Katsaros and Y. Manolopoulos. Broadcast Program Generation for Webcasting. *Data & Knowledge Engineering* 49(1):1–21, 2004.
10. W. C. Lee and D. L. Lee. Using Signature Techniques for Information Filtering in Wireless and Mobile Environments. *DPDB* 4(3):205–227, 1996.
11. Microsoft Corporation. DirectBand Network. Microsoft Smart Personal Objects Technology (SPOT), 2005, http://www.microsoft.com/resources/spot.
12. W.-C. Peng and M.-S. Chen. Efficient Channel Allocation Tree Generation for Data Broadcasting in a Mobile Computing Environment. *Wireless Networks* 9(2):117–129, 2003.
13. A. Seifert and J.-J. Hung. FlexSched: A Flexible Data Schedule Generator for Multi-Channel Broadcast Systems. Tech. Rep. 211, University of Konstanz, 2005.
14. N. Shivakumar and S. Venkatasubramanian. Energy-Efficient Indexing for Information Dissemination in Wireless Systems. *MONET* 1(4):433–446, 1996.

15. SkyTel Corporation. Timex Internet Messenger, 2005, http://mobile.timex.com/indexENTER.html.
16. K. L. Tan and J. X. Yu. Energy Efficient Filtering of Nonuniform Broadcast. *16th International Conference on Distributed Computing Systems*, pp. 520–528, 1996.
17. M. A. Viredaz, L. S. Brakmo, and W. R. Hamburgen. Energy Management on Handheld Devices. *Queue* 1(7):44–52, 2003.
18. J. Xu, W.-C. Lee, and X. Tang. Exponential Index: A Parameterized Distributed Indexing Scheme for Data on Air. *MobiSys 2004*, pp. 153–164, 2004.
19. G. K. Zipf. *Human Behavior and Principle of Least Effort: An Introduction to Human Ecology*. Addison-Wesley, 1949.

# Multi-query SQL Progress Indicators

Gang Luo[1], Jeffrey F. Naughton[2], and Philip S. Yu[1]

[1] IBM T.J. Watson Research Center
[2] University of Wisconsin-Madison
luog@us.ibm.com, naughton@cs.wisc.edu, psyu@us.ibm.com

**Abstract.** Recently, progress indicators have been proposed for SQL queries in RDBMSs. All previously proposed progress indicators consider each query in isolation, ignoring the impact simultaneously running queries have on each other's performance. In this paper, we explore a multi-query progress indicator, which explicitly considers concurrently running queries and even queries predicted to arrive in the future when producing its estimates. We demonstrate that multi-query progress indicators can provide more accurate estimates than single-query progress indicators. Moreover, we extend the use of progress indicators beyond being a GUI tool and show how to apply multi-query progress indicators to workload management. We report on an initial implementation of a multi-query progress indicator in PostgreSQL and experiments with its use both for estimating remaining query execution time and for workload management.

## 1 Introduction

Recently, [4, 6, 11, 12] proposed progress indicators (PIs) for SQL queries in RDBMSs. For a SQL query, a PI keeps track of the work completed and continuously estimates the remaining query execution time. [4, 6, 11, 12] proposed a set of techniques to implement single-query PIs. By single-query, we mean that in estimating the progress of a SQL query $Q$, these estimators only consider the current load and the progress of query $Q$ itself, ignoring the effect of concurrently running queries and future queries. The main contributions of this paper are the first proposal of a multi-query PI, the exploration of its performance as compared to single-query PIs, and an application of the multi-query PI to problems arising in workload management.

Clearly there are cases where a single-query PI gives bad estimates. For example, if one query is substantially impeding the progress of another, but the first query is about to finish, a single-query PI will grossly overestimate the remaining execution time of the second query. Avoiding such behavior was our original motivation for developing multi-query PIs.

When estimating the remaining execution time for a query $Q$, a multi-query PI considers $Q$, other concurrently running queries, and, if available, predictions about new queries that can be expected to arrive while $Q$ is running. As multi-query PIs consider more information than single-query PIs, they can provide more accurate estimates. A reasonable concern is whether we are depending on accurate predictions of the future. The answer is no – our multi-query PIs continuously monitor the system and adjust their predictions as time progresses. The closer the predictions about future queries are to reality, the better the initial estimates – but eventually the PIs will detect and correct their estimates even in situations in which their initial estimates were based on highly inaccurate information about the future.

In the published literature, SQL PIs have been proposed as a graphical user interface (GUI) tool [6, 11]. In this paper, we also present a new motivation for considering multi-query PIs: workload management. We formulate several workload management problems and show how to solve them by using information provided by multi-query PIs. Traditionally, workload management is static in that once workload management decisions are made, they are not changed. In this paper, we exploit multi-query PIs to facilitate more dynamic workload management. PIs are used to continuously monitor the system status. If the system status differs significantly from what was predicted, the original workload management decisions are revised accordingly. That is, our workload management methods are adaptive, hence they are consistent with the industry trend of autonomic computing [8] and automatic administration [13].

The rest of the paper is organized as follows. Section 2 describes our multi-query PI. Section 3 discusses three workload management problems, and describes our solution to each workload management problem by using the information provided by our multi-query PIs. Section 4 discusses some practical considerations for building multi-query PIs. Section 5 presents results from an initial implementation of our techniques in PostgreSQL. We discuss related work in Section 6 and conclude in Section 7.

## 2 Multi-query Progress Indicator

In this section, we describe our multi-query PI. The single-query PIs in [11, 12] (the PIs described in [4, 6] predict only percentage of completion, not remaining query execution time) work roughly as follows. For a query $Q$, the PI initially takes the optimizer's estimated cost for $Q$ measured in some unit we call $U$'s. The choice of $U$ can be somewhat arbitrary, so for concreteness we let $U$ represent the amount of work required to process one page of bytes. At any time during $Q$'s execution, based on the statistics collected so far, the PI refines the estimated remaining query cost $c$. The PI also continuously monitors the current query execution speed $s$, and the remaining query execution time is estimated as $t=c/s$.

Although monitoring the current query's execution speed means that the single-query PI implicitly considers the impact of other queries running in the system (since the measured speed will be slower if other queries are running), the single-query PI does not explicitly consider other queries in that it has no idea how long they will run. In the following, we show how to build a multi-query PI that explicitly considers other queries. The main idea in multi-query PIs is that they should predict future execution speeds by considering the expected remaining execution time for concurrently running queries, and, if statistics are available, they should even attempt to predict the impact of queries that might arrive while the current query is running.

## 2.1 Initial Simplifying Assumptions

We first describe some simplifying assumptions that enable a framework for describing and analyzing multi-query PIs. This framework is useful even when they only roughly approximate true system behavior. Section 4 gives our rationale for these assumptions and discusses how our PI is affected when they are relaxed.

**Assumption 1:** The RDBMS processes work units at a constant rate $C$ (work units per second) that is independent of the number of running queries.

**Assumption 2:** The PI has perfect knowledge about the remaining cost $c_i$ of each running query $Q_i$.

**Assumption 3:** Queries execute at speed proportional to the weights associated with their priorities. In more detail, suppose $n$ queries $Q_1, Q_2, \ldots,$ and $Q_n$ are running in the RDBMS concurrently. $Q_i$ ($1 \leq i \leq n$) has priority $p_i$. The corresponding weight for priority $p_i$ is $w_i$. Then each $Q_i$ ($1 \leq i \leq n$) is executed at speed $s_i = C \times w_i / W$, where

$$W = \sum_{j=1}^{n} w_j .$$

## 2.2 Multi-query Progress Estimation

We first consider the simple case where no new queries arrive while the current queries are executing. Although this is an artificial case, it is useful in providing insight for the more general case we discuss in Section 2.4. Also, as we will see, this case turns out to be important in its own right in the context of workload management.

Suppose $n$ queries $Q_1, Q_2, \ldots,$ and $Q_n$ are running in the RDBMS, where $Q_i$ ($1 \leq i \leq n$) has priority $p_i$ and weight $w_i$. The current time is time 0. To estimate the remaining query execution time, the $n$ queries $Q_1, Q_2, \ldots,$ and $Q_n$ are first sorted in the ascending order of $c_i/s_i$. That is, after sorting, we have $c_1 / s_1 \leq c_2 / s_2 \leq \cdots \leq c_n / s_n$ (or equivalently,

$$c_1 / w_1 \leq c_2 / w_2 \leq \cdots \leq c_n / w_n \qquad (1)$$

This order will be useful in the discussion below.

The execution of the $n$ queries is divided into $n$ stages. At the end of each stage, a query finishes execution. Stage $i$ ($1 \leq i \leq n$) lasts for time $t_i$. We call this *the standard case* in the remainder of this paper.

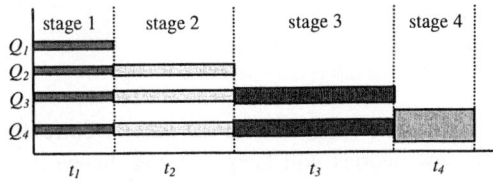

**Fig. 1.** Sample execution of $n=4$ queries

To give the reader a feeling of how the $n$ queries will behave, Figure 1 shows a sample execution of $n=4$ queries. All these queries have the same priority. At the end of stage $i$ ($1 \leq i \leq n$), query $Q_i$ finishes execution. During each stage $i$, the amount of work completed for $Q_j$ ($i \leq j \leq n$) is re-presented as a rectangle, where the height of the rectangle represents the execution speed of $Q_j$.

Now we describe our algorithm in detail. We first discuss stage 1. Recall that $c_1/s_1 \leq c_2/s_2 \leq \cdots \leq c_n/s_n$. Hence, among all the $n$ queries $Q_1, Q_2, \ldots,$ and $Q_n$, $Q_1$ will be the first one to finish, and it will finish at time $t_1 = c_1/s_1$.

During stage 1, for each $i$ ($2 \leq i \leq n$), the amount of work completed for query $Q_i$ is $a_i^{(1)} = s_i \times t_1 = s_i \times c_1/s_1 = c_1 \times w_i/w_1$. Hence, at the end of stage 1, the remaining cost of $Q_i$ ($2 \leq i \leq n$) is $c_i^{(1)} = c_i - a_i^{(1)} = c_i - c_1 \times w_i/w_1$.

Now we discuss stage 2. During this stage, there are $n-1$ queries running: $Q_2, Q_3, \ldots,$ and $Q_n$. Each $Q_i$ ($2 \leq i \leq n$) executes at speed $s_i^{(1)} = C \times w_i / W^{(1)}$, where $W^{(1)} = \sum_{j=2}^{n} w_j = W - w_1$. For each $i$ ($2 \leq i \leq n$), $c_i^{(1)}/s_i^{(1)} = (c_i/w_i) \times W^{(1)}/C - (c_1/C) \times W^{(1)}/w_1$. According to (1), $c_2/w_2 \leq c_3/w_3 \leq \cdots \leq c_n/w_n$. Hence, $c_2^{(1)}/s_2^{(1)} \leq c_3^{(1)}/s_3^{(1)} \leq \cdots \leq c_n^{(1)}/s_n^{(1)}$. That is, among the queries $Q_2, Q_3, \ldots, Q_n$, $Q_2$ will finish first, and it will take time $t_2$, where $t_2 = c_2^{(1)}/s_2^{(1)}$.

During stage 2, for each $i$ ($3 \leq i \leq n$), the amount of work completed for query $Q_i$ is $a_i^{(2)} = s_i^{(1)} \times t_2 = s_i^{(1)} \times c_2^{(1)}/s_2^{(1)} = c_2^{(1)} \times w_i/w_2$. Hence, at the end of stage 2, the remaining cost of $Q_i$ ($3 \leq i \leq n$) is $c_i^{(2)} = c_i^{(1)} - a_i^{(2)} = c_i^{(1)} - c_2^{(1)} \times w_i/w_2 = c_i - c_1 \times w_i/w_1 - (c_2 - c_1 \times w_2/w_1) \times w_i/w_2 = c_i - c_2 \times w_i/w_2$.

This procedure is repeated for all the $n$ stages to compute all the $t_i$'s ($1 \leq i \leq n$). By induction, we find that $Q_1, Q_2, \ldots,$ and $Q_n$ will finish in the order $Q_1, Q_2, \ldots,$ and $Q_n$. That is, at the end of each stage $i$, $Q_i$ finishes execution. At time 0, the remaining execution time of $Q_i$ is $r_i = \sum_{j=1}^{i} t_j$.

The time complexity of the above algorithm is $O(n \times \ln n)$, and the space complexity is $O(n)$. (The derivation details are omitted due to space constraints.)

### 2.3 Non-empty Query Admission Queues

An RDBMS typically contains a query admission queue. If the RDBMS is overloaded, newly arrived queries will be put into the query admission queue rather than starting execution immediately. Since queries already in the query admission queue are also "known" queries, a multi-query PI can extend its visibility into the future by examining this queue. An example of this is given in our experimental evaluation in Section 5.

### 2.4 Considering Future Queries

The above discussion assumed that no new queries arrive while the queries currently in the RDBMS are running. In general, new queries will keep arriving, hence they will influence the load on the RDBMS, and a PI must somehow account for these queries. These queries are different from those in the admission queue – they have not yet arrived and predictions about them necessarily involve speculation.

If nothing at all is known about the future, then one guess about future loads is as good as another, and there is no point in trying to do any forecasting. However, in practice we think it is rare that absolutely nothing can be predicted about the future, and that rough approximate information is likely to be available. The goal of the PI then is to use such approximate information to improve its guesses about the future.

In our approach, we assume that we know the average query priority $\bar{p}$, the average cost $\bar{c}$, and the average arrival rate $\lambda$. (The average inter-arrival time is then $\bar{\iota} = 1/\lambda$.) Of course such predictions are only approximate, and as will be shown in our experimental section, they need not be very accurate for the multi-query PI to outperform a single-query PI. In many applications, the overall load on the system over time is at least partially predictable, and these numbers can be obtained from past statistics. Then we proceed in a way similar to that in Section 2.2. The only difference is that every $\bar{\iota}$ seconds, we predict that a new query with priority $\bar{p}$ and cost $\bar{c}$ will arrive at the RDBMS, and it is considered in the PI's estimates.

## 3 Workload Management

Workload management for RDBMS has been extensively studied (e.g., [3, 7, 14, 19, 23]), and major commercial RDBMSs come with workload management tools [8, 10, 13, 15]. However, due to a lack of information about the progress of queries running in the RDBMS, these tools cannot always make intelligent decisions.

For example, consider the following scheduled maintenance problem. Suppose at time 0, we need to schedule maintenance (e.g., we need to install some new software, or add several new data server nodes to a parallel RDBMS), and that the maintenance is scheduled to begin at time $t$. A common practice is to perform two operations [22]:

*O1*: Starting from time 0, no new queries are allowed to enter the RDBMS.
*O2*: The existing queries are allowed to run until time $t$, when any queries that have not completed are aborted.

The challenge is how to choose the maintenance time $t$ so as to minimize the amount of lost work without over-delaying the maintenance. In general, workload management tools do not know which queries can finish by time $t$, so the DBA needs to guess an arbitrary time that he/she thinks is appropriate. However, if we can estimate query running times, then more intelligent decisions can be made. For example, operation *O2* can then be replaced with the following two operations:

*O2'*: Predict which queries cannot finish by time $t$ and abort them at time 0. (Note: aborting queries will reduce the load on the RDBMS and hence change the estimate about which queries cannot finish by time $t$.)
*O3*: Let other queries in the RDBMS keep running. Suppose at time $t$, some of these queries have not finished execution (this is possible if our estimation has errors). Then they are either aborted or allowed to run to completion – the appropriate action depends on both the application requirement and the estimate of how soon those queries are going to finish.

Compared to operation *O2*, operations *O2'* and *O3* have the following advantages. First, even for the same maintenance time *t*, by aborting some "hopeless" queries, more queries can finish. Second, the amount of lost work can be controlled by adjusting the maintenance time *t*.

As a second example, suppose that for some reason, the DBA needs to speed up the execution of a target query *Q*. The DBA decides to do this by choosing one running query (the victim query) and blocking its execution. In this case, a common approach is to choose the victim query to be the heaviest resource consumer. However, if it happens that this victim query will finish quickly, then blocking the execution of this query will not speed up the execution of *Q* as much as blocking some other query that has a longer remaining execution time. If the remaining execution time of the running queries can be estimated, we can avoid choosing a victim query that is about to finish.

From the above discussion, we can see that it is desirable to give the workload management tool more information about the remaining execution time of running queries, and to use this information to make more intelligent decisions.

In this section, we discuss how to do this for three workload management problems. Variants of these workload management problems are frequently encountered in practice. Our goal is not to give an exhaustive account of all ways that PIs could be useful for workload management; rather, it is to demonstrate by example that the information provided by multi-query PIs can improve the quality of decisions made by workload management tools.

In our discussion, for ease of description, we assume that the *n* queries $Q_1, Q_2, \ldots,$ and $Q_n$ are numbered so that $c_1/s_1 \leq c_2/s_2 \leq \cdots \leq c_n/s_n$. Furthermore, we present our techniques for making workload management decisions based on the current system status (the *n* queries $Q_1, Q_2, \ldots,$ and $Q_n$).

## 3.1 Single-Query Speed Up Problem

Suppose we want to speed up the execution of a target query $Q_i$ ($1 \leq i \leq n$). A natural choice is to increase the priority of $Q_i$. However, if $Q_i$ is already of highest priority, then we must either block one or more other queries, or lower the priority of one or more other queries. In this paper, the first alternative is considered.

Assume that at time 0, we want to speed up the execution of query $Q_i$ by blocking $h \geq 1$ victim queries. Which *h* queries should be blocked? This is our single-query speed up problem. We first consider the simple case where $h=1$, and then discuss $h \geq 1$. Intuitively, the optimal victim query $Q_v$ should satisfy the following two conditions:

*C1*:   $Q_v$ should be the heaviest resource consumer.
*C2*:   If not blocked, $Q_v$ should run for the longest time (at least longer than $Q_i$).

In other words,

*C1*:   The weight of $Q_v$, $w_v$, should be the largest.
*C2*:   $c_v/s_v$, or *v* (since all queries are sorted in the ascending order of $c_j/s_j$), should be the largest.

It is not always possible to find a victim query that satisfies both conditions. Rather, the optimal victim query should be chosen based on a tradeoff between these two conditions. This tradeoff leads to a mathematical optimization problem.

The sketch of our method is as follows. The $n$-$1$ queries $Q_1, Q_2, \ldots, Q_{i-1}, Q_{i+1}, Q_{i+2}, \ldots,$ and $Q_n$ are divided into two sets: $S_1=\{Q_1, Q_2, \ldots, Q_{i-1}\}$ and $S_2=\{Q_{i+1}, Q_{i+2}, \ldots, Q_n\}$. In either set $S_j$ ($j=1, 2$), the best candidate victim query $Q_{v_j}$ is picked. This is achieved by quantifying the "benefit" of speeding up the execution of the target query $Q_i$ that is gained by blocking the execution of the victim query. Then the optimal victim query $Q_v$ is the better one of $Q_{v_1}$ and $Q_{v_2}$.

Our algorithm contains three steps.

**Step 1:** The queries in set $S_2$ are examined first. In this case, condition $C2$ does not matter, as each $Q_j$ ($i+1 \leq j \leq n$) runs longer than $Q_i$. To satisfy condition $C1$ as much as possible, a natural choice is to choose query $Q_{v_2}$ to be the query with the highest weight. That is, $w_{v_2} = \max\{w_j \mid i+1 \leq j \leq n\}$.

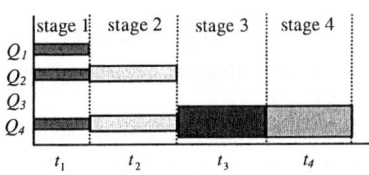

**Fig. 2.** Sample execution of $n=4$ queries (the execution of $Q_3$ is blocked at time 0)

We justify this choice formally. Suppose $Q_m$ ($i+1 \leq m \leq n$) is chosen as the victim query. To compute the "benefit" of blocking $Q_m$, the following key technique is used. The entire period of executing the $n$-$1$ queries $Q_1, Q_2, \ldots, Q_{m-1}, Q_{m+1}, \ldots,$ and $Q_n$ is divided into $n$ stages. During each stage $j$ ($1 \leq j \leq n$), except for $Q_m$, the amount of work completed for $Q_k$ ($1 \leq k \leq n, k \neq m$) remains the same as that in the standard case (recall that the standard case is defined in Section 2.2).

It is easy to see that except for stage $m$, at the end of each stage $j$ ($1 \leq j \leq n, j \neq m$), a query ($Q_j$) finishes execution. Also, at stage $j$ ($1 \leq j \leq i$), compared to the standard case, the execution of each $Q_k$ ($j \leq k \leq n, k \neq m$) is sped up by a factor of $\sum_{p=j}^{n} w_p / (\sum_{p=j}^{n} w_p - w_m)$. As a result, the duration of stage $j$ is shortened from $t_j$ to $t'_j = t_j \times (\sum_{p=j}^{n} w_p - w_m) / \sum_{p=j}^{n} w_p$. In other words, the duration of stage $j$ is shortened by $\Delta t_j = t_j - t'_j = t_j \times w_m / \sum_{p=j}^{n} w_p$.

Hence, the remaining execution time of query $Q_i$ is shortened by $T_m = \sum_{j=1}^{i} \Delta t_j = \sum_{j=1}^{i} (t_j / \sum_{p=j}^{n} w_p) \times w_m$. In order to maximize $T_m$, $w_m$ needs to be maximized.

**Step 2:** Now the queries in set $S_1$ are examined. Suppose $Q_m$ ($1 \leq m \leq i-1$) is chosen as the victim query. To compute the "benefit" of blocking $Q_m$, the technique of Step 1 is used again. The entire period of executing the $n$-$1$ queries $Q_1, Q_2, \ldots, Q_{m-1}, Q_{m+1}, \ldots,$ and $Q_n$ is divided into $n$ stages. During each stage $j$ ($1 \leq j \leq n$), except for $Q_m$, the amount of work completed for $Q_k$ ($1 \leq k \leq n, k \neq m$) remains the same as that in the standard case.

The remaining execution time of query $Q_i$ is shortened by $T_m = c_m/C$. This is because in the first $i$ stages, by blocking the execution of $Q_m$ at time 0, $c_m$'s work is saved. To maximize $T_{v_1}$, we should choose $Q_{v_1}$ such that $c_{v_1} = \max\{c_m \mid 1 \leq m \leq i-1\}$.

**Step 3:** The optimal victim query $Q_v$ is the better one of $Q_{v_1}$ and $Q_{v_2}$. That is, $T_v = \max\{T_{v_1}, T_{v_2}\}$.

From the above analysis, it can be seen that at time 0, by blocking a query $Q_m$ ($1 \leq m \leq n$) whose remaining execution time is $r_m$, no more than $r_m$ can be saved from the execution of other queries. This agrees with our assertion at the beginning of Section 3 that if the victim query will finish soon, blocking its execution will not help much. The time complexity of the above algorithm is $O(n \times \ln n)$, while the space complexity is $O(n)$.

We now consider the special case where all $n$ queries $Q_1, Q_2, \ldots,$ and $Q_n$ have the same priority. In this case, the solution to the problem is greatly simplified:

(1) If $i < n$, the optimal victim query is any $Q_j$ ($i+1 \leq j \leq n$).
(2) If $i = n$, the optimal victim query is $Q_{n-1}$.

The time complexity of this solution algorithm is $O(n)$. This is because in this case, there is no need to either sort the $n$ queries $Q_1, Q_2, \ldots,$ and $Q_n$ in ascending order of $c_j/s_j$ or compute all the $t_j$'s. Rather, given the target query $Q_i$ whose remaining cost is $c$, to find the optimal victim query, all the other queries need to be scanned (at most) once. If we find a query whose remaining cost is no less than $c$, we are done. Otherwise the query with the largest remaining cost is picked.

Now we return to the general case of our single-query speed up problem, where $h \geq 1$. Suppose the $h$ victim queries are chosen to be $Q_{g_1}, Q_{g_2}, \ldots,$ and $Q_{g_h}$, where $\{g_1, g_2, \ldots, g_h\} \subseteq \{1, 2, \ldots, n\} - \{i\}$. Assume by blocking $Q_{g_j}$ ($1 \leq j \leq h$) at time 0, the remaining execution time of $Q_i$ is shortened by $T_{g_j}$. Then from an analysis similar to that above, it can be shown that by blocking the $h$ victim queries $Q_{g_1}, Q_{g_2}, \ldots,$ and $Q_{g_h}$ at time 0, the remaining execution time of $Q_i$ is shortened by $\sum_{j=1}^{h} T_{g_j}$.

Based on this observation, the following greedy method can be used to deal with the general case of our single-query speed up problem. First, the optimal victim query is chosen according to the algorithm presented previously. Then, among the remaining queries, the next optimal victim query is chosen. This procedure is repeated $h$ times to get $h$ victim queries. These $h$ victim queries are the optimal $h$ victim queries.

## 3.2 Multiple-Query Speed Up Problem

Suppose now that we want to block a single query to speed up the execution of the other $n-1$ queries. Which query should be blocked? This is the multiple-query speed up problem.

Suppose $Q_m$ ($1 \leq m \leq n$) is chosen as the victim query. From an analysis similar to that in Section 3.1, we know that for each $j$ ($1 \leq j \leq m$), compared to the standard case, the duration of stage $j$ is shortened by $\Delta t_j = t_j \times w_m / \sum_{p=j}^{n} w_p$. Also, each stage $j$ ($m+1 \leq j \leq n$) is the same as that in the standard case.

At each stage $j$ ($1 \leq j \leq m$), $n$-$j$ queries $Q_j$, $Q_{j+1}$, ..., $Q_{m-1}$, $Q_{m+1}$, ..., and $Q_n$ are running, and their total response time is improved by $(n-j) \times \Delta t_j$. Hence, by blocking $Q_m$ at time 0, the total response time of all the other $n$-$1$ queries $Q_1$, $Q_2$, ..., $Q_{m-1}$, $Q_{m+1}$, ..., and $Q_n$ is improved by $R_m = \sum_{j=1}^{m}(n-j) \times \Delta t_j = \sum_{j=1}^{m}(n-j) \times t_j \times w_m / \sum_{p=j}^{n} w_p$. To maximize $R_m$, we should choose the optimal victim query $Q_v$ such that $R_v = \max\{R_m \mid 1 \leq m \leq n\}$. The time complexity of the above algorithm is $O(n \times \ln n)$. Also, the space complexity of the above algorithm is $O(n)$.

## 3.3 Scheduled Maintenance Problem

In this section, we discuss the problem mentioned at the beginning of Section 3: how can we choose the maintenance time $t$ and the queries to abort so that the amount of lost work can be minimized without over-delaying the maintenance? In practice, the amount of lost work $L_w$ can be defined in multiple ways. Due to space constraints, in this paper, only the following two cases are discussed:

**Case 1**: $L_w$ is the total amount of work that has been completed for the queries that will be aborted.

**Case 2**: $L_w$ is the total cost of the queries that will be aborted. In this case, it is more appropriate to call $L_w$ the amount of unfinished work, since the aborted queries need to be rerun after the RDBMS is restarted.

For each $i$ ($1 \leq i \leq n$), let $e_i$ denote the amount of work that has been completed for query $Q_i$ at time 0. We only describe the solution to Case 1. For Case 2, the solution is the same except that for each $i$ ($1 \leq i \leq n$), $e_i$ needs to be replaced with $e_i + c_i$. Recall that $c_i$ is the remaining cost of query $Q_i$ at time 0.

In our discussion, we assume that the overhead of aborting queries is negligible compared to the query execution cost. This will be true in a primarily read-only environment. In general, aborting jobs may introduce non-negligible overhead. How to handle this case is left as an interesting area for future work.

We define the *system quiescent time* to be the time when all the $n$ queries $Q_1$, $Q_2$, ..., and $Q_n$ (except for those queries that are aborted, if any) finish execution. The estimated system quiescent time is our estimation of the earliest time when the system maintenance can start. Suppose for each $i$ ($1 \leq i \leq n$), by aborting $Q_i$ at time 0, the system quiescent time is shortened by $V_i$. It is easy to see that $V_i = c_i / C$. Also, by aborting $h$ queries $Q_{g_1}$, $Q_{g_2}$, ..., and $Q_{g_h}$ at time 0, where $1 \leq h \leq n$ and $\{g_1, g_2, ..., g_h\} \subseteq \{1, 2, ..., n\}$, the system quiescent time is shortened by $\sum_{j=1}^{h} V_{g_j}$.

Our goal is to maximize $\sum_{j=1}^{h} V_{g_j}$ while minimizing $\sum_{j=1}^{h} e_{g_j}$. This is the standard knapsack problem [5]. Consequently, we use a greedy method to solve it. First the $n$ queries $Q_1$, $Q_2$, ..., and $Q_n$ are re-sorted in ascending order of $e_i / V_i$ (recall that we assume that originally, the $n$ queries $Q_1$, $Q_2$, ..., and $Q_n$ are sorted in ascending order of $c_i / s_i$). After re-sorting, we have $e_{f_1} / V_{f_1} \leq e_{f_2} / V_{f_2} \leq \cdots \leq e_{f_n} / V_{f_n}$ (or equivalently,

$e_{f_1}/c_{f_1} \le e_{f_2}/c_{f_2} \le \cdots \le e_{f_n}/c_{f_n}$), where $\{f_1, f_2, ..., f_n\}$ is a permutation of $\{1, 2, ..., n\}$. Then we keep aborting $Q_{f_1}$, $Q_{f_2}$, ..., until the system quiescent time becomes satisfactory.

## 4 Revisiting the Assumptions

Sections 2 and 3 are based on the three assumptions in Section 2.1. Although we believe that these assumptions approximate reasonable system behavior, in practice, the system behavior will deviate from that predicted by these assumptions. Overall, the impact of relaxing these assumptions is that the multi-query PI now gives only approximate estimates, and for this reason the "advice" it gives for workload management becomes heuristic rather than provably optimal. As mentioned in the introduction, our method is adaptive and can make dynamic adjustments to ameliorate previous errors. This can mitigate the effect of imprecise estimates. We discuss this in more detail in the following subsections.

### 4.1 Assumptions 1 and 2

Assumption 1 says that for all the running queries, the RDBMS processes $C$ units of work per second in total. When Assumption 1 is not valid, the PI may either underestimate the speedup that will occur when a query terminates (if, for example, the system was thrashing until that query finished), or overestimate the speedup that will occur when a query terminates (if, for example, a CPU-intensive query terminates and the other queries are all I/O-intensive). While this will hurt the accuracy of the multi-query PI, it is still likely to be superior to that of a single-query PI, which pays no attention whatsoever to other queries.

Assumption 2 says that for each running query, the exact remaining cost is known. If these estimates turn out to be far off, the accuracy of the multi-query PI will again be harmed, although again it is likely to be better than that of a PI that completely ignores these other queries. These scenarios could be dealt with in a number of ways, including augmenting the PI to have a more accurate performance model (including better modeling of a lightly loaded system), being willing to tolerate inaccuracies in the PI's estimates, or even revisiting the workload management decisions periodically if the inaccuracies of the model have resulted in suboptimal decisions. Which approach is best under which circumstances is an interesting question for future research. We suspect that because the PI adjusts its estimates "on the fly" as it discovers that they are inaccurate, it may not be worth the effort to improve the precision of these estimates – but this is still an open question and also scope for interesting future research.

### 4.2 Assumption 3

Assumption 3 says that each query's execution speed is proportional to the weight associated with its priority. This assumption is mainly for concreteness, for to discuss workload management problems in the context of queries with priorities, some policy needs to be specified for how priority affects execution speed. If a system implements a different approach to priorities, a priority model for the multi-query PI would need to be developed for that approach. Even if the system attempts to implement a policy where execution speed is proportional to priority, the true behavior may be different for a variety of reasons – one example is the details of query interactions (e.g., a high-priority I/O-intensive query might not substantially block a low-priority CPU-intensive query, or two queries compete for/share buffer pool pages and thus slow down/speed up each other's execution). As was the case in Section 4.1, these factors will harm the accuracy of the multi-query PI, and ways to deal with this include building a more accurate model, tolerating errors, or periodically revising decisions.

### 4.3 Other Practical Considerations

The time complexity of most algorithms described in this paper is $O(n \times \ln n)$, where $n$ is the number of queries in the RDBMS. This is a cause for some concern if $n$ is large. However, in general, we would expect that the majority of queries are short (i.e., queries that can finish in a few seconds) and not really candidates for progress estimation or relevant individually for workload management. For this reason we think it is reasonable for the purposes of workload management and progress estimation to ignore these short queries and focus on long-running queries. Thus the effective $n$ in the preceding formula is likely to be small and the computational cost will be small.

## 5 Performance Evaluation

In this section, we present results from a prototype implementation of our techniques in PostgreSQL Version 7.3.4 [17].

### 5.1 Experiment Environment

Our measurements were performed with the PostgreSQL client application and server running on a Dell Inspiron 8500 PC with one 2.2GHz processor, 512MB main memory, one 40GB disk, and running the Microsoft Windows XP operating system. The relations used for the experiments followed the schema of the standard TPC-R Benchmark relations [21]:

lineitem (partkey, quantity, extendedprice, ...),
part_i (partkey, retailprice, ...) ($i \geq 1$).

**Table 1.** Test data set

|  | number of tuples | total size |
|---|---|---|
| lineitem | 24M | 3.02GB |
| part_i ($i \geq 1$) | 10×$N_i$ | 1.4×$N_i$ KB |

In our experiments, each *part_i* relation ($i \geq 1$) contains $10 \times N_i$ tuples. (How the $N_i$'s are chosen is discussed later.) The *partkey* attribute values in the *part_i* relations are randomly distributed between the minimal *partkey* attribute value and the maximal *partkey* attribute value in the *lineitem* relation. In a given *part_i* relation, all the tuples have different *partkey* attribute values. On average, each *part_i* tuple matches with 30 *lineitem* tuples on the attribute *partkey*. We built an index on the *partkey* attribute of the *lineitem* relation.

The following queries were tested, which find parts that are on average selling for 25% below suggested retail price:

**Query $Q_i$** ($i \geq 1$): select * from part_i p where p.retailprice×0.75>
(select sum(l.extendedprice)/sum(l.quantity) from lineitem l where l.partkey=p.partkey);

Each query is a nested query that contains a correlated sub-query. The query plan chosen by PostgreSQL for the correlated sub-query is an index-scan on the *lineitem* relation. We repeated our experiments with other kinds of queries. The results were similar and thus not presented here.

Before we ran queries, we ran the PostgreSQL statistics collection program on all the relations. PostgreSQL does not support priorities for queries. Hence, all the queries $Q_i$ ($i \geq 1$) have the same priority. In all experiments, the outputs from each PI were stored into a separate file.

## 5.2 Multi-query Progress Indicator

Three experiments were performed to compare single-query PIs with multi-query PIs. In the first two experiments, we ensure that no new queries arrive at the RDBMS while the queries under consideration are running. In the third experiment, we explore the situation in which new queries keep arriving at the RDBMS.

### 5.2.1. Multiple Concurrent Query (MCQ) Experiment

In this experiment, ten queries were used: $Q_i$ ($1 \leq i \leq 10$). Their $N_i$'s followed a Zipfian distribution with parameter $a=1.2$. At time 0, each of these ten queries was at a random point of its execution.

This experiment was performed multiple times. A typical run is examined here. In this run, among the $n=10$ queries $Q_i$ ($1 \leq i \leq 10$), we focus on a typical large query $Q$. For this $Q$, Figure 3 shows the remaining query execution time estimated by the PI over time. Figure 4 shows the query execution speed monitored by the PI over time. In Figure 3, the actual remaining query execution time is represented by the dashed line, the

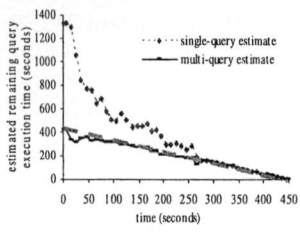

**Fig. 3.** Remaining query execution time estimated over time for Q (MCQ experiment)

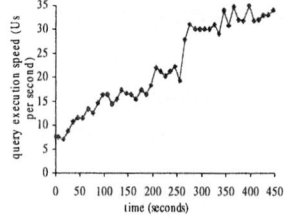

**Fig. 4.** Query execution speed monitored over time for Q (MCQ experiment)

single-query estimate is provided by the single-query PI, and the multi-query estimate is provided by the multi-query PI.

From time 0 to the completion time of query $Q$, due to the completion of other concurrent queries, the execution speed of $Q$ gradually increases by almost a factor of five. The multi-query PI is able to predict the change in the load on the RDBMS while the single-query PI cannot. As a result, the multi-query estimate is fairly close to the actual remaining query execution time, while the single-query estimate differs from the actual remaining query execution time by almost a factor of three at the beginning.

### 5.2.2. Non-empty Admission Queue (NAQ) Experiment

In this experiment, three queries were used: $Q_1$, $Q_2$, and $Q_3$, with $N_1=50$, $N_2=10$, $N_3=20$. The query admission policy was that at any time, at most two queries could run concurrently in the RDBMS. At time 0, $Q_1$, $Q_2$, and $Q_3$ entered the RDBMS admission queue. $Q_1$ and $Q_2$ started execution first, with $Q_3$ blocked until $Q_2$ finishes.

The purpose of this experiment is to show that when the admission queue is not empty, multi-query PIs that consider the admission queue can provide more accurate estimates than either single-query PIs or multi-query PIs that do not consider the admission queue. In effect, examining the admission queue lets the PI see farther into the future.

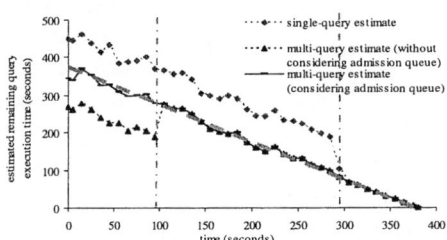

**Fig. 5.** Remaining query execution time estimated over time for $Q_1$ (NAQ experiment)

For query $Q_1$, Figure 5 shows the remaining query execution time estimated by the PIs over time. There, the actual remaining query execution time is represented by the dashed line. Two vertical dashed-dotted lines are used, one representing the start time of $Q_3$, and another representing the finish time of $Q_3$.

The execution time of query $Q_1$ is longer than the sum of the execution time of $Q_2$ and the execution time of $Q_3$. Before $Q_2$ finishes, without considering $Q_3$ that is waiting in the admission queue, neither the single-query PI nor the multi-query PI can accurately predict the load on the RDBMS after the completion of $Q_2$. Hence, the multi-query estimate considering the admission queue is more precise than the other approaches.

At the 97th second, query $Q_2$ finishes and $Q_3$ starts. The query admission queue becomes empty. The multi-query PI is able to predict that $Q_3$ will finish before $Q_1$ and then the execution speed of $Q_1$ will increase, while the single-query PI incorrectly assumes that the execution speed of $Q_1$ will remain the same during the execution of $Q_1$. As a result, the multi-query estimate becomes more precise than the single-query estimate until $Q_3$ finishes at the 291st second.

### 5.2.3. Stream Concurrent Query (SCQ) Experiment

In this experiment, at time 0, ten queries $Q_i$ ($1 \leq i \leq 10$) were running in the RDBMS and each of them was at a random point of its execution. New queries kept arriving at the

RDBMS according to a Poisson process with parameter $\lambda$. (The unit of $\lambda$ is second$^{-1}$.) For both $Q_i$'s ($1 \leq i \leq 10$) and new queries, their $N_i$'s followed a Zipfian distribution with parameter $a=2.2$. (We also tested other values of $a$. The results are similar and thus omitted.)

Consider any $Q_i$ ($1 \leq i \leq 10$). Suppose the actual remaining query execution time is $t_{actual}$. At time 0, the multi-query PI estimates the remaining query execution time to be $t_{multi}$. The relative error of the multi-query estimate is defined as $|t_{multi} - t_{actual}|/t_{actual} \times 100\%$. The relative error of the single-query estimate is defined in a similar way.

Among all $Q_i$'s ($1 \leq i \leq 10$), the one with the largest remaining cost at time 0 will finish last and is thus called the *last finishing query*. The test was repeated one hundred times (one hundred runs). Unless otherwise specified, all the reported numbers are averaged over these one hundred runs.

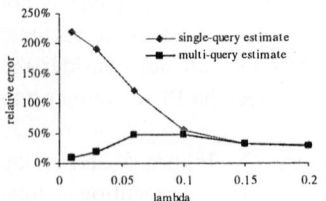

**Fig. 6.** Relative error of estimated remaining execution time for the last finishing query ($a=2.2$)

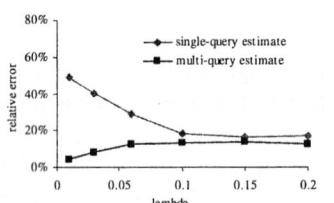

**Fig. 7.** Average relative error of estimated remaining execution time for all ten queries ($a=2.2$)

We first discuss the case where the multi-query PI knows the exact average arrival rate $\lambda$ and the exact average cost $\bar{c}$ of future queries. For the last finishing query, Figure 6 shows the relative error of the estimated remaining execution time. For all $Q_i$'s ($1 \leq i \leq 10$), Figure 7 shows the average relative error of the estimated remaining execution time.

When producing estimates, the multi-query PI considers both concurrently running queries and future queries. In contrast, the single-query PI incorrectly assumes that the load will remain stable in the future. As a result, the relative error of the multi-query estimate is always smaller than that of the single-query estimate.

When the system is stable, the relative error of the single-query estimate decreases as $\lambda$ increases. This is because the larger the $\lambda$, the closer to reality the assumption made by the single-query PI. In contrast, the relative error of the multi-query estimate increases with $\lambda$, as the faster new queries arrive, the larger and the more random their influence on existing queries. Note that the stable system case is the most common case encountered in practice. In this case, the relative error of the multi-query estimate is much smaller than that of the single-query estimate.

When $\lambda>0.07$, new queries come faster than the RDBMS can process them and thus the system becomes unstable. In this case, the influence of new queries on existing queries becomes fairly large and random. Hence, single-query and multi-query estimates have roughly the same (large) relative error.

Among all $Q_i$'s ($1 \leq i \leq 10$), the last finishing query gets the largest and most random influence from new queries. Consequently, PIs provide the least precise estimate for the last finishing query. This leads to the effect that for both single-query and multi-query estimates, the average relative error for the ten queries is smaller than the relative error for the last finishing query.

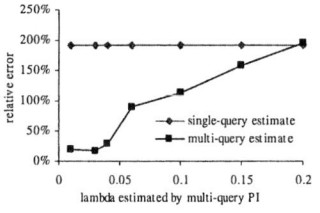

Fig. 8. Relative error of estimated remaining execution time for the last finishing query ($a=2.2$, $lambda=0.03$)

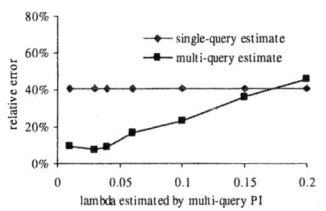

Fig. 9. Average relative error of estimated remaining execution time for all ten queries ($a=2.2$, $lambda=0.03$)

Now we discuss the case where the multi-query PI cannot estimate $\lambda$, the average arrival rate of future queries, precisely. We include this experiment to illustrate one example of the multi-query PI detecting when its estimates were wrong and then adapting and correcting its estimates. This is not the only way it does so; like single-query PIs, multi-query PIs also react to incorrect cost estimates (due perhaps to bad cardinality estimates or an inaccurate hardware cost model) and incorrect assumptions about how concurrently executing queries affect the performance of a given query (even single-query PIs notice, e.g., that they have slowed down when another query starts, even though they do not know why, or how long the slowdown might last, or if a similar slowdown might occur again in the future from a yet-to-arrive query.) Because we have explored this sort of adaptivity in our prior work [11, 12], we do not explore it here. Instead, we focus on a kind of adaptivity unique to multi-query PIs, i.e., adapting to errors in expected query arrival rate.

Let $\lambda=0.03$. The multi-query PI makes its estimate based on $\lambda'$ while $\lambda' \neq \lambda$. For the last finishing query, Figure 8 shows the relative error of the estimated remaining execution time. For all $Q_i$'s ($1 \leq i \leq 10$), Figure 9 shows the average relative error of the estimated remaining execution time.

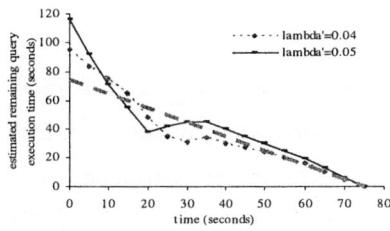

Fig. 10. Remaining query execution time estimated by multi-query PI over time (lambda=0.03)

The bigger the difference between $\lambda'$ and $\lambda$, the more inaccurate the multi-query estimate. However, unless $\lambda'$ is more than five times larger than $\lambda$, the relative error of the multi-query estimate is always smaller than that of the single-query estimate. This shows that, at least in these tests, even somewhat inaccurate information about the future is better than no information about the future.

We pick a typical run among the one hundred runs. In this run, for the last finishing query, Figure 10 shows the remaining query execution time estimated by the multi-query PI over time. There, the actual remaining query execution time is represented by the dashed line. At the beginning, due to the incorrectly estimated arrival rate $\lambda'$, the multi-query estimate is quite different from the actual remaining query execution time. The bigger the difference between $\lambda'$ and $\lambda$, the more inaccurate the multi-query estimate. However, the multi-query PI is adaptive and can correct its own errors. The closer to query completion time, the more precise the multi-query estimate is.

In summary, as long as there is some reasonable (approximate) information about the future load, the multi-query PI can provide (often much) more accurate estimate of remaining query execution time than the single-query PI. This information need not be extremely accurate - the multi-query PI is adaptive and can correct its own errors over time.

## 5.3 Workload Management

Section 3 discussed three workload management problems. The experiment results for these three workload management problems were similar, since similar techniques were used for each problem. Accordingly, in this section, only the experiment results for Case 2 of the scheduled maintenance problem are presented, where the amount of unfinished work is defined as the total cost of all queries that will be aborted.

### 5.3.1. Experiment Description

We wanted to simulate a typical situation in practice, where the number of small queries submitted to the RDBMS is much larger than the number of large queries submitted to the RDBMS. To achieve this, a large number of queries $Q_i$ ($i \geq 1$) are used. We let all the $N_i$'s follow a Zipfian distribution with parameter $a=2.2$. (We also tested other values of $a$. The results were similar and thus are omitted.) Note that $N_i$ "represents" the cost of $Q_i$. Each $Q_i$ ($i \geq 1$) has the same probability to be submitted to the RDBMS.

We evaluated the performance of our workload management techniques in the following way. At any time, $n=10$ queries $Q_{f_j}$ ($f_j \geq 1$, $1 \leq j \leq 10$) are running in the RDBMS. At the time that a query $Q_{f_j}$ finishes execution, a random $k$ ($k \geq 1$) is picked and query $Q_k$ is submitted to the RDBMS for execution. Hence, for all the queries $Q_k$ submitted to the RDBMS, the $N_k$'s follow a Zipfian distribution with parameter $a$.

A random time $r_t$ is chosen. At time $r_t$, the RDBMS is inspected and decisions are made to prepare for system maintenance scheduled for $t$ seconds later. By a simple mathematical derivation, it can be shown that for the $n=10$ queries $Q_{g_j}$ ($g_j \geq 1$, $1 \leq j \leq 10$) running at time $r_t$, their $N_{g_j}$'s follow a Zipfian distribution with parameter $a-1$. Due to space constraints, we only describe the main ideas in the derivation while omitting the details. For a particular $Q_k$ ($k \geq 1$), the probability that $Q_k$ is running at time $r_t$ is proportional to both the probability that $Q_k$ is submitted and the cost of $Q_k$ (larger queries will run longer and hence are easier to be "seen"). Thus, $probability(N_{g_j} = m) \propto (1/m^a) \times m = 1/m^{a-1}$.

We compare the following three methods:

**No PI method:** No PI was used. Rather, we performed operations *O1* and *O2* described in Section 3.

**Single-query PI method:** We used the single-query PI and performed operations $O1$, $O2'$, and $O3$. When operation $O2'$ was performed, the query with the largest estimated remaining cost was first aborted. Then if necessary, we further aborted the query with the second largest estimated remaining cost, and so on.

**Multi-query PI method:** We used the multi-query PI and performed operations $O1$, $O2'$, and $O3$. When operation $O2'$ was performed, the algorithm described in Section 3.3 was used.

In all three methods, at the scheduled maintenance time $r_t+t$, the queries that had not finished execution were aborted. The test was repeated ten times (ten runs). Unless otherwise specified, all the reported numbers are averaged over these ten runs.

For the $n=10$ queries $Q_{g_j}$ ($g_j \geq 1$, $1 \leq j \leq 10$) running at time $r_t$, the total work $TW$ is defined to be their total cost. The unfinished work $UW$ is defined to be the total cost of those queries that are aborted between time $r_t$ and the scheduled maintenance time $r_t+t$. (Recall that unfinished queries are aborted at time $r_t+t$.) Finally, $t_{finish}$ is defined to be their remaining execution time under the *no interruption condition*. That is, under the condition that no new queries enter the RDBMS for execution and there is no scheduled maintenance so that none of the existing $n=10$ queries is aborted, all the existing $n=10$ queries can finish by time $r_t+t_{finish}$.

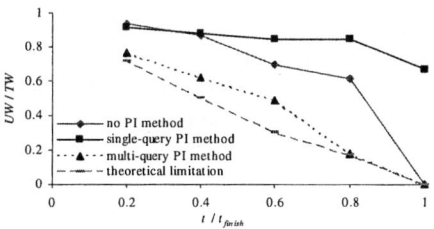

**Fig. 11.** Unfinished work of the three methods ($a=2.2$)

Figure 11 shows the unfinished work of the three methods. Note that the x-axis is $t/t_{finish}$. The y-axis is $UW/TW$. That is, both the x-axis and the y-axis have been "normalized," as the specific values of $t_{finish}$ and $TW$ vary from one run to another. In the rest of Section 5.3, when we refer to the amount of unfinished work, we always mean $UW/TW$.

Figure 11 also shows the theoretical limit that any method can achieve. This limit is computed using the exact information that comes from the actual run-to-completion execution of the $n=10$ queries. That is, based on this exact information, we compute the optimal set of queries that should be aborted at time $r_t$ so that all the other queries can finish by the scheduled maintenance time $r_t+t$.

If $t=t_{finish}$, then in both the no PI method and the multi-query PI method, all queries can run to completion and there is no unfinished work. However, in the single-query PI method, 67% of the total work $TW$ is not finished. The reason is as follows. In general, as can be seen from the experiment results in Section 5.2.1, the single-query PI tends to significantly overestimate the remaining execution time of those queries whose remaining costs are large at time $r_t$. Consequently, the single-query PI method thinks that a large portion of those queries cannot meet the scheduled maintenance time and aborts them unnecessarily at time $r_t$.

If $t<t_{finish}$, each of the three methods needs to abort queries. Among the three methods, the multi-query PI method has the least amount of unfinished work.

Compared to the no PI method, the multi-query PI method reduces the amount of unfinished work by 18%~44%. Compared to the single-query PI method, the multi-query PI method reduces the amount of unfinished work by 15%~67%. The reason for this reduction of work is as follows. First, in this case the multi-query PI can estimate the remaining query execution time fairly precisely. As a result, the multi-query PI method can estimate which queries cannot finish in time and abort them early so that more queries can meet the scheduled maintenance time. Second, as explained above, the single-query PI method aborts a large number of queries unnecessarily. Finally, the no PI method does not abort any query until the scheduled maintenance time. As a result, before the scheduled maintenance time, queries compete with each other for resources and are executed relatively slowly. Hence, compared to the multi-query PI method, fewer queries can meet the scheduled maintenance time.

In general, the no PI method has less unfinished work than the single-query PI method. However, when $t$ is small (say, $t=0.2 \times t_{finish}$), the no PI method has a little bit more unfinished work than the single-query PI method. This is because in this case, at time $r_t$, the single-query PI method aborts those queries whose remaining costs are large. Then other queries can run faster and finish by the scheduled maintenance time. In contrast, the no PI method does not abort any query at time $r_t$. This leads to the effect that all queries are executed very slowly. As a result, very few queries can meet the scheduled maintenance time. Note that if $t$ is large, this effect is not so significant. This is because those queries whose remaining costs are small at time $r_t$ are going to finish in a small amount of time. Then other queries can run faster.

In all ten runs, in most cases, the multi-query PI method performs better than both the no PI method and the single-query PI method. In the extreme case, compared to the no PI method and the single-query PI method, the multi-query PI method reduces the amount of unfinished work by 73% and 94%, respectively. (Note: the maximum percentage by which the multi-query PI method can reduce the amount of unfinished work is at most 100%.)

Occasionally, the multi-query PI method performs worse than either the no PI method or the single-query PI method. In the worst case, compared to the no PI method and the single-query PI method, the multi-query PI method increases the amount of unfinished work by 12% and 3%, respectively. This is because in the multi-query PI method, the greedy method only provides an approximate solution to the knapsack problem (finding the optimal solution to the knapsack problem is NP-hard). Also, the estimates provided by multi-query PIs have errors, mainly due to the imprecise statistics collected by PostgreSQL.

Among all the three methods, the multi-query PI method performs the closest to the theoretical limitation. When $t<t_{finish}$, compared to the theoretical limitation, on average, the multi-query PI method increases the amount of unfinished work by 3%~12%. In the worst case, the multi-query PI method increases the amount of unfinished work by 60%.

In summary, the average performance of the multi-query PI method is better than both that of the no PI method and that of the single-query PI method. The multi-query PI method can avoid extremely bad decisions. In the best case, the multi-query PI method can perform much better than both the no PI method and the single-query PI method. In the worst case, compared to both the no PI method and the single-query PI method, the multi-query PI method performs only a little worse. Moreover, in a large number of cases, the multi-query PI method performs fairly close to the theoretical limitation.

## 6 Related Work

As mentioned in the introduction, all previous work on PIs has considered only single-query PIs, and none of the previous work has considered the application of PIs to workload management. Of course, there is a great deal of related work dealing with workload management. In general, the workload management problems discussed in Section 3 are scheduling problems. In this section, we give a brief survey of existing work related to scheduling.

Process scheduling has been exhaustively studied in the context of operating systems. In general, the process scheduler in the operating system does not know the job sizes [20]. By contrast, in our workload management environment, the query costs are known (or at least the query costs can be roughly estimated).

Process scheduling and transaction scheduling have been extensively studied in real-time operating systems [9, 24] and real-time database systems [1, 18]. In general, the main concern there is to meet deadlines rather than to maximize resource utilization. Most real-time systems are memory resident and the jobs there can be finished in a short amount of time (say, less than a few seconds). Hence, they need special time-cognizant protocols (e.g., to handle critical sections). Many real-time systems use hard deadlines. As a result, the jobs there are usually pre-defined (i.e., "canned" jobs). Also, almost all jobs there have deadlines.

In our workload management environment, we do not want to sacrifice resource utilization ratio in our general-purpose RDBMS. Queries may incur substantial I/Os and run for a long time. Therefore, short-term effects can be ignored and no special time-cognizant protocol is needed. Before queries are submitted to the RDBMS, we have only approximate knowledge of their resource requirements. Also, most queries do not have hard deadlines.

Job scheduling has been extensively studied in operations research and in computer science theory [2, 16]. In these studies, jobs usually have precedence constraints. On a single machine, jobs are typically executed one after another. Also, the main concern is to maximize the throughput/utilization ratio of the machines. In our database workload management environment, queries do not have precedence constraints and are executed concurrently.

## 7 Conclusion

In this paper we considered going beyond the state of the art in RDBMS PIs by considering the impact queries have on each other's progress and eventual termination. Our multi-query PIs consider not only currently executing queries, but also predictions about queries that might arrive in the future. Even approximate information about future queries is helpful, and the PIs are adaptive in that they detect when they were given "bad" information about the future and correct their estimates as they learn more about the true query workload. We also demonstrated how to apply the resulting multi-query PIs to several workload management problems. As shown in experiments with a prototype implementation, for both estimating remaining query execution time and workload management purposes, the proposed multi-query PIs have significant advantages over single-query PIs or no PIs, suggesting that multi-query PIs may be a useful addition to RDBMSs.

## Acknowledgements

We would like to thank Curt J. Ellmann and Michael W. Watzke for helpful discussions. This work was supported in part by NSF grants CDA-9623632 and ITR 0086002.

## References

1. R.K. Abbott, H. Garcia-Molina. Scheduling Real-time Transactions: a Performance Evaluation. VLDB 1988: 1-12.
2. J. Blazewicz, K.H. Ecker, and E. Pesch et al. Scheduling Computer and Manufacturing Processes, Second Edition. Springer-Verlag, 2001.
3. M.J. Carey, S. Krishnamurthi, and M. Livny. Load Control for Locking: The 'Half-and-Half' Approach. PODS 1990: 72-84.
4. S. Chaudhuri, R. Kaushik, and R. Ramamurthy. When Can We Trust Progress Estimators for SQL Queries? SIGMOD Conf. 2005.
5. T.H. Cormen, C.E. Leiserson, and R.L. Rivest et al. Introduction to Algorithms, Second Edition. MIT Press, 2001.
6. S. Chaudhuri, V.R. Narasayya, and R. Ramamurthy. Estimating Progress of Long Running SQL Queries. SIGMOD Conf. 2004: 803-814.
7. C. Faloutsos, R.T. Ng, and T.K. Sellis. Predictive Load Control for Flexible Buffer Allocation. VLDB 1991: 265-274.
8. IBM Autonomic Computing homepage. http://www.research.ibm.com/autonomic.
9. S. Khanna, M. Sebree, and J. Zolnowsky. Realtime Scheduling in SunOS 5.0. USENIX Winter 1992: 375-390.
10. G.M. Lohman, S. Lightstone. SMART: Making DB2 (More) Autonomic. VLDB 2002: 877-879.
11. G. Luo, J.F. Naughton, and C.J. Ellmann et al. Toward a Progress Indicator for Database Queries. SIGMOD Conf. 2004: 791-802.
12. G. Luo, J.F. Naughton, and C.J. Ellmann et al. Increasing the Accuracy and Coverage of SQL Progress Indicators. ICDE 2005: 853-864.
13. Microsoft AutoAdmin Project homepage. http://research.microsoft.com/dmx/autoadmin.
14. D.T. McWherter, B. Schroeder, and A. Ailamaki et al. Priority Mechanisms for OLTP and Transactional Web Applications. ICDE 2004: 535-546.
15. Oracle Database: Manageability. http://www.oracle.com/database/index.html?db_manageability.html.

16. M. Pinedo. Scheduling: Theory, Algorithms, and Systems, Second Edition. Prentice Hall, 2001.
17. PostgreSQL homepage, 2005. http://www.postgresql.org.
18. K. Ramamritham. Real-Time Databases. Distributed and Parallel Databases 1(2): 199-226, 1993.
19. D. Shasha, P. Bonnet. Database Tuning: Principles, Experiments, and Troubleshooting Techniques. Morgan Kaufmann Publishers, 2002.
20. A. Silberschatz, P. Galvin, and G. Gagne. Operating System Concepts, Sixth Edition. John Wiley, 2002.
21. TPC Homepage. TPC-R benchmark, www.tpc.org.
22. Michael W. Watzke. Personal communication, 2005.
23. G. Weikum, C. Hasse, and A. Moenkeberg et al. The COMFORT Automatic Tuning Project. Inf. Syst. 19(5): 381-432, 1994.
24. W. Zhao. Editor. Special Issue on Real-Time Computing Systems. Operating Systems Review 23(3), 1989.

# Finding Equivalent Rewritings in the Presence of Arithmetic Comparisons

Foto Afrati[1,*], Rada Chirkova[2,**], Manolis Gergatsoulis[3], and Vassia Pavlaki[1,*]

[1] Department of Electrical and Computing Engineering,
National Technical University of Athens (NTUA), 15773 Athens, Greece
{afrati, vpavlaki}@softlab.ntua.gr

[2] Computer Science Department, North Carolina State University,
Campus Box 7535, Raleigh, NC 27695-7535
chirkova@csc.ncsu.edu

[3] Department of Archive and Library Sciences, Ionian University,
Palea Anaktora, Plateia Eleftherias, 49100 Corfu, Greece
manolis@ionio.gr

**Abstract.** The problem of rewriting queries using views has received significant attention because of its applications in a wide variety of data-management problems. For select-project-join SQL (a.k.a. conjunctive) queries and views, there are efficient algorithms in the literature, which find equivalent and maximally contained rewritings. In the presence of arithmetic comparisons (ACs) the problem becomes more complex. We do not know how to find maximally contained rewritings in the general case. There are algorithms which find maximally contained rewritings only for special cases such as when ACs are restricted to be semi-interval. However, we know that the problem of finding an equivalent rewriting (if there exists one) in the presence of ACs is decidable, yet still doubly exponential. This complexity calls for an efficient algorithm which will perform better on average than the complete enumeration algorithm. In this work we present such an algorithm which is sound and complete. Its efficiency lies in that it considers fewer candidate rewritings because it includes a preliminary test to decide for each view whether it is potentially useful in some rewriting.

## 1 Introduction

The problem of answering queries using views (i.e. rewriting queries using views) is as follows. Suppose we are given a query $Q$ over a database schema, and a set of view definitions $V_1, V_2, \ldots, V_k$ over the same schema. We want to know whether and how we can answer the query $Q$ using only the answers to the views

---

* The project is co-funded by the European Social Fund (75%) and National Resources (25%)- Operational Program for Educational and Vocational Training II (EPEAEK II) and particularly the program PYTHAGORAS.
** This author's work on this material has been supported by the National Science Foundation under Grant No. 0307072.

$V_1, V_2, \ldots, V_k$. The problem has recently received significant attention because of its applications in a wide variety of data management problems, query optimization, maintenance of physical data independence, data integration, data warehousing, global information systems and mobile computing.

When answering queries using views we often need either find *equivalent rewritings* for a query or *maximally contained rewriting* (MCR). In data integration, where views describe a set of autonomous heterogenous data sources, we search for a maximally-contained rewriting, which provides the best answer, given the available sources. In query optimization or maintenance of physical data independence we search for a solution that uses the views and is equivalent (instead of contained) to the original query. When the query and views are conjunctive (i.e., select-project-join) without comparison predicates, the maximally-contained rewriting is a union of conjunctive queries over the views [2].

The original definition of conjunctive queries does not allow for comparisons between data values. However, in practice users often ask select-project-join queries that do involve comparisons in the selection condition (e.g. $price \leq 100$). For this reason, we extend the class of conjunctive queries by allowing built-in predicates which are arithmetic comparisons (ACs). So the problem of answering queries using views in the presence of arithmetic comparisons becomes more important, yet more complex. The following example illustrates this complexity.

*Example 1.* Consider the following query $Q$ and set of views $V_1$, $V_2$:

$Q : q(X, X) \text{ :- } a(X, X), b(X), X < 7$
$V_1 : v_1(T, U) \text{ :- } a(S, T), b(U), T \leq S, S \leq U$
$V_2 : v_2(T, U) \text{ :- } a(S, T), b(U), T \leq S, S < U$

The query $Q' : q(A, A) \text{ :- } v_1(A, A), A < 7$ is an equivalent rewriting of $Q$ using $V_1$. To see why, suppose we expand $Q'$ by replacing the view subgoal $v_1(A, A)$ by its definition. We get the expansion $Q'^{exp} : q(A, A) \text{ :- } a(S, A), b(A), A \leq S, S \leq A, A < 7$. By equating $S$ and $A$ we see that the expansion is equivalent to $Q$. Notice that the definitions of the views $V_1$, $V_2$ differ only on their second inequalities. However $V_2$ can not be used to answer $Q$. Thus, it is the comparison predicate that affects the existence of the rewriting.

Equivalent and contained rewritings use the containment test. Several algorithms have been proposed for testing containment in the presence of arithmetic comparisons [12, 10, 25, 4]. Some of these algorithms [10, 25] first normalize the queries by replacing constants and shared variables, each with new unique variables, and add arithmetic comparisons to equate those new variables to the original constants or shared variables. The containment is tested by checking a logical implication using multiple containment mappings. Another containment test existing in the literature is based on canonical databases [17, 12].

The problem of finding an equivalent rewriting (if there exists one) in the general case of ACs is decidable, yet still doubly exponential [3]. This complexity calls for an efficient algorithm which will perform better on average than the complete enumeration algorithm.

In this work we present an algorithm that, given a query and a set of views which are conjunctive queries with arithmetic comparisons, finds an equivalent rewriting if there exists one. The algorithm is sound and complete. Its efficiency lies in that it considers fewer candidate rewritings because it includes a preliminary test to decide for each view whether it is potentially useful in some rewriting. One of the challenges of our work consists in finding the relationship between the two problems; a) finding equivalent rewritings in the case of conjunctive queries with arithmetic comparisons and b) finding equivalent rewritings in the case of simple conjunctive queries. Such relation would allow us to leverage on existing algorithms for the latter problem. However this is not easy as we explain in detail in Subsection 3.1.

Another challenge comes from the following observation. In the case of conjunctive queries, if an equivalent rewriting exists in the language of union of conjunctive queries, then there exists one which is a single conjunctive query. However, in the case of conjunctive queries with arithmetic comparisons this property does not hold. Indeed even for very simple cases of conjunctive queries and views with arithmetic comparisons, it is often not possible to find equivalent rewritings in the form of a single conjunctive query with arithmetic comparisons. Instead, it is possible to find equivalent rewritings in the form of unions of conjunctive queries with arithmetic comparisons, as the following example illustrates.

*Example 2.* Consider the following query $Q$ and set of views $V_1$, $V_2$:

$Q : q() \mathbin{:\!-} p(X), X \geq 0$
$V_1 : v_1() \mathbin{:\!-} p(X), X = 0$
$V_2 : v_2() \mathbin{:\!-} p(X), X > 0$

It is easy to see that there is no conjunctive query which is an equivalent rewriting of $Q$ using $V_1$, $V_2$. Instead, the following union of conjunctive queries is an equivalent rewriting:

$r_0() \mathbin{:\!-} v_1()$
$r_0() \mathbin{:\!-} v_2()$

## 1.1 Related Work

The problem of answering queries using views is closely related to the problem of testing for query containment. Chandra and Merlin [6] have shown that the problems of containment, minimization, and equivalence of conjunctive queries are NP-complete. Klug in [12] showed that the containment problem for the class of conjunctive queries with arithmetic comparisons is in $\Pi_2^P$ which is the second level of the polynomial hierarchy introduced by Stockmeyer [23]. In the same work was also proved that when only left (or right) semi-interval comparisons are used, the containment problem is shown to be in NP. In a more recent work Afrati et al. [4] showed more classes of conjunctive queries with arithmetic comparisons for which the problem of query containment is in NP. Van der Meyden in [24] proved Klug's conjecture that containment for conjunctive queries with inequality arithmetic comparisons is $\Pi_2^P$-complete. He also pointed out that the containment problem for conjunctive queries with inequalities ($\neq$) is also $\Pi_2^P$-complete. The work in [13] studies the computational complexity of the query containment problem of queries with inequality ($\neq$). In fact, Kolaitis et al. proved that the complexity for the containment problem for safe conjunctive queries with inequalities ranges between coNP and $\Pi_2^P$-completeness depending on how many times each database predicate occurs in the body of the contained query. They also showed that when one of the two queries is fixed the problem can be DB-complete, where DB is the class of all decision problems that are the conjunction of a problem in NP and a problem in coNP.

The problem of finding whether there exists an equivalent rewriting for a query using views was studied in [14]. An efficient algorithm for finding equivalent rewritings with the smallest number of subgoals is given in [5]. The work in [16] considers the problem of answering conjunctive queries using infinite sets of views and they extend their results to cases when the query and the views use the built-in predicates $<, \leq, =$ and $\neq$.

The work in [1] shows how to find a Datalog maximally-contained rewriting (MCR) for a special case of Datalog queries and views that are unions of conjunctive queries. Several algorithms have been developed for finding rewritings of queries using views. The bucket algorithm [9, 15], the inverse-rule algorithm [8, 21, 1], the MiniCon algorithm [20], and the Shared-Variable-Bucket algorithm [18] are some of them (see [11] for a survey.) These algorithms aim at generating contained rewritings for a query that compute a subset of the answer to the query, and take the open-world assumption.

Afrati et al. in [2, 3] study the problem of query rewriting in the presence of arithmetic comparisons. They show that it is decidable to tell whether there exists an equivalent rewriting which is the union of conjunctive queries with arithmetic comparisons. They also investigate the existence of maximally contained rewritings in the presence of arithmetic comparisons and prove that for a special case of semi-interval comparisons there is a maximally contained rewriting.

## 2 Preliminaries

In this section we review the problem of query rewriting using views and summarize results in the literature on conjunctive queries with arithmetic comparisons. In the remainder of the paper we shall use names beginning with lower-case letters for constants and relations, and names beginning with upper-case letters for variables. We use $V, V_1, \ldots, V_m$ to denote views that are defined by conjunctive queries on the base relations. Moreover, for the sake of simplicity, we use "CQ" to represent "conjunctive query", "AC" for "arithmetic comparison", and "CQAC" for "conjunctive query with arithmetic comparisons".

### 2.1 Answering Queries Using Views

We start by reviewing the problem of answering queries using views for conjunctive queries (i.e., select-project-join queries). A conjunctive query CQ is a query of the form: $h(\overline{X}) \colonminus e_1(\overline{X}_1), \ldots, e_k(\overline{X}_k)$, where the head $h(\overline{X})$ represents the results of the query, and $e_1 \ldots e_k$ are database relations. Each atom in the body of a conjunctive query is said to be a *subgoal*. Every argument in the subgoal is either a variable or a constant. The variables in $\overline{X}$ are called *head* or *distinguished* variables, while the variables in $\overline{X}_i$ are called *body* variables of the query. A conjunctive query is said to be *safe* if all its distinguished variables also occur in its body. A query $Q_1$ *is contained* in a query $Q_2$, denoted $Q_1 \sqsubseteq Q_2$, if for any database $D$ of the base relations, the answer computed by $Q_1$ is a subset of the answer computed by $Q_2$, i.e., $Q_1(D) \subseteq Q_2(D)$. The two queries are *equivalent*, denoted $Q_1 \equiv Q_2$, if $Q_1 \sqsubseteq Q_2$ and $Q_2 \sqsubseteq Q_1$.

Chandra and Merlin [6] show that a conjunctive query $Q_1$ is contained in another conjunctive query $Q_2$ if and only if there is a containment mapping from $Q_2$ to $Q_1$. The containment mapping maps the head and all the subgoals in $Q_2$ to $Q_1$. It maps each variable to either a variable or a constant, and maps each constant to the same constant. Concerning unions of CQs, the following containment test is from [22]; a union of CQs $P_1 \cup \ldots \cup P_k$, is contained in a union of CQs $Q_1 \cup \ldots \cup Q_n$, denoted $P_1 \cup \ldots \cup P_k \sqsubseteq Q_1 \cup \ldots \cup Q_n$, iff for all $P_i$ there exists some $Q_j$ such that $P_i \sqsubseteq Q_j$.

Let $Q$ be a query defined on a database schema $S$, $V$ be a set of views defined on $S$, and $D$ be a database with the schema $S$. A query $R$ is a rewriting of the query $Q$ using the views in $V$ if the subgoals of $R$ are only view predicates defined in $V$ or interpreted predicates. The *expansion* of a query $P$ on a set of views $V$, denoted by $P^{exp}$, is obtained from $P$ by replacing all the views in $P$ with their corresponding base relations. Note that in the case of union of CQs the following holds: if $R = \cup R_i$, then $R^{exp} \equiv \cup(R_i^{exp})$.

Given a query $Q$ and a view set $V$, a query $P$ is a *contained rewriting* of query $Q$ using $V$ if $P$ uses only the views in $V$, and $P^{exp} \sqsubseteq Q$. That is, $P$ computes a partial answer to the query. Given a rewriting language $L$ (e.g., unions of conjunctive queries), we call $P$ an *equivalent rewriting* of $Q$ using $V$ w.r.t. $L$ if $P$ is in $L$, and $P^{exp} \equiv Q$. We call $P$ a *maximally-contained rewriting (MCR)* of $Q$ w.r.t. $L$ if (1) $P$ is a contained rewriting (in $L$) of $Q$, and (2) there is no contained rewriting $P_1$ (in $L$) of $Q$ such that $P_1$ properly contains $P$.

## 2.2 Conjunctive Queries with Arithmetic Comparisons

In this work we study the problem of rewriting a query using views when both the query and the views are of the following form:

$$h(\overline{X}) :\!- e_1(\overline{X}_1), \ldots, e_k(\overline{X}_k), C_1, \ldots, C_m$$

where each $C_i$ is an arithmetic comparison in the form $A_1 \theta A_2$, where $A_1$ and $A_2$ are variables or constants. The operator $\theta$ is one of the following: $<, \leq, =, >,$ or $\geq$. We call an arithmetic comparison *open* if its operator is $<$ or $>$ and *closed* if its operator is $\leq$ or $\geq$. We call the $e_i$'s *ordinary subgoals*, and the $C_i$'s *arithmetic comparison subgoals* (AC subgoals). In addition, the following assumptions must hold:

1) Values for the arguments in the arithmetic comparisons are chosen from an infinite, totally densely ordered set, such as the rationals or reals.

2) The arithmetic comparisons are not contradictory; that is, there exists an instantiation of the variables such that all the arithmetic comparisons are true.

3) All the comparisons are safe, i.e., each variable in the comparisons also appears in some ordinary subgoal.

## 2.3 Testing Containment of CQACs

When the queries and views are expressed as conjunctive queries (without arithmetic comparisons), we know how to find equivalent rewritings (if they exist) and maximally-contained rewritings (MCRs) that are unions of conjunctive queries (see [11] for a survey). However, arithmetic comparisons introduce many complications to the problem. In particular, both the containment mapping theorem [6] and the theorem for unions of CQs [22] no longer hold.

Let $Q_1$ and $Q_2$ be two conjunctive queries with arithmetic comparisons (CQACs). To test whether $Q_2 \sqsubseteq Q_1$ there are two most popular methods: a) the test of canonical databases [17, 12] and b) the test of Gupta and Zhang-Ozsoyoglu [10, 25]. In the following paragraphs we shortly review the first test, which we use extensively throughout the paper. Due to space limit, we refer the reader to [4] for more details about the second test. Before presenting the test, we briefly explain how to obtain a canonical database $D$ given a query $Q$: we turn each ordinary subgoal into a fact by replacing each variable in the body by a distinct constant, and treating the resulting subgoals as the only tuples in $D$.

We now describe the test of canonical databases [17, 12]. When dealing with CQACs we must consider the set of values in the database as belonging to a totally ordered set, e.g. the rationals or reals. This test produces an exponential number of canonical databases any one of which could be a counterexample to the containment. Suppose we want to test $Q_1 \sqsubseteq Q_2$. We do the following:

1) Consider all partitions of the variables of $Q_1$. For each partition $P$ consider all possible total orders of the members of the partition and assign to each member $b_i$ of $P$ a unique positive integer $n_i$ such that if $b_k, b_l \in P$ and $b_k < b_l$, then $n_k < n_l$. Then, substitute (freeze) every variable in each member $b_i$ of $P$ by the corresponding constant $n_i$. Thus we obtain a number of canonical databases $D_1, D_2, \ldots, D_n$, one database for each different order in each partition. Each $D_i$ consists of the frozen subgoals of $Q_1$ excluding the subgoals having comparison predicates.

2) Test whether for all $D_i$ that make the body of $Q_1$ true, $Q_2(D_i)$ includes the frozen head of $Q_1$. The frozen head of $Q_1$ is obtained by making the same substitution of constants for variables that yielded $D_i$.

3) $Q_1 \sqsubseteq Q_2$ if and only if (2) holds.

## 2.4 Known Decidability Results

The following two theorems from [2] prove the decidability of the problem we study in this work.

**Theorem 1.** *(CQAC equivalent rewritings) For a query and views that are conjunctive queries with arithmetic comparisons, it is decidable whether there is an* equivalent rewriting for the query using the views, where the rewriting is also a conjunctive query with arithmetic comparisons. If such an equivalent rewriting exists, there is an algorithm to find it.

**Theorem 2.** *(Union of CQAC equivalent rewritings) For a query and views that are conjunctive queries with arithmetic comparisons, it is decidable whether there is an equivalent rewriting for the query using the views, where the rewriting is a finite union of conjunctive queries with comparisons. If such an equivalent rewriting exists, there is an algorithm to find it.*

### 2.5 Technical Details

This subsection contains some technical points that are needed to understand the details of our algorithm. Let $D$ be the canonical database of the query $Q$ when ignoring the ACs and let $V(D)$ be the result of applying the view definitions $V$ on database $D$. For each tuple in $V(D)$, we "unfreeze" each introduced constant back to the original variable of $Q$, and obtain a set of view tuples $T(V)$.

A head homomorphism [20] of the head variables in a view is a partitioning of these variables, such that all the variables in each member of the partition are equated to a single variable. For a specific view, different head homomorphisms result in different view tuples.

Now we consider containment mappings from the ordinary subgoals of the query to the ordinary subgoals of the view. Let $\mu$ be one such mapping from some query subgoals to view subgoals. The definition of the *shared variable property* for $\mu$ is the following: whenever a query variable $X$ is mapped on a nondistinguished view variable, then all query subgoals that contain $X$ are in the domain of the mapping.

**Definition 1.** *We assume that the sets of variables in the query and the view definitions are disjoint. An MCD mapping (MiniCon Description [20]) $\mu$ is an one-to-one[1] containment mapping from the ordinary subgoals of the query to the ordinary subgoals of view $V$ which satisfies the shared variable property. Let $S$ be the set of query variables that are mapped to head variables of view $V$ under $\mu$. We rename each variable $X$ in $\mu(S)$ to $\mu^{-1}(X)$. Let $v$ be the head of view $V$ after this renaming. Then, we say that $\mu$ is an MCD mapping for view tuple $v$.*

Intuitively, an MCD mapping represents a fragment of a containment mapping from the query to the expansion of the rewriting. The way in which MCDs are constructed guarantees that these fragments can be combined seamlessly.

**Definition 2.** *Let $v_i$ and $v_j$ be view tuples of $V$ such that there is a containment mapping from $v_i$ to $v_j$. We say that $v_i$ is a more relaxed form of $v_j$.*

---
[1] This is the only difference with the algorithm in [20]. Here we consider one-to-one mappings because we are searching for equivalent rewritings whereas in [20] they are searching for MCR's.

**Definition 3.** *We call a nondistinguished variable $X$ in a view $V$ exportable if there is a head homomorphism $h$ for $V$, such that the inequalities in $h(V)$ imply that $X$ is equal to a distinguished variable in $V$.*

To find exportable nondistinguished variables in a view $V$, we use the ACs in $V$ to construct its inequality graph [12], denoted by $G(V)$. That is, for each variable or constant $A$ in ACs we create a node in the graph labelled with $A$. Then, for every comparison predicate $A\theta B$ where $\theta$ is $<$ or $\leq$, we introduce an edge labeled $\theta$ from $A$ to $B$. If there is a path from node $A$ to $C$, we have $A \leq C$. If there is a $<$-labeled edge on any path between $A$ and $C$, then $A < C$. We need the following concepts to show how to export a nondistinguished view variable.

**Definition 4.** *Let $X$ be a nondistinguished variable in a view $V$. The leq-set (less-than-or-equal-to set) of $X$, denoted by $S_\leq(V, X)$, includes all distinguished variables $Y$ of $V$ that satisfy the following conditions. There exists a path from $Y$ to $X$ in the inequality graph $G(V)$, and all edges on all paths from $Y$ to $X$ are labeled $\leq$. In addition, in all paths from $Y$ to $X$, there is no other distinguished variable except $Y$.*

Correspondingly, we define the geq-set (greater-than-or-equal-to set) of a variable $X$, denoted by $S_\geq(V, X)$. The following lemma from [2] can help us decide if a variable in a view $V$ is exportable.

**Lemma 1.** *A nondistinguished variable $X$ in view $V$ is exportable if and only if both $S_\leq(V, X)$ and $S_\geq(V, X)$ are nonempty.*

## 3 Finding Equivalent Rewritings of CQAC Queries Using CQAC Views

In the following paragraphs we present an algorithm that finds an equivalent rewriting (if there exists one) for queries that are CQAC using views that are also CQAC. Our algorithm consists of two phases. In the first phase we find all candidate rewritings that contain the query, while in the second phase we add constraints to the rewritings (obtained in the first phase) and we check whether these rewritings are contained in the query.

The efficiency of our algorithm is mainly based on the observations that if there exists an equivalent rewriting then there exists one which uses view subgoals out of a restricted search space of potentially useful view subgoals. These useful view subgoals are found by using techniques for finding rewritings of queries and views without arithmetic comparisons. In more detail, we use chase-like techniques [7,19,5] to find candidate useful subgoals and then we prune the space even further by using techniques used in finding maximally contained rewritings [20].

The main challenge of our algorithm however comes from the presence of arithmetic comparisons and the complications in testing query containment in this case. Due to these complications, existing algorithms cannot be used without modification as the discussion in the next subsection shows.

### 3.1 Technical Challenges

In the first phase of our algorithm we find rewritings using the views $V$ that contain the query $Q$. We begin by considering query $Q'$ and view $V'$ which result from $Q$ and $V$ after dropping the ACs. Then, we find maximally contained rewritings of $Q'$ using $V'$ and we ensure that these are also equivalent rewritings of $Q'$ using $V'$ by deleting the view tuples that are not more relaxed. In particular, we use the algorithm proposed in [20] adjusted to our setting as described in Subsection 3.2. Other known algorithms which compute either equivalent rewritings or maximally contained rewritings might also be used. In any case it is not straightforward how they can be useful. The reason is that these algorithms focus on rewritings which do not use redundant view subgoals or that are containment minimal [5]. The following two examples illustrate this point.

*Example 3.* Consider query $Q$ and set of views $V = \{V_1, V_2, V_3\}$:

$Q: q() \coloneq a(X_1, X_2), a(X_2, X_3), a(X_3, X_4), a(X_4, X_5), a(X_5, X_6), a(X_6, X_7),$
$\qquad a(X_7, X_1), X_2 > 5, X_7 < 8$
$V_1: v_1(X_1, X_4) \coloneq a(X_1, X_2), a(X_2, X_3), a(X_3, X_4), a(X_4, X_5), a(X_5, X_6),$
$\qquad a(X_6, X_7), a(X_7, X_1), X_3 > 5$
$V_2: v_2(X_3, X_5) \coloneq a(X_1, X_2), a(X_2, X_3), a(X_3, X_4), a(X_4, X_5), a(X_5, X_6),$
$\qquad a(X_6, X_7), a(X_7, X_1), X_4 < 8$
$V_3: v_3(X, Y) \coloneq a(X, X_2), a(X_2, Y)$

Note that $Q$ evaluates to *true* whenever there exists a closed path of length 7 in the database $D$ such that the conditions shown in Figure 1(a) hold for that path. We consider also the query $Q'$ which is defined as $Q$ with the ACs dropped and the views $V_1'$, $V_2'$, and $V_3'$ (with predicates $v_1'$, $v_2'$ and $v_3'$ respectively) which are the views $V_i$ without the ACs in their definition. For this last query $Q'$ the CoreCover algorithm [5] will find an equivalent rewriting $R'$ where:

$R': r() \coloneq v_1'(X, Y)$

However, if we use this rewriting and simply add ACs, we will not find an equivalent rewriting of the original query $Q$ using views $V_i$. Note that such an equivalent rewriting $R$ does exist and is the following:

$R: r() \coloneq v_1(X, Y), v_2(Z, X), v_3(Y, Z)$

This comes easily from Figure 1(b) which shows the two heptagons corresponding to the (expansions of the) atoms $v_1(X, Y)$ and $v_2(Z, X)$ with a common vertex labelled $X$. Notice also the path formed by the arcs $Y \to X_2''$ and $X_2'' \to Z$ corresponding to the (expansion of the) atom $v_3(Y, Z)$. Thus the Figure 1(b) represents the expansion of $R$. It is easy to see that $Q \sqsubseteq R$ since whenever $Q$ evaluates to true then so does $R$ (we can check it by considering twice the heptagon corresponding to instance of the body of $Q$). To check

# Finding Equivalent Rewritings in the Presence of Arithmetic Comparisons 951

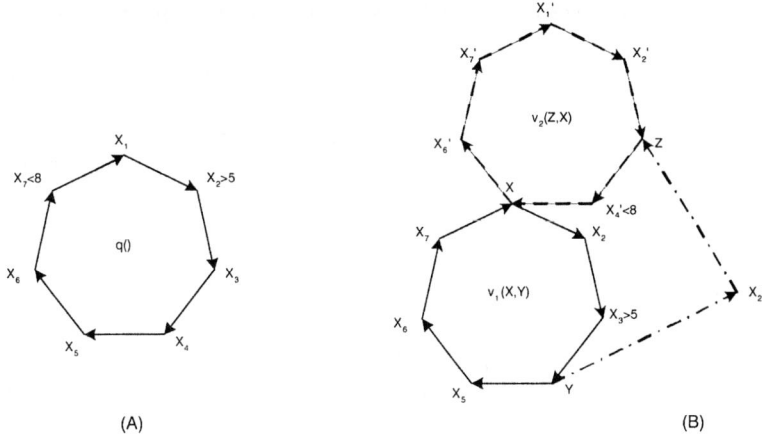

**Fig. 1.** Example 3

that $R \sqsubseteq Q$ notice that the heptagon with vertices $Z, X_4', X, X_2, X_3, Y, X_2''$ which is formed by the expansion of $R$ satisfies the properties required by the query $Q$. It is not straightforward that the heptagon fulfills the conditions of $Q$.

The rewriting: $R'' : r() :- v_1'(X,Y), v_2'(Z,X), v_3'(Y,Z)$ is an equivalent rewriting of $Q'$ using $V'$ and in fact it is the rewriting that our algorithm needs to use in order to find an equivalent rewriting of the given CQAC $Q$ using the views $V$. However, this rewriting would not have been computed by the existing algorithms since it contains the redundant subgoals $v_2'(Z,X)$ and $v_3'(Y,Z)$.

*Example 4.* Suppose we are given the following query and set of views:

$Q: q(X,Y) :- a(X,Z_1), a(Z_1,2), b(2,Z_2), b(Z_2,Y), Z_1 < 5, Z_2 > 8$
$V_1: v_1(X,Y) :- a(X,Z_1), a(Z_1,2), b(2,Z_2), b(Z_2,Y), Z_1 < 5$
$V_2: v_2(X,Y) :- a(X,Z_1), a(Z_1,2), b(2,Z_2), b(Z_2,Y), Z_2 > 8$

Note that an equivalent rewriting is

$R: r(X,Y) :- v_1(X,Y'), v_2(X',Y)$

We consider the query $Q'$ which is defined as query $Q$ with the ACs dropped and the views $V_1'$ and $V_2'$ which are the two views again without the ACs in their definition. In this case the rewriting of $Q'$ using $V'$ does not contain redundant subgoals. Still, it is not a containment minimal rewriting [5], i.e. there is another equivalent rewriting of $Q'$ using $V'$ which is the following:

$R' : r(X,Y) :- v_1(X,Y).$

However we cannot obtain from $R'$ an equivalent rewriting of $Q$ using $V$. Therefore we cannot use the algorithm in [5].

## 3.2 Phase 1: Construct Rewritings that Contain the Query

In Phase 1 we begin by creating all canonical databases of the query. For this we consider all total orders of the variables of the query and the constants of both the query and the views. Thus we obtain a number of canonical databases. Notice that the number of canonical databases is exponential in the number of variables. From these canonical databases we keep only those that compute the head of the query, or if the query is boolean, that make the body of the query true. Suppose $D_1, D_2, \ldots, D_k$ are these canonical databases. For every $D_i, i = 1, \ldots, k$ we compute the view tuples $T_i(V)$ by applying the view definitions $V$ on $D_i$ and restoring back the variables in the tuples. Note that the total order of each canonical database must satisfy the ACs of views; otherwise we omit the view tuples corresponding to the specific canonical database and view definition.

*Example 5.* Suppose we are given the following query $Q$ and the view $V$:

$Q: \; q(A) \;\text{:-}\; r(A), s(A, A), A \leq 8$
$V: \; v(Y, Z) \;\text{:-}\; r(X), s(Y, Z), Y \leq X, X \leq Z$

(Note that $P: \; p(A) \;\text{:-}\; v(A, A), A \leq 8$ is an equivalent rewriting of $Q$). To compute the sets of view tuples we first construct the canonical databases of $Q$ by considering all variables of $Q$ and all constants of both query and views:

$D_1 = \{r(a), s(a, a)\} : a < 8$
$D_2 = \{r(a), s(a, a)\} : a = 8$
$D_3 = \{r(a), s(a, a)\} : a > 8$

From these canonical databases we keep only $D_1, D_2$ as they compute (taking also into account the comparison predicates) the head of the query. To compute the view tuples corresponding to $D_1$ we apply the view definitions to $D_1$. We get $V(D_1) = \{v(a, a)\}$. Then, by restoring the constant $a$ back to the variable $A$ we get the set of view tuples $T_1(V) = \{v(A, A)\}$. Similarly, for the canonical database $D_2$, we get $T_2(V) = \{v(A, A)\}$.

Having computed $T_i(V)$ we proceed as follows. Let $Q_0$ be the query obtained by deleting the comparisons from $Q$, and let $V_0$ be the view obtained by deleting the comparisons from $V$ and exporting in the head of the view definition the *exportable variables* (Subsection 2.5, or see [4] for more details). Due to the different ways of exporting variables, it is possible that to one view in $V$ may correspond more than one view in $V_0$. The following example illustrates this point.

*Example 6.* Suppose we are given the following view definition:

$V: \; v(X, Y, W) \;\text{:-}\; a(X, Z_1), a(Z_1, Z_2), b(Z_2, Y, W), X \leq Z_1, W \leq Z_1, Z_1 \leq Y.$

By equating variable $X$ to variable $Y$ we obtain the view tuple $v_1$ and by equating variable $Y$ to variable $W$ we obtain the view tuple $v_2$. In both cases we export variable $Z_1$, in $v_1$ by equating $Z_1$ to $X$ and in $v_2$ by equating $Z_1$ to $Y$. That is:

$V_1: \; v_1(X, X, W) \;\text{:-}\; a(X, X), a(X, Z_2), b(Z_2, X, W)$
$V_2: \; v_2(X, Y, Y) \;\text{:-}\; a(X, Y), a(Y, Z_2), b(Z_2, Y, Y)$

We continue with an overview of the algorithm presented by Pottinger and Levy in [20] in order to make clear the contribution of our work. The algorithm in [20] consists of two phases. The first phase computes MCDs and populates the buckets accordingly. In the second phase the algorithm combines the content of the buckets to create MCRs. Our algorithm starts as the first phase of [20] but after this we do not proceed directly to the second phase. First, we delete those view tuples in the buckets that are not more relaxed forms of view tuples in $T_i(V)$. Then, we proceed to the second phase of [20] but only to get an answer to whether there exists an MCR. If it does not exist, our algorithm stops. If it does exist, then we output a rewriting $PR_i$ consisting of a conjunctive query with subgoals the content of all buckets. So to every canonical database corresponds only one rewriting.

The above procedure is repeated for every canonical database. If there exists a canonical database $D_i$ for which there is no maximally contained rewriting, then the algorithm stops and there is no equivalent rewriting of the query. If there is at least one maximally contained rewriting, then the output of the first phase of our algorithm is a set of *Pre-Rewritings* (denoted $PR_1, PR_2, \ldots, PR_k$), one for each canonical database. Figure 2 summarizes the steps of the first phase of our algorithm.

*Example 7.* (Continued from Example 5) There are two Pre-Rewritings $PR_1$, $PR_2$ corresponding to the two canonical databases $D_1$, $D_2$:

$PR_1(A) : -v(A, A)$
$PR_2(A) : -v(A, A)$

---

**Procedure Pre-Rewritings:**
Input: A CQAC $Q$ and a set $V$ of CQAC views.
Output: A set of Pre-Rewritings $PR_1, PR_2, ..., PR_k$ together with the corresponding canonical databases $D_1, D_2, ..., D_k$.
Method:
(1) Construct all canonical databases for $Q$ by taking into account the variables of $Q$ and all constants of the query and views. Construct also query $Q_0$ which is $Q$ with the ACs dropped, and a set $V_0$ of CQ views which is $V$ with the ACs dropped.
(2) Keep only those canonical databases which compute the head of $Q$.
(3) For every canonical database $D_i$ do:
  1. Compute the view tuples $T_i(V)$ by applying the view definitions $V$ on $D_i$.
  2. If for a canonical database $D_i$ it holds $T_k(D_k) = \emptyset$ then stop (as there is no rewriting).
  3. Run the first phase of [20] with respect to $Q_0$ and $V_0$ which populates the buckets.
  4. Delete from the buckets those tuples that are not more relaxed forms of view tuples in the $T_i(V)$.
  5. Run the second phase of [20]. If it produces an MCR continue, otherwise stop.
  6. Produce a Pre-Rewriting whose subgoals are all view tuples contained in the buckets.
  7. Output the Pre-Rewriting together with the corresponding canonical database.

---

**Fig. 2.** Phase 1 of our algorithm

In Proposition 1 we prove that each canonical database $D_i$ of the query must correspond to one CQAC $P_j^{exp}$ of $P$ which computes the query head on this canonical database.

**Proposition 1.** *Let $Q$ be a CQAC query. If there exists a union of CQAC $P = \cup P_i$ which is an equivalent rewriting of $Q$, then for every canonical database $D_i$ of $Q$, there exists a $P_j$ such that $P_j^{exp}$ computes the head of $Q$ in $D_i$.*

*Proof.* (sketch) The reason is that for every canonical database $D_i$ of the query, $P^{exp}$ must compute the head of the query on this canonical database. Therefore, there must exist a $P_j$ such that $P_j^{exp}$ computes the head of the query.

The view subgoals in the body of $P_j$ (the corresponding CQAC of canonical database $D_i$) as a consequence of Proposition 1 are necessarily more relaxed forms of view tuples in $T_i(V)$. Therefore, it suffices to restrict our search to view tuples in more relaxed forms than tuples in $T_i(V)$. Proposition 2 shows that by restricting ourselves to view tuples, that we compute in Phase 1, we do not lose solutions.

**Proposition 2.** *Let $Q$ be a CQAC query. Suppose there is an equivalent rewriting $P$ of $Q$ in the language of unions of CQACs using a set of CQAC views $V$. Then, there is a $P' = \cup P'_i$ which is an equivalent rewriting of $Q$ using views $V$ with the following property. There exists a canonical database $D$ on which $Q$ computes the head tuple such that any view (hence ordinary) subgoal of $P'_i$ maps on a view tuple in $D$.*

Proposition 3 shows that by restricting ourselves to view tuples in their more relaxed form that are part of an MCR CQAC we do not lose solutions.

**Proposition 3.** *Let $Q$ be a CQAC query. Suppose there is an equivalent rewriting $P$ of $Q$ in the language of union of CQACs using a set of CQAC views $V$. Then there is a $P'$ which is an equivalent rewriting of $Q$ using views $V$ with the following property. Let $P'_i$ be a CQAC in $P'$. Let $P'_i = P'_{i,0} + \beta_i$. Then $P'_{i,0}$ is a CQ in the MCR of $Q_0$ using $V_0$ possibly with redundant subgoals.*

Propositions 2 and 3 are partial results of the completeness of our algorithm and Lemma 2 is a partial result of soundness so far.

**Lemma 2.** *Let $Q$ be a CQAC query and $V$ a set of CQAC views. Let $D_i$, with $i = 1, \ldots, k$, be the canonical databases and $PR_i$, with $i = 1, \ldots, k$, the corresponding Pre-Rewritings obtained by procedure of Figure 2. Let $PR_i^{exp,V}$ be the expansion of $PR_i$ wrt $V$. Then $Q \sqsubseteq \cup PR_i^{exp,V}$.*

*Proof.* The proof of the lemma follows from the containment test for CQACs.

## 3.3 Phase 2: Construct Rewritings that Are Contained in the Query

The second phase performs two tasks: a) it constructs the candidate rewritings by adding constraints to the Pre-Rewritings $PR_i$ obtained in Phase 1, still preserving that the union of the new Pre-Rewritings still contains the query, b) it checks that the candidate rewritings are also contained in the query. In task a) to every $PR_i$ we add the constraints of the canonical database of $Q$ to which this Pre-Rewriting corresponds. We call these new Pre-Rewritings $PR'_i$. Then, in task b) we check the containment in the query by considering the expansions of all $PR'_i$s w.r.t. $V$ and constructing the canonical databases of these expansions. We keep only those canonical databases that compute the head of the expansion (or if the expansion is boolean, that make the body true). Note that the expansion contains constraints coming from the bodies of the view definitions too. So fresh variables may also appear. However these variables are used only for checking the containment in the query.

*Example 8.* (Continued from Example 7). To those Pre-Rewritings obtained in Phase 1 we add the total order of the corresponding canonical database. So we have the following Pre-Rewritings:

$PR'_1(A) :\!\!- v(A,A), A < 8$
$PR'_2(A) :\!\!- v(A,A), A = 8$

We then consider the expansion of $PR'_1$, and $PR'_2$:

$PR_1^{'exp}(A) :\!\!- r(X), s(A,A), A < 8, A \leq X, X \leq A$

which simplifies to

$PR_1^{'exp}(A) :\!\!- r(A), s(A,A), A < 8$

and,

$PR_2^{'exp}(A) :\!\!- r(X), s(A,A), A = 8, A \leq X, X \leq A$

which simplifies to

$PR_2^{'exp}(A) :\!\!- r(A), s(A,A), A = 8$

We proceed to the construction of the canonical databases of every $PR_i^{'exp}$ by considering all variables and constants of the expansion. Here, both $PR_i$'s have the same set of canonical databases.

$D_{1,1} = \{r(a), s(a,a)\} : a < 8$
$D_{1,2} = \{r(a), s(a,a)\} : a = 8$
$D_{1,3} = \{r(a), s(a,a)\} : a > 8$
$D_{2,1} = \{r(a), s(a,a)\} : a < 8$
$D_{2,2} = \{r(a), s(a,a)\} : a = 8$
$D_{2,3} = \{r(a), s(a,a)\} : a > 8$

We keep only the canonical databases that compute the head of the expansion of the rewriting. In this example we keep only the canonical databases $D_{1,1}, D_{2,2}$.

The last step of Phase 2 consists in checking the constraints for each $PR'_i$ through a two-column tableau constructed as follows. Each row corresponds to a canonical database of the expansion of $PR'_i$. We apply the query $Q$ on this canonical database and if the expansion head is computed, we place the

**Procedure Equivalent_rewritings:**
(1) Input: A set of Pre-Rewritings $PR_1, PR_2, ..., PR_k$ together with the corresponding canonical databases $D_1, D_2, ..., D_k$
(2) Output: An equivalent rewriting $R$
(3) Method:
1. For each $PR_i$ do:
   (a) Construct $PR'_i$ by adding the ACs of the canonical database $D_i$ to which $PR_i$ corresponds.
   (b) Consider the expansion $PR'^{exp}_i$ wrt V of $PR'_i$ and all its canonical databases.
   (c) Make a two-column tableau as follows: in the left column place the total order of all canonical databases created from the $PR'^{exp}_i$ in which $Q$ computes the head variable of $PR'^{exp}_i$. In the right column place the total order of the canonical databases created from the $PR'^{exp}_i$s in which $Q$ does not compute the head variable of $PR'^{exp}_i$.
2. If a constraint appears on the right column of the tableau, then the algorithm fails (there is no rewriting). If not, then output $R = \cup PR'_i$.

**Fig. 3.** Phase 2 of our algorithm

constraint corresponding to the total order of the canonical database in the left column of the tableau. Otherwise, we place the constraint in the right column. In the end, if there is at least one constraint on the right column of the tableau there is no equivalent rewriting to the query. Otherwise, the equivalent rewriting of $Q$ is the union of $PR'_i$. Figure 3 presents the steps of Phase 2.

*Example 9.* (Continued from Example 8). For every canonical database that we finally keep, we check the corresponding total order through the following tableau:

|           | Q satisfies db | Q does not satisfy db |
|-----------|----------------|----------------------|
| $D_{1,1}$ :| $a < 8$        |                      |
| $D_{2,2}$ :| $a = 8$        |                      |

Since no constraint appears on the right column of the tableau, then the equivalent rewriting $R$ to the query $Q$ consists of the union:

$r(A) :\!- v(A, A), A < 8$
$r(A) :\!- v(A, A), A = 8$

*Example 10.* This example illustrates the case when the algorithm detects that there is no equivalent rewriting and stops. Consider the query and view:

$Q : q(A) :\!- r(A), s(A, A), A \leq 8$
$V : v(Y, Z) :\!- r(X), s(Y, Z), Y \leq X, X < Z$

Phase 1: We construct the canonical databases of Q by considering all variables of Q and all constants of the query and views:

$D_1 = \{r(a), s(a, a)\} : a < 8$
$D_2 = \{r(a), s(a, a)\} : a = 8$
$D_3 = \{r(a), s(a, a)\} : a > 8$

We keep those canonical databases on which we compute the head of the query. That is, we keep only $D_1$, $D_2$. As $V(D_1) = V(D_2) = \emptyset$, the algorithm would stop in Phase 1, and the query has no equivalent rewriting.

### 3.4 Soundness and Completeness

To prove soundness and completeness of our algorithm we use Lemma 2 and Propositions 2 and 3 from Phase 1.

**Proposition 4.** *Let $PR_i$ be the Pre-Rewriting computed in Phase 1 of the algorithm corresponding to the canonical database $D_i$ of $Q$. Then, every $PR_i'^{exp}$ constructed in Phase 2 still computes the head of $Q$ in $D_i$. Hence, $Q \sqsubseteq \cup PR_i'^{exp}$.*

*Proof.* (sketch) The $PR_i'$s in Phase 2 are constructed from $PR_i$s by adding the constraints implied by the total order of the corresponding canonical database $D_i$ of $Q$. So the new constraints do not harm, and $\forall i$ $PR_i'^{exp}$ still computes the head of $Q$ in $D_i$.

So far we have proved that our algorithm is complete i.e. if there are rewritings equivalent to $Q$ with respect to the views in $V$, then our algorithm finds at least one. Lemma 3 proves that whenever our algorithm produces a rewriting then this rewriting is equivalent to the query.

**Lemma 3.** *Let $Q$ be a CQAC query and $V$ a set CQAC views. Let $PR = \cup PR_i$ be the set of Pre-Rewritings. When the algorithm does not fail then the output $R$ of the algorithm in Figure 3 is an equivalent rewriting of $Q$ using $V$.*

**Theorem 3.** *Given a query and views that are CQACs, our algorithm finds an equivalent rewriting (if there exists one) in the language of unions of CQACs.*

*Proof.* (sketch) Completeness: a consequence of Propositions 2, 3 and 4.
Soundness: a consequence of Lemma 3.

## 4 Experimental Results

In this section we present some of the experiments conducted to evaluate the efficiency of our algorithm. All the experiments were run on a machine with 3GHz Intel Pentium 4 processor with 512MB RAM and a 80GB hard disk, running the Windows XP operating system. Figure 4(a), (b) and (c) show that the runtime of the algorithm depends strongly on the number of distinct variables and constants in the CQAC queries and CQAC views rather than on the number of views.

Note that a completely naive full-enumeration algorithm would not have a chance because it would have to enumerate thousands of combinations of view tuples for a typical query. In simple words, we would not be able to draw the curves in the graphs as they would go nearly vertically.

In more detail, Figure 4(a) shows the dependence of the runtime on the number of views where the number of variables is kept constant (6 variables and

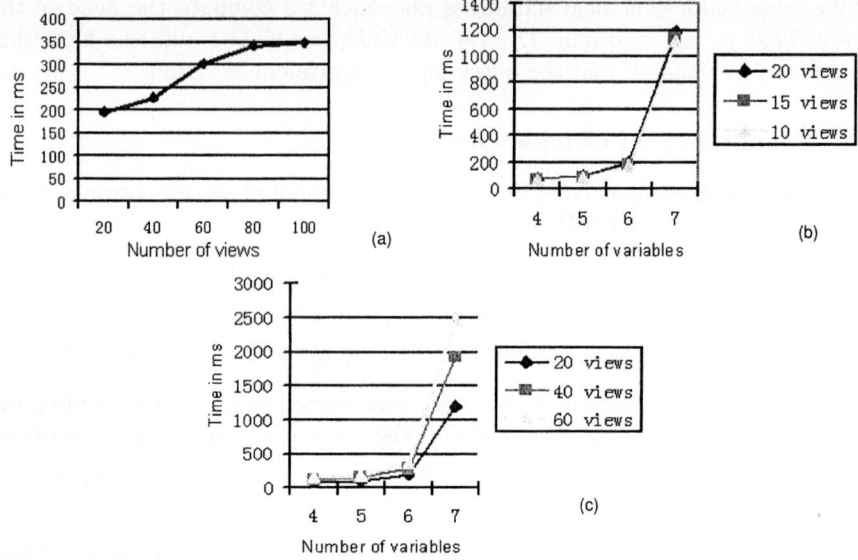

**Fig. 4.** Experimental results

constants). The graphs in Figures 4(b) and 4(c) present the dependence of our algorithm on both the number of the variables and the number of views. To be more precise, graph (b) gives the dependence for 10-20 views whereas graph (c) for 20-60 views.

## 5 Conclusions

The problem of rewriting queries using views in the presence of arithmetic comparisons is an important problem since users often need to pose queries containing inequalities. However the presence of arithmetic comparisons adds more complexities. The problem of finding an equivalent rewriting (if there exists one) in the presence of ACs is decidable. The doubly exponential complexity though calls for an efficient algorithm which will perform better on average than the complete enumeration algorithm.

In this work we present an algorithm which finds equivalent rewritings for conjunctive queries with arithmetic comparisons, and prove its correctness. Its efficiency lies in that it considers fewer candidate rewritings because it includes a preliminary test to decide for each view whether it is potentially useful in some rewriting. Experiments conducted to evaluate our algorithm proved its efficiency. In future work it would be interesting to investigate special cases in which our algorithm may have lower complexity, such as acyclic queries.

**Acknowledgments.** The authors would like to thank the students Manik Chandrachud and Dongfeng Chen who ran the experiments presented in this work.

# References

1. F. Afrati, M. Gergatsoulis, and T. Kavalieros. Answering queries using materialized views with disjunctions. In *ICDT*, pages 435–452, 1999.
2. F. Afrati, C. Li, and P. Mitra. Answering queries using views with arithmetic comparisons. In *PODS*, pages 209–220, 2002.
3. F. Afrati, C. Li, and P. Mitra. Rewriting queries using views in the presence of arithmetic comparisons. Technical report, UC Irvine, 2002.
4. F. Afrati, C. Li, and P. Mitra. On containment of conjunctive queries with arithmetic comparisons. In *EDBT*, pages 459–476, 2004.
5. F. Afrati, C. Li, and J. D. Ullman. Generating efficient plans for queries using views. In *SIGMOD*, pages 319–330, 2001.
6. A. K. Chandra and P. M. Merlin. Optimal implementation of conjunctive queries in relational data bases. In *STOC*, pages 77–90, 1977.
7. A. Deutsch. *XML Query Reformulation over Mixed and Redundant Storage*. PhD thesis, University of Pennsylvania, 2002.
8. O. M. Duschka and M. R. Genesereth. Answering recursive queries using views. In *PODS*, pages 109–116, 1997.
9. G. Grahne and A. O. Mendelzon. Tableau techniques for querying information sources through global schemas. In *ICDT*, pages 332–347, 1999.
10. A. Gupta, Y. Sagiv, J. D. Ullman, and J. Widom. Constraint checking with partial information. In *PODS*, pages 45–55, 1994.
11. A. Y. Halevy. Answering queries using views: A survey. *VLDB Journal*, 10(4):270–294, 2001.
12. A. Klug. On conjunctive queries containing inequalities. *Journal of the ACM*, 35(1):146–160, 1988.
13. P. G. Kolaitis, D. L. Martin, and M. N. Thakur. On the complexity of the containment problem for conjunctive queries with built-in predicates. In *PODS*, pages 197–204, 1998.
14. A. Levy, A. O. Mendelzon, Y. Sagiv, and D. Srivastava. Answering queries using views. In *PODS*, pages 95–104, 1995.
15. A. Levy, A. Rajaraman, and J. J. Ordille. Querying heterogeneous information sources using source descriptions. In *VLDB*, pages 251–262, 1996.
16. A. Levy, A. Rajaraman, and J. Ullman. Answering queries using limited external processors. In *PODS*, pages 227–234, 1996.
17. A. Levy and Y. Sagiv. Queries independent of updates. In *VLDB*, pages 171–181, 1993.
18. P. Mitra. An algorithm for answering queries efficiently using views. In *Proceedings of the Australasian Database Conference*, pages 99–106, 2001.
19. L. Popa. *Object/Relational Query Optimization with Chase and Backchase*. PhD thesis, University of Pennsylvania, 2000.
20. R. Pottinger and A. Halevy. A scalable algorithm for answering queries using views. *VLDB Journal*, 10(2-3):182–198, 2001.
21. X. Qian. Query folding. In *ICDE*, pages 48–55, 1996.

22. Y. Sagiv and M. Yannakakis. Equivalences among relational expressions with the union and difference operators. *Journal of the ACM*, 27(4):633–655, 1980.
23. L. J. Stockmeyer. The polynomial-time hierarchy. *Theoretical Computer Science*, 3:1–22, 1977.
24. R. van der Meyden. The complexity of querying indefinite data about linearly ordered domains. In *PODS*, pages 331–345, 1992.
25. X. Zhang and M. Z. Ozsoyoglu. On efficient reasoning with implication constraints. In *DOOD*, pages 236–252, 1993.

# Fast Computation of Reachability Labeling for Large Graphs

Jiefeng Cheng[1], Jeffrey Xu Yu[1], Xuemin Lin[2], Haixun Wang[3], and Philip S. Yu[3]

[1] The Chinese University of Hong Kong, China
{jfcheng, yu}@se.cuhk.edu.hk
[2] University of New South Wales & NICTA, Australia
lxue@cse.unsw.edu.au
[3] T. J. Watson Research Center, IBM, USA
{haixun, psyu}@us.ibm.com

**Abstract.** The need of processing graph reachability queries stems from many applications that manage complex data as graphs. The applications include transportation network, Internet traffic analyzing, Web navigation, semantic web, chemical informatics and bio-informatics systems, and computer vision. A graph reachability query, as one of the primary tasks, is to find whether two given data objects, $u$ and $v$, are related in any ways in a large and complex dataset. Formally, the query is about to find if $v$ is reachable from $u$ in a directed graph which is large in size. In this paper, we focus ourselves on building a reachability labeling for a large directed graph, in order to process reachability queries efficiently. Such a labeling needs to be minimized in size for the efficiency of answering the queries, and needs to be computed fast for the efficiency of constructing such a labeling. As such a labeling, 2-hop cover was proposed for arbitrary graphs with theoretical bounds on both the construction cost and the size of the resulting labeling. However, in practice, as reported, the construction cost of 2-hop cover is very high even with super power machines. In this paper, we propose a novel geometry-based algorithm which computes high-quality 2-hop cover fast. Our experimental results verify the effectiveness of our techniques over large real and synthetic graph datasets.

## 1 Introduction

Consider a reachability query querying whether a node $v$ is reachable from node $u$ in a large directed graph, $G$. There are several possible yet feasible solutions for efficiently answering such a query, as indicated in [2]. Those solutions include i) maintaining the transitive closure of edges, which results in high storage consumption, and ii) computing the shortest path from $u$ to $v$ over such a large graph on demand, which results high query processing cost. A 2-hop reachability labeling, or 2-hop cover, was proposed by Cohen et al, as a feasible solution, to answer such reachability queries [2]. The key issue is how to minimize such a 2-hop cover, because the minimum 2-hop cover leads to the efficiency of answering reachability queries. The problem is shown to be NP-hard, because minimum 2-hop cover is a minimum set cover problem. Cohen et al proposed an approximation solution. The theoretical bound on the size of 2-hop cover is also provided. Despite the excellence of the theoretical bound on the time complexity, the cost for computing the minimum 2-hop cover is high when dealing with large graphs. In [19], Schenkel, Theobald and Weikum run Cohen et al's algorithm on a 64 processor Sun Fire-15000 server with 180 gigabyte memory for a subset of *DBLP* which consists of 344,992,370 connections. It took 45 hours and 23 minutes using 80 gigabytes of memory to find the 2-hop cover which is in size of 1,289,930 entries. The long construction time makes it difficult to construct such a 2-hop cover for large graphs.

The main contribution of our work in this paper are summarized below.

- We propose a set cover I solution (*SCI*) instead Cohen et al's set cover II solution (*SCII*) [8], where *SCI* minimizes the number of subsets in a set cover and *SCII* minimizes the overlapping among subsets in a set cover. We show evidences that *SCI* can achieve a similar satisfactory level as *SCII* as to minimize the 2-hop cover for a large graph, and at the same time can compute 2-hop cover efficiently.
- We propose a novel geometry-based algorithm to further improve the efficiency of computing 2-hop cover. The two main features of our solution are given below. First, we do not need to compute transitive closure as required in all algorithms that need to compute 2-hop. Second, we map the 2-hop cover problem onto a two-dimensional grid, and compute 2-hop using operations against rectangles with help of a R-tree.
- We conducted extensive experimental studies using different graph generators, and real datasets, with different parameter settings. Our results support our approach as it can significantly improve the efficiency of finding 2-hop cover for large graphs.

The remainder of this paper is organized as follows. Section 2 gives the definition of the 2-hop cover problem. Section 3 discusses our motivation of solving the 2-hop cover problem using a set cover I solution [8] instead of the set cover II solution used in Cohen et al's study [2]. Our work is motivated by the main requirements of the 2-hop cover problem: minimization of the 2-hop cover and minimization of processing time. Section 4 discusses a new geometry-based approach as a set cover I solution to the 2-hop cover problem. Experimental results are presented in Section 5 followed by related work in Section 6. Finally, Section 7 concludes the paper.

## 2 Problem Definition

The 2-hop reachability labeling is defined in [2]. We introduce it below in brief. Let $G = (V, E)$ be a directed graph. A 2-hop reachability labeling on graph $G$ assigns every node $v \in V$ a label $L(v) = (L_{in}(v), L_{out}(v))$, where $L_{in}(v), L_{out}(v) \subseteq V$ such as every node $x$ in $L_{in}(v)$ connects to every node $y$ in $L_{out}(v)$ via the node $v$. A node $v$ is reachable from a node $u$, denoted $u \leadsto v$, if and only if $L_{out}(u) \cap L_{in}(v) \neq \emptyset$. The size of the 2-hop reachability labeling over a graph $G(V, E)$, is given as $L$, below.

$$L = \sum_{v \in V(G)} |L_{in}(v)| + |L_{out}(v)| \qquad (1)$$

In order to solve the 2-hop reachability labeling, Cohen et al. introduced 2-hop cover, which is given below [2].

**Definition 1.** *(2-hop cover) Given a directed graph $G = (V, E)$. Let $P_{u \leadsto v}$ be a set of paths from node $u$ to node $v$ in $G$, and $P$ be a set of all such $P_{u \leadsto v}$ in $G$. A hop, $h_u$, is defined as $h_u = (p_u, u)$, where $p_u$ is a path in $G$ and $u$ is one of the endpoints of $p_u$. A 2-hop cover, denoted $H$, is a set of hops that covers $P$, such as, if node $v$ is reachable from node $u$ then there exists a path $p$ in the non-empty $P_{u \leadsto v}$ where the path $p$ is concatenation of $p_u$ and $p_v$, denoted $p = p_u p_v$, and $h_u = (p_u, u)$ and $h_v = (p_v, v)$.*

The 2-hop reachability labeling can be derived from a 2-hop cover [2]. In addition, the size of the 2-hop cover, $|H|$, for a graph $G$, is the same as that of 2-hop reachability labeling ($|H| = L$).

The 2-hop cover problem is to find the minimum size of 2-hop cover for a given graph $G(V, E)$, which is proved to be NP-hard [2]. Cohen et al show that a greedy algorithm exists to compute a nearly optimal solution for the 2-hop cover problem. The resulting size of the greedy algorithm is larger than the optimal at most $O(\log n)$. The basic idea is to solve the minimum 2-hop cover problem as a minimum set cover problem [8]. Note: in the corresponding minimum set cover problem, a set is a set of edges.

We illustrate Cohen et al's algorithm in Algorithm 1. We call it *MaxDSCovering*. In Algorithm 1, it initializes the 2-hop cover $H$ (line 1), and computes the transitive closure, $T$, for the given graph $G$ (line 2). Here, $T$ is treated as the ground set of the minimum set cover problem. The main body of the algorithm is a while loop, which repeatedly finds hops until $T$ becomes empty (line 3-14). The 2-hop cover is returned in line 15. In line 5-10, it finds a densest bipartite graph, $B$, which has node $w$ as its virtual center, by calling a function *denSubGraph*. In *denSubGraph*, the densest bipartite graph is constructed, based on a node $w$, in two main steps.

- Construct a bipartite graph $B_C(V_C, E_C)$ where $V_C = V_{C_{in}} \cup V_{C_{out}}$, based on node $w$, such as

$$V_{C_{in}} = \{u \mid (u, w) \in T\} \cup \{w\} \quad (2)$$
$$V_{C_{out}} = \{v \mid (w, v) \in T\} \cup \{w\} \quad (3)$$

and

$$E_C = V_{C_{in}} \times V_{C_{out}} \quad (4)$$

The sets, $V_{C_{in}}$ and $V_{C_{out}}$, are all connected via the virtual center $w$, respectively.
- Find the densest bipartite graph, denoted $B(V, E)$, where $V = V_{in} \cup V_{out}$, from $B_C$, such as

$$\max_{\substack{V_{in} \subseteq V_{C_{in}} \\ V_{out} \subseteq V_{C_{out}} \\ E \subseteq E_C}} \frac{|E \cap T'|}{|V_{in}| + |V_{out}|} \quad (5)$$

where $T'$ is the set of uncovered edges. Note: finding the minimum set over is equivalent to find the densest subgraph [2], as illustrated in Eq. (5). As a densest subgraph problem, it can be solved in polynomial time [5].

The candidate bipartite graph $B$ with the highest score (Eq. (5)), after checking every node in $G$, is identified after line 10. In line 11-12, new hops are added into the 2-hop cover, based on $B$. After it, the set of edges of $B$, denoted $\mathcal{E}(B)$ will be removed from $T'$.

**Algorithm 1.** *MaxDSCovering(G)*

**Input:** graph, $G(V, E)$.
**Output:** 2-hop cover, $H$.

1: $H \leftarrow \emptyset$;
2: $T' \leftarrow T \leftarrow \{(u, v) \mid P_{u \rightsquigarrow v} \neq \emptyset\}$;
3: **while** $T' \neq \emptyset$ **do**
4:     $\tau \leftarrow 0$;
5:     **for all** $w \in V$ **do**
6:        $\mathcal{B} \leftarrow denSubGraph(w, T, T')$ with a score $c_w$; $\{B(V, E)$ is a bipartite graph with $V = \mathcal{V}_{in} \cup \mathcal{V}_{out}.\}$
7:        **if** $c_w > \tau$ **then**
8:           $v_b \leftarrow w$;    $\tau \leftarrow c_w$;    $\mathcal{B} \leftarrow B$;
9:        **end if**
10:    **end for**
11:    **for all** $u \in \mathcal{V}_{in}$ of $\mathcal{B}$ **do** $H \leftarrow H \cup \{(u \rightsquigarrow v_b, u)\}$;
12:    **for all** $v \in \mathcal{V}_{out}$ of $\mathcal{B}$ **do** $H \leftarrow H \cup \{(v_b \rightsquigarrow v, v)\}$;
13:    $T' \leftarrow T' \setminus \mathcal{E}(\mathcal{B})$;
14: **end while**
15: **return** $H$;

## 3 A Set Cover I Solution

Cohen et al. solve (approximate) the minimum 2-hop cover problem as a minimum set cover problem with a theoretical bound on the time complexity, $O(n^4)$ where $n$ is the number of nodes in the graph $G$. However, it is challenging to compute such a 2-hop cover for very large graphs because the algorithm is CPU intensive as reported in [18, 19]. Also, it needs to precompute the transitive closure which requires large memory space. Recall, in [19], Schenkel, Theobald and Weikum run Cohen et al's algorithm on a 64 processor Sun Fire-15000 server with 180 gigabyte memory for a subset of *DBLP* which consists of 344,992,370 connections. It took 45 hours and 23 minutes using 80 gigabytes of memory to find the 2-hop cover which is in size of 1,289,930 entries.

The minimum set cover problem used in *MaxDSCovering* is called a minimum set cover II problem, denoted *SCII*, in [8]. *SCII* is to find a set cover which has the least overlapping, and shares the same goal as 2-hop cover problem's. In [8], Johnson also gave a set cover I problem, denoted *SCI*, which is to minimize the cardinality. Here, consider a set of subsets $S_1, S_2, \cdots, S_m$, over a finite set $S \ (= \cup_i S_i)$. The minimum set cover I (*SCI*) is to find a smallest set of sets, denoted $\mathcal{S}$, such as $\cup_j S_j = S$ for $S_j \in \mathcal{S}$. The two set cover problems, *SCI* and *SCII*, are different. The optimal solution for one may not be the optimal solution for the other.

In this paper, we show that the minimum 2-hop cover problem can be solved using *SCI* effectively. By effectiveness, we mean that the size of 2-hop set identified by *SCI* is very similar to the size of 2-hop set identified by *SCII*, in practice, using greedy algorithms, when handling large graphs.

We propose an algorithm called *MaxCardinality*. The algorithm is the same as *MaxDSCovering* after replacing Eq. (5) with the following equation Eq. (6), for finding

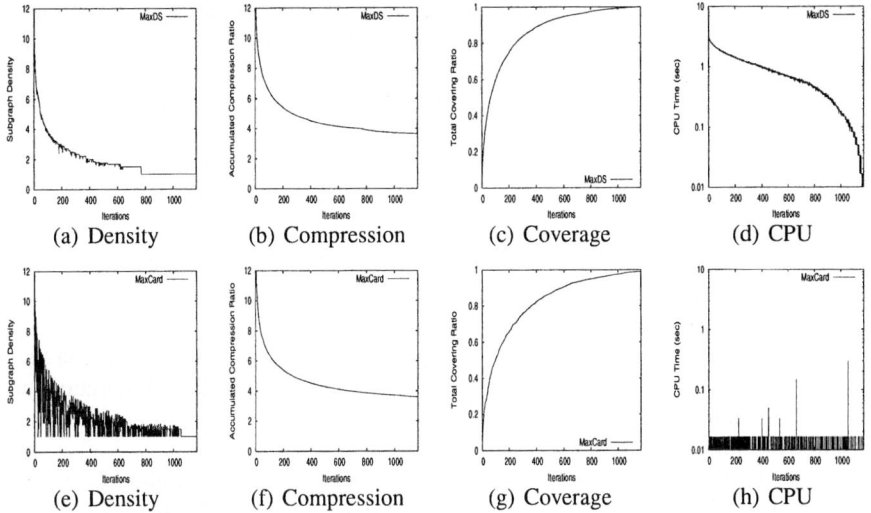

**Fig. 1.** *SCII* vs *SCI* over a Directed Acyclic Graph ($|V| = 2,000, |E| = 4,000$)

a bipartite subgraph $B(V, E)$ from a bipartite graph $B_C(V_C, E_C)$ where $V = V_{in} \cup V_{out}$. As the name of the algorithm indicates, it is to maximize the cardinality of the edges (uncovered paths) in each bipartite graph.

$$\max_{\substack{V_{in} \subseteq V_{C_{in}} \\ V_{out} \subseteq V_{C_{out}} \\ E \subseteq E_C}} |E \cap T'| \quad (6)$$

where $T'$ is the uncovered set.

We show the similarities and differences between the two solutions, namely, *SCI* and *SCII*, in Fig. 1, using a random graph, $G(V, E)$ where $|V| = 2,000$ and $|E| = 4,000$, generated by a graph generator [9]. In Fig. 1, it compares *MaxCardinality* (a *SCI* solution) with *MaxDSCovering* (a *SCII* solution). The figures (a)-(d) are for *MaxDSCovering*, and the figures (e)-(h) are for *MaxCardinality*. Note: both algorithms are the same as shown in Algorithm 1 except that *MaxDSCovering* uses Eq. (5) and *MaxCardinality* uses Eq. (6) for identifying a subgraph.

– In Fig. 1 (a) and (e), we show the density of the subgraph found in *MaxCardinality* and *MaxDSCovering* ($\mathcal{B}(\mathcal{V}, \mathcal{E})$ in Algorithm 1). The density (y-axis) is $|\mathcal{E}|/(|\mathcal{V}_{in}|+|\mathcal{V}_{out}|)$ where $\mathcal{V} = \mathcal{V}_{in} \cup \mathcal{V}_{out}$. It is important to note that *MaxCardinality* does not use it to compute, but uses it to measure its density per iteration, in comparison with *MaxDSCovering*.

*MaxDSCovering* decreases monotonically, because it always finds the best densest subgraph per iteration (Fig. 1 (a)). *MaxCardinality* decreases globally, but shows fluctuation patterns (Fig. 1 (e)), because it cannot find the best densest subgraph per iteration. However, one very important observation is that *MaxCardinality* can find a more dense graph than former selected ones in one of the following iterations

after it misses a densest graph in some iteration. If we compare the two subfigures, *MaxCardinality* sometime outperforms *MaxDSCovering* in many iterations for this reason.
- In Fig. 1 (b) and (f), we show the accumulated compression ratio, $|T_i|/H_i$, where $T_i$ is the transitive closure that has been covered already at the $i$-th iteration, and $H_i$ is the 2-hop cover for $T_i$. Both figures are almost the same. It shows that the 2-hop cover can be solved effectively using a *SCI* solution. For this graph, the size of the transitive closure, $T$, is $|T| = 24,888$. The sizes of the 2-hop covers found by *MaxDSCovering* and *MaxCardinality* are, 6,840 and 7,089. The difference is 249. The compression rate of the 2-hop covers by *MaxDSCovering* and *MaxCardinality* are, 0.27 (6,800/248,88) and 0.28 (7,089/24,888).
- In Fig. 1 (c) and (g), we show the coverage of the graph up to the $i$-th iteration, $|T_i|/|T'_i|$, where $T_i$ is the transitive closure being covered at the $i$-th iteration, and $T'$ is the transitive closure that has not been covered up to the $i$-th iteration. Both share the similar trend.
- In Fig. 1 (d) and (h), we show the CPU time spent in every iteration. Due to the difference between *SCI* (Eq. (5)) and *SCII* (Eq. (6)), *MaxCardinality* spends much less time than *MaxDSCovering*.

The above discussions show that a *SCI* solution can effectively and efficiently solve the minimum 2-hop cover problem.

## 4 A Fast Geometry-Based Algorithm for the Set Cover I Solution

In this section, we show that we can significantly improve the efficiency of *MaxCardinality* (a *SCI* solution) by solving it over a 2-dimensional space using simple operations against rectangles.

The outline of our approach is given below. First, for a given directed graph $G$, we construct a directed acyclic graph, denoted $G_\downarrow$. Second, we compute the 2-hop cover for the directed acyclic graph $G_\downarrow$. Third, we compute the 2-hop cover for the directed graph $G$ using the 2-hop cover obtained for $G_\downarrow$, in a simple post-processing step. Below, we discuss the first step, and the third step and will discuss the second step in the following subsections.

**Directed acyclic graph construction:** Given a directed graph $G(V, E)$, we identify its strongly connected components, $C_1, C_2, \cdots$ efficiently, in the order of $O(|V| + |E|)$ [4]. Note: any two nodes are reachable if they are in the same strongly connected component, $C_i$. The directed acyclic graph $G_\downarrow(V_\downarrow, E_\downarrow)$ is constructed as follows. A node $v \in V_\downarrow$ represents either a strongly connected component, $C_i$ or a node in $G$. If $v$ represents a strongly connected component $C_i$, we randomly select one of the nodes in $C_i$, denoted $v'$, as the representative in $V_\downarrow$. All other nodes in $C_i$ will not appear in $V_\downarrow$. All the edges between the nodes in the strongly connected component $C_i$ will not appear in $E_\downarrow$; all edges going into/from the strongly component, $C_i$, will be represented as edges going into/from the node $v'$ in $E_\downarrow$. If $v$ represents a node in $G$, which is not involved in any strongly connected component, the node will be added into $V_\downarrow$, and the corresponding edges going into/from $v$ appear in $E_\downarrow$. The conversion of $G$ to $G_\downarrow$ can be done as the same time when finding strongly connected components as a by-product.

**Generation of 2-hop cover for $G$ upon the 2-hop cover for $G_\downarrow$:** Recall in a strongly component $C_i$, any two nodes, $u$ and $v$, are reachable such as $u \rightsquigarrow v$ and $v \rightsquigarrow u$. Therefore, they share the same 2-hop. Suppose that we know the 2-hop for a node $u$ in a strongly connected component, $C_i$, all the nodes in $C_i$ should have the same 2-hop. The 2-hops can be simply added for connecting nodes in a single strongly component.

## 4.1 Computing 2-Hop Cover for a Directed Acyclic Graph

In the following subsections, we explain how to compute 2-hop cover for a directed acyclic graph. The main techniques are: 1) to map a reachability between $u \rightsquigarrow v$ onto a grid point in a 2-dimensional grid, 2) map a bipartite graph with a virtual center into rectangles, and 3) compute the densest bipartite graph, based on Eq. (6), as to compute the largest area of rectangles. Note: R-tree can be used to assist the last step.

Below, in Section 4.2, we introduce an efficient approach [1] which computes an interval labeling for reachability over a directed acyclic graph. Note: there is no need to compute transitive closure. We will discuss space complexity between the interval labeling and 2-hop labeling in our experimental studies. In Section 4.3, we discuss a 2-dimensional reachability map, which is constructed using the interval labeling [1]. The reachability information is preserved completely in the map. In Section 4.4, we give our algorithm, and explain it using an example.

## 4.2 An Interval Based Reachability Labeling for Directed Acyclic Graphs

Agrawal et al [1] proposed a method for labeling directed acyclic graphs using intervals. The labeling is done in three steps for a directed acyclic graph, $G_D$. 1) Construct an optimum tree-cover $\mathcal{T}$. An optimum tree-cover is defined as to minimize the number of intervals. 2) Every node, $v$, in $\mathcal{T}$ is labeled using an internal $[s, e]$. A node $v$ has a unique *postorder number*, denoted $po$, which is the number assigned following a postorder traversal of the tree starting from 1. The $e$ value in $[s, e]$ for a node $v$ is the postorder number of the node $v$, and the $s$ value in the interval is the smallest postorder number of its descendants, where $s = e$ if $v$ is a leaf node. 3) After $\mathcal{T}$ is labeled, it examines all nodes of $G_D$ in the reverse topological order. During the traversal, for each node $u$, add all the intervals associated with $v$, if there exists an edge $(u, v)$, into the interval associated with $u$. An interval can be eliminated if it is contained in another. Let $I_u$ be a list of intervals assigned to a node $u$. Suppose there are two nodes $u$ and $v$ where $I_u = \{[s_1, e_1], [s_2, e_2], \cdots, [s_n, e_n]\}$, and $I_v = \{[s'_1, e'_1], [s'_2, e'_2], \cdots, [s'_m, e'_m]\}$. There exists a path from $u$ to $v$ iff the postorder of $v$ is in an interval, $[s_j, e_j]$, of $u$.

## 4.3 A 2-Dimensional Reachability Map

First, we show how to construct a 2-dimensional reachability map, $M$. With the help of $M$, we want to check $u \rightsquigarrow v$ in a directed acyclic graph, $G_\downarrow$, quickly, using a function $f(u, v)$, such as $f(u, v) = 1$ iff $u \rightsquigarrow v$, and $f(u, v) = 0$ iff $u \not\rightsquigarrow v$.

The construction of the reachability map is done using two interval labelings obtained on the directed acyclic graph, $G_\downarrow(V_\downarrow, E_\downarrow)$, on which we are going to compute its 2-hop cover, and another auxiliary directed acyclic graph, $G_\uparrow(V_\uparrow, E_\uparrow)$, respectively.

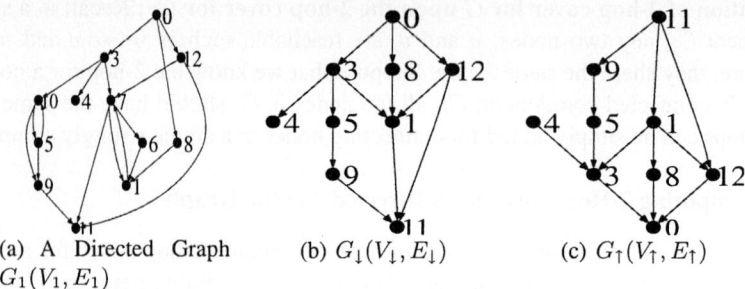

(a) A Directed Graph $G_1(V_1, E_1)$

(b) $G_\downarrow(V_\downarrow, E_\downarrow)$

(c) $G_\uparrow(V_\uparrow, E_\uparrow)$

**Fig. 2.** A directed graph, and its two directed acyclic graphs, $G_\downarrow$ and $G_\uparrow$

**Table 1.** A Reachability Table for $G_\downarrow$ and $G_\uparrow$

| $w$ | $G_\downarrow$ | | $G_\uparrow$ | |
|---|---|---|---|---|
|  | $po_\downarrow(w)$ | $I_\downarrow(w)$ | $po_\uparrow(w)$ | $I_\uparrow(w)$ |
| 0 | 9 | [1,9] | 4 | [4,4] |
| 1 | 1 | [1,1],[3,3] | 3 | [1,5] |
| 3 | 6 | [1,6] | 5 | [4,5] |
| 4 | 2 | [2,2] | 9 | [4,5],[9,9] |
| 5 | 5 | [3,5] | 6 | [4,6] |
| 8 | 7 | [1,1],[3,3],[7,7] | 1 | [1,1],[4,4] |
| 9 | 4 | [3,4] | 7 | [4,7] |
| 11 | 3 | [3,3] | 8 | [1,8] |
| 12 | 8 | [1,1],[3,3],[8,8] | 2 | [2,2],[4,4] |

Note: $G_\uparrow(V_\uparrow, E_\uparrow)$ can be easily obtained from $G_\downarrow(V_\downarrow, E_\downarrow)$, such as $V_\uparrow = V_\downarrow$, and a corresponding edge $(v, u) \in E_\uparrow$ if $(u, v) \in E_\downarrow$. In brief, for a node, $u$, the former can tell which nodes $u$ can reach, and the latter can tell which nodes can reach $u$, fast. For the pair of graphs, $G_\downarrow$ and $G_\uparrow$, we compute the postorder numbers ($op_\downarrow$ and $op_\uparrow$) and interval labels ($I_\downarrow$ and $I_\uparrow$), using Agrawal et al's algorithm efficiently [1]. We store them in a table, called a *reachability table*.

**Example 1.** *As a running example, a random directed graph, $G_1(V_1, E_1)$, with 12 nodes and 19 edges, is shown in Fig. 2 (a). There are two strongly connected components. One is among nodes 10 and 5, the other is among nodes 1, 6 and 7.*

Consider the example graph $G_1$ (Fig. 2 (a)). Its two directed acyclic graphs, $G_\downarrow$ and $G_\uparrow$, are shown in Fig. 2 (b) and (c), respectively. In $G_\downarrow$, there are only 9 nodes out of 12 nodes in $G_1$, because there are two strongly connected components. One is among nodes 5 and 10, and the other is among 1, 6 and 7. We select 5 and 1 as the representatives for the former and latter strongly connected components in $G_\downarrow$. The corresponding reachability table is shown in Table 1. In Table 1, the first column is the node identifiers in $G_1$ (Fig. 2 (a)). The second and third columns are the postorder number and the intervals for $G_\downarrow$, and the fourth and fifth columns are the postorder number and the intervals for $G_\uparrow$.

We can virtually represent the reachability table, as an $n \times n$-grid reachability map $M$, where $n = |V_\downarrow| = |V_\uparrow|$. The x-axis represents the postorder numbers of the nodes in the graph $G_\downarrow$, and the y-axis represents the postorder numbers of the same nodes in the graph $G_\uparrow$. Note, the postorder numbers are in the range of $[1, n]$. Given a pair of nodes, $u$ and $v$ in $G_\downarrow$, a function $f(u,v)$ maps it onto a grid $(x(v), y(u))$ in $M$, where $x(w) = op_\downarrow(w)$ and $y(w) = op_\uparrow(w)$. Here, $op_\downarrow(w)$ represents the postorder number of $w$ in $G_\downarrow$ and $op_\uparrow(w)$ represents the postorder number of $w$ in $G_\uparrow$. The grid value of $f(u,v)$ is 1, if $u \rightsquigarrow v$, otherwise 0.

The reachability map $M$ for $G_\downarrow$ (Fig. 2 (b)) is shown in Fig 3, where a shaded grid shows a reachability $u \rightsquigarrow v$. The details for all possible $u \rightsquigarrow v$, such as $u \neq v$, $G_\downarrow$, are given in Table 2. For example, $3 \rightsquigarrow 9$, is mapped onto $(4, 5)$ in $M$, and $(4, 5)$ represents $3 \rightsquigarrow 9$, because it is shaded.

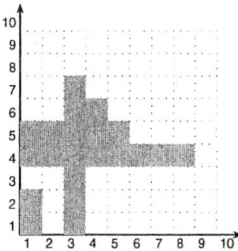

**Table 2.** All $u \rightsquigarrow v$ in $G_\downarrow$

| $p$ | $f(p)$ | $p$ | $f(p)$ | $p$ | $f(p)$ |
|---|---|---|---|---|---|
| $0 \rightsquigarrow 1$ | $(1,4)$ | $0 \rightsquigarrow 3$ | $(6,4)$ | $0 \rightsquigarrow 4$ | $(2,4)$ |
| $0 \rightsquigarrow 5$ | $(5,4)$ | $0 \rightsquigarrow 8$ | $(7,4)$ | $0 \rightsquigarrow 9$ | $(4,4)$ |
| $0 \rightsquigarrow 11$ | $(3,4)$ | $0 \rightsquigarrow 12$ | $(8,4)$ | $1 \rightsquigarrow 11$ | $(3,3)$ |
| $3 \rightsquigarrow 1$ | $(1,5)$ | $3 \rightsquigarrow 4$ | $(2,5)$ | $3 \rightsquigarrow 5$ | $(5,5)$ |
| $3 \rightsquigarrow 9$ | $(4,5)$ | $3 \rightsquigarrow 11$ | $(3,5)$ | $5 \rightsquigarrow 9$ | $(4,6)$ |
| $5 \rightsquigarrow 11$ | $(3,6)$ | $8 \rightsquigarrow 1$ | $(1,1)$ | $8 \rightsquigarrow 11$ | $(3,1)$ |
| $9 \rightsquigarrow 11$ | $(3,7)$ | $12 \rightsquigarrow 1$ | $(1,2)$ | $12 \rightsquigarrow 11$ | $(3,2)$ |

**Fig. 3.** Reachability Map

Second, we show that, for a node $w$ as a virtual center, all the the nodes that $w$ can reach and the nodes that can reach $w$, can be represented as rectangles in the reachability map, $M$. We explain it below. Given a node $w \in G_\downarrow$. Suppose that $I_\downarrow(w) = ([s_1, e_1], [s_2, e_2], \cdots, [s_n, e_n])$ and $I_\uparrow(w) = ([s'_1, e'_1], [s'_2, e'_2], \cdots, [s'_m, e'_m])$. It is important to note that a pair $[s_i, e_i]$ in $I_\downarrow(w)$ indicates that the corresponding nodes in $[s_i, e_i]$ can be reached from $w$ and a pair $[s'_j, e'_j]$ in $I_\uparrow(w)$ indicates that the corresponding nodes in $[s_i, e_i]$ can reach $w$. Therefore, all the possible pairs of $[s_i, e_j]$ and $[s'_j, e'_j]$ represent the reachability with $w$ as the center.

We define a function $Rect(w)$ which maps the all reachability, with $w$ as the virtual center, onto $n \times m$ rectangles in $M$, such as $((s_i, s'_j), (e_i, e'_j))$ for every $1 \leq i \leq n$ and $1 \leq j \leq m$. Note: a rectangle being contained in another can be eliminated. Two adjacent rectangles can be merged into a single rectangle.

The rectangular representation of the reachability of the nine nodes in $G_\downarrow$ (Fig. 4 (b)) are shown in Fig. 4. For example, consider node $w = 1$ in $G_\downarrow$. The cross in Fig. 4 (b) represents node $w = 1$ as $1 \rightsquigarrow 1$ at the grid $(x, y) = (1, 3)$ in $M$. Here, $I_\downarrow(1)$ has two intervals, $[s_1, e_1] = [1, 1]$ and $[s_2, e_2] = [3, 3]$, and $I_\uparrow(1)$ has an interval $[s'_1, e'_1] = [1, 5]$. The two rectangular representations become $((s_1, s'_1), (e_1, e'_1)) = ((1, 1), (1, 5))$ and $((s_2, s'_1), (e_2, e'_1)) = ((3, 1), (3, 5))$.

Third, we show that $Rect(w)$ represents a bipartite graph $B_C(V_C, E_C) \subseteq G_\downarrow$, which has $w$ as its virtually center, in the reachability map, $M$. Recall: $V_C = V_{C_{in}} \cup V_{C_{out}}$, $V_{in}$ (Eq. (2)) and $V_{out}$ (Eq. (3)) can be computed as follows.

$$V_{C_{in}} = g_\uparrow(Rect(w)) \qquad (7)$$
$$V_{C_{out}} = g_\downarrow(Rect(w)) \qquad (8)$$

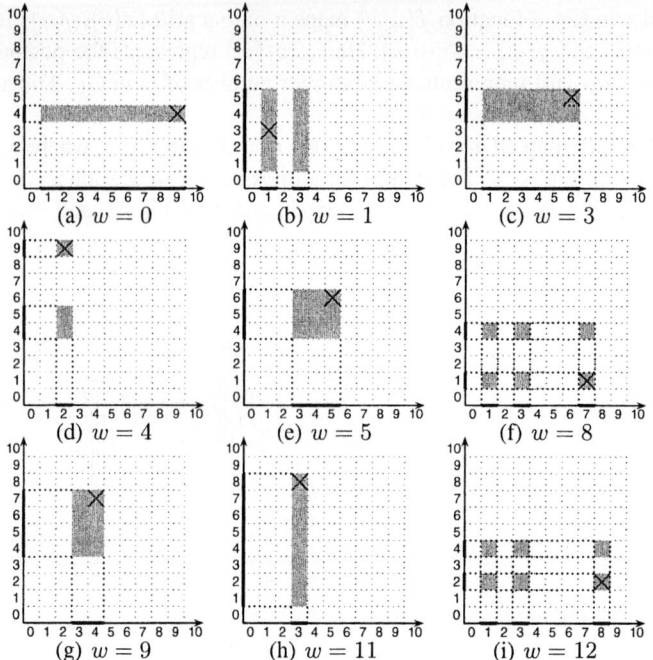

**Fig. 4.** Rectangular representations of bipartite graphs for nodes $w \in G_\downarrow$

where $g_\downarrow$ and $g_\uparrow$ are functions that return a set of node identifiers represented as postorder numbers in the $y$-axis and $x$-axis. We explain the two functions, $g_\downarrow$ and $g_\uparrow$, using an example.

Reconsider node $w = 1$ again in $G_\downarrow$ (Fig. 2 (b)). $Rect(w)$ represents two rectangles, $((1,1),(1,5))$ and $((3,1),(3,5))$. $Rect(w)$ covers $x$-values in $X = \{1,3\}$ and $y$-values in $Y = \{1,2,3,4,5\}$. As shown in Table 1, $V_{out} = \{1,11\}$, because $1 = op_\downarrow^{-1}(1)$ and $11 = op_\downarrow^{-1}(3)$. In a similar fashion, $V_{in} = \{8,12,1,0,3\}$, because every value, $k \in V_{in}$, is obtained by a value $l \in Y$, such as $k = op_\uparrow(l)$. The corresponding bipartite graph is shown in Fig. 5.

Fourth, we show that we can compute densest bipartite graphs using rectangles. Let $B_{C_1}$ and $B_{C_2}$ be two bipartite graphs for nodes $w_1$ and $w_2$. We have the following three equations.

$$Rect(B_{C_1} \cap B_{C_2}) = Rect(B_{C_1}) \cap Rect(B_{C_2}) \tag{9}$$

$$Rect(B_{C_1} \cup B_{C_2}) = Rect(B_{C_1}) \cup Rect(B_{C_2}) \tag{10}$$

$$Rect(B_{C_1} - B_{C_2}) = Rect(B_{C_1}) - Rect(B_{C_2}) \tag{11}$$

The above equations state that the rectangle of union/intersection/difference of two bipartite graphs is the union/intersection/difference of the rectangles of the two bipartite graphs. Based on them, we can fast compute *SCI* using rectangles. We omit the proof, because it is trivial. An example is shown in Fig. 6. Here, $B_{C_1}$ is mapped onto $((x_1,y_1),(x_2,y_2))$ by $Rect(B_{C_1})$, and $B_{C_2}$ is mapped onto $((x_3,y_3),(x_4,y_4))$

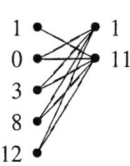
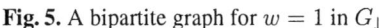
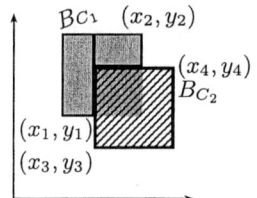

**Fig. 5.** A bipartite graph for $w = 1$ in $G_\downarrow$

**Fig. 6.** $B_{C_1} - B_{C_2}$

by $Rect(B_{C_2})$. $Rec(B_{C_1} - B_{C_2})$ is the two rectangles: $((x_1, y_1), (x_3 - 1, y_2))$ and $((x_3, y_4 + 1), (x_2, y_2))$.

### 4.4 The Algorithm

We discuss our new fast 2-hop algorithm, called *MaxCardinality-G*, because it can result in the same set of 2-hop cover as *MaxCardinality*. The efficiency of *MaxCardinality-G* is achieved due to the introduction of reachability map and the operations over rectangles (Eq. (9), (Eq. (10) and (Eq. (11)). We do not need to compute bipartite graphs, $B_C$, with a node $w$ as its virtual center, and we do not need to compute sets. Instead, we use $I_\downarrow$ and $I_\uparrow$ to obtain $B_C$, and use rectangles to determine the densest subgraph based on SCI.

In *MaxCardinality-G* (Algorithm 2), it takes $G$ as an input directed graph. It constructs a directed acyclic graph $G_\downarrow$ for $G$ (line 1), and computes its reachability table and its reachability map (line 2). The 2-hop cover, $H_\downarrow$, will be obtained after line 12. In line 13, it computes a 2-hop cover for the given graph $G$ based on the 2-hop cover, $H_\downarrow$, for $G_\downarrow$. The 2-hop cover $H$ is returned in line 14. The main body of *MaxCardinality-G* is to compute the 2-hop cover $H_\downarrow$ for the directed acyclic graph $G_\downarrow$. For computing $H_\downarrow$, it initializes $H_\downarrow$ in line 3. Also, in line 4, it initializes $\Delta$ as empty which is used to maintain all the rectangles covered by the algorithm. A rectangle represents a bipartite subgraph in $G_\downarrow$. In line 6, it finds the densest bipartite subgraph, with node $w$ as its center in $G_\downarrow$, in terms of Eq. (5), using operations (Eq. (9), (Eq. (10) and (Eq. (11)) upon its corresponding rectangles, $Rect(w)$, over the reachability map $M$. In line 6, it finds the largest area of $Rect(w) - \Delta$. Suppose the largest rectangle is for node $w$, in line 7-9, it add hops into $H_\downarrow$. Afterward, it adds the covered rectangles into $\Delta$ (line 10), and removes node $w$ from the set of nodes $V_\downarrow$ (line 11).

We explain *MaxCardinality-G* using the directed acyclic graph example $G_\downarrow$ (Fig. 2) (b). Below, we show the details of the algorithm *MaxCardinality-G*, in comparison with its counterpart algorithm *MaxCardinality*. The 4 bipartite graphs, generated in the 4 iterations of the algorithm *MaxCardinality* are shown in Fig. 8, using Eq. (6). In the 1st iteration, it finds a bipartite graph with $w = 3$ as its virtual center (Fig. 8 (a)); in the 2nd iteration, it finds a bipartite graph with $w = 1$ as its virtual center (Fig. 8 (b)); in the 3rd iteration, it finds a bipartite graph with $w = 9$ as its virtual center (Fig. 8 (c)); and in the 4th iteration, it finds a bipartite graph with $w = 0$ as its virtual center (Fig. 8 (d)).

Recall the reachability map, which preserves the complete reachability information is given in Fig. 3. Therefore, the algorithm *MaxCardinality-G* needs to find all rectangles $Rect(w)$, for node $w$, that cover all the valid points in the reachability map. We

## Algorithm 2. *MaxCardinality-G*

**Input:** a graph, $G(V, E)$
**Output:** a 2-hop cover, $H$

1: Construct a directed acyclic graph $G_\downarrow(V_\downarrow, E_\downarrow)$;
2: Compute the reachability table, and consider it as a virtual reachability map;
3: $H_\downarrow \leftarrow \emptyset$ {2-hop cover for $G_\downarrow$}
4: $\Delta \leftarrow \emptyset$; {covered rectangles}
5: **while** $V_\downarrow \neq \emptyset$ **do**
6: let $w$ be the node with the max area of $Rect(w) - \Delta$; {Densest subgraph in terms of *SCI*}
7: let $u$ and $v$ be two nodes in $G_\downarrow$;
8: **for all** $(x(w), y(u)) \in Rect(w)$ **do** $H_\downarrow \leftarrow H_\downarrow \cup \{(u \rightsquigarrow w, u)\}$;
9: **for all** $(x(v), y(w)) \in Rect(w)$ **do** $H_\downarrow \leftarrow H_\downarrow \cup \{(w \rightsquigarrow v, v)\}$;
10: $\Delta \leftarrow \Delta \cup (Rect(w) - \Delta)$;
11: $V_\downarrow \leftarrow V_\downarrow \setminus \{w\}$;
12: **end while**
13: Compute $H$ over $H_\downarrow$ for $G$;
14: **return** $H$;

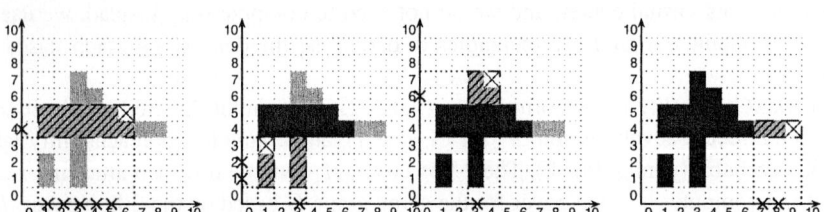

**Fig. 7.** *MaxCardinality-G* Steps for $G_\downarrow$

show how it is done using Fig. 7. In Fig. 7 (a), all the shaded points are the valid points; the cross point show the node $w = 3$, which is the same node selected in the 1st iteration of *MaxCardinality* (Fig. 8 (a)); and the striped points shows the largest area of $Rect(w)$, for $w = 3$, among all the other nodes. The $Rect(3)$ corresponds to Fig. 8 (a). After this step, the covered area, $\Delta$, is shown as dark points in Fig. 8 (b)-(d)). In the second iteration, the algorithm *MaxCardinality-G* will select a node $w = 1$ which has largest area of $Rect(w) - \Delta$. As shown above, the algorithm *MaxCardinality-G* finds the exact bipartite graphs as the algorithm *MaxCardinality* but performs more efficiently, because

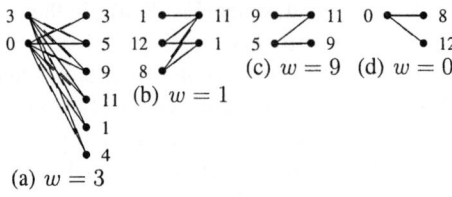

**Fig. 8.** *MaxCardinality* Steps for $G_\downarrow$

**Table 3.** 2-hops

| $w$ | 2-hops |
|---|---|
| 3 | $(0 \rightsquigarrow 3, 0), (3 \rightsquigarrow 5, 5), (3 \rightsquigarrow 9, 9)$, $(3 \rightsquigarrow 11, 11), (3 \rightsquigarrow 1, 1), (3 \rightsquigarrow 4, 4)$ |
| 1 | $(12 \rightsquigarrow 1, 12), (8 \rightsquigarrow 1, 8), (1 \rightsquigarrow 11, 11)$ |
| 9 | $((5 \rightsquigarrow 9), 5), (9 \rightsquigarrow 11, 11)$ |
| 0 | $(0 \rightsquigarrow 8, 8), (0 \rightsquigarrow 12, 12)$ |

it only needs to use operations against rectangles. The hops found in every iteration are given in Table 3.

We give implementation details for the algorithm *MaxCardinality-G*. The reachability table for the directed acyclic graph $G_1$ is maintained in memory. The rectangles for the covered areas, $\Delta$, are maintained in a R-tree [6]. The area of a node $w$ with $Rect(w) - \Delta$ is done as follows. 1) use $Rect(w)$ to retrieve all the areas in $\Delta$ that overlap with $Rect(w)$. 2) Suppose there are $n$ rectangles, $R_1, \cdots, R_n$, returned. It does $Rect(w) - R_i$ for all $1 \leq i \leq n$. 3) The area of the $Rect(w) - \Delta$ can be computed.

## 5 Experimental Studies

We conducted extensive experimental studies to study the performance of the three algorithms, namely, the algorithm *MaxDSCovering*, *MaxCardinality*, and *MaxCardinality-G*. We have implemented all the algorithms using C++. In the following, denote them as D, C and C-G, respectively.

Both D and C compute set cover, for a graph $G(V, E)$, upon its transitive closure, $T$, whose size can be very large, in the worst case, $O(|V|^2)$. We compute the transitive closure using the algorithm [7], and precompute all bipartite graphs, $B_C(V_C, E_C)$ which has $w$ as its center. All those precomputed bipartite graphs are stored in a B-tree on disk. For a given node $w \in G$, we can efficiently retrieve its corresponding bipartite graph $B_C$ from disk through a simple buffering mechanism from the B-tree. For D and C, all the other data, except the transitive closure $T$, are maintained in main memory. We also implemented a variation for D and C by the procedure of DAG conversion, that is: 1) converting a directed graph into a directed acyclic graph, 2) finding 2-hop cover for the directed acyclic graph using D and C respectively, and 3) generating 2-hop cover for the directed graph using a simple post-processing step, based on the 2-hop obtained in step 2). We denote them as D* and C*, respectively. For C-G, we maintain data structures in main memory where possible including the reachability table and R-tree. We use Antonin Guttman's R-tree code[1]. We also implemented a ranking adopted from [19], which is used to reduce the cost for computing densest bipartite graphs in every iteration. Table 4 summarizes the processing involved in each algorithm.

**Table 4.** Algorithms in Testing

| Processing Involved | MaxDSCovering | | MaxCardinality | | |
|---|---|---|---|---|---|
| | D | D* | C | C* | C-G |
| Transitive Closure Computation | √ | √ | √ | √ | × |
| DAG Conversion | × | √ | × | √ | √ |
| Geometry-based Approach | × | × | × | × | √ |

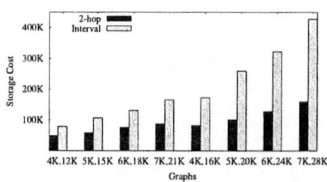

**Fig. 9.** Interval-Code vs 2-Hop Cover

We generated various synthetic data using two graph generator, namely, the random directed graph generator *GraphBase* developed by Knuth [14] and the random directed

---
[1] http://web.archive.org/web/20020802233653/es.ucsc.edu/tonig/rtrees

acyclic graph generator *DAG-Graph* developed by Johnsonbaugh [9]. We vary two parameters, $|V|$ and $E|$, used in the two generators, while the default values for the other parameters. We also tested several large real graph datasets.

We conducted all the experiments on a PC with a 3.4GHz processor and 2GB memory running Windows XP.

### 5.1 Exp-1: Comparison of the Five Algorithms over Directed Graphs

Because the focus of this paper is to compute 2-hop cover for general directed graphs, we first generate 10 random directed graphs using *GraphBase*, where $|V| = 5,000$ and $|E| = 10,000$, with different seeds. We compare five algorithms, namely, two *SCII* algorithms and three *SCI* algorithms. Note: D and D* are a *SCII* solution, and C, C* and C-G are a *SCI* solution. We report the size of 2-hop cover, $H$, processing time (sec), memory consumption (MB), and the number of I/O accesses. Figure 10 shows the details for D, C, D*, C*, and C-G in that order, using 10 random directed graphs. In terms of quality, they all performed in a similar way. All algorithms achieved the similar size of 2-hop cover and hence the similar compression ratio. In terms of efficiency (CPU, Memory, I/O), D and C performed worst because they compute 2-hop cover for a directed graph by first computing transitive closure. D* and C* performed better because they compute 2-hop cover by first converting a directed graph into a smaller directed acyclic graph. The cost can be reduced because the cost of computing transitive closure is reduced, and less computational cost is needed for the 2-hop cover. C-G performed the best, and significantly outperformed the others, because it does not need to compute transitive closure and it computes the bipartite graphs using rectangles. Averagely, D uses as much time as 364 times of C*'s and 70,065 times of C-G's.

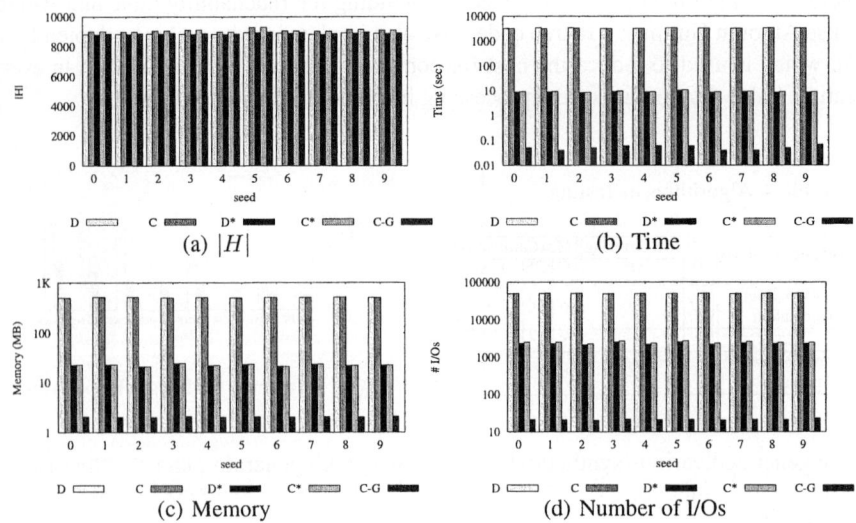

**Fig. 10.** Compare of 5 Algorithms over Directed Graphs

As expected, as shown in Fig. 10, the strategy of converting a directed graph onto a directed acyclic graph is beneficial. As a *SCII* solution, D* performed the best, and as a *SCI* solution, C-G performed the best. In the following, we focus on D* and C-G, and report our testing results using D* and C-G.

## 5.2 Exp-2: Scalability Testing on Directed Acyclic Graphs

As discussed above, for increasing efficiency, a directed graph can be first converted onto a directed acyclic graph to compute 2-hop cover. In this testing, we focus on scalability testing, for D* and C-G, over directed acyclic graphs. We use the *DAG-Graph* generator to generate directed acyclic graphs, using various $|V|$ and $|E|$. We fix $n = |E|/|V|$ to be 3, 4, 5 and 6, and increase $|V|$ from 4,000 to 6,000. Such a setting is due to the fact that D* consumes much time to complete for larger graphs.

The results are shown in Fig. 11. In terms of quality (the size of 2-hop cover, $H$), D* marginally outperforms C-G. As shown in Fig. 11 (a-d), when $n = |E|/|V|$ increases from 3 to 6, the difference between C-G and D* becomes smaller in terms of the size of the 2-hop cover. As also confirmed in other testing, C-G and D* becomes very similar when the density of directed acyclic graphs becomes higher. In terms of efficiency, C-G significantly outperforms D*, in particular, when the density of a directed acyclic graph is high, e.g. $n = 6$ in this testing. It is worth noting that D* consumes more 2,387 sec. than C-G to gain a compression ratio larger than C-G by 2.12, about 0.539% of $T$.

In Fig. 9, we also compared the code size between the 2-hop labeling and the interval labeling [1] over directed acyclic graphs. The 8 directed acyclic graphs are labeled $|V|, |E|$ on the x-axis. Let $n = |E|/|V|$, the first four pairs are with $n = 3$, and the remaining pairs are with $n = 4$. We compare the size by the number of units where a unit can be an integer. Note for the interval code, 2 units for start and end numbers and 1 unit for postnumber. The 2-hop labeling outperforms interval labeling in all the 8 graphs. As the $n = |E|/|V|$ and $|V|$ increase, the size of the interval code increases significantly, while the size of 2-hop cover remains similar.

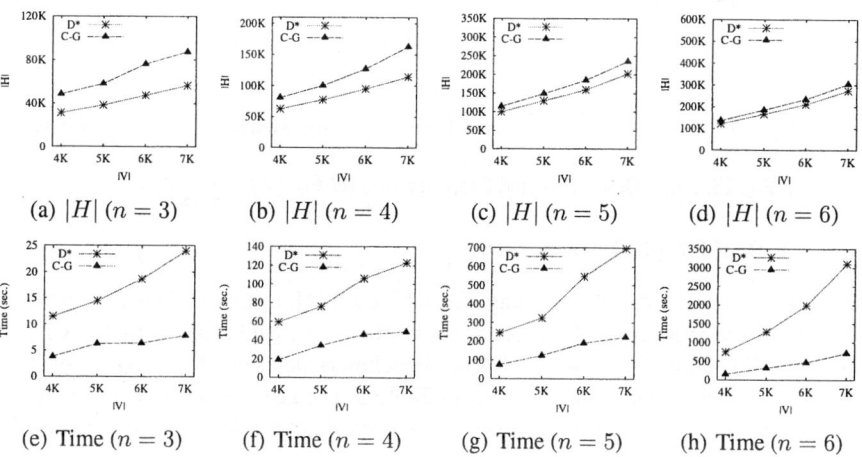

**Fig. 11.** Scalability Testing: Increase $|V|$ with Various $n = |E|/|V|$

### 5.3 Exp-3: Test Dense Graphs

We test dense directed acyclic graphs using the *DAG-Graph* generator. We fix $|V| = 1,000$, and vary $|E|$, based on $|E| = n \cdot |V|$, where $n$ is in range from 120 to 480. The results are shown in Fig. 12 where $n = |E|/|V|$ is shown in the $x$-axis. Note, let $|V| = 1,000$, $|E| = 480,000$ when $n = 480$. C-G significantly outperforms D* in terms of efficiency, and achieves the similar quality as D* does.

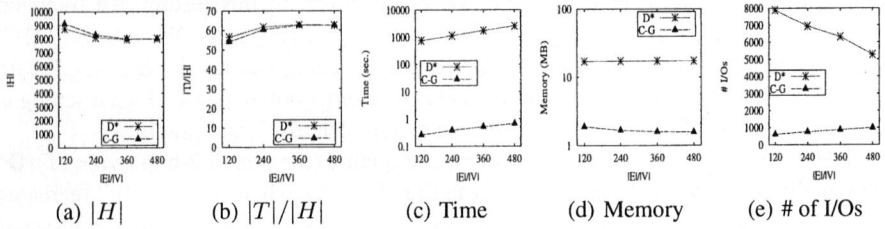

**Fig. 12.** Dense Directed Acyclic Graph Testing: Vary $|E|$ while $|V| = 1,000$ is fixed

We also conducted experiments on C-G using large directed graphs. We fix $|V| = 100,000$ and vary $|E|$ from 120,000 to 180,000. The graphs are randomly generated by the *Graph-Base* generator [14]. The processing time decreases while $|E|$ increases, because the number of strongly connected components increases. When the number of strongly connected components is larger, the generated directed acyclic graph becomes smaller. Therefore, the processing time becomes smaller. For the fast one, we only use 6.99 sec. to compute the 2-hop cover for a directed graph with 10,000 nodes and 180,000 edges.

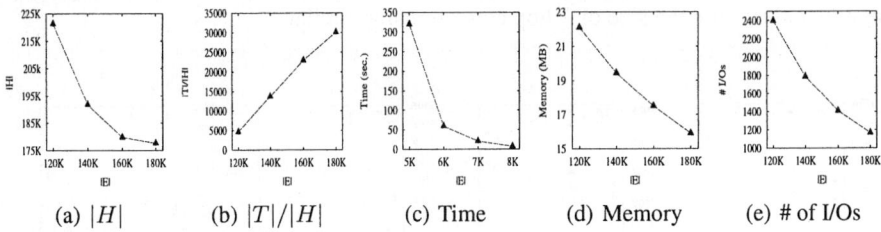

**Fig. 13.** Large Dense Directed Graph Testing (C-G): $|V| = 100,000$

### 5.4 Exp-4: Real Graph Datasets Testing

We tested several real datasets including Ecoo157 used [1], a subset of DBLP[2], which consists of all the records for 5 international conferences, SIGMOD, VLDB, ICDE, EDBT and ICDT, until 2004, and two XMark benchmark datasets [20] using factor 0.1 and 0.2. We only show the results of C-G in Table 5, because the others consume too much resources to compute. For example, for XMark dataset with factor 0.2, denoted

---
[2] A snapshot of http://dblp.uni-trier.de/xml/dblp.xml in Mar/2004

XMK.02, the number of nodes is is 336K, and the number of edges is 398K. It is a sparse graph, the compression rate achieves up to 3,565. The processing time is 3,600 seconds, and the memory consumption is 223MB at most, because C-G does not need to compute transitive closure, and uses rectangles. For the small real dataset Ecoo157 with 12,620 nodes and 17,308 edges, C-G only takes 0.36 seconds, and consumes 10MB memory.

**Table 5.** Performance on real graphs

| Data Set | $|V|$ | $|E|$ | Time(sec.) | Mem.(MB) | # of I/Os | $|H|$ | $|T|$ | $|T|/|H|$ |
|---|---|---|---|---|---|---|---|---|
| Ecoo157 | 12,620 | 17,308 | 0.36 | 9.83 | 237 | 23,913 | 2,402,260 | 100.46 |
| DBLP | 140,005 | 157,358 | 737.05 | 99.67 | 11,628 | 653,184 | 198,008,864 | 303.14 |
| XMK.01 | 167,865 | 198,412 | 831.87 | 114.66 | 4,866 | 583,706 | 2,009,963,198 | 3,443.45 |
| XMK.02 | 336,244 | 397,713 | 3,598.69 | 222.52 | 9,418 | 1,165,683 | 4,156,191,411 | 3,565.46 |

## 6 Related Work

Agrawal et al studied efficient management of transitive relationships in large databases [1]. The interval based labeling in [1] for directed acyclic graphs are reexamined for accessing graph, semistructured and XML data. Kameda [10] proposed a labeling scheme for reachability in planar directed graphs with one source and one sink. Cohen et al studied reachability labeling using 2-hop labels [2]. Schenkel et al [18, 19] studied 2-hop cover problem and proposed a divide-conquer approach. They attempted to divide a large graph into a set of even-partitioned smaller graphs, and solve the 2-hop cover problem for the large graph by post-processing the 2-hop covers for the small graphs. The work presented in this paper suggests that we can compute a large entire graph efficiently without the need to divide a graph into a large number of smaller graphs. Also, when there is a need to compute a large graph using the divide-conquer approach [18, 19], using our approach, it only needs to divide a graph into a rather small number of large graphs. In [22], we proposed a dual labeling scheme, in order to answer reachability queries in constant time for large sparse graphs. The work in [22] is different from the work presented in this paper. In this paper, we focus on computing 2-hops for arbitrary graphs which can be either sparse or dense. Several numbering schema were proposed for processing structural joins over tree structured data (XML data) including region-based [25, 24, 17, 12], prefix-based [3, 16, 11, 13, 21], and k-ary complete-tree-based [15, 23].

## 7 Conclusion

In this paper, we studied a novel geometry-based algorithm, called *MaxCardinality-G*, as a set cover I solution, to solve the 2-hop cover problem. Our algorithm utilizes an efficient interval based labeling for directed acyclic graphs, and builds up a reachability map which preserves all the reachability information in the directed graph. With the reachability map, our algorithm uses operations against rectangles to solve the 2-hop cover efficiently. As reported in our extensive experimental studies using synthetic datasets and large real datasets, our algorithm can compute 2-hop cover for large directed graphs, and achieve the similar 2-hop cover size as Cohen's algorithm can do.

**Acknowledgment.** The work described in this paper was supported by grant from the Research Grants Council of the Hong Kong Special Administrative Region, China (CUHK418205).

# References

1. R. Agrawal, A. Borgida, and H. V. Jagadish. Efficient management of transitive relationships in large data and knowledge bases. In *Proc. of SIGMOD'89*, 1989.
2. E. Cohen, E. Halperin, H. Kaplan, and U. Zwick. Reachability and distance queries via 2-hop labels. In *Proc. of SODA'02*, 2002.
3. E. Cohen, H. Kaplan, and T. Milo. Labeling dynamic XML trees. In *Proc. of PODS'02*, 2002.
4. T. H. Cormen, C. E. Leiserson, R. L. Rivest, and C. Stein. *Introduction to algorithms*. MIT Press, 2001.
5. G. Gallo, M. D. Grigoriadis, and R. E. Tarjan. A fast parametric maximum flow algorithm and applications. *SIAM J. Comput.*, 18(1):30–55, 1989.
6. A. Guttman. R-trees: A dynamic index structure for spatial searching. In *Proc. of SIGMOD'84*, 1984.
7. Y. E. Ioannidis. On the computation of the transitive closure of relational operators. In *Proc. of VLDB'86*, 1986.
8. D. S. Johnson. Approximation algorithms for combinatorial problems. In *Proc. of STOC'73*, 1973.
9. R. Johnsonbaugh and M. Kalin. A graph generation software package. In *Proc. of SIGCSE'91, (http://condor.depaul.edu/rjohnson/algorithm)*, 1991.
10. K. Kameda. On the vector representation of the reachability in planar directed graphs. *Information Processing Letters*, 3(3), 1975.
11. H. Kaplan, T. Milo, and R. Shabo. A comparison of labeling schemes for ancestor queries. In *Proc. of SODA'02*, 2002.
12. D. D. Kha, M. Yoshikawa, and S. Uemura. An XML indexing structure with relative region coordinate. In *Proc. of ICDE'01*, 2001.
13. W. E. Kimber. HyTime and SGML: Understanding the HyTime HYQ query language 1.1. Technical report, IBM Corporation, 1993.
14. D. E. Knuth. *The Stanford GraphBase: a platform for combinatorial computing*. ACM Press, 1993.
15. Y. K. Lee, S. J. Yoo, and K. Yoon. Index structures for structured documents. In *Proc. of ACM First International Conference on Digital Libraries*, 1996.
16. S. Lei and G. . a. Z. M. ãzsoyoglu. A graph query language and its query processing. In *Proc. of ICDE'99*, 1999.
17. Q. Li and B. Moon. Indexing and querying XML data for regular path expressions. In *Proc. of VLDB'01*, 2001.
18. R. Schenkel, A. Theobald, and G. Weikum. Hopi: An efficient connection index for complex xml document collections. In *Proc. of EDBT'04*, 2004.
19. R. Schenkel, A. Theobald, and G. Weikum. Efficient creation and incremental maintenance of the HOPI index for complex XML document collections. In *Proc. of ICDE'05*, 2005.

20. A. Schmidt, F. Waas, M. Kersten, M. J. Carey, I. Manolescu, and R. Busse. Xmark: A benchmark for xml data management. In *Proc. of VLDB'02*, 2002.
21. I. Tatarnov, S. D. Viglas, K. Beyer, J. Shanmugasundaram, E. Shekita, and C. Zhang. Storing and quering ordered XML using a relational database system. In *Proc. of SIGMOD'02*, 2002.
22. H. Wang, H. He, J. Yang, P. S. Yu, and J. X. Yu. Dual labeling: Answering graph reachability queries in constant time. In *Proc. of ICDE'06*, 2006.
23. W. Wang, H. Jiang, H. Lu, and J. Yu. Pbitree coding and efficient processing of containment join. In *Proc. of ICDE'03*, 2003.
24. M. YoshiKawa and T. Amagasa. XRel: A path-based approach to storage and retrieval of XML documents using relational databases. *ACM Transactions on Internet Technology*, 1(1), 2001.
25. C. Zhang, J. F. Naughton, D. J. DeWitt, Q. Luo, and G. M. Lohman. On supporting containment queries in relational database management systems. In *Proc. of SIGMOD'01*, 2001.

# Distributed Spatial Clustering in Sensor Networks

Anand Meka and Ambuj K. Singh

Department of Computer Science,
University of California, Santa Barbara,
Santa Barbara, CA
{meka, ambuj}@cs.ucsb.edu

**Abstract.** Sensor networks monitor physical phenomena over large geographic regions. Scientists can gain valuable insight into these phenomena, if they understand the underlying data distribution. Such data characteristics can be efficiently extracted through *spatial clustering*, which partitions the network into a set of spatial regions with similar observations. The goal of this paper is to perform such a spatial clustering, specifically $\delta$-*clustering*, where the data dissimilarity between any two nodes inside a cluster is at most $\delta$. We present an *in-network* clustering algorithm *ELink* that generates good $\delta$-clusterings for both synchronous and asynchronous networks in $O(\sqrt{N}\log N)$ time and in $O(N)$ message complexity, where $N$ denotes the network size. Experimental results on both real world and synthetic data sets show that ELink's clustering quality is comparable to that of a centralized algorithm, and is superior to other alternative distributed techniques. Furthermore, ELink performs 10 times better than the centralized algorithm, and 3-4 times better than the distributed alternatives in communication costs. We also develop a distributed index structure using the generated clusters that can be used for answering range queries and path queries. The query algorithms direct the spatial search to relevant clusters, leading to performance gains of up to a factor of 5 over competing techniques.

## 1 Motivation

Sensor networks are being deployed over large networks to monitor physical phenomenon: to collect, analyze, and respond to time-varying data. The analysis and querying of sensor data should be done in a distributed manner in order to remove the performance bottlenecks and to avoid the single point of failure of a centralized node. We address the problem of discovering spatial relationships in sensor data through the identification of clusters. This clustering is achieved through in-network distributed algorithms.

Sensing phenomena such as temperature [2] or contaminant flows [5] over large spatial regions helps scientists explain phenomena such as wind patterns, and varying disease rates in different regions. For example, Fig. 1 shows the varying sea surface temperature regions in the Tropical Pacific [2]. Given such a heat map, a geologist can explain that the wind currents shown in the figure arise due to the pressure variations among the underlying temperature zones.

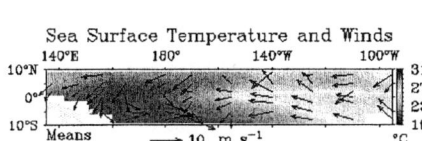
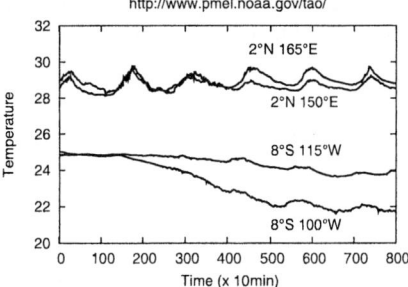

**Fig. 1.** Tao: Ocean monitoring with sensors

**Fig. 2.** Correlations in time series from four sensors

The goal of this paper is to partition the network into such a set of zones or *clusters*, which have observed similar phenomena. For example, consider the time series of four sensors (from Fig. 1) that are shown in Fig. 2. Notice that the spatially proximate sensors follow similar trends. Since our objective is to cluster regions based on the underlying trend, spatial clustering would group the top pair of sensors (shown in Fig. 2) into one cluster and the bottom pair into another.

Spatial clustering also serves to prolong network lifetime. Instead of gathering data from every node in the cluster, only a set of cluster representatives need to be sampled based on their spatio-temporal correlations. This reduces data acquisition and transmission costs [9, 14] in a sensor network constrained by storage, communication and power resources. Furthermore, there exists a need in the sensor network community to identify such clusters where *space-stationarity* holds. Eiman et al. [10] assume spatial stationarity of data in order to remove faults and outliers based on neighborhood and history. Guestrin et al. [14] perform in-network regression using kernel functions assuming rectangular *regions of support*. Our work addresses this important necessity to discover clusters that are both spatially stationary and are natural regions of support.

Clustering can be done off-line at the base station, if every node transmits its data to the central base station. But, this leads to huge communication costs. Besides, the power consumption for communication is up to three orders of magnitude higher than that for computation on a sensor node (such as a Crossbow Mica2 mote [3]). Therefore, for power efficiency, we propose *in-network* clustering. Furthermore, we regress time-series data at each node to build models. Clustering on model coefficients not only captures global spatio-temporal correlations, but also reduces transmission and memory costs. Overall, the contributions of the paper are:

1. We prove that $\delta$-clustering is NP-complete and hard to approximate.
2. We present and design a distributed clustering algorithm called ELink that generates high quality clusterings in $O(\sqrt{N} \log N)$ time and in $O(N)$ message complexity, for both synchronous and asynchronous networks.
3. We present an efficient slack-parameterized update algorithm that trades quality for communication. Furthermore, we employ the spatial clusters to efficiently answer both range queries and path queries.

4. Our experimental results on both real world and synthetic data sets show that ELink's clustering quality is comparable to that of a centralized algorithm and is superior to other distributed alternative techniques. Furthermore, ELink performs 10 times better than the centralized algorithm, and 3-4 times better than other distributed alternative techniques in communication costs. For the query algorithms, the average communication gains were up to a factor of 5 over competing techniques.

## 2 Parameterized Clustering

We first define the clustering problem and discuss its complexity. Then, we briefly discuss the distance measure used for clustering.

### 2.1 Clustering: Definition and Complexity

A good spatial clustering algorithm should group nodes in a sensor network based on data characteristics. In order to achieve this, data is regressed locally at each node to build models [26]. We adopt an auto-regression framework for defining the models (discussed in Section 2.2). The coefficients of this model are used as the *features* [15] at each node. We denote the feature at a sensor node $i$ by $F_i$. The (dis)similarity between any two features $F_i$ and $F_j$ is captured by distance $d(F_i, F_j)$. We assume that the distance is a metric, i.e., it satisfies positivity, symmetry and triangle inequality. For example, consider the communication graph $CG$ of a sensor network $S$ as shown in Fig. 3a). Fig. 3b) shows an example of a distance metric $d()$ between the features of the nodes in $S$.

Using the dissimilarity threshold $\delta$, a cluster is defined as follows:

**Definition 1.** *($\delta$-cluster) Given a set of sensors $S$, their communication graph $CG$, distance metric d, and a real number $\delta$, a set of sensors $C$ is called a $\delta$-cluster if the following two conditions hold.*

1. *The communication subgraph induced by $C$ on $CG$ is connected.*
2. *For every pair of nodes $i$ and $j$ belonging to $C$, $d(F_i, F_j) \leq \delta$. We refer to this property as the $\delta$-condition or $\delta$-compactness.*

$\delta$-*Clustering* is defined as the partition of the communication graph $CG$ into a set of disjoint $\delta$-clusters. Our goal is to find the optimal $\delta$-Clustering, i.e., the clustering with the minimum number of $\delta$-clusters.

Consider the network in Fig. 3a). If $\delta = 5$, then nodes $c$ and $e$ cannot belong to the same cluster since $d(F_c, F_e) = 6 > 5$, and for the same reason, nodes $c$ and $d$ cannot belong to the same cluster. Hence, the two possible minimal clusterings are as shown in Fig. 3c). Next, we present the complexity results for *optimal* clustering.

**Theorem 1.** *Given a set of sensors $S$, a communication graph $CG$, a metric distance d, and a real number $\delta$:*

1. *The decision problem "Does there exist a partition of graph $CG$ into $m$ disjoint $\delta$-clusters?" is NP-complete.*

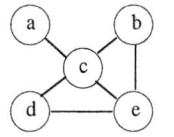
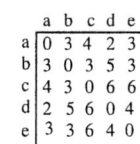
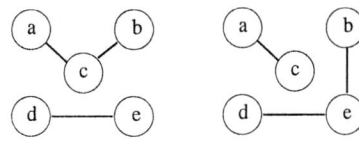

a) Communication graph (CG)   b) Distance matrix   c) Two minimal clusterings

**Fig. 3.** For the communication graph in a) and distance matrix b), and $\delta = 5$, the minimal possible clusterings are shown in c)

2. It is not possible to approximate (in polynomial time) the optimal solution to $\delta$-clustering within ratio $n^\phi$ where $\phi > 0$, unless P=NP.

*Proof.* The proof is based on a reduction from the *clique cover* [19] problem. The clique-cover problem $(G = (V, E), c)$ states that the decision problem "Does there exist a partition of graph $G$ into $c$ disjoint cliques?" is NP-complete.

Given an instance $I$ of the clique-cover $(G = (V, E), c)$, we map it into an instance $I'$ of $\delta$-clustering $(CG, d, \delta, m)$ as follows: Define $CG$ as a clique of size $|V|$. Set $\delta$ equal to 1 and $m$ equal to $c$. For every pair of vertices $i, j \in V$, define $d()$ as shown.

$$d(F_i, F_j) = \begin{cases} 1 & \text{if } e_{ij} \in E, \\ 2 & \text{otherwise.} \end{cases}$$

Note that $d()$ satisfies the metric properties. Output the solution of $I'$ as the solution for $I$. From the above mapping, we can see that $I$ has a solution iff $I'$ has a solution. Also, there exists a one to one correspondence between the solutions of $I$ and $I'$; so, the above reduction is approximation preserving. Since clique cover denies any approximation within ratio $n^\phi$, therefore the same bound holds for $\delta$-clustering as well. □

Since optimal $\delta$-clustering is a hard problem, even in a centralized setting, we propose an efficient distributed algorithm that generates high quality clusterings. But first, we explain features and distance measures.

### 2.2 Feature Model and Distance

In order to discover the global spatio-temporal patterns in a sensor network, spatial clustering should be performed on the underlying trend rather than on the raw time-series data. Therefore, we construct a data model at each node to capture the structure in the data (e.g., the trends and cycle in the four sensors observed in Fig. 1). Each node models data using an Auto-Regression (AR) model. The general ARIMA model [26] captures the seasonal moving averages (MA) along with the daily up and down trends (AR). At a node $i$, the set of model coefficients represent the feature $F_i$.

In an AR(k) model, the time series of an attribute $X$ at any node is modeled as $X_t = \alpha_1 X_{t-1} + \ldots + \alpha_k X_{t-k} + \epsilon_t$ where $\alpha_1, \ldots, \alpha_k$ are the auto-regression coefficients and $\epsilon_t$ is white noise with a zero mean and non-zero variance. Given $m$ such data measurements at a single sensor node, the problem of finding auto-regressive coefficients can be stated in matrix notation as $\mathbf{Y} = \mathbf{X}^T \alpha + \mathbf{e}$ where $\mathbf{Y}$ is a $m \times 1$ column of known $X_t$ values, $\mathbf{X}$ is $k \times m$ matrix of known explanatory variables $(X_{t-1}, \ldots, X_{t-k})$ and $\alpha$ is a $k \times 1$ column of unknown regression coefficients. Under basic assumptions of $\mathbf{e} = N(0, \sigma^2 I)$, the minimization of least squares errors leads to the solution $\hat{\alpha} = (\mathbf{XX^T})^{-1}\mathbf{XY}$.

Next, we discuss the distance $d()$, between models. Consider the models at three nodes:

$$N_1 : x_t = 0.5x_{t-1} + 0.4x_{t-2} + \epsilon_t \quad (1)$$
$$N_2 : x_t = 0.5x_{t-1} + 0.3x_{t-2} + \epsilon_t \quad (2)$$
$$N_3 : x_t = 0.4x_{t-1} + 0.4x_{t-2} + \epsilon_t \quad (3)$$

Node $N_1$ is more correlated to $N_2$ than to $N_3$, because of the importance of higher order coefficients. Therefore, simple euclidean or Manhattan distance between the coefficients will not suffice. We need to consider a weighted euclidean distance on the model coefficients. Such distances are metrics. This motivates us to formulate the clustering problem in the context of metric spaces, rather than euclidean spaces.

## 3 Distributed Clustering Algorithm

In this section, we present and analyze a distributed algorithm, ELink, for *in-network* clustering. In the experimental section, we present three other alternative techniques: a centralized *spectral clustering* algorithm, and two other distributed clustering techniques, *Spanning forest* and *Hierarchical* for comparison. Section 9 discusses the drawbacks of extending the traditional clustering algorithms such as k-medoids-, hierarchical-, and EM- [8, 13, 23] based algorithms to this particular problem setting.

At the termination of the ELink algorithm, the communication graph $CG$ is decomposed into disjoint $\delta$-clusters. Each cluster is organized as a tree, referred to as a *cluster tree*, with the root as the designated leader. A node $i$ inside a cluster $C_i$ maintains a 3-tuple $\langle r_i, F_{r_i}, p \rangle$. The first is the root id, $r_i$; the second is the root feature, $F_{r_i}$; the third is the id of the parent, $p$, in the cluster tree.

### 3.1 ELink Clustering

The key idea behind ELink is to grow clusters from a set of *sentinel* nodes to the maximal extent, i.e., until they are $\delta$-compact, and then start growing another set of clusters from a different set of sentinel nodes, reiterating this process until every node is clustered. A definite order is imposed on the scheduling of the different sentinel sets; and moreover, a new sentinel set begins expanding only after the previous set has finished clustering. A node in the new sentinel set does not start expanding either until it is contacted by a node in the previous sentinel set (in an explicit signalling approach), or until its predefined timer expires (in an implicit signalling approach). Although both the techniques are guaranteed to run in $O(\sqrt{N} \log N)$ time and in $O(N)$ message complexity, the implicit signalling technique is designed for synchronous networks, whereas the explicit signalling technique is designed for asynchronous networks. We first give an overview of the general ELink algorithm, and then explain both the techniques in detail.

## 3.2 Algorithm

In order to understand the sentinel sets, we begin with a decomposition of the sensor network. To simplify the discussion, we assume a square grid of $N$ nodes. Spatially, the entire topology is recursively broken down into cells at different resolutions (*levels*) in a quadtree like structure. The root cell is at level 0. Every cell elects a leader node [11, 16].[1] Sentinel set $S_l$ comprises of all the cell leaders at a particular level $l$ (as shown in Fig. 4), for $0 \leq l \leq \alpha$, such that $\sum_{l=0}^{\alpha} |S_l| = N$. Since $|S_l| = 4^l$, the depth of the hierarchy, $\alpha$, evaluates[2] to $\log_4(3N+1) - 1$. The parents of all the nodes in the sentinel set $S_l$ comprise the set $S_{l-1}$. Initially, the single sentinel in $S_0$ begins expanding its cluster until it is $\delta$-compact. Then, all the sentinels in $S_1$ are either explicitly or implicitly signalled to start expanding. This process is carried recursively at every level. The expansion of each sentinel is carried out only using the edges of the communication graph $CG$.

We use the term *root* (and *tree*) in two different contexts. The quadtree has a root, sentinel $S_0$. Every cluster $C_i$ also has a root, cluster leader $r_i$, which is one of the sentinels belonging to $S_0, S_1, \ldots, S_\alpha$. The quadtree is used for the definition of the sentinels and their signalling. The cluster tree is used for defining the clusters.

The underlying idea behind the ELink algorithm is as follows. We first suppose that the whole network can be placed in a single $\delta$-cluster; hence, we allot sufficient time for the cluster from $S_0$ to expand and include every node in the network. In that case, none of the lower level sentinels in $S_1, \ldots, S_\alpha$ start, and the single cluster remains intact. Otherwise, we suppose that the whole network can be partitioned into *at most* five clusters. So, cluster formation is initiated from each of the four sentinels in $S_1$. We allow nodes to switch cluster memberships a limited number of times. This handles the case when the number of clusters should be less than 5. Now, if the whole network is still not clustered after sentinel set $S_1$'s expansion, we assume that the network can be decomposed into at most twenty one clusters (five from the previous levels), and start growing each of the sixteen sentinels in $S_2$. A sentinel set $S_l$'s expansion begins *only* after sentinel set $S_{l-1}$ terminates clustering. The implicit and explicit signalling techniques ensure that expansion happens strictly as above. Next, we explain how a sentinel node grows its $\delta$-cluster.

Once a sentinel node $i$ at level $l$ has been signalled, it examines if it is already clustered. If so, it does nothing. Else, it elects itself as the leader (root) of cluster $C_i$ and sets $F_{r_i} = F_i$. Then, it attempts to include every neighbor $j$ in its cluster, if $d(F_{r_i}, F_j) \leq \delta/2$. If node $j$ is unclustered, it joins cluster $C_i$. If it is already clustered, we ensure that its reclustering does not destroy clusters grown from a lower level and that the gain in the clustering quality (measured by a distance in the metric space) is above a certain predefined threshold $\phi$. Furthermore, we allow node $j$ to switch clusters at most $c$ times, where $c$ is again a predefined constant. This is done in order to reduce the communication overhead. Constant $c$ is application specific and is usually small, around 3–5.

---

[1] For routing purposes, the node closest to the cell centroid is elected as the leader.
[2] This is precise for a grid network. But, even under the general assumption of uniform network density [11, 18], $\alpha$ can be bounded by $\log_4(3N+1) + k$, for some small positive integer $k$, which is sufficient for all the subsequent theorems to hold.

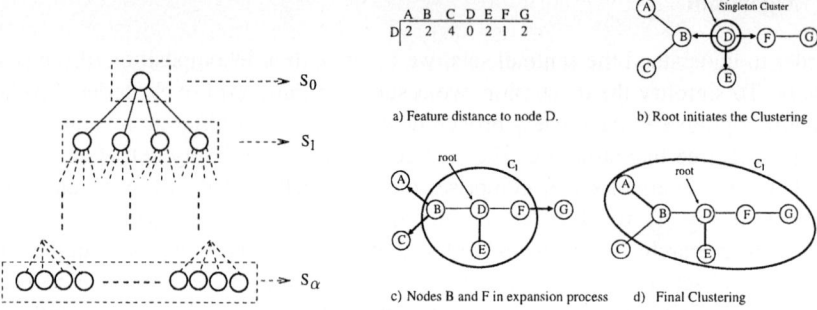

**Fig. 4.** Sentinel set $S_0$ comprises of the quadtree root. Sentinel set $S_l$ comprises of all the leaders at level $l$.

**Fig. 5.** For $\delta = 6$, the feature distances of every other node to sentinel node $D$ are shown in a). The expansion of cluster $C_1$ starts as shown in b), continues as shown in c), and terminates as shown in d).

If node $j$ decides to be a member of cluster $C_i$, then $j$ sets its root id to $i$, and stores the root feature $F_{r_i}$. It now attempts to expand cluster $C_i$. This process repeats until no new nodes can be added. Since the distance between the feature value of any node in the cluster and the root feature $F_{r_i}$ is at most $\delta/2$, triangle inequality ensures that the distance between the feature values of any two nodes in the cluster is at most $\delta$.

The following example (Fig. 5) illustrates the clustering by a sentinel node $D$, for $\delta = 6$. The metric distance of every node to sentinel $D$ is shown in Fig. 5a). Initially, $D$ sets itself as the root, as shown in Fig. 5b). Since $d(F_D, F_F) = 1 \leq 3 = \delta/2$, node $D$ includes neighbor $F$ in its cluster $C_1$, and transmits its root feature $F_D$ to it. Similarly, neighbors $B$ and $E$ are included in cluster $C_1$, as shown in Fig. 5c). Nodes $D$ and $E$ cannot expand further, since all their neighbors are already clustered. Now, node $F$ expands $C_1$ to include node $G$, since $d(F_D, F_G) = 2 \leq 3$. In a similar way, node $B$ includes node $A$ in $C_1$, but does not include node $C$, since $d(F_D, F_C) = 4 > 3$. After this step, none of the nodes in the cluster can expand, and so the clustering terminates. The final cluster $C_1$ is shown in Fig. 5d). The complete algorithm is outlined in Fig. 16 (Appendix B).

## 4 Implicit Signalling Technique

The implicit signalling technique is designed for synchronous networks. This algorithm ensures that the sentinel set $S_l$ is granted sufficient time to complete expansion, before sentinel set $S_{l+1}$ starts growing. Consider the bounding rectangle $[L \times L]$ of the entire $N$ node network on the $x$-$y$ plane. If $\rho$ denotes the node density, then $\rho L^2 = N$. For the sake of simplicity, we assume $\rho = 1$ implying $L = \sqrt{N}$. We assume that the every node has at most $d$ neighbors. In sensor networks [12], $d$ is assumed to be a constant and very small compared to $N$. Let stretch factor $\gamma$ denote the ratio of the worst case increase in path length of "expand" messages (for cluster expansion) to the shortest path length between two nodes using multi-hop communication. Constant $\gamma$ is usually small, around 0.2–0.4 [18]. For simplicity, assume that the worst-case delay over a hop is a single time unit. This blurs the distinction between path length and end-to-end communication delay between two nodes. Let $\kappa$ denote the worst-case message cost or time (in a synchronous network) for the root sentinel $S_0$ to cluster with any other node in its level 0 cell (the whole network).

Note that $\kappa = (1+\gamma)\sqrt{\frac{N}{2}}$. Similarly, the worst-case time for a sentinel in $S_m$ to cluster with any other node in its level $m$ cell is $\kappa/2^m$. Extending this reasoning, a sentinel in $S_l$ can cluster with any other node in the entire network in time $t_l = \kappa(1+1/2+..1/2^m+..+1/2^l)$. Therefore, every node in $S_l$ is allotted a time interval $t_l$ to finish expansion. Fig. 6 illustrates the interval $t_1$ of a sentinel node $A \in S_1$. Hence, scheduling of the sentinel set is done as follows. At time $T = 0$, sentinel set $S_0$ starts expanding, and every other sentinel set $S_l$ starts its expansion at time $T = \sum_{i=0}^{l-1} t_i$. The algorithm is outlined in Fig. 17 (Appendix B).

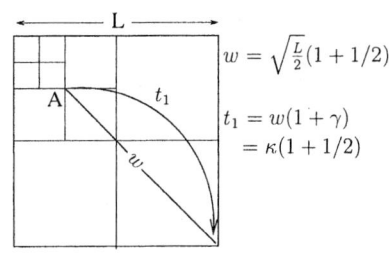

**Fig. 6.** The worst case path length from node $A \in$ sentinel set $S_1$ to cluster any node in the network is $t_1$

**Theorem 2.** *The implicit signalled ELink algorithm runs in $O(\sqrt{N} \log N)$ time and requires $O(N)$ messages.*

*Proof.* First, we prove the bound on time. Since every sentinel set $S_l$ terminates expansion before $S_{l+1}$ starts growing, the total running time of the algorithm is bounded by the scheduling time for the sentinel set for the last level $\alpha$, combined with its allotted expansion duration. Therefore, the total running time is $T = (\sum_{l=0}^{\alpha-1} t_l) + t_\alpha$. Since $t_1 < t_2 < t_3 \ldots < t_{\alpha-1} < t_\alpha$, and $t_\alpha < 2\kappa$, $T$ is at most $2\kappa\alpha$. Hence, ELink runs in time $O(\sqrt{N} \log N)$.

Next, we consider the message complexity. A node sends out a message only in two cases; first, when it is scheduled as a sentinel, and second, when it has received a message from a neighbor, which is a member of a different cluster. In the first case, a sentinel node sends messages to all its neighbors, and since every node has at most $d$ neighbors, the total cost over all nodes is at most $dN$. In the second case, a node sends a message only if it has switched clusters, or has just been clustered for the first time. As a node is restricted to switch cluster membership at most $c$ times, it will send no more than $c + 1$ messages to each of its neighbors. Hence, the $N$ nodes will send at most $d(c+1)N$ messages. Therefore, ELink's message complexity is $O(N)$. □

## 5 Explicit Signalling Technique

The running time and message complexity of the implicit technique are guaranteed only for a synchronous network. In order to retain these complexities for an asynchronous network, we designed the explicit signalling technique, incorporating additional synchronization [4] into ELink. In this technique, a sentinel in $S_{l+1}$ does not begin cluster expansion until it is explicitly contacted by its parent in $S_l$. This does not happen until every sentinel in $S_l$ completes expansion; thus, maintaining the order in sentinel set expansion: $S_0 \to S_1 \to \cdots \to S_\alpha$. Next, we give an overview of the synchronization that ensures this ordering.

The synchronization at every level $l$ is divided into two phases. After realizing the completion of its cluster expansion, each sentinel in $S_l$ begins the first phase, *phase 1*, by contacting its quadtree parent. This parent, after being contacted by all its children, notifies its own parent. This is carried recursively up till the root sentinel, $S_0$. When the root is contacted by all its quadtree children, implying that all the nodes in $S_l$ have finished expansion, it starts the second phase, *phase 2*, by propagating messages recursively down the quadtree to notify all the nodes in $S_l$. After receiving such a *phase 2* message, each node in $S_l$ instructs its children in $S_{l+1}$ to start ELink.

The complete algorithm is shown in Fig. 18. During the ELink expansion of a sentinel in $S_l$, an intermediate node $i$ along every path of cluster expansion, maintains a *children* counter to denote the number of children it has in the cluster tree. Node $i$ receives an $ack2$ message from a child $j$, when the cluster expansion of subtree rooted at $j$ is complete. Then, node $i$ decrements the *children* counter by 1, and if the counter equals 0, then node $i$ realizes the completion of cluster expansion of the tree rooted at $i$. Now, if node $i$ is not the cluster root, it transmits an $ack2$ to its parent $p$. Else, it realizes that the entire cluster expansion has been completed, and contacts its quadtree parent by a *phase 1* message.

**Theorem 3.** *The explicit signalled ELink algorithm runs in $O(\sqrt{N}\log N)$ time and requires $O(N)$ messages.*

*Proof.* First, we prove the bound on time. A node $i$ in the sentinel set $S_l$ completes expansion in time interval $t_l$ (defined in Section 4). Therefore, within $2*t_l$ time, all $ack2$ messages denoting the completion of cluster expansion arrive at the sentinel. After this, there is the additional time of contacting the root sentinel $S_0$ with *phase 1* messages, and then, $S_0$ responding back with *phase 2* messages. The worst-case path length from a sentinel in $S_m$ to its quadtree parent in $S_{m-1}$ is bounded by $\kappa/2^m$. Thus, the total time for a sentinel in $S_l$, to contact $S_0$ in *phase 1* is at most $\kappa(1/2 + 1/2^2 + .. + 1/2^m + .. + 1/2^l)$, which is the same as $t_{l-1}/2$. Similarly, the time taken by *phase 2* can also be bounded by $t_{l-1}/2$. After the completion of two phases, sentinel $i$ contacts the children in $S_{l+1}$ via *start* messages. This delay is bounded by $\kappa/2^{l+1}$. Hence, the total running time for all the sentinel sets is $T = \sum_{l=0}^{\alpha} 2*t_l + \sum_{l=1}^{\alpha} t_{l-1} + \sum_{l=0}^{\alpha-1} \kappa/2^{l+1}$. In a manner similar to the implicit technique, the first and second summations evaluate to $O(\sqrt{N}\log N)$, whereas the third summation evaluates to $O(\sqrt{N})$. Hence, the time complexity is $O(\sqrt{N}\log N)$.

Now, consider the message complexity. In addition to the two types of clustering messages transmitted as in the implicit technique, nodes have to deal with four other types of messages— first, to inform the parents in the cluster tree ($ack1$) about their children; second, to inform the sentinel node about the completion of cluster expansion ($ack2$); third, the messages sent up the quadtree while notifying the root (*phase 1*), and down the quadtree while receiving a reply (*phase 2*); fourth, the messages sent to instruct the children (*start*) to invoke ELink. In the first and second cases, the total number of messages will be the same as those needed for cluster expansion as in the implicit technique, which is $O(N)$. We will now bound the total number of messages in *phase* 1 and *phase* 2, $\mu$, over all levels. Let $\beta_l$ denote the message cost of notifying the root by all the nodes in $S_l$ in *phase* 1. Then $\beta_l$ can be recursively expressed as $\beta_l = \beta_{l-1} + |S_l| * \kappa / 2^l$. Since $|S_l| = 4^l$, this recurrence yields the solution $\beta_l = (2^{l+1} - 1) * \kappa$. Hence summing over all sets $S_l$, the total cost of *phase* 1 and *phase* 2 messages, $\mu$, can be expressed as shown below in equation (1).

$$\mu = \sum_{l=1}^{\alpha} 2 * \beta_l = 2 \sum_{l=1}^{\alpha} (2^{l+1} - 1) * \kappa$$
$$= 2\kappa \left(4(2^\alpha - 1) - \alpha\right)$$
$$= 2\kappa \left(2\sqrt{(3N+1)} - \log_4(3N+1) - 3\right) \quad (4)$$

Since $\kappa = O(\sqrt{N})$, the total cost of the above term is $O(N)$. The total cost of *start* messages is $\sum_{l=0}^{\alpha-1} |S_l| * \kappa / 2^{l+1}$. In a manner similar to Equation 4, this term also evaluates to $O(N)$. Hence, the explicit technique's message complexity is $O(N)$. □

Note that if optimizing the time complexity was our sole concern, then an unordered expansion of the sentinel suffices. We can expand all the sentinels simultaneously, subject to the constraint that a node can switch clusters at most $c$ times. Since $2\kappa$ is the worst-case time for any node to reach any other node in the network, this algorithm will terminate in $O(\sqrt{N})$ time. The message complexity of this algorithm can be bounded by $O(N)$. However, this algorithm has poor clustering quality due to excessive contention across sentinel levels.

## 6 Dynamic Cluster Maintenance

After the clustering of distributed data sources has been carried out, the underlying data distribution may change.[3] This may lead to violations of the $\delta$-compactness conditions within a cluster, necessitating an expensive re-clustering. In this section, we show that introducing a small slack [25] locally at each node avoids such global computations. Although this leads to a degradation in clustering quality, the resulting benefits in communication are huge.

Given a slack parameter $\Delta$, the maximum divergence within a cluster, $\delta$, is reduced to $(\delta - 2\Delta)$ during the initial clustering, and during any global cluster re-computation. Such a reduction gives a $\Delta$ slack for the feature update at node $j$ for the $\delta$-compactness condition.

Let $F_i$ the feature at node $i$ be updated to $F_i'$ with the arrival of a new measurement. Similarly, let the feature at the root of node $i$, $F_{r_i}$ be updated to $F_{r_i}'$. The root node verifies locally that $d(F_{r_i}, F_{r_i}') \leq \Delta$. Node $i$ verifies the conditions $\mathbf{A_1}$, $\mathbf{A_2}$ and $\mathbf{A_3}$.

$$d(F_i, F_i') \leq \Delta \quad (\mathbf{A_1})$$
$$d(F_i', F_{r_i}) - d(F_i, F_{r_i}) \leq \Delta \quad (\mathbf{A_2})$$
$$d(F_i', F_{r_i}) \leq \delta - \Delta \quad (\mathbf{A_3})$$

---
[3] On the arrival of a new measurement, each node updates its AR model as shown in Appendix A.

If any of these conditions holds then it follows from triangle inequality that the $\delta$-compactness property is not violated. If all the three conditions are violated, a reclustering needs to occur. Node $i$ propagates a message up the cluster tree to the root to obtain the updated root feature $F'_{r_i}$. After obtaining this feature, node $i$ evaluates $d(F'_i, F'_{r_i}) \leq \delta$. If the condition is violated, node $i$ detaches from the cluster, and merges with the cluster of a neighbor $k$ if $d(F'_i, F_{r_k}) \leq \delta$. Else, it becomes a singleton cluster.

If the condition $d(F_{r_i}, F'_{r_i}) \leq \Delta$ is violated at the root, then the root propagates $F'_{r_i}$ down to every node in the cluster tree. Every intermediate node computes its distance to this feature and decides if it should remain in the same cluster. The details of the update algorithm are deferred to the full paper [21].

## 7 Index Structure and Queries

In this section, we first discuss how a distributed index structure is built on the models, and then, describe how this index structure along with the $\delta$-compactness property is employed to prune large portions of the sensor network for range and path queries.

### 7.1 Index Structure

The ELink algorithm partitions the network into cluster trees that provide a natural way to build a hierarchical index structure. Our index structure is similar to a distributed *M-tree* [7] built on the feature space, but physically embedded on the communication graph. An index at node $i$ maintains a *routing feature*, $F_i^R$, and a *covering radius*, $R_i$ such that the feature of every node in the subtree rooted at $i$ is within distance $R_i$ from $F_i^R$. A leaf in the cluster tree propagates its routing feature $F_i^R = F_i$ and covering radius $R_i$ (set to 0 for a leaf node) to its parent. The parent uses its own feature and the information from all its children to compute its own routing feature and covering radius. This process is carried on recursively up to the root of the cluster.

A range query $q$ with radius $r$ on an M-tree retrieves all the nodes whose feature values are within distance $r$ from the query feature $q$. The range search starts from the root and recursively traverses all the paths leading to nodes which cannot be excluded from the answer set. A subtree rooted at node $i$ can be safely pruned from search, if $d(q, F_i^R) > r + R_i$. The whole subtree satisfies the query, if $d(q, F_i^R) \leq r - R_i$. Since, each node stores the information of all its children, node $i$ can prune a child-subtree rooted at $j$, if the condition $|d(q, F_i^R) - d(F_i^R, F_j^R)| > r + R_j$ holds; or it can include the subtree completely in the query if the condition $d(q, F_i^R) + d(F_i^R, F_j^R) \leq r - R_j$ holds. All the above follow from triangle inequality. Next, we discuss the range and path query algorithms.

### 7.2 Range Querying in Sensor Networks

Geographic regions exhibiting abnormal behavior similar to that of the El Nino pattern [2] are of critical interest to scientists. These regions can be discovered by posing range queries of the form: *"Which are the regions behaving similar to node $x$?"* or

"Given a query model $q$, find all the regions whose behavior is within a specified distance $r$ (measured in terms of model coefficients) of $q$?".

A spanning tree connecting the leaders of different clusters (a *backbone* network) is built in order to efficiently route the query to every cluster. A range query can be initiated from any node in the network. The initiator routes the query to its cluster root, which forwards it to other cluster roots using the backbone tree. Every root first prunes using the $\delta$-compactness property (explained next), and then employs the hierarchical index structure to selectively propagate the query to its children. Results are aggregated, first within the cluster tree, and then on the backbone network, and returned to the query initiator.

Pruning by the $\delta$-compactness property is achieved as follows. No node in a cluster will satisfy the query $q$ with radius $r$ if query $q$'s distance from the root $d(q, F_{r_i}) > r + \delta/2$. On the other hand, every node inside the cluster will satisfy the query if $d(q, F_{r_i}) \leq r - \delta/2$. (These follow from triangle inequality). If the query doesn't satisfy either of these conditions, the root employs the M-tree to prune the query (as mentioned in 7.1) in order to retrieve the answer set.

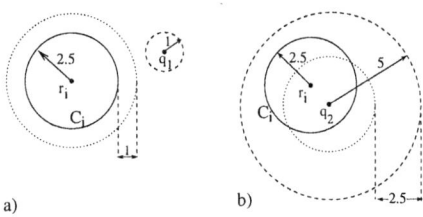

**Fig. 7.** Pruning conditions for $\delta = 5$: a) cluster $C_i$ is *excluded* from the query $q_1(8,9)$ with $r = 1$, b) cluster $C_i$ is *included* in query $q_2(4,6)$ with $r = 5$

The above pruning is now illustrated using an example in which a model is represented by a tuple of two coefficients. For the sake of simplicity, assume euclidean distances. Let the root of cluster $C_i$ (shown in Fig. 7) be $F_{r_i}:(3,7)$ where $\delta = 5$. Fig. 7a) shows that no node inside cluster $C_i$ can intersect the query $q_1:(8,9)$ with radius $r = 1$ because $d(q_1, F_{r_i}) = 5.38 > 1 + 5/2$. Therefore, $C_i$ can be completely pruned. On the other hand, every node in the cluster $C_i$ will satisfy the query $q_2:(4,6)$ with radius $r = 5$ as shown in Fig. 7b), since $d(q, F_{r_i}) = 1.414 \leq 5 - 5/2$. Query $q_3:(3,7)$ with $r = 1$ does not fall into either of the cases since $d(q_3, F_{r_i}) = 0 > 1 + 5/2$ is *false* and $d(q_3, F_{r_i}) = 0 \leq 1 - 5/2$ is also *false*. Therefore, it is injected into the M-tree root of cluster $C_i$. The M-tree pruning conditions are employed in this case.

### 7.3 Path Querying in Sensor Networks

During pollutant leaks and fire hazards, rescue missions need to navigate a safe path from a source node to a destination node. Ensuring the safety of mission implies that the exposure to chemical along the path is at least a *safe* $\gamma$ distance away from the danger (represented as a feature) $F_D$. Formally, a path query is posed as "*Return a path from the source node $x$ to destination node $y$, such that for all the nodes $j$ along the path, $d(F_j, F_D) \geq \gamma$*".

Path querying employs pruning similar to a range query. A cluster $C_i$ with root $r_i$ is *safe* for traversal if $d(F_{r_i}, F_D) > \gamma + \delta/2$; it is *unsafe* for traversal if $d(F_{r_i}, F_D) \leq \gamma - \delta/2$. Otherwise, the *safe* and *unsafe* regions inside a cluster are identified by drilling down the index structure, as safe and unsafe *sub-clusters*. Then, every set of spatially contiguous safe clusters (and sub-clusters) is connected using a *safe* backbone tree. Thus, the whole network is partitioned into disjoint set of safe trees.

The source node $x$ forwards the query to the root of its cluster. If the cluster is evaluated to be *unsafe*, the root suppresses the query. Else, it dispatches a BFS query using the safe backbone tree to the root of the cluster (or sub-cluster), which contains the destination $y$. The whole path from the destination node $y$ to source node $x$ can be traced back. If node $y$ does not belong to the same safe backbone tree as node $x$, then there does not exist a safe path between these two nodes.

## 8 Experimental Results

In this section, we first explain our real-world and synthetic datasets, then present interesting alternatives for clustering and querying, and finally evaluate a) the quality and the communication gains of ELink clustering, and b) the communication benefits achieved by the query pruning techniques over the presented alternatives. We only report the results for range queries. Results for path queries are deferred to the full paper [21].

### 8.1 Data Sets

**Tao (Spatially correlated dynamic data set):** This data consists of daily sea surface temperature measurements of Tropical Pacific Ocean [2]. We obtain a 10-minute resolution data for a month (December 1998) from each sensor in a $6 \times 9$ grid. The sensors are moored to the buoys between $2S$–$2N$ latitudes and $140W$–$165E$ longitudes. The temperature range was $(19.57, 32.79)$ with $\mu = 25.61$ and $\sigma = 0.67$. The neighbors in the communication graph were defined by the grid. Each node is initialized with a model trained on the previous month's data. The temperatures within a day follow regular upward and downward trends, i.e, AR(1), whereas the daily variations in mean were observed to follow an AR(3). Hence, the temperature at every node is modelled as $x_t = \alpha_1 x_{t-1} + \beta_1 \mu_{T-1} + \beta_2 \mu_{T-2} + \beta_3 \mu_{T-3} + \epsilon_t$. The weight vector for distance computation is $(0.5, 0.3, 0.2, 0.1)$. Coefficient $\alpha_1$ is updated for every measurement whereas $\beta$'s are updated every day.

**Death Valley data (Spatially correlated static data set):** This data consists of geographic elevation of Death Valley [1]. Sensors are assumed to be scattered over the terrain and the elevation of the terrain at a sensor location is assigned as the sensor feature. The altitude range was $(175, 1996)$. Our performance results are averaged over 5 different random topologies, each consisting of 2500 samples.

**Synthetic data (Spatially uncorrelated dynamic data set):** Experiments were conducted on network sizes ranging from 100 nodes to 800. We used a random placement of nodes with a uniform probability distribution. Node densities were varied from 0.7 to 0.9. Each node has on the average 4 nodes within its radio range. Data at every node $i$ is modeled as, $x_t = \alpha_i x_{t-1} + e_t$ where $e_t \sim U(0, 1)$ and $\alpha_i \sim U(0.4, 0.8)$. $100,000$ readings were generated at each node. The range was $(10.00, 132.93)$ with $\mu = 69.27$ and $\sigma = 48.19$. Every node is initialized with $\alpha_1 = 1$. This model is updated for every measurement.

## 8.2 Performance Metrics

**Clustering:** The clustering quality is measured by the number of clusters generated by each algorithm.

**Communication:** Communication overhead is measured by the total number of messages exchanged for each algorithm. A message can transmit a single coefficient or a data value. The query cost is the average number of messages required to route the query, and to aggregate the results back at the originator. The cost of building the intercluster leader backbone network is accounted in the ELink algorithm.

## 8.3 Alternative Clustering and Querying Techniques

The performance of the ELink algorithm is compared against a centralized algorithm [22] and two other distributed algorithms that we propose. Our range query algorithm is compared against TAG [20] and our path query algorithm is compared against BFS.

**Centralized clustering:** There are two kinds of centralized algorithms. In the first, every update to the raw data is sent to the centralized base station (for baseline comparison in communication). In the second, an AR model is built at each node, and the model coefficients are sent to the centralized base station if the coefficient changes by more than a certain threshold [25]. We explain how this threshold is set in Section 8.5. At the base station, a *spectral decomposition algorithm* [22] is used for clustering. It computes the Laplacian $L$ of the affinity matrix and then partitions the network into $k$ clusters using the $k$ largest eigenvectors of $L$. If $x$ denotes the distance $d(F_i, F_j)$ between any two nodes $i$ and $j$, then we define the affinity matrix $a()$ as follows:

The algorithm is repeated with different values of $k$ and the smallest $k$ is chosen such that each cluster satisfies the $\delta$-condition.

$$a(i,j) = \begin{cases} x & \text{if } e_{ij} \in CG, \\ 0 & \text{otherwise.} \end{cases}$$

**Spanning forest based clustering:** This algorithm generates sub-optimal clusters in a greedy manner, but incurs a low communication cost. It consists of two phases. In the first phase, the algorithm decomposes the network into a spanning forest of trees, and in the second phase, it partitions each tree greedily into subtrees which satisfy the $\delta$-compactness property.

In the first phase, each node selects the neighbor with the smallest feature distance, and an id smaller than its own id as its parent (to ensure a partial order). By iterative expansion, this phase decomposes the network into a forest of trees. In the second phase of the algorithm, these trees are checked for $\delta$-compactness. Variable *height* at a node stores an upper bound on the feature distance between the node and any leaf belonging to the cluster subtree of the node. Every node initializes its *height* to 0. Beginning with the leaves, each leaf $i$ sends its *height* (0) and its feature $F_i$ to its parent $p$. Each parent node $p$ maintains its own *height*, its local feature $F_p$, and the identifier of the child with the maximal height in a variable *highest_child*. When it receives a new $height$ from one of its children $i$, it uses a temporary variable $h$ to store the value $height + d(F_i, F_p)$, and then examines if the sum of $h$ and the local $height$ variable at node $p$ exceeds $\delta$.

If it does, then node $p$ instructs the child whose height is the largest (*highest_child*) to detach. Otherwise, node $p$ updates its *height* and *highest_child* variables. After receiving the heights of all its children, $p$ sends its own height and feature $F_p$ to its parent. Every detached subtree forms a new cluster with the *highest_child* as the root. The time and message complexity of this algorithm is $O(N)$.

**Hierarchical clustering:** The second distributed algorithm, Hierarchical clustering, grows the clusters in a hierarchical fashion using a notion of optimality absent in the spanning forest algorithm. Every cluster maintains a feature diameter and spatially neighboring clusters whose merger increases the diameter the least are merged in a bottom-up hierarchical fashion [23].

For a given cluster, every neighboring cluster is a candidate for merger if it does not violate the $\delta$-condition. A *fitness* value is defined for all the candidates. The candidate with the minimum *fitness* is called the *best_candidate*. A pair of clusters merge if they are the *best_candidates* with respect to each other. This merger continues recursively until there is a single cluster in the whole network or no further mergers are possible.

Assuming that $k$ clusters (trees) have been generated, we now explain how two neighboring trees $C_i$ and $C_j$ merge. Every cluster $C_i$ maintains its diameter $m_i$. Clusters $C_i$ and $C_j$ verify the condition: $m_i + d(F_{r_i}, F_{r_j}) + m_j \leq \delta$. If they violate the condition, then $C_i$ and $C_j$ rule each other out as candidates for merger; else, they evaluate the *fitness* of the possible merger. The fitness of the merger is determined by $m_{ij}$, the diameter of the merged cluster. If $m_i \geq m_j$ then $m_{ij}$ is set to $\max(m_i, m_j + d(F_{r_i}, F_{r_j}))$, else it is set to $\max(m_j, m_i + d(F_{r_i}, F_{r_j}))$. Cluster $C_i$ chooses the optimal candidate based on these values: $best\_candidate_i = \text{argmin}_j\ m_{ij}$. Clusters $C_i$ and $C_j$ merge if $best\_candidate_i = j$ and $best\_candidate_j = i$. The time and message complexity of this algorithm is $O(N^2)$.

**TAG querying:** TAG [20] is a tiny aggregation scheme, distributed as a part of the TinyDB (Tiny Database) package that runs on motes [3]. TAG uses a SQL like declarative query interface to retrieve data from the network. It consists of two phases. In the *distribution* phase, the query is pushed down into the network using an overlay tree network, and in the *collection* phase, the results are aggregated continually up from the children to parents and reported to the base station. We evaluate the pruning benefits achieved by our range query algorithm by comparing it to TAG.

## 8.4 Clustering Quality

Figs. 8 & 9 compare the clustering quality of ELink with the competing schemes, for varying $\delta$. The threshold decrease required to switch a cluster, $\phi$, was set to $0.1\delta$, and the maximum number of switches allowed, $c$, was set to 4. The Implicit and Explicit signalled ELink algorithms output the same clusters, except that the Explicit ELink has a higher communication cost than the Implicit one due to additional synchronization. The clustering quality of these algorithms is almost as good as the centralized scheme for all the data sets. Notice that ELink generates better clustering quality than the Hierarchical and Spanning forest algorithms. The Hierarchical algorithm performs better

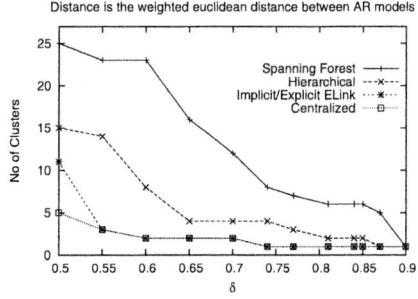

**Fig. 8.** Clustering quality for Tao data     **Fig. 9.** Clustering quality for Death Valley data

than Spanning forest, as it employs the *fitness* function to optimize the diameter. Results for the synthetic data set [21] were similar, except that there was an increase in the number of clusters due to little data correlations among spatial neighbors.

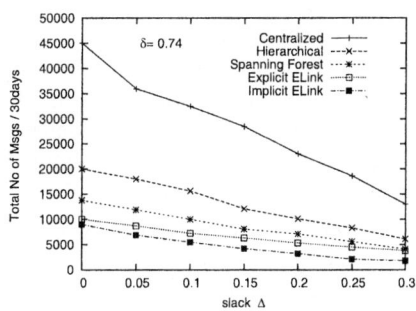
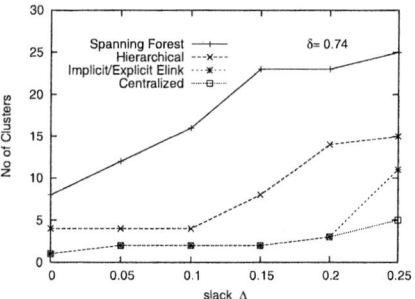

**Fig. 10.** Update costs with varying slack     **Fig. 11.** Clustering quality with varying slack

## 8.5 Communication Costs

In this section, we evaluate the cluster update handling algorithm and the scalability of our algorithms in terms of their communication costs. Computational costs are negligible compared to communication costs in a sensor network. For brevity, we only report the representative results.

**Update Handling:** Every node in the centralized algorithm has to update the base station if the local model violates the slack $\Delta$; hence, the algorithm incurs a huge communication overhead. Even if the slack condition ($\mathbf{A_1}$) is violated locally, the ELink update algorithm (in section 6) does not generate any messages if the conditions $\mathbf{A_2}$ and $\mathbf{A_3}$ are satisfied. Since these conditions require the cluster root feature $F_{r_i}$, and a node in the centralized algorithm does not maintain $F_{r_i}$ locally, the centralized algorithm cannot prune by conditions $\mathbf{A_2}$ and $\mathbf{A_3}$. Due to these reasons, the communication cost of ELink algorithms is 10 times lower than the centralized algorithm as seen in Fig 10. As the slack is increased (effectively reducing the $\delta$ parameter), the quality of clustering decreases for all the algorithms as shown in Fig 11.

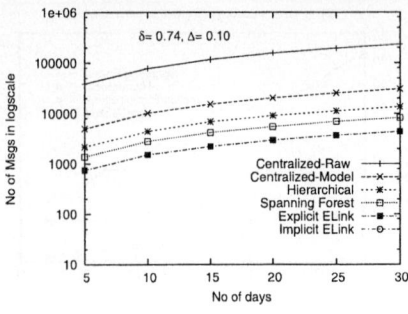
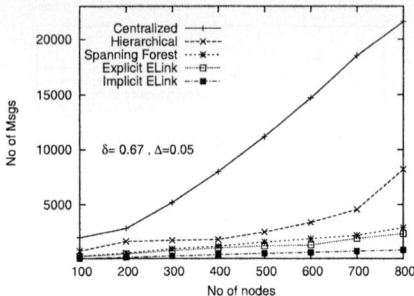

**Fig. 12.** Scalability with time on Tao data (shown in logscale plot)

**Fig. 13.** Scalability with network size on synthetic data

**Scalability:** Fig. 12 & 13 depict the scalability of the algorithms with time, and with the size of network. Fig. 12 shows the *log scale plot* of the scalability of algorithms on the Tao data set. We have included an extra plot for the centralized algorithm, in which every update to a raw value at a node is sent to the centralized base station. This figure illustrates that communication benefits obtained by modeling alone are an order of magnitude compared to raw data updates, whereas modeling combined by *in-network* clustering brings the cost down by another order of magnitude. Fig. 13 shows the scalability of algorithms with network size. We see the superior scalability of ELink based algorithms. This is because all the distributed techniques confine the updates locally, whereas the centralized scheme incurs a huge overhead of transmitting the model coefficients to the base station. Furthermore, Hierarchical clustering also incurs a huge cost since every merger decision has to be propagated to the cluster leader in order to evaluate the $best\_candidate$. Since Explicit ELink algorithm has additional synchronization costs, it incurs a larger overhead than the Implicit ELink algorithm.

### 8.6 Range Querying

Figs. 14 & 15 show the average per-query cost when the range query algorithm is run separately on each clustering algorithm on both the data sets. The query point was sam-

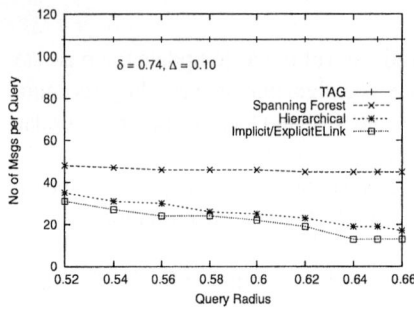
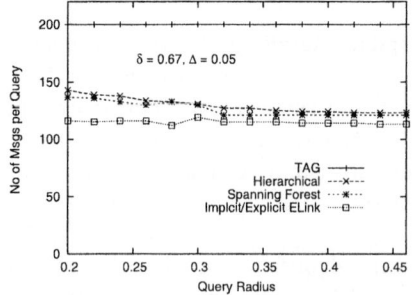

**Fig. 14.** Range query cost on Tao data

**Fig. 15.** Range query cost on synthetic data

pled uniformly from the nodes. The query radius $r$ was varied from $(0.7\delta, 0.9\delta)$ for the real data and $(0.3\delta, 0.7\delta)$ for the synthetic data. TAG is shown for comparison. Since TAG builds an overlay tree and aggregates the results back, the average number of messages per query is fixed and is equal to twice the number of edges in the spanning tree. In the real data set in Fig. 14, the clustering was compact, and hence ELink and Hierarchical pruned many clusters using the $\delta$-compactness property, thus decreasing the query cost 5 times. But, as the query radius increased, the benefits of pruning by the $\delta$-compactness property decreased, the pruning was now primarily due to the distributed index structure. Fig. 15 shows that there were less communication benefits for the synthetic data set. This is because the data was not spatially correlated.

## 9 Related Work

The general problem that the paper addresses—*clustering of data distributions*—has been extensively studied in statistics, machine learning and pattern recognition literature. There are three basic types of clustering algorithms: partitioning, hierarchical and mixture of Gaussian models. Partitioning algorithms such as $k$-means for euclidean spaces, or $k$-medoids for metric spaces (e.g. PAM, CLARANS [23]) represent each of the $k$ clusters by a centroid or an object. For our problem, distributed $k$-medoids would be communication intensive because in every iteration, all the medoids would have to be broadcast throughout the network so that every node computes its closest medoid. In hierarchical clustering (e.g. CURE [24]), the most similar pair of clusters are merged in each round, finally resulting in a single cluster. Our distributed hierarchical clustering technique is based on the same idea. But, this incurred a huge communication cost because of the exchange of data in in every round of merger.

Spatial data mining discovers interesting patterns in spatial databases. STING [28], a spatial clustering technique, captures the statistics associated with spatial cells at different resolutions, in order to answer range-queries efficiently. But it generates *isothetic* clusters whose boundaries are aligned to horizontal or vertical axis. WaveCluster [27] finds the densely populated regions in the euclidean space using the multi-resolution property of wavelets. It is a centralized scheme. In sensor networks distributed clustering has been studied for effcient routing purposes rather than for discovering data correlations [30]. Chintalapudi et al. [6] detect the edges of clusters (or phenomenon) in the specific setting where a sensor node emits only binary values. Instead of clustering, Kotidis [17] aims to determine the representatives among groups of sensors with similar observations.

## 10 Conclusions

We considered the problem of spatial clustering in sensor networks, and showed that is both NP-complete and hard to approximate. We presented a distributed algorithm, ELink, based on a quadtree decomposition and a level by level expansion using sentinel sets. Our algorithm generated good quality clustering, comparable to those achieved by centralized algorithms. Our algorithm is also efficient: it takes $O(N)$ messages and

$O(\sqrt{N} \log N)$ time for both synchronous and asynchronous networks. Our experiments showed that ELink outperforms a centralized algorithm (10 times) and competing distributed techniques (3-4 times) in communication costs of clustering. We also answered range queries and path queries efficiently based on the $\delta$-compactness property and by using a hierarchical index, resulting in communication gains of up to a factor of 5 over competing techniques.

**Acknowledgements.** This work was supported by the Army Research Organization grant DAAD19-03-D-004 through the Institute of Collaborative Biotechnologies.

# References

1. The EROS data center for geological survey. *http://edc.usgs.gov/geodata/*.
2. Tropical atmosphere ocean project. *www.pmel.noaa.gov/tao/*.
3. *Crossbow, Inc. Wireless sensor networks*, http://www.xbow.com/.
4. B. Awerbuch. Complexity of network synchronization. *JACM*, 32(4):804–823, 1985.
5. J. Berry, L. Fleischer, W. E. Hart, and C. A. Phillips. Sensor placement in municipal water networks. *World Water and Environmental Resources Congress*, 2003.
6. K. K. Chintalapudi and R. Govindan. Localized edge detection in a sensor field. *SNPA*, 2003.
7. P. Ciaccia, M. Patella, and P. Zevula. M-tree: An efficient access method for similarity search in metric spaces. *VLDB*, 1997.
8. A. P. Dempster, N. M. Laird, and D. B. Rubin. Maximum likelihood from incomplete data via the expectation-maximization algorithm. *Journal of Royal Statistical Society*, 9(1):1–38, 1999.
9. A. Deshpande, C. Guestrin, W.Hong, and S. Madden. Exploiting correlated attributes in acquisitonal query processing. *ICDE*, 2005.
10. E. Elnahrawy and B. Nath. Context-aware sensors. *EWSN*, 2004.
11. D. Estrin, R. Govindan, and J. Heidemann. Next century challenges: Scalable coordination in sensor networks. *MOBICOM*, 1999.
12. D. Ganesan, D. Estrin, and J. Heidemann. Dimensions: Why do we need a new data handling architecture for sensor networks? *SIGCOMM*, 2003.
13. V. Ghanti, R. Ramakrishnan, and J.Gehrke. Clustering large datasets in arbitrary metric spaces. *ICDE*, 1999.
14. C. Guestrin, P. Bodik, R. Thibaux, M. Paskin, and S. Madden. Distributed regression: An efficient framework for modeling sensor network data. *IPSN*, 2004.
15. J. Han and M. Kamber. Data mining: Concepts and techniques. *Morgan Kaufmann*, 2001.
16. B. Karp and H. T. Kung. GPSR: Greedy perimeter stateless routing for wireless networks. *MOBICOM*, 2003.
17. Y. Kotidis. Snapshot queries: Towards data-centric sensor networks. *ICDE*, 2005.
18. Q. Li, M. DeRosa, and D. Rus. Distributed algorithms for guiding navigation across a sensor network. *MOBICOM*, 2003.
19. C. Lund and M. Yannakakis. On the hardness of approximating minimization problems. *JACM*, 41(5):960–981, 1997.
20. S. Madden, M. Franklin, J. Hellerstein, and W. Hong. The design of an acquisitional query processor for sensor networks. *SIGMOD*, 2003.
21. A. Meka and A. K. Singh. Distributed algorithms for discovering and mining spatial clusters in sensor networks. *UCSB TechReport*, 2005.

22. A. Y. Ng, M. Jordan, and Y. Weiss. On spectral clustering: Analysis and an algorithm. *NIPS*, 2002.
23. R. T. Ng and J. Han. Efficient and effective clustering methods for spatial data mining. *VLDB*, 1994.
24. R. T. Ng and J.Han. Efficient clustering methods for spatial data mining. *VLDB*, 1997.
25. C. Olston, B. T. Loo, and J. Widom. Adaptive precision setting for cached approximate values. *SIGMOD*, 2001.
26. M. Pourahmadi. Foundations of time series analysis and prediction theory. *Wiley*, 2001.
27. G. Sheikholeslami, S. Chatterjee, and A.Zhang. WaveCluster: A multi-resolution clustering approach for very large spatial databases. *VLDB*, 1998.
28. W. Wang, J. Yang, and R. R. Muntz. STING: A statistical information grid approach to spatial data mining. *VLDB*, 1997.
29. B. K. Yi, N. D. Sidiropoulos, T. Johnson, H. V. Jagadish, and C. Faloutsos. Online data mining for co-evolving time sequences. *ICDE*, 2000.
30. O. Younis and S. Fahmy. HEED: A hybrid energy-efficient distributed clustering for adhoc sensor networks. *INFOCOM*, 2004.

## Appendix A. Online Updates to a Model

In this section we show how our model coefficients are updated incrementally. Let us assume that $X$ is an $k \times m$ matrix of $m$ measurements (one set of $k$ input variables per column), $\alpha$ is the $k \times 1$ vector of regression coefficients and $y$ the $m \times 1$ vector of outputs. The Least Squares solution to the over-determined system $X^T \alpha = y$ is the solution of $XX^T \alpha = Xy$. Let $P$ denote $XX^T$ and $b$ denote $XY$. We can compute $\hat{\alpha} = P^{-1} b$, where

$$P_k = [\sum_{i=1}^{k} x_i x_i^T]^{-1} \text{ and } b_k = \sum_{i=1}^{k} x_i y_i \quad (5)$$

The operations above will be performed once. When a new vector $x_{m+1}$ and output $y_{m+1}$ arrive, the recursive equations for online model computation can be derived from [29] as:

$$b_k = b_{k-1} + x_k y_k \quad (6)$$
$$P_k = P_{k-1} - P_{k-1} x_k [1 + x_k^T P_{k-1} x_k]^{-1} x_k^T P_{k-1} \quad (7)$$
$$\hat{\alpha}_k = \hat{\alpha}_{k-1} - P_k (x_k x_k^T \alpha_{k-1} - x_k y_k) \quad (8)$$

## Appendix B. ELink Algorithms

---

▷ **ELink clustering at node i** $(0 \leq i < N)$

$l$ : level of node $i$ in the quadtree.
$clustered$ : boolean variable. Initially false.
$m$ : level of the sentinel it is clustered by.
$p$ : parent of $i$ in the cluster tree. Initially set to $i$.
$r_i$ : root of cluster to which $i$ belongs.
$F_i$ : feature value at node $i$.
$F_{r_i}$ : feature value at root $r_i$.
$counter$ : number of times a node can switch clusters. Initialized to $c$.
$\phi$ : threshold for switching clusters.

// Procedure executed upon receiving a signal
ELink (i) ::
  if ($\neg clustered$) then
    $r_i := i$;
    $clustered := true$;
    $F_{r_i} := F_i$;
    $m := l$;
    send <"expand", $F_{r_i}, r_i, m$> to all neighbors.

receive <"expand", $F_{r_j}, r_j, n$> from a neighbor $j$ ::
  if $(d(F_{r_j}, F_i) \leq \delta/2$ & $(\neg clustered \parallel (n = m$
  & $d(F_{r_j}, F_i) < d(F_{r_i}, F_i) + \phi$ & $counter \geq 0)))$
  then
    $p := j$;
    $r_i := r_j$;
    $F_{r_i} := F_{r_j}$;
    $m := n$;
    if ($clustered$) then
      $counter := counter - 1$;
    $clustered := true$;
    send <"expand", $F_{r_i}, r_i, m$> to all neighbors;
    // Explicit Signalling: send <"ack1"> to $p$.

**Fig. 16.** ELink clustering algorithm

---

▷ **Implicit signalling at node i** $(0 \leq i < N)$

$S_l$ : Sentinel set to which $i$ belongs.
$\kappa := (1+\gamma)\sqrt{\frac{N}{2}}$ // Worst-case time for the quadtree root to cluster with any node in the network.
$t_l := \kappa(1 + 1/2 + \ldots + 1/2^l)$ // Duration for $i$ to expand.
$Timer := \sum_{j=0}^{l-1} t_j$ // Time after which $i$ starts Elink.

$TimerExpires$ ::
  ELink (i).

**Fig. 17.** Implicit signalling technique

---

▷ **Explicit signalling at node i** $(0 \leq i < N)$

$children$ : number of $i$'s children in the cluster tree. Initially 0.
$quad\_children$ : number of $i$'s children in the quadtree. Initially 4.
$quad\_parent$ : $i$'s parent in the quadtree.
// The rest of the variables are from ELink algorithm.

// A node after sending the $expand$ messages (Fig. 16),
determines that it is a leaf in the cluster tree
if it does not receive any $ack1$ messages from its
neighbors within a conservative time-out period.

if ($i$ is a leaf)
  send <"ack2"> to $p$.

$MessageHandler$ ::

// This message is received during
// ELink's cluster expansion.
receive <"ack1"> from j ::
  $children := children + 1$.

receive <"ack2"> from j ::
  $children := children - 1$;
  if ($children = 0$)
    if ($i = r_i$) // $i$ is the cluster leader.
      send <"phase 1", $l$> to $quad\_parent$;
    else
      send <"ack2", $l$> to $p$.

receive <"phase 1", $n$> from j ::
  $quad\_children := quad\_children - 1$;
  if ($quad\_children = 0$)
    if ($i \in S_0$) // the quadtree root
      send <"phase 2", $n$> to all quadtree children;
    else
      send <"phase 1", $n$> to $quad\_parent$ ;
    $quad\_children := 4$. // Reset for the next round.

receive <"phase 2", $n$> from j ::
  if ($l = n$)
    send <"start"> to all quadtree children;
  else
    send <"phase 2", $n$> to all quadtree children.

receive <"start"> from j ::
  $quad\_parent := j$;
  ELink (i).

**Fig. 18.** Explicit signalling technique

# SCUBA: Scalable Cluster-Based Algorithm for Evaluating Continuous Spatio-temporal Queries on Moving Objects

Rimma V. Nehme[1] and Elke A. Rundensteiner[2]

[1] Department of Computer Science, Purdue University
[2] Department of Computer Science, Worcester Polytechnic Institute
rnehme@cs.purdue.edu, rundenst@cs.wpi.edu

**Abstract.** In this paper, we propose, SCUBA, a Scalable Cluster Based Algorithm for evaluating a large set of continuous queries over spatio-temporal data streams. The key idea of SCUBA is to group moving objects and queries based on common spatio-temporal properties at run-time into moving clusters to optimize query execution and thus facilitate scalability. SCUBA exploits shared cluster-based execution by abstracting the evaluation of a set of spatio-temporal queries as a spatial join first between moving clusters. This cluster-based filtering prunes true negatives. Then the execution proceeds with a fine-grained within-moving-cluster join process for all pairs of moving clusters identified as potentially joinable by a positive cluster-join match. A moving cluster can serve as an approximation of the location of its members. We show how moving clusters can serve as means for intelligent load shedding of spatio-temporal data to avoid performance degradation with minimal harm to result quality. Our experiments on real datasets demonstrate that SCUBA can achieve a substantial improvement when executing continuous queries on spatio-temporal data streams.

## 1 Introduction

Every day we witness technological advances in wireless communications and positioning technologies. Thanks to GPS, people can avoid congested freeways, businesses can manage their resources more efficiently, and parents can ensure their children are safe. These developments paved the way to a tremendous amount of research in recent years in the field of real-time streaming and spatio-temporal databases [11, 14, 20, 29, 33]. As the number of users of location-based devices (e.g., GPS) continues to soar, new applications dealing with extremely large numbers of moving objects begin to emerge. These applications, faced with limited system resources and near-real time response obligation call for new real-time spatio-temporal query processing algorithms [23]. Such algorithms must efficiently handle extremely large numbers of moving objects and efficiently process large numbers of continuous spatio-temporal queries.

Many recent research works try to address this problem of efficient evaluation of continuous spatio-temporal queries. Some focus on indexing techniques

[14, 20, 32, 37], other on shared execution paradigms [24, 29, 39], yet others on special algorithms [34, 27]. A major shortcoming of these existing solutions, however, is that most of them still process and materialize every location update individually. Even in [24, 39] where authors exploit a *shared execution* paradigm among all queries, when performing a join, each moving object and query is ultimately processed individually. With an extremely large number of objects and queries, this may simply become impossible.

Here we now propose a two-pronged strategy towards combating this scalability problem. Our solution is based on the fact that in many applications objects naturally move in clusters, including traffic jams, animal and bird migrations, groups of children on a trip or people evacuating from danger zones. Such moving objects tend to have some common motion related properties (e.g., speed and destination). In [41] Zhang et. al. exploited *micro-clustering* for data summarization i.e., grouping data that are so close to each other that they can be treated as one unit. In [22] Li et. al. extended this concept to *moving micro-clusters*, groups of objects that are not only close to each other at a current time, but also likely to move together for a while. These works focus on finding interesting patterns in the movements. We take the concept of *moving micro-clusters*[1] further, and exploit this concept towards the optimization of the execution of the spatio-temporal queries on moving objects.

We propose the <u>S</u>calable <u>Cl</u>uster-<u>B</u>ased <u>A</u>lgorithm (SCUBA) for evaluating continuous spatio-temporal queries on moving objects. SCUBA exploits a *shared cluster-based execution* paradigm, where moving objects and queries are grouped together into moving clusters based on common spatio-temporal attributes. Then execution of queries is abstracted as a *join-between* clusters and a *join-within* clusters executed periodically (every $\Delta$ time units). In *join-between*, two clusters are tested for overlap (i.e., if they intersect with each other) as a cheap pre-filtering step. If the clusters are filtered out, the objects and queries belonging to these clusters are guaranteed to not join at an individual level. Thereafter, in *join-within*, individual objects and queries inside clusters are joined with each other. This two-step filter-and-join process helps reduce the number of unnecessary spatial joins. Maintaining clusters comes with a cost, but our experimental evaluations demonstrate it is much cheaper than keeping the complete information about individual locations of objects and queries and processing them individually.

If in spite of our cheap pre-filtering step, the query engine still cannot cope with the current query workload due to the limited system resources, the results may get delayed and by the time they are produced probably become obsolete. This can be tackled by shedding some data and thus reducing the work to be done. The second contribution of this work is the application of moving clusters as means for intelligent load shedding of spatio-temporal data. Since clusters serve as summaries of their members, individual locations of the members can be discarded if need be, yet would still be sufficiently approximated from the location of the their cluster centroid. The closest to the centroid members are

---

[1] We use the term *moving clusters* in this paper.

abstracted into a nested structure called *cluster nucleus*, and their positions are load shed. The nuclei serve as approximations of the positions of their members in a compact form. To the best of our knowledge this is the first work that exploits moving clustering as means to perform intelligent load shedding of spatio-temporal data.

For simplicity, we present our work in the context of continuous spatio-temporal range queries. However, SCUBA is applicable to other types of spatio-temporal queries (e.g., *knn* queries, trajectory and aggregate queries). Since clusters themselves serve as summaries of the objects they contain (i.e., aggregate) based on objects' common properties. This can facilitate in answering some of the aggregate queries. For knn queries, moving clusters that are not intersecting with other moving clusters and contain at least k members can be assumed to contain nearest members of the query object.

The contributions of this paper are the following:

1. We describe the incremental cluster formation technique that efficiently forms clusters at run-time. Our approach assures longevity and quality of the motion clusters by utilizing two key thresholds, namely distance threshold $\Theta_D$ and speed threshold $\Theta_S$.
2. We propose SCUBA - a first of its kind cluster-based algorithm utilizing dynamic clusters for optimizing evaluation of spatio-temporal queries. We show how the cluster-based execution with the two-step filtering approach reduces the number of unnecessary joins and improves query execution on moving objects.
3. We describe how moving clusters can naturally be applied as means for intelligent load shedding of spatio-temporal data. This approach avoids performance degradation with minimal harm to result quality.
4. We provide experimental evidence on real datasets that SCUBA improves the performance when evaluating spatio-temporal queries on moving objects. The experiments evaluate the efficiency of incremental cluster formation algorithm, query execution and load shedding.

The rest of the paper is organized as follows: Section 2 is background on the motion model. The essential features of moving clusters are described in Section 3. Section 4 introduces join algorithm using moving clusters. Moving cluster-driven load shedding is presented in Section 5. Section 6 describes experimental evaluation. Section 7 discusses related work, while Section 8 concludes the paper.

## 2  Background on the Motion Model

We employ a similar motion model as in [22,34], where moving objects are assumed to move in a piecewise linear manner in a road network (Fig. 1). Their movements are constrained by roads, which are connected by *network nodes*, also known as *connection nodes*[2].

---

[2] Our solution relies on the fact that objects have common spatio-temporal properties independent of whether objects move in the network or not, and is applicable to both constrained and unconstrained moving objects.

We assume moving objects' location updates arrive via data streams and have the following form ($o.OID$, $o.Loc_t$, $o.t$, $o.Speed$, $o.CNLoc$, o.Attrs), where $o.OID$ is the id of the moving object, $o.Loc_t$ is the position of the moving object, $o.t$ is the time of the update, $o.Speed$ is the current speed, and $o.CNLoc$ is the position of the connection node in the road network that next be reached by the moving object (its current destination). We assume that an $CNLoc$ of the object doesn't change before the object reaches this connection node, i.e., the network is stable. $o.Attrs$ is a set of attributes describing the object (e.g., child, red car).

A continuously running query is represented in a similar form ($q.QID$, $q.Loc_t$, $q.t$, $q.Speed$, $q.CNLoc$, $q.Attrs$). Unlike for the objects, $q.Attrs$ represents a set of query-specific attributes (e.g., size of the range query)

## 3 Overall Moving Cluster Framework

### 3.1 The Notion of Moving Clusters

A *moving cluster* (Fig. 2) abstracts a set of moving objects and moving queries. Examples include a group of cars travelling on a highway, or a herd of migrating animals. We group both moving objects and moving queries into *moving clusters* based on common spatio-temporal properties i.e., with the intuition that the grouped entities[3] travel closely together in time and space for some period. We consider the following attributes when grouping moving objects and queries into clusters: (1) speed, (2) direction of the movement (e.g., connection node on the road network), (3) relative spatial distance, and (4) time of when in that location. Moving objects and queries that don't satisfy conditions of any other existing clusters form their own clusters, *single-member moving clusters*. As objects and queries can enter or leave a moving cluster at any time, the properties of the cluster are adjusted accordingly (Section 3.2).

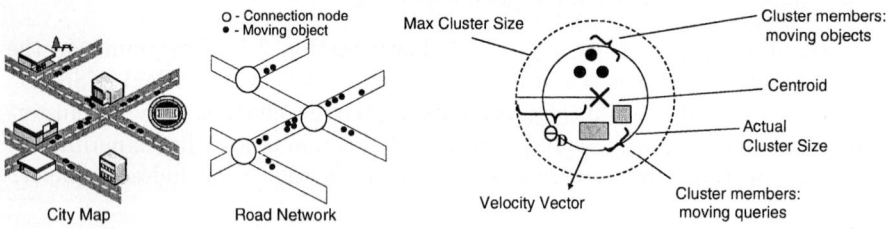

**Fig. 1.** Road Network Representation    **Fig. 2.** Moving Cluster in SCUBA

A moving cluster $m$ at time $t$ is represented in the form ($m.CID$, $m.Loc_t$, $m.n$, $m.OIDs$, $m.QIDs$, $m.AveSpeed$, $m.CNLoc$, $m.R$, $m.ExpTime$), where $m.CID$ is the moving cluster id, $m.Loc_t$ is the location of the centroid of the cluster at time $t$, $m.n$ is the number of moving objects and queries that belong to this

---

[3] By entities we mean both moving objects and queries.

cluster, $m.OIDs$ and $m.QIDs$ are the collections of id's and relative positions of the moving objects and queries respectively that belong to this moving cluster, $m.AveSpeed$ is the average speed of the cluster, $m.CNLoc$ is the cluster destination, $m.R$ is the size of the radius, and $m.ExpTime$ is the "expiration" time of the cluster (for instance, this may be the time when the cluster reaches the $m.CNLoc$ travelling at $m.AveSpeed$). The motivation behind the "expiration" time of the cluster is the fact that once a cluster reaches its $m.CNLoc$ (which may represent a major road intersection) its members may change their spatio-temporal properties significantly (e.g., move in different directions) and thus no longer belong to the same cluster. Alternate options are possible here (e.g., splitting a moving cluster). We plan to explore this as a part of our future work.

Individual positions of moving objects and queries inside a cluster are represented in a relative form using polar coordinates (with the pole at the centroid of the cluster). For any location update point $P$ its polar coordinates are $(r, \theta)$, where $r$ is the radial distance from the centroid, and $\theta$ is the the counterclockwise angle from the x-axis. As time progresses, the center of the cluster might shift, thus making it necessary to transform the relative coordinates of the cluster members. We maintain a transformation vector for each cluster that records the changes in position of the centroid between the periodic executions. We refrain from constantly updating the relative positions of the cluster members, as this info is not needed, unless a *join-within* is to be performed (Fig. 3).

We face the challenge that with time clusters may deteriorate [15]. To keep a competitive and *high quality* clustering (i.e., clusters with compact sizes), we set the following thresholds to limit the sizes and deterioration of the clusters as the time progresses: (1) *distance threshold* ($\Theta_D$) and (2) *speed threshold* ($\Theta_S$). Distance threshold guarantees that the clustered entities are close to each other at the time of clustering, while the speed threshold assures that the entities will stay close to each other for some time in the future. The thresholds prevent dissimilar moving entities from being classified under the same cluster and ensure that good quality clusters will be formed.

Clusters are *dissolved* once they reach their destination points. So if the distance between the location where the cluster has been formed and its destination is short, the clustering approach might be quite expensive and not as worthwhile. The same reasoning applies if the average speed of the cluster is very fast and it thus reaches its destination point very quickly, then forming a cluster might not give very little, if any, advantages. In a typical real-life scenario though, moving objects can reach relatively high speeds on the larger roads (e.g., highways), where connection nodes would be far apart from each other. On the smaller roads, speed limit, and the proximity of other cars constrains the maximum speed the objects can develop, thus extending the time it takes for them to reach the connection nodes. These observations support our intuition that clustering is applicable to different speed scenarios for moving objects in every day life.

## 3.2 Moving Cluster Formation

We adapt an incremental clustering algorithm, similar to the *Leader-Follower* clustering [8, 16], to create and maintain moving clusters in SCUBA. Incremental clustering allows us not to store all the location updates that are to be grouped into the clusters. So the space requirements are small compared to the non-incremental algorithms. Also once $\Delta$ expires, SCUBA can immediately proceed with the query execution, without spending any time on re-clustering the entire data set. However, incremental clustering makes local one-at-a time decisions and its outcome is in part dependent on the arrival order of updates. We experimentally evaluate the tradeoff between the execution time and clustering quality when clustering location updates incrementally as updates arrive vs. non-incrementally when the entire data set is available (Sec. 6.4).

We now will illustrate using an example of a moving object how moving entities get clustered. A spatial grid index (we will refer to it as *ClusterGrid*) is used to optimize the process of clustering. When a location update from the moving object $o$ arrives, the following five steps determine the moving cluster it belongs to:

**Step 1:** Use moving object's position to probe the spatial grid index *ClusterGrid* to find the moving clusters ($S_c$) in the proximity of the current location (i.e., clusters that the object can potentially join).

**Step 2:** If there are no clusters in the grid cell ($S_c = \emptyset$), then the object forms its own cluster, with the centroid at the current location of the object, and the radius $= 0$;

**Step 3:** If otherwise, there are clusters that the object can potentially join, we iterate through the list of the clusters $S_c$ and for each moving cluster $m_i \in S_c$ check the following properties:

1. Is the moving object moving in the same direction as the cluster $m_i$ ($o.CNLoc == m_i.CNLoc$)?
2. Is the distance between the centroid of the cluster and the location update less than the distance threshold, that is $|o.Loc_t - m_i.Loc_t| \leq \Theta_D$?
3. Is the speed of the moving object less than the speed threshold, that is $|o.Speed - m_i.AveSpeed| \leq \Theta_S$?

**Step 4:** If the moving object $o$ satisfies all three conditions in Step 3, then the moving cluster $m_i$ *absorbs* $o$, and adjusts its properties based on $o$'s attributes. The cluster centroid position is adjusted by considering the new relative position of object $o$. The average speed gets recomputed. If the distance between the object $o$ and the cluster centroid is greater than the current radius, the radius is increased. Finally, the count of the cluster members is incremented.

**Step 5:** If $o$ cannot join any existing cluster (from Step 4), $o$ forms its own moving cluster.

Critical situations (e.g., each moving cluster contains one object or one big moving cluster contains all moving objects) are rare to happen. If such situation does in fact occur, then our solution can default to any other state-of-the-art moving objects processing technique without any savings offered by our solution.

# 4 Join Algorithm Using Moving Clusters

In this section, we describe the joining methods utilized by SCUBA to minimize the cost of execution of spatio-temporal queries. The main idea is to group similar objects as well as queries into moving clusters, and then the evaluation

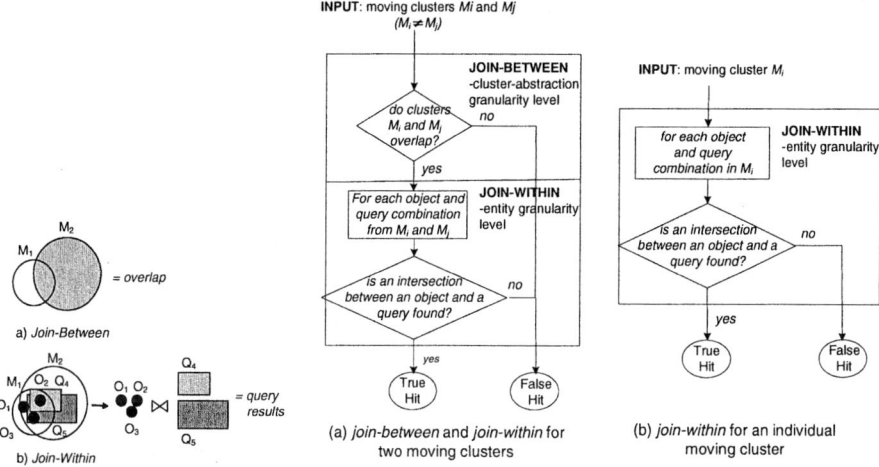

**Fig. 3.** *Join-Between* and *Join-Within* moving clusters

**Fig. 4.** *Join-Between* and *Join-Within* workflows

of a set of spatio-temporal queries is abstracted as a spatial join, first *between* the moving clusters (which serves as a filtering step) and then *within* the moving clusters (Fig. 3). To illustrate the idea, traditionally each individual query is evaluated separately. In the *shared execution* paradigm the problem of evaluating numerous spatio-temporal queries is abstracted as s spatial join between the set of moving objects and queries [39]. While a shared plan allows processing with only one scan, however objects and queries are still joined individually. With large numbers of objects and queries, this may still create a bottleneck in performance and may cause us to potentially run out of memory. The *shared cluster-based execution* groups moving entities into moving clusters and a spatial join is performed on all moving clusters. Only if two clusters overlap, we have to go to the individual object/query level of processing, or automatically assume that objects and queries within those clusters produce join results (Fig. 4).

### 4.1 Data Structures

In the course of execution, SCUBA maintains five in-memory data structures (Fig. 5): (1) *ObjectsTable*, (2) *QueriesTable* (3) *ClusterHome*, (4) *ClusterStorage*, and (5) *ClusterGrid*.

*ObjectsTable* stores the information about objects and their attributes. An object entry in the *ObjectsTable* has the form $(o.OID, o.Attrs)$, where $o.OID$ is the object id and $o.Attrs$ is the list of attributes that describe the object. Similarly, *QueriesTable* stores the information about queries, and has the form $(q.QID, q.Attrs)$ where $q.QID$ is the query id, and the $q.Attrs$ is the list of query attributes. *ClusterHome* is a hash table that keeps track of the current relationships between objects, queries and their corresponding clusters. A moving object/query can belong to only one cluster at a time $t$. An entry in the *ClusterHome* table is of the following form $(ID, type, CID)$, where $ID$ is the id of a moving entity, *type* indicates whether it's an object or a query, and the *CID* is the id of the cluster that this moving entity belongs to. *ClusterStorage* table stores the information (e.g., centroid, radius, member count, etc.) about moving clusters. *ClusterGrid* is a spatial grid table dividing the data space into N x N grid cells. For each grid cell, *ClusterGrid* maintains a list of cluster ids of moving clusters that overlap with that cell.

### 4.2 The SCUBA Algorithm

SCUBA execution has three phases: (1) *cluster pre-join maintenance*, (2) *cluster-based joining*, and (3) *cluster post-join maintenance* as depicted in Fig. 6. The cluster pre-join maintenance phase is continuously running where it receives incoming information from moving objects and queries and applies in-memory clustering. In this phase, depending on the incoming location updates, new clusters may be formed, "empty" clusters may be dissolved, and existing clusters may be expanded. The cluster-based joining phase is activated every $\Delta$ time units where join-between and join-within moving clusters is executed. The cluster post-join phase is started by the end of the joining phase to perform a cluster maintenance for the next query evaluation time.

Algorithm 1 shows the pseudo code for SCUBA execution. For each execution interval, SCUBA first initializes the interval start time (Step 3). Before $\Delta$ time interval expires, SCUBA receives the incoming location updates from moving objects and queries and incrementally updates existing moving clusters or creates new ones (Step 6).

When $\Delta$ time interval expires (location updating is done), SCUBA starts the query execution (Step 8) by performing *join-between* clusters and *join-within* clusters. If two clusters are of the same type (all objects, or all queries), they are not considered for the *join-between*. Similarly, if all of the members of the cluster are of the same type, no *join-within* is performed. The *join-between* checks if the circular regions of the two clusters overlap (Algorithm 2), and *join-within* performs a spatial join between the objects and queries of the two clusters (Algorithm 3). If *join-between* does not result in intersection, *join-within* is skipped.

After the joining phase, cluster maintenance is performed (Step 23). Due to space limitations, we don't include the pseudo-code for *PostJoinClustersMainte-*

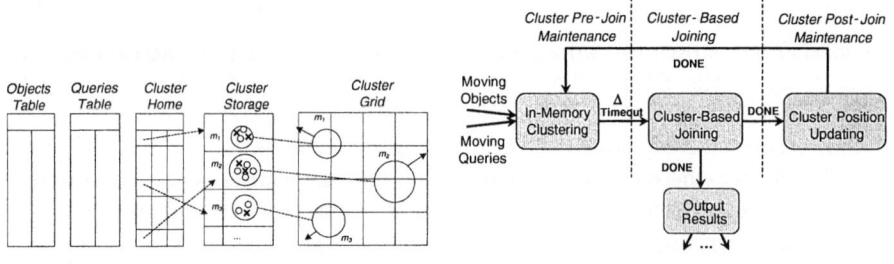

**Fig. 5.** Data Structures in SCUBA          **Fig. 6.** State Diagram

**Algorithm 1.** *SCUBA()*

```
1:  loop
2:    //*** CLUSTER PRE-JOIN MAINTENANCE PHASE ***
3:    T_start = current time //initialize the execution interval start time
4:    while (current time - T_start) < Δ do
5:      if new location update arrived then
6:        Cluster moving object o/query q //procedure described in Section 3.2
      // Δ expires. Begin evaluation of queries
7:    //*** CLUSTER-BASED JOINING PHASE ***
8:    for c = 0 to MAX_GRID_CELL do
9:      for every moving cluster m_L ∈ G_c do
10:       for every moving cluster m_R ∈ G_c do
11:         //if the same cluster, do only join-within
12:         if (m_L == m_R) then
13:           //do within-join only if the cluster contains members of different types
14:           if ((m_L.OIDs > 0) && (m_L.QIDs > 0)) then
15:             Call DoWithinClusterJoin(m_L,m_L)
16:         else
17:           //do between-join only if 2 clusters contain members of different types
18:           if ((m_L.OIDs > 0) && (m_R.QIDs > 0)) ||
                 ((m_L.QIDs > 0) && (m_R.OIDs > 0)) then
19:             if DoBetweenClusterJoin(m_L,m_R) == TRUE then
20:               Call DoWithinClusterJoin(m_L,m_R)
21:   Send new query answers to users
22:   //*** CLUSTER POST-JOIN MAINTENANCE PHASE ***
23:   Call PostJoinClustersMaintenance() //do some cluster maintenance
```

**Algorithm 2.** *DoBetweenClusterJoin(Cluster $m_L$, Cluster $m_R$)*

```
1:  //Check if two circular clusters m_L and m_R overlap
2:  if ((m_L.Loc_t.x - m_R.Loc_t.x)^2 + (m_L.Loc_t.y - m_R.Loc_t.y)^2) < (m_L.R - m_R.R)^2 then
3:    return TRUE; //the clusters overlap
4:  else
5:    return FALSE; //the clusters don't overlap
```

*nance()*. The operations performed during post-join cluster maintenance include dissolving "expiring" clusters and re-locating the "non-expiring" clusters (in the ClusterGrid) based on their velocity vectors for the next execution interval time (i.e., $T + \Delta$). If at time $T + \Delta$ the cluster passes its destination node, the cluster gets dissolved.

**Example.** Fig. 7 gives an illustrative example for the SCUBA algorithm. There are two moving clusters $M_1$ and $M_2$ (Fig. 7a). $M_1$ contains four moving objects ($O_1, O_2, O_3, O_5$) and no moving queries. $M_2$ contains one moving object ($O_4$) and two moving queries ($Q_1, Q_2$). New moving object $O_6$ and a new moving query $Q_3$ send their location updates (Fig. 7b). $Q_3$ has common attributes with moving cluster $M_1$ and $O_6$ has common attributes with $M_2$. Thus $M_1$ adds query $Q_3$ as its member (which causes its radius to expand). $M_2$ adds object $O_6$ as its member (no radius expansion here) (Fig. 7c). In Fig. 7d, we differentiate the members of the two clusters using color[4]. At time T the cluster joining phase begins (Fig. 7e). *Join-between* $M_1$ and $M_2$ returns a positive overlap. Thus the *join-within* the two clusters must be performed which produces a result ($Q_2, O_3$). *Join-within* for the cluster $M_1$ returns a result ($Q_3, O_5$). After the cluster joining phase,

---
[4] We do it for visibility purpose for the reader. No such step is executed in SCUBA.

**Algorithm 3.** *DoWithinClusterJoin(Cluster $m_L$, Cluster $m_R$)*

1:  $R = \emptyset$; //set of results
2:  $S_q$ = Set of queries from $m_L \cup m_R$ //query members from both clusters
3:  $S_o$ = Set of objects from $m_L \cup m_R$ //object members from both clusters
    //join moving objects with queries from both clusters
4:  **for** every moving object $o_i \in S_o$ **do**
5:     **for** every moving query $q_j \in S_q$ **do**
6:        spatial join between object $o_i$ with query $q_j$ ($o_i \bowtie q_j$)
7:        $S_r$ = Set of queries from joining $o_i$ with queries in $S_q$
8:        **for** each $Q \in S_q$ **do**
9:           add $(Q, o_i)$ to $R$
10: return $R$;

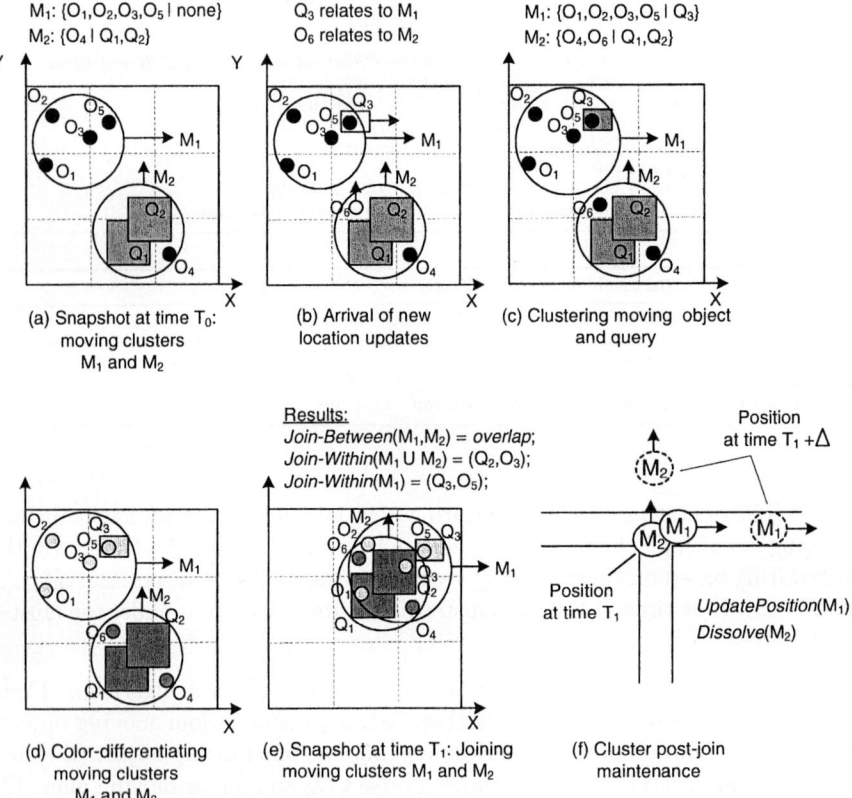

**Fig. 7.** SCUBA execution example

the maintenance on the clusters is performed (Fig. 7f). Based on the velocity vectors, SCUBA calculates the positions of the clusters at the next joining time (T+$\Delta$). Since $M_1$ still hasn't reached its destination node at time T+$\Delta$, it is not dissolved, but moved to its expected position based on the velocity vector. $M_2$ will pass its destination at the next join time. It will be dissolved at this stage.

## 5 Load Shedding Using Moving Clusters

Load shedding is not a new idea. It has been well explored in networking [18], multimedia [6], and streaming databases [2, 36, 35]. Typically, there are two fundamental approaches distinguishing which data tuples to load shed, namely random tuples or semantically less important ones [36]. Thereafter, most works thus far primarily focus on the easy case, namely random drops, treating all tuples equally in terms of value to users [28, 35]. We instead here follow the idea of semantic load-shedding, however now as applied to the spatio-temporal context. That is, our proposal is to use moving clusters to identify and thus subsequently discard the less important data first (i.e., the data that would cause the minimal loss in accuracy of the answer). Specifically, we consider for this purpose relative positions of the cluster members with respect to their centroids.

Depending on the system load and the accuracy requirements, SCUBA employs the following methods for handling cluster members (Fig. 8). Namely, all cluster members' relative positions are maintained (i.e., no load shedding) (Fig. 8a), none of the individual positions are maintained (i.e., full load shedding) (Fig. 8b), or a subset of relative positions of the cluster members are maintained (partial load shedding) (Fig. 8c). The members near the center are abstracted into a structure inside a cluster called *nucleus*, a circular region that approximates the positions of the cluster members near the centroid of the cluster. The size of the nucleus is determined by its radius threshold, $\Theta_N$ parameter where $(0 \leq \Theta_N \leq \Theta_D)$. The larger the value of $\Theta_N$, the more data is load shed.

If the system is about to run out of memory, SCUBA begins load shedding of cluster member positions and uses a *nucleus* to approximate their positions. If memory requirements are still high, then SCUBA load sheds positions of all cluster members. In this case the cluster is the sole representation of the movement of the objects and queries that belong to it. Such abstraction of cluster members positions by nucleus/cluster corresponds to a tradeoff between accuracy and performance. The accuracy depends on how compact the clusters are. The larger the size of the clusters, the more false positives we might get for answers when

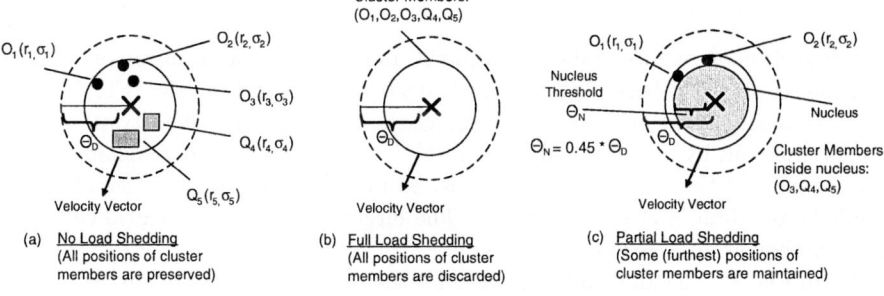

**Fig. 8.** Moving cluster-driven load shedding

performing the join-between. If individual positions are load shed, then when two clusters intersect (in *join-between*), we assume that the objects from the clusters satisfy the queries from both clusters. Making the size of the clusters compact will give more accurate answers, but also will increase the overall number of clusters, hence the join time. Increasing the size of clusters would make the processing faster, but with less accurate results. In Section 6.6 we evaluate all three schemes (i.e., no load shedding, full load shedding, and partial load shedding) in terms of its impact on performance and accuracy.

## 6 Experimental Evaluation

In this section, we compare SCUBA with a traditional grid-based spatio-temporal range algorithm[5], where objects and queries are hashed based on their locations into an index, say a grid. Then a cell-by-cell join between moving objects and queries is performed. Grid-based execution approach is a common choice for spatio-temporal query execution [9, 24, 27, 39, 29]. In all experiments queries are evaluated periodically (every $\Delta$ time units).

### 6.1 Experimental Settings

We have implemented SCUBA inside our stream processing system CAPE [31]. Moving objects and queries generated by the *Network-Based Generator of Moving Objects* [5] are used as data. The input to the generator is the road map of Worcester, USA. All the experiments were performed on Red Hat Linux (3.2.3-24) with Intel(R) XEON(TM) CPU 2.40GHz and 2GB RAM. Unless mentioned otherwise, the following parameters are used in the experiments. The set of objects consists of 10,000 objects and 10,000 spatio-temporal range queries. Each evaluation interval, 100% of objects and queries send their location updates every time unit. No load shedding is performed, unless noted otherwise. For the *ClusterGrid* table we chose a 100x100 grid size. $\Delta$ is set to 2 time units. The distance threshold $\Theta_D$ equals 100 spatial units, and the speed threshold $\Theta_S$ is set to 10 (spatial units/time units).

### 6.2 Varying Grid Cell Size

In this section, we compare the performance and memory consumption of SCUBA and the regular grid-based algorithm when varying the grid cell size. Fig. 9 varies the granularity of the grid (on x-axis). Since the coverage area (the city of Worcester) is constant, by increasing/decreasing the cell count in each dimension (x- and y-), we control the sizes of the grid cells. So in the 50x50 grid the size of a grid cell is larger than in the 150x150 grid. The larger the count of the grid cells, the smaller they are in size and vice versa.

From Fig. 9a, the join time decreases for the regular operator when decreasing the grid cell size. The reason for that is that smaller cells contain fewer objects

---
[5] For simplicity, we will refer to it as *regular execution* or *regular operator*.

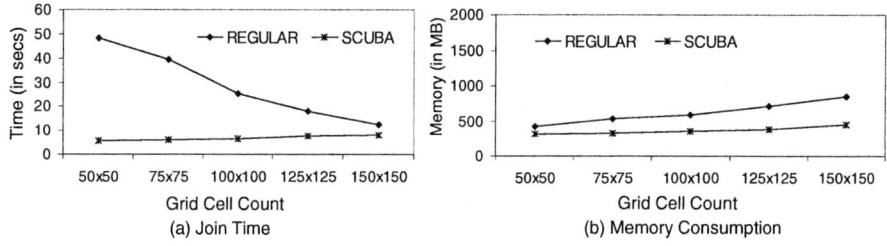

**Fig. 9.** Varying grid size

and queries. Hence, fewer comparisons (joins) need to be made. But the fine granularity of the grid comes at a price of higher memory consumption, because of the large number of grid cells, each containing individual location updates of objects and queries.

The join time for SCUBA slightly goes up as the grid cell sizes become smaller. But the change is minimal, because the cluster sizes are compact and even as the granularity of the cells is increasing, the size of grid cells is frequently larger than the size of clusters. So unless many clusters are on the borderline of the grid cells (overlapping with more than one cell), the performance of SCUBA is not "hurt" by the finer granularity of the grid. Moreover, only one entry per cluster (which aggregates several objects and queries) needs to be made in a grid cell vs. having an individual entry for each object and query. This provides significant memory savings when processing extremely large numbers of densely moving objects and queries.

### 6.3 Varying Skewness to Facilitate Clustering

Now we study the impact of the skew in the spatio-temporal attributes of moving objects and queries. By varying the cluster-related attributes causing objects and queries to be very dissimilar (no common attribute values) or very much alike (i.e., clusterable). This determines the number of clusters and the number of cluster members per cluster.

In Fig. 10, the *skew factor* on x-axis represents the average number of moving entities that have similar spatio-temporal properties, and thus could be grouped

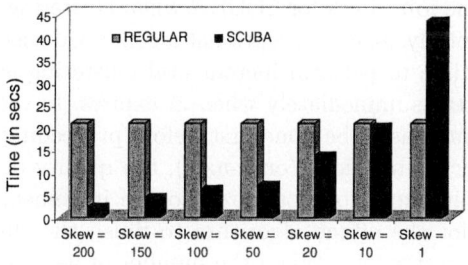

**Fig. 10.** Join time with skewing factor

into one cluster. For instance, when skew factor = 1, each object and query moves in a distinct way. Hence each forms its own cluster. When the skew factor = 200, every 200 objects/queries send their updates move in a similar way. Thus they typically may form a cluster. In Fig. 10, when not many objects and queries are clusterable, the SCUBA performance suffers due to the overhead of many single-member clusters. Thus more join-between clusters are performed as the number of clusters goes up. If many single member clusters spatially overlap, the join-within is performed as well. This increases the overall join time. In real life this scenario is highly unlikely as with a large number of moving objects the chance increases that common motion attributes for some duration of time are present (e.g., increase in traffic on the roads). As the skew factor increases (10-200), and more objects and queries are clusterable, the join time for SCUBA significantly decreases. The overall join time is several orders of magnitude faster compared to a regular grid-based approach when the skew factor equals 200, i.e., approximately 200 moving entities per cluster.

## 6.4 Incremental vs. Non-incremental Clustering

In this section we study the tradeoff between the improved quality of the clusters which can be achieved when clustering is done non-incrementally (with all data points available at the same time) and the performance of SCUBA. As proposed, SCUBA clusters location updates incrementally upon their arrival. We wanted to investigate if clustering done offline (i.e., non-incrementally, when all the data points are available) and thus producing better quality clusters and facilitating a faster join-between the clusters outweighs the cost of non-incremental clustering. In particular, we focus on the join processing time, and how much improvement in join processing could be achieved with better quality clusters.

We implemented a *K-means* (a common clustering algorithm) extension to SCUBA for non-incremental clustering. The K-means algorithm expects the number of clusters specified in advance. We used a tracking counter for the number of unique destinations of objects and queries for a rough estimate of the number of clusters needed. Another disadvantage is that K-means needs several iterations over the dataset before it converges. With each iteration, the quality of clustering improves, but the clustering time increases. We varied the number of iterations from 1 to 10 in this experiment to observe the impact on quality of clusters achieved by increasing the number of iterations.

Fig. 11 presents the join times for SCUBA when clustering is done incrementally vs non-incrementally. The bars represent a combined cost of clustering time and join time. The time to perform incremental clustering is not portrayed as the join processing starts immediately when $\Delta$ expires. In the offline clustering scenario, the clustering has to be done first before proceeding to the join. With the increased number of iterations (on x-axis), the quality of clusters improves resulting in faster join execution compared to the incremental case. However, the cost of waiting for the offline algorithm to finish the clustering outweighs the advantage of the faster join. When the number of iterations is 3 or greater, the clustering time in fact takes longer than the actual join processing. The

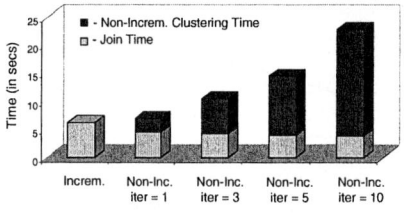 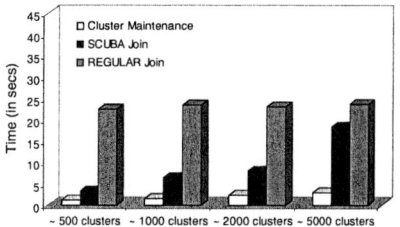

**Fig. 11.** Incr. vs. Non-Incr. Clustering     **Fig. 12.** Cluster Maintenance

larger the dataset the more expensive each iteration becomes. Offline clustering is not suitable for clustering large amounts of moving objects when there are constraints on execution time and memory space. Even with a reduced number of scans through the data set and improved join time, the advantage of having better quality clusters is not amortized due to the amount of time spent on offline clustering and larger memory requirements. This justifies the appropriateness of our incremental clustering as an efficient clustering solution.

### 6.5 Cluster Maintenance Cost

In this section, we compare the cluster maintenance cost with respect to join time in SCUBA and regular grid-based join time. Fig. 12 gives the cluster maintenance time when the number of clusters is varied. By cluster maintenance cost we mean the time it takes to pre- and post-process the clusters before and after the join is complete (i.e., form new clusters, expand existing clusters, calculate the future position of the cluster using its average speed, dissolve expired clusters, and re-insert clusters into the grid for the next evaluation interval).

For this experiment, we varied the skew factor to affect the average number of the clusters (the number of objects and queries stays the same). The x-axis represents the average number of clusters in the system. Fig. 12 shows that the cluster maintenance (which is an overhead for SCUBA) is relatively cheap. If we combine cluster maintenance with SCUBA join time to represent the overall join cost for SCUBA, it is still faster than the regular grid-based execution. Hence, even though maintaining clusters comes with a cost, it is superior over processing objects and queries individually.

### 6.6 Moving-Cluster-Driven Load Shedding

Here we evaluate the effect of moving cluster-based load shedding on the performance and accuracy in SCUBA. Figures 13a and 13b respectively represent the join processing times and accuracy measurements for SCUBA when load shedding positions of the cluster members. The x-axis represents the percent of the size of the *nucleus* (i.e., circular region in the cluster approximating cluster members whose positions are discarded) with respect to the maximum size of the cluster. For simplicity, we will refer to percent of the nucleus-to-cluster size as $\eta$. When $\eta = 0\%$, no data is discarded. On the opposite, when $\eta = 100\%$,

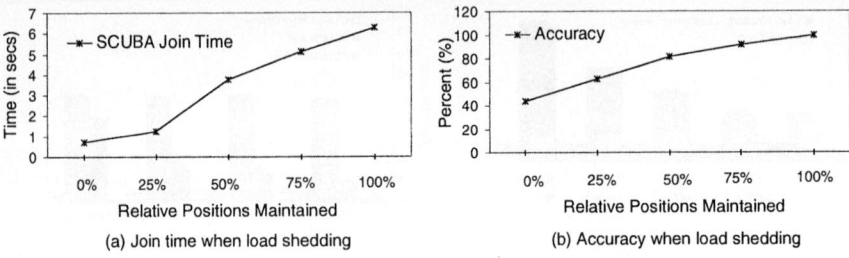

**Fig. 13.** Cluster-Based Load Shedding

all cluster members' positions are discarded, and the cluster solely approximates the positions of its members. The fewer relative positions are maintained, the fewer individual joins need to be performed when executing a join-within for overlapping clusters.

As expected load shedding comes at a price of less accurate results (Fig. 13b). To measure accuracy, we compare the results outputted by SCUBA when $\eta = 0\%$ (no load shedding) to the ones output when $\eta > 0\%$, calculating the number of false-negative and false-positive results. The size of the nucleus has a significant impact on the accuracy of the results when performing load shedding. Hence it must be carefully considered. When $\eta = 50\%$, the accuracy $\approx 79\%$. So relatively good results can be produced with cluster-based load shedding even if 50 % of a cluster region is shed. If random load shedding were to be performed, the same number of tuples - but just not the same tuples would be load shed. Instead the shedding mechanism would randomly pick which ones to shed, potentially throwing away more important data and significantly degrading the results' accuracy.

## 7 Related Work

**Related Work on Spatio-Temporal Query Processing:** Efficient evaluation of spatio-temporal queries on moving objects has been an active area of research for quite some time. Several optimization techniques have been developed. These include Query Indexing and Velocity Constrained Indexing (VCI) [29], shared execution [24, 38, 39], incremental evaluation [24, 39], and query-aware moving objects [17]. Query Indexing indexes queries using an R-tree-like structure. At each evaluation step, only those objects that have moved since the previous evaluation step are evaluated against the Q-index. VCI utilizes the maximum possible speed of objects to delay the expensive updates to the index. To reduce wireless communication and query reevaluation costs, Hu et. al [17] utilize the notion of safe region, making the moving objects query aware. Query reevaluation in this framework is triggered by location updates only. In the similar spirit [29] and [38] try to minimize the number of unnecessary joins between objects and queries by using the *Safe* and *No-Action* regions respectively. In the latter case, the authors combine it with different join policies to filter out the objects and queries that are guaranteed not to join.

The scalability in spatio-temporal query processing has been addressed in [11, 23, 24, 29, 39]. In a distributed environment, such as MobiEyes [11], part of the query processing is send to the clients. The limitations of this approach is that the devices may not have enough battery power and memory capacity to perform the complex computations. The shared execution paradigm as means to achieve scalability has been used in SINA [24] for continuous spatio-temporal range queries, and in SEA-CNN [39] for continuous spatio-temporal kNN queries. Our study falls into this category and distinguishes itself from these previous works by focusing on utilizing moving clusters abstracting similar moving entities to optimize the execution and minimize the individual processing.

**Related Work on Clustering:** Clustering has been an active field for over 20 years [1, 25, 41]. Previous work typically uses clustering to analyze data to find interesting patterns. We instead apply clustering as means to achieve scalable processing of continuous queries on moving objects. To the best of our knowledge, this is the first work to use clustering for shared execution optimization of continuous queries on spatio-temporal data streams.

In this work we considered clustering algorithms in which clusters have a distinguished point, a center. The commonly used clustering algorithm for such clustering, k-means, is described in [8, 13, 30]. Our concentration was on incremental clustering algorithms only [4], [7], and [40]. Some of the published clustering algorithms for an incremental clustering of data streams include BIRCH[41], COB-WEB [10], STREAM [12, 26], Fractal Clustering [3], and the Leader-Follower (LF) [16]. Clustering analysis is a well researched area, and due to space limitations we do not discuss all of the clustering algorithms available. For an elaborate survey on clustering, readers are referred to [19]. In our work, we adapt an incremental clustering algorithm, similar to the Leader-Follower clustering [16]. The extensibility, running time and the computational complexity of this algorithm is such that makes it attractive for processing streaming data.

Clustering of spatio-temporal data has been explored to a limited degree in [21]. This work [21] concentrates on discovering moving clusters using historic trajectories of the moving objects. The algorithms proposed assume that all data is available. Our work instead clusters moving entities at run-time and utilizes moving clusters to solve a completely different problem, namely, efficient processing of continuous spatio-temporal queries.

## 8 Conclusions and Future Work

In this paper, we propose a unique algorithm for efficient processing of large numbers of spatio-temporal queries on moving objects termed SCUBA. SCUBA combines motion clustering with shared execution for query execution optimization. Given a set of moving objects and queries, SCUBA groups them into moving clusters based on common spatio-temporal attributes. To optimize the join execution, SCUBA performs a two-step join execution process by first pre-filtering a set of moving clusters that could produce potential results in the join-between moving clusters stage and then proceeding with the individual join-within execution on those selected moving clusters. Comprehensive experiments show that the performance of SCUBA is better than traditional grid-based approach where moving entities are processed individually. In particular the experiments demonstrate that SCUBA: (1) facilitates efficient execution of queries on moving objects that have common spatio-temporal attributes, (2) has low cluster maintenance/overhead cost, and (3) naturally facilitates load shedding using motion clusters while optimizing the processing time with minimal degradation in result quality. We believe our work is the first to utilize motion clustering to optimize the execution of continuous queries on spatio-temporal data streams. As future work, we plan to further refine and validate moving cluster-driven load shedding, enhance SCUBA to produce results incrementally and explore further through additional experimentation.

# References

1. R. Agrawal and et. al. Automatic subspace clustering of high dimensional data for data mining applications. In *SIGMOD*, pages 94–105, 1998.
2. B. Babcock, M. Datar, and R. Motwani. Load shedding techniques for data stream systems, 2003.
3. D. Barbará. Chaotic mining: Knowledge discovery using the fractal dimension. In *SIGMOD Workshop on Data Mining and Knowl. Discovery*, 1999.
4. D. Barbará. Requirements for clustering data streams. *SIGKDD Explorations*, 3(2):23–27, 2002.
5. T. Brinkhoff. A framework for generating network-based moving objects. *GeoInformatica*, 6(2):153–180, 2002.
6. C. L. Compton and D. L. Tennenhouse. Collaborative load shedding for media-based applications. In *Int. Conf. on Multimedia Computing and Systems*, 1994.
7. P. Domingos and G. Hulten. Catching up with the data: Research issues in mining data streams. In *DMKD*, 2001.
8. R. O. Duda, P. E. Hart, and D. G. Stork. *Pattern Classification*. Wiley-Interscience Publication, 2000.
9. H. G. Elmongui, M. F. Mokbel, and W. G. Aref. Spatio-temporal histograms. In *SSTD*, 2005.
10. D. H. Fisher. Iterative optimization and simplification of hierarchical clusterings. *CoRR*, cs.AI/9604103, 1996.
11. B. Gedik and L. Liu. Mobieyes: Distributed processing of continuously moving queries on moving objects in a mobile system. In *EDBT*, pages 67–87, 2004.
12. S. Guha, N. Mishra, R. Motwani, and L. O'Callaghan. Clustering data streams. In *FOCS*, pages 359–366, 2000.
13. S. K. Gupta, K. S. Rao, and V. Bhatnagar. K-means clustering algorithm for categorical attributes. In *DaWaK*, pages 203–208, 1999.
14. S. E. Hambrusch, C.-M. Liu, W. G. Aref, and S. Prabhakar. Query processing in broadcasted spatial index trees. In *SSTD*, pages 502–521, 2001.
15. S. Har-Peled. Clustering motion. In *FOCS '01: Proceedings of the 42nd IEEE symposium on Foundations of Computer Science*, page 84, 2001.
16. J. A. Hartigan. *Clustering Algorithms*. John Wiley and Sons, 1975.
17. H. Hu, J. Xu, and D. L. Lee. A generic framework for monitoring continuous spatial queries over moving objects. In *SIGMOD*, 2005.

18. V. Jacobson. Congestion avoidance and control. *SIGCOMM Comput. Commun. Rev.*, 25(1):157–187, 1995.
19. A. K. Jain, M. N. Murthy, and P. J. Flynn. Data clustering: A review. Technical Report MSU-CSE-00-16, Dept. of CS, Michigan State University, 2000.
20. D. V. Kalashnikov and et. al. Main memory evaluation of monitoring queries over moving objects. *Distrib. Parallel Databases*, 15(2), 2004.
21. P. Kalnis, N. Mamoulis, and S. Bakiras. On discovering moving clusters in spatio-temporal data. In *SSTD05*, 2005.
22. Y. Li, J. Han, and J. Yang. Clustering moving objects. In *KDD*, pages 617–622, 2004.
23. M. F. Mokbel and et. al. Towards scalable location-aware services: requirements and research issues. In *GIS*, pages 110–117, 2003.
24. M. F. Mokbel, X. Xiong, and W. G. Aref. Sina: Scalable incremental processing of continuous queries in spatio-temporal databases. In *SIGMOD*, pages 623–634, 2004.
25. R. T. Ng and J. Han. Efficient and effective clustering methods for spatial data mining. In *VLDB*, pages 144–155, 1994.
26. L. O'Callaghan and et. al. Streaming-data algorithms for high-quality clustering. In *ICDE*, page 685, 2002.
27. D. Papadias and et. al. Conceptual partitioning: An efficient method for continuous nearest neighbor monitoring. In *SIGMOD*, 2005.
28. Y. C. Philip. Loadstar: A load shedding scheme for classifying data streams.
29. S. Prabhakar and et.al. Query indexing and velocity constrained indexing: Scalable techniques for continuous queries on moving objects. *IEEE Trans. Computers*, 51(10), 2002.
30. E. M. Rasmussen. Clustering algorithms. In *Information Retrieval: Data Structures & Algorithms*, pages 419–442. 1992.
31. E. A. Rundensteiner, L. Ding, and et.al. Cape: Continuous query engine with heterogeneous-grained adaptivity. In *VLDB*, pages 1353–1356, 2004.
32. S. Saltenis, C. S. Jensen, S. T. Leutenegger, and M. A. Lopez. Indexing the positions of continuously moving objects. In *SIGMOD*, pages 331–342, 2000.
33. A. P. Sistla, O. Wolfson, S. Chamberlain, and S. Dao. Modeling and querying moving objects. In *ICDE*, pages 422–432, 1997.
34. Y. Tao and D. Papadias. Time-parameterized queries in spatio-temporal databases. In *SIGMOD*, pages 334–345, 2002.
35. N. Tatbul. Qos-driven load shedding on data streams. In *EDBT '02: Proceedings of the Worshops XMLDM, MDDE, and YRWS on XML-Based Data Management and Multimedia Engineering-Revised Papers*, London, UK, 2002. Springer-Verlag.
36. N. Tatbul, U. Çetintemel, S. B. Zdonik, M. Cherniack, and M. Stonebraker. Load shedding in a data stream manager. In *VLDB*, pages 309–320, 2003.
37. J. Tayeb, Ö. Ulusoy, and O. Wolfson. A quadtree-based dynamic attribute indexing method. *Comput. J.*, 41(3):185–200, 1998.
38. X. Xiong and M. F. M. et.al. Scalable spatio-temporal continuous query processing for location-aware services. In *SSDBM*, pages 317–, 2004.
39. X. Xiong, M. F. Mokbel, and W. G. Aref. Sea-cnn: Scalable processing of continuous k-nearest neighbor queries in spatio-temporal databases. In *ICDE*, pages 643–654, 2005.
40. N. Ye and X. Li. A scalable, incremental learning algorithm for classification problems. *Comput. Ind. Eng.*, 43(4):677–692, 2002.
41. T. Zhang, R. Ramakrishnan, and M. Livny. Birch: An efficient data clustering method for very large databases. In *SIGMOD*, pages 103–114, 1996.

# Caching Complementary Space for Location-Based Services

Ken C.K. Lee[1], Wang-Chien Lee[1], Baihua Zheng[2], and Jianliang Xu[3]

[1] Pennsylvania State University, University Park, USA
{cklee, wlee}@cse.psu.edu
[2] Singapore Management University, Singapore
bhzheng@smu.edu.sg
[3] Hong Kong Baptist University, Hong Kong
xujl@comp.hkbu.edu.hk

**Abstract.** In this paper, we propose a novel client-side, multi-granularity caching scheme, called *"Complementary Space Caching"* (CS caching), for location-based services in mobile environments. Different from conventional data caching schemes that only cache a portion of dataset, CS caching maintains a global view of the whole dataset. Different portions of this view are cached in varied granularity based on the probabilities of being accessed in the future queries. The data objects with very high access probabilities are cached in the finest granularity, i.e., the data objects themselves. The data objects which are less likely to be accessed in the near future are abstracted and logically cached in the form of complementary regions (CRs) in a coarse granularity. CS caching naturally supports all types of location-based queries. In this paper, we explore several design and system issues of CS caching, including cache memory allocation between objects and CRs, and CR coalescence. We develop algorithms for location-based queries and a cache replacement mechanism. Through an extensive performance evaluation, we show that CS caching is superior to existing caching schemes for location-based services.

## 1 Introduction

Due to the rapid advances in wireless and positioning technologies, location-based services (LBSs) [1] have emerged as one of the killer applications for mobile computing. To improve the access efficiency and alleviate the contention of limited wireless bandwidth in mobile environments, data caching techniques are particularly important for LBSs.

Conventional caching techniques cache a portion of a database in units of tuples or pages. Due to the lack of data semantics, clients cannot be sure whether the cached data alone can sufficiently satisfy some complex queries, forcing them to submit requests to the server even if the answers are completely available in the cache. Semantic caching addresses this problem by caching query results along with their corresponding queries (which serve as the semantic descriptions of the cached query results) [2, 3, 4]. Thus, a query and its result form a semantic

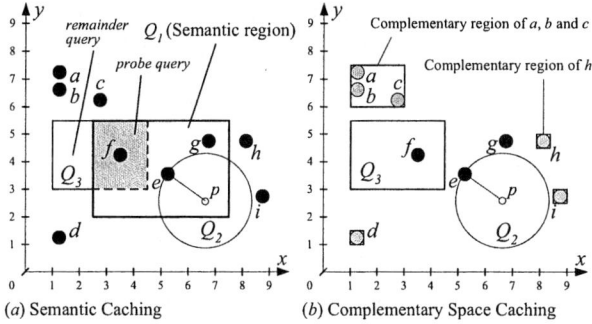

**Fig. 1.** Semantic caching and Complementary space caching

region. By consulting cached semantic regions, a new query can be decomposed into a *probe query* which can be answered locally by the cache and a *remainder query* which is only answerable by the server. If a query is fully covered by cached semantic regions, no contact with the server is needed.

However, the representation of semantic regions is highly query-dependent. If a query is of different type from the queries captured by semantic regions, the cached data objects cannot be reused. Besides, because clients' knowledge about data objects is constrained by cached semantic regions, the clients are unable to determine whether there are objects beyond the cached semantic regions. Therefore if a query is partially covered by semantic regions, remainder queries (i.e., uncovered portions of the query) must be formed and submitted to the server to retrieve possibly missing objects. The following example (as shown in Fig. 1(a)) illustrates the above described deficiencies.

*Example 1.* Suppose that a database server contains 9 objects, namely, '$a$' through '$i$'. A client with an empty cache submits a window query, $Q_1$, to the server. A result set of three objects $\{f, e, g\}$ is returned and cached along with the query window as a semantic region. Later, a nearest neighbor (NN) query, $Q_2$ (with a query point $p$), is issued. Due to incompatibility between window and NN queries, the cached semantic region cannot answer the query even though the result (i.e., $e$) is in the cache. Consequently, $Q_2$ is submitted to server and $e$ is retrieved again. Later, the client issues another window query, $Q_3$, which is partially covered by the semantic region. Thus, a remainder query is submitted to the server even though this query actually retrieves no object. ∎

These deficiencies are due to the lack of a *global view* of data in the cache. For a cache designed to support various kinds of queries, it is desirable to maintain certain auxiliary location information that provides a global view of all data objects in the database. Motivated by this observation, we propose a novel multi-granularity data caching scheme for mobile clients called *Complementary Space Caching* (CS caching). The CS caching distinguishes itself from other caching schemes by having a global view of the whole dataset. Different portions of this cached view have varied granularity based on the probabilities of corresponding data objects to be accessed in the future queries. The data objects with very high access probabilities are cached in the finest granularity, i.e., the actual data objects. Those data objects less likely to be accessed in the near future are not physically cached, rather are abstracted and logically cached in the form of *complementary regions (CRs)* in a coarse granularity. In our design, CRs present auxiliary location information regarding to *missing objects*, i.e., those objects in the server but not kept in the cache. This auxiliary information can facilitate the local processing of various location-dependent queries and alleviate unnecessary queries to the server. Fig. 1(b) shows that same scenario as Example 1 except that CS caching is adopted (where black dots are objects and rectangle boxes are CRs). Since the result of $Q_1$ is cached, object $e$ in the cache can answer $Q_2$ because no other object or CR is closer than $e$ to $p$. $Q_3$ finds only object $f$ inside the query window so no additional objects are needed from the server.

Due to limited cache memory, there is a trade-off between keeping objects and keeping CRs in the cache. Storing more data objects in the cache can potentially provide a higher cache hit rate but reduce the precision of the auxiliary location information in CRs (because more CRs need to be merged and stored in a coarse granularity in order to make rooms for objects). This could lead to more *false misses*, i.e., a query finds a CR for potentially answer objects but no objects are returned. On the other hand, taking more cache memory to maintain fine-granularity CRs will reduce the number of data objects cached physically and thus reduce the cache hits. The design of CS caching strives to optimize the cache memory allocation for physical data objects and CRs in order to achieve a high cache hit rate and a low false miss rate (which leads to the excellent performance in terms of response time and bandwidth consumption). In this paper, we explore several design and system issues of CS caching. We develop and implement algorithms for processing window, range, and $k$ nearest neighbor queries based on CS caching, and develop a very efficient cache replacement mechanism for cache maintenance. Through comprehensive experiments based on simulation, we validate our proposal and show that CS caching is superior to existing caching schemes for location-based services.

The rest of this paper is organized as follows. Section 2 gives an overview of the CS caching model and reviews related work. Section 3 describes the query processing in CS caching. Section 4 discusses CR coalescence, an important technique for reducing transmission overhead. Section 5 describes the cache management. Section 6 reports the simulation result. At last, Section 7 states our future directions.

## 2 Complementary Space Caching

In this section, we first briefly review the R-tree and the notion of minimum bounding boxes that we adopt to represent complementary regions. We then describe the CS caching model and discuss some relevant research.

## 2.1 Preliminaries

In many spatial databases, objects are very often indexed using R-tree [5] or its variants for its efficiency and wide acceptance. In R-tree, objects close in space are clustered in a leaf node represented as a *minimum bounding box (MBB)*. Nodes are then recursively grouped together following the same principle until the top level, which consists of a single root. To process a query, a search algorithm starts traversal at the root and recursively visits index nodes and objects. By simply examining MBBs of index nodes or objects (e.g., by checking the intersection of the query and an MBB for window queries or the *mindist* between a query point and an MBB for $k$NN queries [6]), whether the enclosed objects are candidates of the query can be quickly determined. If an MBB does not satisfy the query requirement, the corresponding subtree (i.e., the enclosed group of objects) can be safely discarded from further investigation. The query traversal ends when all objects are retrieved and all irrelevant subtrees are pruned.

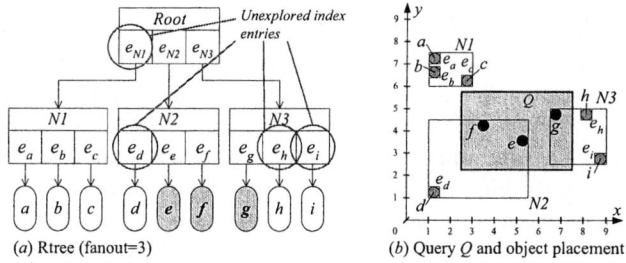

**Fig. 2.** R-tree example

Fig. 2($a$) depicts an R-tree (with a fanout of 3) that has 3 leaf nodes, labeled $N1$, $N2$ and $N3$, and 9 objects labeled '$a$' through '$i$'. The corresponding object placements are shown in Fig. 2($b$). Suppose a window query $Q$ is evaluated. It first traverses the root and skips its child entry $e_{N1}$ whose MBB does not overlap with the query. Next, $N2$ is explored. Entry $e_d$ is not explored since it is outside $Q$. Then objects $e$ and $f$ are collected. Similarly for $N3$, object $g$ is retrieved while $e_h$ and $e_i$ are not explored. Finally, objects $e$, $f$ and $g$ are collected as the query result while the unexplored entries are $\{e_{N1}, e_d, e_h, e_i\}$.

It can be observed from the above index traversal that the unexplored entries exactly represent the complement set of objects to queried objects. In other words, both queried objects and those unexplored entries' MBBs cover the entire data space. If such information is available in mobile clients, a new query, $Q'$, of any type can be supported and resolved at the client side by simply examining the previous queried objects and by checking whether the areas covered by MBBs need to be further explored (i.e., by sending requests to the server). This observation inspires the ideas we proposed for the design of CS caching.

## 2.2 Complementary Space Caching Model

We assume that the server is stateless and a point-to-point communication channel is established between the server and a client. We also assume that the database is indexed by R-tree. To simplify our discussion, we assume all updates occur in the server and the update is infrequent. The issue of cache coherence is out of scope of this study and will be the extension of this work.

Formally, we consider a database at the server composed of a set of objects, $\mathcal{O}$. All object locations ($x$-,$y$-coordinates) constitute a bounded geographical space, $\mathcal{S}$. Data objects $O \subseteq \mathcal{O}$ residing in a subspace $S \subseteq \mathcal{S}$ can be determined by a function, $m$, i.e. $m(S) \to O^1$. Conversely, given a set of objects $O$, the corresponding (minimal) subspace $S$ can also be determined.

The CS cache $C$ is defined as $(O, R)$, where $O$ is a set of cached objects and $R$ is a set of subspaces that is *complementary regions* (CRs). The CRs are presented in a form of MBBs[2]. Initially, a client cache is empty and is initialized as $(\emptyset, \{\mathcal{S}\})$. After the first query is processed by the server, queried objects along with MBBs of unexplored entries are returned to the client and are cached. There is obviously an overhead for maintaining the MBBs in the client cache, but it is justifiable for the following reasons: (1) collection of unexplored entries and their MBBs via R-tree based query processing at the server is almost effortless; (2) individual MBBs are compact in size and thus do not consume a lot of bandwidth and cache memory; (3) the number of unexplored entries (and MBBs) is reasonably small since most of irrelevant data objects are pruned at high-level branches of the R-tree due to its nice clustering property; (4) It is only a one-time cost, which will be amortized over subsequent queries; and (5) as shown previously, keeping MBBs in the cache can effectively avoid sending unnecessary queries to the server. As to be discussed in Section 6, our evaluation demonstrates that the performance gain outweighs the overhead cost.

With both objects and CRs kept in the cache to preserve a global view of the dataset, query processing and cache management in CS caching behave differently from the conventional ones. Fig. 3 that continues the running example in Fig. 2(b) gives the overview of query processing and cache replacement. Suppose after $Q$, the cache content of a client becomes $(\{e, f, g\}, \{r_{N1}, r_h, r_i, r_d\})$ (where $r_x$ is the MBB of $e_x$). Suppose the client moves and issues a query that covers $r_{N1}$ (see Fig. 3(a)). The client explores $r_{N1}$ by querying the server. Then an object $c$ together with two MBBs, $r_a$ and $r_b$, that are part of $r_{N1}$ are received. Both are in a finer granularity and they represent other areas of current client interest. In that sense, query processing resembles as a *zooming-in* action that brings more details about queried area into the cache. Memory should be reclaimed to accommodate new coming objects and other finer CRs if the cache is full. Suppose an object $g$ is chosen to be removed from the cache (see Fig. 3(b)). First, $r_g$, a CR for object $g$ is introduced in the $g$'s position (so that the global view is preserved) and then $g$ is physically deleted. Further, if more free space is demanded, $r_g$, $r_h$ and $r_i$, three closely located CRs, are coalesced into a single

---
[1] This function is logically supported by the database.
[2] If no ambiguity caused, we would use CR and MBB interchangeably.

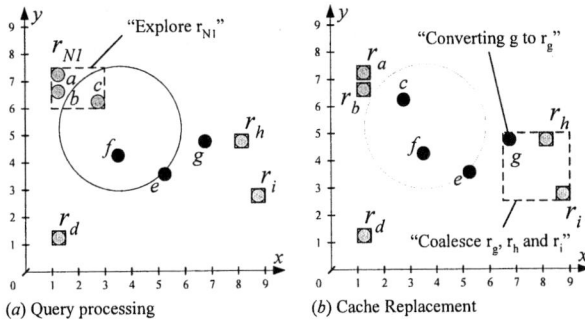

**Fig. 3.** Overview of query processing and cache replacement with CS caching

CR that is cached in a coarser granularity. This cache replacement is analogous to a *zooming-out* action that removes the details of an area that is currently not interested by the client.

In order for query processing and cache replacement to maintain a global view of the dataset, CS caching reinforces the following integrity requirements:

**Requirement 1** **Full dataset coverage.** *At any time, the union of cached objects, $O$, and missing objects captured by the set of CRs, $R$, must equal $\mathcal{O}$, formally $(\bigcup_{r \in R} m(r)) \cup O = \mathcal{O}$.* ∎

This integrity requirement assures that every missing object ($\notin O$) is captured by one of the CRs, $r \in R$. Based on $R$, a client can determine whether there are potentially missing objects for a query.

**Requirement 2** **No CR-object overlap.** *A CR should not cover any cached object, formally $\forall r \in R, m(r) \cap O = \emptyset$.* ∎

**Requirement 3** **No full CR-CR containment.** *No CR is contained in another CR, formally, $\forall r_i \in R, r_j \in R, i \neq j, m(r_i) \not\subseteq m(r_j)$.* ∎

The second requirement aims at reducing false misses. The third requirement eliminates redundant CRs. A CR is redundant if it is already covered by another CR and thus is safe to remove.

## 2.3 Related Work

As discussed earlier, semantic caching [2,3,4] is query-dependent and provides limited knowledge about the cached subspace. By fixed space partitioning, chunk-based caching [7] partitions the semantic space into *chunks*, independent of query and object distribution. Every window query is mapped into a set of chunks. Query fetches chunks from the server if they are not in the cache, regardless of whether the chunks have objects or not. Without keeping an entire view of semantic space, chunk-based caching cannot support various kind of queries.

Similar to CS caching, proactive caching [8] supports a number of different types of spatial queries. It is important to note that these two caching schemes are conceptually and functionally different. Proactive caching tightly adheres to R-tree, yet CS caching does not. Proactive caching maintains traversed index paths (a portion of index) and a set of objects below the cached index paths in the cache. The cached partial index enables a client to execute query processing algorithms as the server does. If a query needs to find any missing index nodes or objects, the query and all intermediate execution states are shipped to the server for remaining execution. The cached index path in proactive caching is the only means to access underlying objects so implicitly the index nodes are granted higher priority than objects to cache. This has an impact on cached hit rate because cached index nodes alone (without beneath objects) cannot make query locally answered. Besides, excessive bandwidth is taken to transmit index structures which in fact can be reconstructed using objects and CRs as shown in CS caching. Without the necessity to conform to the R-tree at the server, CRs can be flexibly coalesced and partitioned for optimizing the cache performance.

## 3 Location-Based Query Processing

With the global view maintained in the cache, a location-based query of any kind can be answered by reusing cached objects and exploring some involved CRs for missing objects from the server. Generally speaking, query processing with CS caching is a three-step procedure:

1. *Cache probing:* Qualified objects in the cache are collected as a tentative query result and CRs that could contribute to the query result are identified. The cache probing varies with different types of queries and will be discussed shortly in Section 3.1.
2. *Remainder query processing:* If no CR is identified for the query meaning the query is fully covered by the cache, the query processing terminates here. Otherwise, the missing objects in the identified CRs need to be requested from (and possibly checked by) the server. This will be discussed in Section 3.2.
3. *Cache maintenance:* After the remainder query is answered, the newly returned data objects and CRs are admitted to the cache. This invokes the cache maintenance operations such as cache replacement and CR coalescence that will be discussed in Section 5.

### 3.1 Cache Probing

In the following, we informally describe the cache probing for some typical location-based queries such as window, range, and $k$ nearest neighbors ($k$NN) queries[3]. They are incompatible in nature but can be processed in a similar fashion using CS caching. The outputs of cache probing are cached objects in the answer set and CRs to be explored in the server via remainder query processing.

---

[3] A range query is specified by a query point and a radius.

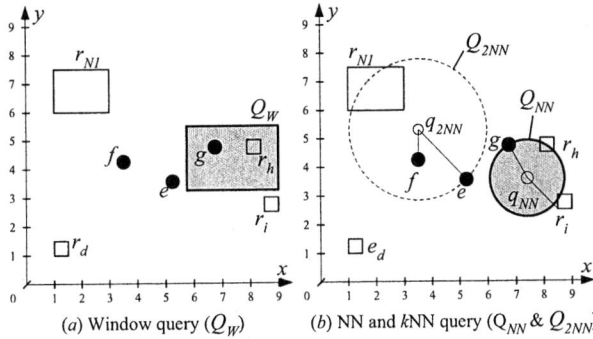

**Fig. 4.** Examples of lookup mechanism for various types of queries

Cache probing for a window (or range) query is pretty straightforward. The client scans the cached objects and CRs to return those overlapped by the query window (or range). Figure 4(a) shows an example of a window query, $Q_W$. In this example, cached object, $g$, and CR, $r_h$, are identified. Without an explicit search range, cache probe for an NN query expands a search range from a query point outwards until one object is touched. Then, all CRs within the search range are identified for further exploring. The extension to handle $k$NN query is straightforward by extending the search range to first $k$ covered objects. Fig. 4(b), the client finds objects $f$ and $e$, the two closest objects to $q_{2NN}$ of the query $Q_{2NN}$. The CR $r_{N1}$ overlapped with the vicinity circle across $e$ is identified for further exploring.

## 3.2 Remainder Query Processing

A remainder query is submitted to the server to retrieve missing objects if some CRs are identified for a query. Besides, refined CRs (i.e., MBBs of those entries inside submitted CRs but not explored by a query) may be returned. One of the primary issues in processing remainder queries is "how to express the query" which has a major impact on the processing cost (in terms of response time and bandwidth overhead) and the quality of cached information. We examine two possible approaches: 1) CRs only, and 2) Query+CRs.

The first approach is to submit only the identified CRs treated as window queries in the server. As shown in Fig. 5(a), a query, $Q$, overlaps with three objects, $e$, $f$, $g$ and three CRs, $r_{N1}$, $r_h$, $r_i$. The remainder query in this approach is expressed as $(r_{N1}, r_h, r_i)$. Because $r_{N1}$ covers a large area outside $Q$'s range, some extra objects may be returned to the client. Even worse, they would not be used at all eventually. This approach consumes minimal uplink bandwidth.

The second approach is to submit the original query along with the identified CRs. The CRs are used as filters for processing of $Q$ in the server. When the R-tree index is traversed, only the branches overlapped with the CRs are further explored. The MBBs unexplored by $Q$ and intersecting with the CRs are also returned (as refined CRs in the original CRs) along with qualified data objects to the client. As shown in Fig. 5(a), a remainder query in this approach is

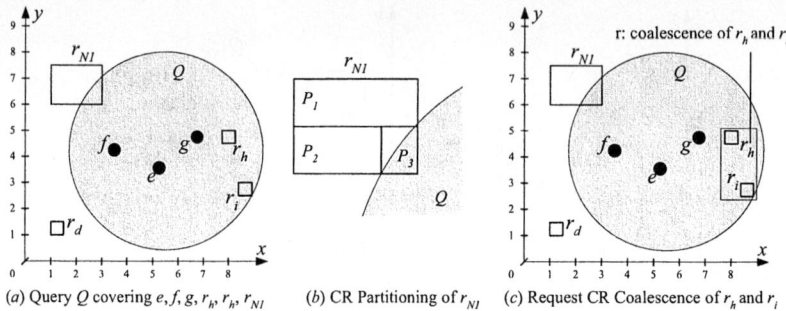

(a) Query $Q$ covering $e, f, g, r_h, r_h, r_{NI}$   (b) CR Partitioning of $r_{NI}$   (c) Request CR Coalescence of $r_h$ and $r_i$

**Fig. 5.** Remainder query

expressed as $Q + (r_{N1}, r_h, r_i)$. With this approach, the downlink cost is expected to be reduced because a precise set of required objects and a smaller number of CRs are downloaded.

Delivering a large number of fine-granularity CRs back to the clients may incur an excessive downlink overhead (and the additional energy consumption of clients). To address this issue, a client can partition CRs if they are only partially covered by a query during remainder query preparation. An example is depicted in Fig. 5(a), CR $r_{N1}$ is partially covered by a query $Q$ and thus can be partitioned into three parts, namely, $P_1$, $P_2$ and $P_3$ (as shown in Fig. 5(b)). The portion, $P_3$, enclosing the overlap between $r_{N1}$ and $Q$, is taken to formulate a remainder query. Thus, $r_{N1}$ is removed while $P_1$ and $P_2$ are retained as CRs in the cache. This partitioning may result in some savings of download overhead because the number of refined CRs in $P_3$ is expected to be smaller than those in $r_{N1}$. However, a low precision CR will be resulted like $P_1$ and $P_3$ having not exact bounding box of enclosed objects. It is also probable that the partitioned CRs have no missing object inside. Examining them definitely causes false misses.

On the other hand, a large number of CRs could be covered by a query. Submitting all those individual CRs to the server incurs a high upload cost. Thus, CRs can be merged into a few coarse CRs. This merging of CRs is called *CR coalescence*. As shown in Fig. 5(c), $r_h$ and $r_i$ are coalesced to a coarse CR $r$. $r_{N1}$ and $r$ can be submitted instead, i.e., the remainder query is $Q + (r, r_{N1})$. However, the newly formed CR may overlap with some answer objects already found in the cache. For example, further coalescence of $r$ and $r_{N1}$ may form a larger CR, $r'$, that overlaps with cached objects $e$, $f$, and $g$. Using $r'$ as request CR will redundantly fetch these already cached objects.

To tackle this problem, we supplement IDs of overlapped cached objects in the remainder query as a result filter that removes the objects already cached from the downlink. Then, the new remainder query becomes $Q + (r') + (\{e, f, g\})$ and is sent to the server. It raises a question if an expression $Q + (r') + (\{e, f, g\})$ saves more uplink bandwidth than $Q + (r, r_{N1})$ or other expressions else. This is an optimization issue in CR coalescence, which will be discussed in Section 4. Finally, for NN or $k$NN query processing, instead of exploring all potential CRs covered by the conservative vicinity circle as described above, we can take an incremental approach to explore the identified CRs one by one until the answer set is obtained.

## 4  CR Coalescence

CRs are essential information to transmit between the client and the server. An efficient CR coalescence algorithm is needed to condense those overly fine CRs to save bandwidth. In this section, we first devise a generic CR coalescence algorithm, based on which two specializations for coalescing CRs in request messages and in reply messages are derived.

### 4.1  Generic CR Coalescence Algorithm

Given a set of CRs, $R$, a coalescence algorithm selects $n$ subsets of $R$, that is $R'_1, \cdots, R'_n$ ($R'_i \subseteq R$), to coalesce. Each $R'_i$ is replaced by a newly formed CR called *coalescing CR*, denoted by $r_{R'_i}$, that is an MBB of all original CRs in $R'_i$. Hence, the coalescence operation on $R$ can be described as $(R - \cup_i R'_i) \cup (\cup_i \{r_{R'_i}\})$.

The key issue here is to determine the optimal subsets of CRs to be coalesced. In order to tackle this selection problem, we first formulate a cost model. Every CR, $r$, bears a cost, $c(r)$, which measures the performance loss due to missing objects. The definition of cost function varies with the operation scenario (to be detailed later in this section). In general, the larger is the region, the higher is the cost, and the more is the potential performance loss. Therefore, after coalescing $R'_i$'s ($i = 1, 2, \cdots, n$), the cost increase is:

$$\text{total cost increase} = \sum_{1 \leq i \leq n} \left( c(r_{R'_i}) - \sum_{r \in R'_i} c(r) \right), \qquad (1)$$

but the number of CRs is reduced by:

$$\text{total CR saving} = \Big( \sum_{1 \leq i \leq n} |R'_i| \Big) - n \qquad (2)$$

Given an expected CR saving, the optimal selection algorithm should minimize the cost increase. Here, we propose a greedy algorithm to choose CRs to coalesce until an application-dependent termination condition is met. The algorithm is outlined in Fig. 6. At each step, it selects the best pair of CRs to merge. The "best" means the least cost increase after coalescing the pair of CRs. A priority queue is used to keep track of the possible CR pairs. Initially, we determine the best counterpart for each CR in $R$ and coalesce the best pair of CRs. After coalescence, the original CRs $r_i$ and $r_j$ are replaced with the coalescing CR, $r_{\{r_i, r_j\}}$; the CR saving and cost increase are 1 and $c(r_{\{r_i, r_j\}}) - c(r_i) - c(r_j)$, respectively. Based on $r_{\{r_i, r_j\}}$, a new candidate pair is inserted to the queue. The algorithm continues until the termination condition is satisfied. The termination condition can be specified by limiting the number of CRs coalesced so

```
Algorithm. GenericCRCoalescence(R: a set of CRs)
Input/output: R: a set of CRs;
Local:         Q: priority queue;
Begin
1     foreach r ∈ R do
2        find r's best counterpart CR, r' from R − {r};
3        push (r, r', anticipated cost increase) into Q;
4     while (termination condition is not satisfied) do
5        pop (r_i, r_j, anticipated cost increase) from Q;
6        r ← coalesce(r_a, r_b);
7        replace r_i and r_j with r in R;
8        find r's best partner CR, r' from R − {r};
9        push (r, r', anticipated cost increase) into Q;
10    output R;
End.
```

**Fig. 6.** Generic CR coalescence algorithm

that the remaining number of CRs can be controlled or by setting a threshold on cost increase metric that guarantees the CR fineness. In the following two subsections, we shall derive specific coalescence techniques for coalescing CRs in requests (request CRs) and CRs in replies (reply CRs).

### 4.2 Client Request CR Coalescence

In Section 3.2, we briefly discussed the issue of request CR coalescence and raised the question about what CRs should be coalesced. Here, we address this problem with our generic coalescence algorithm described above. Let $r$ be a CR. We set the cost of $r$, $c(r)$, as the number of objects covered by $r$. As the size of remainder query is our main concern in coalescing request CRs, we aim at maximizing the overhead reduction specified below:

$$\text{overhead reduction} = \text{total } CR \text{ saving} \times CR \text{ size} - \text{total cost increase} \times \text{object ID size.} \quad (3)$$

This expression considers the volume saved by CR coalescence (CR saving) and the overhead of including additional object IDs (cost increase). Reconsider the situation in Fig. 5(c), $r_h$ and $r_i$ can be coalesced to form a coalescing CR, $r$, with 1 CR saved and no object included, i.e., $c(r) = 0$. Further, coalescing $r$ and $r_{N1}$ into $r'$ has 1 more CR saved but covers three objects, i.e., $c(r') = 3$. As a CR and an object ID respectively take 16 bytes and 4 bytes, the total overhead reduction for taking $r'$ and $\{e, f, g\}$ is $32 - 12 = 20$ and that for taking $r$ and $r_{N1}$ is 16. Thus, both $r'$ and $\{e, f, g\}$ are used to express the remainder query.

### 4.3 Server Reply CR Coalescence

Very often, portions of CRs, submitted as remainder queries, might not be fully explored for answering queries in the Query + CRs approach. Thus, refined CRs are returned to the client along with the answer objects. To save the downlink cost, the server reply CRs can be coalesced. The optimization should consider reducing the number of CRs while retaining the quality of CRs such that a low false miss rate can be achieved. We associate CR quality with some quantitative metrics by defining cost function $c(r)$ for a CR $r$ based on different heuristics:

- **Area.** Generally, the larger the area of a CR, the more likely the CR provides a higher false miss rate since it may include more empty regions in which no objects exist. Therefore, $c(r)$ is set to the area of $r$, $area(r)$. In this case, we expect a smaller average size of coalescing CRs.
- **Distance.** With spatial access locality, the closer is the CR located to the user location, the more likely is the CR to be accessed in the near future. It is thus important to have a fine granularity for those nearby CRs. Hence, we model $c(r)$ as the inverse of its distance to the user, i.e., $1/dist(r)$. In this case, we expect to coalesce farther CRs.
- **Area By Distance.** Area and distance are two orthogonal factors and they can be used in setting the cost $c(r)$, i.e., $area(r)/dist(r)$.

Server reply CR coalescence can save download cost but it also haunts the CR quality. To balance the transmission overhead saving and the quality of coalesced CRs, we limit the CR saving. In our implementation, we set a threshold that is the percentage of the total number of CRs before coalescence. When the number of remained CRs falls below the threshold, the coalescence terminates. Note that server reply CR coalescence has an additional constraint in coalescing CRs. If a coalesced CR contains some returning objects, the corresponding coalescence is prohibited because the resultant CR is highly possible to give a false miss if the client issues the same queries later (see Requirement 2 in Section 2.2).

## 5 Cache Management

As CS caching keeps both objects and CRs to preserve the global view of a dataset, its cache management is totally different from conventional ones that cache homogeneous caching units such as data objects. In this section, we discuss the CS cache organization and two cache space allocation strategies, followed by description of the cache CR coalescence and the cache replacement algorithm.

### 5.1 Cache Organization

The cache memory is structured as a table. Each table entry is of equal size and large enough to accommodate either one object or a collection of CRs. A table entry assigned to maintain CRs (called *CR entry*) keeps at most $n$ CRs and one *coalescing CR*, which is an MBB enclosing all the CRs within this entry with $n$ the capacity of a CR entry. Each stored CR has a timestamp about the latest access time. The coalescing CR facilitates fast CR lookup and CR coalescence in the cache, serving cache replacement.

The admission of an object is straightforward, i.e., finding a vacant entry to accommodate the object. The admission of CRs is handled in a way similar to R-tree insertion. A CR entry is chosen to store the admitted CRs if the expansion of its coalescing CR after insertion is the smallest among all candidate CR entries. If a CR entry overflows after insertion, all CRs (except the coalescing CR) are migrated to other CR entries with free space. If the space is insufficient, the collection of CRs in a CR entry are split into two groups and each group is placed into two CR entries. Deletion removes a CR from an entry. To maintain high occupancy, an occupancy threshold is set[4]. An underflowed entry (i.e., its occupancy below the threshold) is removed and all its CRs (except the coalescing CR) are re-inserted to other CR entries.

We propose two possible space allocation strategies, namely *static allocation* and *dynamic allocation*. For static allocation, cache memory is split into two portions with each dedicated to caching objects or CRs. Dynamic allocation has no fixed portions and treats objects and CRs in the same way to exploit higher flexibility in space utilization.

## 5.2 Cache CR Coalescence

Cache CR coalescence replaces a set of fine CRs with a bounding CR in a coarser granularity to release cache space. The efficiency of CR coalescence is crucial to the performance when cache replacement occurs frequently. Therefore, instead of using the generic algorithm described in Section 4, we adopt a pre-clustering technique that groups CRs in the same CR entry into their corresponding coalescing CR.

The pre-clustering of CRs is performed when CRs are admitted to the cache (as described in Section 5.1). We use minimal expansion of coalescing CRs as the criteria to determine which CR entry a new CR can be inserted into. Since the coalescing CR in a CR entry readily represents the result of coalescing all CRs in the entry, we can quickly perform CR coalescence to release a CR entry by looking up the coalescing CRs only.

## 5.3 Cache Replacement

Cache replacement in CS caching is responsible not only for fitting objects and CRs in the cache but also for balancing the granularity of different portions of the global view (in terms of objects and CRs) maintained in the cache. An object removal is performed as converting the object to a CR. A CR removal implies coalescence of a set of CRs. However, to make cache replacement efficient, usually all CRs in a victim CR entry will be removed by inserting its coalescing CR into another CR entry. In the following, we discuss the replacement algorithms corresponding to both static allocation and dynamic allocation.

**Static allocation.** Replacement starts in the object portion. If the object portion is full, victim objects are removed by transforming them into CRs, which

---

[4] Our simulation uses $n/2$ where $n$ is the capacity of a CR entry.

are put to the CR portion. If a CR portion is full, victim CR entries are chosen to remove and their coalescing CRs are re-inserted to the CR portion. The victim selection (i.e. cache replacement policy) is based on LRU and FAR [9] heuristics. For FAR heuristic, distance is measured between the current client position and the anticipated CR (either resulted from object deletion or CR coalescence).

**Dynamic allocation.** Both object replacement and CR coalescence can make room for new objects and CRs. Cache replacement policy for both operations is crucial for ensuring the overall cache performance. In order to prioritize object replacement and CR coalescence which are totally different in nature, we use a replacement score based on the expected reloading cost of objects or CRs. Let $size_o$ and $size_r$ denote the object size and the CR size respectively, and $\rho$ denote the access probability of an entity (either an object or a CR). In this work, we consider access probability based on LRU and FAR. The communication cost of reloading an object from the server is $\rho \times size_o$ and that of reloading CRs is $\rho \times m \times size_r$, where $m$ is the number of CRs involved in the CR coalescence. Taking the reloading cost as a replacement score, we describe our cache replacement operation as follows. We maintain a priority queue of existing table entries. The queue always returns one entry with the least reloading cost. If a table entry is retrieved from the queue, it is freed to accommodate the new object and the newly formed CR (resulted from conversion of object or CR coalescence) is inserted back to an appropriate CR entry. Similarly, CRs downloaded from the server are inserted to CR entries. It may be the case that a CR entry overflows and additional entry space is required. Then, an additional entry space is reclaimed as that for a new incoming object. It might be possible that the newly formed CR entry whose reloading cost is less than those in the queue. In this case, CR coalescence is immediately performed and the coalescing CR is re-inserted to the cache.

## 6 Performance Evaluation

We conduct a performance evaluation on our proposal based on a simulation developed in C++. In the simulation, there are only one client and one server communicating via a point-to-point wireless channel with bandwidth of 384Kbps, the typical capacity of 3G network. The server maintains a synthetic dataset with 100,000 point objects uniformly distributed in a unit square of $[1, 1]$ and indexed with a R*tree [10] which has a node page size of 1Kbytes and its maximum fanout is 50. The size of each object is ranged from 64, 128, 256 to 512 bytes. The client has 128 Kbyte cache memory. In the experiments, client movement patterns are generated based on two well known mobility models, Manhattan Grid model and Random Waypoint, using BonnMotion [11]. For Manhattan Grid model, we set the mean speed to $1 \times 10^{-3}/sec$ and standard deviation to $0.2 \times 10^{-3}/sec$. For Random Waypoint model, we set the speed ranging between $0.5 \times 10^{-3}/sec$ to $1.5 \times 10^{-3}/sec$. The maximum think times (i.e., time duration that the client remains stationary during moving path change) for both models are set to 60 seconds. Meanwhile, we generate a query workload with query inter-arrival time following the exponential distribution with mean varying from 10 to 30 at step of 10 (seconds). We assume that the client issues queries along her journey. We examine three types of queries: 1) range queries (with radius of $5 \times 10^{-3}$ to $10 \times 10^{-3}$), 2) window queries (with window size of $(10 \times 10^{-3})^2$ to $(20 \times 10^{-3})^2$), and 3) $k$NN (with $k \in [10, 20]$). Each type of queries has the same weight in our experiments. The simulation runs for 10,000 seconds.

The performance metrics used in our evaluation include *response time*, *bandwidth consumption*, *cache hit ratio* and *answerability* while the answerability measures how many queries can be completely answered by the client cache without the server help. In addition to our proposed CS caching scheme, we implement *Chunk-based caching* [7], *Semantic caching* [2, 12], and *Proactive caching* [8] for comparison. Note that the chunk-based caching only supports window queries. Semantic caching supports window and $k$NN queries by caching two types of semantic regions. However, each type of semantic regions can only support queries of the same type. Proactive caching keeping a portion of R-tree index can support all queries we considered. When a client receives a query that is not supported, it requests the server to process it and results of these queries are not cached.

### 6.1 Evaluation 1. Performance of Caching Schemes

We first examine the performance of different caching schemes, namely, Semantic, Chunk-based, Proactive and CSC in terms of *response time*, *bandwidth* (both upload and download) and *cache hit ratio*. For CSC, remainder queries are expressed as Query + CRs, with CR partitioning and both request and reply CR coalescence. The Manhattan Gird model is adopted. The result is depicted in Fig. 7 (where the cache size and object size are fixed at 128KByte and 256 bytes, respectively).

From the plots, we can see that CSC outperforms the rest in all metrics for its effectiveness in supporting different queries, the efficient use of cache memory, and the low overhead in data transmission. Semantic is the weakest among all because it maintains two types of semantic regions that may result in an overlap of cached objects, in turn degrading the effective use of cache (as indicated by its low cache hit ratio). Chunk-based performs better since chunks contain extra objects that can be used to answer later window queries, thus outweighing some loss in processing $k$NN and range queries. Proactive performs worse than Chunk because the cached partial server index reduces the availability of cache memory for data objects. This evaluation validates CSC for location-based services.

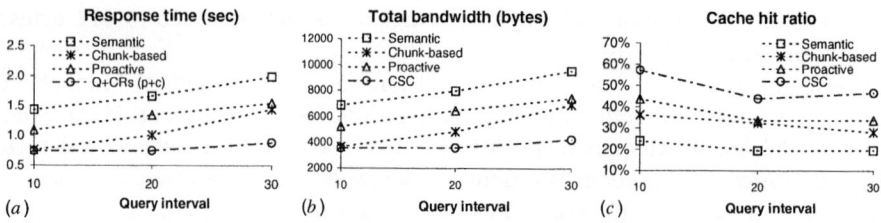

**Fig. 7.** Performance of caching schemes on query interval

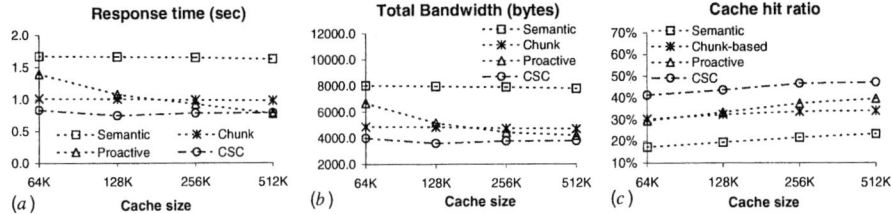

**Fig. 8.** Performance of caching schemes on cache size

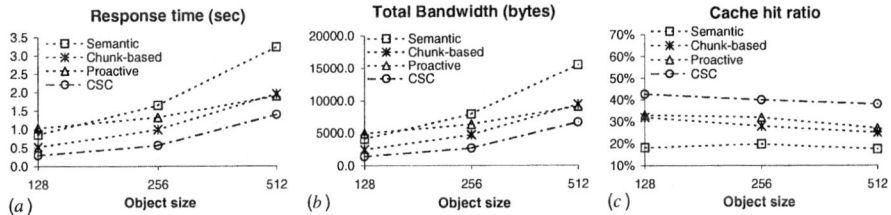

**Fig. 9.** Performance of caching schemes on object size

In addition, we study the impact of cache size on caching schemes. In Fig. 8 (where the object size is fixed at 256 bytes and the mean query inter-arrival time is 20 seconds), the response time of Semantic and Chunk-based is shown to be more or less invariant since they use cache space to maintain the query results they support. In effect, they may not fully utilize the space. For CSC, response time is a bit higher when cache size is 64K. For Proactive, response time drops when more space is available to store the index nodes.

In Fig. 9 (where the cache size is 128K and mean query inter-arrival time is 20 seconds), all caching schemes show that the larger the object size, the longer the expected response time. As the object size is increased, the cache hit is reduced accordingly because less objects are cached. The download cost, a major time consuming component, also increases when larger objects are experimented. For the same reasons discussed in above two settings, CSC is shown superior to others.

### 6.2 Evaluation 2. Performance of Remainder Query Expressions

Here we evaluate three different forms of remainder queries, i.e., original query plus CRs (denoted as Q+CRs), Q+CRs with partitioning (denoted as Q+CRs (p)), and Q+CRs with both partitioning and client request CR coalescence (denoted as Q+CRs (p+c)). These three forms of remainder queries have the same cache hit (so the plot is not shown to save space). Also, we have evaluated the remainder query with CRs only but its performance is much worse. The plot is not shown for space saving. The difference in their performance is due to the compression and improved precision of CRs. Using partitioning (i.e., Q+CRs (p) and Q+CRs (p+c)), the client avoids downloading extra CRs (see Fig. 10(c)). The response

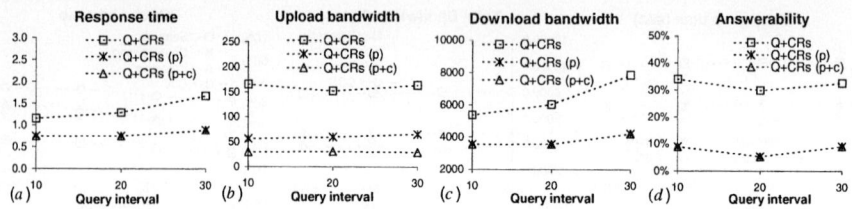

**Fig. 10.** Performance of using all remainder query expressions

time is also shortened in Fig. 10(a). However, the answerability is much lower than the basic Q+CRs because the CRs partitioned by the client are less precise (see Fig. 10(d)). Both of Q+CRs (p) and Q+CRs (p+c) can only answer 10% of queries without the server help while the Q+CRs needs to do that for 33% of time. Finally, the CR coalescence Q+CRs (p+c) is shown to be very effective in reducing the uplink bandwidth (see Fig. 10(b)). It saves almost 50% uplink bandwidth compared with Q+CRs (p). This saving is important because mobile clients consume more energy in sending packets than receiving packets.

### 6.3 Evaluation 3. Performance of Server Reply CR Coalescence

We study three heuristics, Area, Distance, and Area By Distance, used in coalescing CRs in server replies (see Fig. 11). We assume that remainder queries are sent in form of Q+CRs. We vary the percentage of CRs coalesced (where 0% means no coalescence) to observe its impact on response time and total bandwidth. Area is generally not a good heuristic because CRs close to the query are often of smaller area. Forming coarse CRs with those close CRs will degrade the cache performance since those close CRs are likely to be accessed. However, Area By Distance can provide very good performance (even better than Distance). Balancing on client location and CR size renders an appropriate granularity for returned CRs.

### 6.4 Evaluation 4. Performance of Cache Management

Finally, we study the two space allocation strategies, i.e., static allocation (Static) and dynamic allocation (Dynamic). For Static, we allocate $x$ percent of cache storage for CRs. As shown in Fig. 12(a), Dynamic generally performs the best in term of response time. For Static, we can see that increasing cache space for CRs from 10% to 20% improves the response time but not when it is increased 25% as reflected by their corresponding cache hit ratios (shown in Fig. 12(a)). The more cache space allocated to CRs, the less cache space is available for objects, so the cache hit ratio drops when the CR portion of cache expands. Though Static 10% and Static 20% by allocating less space to CRs have higher cache hit ratios than Dynamic, they hold overly coarse CRs and result in a high false miss rate, which in turn increases the response time. For cache management, we also tested cache replacement using FAR and LRU policies upon different moving model. FAR generally outperforms LRU. The results are not shown due to limited space.

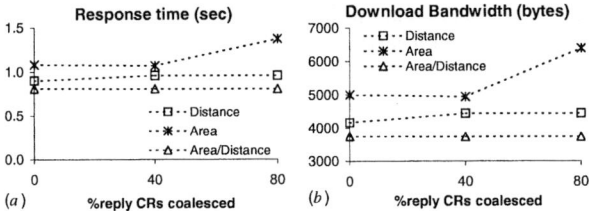

**Fig. 11.** Performance of heuristics in server reply CR coalescence

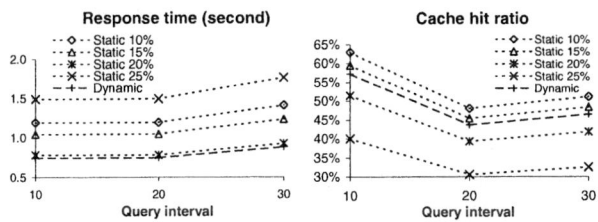

**Fig. 12.** Performance of cache allocation strategies

# 7 Future Works

As for the next steps of this research, we plan to study the issues of cache coherence caused by updates. We also plan to perform a more extensive performance evaluation to bring out more insights. Finally, we plan to prototype the system and to perform the feasibility test in a realistic mobile computing environment.

## Acknowledgements

In this research, Wang-Chien Lee and Ken C.K. Lee were supported in part by US National Science Foundation grant IIS-0328881. Baihua Zheng's work was partially supported by the Office of Research, Singapore Management University. Jianliang Xu's work was partially supported by grants from the Research Grants Council, HKSAR, China (Project Nos. HKBU 2115/05E and FRG/04-05/II-26).

## References

1. Schiller, J.H., Voisard, A., eds.: Location-Based Services. Morgan Kaufmann (2004)
2. Dar, S., Franklin, M.J., Jónsson, B.T., Srivastava, D., Tan, M.: Semantic data caching and replacement. In: Proc. of 22th International Conference on Very Large Data Bases (VLDB), Bombay, India, Sep 3-6. (1996) 330–341
3. Lee, K.C., Leong, H.V., Si, A.: Semantic query caching in a mobile environment. ACM Mobile Computing and Communication Review ($MC^2R$) **3** (1999) 28–36
4. Ren, Q., Dunham, M.H., Kumar, V.: Semantic Caching and Query Processing. IEEE Trans. on Knowledge and Data Engineering (TKDE) **15** (2003) 192–210

5. Guttman, A.: R-Trees: A Dynamic Index Structure for Spatial Searching. In: Proc. of the ACM SIGMOD International Conference on Management of Data, Boston, MA, Jun 18-21. (1984) 47–57
6. Roussopoulos, N., Kelly, S., Vincent, F.: Nearest Neighbor Queries. In: Proc. of the 1995 ACM SIGMOD International Conference on Management of Data, San Jose, CA, USA, May 22-25. (1995) 71–79
7. Deshpande, P.M., Ramasamy, K., Shukla, A., Naughton, J.F.: Caching Multi-dimensional Queries Using Chunks. In: Proc. of the ACM SIGMOD International Conference on Management of Data, San Diego, CA, USA, Jun 9-12. (1998) 259–270
8. Hu, H., Xu, J., Wong, W.S., Zheng, B., Lee, D.L., Lee, W.C.: Proactive Caching for Spatial Queries in Mobile Environments. In: Proc. of the 21st International Conference on Data Engineering (ICDE), Tokyo, Japan, Apr 5-8. (2005) 403–414
9. Ren, Q., Dunham, M.H.: Using Semantic Caching to Manage Location Dependent Data in Mobile Computing. In: Proc. of the International Conference on Mobile Computing and Networking (Mobicom), Boston, MA, USA, Aug 6-11. (2000) 210–221
10. Backmann, N., Kriegel, H.P., Schneider, R., Seegar, B.: The R*-Tree: An Efficient and Robust Access Method for Points and Rectangles. In: Proc. of the ACM SIGMOD International Conference on Management of Data, Atlantic City, NJ, USA, May 23-25. (1990) 322–331
11. BonnMotion: A mobility scenario generation and analysis tool. (website: http://web.informatik.uni-bonn.de/IV/Mitarbeiter/dewaal/BonnMotion/)
12. Zheng, B., Lee, W.C., Lee, D.L.: On Semantic Caching and Query Scheduling for Mobile Nearest-Neighbor Search. Wireless Networks **10** (2004) 653–664

# Evolving Triggers for Dynamic Environments

Goce Trajcevski[1,*], Peter Scheuermann[1,**], Oliviu Ghica[1],
Annika Hinze[2], and Agnes Voisard[3]

[1] Northwestern Univ., Dept. of EECS
{goce, peters, oliviu}@eecs.northwestern.edu
[2] Univ. of Waikato, Computer Science Dept.
hinze@cs.waikato.ac.nz
[3] Fraunhofer ISST and FU, Berlin
Agnes.Voisard@isst.fhg.de

**Abstract.** In this work we address the problem of managing the reactive behavior in distributed environments in which data continuously changes over time, where the users may need to explicitly express how the triggers should be (self) modified. To enable this we propose the $(ECA)^2$ – *E*volving and *C*ontext-*A*ware *E*vent-*C*ondition-*A*ction paradigm for specifying triggers that capture the desired reactive behavior in databases which manage distributed and continuously changing data. Since both the monitored event and the condition part of the trigger may be continuous in nature, we introduce the concept of *metatriggers* to coordinate the detection of events and the evaluation of conditions.

## 1 Introduction and Motivation

Many application domains deal with data that changes very frequently and is generated by distributed and heterogeneous sources. These data-properties have spurred extensive research efforts in several fields. In Event-Notification Systems (ENS), and Publish-Subscribe (P-S) systems [3, 11], typically an instance user's profile is matched against the current status of continuously evolving data sources, and appropriate notifications are sent to the user. The main focus of Continuous Queries (CQ) processing [6, 12] is on efficient management of user queries over time, without forcing the users to re-issue their queries. The data values may arrive as streams which the system has to process on the fly [5, 4, 14] and, furthermore, the data may be multidimensional in nature, as is the case in Location-Based Services (LBS) [16] and Moving Objects Databases (MOD) [10]. In some applications, e.g sensor networks, the data management must consider other constraints such as the limited battery-lifetime of the nodes [22].

One may observe that in the majority of the applications, there is a need for some form of a *reactive* behavior. The database community has provided many results on the topic of Active Databases (ADb), which manage triggers operating under the Event-Condition-Action (ECA) paradigm [8, 15, 20]. In the

---

* Research supported by the Northrop Grumman Corp., contract: P.O.8200082518.
** Research supported by the NSF grant, contract: IIS-0325144/003.

recent years there have been works incorporating ECA-like triggers in novel, highly-heterogeneous, distributed and dynamic data-driven application domains, e.g., the Web [9], peer-to-peer (P2P) systems and sensor networks [22]. Despite the co-existence of the large body of works in ENS, CQ, Data Streams, MOD [3, 5, 4, 6, 12, 11, 16, 10], all of which have the common need of dealing with dynamically changing information, and the rich history of ADb results [8, 15, 20] – there is a lack of tools that would enable using the "best of all the worlds". Namely, there is no paradigm that allows the users to seamlessly tie: (1) Detection of (composite) events obtained by monitoring continuously changing data with (2) Evaluation of conditions that are continuous queries and with (3) Dynamical adjustment of the triggers themselves – all for the purpose of executing a desired policy in a constantly evolving domain of interest.

In order to illustrate our motivation better, we present two scenarios and we analyze the requirements posed by each of them.

**I. Rq1:** *"When a moving object is continuously_moving_towards the region R for more than 5 minutes, if there are less than 10 fighter jets in the base B1, then send* `alert_b` *to the armored unit A1. Also send* `alert_a` *to the infantry regiment I1, when that object is closer than 3 miles to R, if all the marine corps units are further then 5 miles from R".*

**Rq1** needs to detect a composite event *(moving continuously towards...)*, using the individual *(location,time)* updates as simple events. These can be obtained, e.g., by tracking sensors [22], and in [18] we provided efficient algorithms for detecting the *continuously moving towards* predicate. **RQ1** also needs to initiate a continuous query at a remote system – the one monitoring the status of the air-base $B1$. However, **Rq1** has some other subtleties:

• It needs the status of the air-base $B1$ for as long as the original enabling event *moving towards* is still valid. After detecting its enabling event, **Rq1** requires that the system "spans" its attention to monitoring one more event *(closer than 3 miles to R)* and, upon its detection, request an evaluation of another remote condition-query, which happens to be instantaneous. Observe that there is a *binding* between the new event to the original event – the new one needs to focus on the distance pertaining to the particular object that satisfied the original enabling event.

**II. Rq2:** *"When the IBM stock in New York stock exchange has three consecutive increases of its value within 30 minutes with a total increase of at least 5%, if there is a stock exchange at which both IBM and Intel stocks within 15 min. from the originating event have achieved a one hour interval without dropping, then execute portfolio P1 for purchasing IBM shares at that stock exchange. Otherwise, if there is a non-decrease of the Google stock for 45 minutes, while the IBM increase is still valid on any other stock exchange, execute portfolio P2 for purchasing IBM shares at that other stock exchange. Subsequently, only execute portfolio B for purchasing Motorola shares, when its stock has two consecutive increases by a total of at least 8% in London, if its average daily increase on any other exchange market is non-negative".*

- Unlike **Rq1**, now the validity of the composite event related to the IBM values, which is detected based on the primitive events that are updates of the value of the its stock, is limited by an explicit time-value – *15 min*. The system requests an evaluation at another site of the if condition, however, this condition is peculiar in that it combines a continuous query with the one-hour past history of the system [5] of the IBM and Intel stocks, but allows for a portion of that history to be satisfied within the continuous query itself, for as long as it is within 15 minutes after the detection of the IBM-increase event.
- In **Rq2** the user has an "alternative plan" of reacting, if the first condition fails. This alternative depends on the outcome of another continuous query *(Google stock)*, which is tying the duration of interest for evaluating the continuous query with the "native" enabling event. **Rq1** requires the system to span its attention, but **Rq2** in its last part requires the system to completely *shift* the focus of its reactive behavior. After the failure of the respective Intel and Google-related criteria, the user is no longer interested in reacting to the events related to the increases of the IBM stock and wants to focus on the Portfolio B for Motorola shares.

The observations related to **Rq1** and **Rq2** have motivated our research towards the new paradigm for reactive behavior. Our main contributions are:

- We introduce a paradigm for specifying reactive behavior, called $(ECA)^2$ (Evolving and Context-Aware Event-Condition-Action), that enables the users to specify triggers that pro-actively evolve so that they can ensure a desired policy.
- We introduce the concept of a *metatrigger* for the purpose of minimizing the communication overhead and ensuring behavioral correctness in distributed setting. We observe that there is a duality in the nature of events and conditions that can be exploited in the functioning of the the metatriggers.

In the rest of this paper, Section 2 introduces the $(ECA)^2$ paradigm and its syntactic elements. The concept of the metatriggers is presented in Section 3, and Section 4 concludes the paper.

## 2 Evolution of the Triggers

In this section, we explain the main aspects of the specification of the triggers under the $(ECA)^2$ paradigm. The syntactic components are presented in Figure 1. Firstly, observe that in the events, conditions and actions we allow variables to be used. Thus, for example, $E_p(EV_p)$ denotes that the event of the parent-trigger $E_p$ has the (vector of) variable(s) $EV_p$ in its specification; similarly, $C_{p1}(VC_p1)$ denotes the query and the variables used in the first condition of the parent trigger. We assume that the usual rules for *safety* [19] of the variables apply, in the sense that each variable that appears in a negative literal, must also appear in a positive literal, or have a ground value at the time of the invocation/evaluation of the corresponding (negated) predicate. Secondly, observe that we allow two types of children-triggers to be specified within the scope of a given (parent) trigger. As is commonly done in the programming languages, we use rectangles

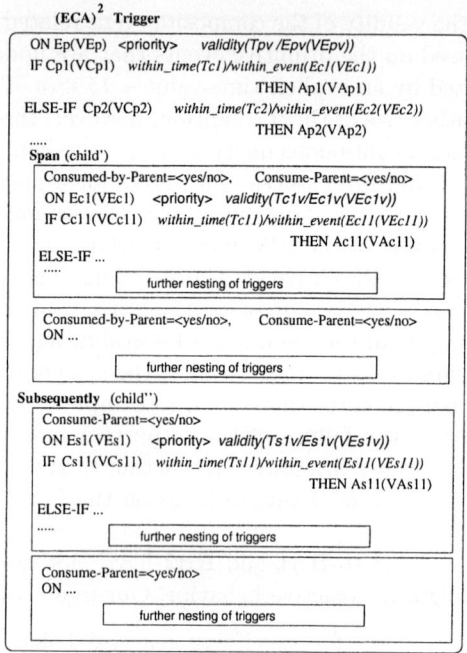

**Fig. 1.** Evolving Triggers Specification

to visualize the nesting of the relative scope of children-triggers within the scope of the parent-trigger. As indicated in Figure 1, the user can specify an arbitrary level of nesting of descendants within the children-triggers.

Before we give detailed explanation of the syntax of the $(ECA)^2$ triggers, we provide an example for the **Rq2**, illustrated in Figure 2. Using variables, one can express the desired relationships among the locations of the stock exchanges for evaluating the criteria of interest. Thus, when evaluating the condition for the alternative policy regarding the *Google* stock, the variable $SE_2$ denotes a stock exchange which is different from *New York*. By using $SE2$ as a variable in the action that executes the Portfolio $P2$, we ensure that the purchase is executed at "that other" stock exchange. The important observation here is that whenever the value of the IBM stock in New York stock exchange decreases it terminates the validity of the enabling event for the (parent) trigger. Past that point, the *child* trigger which implements the reactive policy for Motorola stock exists on its own, monitoring its respective event. Now we proceed with explaining the elements in the syntax of the $(ECA)^2$ triggers:

1. The option `validity` in the trigger's specification allows the user to state *how long* should the trigger be considered "alive". It reflects the user's policy, and it can be either an explicit time-value, or an event which, when detected causes the particular trigger's instance to be disabled. As a special case, one is able to specify *for as long as the original enabling event is valid*, by utilizing proper expressions of the available event algebra. For example, in the case of **Rq2** one

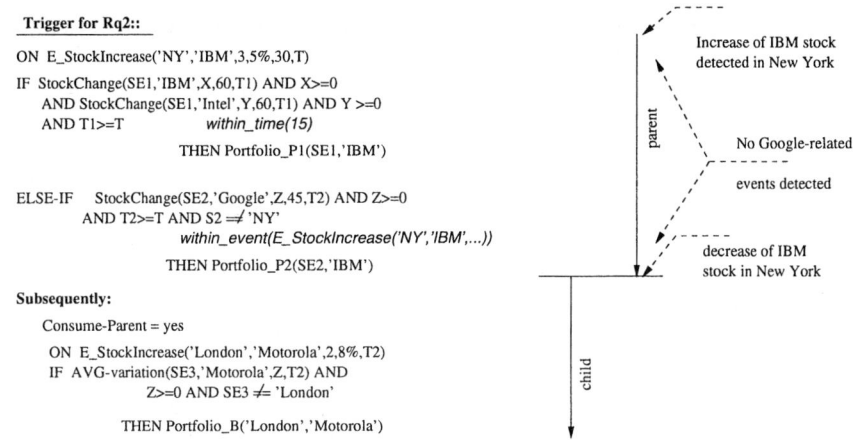

**Fig. 2.** Example Trigger for **Rq2**

may specify a composite event which is (a sequence of) IBM-increase events that enabled the trigger, followed by an IBM-decrease related event.

2. The *Else-If* parts at each level of nesting of the triggers correspond to alternative policies, based on the value of the respective conditions, once an instance of a particular trigger is "awaken". Clearly, these can be written as conditions of separate triggers with the same enabling event. We use the way depicted in Figure 1 for compactness, assuming that the ordering of the conditions actually corresponds to the users' preference when it comes to their evaluation. Some prototype systems (e.g., Starburst [21]) enable the users to explicitly state their ranking for (partial) ordering among the triggers (e.g., PRECEDES), but some commercial systems conforming to the ANSI standard (e.g., Oracle 9i [2]) do not allow this – triggers are ranked based on their time-stamps and that ranking is not always ensured at run-time. As indicated in Figure 1, we do consider the option of an explicit numeric priority specification for the triggers, which can be straightforwardly extended to the conditions.

3. Each condition has two options for indicating for how long its corresponding continuous query should be evaluated. One option is to explicitly list a time-interval value, as commonly done in CQ systems (e.g., [6]). An example for this is the statement *within_time(15)* in the trigger for **Rq2**. The other option is to specify an event which will confirm the termination of the user's interest in that condition. In the case of **Rq1**, the user is interested in getting updates about the state of the air-base for as long as the composite event $E\_moving\_towards$ is satisfied, based on the *(location,time)* update-events [18].

4. There are two types of *child-triggers*:

4.1. The first type – *child'*, enables a reaction to subsequent occurrences of other events that could potentially request monitoring of other conditions. This is the case in **Rq1**, where the user is also interested in detecting the proximity of that particular object to the region $R$. The value $Consumed\text{-}by\text{-}Parent = yes$ indicates that the child-trigger should terminate when the parent-trigger terminates. Conversely, *Consumed-by-Parent = no*, specifies that the child-trigger should continue its execution even though the parent has ceased to exist. As an example, in **Rq1** the value *Consumed-by-Parent = no* specifies that, although the particular moving object may no longer be *moving_continuously_towards* the region $R$ (e.g., it is following a zig-zag route), which disables the original (parent) trigger, the user is still interested in monitoring the *distance* of that particular object. Both consumption parameters provide means to dynamically `enable` and `dissable` instances of the triggers.

4.2. The second type of a child-trigger – *child"*, is specified with the **Subsequently** option, and its intended meaning is that, after the particular parent-trigger has been enabled, and all its "options have been exhausted" (e.g., expiration of the interval of interest for the continuous queries; no occurrence of the events for the *child'*-triggers), the user wants to focus on other aspects of the possible subsequent evolutions of the domain of interest. In the case of **Rq2**, the user shifts his interests to the properties related to the *Motorola* stock. However, the user has the option of stating whether in the future, the system should consider "waking-up" the parent trigger again or not. This is achieved by the statement *Consume-Parent*. *Consume-Parent = yes* reflects the user's intention not to consider the parent-trigger in the future at all. In the context of our **Rq2** example, the user does not want to bother with the future variations related to the IBM. In a sense, this is an equivalent to the SQL `drop` trigger rule, as no further instances of the parent-trigger are desired. *Consume-Parent = no* has the opposite effect.

Having the instances of the child-triggers active is similar in effect to the SQL `enable` command. However, in practice it is very unlikely to expect that the desired behavior can be achieved if the users are to manually execute it. Furthermore, attempting to write a child-trigger as a separate trigger from (and at the same scoping/nesting level as) its parent, with an enabling event which is a sequence of the *parent_event* followed by the *own_event*, may yield an unintended behavior. For example, in **Rq2** if, instead of being a child, the trigger related to *Motorola* stock is specified independently, with the event *E_StockIncrease('NY', 'IBM',3,...)* ; *E_StockIncrease('London', 'Motorola',2,...)*, the user may end up executing the Portfolio B in the settings in which, according to his preferences, he should have executed portfolio P1. The reason for this is that the condition of the *Motorola*-related trigger is an *instantaneous* query, which may be satisfied as soon as the composite event which enables the corresponding trigger is detected.

## 3 Metatriggers

The *metatrigger* is a module that is in charge of coordinating the detection of events and evaluation of the conditions in distributed environments, in a manner that ensures behavioral correctness and minimizes the communication overhead. To better motivate it, observe the following detailed example in the context of **Rq1** assuming, for the sake of argument that the *(location,time)* are detected every two minutes.

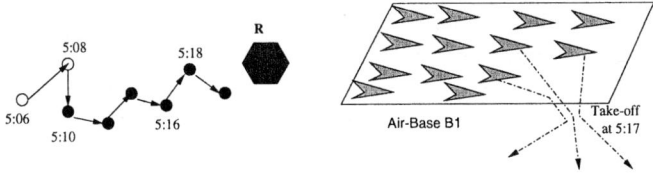

**Fig. 3.** Dynamics of Events and Conditions

As illustrated in Figure 3, the system began monitoring the object at 5:06, however, the *(location,time)* updates at 5:06 and 5:08, depicted with blank circles, were discarded because they were of no use for detecting the event of interest. Starting at 5:10, the system can detect the occurrence of the desired composite event *moving towards*) at 5:16 [18] which, in turn, "awakes" an instance of the corresponding trigger for **Rq1**. Upon checking the condition *(less than 10 airplanes in B1)*, the system will find out that there are actually 12 airplanes there and will not execute the action part *(alert)*. However, as illustrated in Figure 3, in a very short time-span, three jets have left the air-base and, by 5:17 it has only 9 jets available. Intuitively, the trigger for the **Rq1** should fire and raise the alert. However, this may not happen until 5:18 at which time the event *moving towards* is (re)detected. In many time-critical applications, this may cause unwanted effects. One possible solution is to periodically poll the remote database, however, this may incur a lot of unnecessary communication overhead[1] and, moreover, may still "miss" the actual time-point at which the condition became satisfied.

The main role of the metatriggers is the management of the type of behavior as described above in distributed environments. Figure 4 illustrates the position of the metatrigger module in the context of a typical ADb architecture, extended with an Event-Base (EB) (c.f. [8]). The arrowed lines indicated the data flow among the modules. Note that the module for the Continuous Queries Processing (CQP), is coupled with the Query Processing (QP) and the Rule (trigger) Processing (RP) modules [6].

When it comes to managing the reactive behavior in distributed settings, the crux of the metatriggers is the *Event and Conditions Manager* (ECM) component. This component translates the original specifications of the user and generates a new set of triggers, events and conditions that achieve the desired behavior, but are much more efficient for distributed environments. To describe this task more formally, consider the following simplified version of a trigger:

**TR1: ON** $E_1$
    **IF** $C_{1i} \wedge C_{1c}$
    **THEN** $A_1$

Its condition part consists of two conjuncts:

---

[1] Observe that the user may insist on a particular frequency of re-evaluation of the continuous query (c.f. [6]).

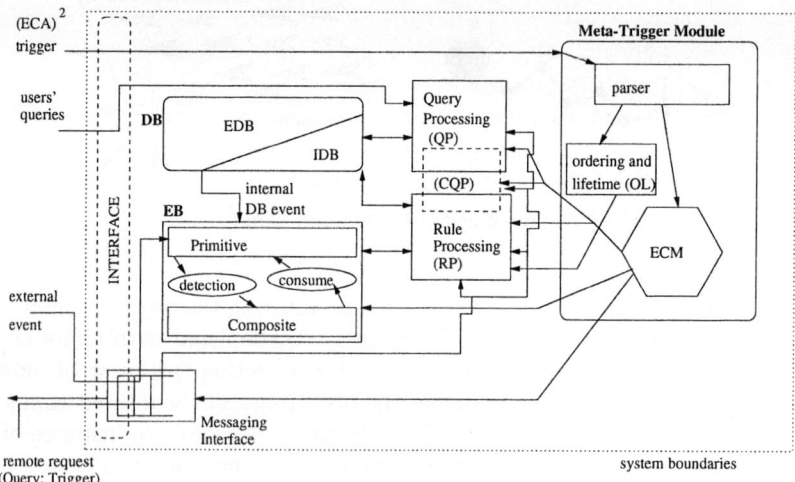

**Fig. 4.** Metatriggers Activities

- $C_{i1}$-instantaneous conditions, whose evaluation may be bound to various states. Such bindings have already been identified as a *semantic dimension* of the active databases [8,15] and there are syntactic constructs that can specify particular states for evaluating the condition of the triggers (e.g., *referencing old/new*).
- $C_{1c}$- a condition which expresses a continuous query.

The ECM component of the metatrigger performs the following activities:

1. Translate the specifications of the original trigger into:

**TR1':**    ON    $E_1$ ;    $(E_{\overrightarrow{C_{1c}}} ; E_{\overleftarrow{C_{1c}}})$
         IF    $C_{1i}$
         THEN    $A_1$

Where $E_{\overrightarrow{C_{1c}}}$ and $E_{\overleftarrow{C_{1c}}}$ are two new events with the following semantics:

1.1. $E_{\overrightarrow{C_{1c}}}$ – an event denotes the request for evaluating $C_{1c}$, which may have to be sent to a remote site – e.g., in the case of **Rq1** it is send to the air-base.

1.2. $E_{\overleftarrow{C_{1c}}}$ – an event (external in case of **Rq1**), which denotes that the continuous condition has been evaluated to true, and the notification about it has been received. Observe that the new local trigger **TR1'** is now enabled by the composite event which is the sequence of events $E_1$ ; $(E_{\overrightarrow{C_{1c}}} ; E_{\overleftarrow{C_{1c}}})$

2. It translates the continuous query $C_{1c}$ of the condition into:

2.1. A message for the remote site, requesting immediate evaluation and notification if true;

2.2. A trigger that is transmitted to the remote site, which essentially states:

**TR1c:**    ON    $E_1$; $E_{\overrightarrow{C_{1c}}}$
         IF    $C_{1c}$
         THEN    $A(\text{Send\_Notification}(E_{\overleftarrow{C_{1c}}}))$

3. Lastly, the ECM generates the specification of another local trigger **TR1"**, whose description we omit – but whose purpose is to detect when the original

trigger **TR1**, as specified by the user, has "expired", i.e., the criteria used in the validity specification, temporal or event-based, is satisfied, and:
3.1. disable the current instance of the local trigger **TR1'**.
3.2. Send a notification that the instance of the **Tr1c** in the remote site should be disabled.

What we described above exemplifies how something that was initially perceived as a pure query-like condition, becomes a "generator" of a several new events/triggers. We only explained the basic functionality of the ECM as a translator for a simplified version of the original specifications of the user's trigger. Clearly, in reality, one may expect more sophisticated queries whose translation and generation of the equivalent new events, triggers, and messages to the remote sites will be more complicated. In the settings of the **Rq1**, one may observe another motivation for translating the original condition's query: the predicate JetsCount (c.f. Figure 2), say, for security purposes, may be a *view* and the user cannot express much at the specification time of the corresponding trigger.

Although the ECM is the most relevant component of the metatrigger module, it has few other components. The parser extracts the constructs of the syntax that define the corresponding events and conditions, as well as user's preferences for priority/ordering. The *Ordering and Lifetime* (OL) component of the metatrigger works in conjunction with the RP component. It ensures that, whenever a particular event is detected, the order of evaluating the conditions and executing the actions among all the triggers "awaken" by that event, conforms with the user's specifications. We re-iterate that although some prototype ADb systems, such as Starburst [20] provide the option for priorities among the triggers ([8, 15]), the commercial DBMS with active capabilities, conforming with the ANSI SQL99 standard specifications [1] do not. Since we are using Oracle 9i [2], we needed to write a separate PL/SQL routine (c.f. [17]). The OL component of the metatrigger is also in charge of enable-ing the (instances of the) child-triggers in the proper states of the evolution of the system. Upon "ceasing" of a particular trigger, OL ensures that the appropriate clean-up actions are performed which, based on the values of the *Consumed-by-Parent* and *Consume-Parent* parameters, are either disable or drop.

## 4 Related Works and Concluding Remarks

There is a large body of existing results in several research areas that address managing of (re)active behavior [3, 5, 7, 8, 11, 13, 15, 21, 22]. These works provide a technical foundations for, and in turn, can benefit from our work, however, their detailed discussion is well beyond the scope of this paper.

We presented a novel paradigm $(ECA)^2$, for triggers that are aware of the dynamic correlation between the events and conditions and, in a sense, can "react in a proactive manner" – by modifying themselves. We also provided syntactic constructs for specifying the triggers under this paradigm and enable using the $(ECA)^2$ paradigm in dynamic distributed environments, and we proposed the concept of the metatriggers as a possible tool for their management.

Currently, we are focusing on further incorporating the $(ECA)^2$ in heterogeneous/multidatabase settings, and we would like to believe that, in a near future, our work will motivate a wide spectrum of new challenges, ranging from theoretical aspects (e.g., termination/expresiveness [21]) up to intricate details that depend on the application/problem domain constraints (e.g., power-limitations in sensor networks [22]; interplay among context variables in LBS [16]).

# References

1. ANSI/ISO International Standard: Database language SQL. http://webstore.ansi.org.
2. Oracle 9i. www.oracle.com/technology/products/oracle9i.
3. A. Carzaniga, D.S. Rosenblum, and A.L. Wolf. Design and evaluation of a wide-area event notification service. *ACM-TOCS*, 19(3), 2001.
4. S. Chandrasekaran and M.J. Franklin. Streaming queries over streaming data. In *VLDB Conference*, 2002.
5. S. Chandrasekaran and M.J. Franklin. Remembrance of streams past: Overload-sensitive management of archived streams. In *VLDB Conference*, 2004.
6. J.J. Chen, D.J. DeWitt, F. Tian, and Y. Wang. NiagaraCQ: A scalable continuous query system for internet databases. In *ACM SIGMOD Conference*, 2000.
7. Y. Diao, S. Rizvi, and M.J. Franklin. Towards an internet-scale XML dissemination service. In *VLDB Conference*, 2004.
8. P. Fraternali and L. Tanca. A structured approach for the definition of the semantics of active databases. *ACM TODS*, 20(4), 1995.
9. G.Papamarkos, A.Poulovassilis, and P.T.Wood. Event-condition-action rule languages for the semantic web. In *SWDB Workshop (at VLDB)*, 2003.
10. R.H. Güting and M. Schneider. *Moving Objects Databases*. Morgan Kaufmann, 2005.
11. A. Hinze and A. Voisard. Location-and time-based information delivery in tourism. In *SSTD*, 2003.
12. L. Liu, C. Pu, and W. Tang. Continual queries for internet scale event-driven information delivery. *IEEE-TKDE*, 11(4), 1999.
13. S. Madden, M.A. Shah, J.M. Hellerstein, and V. Raman. Continuously adaptive continuous queries over streams. In *ACM SIGMOD Conference*, 2002.
14. C. Olston, J. Jiang, and J. Widom. Adaptive filters for continuous queries over distributed data streams. In *ACM SIGMOD*, 2003.
15. N. Paton. *Active Rules in Database Systems*. Springer-Verlag, 1999.
16. J. Schiller and A. Voisard. *Location-based Services*. Morgan Kaufmann Publishers, 2004.
17. G. Trajcevski, H. Ding, and P. Scheuermann. Context-aware optimization of continuous range queries for trajectories. In *MobiDE Workshop (at SIGMOD)*, 2005.
18. G. Trajcevski, P. Scheuermann, H. Brönnimann, and A. Voisard. Dynamic topological predicates and notifications in moving objects databases. In *MDM*, 2005.
19. J. D. Ullman. *Principles of Database and Knowledge – Base Systems*. Computer Science Press, 1989.
20. J. Widom. The Starburst active database rule system. *IEEE TKDE*, 8(4), 1996.
21. J. Widom and S. Ceri. *Active Database Systems: Triggers and Rules for Advanced Database Processing*. Morgan Kaufmann, 1996.
22. F. Zhao and L. Guibas. *Wireless Sensor Networks: an Information Processing Approach*. Morgan Kauffman, 2004.

# A Framework for Distributed XML Data Management

Serge Abiteboul[1], Ioana Manolescu[1], and Emanuel Taropa[1,2]

[1] INRIA Futurs & LRI, France
firstname.lastname@inria.fr
[2] CS Department, Yonsei University, Korea

**Abstract.** As data management applications grow more complex, they may need efficient distributed query processing, but also subscription management, data archival etc. To enact such applications, the current solution consists of stacking several systems together. The juxtaposition of different computing models prevents reasoning on the application as a whole, and wastes important opportunities to improve performance.

We present a simple extension to the AXML [7] language, allowing it to declaratively specify and deploy complex applications based solely on XML and XML queries. Our main contribution is a full algebraic model for complex distributed AXML computations. While very expressive, the model is conceptually uniform, and enables numerous powerful optimizations across a distributed complex process.[1]

## 1 Introduction

Distributed data management has been an important domain of research almost since the early days of databases [15]. With the development of the Web and the existence of universal standards for data exchange, this problem arguably became the most essential challenge to the database community. The problem as considered in distributed relational systems was already very complex. With the heterogeneity and autonomy of sources, it is now even more difficult.

The language Active XML based on the embedding of service calls inside XML documents has been proposed for distributed data management. Several works have shown that the exchange of such documents provides a powerful support for distributed optimization [1, 2, 3]. However, these works proposed isolated solutions for isolated tasks, and had to rely on features not present in the language. In this paper, we isolate the missing components and propose an extension that could serve as a unified powerful language for describing, in a very flexible manner the deployment and evaluation of queries in a collaborative manner. The aforementioned techniques, as well as standard distributed query optimization techniques, can all be described based on rewrite rules in the language.

To pursue the analogy with (centralized) relational database, Active XML as originally proposed, is a *logical* language for describing distributed computation,

---
[1] This work was partially supported by the French Government ACI MDP2P and the *eDos* EU project.

to which we associated a fixed simple evaluation strategy. Its extension proposed here is an *algebraic* counterpart that provides for more efficient evaluation.

One missing aspect from Active XML (as originally described) is the capability to control explicitly the shipping of data and queries, although we did use this feature [1]. We explicitly add it here, to allow delegating computations to other peers. We also explicitly introduce *generic* data and service, which are available on several sites; a particular flavor of this feature was used in [3].

This paper is organized as follows. Section 2 introduces AXML, and shows how the application could be deployed based on AXML. Section 3 holds our main contribution: an algebra for distributed computations, with associated equivalence rules and an optimization methodology. Section 4 concludes.

An application of our methodology to a real-life software distribution application is described in the full version of this paper [4].

## 2 Preliminaries: AXML Documents and Queries

In this section, we briefly introduce the features of the pre-existing ActiveXML model (AXML, in short) [5, 7]. We use the following notations:

- a set $\mathcal{D}$ of *document names*. Values from $\mathcal{D}$ are denoted: $d$, $d_1$, $d_2$ etc.
- a set $\mathcal{S}$ of *service names*. Values from $\mathcal{S}$ are denoted: $s$, $s_1$, $s_2$ etc.
- a set $\mathcal{P}$ of *peer identifiers*. Values from $\mathcal{P}$ are denoted: $p$, $p_1$, $p_2$ etc.
- a set $\mathcal{N}$ of *node identifiers*. Values from $\mathcal{N}$ are denoted: $n_1$, $n_2$ etc.

We assume given a finite set of peers, each of which is characterized by a distinct peer identifier $p \in \mathcal{P}$. Intuitively, a peer represents a context of computation; it can also be seen as a hosting environment for documents and services, which we describe next. We make no assumption about the structure of the peer network, e.g. whether a DHT-style index is present or not. We will discuss the impact of various network structures further on.

### 2.1 XML Documents, Types, and Services

We view an XML tree as an unranked, unordered tree, where each leaf node has a label from $\mathcal{L}$, and each internal nodes has a label from $\mathcal{L}$ and an identifier from $\mathcal{N}$. Furthermore, each tree resides on exactly one peer identified by $p \in \mathcal{P}$. We will refer to the tree as $t@p$. An *XML document* is a tuple $(t, d)$ where $t$ is an XML tree, $d \in \mathcal{D}$ is a document name. No two documents can agree on the values of $(d, p)$. We will refer to a document as $d@p$.

We denote by $\Theta$ the set of all XML tree types, as expressed for instance in XML Schema [18], and we refer to individual types as $\tau, \tau_1, \tau_2$ etc.

We model a *Web service* as a tuple $(p, s)$, where $p \in \mathcal{P}$ is the identifier of the peer providing the service, and $s \in \mathcal{S}$ is the service name. The service is associated an unique type signature $(\tau_{in}, \tau_{out})$, where $\tau_{in} \in \Theta^n$ for some integer $n$, and $\tau_{out} \in \Theta$. We use $s@p$ to refer to such a service; it corresponds to a (simplified) WSDL request-response operation [17].

When a Web service $s@p$ receives as input an XML forest of type $\tau_{in}$, it reacts by sending, successively, one or more XML trees of type $\tau_{out}$. If the service may send more than one such tree, we term it a *continuous service*.

## 2.2 AXML Documents

An AXML document is an XML document containing some nodes labeled with a specific label sc, standing for service calls. An sc node has several children. Two children, labeled peer and service, contain, respectively, a peer $p_1 \in \mathcal{P}$ and a service $s_1 \in \mathcal{S}$, where $s_1@p_1$ identifies an existing Web service. The others are labeled $\text{param}_1,...,\text{param}_n$, where $n$ is the input arity of $s@p$.

Assume an AXML document $d_0@p_0$ contains a service call to a service $s_1@p_1$ as above. When the call is *activated*, the following sequence of steps takes place:

1. $p_0$ sends a copy of the $\text{param}_i$-label children of the sc node, to peer $p_1$, asking it to evaluate $s_1$ on these parameters.
2. $p_1$ eventually evaluates $s_1$ on this input, and sends back to $p_0$ an XML subtree containing the response.
3. When $p_0$ receives this subtree, it inserts it in $d_0$, as a sibling of the sc node.

AXML supports several mechanisms for deciding when to activate a service call. This control may be given to the user via some interactive hypertext. Alternatively, a call may be activated only when the call result is needed to evaluate some query over the enclosing document [2], or in order to turn $d_0$'s XML type in some other desired type [6]. It is also possible to specify that a call must be activated *just after* a response to another activated call has been received.

AXML also supports *calls to continuous services*. When such a call is activated, step 1 above takes place just once, while steps 2 and 3, together, occur repeatedly starting from that moment. In this paper, we consider that the response trees successively sent by $p_1$ accumulate as siblings of the sc node [5]. If a service call $sc_1$ must be activated just after $sc_2$ and $sc_2$ is a call to a continuous service, then $sc_1$ will be activated after handling every answer to $sc_2$. We consider all services are continuous.

Sc nodes may reference any WSDL-compliant Web service. Of particular interest for us are *declarative Web services*, whose implementation is a declarative XML query or update statement, possibly parameterized. The statements implementing such services are visible to other peers, enabling many optimizations. Our goal is thus: given a set of AXML documents and declarative services, and a query $Q$, find alternative evaluation strategies (possibly involving new documents and services dynamically created) which compute the same answers for $Q$, and are potentially more efficient. We first make some extensions to AXML.

## 2.3 AXML Extensions

We introduce *generic* documents and services, and define a notion of tree, document, and service equivalence. Then, we make some extensions to the syntax of sc elements, central in AXML, to allow for more communication patterns.

A *generic document* $ed@any$ denotes any among a set of regular documents which we consider to be *equivalent*; we say $ed$ is a *document equivalence class*. We consider a specific notion of document equivalence denoted $\equiv$, suited for AXML. Two documents are equivalent *iff* their trees are equivalent. Two trees $t_1$ and $t_2$ are equivalent *iff* their potential evolution, via service call activations, will eventually reach the same fixpoint. This notion has been formally defined in [5] for the purpose of studying confluence and termination for AXML; we use it here as a basis for optimization. We introduce *generic services* similarly [4].

We allow queries to refer to generic documents as well as regular ones, and sc nodes to refer to generic services as well as regular ones. The semantics of such queries and calls will be defined shortly.

We add to an sc element some optional forw children, each of which contains a *location to which the service results(s) should be forwarded*. Each forw element encapsulates a node identifier of the form $n@p$, where $p \in \mathcal{P}$ and $n \in \mathcal{N}$. The semantics is that the response should be added as a child of node $n$, which resides on peer $p$. If no forw child is specified, a default one is used containing the ID of the sc's parent, just like in the existing AXML model.

We will refer to a document as $d@p$ or alternatively as $d@any$, and similarly for services. We will denote a service call in our extended AXML model as:

$$\text{sc}((p_{prov}|any), serv, [\text{param}_1, \ldots, \text{param}_k], [\text{forw}_1, \ldots, \text{forw}_m])$$

where $p_{prov} \in \mathcal{P}$ is a peer providing the service $serv$.

## 3 An Algebra for Extended AXML Computations

### 3.1 AXML Expressions

To model the various operations needed by our distributed data management applications, we introduce here a simple language of AXML expressions, denoted $\mathcal{E}$. In the following, $p$, $p_1$, $p_2$ are some peers from $\mathcal{P}$.

Any tree $t@p$ or document $d@p$ is in $\mathcal{E}$. Also, let $q@p$ be a query of arity $n$ defined at $p$, and let $t_1@p, t_2@p, \ldots, t_n@p$ be a set of trees at $p$. Then, $q@p(t_1@p, t_2@p, \ldots, t_n@p) \in \mathcal{E}$.

Let $t@p_1$ be a tree. Then, $send(p_2, t@p_1) \in \mathcal{E}$, where $send(\cdot)$ is an expression constructor. This expression denotes the sending of a piece of data, namely $t$, from $p_1$ to $p_2$. Similarly, if $d@p_1$ is a document, $send(p_2, d@p_1) \in \mathcal{E}$. The exact place where $t$ (or $d$) arrives at peer $p_2$ is determined when evaluating the expression, as the next sections explains.

$\mathcal{E}$ also allows to specify the exact location(s) where a tree should arrive. The expression $send(n_2@p_2, t@p1)$ says that $t$ should be added as a child of the node $n_2@p_2$. The expression $send([n_2@p_2, n_3@p_3, \ldots, n_k@p_k], t@p1)$ corresponds to the operation of sending the same tree to several destinations. Finally, $send(d@p_2, t@p_1)$ states that $t$ is installed under the name $d$ as a new document at $p_2$ (where $d$ was not previously in used on $p_2$).

$\mathcal{E}$ also allows sending queries (in the style of code shipping). Let $q@p_1$ be a query. Then, $send(p_2, q@p_1) \in \mathcal{E}$, where $send(\cdot)$ is the same (slightly overloaded) expression constructor. This denotes the sending of the query $q$ on peer $p_2$.

An expression can be viewed (serialized) as an XML tree, whose root is labeled with the expression constructor, and whose children are the expression parameters. An expression located at some peer, denoted $e@p$, is an XML tree.

## 3.2 Evaluating AXML Expression Trees

The expression language $\mathcal{E}$ *describes* some computations to be performed. In this section, we define the *evaluation* of an expression tree $e@p$, where $e \in \mathcal{E}$.

Intuitively, $eval@p(e)$ may do one or more of the following: (*i*) *return* another XML tree (or, more generally, a stream of XML trees, where a stream is a flow of XML trees which accumulate, as children of a given node on some peer); (*ii*) *return* a new service; (*iii*) *as a side effect, create one or more XML streams*, accumulating under some well-specified nodes on one or more peers.

This is best illustrated by the following *eval* definitions, where $p, p_i$ designates a peer, $t_j@p$ is a tree at peer $p$, and $n_l@p$ a node at $p$.

We first define *eval* for tree expressions. Let $t@p_0$ be a tree, whose root is labeled $l \in \mathcal{L}, l \neq \mathsf{sc}$, and let $t_1, \ldots, t_n$ be the children of the root in $t$. We define:

$$eval@p_0(t@p_0) = l(eval@p_0(t_1), eval@p_0(t_2), \ldots, eval@p_0(t_n)) \qquad (1)$$

The evaluation copies $t$'s root and pushes the evaluation to the children. Evaluating one XML tree (the expression tree on the left) yields the (partially evaluated) XML tree at right, into which the expressions to evaluate are smaller.

As a consequence of (1), for any tree $t@p_0$ containing no $\mathsf{sc}$ node, we have $eval@p_0(t@p_0) = t@p_0$: evaluating the expression simply returns the data tree.

Now consider what happens if we replace the (static) tree $t@p_0$ with a stream of successive XML trees, accumulating as children of some node $n@p_0$. Clearly, in this case, definition (1) applies for every tree in the stream, thus *eval* over the stream of trees returns another stream of (partially evaluated) trees.

Definition (1) covers a particular class of $eval@p(t)$ expressions; we will define *eval* for the other cases gradually. For the time being, we turn to defining the evaluation of (a particular class of) query expression trees:

$$eval@p(q(t_1@p, \ldots, t_n@p)) = q(eval@p(t_1@p), \ldots, eval@p(t_n@p)) \qquad (2)$$

Evaluating a local query expression tree amounts to evaluating the query parameters, and then evaluating the query (in the usual sense) on these trees.

Recall that all queries are continuous. If we take $t_i@p$ to be streams of trees arriving at $p$, definition (2) captures the intuitive semantics of continuous incremental query evaluation: $eval@p(q)$ produces a result whenever the arrival of some new tree in the input streams $t_1, t_2, \ldots, t_n$ leads to creating some output. This generalization reasoning (from trees to streams of trees) applies to all remaining *eval* definitions, and we will consider it implicit in the sequel.

We next define the evaluation of a simple class of *send* expressions.

$$eval@p_0(send(p_1, t@p_0)) = \emptyset \qquad (3)$$

Evaluating a *send* expression tree at $p_0$, hosting $t$, returns at $p_0$ an empty result. Intuitively, the message encapsulating the copy of $t$ has left $p_0$, and moved to $p_1$.

However, as a side effect, a copy of $t@p_0$ is made, and sent to peer $p_1$. From now on, all evaluations of *send* expression trees are implicitly understood to copy the data model instances they send, prior to sending them.

**Notation.** From now on, we will use the shorthand $send_{p_1 \to p_2}(e)$ to denote $eval@p_1(send(p_2, e))$, where $p_1, p_2 \in \mathcal{P}$ and $e \in \mathcal{E}$, and we use $send_{p_1 \to fwList}(e)$ to denote $eval@p_1(send(fwList, e))$, where $fwList$ is a list of nodes.

If $p_2 \neq p_0$, $send_{p_2 \to p_1}(t@p_0)$ is undefined. The intuition is that $p_2$ cannot send something it doesn't have. More generally, for any tree $x@p_0$, $send_{p_2 \to p_1}(x@p_0)$ is undefined if $p_2 \neq p_0$. Similarly, we define:

$$send_{p_0 \to [n_1@p_1, n_2@p_2, \ldots, n_k@p_k]}(t@p_0) = \emptyset \qquad (4)$$

Sending $t@p_0$ to the locations $n_i@p_i$ returns an empty result at $p_0$, and as a side effect, at each $p_i$, the result of $eval@p_i(t@p_i)$ is added as a child of $n_i@p_i$. We use $t@p_i$ to denote the copy of $t@p_0$ that has landed on $p_i$.

We now define *eval* at some peer, of a data expression of a remote tree.

$$eval@p_1(t@p_2) = send_{p_2 \to p_1}(eval@p_2(t@p_2)) \qquad (5)$$

We assume $p_1 \neq p_2$, thus $p_1$ initially doesn't have $t$. In order for $p_1$ to get the evaluation result, $p_2$ is asked to evaluate it[2], and then send it at $p_1$. Overall, $p_2$ has received the expression tree $t@p_2$ as some local tree, has replaced this local tree with the result of $eval@p_2(t)$, and has sent this result to $p_1$. After this send evaluation, the local send expression tree on $p_2$ becomes $\emptyset$, by (3). Setting a tree to $\emptyset$ amounts to deleting it, thus, $p_2$'s set of documents and services is unchanged after the evaluation. The overall effect on $p_1$ is that the expression tree $eval@p_1(t@p_2)$ has been replaced with the desired evaluation result.

We now have the ingredients for defining the evaluation of a tree $t@p_0$, whose root is labeled **sc**. We denote by $parList = [t_1, t_2, \ldots, t_n]$ the list of $\texttt{param}_i$-labeled children of the **sc**, and by $fwList$ the list of their $\texttt{forw}_j$-labeled siblings.

$$\begin{aligned}&eval@p_0(\texttt{sc}(p_1, s_1, parList, fwList)) = \\ &send_{p_1 \to fwList}(q_1(send_{p_0 \to p_1}(eval@p_0(parList))))\end{aligned} \qquad (6)$$

where $eval@p_0(parList)$ stands for $[eval@p_0(t_1), eval@p_0(t_2), \ldots, eval@p_0(t_n)]$.

The second part of the definition (6) is best read from the innermost paranthesis to the outer. To evaluate **sc**, $p_0$ first evaluates the parameters (innermost *eval*), then sends the result to $p_1$, as denoted by $eval@p_0(send(p_1, \ldots))$. Peer $p_1$ evaluates, in the usual sense, the query $q_1$ (the one which implements its service $s_1$), and sends the result to the locations in the forward lists.

We do not need to define the evaluation of a tree $t@p_0$, whose root is labeled **sc**, at some peer $p_1 \neq p_0$; this case is already covered by definition (5).

---

[2] This is performed at $p_2$ by applying successively definitions (1), (5) and (6), see next.

The evaluation at some peer $p_1$, of a query defined at another peer $p_2$, is:

$$eval@p_1(q(t_1@p_2, t_2@p_2, \ldots, t_n@p_2)) = \\ eval@p_1((send_{p_2 \to p_1}(q))\,(send_{p_2 \to p_1}([t_1@p_2, \ldots, t_n@p_2]))) \quad (7)$$

This states that $p_2$ should send both $q$ and its arguments to $p_1$, as shown by the two $send_{p_2 \to p_1}$, and $p_1$ can then evaluate locally as per definition (2).

What happens when evaluating a send expression of some query?

$$eval@p_1(send(p_2, q@p_1)) = send_{p_1 \to p_2}(q@p_1) = \emptyset \quad (8)$$

Evaluating the send expression tree erases it from $p_1$ and, as a side effect, deploys query $q$ on peer $p_2$ as a new service. Rather than giving it an explicit name, by a slight abuse of notation, we may refer to this service as $send_{p_1 \to p_2}(q@p_1)$.

So far, we have defined $eval$ on expressions involving precise documents and queries. We now turn to the case of generic documents and queries. We have:

$$eval@p(expr(d@any)) = eval@p(expr(eval@p(pickDoc(d@any)))) \quad (9)$$

where $expr$ is some $\mathcal{E}$ expression, and the functions $pickDoc$, present on all peers, return the name of some document from the equivalence class $d@any$. A similar rule applies for generic services [4]. Definition 9 states that $p$ should find the name of a regular document corresponding to the equivalence class $d@any$, then proceed to evaluate $expr$ where references to $d@any$ have been replaced with that name. The implementation of an actual $pick$ function at $p$ depends on $p$'s knowledge of the existing documents and services, $p$'s preferences etc. [4].

We have so far specified a procedure for expression evaluation: for any $e \in \mathcal{E}$, to evaluate $e@p$, identify the definition among (1)-(9) which fits $e$'s topmost node and $p$, apply this definition, and so on recursively down $e$'s structure until a plain data tree is obtained at $p$. This strategy extends the basic AXML one, to deal with the AXML extensions we introduced in Section 2.3. As we have argued, however, this strategy will not necessarily lead to best performance.

### 3.3 Equivalence Rules

In this section, we explore equivalent, potentially more efficient strategies for evaluating an expression tree $eval@p(e)$, where $p \in \mathcal{P}$ and $e \in \mathcal{E}$.

We call *state of an AXML system* over peers $p_1, p_2, \ldots, p_n$, and denote by $\Sigma$, all documents and services on $p_1, p_2, \ldots, p_n$. Evaluating an expression $e@p$ over an AXML system in state $\Sigma$ brings it to a possibly different state, which we denote $eval@p(e)(\Sigma)$. We say two expression evaluations $e_1@p_1$ and $e_2@p_2$ are equivalent, denoted $e_1@p_1 \equiv e_2@p_2$, if for any AXML system state $\Sigma$, $eval@p_1(e_1)(\Sigma) = eval@p_2(e_2)(\Sigma)$.

Our first equivalence rule refers to query delegation:

$$eval@p_1(q(t@p_1)) \equiv send_{p_2 \to p_1}((send_{p_1 \to p_2}(q))(send_{p_1 \to p_2}(t))) \quad (10)$$

This rule says that evaluating a query $q(t)$ at $p_1$ gives the same result as: sending $q$ and $t$ to another peer $p_2$, evaluating $q(t)$ at $p_2$, and sending back the results to $p_1$. The rule derives from the definitions (2), (4) and (8).

A second very useful rule refers to query composition/decomposition. Let $q$, $q_1, q_2, \ldots, q_n$ be some queries, such that $q$ is equivalent to the composed query $q_1(q_2, q_3, \ldots, q_n)$ (in the sense defined in Section 2.3). We have:

$$eval@p(q@p) \equiv eval@p(q_1(eval@p(q_2@p), \ldots, eval@p(q_n@p))) \qquad (11)$$

Intuitively, the rule states that $eval$ distributes over query composition. It is a direct consequence of the query equivalence hypothesis, and of the definition (2).

The query decomposition and query delegation rules, together, capture many existing distributed query optimization techniques, as Example 1 illustrates.

*Example 1 (Pushing selections).* Let $q_1$ be a query equivalent to $q_1(\sigma(q_2))$, where $\sigma$ is some logical selection, and $q_1$ and $q_2$ are chosen so that $\sigma$ has been pushed down as far as possible. Denoting by $q_3$ the query $\sigma(q_2)$, we have $q \equiv q1(q_3)$). Let $t@p_2$ be a tree, and $p$ be some peer other than $p_2$. We have:

$eval@p(q(t@p_2)) = eval@p(q_1(q_3(d@p_2))) \equiv_{(11)}$
$eval@p(q_1(eval@p(q_3(t@p_2)))) \equiv_{(10)}$
$eval@p(q_1(send_{p_2 \to p}(eval@p_2(q_3(t@p_2))))) =_{(2)} eval@p(q_1(send_{p_2 \to p}(q_3(t@p_2))))$

The definition or rule used at each step above is shown by a subscript. The first $eval$ designates the evaluation of $q$ on the remote tree $t$. Definition (7) suggests sending the whole tree $t$ to $p$ and evaluating there. However, the last $eval$ above delegates the execution of $q_3$ (which applies the selection) to $p_2$, and only ships to $p$ the resulting data set, typically smaller. □

Other classical distributed optimizations may be similarly derived.

The following rules allow for powerful optimizations of data transfers, and can be derived easily from the definitions of $send$ evaluation:

$$send_{p_1 \to p_2}(eval@p_0(send(p_1, t@p_0))) \equiv send_{p_0 \to p_2}(t@p_0) \qquad (12)$$

$$\begin{array}{l} eval@p(e_1(e_2(send_{p_1 \to p}(t@p_1)), e_3(send_{p_1 \to p}(t@p_1)))) \equiv \\ eval@p(e_1(e_2(send_{p_1 \to p}(t@p_1, d@p)), e_3(d@p))) \end{array} \qquad (13)$$

Rule (12), read from right to left, shows that data in transit from $p_0$ to $p_2$ may make an intermediary stop to another peer $p_1$. Read from left to right, it shows that such an intermediary halt may be avoided. While it may seem that rule (12) should always be applied left to right, this is not always true [4] !

In rule (13), subexpressions $e_2$ and $e_3$ need to transfer $t@p_1$ to $p$. If $t$ is transferred for the needs of $e_2$ and stored in a document $d@p_1$, $e_3$ no longer needs to transfer $t$, and can use $d@p$ directly. The rule holds assuming that the evaluation of $e_3$ is only enabled when $d$ is available at $p$, which breaks the parallelism between $e_2$ and $e_3$'s evaluations. This may be worth it if $t$ is large.

Another powerful rule concerns delegation of expression evaluation:

$$eval@p(e) \equiv eval@p_1(send(p, eval@p(e))) \qquad (14)$$

Some specific rules apply to trees rooted in sc nodes:

$$\begin{array}{l} eval@p(\text{sc}(p_1, s_1, parList, fwList)) \equiv \\ eval@p_2(send_{p \to p_2}(\text{sc}(p_1, s_1, parList, fwList))) \end{array} \qquad (15)$$

$$eval@p(q@p(\mathtt{sc}(p_1, s_1, parList@p, fwList))) \equiv \\ send_{p_1 \to fwList}(eval@p_1((send_{p \to p_1}(q@p))\ (q_1(send_{p \to p_1}(parList@p))))) \quad (16)$$

Rule (15) shows that the peer where an sc-rooted tree is evaluated does not impact the evaluation result. Notice there is no need to ship results back to $p_1$, since results are sent directly to the locations in the forward list $fwList$.

Rule (16) provides an interesting method to evaluate a query $q$ over a sc-rooted tree. Here, sc refers to service $s_1@p_1$, implemented by the query $q_1$. The idea is to ship $q$ and the service call parameters to $p_1$, and ask it to evaluate $q$ directly over $q_1(parList)$. We call this rule *pushing queries over service calls*.

## 4 Concluding Remarks

The work presented here follows the footsteps of previous works on distributed query processing [12, 15], and is particularly related to query optimization in mediator systems [10, 16] and in peer-to-peer environments [3, 8, 9, 11]. Our work brings the benefits of declarativeness and algebraic-based optimization to AXML, a language integrating queries and data in a single powerful formalism. Our algebra can be seen as a formal model for mutant query plans [13], extended to continuous XML streams. AXML algebraic optimization has first been explored in [14].

Our ongoing work focuses on refining our algebraic formalism, extending it to AXML type-driven rewriting [6], designing and implementing in the AXML system efficient and effective distributed optimization algorithms.

## References

1. S. Abiteboul, Z. Abrams, S. Haar, and T. Milo. Diagnosis of asynchronous discrete event systems: Datalog to the rescue! In *PODS*, 2005.
2. S. Abiteboul, O. Benjelloun, B. Cautis, I. Manolescu, T. Milo, and N. Preda. Lazy query evaluation for Active XML. In *SIGMOD*, 2004.
3. S. Abiteboul, A. Bonifati, G. Cobéna, I. Manolescu, and T. Milo. Dynamic XML documents with distribution and replication. In *SIGMOD*, 2003.
4. S. Abiteboul, I. Manolescu, and E. Taropa. A framework for distributed XML data management. Extended version (Gemo technical report no. 436), 2005.
5. S. Abiteboul, T. Milo, and O. Benjelloun. Positive Active XML. In *PODS*, 2004.
6. S. Abiteboul, T. Milo, and O. Benjelloun. Regular and unambiguous rewritings for Active XML. In *PODS*, 2005.
7. ActiveXML home page. Available at http://www.activexml.net.
8. S. Ceri, G. Gottlob, L. Tanca, and G. Wiederhold. Magic semi-joins. *Information Processing Letters*, 33(2), 1989.
9. L. Galanis, Y. Wang, S. Jeffery, and D. DeWitt. Locating data sources in large distributed systems. In *VLDB*, 2003.
10. L. Haas, D. Kossmann, E. Wimmers, and J. Yang. Optimizing queries across diverse data sources. In *VLDB*, 1997.
11. A. Halevy, Z. Ives, P. Mork, and I. Tatarinov. Piazza: data management infrastructure for semantic web applications. In *WWW*, 2003.

12. D. Kossmann. The state of the art in distributed query processing. *ACM Computing Surveys*, 32(4), 2000.
13. V. Papadimos, D. Maier, and K. Tufte. Distributed query processing and catalogs for peer-to-peer systems. In *CIDR*, 2003.
14. N. Ruberg, G. Ruberg, and I. Manolescu. Towards cost-based optimizations for data-intensive web service computations. In *SBBD*, 2004.
15. P. Valduriez and T. Ozsu. *Principles of Distributed Database Systems*. Prentice Hall, 1999.
16. V. Vassalos and Y. Papakonstantinou. Describing and using the query capabilities of heterogeneous sources. In *VLDB*, 1997.
17. W3C. WSDL: Web Services Definition Language 1.1.
18. XML Schema. http://www.w3.org/TR/XML/Schema.

# Querying and Updating Probabilistic Information in XML

Serge Abiteboul and Pierre Senellart*

INRIA Futurs & LRI, Université Paris-Sud, France
serge.abiteboul@inria.fr, pierre@senellart.com

**Abstract.** We present in this paper a new model for representing probabilistic information in a semi-structured (XML) database, based on the use of probabilistic event variables. This work is motivated by the need of keeping track of both confidence and lineage of the information stored in a semi-structured warehouse. For instance, the modules of a (Hidden Web) content warehouse may derive information concerning the semantics of discovered Web services that is by nature not certain. Our model, namely the fuzzy tree model, supports both querying (tree pattern queries with join) and updating (transactions containing an arbitrary set of insertions and deletions) over probabilistic tree data. We highlight its expressive power and discuss implementation issues.

## 1 Introduction

If the problem of discovering information on the surface Web is facilitated by a number of directories and search engines, the discovery, understanding and use of databases published on the Web (typically via HTML forms) is still cumbersome. It is therefore important to develop automatic tools to capture the semantics of this so-called *Hidden Web*. Such tools require a combination of techniques, e.g. from information extraction or natural language processing. We are concerned with combining such tools to develop a content warehouse to manage tree data coming from both the surface and Hidden Web [1]. Since such a system relies on techniques that are by nature imprecise, we need a model for imprecise tree data. The main contribution of this paper is such a model, the *fuzzy tree model*.

Models for managing imprecise information are not new. In particular, a large literature exists for the relational model, typically based on two approaches: (*i*) a probabilistic approach, e.g. [2,3], and (*ii*) a logic approach, e.g. [4]. An originality of our model is that it is based on a tree model, primarily to meet the needs of the standard for data exchanges, XML. Another originality is that our model combines the two aforementioned approaches. Probabilities are attached to pieces of data to capture the confidence the warehouse may have about the semantics of such pieces, while we rely on probabilistic events that are in the spirit of the logical conditions of [4], e.g. to capture choices performed during the extraction of information or its analysis. These probabilistic events capture dependencies between the probabilities of distinct pieces of data. Finally, while

---

* This work was developed in the framework of the RNTL Project WebContent.

most works on incomplete information focus on queries, updates play a central role in the present work as, for instance, in [5].

The fuzzy tree model arises quite naturally when considering the management of information discovered on the Web. The model is at the same time expressive (it captures complex situations) and concise (it provides compact representations). This will be shown by comparing the fuzzy tree model with two more standard models for describing imprecision. Most importantly, we will show that the model supports queries (tree pattern queries with joins, a standard subset of XQuery) and updates. Queries provide the means for a user to obtain information. Updates form the core component for the building of knowledge. The global system consists in a number of modules (crawlers, classifiers, data extractor, etc.). These tools introduce probabilistic knowledge in the content warehouse by updating it.

The paper is organized as follows. In Sect. 2, we present more motivation. In Sect. 3, we briefly present preliminary notions used throughout the paper. Section 4 discusses two simple models. The fuzzy tree model is the topic of Sect. 5. Before discussing related work and concluding, we present in Sect. 6 an on-going implementation of the fuzzy tree model. **An extended version of this paper is available in [6].**

## 2 Motivation

Since its creation in 1991, the World Wide Web has considerably grown, with billions of freely accessible pages. It is generally assumed that the Hidden Web (also known as Deep Web or Invisible Web) that consists of databases accessible through HTML forms or Web services, is even much larger (see, e.g., [7]) and that its content is typically of better quality than that of the surface Web. The Hidden Web is undoubtedly an invaluable source of information.

We want to provide access to the Hidden Web via high-level queries. To illustrate, consider a Web user interested in available options for a particular car. A current search engine will return a list of HTML pages including the constructor's website. We would like our system to discover that a particular form on a given site provides the desired information, fill that form, get the answer and directly provide the desired information. Such a semantic interpretation of the Hidden Web implies that the system has to discover the service, understand it, and index it so that, at query time, the proper data may be retrieved.

Imprecision is inherent in such a process: the inference performed by most modules typically involves some level of confidence. For instance, the system may be rather confident (but not certain) that a site is that of the constructor. Any module participating in the construction of the warehouse must then be able to insert, modify or delete information *with a given confidence.* This confidence or, in other words, the *probability* that the information is true, should be handled throughout the entire process. It is essential for informing the user of the confidence of portions of an answer as well as for ranking query results.

Three aspects, namely (*i*) the independent agents, (*ii*) the need to monitor the derivation of knowledge, and (*iii*) the non-sequentiality of the entire

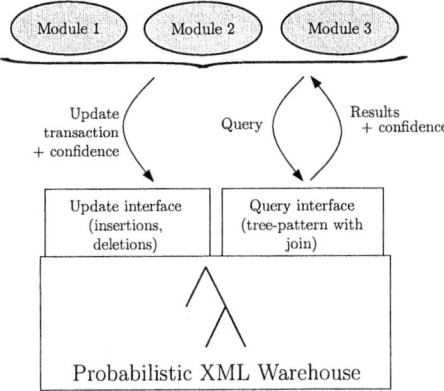

**Fig. 1.** Queries and Updates on a Probabilistic XML Warehouse

process, suggest the design of a *content-centric* system, as shown on Fig. 1 in the style of [1]. More precisely, the system is built on top of a content (semi-structured) warehouse, with querying and updating capabilities supporting imprecise information. Probabilistic information is stored in the warehouse and confidence tracking is directly provided through the query and update interfaces. Each query result and update transaction comes with confidence information. The purpose of this paper is to detail the model used to describe, query and update the probabilistic information stored in the warehouse.

## 3 Preliminary Definitions

In this section, we present preliminary definitions that are used in the remaining of the paper. We assume the existence of a set $N$ of labels and a set $V$ of values (say, the set of strings, with a particular value $\varepsilon$, the empty string). Although we are typically interested in XML, the standard for data exchange on the Web, we consider a simpler tree model that in particular ignores ordering of siblings.

**Definition 1.** *An (unordered) data tree $t$ is a 5-uple $t = (S, E, r, \varphi, \nu)$ where $S$ is a finite set of nodes, $E \subseteq S^2$ a tree rooted in $r \in S$, $\varphi : S \to N$ associates a label to each node in $S$ and $\nu$ associates a value in $V$ to leaves of the tree (where a leaf is a node in $S - \{r\}$ that has no child.)*

**Definition 2.** *A Tree-Pattern-With-Join (TPWJ) query is a 3-uple $(t, \mathcal{D}, J)$ where $t = (S, E, r, \varphi, \nu)$ is a data tree, $D \subseteq E$ is a set of descendant edges (the other edges are interpreted as child edges) and $J \subseteq S^2$ is a set of join conditions, such that for all $(s, s')$ in $J$, $s$ and $s'$ are two leafs of $t$ and $s \neq s'$.*

**Definition 3.** *Let $Q = (t, D, J)$ with $t = (S, E, r, \varphi, \nu)$ be a TPWJ query and $t' = (S', E', r', \varphi', \nu')$ a data tree. Then a valuation $\Psi$ (from $Q$ in $t'$) is a mapping from $S$ to $S'$ verifying: (i) (root) $\Psi(r) = r'$ (ii) (labels) $\forall s \in S, \varphi(\Psi(s)) = \varphi(s)$ (iii) (edges) $\forall (s_1, s_2) \in E$, if $(s_1, s_2) \in D$, $\Psi(s_2)$ is a descendant of $\Psi(s_1)$,* otherwise it is a child of $\Psi(s_1)$ *(iv)* (values) *For each leaf $s$ of $t$ with $\nu(s) \neq \varepsilon$, $\Psi(s)$ is a leaf of $t'$ and $\nu'(\Psi(s)) = \nu(s)$ (v)* (join conditions) *For each $(s1, s2) \in J$, both $\Psi(s1)$ and $\Psi(s2)$ are leaves of $t'$ and $\nu'(\Psi(s_1)) = \nu'(\Psi(s_2))$.*

Let $\Psi$ be such a valuation. Then the minimal subtree of $t'$ containing $\Psi(S)$ is called an answer *(we consider that a subtree is defined by a connected subset of the set of nodes containing the root)*. The set of all answers is denoted $Q(t')$.

We next define update operations, whose basic components are *insertions* and *deletions*. Let $t = (S, E, r, \varphi, \nu)$ and $t' = (S', E', r', \varphi', \nu')$ be two data trees. Assume without loss of generality that they use different IDs, i.e. $S \cap S' = \emptyset$. An *insertion* is an expression $i(t, n, t')$ where $n$ is in $S$, the node where $t'$ is to be inserted. A *deletion* is an expression $d(t, n)$ where $n$ is in $S - \{r\}$. Node $n$ is removed as well as all its descendants. Insertions and deletions are *elementary* updates that are used to define *update transactions*. Typically, one want to perform a number of update operations based on the result of a query. This motivates the following definition.

**Definition 4.** *An* update transaction *is a pair $\tau = (Q, U)$ where $Q = (t_Q, D, J)$ is a TPWJ query and $U$ is a set $\{i_1 \ldots i_p, d_1 \ldots d_q\}$ where $i_1 \ldots i_p$ are insertions on $t_Q$ and $d_1 \ldots d_q$ are deletions on $t_Q$.*

Queries are used to select the nodes of the trees where insertions or deletions are made. Intuitively, when one applies a transaction on a data tree $t$, one operation, say $d_i$, results in the deletion of a subtree for each valuation of $Q$.

**Definition 5.** *Let $\tau = (Q, U)$ be an update transaction. Let $t$ be a tree matched by $Q$ and let $\Psi_1 \ldots \Psi_n$ be the valuations of $Q$ on $t$. Let $(n^{i_1} \ldots n^{i_p}, n^{d_1} \ldots n^{d_q})$ be the nodes of $Q$ of the insertions and deletions of $U$. For each $k$ with $1 \leq k \leq p$, we define the set $I_k = \bigcup_{1 \leq j \leq n} \{\Psi_j(n^{i_k})\}$. For each $k$ with $1 \leq k \leq q$, we define the set $D_k = \bigcup_{1 \leq j \leq n} \{\Psi_j(n^{d_k})\}$.*

*The result of the transaction $\tau$ on $t$, denoted $\tau(t)$, is the result of the insertions $i_1 \ldots i_p$ on, respectively, each of the nodes of $I_1 \ldots I_p$ and the deletions $d_1 \ldots d_q$ on, respectively, each of the nodes of $D_1 \ldots D_q$.*

## 4 Two Simple Models

A natural way of representing probabilistic information is to list all *possible worlds*, each with its probability. See the example in Fig. 2. More formally:

**Definition 6.** *A* Possible Worlds (PW) set *$T$ is a finite set of pairs $(t_i, p_i)$ where each $t_i$ is a data tree, each $p_i$ is a positive real and $\sum_{i=1}^{n} p_i = 1$.*

If $(t, p)$ is in a PW set $T$, this means that there is a probability $p$ that the information contained in $T$ is indeed $t$. This is a rather general, if not practical, way of representing probabilistic semi-structured information.

A PW set $T = \{(t_i, p_i)\}$ is said to be *normalized* if there is no $i, j$ distinct such that $t_i, t_j$ are identical (up to node isomorphism). The *normalization* of

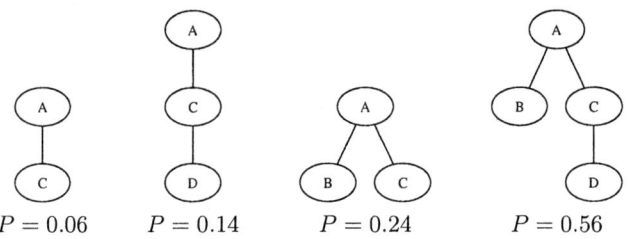

**Fig. 2.** Example Possible Worlds set

a PW set $T$ is obtained by regrouping the identical component trees into one component and summing their probabilities. In the remaining of this paper, we will assume that all PW sets are normalized. The definition of TPWJ query on a data tree can be extended in a quite natural way to PW sets.

**Definition 7.** *Let $Q$ be a TPWJ query and $T = \{(t_i, p_i)\}$ a PW set. The set of probabilistic possible answers is $\mathcal{P} = \{(t, p_i) \mid (t_i, p_i) \in T, t \in Q(t_i)\}$. The result of $Q$ for $T$ is the normalization $Q(T)$ of $\mathcal{P}$.*

Note that by construction $Q(T)$ is not always a PW set since the sum of probabilities is not 1 in the general. The fact that $(t, p) \in Q(T)$ is interpreted as there is a probability $p$ that $t$ is a result of the query $Q$ over $T$. So, for instance, the query "Who are the children of John?" may return "Alice" with a probability 0.9 and "Bob" with a probability 0.4. Note that the sum is greater than 1.

Now consider updates. A *probabilistic update transaction* is a pair $(\tau, c)$ where $\tau$ is an update transaction and $c \in ]0; 1]$ is the *confidence* we have in the transaction.

**Definition 8.** *Let $T = \{(t_i, p_i)\}$ be a PW set, $(\tau, c)$ a probabilistic update transaction, $\tau = (Q, Seq)$. The result of $(\tau, c)$ on $T$, denoted $(\tau, c)(T)$, is a PW set obtained by normalizing:*
$\{(t, p) \in T \mid t \text{ is not selected by } Q\}$
$\bigcup \{(\tau(t), p \cdot c) \mid t \text{ is selected by } Q\}$
$\bigcup \{(t, p \cdot (1 - c)) \mid t \text{ is selected by } Q\}$

Note that in the worst case, the number of components is multiplied by 2. This may occur for instance if one inserts a node as a child of the root. Then $Q$ matches all data trees. Thus, the number of components grows, in the worst case, exponentially in the number of update transactions performed.

Note that the PW model is not practical storage-wise. It is neither practical for query and update processing (in particular because of the potential exponential explosion). We next look at alternative ways of representing probabilistic tree information. The possible world semantics is natural and will provide guidelines for more complex models.

In the remaining of this section, we discuss another natural model, namely the Simple Probabilistic tree model.

In the spirit of probabilistic models for the relational model, we can attach a probability to each node in the tree. The intuition is that it captures the probability of that node to be present assuming its parent is. A limitation of

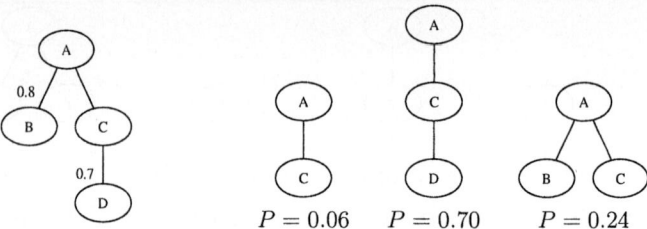

**Fig. 3.** Example SP tree    **Fig. 4.** More complex PW set

this model is that the only probability dependency captured is between the dependencies of nodes in a parent/child relationship.

**Definition 9.** *A* Simple Probabilistic (SP) tree *$T$ is a pair $(t, \pi)$ where $t = (S, E, r, \varphi, \nu)$ is a data tree and $\pi : S - \{r\} \to ]0; 1]$ assigns probabilities to tree nodes.*

Such an SP tree is represented as in Fig. 3.

We can give a *possible worlds semantics* to an SP tree as follows. Choose an arbitrary $X \subseteq S$. Consider $t_X$ the tree obtained by removing from $t$ all nodes not in $X$ (and their descendants). We assign to this tree the probability $p_X = \prod_{s \in X} \pi(s) \times \prod_{s \in S - X} (1 - \pi(s))$.

The possible world semantics of $T$, denoted $[\![T]\!]$, is defined as the normalization of the set $\{(t_X, p_X) \mid X \subseteq S\})$. Note that, as $X$ is an arbitrary subset of $S$, a given tree $t'$ can be obtained from various subsets $X$, including subsets which contain nodes not in $t'$. The normalization, by summing on the different $X$ leading to the same tree, ensures that the probability of $t'$ is correct. As an example, the semantics of the SP tree of Fig. 3 is the PW set on Fig. 2.

A natural question is then whether the SP tree model is as expressive as the PW set model. The answer is no. Figure 4 is an example of a PW set that has no equivalent SP tree. This negative result is not a sufficient reason for rejecting the SP model, since one might argue that PW sets not representable in the SP model are of little practical interest. The following result, however, demonstrates that the SP tree model does not meet basic requirements in terms of update, so motivates the model we introduce in the next section.

**Proposition 1.** *There exists an SP tree $T$ and a probabilistic update transaction $(\tau, c)$ such that there is no SP tree whose semantics is $(\tau, c)([\![T]\!])$.*

In other words, "SP trees are not closed under updates". This comes from the fact that dependencies between nodes are not expressible in the SP model. Indeed, a simple *modification* that can be seen as an interdependent succession of an insertion and a deletion, cannot be represented in the SP model. We next present a model that overcomes this limitation.

## 5 The Fuzzy Tree Model

In this section, we propose an original model for representing probabilistic information in semi-structured databases, that we call the *fuzzy tree model*. This model is inspired by the SP model from the previous section and enriches it using conditions à la [4], that are called probabilistic conditions here.

The conditions we use are defined using the auxiliary concept of *probabilistic event*. Given a set $W$ of event names, a probability distribution $\pi$ assigns probabilities, i.e. values in $]0;1]$ to elements of $W$. An *event condition* (over $W$) is a finite (possibly empty) set of *event atoms* of the form $w$ or $\neg w$ where $w$ is an event in $W$. The intuition is that we assign probabilistic conditions to nodes in the trees, instead of assigning them simple probabilities like in the SP model. This mechanism captures complex dependencies between nodes in the database.

**Definition 10.** *A fuzzy tree $T$ is a 3-uple $(t, \pi, \gamma)$ where $t = (S, E, r, \varphi, \nu)$ is a data tree, $\pi$ is some probability distribution over some set $W$ of events and $\gamma$ assigns event conditions to nodes in $S - \{r\}$.*

**Definition 11.** *Let $T = (t, \pi, \gamma)$ with $t = (S, E, r, \varphi, \nu)$ be a fuzzy tree. Let $W$ be the event names occurring in $T$. The possible worlds semantics of $T$ is the PW set, denoted $[\![T]\!]$, defined as the normalization of:*

$$\bigcup_{V \subseteq W} \{(t_{|V}, \prod_{w \in V} \pi(w) \prod_{w \in W - V} (1 - \pi(w)))\}$$

*where $t_{|V}$ is the subtree of $t$ where all nodes conditioned by a '$\neg w$' atom with $w \in V$ or a '$w$' atom with $w \notin V$ are removed (as well as their descendants).*

Example of PW semantics of fuzzy trees are given in Fig. 2 and 4, respectively, for the fuzzy trees of Fig. 5. Observe that the fuzzy tree model is more expressive than the SP model, since the latter did not have an equivalent of the PW set represented in Fig. 4. Actually, the following important result states that the fuzzy tree model is as expressive as the PW model.

**Theorem 1.** *For each PW set $X$, there exists a fuzzy tree $T$ such that $X = [\![T]\!]$.*

We now define queries on fuzzy trees:

**Definition 12.** *The result of $Q$ on a fuzzy tree $T = (t, \pi, \gamma)$, denoted $Q(T)$, is the normalization of $\bigcup_{u \in Q(t)} \{(u, eval(\bigcup_{n \text{ node of } u} \gamma(n)))\}$ where $eval(cond)$ returns $0$ if there is an event $w$ such that both '$w$' and '$\neg w$' are in cond, and $\prod_{w \in cond} \pi(w) \cdot \prod_{\neg w \in cond} (1 - \pi(w))$ otherwise.*

*When normalizing the set, if one of the probabilities is $0$, the element is removed. If the resulting set is empty, $Q$ does not match $T$.*

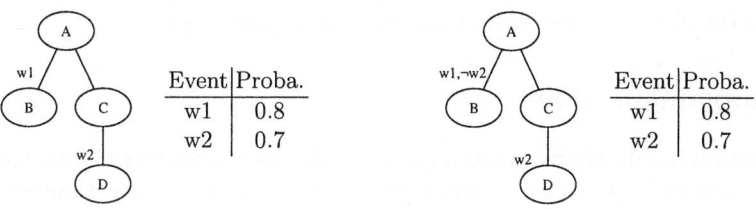

**Fig. 5.** Sample fuzzy trees

**Theorem 2.** *Let $T$ be a fuzzy tree and $Q$ be a TPWJ query. $Q$ matches $T$ if and only if $Q$ matches $[\![T]\!]$. Moreover, $Q(T) = Q([\![T]\!])$.*

Finally, we show that unlike the SP model, the fuzzy tree model supports arbitrary probabilistic update transactions. Let $(\tau, c)$ with $\tau = (Q, U)$ be a probabilistic update transaction and $T = (t, \pi, \gamma)$ a fuzzy tree. Let $w$ be a fresh event variable.

Consider the case where $|Q(T)| = 1$, that is where the position of update operations is uniquely defined (the extension when $|Q(T)| > 1$ is straightforward and detailed in [6]). Let $u$ be the unique element of $Q(T)$ and $cond = \bigcup_{n \text{ node of } u} \gamma(n)$; $cond$ is the set of conditions to be applied to the inserted and deleted nodes. The result of $(\tau, c)$ on $T$ is denoted $(\tau, c)(T)$, is the fuzzy tree obtained from $t$ by applying insertions and deletions in the following way.

Insertions are performed at the position mapped by $Q$ on $t$ in $u$. If $n$ is the position to insert a subtree $t'$, and $cond_\text{ancestors}$ is the union of the event conditions on the (strict) ancestors of $n$, $t'$ is inserted and its root is assigned the condition $\{w\} \cup (cond - (\gamma(n) \cup cond_\text{ancestors}))$.

Deletions are performed at the position mapped by $Q$ on $t$. Let $n$ be the node to be deleted and $cond_\text{ancestors}$ be the union of the event conditions on the (strict) ancestors of $n$. Let $cond_\text{new} = \{w\} \cup cond - (\gamma(n) \cup cond_\text{ancestors})$. The original $n$ node is replaced by as many copies as elements of $cond_\text{new}$. Let $a_1 \ldots a_p$ be the $p$ elements of $cond_\text{new}$. The first copy of $n$ is annotated with condition $\gamma(n) \cup \{\neg a_1\}$. The second copy of $n$ is annotated with condition $\gamma(n) \cup \{a_1, \neg a_2\} \ldots$ The last copy of $n$ is annotated with conditions $\gamma(n) \cup \{a_1 \ldots a_{n-1}, \neg a_n\}$.

**Theorem 3.** *Let $(\tau, c)$ be a probabilistic update transaction and $T$ a fuzzy tree. Then $[\![(\tau, c)(T)]\!] = (\tau, c)([\![T]\!])$.*

The fuzzy tree model provides a concise representation of imprecision. Updates can be captured in the model. Simple updates (insertions, or deletions without dependency on another branch of the tree) do not yield an exponential growth, as it is the case for the PW model. Complex updates may still be costly.

An interesting side benefit of using the fuzzy tree model is the possibility to keep *lineage* (or *provenance*) information about the data. Since every node is conditioned by event variables corresponding to update transactions, we can associate meta-data to these variables to record information about the origin of the corresponding transaction. Note that these variables are preserved throughout the whole process; a fuzzy tree system is able to deliver, along with query results and probabilities, information about the lineage associated with a piece of data (possibly updated more than once) and query results.

## 6 Implementation

This section briefly discusses our implementation of a fuzzy tree system that will soon be available at http://pierre.senellart.com/software/fuzzyxml/

XML documents are stored in a file system. (The use of an XML repository will be considered in the future.) TPWJ queries themselves are represented as XML fragments. The query evaluation over fuzzy trees is implemented using the Qizx/open Java XQuery engine [8]. TPWJ queries are compiled into XQuery queries, whose results are converted to the minimal subtrees referred to in Definition 2. A post-processing step is performed on the resulting subtrees to compute the associated probabilities. For optimization, query processing relies on a dataguide of the document obtained by using the XML Summary Drawer described in [9]. Finally, updates are performed directly on the XML tree, following the rules described in Sect. 5.

## 7 Conclusion

The topic of probabilistic databases has been intensively studied, see for instance [4, 3, 10, 11, 12], and [2, 13] for more recent works. In [13], Widom stresses the need for a system maintaining both *probability* and *lineage* of the data. In that paper, imprecision comes from three distinct sources: inaccuracy of the values, confidence in the tuples of the relations and incompletude in the coverage of relations. We were only interested here in this second source of imprecision. The idea of associating probabilistic formulas to data elements comes from the *conditional tables* of [4].

A relatively small number of works have dealt with the representation of probabilistic semi-structured data. In [14], Dekhtyar et al. use a semi-structured database to store complex probabilistic distributions of data which is essentially relational. Works closer to ours are [15, 16, 17]. Nierman et al. [15] describe a variant of the SP model and present strategies for efficient evaluations of logical queries. In [16], a complex model, based on directed acyclic graphs, is developed, along with an algebraic query language. Finally, Keulen et al. [17] present an approach to data integration using probabilistic trees; their model is a mix of the PW and SP model, which allows both extensive descriptions of the possible worlds and node-based factorization. Querying and the way to present data integration results on this model are also shown. It is to be noted that none of the previous works, to the best of our knowledge, describes in an extensive way how to do updates on a probabilistic semi-structured database, one main contribution of this paper.

The work presented here is part of a larger project on the construction of content warehouses from (Hidden) Web resources as described in Sect. 2. While working on this topic, we realized that imprecision has to be a core part of the XML-based warehouse since ad-hoc processing of imprecision simply does not scale. This observation motivated the present work. We need now to complete the implementation of the fuzzy tree system, move it to an efficient XML repository and experiment with a real application.

A most important direction of research is to develop optimization techniques tailored to the fuzzy tree model. In particular, one would like to trim query evaluation branches that would provide data with too low confidence. Also, we want to study fuzzy tree simplification, i.e. finding more compact representations of imprecise data. As it is defined, the fuzzy tree model is not completely algebraic:

if the result of an update is a tree, the result of a query is a set of tree/probability pairs. Actually, a similar construction can provide a representation of the answer as a fuzzy tree; the details are omitted. Finally, an interesting aspect is schema validation. Suppose we have a fuzzy tree representation $T$ of some data, conforming to some DTD $D$. Its semantics can be seen as $X = \{[\![T]\!] \cap sat(D)\}$ where $sat(D)$ is the set of documents validating $D$. An issue is to efficiently compute a fuzzy tree for $X$. Of course, we will have to ignore order-related typing issues. But other aspects such as cardinalities are already quite challenging.

# References

1. Abiteboul, S., Nguyen, B., Ruberg, G.: Building an active content warehouse. In: Processing and Managing Complex Data for Decision Support. Idea Group Publishing (2005)
2. Dalvi, N.N., Suciu, D.: Efficient query evaluation on probabilistic databases. In: Very Large Data Bases, Hong Kong, China (2004) 864–875
3. de Rougemont, M.: The reliability of queries. In: Principles Of Database Systems, San Jose, United States (1995) 286–291
4. Imieliński, T., Lipski, W.: Incomplete information in relational databases. J. ACM 31 (1984) 761–791
5. Abiteboul, S., Grahne, G.: Update semantics for incomplete databases. In: Very Large Data Bases, Stockholm, Sweden (1985)
6. Abiteboul, S., Senellart, P.: Querying and updating probabilistic information in XML. Technical Report 435, GEMO, Inria Futurs, Orsay, France (2005)
7. BrightPlanet: The Deep Web: Surfacing hidden value. White Paper (2000)
8. Franc, X.: Qizx/open (2005) http://www.xfra.net/qizxopen/.
9. Arion, A., Bonifati, A., Manolescu, I., Pugliese, A.: Path summaries and path partitioning in modern XML databases. Technical Report 437, Gemo (2005)
10. Cavallo, R., Pittarelli, M.: The theory of probabilistic databases. In: Very Large Data Bases. (1987) 71–81
11. Barbará, D., Garcia-Molina, H., Porter, D.: The management of probabilistic data. IEEE Transactions on Knowledge and Data Engineering 4 (1992) 487–502
12. Fuhr, N., Rölleke, T.: A probabilistic relational algebra for the integration of information retrieval and database systems. ACM Trans. Inf. Syst. 15 (1997)
13. Widom, J.: Trio: A system for integrated management of data, accuracy, and lineage. In: Biennal Conference on Innovative Data Systems Research, Pacific Grove, USA (2005)
14. Dekhtyar, A., Goldsmith, J., Hawkes, S.R.: Semistructured probabilistic databases. In: Statistical and Scientific Database Management, Tokyo, Japan (2001) 36–45
15. Nierman, A., Jagadish, H.V.: ProTDB: Probabilistic data in XML. In: Very Large Data Bases, Hong Kong, China (2002)
16. Hung, E., Getoor, L., Subrahmanian, V.S.: PXML: A probabilistic semistructured data model and algebra. In: International Conference on Data Engineering, Bangalore, India (2003) 467–478
17. van Keulen, M., de Keijzer, A., Alink, W.: A probabilistic XML approach to data integration. In: International Conference on Data Engineering. (2005) 459–470

# An ECA Rule Rewriting Mechanism for Peer Data Management Systems

Dan Zhao[1], John Mylopoulos[1], Iluju Kiringa[2], and Verena Kantere[3]

[1] University of Toronto, Toronto, Canada
{dzhao, jm}@cs.toronto.edu
[2] University of Ottawa, Ottawa, Canada
kiringa@site.uottawa.ca
[3] National Technical University of Athens, Athens, Greece
verena@dblab.ece.ntua.gr

**Abstract.** Managing coordination among peer databases is at the core of research in peer data management systems. The Hyperion project addresses peer database coordination through Event-Condition-Action (ECA) rules. However, peer databases are intended for non-technical end users, such as a receptionist at a doctor's office or an assistant pharmacist. Such users are not expected to know a technically demanding language for expressing ECA rules that are appropriate for coordinating their respective databases. Accordingly, we propose to offer a library of "standard" rules for coordinating two or more types of peer databases. These rules are defined in terms of assumed standard schemas for the peer databases they coordinate. Once two acquainted peers select such a rule, it can be instantiated so that it can operate for their respective databases.

In this paper, we propose a mechanism for rewriting given standard rules into rules expressed in terms of the schemas of the two databases that are being coordinated. The rewriting is supported by Global-As-View mappings that are supposed to pre-exist between specific schemas and standard ones. More specifically, we propose a standard rule rewriting algorithm which we have implemented and evaluated.

## 1 Introduction

A peer system is an open-ended network of distributed computational peers (nodes), where peers can join or leave the network at any time without central control. Moreover, each peer is acquainted with a number of other peers - its acquaintances. Acquaintance relationships are dynamic and ever-changing.

Existing peer systems, such as Napster, Gnutella, Freenet [3], Chord [7], CAN [12], and Pastry [11] were designed specifically for file sharing, and cannot accommodate relational databases. For example, it is difficult to search for some files whose contents satisfy a given predicate, the way one can with relational databases. Thus, along a different path, a few projects are focusing on data semantics by using queries, views, and schema mappings for data sharing and coordination among peer databases [6, 5, 4].

The Hyperion project has proposed a distributed Event-Condition-Action (ECA) rule language as a coordination mechanism for peer databases [15, 13].

Different peers may, however, have different database schemas. As a result, ECA rules between different peers may also be different according to their respective schemas even when they are intended to capture the same constraint. Moreover, most end-users do not have sufficient professional training to establish ECA rules for their own schemas, and hiring an expert to do the work can be both time consuming and prohibitively expensive. Therefore, it is vital to have a means for generating rules automatically for different schemas.

In this paper, we assume that there exist standard database schemas for classes of peers, and standard coordination ECA rules between these schemas. These rules capture common coordination patterns between different classes of peers, e.g., family doctors and pharmacists. When a peer, such as a family doctor, joins a class of peers, that peer establishes a mapping from the standard database schema of the peer group to his or her own schema. When the peer wants to adopt a standard rule to maintain data consistency with another peer, it uses our rule rewriting algorithm to instantiate the rule for his or her schema so that it will offer the same functionality as the standard rule for the standard schemas.

The main contribution of this paper is to propose an algorithm to instantiate rules according to the mappings between the standard schemas and the instantiated schemas. That is, given a set of standard database schemas $s1$, a standard distributed ECA rule $rule1$ over $s1$, a set of instantiated database schemas $s2$, and a mapping $m$ from $s2$ to $s1$, the algorithm outputs a new rule, $rule2$, for $s2$, which display the same functionality as $rule1$ for $s1$. In general, the mapping $m$ from $s2$ to $s1$ can relate several relations in $s1$ to several other relations in $s2$. In this paper however, we restrict our attention to the special cases where the two schemas $s1$ and $s2$ have isomorphic relations or the instantiated schema $s2$ has more relations than the standard schema $s1$, whereby one relation in $s1$ is mapped into several in $s2$. The algorithm does not support those cases where several relations in $s1$ map into one schema in $s2$, neither does it support many-to-many mappings.

## 2 Background: ECA Rules and Schema Mappings

### 2.1 ECA Rules

An Event-Conditon-Action(ECA) rule is composed of three parts:

**WHEN**$< event >$, (**IF**$< condition >$,) **THEN**$< action >$.

The 'when' part describes the event which is meant to trigger the rule. The event can be as simple as an insertion or a deletion of a tuple in table, or a time event triggered at a certain time, or it can be a combination of many simple events. The second part describes the condition of the rule. This is optional, and consists of a Boolean expression. After the rule is triggered, the expression is evaluated. If true, the action in the 'then' clause is executed. The action of the rule can be a simple database operation, a composite transaction including many simple database operations, or even a user-defined function.

Kantere et al. [15] have proposed a distributed ECA rule language for peer Data Management Systems. Their rule language allows that the data accessed and/or updated by a rule reside in different peer databases. They also propose a mechanism to implement efficiently the distributed ECA rule language.

The following is an example of an ECA rule. Suppose that our peer network includes peer groups such as a family doctors, pharmacists, and hospitals. Each peer group has a standard - canonical - schema. Here is a fragment of the hospital group standard schema:

**SDHDB:**

**Admission**  (AdmID, OHIP#, ...)
**Patient**      (H#, OHIP#, FName,LName, Sex, Age, FamilyDr, PatRecord)

The following is part of the standard schema for the family doctor group:

**SDFDDB:**

**Patient**       (OHIP#, FName, LName, Phone#, Sex, Age, PatRecord)

A standard rule is defined over one or more standard schemas and is intended to express a generic coordination constraint. For example, when a patient enters a hospital, a record including the OHIP# (a unique patient identification number used in the health care system of Ontario, Canada) of that patient is inserted into the Admission table of the hospital database. This rule involves a single standard schema. Another example rule is triggered when there is an insertion into the Admission relation of the standard hospital schema. Its condition part checks whether the patient with the same OHIP# is a patient of a family doctor who is acquainted with the hospital. If the logical expression in the condition part returns true - that is, the patient is a patient of the acquainted family doctor - then the rule inserts a tuple to the 'Patient' table in the hospital database with the patient's information retrieved from the 'Patient' table of the family doctor. If the logical expression returns false, no action is taken. This rule can be expressed in the rule language of Kantere *et al.* as follows:

**Rule 1:**

**WHEN** SDHDB.('insert', (Admission, ( OHIP#=>OHIP#_value1 )))
**IF**    OHIP#_value1 = OHIP#_value2
        where   SDFDDB.('retrieve', 45, {OHIP#_value2, FName_value, LName_value, Phone#_value, Sex_value, Age_value, PatRecord_value})
**THEN** SDHDB.('insert', (Patient, (OHIP# <= OHIP#_value1, FName <= FName_value, LName <= LName_value, Sex <= Sex_value, Age <= Age_value, PatRecord <= PatRecord_value )))

The Query which retrieves the variables in the 'if' part of Rule 1 is:

**SDFDDB query 45:**

> **SELECT** OHIP#, FName, LName, Phone#, Sex, Age, PatRecord
> **FROM**   Patient

## 2.2  Schema Mappings: LAV and GAV

Data Integration systems address the problem of how to access data from various data sources[16]. A data source can be a database system such as a relational database, an object-oriented database system, or a collection of some unstructured data such as text files or web pages. Accessing a collection of heterogeneous data sources is done through a global schema – used as access point for all the integrated data sources – along with a set of formal mappings between the global schema and each local schema. Many languages are available to define such mappings - datalog, description logics, views and so on. In this paper, we use views, because they are both expressive and simple. There are two main approaches for expressing mappings using views: local-as-view (LAV) and global-as-view (GAV), which are described in the following subsections.

The LAV approach treats the source data as views of the global schema – that is, LAV describes source data in terms of the global schema. In this approach, the integrated system is seen from a local view.

The GAV approach, on the other hand, treats the global schema as a view of the local schemas - that is, the global schema is defined in terms of the local ones. Here, each element of the global schema is associated with a query over the sources.

Two assumptions generally accepted by many data integration systems are: to not allow for integrity constraints over the global schemas and to consider only exact views. A view used as a mapping in this setting is said to be exact if it defines the same set of tuples as the associated element of the global schema. Under these assumptions, the GAV query rewriting is reducible to an unfolding mechanism [16]. The unfolding method is a straightforward strategy: whenever a query $q$ is posed against the global schema, every element of the global schema mentioned in $q$ is replaced by the associated query over the sources.

**Table 1.** Local schema and global schema

| Local schema | TGHDB: | Admission | (AdmID, OHIP#, ...) |
|---|---|---|---|
| | | Patient | (TGH#, OHIP#, FName, LName, Sex, Age, FamilyDr, PatRecord) |
| | DavisDB: | PatientInfo | (Pat#, InsuranceType, Insurance#, FName, LName, Phone#, Gender, Age, PatRecord) |
| global schema | SDHDB: | Admission | (AdmID, OHIP#, ...) |
| | | Patient | (H#, OHIP#, FName, LName, Sex, Age, FamilyDr, PatRecord) |
| | SDFDDB: | Patient | (OHIP#, FName, LName, Phone#, Sex, Age, PatRecord) |

Table 1 shows a database schema of Toronto General hospital database (TGHDB) and a database schema of a family doctor - Dr. Davis' database (DavisDB). The interface schemas are a standard hospital database schema (SDHDB) and a standard family doctor database schema (SDFDDB). Table 2 shows a sample GAV mapping for this example.

In this paper, we choose GAV to define mappings between instance (local) schemas and standard (global) ones. The intuition behind this choice is that we only want to perform one-way rewriting; that is, we need only rewrite the standard rules into instantiated ones and never proceed the other way back.

**Table 2.** Sample GAV Mapping

| SDHDB. | Admission: | Select AdmID, OHIP#, ... |
|---|---|---|
| | | From TGHDB.Admission |
| | Patient: | Select TGH# as H#, OHIP#, FName, LName, Sex, Age, FamilyDr, PatRecord |
| | | from TGHDB.Patient |
| SDFDDB. Patient: | | Select Insurance# as OHIP#, FName, LName, Phone#, Gender as Sex, Age, PatRecord |
| | | from DavisDB.PatientInfo |
| | | where InsuranceType = 'OHIP' |

## 3 Problem Definition

When using rules for coordinating data exchange between peers, we face a major problem: since the coordination technology that we are developing is end-user oriented, a non technical user needs only to be aware of pre-existing standard ECA rules, while the system takes care of automatically instantiating those pre-existing rules. Moreover, it is unrealistic to expect that users would design rules for their acquaintances from scratch. Therefore we must produce peer data management systems that have some mechanism to manage coordination among acquaintances by instantiating pre-existing standard rules. We propose to accomplish this by using the existing standard schemas of peers groups as well as the local schemas of peers and the respective GAV mappings that relate the standard schemas to the local ones. Specifically, we propose to solve the following problem:

**Input** Given standard database schemas (a set of schemas) $s1$, and a standard distributed peer rule $rule1$, instantiated database schemas (also a set of schemas) $s2$, and a GAV mapping $m$, $m$ maps $s2$ to $s1$.

**Output** Based on $(s1, s2, m, rule1)$, a new rule $rule2$ for $s2$, which acts the same as $rule1$ for $s1$.

Figure 1 illustrates the problem.

In the Hyperion projext, some standard schemas have been defined for different groups, such as family doctors, hospitals, pharmacists and day care centers. Standard rules describing common inter-peer constraints are also defined among the standard schemas of those groups. After that, whenever a peer joins a group, the peer can choose rules that apply to its own database and those of acquainted peers. These rules can then be instantiated automatically through the instantiation mechanism proposed in this paper.

Standard schemas in our framework clearly play a role analogous to that of global schemas in the data integration literature. It is important to note, however, that a standard schema is not intended to integrate the content of all local (instance) databases. Rather, it is intended to capture common elements of all these schemas in terms of which common coordination constraints can be defined.

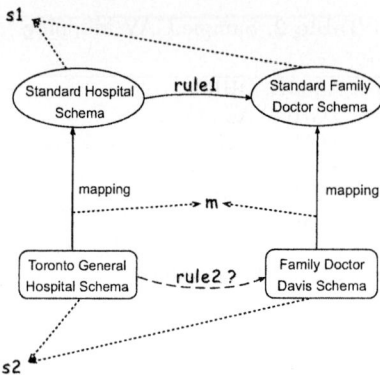

**Fig. 1.** Problem Definition

## 4   Rewriting Algorithm

The main idea behind our algorithm is divide and conquer: We use the unfolding method to rewrite the different parts of rules. If one database event is unfolded to two or more events, we will also rewrite the event into two or more events; if several database events are unfolded to two or more events, we will combine the results of rewriting the result of each database event. When the information in the instantiated schema is missing, we will just ignore it if the information does not appear in the condition part; but if the information does appear in the condition part, then we will get a value from a user through an input statement.

Assume that $s1$ and $s2$ were singletons; we abuse the notation by calling the schemas in these sets $s1$ and $s2$, respectively. Our algorithm works only for view-based mappings. Recall that it works if the two schemas (standard, and instantiated) have isomorphic relations and also if the instantiated schema $s2$ has more relations than the standard schema $s1$ where one relation in $s1$ is mapped into several in $s2$. But it does not support those cases where several relations in $s1$ map into one relation in $s2$, nor does it support many-to-many mappings.

We spell out the details of the algorithm as follows:

- We first use the unfolding; that is, we replace everything in $rule1$ and $s1$ with corresponding fields and tables in $s2$ by using mapping rules included in $m$.
- If a database event in the event part of $rule1$ involves two or more tables in $s2$, which means the related table in $s1$ maps to two or more tables in $s2$, then we try to rewrite the database event into two or more events in which every event leads to a new rule, while the missing information in other tables will be retrieved later using queries.
- If there are more than one database events involving two or more tables, we will produce two or more rules. When the composite event has $m$ database events, and when for every database event the number of related tables in the instantiated schemas is $n_1$, $n_2$, $n_3$, ..., $n_m$, then the number of output rules will be $n_1 * n_2 * n_3 * ... * n_m$. In practice, we seldom have more than

three database events in a rule, which means that the number of resulting rules will not increase too fast.
- If the action part is a composite action, then we directly put all the rewritten actions in the result.
- This relates to a case when some instantiated schemas do not have information in the standard schemas. If the missing field does not appear in the condition part, the missing information will not cause a problem so we just ignore it; otherwise, since the missing field appears in the condition part, we will get the variable through the user's input.

Figures 2-5 present the algorithm in more detail. Figure 2 shows the whole rewriting process, which is implemented by a sequence of processes. The query rewriting part and condition rewriting part both use the unfolding algorithm. The function that implements rewriting the event part is 'rewriteevent' and is shown in Figure 4. The function that implements rewriting the action part is 'rewriteaction' and is shown in Table 5.

Figure 3 shows the function rewriteelement(), which is called in both the function rewriteevent() and the function rewriteaciton(). This function rewrites an element of the event or action. We can do this because the event part and action part have the same structure. If the element is of the form xxx_value,

```
Rulerewrite(){
        rewrite event part;
        rewrite queries in the rule;
        rewrite condition part;
        rewrite action part;
        combine the results of each part
}
```

**Fig. 2.** Pseudo-code for rule rewriting

```
rewriteelement(){
        if the element part is of form xxx_value,
                replace it with the new name of the
                value in the namemaplist
        if the element part is a database event
        or database action{
                \\for example: AllenDB.('insert', (Cust-
                \\ Info, (CustAge => CustAge_value)))
                for each attribute, find the relative
                attribute in s2
                Combain the attributes in same tables;
                return the new DBelement(s);
        }
        if the element part is none of the above,
                keep it same in the new rule;
}
```

**Fig. 3.** Pseudo-code for rewriting an element

```
rewriteevent(){
    oldevents = null event;
    For each event element e{
        newele = rewriteelement(e);
        for i = 1 to oldevents.size
            for j = 1 to newele.size
                newevents[i][j] = oldevents[i]
                    appending newele[j];
        oldevents = newevents;
    }
}
```

**Fig. 4.** Pseudo-code for rewriting event part

```
rewriteaction(){
    newaction = null;
    For each action element a{
        newele = rewriteelement(a);
        for i =1 to newele.size
            newaction = newaction
                appending newele[i];
    }
}
```

**Fig. 5.** Pseudo-code for rewriting action part

we find the new name for the variable in the namemaplist and return the new name. If the element is a simple Database Event or simple Database Action, e.g., AllenDB.('insert', (CustInfo, (CustAge => CustAge_value))), we will find each of the attributes in the new schema $s2$ using the mapping $m$. After that we combine the results by the tables, because one simple database event can only relate to one table. So we will return all the new database event(s) or action(s). Another case is that the element is none of the above cases; here we just keep it unchanged.

Figure 4 shows the functionality of rewriteevent(). We are maintaining a list of the result events, because it is possible we get more than one events in the result. We rewrite each of the elements in the event part, if the rewrite returns one event element, we just append it to the end of each event in the result, if the rewrite returns more than one ($n$) event elements, we will copy the events in the result $n$ times, and append the $n$ event elements at the end of each of them accordingly.

Figure 5 shows the functionality of rewriteaction(). We have a result action variable and we only have one action in the result. Then we rewrite each element in the action, and we append each of the returned elements to the end of the result action variable.

From the pseudo-code, we can notice the difference between event part rewriting and action part rewriting. In the event part, it is possible that one event is rewritten to many events; in the action part, we always get only one action in the new rule.

## 5 Discussion and Future Work

### 5.1 Related Work

It is interesting to compare query rewriting [1, 16] with rule rewriting considered in this paper because both problems have many common features, but also some differences. We do not attempt to review the extensive work done on query rewriting, particularly in the context of data integration [16] and query answering using views [1]. Instead, we briefly discuss how rule rewriting ressembles, but also differs from query rewriting.

The key feature common to rule rewriting and query rewriting is that we want them both to translate a given artifact to another format according to a mapping. Therefore, we can adapt many ideas from query rewriting to rule rewriting. Of course, we must point out that query rewriting is part of rule rewriting, since a query is part of a rule. Consequently, rule rewriting is at least as hard as query rewriting. In recent years, it has been shown how hard query rewriting can be [17, 18]. It was particularly shown in [17] that, in the context of view-based query processing, even for quite simple query languages, rewriting is in general a co-NP function of the size of the extensions of the underlying views. Moreover, a tight connection is found between view-based query processing and constraint satisfaction problems, which, in general, rarely admit PTIME solutions. This suggests the anticipated hardness of ECA rule rewriting.

On the other hand, in our rule rewriting approach, mappings are of the GAV variety, while in query rewriting, most research has been done for the LAV approach.

Another point of interest is that – generally speaking – performance is a major consideration for query rewriting, because the query is rewritten online; i.e., a user or an application is waiting for the result which can not excessively be delayed. Rule rewriting, however, is done offline, when acquainted peers decide to adopt a standard rule, and before the rule is actually put to use. In this setting, performance is not as critical.

### 5.2 Conclusions and Future Work

We have proposed an algorithm for rewriting standard ECA rules in terms of local schemas of peers assuming the existence of GAV mappings between standard schemas of the groups to which the peers belong and the local schemas of the peers. A longer version of the paper reports on the implementation of this algorithm, and an evaluation of it using various samples rules.

The distributed rule mechanism of Kantere et al. [14] is the first known attempt to propose a distributed rule mechanism for peer data management systems. After this rule mechanism was proposed, the rule rewriting problem emerged as an important and open problem. To our knowledge, the work reported here is the first attempt to investigate the rule rewriting problem and give an algorithm for it. More research needs to follow.

In the future, we propose to extend the algorithm by removing some of the current restrictions (e.g., availability of GAV mappings, many-to-many correspondences between relations in local and standard schemas). We also plan to formalize the rule rewriting problem and study its complexity. Formal foundations will allow us to state and prove the correctness and the efficiency of our proposed method.

Query rewriting for LAV is generally intractable [1], making LAV mappings hard for many data integration tasks. However, the Piazza approach [6] has shown that efficient LAV or GLAV query rewriting algorithms can be designed for some practical settings, despite the known discouraging complexity results. Therefore, a next step would be to take a LAV approach towards ECA rule rewriting.

Finally, a particular question of interest is how to develop techniques for discarding unnecessary rules when a standard rule may be rewritten into more than one instantiated rules, some of which are not useful. We propose to extend our algorithm to remove unnecessary rules semiautomatically, and on the fly.

# References

1. A.Y. Halevy. Answering queries using views: A survey. The International Journal on Very Large Data Bases, Volume 10, Issue 4, 2001.
2. A. Kementsietsidis, M. Arenas, and R.J. Miller. Mapping Data in PeertoPeer Systems: Semantics and Algorithmic Issues. SIGMOD, 2003.
3. I. Clarke, O. Sandberg, B. Wiley, and T. Hong. W. Freenet: A distributed anonymous information storage and retrieval system. In Proceedings of the ICSI Workshop on Design Issues in Anonymity and Unobservability, 2000.
4. Context2Context project. http://dit.unitn.it/ p2p/.
5. Hyperion project. http://www.cs.toronto.edu/db/hyperion/.
6. A.Y. Halevy, Z.G. Ives, J. Madhavan, P. Mork, D. Suciu, I. Tatarinov. The Piazza Peer Data Management System. IEEE Trans. Knowl. Data Eng. 16(7): 787-798 2004.
7. I. Stoica, R. Morris, D. Karger, F. Kaashoek, and H. Balakrishnan. Chord: A Scalable Peer-to-peer Lookup Service for Internet Applications, ACM SIGCOMM 2001, San Deigo, CA, August 2001.
8. L. Serafini, F. Giunchiglia, J. Mylopoulos, and P. Bernstein. The Local Relational Model: A Logical Formalization of Database Coordination. CONTEXT 2003.
9. M. Arenas, V. Kantere, A. Kementsietsidis, I. Kiringa, R. Miller, and J. Mylopoulos. The Hyperion Project: From Data Integration to Data Coordination. In SIGMOD Record, Special Issue on Peer-to-Peer Data Management, 32(3):53-58, 2003.
10. N.W. Paton (Ed.). Active Rules in Database Systems. Springer, 1999.
11. A. Rowstron, and P. Druschel. Pastry: Scalable, distributed object location and routing for largescale peer-to-peer systems. in IFIP/ACM Middleware. 2001.
12. S.P. Ratnasamy. A Scalable Content-Addressable Network. PH.D. thesis 2002.
13. W. Xie. Recognizing Composite Events for Event-Condition-Action Rules, Master Thesis 2004.
14. V. Kantere, I. Kiringa, J. Mylopoulos, A. Kementsietsidis, and M. Arenas. Coordinating Peer Databases Using ECA Rules. DBISP2P 2003.
15. V. Kantere, J. Mylopoulos, and I. Kiringa. A Distributed Rule Mechanism for Multidatabase Systems. In Proceedings of the Tenth International Conference on Cooperative Information Systems (COOPIS'03).
16. M. Lenzerini. Data Integration: A Theoretical Perspective. in PODS 2002.
17. D. Calvanese, D. De Giacomo, M. Lenzerini, and M. Vardi. What is Query Rewriting? KRDB 2000.
18. D. Calvanese, D. De Giacomo, M. Lenzerini, and M. Vardi. View-Based Query Processing: On the Relationship Between Rewriting, Answering and Losslessness. ICDT 2005.

# A Metric Definition, Computation, and Reporting Model for Business Operation Analysis

Fabio Casati, Malu Castellanos, Umeshwar Dayal, and Ming-Chien Shan

Hewlett-Packard Laboratories, Palo Alto, CA
firstname.lastname@hp.com

## 1 Introduction and Motivations

This paper presents a platform, called *Business Cockpit*, that allows users to define, compute, monitor, and analyze business and IT metrics on business activities. The problem with existing approaches to metric definition and computation is that they require a very significant development and maintenance effort. The cockpit overcomes this problem by providing users with a set of *abstractions* used to model the problem space, as well as *development* and *runtime* environments that support these abstractions. The cockpit is based on three conceptual models: the *business domain* model defines the business data to be analyzed, the *metric model* defines the business metrics of interest for the user, and the *reporting model* defines how metrics should be aggregated and presented in the reports. The proposed approach provides the following key benefits: i) it allows the definition of many different reports without writing code; ii) it reduces metric computation times; iii) it enables the definition of different ways of computing a metric based on the characteristic of the object being measured; iv) all the code of the cockpit is independent of the business domain to be managed. As such, it can be applied to many scenarios. Domain independence, however, is not achieved at the expense of complexity in the configuration: to apply the cockpit to a given domain, users are simply required to provide an abstract description of the part of their data model that is useful for business operation analysis purposes. The cockpit, and the features described above, have been developed and refined over the past few years. Our research started in the context of business processes, and we have then applied the same concepts to other domains, such as inter-bank transactions.

## 2 Business Cockpit Models

**Business Domain Model.** To provide its functionality, the cockpit must be aware of the structure of the data in the operational system. This is because it needs i) to know on which *entities* users want to define metrics, e.g., "orders", "processes", "resources", etc; ii) to describe how to perform metric aggregations when providing reports; iii) to know how to retrieve data about entities from the operational system. Essentially, in this model users can specify which entities they want to measure, what are their attributes, what are their relationships, and how each of these is mapped to the operational database (e.g., in which table the entity data can be found). Attributes are needed as they are used as filtering criteria for reports. In addition, they are used for context partitioning (see below). Relationships are used to know which aggregations can be computed when providing reports, and how to compute them (this is somewhat similar to linking facts with dimensions in star schemas for reporting). The aggregation logic can be derived by looking at the foreign keys, or it can be user-defined.

**Metric Model.** A metric is a measurable property of the elements of an entity. It can be quantitative (numeric) or qualitative (categorical). The metric computation logic is defined by associating metrics to *mappings*, i.e., reusable functions that label operational data with Boolean or numeric values. The following SQL query example is a function that runs over operational data and returns <quote identifiers, value> pairs where the value corresponds to the time taken to respond to a request for quote:

```
SELECT QUOTE_UUID, DURATION FROM QUOTE_REQUESTS Q
```

The following function returns instead all orders processed in a time that exceeded the one specified as part of the SLA stipulated with the customer:

```
SELECT QUOTE_UUID
FROM QUOTE_REQUESTS Q, SLA, CUSTOMER C
WHERE Q.CUSTOMER_ID=C.ID AND SLA.CUSTOMER_ID=C.ID
    AND Q.DURATION>SLA.MAX_DURATION
```

In general, a mapping is characterized by the following properties:

- A name (e.g., *compute SLA violations*).
- The data type of the values computed by the function. This can be numeric or Boolean. Numeric metrics can be computed by numeric mappings. Taxonomical metrics are instead computed by associating, to each category in the taxonomy, a different Boolean mapping. If the mapping returns *true* for an element, then the element belongs to the category.
- The entity whose elements are labeled. For example, a mapping can associate values to *requests for quotes*.
- The mapping function, that returns a set of pairs <element ID, value>.
- The name and types of the mapping function parameters, if any.

Conceptually, the mapping function can be expressed in any language. In the cockpit, they are defined by means of SQL statements, for performance reasons.

Metrics give semantics to the values computed by the mappings. A metric is characterized by a definition and an implementation part. The definition part states i) the *name* of the metric; ii) the *data type*, that can be numeric, Boolean, or taxonomy; iii) the *entity* whose elements are to be measured (e.g., cost is computed for orders). The implementation part of a metric defines which mapping functions should be used to compute it. For example, a metric *quote request SLA violation* can be computed based on the Boolean mapping described above for those customers that had agreed on a certain SLA. Note that different customers can have different SLA targets. In summary, metrics measure elements of entities via mappings.

The metric model allows a metric to be "polymorphic", i.e., computed via different mappings, depending on the element being measured (i.e., based on the *business context* to which the element belongs). The possibility of associating the same metric to different mappings is very important since it allows the definition of homogeneous metrics over heterogeneous elements. An example is the SLA violation metric discussed above, where the computation logic depends on the customer (SLA logics can be very complex). In this case, the analyst can define one metric, and state that a different mapping should be used based on the context (customer). The analyst will be able to evaluate SLA violations by simply looking at one metric, regardless of the way violations are computed.

Contexts can be identified by any partitioning over the set of elements. However, to simplify modeling, partitioning is specified in terms of relationships to other entities or in terms of an entity's attributes. For example, orders can be partitioned based on the customer or on their priority level. Note that the cockpit knows how to compute if an element belongs to a context, since attributes and relationships have been described as part of the business model.

The key to reducing the development effort consists in allowing the definition of functions that are easily customizable and highly reusable, so that the same function can be leveraged to compute different metrics. For example, a mapping function that returns the value of a quote request attribute is completely generic, in that it does not "hardcode" the definition of the metric it is computing, nor the context to which it applies. As such, this function becomes handy for computing lots of different metrics. It is up to the cockpit, as we will see later, to use mappings in such a way that they can compute the right metric on the right context with the right parameters and in the most efficient way. Hence, the development time for defining a new report tends to zero as the number of metrics grow. This is indeed a very concrete benefit. In a supply chain scenario, only nine mappings were needed to define all the metrics underlying the reporting application, consisting of more than 80 reports. In this way, the software development and testing effort is drastically reduced.

**Reporting Model.** The reporting model defines how we want to look at a metric. A report is characterized by the metric to be reported and by the desired statistics on this metric (e.g., average). In addition, grouping and filtering conditions can be specified, based on entity attributes and relationships. Thanks to the business model, the cockpit knows how to compute these. In addition, users can define the *drill-down* behavior, choosing from several options, including: displaying another specified report; executing a query; executing the code defined in a Java class; accessing a specified Web page. Finally, report definition includes scheduling times and preferred visualization (charting) technique. The definition of reports is done by means of a point-and-click GUI that is aware of the business domain and of the metric definitions, and therefore knows what options (in terms of, e.g., aggregation) can be provided. For example, it is aware that it is possible to aggregate *orders* by *customers*, but not vice versa.

## 3 Mapping Transformations

In the cockpit, definitions of the domain, metric, and reporting schema (along with other configuration information) are performed through a Java or a Web based GUI that accesses the cockpit definition API. The most interesting aspect in the definition process lies in the way mappings are handled. The cockpit keeps all metric definition data into a few database tables. In particular, a table *meters* defines the mappings used by each metric, a table *contexts* stores information about the context for which a certain <metric,mapping> association should be applied, and a table *meter_parameters* defines which values should be given to mapping parameters when the mapping is used to compute a certain metric. For example, meter *meterForCost* may state that metric cost is measured by mapping *numResourcesUsedTimesUnitCost* (which has the unit cost as a parameter). An entry in table context may state that *meterForCost* is only applied to the *purchase* process. An entry in *meter_parameters* may state that for *meterForCost*, a certain cost value (e.g., 20$) should be used.

Mappings as written by the user have no knowledge of the cockpit database schema, as users should not be required to know the intricacies of the cockpit's internals, but just the domain data. The cockpit extends mapping definitions so that they can not only label elements with metric values, but also identify which metrics are being computed, what are the different parameter values, and what are the different contexts to which the mapping should be applied when computing each metric. For example, Figure 1 shows how the cockpit transforms the code of mapping *quote request attribute value*. The modified query accesses the different tables that store metric definition data, and returns, in addition to element IDs and values, also the metric to which these values refer. Also, the *where* clause is extended with the capability of restricting the context as specified by the metric definition. The code that extends the mapping (like all of the cockpit code) is generic and has no a priori knowledge of the business domain. However, due to the way the domain model has been defined, the business domain description contains all the information necessary to perform the mapping transformation mentioned above, that can therefore be executed at mapping definition time. This post-processing of the mapping definition is what enables the creation of queries that are simple and generic, since cockpit dynamically figures out what they should compute and on what data, as opposed to hardcoding this information into the query. Another benefit of this approach is that, thanks to the set oriented nature of SQL, one execution of a given mapping computes all metrics that have been defined on top of it. Since many metrics typically depend on the same mappings, the computation time remains quasi-constant as the number of metrics grows.

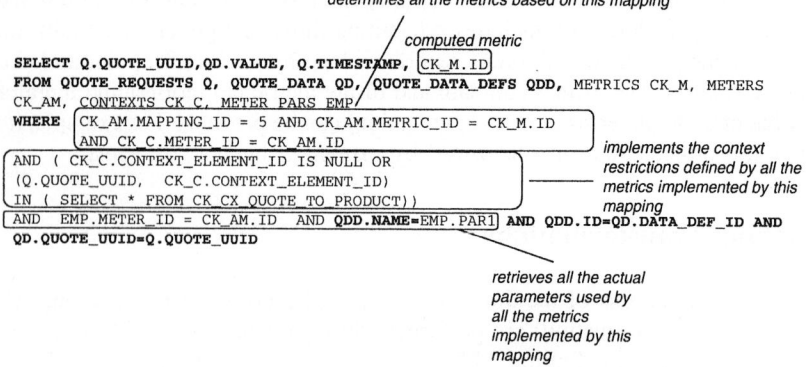

**Fig. 6.** Wrapping of mapping definitions. Original code is in bold.

## 4 Concluding Remarks

In summary, the proposed approach considerably simplifies development of reporting solutions, both for verticals (e.g., for a financial application) and for middleware applications (e.g., it can be used to provide reports for workflows or messaging systems). The use of modules that encapsulate metrics and mappings make such deployments easy to perform and to maintain. Further details and publications on this topic are available at http://www.hpl.hp.com/techreports/ .

# BISON: Providing Business Information Analysis as a Service

Hakan Hacıgümüş, James Rhodes, Scott Spangler, and Jeffrey Kreulen

IBM Almaden Research Center,
650 Harry Road, San Jose, CA 95120, USA
hakanh@acm.org, {jjrhodes, spangles, kreulen}@us.ibm.com

**Abstract.** We present the architecture of a Business Information Analysis provisioning system, BISON. The service provisioning system combines two prominent domains, namely structured/unstructured data analysis and service-oriented computing. We also discuss open research problems in the area.

## 1 Introduction

Today's highly competitive business environment challenges enterprises to push their limits to take advantage of all available information to improve business performance and stay competitive. This challenge becomes more difficult with the ever increasing amount of data from disparate sources. Although there is a glut of data generated by various sources those data mostly are not in a form that could be directly used to support critical business decision making processes. Thus, the essential problem is transforming the data into information that provides insights into the business operations and the competitiveness measures. Typically, the data are available from heterogeneous resources in varied formats. It is well known that the amount of unstructured data in the text form far surpasses the amount of available data in the structured form. Therefore, one important step in exploiting the available resources is structuring the inherently unstructured data in meaningful ways. A well-established first step in gaining understanding is to segment examples into meaningful categories. This leads to the idea of taxonomies. The taxonomies are meaningful hierarchical categorizations of documents into topics reflecting the natural relationships between the documents and their business objectives. Clearly there is need for systems that enable knowledge workers to take full-advantage of available data sources and generate business reports in a timely manner.

We have developed such a system, called Business Insights Workbench (BIW), at the IBM Almaden Research Center. BIW has been used in numerous customer setups to solve complex problems that require understanding and analysis of very large textual data sets to fulfill the business objectives.

Service-oriented computing is a new prominent computing paradigm. It allows organizations to seamlessly integrate heterogeneous resources that are available internally or externally. Services are defined as autonomous, platform-independent elements that are described, implemented, published, and discovered using standard protocols. We envisioned the union of these two technologies; namely the business information analysis and the service-oriented computing, to deliver even grater value for the customers. The resultant computing environment offers scores of new competencies such as better integration with intra- and inter-organization computing capabilities, enhanced and custom computing environments by composing available services from different providers, larger customer base coverage, and solutions to clustering, scalability, extensibility, dynamic provisioning, and fault tolerance.

## 2 Business Insights Workbench (BIW)

In this section we give an overview of our business information analysis system, BIW. The details of the system can be found in [1] and [2]. BIW is a comprehensive data analysis application that allows a knowledge worker to learn from large collections of unstructured documents. The tool can be used to automatically categorize a large collection of text documents and then to provide a broad spectrum of controls to refine the building of an arbitrarily complex hierarchical taxonomy. The applicable tasks are grouped under three categories, namely, Explore, Understand, and Analyze.

**Explore** operation performs the selection of the data of interest via queries or search from the data sources and summarizes structured values via metrics. It includes data specific functions such as full text search, database drill down, data join, intersect, and subset selection.

**Understand** taxonomies uses text mining to extract higher level features from unstructured information. It provides tools to edit generated taxonomies visualize relationships among categories, build text models that can be applied to other data sets, and use nearest neighbor techniques to find related documents.

**Analyze** function examines the intersections between taxonomies and structured information. It is used to discover trends and correlations, visualize data categories over time, analyze relationships between categories in different taxonomies, and compare structured and unstructured information. Analyze function essentially combines the structured and unstructured data sources to provide a complete view.

## 2 Service-Oriented Approach

We have been developing a business information analysis service provisioning system, BISON, based on Business Insights Workbench that is presented above. The architecture diagram of BISON system is shown in Figure 1. We use J2EE standards as the implementation framework. Communications among the system entities, including the clients, are implemented as Web Services.

**Data Sources** may provide structured and unstructured data and metadata information, such as full text indexes. Typical examples for text indexes are indexes created by crawling engines for increased full-text search performance. Data sources expose all the characteristics information, such as name of the source, schema of the database, and types of the data available, and data access mechanisms as web services. Data sources are registered in the services directory so that they can be discovered by the other system entities. The system architecture allows data sources dynamically join or leave the resource pool, or change the service characteristics.

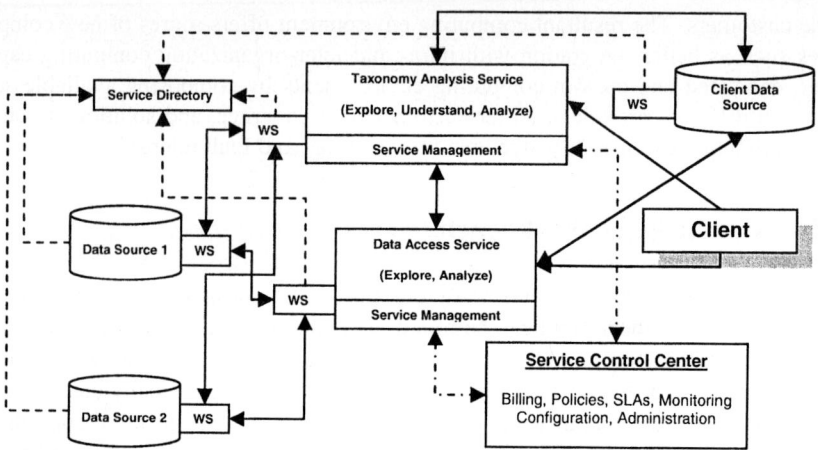

**Fig. 1.** The Architecture of BISON

**Data Access Service** is primarily responsible for querying the data sources to retrieve the data of interest and performing database oriented tasks. It also supports analyze functions over the data sources. The data access service is instrumented to facilitate service provisioning specific tasks. These tasks include, access control, metering, service monitoring for QoS and Service Level Agreements (SLAs). This information, along with the service management information from the other systems entities, is collected, monitored, acted upon by the Service Control Center.

**Taxonomy Analysis Service** provides all of the enhanced analysis capabilities defined over the taxonomies, that is, explore, understand, and analyze functions. The separation of the data access service and the taxonomy analysis service provides service flexibility and scalability.

**Service Control Center** oversees the service provisioning tasks in the system. It monitors and aggregates the system management data provided by the individual services. This aggregate information is used for billing, configuration management, dynamic provisioning, SLA management, and policy enforcement.

**The client** is the consumer of the services. Typically there are two different types of clients in our system. First, the individual users those connect to the service directly by using a web browser. The second category of the clients is the service providers. They use our services to provide additional services to their end-users.

**The Client Data Source** is a temporary data source that is created to maintain the intermediate results between the service calls for the client.

## 2 Current Research and Technology Issues

Combining business information analysis applications and the service-oriented computing presents certain research and technology issues. We describe some those problems in this section.

**Metering.** Metering is important for the cost analysis of the service delivery and generating the billing information. The metering is also important from the system management perspective as it provides valuable information for the performance of the system components. The real challenge is defining the metrics for metering that would be meaningful for the information management functions.

**Monitoring.** Along with the overall service and system monitoring, we need application level monitoring techniques. Application level monitoring helps problem determination and also enables application specific billing. Given that each application has its own characteristics, developing a common monitoring methodology that could be applied to all of the possible service components is a challenging problem.

**Data Security and Privacy.** The security of the data sources includes preventing unauthorized access to the data sources and preventing data disclosure to the parties who are not entitled to use the particular parts of the data. In addition, the clients may be concerned about revealing their identity for their particular interest in certain data sets. As a more challenging problem, if the client actually owns a data source and just uses the information analysis services, then the possible disclosure of confidential information to the service provider becomes an issue.

**Business Integration.** In most of the cases the information analysis is a part of the higher level business processes at the client organizations. Hence, we need to develop methodologies that allow us to model our system processes and tie them into higher level business processes.

## 2 Conclusion

We have presented the architecture of a Business Information Analysis provisioning system, BISON. The service provisioning system combines two very important domains, structured/unstructured data analysis and service-oriented computing. We have also described some open research problems in this area.

## References

1. Scott Spangler, Jeffrey T. Kreulen: Interactive methods for taxonomy editing and validation, CIKM 2002
2. William F. Cody, Jeffrey T. Kreulen, Vikas Krishna, W. Scott Spangler: The integration of business intelligence and knowledge management. IBM Systems Journal 41(4): 697-713 (2002)

# The Design and Architecture of the $\tau$-Synopses System

Yossi Matias, Leon Portman, and Natasha Drukh

School of Computer Science,
Tel Aviv University
matias@cs.tau.ac.il, leon.portman@nice.com,
kreimern@cs.tau.ac.il

**Abstract.** Data synopses are concise representations of data sets, that enable effective processing of approximate queries to the data sets. The $\tau$-Synopses is a system designed to provide a run-time environment for remote execution of multiple synopses for both relational as well as XML databases. The system can serve as an effective research platform for experimental evaluation and comparison of different synopses, as well as a platform for studying the effective management of multiple synopses in a federated or centralized environment.

## 1 Introduction

In large data recording and warehousing environments, it is often advantageous to provide fast, approximate answers to queries, whenever possible. The goal is to provide a quick response in orders of magnitude faster than the time to compute an exact answer, by avoiding or minimizing the number of accesses to the base data.

Approximate query processing is supported by synopses that are compact representations of the original data, such as histograms, samples, wavelet-synopses or other methods [1]. In the AQUA system [2], synopses are precomputed and stored in a DBMS. The system supports approximate answers by rewriting queries originally directed to the base tables to run on these synopses, and it enables keeping synopses up-to-date as the database changes. The question of how to reconcile various synopses for large data sources with many tables was studied in [3].

The $\tau$-Synopses system was designed to provide a run-time environment for execution of multiple synopses. The system can serve as an effective research platform for experimental evaluation and comparison of different synopses, as well as a platform for studying the effective management of multiple synopses. The synopses can be placed at a centralized environment, or they can function as web services in a federated architecture.

A software demo of the system as a federated environment with remote execution of synopses was presented in [5]. A software demo of the system with emphasis on the synopses management in a centralized environment was presented in [4]. The system currently includes several dozens of synopses for both Relational as well as XML databases.

This paper presents a high-level overview of the architecture and functionality of the system. For more details, please refer to the full paper [6].

## 2 The $\tau$-Synopses Functionality

The main operational processes supported by the $\tau$-Synopses system are: constructing and updating multiple pluggable synopses, interception and analysis of query workload, interception and analysis of data updates, approximate query processing, synopses management, and benchmarking.

The user interface provides an administrator user with a capability to manage data sources, synopses specifications, updates and pre-defined workloads. Figure 1 depicts the main administration UI.

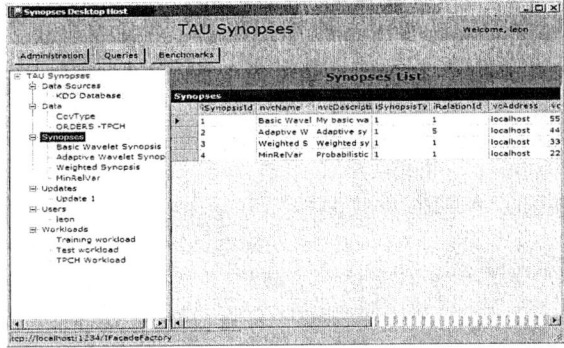

**Fig. 1.** The Administration UI

End users can test and compare different synopses that are registered in the system. In the *Query execution* mode a user can evaluate a single synopsis at a time.

In the *Query Mode*, the user selects the synopsis to be evaluated. Relational queries can be of the following structure:

SELECT Sum(Data) FROM Relation WHERE filter > l AND filter < h . For

XML synopses, the queries are XPath expressions. The system validates the user input expression for the XPath syntax and the tag labels are validated against existing labels of the underlying XML document.

The Query mode also allows the evaluation of multiple queries at a time by specifying a workload to be evaluated. The approximate results obtained using the registered synopses are depicted together with the exact results computed by the system.

The *Benchmark Mode* enables multiple synopses evaluation over pre-defined workloads and their comparison using visual display; see Figure 2. The user selects the synopses to be evaluated and the workload to be used for the evaluation. For the performance measurements, the minimum, maximum and step size

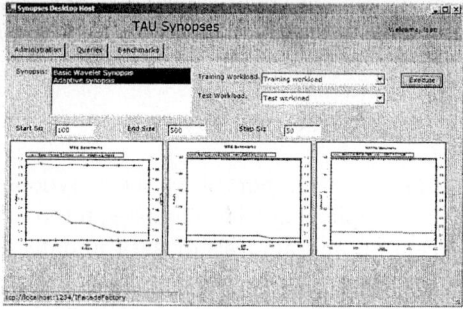

**Fig. 2.** Benchmark Mode

for the synopses construction are set by the user. The system invokes the construction of the different synopses, and these synopses are then evaluated over the selected workload. The system can compute the accuracy of the different synopses using several error metrics.

## 3 Architecture

In order to provide an effective operational and research platform the $\tau$-Synopses system commits to the following design goals:

- Pluggable integration
- Remote execution
- Distributed client-server environment
- Flexibility and scalability
- Low bandwidth requirement

The core of the $\tau$-Synopses system architecture features the following components: Query Execution Engine, Synopses Manager, Updates Logger, and Workload Manager. These modules interact with a relational or XML databases which hold the data sets, and with registered synopses that act as web services. These synopses are connected either locally or remotely through a SOAP-enabled platforms.

The Synopses Manager is used for registration and maintenance of the synopses. A new synopsis is added to the system by registering its parameters (including list of supported queries and data sets) in the Synopses Manager Catalog.

The Query Execution Engine supports an interface for receiving query request from end-users and invoking the appropriate synopsis (or synopses), as determined by the Synopses Manager in order to process such query.

The Updates Logger feeds all data updates to the registered synopses by intercepting data updates information in the data sources.

The Workload Manager captures, maintains and analyzes workload information for building, maintaining and testing synopses.

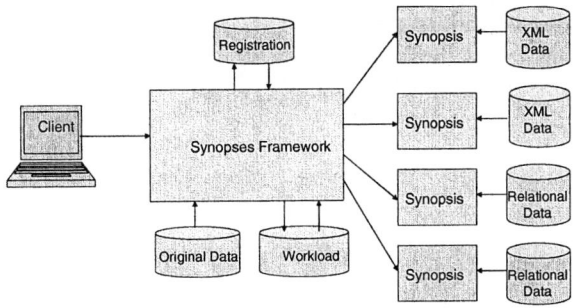

**Fig. 3.** General Architecture

The system provides a light-weight host process, inside which the custom synopses will be running. The host is responsible for all communication with the system and is transparent to the synopsis. This design enables unconstrained deployment. A remote synopsis can be integrated into the system by deploying or adapting such host into the remote system, and connecting the synopsis module locally into the host. Figure 3 illustrates an overall view of the system in a distributed environment, consisting of multiple remote synopses, each representing its local data source.

The system modules were implemented in the .NET framework, with remote modules communicating through the .NET Remoting. Any relational DB can be used as a database provider.

**Acknowledgement.** We thank Yariv Matia and Daniel Urieli for their contributions to the system development. We also thank the students in various classes at Tel Aviv university who have contributed synopses implementations to the system and for their feedback.

# References

1. P. B. Gibbons and Y. Matias. Synopsis data structures for massive data sets. *External Memory Algorithms, DIMACS Series in Discrete Mathematics and Theoretical Computer Science, American Mathematical Society, 50*, A, 1999. Also in SODA'99.
2. P. B. Gibbons, V. Poosala, S. Acharya, Y. Bartal, Y. Matias, S. Muthukrishnan, S. Ramaswamy, and T. Suel. AQUA: System and techniques for approximate query answering. Technical report, Bell Laboratories, Murray Hill, 1998.
3. A. C. Konig and G. Weikum. A framework for the physical design problem for data synopses. In *EDBT 2002 - Advances in Database Technology*, March 2002.
4. Y. Matia, Y. Matias, and L. Portman. Synopses reconciliation via calibration in the $\tau$-synopses system. In *Software Demo, EDBT'06*.
5. Y. Matias and L. Portman. $\tau$-Synopses: a system for run-time management of remote synopses. In *Software Demo, ICDE'04, EDBT'04*.
6. Y. Matias, L. Portman, and N. Drukh. The design and architecture of the $\tau$-synopses system. Technical Report, Tel Aviv University, 2005.

# Integrating a Maximum-Entropy Cardinality Estimator into DB2 UDB

Marcel Kutsch[1], Peter J. Haas[2], Volker Markl[2],
Nimrod Megiddo[2], and Tam Minh Tran[3]

[1] IBM Boeblingen Laboratory, Schoenaicher Str. 220,
71032 Boeblingen, Germany
kutschm@de.ibm.com
[2] IBM Almaden Research Center, 650 Harry Road,
San Jose, CA 95120, USA
{marklv, phaas, megiddo}@us.ibm.com
[3] IBM Silicon Valley Research Laboratory, 555 Bailey Avenue,
San Jose, CA 95141, USA
minhtran@us.ibm.com

## 1 Introduction

When comparing alternative query execution plans (QEPs), a cost-based query optimizer in a relational database management system (RDBMS) needs to estimate the selectivity of conjunctive predicates. The optimizer immediately faces a challenging problem: how to combine available partial information about selectivities in a consistent and comprehensive manner [1]. This paper describes a prototype solution to this problem.

In more detail, suppose that the optimizer needs to estimate the selectivity $s_{1,2,\ldots,n}$ of a predicate of the form $p_1 \wedge p_2 \wedge \cdots \wedge p_n$ defined over a specified relation $R$, where each *simple predicate* $p_i$ (also called a *Boolean factor* or BF) is of the form "*column op literal*." Here *column* is the name of a column in $R$, *op* is a relational comparison operator such as "=", ">", or "LIKE", and *literal* is a value in the domain of the column; e.g., MAKE = 'Honda' or YEAR > 1995. As usual, the selectivity of a predicate $p$ is the fraction of rows in $R$ that satisfy $p$. Estimates are typically available for simple-predicate selectivities of the form $s_i$ and, in modern optimizers, partial information is often available in the form of joint selectivity estimates such as $s_{2,3}$, $s_{1,3,5}$, and so forth. These joint selectivities are computed from *multivariate statistics* (MVS) such as multidimensional histograms, column-group statistics [2], and statistics on views. Gaps in the available information are typically filled using uniformity and independence assumptions. A serious problem now arises in that there may be multiple, non-equivalent ways of estimating the selectivity of a given predicate. E.g., if selectivities $s_1, s_2, s_3, s_{1,2}$, and $s_{2,3}$ are available, then we can estimate $s_{123}$ as (i) $s_{123} = s_1 \cdot s_2 \cdot s_3$, (ii) $s_{123} = s_{1,2} \cdot s_3$, or (iii) $s_{123} = s_1 \cdot s_{2,3}$. Arbitrary, inconsistent choices among non-equivalent selectivity estimates lead to arbitrary, unreliable, and usually suboptimal choices of QEPs. The ad hoc methods for ensuring consistency used in current RDBMS are cumbersome and expensive, and throw away valuable information; as discussed in [1], the net effect is to bias the optimizer toward those QEPs about which it has the least information.

To address the foregoing problems, the authors have proposed a technique called MAXENT [1], which uses the maximum entropy principle to obtain selectivity estimates. MAXENT exploits all available information in a consistent and principled manner, while avoiding imposition of any extraneous assumptions. We illustrate the basic idea for a predicate $p_1 \wedge p_2 \wedge p_3$ having three conjuncts, assuming that partial selectivities $s_1$, $s_2$, $s_3$, and $s_{1,2}$ are available. For a binary string of length 3, denote by $x_b$ the selectivity of the corresponding *atom* associated with the BFs in the predicate. For example, $x_{110}$ is the selectivity of the atom $p_1 \wedge p_2 \wedge \neg p_3$, and so forth. MAXENT provides a principled means of assigning values to the collection of atomic variables $\boldsymbol{x} = \{x_b : b \in \{0,1\}^3\}$, that is, for selecting a relative frequency distribution $\boldsymbol{x}$ over the atoms. Given the MAXENT solution, we can estimate the desired selectivity as $s_{1,2,3} = x_{111}$. MAXENT first expresses the available information as a system of equations; in our example, the equations are:

$$x_{100} + x_{110} + x_{101} + x_{111} = s_1 \tag{1a}$$

$$x_{010} + x_{011} + x_{110} + x_{111} = s_2 \tag{1b}$$

$$x_{001} + x_{011} + x_{101} + x_{111} = s_3 \tag{1c}$$

$$x_{110} + x_{111} = s_{1,2} \tag{1d}$$

$$\sum_b x_b = 1 \tag{1e}$$

There are typically many distributions $\boldsymbol{x}$ that satisfy (1a)–(1e); MAXENT selects the distribution with the highest *entropy* value $H(\boldsymbol{x}) = -\sum_b x_b \log x_b$. Intuitively, $H(\boldsymbol{x})$ is a measure of uncertainty in the distribution $\boldsymbol{x}$; by maximizing entropy, MAXENT selects the "simplest" distribution that is consistent with the constraints in (1a)–(1e). In the absence of information, the MAXENT solution reduces to the classical optimizer assumptions of uniformity and independence. The maximum entropy distribution can be computed using a well known algorithm called Iterative Scaling (IS); see [1] for details.

In this paper we describe our experience in implementing a prototype of MAXENT in DB2 UDB. We found ourselves facing a number of challenges. First, the computational complexity of the IS algorithm grows exponentially in the number of BFs, so we needed to decompose the constrained optimization problem into a multiple small problems, each involving only a subset of the BFs. Our next problem was that the set of constraints as in (1a)–(1e) was inconsistent in many cases, so that there did not exist a feasible solution $\boldsymbol{x}$ to the optimization problem and the IS algorithm failed to converge. Inconsistent constraints can arise both when statistics are gathered at different times and when selectivity estimates are based on erroneous uniformity and/or independence assumptions. Finally, the IS algorithm can fail to converge even when the constraints are consistent, if the set of constraints implies that a given variable $x_b$ must equal 0 in any feasible solution [and hence $\partial H(\boldsymbol{x})/\partial x_b = -1 - \log x_b = +\infty$]. For example, if $p_1 \Rightarrow p_2$, so that $s_{1,2} = s_1$, then $x_{100} = x_{101} = 0$. All such "implied zeros" must be identified and handled explicitly when setting up the constrained optimization problem.

## 2 Implementation Overview

MAXENT fits seamlessly into the existing optimizer architecture. After parsing a query, the optimizer, as in previous versions of DB2 UDB, first precomputes selectivities from single-column statistics and MVS (specifically, column-group statistics and statistics on views). The new MAXENT module then precomputes any missing selectivities using the iterative scaling algorithm. During the final steps of QEP enumeration, costing, and selection, the DB2 optimizer uses the precomputed selectivity estimates to estimate the cardinalities of each partial QEPs that it considers.

We now outline the various steps of our MAXENT implementation and indicate how we have addressed the challenges mentioned in the previous section. These steps, described below, consist of (1) partitioning, (2) inconsistency resolution, (3) implied-zero elimination, (4) iterative scaling, and (5) combination.

*Partitioning:* The partitioning step decomposes the set of BFs into disjoint subsets; the IS algorithm is run independently on each partition in order to reduce overall computation time. Using the available selectivities, the partitioning algorithm first tries to break up the BFs into mutually "independent" subsets that are each as small as possible; here, e.g., the subsets $\{p_1, p_2\}$ and $\{p_3, p_4\}$ are independent if $s_{1,2,3,4} = s_{1,2} \cdot s_{3,4}$. If any of the resulting subsets are still too large to be efficiently processed by the IS algorithm, the subset is partitioned further into (non-independent) subsets, in order to ensure sub-second response time. See [1, Sect. 5] for further elaboration of the partitioning problem. Steps (2)–(4) are now applied separately to each partition.

*Inconsistency resolution:* To detect and resolve inconsistencies in the constraint set, MAXENT solves a linear program (LP) that is obtained by adding a pair of "slack" variables to each constraint. The slack variables represent adjustments (increases or decreases) to the corresponding selectivity that are needed to achieve consistency. In our running example, constraint (1d) becomes $x_{110} + x_{111} + a^+_{1,2} - a^-_{1,2} = s_{1,2}$, and we add the additional constraints $a^+_{1,2}, a^-_{1,2} \geq 0$ and $0 \leq s_{1,2} - a^+_{1,2} + a^-_{1,2} \leq 1$. The other constraints (1a)–(1c) are similarly modified. We then use linear programming to minimize the sum of the slack variables, i.e., $a^+_1 + a^-_1 + a^+_2 + a^-_2 + a^+_3 + a^-_3 + a^+_{1,2} + a^-_{1,2}$, subject to the modified constraints, thereby making the adjustments as small as possible. The selectivities are then modified using the slacks, e.g., we take $s'_{1,2} = s_{1,2} - a^+_{1,2} + a^-_{1,2}$. Our prototype uses the open source COIN LP solver (found at www.coin-or.org).

*Implied-zero elimination:* Implied zeros can be detected using linear programming; the maximum entropy optimization problem is then formulated so that implied zeros appear neither in the objective function nor the constraints. The "exact" solution is computationally expensive, but the following heuristic method is very effective in practice. Write each atomic variable as $x_b = v_b + w_b$, and then maximize $\sum_b v_b$ subject to the usual maximum entropy constraints as in (1a)–(1e), as well as the additional constraints that $0 \leq w_b \leq 1$ and $0 \leq v_b \leq \varepsilon$ for each $b$, where $\varepsilon$ is a small number such as 0.0001. Then $x_b$ is taken as an implied zero if and only if $w_b = v_b = 0$ in the optimal solution. The idea is that setting $x_b = 0$ requires setting $v_b = 0$, which significantly impacts the objective function because of the $\varepsilon$ upper bound; thus, only "true" implied zeros are likely to appear in an optimal solution to the LP.

*Iterative Scaling:* In this step MAXENT computes the solution to the maximum-entropy optimization problem using the IS algorithm, as described in [1].

*Combination:* This step computes the overall maximum entropy solution by multiplying selectivities from different partitions. E.g., given two partitions $\{p_1, p_2\}$ and $\{p_3, p_4\}$, we would set $x_{1101} = x_{11}^{(1)} \cdot x_{01}^{(2)}$, where $x_b^{(i)}$ is a selectivity for the $i$th partition.

## 3 Experimental Evaluation

Figure 1 shows the effect of the preprocessing steps on the quality of the maximum-entropy solution. We used 600 random queries with BFs involving between 3 and 14 columns of a DMV database as in [1]. The first (resp., second) three bars show the effect of the preprocessing without (resp., with) partitioning. With no preprocessing (Bar 1), the IS algorithm fails for 24% of the queries due to inconsistent constraints and for an additional 2% of the queries due to implied zeros. Inconsistency resolution (Bar 2) guarantees the existence of a maximum entropy solution, but IS still converges for only 74% of the queries because of implied zeros. Elimination of implied zeros (Bar 3) produces a maximum entropy solution for every query. Bars 1P–3P show similar results in the presence of partitioning.

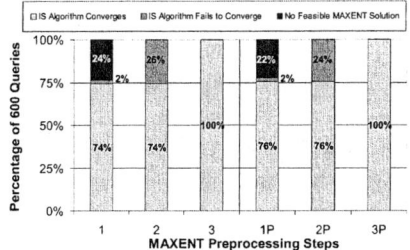
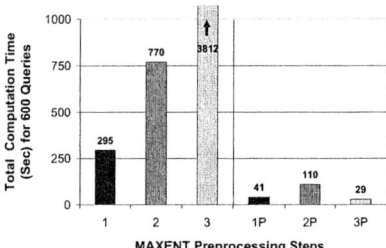

**Fig. 1.** Success rate of MAXENT

**Fig. 2.** MAXENT computation time

Figure 2 shows the total computation time needed to build the maximum entropy model for the 600 queries. The various preprocessing regimes are as in Fig. 1. As can be seen, partitioning reduces the computation time by orders of magnitude. Partitioning also has an impact on the relative effects of the preprocessing strategies; we focus on Bars 1P–3P, since partitioning is the regime used in practice. Bar 2P shows that inconsistency resolution almost triples the computation time, but Bar 3P shows that the speedup due to implied-zero elimination more than compensates for the cost of inconsistency resolution. Overall, the performance impact of the preprocessing steps is negligible—the average time to process a query is 0.05 seconds—whereas the quality of the results is improved dramatically as in Fig. 1.

As shown in [1], use of MAXENT can speed up query processing by orders of magnitude. Our new results show that a careful implementation of MAXENT can achieve these improvements in a commercial RDBMS while barely impacting query compilation time.

## References

1. Markl, V., Megiddo, N., Kutsch, M., Tran, T.M., Haas, P.J., Srivastava, U.: Consistently estimating the selectivity of conjuncts of predicates. In: Proc 31st VLDB. (2005) 373–384
2. Ilyas, I.F., Markl, V., Haas, P.J., Brown, P.G., Aboulnaga, A.: CORDS: Automatic discovery of correlations and soft functional dependencies. In: Proc ACM SIGMOD. (2004) 647–658

# Improving DB2 Performance Expert - A Generic Analysis Framework

Laurent Mignet[1], Jayanta Basak[1], Manish Bhide[1], Prasan Roy[1],
Sourashis Roy[1], Vibhuti S. Sengar[1], Ranga R. Vatsavai[1], Michael Reichert[2],
Torsten Steinbach[2], D.V.S. Ravikant[3,*], and Soujanya Vadapalli[4,**]

[1] IBM India Research Laboratory, IIT Campus, New Delhi, India
{lamignet, bjayanta, abmanish, prasanr, souraroy, visengar,
rvatsava}@in.ibm.com
[2] IBM Information Management Development, Böblingen, Germany
{rei, torsten}@de.ibm.com
[3] Cornell University, USA
[4] IIIT Hyderabad
soujanya@iiit.ac.in

**Abstract.** The complexity of software has been dramatically increasing over the years. Database management systems have not escaped this complexity. On the contrary, this problem is aggravated in database systems because they try to integrate multiple paradigms (object, relational, XML) in one box and are supposed to perform well in every scenario unlike OLAP or OLTP. As a result, it is very difficult to fine tune the performance of a DBMS. Hence, there is a need for a external tool which can monitor and fine tune the DBMS. In this extended abstract, we describe a few techniques to improve DB2 Performance Expert, which helps in monitoring DB2. Specifically, we describe a component which is capable of doing early performance problem detection by analyzing the sensor values over a long period of time. We also showcase a trends plotter and workload characterizer which allows a DBA to have a better understanding of the resource usages. A prototype of these tools has been demonstrated to a few select customers and based on their feedback this paper outlines the various issues that still need to be addressed in the next versions of the tool.

## 1 Introduction

Early detection/prediction of performance problems and potential resource constraints is essential for building robust and adaptive systems. Such prediction systems are also useful in limiting the impact of the failure. Often simple heuristics (rules of thumb) such as - the log size should be three times the raw data size - are often inadequate to address this problem. For example, too small a log size will increase the risk of frequent failures (transaction log full), and too large a log size will prevent proper utilization of the system resources.

---

* Work done during his stay in IRL.
** Work done during her internship in IRL.

Previous attempts to predict system performance include specific models that best characterize the given problem at hand. However, generalizing those models to a broad spectrum of database performance problems is very difficult. In our research we focus on generic tools that address a broad spectrum of DB2 health issues. In other words, instead of problem-specific models we are building a generic suit of models that can be applicable for addressing a broad set of performance problems that arise in day to day DB2 production environments. Our tools analyze the historical temporal data generated by the DB2 Performance Expert [5] (PE) and predict potential resource constraints, performance and specific trends.

## 1.1 Previous Art

Early Warning Mechanism is a very standard mechanism to provide some proactive features. In commercial database software, several products offer such features. DB2 Health Monitor [4] is one such tool and it monitors in background, several gauges and automatically issues an alert when a pre-specified threshold is met. Oracle in its version 10g provides trends analysis via the Automatic Database Diagnostic Monitor (ADDM) [6]. The ADDM includes a trends analysis wizard permitting users to forecast when a particular event may occur by using linear regression mechanism [7].

There are a few third party tools which also provide similar functionalities. BMC Software [2] offers a Connection-Miner tool which is part of their DGI Classic Suite. The tool provides some trend analysis reports showing resource utilization, trends by hour, week, month, or other desired criteria. The same features are also available in their SmartDBA offer [2]. Another third party tool is NORAD DBControl from Bradmark [3] which provides almost the same functionalities as that of the Connection-Miner tool. Finally, BEZ Systems [1] offers BEZPlus software which includes SerView, a database performance and SQL tuning tool and CorpView, an analysis tool that uses a performance data warehouse to track usage of the resources, data and SQL activity on the monitored server. The warehouse is used to perform trend analysis, problem identification and root-cause analysis.

Unlike other database management tools, our current work tries to consolidate all these functionalities in a single tool thereby giving a holistic view to the users. In the rest of the paper we first give a brief description of the components showcased to customers in May 2005. We then outline a few components which were conceived based on their feedback. Finally, we enumerate some problems that we encountered during the preliminary research on the components described in this the paper.

## 2 Components and Features

This section outlines the different modules that could potentially extend the existing tool, DB2 Performance Expert. Explained next are the modules that were showcased to a few select customers.

***Performance Wizard:*** Optimizing DB2 performance involves tuning several parameters which are dependent on the workload characteristics. Due to the dynamic nature of the workload, these parameters might need to be retuned. Hence there is a need for a tool that would suggest optimal parameter values to the DBA depending on the workload. This task is accomplished by the Performance Wizard. To that end it creates a tree of registered performance problems. The intermediate nodes of the tree consists of problems like memory problem, IO problem etc. The leaves of a sub-tree represent the parameter values that can potentially cause the problems represented by the nodes of the tree. The user chooses a branch of the tree on which the problem analysis is to be performed. The performance wizard engine analyzes the sensor values corresponding to the parameters represented by the leaves of the sub-tree (for which the analysis is to be performed). The value of these sensors is compared over time with a predefined threshold, and more than one deviation from the normal behavior of the sensor is necessary to detect a performance problem. If the engine detects a performance problem, in order to fix the problem the engine suggests a new value of the parameter to the user.

***Trends Plotter:*** This component allows the user to plot the trend of several sensors. The user is able to define the workload on which the analysis is to be performed. A workload can be defined based on the queries executed by a specific user, application, location (IP address of the origin of the query) or already defined workloads. The user can then plot the usage of predefined resources one by one or a set at the same time. The component also provides an option to drill-down by workload so as to better understand the way that the resources are being used. Another feature permits the user to plot the trend of the historical data using linear regression techniques. The users are also given an option to analyze the impact of the SQL queries performed by the RDBMS in terms of most used columns, tables, joins etc.

These two extensions were showcased to a few selected customers. Based on their feedback we are investigating the feasibility of their requirements. The additional components being explored are given below:

***Workload characterization:*** This feature involves fitting a mathematical model that best describes the current workloads seen by the database engine. A correlation between the workload characteristics and various system parameters helps in estimating the system resource requirements for an arbitrary workload.

***Discovering correlations between DB2 parameters:*** DB2 PE gathers over hundred parameters and records the current status of each parameter in a database. This component tries to establish the relationships between these parameter values. Various feature selection techniques and correlation analysis might uncover interesting relationships between various subsets of these parameters.

***Long term storage:*** This component involves developing the storage and archival techniques needed to efficiently manage the growing amount of historical runtime performance data present in DB2 PE. Apart from traditional compression techniques, we are also investigating various statistical distributions to represent data very concisely (that is store trends, rather than trend data). Suitable statistical sampling techniques and inverse transformation (decompression) techniques are being investigated to reconstruct the original data.

***Fitting Prediction Models:*** This features exploits the workload characterization and correlation discovery components (explained above) to fit a suitable mathematical model for predicting performance and resource usage. This will provide advisory tools that would guide the user to select a best model based on a given workload. Incremental algorithms are being designed so that analysis and prediction models do not further overburden the system. Figure 1 shows an example trend predicted (red) using one of our prediction model.

## 3 Future Work

During our work on the tool we encountered some problems due to the nature of the data as well as the nature of the application. Monitoring a software always implies a cost both in terms of communication (sending data over the network) as well as processing (gathering the data) on the monitored side. To lower this cost as much as possible, in our tool the data is only gathered using a discrete scheme (i.e., at some intervals). As a result, handling of missing data is an intrinsic part of the solution. This problem not only affects the numerical data extracted from the different sensors, but it has a bigger impact on the retrieval of the SQL statements. In the discreet scheme, the number of possible un-recovered SQL statements is not know and hence it is very difficult to estimate the correctness of the gathered information.

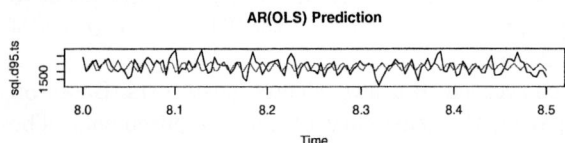

**Fig. 1.** Prediction using AR model

Another problem is related to the analysis of the historical data when seen as numerical time series. The literature on econometrics or digital signal processing is abundant with techniques to analyze time series to extract trends or to predict future values. The basic assumption of these models (for instance AR, ARIMA) is that the time series is stationary or pseudo-stationary. Unfortunately, this assumption does not hold in the case of the sensor data collected during our experimental phases which was generated using the TPC benchmark. We plan to investigate the feasibility of developing each of the components described above by designing new techniques which would overcome the enumerated problems.

## References

1. BEZ Systems. www.bez.com.
2. BMC Software, DGI Classis Suite. http://www.bmc.com/products/products_services_detail/0,,0_0_0_1401,00.html.

3. Bradmark, Norad DB Control. www.bradmark.com/site/products/products.html.
4. DB2 Health Monitor. http://www.db2mag.com/story/showArticle.jhtml?articleID=51200282.
5. DB2PE. http://www-306.ibm.com/software/data/db2imstools/db2tools/db-2pe/.
6. Oracle, ADDM. http://www.oracle.com/technology/oramag/oracle/04-may/-o34tech_talking.html.
7. Oracle, ADDM. http://www.oracle.com/technology/products/oracle9i/datasheets/oem_diagnostic/diagnostic.html.

# Managing Collections of XML Schemas in Microsoft SQL Server 2005

Shankar Pal, Dragan Tomic, Brandon Berg, and Joe Xavier

Microsoft Corporation, Redmond, WA 98052, USA
{shankarp, dragant, branber, joexav}@microsoft.com

**Abstract.** Schema evolution is of two kinds: (a) those requiring instance transformation because the application is simpler to develop when it works only with one version of the schema, and (b) those in which the old data must be preserved and instance transformation must be avoided. The latter is important in practice but has received scant attention in the literature. Data conforming to multiple versions of the XML schema must be maintained, indexed, and manipulated using the same query. Microsoft's SQL Server 2005 introduces XML schema collections to address both types of schema evolution.

## 1 Introduction

Many XML schemas have become standard in vertical industry segments such as ACORD [1] and SportsML [5]. Microsoft's Office products have made their XML schemas openly available [3]. These efforts have lead to better interoperability among loosely connected systems and the development of new applications, such as rich search and data sharing among applications. Standards bodies evolve their schemas, which may require reworking the applications since the XML schema evolution may require database schema changes. The scenarios for schema evolution are:

1. The new schema extends an existing one with new schema components. For example, the new schema can add a top-level element called "language" if a publisher enters a new, foreign market. The application considers existing data to have a default value for the new schema components (e.g. US English).
2. The schema is modified in an incompatible way. This often occurs with change in business needs and merger of systems. The existing data must be mapped to the new schema, using, for example, XSL transformations [8], if it does not conform to the new schema. The data transformation can be avoided in some cases (e.g. maxOccurs of <phone> changes from 7 to 5 but no instance exceeds 5 <phone>s).
3. The schema undergoes modification as government or business rules change. New data must conform to the new schema while old data must be retained in its old form for archival purposes. Examples are tax filing and securities trading. Tax laws change from one year to the next, but old tax returns should not be transformed to conform to the latest version of the XML schema.

While the first two kinds of schema evolution have been studied extensively in the literature, the third kind is a practical problem with a few ad hoc solutions. SQL Server 2005 addresses it using a meta-data notion called an *XML schema collection* –

a container of XML schemas that may be related (e.g. through <xs:import>) or unrelated to one another. Each schema in an XML schema collection C is identified using its target namespace. A new version of an XML schema with a new target namespace can be added to C and is treated like a new schema. This framework is powerful enough to support the other types of schema evolution too.

The XML data is stored in a column of a rich data type called XML, as opposed to decomposing the data into tables and columns. This avoids database schema modification when XML schemas in C are added, dropped or modified. The database engine validates each XML instance according to XML schema specified in the XML instance during data assignment and modification.

## 2 XML Schema Collection

An XML schema collection C is created using the following statement and registering one or more XML schemas:

```
CREATE XML SCHEMA COLLECTION C AS '<xs:schema> …
</xs:schema>'
```

The schema processor identifies and stores in C the schema components supplied in the schemas. An *XML schema component* is anything defined at the top level of an XML schema, such as an element, attribute, type, or group definition. Schema components from multiple XML schemas with the same target namespace are grouped together by the target namespace.

A user can type an XML column using C. The constraint imposed by C is the collective set of the schema constraints imposed by the individual XML schemas in C. The post-schema validation Infoset (PSVI), which adds type information to the Infoset [6], is encoded in the internal representation of the XML data for faster parsing during XQuery [7] processing.

### 2.1 Schema Evolution

Suppose you add an XML schema with target namespace BOOK-V1 to an XML schema collection C. An XML column XDOC typed using C can store XML data conforming to BOOK-V1 schema. To extend the XML schema, the schema designer adds the new schema components to the BOOK-V1 namespace. Adding optional elements and attributes, and top-level elements and type definitions do not require re-validation of the existing XML data in column XDOC. Suppose later the application wants to provide a new version of the XML schema, for which it chooses the target namespace BOOK-V2. This XML schema is added to C without transforming the existing XML instances in XDOC. The XML column can store instances of both BOOK-V1 and BOOK-V2 schemas. This yields significant simplification in data management when C contains a large number of XML schemas. The user can insert and modify XML instances conforming to the latest version of the schema as well as those conforming to the older versions of the schema.

The XML schema collection framework can also support applications that require instance transformation. The application has to supply the modified XML schema and the transform, such as XSL or XQuery, to be applied to the XML data. The system can generate the transform by comparing the old and the new XML schemas.

XML schemas may use a "version" attribute [6] to specify the schema version while using the same target namespace for all versions. There is no language support in XQuery to specify the version of a schema. Furthermore, the XML schemas published by W3C and Microsoft include the year and optionally the month and the day of publication in the target namespace. Hence, our choice has been to rely on a new target namespace to indicate evolving versions of an XML schema.

## 3 Indexing and Querying XML Data

XML indexes [4] are built on XML columns to speed up different classes of queries. Type information from the XML schema collection is stored in the XML indexes for scalar values and element types. Furthermore, tag names and paths are encoded relative to their target namespace. This ensures that a search can distinguish between a <book> element within the target namespace BOOK-V1 from one within the target namespace BOOK-V2. This allows users to restrict their queries to the desired schema namespaces and yet get good performance. However, search for <book> in all namespaces can become a union query or turn into a primary XML index scan.

One of the main benefits of an XML schema collection is the ability to query across multiple XML schemas. The XQuery compiler uses the schema component definitions to perform static type analysis, based on which it can reject a priori some queries that would result in run-time errors (e.g. type mismatch). It can also infer cardinality to assist in static query optimizations. If desired, an XQuery expression can be limited to a specific version of an XML schema. This is desirable since the older data should be as easily searchable as the new data.

Querying over multiple schema versions can be broken down as follows:

- If elementFormDefault or attributeFormDefault is specified as unqualified in an XML schema, the target namespace of non-top level elements and attributes in the schema is absent. A query for those elements and attributes looks for the type definitions in the special no name target namespace. This allows queries over elements and attributes defined in different XML schemas within the XML schema collection C, and yields very good performance.
- If the element or attribute is qualified in the XML schema, then the appropriate target namespace can be used to limit an XQuery expression to the element or attribute definitions within the specified target namespace.
- When an element or attribute is unqualified in an XQuery expression, the query looks for the type definitions in the default target namespace specified in the XQuery prolog. If no definition is found, then the no name target namespace is searched for the type definitions.
- If the element or attribute is qualified in the XML schema, a search is performed over multiple target namespaces using a wildcard for the target namespace. Thus, to search for <book> elements within multiple versions of an evolving XML schema, the user can write the path expression as //*:book. This looks for the definition of the <book> element in all the XML schemas registered with the XML schema collection, including the no name target

namespace. Wildcard namespace queries are slow because they result in a primary XML index scan but some optimizations can be done such as turning it into an "or" query over the different XML schemas in C.

## 4 Conclusions and Future Work

The focus in SQL Server 2005 has been to build up the infrastructure for XML schema evolution using XML schema collection. Most of the common features of XML Schema specification have been implemented to meet customer needs. For future work, incorporating instance transformation is useful. This can be based on XQuery or XSLT, and the system can generate the transform.

Some applications, such as securities trading, require limiting an XML schema collection to the latest version of the XML schemas. In a query such as //*:author, which finds the <author> elements in all the target namespaces within an XML schema collection, the query can be restricted to only the latest schema based upon execution context settings.

The next version of the SQL standard for XML [2] introduces the concept of a registered XML schema which can accommodate multiple XML schemas that are related to one another using <xs:import>. This allows schema evolution as long as the evolved XML schema imports the old schema; the registered XML schema descriptor must be updated as well. By comparison, our XML schema collection accommodates disjoint XML schemas and allows more general schema evolution.

## References

1. ACORD – Global Insurance Standard. http://www.acord.org/standards/StandardsHome.aspx
2. Melton, J.: ISO/IEC 9075-14:2003, Information technology — Database languages — SQL — Part 14: XML-Related Specifications (SQL/XML) (2004)
3. Office 2003: XML Reference Schemas. http://www.microsoft.com/downloads/details-aspx?familyid=fe118952-3547-420a-a412-00a2662442d9&displaylang=en
4. S. Pal et al.: Indexing XML Data Stored in a Relational Database. Proc VLDB (2004).
5. SportsML – Sports Markup Language. http://www.sportsml.org/
6. XML Schema Part 1: Structures and Part 2: Datatypes. W3C Recommendation 2 May 2001. http://www.w3.org/TR/2001/REC-xmlschema-1-20010502, http://www.w3.org/TR/2001/REC-xmlschema-2-20010502
7. XQuery 1.0: An XML Query Language. http://www.w3c.org/TR/xquery
8. XSL Transformations (XSLT) Version 2.0. http://www.w3.org/TR/2005/WD-xslt20-20050915/.

# Enabling Outsourced Service Providers to Think Globally While Acting Locally

Kevin Wilkinson, Harumi Kuno, Kannan Govindarajan, Kei Yuasa,
Kevin Smathers, Jyotirmaya Nanda, and Umeshwar Dayal

Hewlett-Packard Laboratories,
1501 Page Mill Rd.,
Palo Alto, CA 94304

## 1 Introduction

Enterprises commonly outsource all or part of their IT to vendors as a way to reduce the cost of IT, to accurately estimate what they spend on IT, and to improve its effectiveness. These contracts vary in complexity from the outsourcing of a world-wide IT function to smaller, country-specific, deals.

For service providers to realize the economies of scale necessary for them to be profitable, they must "productize" services and work from models that standardize significant aspects of services and the resources required to fulfill them. However, "productization of services" is not simple. Services are inherently different from products. Services organizations are more likely to have significant regional variations when compared to their manufacturing counterparts. Local customers often prefer local service. Global customers expect the same service in all the regions that they operate in, and the service provider must thus leverage local service capabilities in a globally consistent manner. IT technology evolves rapidly, and service offerings, options on existing service offerings, and preferred standard solutions must follow suit.

Finally, large global deals require the service provider to coordinate multiple teams from various regions with different areas of expertise and that use a variety of tools (often implemented using personal productivity applications such as Excel) and highly-manual processes. This leads to information silos where information is trapped in personal documents, making it difficult for management to make informed decisions about the services business.

We introduce here novel techniques that address the unique needs of the IT service domain. Our initial prototype, introduced in [1], used conventional techniques. However, we found this approach was subject to limitations that prevented the wide adoption of our prototype (Section 2). Our new approach leverages metadata technology and the ubiquity of office productivity tools to overcome these barriers (Section 3).

## 2 Initial Approach

Our hypothesis is that a critical factor in these problems is that, fundamentally, the right information is not made available to the right person at the right time.

We believe this is because manual processes simply cannot scale to accommodate the tens of thousands of relationships and details involved in service design.

To address these issues, we look to the manufacturing domain's experience with computer-aided design (CAD) systems [2]. Backed by a library of components and their relationships, a CAD system takes care of tedious details of mechanical design tasks such as version management, component reuse, the validation of design rules, etc., freeing designers to focus on design objectives. Applying the CAD metaphor to the service domain, we hoped that by automating the management of relationship information and configuration processes, by exploiting human input for the difficult tasks of term/value configuration and mapping validation, and by integrating the relationships discovered during the human input phase back into the system, we would manage the information required for the design of service solutions more accurately and efficiently than either a fully-automated system or a non-automated system could.

## 2.1 First Prototype

Our first prototype application connected the stages of a deal lifecycle by providing a central repository that maintains and links between the per-customer data used in each of the stages. We refer readers to [1] for details. We call our prototype system the Service Configurator because it helps design solutions based on standard offerings followed by customer specific configuration. Integrating the lifecycle stages lets us identify and control the amount of unique work required for each customer and deliver low-cost, high-quality service offerings that adapt to changing customer needs.

Our initial instinct was to use traditional design choices, such as a conventional three-tier web-client-server architecture. The data source layer was based upon a global information model, and used fixed schema mappings to provide access to data from domain-specific "authoritative" repositories maintained by the business unit. Each of these repositories was in turn itself global in nature, with relatively stable schema and content.

Our business unit partners tested the prototype with data from an ongoing deal with a major customer, and validated benefits of the Service Configurator's approach, such as information flow continuity and automation [1]. The prototype was reasonably well-received. Our collaborators were intrigued by the possibilities when presented with the concrete demonstrator, and we were chartered to build a second prototype with help from a larger pool of domain experts.

## 2.2 Issues with the First Prototype

Despite its positive reception, the first prototype suffered from issues that prevented it from being transferred directly to the business unit. Most significantly, we came to realize that service configuration is characterized by highly dynamic, distributed, disconnected processes, tools, and data sources. The first prototype was based upon a global perspective, yet its user community spans sub-organizations, roles, and regions. Adopting the first system would have required big changes in the field's processes and data sources, not to mention the creation of a receptor organization to develop the prototype into a complete system and support it. Because we did not accommodate existing regional infrastructures, tools, and practices, regional users could not use our system as-is.

Second, although one of the most significant contributions of the first prototype is the data model, we came to realize that because the information model was exposed implicitly through web forms, the underlying concepts/relationships were not always clear to the system users.

Finally, our system must bridge gaps between global and regional models, deal and service lifecycle stages, organizations and roles in the service business, and service portfolios. We provided only a global view of solutions, and found that the field needs to easily extend/augment the model. Furthermore, there was a need for a means to share those extensions among peers (and eventually promote the extensions to the global model). Our original, centralized, solution offered only limited interchange/interoperability. We needed an easy way to export/import subsets of the information model.

## 3 New (Federated) Approach

Our first system showed how a common information model could enable information sharing and new capabilities across the various dimensions of service outsourcing, e.g., service lifecycle, service offerings, tasks and roles. The goal of our second system is to overcome the barriers to using such a system by the service professionals. We used a two-pronged approach: integrate with familiar user tools and utilize semantic information models.

Service professionals were skeptical how a central repository could maintain up-to-date information in the fast-paced, dynamic and disconnected environment of deal pursuit and delivery. We also observed a reliance on simple office productivity tools such as Excel and Word, which encapsulate information in manageable chunks and are frequently shared in the field. Consequently, we have developed interfaces between our system and Word and Excel. For Excel documents, we support mappings between cells in a spreadsheet and parameters in a service configuration. For Word documents, arbitrary snippets of content can be tagged and associated with a parameter. Transformation programs then exchange information between the Word or Excel documents and the repository.

Our mappings enable repository content to appear in documents and the repository to be updated from the documents. Consequently, service professionals can immediately share and view any changes for a deal. An added advantage is that these documents are mobile, so information is available even when the repository is not accessible. Further, there is no learning curve for getting access to this information since the user interfaces, Word and Excel are familiar. The mappings are expressed in a relatively simple language and can be hidden. As needed, new mappings could easily be defined by a trained user.

This basic capability is necessary but not sufficient because it only enables data sharing. It does not enable the sharing of data definitions, i.e., metadata. The information model in our first system was hidden behind a set of Web forms.

Our second system exposes the information model, and enables the definition and sharing of new concepts and relationships.

We chose RDF/OWL as a representation language for our information model because it provides globally unique identifers for resources (URIs), enables rich semantic descriptions of information, and supports decomposition of models into smaller chunks that can be individually shared and extended. Rather than develop a single, complicated ontology to describe the complete services business, we are using an incremental approach that divides the business into sub-domains. There are a number of core ontologies. We anticipate the development of ontologies specific to regions, task or industry segment.

RDF/OWL enables the extension and sharing of ontologies and facilitates their integration. However, expressed as an RDF graph, an ontology is not an appropriate representation for use by services professionals. We thus provide task-specific views of the ontology, each of which is a projection of the graph onto a tree. A tree provides a more natural presentation of the information, and is easily expressed in XML, facilitating interchange with other tools. E.g., a deal configuration graph might be projected onto a simpler, partonomic tree that lists, for each service, the modules comprising the service and the parameter values for each module. The views are expressed as templates and a transformation program applies the template to a graph to generate an XML tree.

These views are intended for round-trip transformations. E.g., we can use a single view template to create round-trip transformations– from RDF to XML, as well as from XML back to RDF. In this way, we can extract information from a graph representing a configuration, incorporate that into some Word or Excel document, allow users to modify (in a limited way) that content and then update the configuration with the modified information.

## 4 Status and Challenges

Our second prototype has been met with enthusiastic reception from business unit contacts. Thus far, we have won sponsorship all the way up the services organization and have begun to engage with a transfer organization.

In addition, we have identified some challenges to explore next. These include more sophisticated reporting and analysis functions, mechanisms for enabling the government of interactions between global and regional systems, and a workflow framework for analysis and delivery.

## References

1. Kuno, H., Yuasa, K., Govindarajan, K., Smathers, K., Burg, B., Carau, P., Wilkinson, K.: Governing the contract lifecycle: A framework for sequential configuration of loosely-coupled systems. In: DNIS 2005. (2005)
2. Katz, R.H.: Toward a unified framework for version modeling in engineering databases. ACM Comput. Surv. **22** (1990) 375–409

# Another Example of a Data Warehouse System Based on Transposed Files

Antonio Albano[1], Luca De Rosa[2], Lucio Goglia, Roberto Goglia, Vincenzo Minei, and Cristian Dumitrescu[3]

[1] Univ. of Pisa, Dept. of Computer Science,
Largo B. Pontecorvo 3, 56127 Pisa, Italy
[2] Advanced Systems, Via Napoli 159,
80013 Casalnuovo di Napoli (NA), Italy
[3] Sisteme Avanzate Italo-Romane, Calea Victoriei 155,
Bucarest 1, Romania

**Abstract.** The major commercial data warehouse systems available today are based on record-oriented relational technology optimized for OLTP applications. Several authors have shown that substantial improvements in query performance for OLAP applications can be achieved by systems based on transposed files (column-oriented) technology, since the dominant queries only require grouping and aggregation on a few columns of large amounts of data. This new assumption underlying data warehouse systems means that several aspects of data management and query processing need to be reconsidered. We present some preliminary results of an industrial research project which is being sponsored by the Italian Ministry of Education, University and Research (MIUR) to support the cooperation of universities and industries in prototyping innovative systems. The aim of the project is to implement an SQL-compliant prototype data warehouse system based on a transposed file storage system. The paper will focus on the optimization of star queries with group-by.[1]

## 1 Introduction

The most important commercial data warehouse systems are based on record-oriented relational technology optimized for OLTP applications. They have been extended with new kinds of indexes and new optimization techniques for typical OLAP queries that require grouping and aggregation on just a few columns over large amounts of data. Several authors have demonstrated that, since a data warehouse system is query-intensive, an implementation based on a transposed file storage system (also called column-oriented, projection indexes) can achieve substantial improvements in OLAP query performance [7], [4], [3], [1], [6]. In

---

[1] This work was partially supported by the MIUR, under FAR Fund DM 297/99, Project number 11384. The project partners are Advanced Systems, University of Pisa, Department of Computer Science, and University of Sannio, Research Centre on Software Technology.

addition to research prototype systems there are several commercial products that have adopted transposed files as a storage structure, such as Addamark and KDB. Clearly, the idea of changing the way data are stored is not in itself enough to achieve the expected query performance. Other storage structures must be considered and new algorithms for generating access plans must be designed. Although algorithms for join query processing are reported in the above references, the execution of the most typical OLAP query with grouping and aggregation has received less attention. It is well known that a standard way to evaluate this kind of query is to perform all the joins first and then the group-by. However, several authors have shown that an optimizer should also consider doing the group-by before the join [2], [5].[2]

We present some preliminary results of an industrial research project SADAS which began in March 2003 and is being sponsored by the Italian Ministry of Education, University and Research (MIUR) to support the cooperation of universities and industries in prototyping innovative systems. The main contractor is the Italian company Advanced Systems that implemented the commercial system Overmillion in the late 1990s using a completely transposed storage structure. However the system does not support either multi-relation queries or SQL. On the basis of their successful experience, the aim of our project was to redesign and re-implement Overmillion to have a complete SQL-compliant data warehouse system using a transposed file storage system.

The paper is organized as follows. First we outline the main storage structures in SADAS, and then we present the approach adopted in generating query plans for star queries with grouping and aggregations.

## 2 Storage Structures

We briefly present the storage structures implemented in SADAS and the physical operators used in query plans. We consider only those features that are relevant for the group-by optimization, and we make the following assumptions to simplify the presentation: (a) the database has a star schema, where the primary and foreign keys have only one attribute; (b) the database is read-only; (c) a completely transposed structure is used for each table, and so each column is stored in a separate file; (d) each column has fixed length values different from null. The system adopts the following storage structures:

1. each column $A$ of a table with $n$ records is stored in two files with $n$ elements using two representations: (a) a file named A.CLN (column values) which contains the column values for all the records of a table (an index is maintained for this file) and (b) a file named A.CLI (codified column) which contains the column values coded as the position of the values in the corresponding column index;

---

[2] We would like to apologize to other contributors in this area whose work we have not acknowledged due to limitations of space.

2. for each foreign key $f_k$ of the fact table $F$ for the dimensional table $D$ there is a join index, which is a file that contains the RIDs of the matching records in $D$, instead of the corresponding key values;
3. for all the not empty subsets of the fact table foreign keys, the following structures exist:
    (a) a partial multi-column index $G$ where (a) for each column $A$ the values are those stored in the corresponding file A.CLI, and (b) the index contains only the values part and the number of elements for each entry. For example, in the index on columns $A$ and $B$ of $F$, the $k$-th entry that corresponds to the values $(a_1, b_3)$, will contain the values $(1, 3)$ if $a_1$ has code 1 and $b_3$ has code 3;
    (b) a file $G.GDI$ that contains the column values coded as the position of the values in the corresponding column index. For example, if the $i$-th record of the fact table $F$ has columns $A$ e $B$ with values $(a_1, b_3)$, in the file $G.GDI$ the $i$-th entry contains the value $k$.

## 3 Optimization of Star Queries with Grouping and Aggregations

Usually a star query is executed by traditional data warehouse systems using the best of two plans, the one produced in the usual way by relational systems, and the other produced with the following basic phases: (a) the local conditions are applied to the fact table and to the dimensional tables that participate in the join to compute the *local rowsets*. A local rowset is a bitmap representing the selected tuples from a table; (b) using the join indexes and the local rowsets, the *global rowset* is computed, which is a bitmap representing the records from the fact table that belong to the star join. The algorithm to execute this phase depends on the kind of join indexes available; (c) once the relevant fact table records have been retrieved using the *global rowset*, they are joined with the dimension tables to produce the answer to the query.

When a system adopts a completely transposed file solution, the best plan to execute a star query is produced by adopting the same first two phases, using the operators BMIndexFilter and BMJoinIndex, but a different strategy for the third phase: To evaluate a group-by, the optimizer determines if a group-by can be moved on the fact table to use the operator IndexGByJoinFromBM, which exploits the benefits of a specific structure provided to accelerate the operation starting from the *global rowset* produced by the BMJoinIndex operator:

> IndexGByJoinFromBM$(O, \{A_i\}, \{D_j\}, \{R_h\}, \{g_k\})$ groups the records of the fact table that participate in the star join, represented by the global rowset $O$, by a set of foreign keys $\{A_i\}$, and retrieves the values of the dimensional columns $\{D_j\}$. It returns a set of records whose fields are the values of the columns $\{R_h\} \subseteq \{A_i\} \cup \{D_j\}$ and the values of the aggregate functions $\{g_k\}$.

To exploit the benefits of doing the group-by before the join, we decided to consider the three cases studied in [2], [5], which we revised and reformulated in the form of equivalent rules of the relational algebra. Due to limitations of space, we will only show the following case.

**Proposition 1.** *Let $\alpha(X)$ be the set of columns in $X$ and $R \bowtie_{C_j} S$ an equi-join using the primary key $p_k$ of $S$ and the foreign key $f_k$ of $R$. $R$ has the invariant grouping property*

$$_A\gamma_F(R \bowtie_{C_j} S) \equiv \pi_{A \cup F}((_{A \cup \alpha(C_j) - \alpha(S)}\gamma_F(R)) \bowtie_{C_j} S)$$

*if the following conditions hold: (a) the foreign key of $R$ is functionally determined by the grouping columns $A$ in $R \bowtie_{C_j} S$; (b) each aggregate function in $F$ only uses columns of $R$.*

*Example 1.* Consider the star schema and the query:

Product(PKproduct, pName, cost, division),   Keys: {PKproduct}, {pName}
Order(PKorder, FKproduct, FKdealer, price, qty, date),   Key: {PKorder}

```
SELECT      pName, SUM(qty) AS Q
FROM        Order, Product
WHERE       FKproduct = PKproduct AND division = 'D1' AND qty = 100
GROUP BY    pName;
```

Since the fact table Order has the invariant grouping property, the optimizer is aware that the group-by can be moved on Order, and so it considers the following plan:

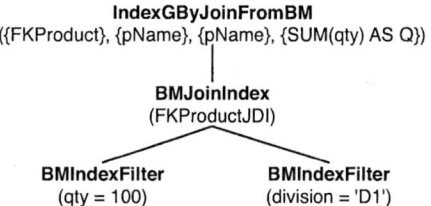

## 4  Conclusions

We have briefly presented (a) some of the features of the SADAS system, a data warehouse management system based on transposed files, and (b) the approach adopted in generating query plans for star queries with grouping and aggregations that benefit from specialized data structures. A single-user version of the system using a subset of SQL is operational and the demonstration at EDBT will show how its query performance compares favorably with that of commercial row-store data warehouse products, as reported by authors of similar projects.

# References

1. P. A. Boncz and M. L. Kersten. MIL Primitives for Querying a Fragmented World. *The VLDB Journal* **8** (1999) 101–119.
2. S. Chaudhuri and K. Shim: Including Group-By in Query Optimization. In *Proc. Intl. Conf. on VLDB*, Santiago, Chile, (1994) 354–366.
3. A. Datta, K. Ramamritham, and H. M. Thomas: Curio: A N ovel Solution for Efficient Storage and Indexing in Data Warehouses. In *Proc. Intl. Conf. on VLDB*, Edinburgh, Scotland, (1999) 730–733.
4. C. D. French: "One size fits all" Database Architectures do not Work for DDS. In *Proc. of the ACM SIGMOD Intl. Conf. on Management of Data*, San Jose, California, USA, (1995) 449–450.
5. C. A. Galindo-Legaria and M. M. Joshi: Orthogonal Optimization of Subqueries and Aggregation. In *Proc. of the ACM SIGMOD Intl. Conf. on Management of Data*, Santa Barbara, California, USA, (2001) 571–581.
6. M. Stonebraker et al.: C-Store: A Column-Oriented DBMS. In *Proc. Intl. Conf. on VLDB*, Trondheim, Norway, (2005) 553–564.
7. M. J. Turner, R. Hammond, and P. Cotton: A DBMS for Large Statistical Databases. In *Proc. Intl. Conf. on VLDB*, Rio de Janeiro, Brazil, (1979) 319–327.

# XG: A Grid-Enabled Query Processing Engine

Radu Sion[1], Ramesh Natarajan[2], Inderpal Narang[3], and Thomas Phan[3]

[1] Stony Brook University
sion@cs.stonybrook.edu
[2] IBM TJ Watson Research Lab
phantom@us.ibm.com
[3] IBM Almaden Research Lab
narang@us.ibm.com
[4] IBM Almaden Research Lab
phantom@us.ibm.com

**Abstract.** In [12] we introduce a novel architecture for data processing, based on a functional fusion between a data and a computation layer. In this demo we show how this architecture is leveraged to offer significant speedups for data processing jobs such as data analysis and mining over large data sets.

One novel contribution of our solution is its data-driven approach. The computation infrastructure is *controlled from within the data layer*. Grid compute job submission events are based within the query processor on the DBMS side and in effect controlled by the data processing job to be performed. This allows the early deployment of on-the-fly data aggregation techniques, minimizing the amount of data to be transfered to/from compute nodes and is in stark contrast to existing Grid solutions that interact with data layers as external (mainly) "storage" components. By integrating scheduling intelligence in the data layer itself we show that it is possible to provide a close to optimal solution to the more general grid trade-off between required data replication costs and computation speed-up benefits. We validate this in a scenario derived from a real business deployment, involving financial customer profiling using common types of data analytics.

## 1 Demonstration Outline

In this demo we will show how integrating a computation grid with a data layer results in significant execution speedups. For example, with only 12 non-dedicated nodes, a speedup of approximately 1000% can be attained, in a scenario involving complex linear regression analysis data mining computations for commercial customer profiling. In this demo we deploy XG with live connections (on-site demo only also possible) to our 70+ nodes CPU Grid located in IBM Almaden. We then demonstrate the data processing scenarios discussed below, including the mining query execution speedup shown in Figure 2. Additionally, we propose to demonstrate some of the more subtle features of our system, opening insights into important underlying design decisions. These features include: (i) the runtime mechanism for on-demand QoS provisioning of data replication and computation (provisioning the right amount of resources per data processing task to meet QoS demands, e.g., deadlines), (ii) the on-the-fly recovery on failure in both computation and data layers, (iii) the automatic discovery of computation resources, (iv) the runtime monitoring of computation and data flows between the data layer and the grid. This demonstration is facilitated by the fact that these features are exposed through a user-friendly GUI.

## 2 Introduction

As increasingly fast networks connect vast numbers of cheaper computation and storage resources, the promise of "grids" as paradigms of optimized, heterogeneous resource sharing across boundaries [2], becomes closer to full realization. It already delivered significant successes in projects such as the Grid Physics Network (GriPhyN) [4] and the Particle Physics Data Grid (PPDG) [10]. While these examples are mostly specialized scientific applications, involving lengthy processing of massive data sets (usually files), projects such as Condor [1] and Globus [3] aim at exploring "computational grids" from a declared more main-stream perspective.

There are two aspects of processing in such frameworks. On the one hand, we find the computation resource allocation aspect ("computational grid"). On the other hand however data accessibility and associated placement issues are also naturally paramount ("data grid"). Responses to these important data grid challenges include high performance file sharing techniques, file-systems and protocols such as GridFTP, the Globus Replica Catalog and Management tools in Globus, NeST, Chirp, BAD-FS , STORK , Parrot , Kangaroo and DiskRouter in Condor. The ultimate goal of grids is (arguably) an increasingly optimized use of existing compute resources and an associated increase of end-to-end processing quality (e.g. lower execution times). Intuitively, a tighter integration of the two grid aspects ("computational" and "data") could yield significant advantages e.g., due to the potential for optimized, faster access to data, decreasing overall execution times. There are significant challenges to such an integration, including the minimization of data transfer costs by performing initial data-reducing aggregation, placement scheduling for massive data and fast-changing access patterns, data consistency and freshness.

In this work we propose, analyze and experimentally validate a novel integrated data-driven grid-infrastructure in a data mining framework. Computation jobs can now be formulated, provisioned and transparently scheduled from within the database query layer to the background compute Grid. Such jobs include e.g., the computation of analytical functions over a data subset at the end of which the result is returned back in a data layer (either by reference to a specific location or inline, as a result of the job execution). We designed and built a specialized experimental grid infrastructure. One of the main design insights behind it is that (arguably) any "global" grid is ultimately composed of clustered resources at the "edge". It is then only natural to represent it as a hierarchy of computation clusters and associated close-proximity data sources. Using our end-to-end solution (data-layer aggregation and compute grid invocation), in our considered application domain (data analysis for predictive modeling) significant speed-ups have been achieved versus the traditional case of data-layer processing.

**Scenario: Customer Analytics.** Let us now explore an important commonly encountered operation scenario for data mining in a commercial framework that yielded significant cost and speed-up benefits from our solution: a large company (i.e., with a customer base of millions of customers), maintains an active customer transaction database and deploys data mining to better customize and/or optimize its customer-interaction response and associated costs. There are two types of customer interactions, each subject to different types of requirements and response mechanisms, namely (i) incoming ("pull" model) inquiries and (ii) outgoing advertisements ("push" model). For space reasons, here we are discussing (i).

*Incoming* inquiries (e.g., over the phone, online) are handled in a real-time or short-notice manner. There are bounds on response-time (e.g., Human-Computer interaction experiences should feature response times of under 7-8 seconds to be acceptable) [11] to be satisfied. An imprecise but fast initial "pre"-response might be often preferable to an exact but slow one, as it is likely that higher waiting-times would result in a drop in overall customer satisfaction.

The company's response data is based on previously recorded customer "profiles", composed of a history of transactions and a set of related predictive models. Such profiles need to be maintained with sufficient (preferably maximal) accuracy and the associated (predictive) models re- computed periodically or as part of an event- driven paradigm in which associate customer events trigger individual model re- computations.

In such an interaction, often the center-point (and likely the most expensive) is processing a function of the immediate input data and the customer predictive models in the stored profile ("model scoring"). Often, also, new models need to be computed on the fly. Because of its real-time nature, and the potential for thousands of simultaneous incoming customer requests, this scenario is extremely challenging.

To understand the size of this problem, let us quantify some of the previous statements with real data. Let us assume a customer base of over 10 million customers. Roughly 0.1% (10k) of them are active at any point in time (interactive and automated phone calls, web access, other automated systems). Preferably, the company response in each and every transaction should be optimally tailored (i.e., through on-demand data mining) to maximize profit and customer satisfaction. On average, only 75% (7.5k) of these active (meta)transactions are resulting in actual data mining tasks and, for each second, only 20% of these task- triggering customers require data mining. To function within the required response-behavior boundary, the company has to thus handle a continuous parallel throughput of 1500 (possibly complex) simultaneous data mining jobs. Achieving this throughput at the computation and data I/O level is very challenging from both a cost and scalability viewpoint.

## 3 System Architecture

The end-to-end solution comprises several major components: modeling, aggregation and computation outsourcing (in the data layer) and grid scheduling and management (grid layer).

**Data Layer.** Designing specifically for data mining over large data sets, requires a careful consideration of network data transfer overheads. As traditional data mining solutions are often based on code directly executed inside the database query processor, these overheads could often be reduced by an initial data aggregation step performed inside the data layer, before outsourcing the more computation heavy model generation tasks.

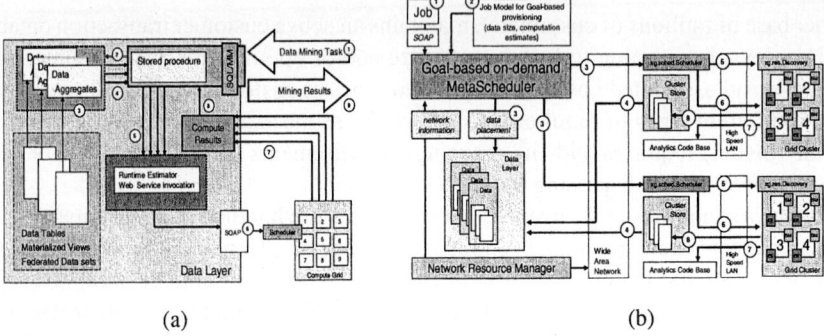

**Fig. 1.** (a) Data Layer Overview: The grid is leveraged transparently from the data side. Mining tasks can execute normally within the query processor (e.g., as stored procedures). (b) Both data replication/placement (to cluster stores) and job scheduling in the hierarchical grid infra-structure is controlled by a meta scheduler.

The solution allows for dispatching of multiple simultaneous data processing tasks from within the query processor (i.e. SQL level) by performing simple calls through a user defined function (UDF) mechanism. At the completion of these tasks, their results become available within the actual data layer, ready for further processing. The interaction between the data layer and compute grid is composed of two elements: job submission control and data placement/replication. Job submission is initiated in the database and forwarded to the main computation grid through a webservice interface exposing the main grid scheduling control knobs. This interaction is enabled by user defined functions (UDF) within DB2, (constructs present also in a majority of big-vendor DBMS solutions including DB2 [6], Oracle [9] and SQL Server [8]).

The grid scheduler controls are exposed through a webservice interface. This is achieved through the XML Extender [7] and its SOAP messaging capabilities which allows the invocation of job submission methods exposed by the schedulers in the compute grid layer (see Figure 1 (a)). The invocation is asynchronous so as to not block the calling thread and to allow actual parallelism in data processing. While extensive details are out of the current scope, for illustration purposes, let us discuss here the query in Figure 2 (a).

After the initial aggregation step (performed by $agg()$) the resulting computations are outsourced to the grid (grouped by customer, $c\_id$) through the $analysis\_grid()$

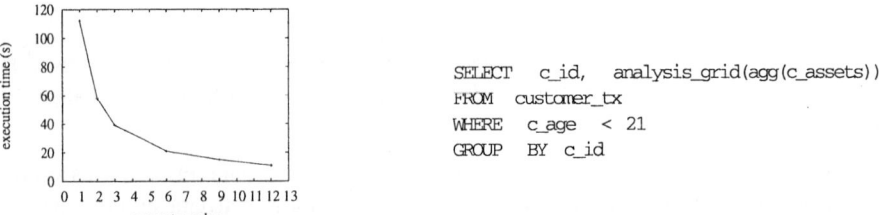

**Fig. 2.** (a) With increasing number of computation nodes, query execution time decreases. (b) Sample Query.

UDF. This constructs the necessary SOAP envelopes, converts the arguments to a serializable format and invokes the grid scheduler with two parameters for each customer: (i) an URL reference to the external regression analysis code (located in the grid code-base, see Figure 1 (b)) and (ii) a reference to the aggregate input data.

There are two alternatives for data transfer to/from the compute grid: *inline* (as an actual parameter in the job submission – suitable for small amounts of input data and close local clusters) and *by-reference* where actual input data sources are identified as part of the job submission – suitable for massive data processing in a global grid. To support the input/output data by reference paradigm, in our design data replication is activated by the meta-scheduler at the grid cluster level, leveraging "close" data stores and linking in with data replication/placement mechanisms (Information Integration [5]) if the data is "far" (see Figure 1 (b)).

**Computation Layer.** XG is a grid management solution designed for tight data-layer integration. It enables a hierarchical grid structure of individual fast(er)-bus compute clusters (at the extreme just a single machine). This design derived from the insight that (arguably) a majority of grid infra-structures are to be composed of multiple high-speed cluster networks linked by lower speed inter-networks. Designing an awareness of this clustering structure in the actual grid allows for location-based scheduling and associated data integration and replication algorithms.

The grid hierarchy is supported by the concept of a meta-scheduler, (Figure 1 (b)) a software entity able to control a set of other individual (meta)schedulers in a hierarchical fashion, composing a multi-clustered architecture. Job submission at any entry-point in this hierarchy results in an execution in the corresponding connected subtree (or sub-graph). At the cluster level a scheduler is managing a set of *computation nodes*. A node is composed (among others) of an Execution Engine and an Execution Monitor.

The scheduler deploys a discovery protocol for automatic discovery of available compute resources, a polling mechanism for monitoring job progress and notifications for job rescheduling (e.g., in case of failures) and a scheduling algorithm for job scheduling. The scheduling algorithm is designed as a plugin within the scheduler, allowing for different scheduling policies to be hot- swapped. For inter-operability, at all levels, the schedulers are designed be invoked (e.g. for job scheduling) through a web-service interface. This interface allows for job submission (with both inline and by-reference data), job monitoring and result retrieval among others. More details are out of scope here.

**Results.** Our experimental test-bed consists of a grid cluster composed of 70 general purpose 1.2GHz Linux boxes with approximately 256MB of RAM each. The data layer deploys IBM DB2 ver. 8.2. with the XML Extender [7] enabled. We evaluated the actual speed-ups of the model generation process with increasing number of grid nodes. Figure 2 (b) illustrates a data mining scenario (for 100 customer profiling jobs) for which execution time went down from roughly 112 seconds for one compute node, to about 11 seconds when 12 nodes where deployed. The deployed code in both the data layer and the grid remained the same. What changed was just the availability of new computation power on the grid side.

## 4 Conclusions

In this work we introduced a novel architecture for data processing, a functional fusion between a data and a computation layer. We then experimentally showed how our solution can be leveraged for significant benefits in data processing jobs such as data analysis and mining over large data sets.

There are significant open avenues for future research including: the integration of a message passing interface solution in the compute grid, more complex failure recovery augmented by check-pointing, the implementation of privacy-preserving primitives for data processing, the exploration of both data placement and computation scheduling as first class citizens in resource scheduling. This becomes especially relevant in on-demand environments where a maximal throughput in data and compute intensive application is not possible using current manual data partitioning and staging methods. Last but not least, we believe *grid-aware query processing* to be an exciting avenue for future research, ultimately resulting in a computation aware grid query optimizer within a traditional DBMS query processor.

## References

1. The Condor Project. Online at http://www.cs.wisc.edu/condor.
2. The Global Grid Forum. Online at http://www.gridforum.org.
3. The Globus Alliance. Online at http://www.globus.org.
4. The Grid Physics Network. Online at http://www.griphyn.org.
5. The IBM DB2 Information Integrator. Online at http://www.ibm.com/software/data/integration.
6. The IBM DB2 Universal Database. Online at http://www.ibm.com/software/data/db2.
7. The IBM DB2 XML Extender. Online at http://www.ibm.com/software/data/db2/extenders/xmlext.
8. The Microsoft SQL Server. Online at http://www.microsoft.com/sql.
9. The Oracle Database. Online at http://www.oracle.com/database.
10. The Particle Physics Data Grid. Online at http://www.ppdg.net.
11. Julie Ratner. *Human Factors and Web Development, Second Edition.* Lawrence Erlbaum Associates, 2002.
12. Radu Sion, Ramesh Natarajan, Inderpal Narang, Wen-Syan Li, and Thomas Phan. XG: A Data-driven Computation Grid for Enterprise-Scale Mining. In *Proceedings of the International Conference on Database and Expert Systems Applications DEXA*, 2005.

# Managing and Querying Versions of Multiversion Data Warehouse

Robert Wrembel and Tadeusz Morzy

Poznań University of Technology,
Institute of Computing Science, Poznań, Poland
{Robert.Wrembel, Tadeusz.Morzy}@cs.put.poznan.pl

## 1 Introduction

A data warehouse (DW) is a database that integrates external data sources (EDSs) for the purpose of advanced data analysis. The methods of designing a DW usually assume that a DW has a static schema and structures of dimensions. In practice, schema and dimensions' structures often change as the result of the evolution of EDSs, changes of the real world represented in a DW, new user requirements, new versions of software being installed, and system tuning activities. Examples of various change scenarios can be found in [1, 8].

Handling schema and dimension changes is often supported by schema evolution [2], temporal extensions [3, 8, 5, 10, 7], and versioning extensions [6]. Schema evolution approaches maintain one DW schema and the set of data that evolve in time. Temporal versioning techniques use timestamps on modified data in order to create temporal versions. In versioning extensions, a DW evolution is managed partially by means of schema versions and partially by data versions. These approaches solve the DW evolution problem partially. Firstly, they do not offer a clear separation between different DW states. Secondly, the approaches do not support modeling alternative, hypothetical DW states required for a *what-if* analysis. In order to eliminate the limitations of the aforementioned approaches, we propose a *multiversion data warehouse*.

## 2 Multiversion Data Warehouse - Supported Features

The *multiversion data warehouse* (MVDW) serves as a framework for: (1) separating various structures and contents of a DW, corresponding to various time periods; (2) creating and managing multiple alternative virtual business scenarios, required for the *what-if* analysis; (3) running queries addressing either a single or multiple DW versions [1].

**Concept.** The MVDW is composed of persistent versions, each of which describes a DW schema and data within a given time period. A *DW version* is in turn composed of a schema version and an instance version. A *schema version* describes the structure of a DW, whereas an *instance version* represents the set of data described by its schema version. Both of them are valid within a certain period of time, represented by validity timestamps. We distinguish real and alternative versions. *Real versions* are used for representing changes in a real business environment, e.g. changing organizational structures, changing geographical borders of regions. Real versions are linearly ordered by the time they are valid within. *Alternative versions* represent virtual business scenarios and are used for simulation purposes. All DW versions form a version derivation graph whose root is the first real version.

**Schema and Dimension Structure Changes.** The structure of a schema version and dimensions is modified by the set of operations that include among others: creating/modifying/dropping/renaming fact and level tables, adding/modifying/dropping/renaming attributes, inserting/updating/deleting fact and dimension records, splitting/merging/reclassifying dimension records.

**Data Sharing.** Multiple DW versions may partially use the same sets of data e.g., two real versions may use the same dimension. In order to eliminate data redundancy and reduce data volume, our prototype system applies data sharing. To this end, an information about all DW versions a given record belongs to is stored with this record in the form of bitmaps. A single bitmap represents one DW version. The number of bitmaps equals to the number of versions sharing data. The number of bits in a bitmap equals to the number of records in a given table. The $i^{th}$ bit in bitmap describing version $V_m$, is set to 1 if the $i^{th}$ record in the table exists in $V_m$. Otherwise the bit is set to 0.

**Querying Multiple DW Versions.** In a MVDW, data of a user's interest are usually distributed among several versions and a user may not be aware of the location of particular data. Moreover, DW versions addressed in queries may differ with respect to their schemata. For the purpose of querying a MVDW we proposed an extension to a standard SQL language that allows to: (1) address either a single version (further called a single-version query - SVQ) or multiple versions (further called a multi-version query - MVQ), (2) present results from various DW versions as if they belonged to a selected DW version, c.f. [9].

A user expresses a MVQ in terms of a selected schema version (usually the current real one), then a MVQ is processed by the parser and executor in the following steps. *St1: Constructing the set of DW versions* that are to be addressed in a MVQ - to this end version validity timestamps are used. *St2: Decomposing MVQ* into $n$ SVQs taking into account schema changes (e.g. domain, attribute name, and table name changes). Each of SVQs addresses its own DW version. *St3: Executing SVQs* in their own DW versions. *St4: Returning results* of every SVQs to a user and presenting them separately. Additionally, every result set is annotated with: (1) information about a DW version the result was obtained from, (2) meta information about schema (e.g. attribute/table renaming, attribute domain modification) and dimension instance changes (e.g. reclassifying, splitting, or merging dimension records) between adjacent DW versions addressed by a MVQ. This meta information allows to analyze and interpret the obtained data appropriately. *St5: Integrating SVQ results* into one common data set (if possible). This set is represented in a DW version specified by a user (the current real version by default). The integration will not be possible if, for example, some attributes are missing in some queried DW versions.

**Transactional Maintenance.** A MVDW is maintained by transactions in order to assure the consistency of its schema and data versions. To this end, we use four basic types of transactions. A *versioning transaction* is responsible for deriving a new DW version. A *schema transaction* is responsible for modifying a schema version. A *data refreshing transaction* is responsible for loading/refreshing fact and dimension level tables. A *user transaction* is applied to analytical processing by end users. The isolation of these transactions is achieved by a standard multiversion concurrency control algorithm.

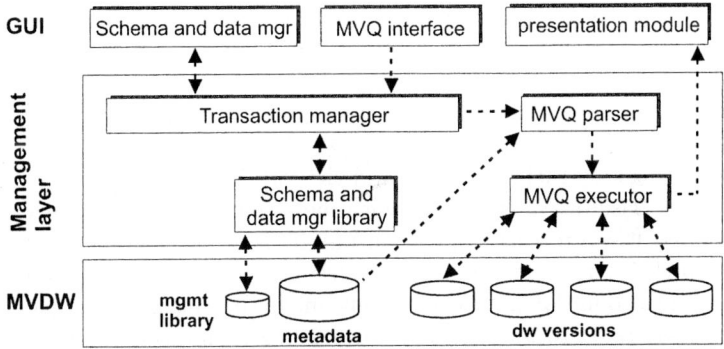

**Fig. 1.** The software architecture of the MVDW prototype

**Metadata Management.** In order to provide schema and data versioning and querying a MVDW, the set of well defined metadata is required. Our system manages metadata on: (1) the structure and content of every DW version, (2) changes applied between adjacent versions, (3) data conversion methods - which are required for MVQs, (4) transactions run in the system.

**Prototype Architecture and Implementation.** Our MVDW has been implemented as a middle layer (cf. Figure 1) on top of Oracle10g DBMS that stores metadata, versions of data, and the library of the system's management software. A user operates on a MVDW by means of a graphical interface implemented in Java. It makes available tools for managing multiversion schema and data, executing multiversion queries, and presenting their results. The middle management layer is composed of four main software modules, i.e. transaction manager, schema and data manager, MVQ parser, and MVQ executor.

## 3 Prototype Demonstration

The demonstration of the prototype MVDW will focus on: (1) showing how multiple DW versions are derived and managed, (2) applying schema and dimension modification operations to selected DW versions, (3) demonstrating how queries can address multiple DW version that differ with respect to their schemata and dimension structures, (4) demonstrating how results of MVQs are visualized and how the results are annotated with meta information, (5) populating DW versions with data and explaining data sharing between multiple DW versions.

## 4 Contribution

To the best of our knowledge, our MVDW prototype is the first system that supports changes not only to the structure of dimensions but also to the structure of a DW schema. Real DW versions can also be used for storing versions of data only, and in this case our MVDW offers the functionality identical to temporal systems. Alternative DW versions are used for simulation purposes within the *what-if* analysis. By physically separating DW versions, one can clearly distinguish between different states of reality or simulation scenarios. A user can query only versions of interest, thus limiting the searched volume of data. Our implementation of a multiversion query language allows to query DW versions that differ with respect to their schemata and the structure of dimensions [9]. Additionally, query results are annotated with meta information on changes applied to the queried DW versions, which is a unique feature. This meta information allows to interpret the obtained results correctly. Changes made between DW versions are traced in the metaschema, but unlike the lineage techniques e.g., [4], our prototype allows to manage the provenience of data and schema elements only inside the MVDW.

## References

1. Bębel B., Eder J., Koncilia Ch., Morzy T., Wrembel R.: Creation and Management of Versions in Multiversion Data Warehouse. Proc. of ACM SAC, Cyprus, 2004
2. Blaschka M., Sapia C., Höfling G.: On Schema Evolution in Multidimensional Databases. Proc. of DaWak, Italy, 1999
3. Chamoni, P., Stock, S.: Temporal Structures in Data Warehousing. Proc. of DaWaK, Italy, 1999
4. Cui Y., Widom J.: Lineage Tracing for General Data Warehouse Transformations. Proc. of VLDB, 2001
5. Eder J., Koncilia C., Morzy T.: The COMET Metamodel for Temporal Data Warehouses. Proc. of CAISE, Canada, 2002
6. Golfarelli M., Lechtenbörger J., Rizzi S., Vossen G.: Schema Versioning in Data Warehouses. Proc. of ER Workshops, China, 2004
7. Microsoft ImmortalDB. Retrieved November 25, 2005 from http://research.microsoft.com/db/ImmortalDB/
8. Mendelzon A.O., Vaisman A.A.: Temporal Queries in OLAP. Proc. of VLDB, Egypt, 2000
9. Morzy T., Wrembel R.: On Querying Versions of Multiversion Data Warehouse. Proc. of DOLAP, USA, 2004
10. Salzberg B., Jiang L., Lomet D., Barrena M., Shan J., Kanoulas E.: A Framework for Access Methods for Versioned Data. Proc. of EDBT, 2004

# Natix Visual Interfaces

A. Böhm*, M. Brantner**, C-C. Kanne,
N. May, and G. Moerkotte

University of Mannheim, Germany
{alex, msb, cc, norman, moer}@pi3.informatik.uni-mannheim.de

**Abstract.** We present the architecture of Natix V2. Among the features of this native XML Data Store are an optimizing XPath query compiler and a powerful API. In our demonstration we explain this API and present XPath evaluation in Natix using its visual explain facilities.

## 1 The Natix System

The Natix Project [3] was among the first to realize the idea of a native XML Data Store (XDS), which supports XML processing down to the deep levels of storage and query execution engine. Such native XDSs are now also being introduced by major database vendors [1]. Natix Version 2.0 provides most features of a native, enterprise-class XDS to application programmers, e.g. ACID transactions, efficient processing of XPath 1.0, and a rich set of APIs. Fig. 1 shows the modules contained in the Natix C++ library.

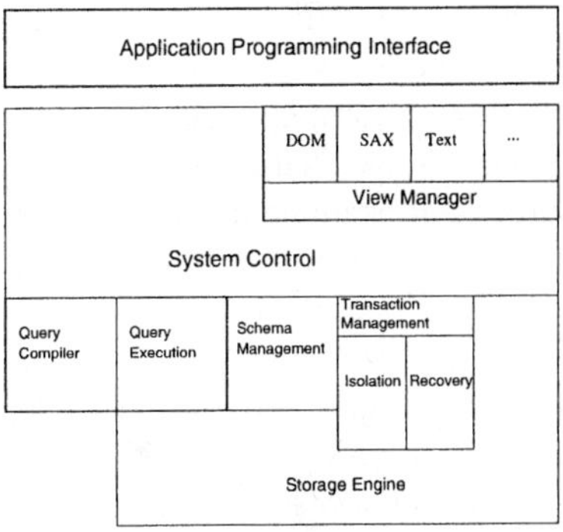

**Fig. 1.** Natix architecture

Applications use Natix' *schema management* facilities to organize their persistent XML data collections. The topmost organizational unit is the Natix *instance*. System parameters, such as main memory buffer sizes, are instance-specific. Both transaction and crash recovery operate at the instance level. Therefore, all operations of a particular transaction must be executed within the context of a single instance. Each instance consists of several *repositories* that contain documents of a particular application domain. For example, the product catalog of an online shop could be stored within one repository, while another one would be used for the business reports. A repository comprises *document collections*. Document collections represent an unordered set of related documents, typically having a similar structure and markup, although they are not required to conform to a conjoint schema. Applica-

---

\* This work was supported by Landesgraduiertenförderung Baden-Württemberg.
\*\* This work was supported by the Deutsche Forschungsgemeinschaft under grant MO 507/10-1.

Y. Ioannidis et al. (Eds.): EDBT 2006, LNCS 3896, pp. 1125–1129, 2006.
© Springer-Verlag Berlin Heidelberg 2006

tions use this hierarchy level for grouping documents together that are processed as a unit, for example, all items belonging to a particular commodity group of an online shop.

## 2 Application Programming Interface

Programming convenience, flexibility, and high performance are crucial for developing universal data management applications. Below, we describe the concepts that enable the Natix API to satisfy these requirements. Natix provides a variety of language bindings for the concepts. We present the C++ binding as an example.

### 2.1 Concepts

The Natix API [4] allows accessing and manipulating entities on all levels of the logical hierarchy through *request* objects. To perform a database operation, an application creates a request object and and forwards it to the system. Instance-level operations such as instance creation and destruction are performed by sending requests to the instance, while transaction-level operations are performed by sending them to corresponding transaction objects.

The API uses *fragments* as an abstract representation of all XML data that is handled by the Natix system. Fragments are an analogy to UNIX file descriptors, which provide a uniform interface to a variety of physical objects such as files, sockets, memory regions, etc. Natix fragments provide a uniform interface to a variety of XML data sources, for example documents stored in Natix, documents stored in the file system, entire document collections, or query results.

Another important concept are *views*. Generally, there are many ways to represent and access XML data, such as the DOM and the SAX API, each of them having their particular benefits and drawbacks depending on the requirements of the respective application. In order to provide maximum flexibility, Natix implements many different interfaces for accessing XML data. To access an XML data source through a particular API, the application opens a corresponding view on a fragment. The current Natix release includes, among others, views for both the DOM and the SAX API, a C++ stream interface, a document metadata view and various sequence views for iterating over elements contained in an organizational unit (for example, all documents of a particular collection).

The convenience and flexibility of the fragment/view concept is complemented by an efficient implementation mechanism. Natix uses a fragment/view matrix to obtain the most efficient implementation of a particular API for a given fragment type. For example, when accessing a document in the file system using a DOM view, a conventional parser is used to create a main-memory DOM representation. In contrast, if a DOM view is requested for a document stored in Natix, an object manager will make sure that only those parts that are actually required by the application are loaded from secondary storage, thereby reducing main memory consumption and avoiding unnecessary I/O overhead. As another example, if a SAX view is opened for a query result, the SAX events can be returned to the application in a pipelined fashion while the query is being evaluated.

## 2.2 C++ Language Binding

We will illustrate the Natix binding for C++ on the basis of the evaluation of XPath queries[1]. Two queries will be used as examples, one for selecting the book with the specific id (`//book[@id='2342']`) from a particular book collection, the other one for gathering all invoices that exceed a specific amount (`/invoice[sum(item/@price) > 200]`) from a document collection.

As proposed by the W3C, query execution in Natix is divided into two phases. We distinguish between a static and a dynamic evaluation phase. During the static phase, the query is compiled and prepared to be executed. A static query context is provided, which allows passing parameters to the compilation process. After the query is successfully prepared, it can be executed. A dynamic query context defines the environment for query execution, in particular the context item (e.g. a document or a collection). Figure 2 shows a few lines of code for executing a query on a single document. At the end, a DOMView

```
// start the transaction
Transaction trans(inst);

// create the query
QueryHandle queryHandle =
  CreateQueryTidy(trans,
                  "//book[@id='2342']");

// prepare the query
PrepareQueryTidy(trans, queryHandle);

// execute it and get a fragment
FragmentDescriptor queryResult =
  ExecuteQueryTidy(trans, queryHandle,
                   "store", "books",
                   "document.xml");

OpenViewTidy<natix::DOMView>
  domView(trans, queryResult);

xercesc::DOMNode *node=domView->getNode();
```

**Fig. 2.** Example for the query API

provides a DOM representation of the requested book element. Note that the actual DOMNode object returned by the DOMView is a binary compatible instance of the C++ DOM binding of Xerces C++ [5].

Executing the second example query on all invoices in one collection and opening a DocumentSequenceView would return an iterator for all qualifying documents.

For programming convenience, the Natix API makes use of several C++ language features such as automatic database resource deallocation when destroying the corresponding objects. In Natix parlance, all of the request objects used in the example are *Tidy* requests, which means that they free any resources when they are destroyed, for example if an exception has been raised.

## 3 Executing XPath Queries in Natix

Next, we give an overview of efficient and scalable XPath query compilation and evaluation. During this process an XPath query runs through different stages. Natix offers one visual explain facility for each of the following three steps of the compilation process.[2]

---

[1] The interface is capable of handling additional query languages such as XQuery or XSLT.
[2] The tool used to trace the compilation process in the demonstration is also available online at http://pi3.informatik.uni-mannheim.de/xpc.html

The result of the first stage — after parsing and normalizing the query — is an internal expression representation. It precisely describes the structure of a query, e.g. relationships between expressions or classification of predicates.

Continuing with this representation, our process departs from the conventional approach of interpreting XPath and enters the realm of algebraic query evaluation. For every expression we apply translation rules that yield an operator tree as a result. Figure 3 shows an operator tree for the first example query.

Besides special operators like unnestmap ($\Upsilon$), this plan uses well-known operators such as a selection ($\sigma$), or aggregation ($\mathcal{A}$). The detailed translation process is described in [2].

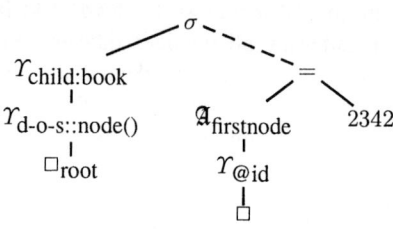

**Fig. 3.** Query evaluation plan

This *query execution plan* (QEP), which is a physical algebra plan, specifies detailed rules for evaluating the query. The last step is called *code generation* and produces code that can be evaluated efficiently in the *Natix runtime system* (RTS). The RTS implements a full-featured algebra as introduced in [2]. To provide scalability all sequence-valued algebra operators are implemented as iterators. The subscripts of these operators are implemented using assembler-like programs that are interpreted by the *Natix virtual machine* (NVM). These provide mechanisms to access the persistent representation of documents in the Natix page buffer or provide comparison and string functions.

## 4 Demonstration

Our demonstration consists of two main components: (1) We provide guidance of how to build XML applications and how to retrieve XML data using the various interfaces offered by Natix. Using several sample programs and a graphical user interface we demonstrate how to create and manage huge XML repositories. Opening views or executing queries shows a variety of possibilities for efficiently accessing the stored data. (2) We explain the internals of the XPath query compiler using the various graphical representations of query plans that are provided by Natix. Several example queries from, for instance, the XMark benchmark help to understand and interpret the facets of our XPath compiler after every compilation step using the different visual explain facilities. The resulting query evaluation plans provide deep insight into the Natix query execution engine.

The Natix XDS is available for download at [4].

## References

1. K. S. Beyer, R. Cochrane, V. Josifovski, J. Kleewein, G. Lapis, G. M. Lohman, B. Lyle, F. Ozcan, H. Pirahesh, N. Seemann, T. C. Truong, B. Van der Linden, B. Vickery, and C. Zhang. System RX: One Part Relational, One Part XML. In *Proc. SIGMOD Conference*, pages 347–358, 2005.

2. M. Brantner, C-C. Kanne, S. Helmer, and G. Moerkotte. Full-fledged Algebraic XPath Processing in Natix. In *Proc. ICDE Conference*, pages 705–716, 2005.
3. T. Fiebig, S. Helmer, C-C. Kanne, G. Moerkotte, J. Neumann, R. Schiele, and T. Westmann. Anatomy of a native xml base management system. *VLDB Journal*, 11(4):292–314, 2002.
4. Chair of Practical Computer Science III. *Natix Manual*. University of Mannheim, 2005. http://pi3.informatik.uni-mannheim.de/natix.html.
5. Apache XML Project. Xerces C++ parser. Project Web Site, 2002.

# Hermes - A Framework for Location-Based Data Management[*]

Nikos Pelekis, Yannis Theodoridis,
Spyros Vosinakis, and Themis Panayiotopoulos

Dept of Informatics, University of Piraeus, Greece
{npelekis, ytheod, spyrosv, themisp}@unipi.gr
http://isl.cs.unipi.gr/db

**Abstract.** The aim of this paper is to demonstrate Hermes, a robust framework capable of aiding a spatio-temporal database developer in modeling, constructing and querying a database with dynamic objects that change location, shape and size, either discretely or continuously in time. Hermes provides spatio-temporal functionality to state-of-the-art Object-Relational DBMS (ORDBMS). The prototype has been designed as an extension of STAU [6], which provides data management infrastructure for historical moving objects, so as to additionally support the demands of real time dynamic applications (e.g. Location-Based Services - LBS). The produced type system is packaged and provided as a data cartridge using the extensibility interface of Oracle10g. The offspring of the above framework extends PL/SQL with spatio-temporal semantics. The serviceableness of the resulting query language is demonstrated by realizing queries that have been proposed in [9] as a benchmarking framework for the evaluation of LBS.

## 1 Introduction

In recent years, we have been witnessing the explosion of emerging non-traditional database applications, such as location-based services. The main components of the underlying database of such applications include stationary and moving objects. The so-called Moving Objects Databases (MODs) are (or soon will be) ubiquitous. As the number of mobile commerce or, in general, mobile services, increases rapidly everyday, the need for robust management systems about location data, as well as the analysis of user movements are vital. In this paper, we present the design and implementation issues of a research prototype for efficient location-based data management, called Hermes (the ancient Greek god of Commerce). Hermes can be considered as a MOD management system with emphasis on the peculiarities of MODs, from representation to querying issues. Someone could mention a series of applications of Hermes at various levels in the context of mobile services. For example, Hermes can be used as a plug-in in telecom companies' data warehouses

---

[*] Research partially supported by the Pythagoras EPEAEK II Programme of the Greek Ministry of National Education and Religious Affairs, co-funded by the European Union.

that include spatio-temporal content. The previous example refers to offline processing of such historical data. Besides, Hermes supports the data management of real-time mobile services, addressing the issues of modern dynamic applications. For instance, imagine a user (tourist, consumer) moving around a city equipped with a next-generation mobile terminal (e.g. 3G cell-phone or PDA enhanced by the presence of a GPS receiver), receiving hints of information, commercial spots etc. Researchers [1], [2], [3], [4], motivated from such kind of application scenarios have tried to model spatio-temporal databases using this concept of moving objects and integrate them into any extensible DBMS. On the other hand, commercial relational or object-relational database systems offer limited capability of handling this kind of non-traditional data (object trajectories, in time and space). Hermes is the partial realization of the above discussed research vision.

## 2 The Prototype

Hermes is developed as a system extension that provides spatio-temporal functionality to Oracle10g's Object-Relational Database Management System (ORDBMS). The system is designed in a way that it can be used either as a pure temporal or a pure spatial system, but its main functionality is to support the modelling and querying of continuously moving objects. Such a collection of data types and their corresponding operations are defined, developed and provided as an Oracle data cartridge. *Hermes Moving Data Cartridge* (*Hermes-MDC*) is the core component of the Hermes system architecture. *Hermes-MDC* provides the functionality to construct a set of moving, expanding and/or shrinking geometries, as well as time-varying base types. Each one of these moving objects is supplied with a set of methods that facilitate the cartridge user to query and analyze spatio-temporal data. Embedding this functionality offered by *Hermes-MDC* in Oracle's DML [5], one obtains an expressive and easy to use query language for moving objects.

In order to implement such a framework in the form of a data cartridge we exploit a set of standard data types together with the static spatial data types offered by the *Spatial* option of Oracle10g [5] and the temporal literal types introduced in a temporal data cartridge, called *TAU Temporal Literal Library Data Cartridge* (TAU-TLL) [6]. Based on these temporal and spatial object data types *Hermes-MDC* defines a series of moving object data types illustrated in the UML class diagram of Figure 1 The interested reader in a detailed discussion for the resulted type system is referred to [7].

## 3 Architecture of Hermes

Figure 2 illustrates the architecture of the Hermes system. A straightforward utilization scenario for a Hermes-MDC user is to design and construct a spatio-temporal object-relational database schema and build an application by transacting with this database. In this case, where the underlying ORDBMS is Oracle10g, in order to specify the database schema, the database designer writes scripts in the syntax of the *Data Definition Language* (DDL), which is the PL/SQL, extended with the spatio-temporal operations previously mentioned.

To build an application on top of such a database for creating objects, querying data and manipulating information, the application developer writes a source program in *Java* wherein he/she can embed *PL/SQL scripts* that invoke object constructors and methods from Hermes-MDC. The *JDBC pre-processor* integrates the power of the programming language with the database functionality offered by the extended PL/SQL and together with the *ORDBMS Runtime Library* generate the application's executable. By writing independent stored procedures that take advantage of Hermes functionality and by compiling them with the *PL/SQL Compiler*, is another way to build a spatio-temporal application.

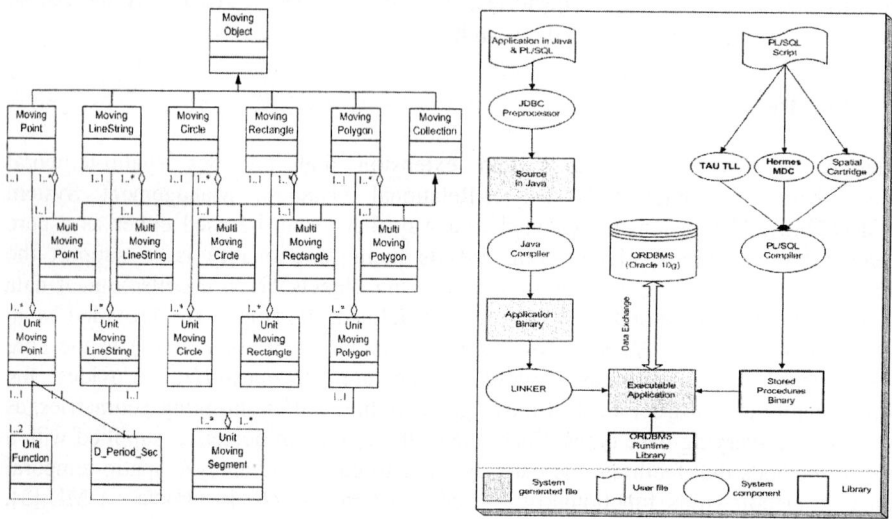

**Fig. 1.** Hermes-MDC Class Diagram     **Fig. 2.** The architecture of Hermes

## 4 The Demonstration Scenario

In order to demonstrate the usefulness and applicability of the server-side extensions provided by Hermes we implement the majority of the benchmark queries for LBS proposed in [9]. Additionally, we specially develop an LBS application scenario for travellers entering the area of an airport, construct a spatial database modeling the ground plan of the airport, and input random trajectories of travellers moving around the area. Then, we pose queries following the same classification as proposed in [9]. Indicative examples include:

- *Queries on stationary reference objects*; examples include point (e.g. does this check-in serve my flight?), range (e.g. are there any fellow travellers in the area in front of this check-in?), distance-based (e.g. find the closer check-in), nearest-neighbor (e.g. find the closest coffee shops to my current location) and topological queries (e.g. find travellers crossed this gate during the past hour);

- *Queries on moving reference objects*; examples include distance-based (e.g. find travellers passed close to me this evening) and similarity-based queries (e.g. find the three most similar trajectories to the one I have followed so far in the airport);
- *Join queries*; examples include distance-join (find the closest check-ins to travellers of this flight) and similarity-join queries (find the two most similar pairs of travellers' trajectories);
- *Queries involving unary operators*, such as travelled distance or speed (e.g. find the average speed of travellers on Saturday nights).

Based on related research work [8] the above queries constitute a minimum functionality a MOD system should provide. The above demonstration scenario is also accompanied (wherever appropriate) by visual illustrations formulated by MapViewer [5] (see Figure 3).

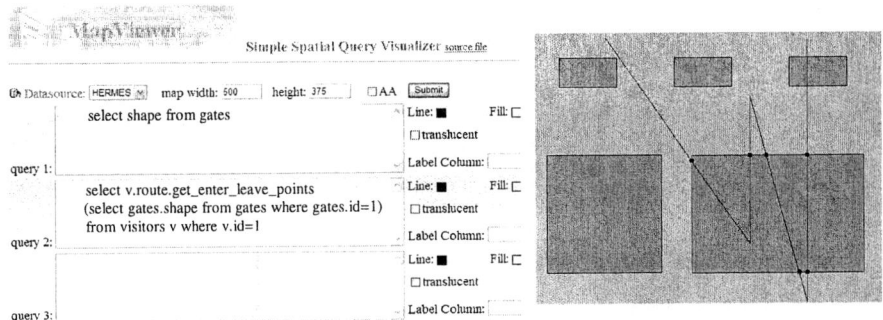

**Fig. 3.** Visualization of entry and exit points in an area of interest

## 5 Conclusions

In this paper, the Hermes prototype system was introduced. Hermes has been designed as a system extension that provides spatio-temporal functionality to state-of-the-art ORDBMS. The usability of the prototype is demonstrated by applying benchmark queries proposed for the evaluation of systems providing location based services. Future work includes knowledge discovery from MODs. Typical examples we plan to incorporate in Hermes framework are: 'characterization of routes as (in)frequent', 'habits in motion with respect to space and/or time constraints' etc.

## References

1. S. Dieker and R. H. Guting, "Plug and Play with Query Algebras: Secondo. A Generic DBMS Development Environment", In *Proc. of the Int. Database Engineering and Applications Symposium (IDEAS)*, p. 380-390, 2000.
2. M. Erwig, R.H. Guting, M. Schneider, and M. Vazirgiannis, "Spatio-Temporal Data Types: An Approach to Modelling and Querying Moving Objects in Databases", *GeoInformatica*, 3(3):265-291, 1999.

3. L. Forlizzi, R. H. Guting, E. Nardelli, M. Schneider, "A Data Model and Data Structures for Moving Objects Databases", In *Proc. ACM SIGMOD Intl. Conf. on Management of Data*, pages 319-330, 2000.
4. R.H. Guting, M. H. Bohlen, M. Erwig, C. S. Jensen, N. A. Lorentzos, M. Schneider, and M. Vazirgiannis, "A Foundation for Representing and Querying Moving Objects", *ACM Transactions on Database Systems*, 25(1):1-42, 2000.
5. Oracle Corp. *Oracle®*. Oracle Database Documentation Library, 10g Release 1 (10.1), URL: http://otn.oracle.com/pls/db10g/.
6. N. Pelekis. STAU: A spatio-temporal extension to ORACLE DBMS, PhD Thesis, UMIST, 2002.
7. N. Pelekis, B. Theodoulidis, Y. Theodoridis and I. Kopanakis. An Oracle Data Cartridge for Moving Objects. UNIPI-ISL-TR-2005-01, March 2005. URL: http://isl.cs.unipi.gr/db.
8. N. Pelekis, B. Theodoulidis, I. Kopanakis and Y. Theodoridis, "Literature Review of Spatio-Temporal Database Models", *Knowledge Engineering Review*, 19(3):235-274, 2005.
9. Y. Theodoridis. "Ten Benchmark Database Queries for Location-based Services", *The Computer Journal*, 46(6):713-725, 2003.

# TeNDaX, a Collaborative Database-Based Real-Time Editor System
## A Word-Processing 'LAN-Party'

Stefania Leone[1], Thomas B. Hodel-Widmer[2],
Michael Boehlen[3], and Klaus R. Dittrich[1]

[1] University of Zurich, Department of Informatics,
Winterthurerstrasse 190, 8057 Zurich, Switzerland
{leone, dittrich}@ifi.unizh.ch
http://www.tendax.net
[2] Swiss Federal Institute of Technology (ETH Zurich),
Leonhardshalde 21, 8092 Zurich, Switzerland
hodel@sipo.gess.ethz.ch
[3] Free University of Bolzano-Bozen, Piazza Domenicani 3,
39100 Bolzano, Italy
boehlen@inf.unibz.it

**Abstract.** TeNDaX is a collaborative database-based real-time editor system. TeNDaX is a new approach for word-processing in which documents (i.e. content and structure, tables, images etc.) are stored in a database in a semi-structured way. This supports the provision of collaborative editing and layout, undo- and redo operations, business process definition and execution within documents, security, and awareness. During document creation process and use meta data is gathered automatically. This meta data can then be used for the TeNDaX dynamic folders, data lineage, visual- and text mining and search.

We present TeNDaX as a word-processing 'LAN-Party': collaborative editing and layout; business process definition and execution; local and global undo- and redo operations; all based on the use of multiple editors and different operating systems. In a second step we demonstrate how one can use the data and meta data to create dynamic folders, visualize data provenance, carry out visual- and text mining and support sophisticated search functionality.

## 1 Introduction

Text documents are a valuable resource for virtually any enterprise and organization. Documents like papers, reports and general business documentations contain a large part of (business) knowledge. Documents are mostly stored in a hierarchical folder structure on file servers and it is difficult to organize them with regard to classification, versioning etc., although it is of utmost importance that users can find, retrieve and edit documents in a user-friendly way.

In most of the commonly used word-processing applications documents can be manipulated by only one user at a time and tools for collaborative document editing and management are rarely deployed. Documents should be seen as a valuable business asset which requires an appropriate data management solution. The need to store, retrieve and edit these documents collaboratively with guaranteed mechanisms for security, consistency, availability and access control is obvious.

In the following, we present the database-based TeNDaX editor system which enables collaborative document editing and management, all within a interactive multi-user database environment.

## 2 The TeNDaX Editor System

TeNDaX stands for a Text Native Database eXtension. It enables the storage of text in databases in a native form so that text editing is finally represented as real-time transactions. Under the term 'text editing' we understand the following: writing and deleting text (characters), copying and pasting, defining layout and structure, inserting notes, setting access rights, defining business processes, inserting tables, pictures, and so on, i.e. all the actions regularly carried out by word processing users. By 'real-time transactions' we mean that editing text (e.g. writing a character/word) invokes one or several database transactions so that everything which is typed appears within the editor as soon as these objects are stored persistently. Instead of creating files and storing them in a file system, the content and all of the meta data belonging to the documents is stored in a special way in the database, which enables very fast transactions for all editing tasks [3]. The database schema and the transactions are designed to be used in a multi-user environment, as is customary in the database context. As a consequence, many of the database features (data organization and querying, recovery, integrity and security enforcement, multi-user operation, distribution management, uniform tool access, etc.) are now, by means of this approach, also available for word processing.

TeNDaX creates an extension of DBMS to manage text. This addition is carried out 'cleanly' and the responding data type represents a 'first-class citizen' [1] of a DBMS (e.g. integers, character strings, etc.).

Since the document data is stored in the database, we automatically gather meta data during the whole document creation process [6]. We gain meta data on document level (creator, roles, date and time, document object ID, document names, structure affiliation, note affiliation, security settings, size, authors, readers, state, places within static folders and user defined properties), on character level (author, roles, date and time, copy-paste references, local and global undo / redo, security settings, version and user defined properties) and from structure, template, layout, notes, security and business process definitions.

## 3 Demonstration: Word-Processing 'LAN-Party'

In our word-processing 'LAN-Party' we focus on the TeNDaX editor system. Editors installed on different operating systems (Windows XP, Linux, Mac OSX) will support the demonstration of the following TeNDaX features:

- **Collaborative editing:** We will concurrently work with multiple users on the same document. Editing a document includes operations like writing and deleting characters [4], inserting pictures, creating tables, applying layout and structure [2], local and global undo- and redo operations, setting access rights etc. All these operations are carried out in a dynamic multi-user database environment.
- **Business process definitions and flow:** We will define and run a dynamic workflow within a document for ad-hoc cooperation on that document [5]. Tasks such as translation or verification of a certain document part can be assigned to specific users or roles. The workflow tasks can be created, changed and routed dynamically, i.e. at run-time.
- **Dynamic Folders**: On the base of the automatically gathered document creation process meta data we will build dynamic folders [6]. Dynamic folders are virtual folders that are based on meta data. A dynamic folder can contain all documents a certain user has read within the last week. Its content is fluent and may change within seconds (e.g. as soon as a document changes). This represents a novel method for document management and text retrieval.
- **Data Lineage**: We can display document content provenance. Meta data about all editing and all copy- and paste actions is stored with the document. This includes information about the source of the new document part, e.g. from which other document a text has been copied (either internal or external sources). We use this meta data to visualize data lineage as depicted in Figure 1.
- **Visual Mining**: The information visualization plug-in provides a graphical overview of all documents and offers a variety of interaction modalities. It is possible to navigate the document and meta data dimensions to gain an understanding of the entire document space. A visualization of a set of documents is shown in Figure 2.
- **Search:** The meta data based searching and ranking plug-in offers sophisticated search options. Documents and parts of documents can either be found based on the document content, or structure, or document creation process meta data. The search result can be ranked according to different ranking options, e.g. 'most cited', 'newest' etc.

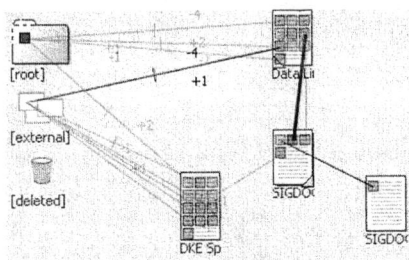
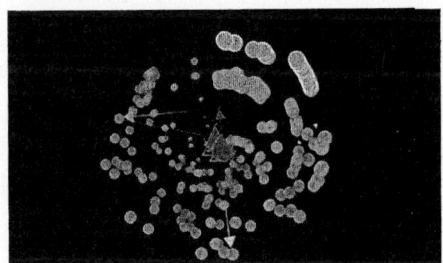

**Fig. 1.** Data Lineage        **Fig. 2.** Visual Mining

## 4 Conclusion

The collaborative database-based real-time TeNDaX editor system enables the storage and management of documents within a database. It natively represents text in fully-fledged databases, and incorporates all necessary collaboration support. It offers functions such as editing, awareness, fine-grained security, sophisticated document management, versioning, business processes, text structure, data lineage, text and visual mining - all within a collaborative multi-user database environment.

Within the above presented TeNDaX editor system we use database technology to provide full word-processing functionality and sophisticated document- and meta data visualization. TeNDaX extends database technology and offers database-based universal data management for text documents.

## References

1. Abiteboul, S., Agrawal, R., Bernstein, P., Carey, M., Ceri, S., Croft, B., DeWitt, D., Franklin, M., Molina, H. G., Gawlick, D., Gray, J., Haas, L., Halevy, A., Hellerstein, J., Ioannidis, Y., Kersten, M., Pazzani, M., Lesk, M., Maier, D., Naughton, J., Schek, H., Sellis, T., Silberschatz, A., Stonebraker, M., Snodgrass, R., Ullman, J., Weikum, G., Widom, J., and Zdonik, S.: The Lowell Database Research Self-Assessment, CACM Vol. 48(5), 111-118 (2005)
2. Hodel, T. B., Businger, D., Dittrich, K. R.: Supporting Collaborative Layouting in Word Processing. IEEE CoopIS (2004) 355–372
3. Hodel, T. B., Dittrich, K. R.: Concept and Prototype of a Collaborative Business Process Environment for Document Processing. Data & Knowledge Engineering, 52, Special Issue: Collaborative Business. Process Technologies (2004) 61–120
4. Hodel, T.B., Dubacher, M., Dittrich, K. R.: Using Database Management Systems for Collaborative Text Editing. ECSCW CEW (2003)
5. Hodel, T.B., Gall, H., Dittrich, K. R.: Dynamic Collaborative Business Process within Documents. ACM SIGDOC (2004) 97–103
6. Hodel, T.B., Hacmac, R., H., Dittrich, K. R.: Using Creation Time Meta Data for Document Management. CAiSE (2005)

# Synopses Reconciliation Via Calibration in the $\tau$-Synopses System

Yariv Matia, Yossi Matias, and Leon Portman

School of Computer Science,
Tel-Aviv University
matiayar@post.tau.ac.il, matias@cs.tau.ac.il,
leon.portman@nice.com

**Abstract.** The $\tau$-Synopses system was designed to provide a run-time environment for multiple synopses. We focus on its utilization for synopses management in a single server. In this case, a critical function of the synopses management module is that of *synopses reconciliation*: given some limited memory space resource, determine which synopses to build and how to allocate the space among those synopses. We have developed a novel approach of *synopses calibration* for an efficient computation of synopses error estimation. Consequently we can now perform the synopses reconciliation in a matter of minutes, rather than hours.

## 1 Introduction

Data synopses are concise representations of data sets, which enable effective processing of approximate queries to the data sets. Recent interest in approximate query processing and in effectively dealing with massive data sets resulted with a proliferation of new synopses.

The $\tau$-Synopses system [6] was designed to provide a run-time environment for local and remote execution of various synopses. It provides the management functionality for registered synopses, and it enables easy registration of new synopses either locally or from remote SOAP-enabled platforms. The $\tau$-Synopses system can serve as an effective research platform for experimental evaluation and comparison of different synopses, as well as a platform for studying the effective management of multiple synopses in a federated or centralized environment.

The system was previously presented in the context of *remote-synopses*, demonstrating how synopses can be managed in a distributed fashion [5]. We now focus our attention on the utilization of the $\tau$-Synopses system for synopses management in a single server. In this case, a critical function of the Synopses Manager module is that of synopses reconciliation: given some limited memory space resource, determine which synopses to build and how to partition the available space among those synopses.

The problem of synopses reconciliation was previously studied and several algorithms were presented (e.g., [3, 2]). A basic operation in all reconciliation algorithms is that of estimating the accuracy of synopses implementations for

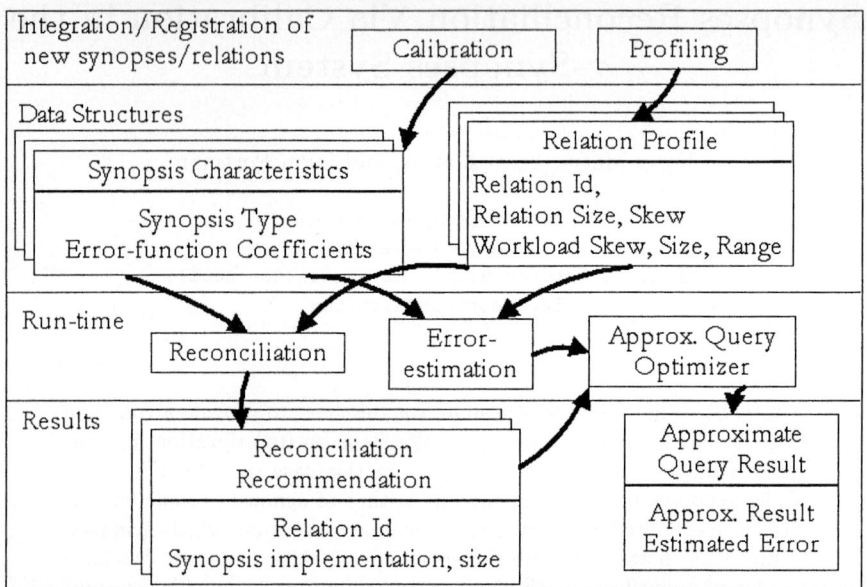

**Fig. 1.** Synopses Manager Architecture

given data sets. The common approach in obtaining such estimation is by invoking expensive queries into the original data. We present a novel approach, in which the reconciliation algorithm can consult with an error-estimation module, which can provide an error estimation without accessing the original data itself. Instead, the error-estimation module computes the synopsis approximation-error based on synopsis characteristics, which are computed by a *calibration* process in integration-time, and statistical data about the data sets, computed by a *profiling* process in registration-time. This results with an effective reconciliation process.

## 2 Synopsis Calibration and Synopses Reconciliation

The *Synopses Manager* module provides an automatic recommendation of which synopses to build and their sizes, based on the available synopses implementations, available memory space, and the registered relations and query workload.

As depicted in Figure 1 the Synopses Manager includes the following types of data structures: (i) *Relation Profile*, which includes statistical information about each registered relation; (ii) *Synopsis Characteristics*, which includes parameters computed at integration time for each synopsis; and (iii) *Reconciliation Recommendation*, which includes the recommendations of synopses to be built for each registered relation. It also includes the following modules: Calibration, Profiling, Error Estimation, Reconciliation, and Approximate Query Optimizer; these modules are described in more details below. A more detailed explanation of the calibration and reconciliation processes can be found in [4].

**The synopsis error-estimation function.** The crux of our approach is a novel calibration technique [4], which associates to every synopsis implementation $T$ an error estimation function, $EE_T$.

We have found, through empirical testing, that the following function quite accurately describes the relative error of synopses implementations w.r.t. their corresponding relations and query workloads:

$$EE_T(L, Z, Q, R, S) = a_1 L^{b_1} + a_2 Z^{b_2} + a_3 Q^{b_3} + a_4 R^{b_4} + a_5 S^{b_5} + a_6 \ .$$

The arguments $L$, $Z$, $Q$, $R$ and $S$, collectively denoted as the *Relation Profile*, are: the relation size ($L$), relation data distribution skew ($Z$), workload query skew ($Q$), workload query range ($R$), and the synopsis size ($S$). The $a_i$ and $b_i$ coefficients, collectively denoted as the *Synopsis Characteristics*, are unique to each synopsis implementation.

**Calibration.** This module is invoked every time a new synopsis implementation $T$ is integrated into the system. The calibration process runs a small number of tests on the synopsis implementation, measuring its behavior under various synthetic relations and workloads. It then derives the $a_i$ and $b_i$ coefficients, of $EE_T$, using a combination of squared linear fitting and the CPLEX commercial solver [1]. The coefficients of the function are stored in the Synopsis Characteristics data structure.

**Error Estimation.** This module is utilized by the Reconciliation and Approximate Query Optimizer modules. Given an approximate query to a relation with synopsis implementation $T$, the module computes the error estimation function $EE_T$ based on the parameters available from the Relation Profile and Synopsis Characteristics data structures, resulting with the estimated approximation-error of the query.

**Approximate Query Optimizer.** This module has two functions: (1) triggers the building of the required synopses based on the recommendations received from the Reconciliation module; and (2) when a user submits an approximate query to the system, this module performs the query on the relevant synopsis, and also invokes the Error-Estimation module, returning both the estimated result, and the estimated approximation-error of the result.

**Profiling.** This module is invoked whenever a new relation or query workload are registered in the system. For relations, this module measures the cardinality of the relation (distinct count), and uses linear-squared-fitting to fit a Zipf parameter to the relation data distribution skew. For query workloads, the number and average range of the queries are calculated, and the Zipf parameter of the query distribution skew is again fitted using linear-squared-fitting. The computed statistical data is stored in the Relation Profile data structure.

**Synopses reconciliation.** Synopses reconciliation is basically an optimization problem – given available synopses implementations, a memory space limit, and a query workload, we would like to know the combination of synopses and their sizes that would yield the minimal error for the entire system.

The Synopses Reconciliation module can accommodate the implementations of any synopses reconciliation algorithm. The module currently has implementations of the algorithms from [3, 2], with the following modification. Whenever the error measurement of a synopsis utilization is required, it uses the Error-Estimation Module, instead of using the straight-forward measurement which involves executing costly queries into the database. The process is invoked on-demand by the administrator, and returns a recommended combination of synopses to build.

Utilizing the same reconciliation algorithms and heuristics as those in [3, 2], but replacing the action of measuring the error with a call to an error-estimation function, significantly reduces the run time of the reconciliation process while maintaining good accuracy.

## 3 System Demonstration

We demonstrate the calibration process for one of these synopses, showing the accuracy of the calculated $EE_T$ function over different relations and workloads. We also demonstrate a full reconciliation process over a complex setup of relations and workloads, showing how a process that would normally take hours to complete, is completed in minutes, and compare its results to those of the optimal combination.

## References

1. iLOG Inc. Ilog cplex 8.0 –user's manual, 2002.
2. H. V. Jagadish, H. Jin, B. C. Ooi, and K. L. Tan. Global optimization of histograms. In *SIGMOD '01*, pages 223–234, 2001.
3. A. C. Koenig and G. Weikum. A framework for the physical design problem for data synopses. In *Proceedings of the 8th International Conference on Extending Database Technology*, pages 627–645, 2002.
4. Y. Matia and Y. Matias. Efficient synopses reconciliation via calibration. Technical report, Tel Aviv University, 2005.
5. Y. Matias and L. Portman. $\tau$-Synopses: a system for run-time management of remote synopses. In *International Conference on Data Engineering (ICDE), Software Demo*, pages 964–865, April 2004.
6. Y. Matias, L. Portman, and N. Drukh. The design and architecture of the $\tau$-Synopses system. In *Proc. EDBT 06', Industrial and Application*, 2006.

# X-Evolution: A System for XML Schema Evolution and Document Adaptation

Marco Mesiti[1], Roberto Celle[2], Matteo A. Sorrenti[1], and Giovanna Guerrini[2]

[1] Università di Milano, Italy
mesiti@dico.unimi.it
[2] Università di Genova, Italy
guerrini@disi.unige.it

## 1 Introduction

The structure of XML documents, expressed as XML schemas [6], can evolve as well as their content. Systems must be frequently adapted to real-world changes or updated to fix design errors and thus data structures must change accordingly in order to address the new requirements. A consequence of schema evolution is that documents instance of the original schema might not be valid anymore. Currently, users have to explicitly revalidate the documents and identify the parts to be updated. Moreover, once the parts that are not valid anymore have been identified, they have to be explicitly updated. All these activities are time consuming and error prone and automatic facilities are required.

A set of primitives that can be applied on an XML schema to evolve its structure has been proposed in [4]. For each primitive we have determined the applicability conditions, that is, when its application produces a schema that is still well-formed. Moreover, we have analyzed when the primitive application alters the validity of the documents instances of the schema. Table 1 reports the evolution primitives classified relying on the object (element, simple type, and complex type) on which they are applied and the kind of operation (insertion, modification, deletion). Primitives marked with "*" do not alter the validity of the document instances. Therefore, their application do not require a revalidation process. Other primitives might only alter the validity of a single element or of a restricted set of elements depending on the schema specification. Therefore, in these cases, the entire revalidation of a document is useless. In [4] we developed an algorithm, based on an element type graph labelling, that minimizes the revalidation process to only the elements affected by the primitives thus making the process more efficient.

A related problem is how to evolve the structure of document instances in order to make them valid for the evolved schema. Suppose to introduce an element in a schema, and this is mandatory for all valid documents. This element should be introduced (maybe with a default or null value) in all the previously valid documents. Suppose now to remove an element from the schema. It should be removed from valid documents. The problem is more complex when the schema modification refers to an operator or to the repeatability of elements, and would often require user intervention. The adaptation process thus

**Table 1.** Evolution primitives

|  | Insertion | Modification | Deletion |
|---|---|---|---|
| Simple Type | $insert\_glob\_simple\_type^*$ $insert\_new\_member\_type^*$ | $change\_restriction$ $change\_base\_type$ $rename\_type^*$ $change\_member\_type$ $global\_to\_local^*$ $local\_to\_global^*$ | $remove\_type^*$ $remove\_member\_type^*$ |
| Complex Type | $insert\_glob\_complex\_type^*$ $insert\_local\_elem$ $insert\_ref\_elem$ $insert\_operator$ | $rename\_local\_elem$ $rename\_global\_type^*$ $change\_type\_local\_elem$ $change\_cardinality$ $change\_operator$ $global\_to\_local^*$ $local\_to\_global^*$ | $remove\_element$ $remove\_operator$ $remove\_substructure$ $remove\_type^*$ |
| Element | $insert\_glob\_elem$ | $rename\_glob\_elem^*$ $change\_type\_glob\_elem$ $ref\_to\_local^*$ $local\_to\_ref^*$ | $remove\_glob\_elem^*$ |

involves subtleties related both to the kind of update performed and to the structure of the updated type. Several updates require the detection of the *minimal substructure* for an element whose insertion is required in documents to validate. Our approach to document adaptation is based on the use of *restructuring structures*, that are an extension of the labelled element type graph employed for document revalidation, in which labels can also be $\Delta_l^\epsilon$, $\Delta_\epsilon^l$, and $\Delta_{l_n}^{l_o}$, with $l, l_n$, and $l_o$ element labels. These structures allow to specify the minimal modifications to be performed on documents invalidated by a schema update and are automatically inferred from the schema update whenever possible (otherwise, user intervention is required). The adaptation process will occur during the revalidation process and the idea is that to validate the special subelement $\Delta_l^\epsilon$, element $l$ should be inserted. Similarly, to validate the special subelements $\Delta_\epsilon^l$ and $\Delta_{l_n}^{l_o}$, element $l$ should be deleted and element $l_o$ should be renamed to $l_n$, respectively.

In this demonstration paper we present X-Evolution, a .NET system developed on top of a commercial DBMS that allows the specification of schema modifications in a graphical representation of an XML schema. It supports facilities for performing schema revalidation only when strictly needed and only on the minimal parts of documents affected from the modifications. Moreover, it supports the adaptation of original schema instances to the evolved schema. The adaptation process is semi-automatic and the required user intervention is minimized. Support is provided to the user for a convenient specification of the required updates.

Commercial tools (e.g. [1, 5]) have been developed for graphically design XML schemas. However, they are not integrated with a DBMS and do not allow the semi-automatic revalidation and adaptation of documents within contained. Schema evolution had been previously investigated for DTDs in [3], where evolution operators were proposed. Problems caused by DTD evolution and the impact on existing documents are however not addressed. Moreover, since DTDs

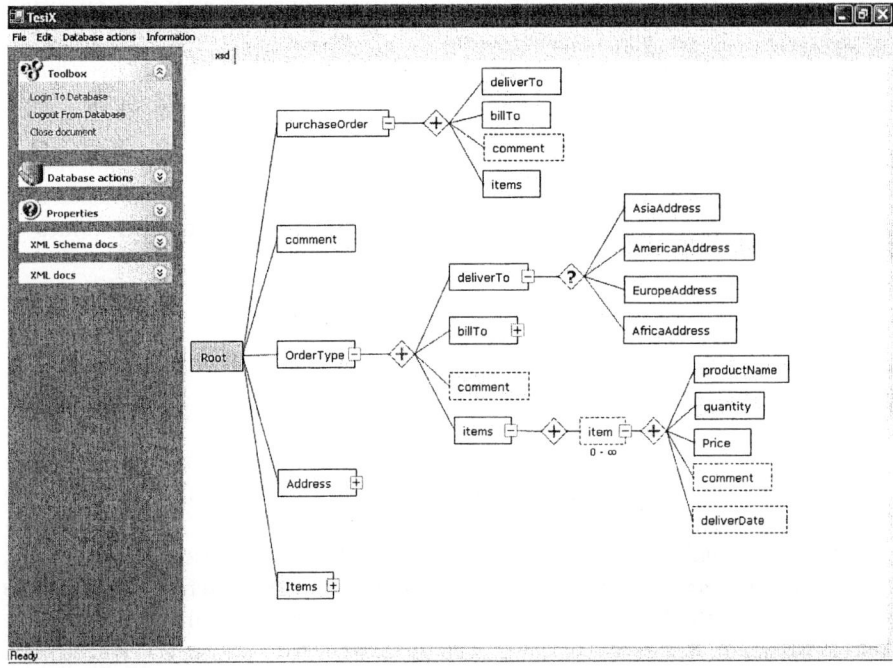

**Fig. 1.** X-Evolution schema modification facility

are considerably simpler than XML Schemas [2] the proposed operators do not cover all the set of schema changes that can occur on an XML Schema.

## 2 X-Evolution Facilities

X-Evolution offers different kind of facilities for handling the evolution of XML schemas, an efficient revalidation of document instances, and the adaptation of document instances to the evolved XML schema.

X-Evolution connects to one or more databases in which the XML schemas and documents are stored. The left side bar of the schema modification facility (Figure 1) presents the identified documents and schemas. Whenever a user clicks on a schema, the system graphically represents the schema and identifies the documents that are valid for such a schema. Whenever a user clicks on a document, the system graphically represents the document and identifies the schemas for which the document is an instance.

By graphically selecting a node of the tree representation of a schema,[1] all the possible schema evolution primitives that can be applied on such a node are visualized. When the user invokes an evolution primitive, X-Evolution

---

[1] Actually a schema should be represented as a direct graph. However, for the sake of readability, we duplicate nodes of the graph with more than one incoming edge.

checks whether the operation can alter the schema consistency. If it is preserved the operation is executed and the evolved schema visualized. Whenever the operation alters (or can alter) the validity of document instances of the schema, X-Evolution points out the documents that are not valid anymore. This operation is performed through an optimized revalidation algorithm detailed in [4]. The user interface helps the user in the adaptation process of non valid documents. For each non valid document the system points out the elements that should be removed or added and allows the specification of default values or structures to be inserted.

## 3 Demonstration

The demonstration of the X-Evolution system consists in four parts.

1. We will show how to connect the graphical interface to a database in which the documents and schemas are stored and how we can easily work with the graphical representation of documents and schemas.
2. We will show how to apply the developed evolution operations on a schema. Specifically, we will show how to construct a schema from scratch and how we can remove all the components from a schema making it an empty schema. Consistency of the resulting schema is checked for each operation, and, if violated, no update is performed.
3. We will show performances of our efficient approach in the revalidation of XML documents against the evolved schema with respect to the naive solution of entirely revalidate the documents instances of the schema.
4. Finally we will show the effectiveness of our adaptation approach by specifying schema modifications and showing the result of the adaptation process.

*Acknowledgement.* The authors wish to thank Daniele Ghelli and Giuseppe Marchi for developing the graphical representation of XML documents and schemas.

## References

1. Altova Inc. XMLSpy, 2005. http://www.altova.com/
2. G.J. Bex, F. Neven, and J. Van den Bussche. DTDs versus XML Schema: A Practical Study. *WebDB*, 79–84, 2004.
3. D. K. Kramer and E. A. Rundensteiner. Xem: XML Evolution Management. *RIDE-DM*, 103–110, 2001.
4. G. Guerrini, M. Mesiti, D. Rossi. Impact of XML Schema Evolution on Valid Documents. In Proc. of WIDM, Germany 2005.
5. Stylus Studio Inc. Stylus XML Editor, 2005. http://www.stylusstudio.com
6. W3C. XML Schema Part 0: Primer, 2001.

# TQuEST: Threshold Query Execution for Large Sets of Time Series

Johannes Aßfalg, Hans-Peter Kriegel, Peer Kröger, Peter Kunath,
Alexey Pryakhin, and Matthias Renz

Institute for Computer Science, University of Munich
{assfalg, kriegel, kroegerp, kunath, pryakhin, renz}@dbs.ifi.lmu.de

**Abstract.** Effective and efficient data mining in time series databases is essential in many application domains as for instance in financial analysis, medicine, meteorology, and environmental observation. In particular, temporal dependencies between time series are of capital importance for these applications. In this paper, we present TQuEST, a powerful query processor for time series databases. TQuEST supports a novel but very useful class of queries which we call *threshold queries*. Threshold queries enable searches for time series whose values are above a user defined threshold at certain time intervals. Example queries are "report all ozone curves which are above their daily mean value at the same time as a given temperature curve exceeds $28°C$" or "report all blood value curves from patients whose values exceed a certain threshold one hour after the new medication was taken". TQuEST is based on a novel representation of time series which allows the query processor to access only the relevant parts of the time series. This enables an efficient execution of threshold queries. In particular, queries can be readjusted with interactive response times.

## 1 Introduction

In this paper, we present TQuEST, a powerful analysis tool for time series databases which supports a novel but very important query type which we call *threshold query*. Given a query time series $q$, a threshold $\tau$, and a time series database $DB$, a threshold query $TQ_{DB}(q, \tau)$ returns the time series $p \in DB$ that has the most similar sequence of intervals of values above $\tau$. In other words, each time series $o \in DB \cup \{q\}$ is transformed into a sequence of disjoint time intervals containing only those values of $o$ that are (strictly) above $\tau$. Then, a threshold query returns for a given query object $q$ the object $p \in DB$ having the most similar sequence of time intervals. Let us note that the exact values of the time series are not considered, rather we are only interested in whether the time series is above or below a given threshold $\tau$. The transformation of the time series into interval sequences is depicted in Figure 1.

Our new query type can for example be applied to pharmacological time series like blood parameters after drug treatment or biological data like gene expression profiles. Another possible application for our tool is the analysis of environmental air pollution which has gained rapidly increasing attention by

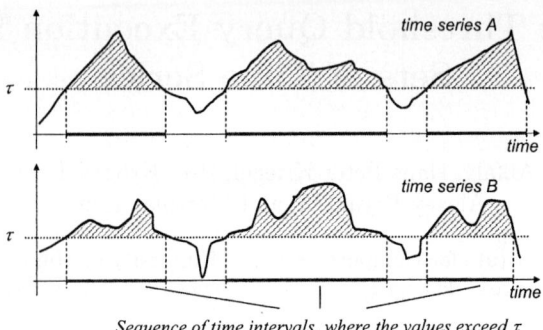

**Fig. 1.** Transformation of time series into sequences of time intervals

many European research projects in recent years. For example, German state offices for environmental protection maintain more than 100 million time series, each representing the daily course of air pollution parameters[1]. It is important to know which parameters nearly simultaneously exceed their legal threshold.

A lot of work on similarity search in time series databases has been published. The proposed methods mainly differ in the representation of the time series, a survey is given in [1]. Standard techniques for dimension reduction include Discrete Fourier Transform (e.g. [2]), Discrete Wavelet Transform (e.g. [3]), Piecewise Aggregate Approximation (e.g. [4]), and Chebyshev Polynomials [5]. However, all techniques which are based on dimension reduction cannot be applied to threshold queries because necessary temporal information is lost.

An effective and efficient processing of queries like "return all ozone time series which exceed the threshold $\tau_1 = 50 \mu g/m^3$ at a similar time as the temperature reaches the threshold $\tau_2 = 25°C$" is of high importance but not supported by the above mentioned techniques. Such a query type has to support the exploration of time series based on user-defined amplitude spectrums. TQuEST not only meets these prerequisites but also enables the user to interactively adjust the query threshold.

## 2  Time Series Representation

As time series objects may be very complex, i.e. contain lots of measurements, we need a data representation of time series objects which allows us to process threshold queries very efficiently. An efficient processing enables interactive query response times, so that the query can be readjusted w.r.t. the last results without causing high response times. In the following, we assume that a time series is described by a sequence of connected segments and each segment denotes the interpolated time series course between a pair of subsequent time series values (measurements).

---

[1] We thank U. Böllmann and M. Meindl for providing us with real-world datasets from the Bavarian State Office for Environmental Protection, Augsburg, Germany.

The query processor is based on a novel data representation of time series. Assume a threshold query with a threshold $\tau$ is given. At query time, the query processor requires for each time series to derive the relevant time intervals, i.e. the time frames where the time series course is above the specified threshold $\tau$. Obviously, those segments of the time series which cross the query threshold $\tau$ suffice to determine the desired time frames. This observation can be used as follows: we decompose the time series into trapezoids where the upper and lower edge is parallel to the time axis, the left side is bounded by an increasing time series segment and the right side is bounded by a decreasing segment. For a certain range of thresholds and a certain range of time, each trapezoid represents all time frames where the time series course is above the threshold. The trapezoids can be described very compactly and can be efficiently accessed by means of a spatial access method (e.g. [6]). The key point of our proposed time series representation is that we do not need to access the complete time-series data at query time. Instead only partial information of the time-series objects suffices to report the results.

## 3  Threshold Query Processor

In this section, we present TQuEST, a JAVA 1.5 application, which supports effective threshold queries efficiently. At first the user has to select the desired *threshold type*. In case of an *Absolute Threshold* $\tau$, all underlying calculations are based on absolute time series values. Our tool also handles *Relative Thresholds* where $\tau$ is given relative to the maximum and the minimum values of the time series. This query mode requires that all time series are also represented in a normalized form. In many application fields, a number of parameters is observed at the same time. Quite often these measurements yield time series with totally different ranges of values. By using relative thresholds, our tool is nonetheless able to detect correlations between certain observed parameters (for example between temperature and ozone concentration).

TQuEST supports two major types of queries: In the *Time Interval Sequence Query* mode, the user can specify a sequence of time intervals on the time bar and a threshold for the query. Our software then retrieves time series that match these parameters best (cf. Figure 2(a)). The *Time Series Query* mode uses a given time series as a query object. Here, the user has to provide a threshold $\tau_1$ for the query time series and a threshold $\tau_2$ for the objects to retrieve. Our software then searches for time series that exceed $\tau_2$ during the same (or similar) time intervals as the query time series exceeds $\tau_1$ (cf. Figure 2(b)).

In both query modes, our tool ranks the resulting time series according to the similarity between the specified time intervals and the time intervals in which the result time series exceed the threshold. Depending on the available metadata for each time series our tool can be configured to display any combination of additional attributes associated with a specific time series (e.g. patient ID, observed parameter, geographical location of the corresponding sensor station, etc.). To get a quick visual impression of the results, multiple time series can be

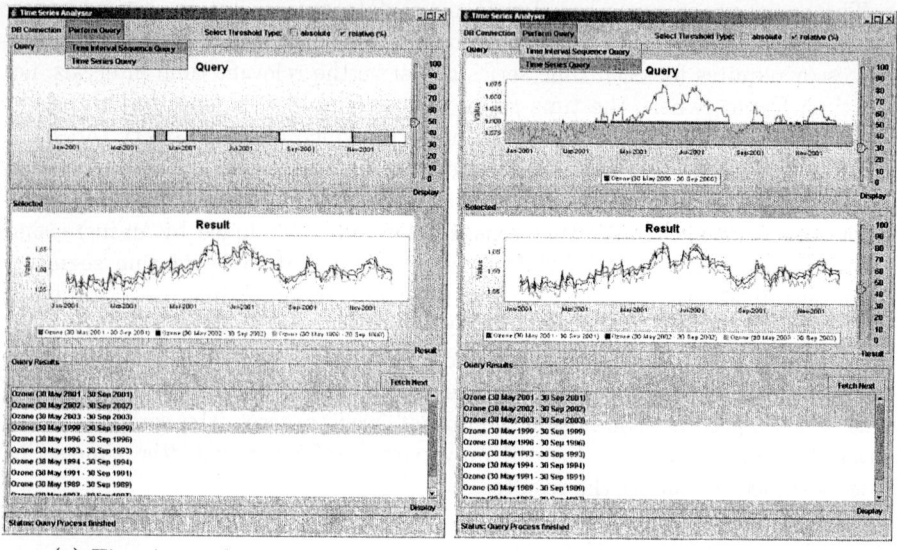

(a) Time interval sequence query  (b) Time series query

**Fig. 2.** Query interface

selected for the graphical display in the middle area of the query GUI. Finally, by clicking the 'Fetch Next' button, the user can retrieve the next results from the database w.r.t. the ranking order.

We demonstrate on real-world data that our prototype TQuEST is very useful. For example, we discovered relationships between meteorological data (e.g. air humidity) and air pollution attributes (e.g. particulate matter). Furthermore we can show that our tool can handle complex threshold queries in adequate time.

# References

1. Keogh, E., Chakrabati, K., Mehrotra, S., Pazzani, M.: "Locally Adaptive Dimensionality Reduction for Indexing Large Time Series Databases". In: Proc. ACM SIGMOD Int. Conf. on Management of Data, Santa Barbara, CA. (2001)
2. Agrawal, R., Faloutsos, C., Swami, A.: "Efficient Similarity Search in Sequence Databases". In: Proc. 4th Conf. on Foundations of Data Organization and Algorithms. (1993)
3. Chan, K., Fu, W.: "Efficient Time Series Matching by Wavelets". In: Proc. 15th Int. Conf. on Data Engineering (ICDE'99), Sydney, Australia. (1999)
4. Yi, B.K., Faloutsos, C.: "Fast Time Sequence Indexing for Arbitrary Lp Norms". In: Proc. 26th Int. Conf. on Very Large Databases (VLDB'00), Cairo, Egypt. (2000)
5. Cai, Y., Ng, R.: "Index Spatio-Temporal Trajectories with Chebyshev Polynomials". In: Proc. ACM SIGMOD Int. Conf. on Management of Data, Paris, France). (2004)
6. Beckmann, N., Kriegel, H.P., Seeger, B., Schneider, R.: "The R*-tree: An Efficient and Robust Access Method for Points and Rectangles". In: Proc. ACM SIGMOD Int. Conf. on Management of Data, Atlantic City, NJ. (1990)

# VICO: Visualizing Connected Object Orderings

Stefan Brecheisen, Hans-Peter Kriegel, Matthias Schubert, and Michael Gruber

Institute for Informatics, University of Munich
{brecheis, kriegel, schubert, gruber}@dbs.ifi.lmu.de

**Abstract.** In modern databases, complex objects like multimedia data, proteins or text objects can be modeled in a variety of representations and can be decomposed into multiple instances of simpler sub-objects. The similarity of such complex objects can be measured by a variety of distance functions. Thus, it quite often occurs that we have multiple views on the same set of data objects and do not have any intuition about how the different views agree or disagree about the similarity of objects. VICO is a tool that allows a user to interactively compare these different views on the same set of data objects. Our system is based on OPTICS, a density-based hierarchical clustering algorithm which is quite insensitive to the choice of parameters. OPTICS describes a clustering as a so-called cluster order on a data set which can be considered as an image of the data distribution. The idea of VICO is to compare the position of data objects or even complete clusters in a set of data spaces by highlighting them in various OPTICS plots. Therefore, VICO allows even non-expert users to increase the intuitive understanding of feature spaces, distance functions and object decompositions.

## 1 Introduction

In modern databases, complex objects like multimedia data, proteins or text objects can be modeled in a variety of representations and can be compared by a variety of distance or similarity functions. Thus, it quite often occurs that we have multiple views on the same set of data objects and do not have any intuition about how the different views on data objects agree or disagree about the similarity of objects. VICO is a tool for comparing these different views on the same set of data objects. Our system is heavily based on OPTICS, a density-based hierarchical clustering algorithm, which is quite insensitive to its parametrizations. OPTICS describes a clustering as a so-called cluster order on a data set. A cluster order can be considered as an image of the data distribution in one representation. The idea of VICO is to select data objects or even complete clusters in one OPTICS plot and additionally highlight the same objects in all other displayed views on the data. VICO has the following three main applications: First, if more than one distance function for a given data set is available, it allows direct comparisons of the distance functions. Second, in a multi-represented setting, where multiple feature transformations for an object are available, the relationships between the given data representations can be examined by comparing the clusterings resulting w.r.t. these representations.

Third, the connection between multi-instance objects and their single instances can be examined by comparing the clustering of multi-instance objects to the clusterings w.r.t. single instances.

## 2 Algorithmic Foundation

In the following, we will introduce the basic concepts behind OPTICS [1] which is the clustering algorithm VICO employs to generate the density plot of a given data representation. OPTICS is a density-based hierarchical clustering algorithm that extends DBSCAN by deriving a cluster hierarchy that is displayed within the so-called reachability plot. The central concepts of OPTICS are the core distance of an object expressing the size of the neighborhood around an object containing at least *MinPts* other objects. In other words, the core distance of object $o$ is the smallest distance for which $o$ would be considered a core point with respect to *MinPts*. The reachability distance of an object $p$ from $o$ denoted as $d_{reach}(p,o)$ is the maximum of the true distance between $o$ and $p$ and the core distance of $o$. OPTICS performs a best first run in a complete directed graph where the objects are the nodes and an edge between the objects $p$ and $o$ is labeled with $d_{reach}(p,o)$. After starting its traversal with an arbitrary node, OPTICS always pursues the edge first that provides the smallest reachability distance and starts with an already reached object. When traversing the data from one object to any other object the reachabilty of the correponding link is collected in the so-called reachability plot. Valleys in this plot indicate clusters: objects having a small reachability value are more similar to their predecessor objects than objects having a higher reachability value.

The reachability plot generated by OPTICS can be cut at any level $\varepsilon$ parallel to the abscissa. It represents the density-based clusters according to the density threshold $\varepsilon$: A consecutive subsequence of objects having a smaller reachability value than $\varepsilon$ belong to the same cluster. An example is presented in Fig. 1: For a cut at the level $\varepsilon_1$, we retrieve two clusters denoted as $A$ and $B$. Compared to this clustering, a cut at level $\varepsilon_2$ would yield three clusters. The cluster $A$ is

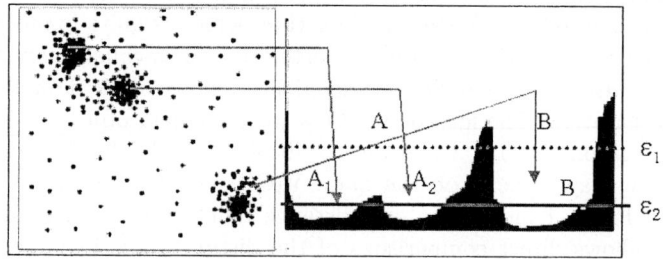

**Fig. 1.** Reachability plot (right) computed by OPTICS for a sample 2-D dataset (left)

split into two smaller clusters denoted by $A_1$ and $A_2$ and cluster $B$ is decreased in size. Usually, for evaluation purposes, a good value for $\varepsilon$ would yield as many clusters as possible.

## 3 Comparing Data Spaces Using VICO

The main purpose of VICO is to compare different feature spaces that describe the same set of data. For this comparison, VICO relies on the interactive visual exploration of reachability plots. Therefore, VICO displays any available view on a set of data objects as adjacent reachability plots and allows comparisons between the local neighborhoods of each object. Fig. 2 displays the main window of VICO. The left side of the window contains a so-called tree control that contains a subtree for each view of the data set. In each subtree, the keys are ordered w.r.t. the cluster order of the corresponding view. The tree control allows a user to directly search for individual data objects. In addition to the object keys displayed in the tree control, VICO displays the reachability plot of each view of the data set.

Since valleys in the reachability plot represent clusters in the underlying representation, the user gets an instant impression of the richness of the cluster structure in each representation. However, to explore the relationships between the representations, we need to find out whether objects that are clustered in one representation are also similar in the other representation. To achieve this type of comparison, VICO allows the user to select any data object in any reachability plot or the tree control. By selecting a set of objects in one view, the objects are highlighted in any other view as well. For example, if the user looks at the reachability plot in one representation and selects a cluster within this plot, the corresponding object keys are highlighted in the tree control and identify the objects that are contained in the cluster. Let us note that it is possible to visualize the selected objects as well, as long as there is a viewable object

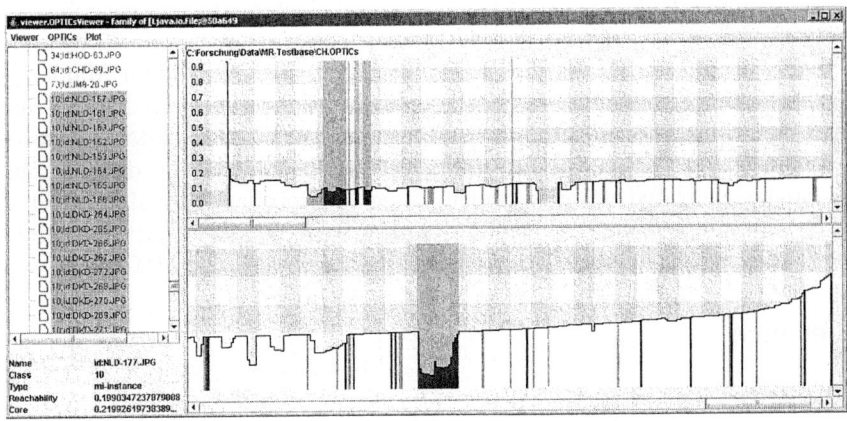

**Fig. 2.** VICO displaying OPTICS plots of multi-represented data

representation. In addition to the information about which objects are clustered together, the set of objects is highlighted in the reachability plots of the other representations as well. Thus, we can easily decide whether the objects in one representation are placed within a cluster in another representation as well or if they are spread among different clusters or are part of the noise. If there exist contradicting reachability plots for the same set of data objects, it is interesting to know which of these representations is closer to the desired notion of similarity. Thus, VICO allows the user to label data objects w.r.t. some class value. The different class values for the objects are displayed by different colors in the reachability plot. Thus, a reachability plot of a data space that matches the user's notion of similarity should display clusters containing objects of the same color. Fig. 2 displays a comparison of two feature spaces for an image data set. Each image is labelled with w.r.t. the displayed motive.

Another feature of VICO is the ability to handle multi-instance objects. In a multi-instance representation, one data object is given by a set of separated feature objects. An example are CAD parts that can be decomposed to a set of spatial primitives, which can be represented by a single feature vector. This way, the complete CAD part is represented by a set of feature vectors, which can be compared by a variety of distance functions. To find out which instances are responsible for clusters of multi-instance objects, VICO allows us to cluster the instances without considering the multi-instance object they belong to. Comparing this instance plot to the plot derived on the complete multi-instance objects allows us to analyze which instance clusters are typical for the clusters on the complete multi-instance object. Thus, for multi-instance settings, VICO highlights all instances belonging to some selected multi-instance object.

## 4 Architecture and Implementation

VICO is implemented in Java 1.5 and thus, runs on any platform supporting the current version of the Java Runtime Environment. VICO includes an integrated version of OPTICS allowing the user to load and cluster data sets described in a variety of file formats like CSV and ARFF files. For this version of OPTICS there are several distance measures already implemented like the Euclidian, Manhattan or Cosine distance. Furthermore, VICO already implements various distance functions for multi-instance objects, e.g. the Hausdorff distance. The system is based on an extensible architecture, so that additional components like new distance functions can be integrated easily by implementing Java interfaces. Finally, VICO can directly load preprocessed reachability plots as well and also export reachability plots that were computed by the integrated implementation of OPTICS.

## Reference

1. Ankerst, M., Breunig, M.M., Kriegel, H.P., Sander, J.: "OPTICS: Ordering Points to Identify the Clustering Structure". In: Proc. ACM SIGMOD Int. Conf. on Management of Data (SIGMOD'99), Philadelphia, PA. (1999) 49–60

# XQueryViz: An XQuery Visualization Tool

Jihad Boulos, Marcel Karam, Zeina Koteiche, and Hala Ollaic

Department of Computer Science,
American University of Beirut,
P.O.Box 11-0236 Riad El-Solh,
Beirut, Lebanon
{jb06, mk62, zak08, hao04}@aub.edu.lb

**Abstract.** We present in this demo the description of XQueryViz: an XQuery visualization tool. This graphical tool can parse one or more XML documents and/or schemas and visualizes them as trees with zooming, expansion and contraction functionality. The tool can also parse a textual XQuery and visualizes it as a DAG within two different windows: the first for the querying part (*i.e.* For-Let-Where clauses) and the second for the "Return" clause. More importantly, users can build XQuery queries with this graphical tool by pointing and clicking on the visual XML trees to build the XPath parts of an XQuery and then build the whole XQuery using visual constructs and connectors. A textual XQuery is then generated.

## 1 Introduction

We present in this demo XQueryViz: a graphical tool for the visualization and construction of XQuery queries. This tool is made of four main parts (Fig. 1) where the first vertical window(s) is(are) dedicated to the visualization of XML documents and schemas. The second vertical window(s) is/are dedicated to the visualization of the "For-Let-Where" (FLW) clauses of a FLWR query and the third vertical window(s) is/are reserved to the "Return" clauses of the (sub)query. The fourth window is a horizontal one where the textual representation of the XQuery is shown and updated dynamically during visual query construction.

The contribution of this tool is its visualization and construction of XQuery queries in a natural data-flow manner where a query block ("FLW" or "Return" in a query or in a sub-query) is represented as a tree—with predicates connecting branches in a tree. The visualization makes it natural for a user to imagine XML data flowing from the root to the leaves of the tree, and hence makes it easier to understand and construct more complex XQuery queries.

Contrary to XQBE [1] where the emphasis is on simplicity and the target users are non-experts, XQueryViz is designed for more advanced users and hence is more complex than XQBE. We explain in the next three sections the three major parts of this graphical tool.

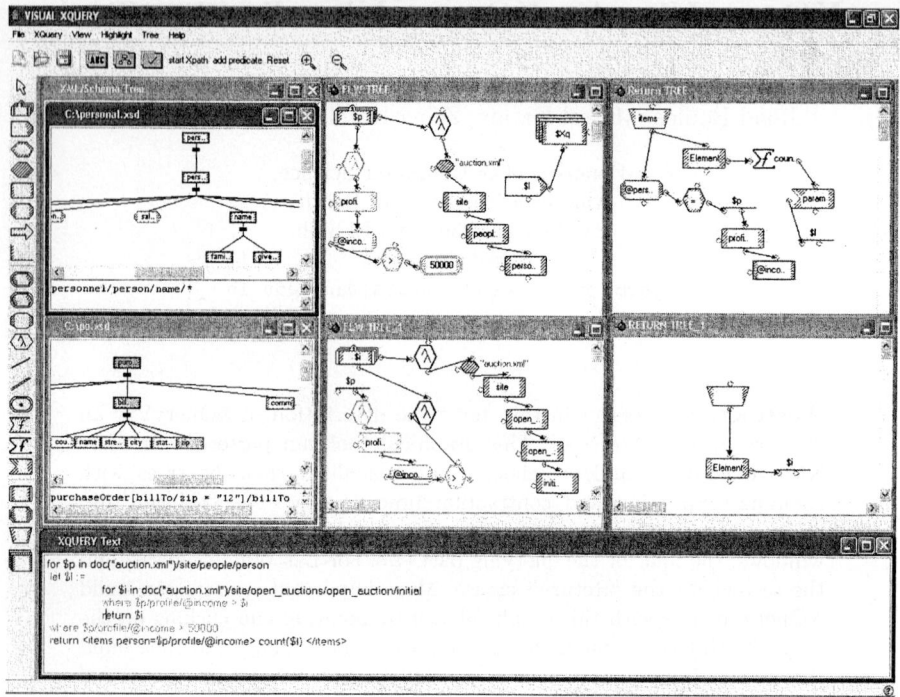

**Fig. 1.** A snapshot of XQueryViz showing an XML schema and an XQuery example

## 2 XML and XPath

The upper-left window(s) of XQueryViz is/are dedicated to XML documents and schemas and XPath visualization. Within these windows, both XML schemas and documents can be visualized as trees. Moreover, and contrary to most graphical interfaces that show XML documents and schemas in directory-like trees, the trees in this window have their natural top-down shapes.

A user can load into this window one or more XML documents and/or schemas. She can then expand and/or contract different branches of a tree and zoom in and out on it. These two facilities are mostly helpful for large documents/schemas. The user can then build one or more XPath queries by pointing and clicking on the nodes of a tree. While working on this visual representation of the document, an XPath query is dynamically generated and updated in the lower (*i.e.* textual) window of the tool. In this way, the user can precisely understand the semantics of her node-clicking and XPath query generation relative to the XML schema/document. Elements, attributes and predicates can be included in the generated XPath expression. Several XPath expressions can be generated and saved, and then included in a larger XQuery that can normally contain several XPath expressions. Moreover, a user can use this part to define and construct new XML schemas.

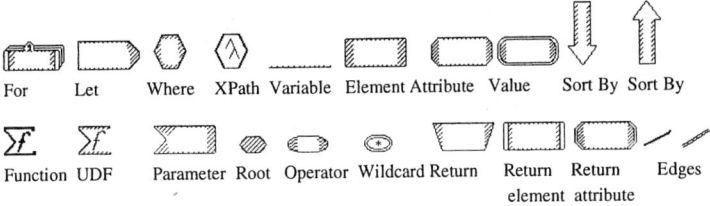

**Fig. 2.** Visual icons

## 3 The Querying Part

The querying part of an XQuery is divided into three visual sub-parts that represent the "For", "Let", and "Where" clauses of that query. This part is visualized in the middle vertical window(s) of the graphical tool. Each clause is written in the textual form with a specific color and shown in the visual window with that specific color. In this case, the user can naturally associate the sub-parts in that window with the clauses in the query.

A user can currently load an XQuery from a file and visualizes it in this middle window and its "Return" clause in the third vertical window. The user has also the option of visually modifying this query and saving its new textual format or visually building a completely new query with or without using the XPath construction facility provided in the first window. With these options, a user can manipulate both textually and visually an XQuery so that it becomes as complicated as that user needs it to be.

Every clause of an XQuery (i.e. For, Let, Where, Return, Order By) has its own visual construct and every component in these clauses has its own visual construct too. The components that XQueryViz currently supports are: elements, attributes, wildcards, variables, XPath, document roots, numbers, strings, parent-child relationships, ancestor-descendant relationships, predicates, functions, and quantifiers. These are shown in a palette list to the left of the three vertical windows in Fig. 1 and are shown is Fig. 2 with their meanings. Sub-queries are recursively constructed in the same manner as explained in the following.

*The "For" Clause:* Multiple "For" clauses in an XQuery can be defined. The first "For" clause binds a variable to an XPath expression that should be applied on a certain XML document. Any subsequent "For" clauses may do the same of binding their variables to previously bound ones, or to the same or newly defined XML documents. The visual construct for the "For" clause has a right diamond that is connected to the tree representing the XPath expression and where the root of the document has its own visual construct and elements, attributes, and predicate expressions can also be visualized/constructed with their respective visual constructs.

*The "Let" Clause:* Here too, multiple "Let" clauses can be defined and they can also be intertwined with "For" clauses. The "Let" clause has its visual construct that binds a variable to another variable with or without extension to its XPath, to an XPath expression on the root of an XML document, or to a constant value.

*The "Where" Clause:* Predicate expressions on the previously defined variables in the "For" and "Let" clauses are applied here. While the previous two clauses contain only XPath expressions with their internal predicates, the user can define here predicates across the different variables and XPath expressions; hence, eventually connecting some XPath trees to produce the general shape of a DAG.

## 4 The Return Part

A user can visualize and construct the result of a query in the third vertical window of the graphical tool. Almost the same visual constructs for using previously defined elements and attributes, and for applying predicates and functions can also be used here. The major new visual constructs are the ones that define new elements. Moreover, defined variables in the "For-Let-Where" clauses (*i.e.* in the middle windows) have their new visual construct that makes them understood as defined earlier.

*Sub-Queries:* We recently extended XQueryViz to handle an XQuery as a sub-query in both the "Where" and the "Return" clauses of a larger query. Our design is based on recursively spanning from the FLW or the "Return" window of the englobing XQuery two new windows that contain the two parts of the querying and returning of the sub-query. The yet unresolved problem here is how to visually connect these new windows to the spanning "Where" or "Return" clause to make it clear for a user how this sub-query is part of that "Where" or "Return" clause.

## 5 Conclusion

We presented in this paper the different functionality of an XQuery visualization tool that can visualize and construct XQuery queries. This tool can also visualize XML schemas and documents and let a user visually builds XPath queries on them. XQuery queries can then be built and manipulated in quite a more natural and easier manner than only textual format. We are currently preparing a usability study of XQueryViz where a certain number of users with different experience with XQuery will be asked to visualize and construct a certain number of XQuery queries and collect feedback and statistics on how effective and ergonomic this tool is.

## Reference

1. D. Barga, A. Campi, and S. Ceri. XQBE (XQuery By Example): A Visual Interface to the Standard XML Query Language. ACM Transactions on Database Systems, Vol. 30, No. 2, June 2005. Also, Demo in Sigmod 2005.

# SAT: Spatial Awareness from Textual Input*

Dmitri V. Kalashnikov, Yiming Ma, Sharad Mehrotra, Ramaswamy Hariharan, Nalini Venkatasubramanian, and Naveen Ashish

Information and Computer Science,
University of California, Irvine

## 1 Motivation

Recent events (WTC attacks, Southeast Asia Tsunamis, Hurricane Katrina, London bombings) have illustrated the need for accurate and timely situational awareness tools in emergency response. Developing effective situational awareness (SA) systems has the potential to radically improve decision support in crises by improving the accuracy and reliability of the information available to the decision-makers. In an evolving crisis, raw situational information comes from a variety of sources in the form of situational reports, live radio transcripts, sensor data, video streams. Much of the data resides (or can be converted) in the form of free text, from which events of interest are extracted. Spatial or location information is one of the fundamental attributes of the events, and is useful for a variety of situational awareness (SA) tasks.

This demonstration will illustrate our approach, techniques and solutions for obtaining spatial awareness from raw input text. There are several challenges that arise in obtaining spatial awareness from raw text input - modeling/ representation, event extraction and disambiguation, querying, reasoning and visualization. We specifically focus on illustrating solutions for (a)modeling and representation that captures spatial uncertainty in text and (b) efficient indexing and processing of various types of spatial queries to support reasoning of spatial information. Our solutions are implemented in the context of a prototype system called SAT (spatial awareness from text)that models and represents (potentially uncertain) event locations described in free text and incorporates several types of spatial queries of interest in SA applications. We demonstrate SAT in the context of 2 real-world applications that derive spatial information from text at different phases of the disaster response process.

- Offline spatial analysis of data from the Sept 11, 2001 WTC attacks to retrieve relevant events and the response as it occurred.
- Online, real-time assistance to field personnel using real time communication transcripts between dispatchers and first responders from 911 call centers in Los Angeles area.

Such tools enable social scientists and disaster researchers to accurately analyze transcribed communication logs and situational reports filed by the first

---

* This work was supported by NSF grants 0331707, 0331690.

responders after major disasters. These techniques can also be used to support real-time triaging and filtering of relevant communications and reports among first responders (and the public) during a crisis. Our primary objective is to design database solutions to support applications where the real world is being monitored (potentially using a variety of sensing technologies) to support tasks such as situation assessment and decision-making.

**An illustrative example.** Consider a scenario during the response to the September 11, 2001 WTC attacks that demonstrates the need for spatial awareness. The following are excerpts from two real reports[1] filed by *Port Authority Police Department* (PAPD) Officers:

1. *"... the PAPD Mobile Command Post was located on West St. north of WTC and there was equipment being staged there ..."*
2. *"... a PAPD Command Truck parked on the west side of Broadway St. and north of Vesey St. ..."*

These two reports refer to the same location, i.e. the same command post – a point-location in the New York, Manhattan area. However, neither of the reports specify the exact location of the events; they do not even mention the same street names. Our objective is to represent and index such reports in a manner that enables efficient evaluation of spatial queries and subsequent analysis using the spatial data. Our system should have efficient supports to commonly used spatial queries, such as range, NN, spatial join, and so on. For instance, the representation must enable us to retrieve events in a given geographical region (e.g., around World Trade Center). Likewise, it should enable us to determine similarity between reports based on their spatial properties; e.g., we should be able to determine that the above events might refer to the same location(assuming a temporal correlation of the events).

To support spatial analyses on free text reports, merely storing location in the database as free text is not sufficient either to answer spatial queries or to disambiguate reports based on spatial locations. For example, spatial query such as 'retrieve events near WTC', based on keywords alone, can only retrieve the first report mentioned earlier. So instead, we need to project the spatial properties of the event described in the report onto the 2-dimensional domain $\Omega$ and answer queries within this domain. In this paper, we model uncertain event locations as random variables that have certain probability density functions (*pdfs*) associated with them. Assisted by GIS and probabilistic modeling tools, we map uncertain textual locations into the corresponding pdfs defined in $\Omega$. Given that a large number of spatially uncertain events can potentially arise during crisis situations[2], the focus of our project is on developing scalable solutions for effective and efficient processing of such spatially-uncertain events.

---

[1] Original audio data available in converted text form.
[2] For instance, more than 1000 such events can be extracted from just 164 reports filed by Police Officers who participated in the disaster of September 11th, 2001.

## 2 Research Challenges and Solutions to Be Demonstrated

Development of an end-to-end approach for spatial awareness from textual input must address four practical challenges – (1) modeling uncertain spatial events, (2) representation, (3) indexing, and (4) query processing. In Figure 1, we show the major components of SAT. In the remaining of this section, we briefly describe the functionalities of SAT components and demonstrate the potentials of SAT in handling these challenges.

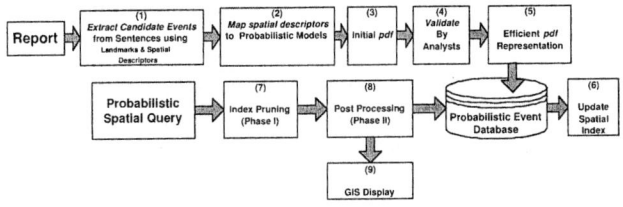

**Fig. 1.** SAT Components

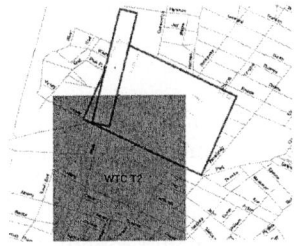

**Fig. 2.** WTC: Data and Query

**Fig. 3.** GIS Interface

**Modeling.** Spatial uncertainty has been explored both in the GIS and in database literature. We extend the probabilistic model for spatial uncertainty developed in [1, 2, 3]. In the probabilistic model, an uncertain location $\ell$ is treated as a continuous random variable (r.v.) which takes values $(x,y) \in \Omega$ and has a certain probability density function (pdf) $f_\ell(x,y)$ associated with it. Interpreted this way, for any spatial region $R$, the probability that $\ell$ is inside $R$ is computed as $\int_R f_\ell(x,y)dxdy$. However, to apply the probabilistic models in our context requires us to solve: (a) event extraction from text, (b) modeling spatial uncertainty in text. The first four components (1–4) of Figure 1 are meant for these tasks. First, automated tools are employed to extract events from text, including their spatial properties. The analyst oversees this process to correct errors arising from this process and also to resolve extraction ambiguities (cf. [4]). Next, we map the extracted textual location into the corresponding probabilistic representation in a semi-supervised fashion. Our modeling solution [5] takes a spatial expression (s-expression) as its input and outputs the desired pdf for the s-expression. It achieves that by analyzing landmarks and spatial descriptors (s-descriptors) mentioned in the s-expression. The analyst oversees these steps and adjusts the models if needed. We integrate this modeling process as a toolkit to the standard GIS system as shown in Figure 3. For example, our extraction and modeling tools can automatically determine the uncertainty regions of the two reports in Section 1, and display them as in Figure 2. An analyst can use the probabilistic modeling toolkit to further enhance the probabilistic models. Besides demonstrating the modeling process, we will also demonstrate the practical significance of using the probabilistic models. Showing together with query processing demonstration, we will show that simple bounding region models are not sufficient to answer analytical queries.

**Representation.** In our context, we need to be able to represent pdfs of complex shapes in the database. There are several known methods for such a representation, such as histograms and modeling pdf as a mixture of Gaussians or of other distributions. However, these solutions cannot scale well. In [6], we have proposed a novel compressed quad-tree representation. We have implemented this representation in the SAT component No. 5 in Figure 1. Coupled with our new indexing strategies, we will demonstrate significant performance boost in query response time. It is interesting to note that the existing solutions that also deal with probabilistic spatial queries [1,2,3] do not address the representation issues directly. The reason is that their empirical evaluation is carried out using only simple densities such as uniform and Gaussian.

**Indexing and query processing.** SAT efficiently supports several spatial query types – such as range, NN, and spatial join – commonly used in SA applications. For example, using a spatial region query, an analyst can express a query such as "find all the events, the location of which are around WTC". Figure 2 shows this query visually (shaded region). The system should compute the probability of the events inside this region, and filter away low probability events. In [6], we have proposed a novel grid base indexing approach. Compared to the state-of-arts techniques proposed in [1, 3], our new indexing scheme has 2–10 times speedup. The new index solution has been incorporated into SAT system as component 6,7 and 8 in Figure 1. In our demonstration, using both real and synthetic data, we will demonstrate the efficiency of the indexing solution on different types of spatial query.

## 3 Concluding Remarks

In this paper we presented a system – SAT – which builds spatial awareness and provides for reasoning with spatial locations from textual input. Such Situational Awareness (SA) applications abound in a variety of domains including homeland security, emergency response, command and control, process monitoring/automation, business activity monitoring, to name a few. We believe that techniques such as ours can benefit a very broad class of applications where free text is used to describe events.

# References

1. Cheng, R., Kalashnikov, Prabhakar, S.: Querying imprecise data in moving object environments. TKDE **16** (2004)
2. Cheng, R., Kalashnikov, D., Prabhakar, S.: Evaluating probabilistic queries over imprecise data. In: SIGMOD. (2003)
3. Cheng, R., Xia, Y., Prabhakar, S., Shah, R., Vitter: Efficient indexing methods for probabilistic threshold queries over uncertain data. In: Proc. of VLDB. (2004)
4. Woodruff, A., Plaunt, C.: GIPSY: Georeferenced Information Processing SYstem. (1994)
5. Kalashnikov, D.V., Ma, Y., Hariharan, R., Mehrotra, S.: Spatial queries over (imprecise) event descriptions. Submitted for Publication (2005)
6. Kalashnikov, D., Ma, Y., Mehrotra, S., Hariharan, R.: Spatial indexing over imprecise event data. (In: Submitted to EDBT 2006)

# MUSCLE: Music Classification Engine with User Feedback

Stefan Brecheisen[1], Hans-Peter Kriegel[1], Peter Kunath[1], Alexey Pryakhin[1], and Florian Vorberger[2]

[1] Institute for Informatics, University of Munich
{brecheis, kriegel, kunath, pryakhin}@dbs.ifi.lmu.de
[2] Florian.Vorberger@detach.de

**Abstract.** Nowadays, powerful music compression tools and cheap mass storage devices have become widely available. This allows average consumers to transfer entire music collections from the distribution medium, such as CDs and DVDs, to their computer hard drive. To locate specific pieces of music, they are usually labeled with artist and title. Yet the user would benefit from a more intuitive organization based on music style to get an overview of the music collection. We have developed a novel tool called MUSCLE which fills this gap. While there exist approaches in the field of musical genre classification, none of them features a hierarchical classification in combination with interactive user feedback and a flexible multiple assignment of songs to classes. In this paper, we present MUSCLE, a tool which allows the user to organize large music collections in a genre taxonomy and to modify class assignments on the fly.

## 1 Introduction

The progress of computer hardware and software technology in recent years made it possible to manage large collections of digital music on an average desktop computer. Thus, modern computer systems are able to compress a piece of music to a few megabytes in very fast time. Easy to use software that automates this process is available. Often, this software stores meta information, such as artist, album or title, along with the audio file. However, the amount and quality of the available meta information in publicly accessible online databases, e.g. freedb.org, is often limited. This meta data is especially useful when searching for a specific piece of music in a large collection. To organize and structure a collection, additional information such as the genre would be very useful. Unfortunately, the genre information stored in online databases is often incorrect or does not meet the user's expectations.

In this demonstration paper, we present MUSCLE, a prototype of a powerful hierarchical genre classification tool for digitized audio. It is often problematic to assign a piece of music to exactly one class in a natural way. Genre assignment is a somewhat fuzzy concept and depends on the taste of the user. Therefore, MUSCLE allows multi-assignments of one song to several classes. The classification is based on feature vectors obtained from three acoustic realms namely

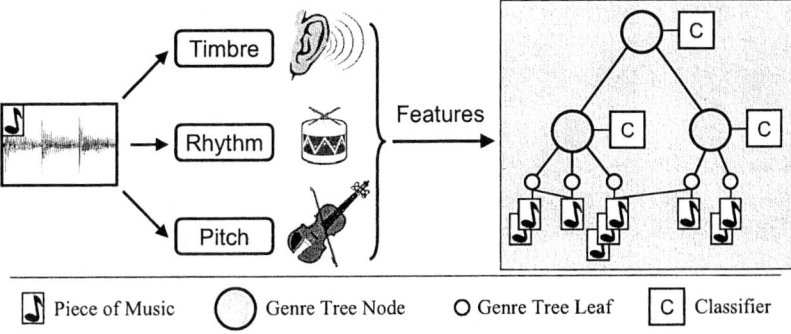

**Fig. 1.** Architecture of MUSCLE.

*timbre*, *rhythm* and *pitch*. Timbre features are derived from the frequency domain and were mainly developed for the purpose of speech-recognition. The extraction of the timbral texture is performed by computing the short time fourier transform. We use the Mel-frequency cepstral coefficients (MFCCs), spectral flux and spectral rolloff as trimbral representations [1]. Rythmic content features are useful for describing the beat frequency and beat strength of a piece of music. In our demo, we use features derived from beat histograms [1] as description of the rhythmic content. Pitch extraction tries to model the human perception by simulating the behavior of the cochlea. Similar to the rhythmic content features, we derive pitch features from pitch histograms which were generated by a multipitch analysis model [2]. To sum up, each song is described by multiple representations and multiple instances, i.e. there exists a set of feature vectors per representation.

The general idea of hierarchical classification is that a classifier located on an inner node solves only a small classification problem and therefore achieves more effective results more efficiently than a classifier that works on a large number of flat organized classes. There exist only a few approaches for automatic genre classification of audio data. In [3], music pieces are classified into either rock or classic using $k$-NN and MLP classifiers. An approach for hierarchical genre classification which does not support user feedback is presented in [1]. Zhang [4] proposes a method for a hierarchical genre classification which follows a fixed schema and where is only limited support for user-created genre folders. Moreover, all above mentioned hierarchical classification methods do not take full advantage of multi-instance and multi-represented music objects. In contrast, MUSCLE handles such rich object representations as well as an arbitrary genre hierarchy, deals with user feedback and supports multi-assignment of songs to classes.

## 2 Theoretical Foundation

In this section, we briefly describe MUSCLE's approach for classifying music pieces into a genre taxonomy (cf. Fig. 1). Support vector machines (SVM) are used as classifiers which achieve superior classification accuracy in various application areas and have received much attention recently. By using kernel functions in combination with SVMs, any kind of data can be classified. Since a music piece is described by a set of feature vectors, we apply a set kernel function [5] for SVMs.

The hierarchical classification problem is handled by performing a two layer classification process (2LCP) on each inner node $N$ of the genre taxonomy. This process distinguishes only descendent nodes of $N$ as classes $C_{single}$ and acts as a guidepost for the hierarchical classification. We train SVMs in the first layer of the 2LCP that distinguishes only single classes in each representation. Since standard SVMs are able to make only binary decisions we apply the so-called one-versus-one (OvO) approach in order to make a classification decision for more than two classes. We argue that for our application the OvO approach is best suitable because the voting vectors provided by this method are a meaningful intermediate description that is useful for solving the multi-assignment problem in the second layer of our 2LCP. In order to perform the multi-assignment we take advantage of the class properties in our application domain. We limit the possible class combinations to a subset $C_{combi} \subset 2^{C_{single}}$ because there exist several combinations that do not make sense, e.g. a piece of music belonging to the class 'classic' is very implausible to be also in the class 'hip-hop'. Thus, the classifier (SVM) in the second layer of the 2LPC uses an aggregation of the voting vectors from the first layer of the 2LPC as input to assign an object to a class $c \in C_{single} \cup C_{combi}$. The voting vectors provided by the first layer SVMs for each representation are aggregated by using a weighted linear combination. The weights in the combination are calculated by using a so called object adjusted weighting. The intuition behind the object adjusted weighting is that the object to be classified needs to have a sufficient distance from any of the other classes. For more details we refer to [6].

## 3 Practical Benefits

MUSCLE is implemented in C/C++ and runs on the Windows platform. Its hierarchical playlist acts as a jukebox. The installation archive of MUSCLE contains a default genre taxonomy including the necessary training data in the form of feature vectors for each song. This data is used in the demonstration. Using aggregated information such as feature vectors makes it possible to share the training data without having to distribute the underlying music data. Classes and training data in the genre taxonomy can be deleted, moved or added by the user. When the user commits the changes of the class hierarchy or of the corresponding training data, MUSCLE trains the affected classifiers. Note that usually only a small subset of the entire classifier hierarchy has to be trained because a modification at a node requires a partial adaptation of the node and all parent nodes only. It is also possible to start the training automatically after each modification or to run the training in the background. When the user is satisfied with the training setup, a folder to automatically classify all contained songs can be selected.

(a) Multi-Assignment of Songs  (b) User Feedback

**Fig. 2.** MUSCLE User Interface

Fig. 2 illustrates MUSCLE's user interface. In the main window the playlist containing the classification result in form of a genre tree is displayed. An example for a multiple assignment of the song 'Anticipating' to the classes 'pop' and 'rhythm & base' can be seen in Fig. 2(a). In case the user wants to manually adjust the genre assignment of a song, entries can be re-arranged using drag & drop as shown in Fig. 2(b).

# References

1. Tzanetakis, G., Cook, P.: Musical genre classification of audio signals. IEEE Transactions on Speech and Audio Processing **10** (2002) 293–302
2. Tolonen, T., Karjalainen, M.: A computationally efficient multipitch analysis model. IEEE Transactions on Speech and Audio Processing **8** (2000) 708–716
3. Costa, C.H.L., Valle, J.D.J., Koerich, A.L.: Automatic classification of audio data. IEEE Transactions on Systems, Man, and Cybernetics **3** (2004) 562–567
4. Zhang, T.: Semi-automatic approach for music classification. In: Proc. of the SPIE: Conf. on Internet Multimedia Management Systems. Volume 5242. (2003) 81–91
5. Gärtner, T., Flach, P.A., Kowalczyk, A., Smola, A.J.: Multi-instance kernels. In: Proc. of the 19th Int. Conf. on Machine Learning (ICML). (2002) 179–186
6. Kriegel, H.P., Kröger, P., Pryakhin, A., Schubert, M.: Using support vector machines for classifying large sets of multi-represented objects. In: Proc. SIAM Int. Conf. on Data Mining (SDM). (2004)

# *i*MONDRIAN: A Visual Tool to Annotate and Query Scientific Databases

Floris Geerts[1,3], Anastasios Kementsietsidis[1], and Diego Milano[2]

[1] School of Informatics, University of Edinburgh, UK
{fgeerts, akements}@inf.ed.ac.uk
[2] Universitá di Roma "La Sapienza", Italy
diego.milano@dis.uniroma1.it
[3] Hasselt University, Belgium

**Abstract.** We demonstrate *i*MONDRIAN, a component of the MONDRIAN annotation management system. Distinguishing features of MONDRIAN are (i) the ability to annotate sets of values (ii) the annotation-aware query algebra. On top of that, *i*MONDRIAN offers an *i*ntuitive visual *i*nterface to annotate and query scientific databases.

In this demonstration, we consider Gene Ontology (GO), a publicly available biological database. Using this database we show (i) the creation of annotations through the visual interface (ii) the ability to visually build complex, annotation-aware, queries (iii) the basic functionality for tracking annotation provenance. Our demonstration also provides a *cheat window* which shows the system internals and how visual queries are translated to annotation-aware algebra queries.

## 1 Introduction

Modern science relies increasingly on the use of database systems to store huge collections of scientific data. These data are generated from laboratory processes or are copied from other scientific databases. To make sense of these data and decide under which circumstances they can be used, scientists need to know their lineage, i.e., the conditions under which the data were generated, the accuracy of the processes that produced them, or how trust-worthy is the source from which the data were copied. These *metadata* are often stored in scientific databases in the form of annotations. In spite of their importance, existing data formats and schemas are not designed to manage the increasing variety of annotations. Moreover, DBMS's often lack support for storing and querying annotations.

Our work in the MONDRIAN[1] annotation management system [1] is motivated by the pressing needs of biologists, some of which are highlighted by the following example. Consider the relation in Figure 1 which lists triples of identifiers belonging to three distinct biological databases. Each triple associates the identifier *gid* of a gene (in the gene database) with the identifier *pid* of the protein (in the protein database) that

---

[1] Piet Mondrian: Dutch painter whose paintings mainly consist of color blocks.

the gene produces, where the sequence of the protein is identified by *sid* (in the protein sequence database). Such relations are widely used in the biological domain and offer a quick way to cross-reference and establish associations between independent biological sources [2, 3].

Given such a relation, a biologist often wants to annotate each triple with any evidence that exist and verify its validity. Such evidence might include a reference to an article that mentions that the indicated gene produces the specified protein, or the name of a curator who verified this association. In the figure, we show possible annotations in the form of blocks and block labels. Blocks are used to indicate the set of values for which an annotation exists, while block labels are used to indicate the annotations themselves. In the figure, the annotations indicate the names of curators who verified that a particular association holds. So, in the first tuple, a block indicates Mary's belief that the gene with GDB id *120231* produces protein with id *P21359*. Notice that parts of a triple can be verified by different curators (e.g. see the first tuple), while other parts are yet to be verified (e.g. see the third tuple).

For annotations to be useful, the biologist must be able to query them. For example, she might want tuples that are annotated by either John or Mary. Or, she might want to find which are annotated, and by whom. Often, the lack of annotations is also of interest. For example, a biologist might want the gene-protein (*gid, pid*) pairs that are not annotated, so as to investigate the validity of these yet unverified pairs.

To the best of our knowledge, MONDRIAN is the first system to support the annotation of sets of values, thus allowing for complex annotations such as the ones shown in the figure. Previous works only allowed for annotations to be attached to a particular value of a specific attribute (e.g., see [4]). Single-value annotations are insufficient since they fail to capture the complex relationships of values, relationships which span across attribute boundaries. Another distinguishing feature of MONDRIAN is the ability to query annotations and values alike. MONDRIAN offers an annotation-aware query algebra which we have shown to be both complete (it can express all possible queries over the class of annotated databases) and minimal (all the algebra operators are primitive) [1]. The expressiveness of our algebra goes well beyond the query capabilities of similar systems like, for example, DBNotes [5]. The algebra is simple and intuitive and is able to express all the queries mentioned earlier, and many more (see [1] for the full syntax and examples). For example, query $q_1$ below retrieves all the tuples that are annotated by either John or Mary, while query $q_2$ only retrieves tuples that have a gene-protein sequence (*gid, sid*) annotated pair.

$$q_1 = \Sigma_{Mary} \cup \Sigma_{Peter} \qquad q_2 = \Pi^L_{gid,sid}$$

In spite of being simple (and very easy to learn by those familiar with relational algebra), we don't expect that biologists would want to learn yet another query algebra. Instead, it seems natural to offer a visual tool through which a biologists can both annotate data and query them. The objective of this demonstration is to present *i*MONDRIAN, a tool that offers the above capabilities. Once more, the simplicity of the algebra is to our favor since it facilitates the direct translation of visual queries to algebra queries.

## 2 The *i*MONDRIAN Demonstration

The demonstration of *i*MONDRIAN shows how the tool can be used by biologists, throught the lifecycle of annotations, starting from their insertion, to their querying and ending with their deletion. The demonstration uses data and annotations from Gene Ontology (GO) [6], a publicly available biological database.

### 2.1 System Architecture

The MONDRIAN architecture, shown in Figure 2. MONDRIAN is built in java and is running on top of MySQL. The *i*Mondrian component is the front-end through which a user interacts with the system. A visually expressed query is translated to a query written in the MONDRIAN query algebra and this is subsequently translated to SQL and is executed over the underlying RDBMS. One advantage of MONDRIAN queries is that they are *storage-model independent* [1]. That is, MONDRIAN queries are at a level of abstraction that is independent of the chosen representation of annotations. Unlike the executed SQL queries, a change in this representation does not require the reformulation of our queries.

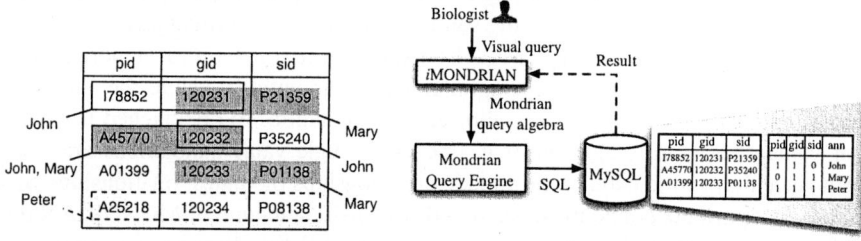

**Fig. 1.** An annotated relation

**Fig. 2.** The MONDRIAN Architecture

### 2.2 Demonstrated Functionality

Figures 3 and 4 show the *i*MONDRIAN interface. For ease of presentation, annotations are represented as colors. Thus, sets of values with the same annotation are colored the same. The same color can appear in a tuple over distinct attributes sets and thus colors do not suffice to tell which attributes are annotated as a set. Therefore, when a user selects an attribute value in a tuple, all the other attributes with which this value is annotated are highlighted. Furthermore, a value can participate in more than one blocks and thus it can have multiple colors. Such values are shown in grey, with a black border, and when a user clicks on them she sees all its colors in a popup window (see Figure 3).

During the demo, we show how users can insert new tuples and annotations. An annotation can be inserted by selecting a set of values and attaching a color to them. This color can be either one that is used already in some tuple or a brand new color (annotation).

The user can query both values and annotations in isolation or in unison. For example, to query annotations, the user can select a color from a value and ask for all the tuples that have the same color (annotation). For example, a visual query $v_1$ might

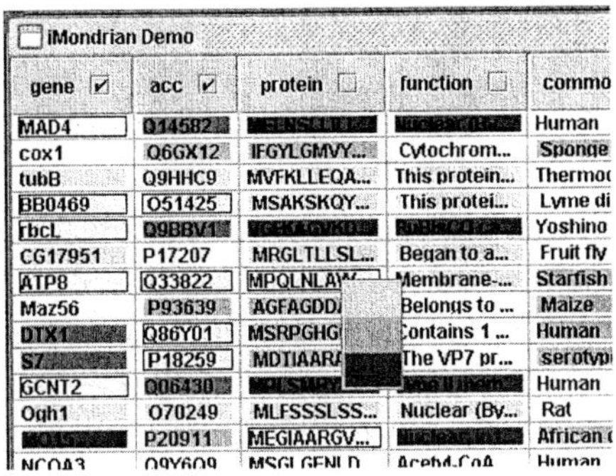

**Fig. 3.** The *i*MONDRIAN interface

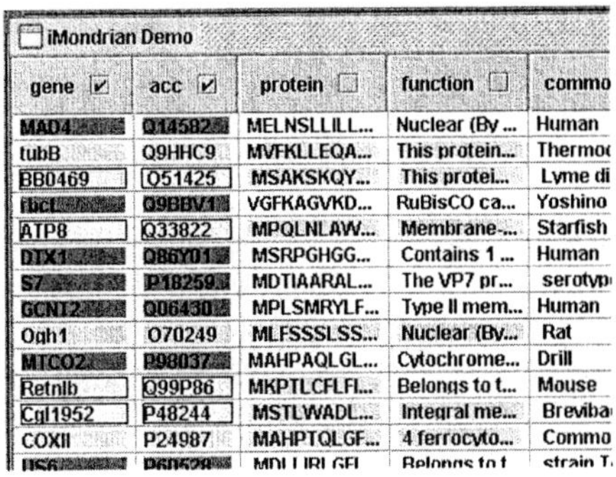

**Fig. 4.** The result of a visual query

ask for all the annotations with a red or green color. Or, the user can select a number of attribute columns (by clicking check boxes next to each attribute name) and pose a visual query $v_2$ that returns all the tuples with annotations that involves all of these columns. Each visual query results in a new window containing the query result. The user can pose queries in the result window of a previous query, thus allowing for building of comlex queries. Figure 4 shows the result of applying visual queries $v_1$ and $v_2$ to the relation of Figure 3. The composed query, written in the MONDRIAN query algebra, is available from the *cheat window*. This is useful if a user wants to execute periodically the same query. Then, she doesn't have to go through the same steps in the *i*MONDRIAN interface. She only needs to copy the algebra query from the cheat window and send it directly to the MONDRIAN query engine.

The demo also illustrates how MONDRIAN supports alternative annotation semantics [1]. For example, we discuss *annotation (non-)inheritance* a property that, given an annotation over a set of values, it determines whether, or not, any subset of these values also inherits the annotation. Finally, the demo illustrates some basic provenance functionality, which allows to trace back the origin of annotations.

## References

1. Geerts, F., Kementsietsidis, A., Milano, D.: MONDRIAN: Annotating and querying databases through colors and blocks. In: ICDE. (2006) (To appear).
2. Kementsietsidis, A., Arenas, M., Miller, R.J.: Data Mapping in Peer-to-Peer Systems: Semantics and Algorithmic Issues. In: ACM SIGMOD. (2003) 325–336
3. Tan, W.C.: Research Problems in Data Provenance. IEEE Data Engineering Bulletin **27** (2004) 45–52
4. Bhagwat, D., Chiticariu, L., Tan, W.C., Vijayvargiya, G.: An Annotation Management System for Relational Databases. In: VLDB. (2004) 900–911
5. Chiticariu, L., Tan, W.C., Vijayvargiya, G.: Dbnotes: a post-it system for relational databases based on provenance. In: ACM SIGMOD. (2005) 942–944
6. Consortium, T.G.O.: The gene ontology (go) database and informatics resource. Nucl. Acids Res **32** (2004) 258–261

# The SIRUP Ontology Query API in Action

Patrick Ziegler, Christoph Sturm, and Klaus R. Dittrich

Database Technology Research Group,
Department of Informatics, University of Zurich,
Winterthurerstrasse 190, CH-8057 Zürich, Switzerland
{pziegler, sturm, dittrich}@ifi.unizh.ch

**Abstract.** Ontology languages to represent ontologies exist in large numbers, and users who want to access or reuse ontologies can often be confronted with a language they do not know. Therefore, ontology languages are nowadays themselves a source of heterogeneity.

In this demo, we present the SIRUP Ontology Query API (SOQA) [5] that has been developed for the SIRUP approach to semantic data integration [4]. SOQA is an ontology language independent Java API for query access to ontological metadata and data that can be represented in a variety of ontology languages. In addition, we demonstrate two applications that are based on SOQA: The SOQA Browser, a tool to graphically inspect all ontology information that can be accessed through SOQA, and SOQA-QL, an SQL-like query language that supports declarative queries against ontological metadata and data.

## 1 Introduction

In current information systems, ontologies are increasingly used to explicitly represent the intended real-world semantics of data and services. Ontologies provide a means to overcome heterogeneity by providing explicit, formal descriptions of concepts and their relationships that exist in a certain universe of discourse, together with a shared vocabulary to refer to these concepts. Based on agreed ontological domain semantics, the danger of semantic heterogeneity can be reduced.

A large number of ontology languages is available to specify ontologies. Besides traditional ontology languages, such as Ontolingua [1] or PowerLoom[1], there is a notable number of ontology languages for the Semantic Web, such as SHOE[2], DAML[3], or OWL[4]. Therefore, ontology languages are nowadays themselves a source of heterogeneity. As ontologies can be specified in a manifold of ontology languages, users looking for suitable ontologies can often be confronted with ontologies that are defined in a language they do not know. To make use of these ontologies, users either have to learn the particular ontology language or to find and employ suitable tools to access the desired ontology. Heterogeneity caused

---

[1] http://www.isi.edu/isd/LOOM/PowerLoom/
[2] http://www.cs.umd.edu/projects/plus/SHOE/
[3] http://www.daml.org
[4] http://www.w3.org/2004/OWL/

by the use of different ontology languages can therefore be a major obstacle in ontology access.

Besides this, building ontologies is a demanding and time-consuming task. Especially in cases where large all-embracing ontologies are built, the development phase can be a substantial investment — for example, more than a person-century has been invested in the development of CYC [2]. Therefore, existing ontologies should be reused so that advantage can be taken of the efforts spent during the ontology development phase. However, heterogeneity caused by the use of different ontology languages can be a considerable impediment to this.

In this demo, we present the SIRUP Ontology Query API (SOQA) [5], which is an ontology language independent Java API for query access to ontological metadata and data that can be represented in a variety of ontology languages. In an example scenario, four publicly available ontologies, each represented in a different ontology language, are accessed through SOQA. It is shown how their contents can be compared fast though concisely with the graphical SOQA Browser and with declarative queries in the SOQA Query Shell.

## 2 Overview of the SIRUP Ontology Query API

In general, ontology languages are designed for a particular purpose and, therefore, they vary in their syntax and semantics. To overcome these differences, we defined the SOQA Ontology Meta Model. It represents modeling capabilities that are typically supported by ontology languages to describe ontologies and their components; i.e., concepts, attributes, methods, relationships, instances, and ontological metadata [5]. Based on the SOQA Ontology Meta Model, the functionality of the SOQA API was designed. The SIRUP Ontology Query API (SOQA) is an ontology language independent Java API for query access to ontological metadata and data that can be represented in a multitude of ontology languages. That is, SOQA provides read access to ontologies through a uniform API that is independent of the underlying ontology language and hardware/software platform. Consequently, accessing and reusing general foundational ontologies as well as specialized domain-specific ontologies can be facilitated. With SOQA, users and applications can be provided with unified access to metadata and data of ontologies according the SOQA Ontology Meta Model. Besides, data of concept instances can be retrieved through SOQA. Note that despite the fact that SOQA is mainly employed for ontology access used for data content explication in the SIRUP integration approach [4], it is intended and designed to be a general-purpose ontology query API that can be used independently of SIRUP. SOQA and all its components are fully implemented in Java 1.5.

From an architectural perspective, the SOQA API reflects the Facade design pattern: SOQA provides a unified interface to a subsystem which is in charge of retrieving information from ontologies that are specified in different ontology languages. SOQA as a Facade shields external clients from the internal SOQA components and represents a single point for unified ontology access (see Fig. 1). Examples for external clients of the API provided by the SOQA Facade are:

- The query language SOQA-QL [5], which supports declarative queries over data and metadata of ontologies that are accessed through SOQA;
- The SOQA Browser [5] that enables users to graphically inspect the contents of ontologies independent of the ontology language they are specified in;
- (Third-party) Java applications that use SOQA as a single point of access to information that is specified in different ontology languages. Possible application areas are virtual organizations, enterprise information and process integration, the Semantic Web, and semantics-aware universal data management.

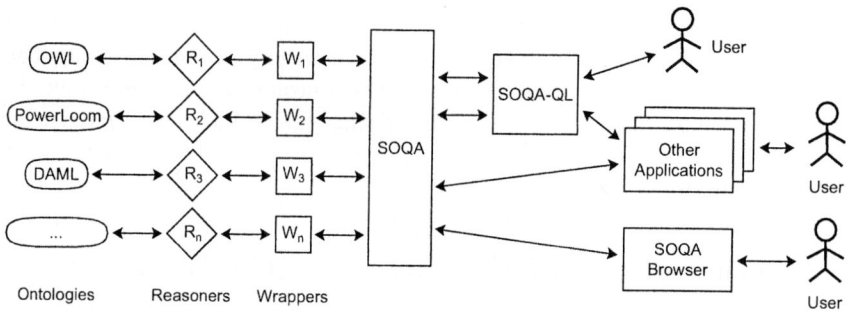

**Fig. 1.** Overview of the SOQA Software Architecture

Based on its Facade architecture, SOQA provides more than 70 Java methods for unified ontology access according to the SOQA Ontology Meta Model (for details, see [5]). Behind the SOQA Facade, ontology wrappers are used as an interface to existing reasoners that are specific to a particular ontology language (see Fig. 1). Up to now, we have implemented SOQA ontology wrappers for OWL, PowerLoom, DAML, and the lexical ontology WordNet [3].

## 3 Demonstration Highlights

To illustrate the capabilities of the SOQA, we assume an example scenario where a developer of an information system is looking for a publicly available ontology concerning persons from the university domain. Therefore, he or she might use a search engine and find (1) the Aktors Portal Ontology[5] that is represented in OWL, (2) the PowerLoom Course Ontology[6] developed in the SIRUP project, (3) the DAML University Ontology[7] from the University of Maryland, (4) and the lexical ontology WordNet. In contrast to the traditional approach, where our developer has to cope with four ontology languages and different ontology tools, we demonstrate uniform access to ontological information through SOQA. In particular, we show the capabilities of our graphical SOQA Browser and the

---
[5] http://www.aktors.org/ontology/portal
[6] http://www.ifi.unizh.ch/dbtg/Projects/SIRUP/ontologies/course.ploom
[7] http://www.cs.umd.edu/projects/plus/DAML/onts/univ1.0.daml

```
SELECT author, documentation, languagename FROM ontology;
SELECT name, documentation FROM attributes(base1_0_daml:Student);
SELECT * FROM directsuperconcepts(wordnet_1:Student);
SELECT name, value(portal:emailAddress)
FROM    instances(subconcepts(portal:Student)) WHERE name < 'C';
```

**Fig. 2.** SOQA-QL Example Queries Against Different Ontologies

declarative SOQA Query Shell for user-friendly access to ontology information independent of the language the four ontologies are represented in:

- The SOQA Browser is presented to quickly survey the concepts and their attributes, methods, relationships, and instances that are defined in a particular ontology, as well as metadata concerning the ontology itself. Thus, fast though concise comparisons of the four ontologies in distinct browser windows are shown.
- In the SOQA Query Shell, SOQA-QL queries are formulated for detailed access to ontological ontology data and metadata (see Fig. 2). Here, we present how the four ontologies and their components can be compared using declarative queries.

Based on this, we demonstrate how ontology access and reuse is enabled and facilitated through SOQA that can, hence, contribute to leverage from database systems to semantics-aware, universal data management.

# References

1. A. Farquhar, R. Fikes, and J. Rice. The Ontolingua Server: A Tool for Collaborative Ontology Construction. *International Journal of Human-Computer Studies (IJHCS)*, 46(6):707–727, 1997.
2. D. B. Lenat. CYC: A Large-Scale Investment in Knowledge Infrastructure. *Communications of the ACM*, 38(11):32–38, 1995.
3. G. A. Miller. WordNet:A Lexical Database for English. *Communications of the ACM*, 38(11):39–41, 1995.
4. P. Ziegler and K. R. Dittrich. User-Specific Semantic Integration of Heterogeneous Data: The SIRUP Approach. In M. Bouzeghoub, C. Goble, V. Kashyap, and S. Spaccapietra, editors, *First International IFIP Conference on Semantics of a Networked World (ICSNW 2004)*, pages 44–64, Paris, France, June 17-19, 2004. Springer.
5. P. Ziegler, C. Sturm, and K. R. Dittrich. Unified Querying of Ontology Languages with the SIRUP Ontology Query API. In G. Vossen, F. Leymann, P. C. Lockemann, and W. Stucky, editors, *Datenbanksysteme in Business, Technologie und Web (BTW 2005)*, pages 325–344, Karlsruhe, Germany, March 2-4, 2005. GI.

# Querying Mediated Geographic Data Sources

Mehdi Essid, François-Marie Colonna, Omar Boucelma, and Abdelkader Betari

LSIS and Université Paul Cézanne, Aix-Marseille 3,
Avenue Escadrille Normandie-Niemen,
F-13397 Marseille Cedex 20
`first.last@lsis.org`

**Abstract.** With the proliferation of geographic data and resources over the Internet, there is an increasing demand for integration services that allow a transparent access to massive repositories of heterogeneous spatial data. Recent initiatives such as Google Earth are likely to encourage other companies or state agencies to publish their (satellite) data over the Internet. To fulfill this demand, we need at minimum an efficient geographic integration system. The goal of this demonstration is to show some new and enhanced features of the VirGIS geographic mediation system.

## 1 Introduction

With the proliferation of geographic data and resources over the Internet, there is an increasing demand for integration services that allow a transparent access to massive repositories of heterogeneous spatial data. Recent initiatives such as Google Earth [5] are likely to encourage other companies or state agencies to publish their (satellite) data over the Internet, while integrating such data still poses several challenges.

The goal of this demonstration is to illustrate the enhanced and new features of VirGIS[3], a geographic mediation/wrapper system that provides the user with an integrated view of the data, and advanced query facilities. Typical mediation approaches are data-driven and do not address the problem of integration of query capabilities. But the exploitation of available query capabilities is critical to a geographic mediation system.

A preliminary version of the VirGIS prototype has been demonstrated at ICDE'2004[2]. This new version will exhibit advanced capabilities, both from the query engine point of view, and from the user interface perspective as well.

## 2 What Will Be Demonstrated

We will show the following aspects:

1. An enhanced GQuery [1] user interface: in the previous prototype, users were able to pose WFS [6] queries and some limited GQuery expressions. WFS

queries or XML/KVP (keyword-value-pair) queries are XML programs sent to WFS servers wrapping data sources. Although it allowed access to any geographic repository that is OpenGIS compliant, i.e., with a WFS interface, the system inherited WFS limitations because it lacked for complex queries expressions. The need for a more expressive and powerful query langage became obvious, and this led to the design and implementation of GQuery, an XQuery based language that allows spatial complex queries over GML data sources.
2. An extended mapping language that allows the expression of complex mappings (not only 1-to-1) in using constraints or functions (either basic ones or topological ones) between corresponding entities, i.e., attributes or features (classes).
3. A smarter query rewriting strategy: previously, when a property of a feature was missing from a source, a null value was returned to the user. In the current rewriting algorithm, feature properties that are missing in a source candidate, are searched in the other (compensating) local sources. More details on our rewriting strategy are given in [4].
4. Performance enhancement: we discovered that 90% of the execution time was devoted to join operations, performed by the underlying XQuery join processor. To speed up query processing, we developed a specific join component, based on a merge-sort join algorithm.

## 3 Demonstration Scenario

### 3.1 Data Sources

The scenario is a simplified version of the satellite catalogue interoperability problem. Consider the global (mediation) relation

$$satellite(\underline{ID}, Name, SatID, Elevation, Date, Geom, Url).$$

describing a catalogue of satellite images. A user may pose a query against the satellite relation schema, asking for a satellite image (stored at Url address) that cover a location described by Geom (coordinates or bounding box), the image (shot) being taken by a satellite named Name and whose id is SatID, at a given Date and with a given sun Elevation.

Relation satellite results from the integration of three relations stored in three different data sources as illustrated in Figure 1, and described as follows:

- the DBC relation, $DBC(\underline{key}, Satellite, Sat\_ID, Sun\_elev, Date\_, The\_Geom)$, stored in a geographic shape format, contains images taken by different satellites (SPOT, ASTER, IKONOS, etc.). In our example, we are interested only in images taken by SPOT *(satellite = 'spot')*.
- the ikonos relation, $ikonos(\underline{key}, Satellite, Sat\_ID, Sun\_el, Date\_acqui, Geometry)$, relates to (IKONOS) data – expressed in a different scale, and

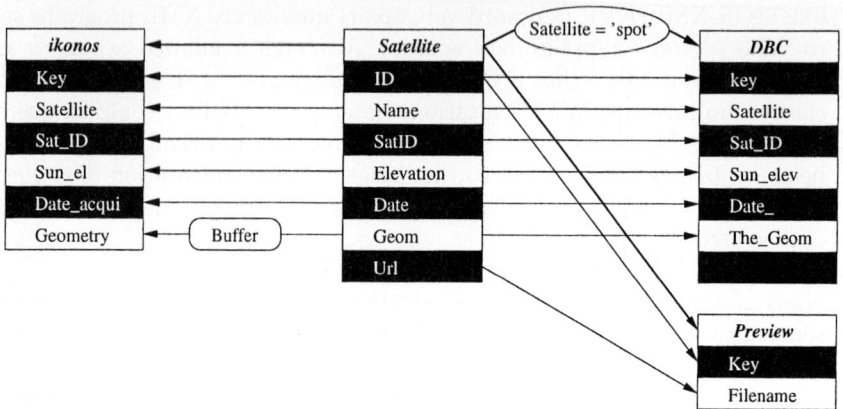

**Fig. 1.** Mapping Between Global and Local Schemas

stored in a PostGIS format. The spatial operator *Buffer* is applied to the *Geometry* attribute to perform scale conversion,
- the preview (*quick_look*) relation, $preview(\underline{key}, filename)$ supplies data stored in a POSTGRES database.

A typical query (denoted $Q_{demo}$) in this scenario could be phrased as follows:
*Given a spatial location, return all satellite images supplied by SPOT and IKONOS, between 2001 and 2004.*

As we already said, this version of VirGIS provides a more expressif mapping language. For example, one can add constraints to express mappings between features (the satellite global feature corresponds to the DBC real feature under the condition satellite = 'spot'). For more expressivity, these constraints may also contain spatial operators (the satellite global feature corresponds to the DBC real feature located in a zone $z$). Another extension of the mapping language allows aggregations between global and local attributes. For example, a global attribute may correspond to the result of an operator (spatial or not) executed over several local attributes (the global geometry attribute corresponds to a buffer built around the geometry of an ikonos feature).

### 3.2 Demonstration Highlights

The query is posed over the satellite relation, either in using GQuery or the graphical interface. When using the GQuery interface, a user can express complex queries over several global features in the same time. This could not be done on the previous prototype due to WFS limitations, that is get one feature at a time. In order to process such complex queries, we developed a three steps algorithm described as follows:

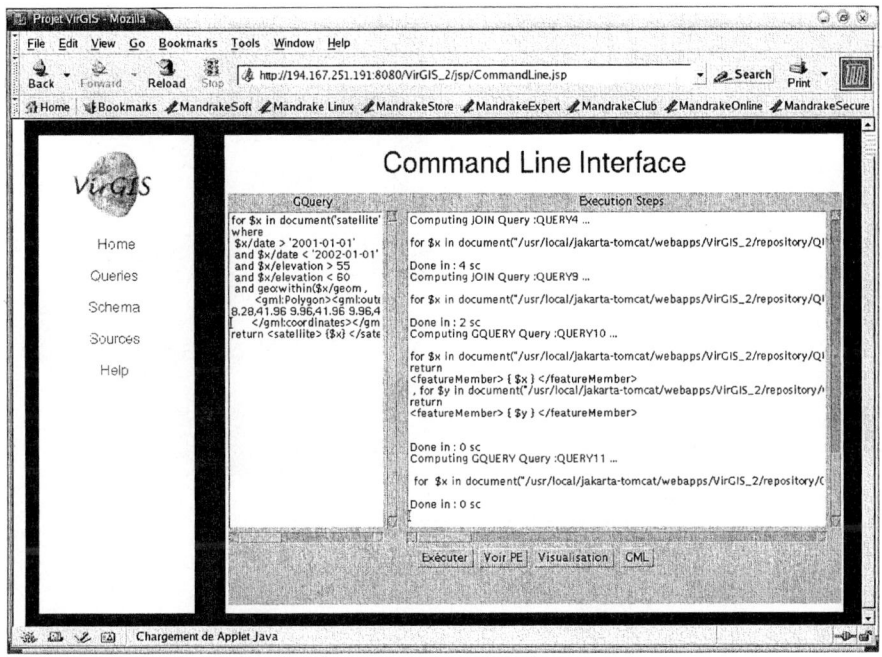

**Fig. 2.** GQuery (Command Line) Interface

1. a decomposition step in which we decompose a complex global query into elementary global queries, each of them dealing with one global feature only. This results in a global execution plan,
2. a rewriting step in which each elementary global query is rewritten in terms of the local schemas. The algorithm relies on key dependencies to return complete answers. This results in an elementary execution plan for each elementary query,
3. a transformation step during which we build the final execution plan. This is done by replacing each elementary query by its elementary execution plan and by adding transformation queries that perform sources to local schema translations.

Figure 2 illustrates the processing of a GQuery expression $Q_{demo}$. The figure highlights three screens: a general menu screen (left), a central screen that allows GQuery expressions to be entered on line, and a right screen that details the step by step query processing.

Figure 3 illustrates the graphical query interface, where a user simply delimits the bounding box target, sets some attribute values and submits the query. The answer may consist of several objects: a simple click on an object (one brick) will display the info attached to it.

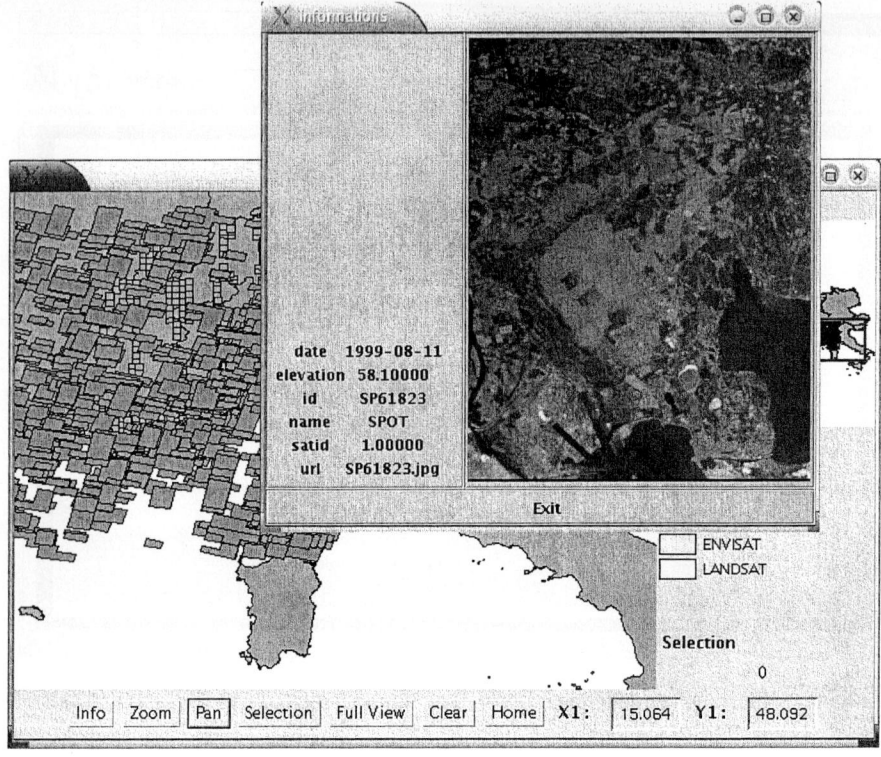

**Fig. 3.** Graphical User Interface

## 4 Conclusion

In this paper, we described the main VirGIS characteristics that will be demonstrated. The system relies on Open GIS standards (data model, GML, WFS, etc.) and represents an advanced mediation system for geographic data. To the best of our knowledge, there is no geographic mediation system that combines both geographic standards with W3C ones.

## References

1. O. Boucelma and F-M. Colonna. Mediation for Online Geoservices. In *Proc. 4th International Workshop, Web and Wireless Geographical Information Systems, W2GIS*, pages 81–93. LNCS 3428, Springer-Verlag, November 2004.
2. O. Boucelma, M. Essid, Z. Lacroix, J. Vinel, J-Y. Garinet, and A. Betari. VirGIS: Mediation for Geographical Information Systems. In *Proc. ICDE 2004, Boston*, March 30 - April 2 2004.
3. Omar Boucelma, Mehdi Essid, and Zoé Lacroix. A WFS-based Mediation System for GIS Interoperability. In *Proceedings of the tenth ACM international symposium on Advances in Geographic Information Systems*, pages 23–28. ACM Press, 2002.

4. M. Essid, O. Boucelma, F.-M. Colonna, and Y. Lassoued. Query Rewriting in a Geographic Mediation System. In *Proceedings of the 12th ACM international symposium on Advances in Geographic Information Systems*, pages 101–108. ACM Press, 2004.
5. Google. Google Earth Beta: A 3D interface to the planet. earth.google.com/.
6. OpenGIS. Web Feature Server Implementation Specification, September 19th 2002.

# FIS-by-Step: Visualization of the Fast Index Scan for Nearest Neighbor Queries

Elke Achtert and Dominik Schwald

Institute for Computer Science, University of Munich, Germany
{achtert, schwald}@dbs.ifi.lmu.de

**Abstract.** Many different index structures have been proposed for spatial databases to support efficient query processing. However, most of these index structures suffer from an exponential dependency in processing time upon the dimensionality of the data objects. Due to this fact, an alternative approach for query processing on high-dimensional data is simply to perform a sequential scan over the entire data set. This approach often yields in lower I/O costs than using a multi-dimensional index. The Fast Index Scan combines these two techniques and optimizes the number and order of blocks which are processed in a single chained I/O operation. In this demonstration we present a tool called FIS-by-Step which visualizes the single I/O operations during a Fast Index Scan while processing a nearest neighbor query. FIS-by-Step assists the development and evaluation of new cost models for the Fast Index Scan by providing user significant information about the applied page access strategy in each step of the algorithm.

## 1 Introduction

A large number of index structures for high-dimensional data have been proposed in previous years, cf. [2] for details. However, for sufficiently high dimensional data the complexity of similarity queries on multidimensional index structures is still far away from being logarithmic. Moreover, simple query processing techniques based on a sequential scan of the data are often able to outperform approaches based on sophisticated index structures. This is due to fact that usual index structures access data in too small portions and therefore cause lots of I/O accesses. The Fast Index Scan proposed in [1] subsumes the advantages of indexes and scan based methods in an optimal way. The algorithm collects accesses to neighboring pages and performs chained I/O requests, where the length of the chains are determined according to a cost model. The benefit of this chained I/O processing is that the seek costs–the main part of the total I/O costs–have to be paid only once. The authors have shown that the Fast Index Scan clearly outperforms both, the sequential scan as well as the Hjaltason and Samet algorithm which is typically used for processing nearest neighbor queries.

In this demonstration we present a tool called FIS-by-Step to visualize the single chained I/O operations during a nearest neighbor query by applying the Fast Index Scan on top of an R-Tree. FIS-by-Step displays the applied page

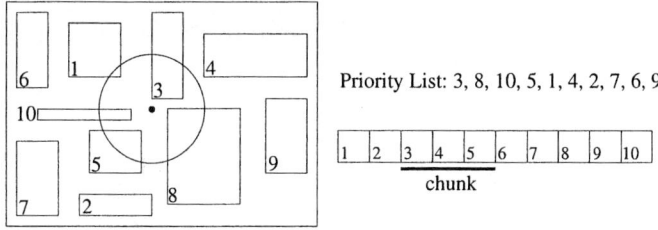

**Fig. 1.** The Fast Index Scan for nearest neighbor queries

access strategy in each step of the algorithm and provides user significant statistical information. The step-by-step visualization is very useful in a lot of cases, e.g. for teaching and explaining the function of the Fast Index Scan, for visual evaluation of the applied strategies or for development of new strategies.

The remainder of this paper is organized as follows: The concepts of the Fast Index Scan are described in Sect. 2. In Sect. 3 we demonstrate our tool FIS-by-Step for visualizing the I/O operations during a Fast Index Scan.

## 2 The Fast Index Scan

As the Fast Index Scan has been evaluated in [1] on top of the IQ-Tree, it can be applied to any R-Tree like spatial index structure that consists of only one directory level. Usually nearest neighbor queries are evaluated by the algorithm of Hjaltason and Samet (HS) [3], which has been proven to be optimal w.r.t. the number of accessed pages. Unlike the original HS algorithm which loads and processes one page after the other, the Fast Index Scan adapts the HS algorithm and tries to chain I/O operations for subsequent pages on disk and optimizes the number and order of pages which are processed in a single I/O-operation.

The HS algorithm keeps a priority list of all data pages in increasing order to their distance to the query point. For all pages $p_i$ in the priority queue there exists a certain probability that $p_i$ has to be loaded to answer the query. The idea of the Fast Index Scan is to load in each step a chunk of neighboring pages with a sufficient high probability instead of loading only one page, as the HS algorithm would do. In [1] the authors proposed a stochastic model to estimate the probability of a page to be accessed during a nearest neighbor query. Based on this access probability the cost balance of a page can be determined. A negative cost balance indicates that it is likely to be "profitable" to load the page in the current chunk additionally. This is given if the additional transfer costs to read the page in the current chunk are less than the estimated costs to read the page later in the algorithm. In Fig. 1 the page strategy of the Fast Index Scan is visualized: starting with page 3 the Fast Index Scan extends the chunk and reads page 4 and 5 additionally, because page 5 has a very high probability to be necessary to answer the query. Thus, reading page 4 and 5 in the current chunk is less expensive than loading page 5 in all probability later and causing additional seek costs.

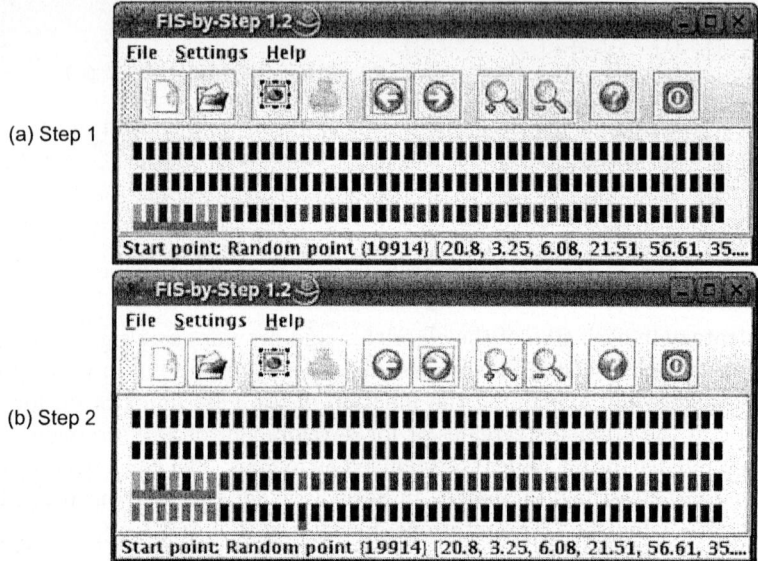

**Fig. 2.** Screenshots of the FIS-by-Step application

## 3 Visualization of the Fast Index Scan

The main purpose of the FIS-by-Step application is to show step-by-step how the Fast Index Scan solves a nearest neighbor query. Figure 2 shows screenshots of our application to explain how FIS-by-Step works.

Before running a query, it is possible to change some settings like the pagesize in order to adjust the application to the data. After choosing a data file (a CSV file of hyperpoints), the first line of black rectangles appears in the main window of the application. Each of these rectangles represents a page on the disk, where the order of the rectangles is identical with the order of the pages on disk. After selecting the query point (which can be the first point of the data, a random point of the data, or any given point) the second line of rectangles appears, again showing all pages, but now there is one blue rectangle: This is the page that is the nearest one to the query point.

The third line appears after using the "Next Step" button. This is the first step of the Fast Index Scan: The access probability is calculated for all pages. The different colors of the rectangles indicate the access probability of the pages: Black indicates an access probability of 0%, i.e. these pages need not to be read. Grey pages have been already processed and thus also have an access probability of 0%. A blue page is the nearest unprocessed page to the query point and therefore has an access probability of 100%. All other pages (with red to green color) have access probabilities between 0% and 100% and might have to be read during the algorithm. As illustrated in Fig. 2(a), in this step of our example 7 pages (underlined magenta) are read by the Fast Index Scan.

|                    | Accessed Pages | Used Time in ms |
|--------------------|---------------:|----------------:|
| Fast Index Scan    | 8              | 23.3104         |
| Hjaltason and Samet| 7              | 52.4216         |
| Sequential Scan    | 46             | 69.9848         |

**Fig. 3.** Statistics about the solved query

After using the "Next Step" button again, two things can happen: Either the query is solved and some statistics are displayed, or the query is not solved yet, so it is necessary to read some more pages as shown in Fig. 2(b). Note that all pages that have been read in the last step are now colored gray, as their access probability is now 0%. A lot of red colored pages from the first step are now black, since they have a larger distance to the query point than the nearest point of the already processed pages. Also there is a new blue page, i.e. a page with an access probability of 100%. This page is the one that is the nearest one to the query point, as all already processed pages are ignored. After this step the example query is solved, thus after using the "Next Step" button there does not appear a new line of rectangles, but a popup window, showing some statistics about the query (cf. Fig. 3). The statistical information consists of the number of accessed pages and the I/O time for solving the query using the Fast Index Scan in comparison to use the HS algorithm or the sequential scan of the data set, respectively. As the statistic shows, the Fast Index Scan outperforms the HS algorithm as well as the sequential scan.

As mentioned above, the primary objective of our FIS-by-Step application is the step-by-step visualization of the Fast Index Scan. This stepwise visualization is very useful in a lot of cases, e.g. for teaching and explaining the Fast Index Scan. FIS-by-Step supports the visual evaluation, comparison and improvement of strategies for building chunks for chained I/O operations, layout of pages on disk, and ordering pages for processing in CPU. Furthermore, FIS-by-Step assists the development of new strategies, as the advantages and disadvantages of a strategy for a given data are shown directly.

# References

1. S. Berchtold, C. Böhm, H. V. Jagadish, H.-P. Kriegel, and J. Sander. Independent Quantization: An index compression technique for high-dimensional data spaces. In *Proc. ICDE*, 2000.
2. C. Böhm, S. Berchtold, and D. A. Keim. Searching in high-dimensional spaces: Index structures for improving the performance of multimedia databases. *ACM Computing Surveys*, 33(3), 2001.
3. G. R. Hjaltason and H. Samet. Ranking in spatial databases. In *Proc. SSD*, 1995.

# *ArHeX*: An Approximate Retrieval System for Highly Heterogeneous XML Document Collections

Ismael Sanz[1], Marco Mesiti[2], Giovanna Guerrini[3], and Rafael Berlanga Llavori[1]

[1] Universitat Jaume I, Castellón, Spain
{berlanga, Ismael.Sanz}@uji.es
[2] Università di Milano, Italy
mesiti@dico.unimi.it
[3] Università di Genova, Italy
guerrini@disi.unige.it

## 1 Introduction

Handling the heterogeneity of structure and/or content of XML documents for the retrieval of information is a fertile field of research nowadays. Many efforts are currently devoted to identifying approximate answers to queries that require relaxation on conditions both on the structure and the content of XML documents [1, 2, 4, 5]. Results are ranked relying on score functions that measure their quality and relevance and only the top-$k$ returned.

Current efforts, however, are still based on some forms of homogeneity on the structure of the documents to be retrieved. The parent-child or ancestor descendant relationship among elements should be still preserved, and the problem of similarity at the tag level (whose solution often requires the use of an ontology) is seldom considered [6, 8]. Consider for example, two entity types Book and Author that are bound by the many-to-many Write relationship. Many XML representations are possible. Someone can model books documents by starting from the Book entity type and listing for each book its authors. Others can model books documents by starting from the Author entity type and listing for each author the books she wrote. Current approaches miss to find relevant solutions in collections containing both kinds of documents because they can relax the structural constraint (book/author becomes book//author) but they are not able to invert the relationship (book/author cannot become author/book). A more general problem is that current systems [3] support only a specific similarity function on XML documents, while in practice the concept of "similarity" strongly depends on the requirements of each particular application. This makes it difficult, if not impossible, to tailor these systems to particular requirements.

In this paper we present *ArHeX*, a system for approximate retrieval in the context of highly heterogeneous XML document collections. Our system is designed to support different similarity functions, including lexical (i.e., tag-oriented) and structural conditions in order to handle a wide variety of heterogeneous collections. In ArHex, a user can specify the pattern of data to be retrieved through

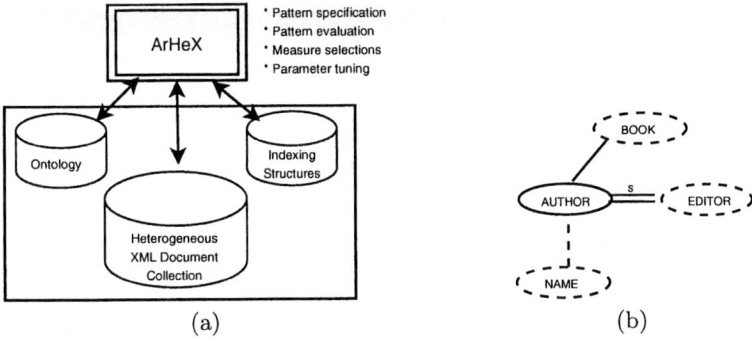

**Fig. 1.** (a) ArHeX architecture, (b) sample pattern

a graphical interface. Moreover, she can specify *mandatory constraints* on some relationships among elements or on the element tags that should be preserved. By means of specifically tailored indexing structures and heuristics, ArHex is able to efficiently identify the approximate answers for the specified retrieval query ranked according to a similarity measure. Several parameters can be set and used to tune the behavior of the system to the application scenario in which it is employed.

## 2 ArHex System

ArHeX allows users to specify a suitable similarity measure for their collection, combining lexical and structural conditions. The lexical measures range from simple techniques based on the overlap of substrings to ontology-based measures. Indexes are tailored to the required measure for an efficient computation, using an inverted file-like structure. A peculiarity of our index is that we do not have an entry for each tag in the collection, but a normalization process is performed to group together similar tags relying on the tag similarity function preferred by the user.

ArHex also supports a set of similarity measures that can be employed in the selection and ranking of query results. The considered measures range from standard information retrieval measures (e.g. occurrence of query tags) to more sophisticated ones (e.g. structure based or sibling order based functions).

The developed system is equipped with the following functionalities.

- *Pattern specification.* The structures of user queries are represented as *patterns* in our system. A pattern is a graph in which the user can specify a "preference" in the parent-child, ancestor-descendant and sibling relationships existing among elements or on the tags of elements (depicted through dashed lines in the graphical representations). "Preference" means that higher scores are given to query answers presenting such a structure but also results that do not (or only partially) present such a structure are returned. Moreover, a user can specify stricter constraints that must occur in the returned results. Our

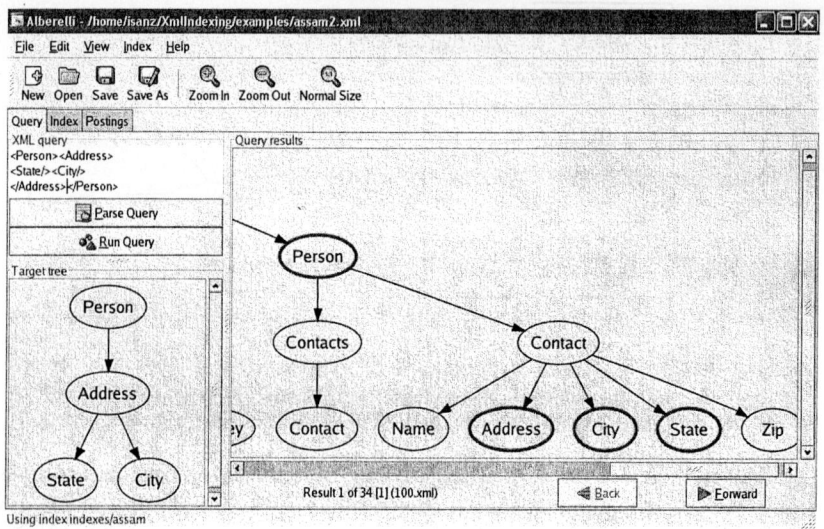

**Fig. 2.** ArHeX pattern evaluation facility

constraints are classified in 3 categories: ancestor-descendant, same level, and tag constraints (as detailed in [7]). Figure 1(b) shows an example of pattern in which we search for books having an author, editor and name elements. The book element can be the parent or the child of the author element. The name element can be the child of the author element but can also appear in other positions. The editor element should be found in the same level of the author element. In ArHeX patterns are specified through a graphical interface and then mapped in an XML document.

- *Pattern evaluation.* The evaluation of a pattern in the collection is performed in different steps (details in [7]). First, through the inverted index, a *pattern index* organized in levels is generated containing the elements in the collection whose tags are similar to those in the pattern. Then, *fragments* are generated by considering the parent-child and ancestor-descendant relationships among elements in the collection. Furthermore, through the use of a similarity measure and the heuristic *locality principle* [6], fragments are combined in regions when the similarity of the pattern with respect to a region is higher than that with respect to each single pattern. Mandatory constraints are checked both during fragment and region construction depending on the category they belong to. Whenever a constraint is not met the corresponding fragment/region can be dropped or penalized according to user preferences. Finally, the similarity measure is employed to rank the top-$k$ results. Figure 2 shows the evaluation of a pattern pointing out a similar region.
- *Measure selection.* Different measures can be applied for the evaluation of similarity between a pattern and a region depending on the application domain. ArHeX allows the selection from a set of predefined measures and the

combination of existing ones. Finally, in the evaluation of a pattern in the collection, a user can visualize the differences of evaluation obtained through a subset of the considered measures.
– *Parameter tuning.* A user can tune the behavior of ArHeX to a specific scenario through a set of parameters that a graphical interface offers. For example, a user can specify the kind of tag similarity to employ (syntactic, semantic or both). Moreover, she can specify an extra weight to assign to elements in the pattern that are not found in similar regions or she can state when regions that do not meet the mandatory constraints should be dropped or penalized (and the weight to apply as penalty in the last case).

## 3 The Demonstration

The demonstration will show the following features:

**Specification of user-defined similarity measures.** The system includes a library of component-based lexical and structural similarity functions, which can be tailored to the user's needs. We will demonstrate the definition of tailored measures.

**Queries on different real and synthetic collections of documents.** The performance of similarity-based queries using the graphical interface will be presented, using different real and synthetic collections of documents. Different similarity measures will be exercised showing the precision and recall results.

**Comparison of different measures.** The system supports the interactive exploration of heterogeneous collection by allowing the use of several distinct similarity measures, in order to compare the results.

## References

1. Amer-Yahia, S., Cho, S., Srivastava, D.: Tree Pattern Relaxation. EDBT. LNCS(2287). (2002) 496–513.
2. S. Amer-Yahia, N. Koudas, A. Marian, D. Srivastava, D. Toman. Structure and Content Scoring for XML. VLDB. (2005) 361–372.
3. G. Guerrini, M. Mesiti, I. Sanz. An Overview of Similarity Measures for Clustering XML Documents. Chapter in A. Vakali and G. Pallis (eds.), Web Data Management Practices: Emerging Techniques and Technologies. Idea Group.
4. A. Marian, S. Amer-Yahia, N. Koudas, D. Srivastava. Adaptive Processing of Top-k Queries in XML. ICDE. (2005) 162–173.
5. A. Nierman, H.V. Jagadish. Evaluating Structural Similarity in XML Documents. WebDB. (2002) 61–66.
6. I. Sanz, M. Mesiti, G. Guerrini, R. Berlanga Llavori. Approximate Subtree Identification in Heterogeneous XML Documents Collections. XSym. LNCS(3671). (2005) 192–206.
7. I. Sanz, M. Mesiti, G. Guerrini, R. Berlanga Llavori. Approximate Retrieval of Highly Heterogeneous XML Documents. Tech. report. University of Milano. (2005).
8. A. Theobald, G. Weikum. The Index-Based XXL Search Engine for Querying XML Data with Relevance Ranking. EDBT. LNCS(2287). (2002) 477–495.

# MonetDB/XQuery—Consistent and Efficient Updates on the Pre/Post Plane

Peter Boncz[1], Jan Flokstra[3], Torsten Grust[2], Maurice van Keulen[3],
Stefan Manegold[1], Sjoerd Mullender[1], Jan Rittinger[2], and Jens Teubner[2]

[1] CWI Amsterdam, The Netherlands
{boncz, manegold, sjoerd}@cwi.nl
[2] Technische Universität München, Germany
{grust, rittinge, teubnerj}@in.tum.de
[3] University of Twente, The Netherlands
{keulen, flokstra}@cs.utwente.nl

## 1 Introduction

Relational XQuery processors aim at leveraging mature relational DBMS query processing technology to provide scalability and efficiency. To achieve this goal, various storage schemes have been proposed to encode the tree structure of XML documents in flat relational tables. Basically, two classes can be identified: *(1)* encodings using *fixed-length surrogates*, like the *preorder ranks* in the *pre/post* encoding [5] or the equivalent *pre/size/level* encoding [8], and *(2)* encodings using *variable-length surrogates*, like, e.g., ORDPATH [9] or P-PBiTree [12]. Recent research [1] showed a clear advantage of the former for efficient evaluation of XPath location steps, exploiting techniques like cheap node order tests, positional lookup, and node skipping in *staircase join* [7]. However, once updates are involved, variable-length surrogates are often considered the better choice, mainly as a straightforward implementation of structural XML updates using fixed-length surrogates faces two performance bottlenecks: *(i)* high physical cost (the *pre*order ranks of all nodes following the update position must be modified— on average 50% of the document), and *(ii)* low transaction concurrency (updating the *size* of all ancestor nodes causes lock contention on the document root).

In [4], we presented techniques that allow an efficient and ACID-compliant implementation of XML updates also on the *pre/post* (respectively *pre/size/level* encoding) without sacrificing its superior XPath (i.e., read-only) performance. This demonstration describes in detail, how we successfully implemented these techniques in *MonetDB/XQuery*[1] [2,1], an XML database system with full-fledged XQuery support. The system consists of the *Pathfinder* compiler that translates and optimizes XQuery into relational algebra [6], on top of the high-performance MonetDB relational database engine [3].

---

[1] MonetDB/XQuery and the Pathfinder compiler are available in open-source: http://monetdb-xquery.org/ & http://pathfinder-xquery.org/; the second version including XML updates will be released well before EDBT 2006.

**Fig. 1.** The impact of Structural Updates on *pre/size/level* XML Storage

## 2 XML Updates

XML updates can be classified as: *(i) value updates*, which include node value changes (be it text, comment or processing instructions), and any change concerning attributes (attribute value changes, attribute deletion and insertion). Other modifications are *(ii) structural updates*, that insert or delete nodes in an XML document. With the *pre/size/level* encoding, value updates map quite trivially to updates in the underlying relational tables. Therefore, we focus on *structural updates* in the remainder.

W3C has not formulated a standard for XML updates, yet. However, we expect that a future standard will include the functionality of the UpdateX language as proposed in [11]. Given that there is no standard XML update language (and hence syntax), yet, we decided to keep the changes in our XQuery parser limited by not using the syntax proposed in [11], but rather implement the same update functionality by means of a series of new XQuery operators with side effects.

**Consistent Bulk Processing.** Semantically, *which* nodes are updated and with *what* values is determined solely using the pre-image (i.e. snapshot semantics). Still, updates need to be applied in the order mandated by XQuery evaluation, which conflicts with the bulk relational query execution employed in MonetDB/XQuery (where optimized query execution may use a different order). To overcome this problem, the update operators initially just produce a *tape* of *intended* updates. This tape is represented by an XQuery item sequence, and thus in the end is yielded in the correct order. Finally, after optimization (in which duplicate updates or updates on deleted nodes are pruned), these updates are applied and committed. In our opinion, this optimized bulk approach to updates is unique to MonetDB/XQuery. Note that the update tape, which separates query evaluation and update execution, bears some resemblance to the idea of monad-based I/O [10] in purely functional programming languages, *e.g.*, Haskell.

**Structural Update Problems.** Figure 1 illustrates how the *pre/size/level* document encoding is affected by a subtree insert (a delete raises similar issues): all *pre* values of the nodes following the insert point change, as well as the *size* of all ancestor nodes. The former issue imposes an update cost of $O(N)$, with

$N$ the document size, because on average half of the document are following nodes. The latter issue is not so much a problem in terms of update volume (the number of ancestors is bound by the tree's height, remaining small even for large XML instances) but rather one of locking: the document root is an ancestor of all nodes and thus must be locked by every update. This problem, however, can be circumvented by maintaining for each transaction a list of nodes of which the *size* is changed, together with the *delta* rather than the absolute changed value. This allows transactions to release locks on *size* immediately, and commit anyway later (even if the *size* of a node has been changed meanwhile by another committed transaction, we can just apply the delta to set it to a consistent state).

With the problem of locking contention on *size* removed this way, in the sequel we concentrate on the problem of the shifts in *pre* here.

**Page-Wise Remappable Pre-Numbers.** Figure 2 shows the changes introduced in MonetDB/XQuery to handle structural updates in the *pre/size/level* table. The key observations are:

- the table is called *pos/size/level* now.
- it is divided into *logical pages*.
- each logical page may contain *unused tuples*.
- new logical pages are appended only (i.e., at the end).
- the *pre/size/level* table is a view on *pos/size/level* with all pages in logical order. In MonetDB, this is implemented by mapping the underlying table into a new virtual memory region.

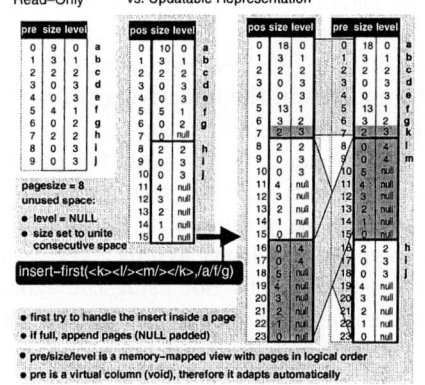

**Fig. 2.** Updates With Logical Pages

Figure 2 shows the example document being stored in two logical pages. The logical size is measured in a number of tuples (here: 8) instead of bytes. The document shredder already leaves a certain (configurable) percentage of tuples unused in each logical page. Initially, the unused tuples are located at the end of each page. Their *level* column is set to NULL, while the *size* column holds the number of directly following consecutive unused tuples. This allows the staircase-join to skip over unused tuples quickly. For the same reason, the *size* of existing nodes now also embraces the unused tuples within the respective subtrees.

The advantage of unused tuples is that structural deletes just leave the tuples of the deleted nodes in place (they become unused tuples) without causing any shifts in *pre* numbers. And since unused tuples are counted in the *size* of their ancestors, deletes do not require updates of the *size* of their ancestors. Also, inserts of subtrees whose sizes do not exceed the number of unused tuples on the logical page, do not cause shifts on other logical pages. Larger inserts, only use page-wise table appends. This is the main reason to replace *pre* by *pos*. The *pos* column is a densely increasing (0,1,2,...) integer column, which in MonetDB can be efficiently stored in a *virtual* (non-materialized) void column.

We introduced new functionality in MonetDB to map the underlying disk pages of a table in a different non-sequential order into virtual memory. Thus, by mapping in the virtual memory pages of the *pos/size/level* table in logical page order, overflow pages that were appended to it, become visible "halfway" in the *pre/size/level* view.

In the example of Figure 2, three new nodes k, l and m are inserted as children of context node g. This insert of three nodes does not fit the free space (the first page that holds g only has one unused tuple at $pos=7$). Therefore, a new logical page must be inserted in-between. Thus, we insert eight new tuples, of which only the first two represent real nodes (l and m), the latter six are unused. Thanks to the *virtual column* feature of MonetDB, in the resulting *pre/size/level* view, all *pre* numbers after the insert point automatically shift, at no update cost at all!

## 3 Conclusion

In our demonstration, we will show the performance and scalability of both read-only and update queries on potentially huge XML databases, provided by MonetDB/XQuery. The demonstration will graphically show how the key techniques described here influence the behavior of the system.

## References

1. P. Boncz, T. Grust, S. Manegold, J. Rittinger, and J. Teubner. Pathfinder: Relational XQuery Over Multi-Gigabyte XML Inputs In Interactive Time. Technical Report INS-E0503, CWI, 2005.
2. P. Boncz, T. Grust, M. van Keulen, S. Manegold, J. Rittinger, and J. Teubner. Pathfinder: XQuery—The Relational Way. In *Proc. VLDB Conf.*, 2005. (Demo).
3. P. Boncz and M.L. Kersten. MIL Primitives For Querying a Fragmented World. *The VLDB Journal*, 8(2), 1999.
4. P. Boncz, S. Manegold, and J. Rittinger. Updating the Pre/Post Plane in MonetDB/XQuery. In *Proc. XIME-P*, 2005.
5. T. Grust. Accelerating XPath Location Steps. In *Proc. SIGMOD Conf.*, 2002.
6. T. Grust, S. Sakr, and J. Teubner. XQuery on SQL Hosts. In *Proc. VLDB Conf.*, 2004.
7. T. Grust, M. v. Keulen, and J. Teubner. Staircase Join: Teach a Relational DBMS to Watch its (Axis) Steps. In *Proc. VLDB Conf.*, 2003.
8. T. Grust, M. van Keulen, and J. Teubner. Accelerating XPath evaluation in Any RDBMS. *ACM Trans. on Database Systems*, 29(1), 2004.
9. P.E. O'Neil, E.J. O'Neil, S. Pal, I. Cseri, G. Schaller, and N. Westbury. ORDPATH: Insert-Friendly XML Node Labels. In *Proc. SIGMOD Conf.*, 2004.
10. S. Peyton-Jones and P. Wadler. Imperative Functional Programming. In *Proc. POPL Conf.*, 1993.
11. G. M. Sur, J. Hammer, and J. Simeon. UpdateX - An XQuery-Based Language for Processing Updates in XML. In *Proc. PLAN-X*, 2004.
12. J. Xu Yu, D. Luo, X. Meng, and H. Lu. Dynamically Updating XML Data: Numbering Scheme Revisited. *World Wide Web Consortium*, 8(1), 2005.

# STRIDER: A Versatile System for Structural Disambiguation*

Federica Mandreoli, Riccardo Martoglia, and Enrico Ronchetti

DII, Università degli Studi di Modena e Reggio Emilia,
via Vignolese, 905/b - I 41100 Modena
{fmandreoli, rmartoglia, eronchetti}@unimo.it

**Abstract.** We present STRIDER[1], a versatile system for the disambiguation of structure-based information like XML schemas, structures of XML documents and web directories. The system performs high-quality fully-automated disambiguation by exploiting a novel and versatile structural disambiguation approach.

## 1 Introduction

In recent years, knowledge based approaches, i.e. approaches which exploit the semantics of the information they access, are rapidly acquiring more and more importance in a wide range of application contexts. We refer to "hot" research topics, like schema matching and query rewriting [2, 5], also in peer data management systems (PDMS), XML data clustering and classification [8] and ontology-based annotation of web pages and query expansion [1, 3], all going in the direction of the Semantic Web. In these contexts, most of the proposed approaches share a common basis: They focus on the structural properties of the accessed information, which are represented adopting XML or ontology based data models, and their effectiveness is heavily dependent on knowing the right meaning of the employed terminology. Fig. 1-a shows the hierarchical representation of a portion of the categories offered by eBay. It is an example of a typical tree-like structure-based information managed in the above mentioned contexts and which our approach is successfully able to disambiguate. It contains many polysemous words, from `string` to which WordNet [6], the most used commonly available vocabulary, associates 16 meanings, to `batteries` (11 meanings), `memory` (10 meanings), and so on. The information given by the surrounding nodes allows us to state, for instance, that `string` is a "stringed instrument played with a bow" and not a "linear sequence of symbols", and `batteries` are electronic devices and not a group of guns or whatever else.

In this paper we propose STRIDER, a system which could be of support to these kinds of approaches in overcoming the ambiguity of natural language, as it makes explicit the meanings of the words employed in tree-like structures. STRIDER exploits the novel versatile structural disambiguation approach we proposed in [4].

---
* This work is partially supported by the Italian Council co-funded project WISDOM.
[1] STRucture-based Information Disambiguation ExpeRt.

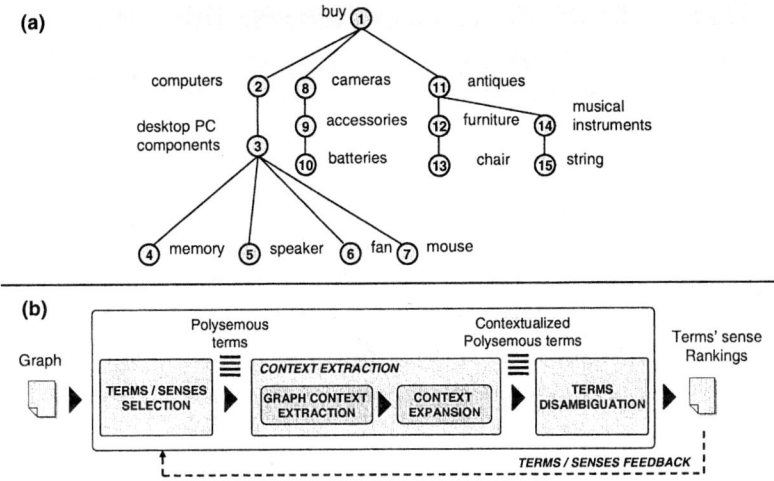

**Fig. 1.** (a) A portion of the eBay categories;(b) The complete STRIDER architecture

## 2   An Overview of the STRIDER System

STRIDER is designed to perform effective disambiguation of tree-like structures. As shown in Fig. 1-b, which depicts the complete architecture of our system, STRIDER takes in input structure-based information like XML schemas, structures of XML documents and web directories and disambiguates the terms contained in each node's label using WordNet as external knowledge source. The outcome of the disambiguation process is a ranking of the plausible senses for each term. In this way, the system is able to support both the completely automatic semantic annotation whenever the top sense of the ranking is selected and the assisted one through a GUI that assists the user providing useful suggestions. The STRIDER system has the following features:

- automated extraction of terms from tree's nodes (**Terms/Senses Selection** component in Fig.1-b);
- high-quality and *fully-automated disambiguation* that:
    - is independent from training or additional data, which are not always available [7];
    - exploits a context which goes beyond the simple "bag of words" approach and preserves the information given by the hierarchy (*graph context*);
    - allows flexible extraction and full exploitation of the graph context according to the application needs (**Graph Context Extraction** component in Fig.1-b);
    - enriches the graph context by considering the *expanded context*, with additional information extracted from WordNet definitions and usage examples (**Context Expansion** component in Fig.1-b);
- *interactive and automated feedback* to increase the quality of the disambiguation results;

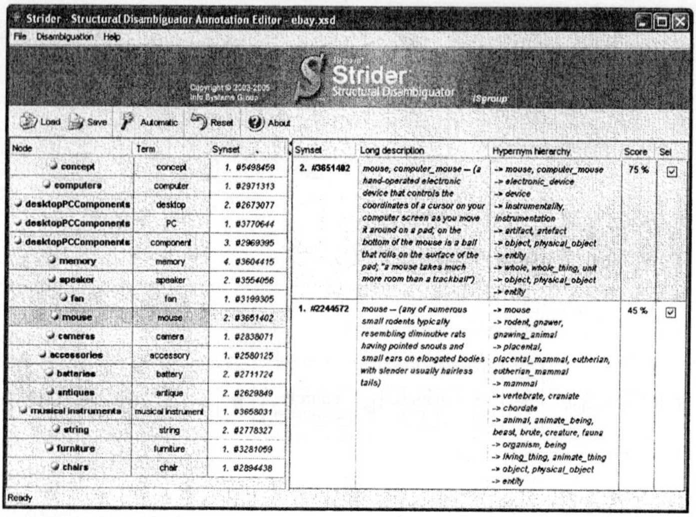

Fig. 2. The Graphical User Interface of the STRIDER System

- user-friendly GUI speeding up the *assisted disambiguation* of trees, providing an easy-to-use layout of the informative components.

Technical details about the implemented techniques for structural disambiguation are available in [4].

## 3 Demonstration

In this section we demonstrate the main features of STRIDER. The effectiveness of the system has been experimentally measured on several trees differing in the level of specificity and polysemy [4] (trees are available online at www.isgroup.unimo.it/paper/strider).

Fig. 2 shows STRIDER's GUI with the results of the disambiguation process for the eBay example (Fig. 1-a). In the left part of the GUI we see columns Node, Term that show the outcome of the automated extraction of terms from the tree's nodes and column Synset that contains the chosen sense for the corresponding term. For flexibility purposes, the GUI allows users to fill it in either by manually choosing one of the senses in the right part or by pressing the *Magic Wand*. This simple act triggers the fully *automatic disambiguation* process of STRIDER which is applied to the entire loaded tree and automatically chooses the top sense in the ranking of each term. When the user highlights a term in the left part of the GUI, the right part shows all the available senses and for each of them the synset's hypernym hyerarchy. One of the major strengths of our system is the versatility of being able to choose the crossing setting that is best suited to the tree characteristics. For instance, when the crossing setting is made up of the whole tree, the term antique of Fig.1-a is not disambiguated as "an old piece of furniture or decorative object", but as "an elderly man" due to the presence of terms like `fan` and `speaker` that could have the meaning of "persons" rather than "objects". This behavior is typical of trees that gather very heterogeneous concepts like web directories. On the other hand, only by using the whole tree as the crossing setting in trees that have a very particular scope, for instance an IMDB tree schema on movies, terms like `episode` and `genre` are correctly disambiguated whereas a restricted crossing setting made of only ancestors and descendants provides wrong results. In general, the performed tests demonstrate that most of the term's senses are correctly assigned straightforwardly with the disambiguation (the mean precision level on the tested trees is generally over 80% [4]). Such good performance is obtained even when the graph context provides too little information, as in generic bibliographic schemas, thanks to the *context expansion* feature which is able to deliver a higher disambiguation precision, by expanding the context with additional related nouns contained in the description and in the examples of each sense in WordNet. To get even better results the user could choose to refine them by performing successive disambiguation runs; for this purpose he/she is able to deactivate/activate the influence of the different senses of the available context words on the disambiguation process. Further, the flexibility of our approach allows the user to benefit from a completely *automated feedback*, where the results of the first run are refined by automatically disabling the contributions of all but the top ranked $X$ senses in the following runs.

## 4 Conclusions

The disambiguation performances achieved by STRIDER are encouraging and demonstrate the very good effectiveness of the adopted approach. The intuitive GUI provides easy interaction with the user; further, the system can also be used in batch mode to meet the needs of the most cutting edge semantic-aware applications, where user intervention is not feasible.

## References

1. P. Cimiano, S. Handschuh, and S. Staab. Towards the self-annotating web. In *Proc. of the 13th WWW Conference*, 2004.
2. H. Do, S. Melnik, and E. Rahm. Comparison of schema matching evaluations. In *Proc. of the 2nd WebDB Workshop*, 2002.
3. Marc Ehrig and Alexander Maedche. Ontology-focused crawling of web documents. In *Proc. of the ACM SAC*, 2003.
4. F. Mandreoli, R. Martoglia, and E. Ronchetti. Versatile Structural Disambiguation for Semantic-aware Applications. In *Proc. of the 14th CIKM Conference*, 2005.
5. F. Mandreoli, R. Martoglia, and P. Tiberio. Approximate Query Answering for a Heterogeneous XML Document Base. In *Proc. of the 5th WISE Conference*, 2004.
6. G. A. Miller. WordNet: A Lexical Database for English. *CACM*, 38(11), 1995.
7. I. Tatarinov and A. Halevy. Efficient Query Reformulation in Peer Data Management Systems. In *Proc. of ACM SIGMOD*, 2004.
8. M. Theobald, R. Schenkel, and G. Weikum. Exploiting Structure, Annotation, and Ontological Knowledge for Automatic Classification of XML Data. In *Proc. of the WebDB Workshop*, 2003.

# An Extensible, Distributed Simulation Environment for Peer Data Management Systems

Katja Hose, Andreas Job, Marcel Karnstedt, and Kai-Uwe Sattler

Department of Computer Science and Automation, TU Ilmenau,
P.O. Box 100565, D-98684 Ilmenau, Germany

**Abstract.** Peer Data Management Systems (PDMS) have recently attracted attention by the database community. One of the main challenges of this paradigm is the development and evaluation of indexing and query processing strategies for large-scale networks. So far, research groups working in this area build their own testing environment which first causes a huge effort and second makes it difficult to compare different strategies. In this demonstration paper, we present a simulation environment that aims to be an extensible platform for experimenting with query processing techniques in PDMS and allows for running large simulation experiments in distributed environments such as workstation clusters or even PlanetLab. In the demonstration we plan to show the evaluation of processing strategies for queries with specialized operators like top-$k$ and skyline computation on structured data.

## 1 Introduction

In recent years research concerning peer-to-peer (P2P) systems has mainly dealt with P2P applications based on environments that are much more sophisticated than those simple file sharing systems that they originate from. Especially Peer Data Management Systems (PDMS) are the focus of current work. They consider the problems arising from peers with different local schemas but appear to be one virtual database.

Research activities in this area do not only include the behavior and topology of a P2P system itself but also query processing strategies, routing indexes[1], schema correspondences[2], etc. All approaches and ideas have to be thoroughly evaluated. For this purpose, simulation environments are built. Such implementations have to meet several requirements in order to allow for reasonable evaluations. In the context of P2P research the primary requirements are: scalability, dynamic behavior, performance, extensibility, arbitrary experimental settings, repeatability, traceability/logging, and control (as mentioned in [3]).

Usually, research groups build their own environments using different data sets, programming languages, application areas and so on. This results in a couple of problems:

- Many environments are implemented rather hastily and have several shortcomings like limited network size, firm index structures and query processing strategies, or even include bugs. Other aspects are simplified and therefore cannot be examined.
- Results gained with different systems are usually not comparable. This leads to unsatisfying evaluations or high reimplementation costs.

- Existing environments are normally based on network simulators like *ns-2* that are too low-level for our purpose.
- Most environments do not have an intuitive user interface let alone a graphical one. Configuring and using the software is difficult. The output is rather cryptic and does not allow for an intuitive result analysis.

In this paper we present SmurfPDMS (SiMUlating enviRonment For PDMS), a simulator that meets all the requirements mentioned above. Furthermore, it tries to overcome the introduced shortcomings of existing simulators. In the following sections we present its architecture (Section 2) and the aspect of extensibility (Section 3). Afterwards, in Section 4, we present the graphical user interface that makes it easy to operate. Finally, in Section 5 we point out what features we are planning to show at the conference.

## 2 Architecture

SmurfPDMS logically consists of two parts that we implemented using Java: the *simulation engine* and an *environment for configuration and experimenting*. The latter uses a graphical interface based on Swing and JGraph (*http://www.jgraph.com*) for visualizing configuration parameters, statistics, networks and so on. Moreover, this environment can generate initial settings like the network topology based on user specified parameters like the number of peers and the average number of connections per peer.

The *simulation engine* simulates peers whose states are represented by peer objects. These objects have local caches and message queues to improve query processing, mappings to describe how to translate queries and data into a neighbor's schema, and indexes to describe a neighbor's data. The simulation environment does not only allow for running simulations locally on a single computer, it also gives the opportunity to run simulations involving a couple of computers - improving scalability. Communication between participating computers is carried out by sending and receiving messages using the JXTA [4] protocols. Simulating only one peer per machine enables the simulator to act like a "real" P2P application. In future work we intend to use *PlanetLab* (*http://www.planet-lab.org*) as the underlying framework.

Each participating computer manages several peer objects that can be connected to others residing on other computers. The localization of peer objects (local or remote) does not have any influence on the implementation of other components like query processing strategies. A central clock mechanism allows for gaining comparable results even in resource-limited environments. Apart from the system architecture like introduced above, Figure 1 shows the implementation architecture of SmurfPDMS. It consists of three layers: the graphical user interface, the simulation layer, and the network communication layer. This architecture considers several central concepts: (i) managers that control the simulation or communication, (ii) messages for information exchange, (iii) hierarchies of inherited objects, and (iv) the distinction of participating JXTA peers between multiple *participators* and one *coordinator*. The *coordinator* runs on a designated computer and coordinates the simulation. Its most important tasks are:

- Determine the setup including calculating a network topology, assigning the peers to the participating computers, calculating data partitions, etc.
- Choose queries and determine peers to initiate them

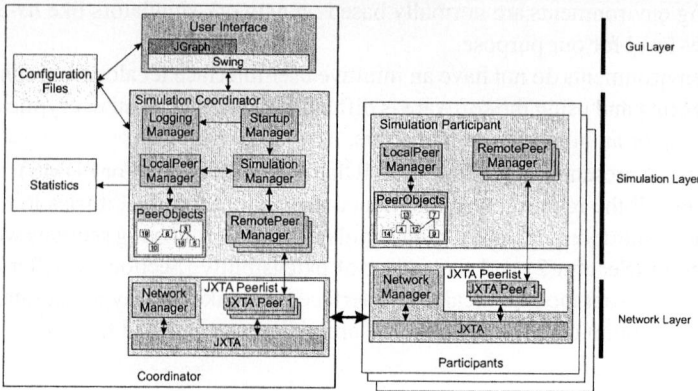

**Fig. 1.** Architecture

- Determine and choose peers to leave or join the network.
- Simulate communication and processing delays, log the initial setup (in order to achieve repeatability) as well as results and statistics.

## 3 Extensibility

We achieve extensibility by a modular architecture. Each of the above mentioned classes (manager, strategy, message, peer, etc.) represents a base class. Thus, the logical *simulation engine* of SmurfPDMS can be easily extended. For example, we have derived queries and answers from messages. If we want to introduce a new message type, we just have to derive a new class from the base class. In order to process such messages correctly, we could extend existing strategies or we could as well introduce a new strategy class as an extension of the corresponding base class.

Just like the *simulation engine*, we can also extend the *environment for configuration and experimenting*. SmurfPDMS has several algorithms for initializing a simulation. Assume we want to test different topology construction algorithms or algorithms for distributing the initial data among peers. Then all we have to do is adding an implementation of these algorithms to the concerned classes. All other parameters can remain the same. This allows us to examine the influence of these algorithms under the same environmental settings.

## 4 Running Experiments

First of all, the simulator has to be configured (*arbitrary simulation settings*). The user has the chance to load configuration files, to reconfigure individual parameters, or to have the simulator compute settings like the network topology, the data distribution, or the query mix. All these parameters and settings can be written to configuration files and reloaded for the next simulation (*repeatability*). Together with the log files we can easily reproduce and reconstruct entire simulations or reuse partial settings like the topology (*traceability/logging*).

Afterwards, the simulator looks for other JXTA peers in the network. The user can select among them those that he or she wants to participate in the simulation (*scalability, performance*). After having selected the JXTA peers the simulation can be started with the computer that the user currently operates on as coordinator (*control*).

Once the simulation has been started, simulations can be halted, canceled, and executed stepwise. Moreover, the *graphical user interface* provides the user with further features for visualization like messages and their details or peers' local statistics. Figure 2 shows the basic principles of visualizing. The simulation either ends after a user

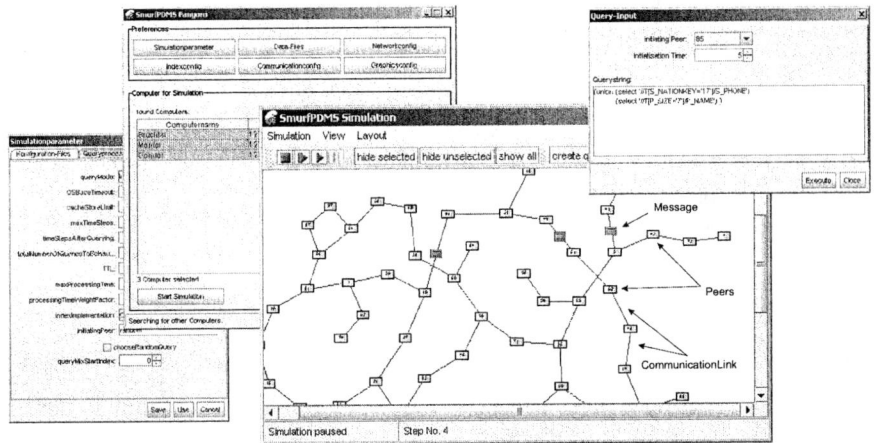

**Fig. 2.** Simulation window

defined number of simulation steps or when no peer has any actions left to perform. In both situations the coordinator sends the break signal to all participating JXTA peers and thus ends the simulation. At the end of a simulation the global statistics are displayed to the user and a file containing that data is created. These results can be used for creating charts like we did for example in [5] and [6].

## 5 Demonstration

We plan to focus our demonstration on the aspect of how to use the simulator for conducting experiments with arbitrary settings. This includes presenting algorithms for automatic topology generation as well as algorithms for distributing data among peers. Furthermore, we will show how to formulate queries by hand or how to have them generated automatically by the simulator. We will also show how to compare different query processing strategies by means of their results and collected statistics. Finally, we will show how we can do all this using a graphical user interface for both configuring the simulator and visualizing the results.

# References

1. Crespo, A., Garcia-Molina, H.: Routing indices for peer-to-peer systems. In: 22nd Int. Conf. on Distributed Computing Systems. (2002) 23–32
2. Tatarinov, I., Halevy, A.: Efficient query reformulation in peer data management systems. In: SIGMOD'04. (2004) 539–550
3. Buchmann, E., Böhm, K.: How to Run Experiments with Large Peer-to-Peer Data Structures. In: IPDPS'04. (2004)
4. Sun Microsystems, I.: JXTA v2.3.x: Java Programmer's Guide – http://www.jxta.org/docs/JxtaProgGuide_v2.3.pdf (2005)
5. Karnstedt, M., Hose, K., Sattler, K.U.: Query Routing and Processing in Schema-Based P2P Systems. In: DEXA'04 Workshops, IEEE Computer Society (2004) 544–548
6. Karnstedt, M., Hose, K., Stehr, E.A., Sattler, K.U.: Adaptive Routing Filters for Robust Query Processing in Schema-Based P2P Systems. In: IDEAS 2005, Montreal, Canada, 2005. (2005)

# Data Management in the Social Web

Karl Aberer

School of Computer and Communications Science,
EPFL, Lausanne, Switzerland
karl.aberer@epfl.ch

An interesting observation relates to the fact that the most successful applications on the Web incorporate some sort of social mechanism. This is true for commercial success stories, such as Ebay with its reputation mechanism, Amazon with its recommendation tool and Google with PageRank, a recommendation-based ranking algorithm. Peer-to-peer file sharing and photo sharing are other recent examples were the essence of the application consists of social interactions. In these applications large numbers of anonymous participants interact, such that mechanisms for social control become increasingly important. This explains the recent interest in reputation-based trust management. The same issues will emerge when large numbers of services will be deployed over the Web through Web services and Grid computing technology.

The goal of the panel is to reflect on these developments, identify important classes of applications involving social interaction which require data management support and information management capabilities, and project from there the potential future impact on the field of data management.

A characteristic property of applications involving social interactions is the large numbers of participants of whom the behavior needs to be tracked and analyzed. This implies a strong need for scalable data management capabilities. Will this require novel approaches in the area of data management or will existing technology be sufficient? The past has shown that new applications frequently open new avenues in data management research. Examples are semi-structured data management responding to the need of managing data on the Web and stream data management responding to the need of managing data in networked environments and sensor data.

Recently, in the context of the Semantic Web, social mechanisms for semantic tagging, so-called folksonomies, have created quite some interest. There the creation and alignment of structured data annotations for Web content becomes a social activity. Similarly as with collaborative filtering in information retrieval the social context is exploited in order to deal with the semantics problem, namely providing proper interpretation of data. Is this a promising approach for dealing with one of the hardest problems in data management, namely dealing with semantic heterogeneity of structured data?

In social settings uncertainty is omnipresent, since intentions and interpretations of autonomous participants cannot be made completely transparent. This holds also true when it comes to the exchange and shared use of data. Is it possible, that the recent growing interest of the database community in applying probabilistic techniques in data management roots also in the need of having appropriate tools for dealing with the uncertainty resulting from interaction in a social context?

Finally, from a more general perspective, new requirements on data management often initiate new directions of interdisciplinary research for the field. Will the need to provide solutions for data management on the Social Web lead database researchers to look into areas such as agent technologies, game theory or micro-economy to better understand the mechanics of social interactions and their impact on data management solutions?

These were some of questions that we will pose to the panel in order to identify interesting directions for future data management research.

# Author Index

Abbadi, Amr El   112
Aberer, Karl   1203
Abiteboul, Serge   1049, 1059
Achtert, Elke   1182
Afrati, Foto   942
Aggarwal, Charu C.   41
Agrawal, Divyakant   112
Agrawal, Rakesh   240
Albano, Antonio   1110
Amer-Yahia, Sihem   349
Ashish, Naveen   1159
Aßfalg, Johannes   276, 1147
Atzeni, Paolo   368

Bai, Yijian   588
Basak, Jayanta   1097
Behrends, Erik   792
Bender, Matthias   149
Berg, Brandon   1102
Bernstein, Abraham   59
Bernstein, Philip A.   368
Betari, Abdelkader   1176
Bhattacharya, Arnab   865
Bhide, Manish   1097
Bijay, Kumar Gaurav   608
Bleiholder, Jens   811
Böhlen, Michael   257, 1135
Böhm, A.   1125
Boncz, Peter   1190
Botev, Chavdar   349
Boucelma, Omar   1176
Boulos, Jihad   755, 1155
Brantner, M.   1125
Brecheisen, Stefan   1151, 1164
Brochhaus, Christoph   204
Broder, Andrei Z.   313
Bruno, Nicolas   386

Camoglu, Orhan   645
Canahuate, Guadalupe   884
Cappellari, Paolo   368
Casati, Fabio   1079
Castellanos, Malu   1079
Celle, Roberto   1143

Chan, Chee-Yong   478
Chaudhuri, Surajit   386
Chen, Ming-Syan   682
Cheng, Jiefeng   961
Chirkova, Rada   942
Chuang, Kun-Ta   682
Colonna, François-Marie   1176
Cormode, Graham   4

Dayal, Umeshwar   1079, 1106
De Rosa, Luca   1110
Demers, Alan   627
Dittrich, Klaus R.   59, 1135, 1172
Drukh, Natasha   1088
Dumitrescu, Cristian   1110

Eiron, Nadav   313
Essid, Mehdi   1176
Ewen, Stephan   847

Feng, Ying   112
Ferhatosmanoglu, Hakan   884
Fletcher, George H.L.   95
Flokstra, Jan   1190
Fontoura, Marcus   313
Fritzen, Oliver   792
Furfaro, Filippo   442

Gamper, Johann   257
Garofalakis, Minos   4
Geerts, Floris   1168
Gehrke, Johannes   627
Gemulla, Rainer   423
Georgiadis, Haris   570
Gergatsoulis, Manolis   942
Ghica, Oliviu   1039
Gibas, Michael   884
Goglia, Lucio   1110
Goglia, Roberto   1110
Golab, Lukasz   608
Govindarajan, Kannan   1106
Gruber, Michael   1151
Grust, Torsten   1190
Guerrini, Giovanna   1143, 1186

Haas, Peter J.   1092
Hacıgümüş, Hakan   1084
Hariharan, Ramaswamy   1159
Herscovici, Michael   313
Hinze, Annika   1039
Hodel-Widmer, Thomas B.   1135
Hong, Mingsheng   627
Hose, Katja   1198
Hu, Haibo   186
Hu, Meng   664
Hua, Kien A.   700
Huang, Jiun-Long   682
Hung, Jen-Jou   902
Hvasshovd, Svein-Olaf   405

Jagadish, H.V.   478, 737
Jensen, Christian S.   257
Jin, Ruoming   533
Job, Andreas   1198

Kache, Holger   847
Kahveci, Tamer   645
Kalashnikov, Dmitri V.   1159
Kanne, C-C.   1125
Kantere, Verena   1069
Kanza, Yaron   222
Karakashian, Shant   755
Karam, Marcel   1155
Karnstedt, Marcel   1198
Kementsietsidis, Anastasios   1168
Kersten, Martin   1
Khuller, Samir   811
Kiefer, Christoph   59
Kiringa, Iluju   1069
Koteiche, Zeina   1155
Koudas, Nick   460
Kreulen, Jeffrey   1084
Kriegel, Hans-Peter   276, 1147, 1151, 1164
Kröger, Peer   276, 1147
Kunath, Peter   276, 1147, 1164
Kuno, Harumi   1106
Kutsch, Marcel   1092

Lee, Dik Lun   186, 515
Lee, Ken C.K.   1020
Lee, Wang-Chien   1020
Lehner, Wolfgang   423
Lempel, Ronny   313
Leone, Stefania   1135

Li, Yunyao   737
Lin, Xuemin   961
Liu, Danzhou   700
Liu, Peiya   588
Liu, Shaorong   588
Ljosa, Vebjorn   865
Llavori, Rafael Berlanga   1186
Lochovsky, Frederick   77
Løland, Jørgen   405
Luo, Gang   921
Luo, Qiong   515

Ma, Yiming   1159
Maier, David   3
Mamoulis, Nikos   167
Mandreoli, Federica   295, 1194
Manegold, Stefan   1190
Manolescu, Ioana   1049
Mansmann, Florian   496
Markl, Volker   847, 1092
Martoglia, Riccardo   295, 1194
Matia, Yariv   1139
Matias, Yossi   1088, 1139
May, N.   1125
May, Wolfgang   792
Mazzeo, Giuseppe M.   442
McPherson, John   313
Megiddo, Nimrod   1092
Mehrotra, Sharad   1159
Meka, Anand   980
Mendelzon, Alberto O.   222
Mesiti, Marco   1143, 1186
Michel, Sebastian   149
Mignet, Laurent   1097
Milano, Diego   1168
Miller, Renée J.   222
Minei, Vincenzo   1110
Moerkotte, G.   1125
Morzy, Tadeusz   1121
Mullender, Sjoerd   1190
Mylopoulos, John   1069

Nanda, Jyotirmaya   1106
Narang, Inderpal   1115
Natarajan, Ramesh   1115
Naughton, Jeffrey F.   921
Naumann, Felix   773, 811
Nehme, Rimma V.   1001
Neven, Frank   829
Ntarmos, Nikos   131

Ollaic, Hala 1155
Özsu, M. Tamer 608

Pal, Shankar 1102
Panayiotopoulos, Themis 1130
Parthasarathy, Srinivasan 533
Pavlaki, Vassia 942
Pelekis, Nikos 1130
Phan, Thomas 1115
Pitoura, Theoni 131
Portman, Leon 1088, 1139
Pryakhin, Alexey 276, 1147, 1164
Puhlmann, Sven 773

Qi, Runping 313

Raghavachari, Mukund 552
Raman, Vijayshankar 847
Raschid, Louiqa 811
Ravikant, D.V.S. 1097
Reichert, Michael 1097
Renz, Matthias 276, 1147
Rhodes, James 1084
Riedewald, Mirek 627
Rittinger, Jan 1190
Ronchetti, Enrico 295, 1194
Roy, Prasan 1097
Roy, Sourashis 1097
Rundensteiner, Elke A. 1001

Sacharidis, Dimitris 4
Sanz, Ismael 1186
Sattler, Kai-Uwe 1198
Schenkel, Ralf 331
Scheuermann, Peter 1039
Schubert, Matthias 1151
Schwald, Dominik 1182
Seidl, Thomas 204
Seifert, André 902
Senellart, Pierre 1059
Sengar, Vibhuti S. 1097
Shan, Ming-Chien 1079
Shanmugasundaram, Jayavel 349
Shekita, Eugene 313
Shmueli, Oded 552
Singh, Ambuj K. 865, 980
Sion, Radu 1115
Sirangelo, Cristina 442
Skopal, Tomáš 718
Smathers, Kevin 1106
Smeaton, Alan F. 2

Sorrenti, Matteo A. 1143
Spangler, Scott 1084
Steinbach, Torsten 1097
Sturm, Christoph 59, 1172
Su, Weifeng 77

Tan, Kian-Lee 478
Tao, Yufei 167
Taropa, Emanuel 1049
Terzi, Evimaria 240
Teubner, Jens 1190
Theobald, Martin 331
Theodoridis, Yannis 1130
Tomic, Dragan 1102
Trajcevski, Goce 1039
Tran, Tam Minh 1092
Triantafillou, Peter 131, 149
Tung, Anthony K.H. 478
Turaga, Deepak S. 23

Vadapalli, Soujanya 1097
Van de Craen, Dieter 829
van Keulen, Maurice 1190
Vassalos, Vasilis 570
Vatsavai, Ranga R. 1097
Venkatasubramanian, Nalini 1159
Venkateswaran, Jayendra 645
Vinnik, Svetlana 496
Vlachos, Michail 23
Voisard, Agnes 1039
Vorberger, Florian 1164
Vosinakis, Spyros 1130
Vu, Khanh 700

Wang, Chao 533
Wang, Fusheng 588
Wang, Haixun 961
Wang, Jiying 77
Weikum, Gerhard 149
Weis, Melanie 773
White, Walker 627
Wichterich, Marc 204
Wilkinson, Kevin 1106
Wrembel, Robert 1121
Wu, Ping 112
Wu, Yao 811
Wyss, Catharine M. 95

Xavier, Joe 1102
Xu, Jianliang 186, 1020

Yang, Huahai    737
Yang, Jiong    664
Yiu, Man Lung    167
Yu, Jeffrey Xu    961
Yu, Ning    700
Yu, Philip S.    23, 921, 961
Yu, Xiaohui    460
Yuasa, Kei    1106

Zhang, Caijie    112
Zhang, Zheng    222
Zhang, Zhenjie    478
Zhao, Ben Y.    112
Zhao, Dan    1069
Zhao, Dyce Jing    515
Zheng, Baihua    1020
Ziegler, Patrick    59, 1172
Zuzarte, Calisto    460

# Lecture Notes in Computer Science

For information about Vols. 1–3808

please contact your bookseller or Springer

Vol. 3923: A. Mycroft, A. Zeller (Eds.), Compiler Construction. XV, 277 pages. 2006.

Vol. 3921: L. Aceto, A. Ingólfsdóttir (Eds.), Foundations of Software Science and Computational Structures. XV, 447 pages. 2006.

Vol. 3903: K. Chen, R. Deng, X. Lai, J. Zhou (Eds.), Information Security Practice and Experience. XIV, 392 pages. 2006.

Vol. 3901: P.M. Hill (Ed.), Logic Based Program Synthesis and Transformation. X, 179 pages. 2006.

Vol. 3899: S. Frintrop, VOCUS: A Visual Attention System for Object Detection and Goal-Directed Search. XIV, 216 pages. 2006. (Sublibrary LNAI).

Vol. 3896: Y. Ioannidis, M.H. Scholl, J.W. Schmidt, F. Matthes, M. Hatzopoulos, K. Boehm, A. Kemper, T. Grust, C. Boehm (Eds.), Advances in Database Technology - EDBT 2006. XIV, 1208 pages. 2006.

Vol. 3895: O. Goldreich, A.L. Rosenberg, A.L. Selman (Eds.), Essays in Theoretical Computer Science. XII, 399 pages. 2006.

Vol. 3894: W. Grass, B. Sick, K. Waldschmidt (Eds.), Architecture of Computing Systems - ARCS 2006. XII, 496 pages. 2006.

Vol. 3890: S.G. Thompson, R. Ghanea-Hercock (Eds.), Defence Applications of Multi-Agent Systems. XII, 141 pages. 2006. (Sublibrary LNAI).

Vol. 3889: J. Rosca, D. Erdogmus, J.C. Príncipe, S. Haykin (Eds.), Independent Component Analysis and Blind Signal Separation. XXI, 980 pages. 2006.

Vol. 3888: D. Draheim, G. Weber (Eds.), Trends in Enterprise Application Architecture. IX, 145 pages. 2006.

Vol. 3887: J. Correa, A. Hevia, M. Kiwi (Eds.), LATIN 2006: Theoretical Informatics. XVI, 814 pages. 2006.

Vol. 3886: E.G. Bremer, J. Hakenberg, E.-H.(S.) Han, D. Berrar, W. Dubitzky (Eds.), Knowledge Discovery in Life Science Literature. XIV, 147 pages. 2006. (Sublibrary LNBI).

Vol. 3885: V. Torra, Y. Narukawa, A. Valls, J. Domingo-Ferrer (Eds.), Modeling Decisions for Artificial Intelligence. XII, 374 pages. 2006. (Sublibrary LNAI).

Vol. 3884: B. Durand, W. Thomas (Eds.), STACS 2006. XIV, 714 pages. 2006.

Vol. 3881: S. Gibet, N. Courty, J.-F. Kamp (Eds.), Gesture in Human-Computer Interaction and Simulation. XIII, 344 pages. 2006. (Sublibrary LNAI).

Vol. 3880: A. Rashid, M. Aksit (Eds.), Transactions on Aspect-Oriented Software Development I. IX, 335 pages. 2006.

Vol. 3879: T. Erlebach, G. Persinao (Eds.), Approximation and Online Algorithms. X, 349 pages. 2006.

Vol. 3878: A. Gelbukh (Ed.), Computational Linguistics and Intelligent Text Processing. XVII, 589 pages. 2006.

Vol. 3877: M. Detyniecki, J.M. Jose, A. Nürnberger, C. J. '. van Rijsbergen (Eds.), Adaptive Multimedia Retrieval: User, Context, and Feedback. XI, 279 pages. 2006.

Vol. 3876: S. Halevi, T. Rabin (Eds.), Theory of Cryptography. XI, 617 pages. 2006.

Vol. 3875: S. Ur, E. Bin, Y. Wolfsthal (Eds.), Haifa Verification Conference. X, 265 pages. 2006.

Vol. 3874: R. Missaoui, J. Schmidt (Eds.), Formal Concept Analysis. X, 309 pages. 2006. (Sublibrary LNAI).

Vol. 3873: L. Maicher, J. Park (Eds.), Charting the Topic Maps Research and Applications Landscape. VIII, 281 pages. 2006. (Sublibrary LNAI).

Vol. 3872: H. Bunke, A. L. Spitz (Eds.), Document Analysis Systems VII. XIII, 630 pages. 2006.

Vol. 3870: S. Spaccapietra, P. Atzeni, W.W. Chu, T. Catarci, K.P. Sycara (Eds.), Journal on Data Semantics V. XIII, 237 pages. 2006.

Vol. 3869: S. Renals, S. Bengio (Eds.), Machine Learning for Multimodal Interaction. XIII, 490 pages. 2006.

Vol. 3868: K. Römer, H. Karl, F. Mattern (Eds.), Wireless Sensor Networks. XI, 342 pages. 2006.

Vol. 3866: T. Dimitrakos, F. Martinelli, P.Y.A. Ryan, S. Schneider (Eds.), Formal Aspects in Security and Trust. X, 259 pages. 2006.

Vol. 3865: W. Shen, K.-M. Chao, Z. Lin, J.-P.A. Barthès (Eds.), Computer Supported Cooperative Work in Design II. XII, 359 pages. 2006.

Vol. 3863: M. Kohlhase (Ed.), Mathematical Knowledge Management. XI, 405 pages. 2006. (Sublibrary LNAI).

Vol. 3862: R.H. Bordini, M. Dastani, J. Dix, A.E.F. Seghrouchni (Eds.), Programming Multi-Agent Systems. XIV, 267 pages. 2006. (Sublibrary LNAI).

Vol. 3861: J. Dix, S.J. Hegner (Eds.), Foundations of Information and Knowledge Systems. X, 331 pages. 2006.

Vol. 3860: D. Pointcheval (Ed.), Topics in Cryptology – CT-RSA 2006. XI, 365 pages. 2006.

Vol. 3858: A. Valdes, D. Zamboni (Eds.), Recent Advances in Intrusion Detection. X, 351 pages. 2006.

Vol. 3857: M.P.C. Fossorier, H. Imai, S. Lin, A. Poli (Eds.), Applied Algebra, Algebraic Algorithms and Error-Correcting Codes. XI, 350 pages. 2006.

Vol. 3855: E. A. Emerson, K.S. Namjoshi (Eds.), Verification, Model Checking, and Abstract Interpretation. XI, 443 pages. 2005.

Vol. 3854: I. Stavrakakis, M. Smirnov (Eds.), Autonomic Communication. XIII, 303 pages. 2006.

Vol. 3853: A.J. Ijspeert, T. Masuzawa, S. Kusumoto (Eds.), Biologically Inspired Approaches to Advanced Information Technology. XIV, 388 pages. 2006.

Vol. 3852: P.J. Narayanan, S.K. Nayar, H.-Y. Shum (Eds.), Computer Vision – ACCV 2006, Part II. XXXI, 977 pages. 2006.

Vol. 3851: P.J. Narayanan, S.K. Nayar, H.-Y. Shum (Eds.), Computer Vision – ACCV 2006, Part I. XXXI, 973 pages. 2006.

Vol. 3850: R. Freund, G. Păun, G. Rozenberg, A. Salomaa (Eds.), Membrane Computing. IX, 371 pages. 2006.

Vol. 3849: I. Bloch, A. Petrosino, A.G.B. Tettamanzi (Eds.), Fuzzy Logic and Applications. XIV, 438 pages. 2006. (Sublibrary LNAI).

Vol. 3848: J.-F. Boulicaut, L. De Raedt, H. Mannila (Eds.), Constraint-Based Mining and Inductive Databases. X, 401 pages. 2006. (Sublibrary LNAI).

Vol. 3847: K.P. Jantke, A. Lunzer, N. Spyratos, Y. Tanaka (Eds.), Federation over the Web. X, 215 pages. 2006. (Sublibrary LNAI).

Vol. 3846: H. J. van den Herik, Y. Björnsson, N.S. Netanyahu (Eds.), Computers and Games. XIV, 333 pages. 2006.

Vol. 3845: J. Farré, I. Litovsky, S. Schmitz (Eds.), Implementation and Application of Automata. XIII, 360 pages. 2006.

Vol. 3844: J.-M. Bruel (Ed.), Satellite Events at the MoDELS 2005 Conference. XIII, 360 pages. 2006.

Vol. 3843: P. Healy, N.S. Nikolov (Eds.), Graph Drawing. XVII, 536 pages. 2006.

Vol. 3842: H.T. Shen, J. Li, M. Li, J. Ni, W. Wang (Eds.), Advanced Web and Network Technologies, and Applications. XXVII, 1057 pages. 2006.

Vol. 3841: X. Zhou, J. Li, H.T. Shen, M. Kitsuregawa, Y. Zhang (Eds.), Frontiers of WWW Research and Development - APWeb 2006. XXIV, 1223 pages. 2006.

Vol. 3840: M. Li, B. Boehm, L.J. Osterweil (Eds.), Unifying the Software Process Spectrum. XVI, 522 pages. 2006.

Vol. 3839: J.-C. Filliâtre, C. Paulin-Mohring, B. Werner (Eds.), Types for Proofs and Programs. VIII, 275 pages. 2006.

Vol. 3838: A. Middeldorp, V. van Oostrom, F. van Raamsdonk, R. de Vrijer (Eds.), Processes, Terms and Cycles: Steps on the Road to Infinity. XVIII, 639 pages. 2005.

Vol. 3837: K. Cho, P. Jacquet (Eds.), Technologies for Advanced Heterogeneous Networks. IX, 307 pages. 2005.

Vol. 3836: J.-M. Pierson (Ed.), Data Management in Grids. X, 143 pages. 2006.

Vol. 3835: G. Sutcliffe, A. Voronkov (Eds.), Logic for Programming, Artificial Intelligence, and Reasoning. XIV, 744 pages. 2005. (Sublibrary LNAI).

Vol. 3834: D.G. Feitelson, E. Frachtenberg, L. Rudolph, U. Schwiegelshohn (Eds.), Job Scheduling Strategies for Parallel Processing. VIII, 283 pages. 2005.

Vol. 3833: K.-J. Li, C. Vangenot (Eds.), Web and Wireless Geographical Information Systems. XI, 309 pages. 2005.

Vol. 3832: D. Zhang, A.K. Jain (Eds.), Advances in Biometrics. XX, 796 pages. 2005.

Vol. 3831: J. Wiedermann, G. Tel, J. Pokorný, M. Bieliková, J. Štuller (Eds.), SOFSEM 2006: Theory and Practice of Computer Science. XV, 576 pages. 2006.

Vol. 3830: D. Weyns, H. V.D. Parunak, F. Michel (Eds.), Environments for Multi-Agent Systems II. VIII, 291 pages. 2006. (Sublibrary LNAI).

Vol. 3829: P. Pettersson, W. Yi (Eds.), Formal Modeling and Analysis of Timed Systems. IX, 305 pages. 2005.

Vol. 3828: X. Deng, Y. Ye (Eds.), Internet and Network Economics. XVII, 1106 pages. 2005.

Vol. 3827: X. Deng, D.-Z. Du (Eds.), Algorithms and Computation. XX, 1190 pages. 2005.

Vol. 3826: B. Benatallah, F. Casati, P. Traverso (Eds.), Service-Oriented Computing - ICSOC 2005. XVIII, 597 pages. 2005.

Vol. 3824: L.T. Yang, M. Amamiya, Z. Liu, M. Guo, F.J. Rammig (Eds.), Embedded and Ubiquitous Computing – EUC 2005. XXIII, 1204 pages. 2005.

Vol. 3823: T. Enokido, L. Yan, B. Xiao, D. Kim, Y. Dai, L.T. Yang (Eds.), Embedded and Ubiquitous Computing – EUC 2005 Workshops. XXXII, 1317 pages. 2005.

Vol. 3822: D. Feng, D. Lin, M. Yung (Eds.), Information Security and Cryptology. XII, 420 pages. 2005.

Vol. 3821: R. Ramanujam, S. Sen (Eds.), FSTTCS 2005: Foundations of Software Technology and Theoretical Computer Science. XIV, 566 pages. 2005.

Vol. 3820: L.T. Yang, X.-s. Zhou, W. Zhao, Z. Wu, Y. Zhu, M. Lin (Eds.), Embedded Software and Systems. XXVIII, 779 pages. 2005.

Vol. 3819: P. Van Hentenryck (Ed.), Practical Aspects of Declarative Languages. X, 231 pages. 2005.

Vol. 3818: S. Grumbach, L. Sui, V. Vianu (Eds.), Advances in Computer Science – ASIAN 2005. XIII, 294 pages. 2005.

Vol. 3817: M. Faundez-Zanuy, L. Janer, A. Esposito, A. Satue-Villar, J. Roure, V. Espinosa-Duro (Eds.), Nonlinear Analyses and Algorithms for Speech Processing. XII, 380 pages. 2006. (Sublibrary LNAI).

Vol. 3816: G. Chakraborty (Ed.), Distributed Computing and Internet Technology. XXI, 606 pages. 2005.

Vol. 3815: E.A. Fox, E.J. Neuhold, P. Premsmit, V. Wuwongse (Eds.), Digital Libraries: Implementing Strategies and Sharing Experiences. XVII, 529 pages. 2005.

Vol. 3814: M. Maybury, O. Stock, W. Wahlster (Eds.), Intelligent Technologies for Interactive Entertainment. XV, 342 pages. 2005. (Sublibrary LNAI).

Vol. 3813: R. Molva, G. Tsudik, D. Westhoff (Eds.), Security and Privacy in Ad-hoc and Sensor Networks. VIII, 219 pages. 2005.

Vol. 3812: C. Bussler, A. Haller (Eds.), Business Process Management Workshops. XIII, 520 pages. 2006.

Vol. 3811: C. Bussler, M.-C. Shan (Eds.), Technologies for E-Services. VIII, 127 pages. 2006.

Vol. 3810: Y.G. Desmedt, H. Wang, Y. Mu, Y. Li (Eds.), Cryptology and Network Security. XI, 349 pages. 2005.

Vol. 3809: S. Zhang, R. Jarvis (Eds.), AI 2005: Advances in Artificial Intelligence. XXVII, 1344 pages. 2005. (Sublibrary LNAI).